THE
KURT DIEMBERGER
OMNIBUS

THE
KURT DIEMBERGER
OMNIBUS

comprising his books:

SUMMITS AND SECRETS
THE ENDLESS KNOT
SPIRITS OF THE AIR

BÂTON WICKS · LONDON

THE MOUNTAINEERS · SEATTLE

Summits and Secrets was first published in Germany in 1970. The first English language edition was published in 1971 (Allen and Unwin. London), relaunched in 1976 (Cordee) with subsequent paperback editions in 1983 and 1991 (Hodder and Stoughton, London).
© Copyright by Kurt Diemberger
The Endless Knot was first published in Italy in 1989. The first English language edition was published in 1991 (Grafton Books, London) and in the United States (The Mountaineers, Seattle).
© Copyright by Kurt Diemberger.
Spirits of the Air was first published in Italy in 1991. The English language edition was published in 1994 (Hodder and Stoughton, London) and in the United States (The Mountaineers, Seattle).
© Copyright by Kurt Diemberger.

The Kurt Diemberger Omnibus: Summits and Secrets, The Endless Knot, Spirits of the Air.
is published simultaneously in 1999 in Great Britain and America by Bâton Wicks Publications, London and The Mountaineers, Seattle.
© 1999 by Kurt Diemberger.
Kurt Diemberger asserts the moral right to be identified as the author of this work.

All trade enquiries in Great Britain, Europe and the Commonwealth (except Canada) to
Bâton Wicks Publications, c/o Cordee, 3a De Montfort Street, Leicester LE1 7HD

All trade enquiries in U.S.A. and Canada to
The Mountaineers • Books, 1001 SW Klickitat Way, Suite 201, Seattle, WA 98134

All rights reserved. No part of this publication may be reproduced, stored in a retrieval system, or transmitted in any form or by any means, without prior permission of the publisher, nor be otherwise circulated in any form of binding or cover other than that in which it is published and without a similar condition being imposed on the subsequent purchaser.

British Library Cataloguing in Publication Data
ISBN 1-898573-26-3   A catalogue records of this book is available in the British Library

United States Library of Congress Catalog Data
ISBN 0-89886-606-3   A catalog record of this book is available at the Library of Congress

Printed and bound in Great Britain by MPG Books Ltd., Bodmin.

PHOTOGRAPHIC ACKNOWLEDGEMENTS
Photos: 3, 5, 8, 9, 11, 12, 13, 14, 15, 20, 21, 24, 25, 27, 29, 30, 32, 33, picture on page 442, 35, 36, 36, 37, 38, 39, 41, 42, 43, 44, 45, 46, 47, 48, 54, 55, 57, 58 – all © Kurt Diemberger; jacket flap, frontis(1), 2, 6, 7, 11, 17, 18, 40, 59, 60, 61, 62, 63, 64, 65 – © Diemberger collection; front cover, 34 – Doug Scott; 4 – Albert Winkler; 10 – Kazimierz Glazek; 22 – Wolfgang Stefan; 23 – Franz Lindner; 26 – Detlef Hecker; 28 – Leo Dickinson; 31 – Lucjan Sadus; 52 – Wojciech Kurtyka; 56 – Ewa Abgarowicz. Others from Diadem Archive.

CONTENTS

Summits and Secrets *5*

The Endless Knot *321*

Spirits of the Air *591*

APPENDICES

between pages 582 and 588
K2 Expeditions, Summit Climbers and Fatalities

between pages 860 and and 864
A Chronology of the Author's Main Climbs and Expeditions
A Note on Terminology
A Selected Bibliography
Note on Heights (Metres to Feet)

PHOTOGRAPHS

between pages 126 and 127
In the Valais; Cima d'Ambiez; Diemberger and Stefan; Lyskamm North Face; Königspitze; Broad Peak/Chogolisa, 1957; Hermann Buhl.

pages 129 and 132
Chogolisa tent; Japanese climbers with Bonatti; The Eiger North Wall.

between pages 256 and 257
Tona Sironi Diemberger; The Peuterey Ridge;
Scenes during the 1960 Dhaulagiri ascent; Hindu Kush, 1967.

pages 322, 442 and 579
K2's South Face; K2 avalanche; K2's East Face; Bauer and Diemberger.

colour pictures between pages 544 and 545
Light aircraft passes Dhaulagiri; On Tirich Mir; The final couloir on Makalu;
On Broad Peak in 1984; Scenes during the 1986 K2 attempts; The Needles.

between pages 672 and 673
K2 from Broad Peak North; K2 from Skyang Kangri; Shartse, 1974;
Gasherbrums II and III; Around Umanak Fjord; Allegri and Diemberger;
Lecturing; Rutkeiwicz with the Diembergers; Messner and Diemberger;
Group with General Zia ul Haq; Group with Mayor Diane Feinstein.

MAPS AND DIAGRAMS

The Baltoro and Broad Peak – *106*; Broad Peak - the route – *111*;
The Peuterey Ridge – *166*; Dhaulagiri and Annapurna – *198*;
Dhaulagiri from the North East – *203*; The Road to Tirich Mir – *256*;
Hindu Kush – *293*; K2 from the north – *359*; Routes on K2 – *585, 586*;
Tirich Mir/Noshaq region – *677, 680*; Greenland *711, 713*.

Summits and Secrets

KURT DIEMBERGER

TRANSLATED BY HUGH MERRICK

First published in Germany in 1970
and in Great Britain in 1971

CONTENTS

PART I

The Astronaut	page 9
Crystals	11

PART II

Grandfather's Bicycle	29
The Matterhorn	42
One Step . . .	47
Book-keeping and Pull-ups	52
Two on a Rope	57
20,000 Feet in Twenty-four Hours	65
Daisies, a Cat and the North Face of the Matterhorn	71
'The Giant Meringue'	85
Tempest	101
My First Eight-thousander: To Broad Peak with Hermann Buhl	102

PART III

The North Face of the Eiger	133
A Lesson in French	161
The Great Peuterey Ridge	165
Alpine Geometry	177
The White Mountain of the Himalaya: Dhaulagiri	186
Herbert Tichy	220
18 to 81: Finals and a Police-sergeant	224

PART IV

The Break-even	233
The Fourth Dimension	238
Ordeal by Fire	243
Higher than the Eagle Soars: Hindu Kush	252
An Apple on Tirich Mir	273
360 Million Years	285

PART V

Three Words from Greenland	288
Between Gran Sasso, Salzburg and . . .	309
Altamira	313
Index	319

It is customary for a book to have a beginning and an end. Not this one; and this page could just as well appear in its middle, or before or after, its contents. It is like my life, which runs its course and I know neither its start nor its conclusion.

In a corner of my room there hangs, by a slender thread, a representation of the world. Consisting of two simple circles of straw, it is transparent. Four star-shaped trimmings are a reminder of Christmas; but it has become almost meaningless, and I see that during the course of the years one of the four stars has fallen off. However, the globe keeps on swinging, slowly, now one way, now the other. It hardly ever comes to rest.

I have christened my circles of straw 'The World'. Sometimes I watch it swinging for quite a time and think about it.

For a naught is nothing; but a naught that has started to swing must, after all, be something . . .

PART I

The Astronaut

When the first man in space caught sight of the earth, his first conclusion was that it really was round. He next observed that it was surrounded by a shimmering blue cloak, clearly defined against the darkness of the void. Not one of the many stars he could see, not the moon, nor the sun, flaming unnaturally there in the black sky, evinced this fairylike feature. Only the earth – man's heaven.

Day and night succeeded one another swiftly. The speed of the flight was breath-taking, but the astronaut was not conscious of it. In the death-like silence, the earth turned beneath him. Now the strip of atmosphere stretched orange-red about the star, veiled in the darkness of night. Scarcely an hour later, cloud-banks were glittering in sunlight. What had become of Time? It was with a sense of irony that the astronaut looked at the face of his watch – except for the capsule, his only fixed point . . . oceans and continents filed past down below. There were people down there whom he could not see, and those he loved were just as remote. All he knew was that they were thinking of him then – there, under the blue glass-dome.

Some day, somebody, perhaps his great grandson, would fly still farther afield, right through the stars, traversing infinite distances away from the earth. He would know no more of nights and days. With him there would only be the stars, space and the fear of death.

What would be that man's thoughts? Must he not be oppressed merely by the idea of his immeasurable distance from the earth? Would he not live, out there among the myriads of the stars, in the sole hope of a safe return to it? To his earth which, for an inexplicable reason that lay in its very self, had created a paradise in the vast loneliness of space?

Our astronaut looked down again at the ever-receding earth. He too belonged to it; to the narrow, precarious space between zero and 8,000 metres, where man can live – in which all the world's miracles and all its bestialities are enacted – the glittering skin of a drop of water.

Down there under the magic carpet of the clouds, men were fighting and making love; in the loud din of war, tanks were roaring through the sands of the desert; ships sailed the seas and cities grew to being; here a mother was bringing her child to life, there a professor was cracking his head over the meaning of existence; forests rustled, and a young girl discovered that her breasts had started to form; and somewhere, somebody, cursing the whole world, died soon after. The earth kept on turning, and there was no end to love . . . for human beings beneath the heavens . . . who have always longed to go to where earth and sky meet.

And so they set out for the horizon, and climbed the highest peaks. Only wise men and lovers stayed where they were; but no one else understood why they had no need to go so far afield. Not even our astronaut, who had not climbed up to heaven, but burst through it, so that he was now outside, and could see the earth in all its limitations – and space in all its infinity.

A turntable was racing round. There were children, holding hands, cutting capers, dancing in a ring, shouting, laughing, clapping, singing in unison with the loud-speaker: 'Little Marcello has gone up into space in his space-ship with a special mission, and is now happily breaking up the stars with his hammer.' A roll of drums, and the stars splinter in the mirror above the gaily-hued pasteboard-box. Manfredo, aged just two, has fetched a chair and is looking on, entranced. '*Ancora!*' howl the others, for the record has run out; the little 'disc-jockey' – yes, he knows how – plants the needle back at the beginning, and for the ninth time the bright-yellow cardboard ship mounts with Marcello to the sky. And the whirling dance goes on . . .

Out here in space all is silence; the earth down there turns soundlessly. The man in the space-capsule knows that the moment for the descent is near – down through the blue cloak of vapour, which protects the earth from death-dealing space. Meteors are quenched in it, so heavy is it; human beings can breathe and move in it, so light it is. The astronaut knows it: in a few minutes he will himself be hurtling through that sky like a meteor. Then the heat-shield will begin to melt, the capsule itself may start to glow . . . and he, will he be burnt to death?

Everything has been worked out to a hair; he will come down safely to earth.

But will he? Nobody knows. Downward tilts the capsule.

Who knows how many urgent prayers have risen to heaven while men were hurtling back through the atmosphere?

Prayers, yes – but to what heaven? Where is that heaven?

The astronaut has landed safely on earth.

Crystals

Suddenly, the first wave of the *föhn* burst upon the silence of the valley. We were on our way to look for crystals, in the night, and the storm howled around us, throwing wave upon shock-wave into the vale.

The wind came from the south, roaring over the sub-alpine ridges, swirling far up to the Marmolata's crest, coursing in wild gusts among the pillars of the Drei Zinnen, and finishing by whistling the whole gamut of the scale among the ridges and towers of the Dolomites.

It was as if the whole sky had burst into turmoil, that March night. Was the storm ushering in the spring; in the night, of all things?

The white wall of the Hohe Tauern, confronting the warm southerly gale on its northward path, drove it high up into the sky. But it was not as easy as that to stop the 'Snowgobbler', as these storms are called in the Salzburg dialect. True, its cloak of cloud, caught between the ice-peaks tarried among the summits – but the storm itself fell with undiminished fury upon the valleys to the north.

There, in the Salzach lowlands, the night-dark meadows stood starred with the first flowers; spring was already here.

Suddenly, the first wave of the *föhn* burst upon the silence of the valley.

We were on our way to look for crystals, and the storm was howling around us. Why had we come here by night?

One of the locals was responsible for that, telling us that he found crystals much more easily by night than by day: they blinked at him from far off in the light of his lantern, as he climbed the gullies in the steep slopes . . .

The *föhn* threw wave upon shock-wave into the vale. They came roaring down from somewhere high up among the glaciers, tearing through the forest, and hastening away from towards the Salzach.

We could see very little, here in the pitch-darkness of the lower Sulzbachtal, which rose, narrowly confined at this point by steep slopes, towards the Gross Venediger – that silvery three-thousander rising above the broad glacier realm of the westerly Hohe Tauern. Even when a gap appeared in the black wall of the forest, we could only guess where the peak stood, high above the head of the valley.

What an idiotic idea, searching for crystals by night ... I should never have thought of it, even in the days when, as a lad, I ranged the valleys with my hammer, dreaming of hidden rifts crammed with crystals. On the other hand if the local was right, it would be like a fairy-story. We had thought of that – already imagining the crystals winking at us in the light of the lantern – when we decided to pursue this fairy-tale.

So here we were, following the narrow path, which I remembered from my young days as a stone-hunter. There was a place where we had to turn up through the forest to the foot of a cliff. It was at a bend in the path, soon after crossing a brook. Could I find it in this darkness?

'How much farther?'

'I'm not sure. Maybe half an hour, maybe an hour. One moves more slowly by night.'

'Can you remember the place?'

'Yes, I shall find it again.'

Things had changed a good deal. Clearings had disappeared, the forest seemed to have grown denser, or was it just the darkness? The path, definitely the only one in the Untersulzbachtal, had not changed at all. Over there, in the next valley, there is a road now; and in the Felbertal – two or three parallel valleys to the east – today you can drive straight through a tunnel, on a splendid motor-way, down to the Dolomites. I am sorry about the Obersulzbachtal – I used to go there on foot ... it was there that, twenty years ago, after a two days' search, I found my first mountain crystal. There it lay on the moss, clear as a drop of dew – just as if everyone knew that crystals always lie on a mossy boulder on a slope. I endowed it with an inner light of its own. Though there was no sun, it was brighter than the snows on the peaks. I can remember how my hand trembled as, at last, I picked it up.

My thoughts were interrupted ...

'Do you think we still need the lamp? The forest isn't so dark here, and you say you know the way. We'll need it when we get there, because we can't find crystals without its light.'

'Quite right,' I agreed. I had a reserve flash-lamp in my rucksack, but it would be a pity if one of us couldn't see anything, up on the slope. So I turned the lamp off.

That moment, with the crystal lying there on the moss, still shines undimmed, whenever I recall it; even though I later found larger and more beautiful ones on the Sonnblick. Not even a shining green emerald in the bed of a stream below an old mine in the Habachtal could oust that small, regular pyramid of quartz from its place in my heart. For it was my first stone.

Today, as I write this, I believe it to be quite wrong simply to believe that the new merely replaces the old. Sometime or other, in some place or other, the past will suddenly surge up – a person, a face, a likeness . . . a tune. And when it does, it is there. All of a sudden you relive something you thought long past. Sometimes it is only a recollection . . . but sometimes that past begins its own strange existence and grows stronger than the present. And so it becomes a new present.

Consciously or unconsciously? Who can tell, for instance, when a 'successful' man starts slaving away at taking a degree; when a dyed-in-the-wool bachelor marries the girl of his childhood, and a barrister decides to become a mountain guide? And then, it is by no means certain whether they themselves know why.

Even I remember an agonized rope-mate, whose ill-fortune it was that crystals suddenly appeared on a ridge we were climbing, and at more than one spot, too. I need hardly say that we did not climb our peak, that day.

'I believe I shall find a great big crystal today . . .' Yes, there was something in the air of this night, but what? I didn't know myself, so I laughed a little and said: 'All crystal-hunters believe that – I thought so myself, every single day. A hunter once told me about a wonderful great crystal in a rock-fissure in the forest; he used to go back every now and then to look at it. Only he knows where, though . . .'

'I can quite understand his keeping it secret. And why shouldn't today be just such a lucky one for us – on my very first search?'

'I hope it will be. It can always happen. But just now it's dark and we have still to find the place. The largest stones found on this face till now were about the length of one's finger – green, brown and sometimes even black ones, of quite unusual brilliance, possibly semi-precious. They are called epidotes, and, so far as I know, no larger ones have been found anywhere; and who knows what else may be hidden in the Tauern, unknown to anyone, even to the old crystal-hunters who clambered about up there for decades . . .' (not like me, for only a few days).

'Once – over there in the Habachtal – I had incredible luck myself. The two-man crew of the old emerald-mine had been washing for emeralds for days outside the half-silted-up hole in the face, at about 8,000 feet. They had already amassed quite a find of "collector's stones" – white or pale green crystals, all full of faults and flaws – but were quite contented. Pure, valuable emeralds are, of course, very rare and hardly ever found. The two men were very amiable, and allowed me to disappear, armed with a little luck and a big bucket, into the darkness of the tunnel. I could fill my bucket once, in the hope that, the muddy deposit might hold a collector's stone, in which case it would be mine to keep. I chose a place that looked likely and filled the bucket, at a venture. Once outside we separated the silvery mud under the jet of water in the sunlight. There, shone a collector's stone . . . and another . . . evidently my luck was in . . . And then, suddenly, we were all three staring in amazement at the mesh: on it lay a glorious emerald, dark green and full of fire, with not a flaw in it . . . Nobody spoke; but I knew what was coming next – I should have to surrender the stone. My luck had lasted just that short moment.'

The whole forest seemed to be in motion by now. The dark trunks swayed slowly back and forth, while the branches moved restlessly up and down, as if they did not belong to them.

'I wouldn't have given it back,' said the voice by my side. I did not reply. Odd characters, these trees all around us.

'How did you, a climber, take to searching for crystals?'

I hesitated. 'That's rather a long story,' I said, 'and had nothing to do with climbing, originally. But if you really want to know . . .?'

'I do.'

'Well, it started like this. When I was a child, my father took me along one day on to the Kumitzberg near Villach – a little, wooded hill at the gates of my home-town in Carinthia. There were supposed to be red garnets up there – whatever they might be; but I realized from the way he spoke that they must be something very special. We got there, after a long time; they weren't anything very special – just red blobs in the rock. What impressed me most was that I had had to walk so far; and my father was very disappointed with me.

'Later, however, at Salzburg, other stones began to mean a great deal to me; there was a big river just outside our windows and its broad rubble-covered flats, which changed in appearance completely after every high-water, seemed to us, when we came out of school, much more important and exciting than all the lovely town, with its parks, churches and fine architecture. On the "Salzach-rubble" nobody read us any lectures; it was our island fastness in the middle of an over-regimented life. No peaceful citizen had ever summoned up the energy to climb down there and interrupt our stony and watery warfare.

'One day I found a fossilized snail as large as a bread-plate in a lump of red rock down there. That gave me a new idea; each flood-water of the Salzach brought something new down with it and, gradually, more and more of it was transferred to our house. At first my mother was none too enthusiastic, but she was a woman who loved the sun and the woods and, indeed all nature; and, after I had shown her the snail, she left me to my own devices. I was soon battling for space; for the Salzach brought quite a lot down on its long journey from the Hohe Tauern to Salzburg. My father, just back from the front, sat in a prisoner-of-war camp, and I could not see him. But I could write to him; so, while I was alternately rustling up food from the Americans and hammering away down on the rubble, I kept him posted about my latest finds. He commented back on them and one day, to my great surprise, he sent me a sketch-map. It seems he knew where the red snails were to be found! I went there the very next day, going on foot with my map, as I did not then possess a bicycle: it was only three miles to the south of Salzburg. At the bottom of a deep red ravine I found quantities of what I was looking for – a whole sea-bed of snails, ammonites, crinoid-stems lay there between the ferns and the roots. Every time I found a new creature, the population of that sea-bed grew in my imagination. Even in the town I went around with staring eyes, and many of those who met me thought I was in a trance. How could they guess that, for me, a nautilus or an ichthyosaurus had just swum across the Residenzplatz? In spite of the heavy traffic, I felt absolutely justified, and certainly no dreamer; it had really happened – only, a couple of million years before. Indeed, someone had once found an ichthyosaurus in my ravine; but that had been a long time ago.

'Every Sunday I scrambled around on the steep cliffs of the gorge; very unsafe ground, slippery with clay, tufted with grass, and at some places dotted with scrubby trees. Twice I lost my hold, but managed each time to grab a branch before going all the way down. As I never met anyone between the walls of the ravine, I soon came to regard it as my own private realm.

'I was wrong, however. I had just gouged an ammonite, the size of my head, out of a newly-discovered ledge – it was narrow and I had to keep my balance by hanging on to a root – just climbed down and stowed it in my rucksack; was just ready, in fact, to whistle my cheerful way home down through the woods, when – as if sprung from the ground, a weatherbeaten old boy popped up, not five paces in front of me, regarding me with a knowing kind of look. Unable to find words I just stood and stared at him, as if he were a ghost; but he was very much alive. "Found owt today, eh?" came the amiable enquiry, emerging from that creased and crinkled face.

'"Oh, just a thing or two—" I stammered, diving into my trouser-pocket for a couple of crinoid stems.

'So there was someone else! The horrid thought crossed my mind that he might know about my ammonite-place up there. I followed an ancient mushroom-hunter's precept: better say nothing. I show him the stems. I could feel the weight of my rucksack tugging at my back.

'"Not much luck, then, today!" said the old man, with an amused smile. "But tha's reet well equipped – so well" (and here he began to chuckle) 'that tha' dids'tna git oop to th' ammonite-layer oop theer – 'cos of t'load tha's wearin' on tha' back . . ."

'"Oh, I see," said I, greatly relieved; and then we both started to laugh. We collectors had reached an understanding.

'Two days later, I was visiting the old man, to see his collection; and with the undeclared intention of picking his brains to the best of my ability. He lived in a somewhat rickety house at the other end of town. Every corner of the room I entered glittered and sparkled, as if the dwarfs of the Grimm Brothers had brought their whole treasure up from the bowels of the earth. There were blue, red, green minerals; stones of every kind, size and shape, and more remarkable, something not to be found anywhere round Salzburg – marvellous crystals, of every shade and colour. At first the old man was just friendly, but said little: only that the crystals came from the Hohe Tauern. Gradually, I dragged more and more out of him; he told me about the old Roman gold-workings near the Bockhardsee, the emeralds in the Habachtal, all about crystals, dark and light, and also about our own epidotes, here in the Untersulzbachtal. He had suddenly become communicative, and told me a great deal about his expeditions to the rim of the glaciers, about ridges which no one visits. Yes, he said, there must be unimaginable treasures still hidden in the Hohe Tauern. As he spoke, my imagination was increasingly seized by the idea of the giant crystal hidden in some rift and waiting for me to find it. At the end of my visit, when the old man presented me with a coloured map of the Venediger Group, I was for starting out that very instant . . .'

'Did you ever find your crystal?'

'No, but only because I did not believe in it long enough. Had I done so, I would simply have gone on till I came across it. But I was lured away by the mountains, the Himalaya, Greenland . . . all the same, it might get a grip on me again any day; if so, I shall just grab my hammer, and go after it.'

For a while, the only sound was that of our footsteps. Then I went on: 'Do you know, there is nothing, however big or mad, you cannot achieve, if you believe in it. You can climb an 8,000-metre peak, cross the Atlantic alone in a boat . . .'

'If your lungs are up to it, and you have a boat, of course.'

'In the end, you can do anything. The only difficult thing is to get across to people. They have to understand you. Their hearts and souls are no mountains, no oceans; they are islands, waiting and hoping for the moment to come. Sometimes, they do understand you . . .

'Of course, not everyone can climb Everest – why should they? They may have discovered quite a different secret: a formula, a work of art – even, perhaps, in so doing – themselves.

'I wonder how many Hillarys and Tensings have never found their way to the heights, simply because they did not believe in them sufficiently? Maybe some descendant of the Vikings, on his Sunday afternoon walk, looks longingly at the waters of some river that winds down to the sea, and knows he is due in the office next morning. That is where he belongs in the "programme" – by his own volition . . . Or *did* he will it? Resigned, he goes home, to watch television, on whose screen he finds what he has lost; the wide, wide sea and far-off, unknown shores. And he waits for something – but what? Finally, he shakes his head, this son of the Vikings, has a look at the papers, and goes to bed. After all, there is always one's leave to look forward to . . .'

'Do you climb mountains, then, just because there is no "programme"?'

'Maybe; but I can't give any precise reason. It is simply that I am happy there, and so have to go back again and again. Sometimes the main attraction is that of the unknown.'

'When did you start?'

'When I was sixteen; soon after I met the old crystal-hunter.'

'And why?'

'I don't really know, now. It just happened, on a day when I wanted to hunt for crystals – in fact I was on my way to a source the old man had suggested to me . . .'

'And then what happened?'

'Nothing – except that I left it unvisited and went straight on to the summit.'

'Do you know why?'

'No.'

The forest had fallen silent. Over on the other side, or down in the valley bed, there was the rushing echo of a torrent.

'If you can't tell me why you went on to your summit, can you describe what it is like to be on a glacier?'

'I love it. For me it is the direct antithesis of a street. It is continually on the move; and you can wander anywhere you like about its ice; for only the glacier itself, with its crevasses and séracs, constrains you. But with enough experience and a good rope-mate, you can climb the most savage ice-falls . . . and how exciting it is to move among these fantastic structures of green ice, over outsize bridges, past towers the height of a house, through a fan-like tracery of blue crevasses, that changes from day to day! There are times when you hear a muffled crack in the giant's cold body; it has moved a little, again; or the roar of collapsing séracs. And when you are jumping a crevasse, you can hear the water down in its depths . . .'

'And you haven't fallen into one yet?'

'No – not yet, surprisingly enough, but, of course, one is always roped. So far, at the moment when I felt the ground give under me, I have always been able to crook my knee and throw myself across. Though I did once fall into a water-hole, quite early on, when I was a boy – and I was alone at the time. I had climbed up on to the ice, out of sheer curiosity, to see what it was like up there, and found it quite fantastic. I wandered about between the glacier-streams and huge mushrooms of rock and ice, occasionally throwing a glance over to the boulders on the moraine, in case there might be a crystal lying among them. It was early morning, and the sun had only just arrived; so the water-holes in the glacier were still hard-frozen. They looked like rare flowers – for the long blue-green stems of ice-crystals had, during the night, grown inwards from the rim to the centre, star-fashion. The sun mounted in the sky, and for once I suppose I was careless: I stepped on to one of those blue flowers, and found myself standing up to my neck in water. For half an hour afterwards – a shivering Adam – I hopped around and did exercises. Fortunately, there was the sun's warmth.'

'And did you note that "blue flowers" can provide a nice cold ruffle for your throat?' came from my side, in gentle irony.

'Naturally,' I answered, unable to suppress a little smile. 'But is that any reason for my not going where they grow?'

How and why did I climb my first peak? I find it difficult to explain it today.

It was the first time that this lad in the Obersulzbachtal, scrambling around at the edge of the ice and on its moraines, saw the great white summits rising opposite him – those great white, shining peaks. He had never seen anything like it before.

Here he was, hunting for crystals, but stopping again and again to look upwards, into the blinding brightness of the peaks. There they lay under a dark sky, so near and so utterly at rest. The snow up there belonged to a different world.

Suddenly, a dull roar filled the air and, from high up on the ridge, a stream of white poured down on to the glacier bed, shaking it far and wide. No, for this lad, there could be nothing more remote than those white summits. They were different from anything in his experience. He looked at them, deeply conscious of their inaccessibility; yet, at the same time, recognizing their beauty of shape – the regular ridges of the Gross Geiger, forming a pyramid – then the iridescent glitter of the Gross Venediger's icefalls, the gentle sweep of its summit, far withdrawn . . .

It was all so unearthly and so vast that he could not understand how anyone could go up there; on that dazzling white world there seemed to lie an absolute taboo. And yet people did go up there. The peaks looked down on him and held their peace.

Disturbed, the lad's thoughts went winging to the highest finding-place of which the old man had spoken; a saddle in a ridge, nearly 10,000 feet up, in between two summits. On it there were phrenitic-crystals to be found – a glittering pale-green lawn of star-points – and he would very much like to have some. Should he really go up there?

The saddle stood high above the Habachtal's glacier-basin and there was a rib running up to quite near it. One evening, he decided to go up. He packed hammer, chisel and some food into his rucksack, and set out at sunrise. The hut-keeper had lent him a pair of snow-goggles.

The white flank below the ridge was scored by avalanche-tracks; the masses of snow had come to rest in the hollow at its foot. Slowly the boy went up towards it. The rib was not very prominent, but looked safe; it consisted more of rock than snow. Right at its start, there lay a lump of crystal, big as a man's head, streaked by little dark-green chlorite blades. What a pity it was broken . . . did it come, he wondered, from the vein of quartz up above? But when he got there, there were only scattered spots. He climbed on, over boulders and pitches; till, presently, the sound of the waterfalls at the glacier's tongue grew fainter. And the silence built up around him.

He put on his goggles, for everything was now dazzling-bright. The snow-diamonds glittered. He had never been up so high before. To the left, above him rose a summit . . . lovely, up there in the morning sun, and in some way secretive, though the boy could not say why. He went on up towards the saddle, which drew nearer. So did the summit.

The air about him sparkled. At every step he felt himself penetrating a realm unlike any he had ever visited; everything seemed marvellous – the view, the depths below, the very air itself. Far below, now, lay the glaciers, the valley, the forests through which he had come, the broad scree-cones, where he had searched for crystals. On the snow-slope down there, he could make out a tiny trail - his own trail.

Yes, he had discovered something, but was not yet sure what. Was it, perhaps, that he could move about up here – move most marvellously? He thought of climbers. Was this it; was he meant to go on up – up into that inaccessible world of summits?

That world of summits . . . one of them stood there above him; had stood all morning, with its brownish-grey individual structure of bare, shattered rock, rising out of dazzling snow-fields. 'A 'three-thousander', this; and, seemingly, quite near ...

As the boy stood there, he could hear water from the melting snow hiccoughing among the boulders. Otherwise there was no sound. Up there, the brown rocks, the highest rocks of the summit, were powdered with the sheen of freshly-fallen snow.

There was something very odd about those rocks ...

Yes.

Suppose he went on up there?

Yes.

And the phrenites? He looked across at the saddle in confusion. Tomorrow, perhaps—?

Yes.

But me? Me, to go up on to a summit? Me? thought the boy, in amazement.

Yes.

And now he wanted it; now he meant to go. Yes, I meant to, and have meant to ever since.

It was wonderful. I was the only being for miles around, and now I was going up the ridge to my summit. It had not changed an iota; but I had. Suddenly I was full of restless excitement about the unknown quantity of those blocks of rock up there. Rock which could, after all, only be rock – rock, above the snow and beneath the sky. I climbed on up the ridge for more than an hour – the summit was not so near as it had seemed – my joy increasing as I saw the intervening distance diminish.

The initial rib had long ago disappeared into the depths and I was working my way up between airy towers, of the strangest stratification; many of them looked as if they would fall down any minute. Far down on the other side I could now see a blue tarn and, much farther down, the Hollerbachtal. There were many peaks all around me, and clouds – everything had opened out into vast distances ...

A step in the ridge pushed me out on to the slope, where there was wet, slushy snow. I traversed cautiously, digging now my hammer and now my chisel into the surface at every step. Suddenly, a little corner of snow broke away under me, grew into a slab of ever-expanding dimensions, broke up and carried away more snow with it. The peace that had reigned was violently replaced by a swelling roar. That is all I saw of it .. but from far down below I heard a wild turmoil and uproar ... the roar of an avalanche. I stood rooted to the spot, unable to grasp it all.

How glad I was when I felt good sound rock under my fingers again.

Crystals

And the summit had drawn appreciably closer. Suddenly, I came upon a green vein in the brown and grey of the rocks of the ridge – a mass of slender, shining needles, all in confusion, or in little delicate clumps like paint-brushes. I wondered what they were, and broke off a lump or two to take along, then continued my climb.

Then came the slab – the slab on which my nailed boots suddenly slipped – and I found myself, I don't know how, sitting a few feet farther down, on the edge of a cliff above the slope. And then I noticed that blood was gushing out of a cut in my wrist – slowly, in spurts, quite a lot of it. There followed long minutes of terrible fear. I lay down and held my hand up high – that might help . . . It stopped.

I lay there for another quarter of an hour, then I wound a handkerchief round my hand and felt my way forward with the other. I was close to the summit now, and sure that I would get there – a wonderful, overpowering certainty. Nothing could stop me now. A few minutes more and I should be there.

There were rocks, lying piled on each other, against the blue. Silent as heaven itself. Heavenly still . . .

My excitement was indescribable, transcending everything. I could feel my heart beating. Only those rocks above me, and then . . .

They were only rocks, after all. But I was up, up on the very top! High above an infinity of air . . . up on my own summit.

Nobody who has ever stood on the 9,885-foot Larmkogel in the Hohe Tauern can have any idea what it meant to me. For it is an insignificant mountain. But it was for me my first summit, and at that moment it belonged entirely to me.

In the south-west a fairy-like gleam broke through the brown of the cloud-wrack: that must be the Gross Venediger. The sun beat down. The silence was absolute, almost oppressive. Only the melting snow gurgled and guggled. How huge the world must be! Those were some of my thoughts at that moment – they have not changed since. Was that the beginning of it all?

To the north, the blue walls of the Limestone Ranges rose above grey-green, slabby hills of the Pinzgau. I recognized the Hochkönig by the light streak of its summit snow-field. Then there was the Steinerne Meer. At my feet lay the Habach and Hollerbach valleys, and far away to the east bulked a snowy peak, with a sharp, slanting summit – the Gross Glockner?

Clouds kept on hiding the view, clouds that came from the south, sweeping through the sky at about 10,000 feet and getting caught up among the loftier summits. I waited a long time for the Venediger to clear, but in vain.

At times a cloud would approach the Larmkogel itself, and then I sat for a while completely wrapped in white mist, till the wind chased it from the peak and it sailed away again, like a ship, over the deep valleys to the north, farther and farther, till it found some other peak to rest on.

'... peaks, unknown to me,' I entered in my diary.

The stars were sparkling and shimmering. There was the scent of soil and snow. We crossed a little stream, but not the one that led to the crystals. Slowly a fish-shaped cloud swam across the starlit sky, and the darkness deepened.

Just for something to say, I remarked: 'You're not saying much today.'

'No, but I see a great deal; have you noticed the cloud?'

'Yes,' I said.

It lay right overhead now, high over the tree-tops, like a baldaquin, vaguely defined and yet regular in shape, an odd cloud. Beyond it, the stars were coming out again. There was no sign of my cliff that housed the crystals. We went on. Wherever could that stream have got to? Perhaps it had ceased to exist?

More and more snow-patches between the trees... We came out into a clearing, giving us an open view up the valley ahead. We saw the dark rocks of a gorge, pale streaks of snow, peaks rising above, hardly distinguishable. Definitely, no!

'What's up? Anyone gone wrong?' came a worried voice through the darkness, as I stood irresolute.

'Yes, we've come too far. Perhaps the stream has vanished – I don't understand it,' I had to admit. Ahead of us, in silence, lay the valley...

'And yet you thought you still knew the way —'

Yes, I had thought so. I did not answer. What should I do now?

'Come, let's turn back, and we'll find it. That cliff is above one of those last ravines.'

We *had* to find it. *I* had to find it. Anything else was unthinkable.

Where was that face above the thick forest covering the slope? We went on up a gully: in vain. And yet it couldn't help being hereabouts ... or was it only a piece of self-deception, some crazy belief? So far, nothing but darkness and tall tree-trunks. Yet something kept on telling me it must be just here. We took to the next slope, a steep groove slashing up through the forest, filled with boulders, piled one on top of the other, often unstable and demanding care. Somewhere I could hear running water – feebly, faintly – a trickle, somewhere up above...

Crystals

The silhouette of a cliff loomed slowly out of the darkness, scattered tree-tops, dark against the sky, a cave . . . a slope . . .

We had found it.

All we needed now was luck.

As we were getting over the last boulders on the slope, we were delighted to find that our old local had been right: for suddenly, between the branches of a bush near by, there flashed a single splinter of crystal, caught in the hardly noticeable light of our lamp. This was the old man's conjuring-trick . . .

Anyone who has ever seen a ring sparkling suddenly in the darkness of a town in this sudden, unexpected way, must have asked himself how it could have happened. It could have been the light of some quite distant street-lamp that the jewel picked up and reflected.

And here, on a slope where every separate crystal lying on the surface reflects the light – how many surprises might lurk between soil and sand, stones, plants and the trunks of the trees? A slope-full of crystals . . . we shed our rucksacks.

Then, without losing another moment, we seized our torches and independently took to the slope. The *föhn* had diminished by now, and only came in occasional waves . . .

I was lucky. Flashes and sparks shone at me out of the darkness everywhere, and I hardly moved as I looked all around me. I have never seen anything quite like it. I only had to bend my head a little and in that instant there was the gleam of dozens of crystals, staring dumbly out of the darkness. I took a short stride, and enjoyed a new display of magic fireworks. It was impossible to think of searching. As I went slowly over the soft, springy ground, I was folded in by a void filled with secret sources of light – flashing, occulting, shimmering, increasing in intensity, vanishing, lighting up again – a sequence as fantastic as it was simple, as unearthly, and yet as of the earth, as is space full of the dust of stars, continually newly-born, flaming, dying out, being reborn – mute up there in the darkness. I was as thrilled as if I had found the crystal of crystals, though I was still empty-handed.

When I moved, this universe circled round me; when I stopped, the glittering orbit froze into immobility. Was I not, at the moment, a little God? And so I did not lay a finger on that magic world – it was beautiful as it was . . .

When, in the end, I approached one of these flashing lights and picked the crystal up, I found only a tiny splinter between my fingers!

I heard a voice saying: 'It's a little like your dreams.'

I couldn't help smiling. 'Yes,' I thought, 'but without them I would never have climbed Dhaulagiri's shining glory, nor travelled to Greenland . . .'

I now started – with varying success – to approach individual points of light. What happens is this: the crystals glitter much more brightly through the dark from a distance than from near by in the light of the lamp. Moreover, it only needs one false movement, however slight, and the crystal disappears into the darkness, mostly for keeps. Nevertheless, there are no exact rules and since everything remains uncertain till the very last moment, what happens, again and again, is this:

You move, and suddenly, at a distance of about ten yards, there is a gleam among the leaves, growing swiftly in intensity – you stop dead, certain that this must be a big crystal. Very cautiously, and taking care not to deviate one inch from a straight course, you approach the alluring glint – for if you deviate, instead of a crystal, there will be nothing there but the darkness of the night. Just as you are getting near, a no less mysterious light shines out from somewhere else.

You remember that consistency is a virtue, and go straight ahead. When, at the end of it all, you hold in your hand a single flat object no thicker than your skin, all you can do is to think of a glow-worm robbed by an electric torch of its magic. Meanwhile, the other crystal has disappeared. Is one likely to remain consistent?

However, the chase of these glinting points of light was not always abortive. I finished with a handful of pretty little crystals. Some of them, poison-green, were like delicate needles, some black and step-shaped, others flat olive-brown prisms; all of them alike had a bright sheen. I remembered that people use these epidotes as jewellery, though not very often.

Shortly after – as the result of a further, highly exciting and successful hunt – I had a shining, empty, crystal-hunter's beer-bottle in my hand, my companion and I were sitting together at the foot of the slope, enjoying an apple or two, bread and bacon, washed down with a carton of milk. Between the silhouettes of the trees a pale glimmer shone down on us from the head of the valley, where rose the Venediger.

'Would you like to see what I found?'

'Yes,' I said, switching the torch on.

There were needles, flakes, prisms – more or less like mine. Not a single large crystal.

'Quite nice,' I conceded, turning a needle in the light of the torch. It shone olive-green and, immediately afterwards, dark-brown.

'Have you noticed how the colour changes?' I asked.

'No – how can it? Let me see!'

Crystals

'Watch,' I said, holding the needle in the blinding cone of light and turning it . . . green . . . brown . . . brown . . . green again.

'How is it possible?'

'It has some connection with the way the light falls on it and through it, and it only happens with very clear crystals – best of all with these small needles. This one will do it too,' I said, handing another one over. 'I have seen much the same thing with icebergs in Greenland; they change colour according to the direction from which the sunlight strikes them.'

The beam of the torch thrust like a finger into the darkness, lighting up a tree, or the ground, without rhyme or reason. Far up the valley we heard the echoing thunder of a springtime avalanche.

'Shall we have a go at the Venediger?'

'Do you think I could do it?'

'Yes, I think so.'

The light of the torch swept the floor almost horizontally. Suddenly there was a movement at my side, a couple of steps and a joyous cry: 'I've got it!'

I jumped up. 'What – a big crystal?'

'Yes, and so close to us. I suddenly caught sight of it, half-hidden under a stone . . .'

'Show me!'

It was a beauty. A dark prism, half the length of one's finger, with smooth, regular surfaces, simply laid against each other – but not symmetrical. A couple of fine lines ran along one edge, underlining its shape. It was a splendid specimen of an epidote.

'You can be unreservedly happy,' I said. 'There isn't a flaw in it.'

'I am,' came the answer.

The find had banished every trace of weariness. Wide awake, we charged up the slope again, as if luck and endurance have anything to do with each other. Or have they?

I have no idea for how many more hours we went up and down that slope. Perhaps it was only a single hour. If you ever ask a crystal-hunter how long he spent digging, or climbing up and down in his search, he will look at you with great surprise and give you a vague answer – for, among the boulders, minutes pass like hours and hours like minutes. One simply hasn't any idea . . .

It was still dark. I had gone back to the top of the slope and was pursuing my search there. I did not have much luck, but it gradually dawned on me that, on this day, it was of no such great importance. For during this night I had found more than ever before. It was as if the whole show-case full of crystals at home had suddenly sprung to life – in a whirling, glittering orbit on that hillside, an orbit that was still continuing. It was part of me now – my great discovery. It was strong as the air blowing down from the mountains, from their summits; the air that blows from up there, where everything is so strong and inexplicable – as inexplicable as what was then being wafted to me on that air . . .

The boy I had once been – it was the same thing as made him go, that first time. A thing indescribable in words. A thing granted me afresh today, as if it had never been before. A thing that had always existed.

Yes, we had both found something – more than ever before. I remembered how I had ranged these valleys, in search of the great unknown. Perhaps a great crystal?

Was that why I had come here today? And you – why have I told you so much already? I hardly know you. Today you found your first crystal. That is almost all I know about you. Down there on the hillside, I can see the light of your torch shining. Why did I bring you here? Is it perhaps that in our very lack of knowledge of each other there lies an element of knowledge?

Down there, on the slope, the light of your torch moves back and forth; a circle of light in which a hand is sorting soil and stones, testing, rejecting, selecting . . .

Who are you? You, who enfold a thousand possibilities?

The light, its circle, moves and moves, erratically. At a movement of your head, your long hair suddenly falls across the light, a shimmering, shining curtain. Then the circle moves on again.

You remain the enigma.

Or have the crystals taught you some of the truth – about that boy? What would it mean to you if I led you up to some high summit tomorrow?

Will you ever be able to understand that the ridge, the icebergs in Greenland, and the Himalayan snows can mean just as much as these crystals? In that case, we shall not have come here in vain. But, perhaps you, down there on the slope, are only looking for a stone for a ring?

The wind had almost dropped; a chill air rose from the ground. I got up and walked up and down for a while.

'How much longer are you going on looking?' came up from below.

'I have stopped looking,' I answered.

'Then we could move on, couldn't we? I am tired and cold – and I shan't find anything more. Besides that one stone is so lovely – what more could I want?'

I slid down to her over the unstable slope in a couple of strides.

'You are right – let's go. But first show me the stone again . . .'

She undid her breast-pocket. 'Of course,' she said.

Crystals

I could feel the nearness of her. The stone was marvellous. I began to think a little less categorically.

'A piece of jewellery,' I remarked; and the description fitted.

'Oh, do you think so?' She held it against her finger, her head tilted sideways, looking at it long and searchingly; and then still longer.

'It would suit you admirably,' I laughed, a little too loudly, and ran my fingers through her hair.

She did not reply. Then a little smile passed over her face. 'Oh no,' she said, looking at me, 'it's not like you think.' Then, suddenly serious and thoughtful, her eyes returning to the stone. 'It would be a shame. I will keep it as I found it – along with today.'

Dawn filtered between the tree-trunks as we came silently out into the Salzach meadows.

Behind us the night seemed far away and yet as real as the grass beneath our feet and the houses we were approaching. Early risers were stirring. The sky was like a turquoise.

We felt, at one and the same time, wide awake and very tired. Down on the road, the ground seemed to give under our feet at every step. I saw crystals – a firmament – full of brilliant flashes. And the day that was coming. The first rays of the sun touching the summit of the Venediger.

A happy certainty. Tomorrow we would be climbing it.

PART II

Grandfather's Bicycle

My grandfather gave me his bicycle, a 1909 'museum-piece'. 'Ride to school on it,' he said; and I can still see the stern but kindly face with its white moustache. He was a headmaster, and headmasters always have to be a little stern . . .

He had covered the whole of the hilly country around the little village in Lower Austria, where he had worked all his life, year in, year out, either on his bicycle or on foot; for he was a keen hunter.

When he was fifty, he thought he had perhaps done enough pedalling, and acquired a motor-cycle; but when the war ended, he had to dispose of it, and started pedalling again. He was still pedalling when he was eighty; and, had not the sight of one eye deteriorated, he would no doubt be pedalling today, when he is over ninety and still facing the world with great confidence.

That bicycle certainly opened up undreamed-of possibilities for me. What matter that this 1909 show-piece was one of the first to be made after the famous 'penny-farthings'? Or that it was still rather taller than normal machines, and a little peculiar to ride? That was just its hall-mark; and there were definitely three people who knew how to ride it – my grandfather, my father and I. Everyone else – and I had a number of friends who wanted to try it out – dismounted in great haste.

'Either you can or you can't,' thought I, and launched out on great adventures. My bike and I crossed the highest passes in the Alps together, journeyed far and wide through Austria, Switzerland and Italy.

I have it no longer. One day I left it outside the railway station, unpadlocked, as always. When I at last remembered it, two days later, it had disappeared, and it has never been seen again. Even now, I just can't understand it. Certainly, nobody can possibly be riding it. Perhaps it graces the private collection of some connoisseur as a vintage exhibit;

or maybe, one of these days, I shall recognize a part of it in an exhibition of Pop-art sculpture.

Nowadays I belong to the majority of the human race – those who either possess, want to possess or have possessed a car. Nowadays, I too take to the available motorway and think in terms of mileage, petrol, cash, and time. A spin in the car? Yes, of course – why not, on a Sunday afternoon?

Yet I wonder whether mountains, valleys and passes really exist any more for the motorist? If anyone says they do, I hand him a bicycle and tell him to get cracking. I am sure he will very soon turn back – and will have understood the message. Poor devils! – he will be thinking – meaning the cyclists. Never again will he attempt a pass on a bicycle; but that will only be because he has sat in a car for too long a time.

Rrrums-treng . . . foot up, look up to see if the hairpin is clear . . . it is . . foot down . . *trrreng* . . then the next hairpin . . *rums-treng* . . . through it . . . left, *treng* . . . right, *treng* . . . left, right, left, right, left . . . ah, here we are at the top of the pass. The motorist is king of the world. He has done it again . . . !

Let's hop out for a couple of minutes and stretch our legs a bit, and look at the view. Noticeably colder up here, but the view is fine, really remarkably fine, the view; a cigarette, eh? Or a quick one at the bar? Yes, the car did very well; the engine still pulls splendidly, well enough, that is – but, of course, such a lot depends on the driver . . .

Then down again on the other side, *rums-treng*, the first hairpin, *rums-trrreng* the second . . . left, right, left, right, left . . . with a new sticker on the windscreen.

What's that I see – a cyclist? And – two more? Dear God, there must still be idealists about the place! The proud motorist at the helm maybe falls silent for a while – or he starts talking about the treadmill of our era, of the shortage of leisure time, of the treadmill from which there is no escape . . . the treadmill . . .

But perhaps, as I have suggested, he falls silent for a while and does some quiet thinking . . .

My grandfather's bicycle was a magnificent treadmill. When you trod on the pedal you took a giant's leap forwards, because the chainwheel was outsize. Later on I changed it for a smaller, more modern one. That produced an additional advantage: for I then had some spare links for my chain again, whereas I had been forced many a time to call in a blacksmith's skill on the old one.

At the outset, I rode to my fossil-beds – what an improvement that was! I was there in next to no time. How mechanical transport can alter one's life ... a quarter of an hour's pedalling and I had covered ground which used to take me a long hour on foot, and reached my Glasenbachklamm, the gorge with the ammonites. Farther north, it only took an hour to the sandstone cliffs of the Haunsberg, where long ago the sea used to break against the near-by coast, and where you could find sea-urchins as big as your head, mussels and a hundred other creatures. And, just before the end of my fossil-hunting days, fate granted me an unusual and highly impressive find. There, on a boulder below a sandstone cliff, in the middle of the woods, sat a crab, which chance had allowed, almost as if intentionally, to fall from high up in the cliff. I couldn't believe my eyes. There it sat, bolt upright, with half-closed claws, between the ferns and the shrubs, as if waiting for something ... for 70 million years.

That sort of thing had, however, become a Sunday-afternoon pastime by now. As soon as I found a little more time, I rode farther afield into the Hohen Tauern, whose realm of peaks now lay open to me, without an upper limit; but I still kept on disappearing into its remotest corners, to look for crystals, minerals, or even gold – for the Romans had discovered the precious metal in the rocks of the Tauern and had mined it high up among them on the steep shores of the Bockart See. I found the gold-galleries, though they were barely recognizable. I must admit at once that I did not make my fortune, for what I lugged down to the valley was pyrites. Of course, I knew that, but I hoped there might be some gold in it. There wasn't. So, in the end, I dragged half a rucksackful – and all I could carry – of silver ore out of a gallery which, for a change, had been worked as recently as the Third Reich. I now felt that I had a great deal of silver at home. True, it had not been minted, but that did not seem to me to be important.

Then I climbed up again towards my summits, traversing the Geiselspitze in fog, armed only with a sketch I had made beforehand; for, having no camera, I had started making sketches of my summits. I had already sketched the Gross Venediger and the Gross Geiger, the first two really white peaks I had ever seen. I was also doing things quite near Salzburg. At Easter, I took a hammer and a chisel, and climbed the north face of the Schafberg, high above the Attersee. There were Christmas roses still blooming down in the woods, snow and ice above that, and finally rock. I felt dreadful, but I could not turn back, and got to the top in the dark. Today I would not dream of tackling it without crampons, and I shudder when I think of it – but young climbers in their early years have all the more need for an outsize guardian angel.

At that moment I discovered for myself a guiding spirit, though a wingless one: it was a book on my father's shelf. He had climbed a little himself in his younger days and later again during his military service. Over and again I had heard the story of his solo climb in army socks – he had left his forage-cap down below – on the Red Tower in the Lienz Dolomites; a story which grew more gripping every time it was repeated. Sometimes, too, when some of his old friends came to see us, I also heard about a certain chimney, up which they had hauled girls from Lienz – by preference fat ones – and how entertainingly Mina had got jammed in it.

The book was called *The Dangers of the Alps* – and it was a fat book at that. There was nothing about Mina in it – but it provided information about absolutely everything else: cornices and avalanches, bad weather, belaying with or without an axe, chimneys and overhangs, snow-slopes and glaciers. 'The Dangers of the Alps' said the jacket, 'by Zsigmondy and Paulcke'. Clearly, at that moment, nothing more interesting could have fallen into my hands . . . It is a certainty that there could be no book of greater interest, and it happened, not infrequently, at school that the margin of some history-book suddenly acquired the picture of a rescue from a crevasse or a snow-contour or the stratification of some mountain – for it was clearly of decisive importance whether one climbed on the top of the strata or toiled painfully up the outward-sloping pitched-roof on the reverse side . . .

My history teacher did not approve at all; but what he naturally could not understand was that it is no use being angry with such people, for they cannot be other than they are. And so I got my usual gamma minus for history again. On the credit side, I owed my life to the three-point rule of climbing when, on an easy but exposed pitch, a foot-hold came away. And it still seemed to me much more interesting to know why a glacier breaks up into crevasses, why in its ice those extraordinary interleavings of blue lie between the paler strata, why and how cornices form, and how to cut a step. When my father presented me with an ice-axe and a rope, I was the happiest person alive. For now I had everything I needed.

And what about grandfather's bicycle?

It was still going splendidly. Why shouldn't it visit Austria's highest mountain-pass, the Glocknerstrasse, which climbs to over 8,000 feet, and where the sharp peak of the Grossglockner soars another 4,000 above the Pasterze glacier at its base?

The trouble was, I had no mountaineering pal, and I didn't dare go up so high by myself. All the same I set off with a school-mate who was at the time a keen cyclist.

We marched and pushed our way up the Mölltal. It rained pitilessly and Erwin and I envied the odd motorist. We were wet to the skin and we never stopped moving all day, so as not to catch cold. In semi-darkness, dead tired, we sought the shelter of an old rick. By morning the hay was wet, and we were dry. When we crept out of our marmot-burrows, we found ourselves in brilliant sunshine. True, it was cold and snow had fallen far down the adjacent slopes, but the road soon had us warm again, rising gradually and steadily as it did, finally in wide hair-pin turns. We dismounted and reverted to pushing.

Suddenly, at the far head of the valley, a white peak appeared. That must be the Glockner! But it was not long before another and higher one gaining in height as we drew nearer, lifted its head. We swore that one must be the Glockner, but we were wrong again. At last it really came into view, unmistakable in its sharp and slender shape, lifting high above everything else in a dazzling mantle of fresh snow. My heart rejoiced at the very sight of it. Then, mastering my excitement, I thought: 'Suppose I could somehow climb it!'

Next day I persuaded my companion (Erwin came from Hanover, in the plains) to embark on the ascent of a neighbouring 'three-thousander'. We made good progress up it and a tiny glimmer of hope for the Gross-glockner awoke in me. Meanwhile, this mountain of ours was appropriately named the 'Sandkopf', which is exactly what it was: miles of debris-slopes and fine scree. Suddenly, I saw a crystal lying in the rubble and progress was abruptly halted. I dug down with both hands, working like a mole, and eventually found a couple more crystals. When I began to dig my fifth 'run', my friend started to show signs of discomfort. I assured him that it was my last but one, and he cheered up a little. After my fifth 'last but one', my finger-tips were wide open and Erwin, by my side, was complaining bitterly. It was late in the afternoon, so we turned back. Erwin was quite reconciled to his fate; far up in the rubble, he had found a horseshoe – heaven knows how it had got up there – and today he is a successful veterinary surgeon . . .

As we left the scree-slopes we saw something else for the first time ever: a whole meadow full of edelweiss, white many-starred clusters shining up at us everywhere, covering the whole meadow with a delicate veil of white. That evening I looked up at the Glockner with growing confidence: I didn't know how and with whom but somehow or other I should get there . . .

That inner feeling about 'yes' or 'no', which I used to have before decisive and often hopeless undertakings, giving me an answer in quite obscure situations, was to remain with me farther and farther into my life. Usually, the answer was 'yes'. Sometimes I did not trust it, and lived to regret my mistrust.

We were still ten miles from the Franz Josefshöhe, ten miles of mountain-road at a gradient of 12 per cent. When we got there, we would be 8,000 feet up and looking down on the grey-green ice-stream of the Pasterze. The Grossglockner would be opposite us, 12,461 feet high. It would take half a day's shoving our heavily-laden bikes, step by step, up those endless hairpins . . .

Next morning, when we left the little village of Heiligenblut, with its slender spire, we had become a threesome. A Viennese, by name Walter, had latched on to us. The important thing about him was that he belonged to the junior membership of the Alpenverein; so the summit of the Grossglockner had moved sensibly nearer. Proudly I showed Walter our edelweiss. 'Not bad,' he said, 'but they are cow-edelweiss – there are proper ones above the Pasterze.'

Cow-edelweiss, indeed . . . that same day we clung to the slabs and found the 'proper ones' – wonderful stars with slender white points. They lay like hoar-frost above their leaves, above the dull green of their stems, with their little yellow suns at the heart of each flower and the soft felt of their starry points, as clean and fresh as if they had just come from the laundry . . . then a clump of grass gave way . . . and I landed backwards on a ledge in the face.

'Stay where you are and don't move,' yelled Walter. I lay gasping for breath, my limbs numbed with fright. In the end, I pulled myself together and climbed up again; but I had had enough of edelweiss. Below where I landed, there was a drop of a hundred feet . . .

During the next two days, while Erwin went on a bicycle-tour over the Hochtor, the 8,200-foot summit of the pass, Walter and I actually climbed the Grossglockner. Even by its normal route it is a regal peak, steep, airy and exposed. No one is ever likely to forget the moment when he stands in the notch between the Klein and Grossglockner, with the Pallavicini Couloir plunging 3,000 feet from his toe-caps; and then, turning round, observes that there is a damnable amount of air below him on the southern face.

That was the first time I ever wore crampons, an ancient set of ten-pointers borrowed at the Franz Josefshöhe. 'Keep your legs wide apart!' Walter instructed me, as we worked our way up the steep slope from the Adlersruhe to the sharp-crested pyramid of the Kleinglockner, with the abyss deepening at every step beneath the soles of our boots. Suddenly – a crampon-point had got caught in the meshes of my stockings. There – oh, hell! – I stood balancing on one leg. Walter, belaying me undisturbed, laughed and said: 'What a thing! Now straighten yourself out and I think you'll have learned a lesson.' He was right, and yet it can happen to anyone at any moment, and there you are, poised on one leg

Grandfather's Bicycle

like a stork. The only difference being that the stork is used to it, while you don't find it amusing. 'Keep calm', is the only answer.

My clothes provided a remarkable contrast to my ice-equipment – consisting as they did of a leather jacket and, of all things, leather shorts, to which I was particularly devoted. Later when, at the cross on the summit, cold mists crept around my knees, I insisted on our starting down again at once. Some hours later a swift descent on their seat had restored my faith in that article of apparel. All the same their days were numbered, and it was the Gross Venediger which finally tipped the scales . . .

Walter disappeared, as he had arrived, and I have never heard a word of him again; but it was he who made a present to me of my Glockner.

I was now seventeen, and my life had undergone a decisive change in a very short time. Ever since, four years earlier, I had found that strange fossil in my trench among the Salzach's rubble, I never let up in my attempts to master more and more of the world. The crystals had led me to the mountains and grandfather's bicycle had laid open for me the road to distant places. I knew I was only at its beginnings, but what joy it was to explore, to guess, to find out everything that might lie along it. The circle in which I knew I had been confined had no limits; it was up to me to extend it ever more widely, to reach out impatiently even beyond it in my imagination, always to be pressing forward to new objectives.

As I rode along the Salzach valley and looked into the lateral valleys opening up to the south, to where the green of the forests took on a bluish tinge, I saw white peaks in the distance. There were more than a dozen such valleys; at the end of each, a high mountain. The road to all of them now lay open to me. I went to one of them, the Gross Venediger, for reasons I need not explain. It was simply the high white peak up above the crystals. There I met some people on their way to the Grosse Geiger and joined up with them. It was an expedition on which I seemed to be breaking out beyond myself, so changed were things since 'a little while ago'.

The Venediger was not at all kind to us. Above 10,000 feet we ran into a blizzard. In spite of all the advice of the nice old keeper at the Kürsinger Hut, I was again wearing my leather shorts – my beloved old gear . . . I was already pretty obstinate, even then.

All the same, we went to the summit, where there was nothing but snow and storm; we had no view at all. My elation at getting to the top was soon chilled and killed by the gale which seared my bare knees. I clamoured for the descent. Very soon my legs were entirely covered by a garment of clinking ice-tassels. 'My poor calves,' I wrote later in my diary, 'lots of little icicles, one hanging from every hair. A proper pelt.'

I ran as much as was possible and, although they say that ice is an excellent insulator, I made a vow, on the spot, never again to go up high wearing the leathern rig of the chamois-hunter and the poacher.

A few days later, however, we saw the summit of 'our' Venediger as we had looked forward to seeing it. No, it was even better than we had imagined it would be; for that sun-drenched day was a very gift from Heaven, up there on the glittering snow, high above the valleys in their autumnal glory. One of those rare days you can hardly dare to hope for, ever again.

Willi, from Vienna, was the leader of our party. I had been deeply impressed, during the preceding days, with his ability to find the way even in the worst weather. He seemed to know exactly what was bound to happen in any given situation. He was pleased with me, the youngest member, who came up last on the rope, because I had twice stopped a fall, over there on the Geiger, by the speed with which I rammed home my ice-axe.

Between us went Eva and Trude, two girls from Berlin – and let me add at once that the mountains have nothing on Berlin girls!

Forgotten was the icy storm on the Venediger, forgotten my frozen knees, as if they had never been. We were all hot with excitement and expectation of the magic mountain rising before us. I remember winding my handkerchief around my axe, so cold was it as we moved across the glacier in the twilight of dawn. The Venediger loomed pale overhead, above the slender ribs of its north face and the curling cornices that swept up with its ridges. Under a velvet sky the snow drew a soft line across the broad saddle towards the Klein Venediger – yet another pyramid. The last stars were flickering. Each of us was alone with his thoughts, the rope our only link. And as we climbed slowly up towards the first icefall, my 'Voice' of those days recorded:

'Away to the east lay a tumultuous cloud-wrack, coloured from a marvellous orange to red and pale green. The sun was not up yet, the pale and misty sky changed from a steely grey to brilliant green and later to bright red and yellow. A dull sheen lay on the ice-armour of the Venediger's summit, lifting above the north face, deeply scored by dark runnels of ice. Where was the sun . . .? As though touched by some ghostly finger, the very tip of the Venediger began to gleam a delicate red; slowly the gentle light flowed farther and farther down the face, till the whole peak hung high above us, bathed in the brilliant morning light,

Grandfather's Bicycle

while we were still in darkness. "The glacier looks as if someone had poured raspberry syrup over it," Trude remarked. The sun was up now; all the summits were now lit by it, only we were still in the shadow of the hollow. Would we too meet light and warmth up there on the saddle? Here it was cracking cold, and my hand and the handkerchief froze to the steel of my axe.

'We were on the last slope leading to the saddle, going slowly up. The angle eased. Thirty yards ahead of me, Willi let out a yell of surprised delight: he was standing in sunshine. As I joined him, I almost had to close my eyes to meet the blinding flood of light that beset me and enveloped me, cancelling out gravity itself. Trude expressed that sensation when she said: "Now I'm floating away on the sunbeams." Our dark-blue shadows alone broke the shimmer and glitter of that virgin snow-slope; for we were the first to come up here since the storm. We were happy beyond description. The remaining peaks of the Venediger group rose out of the flood of light; far away soared the Glockner, and the blue world of spires over there, that must be the Dolomites. A world of savage turrets and walls, with the Drei Zinnen easily recognizable. The shadows, far below us in the valleys, could not even climb up to us; they simply disappeared under the flood of light. We felt weightless as we mounted the summit itself, halting there only briefly. Today there were no limits to the view: one could see right across to the Ötztal Alps.'

For us too there were no limits that day, not even for our cautious Willi. A wild euphoria had seized upon us all, as the four of us strolled, arm-in-arm, down the Venediger to the Rainerhorn, straight into the eye of the sun. The rope behind us dragged on the surface of the snow, but we didn't care. And we sang the song of the Tyrolese girl, which had become our Venediger theme-song: 'Hollariariaholadi – holadio . . .!' There in front of us rose the Rainerhorn. We bagged it, too, and celebrated on its summit with song.

Then across to the Hohen Zaun, the next summit. It was not till we were making our light-hearted way down on the other side to the Defregger Hut that we met people – a whole column of them, coming up, with slow and measured tread, as is right and proper. At least ten of them; a hearty crowd of women-climbers of the 'Touristenclub'. They looked askance and shook their heads at our casual procedures, but we were off and away by then.

That was by no means the end of our day – we dined on a few drops of glacier-water, some porridge-oats, lumps of sugar, and a swig of lemonade – then rubbed sunburn-cream on our lips again, for they were going altogether to pieces today. After lazing about for an hour high above the

Defregger Saddle we crossed the Maurertörl and completed our circuit of the Venediger. By the time we reached the Kürsinger Hut, we had been out for fifteen hours. Our 'Hollariaria – holadi – ho – ladiho' in honour of the Gross Venediger sounded a little subdued. After that it began to snow heavily ... In my excitement I had quite overlooked the fact that school had started three days ago.

If I have strayed somewhat from the theme of grandfather's bicycle, my excuse must be that so important a mountain as the Gross Venediger was responsible – and the blue world of the Dolomite towers rising above the glittering snow of the saddle ...

My friend Peter and I had agreed to leave Salzburg and get to those Dolomites and, once there, to travel the length and breadth of that fairyland of rocky shapes. On our bicycles, of course. Peaks? Yes, some of those too – if possible. I could still see the stark faces of the Lienz Dolomites in my mind's eye.

We were just due to leave, when Peter arrived with death and disaster written all over his face. 'I can't come,' he said. '*She* says I have to choose between her and the mountains!' I was very sorry for him.

He lent me his Leica to take along and I promised to bring back some slides for himself. I had two colour-films – my first – to capture the meadows full of flowers at the foot of the Dolomites and the bright colouring of their rocky walls, as described to me by those who knew.

Milestones, milestones, milestones, rain, rain, rain ... wet roads ... rain ... dense grey clouds, with dark lumps of limestone sticking into them ... soaked through ... all alone ... and the Dolomites as wet as my climbing-slippers ... push the thing uphill again ... would I get to Cortina today? ... anyway, what should I do when I got there? So far as I cared, the devil could scoff the lot.

I wondered whether I could latch on to a lorry, if one came past. Latch on, I did, and the driver didn't notice me. Well, now I should at least cover some ground; though what was the use in this filthy weather?

My goodness, he's stepping on it! Of course, it's level here, but it'll soon be going uphill again. Just you hang on! Crash, bang, splinter ... I found myself hanging on the lorry's tail-board. It had stopped. My bicycle was somewhere underneath it.

The driver came round and helped me to get it out – I was almost in tears. The front wheel had had it in a big way, otherwise ... no damage? Miraculous. What about the main members of the frame? No, only the front wheel. That was bad enough, though.

Grandfather's Bicycle

Two days later I left Cortina, with a bare 3,000 lire in my pocket, and pushed my repaired mount up towards the Falzarego Pass. It was drizzling steadily and the lumps of limestone thrust up into cloud, as usual. The whole of the Dolomites were soaking wet, and so was I.

At last a shape emerged from the veils of cloud – the Cinque Torri. I recognized them from the postcards. At least, and at last, I had seen a peak.

Some hours later, the clouds parted and the gigantic mass of the Tofana rose above them. What a mountain, what a precipice! And then, far to the west, there emerged a white dome. That must be the Marmolata, the only snow-peak in this realm of rock-towers.

At the summit of the pass I remounted, and flew down the wonderful road, with its finely built-out hairpins. Down and down I raced – it was quite fantastic. I was heading straight into the sun, now low in the west, under low banks of cloud. The road had flattened out. I met a few people on it, passed a few houses. A deep valley opened up on my left. There, to the south, rose an immense mountain – glowing ghostly red against the dark background of the sky: a dragon's spine, surmounted by spikes, looming longer and longer, a gigantic wall in the red sunset lave. Breath failed me, my brake squealed, as I drew in to the side of the road, bemused. There, to the south, stood that ghostly mountain, a mass of glowing organ-pipes, barring the whole breadth of the valley. An old peasant came trudging slowly by. 'What is that?' I asked him, and pointed to the great red wall. '*E la Civetta,*' he replied, as if this were an everyday occurrence, and continued on his way.

The Civetta. I never forgot her. Many years later, I was to return and climb that mighty face; but I will never see her again as I saw her at that moment.

Milestones, one after another, in the sunshine, as I pushed my bicycle up towards the Pordoi Pass, among the flowery meadows of the Dolomites, brightly lit by the sun, with the Tofana's summit now far away behind. There were very few cars; the sunny road belonged to me, as did the gigantic rectangular masses of the Sella group above it. So did the grasshopper which crossed the road in great leaps; and the snail sitting at the edge of the road near by, pointing its horns. For some unfathomable reason, it wanted to cross the road too. I picked it up and carried it across. Fancy having as much time as a snail! As a matter of fact I had. It was a gorgeous day.

Step by step, I went up on snow, with my ice-axe and in my rock-climbing slippers, towards the foot of the Boë-spitze, the highest elevation in the Sella group – a rock-peak, with a flat cone lifting above huge rectangular cliffs for its summit. I met more and more snow-fields, of hard frozen snow, with wet fresh snow lying on top of it. My leather shoes got wetter and wetter, and larger and larger – I had taken the 'old master' Paulcke too literally and left my heavy climbing-boots in Salzburg – larger and larger grew my shoes . . .

Finally, having got to the top, I dangled my feet, and my shoes too, in the sunshine. Opposite me, encircled by cloud, flanked by the sharp Vernel ridges, stood the Marmolata, with its broad white glacier, curving steep and massive valley-wards. It was quite irresistible . . . Below it the road twisted like a worm through the gaily-coloured Pordoi meadows.

But what could I do, without boots?

I stood on the Marmolata's summit, in climbing-boots as big as those famous Seven League ones. I had simply gone into a little inn down at the Joch and asked the innkeeper if he would lend me his boots for a climb of the Marmolata. Below me, the South Face plummeted in a fearsome drop to immeasurable depths. It must be awful to plunge to one's death from a Dolomite face . . . they were really no place for anyone but a good rock-climber, and even then they were horrific. Very carefully, hold by hold, I felt my way down from that airy view-point by the way I had come. In deep thought I went down the glacier and across the meadows, redolent with a cloud of cinnamon scent from the small dark-red flowers that covered them, to the Pordoijoch, where I returned his boots to the innkeeper.

The Karersee,* that small tarn, a perfect subject for a colour-slide. I took one for Peter, too. Crystal-clear turquoise water, its dark pine woods and the grey towers of the Latemar above.

I sat by its shore and gave my machine 'full service', surrounded by my pliers, my 'King Dick', ball-bearing-grease, oil-can, a cleaning rag, and a sparrow hopping around and complaining because I had nothing more to give him. This was a lovely place; I would push on in the evening – somewhere. Meanwhile, this spoke needed straightening, and there was the rattling mudguard-ring . . . Somewhere, but where? Perhaps past the Marmolata's southern base . . . look, here's another spoke . . . over the Pellegrino Pass to the Civetta . . . And then the carrier, always getting perilously bent: I should have to load it some other way, or find some additional support for it . . .

* In Italian: Lago di Carezza.

Grandfather's Bicycle

That Latemar, up there ... its towers and turrets looking for all the world like recruits, the first time they are told to fall in and dress their ranks, with a certain natural disorder, a sort of irregular regularity, like the rows of pine-trunks rising from the other shore of the lake ...

I won't move on tonight. I shall traverse the Latemar tomorrow. I want to see it from near by.

I did that, and a great many other things besides; and, wherever I went, everyone exhibited an interest in, and enthusiasm for, cycling which was quite new to me. They were very kind, and let me know that a cyclist was a highly-respected person in the Dolomites – even a cyclist riding his grandfather's bike. I was even asked for which great race I was in training; and I noted in my diary – 'Yesterday, as I sped full-tilt through a village, the children shouted at the top of their voices: "*Evviva Bartale! Evviva Coppi! Evviva!*"' I swung into the next curves with my chest proudly puffed-out, speeding, and feeling, like a champion, only slowing up again as soon as I was out of sight.

Of course, I sent a postcard to my grandfather: 'I have been promoted to the top class. The bicycle is still in one piece. Five Dolomite passes so far, and plan to do three more.' Certainly I had discovered and mastered the Dolomites on a bicycle; experienced, over and over again, the excitement of the unknown view that would unfold beyond the pass – a prize only to be won by long hours of hard work. But then everyone who loves adventure must be prepared to accept hard work – or he will lose both.

And many a motorist – perhaps I should add, many a mountaineer, too? – who thinks on different lines from the cyclist, must none the less realize that he who cheerfully surmounts hairpin after hairpin of a pass under his own steam, yet enjoys a great deal of pleasure in so doing, is totally involved with that 'mountain'; its summit is an aim which he has set himself, and when at last he gets there, great is his joy.

It goes without saying that riding down the other side, free as a bird and motorless, is sheer delight. But that is not all of it. The cyclist has his 'why and wherefor' just as has the mountaineer; though neither of them could explain it. And both earn their 'dimension' again and again.

The Matterhorn

AN EXPEDITION

The Matterhorn, that slender spire, lifting indescribably above the Zermatt Valley – every climber's dream-wish ... sketched, painted, photographed, described in a hundred different accounts, familiar to all ... and yet only really known to those who have actually seen it ...

Erich, Gundl and I had not seen it yet. For us it was a mysterious mountain, clothed in legends, far, far away, somewhere over the horizon, in an unknown land. To reach it meant, for us, a real expedition. We had never been to the Western Alps. We had no money; but we had our dreams – dreams of unknown peaks, in unknown countries – at least, those we could get to on our bicycles.

The Matterhorn ... this legendary Matterhorn ... this 'mountain of mountains', over 13,000 feet high; no, nearly 15,000 – it kept on growing, this *Matterhorn*! Why not make straight for it? It drew us irresistibly; though, of course, we didn't know how we should fare at such an altitude – we had never been on a 'four-thousander'.

By now I believed we could climb it. I had heard a lecture by the 'Dachstein Priest'. I did not know exactly who he was, but he didn't look as tough as all that. If he had climbed it, we could!

It was a splendid lecture, entitled 'The Valaisian Peaks'. We were introduced to the white wall of the Lyskamm, with its perilous cornices – not that it looked dangerous, just white and beautiful – but if he said so ... Yes, after all, its crest did look dangerous, and it too was over 13,000 feet – yet another four-thousander, surpassing that magic level.

Why not combine the two targets – legendary Matterhorn and our first four-thousander, both at the same time? In short, why not go straight for the Matterhorn? If that cosy-looking old gentleman had climbed it, we could. I marvelled at him; as he spoke, the mountain drew ever nearer, acquired rocks, ridges, pitches, arêtes. Yes, we would make a bee-line for this Matterhorn, making no détours, paying no attention to other peaks, on the way ...

The holidays came round. In front of me the big rollers of a colour

The Matterhorn: an Expedition

machine were grinding away, crushing powder in clouds of green, blue and red dust. I fed the mixture, strictly in accordance with the recipe, and dreamed of the Matterhorn. I had taken this temporary job, so as to earn some much-needed money. The firm promptly went into liquidation.

So I went to Aunt Betty, who, I knew, had a kind heart. 100 schillings from her – well, that was a start. Then to Aunt Traudl ('Hallo, Kurty, glad to see you!'). Enough for the three-speed gear for my bike. Then to Uncle Hans ... and ... and ... to all the relatives I could think of. With very few exceptions – and I suppose, in their cases, my failure to visit them before was responsible – they had all heard of the Matterhorn. Even if it wasn't Mount Everest, the expedition's funds grew satisfactorily. To all of them I promised a picture of the Matterhorn, for their living-room, their kitchen, the corridor – it was their problem where to hang it, not mine.

I believe Erich, who was eighteen, a year younger than I, was doing much the same; while our buxom Gundl, with the long plaits, who was only sixteen, was busy working on her mother, in their Styrian home, for the mere permission to come along. It was only when I drew up a detailed list of equipment and provender – 'the thousand minutiae' – that her mother realized on what a serious undertaking we were embarking.

We pedalled and pedalled and pedalled ... we got off and pushed ... we got on again and tore downhill ... then we pedalled, pedalled and pedalled again ... still not less than a week to our Matterhorn.

We entered this unknown Switzerland. Spit-and-polish houses, wonderful hotels, everything neat and tidy. Anyone who slept rough got himself fined. The passes were high, the peaks higher still. And the prices ... ! We post-war Austrians couldn't believe our eyes. That didn't bother us, however. We lived on our rucksacks, boiled our tea at the roadside; our 'bikes' were amply loaded with what we had brought along – everything we needed.

Push, push, push – all the way up the Furka Pass, which we reached on the stroke of midnight. Our impatience to see the Matterhorn knew no bounds – a shepherd over there on the Oberalp Pass had told us that one can pick out its summit from here in clear weather. Well, we should just have to wait till morning. Now, to find a site for our tent ... This was a puzzle, for the heavy rubber-coated 'Special' tent my father had given me had no struts – presumably because its designer was an optimist. It had a loop at the top, so that you could hang it up somewhere ...

We wandered about the dark summit of the Pass – we would gladly have hanged the designer of that loop from the sickle-moon overhead.

We found no hooks; so we lay down and crawled into that chilly skin. The only ray of light was Gundl, in between us, comfortable in the fleece sleeping-bag. My knees were gradually coated in hoar-frost, but my back, at least, was warm. During the early hours, Erich devised several suitable methods for liquidating our clever designer.

Up came the sun . . . we stood there with chattering teeth, looking at the dark rocky summit in the dim distance, hardly distinguishable between white ridges. There it was, at last, the Matterhorn . . . still miles away.

'A cup of hot coffee?' This was unbelievable. A friendly man in field-grey uniform had come out of a house at the roadside and invited us in. However, when Gundl asked him if he could shoot as well as he made coffee, he became distinctly less friendly. Swiss soldiers, he explained, were among the best in the world: they even took their rifles home with them and kept them in a cupboard there, always ready to hand. And he showed Gundl his rifle. On that same day she upset a Swiss woman badly, by innocently referring to the Rhône as a 'brook'.

When, at last, we came close to the Matterhorn, it towered to gigantic heights above us, with a banner of cloud flying from its summit.

We had never imagined it could be so high; and we felt like midgets.

We looked up from time to time at the great spike, at its cloud-banner. Did we really mean to go up there? Ought we not first try the gentler Breithorn?

A man with impressive yellow stockings was coming up the path from near-by Zermatt. By way of small-talk we told him, without any beating around the bush, what our plans were – and that we intended to stay at least a week or ten days. At which point he declared himself as the collector of the local 'Residence-tax'; and could he please have eight days' worth of it, on the spot . . .

'*Residence-Tax?*' Surely our ears were deceiving us – this must be some kind of mistake. We were living in a tent – not much 'residence' about that, surely? In any case, we didn't propose to pay a red cent of our precious money. Indignation, anger, heated argument followed on either side. Nothing would move the man with those jolly stockings. So, off the four of us marched to the police-station.

We consulted among ourselves – suppose the man was right? At the last moment I had a brain-wave. Very politely, we explained to the Police Inspector that it had all been a misunderstanding – true, we were going to spend a week near the Matterhorn, but on its Italian side. *This* was only a short staging-post on our way to the frontier . . .

The Collector looked murder at me. The last barrier was down. Then

The Matterhorn: an Expedition

we proceeded – still on the Swiss side – up to the hut. How would we fare tomorrow, we wondered?

It was dark. Ahead of us we could see electric-torches winking. We could hear ice-axes clinking against rock. The shapes of towers in the ridge were silhouetted around us. Overhead, a gigantic dark mass bulked up – the summit.

The cold air was tense with expectation. We must be sure not to lose contact, in the darkness, with the guided parties in front. The three of us were climbing, roped together, up pitches and over shadowy blocks in the gloom. It wasn't particularly difficult, but a little complicated – and endlessly high. There, now we had lost contact, after all . . .

Daylight came. We were absolutely on our own. Friable slabs, brittle ledges, everything crumbling, crumbling. Were we still really on the right track, following scratch-marks? I had just jumped to safety from a stance that broke away beneath my feet. The blocks went crashing down into the depths . . . Gundl watched them with startled eyes. Erich shook his head – there goes another! This can't be the right way. Then we heard voices coming down from the right, higher up the ridge. Up that way, then – out on to the east face . . .

We were at 12,500 feet. There stood the Solvay Hut, an eagle's eyrie clinging to the edge of the rocks; a shelter should the weather change – but at present it was fine. We drew in deep breaths of the thin air of the four-thousanders for the first time – yes, it was rarer, and cleaner. We felt fine.

Over there, that white comb must be the Lyskamm. I remembered the 'Dachstein Priest's' lecture. That was the Weisshorn, and over there the Obergabelhorn, and there the Dent Blanche, and the cluster of Monte Rosa's five summits. How huge and lovely it all was, and how proud we were to be mounting higher and higher on 'our' Matterhorn and not on the gently-rounded Breithorn. Grey fog was slowly forming a cowl over the sharp outlines of our summit. It was noon. Another thousand feet to go. Then it was afternoon.

How far now? Everything was dim and grey around us. Everything fell away precipitously, like the pitch of a steep roof. Gasping for breath, we were now working our way up on all fours. We glanced timidly downwards, to the horrific abyss yawning below us – the North Face, directly under us.

The ridge flattened, the snow levelled off. Was that a cross over there? Ye sons of man, we were up! We were on top! On the summit ridge. A few yards more. We embraced, hugged each other, danced with joy. We had captured our Matterhorn – we three had done it!

True, we could see nothing, absolutely nothing – no mountains, no valleys – only one another, some rocks, some snow and a cross, ghostly in the fog. But it was the summit-cross on the Matterhorn.

The wind was howling round the Solvay Refuge, rattling its roof, tugging at its planks, in the night. We felt comfortable and safe, up there at 13,700 feet. Everything had gone smoothly on the descent, except for a mishap on the summit's steep roof, when Erich suddenly found himself hanging on one spike of his crampons and shortly afterwards landed on my shoulders after a short tumble. We looked down the abyss of the north face in terror. Fortunately, I was belayed.

Yes, we had been lucky. Our first four-thousander had entailed some risk, and we hardly knew enough to realize all the dangers involved. But when you are eighteen, you are inclined to go straight for what you want, without lengthy détours.

We lay there in the hut, too tired and happy to make any further plans. One thing was quite certain: this was not the last time we should be coming here.

What is it, then, that turns a dream into an aim? Just those little words: 'I want to.' Let us leave insuperable difficulties to those who believe such things exist.

For me, the Matterhorn was a giant's stride into the future. On it, I learned, for the first time, what one can achieve, if one really wants to.

One Step . . .

The old churchyard at Courmayeur is different from other churchyards; at least so it seems to me. The wooden war-crosses stand there like sinister birds of prey, with anonymous, white marble ones between. Mont Blanc and the Dent du Géant look down on it all.

Among those curious crosses stands one that doesn't seem to belong there at all – two simple wooden planks, cruciform. Yet it does belong there . . . Erich. He fell from the Dent du Géant.

Whenever Wolfi and I pass through Courmayeur, we usually go down to the old churchyard. Mostly we go separately, just as it happens to come into one or the other's mind. If I find a few wild-flowers there, I know Wolfi has been. Though it could have been the amiable, white-haired Headmistress of the kindergarten in Entrèves, just as well . . .

Four of us had come to Courmayeur together; all of us on our first visit. Mont Blanc towered gigantic over the green of the valley – almost 13,000 feet above us, draped in thin clouds, in banners of snow. We wheeled our push-bikes happily through the narrow alley-ways, watching the gaily-hued life of the place; buying a few trifles. Erich beamed through his glasses, his whole happy student-face alight with pleasure. 'My children,' he said, 'in a few days we shall be standing on that great mountain up there!' And he looked up at Mont Blanc, high over the roof-tops.

He had come with his Peilstein climbing-partner, Wolfgang Stefan, dark, slight, quiet, though sometimes very funny. He was a student too. They had been training hard recently and had reached a pretty high standard. I had Peter Heilmayer, from Salzburg, with me; he had not been climbing as long as the others, but he was keenness itself. We had all still to get used to the thin air, so we had decided not to make Mont Blanc our first objective.

The first thing we needed was a 'base camp'! We looked around for one, and in due course – in Italy anything can happen – found ourselves sitting in the middle of a kindergarten, cared for and cosseted, adulated and admired – talking broken Italian to the best of our ability. The Headmistress, a friendly old lady, saw to our every need; even the kitchen-staff was glad to take a look at, and to look after, some of these tough guys, who hang on ropes from icy walls, just in order – God knows why! – to climb some savage peak. We were, of course, delighted, explaining what we meant to do, letting them darn our socks, even allowing them – after a little hesitation – to wash our smalls. We tried to jodel, learned the *'Montanara'*, sang the *'Bergvagabunden'* song to them, and the whole kindergarten then proceeded to serenade us with the *'chiesetta alpina'*, which moved me (rapidly promoted to the status of professional photographer) to take a group picture. And, of course, we should be coming back to see them, year after year . . .

Erich was laughing and winking at me, as I had the whole kindergarten lined up in front of us, and unfolded my tripod with true professional skill; a real *fotografo* to the life, posing a few individual figures, with all the vision and assured hand-gestures of a true artist – until, finally, I pressed the shutter. We all laughed as I wiped my forehead with my Sunday-best handkerchief. It was all just too good to be true. Not in the wildest dreams of a mountaineer was there ever such a base camp, so many nice people all gathered in one spot!

We had decided to make the Dent du Géant our first climb. It is a savage rock-tooth, over 13,000 feet high. Well, actually, the figure is a little misleading, for it is the precise altitude reached by the summit. If you approach it by the normal route, all you have to do is less than 3,000 feet of steep but easy snow and rock, to the actual foot of the Tooth itself. Then there is only 700 feet of real climbing, to get to the top. No easy climbing this – Grade III – but we knew there were fixed ropes. We had been told how fearfully airy the climb was; when you clung to the front face of the needle, there was nothing but 3,000 feet or more of thin air under the soles of your boots.

We crossed the bergschrund, and I roped up with Peter, the least experienced member of the party.

'Aren't you going to rope up too?' I asked the others.

'We've got crampons – we'll get along all right.'

They certainly were getting along all right, obviously in tremendous form. Soon they were up there, on the *'Gengiva'*, the 'Gum', at the foot of the Tooth itself, where they had agreed to wait for us.

Our successive rope's-lengths ran out; time moved leisurely by. At last we reached the ridge, close to the huge tower, with its vertical walls of reddish-brown granite. Over there, Wolfi and Erich were traversing the sloping snow-field of the *'Gengiva'*. Then . . . Erich

One Step . . .

slipped . . . threw himself face-down on his axe, braking his slide . . . but, no! . . . he went on sliding . . . Why, in heaven's name, didn't the axe grip? . . . went on sliding . . . sliding . . . sliding . . . out of sight . . .

Wolfi was standing there, shattered, struck dumb. We rushed across to him, arrived breathless. Quick! There was nothing to be seen, but possibly . . . Quick! Wolfi was lowering me on the rope.

There was a score in the snow . . . where he had tried to get a hold with his hands . . . then a couple of rocks – could he have grabbed them? We shouted: silence from the great white abyss. Could he be hanging, caught up in those rocks, having somehow got a grip, somewhere? Unconscious . . . ?

Or? Too horrible to contemplate. It *mustn't* have happened!

The farther I moved down that white surface on the rope – it soon became a sheer gully – the more sure I was of the dreadful truth. It was hard, bone-hard down here, not a chance of checking one's fall, nothing to get a hold on, nothing but a slide at increasing speed.

They added another rope, and I reached the rocks. Nothing . . . no Erich . . . nowhere . . . no answer from the bottomless depths. It had really happened.

Wolfi saw me safely up on the rope, threw me a questioning glance. I looked at him, and he knew.

If we came up from the bottom, we should find him – or would we? He might be lying on the top of a pillar, or in a crevice in that 3,000-foot precipice; or even, over there, on the other side. Could he possibly be alive still? We hurried down the normal route, hoping for a miracle in which we no longer had any faith.

There was a party coming up. Had they seen or noticed anything? Heard anything? No, not a thing; had something happened, then? Yes, one of us had gone, fallen down the face. We left them standing there incredulous, and hurried on, down, down into those awful depths. We looked down on to an old cone of avalanche-snow, far, far down in a bay at the bottom of the face. We saw an elongated black stain on it. Could it be Erich? That kind of snow is not as hard as rock; he might have been lucky – Dear God, grant he had had luck, like Payer when he fell on the Ortler! – but then, of course, it might not be Erich, after all.

We raced down, panting for breath, never seeming to get any nearer. It was a long, long way down – we had already been more than an hour. The stain was the shape of a man. It didn't move. Could be . . .

No way down, here – everything fell away savagely into a hollow, more than a thousand feet, below us. We should have to come round from outside and below, skirting the base of the wall.

There was that dark thing down there on the snow – probably Erich. Nearly 3,000 feet below the '*Gengiva*'. Dear God!

We circled round the base of the rocks, crossing level snow towards the hollow, where the avalanche-cone gradually came into view.

Wolfi ran on ahead up the last 300 feet – I was past following, my knees had gone soft on me. Yes, that bundle up there was a man, was Erich, motionless on the bloodstained snow. Wolfi had reached it. And there he stood, just stood.

At last I arrived. Yes, it was he; his anorak, the grey rift, the . . .

There was a cry in the silence.

It was Erich, his face shockingly disfigured. Wolfi was still standing there, dumb, motionless. I watched the tears running down his face.

That afternoon, we brought him down to Entrèves. Once again he lay in the triangular tent we had used on the Matterhorn. Then we placed him on a bier in the little chapel, over whose slate roof we had looked up at Mont Blanc a few days before.

What was the point of it all —?

We held a vigil over our dead all through the night. I had never seen the stars so big as they were that night; they flickered as though a storm were passing over Heaven itself. Inexplicable.

And most inexplicable of all – there were voices in the air.

Neither Wolfi nor I could give it up. For us the mountains meant everything, as they had for Erich. Not even his death could alter that. Only Peter gave up climbing, later on. Of course we had to ask ourselves whether falling stones, avalanches, a disintegrating hold might not one day dictate an end to it all, however much care we exerted? Could be – but we said 'no' and took great precautions with our belaying. Wolfi and I went climbing together more and more, we were ideally matched, and we became a rope of two – a rope of two equal partners, Diemberger-Stefan or Stefan-Diemberger, each capable of leading it, equally capable of acting as second, according to circumstances. Mostly we led turn and turn about, for our understanding was complete.

Naturally, that did not all come about in a single day. Every mountaineer knows that a real rope partnership is a kind of communal life, in which complete mutual confidence has to be built up. For when one partner, in full knowledge of his own competence, caution or courage, decides to make a move, to use a piton or not, to give up or to go on – his decision absolutely involves the life of the other, bound to him by the same rope. One does not forget that.

One thing is indisputable: everyone you knot-up on a rope with you is different, and on the mountains you will learn to know him. For they reveal each man for what he is.

Without our meticulous and iron-hard training in climbing techniques on Vienna's Peilstein, Wolfi and I could hardly be alive today, after the countless climbs we have done together. And, in spite of everything, it must be admitted that once or twice we both owed our survival to our lucky stars, or to the other's skill. The summer climbing seasons which ensued were long ones: during one, we climbed twenty-five four-thousanders, including some great traverses; the next took us from the Wilde Kaiser to the Bregaglia, on to Mont Blanc, back to the Valais and finally to the Brenta Dolomites. Gradually we grew more and more at home in the whole great sweep of the Alps between Vienna and Marseilles. Then I, too, began to live the greater part of the year in the city of two million inhabitants, which was Wolfi's birthplace.

Fortunately, the Alps begin on its doorstep, in the Wienerwald.

Book-keeping and Pull-ups

Post-war Vienna. From the 'Piaristenkeller' rises the theme-song of 'The Third Man'; the town is punctuated by Russians and Americans, with a few British and French thrown in. Everyone is on his best behaviour, and fraternizes; we have been 'liberated', but unfortunately we are 'occupied'. Some years were still to roll by before Austrian *laissez faire* and Russian Vodka would combine to negotiate a bilateral agreement. 'But,' said the Viennese, 'we'll live it out!'

Early each morning, with a thunderous roar, the No 13 came rolling along the Piaristengasse, in District 8; faded-red, ancient and rust-covered – the tram. Later, at regular intervals, right through till the evening. When it came, the peace of the Alley, in which passers-by and pigeons promenaded happily, for few motor-cars used it, was rudely shattered. And every time No 13, having completed its approach-run the length of the straight road, took the bend opposite the Tröpferlbad, the air was rent by martial sounds – a squealing, a howling, a grating cacophony, which penetrated the topmost storeys as well as the deepest cellars. However, Frau Sedlacek and Herr Navratil, on the ground floor, both dismissed it with the same casual acceptance. 'Only the No 13.' they thought; for the Viennese can get used to anything.

Indeed, No 13 belonged to the very life and being of that thoroughfare. Only the tram-driver registered a protest every morning against his miserable lot. Since I lived directly above the bend, I was able to observe how he deliberately took a run, the whole length of the Piaristengasse, so that he could thunder into the curve with the greatest possible momentum: there could be no doubt that it was done on purpose. Did he want to arouse the conscience of the world? Because he was unhappy with his job? Had he got a grudge against the bend? Or did he simply want to wake us to a new day?

The rails had to be replaced every six months. Fortunately for us, No 13 did not run at night. All the same, it was cruelly early in the morning when it thundered past my window for the first time each day, to be followed immediately by that marrow-shattering screech. Then the Piaristengasse was wide awake. So was I . . .

Surely the man hadn't really meant to be a tram-driver at all; he must have had something quite different in mind?

And that thought brought back to my mind my pages of book-keeping material . . .

What was to become of me – me, the crystal-hunter, the cyclist, the embryo climber? I knew one could achieve anything one really wanted to – but what was I to want? There was no career to fit me.

If all the millions I was transferring from one account to another were really mine, I knew well enough what my goal would be: Exploration . . . Voyages of discovery . . .

There were Sven Hedin and Heinrich Harrer, for instance; how had they managed it? Riches would be the solution but – by Columbus, as I broke an egg into the frying-pan on the electric cooker! – reality was very different. These were the facts of life: a remote back-room in a students' hostel in the Piaristengasse – forty schillings a month, three beds, three chests and a heating-stove that didn't work. There the three of us sat, opposite each other, warmly-clad against the cold, in fleece-jackets, sheepskins and a couple of blankets round our shoulders – the ex-commando parachutist from the North Africa front, now turned sculptor; a book-keeper who would not be finished with his exams for years, though he was fully competent; and I. Our way of life was rather like that of an expedition's base camp; and female visitors were taboo. (According to the latest reports the ladies of Vienna later occupied the hostel by way of a protest: but not in our time.) The parachutist-sculptor carved religious statues; as he said, you have to earn a living somehow. And then, for his own amusement, he made the most wonderful drawings.

As for me, in spite of everything, I had discovered my own little America, one I could manage – the Peilstein in the Wienerwald – that climbers' practice-ground, with its innumerable crannies and climbs. Back there again tomorrow on my bike! According to the Peilstein Song:

> 'There's fever and fun, and the boys and the girls
> Climbing the rocks like flies up a wall;
> And if, in their sport, should one of them fall . . .'

No, no falling for me, thank you; the one taste of it, recently, had been quite enough of a good thing. Railli, supposed to be belaying me, had taken a beautiful header into thin air; however, the piton had held. Now, let's see how fit I am. Twenty – yes, really, twenty – pull-ups on the door-frame! What do I care about non-existent millions in an account-book?

I wondered whether the Career-Consultant, who turned up one day at the Graduation-class, was right: he said I hadn't a hope. After I had filled up the questionnaire ('Would you sooner be a chimney-sweep or a dentist?') with meticulous care, to the great delight of the class, I developed the curved line on a test-sheet, not into a little sponge or even an umbrella, but into a caricature of our Careerist – complete with three tiny hairs on his bald cranium. Not even a staggering likeness between the test-line and that refulgent dome could persuade him that I had great talent. (God is just: and I too count my ultimate blessings.)

And what else didn't I do? I spent six months intoning, in a bass voice, Schubert's songs and Sarastro, to please the lady who taught me singing and was certain that I was a great 'find', for whom she prophesied a splendid future. Vowel-production: 'The rain in Spain falls mainly on the plain' . . . six months of it. Then I rejected other heavier precipitation on the more level parts of Iberia because they told me to give up climbing, for the good of my voice. And Sarastro was converted to mountain-gypsy tunes on the guitar.

What about rocks? A career as a mining-engineer? I left Leoben in a hurry at the end of a single term. Was I to spend the whole of my life sitting near a mine? Quite impossible. Geology? No future in that, they told me in Vienna, at the time. I hesitated and made a big mistake, by not taking up Geology. Business? Not exactly exciting. But business-instructors were always wanted, and teaching was a family tradition. So I would be a business-instructor – that would at least give me time for the mountains. In four years I should have my University of Commerce diploma – and only then could I start to pass the special exams for being a teacher.

Four years sitting in a fleece-jacket in an unheated room in Vienna were undoubtedly good training for the icy giants of the Western Alps. Likewise the pull-ups on the frame of the door . . .

And then, the Peilstein. First with Railli, then with Wolfi, year in, year out, I was always to be found in that exciting realm of smooth towers and walls of superb grey limestone. There, right in the middle of the Wienerwald, amid the first fresh green of early spring on the trees – at first furtively making my trembling way up a Grade IV climb, complaining about one's 'in-and-out' form in April – but happier when I noticed the chap over yonder, who still had that 'sewing-machine' shake in his legs – right through to all the little masterpieces of technique, high above the trees aflame with autumn colours.

Book-keeping and Pull-ups

In between lay our great summer seasons – the Dolomites, the Bregaglia, Mont Blanc. In the autumn we all met again, around camp-fires or at huts, and told each other what great rock-faces we had 'taken apart' – thanks to our iron apprenticeship in the Peilstein school.

Yes, we formed a colourful, venturesome guild, we Peilstein-climbers who, Sunday after Sunday, turned up there from Vienna, twenty-five miles away, on our bicycles – till one or other of us filled everyone else with envy by acquiring a 'machine'. Full of relevant humour, too. One loft traverse high above the tree tops was embellished with a tram-car notice, in black-and-white enamel, which read: 'DON'T LEAN OUT.' And, for occasions when, accompanied by good advice from Wienerwald visitors, spiritually involved in our climbing ('there's a hand-hold, up to the right above you – about seven feet!'), one had safely mastered a difficult overhang and was clinging to nothing more than a few rugosities, 150 feet above the base of the climb, one was greeted by a dentist's placard: 'DON'T SPIT ON THE FLOOR!' Some of the names were very apt, too: you could take your pick from 'Suicide Crack' to 'Poster Pillar'. The rules, though unwritten, of the Peilstein fraternity were strictly observed. The novice started with the 'Balloon' scramble or 'The Slab'; our fair Viennese 'Mizzis' were put on to the easy but deep Schindeltal Chimney. And one universal rule: woe to him who used a piton on a 'free' climb! The unimaginable creature who started knocking his hooks into the superb hand-holds of the almost vertical 'Vegetarian's Arête' – the origin of the name remains obscure for, though the Peilstein brigade like potato salad, their diet is not exactly meatless – sparked off a minor revolution. From the Jahrerkanzel flowed sounds of local vernacular, boos rose from the Couloirs, loud echoes of rage rang from 'Monte Cimone' to the 'Matterhorn', and the sound of many angry voices floated across even to the distant 'Zinnen'; for the Peilsteiners can conceive of no greater crime than to bang a piton into the holds of that arête. Terrified, the ironmonger took to flight (He came, he 'nailed' in the wrong place, and was no more seen). Even so do the Peilsteiners protect the purity of their rocks!

One evening I was poring over my balance-sheets, while the sculptor was at his work close by. Presently he plucked at my sleeve and said: 'Come with me, I want to show you something.' He led me to the window above the dark courtyard: 'Something quite unusual,' he declared, staring raptly up at the nocturnal skies. 'Look!' he said, pointing to a dazzling bright star, 'that's Venus; and the one quite close to it, the pale red one, that's Mars. It is very rare to see them in conjunction.' The two utterly different stars blinked; the one a bluish white, the other emitting occasional flashes of red – a magic spectacle. And then Kloska, the sculptor, began to tell me about the nights, out in the Sahara, under the vast vault of the desert sky.

He told me, too, about the telescope mirror he wanted to make ... I remembered a dusty old telescope and microscope lying unused in Salzburg. Suppose we put them together? We did, and it worked. Now we could see Saturn's ring, Jupiter's moons, Andromeda's gorgeous veil of vapours. Kloska, the parachutist in Rommel's army, the sculptor who carved holy figures and drew so beautifully, the human being who pursued his own quiet life and lived only for his art, was completely at home in the depths of the starlit sky, and now he initiated me into its mysteries. I knew nothing of his life, about which he rarely spoke. But one day he told me, as we were once again exploring the heavens, with that very special gift he had of contented relaxation, that the middle star in Orion's belt was not a star at all, but an indescribably distant cloud of shining vapour, which only looked like a star to the naked eye.

I trained the telescope on that tiny point of light, and saw a marvellous feathery, shimmering cloud ...

'Its light takes ten years to get across from one end to the other of that cloud,' said Kloska.

And then I understood the peace which radiated from him.

Two on a Rope

We had got into a nice mess, damnation take it – properly sewn-up and stuck! There we were, hanging like flies on the three-thousand-foot face of the Croz dell' Altissimo, in the Brenta Dolomites, and nothing made sense any more. Everything was inimical, resistant, grey, smooth, unclimbable and repulsive: below me, a bottomless abyss . . .

The face of the Croz dell' Altissimo is the highest in the Brenta, carved as if by a knife out of a mountain accessible, on its other side, to sheep. It forms the lateral wall of a deep gorge. And there, halfway up it, were Wolfi and I, armed with a route-description in good clear Italian; our 'rock-sense' would, we said, make up for the bits we didn't understand, but since the last passage dictated by that rock-sense, it had all become Greek to us. No, not all: it 'strapiombed' everywhere, which meant it overhung. We had found the start of the route easily enough – a ledge with *mughi*, which assuredly meant little bumps, in it (a striking analogy with our Viennese 'Mugl'); since then it had 'placcted', vertically, 'strapiombed', over us, and 'fissured' – cracked or split – all around. And for the last hour I had had a nasty feeling that the description and the route no longer corresponded. At least, so my 'rock-sense' told me.

Suddenly, the coin dropped. That rusty piton at the adjectival pitch down below there had lured us on to the wrong traverse. It hadn't been the right adjectival pitch – the right one was much higher up. What kind of an adjectival pitch would that be, we wondered? Now it all depended on our 'rock-sense'!

So, now: straight on up, on barely recognizable holds, but fearfully smooth stuff. I banged a piton obliquely into a flake – it wouldn't hold a thing – so, on and up. At last I came to a minute ledge, which might provide a stance. I glued my face against the wall and hammered in another piton. It held!

Wolfi was coming up – clear of the airy slab, like a spider. It looked bizarre; the dark greenish-grey pattern of the wooded gorge, two thousand feet below, straight under his heels and above his shoulders.

'Watch out for that flake!'

'Yes, but the piton —'

Clatteration! Hold him, you've got to hold him! Agony in my knees, the rope cutting my shoulders, Wolfi's brown shock of hair twirling below me in mid-air, his body out over nothingness . . . You've got to hold him! I gritted my teeth, while he paddled in the air with his hands, feeling for the rock, finally got a hand-hold . . . – and that took his weight off my shoulders at last. I drew a deep breath; thanks be, the belaying-piton had held firm . . . but for the moment my tail was well down . . . we hung there on the stance for a few minutes. Then Wolfi led on up.

We did a climb every day. The glowing yellow east face of the Cima di Brenta, the enormous ice-packed chimney of the Cima degli Armi, the stratified mass of the Torre di Brenta, the soaring Campanile Alto, the magnificent rock-pillar of the 'Guglia'. Then more climbs: up the giant staircase of the Brenta Alta's south ridge, the three-thousand-foot arête of the Crozzon – airy routes in a realm of black-and-yellow rock-castles, high above the green carpet of meadows at their feet. We had got used to it; it no longer surprised us to find only a piton or two on vertical faces several hundred feet high; we had got to know the Brenta's rock, with its thousand rough wrinkles, bollards, spikes – often so needle-sharp that they hurt one's fingers – its caves and its 'hour-glasses', behind which one could thread a rope-sling: this peculiar Dolomite, whose amazing horizontal holds demanded great finger-strength. We could smile, now, at our rock-sense of the Croz dell' Altissimo; though we did pursue one more 'Via Fantasia' on the Torre di Brenta.

That same day, on ground not far from the base of the rocks, I found a Roman coin. Had it belonged to a soldier? Or to a hunter? For how long have men climbed up into the mountains?

All that was missing was a Grade VI climb. Cesare Maestri, 'the king of the Brenta', directed us to the Cima d'Ambiez: there was quite a pitch low down on it, he told us – the rest was a dream of a climb. That *was* a rock, a proper rock, he explained, his face lighting up with enthusiasm.

The evening before the climb: the whole face a dim blue shadowy thing, full of questions and surmises. Next morning, 1,200 feet of vertical cliff, brownish-red in the bright sunshine, riddled with holes and crannies. There were coffer-like overhangs, then a crack . . . I gasped for breath, spreadeagled on tiny protuberances; moved up a little and threaded through a piton; up again by a series of split-second decisions; worked my way farther up the face, which did its best to push me out and off – found a stance where I could take a breather. It was a gigantic free-climbing pitch, then; I wonder whether it still is?

Two on a Rope

Then followed the dream of a rock-climb, vertical, overhanging, pitonless, with innumerable small holes and wrinkles – perfect free-climbing on a sheer wall, with an infinity of air around us. At such moments you are gloriously conscious of your fingers, your muscles; of the toes of your boots winning a hold on the rough Brenta rock; of the wall, close to your face, shining black, brown and bright ochre amid the grey – like flower-patterns in a carpet – and all of it high above the combe down there at the foot of the climb. You are enmeshed in a bright web of thoughts, on which you climb ever higher, pulling yourself upwards from hand-hold to hand-hold, foot-hold to foot-hold, towards an ever-increasing freedom, while everything below you falls away – as you exalt yourself all the time.

Down there at the bottom, you see the shadows of the towers lengthen, and feel that you belong to your mountain with every fibre of your being and yet, at the same time, here, high above the abyss, utterly free of mind and spirit, you are acutely aware that you have arms and legs – and a body able to waft you upwards, because you have learned to overcome fear.

I belayed Wolfi up to a stance. We hardly spoke, we just climbed. Occasionally one of us remarked how splendid it was, and how right Cesare's assessment of the climb. I leaned my forehead against the rock; it was sunny and warm. What a joy, what a gift of fortune, it was to climb, to be alive in this lovely world! The very rock in front of me seemed a living thing.

A box of colour-slides. People coming, after their day's work, people who had perhaps a fortnight or three weeks' leave in a year, people who loved the mountains just as much as we did, many of whom the war had robbed of their best days . . . I was giving one of my first lectures. All of a sudden I myself was lost in it all, back in the middle of a summer spent between Mont Blanc and the Drei Zinnen. Everything else was forgotten.

We were at our 'base camp' in the Bregaglia. There were a couple of tents, socks flapping from the rope as they dried in the breeze, flocks of sheep in the distance, 'Peilstein-Joschi' snoozing on the 'post-prandial slab', Friedl sticking some plaster on finger-tips worn raw by climbing, Wolfi immersed in contemplation of the great blue face of Piz Badile, Hilde washing yet more socks in the mountain torrent. Here were to be found the loveliest camping-sites in the world; the most magnificent arêtes; and the worst-behaved sheep. Only yesterday they had devoured some of our savoury West-Alpine socks – one couldn't help laughing, much as the climbers sympathized with the sorely-tried washer-woman: climbing-socks, no mountain stream clear enough to wash them clean, and no representative of the Society for Prevention of Cruelty to Animals within miles!

For a moment I was back in the lecture-room, then I was perched once more two thousand feet above a glacier. 'Come up!' A lay-back up a 'Piaz'-crack. 'You're there!' A still finer lay-back. 'And now it's my turn!' Sunshine, clouds, the Cengalo Arête, with the smooth face of the Badile opposite. Every climber knows that 'Bregaglia' is synonymous with 'Bregaglia granite'. Fantastic rock-forms, incredibly sheer peaks, carved by thousands of years out of the living rock, like monsters in the grey dawn of history, with yellow and black lichens on their rough surfaces, towers, thin sword-blades of rock, spear-heads the size of a house, the smooth flat scoop of a shovel nearly 3,000 feet high – the Badile itself. And next to it the perfect, regular, gigantic curvature of the Cengalo's outline, loftier still by a few hundred feet, raking the sky. The thousand-foot 'Flat-iron', too, complete with hand-holds. Arêtes, arêtes and more arêtes . . .

Wolfi and I did them all, on alternate days, including the Sciora di Fuori and – it goes without saying – the towering North-east Face of the Badile (I had already done that climber's dream, its arête). Then we rode over to the Dolomites, with the Busazza Arête in the Civetta group as our target; but when we got there – once again, needless to say – in spite of our thirst for great ridge-climbs, we went straight up the northwest face of the Civetta herself, the queen of all Dolomite face-climbs, that glowing red screen of organ-pipes; soaring high above a southern valley, which a boy with a bicycle had discovered years before.

How many life-times do we need to make all our dreams come true?

And now the 'Spigolo Giallo' and all the face-climbs on the Zinnen! But when we arrived at the Paternsattel with our last few hellers in our pockets, it rained. We bivouacked in a concrete hut, and sat on our rucksacks, looking at each other, for three days. Then it started to snow.

Autumn had set in. There was nothing for it but to go home.

We always routed our long summer months in the Western Alps from west to east, starting 'over there' in July and finishing up 'over here' in the Dolomites by September. In the end we grew tired of bicycling; hitch-hiking was far more comfortable. Finally, Wolfi acquired a small motor-cycle, by dint of hard saving and, indeed, at the expense of our basic principle not to lose a day of our treasured summer-forays into the mountains by doing a single extra day's work. If it meant living on porridge, it also meant more summits. Meanwhile, I had discovered the

'Grants for Important Ascents', earned lecture-fees, and paid regular visits to my generous 'Aunt Betty'. So yet another Alpine summer was assured.

We were at the start of the south face of the Dent du Géant – a rash of carabiners, the jingle of pitons, rope-slings for the feet, sunshine; and above us the vertical granite wall, with its overhangs.

I started up the first few feet, with a view to reaching the lowest piton, climbing 'free'. Hell, how the thing overhung! ... No use ... I had to come down again. Suddenly I heard a voice, saying in broken German: 'You should put a starting-piton in – it's the drill here. That one up there is the second one.'

A hop-pole of a long Frenchman had arrived at the starting-point, accompanied by a small fat one, and was quietly unpacking his snack-lunch. 'Thanks!' I growled at him, and started up again, ignoring his advice. Nice chap, behaving as if he owned the place – but we would show him! Up I went to within six inches, three inches, of that piton. Blast everything! I had to come down again. There I stood, panting, getting my strength back – I had put everything I had into it, that second time. Wolfi wrinkled his forehead; angrily, I banged in the piton in question; the long slab of a Frenchman sat quietly munching his sandwich. I knew I had seen that type with a woolly cap somewhere before. Never mind that ... off I went, not exactly stylishly, but moving quickly – now we would get clear of the two sandwich-munchers!

I found a stance on an airy pulpit. 'Up you come!' I shouted down, to Wolfi, out of sight. The rope told me how smoothly and swiftly he was coming up; I could see his brown mop appearing around the corner, and – by Friday the thirteenth! – a woolly cap, too. That long slab had arrived at the same time, and was laughing, between a fine set of teeth: '*Alors*, the piton was all right, wasn't it?' – so paternal! – 'You see, I know my way about here; this is the seventh time I've done it.' *Seventh time!* He hauled in his rope – we were hanging out into thin air from that pulpit in all directions – and once again those teeth flashed above a tough chin. 'You don't mind if I go on ahead?' he asked. 'By the way – may I introduce myself? I'm Rébuffat ...' So it was Gaston Rébuffat, the world-famous climber – admittedly the king of the castle in his Mont Blanc group: why, he must know every hold in it! Humbly, we mumbled our names, shook him by the hand – clinging with the other to the rock; then we leaned out even farther into the air to let him pass. Down below us the ropes swung slowly too and fro. Certainly an odd place for such an introduction.

For a while our human bunch of grapes – we were now four – hung out from the sun-baked face, nearly thirteen thousand feet up; then elegant French *étriers* jingled in space and Rébuffat disappeared from sight above an overhang.

A storm was raging on the Peuterey ridge – the weather had broken suddenly. We knew how many had died on the White Mountain, thirty to forty in some seasons – and how often the weather had been responsible for their failing to return from the peaks and faces of the massif.

Snow, and more snow – we had to get down before it was too late. We only had two days' provisions left, a stupid mistake. We groped our way down the Couloir, then through the ice-towers of the Fresnay glacier, valleywards. At last we were down safely, though minus our Peuterey ridge; but we had at least the turreted south ridge of the Aiguille Noire to show for it.

This damned weather! We had lived up there for a fortnight in the bivouac-box under the sharp tooth of the Fourche de la Brenva, before we could finally do the Arête du Diable on the Tacul and the south face of the Dent du Géant . . .

Every day, as we sat there, the gigantic White Brenva face had shimmered down on us, mostly out of the clouds; and the north face of the Aiguille Blanche de Peuterey, with the ice-avalanches roaring down it to shatter the silence.

A thought entered our minds: it must be marvellous to climb those white walls, that difficult ice – those unique ice-faces, huge, forbidding, holdlessly smooth, with their blue bulges, their crystalline towers. For, although we were already committed to rock of every grade of difficulty, we had not yet taken a single step in the world of cold, ice-armoured faces.

Was there something keeping us away? Was rock-climbing to be our whole life? Or was the other thing just something which would come in good time?

When I look back today, the following thoughts spring to my mind: Wolfi had come to the mountains from an apprenticeship on rock, I, who had started as a crystal-hunter, from the white world of snow. All the same, once the day dawned when to climb a peak by the normal route, or in the course of a long traverse, failed any longer to satisfy, I had become a rock-climber, like Wolfi. Rock – with all the difficulties of extreme climbing – that was the thing: cliffs, ridges, arêtes of rock.

Now, in our third Alpine season, we both thought for the first time about an ice-climb: the Brenva face of Mont Blanc. The thought was stifled by masses of snow, falling day after day. Our first intrusion into the world of ice-climbs, into the realm of mountaineering of every grade of difficulty in the white element – never of course, to the exclusion of rock-climbing – would have to wait till next summer.

This process of development in the whole wide field of Alpinism over a lifetime will doubtless repeat itself for many a climber. There is a biological parallel here: in the grey prehistoric days, we all swung from branch to branch. The laws of heredity have repeated the process in our own day. The development is simply that the naked 'hairy ape' has at last invaded the ice-world.

'The standard of a nation's cultural development is recognizable by its table-manners', I read on the page of newspaper in which I had wrapped our tomatoes. Well, well! And we Austrians are supposed to be civilized people. Yet, there, opposite me, Wolfi was sitting on the grass, barefoot, cooking polenta. Were we really a good advertisement for our country? At that moment Wolfi pushed a tomato into his mouth and for several minutes gave a good impersonation of someone trying to swallow a tennis-ball.

'Have you ever considered,' I ask him, 'what kind of an impression of Austria we present when we are abroad?'

Wolfi made a puzzled internal noise corresponding to '*mmmmmh*', the expression in his eyes exactly matching the tennis-ball in his mouth. Then, after swallowing: 'What's wrong with it?' he enquired.

'This paper says you can recognize the standard of a nation's cultural development by its table-manners,' I explained, looking pointedly at the tomatoes. Wolfi laughed, picked another one out of the paper and shoved it into his mouth. It appeared that the recognition of cultural standards lay behind the next tomato. I gave up my attempts at education, fetched my spoon out of my trouser-pocket and immersed myself in polenta. Wolfi did likewise – it is just one of those freaks of chance: he is left-handed, I am right-handed, so we can spoon things out of the same pot at the same time. (This is known as rationalization: arriving at an end by the simplest means.) Anyway, we only had one pot. Wolfi put a finger in his mouth and cleaned his teeth. 'You should use a toothpick,' I reminded him, licking my spoon clean, 'and do it in the loo! You aren't civilized.' (A bronze-coloured millepede was climbing over the polenta-bag.) Wolfi spat scornfully: 'That I suppose is why I developed the system for making do with only one cooking-pot – and with no need for washing up, at that?' (Sequence: polenta or porridge, then a soup-cube, finally tea – and then turn the pot upside down and leave it in the sun.) 'Any objections?'

'None,' I admitted, having exhausted all my arguments. After all, inventive powers are part of civilization, too.

Wolfi looked at me pensively and fired his final shot: 'This seems to be your day for moralizing. Do you know, it's a long time since you trimmed the ragged edges of the holes in your trousers – shall I lend you my knife?'

I did not reply, but, using a piece of newspaper for a napkin, wiped my mouth and raised the aluminium saucer of tea to my lips. After all one must start from small beginnings, and good intentions have their value. See! Wolfi was following my example . . .!

Of the newspaper, there was nothing left.

20,000 Feet in Twenty-four Hours

Had we been seized by some form of madness? Or had we joined the tribe of mere record-hunters? No: we were simply itching to know whether we had the necessary stamina to climb the Obergabelhorn with its crystal-white north face, so difficult of access – as it were, in the original conditions, before there were any club huts – direct from the valley-level.

We were in splendid shape. After various other climbs, we had just done the 4,000-foot north face of the Dent d'Hérens in eight hours. What a gem of an ice-chimney – the crucial key-pitch of the Welzenbach route (how often had it been borne in on us that the name of that great ice-expert stood for climbs of exceptional beauty of form and quality)!

Our fourth and fifth summer seasons in the Western Alps had afforded us an initiation into this new realm of the great ice-faces. We had savoured the crystalline element, in various degrees of steepness and severity, on the Dent d'Hérens, the Obergabelhorn, Breithorn, Lyskamm, Aiguille Blanche and Grands Charmoz; and finally the great Brenva face of Mont Blanc. On our way to the gigantic north face of the Dent d'Hérens, we had cast longing eyes up at one of the greatest 'combined' rock and ice-climbs in the Alps – the north face of the Matterhorn. We had both got over the days of our rock-climbing intoxication in the Brenta Dolomites; we knew now that one could not do everything. Whether on rock or on ice, our minds were turning more and more to the really big climbs. If the actual climbing was less attractive than on many a smaller peak, we now found the very size of the undertaking more impressive and exciting.

20,000 feet without a break: from our tent outside Steinauer's shack at Winkelmatten, near Zermatt, to the top of the 13,365-foot Obergabelhorn, and back down again to our tent. In between lay various ascents and descents; the climax, of course, being the mountain's delicately ribbed North-west Face, an ice-wall whose base is so difficult to approach that, to the best of our knowledge, it had only been climbed five times. Each party had tried to reach its foot, which rises from a savage glacier-cauldron, by a different route. One of them had actually climbed *down* a ridge from the summit in order to get there. And we, starting out from Zermatt, had somehow to find a way over the high intervening range of rock to the west, so as to get down into the cauldron beyond it. Once there, the face is a smooth, finely-drawn slope with an inclination of 55 degrees. The whole thing would normally take three days.

One o'clock in the morning. We fastened the tent-door behind us and left Winkelmatten, its huts shadowy shapes in the moonlight. We went up into the night, past the benches thoughtfully placed by the Tourist Board between the dark trunks of the pines, past the sleeping steinbocks in their enclosure.

By dawn we had negotiated the boulders of the moraine and reached the Rothorn Hut, at 10,500 feet, having come up fully 5,000 feet. The sky was an extraordinary apple-green, above the pale glimmer of the Wellenkuppe's snow-cap. We felt marvellous, and stopped for a cup of tea before continuing the ascent.

The sun came up, painting the rocks a reddish-brown. Our breath turned to a vapour-cloud. What a glorious day this was! Over there rose the Triftjoch, a rocky saddle high above the glacier, our next objective. Up here there was a great deal of fresh snow. The question was whether we should be able to get down from the saddle into that cauldron of ice lying in the valley beyond it, and so reach the foot of our north face?

Nine o'clock, on the saddle . . . opposite us, the Obergabelhorn, shining like a crystal, seamed with bluish-white flutings, still a mile away beyond that deep and ice-filled glacier-bowl, involving a descent of hundreds of feet to its bed of green shadows, blue séracs, huge crevasses and – beyond all doubt – masses of freshly-fallen snow, promising much hard labour. The great white face of our peak flung back the light like a mirror, across the deep ice-blue of the dark network of rock-slopes below us on our side – a miracle of loveliness!

There was certainly no direct way over to it from here. Wolfi bit his lip, as he scanned the surging, long drawn-out corniced ridge to the left, the North-east Ridge of our four-thousander. Could we reach the foot of our face by following it, say, as far as the great *gendarme*, and then cutting diagonally downwards? A steep and most unusual route, surely involving the longest traverse we had ever met? But first we had to turn back and climb the Wellenkuppe.

. . . . .

20,000 Feet in Twenty-four Hours

Late in the morning we were on the 12,796-foot summit of the Wellenkuppe, where the North-east Ridge of the Obergabelhorn begins – an undulating edge, swinging up above the abyss in a long curve, like some narrow suspension-bridge, to the sharp summit of the peak.

By midday we had got to the *gendarme*, and started on our diagonal downward traverse. God, how that slope went plummeting down!

We went on traversing diagonally downwards well into the afternoon, clinging to a 60 degree wall of ice for one hour, two hours; climbing like two tiny spiders across that huge white slope, traversing and traversing diagonally downwards . . .

At last, the bergschrund at the bottom lay only a rope's length below us. Who was going to climb down into it and up out of it again, for the sake of the record, to regularize our ascent of the face? You perhaps, Wolfi? No, not Wolfi. Perhaps you will oblige, Kurt? No, not Kurt . . . we decided that our climb would have to count without that small formality.

So, at last, we could start on our ascent of that enormous crystal, straight up the middle, from its base to its summit, up a face something like 500 yards high. It would be rather nice to have a camp-bed along for rests at the stances!

An endless succession of white ribs, sweeping upwards at 55 degrees, uniform, similar, symmetrical, regular . . . peaceful, and soothing to the mind . . . with a gossamer film of ice-dust rippling down over them.

It was a positive dream of loveliness. One of us moved up, belayed by the other; then the other one moved up, belayed in his turn. Our belaying pitons went in solidly at the stances.

Yes, a camp-bed would have been rather nice . . .

That went on for three hours. Overhead, the ridges were closing in to meet at the summit. Just below it, we were suddenly aware that we had defeated the crucial challenge of that vast white uniformity. Now, straight up and out by the *direttissima* (as a gesture)! Fearfully steep, absolutely smooth ice, with a 70 degree pitch, then a few rocks – and there we were, on our summit. So much for that!

We sat there for a quarter of an hour, while sun-shot mists drifted about us. It was a lovely world! It was also past four o'clock – fifteen hours since we had started out across the meadow down there in Zermatt. We had completed more than half our journey. Somehow, all sense of time seemed to have deserted us. There was the sun, of course, and our watches . . .

We were on our way down, moving steadily along that corniced suspension-bridge of a ridge. Suddenly, the lower half of the Matterhorn's north face loomed out of the mists, glittering in a mantle of freshly-fallen snow. Before us rose our *gendarme*, with thick grey fog all around.

The fog turned yellow, and began to simmer. Light was coming through it – brighter and still brighter, finally dazzling. There was a stir in the air; then, as if by magic, the whole world lay clear. There stood the Dent Blanche and the Obergabelhorn, drenched in the liquid gold of the sunset. Everything was golden-yellow – the mists below us, the mountain-face, our tracks in the snow. The hours had suddenly dissipated into thin air. The sun was going down. We were tired and transfigured – we felt as if we could go on like this for ever. Everything about the day was odd – and now night was drawing in again.

7 p.m.: back at the Rothorn Hut, after eighteen hours and some 13,000 feet of up and down to plague our limbs. How pleasant it would be to stay here at a comfortable hut! Resisting the temptation, we staggered on down towards Zermatt – we *had* to know whether we could achieve the aim we had set ourselves. Boulders, the zig-zag path, darkness, thoughts – I never wanted to be on that mountain-face any more, all I wanted was to be in our tent: in Wolfi's Alpine-Association-Section-Austria double-lined tent, made of material tested in the Himalaya, which always let the rain in, because it doesn't rain in the Himalaya, it snows . . .

Wolfi had stopped. 'I'm waiting for the moon to come up,' he said, and lay down among the boulders. I was waiting for the next bench, above Zermatt, and went on my way towards it . . . *tarum-tumtum* . . . *tarum-tumtum* . . . *tarum tumtum* . . . *hoppla!*

There it was, my bench. Praise be to God and the Tourist Board. Now the moon could come up, if it wanted to.

A pretty young lady with an odd-looking handbag and stiletto-heeled-shoes was coming up the meadows towards me – a sight to cheer one: big almond-eyes, long, dark shining hair, slim legs. She sat down by me and opened her pretty mouth. 'Would you care to take me up with you to the Finch Terrace?' she enquired.

Would I, a guide in this year 2,000, care to – not likely! There was a batting of blue eyelashes. I thought it over: a promenade like that on a chilly ice-terrace? Hadn't people in this day and age anything better to think about, than that one-track North Face of the Dent d'Hérens?

Out loud, I said: 'The coffee isn't at all good up there and they haven't finished the surface-lighting of the crevasses. The kiosk over there on the Tyndall ridge serves a much better Mocca. Of course, we could just eat a Cassata and then climb a few feet, if you really want to;

20,000 Feet in Twenty-four Hours

or we could take the dear old lift to the summit – though I'm afraid it's a bit ancient now.' (Even in 2000 AD, a guide must show at once that he knows his area, if he expects further assignments.)

The sweet young lady got a mirror out of her handbag and redrew her mouth with a lipstick. 'What would you charge?' she asked.

'Hm!' I temporized. Dear old Fiechtl, in whose day everything was so simple, had been dead a long time. I rummaged between punched cards in my rucksack for the latest punched computer-card, which now takes into account, day by day, not only the temperature, air-pressure, wind-force and the state of the weather, but also the guide's fitness. (I had been relegated to Grade I – so many flights up to the terraces had properly grounded me; and all those summit-parties up to the new chapel on top of the Breithorn – these occupational hazards!) If Welzenbach only knew that nowadays one flies up to enjoy a small black coffee in the middle of his ice-wall . . .

But wait a moment; something very odd was happening. The lovely one was pulling an ice-piton out of her little bag, carabiners, rock-pitons and – by Fiechtl and Welzenbach! – a gossamer-thin storm-suit of the new Mars-tested super-skin. Surely she couldn't actually want to *climb* the old route up to the Terrace? Impossible . . . Kurt, pinch your arm, you must be dreaming . . .

I could hear someone running in the woods. Wolfi came past at a jogtrot. The moon was up, too. Down below, a few lights were winking – Zermatt. We stumped on down, and finally – 'by the skin of our teeth' – up the slope that rises to Winkelmatten.

At 1 a.m. we collapsed into the tent like two felled trees – almost exactly 24 hours after leaving it, and after 20,000 feet of height differential. (Later I worked it over again, and it proved to be only 19,300 feet. Nothing is ever complete, not even the most beautiful chapter-heading. We ought, after all, to have done that little extra bit down into the bottom of the bowl.)

We woke up at three o'clock the next afternoon and stretched ourselves in the sun outside the tent. Someone was coming up from Zermatt, through the meadows.

Yellow mists were still floating before my eyes – but now I was suddenly very wide awake. Yellow-stockings: the local collector of the 'residential tax', no doubt about it! I took one big leap into the tent, to resume my residence there. Wolfi continued to lie on the grass, smiling happily. Now for a local gala!

The tax-man arrived. Soon Wolfi was babbling amiably about the

Matterhorn and how long he and his buddy, asleep there in the tent, proposed to stay around that lovely mountain. It was quite a pleasure to listen to him, now he was coming to the point. 'In any case,' he said, making a significant pause – 'we're starting for the Theoduljoch today and going over on to the Italian side . . .'

Perhaps I had not quite slept off the effects of yesterday, but the yellow knee-hose seemed to change colour. I gave a loud yawn, opened the tent-flap and blinked at my old acquaintance. It was worth two whole days of residential tax. He actually recognized me.

We were sitting in the Hörnli Hut, filing the points of our crampons as sharp as possible, for the North Face. Old Kronigk, the hutkeeper, winked at us. He knew us by now and had guessed our intentions; but then he shook his head. 'The weather,' he said. It was beautifully sunny outside. We went on filing. Wolfi had just come back from a solo climb of the Zmutt ridge, from which he had taken a good look at the face. It was in excellent condition: this time we would do it.

By midnight a storm was raging and it was snowing hard – unbelievable masses of snow. Everything had turned white, and the warm wind was coming from the south-west. Not a hope, this time. Next year, perhaps.

Not long afterwards, we were pedalling, as so often before, out into the woods in their autumn glory, to the familiar grey walls and towers of our Peilstein practice-ground, where the local 'Matterhorn' and 'Monte Cimone' stand side by side. Wolfi had acquired a girl-friend. It was really charming to see how careful he was that she didn't fall off – how devotedly he showed her every hand- and foot-hold. But – thought I, what about . . .? Wolfi reassured me about my 'but': he would not let her come along on our next summer's north-face campaign, he promised.

I breathed again, rejoicing. That was how it should be! When one went to the mountains, one should think about mountains and nothing but the mountains. There spoke the true, the genuine mountaineer; he was one of the real ones – *un des purs,* as Samivel has called them. (Anyway, nothing to be surprised about; wasn't he my rope-mate?)

I, of course, had no idea then what fate had in store for me. I did not know that, next summer, I would continually be persuading Wolfi that we needed further supplies of fresh food for our ice-climbs; and that each time, as soon as he had blessed me resignedly with his agreement, I would be hurrying down hot-footed to Zermatt . . .

Just to fetch apples, of course.

Daisies, a Cat and the North Face of the Matterhorn

'She loves me . . . she loves me not . . .'

Daisies on the North Face of the Matterhorn – on its stances?

Shining dark rock, blue glittering ice, light in the bursting bubbles of glassy mountain-waters – marsh-marigolds – veils of ice rippling down the face —

Rébuffat said it: 'A marvellous heap of stones, the Matterhorn.'

Sunshine on the North Face. Hot sun. Ice-blossoms, tinkling down from the rocks, out into the darkness of the valley, flashing yellow and white . . .

Daisies? Anything is possible – if one thinks of it.

Anything is possible, when a determined, resolute Swiss girl packs her bag and says: 'I've got a dog already – now I want a *husband*!' Especially if she knows where to find him: in Vienna. So she travels to Vienna.

Obviously, we Austrians must have a wonderful reputation in foreign parts as husbands; we are supposed to be faithful, reliable, happy-go-lucky, sociable, comfortable and hard-working; if we happen to be a bit slovenly, well, they hope that can always be cured.

I forgot a most important thing: love asks no questions. I asked questions: What is this that comes rolling down on me by Transalpine Express right across the Alps? Apart from what, why just on Vienna (fateful thought!)? I wonder what she looks like . . .?

Wolfi and I were on the Peilstein. 'Your mind doesn't seem to be on climbing today,' he suggested. No, I was thinking about quite a different matter.

It was in the Bernina, three years before. White peaks above the Tschierva Hut; the Biancograt, Piz Roseg opposite, Scerscen in between. Huge cascades of ice. But I, lying totally snow-blind in the darkened dormitory of the hut, could see none of these things. My fate arrived after a six-hour trek up the Rosegtal on pliant espadrilles, with blisters on her soles, gritted teeth, a hard head and a very sweet soul. She wanted, for once, to see the homeland peaks from near by – not only the distant lands in the wide, wide North.

Grit under my eyelids. Dark, confused contours. My lids felt swollen, and now and then came stabbing pain. Damn it, don't rub them! Hardly able to open my eyes, I lay quietly . . . waiting . . . in the darkness . . .

That was the door . . . quiet footfalls . . . someone was there.

A voice said: 'I'll put a couple of bandages on your eyes – cool – it'll do them good.' A damp cloth descended on my eyes and two hands adjusted it gently. What angel was this? The clear voice of a girl, with a Swiss accent, rolled r, hard k and all . . .

'Thanks a lot,' I said. Who was she? The cloth was cool and comforting. Passing my hand pensively over my beard, I considered: one of the hut-staff? Definitely not. No sound; but I knew she had sat down somewhere near by.

'Thanks very much – please tell me —'

'Is it really better?'

'Oh – yes – comfortable.'

Silence. What was there about that voice – clear and gentle at the same time? Of course, a man should not be inquisitive; especially when he can't see.

I could not leave it, though. 'Tell me, who are you?'

She laughed. 'They call me Busle* – the Cat,' she said, in that highly appropriate voice.

That put an end to any thought of further rest. Before my mind's eye, far from blinded, there trooped, on delicate feet, a whole menagerie of cats: grey, tabby, red, blue with greenish markings and humped backs, all on velvet paws —

'I need a fresh bandage,' I said.

The hand was long and slender, I discovered; for, as it adjusted the folds, I held it for a moment.

One thing I knew, now – I must get my sight back immediately. And for that, I definitely needed more bandages. Busle had gone out of the room, but she had promised to come back.

It was dark, and I could see blue, metallic peaks, shimmering outlines of glaciers. I had removed my sun-glasses – things were silhouettes and shadows. However, I was able to establish this much. Busle was tall. Slim down below and rounded high up. Her hair had a bluish gleam in it; it was probably brown, or perhaps darkish-blonde. She had des-

* Busle is a pet name, widely used in Switzerland and really means 'kitten'.

scribed it as: 'Busle-colour, my own colour.' Her face presented itself as a rounded disc with dark eyes in it. Tomorrow she had to go.

I asked her to go to the ice-falls with me, though I could only show them to her, now, in the dark; for by daylight I could see nothing.

The séracs glimmered. Her lips were soft. She was full of warmth and imagination. There could only be one Busle like her, even if I could not see the colour of her eyes.

Three years ago, now.

The train arrived during the evening. Why was I so excited? The neon-tubes of the Westbahnhof vibrated shrilly. I hardly recognized her.

'Really you?'

Up and down the city we went. She was nervous, and walked, as I did, at full tilt. She had a saucy nose and a pony-fringe, and unbelievably long legs.

A café: her hand, her voice. Warmth, clarity, imagination.

Yes, it was really Busle.

Here we were in the grey City by the Danube, with its anonymous masses of people – the blue city by the Danube, with its flowering trees, the Prater, the great wheel; with schnitzel overflowing the plate, with the Wienerwald, its gentle outlines overlapping like stage-settings, right out to the Schneeberg. Trees like in a Japanese painting. And the orange-red sickle of the moon, setting now behind the blue-Danube city's sea of lights.

'How old are you?'

We were under the last of gas-lamps, their gently-hissing light a yellowish-green, on our way down to the city. How old was I? 'Twenty-six,' I said, carefully adding two years to my age; I am usually truthful, but we happened to be the same age, and a man is only a man if he has an age-advantage. Anyway, why ask?

We walked the streets till the sun rose. I knew something more, then. Her eyes were grey-blue-grey-brown. That matched her general colouring – grey-blue-brown-green. Busle-colour. She knew three languages. What a good idea of hers, to come to Vienna!

The sculptor, sculpting, remarked: 'Mars is in conjunction! That's three times I've said it, and you haven't heard me. What ails you?' SO . . . Mars . . . ah, yes. 'Excuse me,' I said. 'But surely it will last for quite a while?' And I went.

She had twenty pairs of high-heeled shoes and travelled all over Europe alone . . . she had an unusually keen colour-sense and collected beer-bottle caps ... she was always full of unexpected ideas ... oh, she was lovely ... and at home she had her own library, she said, fluttering her eyelashes learnedly, full of great, fat books ...

I leaned forward: there were three buttons to her blouse, one of them was open – by Lollo –!

'You aren't paying attention, Kurt. I was telling you about my library,' said she, reproachfully, her face taking on the look of a dyed-in-the-wool State school-marm. I cleared my throat. 'Yes,' I said. 'Lessing was a great man.' That was a big mistake; with a face set in deadly earnest, she promptly gave me a meticulous briefing on Lessing – or was there perhaps a tiny glint of roguishness at the corner of her eyes? I pulled myself together (so was the blouse by now), with great difficulty producing a variety of consenting and disagreeing answers, which laid woefully bare my knowledge of German literature. Why were her eyes so bright? Why did she suddenly smile? Self destructively contrite, I accused myself: 'Kurt, you are a cultural-defective – that has got to be changed.'

'You are a wonderful librarian . . .' I said. And what a fantastic library you are! I thought.

I bought myself a *Signpost to Literature*.

Meanwhile, Busle was gone away.
Situation Report:
1. Season of the year: trees and finances, green (*al verde**).
2. The Book-keeper: misses my daily pull-ups on the door-jamb.
3. The Sculptor: carving a statue of St Antony (though he has seen Busle and knows Wilhelm Busch, who described the terrible 'temptations of that holy man').
4. Wolfi: regards me as if I were a sick horse when, at the 'Vegetarians' Arête', armed with my new learning, I gave him a lecture on Lessing's plays. 'Don't forget the North Face,' he says. 'Don't you let me down over that one!'
5. Me: I regret nothing. The North Face? I shall apply to the Alpine Association for a grant. After all, the North Face is a top-ranking climb.

A letter from Switzerland! It says Busle can come along to the Matterhorn. When I told Wolfi so, on the Peilstein, he groaned.

There was this letter. And another, and another. While the sculptor hewed, I lay on my bed, my face covered with a sheet of business figures, and dreamed – a climber caught between 'ought' and 'has'. Oh,

* i.e. 'the money is finished'.

The North Face of the Matterhorn

Busle how you have changed the life of this book-keeper summit-stormer! 'Ought and Has'? One has what one has.

Eyes deep as the blue-green lakes of the glaciers . . . an ice-wall with a pony-fringe . . . but no, the temperature's all wrong . . . Vesuvius . . . Sophia Loren . . . the desert . . . camels with their rocking gait . . . camels with resolute gait? In high-heeled shoes? That was the trouble, she never walks the same way. *Tarab!* – trot! Daisies, nodding, nodding. The North Face of the Matterhorn, with its nodding gait . . .
The North Face!
My request to the Alpine Association!
I almost choked for want of breath.

Final instalment . . . 'request a grant from the fund for top-ranking climbs'. Well, I had done that.

The North Face of the Matterhorn, with its nodding . . .

Hey! No arguments about its top ranking; it ranked much higher now – wasn't Busle coming along?

Fate moved on rapid feet, now. *Signpost to Literature* in my baggage, off I went to Switzerland.

It all moved so quickly. Helvetia is used to victories. Moorgarten and Sempach: that is where the Austrians were beaten, as every Swiss child knows. Eyelashes flutter knowledgeably, but very sweetly.

There was no doubt about it. She meant it, in good earnest. So, I suppose, did I. None the less a kind of wonder, a sort of amazement fell upon me. I, to marry? That was the question I asked myself, with the instinctive recoil experienced by all sharers of the same fate, down whose back the thought of that unfamiliar legal status has sent coursing a light shudder.

It passed. Remember Moorgarten and Sempach? And now '*Tu, Felix Austria, nube!*' Austria the fortunate, go marry!

I was as radiant as Jove and sent a card to my tame astrologer. As a prudent Austrian, I stipulated a breathing-space – two years. Time to finish my studies.

After that . . . what rapture! What a lovely world! (Only first I shall have to make friends with that dog.)

Permission to make our attempt. Financial aid guaranteed. Our summer of the North Face is guaranteed.

This time we shall get our North Face, you Matterhorn: your top-ranking North Face!

· · · · ·

Foaming breakers; cliffs rising sheer from them. When the waves suck back, all the shingle in the bay rustles. Great and eternal is the Ocean.

I wrote to Wolfi: 'Busle and I will explore the conditions on the North Face and, until you come, I shall get acclimatized to altitude.'

The sweet-scented trees were in blossom and the sun shone. Altitude: zero – a good place to start from. On our napkin-holders was written: '*Signor Lui*' and '*Signora Lei*'. We fed on mussels, Asti Spumante, top-grade '*fritto misto*': top-ranking . . .

Silent stood the Matterhorn and said nothing. Sure, Wolfi and I would climb the North Face.

Dandelions and daisies. Our tent stood close to the glacier's edge, at nearly 10,000 feet. Wolfi was still on a training-course with his Section. A wintry-looking Matterhorn peered through the clouds.

'You needn't come for another ten days,' I wrote to Wolfi. 'There's a horrible mass of fresh snow on all the faces.' All I had left was a big bag of polenta. Top-ranking polenta. And the treasury? Down at sea-level.

That night I dreamed for the first time of the Central Administrative Committee of the Alpine Association. There was a green-clothed table and a great many silent faces around it, looking at me, and still looking at me . . . edelweiss, lulled beneath a black storm-cloud. Postponement of sentence.

A green meadow; dandelions and daisies!

'You moaned something awful in the night – is anything wrong?' Busle questioned me, genuinely worried.

'I dreamed of my record of tours – I think we ought to climb something, you know.'

'Oh, yes – how thrilling – let's go straight for a four-thousander!' she cried, her eyes shining.

'The Breithorn.'

We did it by the ordinary route: six hours of solid slogging.

That night I dreamed of the Association again; the expression on the faces round the table had not altered. They looked sad and troubled. One head was being shaken. Wisps of blue cigarette smoke formed the word: 'top-ranking?'

'But I don't smoke; my solicitor can confirm it!' Busle was shaking me by the arm. 'Have you a law-suit running?' she enquired.

Yellow blew the dandelions – exactly the same colour as the polenta. Yellow, yellow and again yellow.

'I can't look at that stuff you're cooking, ever again. I shall die of starvation' . . . and two great tears welled out of those glacier-lakes. I was at my wit's end. 'I'll make you some porridge'... 'Well, that would be a change,' she sobbed. Something made me cast a glance forward into the future.

'You know, you'll have to learn how to economize,' I said.

'Oh!... xhuatzl ch – Ch – Ch...'

Bluish-green flashes of lightning, and a yellow one, as the polenta-spoon flew towards me...

'Chaibech – ch – ch...' (Please stop it, Busle dear. You are absolutely right. It was *not* the right moment... I'll fetch the spoon)... ch...'

We made our peace.

'I'll go and get a job,' she said, 'down in Zermatt, when Wolfi comes and you start up the face – so we won't have to economize so much.' Oh, you wonderful, wonderful Busle!

But that wasn't enough. Another dream: through yellow polenta a radiant vision of Wolfi in golden corduroys, ringed by a maharajah's aureole. He still had his grant.

He would be arriving in three or four days.

The broad ice-block of the summit, the sheer precipice falling from its skull-cap. There it hung, two thousand feet above our heads, crowning shadows, slabby rock, terrifying grey ice, a whole façade of houses up there, blue, chill, shining in the early light – dangerous...

'To think that Welzenbach survived all his ice-climbs,' growled Wolfi. Under a hanging-glacier one isn't safe even at night. Now was the most dangerous time – soon the sun would have warmed the ice up there, playing havoc with the tensions. Suppose one of those street-car trains came thundering down...

We panted on up the tortuous couloir of the Breithorn's north-west face, crawling on all fours, ice-hammer in one hand, piton in the other, moving simultaneously, not belaying, Wolfi and I, moving as quickly as we knew how. This broke all our rules, but here the danger of a slip was less than that menacing us overhead.

'Look out!' A shadow flew past us, slicing the air quite close to us. Then silence.

It was our first training-climb for the North Face enterprise. We climbed Willo Welzenbach's great route through the North-west Face of the Breithorn in eight hours. Not bad time, but then, not particularly good, either.

Situation report:
1. Wolfi: 'We aren't in top form – more especially you!'
2. Wolfi again: 'Move the tent up from the beautiful meadow

another thousand feet on to rough slabs,' adding, with a meaning glance at me; 'that's the place for an Alpine tent!'
No dandelions. No daisies. Polenta.
3. Busle: Selling apples and pears in a Zermatt fruit-shop. Such is life.
4. Me: Such is life.
5. The North Face: still full of powder-snow. Our next objective would be the Lyskamm.

'Wolfi, believe me, polenta tastes better and is healthier if you add paprika and onions, also apples and pears. Hasn't anyone told you how important fresh foods are for climbers, according to the latest researches?'
'Yes, but . . .'
'Oh, you needn't worry . . .'
'Listen to me . . .'
'All the same . . .'
'But . . .'
'Nevertheless . . .'
The opposition weakened; silence reigned.
'Agreed, then?' 'Agreed!' 'Wolfi you are a decent climbing-partner. I award you the Golden Edelweiss and bars. I'll hurry down to Zermatt . . .' I know the way . . .
'Goodbye, Busle!' I said, as, my rucksack stuffed with Zermatt apples, I hurried off again, up to the Bétemps Hut, in the shadow of the Lyskamm; there was also a sweet melon for Wolfi, No disappointments for him; here I was, though I am not sure that he was convinced by my theory of condition-training, adapted from that of the marathon-runner to the mountaineer.

The icy upsurge of the Lyskamm. Huge white balconies, their surfaces marvellously sculptured. Above them, corniced ridges, against the blue. A thrilling peak!
The North-east Face of the west summit is 3,000 feet high. We climbed it, arrow-straight, by the most direct line we could find. It was a first-ascent, and only seven and a half hours.
A marvellous climb. Wolfi was radiant and so was I. Now we could really think about our Matterhorn North Face!
It was evening, we were down in Zermatt. Busle had gone on ahead, up to Schwarzsee, underneath the Matterhorn. 'You go up to the hut,' I had told her, 'I'll be following quite soon.' That iron man, Wolfi, on the other hand, was lying in the tent somewhere, breathing mountain-

air. Wolfi – *un des purs* as Samivel has it – one of the 'real' ones: every fibre of body and brain now concentrated on the North Face, speaking of nothing else. Two days from now we would be starting up it . . .

I had told Busle I would be coming soon. So I bought a few small things for the North Face; and then, unexpectedly, ran into some old friends. It got late, and later: no question of 'soon' any more. But it is nice to feel comfortably sure that, whatever happens, one is being waited for.

It was midnight when I knocked at the hut door. The place was shut, every bit of it. 'Busle!' I called, in a half-voice. No answer. 'Busle!' – a little louder this time. There were plenty of windows (but which one?); they were all dark, and the wall of the hut smooth.

Surely she must be awake? How could she be sleeping peacefully while I was standing out here in the cold? A dog trotted across the meadow; I did a few knee-bends. She must be sufficiently worried about me to open the window at least every quarter of an hour, to see whether I had arrived? Well, say, at least every half hour! Really, one shouldn't put one's faith in women . . .

In the moonlight a striped cat was promenading through the grass; it sat down to gaze at me with a kind of scornful nonchalance. 'Busle!' The cat gave a jump. My fury kept me warm for another quarter of an hour; then I set about finding a place to bivouac in. No anorak, no bivouac-bag, nothing. What a pitiful object! Wolfi, of course, always has something along with him.

Cardboard-boxes, lumber, pitch darkness – I had got into the wood-shed. Hard beechwood logs, of course . . . how unkind can Providence be?

I couldn't aspire to any higher storey. The outline of the cat showed up again in the door-frame. 'Gschschsch!' It made another jump. No, really – before I let myself remember the whole long night . . . yet freezing isn't much fun either . . .

What about the boxes?

'Oh, Busle' – I wrap myself in corrugated cardboard – 'how can you bear' – I wedge myself into a big rectangular box – 'my getting frozen feet' – a dust of pudding powder, smelling of strawberries comes out of the box, as I push my feet through its bottom and stick my legs into the next carton – 'instead of staying awake' – I cram a reasonably soft macaroni-box over my head – 'unable to sleep, and only waiting for me to come?'

Hard and horrible are the dictates of fate. But I am beginning to believe it was done on purpose. 'Gschschsch!' Is that brute there again?

Hop it – my requirement for cats is fully catered for. I am a climber, in training for the North Face. One of the 'real' ones, at that . . . !

What? Can't even turn round any more? This blasted pudding-box! I've grown four-cornered. What if I force it? That's just about all that was needed. What a smell of strawberries . . .

Life is very hard – hard and four-cornered.

Comes the dawn. Bitterly cold. The surroundings begin to take shape and colour . . . SWISS NOODLE PRODUCTS: UNSURPASSABLE . . . In large letters before my eyes. I try to wriggle my toes. OVOMALTINE, THE NATURAL BRINGER OF STRENGTH . . . I have discovered a kind of rocking motion, inside my cardboard fortress, which provides calories. The morning hours are the chilliest. Ah, a ray of sunlight, falling square across the beech-logs, with little points of light dancing in it. Look at those boxes and logs! You just wait, my Busle, for today's thunderstorm, Austrian pattern!

Half a moment, though. No, I must never give her the pleasure of amusing herself at my expense, about my bivouac! Why, I met friends down in Zermatt, and so I stayed there. So sorry, Sweetie, that you waited for me . . . A much better version than my first idea. Ha! Ha!

I climb out of my boxes and emerge. There is Busle, sitting in the sun outside the door. 'Good morning,' says she, quietly, her eyes shining. My words stuck in my throat. Should it be version One or Two?

'Have you developed a sudden passion for Macaroni?' she asked, amiably. I removed the box from my head. Moorgarten . . .

'Sweetie,' she smiled, 'how you do pong of strawberries!'

Sempach . . .

I took my drubbing as well as I could. (No wonder: for the Swiss army is one of the best in the world; but Helvetia decides which corner of the home shall house the rifle.)

It was midday. I was affectionately occupied with Sunspray and Busle's back (we Austrians are reckoned as helpful, unselfish, always ready to atone for a little slovenliness by attention to detail). Suddenly Wolfi came on the scene, clinking with pitons – actually our 'real' one had the pitons in his rucksack, but I could hear their spiritual clatter, as he found me occupied in such unalpine activities, the day before our face-climb – so excuse the poetic licence.

Said Wolfi, wearing his North Face expression: 'You do know we are starting tomorrow?'

I nodded and went on creaming.

Wolfi threw a first warning look at me, then a second slightly oblique one just brushing Busle's back (she never got a mention in his written

The North Face of the Matterhorn

accounts). 'I think,' he said, 'we should be getting on up to the Hörnli Hut.'

Busle beamed at him. 'Good luck, Wolfi,' she smiled (not without emphasis) 'my Sweetie will soon be finished, and then he'll come.' Wolfi drew a deep breath and looked up at the North Face. Then he sat down.

And now let him carry on with the story:

'... at our feet lay the little mountain lake in which this proud peak mirrors itself. It was not very late yet, so we stretched out in the sun and enjoyed the beauty of the afternoon.

'The mountain soared majestic above us. Its sharply-defined ridges and flanks fall steeply away on all sides. But the most savage and withdrawn of them all is the North Face. The sun only penetrates that wall, almost 4,500 feet high, for four hours a day. There is not much hard snow on that face; for the most part only treacherous powder-snow covers the smooth rock. Two frightening questions kept on recurring to our minds: would we be above the ice-field before the sun loosened the stones, held fast by the frost? Would there be heavy icing on the rocks?

'Time passed. We shouldered our rucksacks. We met people who took smiling stock of us. Our small climbing-rucksacks were topped by a mountain of clothing and other things carefully tied-on with line; and a miner's helmet shone from Kurt's. [Wolfi was always highly scornful about it, likening it to a useful porcelain article – never would he don such a thing in his lifetime! He was to change his mind later on.] Once again we approached the Hörnli Hut looking like two mountain tramps. Everything good happens in threes. [Wolfi, of course, means that this was our third attempt on the North Face; we had been there twice before, during the previous summer.] All around the Hörnli Hut, close to the foot of the Matterhorn, one can hear every language under the sun. There are people examining the Hörnli Ridge through the telescope, trying to discover today what awaits them up there tomorrow. Tired climbers with happy faces passed us on their way down to the valley. They had had their wish. We did not want to attract any attention and did our best to get our equipment into the sleeping-quarters unnoticed. The guardian of the hut came up to us and asked us straight out whether we intended to try the North Face in the morning. It was late, and I tried to sleep, but I couldn't; I was far too excited. I kept on looking at my watch, hour by hour. Once Kurt said to me: "Oh, do stop being so strung-up!" But he must have been feeling just the same.

81

'At last it was midnight. A glance out at the wonderful sky, full of stars, encouraged us not to lose a moment. We climbed cautiously up old, eroded avalanche-cones, with the North Face, deep in shadow, looking eerily down on us, like a ghost. From below, our route had looked unmistakable; now, we had to search around for quite a time before we found our bearings. At about 2.30 a.m. we reached the lower edge of the bergschrund. It was still so dark that we could not see for certain where it was easiest to get across. Kurt settled it by going straight for it, up the cliff. We came to the ice-slope. A stone whistled past us like a bullet, then utter silence again; the only sound was the crunch of the frozen snow under the pressure of our crampons, and the occasional sharp ring of one piton striking against another.

'Above us, the first rays of the sun were already falling on the rocks. Rope's length by rope's length we climbed on steepening ice at an even pace. Up here our twelve-point irons got little purchase on the hard ice. And now we were getting the first morning salute from overhead. Small fragments of ice, loosened by the sun, went humming past our heads. [The daisies! It really looked like a shower of flowers; but then, of course, *I* was wearing my miner's helmet.] We had to watch out for them very carefully. We kept on diagonally to the right, towards the great concavity in the middle of the face, which provided our route for the next 1,400 feet. We changed the lead after nearly every rope's length. The next time I wanted to bang in a piton as a belay, it struck rock after only a few centimetres. I tried another spot, but there was simply nothing to be done. I shouted to Kurt to take great care. Presently we came to a steep rock-step below the great bay in the wall. I tied myself to a piton, took off my crampons and climbed a rope's length up steep rock. Kurt kept his crampons on. In this way we contrived that one of us was always ready for difficult rock, the other equipped for ice.

'In due course, the stratification of the rock became very awkward and there was a heavy layer of ice on it, so I had to put my crampons on again. Although we were warmly clad, the cold up here was biting, for not a ray of sun had yet penetrated this huge, slanting, open gully. To our right, the wall went winging sheer into the depths to where the crevasses in the Matterhorn glacier looked like tiny cracks. Above us to the left it loomed up, starkly unclimbable. Against these measurements of terrifying might and size, a human being feels very small and forsaken.

'We pressed on, slowly but steadily, upwards. The climbing became very unpleasant, on a regular, thin sheet of ice, frozen bone-hard, overlaying a mass of loose stones. [Hiebeler commented later that the

The North Face of the Matterhorn

photographs made it look like winter-conditions.] I looked longingly up at a little rock-spur, up there in the sun, where the Schmid brothers had bivouacked.

'At 11 o'clock, we tied on to two belaying pitons and swallowed a couple of lumps of sugar and a lemon. The way ahead did not look too bad at first. The best of it was that the angle seemed at last to be easing-off a little. But how wrong we were! Ahead lay smooth slabs, without a single hand- or foot-hold, furnished with minute irregularities and heavily iced over. As I none the less started another stroke with my ice-hammer, the slip-ring slipped off the shaft, and the whole hammer out of my frozen mitten. A cold shiver ran down my spine and I held my breath. The hammer was caught by a minute projection and hung there, just below my feet. I climbed down three feet and, to my delight, got a grip on it . . .'

[After that exciting mishap, we reached a traverse in deep powder-snow, which brought us on to that part of the wall which is known as the Roof. We were now well above 13,000 feet.]

'The big snowfield lay ahead of us. Just above us the face looked savagely shattered and rocky. We could already make out the fixed-ropes on the Hörnli Ridge, over there. The terrain became more broken and therefore easier. Towards the top the rock became so good that, in spite of our great exertions, we really enjoyed the climbing. We could hear voices on the Zmutt Ridge . . .

'We climbed a last steep gully of shattered, rough rock, and then over a short snow-slope, straight up to the cross on the summit. It was 7.30 p.m. and the sun was very low. Together on the Matterhorn's summit, we revelled in an unforgettable sunset. An enormous sense of joy enveloped me . . .'

Those minutes enveloped all three of us in it. Busle, who had lost sight of us against the sheer size of the face, now spotted us all the way from Schwarzsee as tiny spotlighted figures on the summit. After seventeen hours on the face, we unroped and in the dying light of an undying day started down towards the Solvay Refuge. All our dreams had been fulfilled – we could hardly believe or grasp it yet – for, three times before, I had been on the Matterhorn in cloud. Today everything was clear. At last we had got our North Face. No bivouac, not a cloud in the sky all day . . . Yes, today, all our dreams had come true.

I did an idiotic thing. Dark though it already was, with the lights of Zermatt quivering down in the valley, there in the darkness of the dark rock-world, I leaned against a black boulder with my camera and pointed it towards the horizon. My hand was shaking, the camera slipped on the rock: over the double-edged silhouette of the Dent Blanche, the colours fuse in a wide band of dark blue, red and yellow.

'Cheerio, Busle!'
The little red train was pulling out of Zermatt and moving away along the valley slope, a small red streak . . . then a dot.
The platform . . . suddenly I was surrounded by nothing but strange faces. I grabbed my ice-hammer and started off for the Theodul Pass, in Wolfi's wake, bound for far-off Mont Blanc.

Nobody else climbed the North Face that year. The slopes below the Matterhorn slowly turned brown. One day the soft, broad, white blanket of the snow unfolded itself on them and on the mountain above them. It was winter once more.

The following summer did not see me in Zermatt. I was living in a tent on the rubble-covered Baltoro Glacier, far away in the Karakorum. Another summer came; I was at the foot of the Eiger's North Wall. Yet another and another summer, as the Earth kept turning . . . I never came back to Zermatt.

There is a meadow, packed with daisies. The sky above it is clear and the air is deep, and transfused with light. The wind caresses the slopes. The daisies lift and droop their little heads. They say 'Yes'.

It is . . . it is . . . it is . . .

I wonder, will any one else ever again discover flowers on the North Face?

The daisies lift and droop their little heads.

They say 'Yes'.

And yet, in a thousand years, no single day passes away.

Himalaya: 'The Gift of the Gods' . . . so said Herbert Tichy, as he and his friends stood on Cho Oyu's summit.

It is in truth, a gift of the Gods to stand so high above the world. I ask myself this: does the intrusion into those ultimate heights change a man? Do the Gods, in return for what they grant, exact something from the best-beloved?

No one knows the answer.

The 'Giant Meringue'

Once in his life – irrespective of age – everyone suddenly does something quite crazy; nor does he normally regret it.

The *direttissima* of the Königswand, the hardest of my first-ascents was a fantastically crazy performance, which still gives me pleasure today, though I would not care to repeat it. But then, I couldn't, for it is no longer possible; the key-pitch has since collapsed into the abyss.

That is not to say one couldn't do the *direttissima*, without the 'meringue', today. It could be easier, but I am not sure. For that summit is a Sphinx; and that enormous cornice of ice, into which they carved a complete defence-position during the First World War, and which fell off the mountain after the second climb, is building up again. Who knows what it will look like tomorrow, or in twenty years' time?

Before the cornice fell, my route was repeated, by none other than Wolfgang Stephan, my regular climbing-partner, who for once was missing on the first occasion. For him, that absence had been too much to stomach . . .

He and two others had an even more disturbing passage than we did. One of them came off, though without hurting himself. The following few sentences from my friend's report of their climb will give some small idea of their venture close to the limits of the possible:

'The "Meringue" loomed like a giant balcony above us . . . the nearer we moved to it, the more impossible it looked. . . we couldn't hide our anxiety from one another . . . in the end, a perfect hedgehog of pitons . . . sheer over the abyss; an amazing sensation to be hanging there from those tiny iron shafts, 12,500 feet up, above nothing . . . getting more and more impossible to communicate with the others, planted below the overhang . . . at last my hand was able to touch the rim of the cornice.'

They had climbed the face and reached the bottom of the barrier, that is the 'Meringue', at about midday. Not till seven hours later, about 6 p.m., did they set foot on the summit. It had taken all that time to master the key-pitch. The third man came off while retrieving the pitons, and found himself hanging in thin air, 2,600 feet above the Königswand glacier . . .

'There was our companion, swinging far out from the face, remote from all possible contact with it. So we threw a rope across to him and tried, without the least success, to haul him up. Then Götz hastily constructed a block and tackle hoist.' Thus Wolfgang's report.

I do not know whether anyone attempted it again after that; certainly, no one succeeded. A few parties have climbed the face and reached the summit by a traverse to one of the ridges on either hand.

And how did we fare? I have an ancient account in front of me. Let it take us back to those fantastic September days, when that blue pavilion of ice still thrust far out over the gulf below, when the summit was still 'in one piece', and I myself all of twenty-four years old. I was both a dreamer and a realist then: bewitched by those white lines of crystal, ready to take any risk to realize the route my imagination showed me, up that loveliest of ice-faces in the Alps. At least, that is how I – lured by a mountain's magic – saw it.

A soft wind caresses the summit of the Königsspitze, soughing among the rocks, sporting with the powdery snow, now and then whirling it in glittering banners skywards, then falling again to leave the mountain quiet in the still air.

It is very quiet up here now. It is autumn, with a hint of winter on many a day. Very rarely does anyone come up here. It is late in the afternoon: the wide blue vault of the heavens arches overhead, from the distant cluster of the Dolomite spires to the white heads of the Bernina. Far down below, in the Sulden valley, the fires of day are quenched and a dim twilight reigns. The icy sweep of the Königswand, too, grows darker, that face plunging away from here to the north-east, overhung by the blue shimmer of untrodden ice-bulges. Slowly the mountain's shadow grows out into the east. The gnomon of the sundial. Minutes on the horizon . . .

The wind starts up again, keen in the stillness, plays about the slender topmost seam of the cornice, leaving a line of glittering dust, outlining the huge buttress of ice and snow. The sun's rays slant to the summit. What was that? From the inner recesses of the mountain comes a soft, almost inaudible thumping. Again, clearer this time, coming from the north-east, where the giant roll bulks far out over the face. Then silence again; till, suddenly, glistening white at the farthest rim, the snow

The 'Giant Meringue'

whirls up, farther over now, quite close to the highest point. Lumps of snow go flying, an ice-axe flashes in the sun . . . a head appears, joy written large on its countenance. Up into the sunlight, and on to the summit!

For two hours there is no rest up here, on top. The air is full of shouts, deep holes are carved out of the snow, ropes run out and taken in; till only the last red gleam of the sun lingers on the summit and the darkness of night comes creeping up those mighty flanks. It is all over: here the three of us sit in the snow, exhausted, dead-tired.

And the *direttissima* up the Königswand is fact, now!

I had discovered the mountain years before, when I was still a boy. We were standing on the summit of the Weisskugel in the Ötztal Alps – I had just acted as guide for a Viennese and two girls from Berlin (the latter we already know; but the man from Vienna was, incidentally, not Willi, the hero of our Venediger story); and we were quite excited because we wouldn't make out what the odd-looking peak, sticking out of the clouds to the south, could be. In the end someone told us: 'It's the Königsspitze.' The name is apt, for the peak is regal, and 12,655 feet high.

My next view was a close-up from the top of the Ortler. I was on my own, having just come across the Stelvio on my grandfather's old boneshaker, making my way home from the Western Alps. There she stood in the morning sun, in all her magic beauty. The light fell slantwise on the delicately-fluted crystal smoothness of the north face. 'That man Ertl,' I thought to myself, 'had a pretty fair idea of what to tackle!' For it was in the thirties that the Munich 'Mountain Vagabond', Hans Ertl, with Hansl Brehm for partner, had made the first direct ascent of the face. High up on the climb, the huge summit ice-bulge had forced him away on to the left-hand ridge. This ridge had been reached, as long ago as 1881, though lower down, by another victim of the spell cast by that face – for once that overdone word is justified in this context; this was Graf Minnegerode, who achieved the first ascent with the brothers Piggera and Peter Reinstadler, three of the best guides in Sulden. They climbed the left-hand side of the face, a less direct route; but without crampons, without pitons – simply in nailed boots and with an ice-axe clutched in their fists. Fifteen hundred steps they cut. And they were the first to climb it.

Albert and I were standing at the foot of the Königswand in the broad, white cauldron of the upper Königswand glacier. It is difficult of access, for huge crevasses and walls of séracs bar the way from below. That is why we had come by daylight, so as to mark our night-time route in advance, for we wanted to be well on to the face by sunrise.

We were tired, and sat down at the edge of a crevasse. We had been stumbling around on the débris of the moraine for hours in the noonday heat, sweating as we built one cairn after another; perhaps a hundred, particularly important among the rocks at the base of the wall, where the route goes up and down, back and forth, in this confusing approach to the white cauldron and above the sérac-walls. We had finally got in from the side. Now we sat, letting the September sunshine scorch our hides – a treat after the snowfalls of the previous days – and taking a look at the face.

Yes, that Ertl, the mountain-vagabond, a man of Nanga Parbat, explorer of jungles, he knew a thing or two...

Then we went into details. A couloir, flanked on either side by rocks, leads up the lower part of the face; above it, a diagonal rib sweeps far up towards the ice-buttresses of the summit region. Hans Ertl had gone up it; we intended to climb straight up from the top of the couloir, following a narrow rib of snow which, mounting in a soft curve and growing even more slender as it mounts, soars right up to the first balcony of blue ice, plumb in the middle of the face.

And then, what?

What a route that would be, straight up to the top over the bulge and the cornice! A dream route, forbidden, impossible... fascinating. Could we do it? Boring a way through, like moles? Perhaps there was a secret crack? Or a way right over its outside? A way over that giant roll of frozen snow – straight from the confectioner's – a 'meringue'! And so the name was born.

Hans Ertl, too, had wanted to go straight on up. But he had only four pitons, and then – he fell off, as can, alas, so easily happen. The fall quenched the joy of climbing, blunted the drive to press on; and so they turned aside. 'Glued to the smooth, cold wall of ice,' he reported, 'it took us four hours to master this very difficult pitch, the traverse below the summit-overhang.' They reached the left-hand ridge quite near the summit, but the great bulging obstacles remained unclimbed. Never yet had a man reached the summit straight up the face. The King's crown was still untouched.

Albert was no less enthusiastic about the idea of the *direttissima* than I. He was one of those 'old hands', an experienced ice-man, a blue-eyed giant – one of those who surprised us youngsters by not 'doing' anything for long periods and then suddenly, with no fuss at all, tackling some-

The 'Giant Meringue'

thing really difficult, as if it were the most natural thing in the world. How then did I suddenly team up with him? This throws some light on the working of our vagabond nature, which is not always the result of planning ahead. A whole summer's climbing in the Western Alps had gone by, and Wolfgang's time had simply run out; he just had to go home. And so, all at once, there I was, partnerless. Should I go home? Well – no. I spent a couple of days messing about on the Drei Zinnen with a young man from Tyrol – Karl Schönthaler, later to be known as 'Charlie'. Then I was on my own again. Should I go home? Instead, I telegraphed the Edelweissklub in Salzburg: 'Send me someone at least up to Pallavicini Couloir standard.' Albert Morocutti mounted his motor-bike – and now he is sitting next to me, quiet, thoughtful, blinking up at the slopes. He is one hundred per cent committed. Yesterday we put in some training on the ice-fall. Tomorrow we are going to start up the face... though we did not know it would be in vain.

Someone knocked. It must be the hut-keeper. 'Thanks!' Two-thirty. One leap out of my bunk and across to the window. Yes, the stars are out. Fine weather.

Then the familiar humming of the Primus-stove, the flicker of the candle, breakfast. The last items go into the pack. That's the lot!

Out we go into the clear night, where not a breath stirs. In the cold out there, our footsteps are the only sound. Abnormally tense, we kept on glancing up at the mountain's dark silhouette. Then the glow of our lamp showed up our first cairn; there it stood on the grass, built of red and blue jam-tins, slightly crooked and helpless-looking, but a masterpiece of our own making. We had to laugh. 'Now for the genuine Chianti flask, which we finished yesterday!' 'Oh, I thought the next one was the tin of donkey in oil?' Over there, something was fluttering, almost ghostly, in the darkness: the economics section of yesterday's paper – in black and white, such a help towards spotting a cairn in the middle of the night! Slowly we lost height, till we met the glacier's level. There, on a particularly lovely cairn, was the Lollobrigida in all her beauty. We began to move upwards again, finding our way easily enough, thanks to the decorated cairns, drawing ever nearer to the mass of dark rocks on the other side. We reached them in about an hour from the hut. It was still pitch-dark.

We stumble upwards in rubble and sand, finally roping up on a small shoulder of rock. In the first pale light of dawn I start up a brittle chimney, feeling my way up, my pocket-lamp in my mouth. Almost at once, out comes a hand-hold. 'Look out!' I yell; but it had already reached the bottom with a crash. Luckily, Albert was safely under cover, and there was no damage to the rope.

Up on the glacier there was already a fair amount of light. The whole face of the Königswand rose bathed in a peculiar greenish-yellow hue. On we went, across the smooth, hard surface; when it steepened, we stopped to put on our crampons. A shout from my companion drew my glance upwards – the sun was coming up. The icy summit ramparts glowed a brilliant red; slowly, softly, the lave flowed down from rib to rib, from hump to hump, leaving only the deep runnels in greenish blue shadow. Even around us, down below, the slopes and séracs caught a faint shimmer, reflected from the shining wall above. Presently the first rays met us, as we were busy adjusting our crampon-straps, and a golden, glittering stream of thousands of tiny crystals shot up towards the sun . . .

A puff of wind came across the glacier. The air was set in motion, gently stroking the slopes – and it was daylight. As we traversed below the Mitscherkopf, the first stones began to fall, counselling us to keep on the move. Threading our way through huge crevasses, we reached the foot of the wall, at the base of the couloir; nothing to be seen above it from where we stood.

At 7 a.m., later than we had hoped, we were at the bergschrund. We stopped to empty a tin of milk, chewed a couple of dried prunes, and got the ironmongery ready. The upper lip overhung a long way, protecting us; but only a little snow came trickling down, not a stone, not a fragment of ice. It was all lovely and quiet? Well, we should see, later on.

I went at the slope above the gash, with an ice piton in my left hand, the ice-hammer in my right; to get over the bergschrund I cut some steps and hand-holds. Then came the first surprise: 'Wash-board snow!' It was fantastic: the surface consisted of innumerable little transverse ripples, hard as bone, some white, some blue, forming a pattern like Grandma's washing-board. Something between snow and ice, sometimes both. What mattered was that this concoction provided a veritable Jacob's ladder to the sky. What incredible luck! Never before in my life . . .

We gained height rapidly, in those ideal conditions. Those blue and white ripples were so fashioned as to afford ample foot- and hand-holds. It was only at stances that we hacked out a step. Albert beamed, and I beamed back at him. There were a few vertical pitches – rock-islands hidden beneath the ice – quite a lumpy world. But what a joy! For several rope's lengths we forgot any question-marks hanging over this marvellous blue September day.

The 'Giant Meringue'

There was a yellow knob of rock above me; to its right, in the sunshine, everything above shone white. The couloir above us was barred by insurmountable pitches; we had to move across, up that way. I worked my way up towards the knob, zig-zagging between sheer ice, snow and passages of rock. The face had become pretty steep hereabouts: I looked diagonally down the couloir below me. I stopped to knock a piton in and snapped a carabiner into it . . . At that moment the 'meringue' came into view – way above us, 1,500 feet or more overhead, a great pavilion, hanging repulsively in thin air, tons of ice balanced out in the blue of the sky, so simple, so motionless – and oh, how it overhung! It seemed quite crazy that it could hold firm, that not a morsel of it came down; but then, it was autumn.

One summer's day it swept two to their death just here, when some of it broke away. I thought of the seconds while they waited helplessly. Today only a few small snow-crystals came dancing down the slope. Today there was magic in the air – and that giant bulge hung up there, as if under some spell.

Are we climbers fatalists? I suppose, in certain situations, we sometimes come fairly near it . . .

Meanwhile, 1,500 feet above our heads, the thing still hung quietly in thin air.

Hours went by. We were in the midst of an extraordinary world of ribs and more ribs and flutings, all going upwards. We chose one and crawled up it, as usual, on all fours; two tiny black dots on that vast face.

Now and then we glanced up at the ice-ramparts above: over the first blue bulge, to the 'meringue' itself. We had got used to it by now, but the nearer we drew to it, the more dauntingly the question hung over us – where was there a way through? A fine powdering of snow and ice came rippling down, but nothing worse; the sun had disappeared behind our mountain and we were in shadow, as we pushed on up towards that first blue bulge. It seemed close enough to grasp, but we never seemed to get noticeably nearer to it. Rope's length after rope's length ran out. Time had lost all meaning. Below us our snow rib lost itself in the gulf, our footsteps up it looking like a column of windows in a skyscraper. Everywhere around us, similar slender ribs swept down into the depths, concentric, like the rays of some gigantic fan, whose top we were trying to reach. Down at the very bottom flashed the mirror of the Königswand glacier's sunlit floor, the overhangs above our heads reflecting its sunny brightness.

At last the snow on our seemingly endless rib grew thinner. Then it petered out into sheer ice. Now down below, I hadn't really bothered my head very much about that first ice-bulge. Just an ice-bulge – so what? Here, the old story was repeating itself: an ice-pitch, at a distance, is just that; close-to, it is something quite different, something that only shows its teeth when your nose is literally jammed against it. And what teeth! This has happened over and over again to every ice-climber who ever lived. A little farther over there, Hans Ertl once had had to fight it out with this self-same bulge . . .

I worked my way up towards the bulge with the utmost caution over a steep slab of black water-ice, of execrable toughness. It took all I knew to cut holds in it. High time, now, to bang a piton in. I tried; but before it even held, there was a sudden crack and an ice-cake a yard long went hurtling down into the depths, almost upsetting my balance. A damned near thing that! At last I managed to get it in with innumerable tiny strokes of the hammer; but on the bulge itself, no matter how I tried, no piton would hold: not the thin flat ones, not the hollow-stemmed ones, not even the extra-short ones . . . Resigned as a burglar might be, finding himself unable to force the glassy security of the König's impregnable keep, I felt my way, with a clatter of ironmongery, back down the smooth slab again. 'No use!' I reported. Our first attack had been repulsed.

It was noon. There we sat on two nicks we had hacked out of the ice, chewing a couple of dry biscuits. What now? Should we take Ertl's route, leftwards, up to the ridge, abandoning the *direttissima*? Or should we have a go, in spite of the wretched ice there, a little to the right, where the bulge broke up into a succession of little pitches, like a blue-tiled roof?

The biscuits tasted horrible. We were only 350 feet from the summit. Three hundred and fifty feet that were the crux of the whole climb . . . Why had the ice to be so bad, just at the crucial point!

Down below, the light was gone from the burnished mirror of the glacier, the shadow of our peak had begun to reach out across the valley. Down there, in the shadowy green, the tiny houses of Sulden shone bright with small points of light. Look, let's get on with it! I got up, slightly stiff from sitting, and started to traverse slowly out to the right . . .

Down in the valley the Sulden guides were astir, and a few end-of-season visitors with them.

'You've lost the litre of red you bet me – they're going up to the right, the Devil they are, as I said; and now it's going to be tough!' Alfred Pinggera bit his lip, jammed his eye to the telescope and nodded. A dyed-in-the-wool mountain guide like him knew just what a hazardous

The 'Giant Meringue'

game was starting, up there. And Alfred grinned with pleasure all over his sun-browned face, because he had been sure that those chaps wouldn't turn it in. The other one, who had lost his bet, nodded, too, a little more doubtfully. 'There's something tough doing up there today, all right! The Giant Roll on the König, of all things! Wonder if the pair will do it – the one with the beard, whom you call "The Spirit of the Hills" and that long slab of an Albert, who only blew in here a couple of days ago? It looks barmy to me – those two little dots below the summit.'

As I began my traverse out to the right, I could not guess how many ice-bosses I was going to meet, nor did I know how many litres of 'red' had been wagered... It seemed better that way, at any rate, for I was still choking with those dry biscuits.

There, in the shadow, a shining tablet of ice, high above the sunlit world, and steep as a church roof! Never in my life had I hung on such a slab. It affronted my nose, shimmering-blue everywhere, all round me, broken up by almost vertical pitches several feet high.

Taking the greatest care of my equilibrium – not a place to come off, this – I leaned against the wall and hacked out a couple of hand-holds in front of my face: very cautiously, so as not to shatter the brittle ice. A couple more, higher up for my hands. Gripping them, I lifted a foot and climbed gingerly with the front teeth of its crampons into one of the first two nicks, now transformed to a foot-hold, threw my weight on the top two, then on my foot. It held, and so I pushed upwards, straightening myself slowly against the face, and started to gouge out another hand-hold. Over and over again, with the need for the occasional piton; but only Albert's special short ones were any good here, the others simply bent. And so, hold by hold, I wormed my way upwards, nearer and nearer to the great Roll of the 'Meringue'...

The tension increased. I hadn't the least idea where we could get through, nor could Albert see a way. All we knew was that those horrid tons of ice hung just above our heads, poised motionless. The excrescence barred the whole face with its stratified layers, an insurmountable obstacle, some eighty feet high, either vertical or overhanging. And so it stretched away, unbroken, to the Sulden ridge, away to the right: only there it was a shade less high.

The main overhang, the pent-house of the 'meringue', was directly to our left, with further balconies behind it, not so easy to see from here. And just behind the great protrusion there was a slight re-entrant. Could it be a shallow groove which would offer a route through those overhangs? Well, it seemed the only faint hope. So: up through the 'meringue' itself...'

Easier said than done . . . Hand-holds, belaying pitons, the lot. At last I am directly below the huge wall, with a balcony chest-high in front of me. Very cautiously I push my arms over it to full stretch, and what do I find – a column of ice, with a gap behind it, a real stroke of luck! With cold fingers, I thread a sling through it, snap in a carabiner and, thanks to a pull on the rope and a couple of snake-like wriggles, there I am sitting in a niche above the balcony. The next bit isn't very amusing: head-first, on my stomach, I wallow my snowy way along a closely over-hung ledge. A few more strides, and I am right inside the 'meringue' itself!

All blue. Extraordinary traceries, their curving lines making a graceful sweep. I stand, looking up. The vertical has become a meaningless word . . .

The great roof of ice goes winging over my head like some huge dome, jutting out fully twenty feet, then rolling gradually into the depths, drawn downwards by its own weight. I can almost touch the icicles hanging from its lower rim. I stand there, gazing, for minutes on end, overwhelmed by this miraculous blue dome, inside which I am, at the world's most inaccessible place; this dome, a fantastic creation of the winds and of gravity. All the day's targets are forgotten. I am the first to penetrate this shrine.

Albert followed me up, experiencing much the same difficulties as I had. Then off I moved again, tense beyond words as to the possibilities of finding any way ahead. The corner, the 'groove', might be the key; but after a very few steps I could see that our dream of the summit-prize was over. Another balcony, of mushy yellow snow, in which no piton could possibly hold, barred any hope of further progress. The pity of it! Looking up, I could see – hardly fifty feet above me – a narrow seam of gold, the sun lighting the rim of the summit.

We turned back without a word, repeating the crawl along the snow-ledge, the balcony and the traverse to our stance, in silence. Then, foot by foot, as the shadow of the 'König' lengthened over the valleys far below, we worked our way across to the Sulden ridge, looking back again and again.

And then, all of a sudden, I spotted it . . . surely, there, just above the snow-crawl, one small weakness in the ice-armour, and the only one! Three bulging overhangs, but definitely of good ice; higher up, it deteriorated, but only where it was no longer overhanging. Yes – just at the most improbable spot – there was a way up under the beetling roof of the 'meringue'; then a traverse on a repulsive-looking ledge below the

The 'Giant Meringue'

overhangs, a diagonal climb over them to the upper rim of the dome itself, a narrow seam of snow – and the summit could be won! I knew I should have to try it, however long I might have to hang in the ice; that last link in the *direttissima*. But not today. It had been a day in a thousand. There we stood on the Sulden ridge, looking back, across to the 'meringue', looking down the immense sweep of the Königswand. And there, immune, stood the summit . . .

More snowy days, putting the 'meringue' out of court; at least, in my opinion. Albert and I climbed the North Face of the Ortler. His leave was over, and home he had to go.

And I was alone again. Go home? Impossible. Not without my 'meringue'. Besides, I had the cash for a week more. 'The "meringue", the "meringue", the "meringue"': round and round in my mind. The weather was perfect. The König soared crystal-clear to the sky. Everything was set for the last, decisive effort to make him mine. But I was alone, and the 'meringue' could not be done solo. I simply didn't trust myself. On the other hand, I couldn't leave without it: *suppose someone else were to come and bag it!* I should never forgive myself! It just wasn't on. It was I who had to bag that 'meringue'. Furiously, I washed last summer's socks, trimmed my beard, darned the holes in my pants and sat down beside the path to the hut.

'How about a climb?' I asked the first one to come that way, who looked at all qualified – having first exchanged a few opening gambits about the weather and the surrounding mountains. No joy at all. As soon as I began to unfold my plan in detail, my opposite number lost all interest, or remembered a previous assignment, or had to look after his girl-friend's interests. I started to seethe: 'These damned women in the mountains! How many first-ascents have been scrapped on their account?' It was beyond endurance – though, of course, only an excuse. And this 'meringue' was such an obvious thing!

I went back to Sulden in despair. Alfred was my last hope – the guide. Alfred promptly agreed; indeed, he was enthusiastic. But Alfred's wife, in the next room, had overheard, and invited him to a tête-à-tête. I began to see red – flaming, crimson red.

I am sure Alfred would have come along just the same; but I was not prepared to let my 'meringue' shatter the peace of a whole, long family-happiness. So I passed on – up to the Hintergrat Hut. I knew Fritz Dangl, the guardian up there, a tough nut and a guide, too. Perhaps he would join me?

Up there, a vision of utter peace met my eyes. There on the bench outside the hut sat Fritz, smoking his pipe, with his grandfather beside him. The children and a dog were playing around the place. No wife in sight.

Fritz agreed at once; but he couldn't leave the hut for a few days, till his wife got back. 'Can't you come sooner?' I urged. No, not till then. Abandoning myself to my fate, next day I climbed the North Face of the Little Zebru, so as to keep my hand in. I soon realized that, in spite of my days of enforced idleness – or because of them? – I was at the top of my form. So I opened up a new route to the north-western peak of the main summit and, after a restful little nap up on the south summit, came down by its north face. That turned out to be a rather dicey trip, and I was glad when I got to the bottom. I got back to the hut in the evening, with two solo 'first-ascents' – one up, one down – in the bag. Enough to make one happy. But I hadn't bagged that 'meringue' yet...

By now, I knew every inch of it by heart – Fritz has a super-telescope – and I was banging the pitons home where they belonged, in my dreams.

I heard that a couple of youngsters – probably 'Extremists' – with heavy rucksacks, were on their way from Sulden to the hut. I went to look, and came upon a tent. Here they were, two Austrians. We reached agreement in no time. Tomorrow we would meet on the summit and attack the 'meringue', approaching it from the Sulden ridge, by which they intended to reach the top. I informed Fritz Dangl of the latest turn of events. Then I went over to the Schaubach Hut.

Some reader or other may confront me with the proposition that a true first-ascent should be made in one piece, all the way up from the bottom. Ideally, that would, of course, be the most satisfactory way. However, on some first-ascents of extreme difficulty, one dispenses with a repetition of the pitches one has already successfully pioneered oneself, as superfluous; and traverses in again on another day, to start at the point where one left off before. That is how the West Face of the Dru was first mastered, the Gemelli Arête, the North Face of the Eiger in winter conditions. Nor had I any doubts about the practice, having regard to the extreme difficulties of my *direttissima*. Only the last bit was missing, and it was that bit which still had to be done.

The Königswand was bathed in morning sunshine. I had packed all my ice-equipment and was sitting quietly outside the Schaubach Hut, enjoying a rare little moment of idleness. By rights, those two ought to be in sight on the Sulden ridge by now...

The 'Giant Meringue'

Not a sign of anyone. Had they been taken ill, or could there be some misunderstanding? Or had they, after all, changed their minds at the last moment – everyone is entitled to. In thoughtful mood, I looked up at our own route on the Königswand, where I knew each separate boulder. Suddenly, I saw two new ones . . . there they were, my young friends . . .

Nobody has ever got up to the summit of the König as quickly as I did then.

When I reached it, my pair were already just under the 'meringue', having made good use of the steps we had left. But something had happened somewhere on the way up – a hammer had broken and was quite useless. Moreover, they had only five pitons. Hans Ertl himself couldn't have got up here with those. At shouting-distance we joined up. I would bring my equipment across to them. One condition: *I* was going to lead on that 'meringue' – *my* 'meringue!'

Down in Sulden, the guides' hearts missed a beat. That tiny black dot up there was slowly pushing its way across the face – up there, under the giant bulge, 2,500 feet above the foot of the wall . . .

That appalling gulf below my feet! I had dithered before taking the first steps out on to the precipice. However, a look across at the 'meringue' drove me on.

Ice in front of my face. Two thousand five hundred feet of emptiness under me. I dare not look down. Utterly alone. Sheer madness, this.

I am stuck; my nerves have let me down. Trembling, I bang a piton in and hang myself on to a line. Deep breaths. My God! Out with the spare rope, and into the piton, hanging on it, and moving on again . . .

The rope has run out. I have got to untie. The rope goes rolling slowly across the sheer face to the piton, with the lazy swing of a pendulum; obedient to the laws of gravity, it hangs straight down the precipice now, over there, like the second-hand of a stopped wrist-watch.

All on my own again. Only my fingers to rely on, and my nerves. Mustn't think. One step, and a compulsory rest. Another. My life depends on the precision with which I make them.

I have got there. Above me, on a narrow ledge, stands Hannes, airborne, it seems. A fine piece of work, his traverse across, under the overhangs. At all events he has retrieved the pitons behind him. How could a second follow him now, unless he 'pendulum'd' across? Unnecessary, now, anyway. Much better like this.

I sent a couple of extra-long pitons up the rope to Hannes. No one could say what his stance might still have to put up with. We both felt a lot better after that. Very soon I attached myself to the rope again, belayed this time by Herbert. Here I am, at last, under that immense roof again. This time, it has simply got to go!

The first thing was to get up to Hannes, and, seeing what this involved, I plumped for the double-rope. Herbert belayed me along the ledge – thirty feet of traverse with a cold, overhanging swell of ice at chest-level, pushing the upper part of my body out into the void. With the aid of a couple of pitons I reached Hannes on his incredibly airy stance. Now Herbert could let my doubled rope run out, swinging across to us pendulum-fashion. There it hung loose below us, moving slowly back and forth. We looked at the overhangs and I fetched a lemon out of my pocket. 'Have a bit?' I asked. 'Thanks,' came the slightly grudging answer: for these two had really wanted to complete the climb on their own, and had, like as not, sat below the 'meringue' for a while, contemplating it. Anyway, here the three of us were now, and none of us would get up without help from the others. For better or worse, we were all in it together – as in some familiar political situations. There Hannes and I sat sucking our lemon, each his own half, looking up at where we wanted to be, guessing where the top might be, hidden behind an ice-bulge. How glad I was to have *étriers* with me; free-climbing on the outward pull of the rope on this mighty cornice could only lead, sooner or later, to falling off. It was bitterly cold up here at 12,500, in the September shadow. With a clatter of pitons, I was off again, and banged the first one in. Hannes kept on belaying me to perfection, which cheered me up. No one wanted to become airborne – down that face – at this point. I kept on hammering away at that piton. The minutes prolonged themselves into hours. This was the toughest ice-climb I had yet met . . .

To me, dependent from the overhang, everything looked crazy! The sun stood crooked above, hidden from sight. In went the next piton: now for the *étrier* . . .

As I lifted my foot, I could for a split second glimpse the spare rope, far down below, on the slanting face of the wall, seen diagonally below my crampon points, a thin line like a forgotten shoe-lace. I felt for the *étrier* with my points – the thin sliver of my wrist-watch's second-hand circling before my eyes. I got hold of the rope again, found a new footing in a space above the slant below me. Thin air, ice-waves, everything at a tilt. Gravity alone told me where the vertical was. Another piton; another ice-cake went clattering down into the deeps. At a certain point

The 'Giant Meringue'

I realized that I hadn't enough pitons. With the greatest difficulty I retrieved those behind me, only to bang them in again above.

A pull on the doubled rope! Worn out, I rest for a moment against the slope. Then up again over a bulge, a small one this time. What a grind! but I feel good all the same. I have got so far, and now it is only a question of time. There is only one more vertical pitch ahead, then the slope eases back.

Blue flakes of ice. One of them goes shattering down into the gulf. A fine cake, this! I had thought the pastry up here would be solider stuff. But, even if I wanted to, I could no longer go back now. So, now for a short breather.

I take a look under my arm at the slope below, deep in shade. One huge funnel of ribs and runnels, a gigantic blue fan. And there in the middle of it Hannes' face, drawn with the icy cold. Time to move on! In goes another long piton, at an angle, between two flakes. Cautiously, I trust my weight to it, and it holds. In goes an *étrier*, and I am dangling clear, relying entirely on two small flakes, damn it! But it's no better *inside* the bulge; I know because I've tried it. This is the wind's handiwork. So, on with the dance . . .

God, the piton's . . . coming out . . . !

Down! Seconds prolong themselves into an eternity. I gasp for breath, cling madly to the piton below, hanging crookedly, and start to lower myself. More second, long ones. Fighting . . . hanging . . . standing. Standing arched in space, but standing again. That was close to the ultimate limit, that was! Curse those bellying flakes, curse them! I lean my head against the wall. There, dangling from the carabiner, swings the faithless piton.

Now things are getting really difficult. The ice here begins to be rotten. And it is still vertical, too; the last swell of the face, before it eases off. Here I am pushed out farther than ever, trying to lean as little as possible on the pitons and still somehow to keep contact with the wall on hand- or finger-holes. Presently I find I can occasionally force the shaft of my axe in, and, with a circular motion, hollow out a wedge-shaped hole. Into it I plunge my arm up to the elbow, put my whole weight on it, then repeat the movement on the other side. It is terribly exhausting and I am pretty near the end of my tether. Panting, I lay my face against the vertical snow-cliff. Careful, though! I feel as if I might go flying down any moment. No chance of turning round, either, any more. It's either up, or the long, airy flight, now . . .

On again. Six feet more and I am over that flaky belly. At last the slope begins to ease. At last I can't see anything down below me any more. Less agitated, I lean my face against the slope again.

Hannes was shouting up from below: Why wasn't the rope moving any more? Did I know it was perishing cold? All this in a beseeching tone. After all, he had been hanging from his piton for more than two hours, hardly daring to move, alone on that ice-ledge. He must be shivering to death. Of Herbert, not a sound for long ages, now.

I screamed down to him that the worst was over.

Of my dozen pitons, I have only one left. This one is not for the hammering, I use it in order to make progress. I grip it in my fist, this my sole life-insurance. And now for the diagonal move up to the rim of the cornice. Above me there, a snow overhang, with sunlight playing at its edge – the summit.

Tougher again, as I hack out a few holds in the seam of the cornice. I try to beat a way through it; great masses of white, ice-cold, powdery snow crash on to my face. Spitting and gasping for air, I can feel the strength ebbing from my arms. The blade of my axe flashes in the sunlight above me . . . but, hell and damnation, I'm all in . . .

Try farther out to the left, on the very crest of the 'meringue' . . . Pull yourself together; you know your last belay is miles away down below there! I move across, plunging my piton into the snow at every step – my very last piton, my lucky mascot . . .

Now I am on the very crest of the 'meringue'. The summit *must* be close overhead. With great care I batter down the last small rim of snow. Just above me, the wind is whirling glittering snow-dust high into the air. I ram my axe in and haul myself up. One last little bit, one last output of strength and then – I am up on the summit in the full blaze of the sun!

Later, we were all three together up there. We did not hurry away, for our coming descent in the darkness gave us no qualms; we were much too strongly under the influence of the events of the past few hours. We sat in the snow, eating a bit, talking – always coming back to those incredible hours, to the same marvellous thing . . .

The summit is empty now, quiet as it was before we came. True, the snowy surface is disturbed, and there is a deep breach in the narrow outer hem of the cornice. But the wind will come rustling there again, stroking the snow, softly smoothing the hollows, and getting on with his eternal architectural work. And in time he will efface every trace of us.

Tempest

Today the giant banners of the storm are flying from the Lyskamm's summit; the cornices asmoke with blown snow. Pressure-waves go buffeting through the air, there is a rattle of ice-darts, pain numbs your face. The blue, blue sky is filled with the organ-notes of some mighty symphony. This is the soaring tempest of the high places!

One of nature's most stupendous manifestations, it clutches at your very heart. Bent double, you almost float on the waves of air, staggering to keep your balance, covering your face against the stinging volleys of those icy particles . . .

This may all be happening on the Lyskamm – but today's fury is the great storm of the Himalaya: the mighty tempest of the high places, ice-cold, merciless, tremendous, under the wide blue vault of the sky.

See to it that you don't lose your gloves! Take care not to be blown bodily off the ridge into limbo!

Safely back in the valley, the rushing roar of the air is still in your ears and the joy of it remains with you: for that is just how it must be in the far-off Himalaya – as tremendous as it was up there today . . .

My First Eight-thousander
TO BROAD PEAK WITH HERMANN BUHL

Day was drawing to its close over the Baltoro peaks. The shadows of the giants lengthened slowly across the broad floor of the glacier, merging to form a silent sea of darkness, from which the mountains rose like fiery islands. The sun drew down in its quivering, flaming glory towards the horizon. Then – in a magical interplay of lovely colour – only the summits of the eight-thousanders shone high above the world, their snows glowing a deep orange hue, their rocks brownish-red, lit with an unearthly brilliance. Two men were standing on a peak, still breathing heavily from the ascent, their limbs weary – but they did not notice it; for the all-enveloping glory of the sun's low light had encompassed them, too.

Deeper and deeper grew the colours. The last rays of light now rested only on the topmost summit-crests. Then, suddenly, as they looked eastwards beyond the rim of snow at their feet, they saw the wide shadow of the mountain cut a swathe out into space, till it lay as an immense pyramid athwart the Tibetan haze and thrust beyond it, far out into the infinite.

No dream-picture, this. It was real enough, and it happened on the 26,404-foot summit of Broad Peak.

I owe it to Kurt Maix, the writer about mountains, the climber, the man who understood the young and had himself remained young – as anyone who has read his book about the South face of the Dachstein knows – that Hermann Buhl invited me to join his 1958 Karakorum Expedition. Maix was president of the 'Reichensteiners', that small, intimate Viennese section of the Alpine Association, of which I was already a member; and when I came back from doing the 'Giant Meringue' on the Königsspitze, it was he who said: 'You ought to go to the Himalaya, that's where you belong.'

The peaks of the Himalaya – they had always been my dream.

So they had, too, for Hermann Buhl, the man who had climbed Nanga Parbat solo, the man who looked so small and light, not in the least like one's idea of a mountaineer. At first sight, one hardly noticed

My First Eight-thousander

his tremendous will-power; yet he had set out alone from the last high camp below the Silbersattel to climb the summit of that ice-clad giant, on which attempt after attempt had failed over the years and which had already claimed more than thirty lives. Without oxygen, taking only his rucksack, an ice-axe and ski-sticks, he went up alone into the dark skies of the death-zone, into a world where none can exist for long. Hermann Buhl, the 'loner', got to the summit and came back; badly frostbitten, after unimaginable efforts and perils; after spending a night, at over 26,000 feet, standing erect on a narrow stance; hearing weird voices, tottering with exhaustion, at the very limits of his being. For his safe return to the valley-levels he had to thank, first and foremost, his incredible will-power. So long as a spark of life was left in him, he would never give in.

I only knew him from a distance – I had seen him once or twice at lectures, and heard much about him. He had some of the quality of the great Himalayan peaks – for me there was something unapproachable about him. Once, after a lecture, he wrote 'Berg Heil!' on my Alpine identity-card, and from that day I regarded it as a mascot.

So Kurt Maix introduced me to his friend, Hermann Buhl, and suggested me as a candidate for his expedition, which was due to leave in a few months, in the following March. I shall never forget that moment in the room where Kurt Maix wrote his books, when for the first time I stood face to face with Hermann, fearing the wrong answer to the dream of my life, opposite the slim, light-limbed mountaineer with the lively, dark eyes, the thick mop of hair, the prominent nose – and, in the background, Kurt Maix's cheerful, weatherbeaten face. It all happened so quickly. Buhl talked to me briefly . . . the North Face of the Matterhorn, eh? . . . so you are a student; do you think you could act as an expedition doctor? . . . that 'Giant Meringue' was a bit dicey, wasn't it? I agreed: it hadn't been easy, but magnificent stuff. He gave me a cursory but friendly glance; then he said, 'All right, you must join us.' Cloud-capped ridges, an endless ocean of peaks burst on my eyes – what had happened to the walls of that room . . . ?

Maix was already telephoning through to the Press. The Austrian Karakorum Expedition had acquired a fourth member. Name: Kurt Diemberger. All right: D for Dora . . . and berger like Berg – mountain. Yes, in March . . .

Again, no dream, this; it had really happened.

We went by sea, all round Africa, for the Suez canal was shut. To Fritz Wintersteller and myself it made no difference, the ticket was good for either way; we were accompanying the two tons of our Expedition's baggage to Karachi. Fritz came from Salzburg and was a first-class climber, as was Markus Schmuck, the fourth leaf in our four-leaved clover. At twenty-five I was the Benjamin of the party by some years. Fritz, a quiet easy-going type, who rolled his own cigarettes even on the summit of Mont Blanc, was our 'Minister of Food'. The smaller, quick, wiry Markus possessed a first-rate administrative talent – in the end, Hermann had handed the over-all leadership of the expedition to him. He himself remained in charge of all climbing matters, and while actually at work on the mountain; then, even the leader of the expedition became subordinate to him. Hermann and Markus were to follow us by air; in the meantime they were still busy at home whipping up the last money that had not come in yet.

So we sailed on – right round Africa – soaking-in a thousand impressions – the sea, an occasional glimpse of the coast, the colourful life on board, the wide horizons, a visit to the top of Table Mountain. Every day, for a whole month, the ship travelled the length of Austria – it made one realize the immensity of the Dark Continent. Secretly, when there was no special celebration aboard, we toasted Nasser – for having closed the Canal. Then we did another thirty laps of the main-deck, at a trot, so as to keep fit.

Our approach-route lay through the valleys of Kashmir's Baltistan. Each day we and our sixty-eight porters covered a stage of about ten miles, sometimes even less. The tempo was typically Asian; we were destined to get used to it during the next three weeks. The porters normally carried a 60-lb. load, though a few of them humped slightly larger ones. Every mile or so, sometimes even sooner, they took quite a long rest. Then the word 'Shabash!' ran down the long, irregularly dispersed groups of our column of bearded men, and they set down their loads supported by cords running across their shoulders, either on some wayside boulder or on a thigh-high, T-shaped wooden prop – a kind of rudimentary walking-stick – which each of them carried. Or else they sat down, made tea, heated stone slabs and baked chapattis on them – unsalted flat-cakes consisting simply of flour and water – sang and danced to a rhythmic clapping of hands.

We had travelled north from Karachi by train, through the wide, endless plain of Pakistan. From Rawalpindi we continued our journey by air, across the main Himalayan chain. We flew past Nanga Parbat, but saw nothing of that mighty peak, for clouds enveloped it entirely. After a flight of two hours we touched down on a runway of sand at Skardu, capital of Baltistan, a place which boasted 5,000 inhabitants. There we waited some days for the porters to put in an appearance,

My First Eight-thousander

which they did eventually; we were assured that this represented a fair degree of punctuality. Then we set off northwards, on our way to the great ice-fortresses of the Karakorum, whose distant gleam Hermann had glimpsed from the summit of Nanga Parbat . . .

'Shabash!', the slogan of our 130 mile-long approach-march. However, one acquired the virtue of patience, shedding the vice of Europe's frantic haste. From the Indus we followed the Shigar, and after that the Braldu, through desert-like, arid valleys, barely reached by the monsoon that breaks on the main chain of the Himalaya (actually their water comes down from high and distant glaciers); valleys full of sand- and débris-flats, shimmering in the heat of the noonday sun, while unnamed white peaks floated in the sky like some mirage.

Then, suddenly, we would come on an oasis, rich with early green and pink clouds of apricot trees in blossom – hundreds of them, foreshadowing the ripe fruit we should find on our return journey. It was spring now, early April; we should not be passing this way again till summer.

The broad valley of the Shigar gave way to the savage gorges of the Braldu. The picture of a suspension-bridge consisting of three interwoven plaits of willow-branches still reminds me of the following conversation between a traveller in the Himalaya, well known to me, and the mayor of a local village . . .

'We shall be crossing that bridge tomorrow. Is it safe?'

'Perfectly safe. You need not worry: it will hold.'

'How often do you rebuild it?'

Quoth the mayor, after a short pause: 'There is no need to worry. We always rebuild it just before it gives way.'

A lover of the truth, at all events.

At every place we came to, I found myself fully occupied – in my capacity as 'doctor'.

Doctor? 'Well, you have been a student,' Hermann Buhl had said. 'Someone has got to act as our doctor!'

I had indeed studied – international trade. So I bought a book called '*Vademecum*' (literally, 'come along with me'), took a short course in administering injections, persuaded a doctor to explain the more important diseases, and presently found myself the proud possessor of 60 lbs. of medical supplies, neatly done up in bags labelled: 'Nose, ears, eyes, frostbite, pneumonia', and so on. For dentistry I was equipped with a single pair of all-purpose forceps. I never used it.

Now, my poor confiding patients waited in a queue – the healthy and the sick – while I punctured blisters, squeezed drops into eyes and ears, sounded chests. Fortunately, I had a good supply of pain-killing tablets,

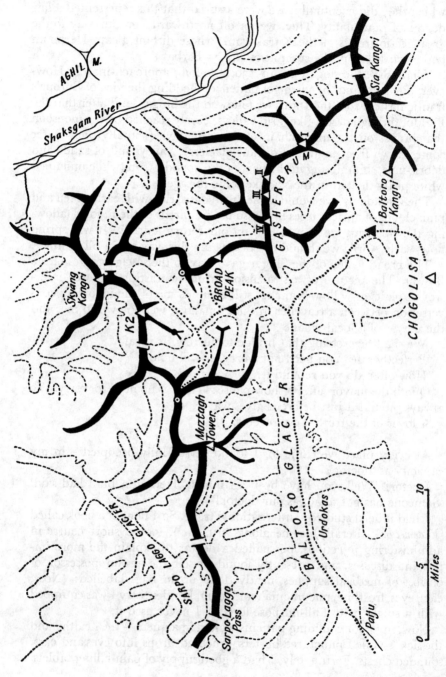

1. The Baltoro and Broad Peak

My First Eight-thousander

for doubtful cases. You see, unlike at home, nothing could be allowed to go wrong, and I had to exert special care in my therapy – for I knew we had to come out again by this same route.

There were, however, occasions when I really could do some good.

After marching nearly a hundred miles, we arrived at Paiju, the last pathetic clump of trees and flowers. Before us, huge and rubble-covered, lay the tongue of the Baltoro glacier, bordered by its sharp containing peaks.

Alpine Technique on an Eight-thousander

Hermann Buhl was well-disposed towards me. I knew it from frequent small touches, such as suggestions he might throw out, and I was glad. He would sometimes explain to me, in a paternal manner, things I knew perfectly well already; but when I saw what pleasure he took in imparting the knowledge, I refrained (sometimes with difficulty) from saying anything. Certainly, I came to know Hermann in a very different light from that in which many of those with whom he 'crossed swords' picture him. Of course he was a difficult man – that did not escape me, either – an extrovert individualist, thin-skinned, and sensitive as a mimosa – but a man in whom there burned an eternal flame for his mountains. Many who did not possess the same degree of burning vision tried in their own fashion to explain things that were crystal-clear to a Hermann Buhl. He never compromised. His zeal knew no limits – and in pursuing his aims he could be unbelievably tough with himself and with others. Not everybody understands such a man.

I wrote, and dedicated to him, a final chapter for his book *'Achttausend, drüber and drunter'*.

One morning, at Paiju, Hermann issued me a light-hearted invitation to go on a reconnaissance with him, and I gladly agreed ... We stood on a high shoulder of the savage granite pinnacles of the Uli-Biaho group, looking up at the huge Paiju Peak, across at the rusty-brown cathedrals of the Trango Towers, and up the Baltoro glacier's immeasurable length, farther and ever farther – to where, twenty-five miles away, soaring above the stratifications and bosses of its rubble-covered icestream, the eight-thousanders stood ghostly, unapproachable, incredibly high, not of this world. And there we saw our mountain, our Broad Peak. And two hearts leaped for the joy of such a day.

Now we began talk about our mountain much more frequently. We were all full of enthusiasm and zeal, as was indeed essential, for the undertaking which lay before us would demand the last ungrudging effort each of us could contribute. No one had yet succeeded in climbing an eight-thousander without using high-altitude porters; this is what Hermann wanted to attempt. His plan was that from base camp onwards there would only be climbers on the mountain; they would do everything, load-carrying, establishment of camps and, finally, the assault on the summit. And it was all to be done without the use of oxygen; we were all to achieve high-altitude acclimatization during our load-carrying up to the high camps.

It was certainly a novel concept, tough and not without its risks; but we all looked forward confidently to the day that would see all four of us on our summit. Hermann, the only one of us with previous experience in the Himalaya, thought it could be done, and he must be right. At home the plan had led to the shaking of many a head; but then, Buhl's plans and achievements had always been more daring than anyone else's. No one knew where, for him, lay the limits of the possible; nor had he yet found out for himself. Broad Peak, without high-altitude porters, without oxygen: 'The ascent of an eight-thousander, using the technique of the Western Alps,' he had called it. It was a typical Hermann Buhl plan.

And the route to the summit? It was just as daring as the plan itself: it would simply go straight up the steep ten thousand-foot face of the mountain, over a col at 25,600 feet and thence up a short terminal ridge to the summit-crest. It was a splendid, direct route, which had already been recognized as possible and described in the 'thirties by that famous Himalayan explorer, Prof. G. O. Dyhrenfurth. Buhl had chosen that route up the 'West Spur' not only for its directness, but because it was less dangerous than the route by which Herrligkoffer had attempted the peak some years before, leading as it did for quite a long stretch, known as the 'Gun-barrel', through the tracks of ice-avalanches. To be sure, Herrligkoffer's expedition had had no choice, because the West Spur was as good as impassable for its laden high-altitude porters – a consideration which of course caused us no worries. Farther up, our route, and his ran together for a little way; but above 23,600 feet, ours broke absolutely fresh ground, on which nobody had ever set foot.

As to the high camps, the intention was to equip them relatively lightly and with no view to lengthy occupation, in keeping with the character of the summit assaults, which were to start as rapid thrusts from base camp, as soon as the 'ladder' of camps was complete.

One day followed another. We and our porters moved on and on over the Baltoro's world of humps. We were now more than 13,000 feet up,

My First Eight-thousander

and the halts multiplied increasingly. It snowed during the nights and the cold was icy. We had already survived one strike on the part of the porters; it was clear that the next one was not far off. The shape of the peaks on either hand was beyond all imagination: the needle-sharpness of Mitre Peak, the fantastic surge of the Mustagh Tower, the huge, shining rhombus of Gasherbrum IV, only just short of the eight-thousand metre line – Gasherbrum, appropriately means 'the gleaming wall' – and, last of all, Chogori, 'the great mountain' – known to the world as K2. I have not calculated it exactly, but I am sure that this gigantic pyramid could contain a dozen Matterhorns. Our Broad Peak, the Breithorn of the Baltoro, with its three summits of 24,935, 26,248 and 26,414 feet, bulked ever more massive ahead of us. Ever colder and more hostile loomed its huge west face; it had been the cold and the storms which had forced Herrligkoffer's expedition, in spite of the presence of such experienced men as Kuno Rainer and Ernst Senn, to abandon the attempt. (Senn had gone flying down over the mirror-smooth 'ice-wall', halfway up the face, for about 700 feet, and would not still be climbing had there not been the soft snow of the 'high plateau' to check his fall at about 21,000 feet.)

At 'Concordia', in fresh snow up to our knees, we met with the expected strike on the part of our porters. All attempts at negotiation proved abortive; this time no pay-rise could shake their decision to go home. Too cold, too much snow, they said.

So there we were sitting on our cases – we four climbers, two mail-runners and Captain Quader Saeed, our liaison officer, left, at this moment, with very little to *liaise*. From now on, we were all porters – shuttling our baggage and finally establishing our base camp, at 16,000 feet. 'Very good training for later on,' remarked Hermann.

Four Men on the Spur

Get yourself fit by carrying loads, and get acclimatized in the process... in other words, accustom yourself to the altitude by humping a fully-laden rucksack up the mountain so often, and for such long hours, that eventually it does not grind you into the ground, your headaches disappear and you cease to gasp for every breath. At that point you will be going like a bomb; and incidentally the high-altitude camps will also have been established.

On May 13th, a lovely morning, we set foot on the face of our mountain for the first time and pushed on up the gullies and slopes of the West Spur to about 19,000 feet, where we discovered an airy but otherwise fairly suitable platform in the ridge, just roomy enough to take a tent. It lay about 3,000 feet above base camp, and three days later our camp I was in being. We found the long stint up to it easier each day and the process of acclimatization was noticeable; all the same we high-altitude-porter-sahibs all agreed that the West Spur was a pretty steep assignment, and our relief was obvious each time we dumped our 35-to 50-lb. loads at the platform. At that stage, however, the advantage of climbing on so steep a spur became manifest; for, instead of a slow, laborious descent, we were able to go tearing down to the bottom, some 2,500 feet, in a sitting glissade on the seat of our pants, a method which took only half an hour and saved us much time and expenditure of effort.

By May 9th we had already established camp II at about 20,992 feet, under the icy overhang of the high plateau's giant cornice. Hermann and Fritz pitched the tent, while Markus and I brought up the supplies from base camp. During this operation, Hermann and Fritz made a valuable discovery: in the natural refrigerator of the 1,500-foot high 'ice-wall' above the Plateau they caught the glint of a salami, a bottle of egg-liquor and a tin of bacon belonging to the Italian K2 expedition; the last item having been fetched by Herrligkoffer's team from the Italians' base camp. Surely it was by an unexampled circular-tour that the bacon found its way into our cook-pot; the liquid was still excellent and even the three-year-old salami had been perfectly preserved up there, as we confirmed after our first hesitation. At our 'ice-palace' (camp II), below the cornice, we later on replaced a tent which had been crushed by snow-pressure by one belonging to the earlier expedition, found by us on the ice-wall; and we built their fixed ropes into our veritable handrail between high-camps II and III, on that very cliff.

We were still short of one camp, the assault camp from which our attempt on the summit would be launched, a camp III at about 23,000 feet: the last rung in the ladder of camps we were in this way pushing up the face. Unfortunately, on May 21st, the weather broke, with devastating days of blizzards and gales. We sat in our base camp and waited; but on the 26th we were all four on our way up the Spur again in beautiful weather. Although camp III had not yet been established, we had decided to go for the summit. After Hermann and I had prepared the slope of polished ice above the Plateau so that loads could be brought up it, while Markus and Fritz looked after the supplies, we finally joined up and established our assault-camp, at just under 23,000 feet, on the evening of the 28th. Fearing that the weather might turn bad again soon, we dispensed with a rest-day and started out at first light the next morning.

We made good progress at first, but higher up we were greatly

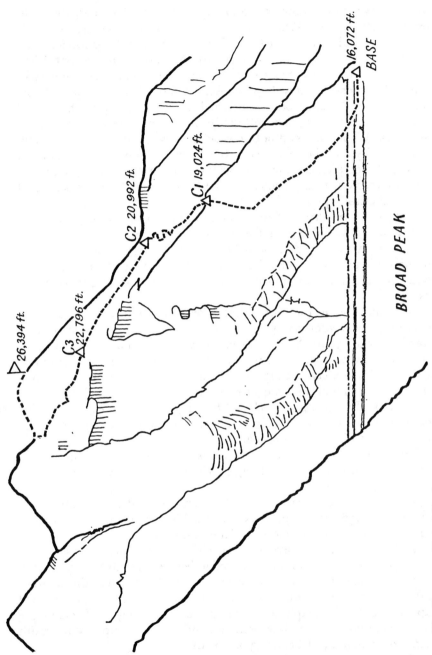

2. The Route on Broad Peak

troubled by the deep-powder snow lying on the steep face and, above all, by the fearsome cold. When the sun's rays at last reached us, we all felt as if we had undergone some kind of a redemption; but this was followed by an ever-growing, leaden sense of lassitude as we gained height. Were we suffering from lack of oxygen? Or was it the effect of the cold we had suffered earlier? Whatever the cause, we moved more slowly all the time. During the afternoon we reached the saddle between the central and main summits, 25,600 feet up! Before us lay a steep ridge of snow and rock. We felt it could not be very far now; perhaps we should still pull it off. By now, however, each step demanded four or five breaths. A couple of rock-pitches called for our last reserves of strength; only will-power forced our weary bodies up, foot by foot, and time was passing at an unbelievable speed.

Fritz was just ahead of me, Hermann and Markus about 150 feet behind us. At last! There, in the level rays of the late sun, above a steep snow-slope, we could see dark rocks clean-cut against the sky. There was nothing higher. We made a last effort. Fritz and I stood on the rocks, with clouds drifting around us. There was really nothing more above us . . .

In front of us, to the south, Broad Peak's summit-crest fell away in gentle curves, swung away widely beyond them – and then – yes – started to rise again! Went on rising, up and up, to form a shining cone of snow, way over there, probably an hour away – the true summit! Perhaps fifty or sixty feet higher than our vantage-point, no more than that . . . but an hour away, over there. It was 6 p.m. – much too late to go on now. Bright mists enveloped the ridge, darkness came climbing out of the abysmal depths. If anyone went on over there now, the odds were against his ever getting back . . .

Down we plodded, 3,000 feet down, back to our assault-camp. By the time we reached it we were all in, utterly spent. Two days later we were all down at base again.

There we were, repeating to each other, over and over again: 'Sixty miserable feet short . . . only sixty vertical feet in height . . . but those sixty feet were at the other end of the mountain!'

Well, we would just have to capture them next time.

Markus and Hermann had suffered a degree of frostbite in their toes. We ate heartily and recovered from our exertions. Then the weather turned marvellous again, clear and beautiful, but icy-cold. We dashed up the spur again, leapfrogging camp I and sleeping at II, below the plateau. The following afternoon, June 8th, we were up at our assault camp once more, just below 23,000 feet.

'Tomorrow, and tomorrow and tomorrow . . .'

My First Eight-thousander

To the Summit

It was unusually light in the tent; the moon was up outside. I kept on thinking about the morning and couldn't sleep much. Hermann kept on turning over next to me. The hours simply crawled. We dozed off for a while . . .

Hermann woke up at 2.30. So did life in the tents. Just getting up was a job, for there isn't much room. Nor was there much time for breakfast. Thermos containers changed hands from tent to tent. Then at last we were off!

It was unbelievably cold. Our fingers stuck to our crampons. Ice-fragments went clattering down the slope outside the tent. The thermometer at the tent-door read $-25°$ C. So it must be $-30°$ outside. But it was a fine morning.

We went up over ice and wind-packed snow in the half-light. Not a breath of wind was stirring. Every now and then our crampons grated on the hard ice. Soon it grew lighter; the first gleam lit the high summit of K2. As if by magic, a little later, hundreds of peaks all around us had caught the new day.

High overhead, the Broad Peak summits stood dark, seamed here and there with bright patches. We looked longingly up, to where there was light and there must be warmth, too. The whole of our western slope lay in deep shadow, and the cold increased every minute.

Down there the tents grew smaller at every step, as we moved into deeper powder-snow alternating with wind-caked hard surface. The cold was pitiless, penetrating everything – our huge Himalayan boots, our fur socks, paper linings, everything. Nothing could stop our toes from losing all feeling. The only thing to do was to halt every 200 feet, and swing our legs for a couple of minutes as hard as we could – an exhausting exercise at that altitude. For all our early progress we were now moving forward very slowly. Hermann, who lost two toes on Nanga Parbat, soon had no sensation at all in his right foot. I wasn't quite so badly affected, yet we had been climbing for four hours in this murderous cold. It was 8 o'clock before the first rays of the sun came to us over the col. High time, too; especially for Hermann, though by now I couldn't feel my toes at all, either. The only thing now was to get out of our boots and resort to massage. Presently Markus and Fritz, who had taken a line rather to the left for the last part, joined us and we were all sitting in the morning sun at 25,000 feet. Hermann and I went on rubbing our feet, but it took a long time to get any feeling back into them. Markus and Fritz were the first to get sensation restored, so they took over the lead from us. Eventually we put our boots on and started up after them. My own feet were perfectly all right again and I felt in good form. Not so Hermann's – he had fierce pains in his right one and went more slowly every minute. His old Nanga Parbat injuries were throbbing unbearably in his veins.

The last 700 feet up the final slope to the col is steep, bare ice; the end bit, consisting of some rocks, is very hard work indeed. We got to the col at 1.30, half an hour behind the others. Hermann was in such a bad state that he had to lie down. He didn't think he could get to the top in his condition. I suggested a rest and some food, which might help; but he only took a handful of dried prunes, some glucose and a drop of tea. His foot was hurting him fearfully.

I stared out far into the west. There in the distance rose that solitary giant, which we had already seen from the plateau, the peak where Hermann had been frostbitten, during his bivouac at 26,000 feet. But he had been to the summit first: all by himself, to that 26,620-foot summit of Nanga Parbat. He had paid a great price . . .

There was hardly a breath of air moving over the col, nor a tiny cloud anywhere in the sky. The sun struck down with full force. We had been there an hour, and Hermann felt a little better.

So off we went again.

We hadn't much time left, but it ought to be enough, if we didn't have to stop too often. Our only chance of getting to the top was a steady, unbroken pace. At all events, there was no doubt that our other pair would get there; for, a little earlier, we had seen the tiny figures of Markus and Fritz disappearing high up on the ridge into the almost black blueness of the sky.

Very slowly we moved on up the steep rock- and snow-ridge leading to the subsidiary summit. The ridge was plastered with huge mushroom-like cornices. The horrific precipices plunging from the east side of the central and main summits were clothed in similar amazing snow-structures – mushrooms, ribs, enormous pilasters of snow. The great wall along whose top we were moving dives fully 10,000 feet into the abyss. It almost made one giddy to look down on unnamed peaks 20,000 feet high and the broad rivers of glaciers flowing away to the far horizon. We had the sensation of being incredibly high in the earth's surface. But it was still a long way to the summit . . .

We stopped again to rest. We went on again, fighting for oxygen for our lungs. A few yards farther on, we stopped again. Then, on again. The intervals between rests grew shorter and shorter. Our neighbour, the Central Summit, roughly 26,250 feet high, showed us how slowly we were gaining height, for it was still well above us. At last we reached the

My First Eight-thousander

rocky step in the ridge. The chimney by which it is climbed demands an output of effort. Hermann braced himself and got up it, but after that we hardly moved forward at all. And we had still not got up to the 26,000-foot level.

We stopped on a little shoulder of snow. It was a quarter to five. Two more hours before the sun goes down. And we had been more than two hours over the short bit from the col up here. The summit was still a long way away. If we ever got to it, it would be in the dark. And then what?

We admitted then that it was too late, and it was a sad and bitter realization. The fact was that it would be lunacy to go on, at our pace.

Could I do it alone? I wondered. I asked Hermann's permission to have a go. He knew how set I was on it, and said yes. I thanked him, promising he wouldn't have to wait very long. I would be back as soon as possible and then we could go down together.

I wanted to say something to cheer him up, but knew there was nothing to be said. There he sat in silence on the snow, staring out into the distance, staring at Nanga Parbat – and, as he sat staring at his own mountain, I knew what he was thinking . . .

If I was to get to the top, I must move quickly; there might just be time. I felt pretty good, as I started off up the ridge again, alone.

That slope up to the subsidiary summit is steep. I was soon gasping for breath. But presently I was above the Central Summit. I gritted my teeth, climbing much too quickly; but I couldn't afford to go slower. I stopped, leaning on my sticks, panting. For a moment everything went round and round. Then I saw Hermann sitting down there, still gazing out into nothingness. Never mind, I thought, I'll soon be back with you again. But now, there's the top up there, and I must get on with it. I wonder how far it is – maybe an hour? I wonder where Fritz and Markus have got to? Perhaps I shall be meeting them soon, now . . .

There they were, two dots on the snow of the summit slope. That's them, and they're still going up. It was a little after 5 o'clock. Come on, I said, don't hang about, there's no time to spare, and Hermann's waiting for you down there. I went at the first great humps like a madman. Then the ridge flattened out, giving way to a mixture of rock and snow. I moved as quickly as I could, shoving myself forwards with my skisticks, my eyes fixed on the next two yards ahead. No time now for looking to right or to left. Now at last the summit was coming down to me at a fair pace. My breath was coming in great gusts. I was puffing like an engine. I knew I mustn't stop, or everything would go swimming around me, like a little while ago. Then I was at the last little rise to the summit. My knees wanted to sag. On you go! Only a few yards more. Steep now.

My heart thumping like mad. But there are the last few rocks, the summit snow slope, just over there . . . and Markus and Fritz . . .

They had just finished taking their summit photographs and were on the point of starting down. A minute later I was alone. I stood there, utterly exhausted, and looked back to the subsidiary summit. I had only taken half an hour to come up from it, so I felt I had earned a short rest. I moved up the few yards to the last steps in the trail, at the edge of the mighty summit-cornice, and dropped my rucksack on the snow. What a relief to be sitting down again! My breathing soon settled down to normal and in a very short time the atmosphere didn't even seem thin any more.

Wherever I looked, a sea of peaks met my eye. Far away, over there, the Pamirs; farther to the left, all by itself, Nanga Parbat, 125 miles away as the crow flies. K2 bulked enormous, just above the subsidiary summit – 28,250 feet of it. I looked up at it in awe, realizing that my 26,400-ft. perch was so noticeably lower. To balance that, I looked down and far, far below me recognized a fairly hefty dwarf; it was, in fact, the proud sharp head of Mitre Peak, 20,000 feet high. Beyond, soared Masherbrum, which had lost nothing of its magnificence. Close at the feet of Mitre Peak lay 'Concordia', my eye plunging almost 12,000 feet down upon it. Then I began to look for our route up the long waves of the Baltoro. That browny-green spot at its far end must be Paiju, the last little oasis before we took to the ice. I couldn't take my eyes off it; I hadn't seen a living green thing for six weeks . . . Why, today must be Whit Sunday! At home, now, the trees must be in blossom, the meadows green with lush spring grass; at home, they will be thinking of us. All about me the great peaks stood in an immense silence. I suddenly felt terribly lonely . . .

I got up. From behind the cornice those two magnificent eight-thousanders, Gasherbrum II and Hidden Peak, lifted their heads. Then I looked out to the left of the cornice, eastwards, where the ranges were lower: brown ridges with snow on them, giving way to greyish-brown plateaux, stretching away into the distance – Tibet? That cornice in front of me annoyed me. If one could look out over it without hindrance, it would feel just like looking down out of the sky; a unique sensation, to be up above everything, with nothing but air and empty, infinite space round and about. I wondered whether it would be safe? When I tested it, I found the cornice was solid névé, a nice permanent structure. Finally I stood clear, with nothing between me and the view, nothing but thin air all round me. I gazed eastwards for a long time over those extraordinary depths, far into the unknown, which must be Tibet. An unbounded loneliness lay on that landscape. There was something in-

My First Eight-thousander

comprehensible about it, though what, I could not say. Then I brought my eyes down to the glittering rim of snow at my feet, which was the ultimate edge of Broad Peak. I let my ski-stick roam over the curve of it, but that was the limit of my climbing.

It was time to go. Hermann would be waiting down there. I was on my way down the summit snow-slope, when I stopped in my tracks and took another look around. What more could I want? I had seen everything. I had been on the summit. What was I waiting for? I didn't even know myself.

I hurried on down, leaving the topmost rocks and the summit snows farther and farther behind. At my feet lay the undulations of the long, almost level crest. It was all over. Was I really happy? Was that the hour of which I had dreamed ever since I first set foot on a mountain? Down there on the ridge, my rope-mate was sitting, the man with whom I had hoped to climb the summit. And what about the summit itself? It had been impressive, the prospect from it overpowering; but the picture in my imagination, my fantasy-summit, outshone it by far.

I stopped again and looked back towards the top, with the trail clearly etched in the snow. Yes, it was all over. I had been up there. It was the climax of a climbing-life – it was the Thing itself. But how utterly different. What a pity! My dream-picture was fading into paleness. It is so still and silent up here, and I am tired and very lonely . . .

I hurried down as fast as I could go; but I was no longer moving as quickly as I should have liked. All the same, half of the crest was behind me now; in a moment the subsidiary summit must pop up behind a rib of rock. Hermann wouldn't have too long to wait now. We should be able to get well below the precipice under the col before daylight failed for he would be rested now . . .

Hermann had remained sitting on the shoulder for a while, then he had felt better; so he took an expert's survey of the steep slope to the subsidiary summit. It didn't look so bad, after all. Yes, he must get up as far as that, at all costs. And after that? Suddenly he knew he would go on beyond it too. Slowly, with all that incredible strength of his will, he started to move, very slowly, upwards. The slope was inhuman and never seemed to end. But Hermann's will-power was even more endlessly inconquerable. Yard by yard he drew nearer to the subsidiary summit, and there on its crest he met his two team-mates, Fritz and Markus, coming down. 'How much farther?' 'Oh, a good hour.' And so, trusting to his Nanga Parbat luck, Hermann went on. He was determined to get to the top now, even if it was in the dark.

The Summit of Dreams

I was still up at 26,000 feet, breathing several times to each step I took. It was slightly uphill again. There were the now familiar rocks. Then the subsidiary summit came into view again, with K2 bulking high above it. I took note of it vaguely and looked down over the hump in the ridge ahead of me. What on earth was that? I stood rooted to the spot. A yellow dot? It must be a hallucination. But it was moving, and it was an anorak. It was Hermann. 'Hermann!' I shouted.

How on earth had he managed it? In the state he was in? Nobody else could have done it. I was amazed, no almost shattered, by such an incredible exhibition of will-power. And now, surely, we would be able to go up to the summit together . . .

Hermann kept on coming up, slowly, step by step, his face drawn, his eyes set straight ahead. Then he was with me. I wanted to say what I felt, but the words wouldn't come. I was just glad that he was here, with me.

It was close on half past six. The sun's light lay quite flat on the crest of the ridge. The Baltoro lay swamped in shadow. The peaks below us seemed incredibly plastic in the horizontal illumination. The sun would be down any minute now.

Surely it would be madness to go on to the summit now? I started worrying about it. Our assault camp was 3,600 feet down there; and here we were climbing up into the night. But Hermann Buhl was going on ahead of me. Hermann, who had already once spent a night at 26,000 feet. Why not this one, too? True enough, he had had unbelievable luck that time. Would we have the same good fortune now? And if we didn't – what matter? I spent a moment savouring the thought; then an extraordinary thing happened.

Suddenly everything was so natural that I could laugh about it all; about the fears of all the others down below there, their fears about their lives, my own fear of a little moment ago. Now, for the first time, I was truly at one with the heights up here. The world down there lay bottomlessly far below, and utterly devoid of meaning. I no longer belonged to it. Even my first climb to the summit was already remote beyond words. What had it brought me? Boundless astonishment that it had all been so different from my anticipation, utter disappointment. That was all, and it was all forgotten already. But now the true summit was up there, bathed in unearthly light, as in a dream.

The shapes of the huge snow-mushrooms grew ever more ghostly, their shadows strangely like faces. Everything seemed alive; and there in front of me on the level snow went Hermann's long shadow, bending, straightening, even jumping. It was deathly still. The sun was almost down. Could anything in life be so beautiful?

I stopped for a moment, leaning heavily on my sticks, then moved on, smiling to myself. There was Hermann going on ahead. We were going on to the top together. Yes, we were going to it in the dark; but ahead of us gleamed a radiance, enfolding every wish life could conjure, enfolding life itself.

Now was the moment of ineffable truth – the silence of space around us, ourselves silent. This was utter fulfilment. The sun bent trembling to the horizon. Down there was the night, and under it the world. Only up here, and for us, was there light. Close over yonder the Gasherbrum summits glittered in all their magic; a little farther away, Chogolisa's heavenly roof-tree. Straight ahead, against the last light, K2 reared its dark and massive head. Soft as velvet, all colours merging into a single dark gleam. The snow was suffused with a deep orange tint, while the sky was a remarkable azure. As I looked out, an enormous pyramid of darkness projected itself over the limitless wastes of Tibet, to lose itself in the haze of impalpable distance – the shadow of Broad Peak.

There we stood, speechless, and shook hands in silence. Down on the horizon a narrow strip of sunlight flickered – a beam of light reached out above and across the darkness towards us, just caressing the last few feet of our summit. We looked down at the snow underfoot, and to our amazement it seemed to be aglow.

Then the light went out.

The west face of Broad Peak lay drenched in the pale illumination of the moon. There were deep shadows among the rocky steps of the subsidiary summit. Presently we were among them, looking for the way down. It was not easy and we roped up for safety. The chimney was particularly difficult in the darkness, but just before the col we were out in the full light of the moon. Then we started down the steep face.

Camp was still nearly 3,000 feet below. Hermann felt a little better now, but we were both dog-tired; too tired to risk a bivouac. So, on we went, down and down.

We must have been going for untold aeons. We halted at the edge of a crevasse, nodding. The ascent was a dark memory now. There was still half the descent to be negotiated. Down in the depths there was a vague gleam, which must be the plateau. It gave us the rough direction, but it never seemed to come any nearer. It seemed quite impossible to get any nearer to it.

'What are we sitting here for? We ought to go on down. It would be lovely to go to sleep.' Somehow we staggered to our feet and started down again. Down and down. Endlessly, eternally down . . .

It was half past one before we got to the tents. We opened the flap and crawled in. In, and into the blessed haven of our sleeping-bags. 'Oh, sleep it is a gentle thing . . .'

Safely back at base camp together, we were all looking up at our mountain, as the evening sun turned its high summit to molten gold. And I gave thanks to fortune for the fulfilment of the greatest wish in my life.

The shining radiance of that great peak will be with me all my days.

Chogolisa

It was by now mid-June. There was a fly sitting on the tent-roof and a spider mountaineering on a boulder. The ice had melted steadily and our base-camp tents were perched on lofty plinths. We were slowly recovering from our exertions and spent the time writing reports and letters: 'All four members of the expedition reached the summit of Broad Peak on June 9th by the shortest and best route, employing neither high-altitude porters nor oxygen equipment . . .' The sun was beating down on the roof of our tent. We were surrounded by the white glitter of high peaks. 'We intend to stay here a little longer and do a few gentle climbs – maybe one or other of the six- or seven-thousanders . . .'

Down there in the valleys it must be high summer. It even makes itself felt a little up here. I lay in my sun-warmed tent and, while the melting ice-streams gurgled away outside, I kept on picking out from among my home mail (we were so much at world's end that the latest the mail-runners had brought up the glacier were six weeks' old) a picture post-card, with a meadow, a tree and, in the background, a little lake on it. On the back was written: 'I am here on a little walking-tour. Tchau!' The card was from Busle, and the tree was a real tree. (How long since I saw a real tree?) Then I re-read her last letter, which came from Norway. 'I have come to the far north,' she wrote, 'I can't describe to you how big that world is – something that I can't explain.' She could not describe that great world of the north, which I had never seen. An odd idea occurred to me. Hadn't I, too, penetrated a great world which I could not describe to anyone, not even to her? Up there on the summit-ridge of an eight-thousander? When I got home would I be the same person I was before I came out here? I took another thoughtful look at that tree. Oh, I should like to be going home this very minute! I looked up and saw the great peaks that ringed us, Chogolisa's heavenly roof-

My First Eight-thousander

tree, the séracs of the Baltoro glacier. Here I was, once in a lifetime. I wrote her a letter from one remote world to another.

Chogolisa is a magic mountain.

It is so lovely that the statistic of its height, 25,110 feet, seems irrelevant. The British had long ago christened it 'Bride Peak', because it is always entirely clad in white. A white rhombus, an icy roof, high up in the heavens. Dyhrenfurth, when he wrote his book about the Baltoro, remarked: 'Its classic beauty of form and the repose of its outlines stamp it as the ideal ice-mountain.' Only when seen from a distance of some twenty miles does it reveal, at the left-hand end of its great pitched-roof, a minute dark tooth, the small rock-turret of its summit. The mighty south-east ridge, sweeping up for something like three miles, catches the full sun from early morning onwards – a great advantage – and it was as long ago as 1909 that the Duke of the Abruzzi's expedition attempted to reach the summit by it. At 24,600 feet, only 500 below the top of that immense roof, they were forced by a storm to retreat; and, for a long, long time that remained the greatest height achieved by man. Nor had anyone reached the summit since.

On our ascent of Broad Peak we had all marvelled at that beautiful mountain to the south of us; but much nearer, to the west, there had been splendid peaks in the Savoia group which had caught our eye as possible secondary objectives. In the end Hermann, who like the rest of us had made a good recovery while resting at base camp, was especially attracted by Mitre Peak and the Trango Tower; besides which we also wanted to visit the Gasherbrum glacier and reconnoitre Gasherbrum IV – or at least take a close look at it from there.

However, the first consideration was to evacuate the Broad Peak camps. Markus and Fritz, taking Captain Quader with them, cleared camp I; and while Hermann and I went all the way up again to deal with II and III, Markus and Fritz, on short skis, went over to the Savoia glacier and climbed the group's highest peak, a fine summit over 23,000 feet high. This lightning foray came as a great surprise to Hermann and myself, who had no idea they had such a venture in mind. We turned our eyes southwards: we would make Chogolisa and the Gasherbrum glacier our programme. And we, too, would carry it out as a two-man expedition.

The One-Runged Ladder

Chogolisa would demand several high camps, that was obvious. Yet we could not carry more than one tent. The solution was daring: a single transportable high camp – a ladder of camps consisting of a single tent. Herbert Tichy and his Sherpa had worked their way up Gurla Mandhata in Tibet that way. So our single tent should serve as our base camp and all succeeding camps, I, II and III, as necessary; a single rung in a ladder which we would push up the mountain day by day.

After Hermann and I had decided, during the course of June 20th, exactly what we should need for our attempt on the peak, I went on ahead that evening towards Concordia, carrying about 80 lbs. Hermann who still had some things to fetch from the foot of Broad Peak, followed me early next morning, humping a similar load. Thanks to the marker-pennants I had planted, there was no difficulty about rejoining one another, and we were able to push on together, late in the afternoon, over the endless humps of the Baltoro's central moraine. By evening we had found a marvellous site for our base camp close to the enormous icefalls at the bottom of Chogolisa, and there we pitched our tent. High overhead soared the mountain's fantastic roof; wherever we looked, we saw nothing but ice and snow.

In spite of that, Hermann thought our climb would only take a few days; after it, we might still turn our attentions to Mitre Peak. The Gasherbrum glacier and more especially Gasherbrum IV were perhaps rather too far to contemplate.

On the 22nd we were already halfway up Chogolisa's ice-falls and laid a depot down on a ridge of hard snow we found there. The next day, the weather was bad; we decided not to wait too long, but to push on as far as we could get.

'June 24th: 4.30 a.m. off with tent; snowing gently; weather nothing special; going very well; 7.30 a.m. depot at 18,000 feet; rucksack, with depot material, about 55 lbs; on up the Spur in knee-deep snow; trail broken all the way to the Kaberi Saddle; about 5 p.m., pitched camp at 20,900 feet; whole route marked with pennants.'

What was the story behind these cryptic entries of Hermann's? First of all, that he was in splendid condition. In spite of the deep snow, he broke the trail all the way up to the Kaberi Saddle and would not hear of my relieving him in the lead. Secondly, that on that first day of ours we climbed 4,600 feet. (These facts should, I hope, convince anyone who imagines that it was an enfeebled Hermann Buhl who tackled Chogolisa, beyond any doubt, that the contrary was the case. Certainly every mountaineer will recognize it.) Moreover we were carrying anything up to 65 lbs on our backs and, in view of our rapid progress in spite of poor weather, our spirits were very high. After heating a drink on our hissing cooker with great difficulty, we went happily to sleep in our first Chogolisa camp.

My First Eight-thousander

Next day, Tuesday the 25th, the weather was bad again. We stayed in our sleeping-bags till 10 o'clock, cooked a meal and, at 1 p.m. struck our tent and, in spite of knee-deep snow, climbed to the shoulder in Chogolisa's South-east Ridge, at a height of 22,000 feet. There we erected our tent again, this time as camp II. We were now high enough to warrant a direct attempt on the summit. All we had to do was to wait for fine weather ...

Towards dawn on the 26th a furious storm blew up. It leaned against the outside of the tent and we against its inside. Luckily we had anchored it well. A few feet higher up, bedlam had broken loose. The wind was screaming over the shoulder with unremitting fury. When at last, after several hours, the walls of the tent stopped flapping, we went out, intending to go up a little way towards the crest we called 'Ridge Peak' and stretch our legs. It was only then that we realized how sheltered our tent-site was. Up on the shoulder we were almost blown away. The rope curved out in a wide festoon, parallel with the ground, weightless, airborne. Ridge Peak looked down on us through clouds of blown snow, flecked here and there by the sun, and the air was full of the howling of the storm, a mighty symphony.

We were soon back in our sleeping-bags, hatching out future plans. In the autumn, Hermann wanted me to come with him on a double-traverse of Mont Blanc, by all its great ridges. Then, the following year, perhaps, we would have a go at Rakaposhi ...

Towards evening the barometer began to rise again and we cheerfully fell to packing our things for the morrow. Then it suddenly cleared, and through the entrance to the tent we saw Baltoro Kangri, sublime in the light of the evening sun ... we might climb it after Chogolisa ...

The Last Day

June 27th dawned clear, fine and calm, a veritable gift of the Gods. We were happy beyond words. Our rest-day had done us good, and we felt brimming over with fitness, and a burning zeal to bag the summit.

We were off at about a quarter to five. It was still very cold, but we knew it couldn't be for very long. The sky grew lighter and lighter above Baltoro Kangri. To the south lay a sea of summits, peaks about 20,000 to 23,000 feet high, and hardly even explored. To the north the sun was already touching K2. Between us and it, Broad Peak displayed only its main summit, masking the other two.

Almost as soon as we had got our legs moving, the warmth of the sun reached us. We tramped happily up over the glittering snow. Free of our loads, we made unbelievably easy progress. The going was excellent on the very crest of the ridge, but the snow was deep and trying on either side; besides which, the wind had formed dangerous wind-slabs on the slope. One of them broke away quite close to us and went thundering down in a fair-sized avalanche to the level plateau of the Kaberi Saddle below. It made quite an impression on us and we stuck carefully to the crest of the ridge, which was so far uncorniced. But how would things go up there on Ridge Peak, where we could see cornices several yards wide projecting unpleasantly in a continuous hem? No doubt the storm of the previous day had notably increased their size.

At 23,000 feet we left the ridge, by now corniced, and traversed a little way across a smooth ice-slope to reach a projection farther up. There were actually a few rocks here, quite a curiosity on this mountain. And what about the route above? Ye Gods! There was the summit, just over there! It couldn't be any great distance and it certainly didn't look difficult. We ought to be up on it by midday, we thought.

Indeed, the next bit was easy; the slope flattened out appreciably and all we had to do was to keep along it to the deep notch beyond Ridge Peak. We made light of turning the huge cornices which towered over us to the right. Chogolisa's immense roof drew rapidly nearer, but after a quarter of an hour we had to admit it wasn't going to be easy. The slope grew steeper and the sector of ridge rising behind it had a distinctly airy look. Then suddenly we could see the whole route, and there was nothing about it to be lightly dismissed. The ridge down to the notch was as sharp as a knife-blade, its left-hand side a giddily steep precipice of rock and ice, to its right great cornices hanging far out over the North Face. We should have to be very careful there. The rock precipices below us kept on forcing us farther up towards the jagged white crest. We belayed carefully with the rope, watching for avalanches. A small wind-slab did in fact break away and went sliding away into the abyss. The snow conditions were really a curse. Just as we got to the rocks, Hermann went through to his waist, and hardly had he scrambled out when he was sitting in another hole. Damn it, the slope was a positive honey-comb! Hermann balanced his way forward as if walking on eggshells – lucky man, he didn't weigh much. He reached ice-plastered rocks and moved from foot-hold to foot-hold with incredible delicacy of balance, hardly touching the holds as he moved. A moment later he disappeared over a rib. 'Up you come!' I could hear him calling.

Rope's length by rope's length, we worked our way along the ridge, sometimes on the slope, sometimes right up at the edge of the cornices. Steadily, the wind passed over the crest; glittering snow rose towards the

My First Eight-thousander

deep blue dome of the sky. Down in the south there were huge clouds now. But they did not move.

We had made good time in spite of the unexpected difficulties. It was only 9 o'clock when we reached the saddle at 23,000 feet. And there, only 2,000 feet above us, was the sharp tip of the turret on the long crest of the summit-ridge. A steep, but for the most part broad, ridge of snow led up to it.

We sat down in a sheltered hollow, in glorious warm sunshine, and took off the rope. We were ravenous; what about a drop of tea and those delicacies we had saved up for our trip to the top? 'This is the best day for me since I came out with the expedition,' mused Hermann. How well I understood him. Climbing a seven-thousander in three days . . . not in three weeks!' This was just his pigeon – very different from what he went through on Broad Peak. I shared his obvious delight.

We didn't move on for a whole long hour. When we did, we took alternate leads in deep snow. We were unroped now. It was enough to carry the rope with us in the rucksack, Hermann said, so I did not think much about it. A steep pitch with a short ice-cliff called for work with the axe; after that it was easy again. Occasional cracks in the slope spelled avalanche-danger. They pushed us out farther on to the brink of the precipice than we had intended.

Ridge Peak was gradually sinking below and behind us. To the south, the great mountainous banks of cloud were moving very slowly nearer. The sky was calm and of a deep, deep blue. The banner of snow blowing from Ridge Peak seemed to have grown a little. To the north lay a tremendous prospect: all the giants of the Baltoro lined up in a row, a whole chain of peaks 26,000 feet high or only just less. We let our gaze range in wonderment from K2 to Hidden Peak. We took photographs and then moved on again.

How quickly the clouds were coming towards us now! We hoped they wouldn't interfere with our view from the top. We quickened our pace. The last steep pitch began a little way up there, and close above it we could see the tower that was the summit – 1,500 feet at the most – *that* couldn't take so very long.

Presently a little cloud came climbing up the slope below us. It grew larger, enveloping us, enveloping the peak. Without any warning, all hell broke loose. Grey veils of mist scurried across the ridge. Unnatural darkness swamped us. We fought our way forward through clouds of blown snow, bending double to meet the fury of the gale. On the crest of the ridge it flung itself upon us in full blast, snatching at our clothes, trying to claw us from our footing. It was terribly cold and the needles of ice blowing down into our faces hurt savagely. We could only see the next yard or two ahead. We kept on changing the lead, struggling grimly upwards.

It didn't seem possible. I thought of the blue sky such a short time back. It had all been so quick. I had an uncanny feeling – hadn't exactly the same thing happened to the Duke of the Abruzzi, quite close to the summit? Were we going to be robbed, too? Away with such stupid thoughts; it was only a few hundred feet, and we had *got* to do it.

It grew lighter for a moment, as the wind parted the driving clouds. We stood rooted, looking up to where the summit must be. There it was, near enough to touch, looming darkly above us. An instant later the wrack had swallowed it up again.

The storm continued its horrific din. Laboriously we moved up, with a steep, bottomless precipice below us, keeping close to the ridge crest. Everything was white now and we could hardly see.

We were at about 24,000 feet. Only another thousand to the summit-tower. Suddenly Hermann spoke: 'We've got to turn back at once, or the wind will cover our tracks up, and then we shall stray out on to the cornices!' He was quite right. We hadn't given a thought to it; and now visibility was almost nil.

We should have to hurry. We turned then and there. Hermann had been leading, so I was in front now. He followed at a safe distance of ten to fifteen yards, which was all that visibility would permit.

Bent double, I felt my way downwards. It was incredible – only 150 feet down, there was no trace to be seen of our upward trail, except the deep holes made by our axes. Very soon there wouldn't be very many of *them*. And still the tempest kept up its infernal din.

I reckoned we must be at about 23,600 feet, and that we must be near the steep avalanche slope which had pushed us so close to the cornices. If only one could see a bit more! I turned and saw Hermann coming after me, keeping the distance unaltered, following in my actual steps. As I moved down, I kept on looking across to the left, trying to see through the mist. All I could see was that it was getting a bit darker overhead and a bit lighter below. That must be the edge of the cornices. It seemed a safe distance away, but in mist distances can be deceptive. Perhaps it would be better to keep a bit to the right, but then I should have to look out for the precipice. It ought to be here by now. Ah, there's another axe-hole . . .

I looked anxiously to the left and then down to the surface at my feet. I was at a loss; it was almost impossible to see anything at all. *Crack!* Something shot through me like a shock. Everything shook, and for a

2, 3. The author, heavily laden, in the Valais in 1955 and leading on the classic Fox/Stenico route (grade VI) on the Cima d'Ambiez, Brenta Dolomites, in 1954 (right). Wolfgang Stefan took this picture of one of the steep and solid wall pitches high on the face . . . "It was a gigantic free-climbing pitch, then; I wonder whether it still is?" The Fox/Stenico route (1939) was enthusiastically commended to them by Cesare Maestri as one of the best Dolomite climbs.

4. The author with Wolfgang Stefan after their rapid (storm-lashed) ascent of the Eiger Nordwand in 1958. *Photo: Albert Winkler (Diemberger collection)*

5. *(left)* This direct route up Lyskamm's North Face was found by the Stefan/Diemberger team in 1956.

6. *(right)* The ice overhang (the Giant 'Meringue') at the top of the North Face of the Königspitze (Ortler Alps) was climbed by the author (partnered by Albert Morocutti) in 1956, in the days before modern ice tools. The first third involved aid-climbing using long ice pitons (see photo 4) but the upper part was a struggle through sugary ice. This first ascent led to an invitation to join the Broad Peak expedition.

BROAD PEAK, 1957

7. *(above)* Hermann Buhl, famed throughout Europe after his Nanga Parbat ascent in 1953, leaves Salzburg station, en route to Genoa, and thence by ship to Pakistan. Accompanying him are Kurt Diemberger and Fritz Wintersteller (plus Marcus Schmuck, not illustrated), sprucely dressed in trilby hats and gaberdine mackintoshes, the norm in the late 1950s.

8. *(right)* Buhl's plan was for four well-trained alpinists to tackle an 8000m peak without porters in a lightweight *Westalpinstil* push. Here Buhl recuperates at Camp 3 (6950m), the final camp before the summit attempt. K2 is seen in the background.

9. Using a steep approach from the Godwin-Austen Glacier at 4900m (a previous attempt having approached by the Broad Glacier) the climbers placed and stocked three camps, a process that provided an ideal training and acclimatisation programme. Here Hermann Buhl, makes a supply trip to Camp 2 (6400m). These were the slopes that Diemberger and Tullis descended after their avalanche escape in 1984.

10. *(above)* The west flank of Broad Peak. From the obvious high glacial slopes, the route gained the col and thence moved right, along the skyline ridge, to the summit (see also cover and diagram on p.111). *Photo: Kazimierz Glazek* (one of the two survivors of the five that climbed the lower but harder Broad Peak Central, on the left, in 1975).

11. *(left)* On the steep slopes above Camp 3.

12. *(top right)* Hermann Buhl on the summit of Broad Peak on 9 June, 1957. In the background, Gasherbrum 4 catches the last rays of sunlight.

13. *(right)* Buhl, slowed by his Nanga Parbat injuries, moving up the ridge above the col.

14. *(far right)* Buhl working carefully along the corniced ridge of Chogolisa on 27 June, 1957.

15, 16. Diemberger and Buhl were tackling Chogolisa's South-East Ridge when a sudden storm forced a hurried retreat. In a near white-out, unroped, with Diemberger leading, they groped back along their fading tracks. Near the cornice edge, Diemberger felt the snow give way and swiftly bounded to the right, whereas Buhl *(inset)* was less lucky (see page 123). The dashed line on the diagram shows where Diemberger worked back trying to find his missing partner, and the arrows indicate the fall and the jump. Later the storm cleared and the author took this photograph of the tracks leading to disaster.

second the surface of the snow seemed to shrink. Blindly, I jumped sideways to the right – an instantaneous reflex action – two, three great strides, and followed the steep slope downwards a little way, shattered by what I had seen at my feet – the rim of the cornice, with little jagged bits breaking away from it. My luck had been in, all right! I had been clean out on the cornice. What would Hermann have to say about that, I wondered? I stopped and turned, but the curve of the slope prevented my seeing over the crest as I looked up. The light was improving a little. Hermann must bob up any moment up there. I still couldn't fathom that extraordinary shaking sensation; had the snow really settled under my weight?

Still no Hermann. 'Hermann!' I shouted. 'For God's sake, what's up? Hermann!' I rushed, gasping up the slope. There it was, the crest . . . and beyond it, smooth snow . . . and it was empty . . . Hermann . . . You! . . .

Done for . . .

I dragged myself up a little farther. I could see his last footmarks in the snow, then the jagged edge of the broken cornice, yawning. Then the black depths.

The broken cornice – that had been the quaking beneath my feet, then.

I couldn't get a sight of the North Face from anywhere near. I should have to get down to Ridge Peak for that. As I went down, the storm gradually abated, and the mists lifted from time to time. I was utterly stunned. How could that have happened just behind me? I had the greatest difficulty in getting up the short rise to Ridge Peak, but even before I got there it had cleared up. I hurried out to the farthest edge of the cliffs.

The storm was hunting the clouds high into the heavens. Above the veils of mist and through them a ridge loomed up – a tower – a great roof with tremendous banners of blown snow streaming from it. Chogolisa, the horrible. I could see the spot where we had turned at about 24,000 feet. Our trail down the broad snow-field below was crystal clear. Then that fearsome drop to the north – into the clouds. And there, even closer to our tracks as they ran straight downwards, the encroaching precipice. And then I could see it all with stark and terrible clarity. Just at that point, Hermann had left my tracks at a slight bend, where I was hugging the rim of the precipice, and gone straight on ahead, only three or four yards – straight on to the tottering rim of the cornice – straight out into nothingness. Of the foot of the wall I could see nothing. Stupidly, I stared upwards again.

If we had been roped . . .

I looked down along the face, shuddering . . .

No, I should never have been able to hold him there; at the moment of his fall I myself was too far out on the overhanging snow.*

At last I could see clearly down below, where the broad snow-masses of an avalanche fanned out. The crashing cornice had set it off and it had swept the face clean. Hermann was nowhere to be seen. He must have fallen at least 1,000, maybe 2,000 feet and was lying there buried under the piled-up snow. Could he have survived that? There was no answer to my shouts and I had no way of getting down there. I should have to fetch the others and we should have to come from below. That was the only faint possibility. I strained my eyes, searching every cranny, searching for a rucksack, a ski-stick, a dark blob. But there was nothing to be seen – absolutely nothing. Only our tracks – up there . . .

Clouds blotted the mountain out again. I was alone.

Mists and a high wind were sweeping the corniced ridge as I tried to find the way down. At times I could see nothing at all and could only tell from rifts in the snow that I had strayed too far down the slope. After what seemed an age, I found our tent. It was a horror of emptiness. I took the absolute essentials for the descent and went on down. At the Kaberi Saddle there was knee-deep fresh snow, through which only a tiny corner of the marker-pennants showed. I probed with my feet under that smooth expanse of white to find out from which side our ascent-route had come, then went straight on into the whiteness . . . to the next pennant. I wandered vaguely down endless hollows, over crevasses, through fog, then into the darkness of night. For long, indescribable hours of horror – during which I at times had a feeling that Hermann was still with me – I managed, by some miracle, to find my way, on-wards, downwards. Then, just before the great ice-falls, my pocket-lamp failed; so I had to bivouac at 18,000 feet. In the first pale light of dawn I made my way down the ice-falls. On and on . . . endlessly on . . . till, 27 hours after Hermann's fall, I tottered into base camp.

The search which followed found absolutely nothing.

Once again, the monstrous rubble-covered river of ice lay freed of all human presence. The sun burned down on it with scorching intensity. The snow was rapidly vanishing, melting into the waters of gurgling glacier-streams. Chogolisa's white roof-tree seemed to lift into the very

* Though, perhaps, the pull of the rope would have kept him in my tracks, and he might never have strayed from the right line of descent. – K.D.

A similar thought was expressed by Othmar Gurtner, commenting on the author's account in *The Mountain World*, 1958–9. – Translator's note.

My First Eight-thousander

sky itself. The great peaks stood silently all around. Were they, too, mourning? Or was this only the great healing silence which eternally enfolds all living and dying?

The engines droned as we flew down the Indus Valley, with mountains close on either hand, sharp spires past which we floated. Steep ridges thrusting up; an occasional glimpse back to the giant Baltoro peaks ... K2, Broad Peak ... already distant, as the minutes sundered us from the months. We should soon be seeing Nanga Parbat.

My thoughts went back to our inward flight, when the weather had been bad. I could see Hermann's face, as his eyes bored into the grey clouds for a sight of *his* mountain. At last he had spoken. 'We'll only fly back on a fine day,' he said.

Today was a fine day.

The savage peaks ahead parted, and only then did we realize that they were only low wing-pieces to that great stage-setting. High above them there was a shimmer of white; snow banners rose to the heavens. There it stood, the mountain – immutable, immense, imperishable – Nanga Parbat.

We could see its dazzling glaciers, and the summit crowning them. Above it the sky stretched blue-black and deep – as if yet another sky were climbing, incessantly, over and up it – up to an infinity of heights and depths.

Hermann Buhl.

Silver banners, ever-growing up into that dark vault.

17, 18. In 1958 Takeo Kuwabara's Chogolisa group found the 1957 camp and later gave Buhl's notebooks to Walter Bonatti (Gasherbrum 4 exp.) for return to his family.

19. An aerial view of The North-West Face of the Eiger *Photo: Swiss National Tourist Office*

PART III

The North Face of the Eiger

A child was playing snowballs.

It was dirty, grey snow, the last relics of winter on the flower-strewn meadows of a slope, high in the Bernese Oberland. The child ran from one patch of snow to the next, made snowballs and threw them into the flowers, where they broke into glittering dust.

We went on, up over the meadows. Tona, Hilde and I had come up from Grindelwald by chair-lift. It was a gloriously fine day.

Tona is my fair-haired wife. I met her in Milan on a lecture tour; she was studying geology then. We went up into the mountains, we fell in love, we married – three years after my Broad Peak adventure. And now we were taking Hildegard, our equally blonde daughter, on an excursion.

Over there, across the valley, the Eiger stood sombre, only the long sweep of the Mittelegi Ridge and the snow on the very summit brightly lit by the sun's rays, dazzling white, making the North Face seem darker still by contrast.

I would not try it again; once was enough. Yet I understood well enough why I had done it, as I looked up at the Mittelegi, glittering white, and the dark North Face winging upwards.

'Papa – why did you climb the Eiger?' Hilde asked me. Tona was smiling; the green slopes lay warm under the sun. What should I say?

'I can't explain it exactly,' I replied. 'But the Eiger is big and high.'

'M'm . . .' She did not seem very convinced, and nor was I. Then she laughed and started all over again to run from one patch of snow to another, making snowballs, throwing them into the green grass. Ah, thought I, she can't be racking her brains about it any longer . . .

Then, suddenly, she came back, stopped, and looked at me with a little smile. 'Do you know,' she asked, 'why I should like to climb the Eiger?'

'No,' I said, deeply curious now to know. 'Tell me, then.'

She laid that fair head of hers a little on one side, crushed the last remnants of a snowball in her palms, and looking up at the summit with her bright eyes, spoke deliberately, pausing several times, as if carefully weighing the meaning of her words.

'I . . . the Eiger . . . I should go up . . . to make snowballs . . . you see . . . the snow is much whiter up there.'

That is just how she said it.

Why do we do these things? Because we enjoy them? Standing at the foot of the Eiger's North Face, I very much doubted it.

A huge, dark triangle rises sheer above the meadows of Alpiglen. There is no life in it, only cold rock. A monstrous slab composed of stone; of grey, riven ice-fields, of crumbling bastions . . . a labyrinth of glassy runnels and ice-encrusted niches between polished steps of rock, rising vertical – like storeys of a house set one on top of the other – right up into the clouds.

That is the Eiger – a world of shadow, ice and silence: a silence broken occasionally by the rattle of falling stones, audible right down to the meadows at its foot.

Rébuffat once described it as 'a stone standing in a flower-garden'. It has never been better described. The base of the 'stone' is two and a half miles long, about half of which is occupied by the North Face. As to its height – if you could lodge the three Zinnen like a child's bricks, one on top of the other, the Western on the Grosse, and the Kleine on top of that – they would still fail to reach the Eiger's summit by hundreds of feet. So it is not surprising that, when you look up it from its base, the ground seems to give way beneath you – for that face is 6,000 feet high.

Six thousand feet . . . between the meadows at its feet and the clouds on its 13,000-foot summit rises a surface which, on the flat, could accommodate a city. Yet, a city is an expression of man's life and activity; the Eiger was not made for human-beings. Because it stands entirely on its own and wide-open to the west, every break in the weather smites it first and with insensate fury. Its inward-curving cavity is like a dark, empty shell tilted against the sky. The clouds which get trapped in it cannot get out again; they cling to the face, circling endlessly between the tremendous ribs enclosing that hollow space, until they eventually dissipate or are sucked up over the summit by the north-westerly gale. Even when the face is clear and windless again, everyone who stands at its foot and looks up into the curved recess feels that something defying

The North Face of the Eiger

all description lies locked in that hushed amphitheatre. Does that concave face embrace the dimension of death itself; of the negation of everything?

The Eiger's face was not made for human beings; its artillery of falling stones strikes blindly. That wall transcends all concepts of battle and victory, of life and death. At least it did till men came and imported them. Men who lived and thought there under that hail of stones, in the whirling fury of the tempest, at the very limits of their being. Men who sought to penetrate that inhuman dimension of the North Face, by trying to climb it . . .

It is an unnatural, outsize dimension, beyond human ken. It is also a dimension whose secret no one can resist.

Certainly I, for one, could not.

Wolfi and I were determined to climb the North Face – we two together, and alone together; neither of us wanted to do it with anyone else. For if we understood anything it was that this would stretch us to the utmost.

During the years when succeeding summers had seen us climbing together in the Western and Eastern Alps, we had become a partnership on the rope in which each of us knew he could depend utterly on the other, no matter what situation might arise. A rope like that can tackle anything . . .

We had become friends.

When we arrived to try our luck, there had been twelve successful attempts. It might have been thirteen, but no one knew for certain – Notdurft and Mayer were 'presumed dead' in the exit-cracks. Gonda and Wyss, too, had all but got to the top, when a small snow-slide swept them to their death from the last few easy feet of the summit-slope. The historians had disallowed the climb because they had not actually stood on the summit of the mountain. So the total remained at twelve, during which thirty-eight people had reached the summit; seventeen had died in the attempt. For the last five years before we came, one vain attempt after another had been made to achieve the thirteenth successful climb. Stefano Longhi's body was still hanging roped to the face. Nobody had been able to reach him, for he had died in a rather inaccessible place, way off the normal route, high up on the level of the 'Spider', that notorious ice-funnel, from which curving gullies, likewise filled with ice, reach out into the dark face in all directions like the legs of an insect.

Obviously, Wolfi and I could not shut our eyes to all those facts, and we were just as anxious to go on living as any one else. Nor did we want to take any risks – so far as it is possible to avoid them on the Eiger's

North Face. We had always climbed with the greatest care, and now we intended to apply an even greater degree of caution to our formidable task. What we did not intend to do, was to abandon our plan – nor, we knew, would the others who were here with the same objective in mind...

And who were these others?

One of the great attractions, when one arrives at the foot of the Matterhorn or Mont Blanc, the Civetta's gigantic wall, the Drei Zinnen or the Bregaglia peaks; as one strolls through the streets of Chamonix or Courmayeur – or, in this case, Grindelwald – is to see who is there; for one knows that one may at any moment meet old acquaintances, climbers with whom one has stood on some peak or other, or even friends whom one has not seen for years past.

So we were soon exchanging greetings with Ante Makohta and the slim, fair-haired Nadja from Ljubljana – Nadja Fajdiga, one of the best women-climbers anywhere, not only in Jugoslavia. They too were waiting for their great chance – settled weather-conditions. Their much-patched, sun-bleached tent was meanwhile pitched on an alp high up near Alpiglen. The only things that could disturb a climber's idyllic peace up there at the foot of the Eiger were cows, and inquisitive people, who wanted to know what the rope was for. And so, as every summer, there were quite a few tents to be seen about the place.

One of them belonged to Hias Noichl, that indestructible guide and proprietor of a ski-school at St Johann-in-Tirol. He and those two cheerful cosmopolitans, Herbert Raditschnig and Lothar Brandler had also set their sights on the Eiger. At the moment, Herbert and Lothar were busy serving savoury rarebits, good solid *Berner Röschti* or a Swiss fondue to the guests of the Hotel Gletschergarten in Grindelwald. To see them in their white jackets and black bow-ties hurrying hither and thither, light-footed – with a smiling 'of course' . . . 'thank-you' . . . 'immediately' . . . 'ready now!' on their lips, you would have thought they had never done anything else in their lives. Today Lothar is a film-producer and Herbert travels the world year in, year out, as a camera-man.

They too were waiting to tackle the Eiger. Their rucksacks were ready, packed; they could exchange their white jackets for anoraks any day, but the weather gave them no encouragement. It had not only to be fine; it had to be settled. For they too wanted to take as few risks as possible – the Eiger was dangerous enough under a blue sky; and even if you wore a helmet, you couldn't crawl under it for complete protection. So they were biding their time, and had gone into the hotel-business for a change.

I saw a quiet middle-aged man sitting in a corner, writing. He had a

The North Face of the Eiger

high forehead and craggy features. It was Heini Harrer, who in the summer of 1938, with his friends, Anderl Heckmair, Wiggerl Vörg and Fritz Kasparek, had been the first to find the way to the summit up the North Face, after a bitter struggle lasting three days – the last part in appalling weather, but then the Eiger has spared nobody so far in that respect. Now he was working on his history of the North Face, which turned out to be a splendid book and a best-seller, not only in mountaineering circles; for today Frau Schulze in Hamburg and Signor Rossi in Milan have read all about the North Face.* It is not without good cause that so many telescopes are to be seen everywhere around Grindelwald, trained on the Eiger, and surrounded by the gay tribe of holiday-makers.

Does that bother the climbers on the face, as he crouches against the rock, his nose pressed against cold ice, with the stones hailing down on him? Not in the least: he has plenty of other things to worry about.

Our base camp was in the cellar of a carpenter's shop at Grund, just below Grindelwald.

It was an ideal lodging; we were wonderfully comfortable among empty packing-cases and racks, which enabled us to sort and separate to our heart's content the considerable baggage our small expedition had brought along. But first we did something even better; we carried an old armchair, a packing-case and a table out into the garden. There, surrounded by flowers and a variety of vegetables, we could sit in the sun, with the Eiger high overhead. Then we bought a few postcards with harmless views of the neighbourhood – huts up on the alps, the gentlemen who blow the alpine horn, a stream with clouds above it and – yes, we even found one in the end! – Grindelwald minus the Eiger. These we dispatched to uncles and aunts, and to all our near and dear ones who, we knew, might worry if they heard that anyone was on the North Face again. 'We are having a lovely time,' we wrote. 'We have done a couple of amusing climbs and are now resting here. After that we want to do the traverse of a splendid ridge. Don't worry about us.' It was all perfectly true, even the bit about the Schreckhorn-Lauteraarhorn traverse. This was to be our final training-climb before we commited ourselves to the face; a fact we naturally didn't mention.

With us at the time were our friends, Franz Lindner and 'Charlie' Schönthaler. Franz, that calm, imperturbable character, we shall meet again in this book, on the Peuterey Ridge of Mont Blanc. Charlie, a carefree enthusiast in every aspect of life, who came from the Tyrol, has

* So has John Smith in Birmingham. In 1959, the translator of this book had the great pleasure of converting Harrer's *Die Weisse Spinne* into *The White Spider*, widely read by the general public here too. – H.M.

just returned with me from the great faces of the Bernina Group. After his very first experience of digging crampons into the sheer ice of the Klucker route on the North-east Face of Piz Roseg, he had struck brilliant form, as we did the North Face of Piz Palü, the North-east Face of Piz Bernina, the ice-nose on Piz Scerscen and, to crown everything, the first-ascent of the *direttissima* on the North-east Face of Piz Roseg's main summit. He was fully qualified for the Eiger, but he knew I wanted to go with Wolfi and fully understood. During the following days he helped me, in the most unselfish manner, to transport all our equipment up to our 'high camp' at the foot of the face, while Wolfi was doing one more climb with Franz. Today Charlie is a ski-instructor, alternating between Australia, Squaw Valley and Kitzbühel and, if you are lucky, you may even meet him in Munich, which is supposed to be his home-town.

There was not much more to be done, now. The rocks of the Wetterhorn glowed reddish-brown in the sunset, but a huge fish-shaped cloud was drifting through the pale sky. Still anything but 'Eiger-weather . . .'

All the same, I wanted to go up with Charlie next day to the foot of the face.

The Bernese Oberland, with its streaming glaciers and proud four-thousanders – Finsteraarhorn, Mönch and Jungfrau – lay under a clear blue sky. The weather looked really good at last.

The long line of the huge Mittelegi Ridge was bathed in sunshine; from the massive rock buttresses at its start in the valley to the shining white of the Eiger's summit, where it ends. A few little tufts of cotton-wool were playing tag in the dark hollow of the North Face. The little red cars of the Jungfrau railway climbed the steep rack and pinion track between the meadows . . .

'Alpiglen!'

Out with my pack . . . and then another sack, and the cardboard-box, and the long sailor's sack, and the carrier-frame . . . the conductor was getting impatient. How could anyone be carting so much stuff with him in a summer-holiday resort?

Luckily, the station-master seemed to understand perfectly; for we certainly couldn't take everything up with us at one go. While the bustle of the trippers faded away and the little train climbed on its way, he stood there, taking stock of our pile of goods. Then he looked at us and muttered: 'The Eiger, of course!' and shook his head. 'If you like, you can park some of it here,' he said. 'I have often done it before.' He straightened his cap and pointed to a door: 'In the corner, on the right there,' he advised. We were only too pleased at the offer; we had been on the point of asking for it. Charlie carried everything we could not

The North Face of the Eiger

manage to the place indicated, while I was tying one sack to the wire-frame.

The stationmaster was still standing there, watching us. He was a slow, comfortable, pleasant Bernese type. 'Many thanks,' we said, when we had finished: 'We'll be back for the rest today.'

'Today or tomorrow, whenever you like,' he nodded. Then he suddenly knitted his brows and looked hard at me. Just as I was beginning to wonder what was coming, he said, very quietly: 'Do you have to do that thing?'

I searched around for words. 'Yes,' I said, ' . . . you see . . .'

'Nowt happened to us as yet!' said Charlie with a cheerful grin. 'Come on,' he said, tapping me on the shoulder.

I was still thinking of the man as we slowly climbed far up the green, flowery slopes; and once, when I turned to look back, I felt sure he was still standing down there, looking up at us.

The sacks weighed a ton, and the ascent was a long one. But what a morning it was: sunny and green, everywhere. This Alpiglen was a lovely corner of the world! In front of us rose a broad tongue of forest; above it the North Face hung like a blue shadow. Not till just under the summit did the sun gild a snowfield, the white veins of ice in dark rock – the very last bit of the climb. There didn't seem to be any distance between it and the sky above.

Lothar, Hias and Herbert must have pitched their tent somewhere in this wood, but we couldn't see it. We meant to site ours much higher up, indeed as high as possible; for it was still a long way from here to the start of the climb, at least an hour by night. We were resting again and, with all this gear to cart, we should have found it much more comfortable to stop here. Then we remembered our friends, whom the vicar of Grindelwald came up to visit one day, with the idea of trying to talk them out of the Eiger. So on we went, up the hill.

We found a tiny, steep-sided patch of grass just below the first slabby steps of the face. This was at 6,600 feet, and no one could get a tent farther up. When we looked up, with our heads tilted right back, we could see, way up there, the big icicles hanging down the greyish-brown wall below the 'Spider'. The summit itself was out of sight, high above.

We used moss and slates to build a level platform into the slope and planted our fabric-house on it. We were protected from any odd stones falling from above by a projecting rock. From here it was no distance to the start of the climb; we could get there without expending any effort.

A few days later, after Wolfi had rejoined me in our 'Alpine Week-end Cottage', as we called it, we enjoyed a really priceless experience. We had just been checking our supply of pitons, when he suddenly nudged me and said: 'Look! There's someone coming up!'

I saw a dark figure coming slowly up the slopes, still a long way down. I recognized a uniform. 'A policeman,' I said. We looked around us, but there was no other tent, nobody else; there could be no doubt he was coming to see us. All the way up from Alpiglen, an hour away down there . . .

'Any guesses, Wolfi?'

'Not a thing.'

The uniformed figure continued to climb resolutely, straight for us.

'Anything to do with your motor-bike?' I suggested.

'Certainly not!' replied Wolfi with an ugly look. 'My motor-bike, indeed!' Wolfi is very touchy about his skill as a rider.

The facings on the uniform were now clearly recognizable. Another quarter of an hour or so . . .

Wolfi had an idea. 'Do you think they have put the North Face out of bounds?' he asked.

'Nonsense!' I retorted. 'Anyway, we'll soon know now.'

Then I had a bright idea. 'Do you think we look like someone else?'

'Possibly,' said Wolfi glancing at me and grinning amiably. 'They may have seen your passport photo, taken on that machine at the railway station.' Tit-for-tat, for the motor-bike, eh? I thought of that photo. Never again would I try to save money.

'In any case, don't look so agitated,' said Wolfi. 'Sit down and relax.'

We relaxed, in that expectant frame of mind in which everyone waits, when the eye of the Law falls on them.

Here he was at last, sweating heavily, touching his cap and assuming an official attitude.

'Your passports, please, gentlemen!'

Oh, so that was it. We handed him our passports.

He ran his fingers through the pages, looked briefly at me, then at Wolfi, addressing his question to him: 'You're going up there, eh?' he asked. He pointed up at the shining curtains, which had been moving slowly up the face all morning.

'H'm,' said Wolfi. What *can* one say when one has planted a tent at the foot of the wall?

'It depends on the weather,' I interposed.

Our policemen nodded. 'Yes, I know,' he said and pocketed our passports. 'You can fetch them down in Grindelwald,' he explained, 'afterwards – when you have got back safely.' He paused for a moment, before adding: 'You see, we always do that nowadays – it often helps us with the question of identification.'

The North Face of the Eiger

He wished us good-day most amiably, touched his cap again and turned to go, visibly relieved that it would now be all downhill.

'H'm,' said Wolfi, and made his 'funny' face – thrusting out his lower lip, biting it and creasing his face, as if to laugh. But when he does that it usually means he is not at all happy.

A wild gale was raging across the Oberland. Ice-blossoms formed on the ridges, but it was a glorious day, with the sun flashing on the rocks, marvellously beautiful to look at in the magic clothing conjured by the storm.

We were on the ridge leading from the Schreckhorn to the Lauteraarhorn, in the course of our last training-climb before tackling the face. Franz was still with us, but Charlie had gone home. Wolfi and I had decided to start up at the first opportunity, once we were back in Grindelwald.

When we got there, we heard that Hias, Lothar and Herbert had made an attempt while we were away. They were down below again, after an indescribably difficult retreat, without any assistance from anyone almost all the way. The photographs in the papers showed Hias's face drawn with pain; he had one arm in a sling. They had reached the 'Flatiron', when a small stone falling clear from the Spider a thousand feet above struck him on his hand as he gripped a hold.

Poor Hias – what devilish luck! Now he was in hospital at Interlaken, where they were trying to save what remained of his hand. The hardships of that retreat had left their mark on Herbert and Lothar's faces. They had had enough of the Eiger for the time being. Later on, they worked out a plan to climb the face in winter, when there are no falling stones, when the cold freezes everything into immobility. But Hiebeler and three others beat them to it.

We visited Hias in hospital; it was all we could do for him.

At last the weather had turned fine. The snow high up was melting. The North Face looked even darker than usual, a sure sign that the rock-pitches would be dry, free from snow and ice, and that much easier at least. To balance that, the ice-fields in the middle section would be glassy and tough, with no snow-crust; and more stones would come down by day – the bombardment would only cease at night and into the early morning.

I called up Zürich on the telephone and asked the Met Station if one could trust the weather. 'Well, it was a temporary "high" – not too bad.' Could it last a couple of days? 'It might . . .' What were we to do? Yesterday's report from the Tourist Office had sounded much more promising, and the weather certainly looked good. We decided to go up to our 'high camp' and see what happened. Two days ought to see us through our climb.

We packed up. Everything lay strewn on the grass round the tent – pitons, provisions, ropes. We were starting this very night, so as to be climbing tomorrow. Should we take that ring-piton, it was a bit heavy? How much petrol? The small tin. 'But you *must* take your big gauntlets.'

The result? Enormous rucksacks – much too heavy for Grade V severities; but holding everything necessary for a week on the face – one never can tell . . .

No use: it was simply too much. We stood the rucksacks on their heads and started sifting everything all over again.

The slight, blonde Nadja had come up from her tent. 'I see you're busy packing. Starting up tomorrow, then?' she enquired.

'Yes,' said Wolfi, laconically, and went on rolling up the bivouac-bag. It just had to get smaller, somehow.

'O.K.,' said Nadja. 'Then I'll go and cook you a real meal.'

Darkness and silence. Somewhere up there the face frowned on our tent, unseen, but seeming to claw down into it with invisible fingers. We had set the alarm for midnight – for we wanted to be early on our way. Slowly, the minutes ebbed.

We were taking twenty pitons, five of them for ice; an equal number of carabiners; two 130-foot ropes, one of them a light reserve one, in case a retreat was forced on us; a quarter of a pint of petrol, for the small extra-lightweight cooker – enough for five days if it came to the worst; also the rest of our equipment, well tested on any number of face-climbs. Our provisions, weighed to the last ounce, concentrated and worked out more than ever on this occasion, consisted of a small bag of corn-flakes, baked in sugar, nuts and raisins – about two pounds in all. A handful of this special food keeps one satisfied for quite a time – possibly it swells in one's stomach. For the rest – fruit juice, chocolate, glucose and quite a hunk of smoked bacon, filling and satisfying; add a little bread, a luxury if one considers its weight, but a necessity. Then bivouac candles for the night; for if anything was certain, we should have to bivouac. A few other trifles . . .

I had fallen into a deep and dreamless sleep. I woke and looked at the dial. Still an hour to go. Well, I was hardly likely to sleep any more, now.

I got out the sketch of our route and quietly turned on my torch, laying my hand over it with great care, for Wolfi was still asleep. A narrow crack of light glowed red between my fingers . . .

The North Face of the Eiger

It was a fairly large photograph of the face, on which we had pencilled in the route. I skipped the first 2,600 feet of the plinth, with its horizontal stratification. It was not difficult, and we wanted to deal with it before daybreak; Wolfi had been up it during an attempt last summer; he knew the way. After that massive stratified plinth, there are 3,000 feet of sheer and at times vertical rock-face, with long traverses to be made, gaining little height and costing much time and labour. In the central section we would have to cross the three ice-fields, steep as church roofs, each of them poised above vertical cliffs, and with their ice pitched at from 55 degrees to 60 degrees. The traverse of the second ice-field in itself is a matter of twenty rope's-lengths. During all this, the main danger is from falling stones, from which there is no respite till, after the third ice-field, one reaches the 'Ramp'; there they fall clear through thin air, missing it in their flight. After that, we should have to take great care not to continue too straight up the face, as Mayer and Notdurft did last year, and Longhi and Corti too, a mistake to be avoided at all costs. Our job would be to find the 'Traverse of the Gods', a crumbling ledge leading to the Spider's huge funnel. Once through that, another place demanding the greatest care; for, above the Spider there are countless runnels, cracks, twisting gullies, not all of which take one out to the summit.

Yes, we would be taking that photograph with us and looking after it as if it were a talisman; for if mists and blizzards robbed us of all visibility, it would be our only guide to escape from the face. On it we could measure rope's lengths with our fingers, find the route, either up or down; for there is no way of getting out of that enormous shell to left or to right. I folded the picture up carefully and put it away.

A quarter of an hour to go. In the red light glowing through my fingers I held a small medal, its dull gleam bitten into by tiny lettering. Busle had given it to me when we parted. The Protestant Paternoster in English: 'For Thine is the Kingdom, the power and the glory, for ever...' Her prayer – she was a Protestant. To me it was not less precious for that; in this whole world there is only one of it.

Overhead, in the darkness, soared the North Face.

Almost midnight, now. I pushed my head out of the tent entrance to see what the weather was doing. Stars and more stars; not a cloud in the sky; dew on the grass. The Eiger in impenetrable darkness.

Crawling in again, I shook Wolfi. 'Just on twelve!' I said.

'O.K. – O.K. I know. Just five more minutes...'

Presently: 'Is it fine outside?' he asked.

'Yes, a clear sky and dew on the grass.'

'Well, I suppose that means we go. What does the altimeter say?'

'You've got it in your pocket,' I replied, handing him the torch. The brilliance of its beam made me shut my eyes for a moment. 'Well, what does it say?'

'Very odd,' said Wolfi, tapping its dial. 'Ten feet higher than yesterday, and that should mean bad weather. Yet it's really fine, and cold, outside – couldn't look better. The dial could have slipped round in my pocket, or it might just have gone wrong.' We had had trouble with it once before. 'Anyway, I say we should go . . .'

1 a.m. Up over the patches of grass, towards the start of the climb, traversing, going up and down, to the débris-cone we knew rose above us. Every now and then we caught sight of the first crags, in the light of our torches. Above them stretched an impenetrable curtain of darkness, a black mass, whose upper edge cut into the starry sky – immense and unknown. What had we to offer against that? All I knew was that I would not want to tackle it with anyone but Wolfi.

'Here we are!' He had recognized the place from his attempt the year before, when I was in the Karakorum. We climbed the débris-cone and a crag or two till a patch of snow shone white in the beam of the torch.

'There's a slab off to the right, here,' said Wolfi, locating it presently, as the beam moved over the rock. 'Only Grade III!'

I followed him as he crossed the little *schrund*, where the snow had melted, and disappeared up the rocks above. All right! Only Grade III it might be, but with a rucksack weighing a ton . . . no ballet-dancing here.

On we went, up crumbling rock-pitches, ledges, precipitous sandy rubble. It wasn't difficult, but it was damnably tricky work, for we could only see the next few feet ahead in the light of our torches. By 3 o'clock, we were at the foot of the First Pillar, up on our left; we couldn't see it, but Wolfi knew it was there. No moon, only the light of the stars; the mountain was asleep, utter silence reigned on its face. We continued our strange, ghost-like ascent, hardly exchanging a word. Every now and then the beam of one head-lamp or the other slashed through the darkness. Occasionally a stone went clocketing down into the void, reminding us, surprisingly, that the face did not consist merely of a few feet of rock on which one happened to be climbing at the moment, but that there was already a great deal of it below us.

We climbed unroped, each of us alone with the light of his lamp, the sound of his boots on the rock, the feel of his hands on it. From time to time, a flash of light, or a word – the only communication with the other man.

It was 4 a.m. and still dark. 2,000 feet of the face lay behind us. Wolfi stopped at the foot of a step, barring the way, not very high but vertical. 'I don't remember that one,' he said. 'Never mind, let's get up it, and not waste time searching around. Make a back for me.' I planted myself firmly on the ledge. Oops! – and again: we were up, not exactly elegantly, but what did style matter, if we could save time and strength? What mattered was getting as high up as possible before the sun was on the rocks.

Another step, another back-up, this time superfluous.

'Up to the left,' said Wolfi. 'We're above the "Shattered Pillar" now.' And he pointed across to where a profile was looming vaguely out of the first grey light of dawn, the shadowy, threatening overhangs of the 'Rote Fluh'. The stars were paling now – fewer and fewer, till there were only three big ones.

'We'll be at the "Difficult Crack" in a moment,' said Wolfi, as we traversed to the left up the slabs.

The sky turned blue above a red streak on the horizon; not the tiniest of clouds in it. The rocks around us were beginning to reflect the new day. And what a marvellous one!

Wolfi was beaming: 'Suppose we had believed the altimeter!'

'Yes,' I answered. 'It's just like our Matterhorn day!'

What a day that had been! The sun had met us on the ice-field, dazzling-bright, to shine on us all the rest of the day. And as the points of our crampons bit into the snow, we kept on thinking: 'Here we are on the North Face of the Matterhorn, *our* North Face . . . at last . . . and on just such a day as this . . . on the North Face . . .'

And now we were on the North Face of the Eiger.

'You see if we're not the first to get right up the Face in fine weather,' I shouted across to Wolfi, who was traversing along a ledge in the rock, now brightly lit by the reflected daylight. Above us towered the face, smooth and overhanging. It would not be long before we were in deep shadow again.

We came to the Difficult Crack, one of the Grade V pitches. Ten feet straight up, there was a piton below a projecting roof. Wolfi clipped himself on and straddled out on to the slab to its left – cautiously, slowly not altogether easily, for his rucksack was heavy. This was no place for ballet-dancing, no matter how good the climber. By now Wolfi had got to the overhang thirty feet farther up, not a very big one, but . . .

Wolfi was cursing his rucksack: 'Damnable, the way this lump pulls one outwards!' He was panting, and I kept a close eye on his every movement. There, he's done it, he's up! I have never seen Wolfi 'come off' yet; he doesn't like the idea, so he never takes a risk. Of course I belay him carefully in spite of that, but it is a comfortable feeling to be on the rope with him. That is probably why we have climbed together so often.

As it happens I don't like the idea of 'coming off' either.

Wolfi had moved on up, straddling widely in a groove, his red anorak a bright spot in the morning sunlight. I took a picture of him, with the overhangs of the 'Rote Fluh' overhead. The Rote Fluh – a face in its own right, a face in the Eiger's great face, leaning far out over our heads, unclimbable by normal means, impossible.

What must Hinterstoisser and his friends have felt that day, years ago, when they looked up from this point? . . . Would it be possible to traverse below that smooth, solid wall, across to the first ice-field; could they get there without having to climb that first enormous cliff? Would the Eiger unlock its gate for them?

The Eiger unlocked the gate. They found the traverse, that 'Hinterstoisser Traverse', which is the gate to the North Face. And then it locked it again behind them.

For, when they were forced to retreat, they found the traverse – heavily iced by the break in the weather – impossible to negotiate; a withdrawal over its glassy slabs is only feasible if the traversing-rope is left in position . . . and they had taken it with them . . .

Very soon we should have dealt with the first 2,600 feet of this gigantic face. It was by now 7 a.m. Everything down in the valley was bathed in sunshine, the meadows shone green, the houses in Grindelwald small and cosy. Where we were, it was cold and grim. We were out of the sun now, and there was ice wedged between the rocks in places. The climbing was not hard and we gained height rapidly; but the area of what was climbable was continually shrinking, swallowed up by the might of the Rote Fluh above us and ahead of us and by the rim of the fearsome precipice pushing up on our left. Finally, it narrowed to a wedge of a snow-crest and then – petered out.

We were out on the smooth sweep of the face, surrounded everywhere by almost vertical slabs. The first few feet were covered by a veneer of ice, above which we could see a piton and an old hemp-rope, curving out in a wide loop, then disappearing from view. 'One of its strands is broken,' growled Wolfi.

That rope had been hanging there for a week, ever since the retreat of the Hias, Lothar, Herbert trio. Poor Hias . . . all because of these blasted stones! All hell must break loose here when the sun is shining on the upper part of the face; the slabs and the rounded limestone cliffs are in places scored with a network of white scars where the stones have struck. At the moment all was quiet. 'A somewhat hostile district,' growled Wolfi, and moved off with great care out on to the slabs.

The North Face of the Eiger

The Hinterstoisser Traverse is 130 feet long. Wolfi had disappeared from view. Out ran the rope in little jerks, quicker than I had expected, but then the rock was dry and in excellent condition. It was a hot summer and so the Eiger was 'dark' for us, and I have already explained the advantages and drawbacks of that – easier climbing on the difficult rock sectors because they are free from snow and ice, but heavier falls of stone, and tough polished ice, hard as glass, on the ice-fields above.

I could just catch Wolfi's 'come on!' from the far end of the traverse. It is a most impressive place. Below me was an appalling drop of 2,600 feet to the meadows, above me 3,000 feet more of the face. Between the two there was a rope, a piton and a small stance, on which I rejoined Wolfi.

He looked at me and said: 'I'll go on, as far as the "Swallows' Nest".' It was almost a question, but he had already hung a sling into the next piton. 'All right,' I said. 'I'll take over from there.' He moved up on the piton, while I belayed him.

'Don't forget to retrieve the sling – it's ours. I don't want to waste any time here,' he called down, almost as if apologizing for his technical inelegance; the pitch really didn't call for a sling, he could have climbed it 'free'. But now time was of the essence . . .

The Swallows' Nest. There we sat, with our legs dangling over nothingness. I tried to spot our tent, without success. Anyway, we had to be moving on. So, on with crampons, for the ice-field. It was my turn to lead now, even if it would have been pleasant to sit in this nice, comfortable niche a little longer . . .

'It's as exposed as any face in the Dolomites,' Wolfi remarked, adding: 'Rebitsch was the first to get down safely from here.'

I tightened my crampon straps a little, looking down into those blue depths at the same time. It was from somewhere round here, it occurred to me, that Toni Kurz had made his last despairing effort to reach the rescue party below. From here he had let himself down, with the last failing remnants of his strength, on the rope, still ready – the only survivor of a party of four – to fight for his life; let himself down (and I leaning out as far as I dared, could see no end to it, for down there the face overhung) to within six feet of his rescuers, where the knotted rope jammed in the carabiner . . .

Six feet from succour and life . . . and there it all ended . . . there Toni Kurz fell backwards on the rope and died.

Wolfi was addressing me: 'I thought you said you wanted to take over the lead?'

'So I do,' I said. 'I'm off – but watch me carefully up the first few feet.'

147

Those first few feet were steep slabs of limestone scoured absolutely smooth; the ice-field must have been much bigger at one time and this was its old, polished floor. I remembered the description: 'Millimetre precision work for a pedant'; it really was abominably smooth hereabouts. I breathed a sigh of relief when at last I was able to dig my points into grey ice. It was tough and in places smooth as a mirror, but they managed to grip. Bless the blacksmith down in Grindelwald who let us use his emery-wheel!

If only we had not got to climb rock to get up to the second ice-field, and so blunt the new, keen edges on our spikes! Yet it didn't look very promising without crampons; a barrier of solid rock, down part of which comes pouring a kind of frozen waterfall – a glistening curtain of black, glassy bubbles – the 'Ice-hose'.

We decided it was better to try the dry end of the barrier, without crampons. Wolfi started up it, climbed the first few feet, disappeared over an edge, said something about slabs, then complete silence. It must have got hellishly difficult up there. The rope kept on coming down, going up again, down again, up again. Somewhere up on that roof Wolfi was obviously hard at it, but the waiting seemed endless. There was, of course, the view to look at, nice green meadows down below; but what in God's name was going on up above? Wolfi had stopped moving altogether; only a few fragments of ice came tinkling down. The sun was gradually invading the rocks high up near the West Ridge, but as yet not a stone had fallen, though it was half past eight. What on earth could be the matter with Wolfi?

As I went up, five minutes later, I found out. It was a thing like a steep roof, covered in places by a thin skin of polished ice. I looked diagonally downwards . . . not a pleasant place to go sliding down . . . At last I got up to Wolfi, on a bad stance, with a fairly useless belay – but the only one available. 'I shall be glad when we're away from here,' he confided.

We could see the second ice-field above us, a gleam of greyish-green. All I could think of at the moment was that, up there, one could bang pitons in anywhere one liked. But we had to get there first . . .

A tongue of ice stretched down towards us, but at least thirty feet overhead. Till then there was only a glittering, glassy layer of black water-ice, less than an inch thick, on the solid rock. Not a hope of fixing a piton or cutting a step in that. As I put my crampons on again I couldn't help thinking how stupid we had been to get ourselves into this hole: if we had only kept on, up to the right! Well this is where we were, so thinking wouldn't do any good . . .

'I'm off,' I said.

'Yes – and you know . . .' Wolfi indicated the rope, lying loose in his hand, by a movement of his head.

Yes, I knew well enough what kind of a belay it was.

I placed my crampon against the glassy surface. Could I get a purchase? No, not here. What about there? Yes, there. Now for the next step: I had managed to clear a grip for my left hand. I moved up. The layer of ice was a little thicker, and I moved a step higher on it. I found another place where my spikes gave me a purchase. The seconds went ticking away, each of them vital, none of them bring any respite. Each of them might have been an hour, or more. Here was the slab, the little hollow in the ice, and here was my foot. The only thought in one's mind, how to put it down properly. Good: that one had got a firm hold!

After an eternity there was proper thick ice, good enough to cut a hand-hold, but lying hollow over the rock, giving out a dull sound; not thick enough for a piton, it would simply shatter. Up again, another hand-hold – getting better now.

And then, at last, decent ice. In went a piton. I gave a sigh of relief, so did Wolfi. The world immediately looked a friendlier place.

'Just a moment's rest,' I said, 'then I'll move on.'

'Yes, you take a rest, by all means.'

I took a rest, looking at the piton, the ring, the snap-link, the rope and the grey ice before me. God, those last minutes had been quite a thing!

I went on resting. There was a niche in the ice up above, followed by a crack at the side of a rock-rib. That must be the best line to take. Off I went again.

I reached the niche, a hole in the ice, through which I hung a sling – an additional belay; then came the crack, which went easily, backing-up between ice and rock. As I emerged, I could see the steep slope of the second ice-field just ahead.

'Only another twenty feet,' I shouted down to Wolfi.

There was a little rock-island just above me, which I should be able to use as a stance. I treated myself to the luxury of cutting a couple of steps, great big comfortable steps . . . the ice splintered, the fragments clinked as they flew, till their sound died away down below; potsherds, tough and glassy, toughened by the cold and the eternal shadow which enveloped us.

Ssssssssssss . . .!

A stone whizzing past, not very far off – the first sign of life on the face. Then all quiet again, here in the shadow; utter silence. High above, rock and snow lay bright in the sunshine, quiet, peaceful, warm-looking. And that was precisely where the menace hung – the menace that could at any moment shatter the cold silence down here, the menace of that beautiful warm glow.

Tick . . . tick . . . ssst. Just a baby stone, hopping harmlessly, dancing down the rocks, whispering past like an insect, small and no danger to anyone. But how long before the cannonade would start, to shatter the peace and quiet down here? It could be minutes, it could be half an hour . . . It was 9 a.m.

I looked up at the warm, even light on those rocks. Then I started cutting steps again, smaller ones, quicker than before. I was up. In went a piton and then I hacked out a stance.

I shouted down to Wolfi: 'You can come now – but look out! The first stones are arriving.'

'So I noticed,' came up from below. 'One has just gone past me.'

Wolfi was coming up – the traverse, the piton, retrieving the sling, pushing a leg into the crack, reaching up with his arm. At that moment there was a 'click' on my helmet, and I enjoyed an instant's satisfaction at the thought that I was wearing it. Then Wolfi joined me.

'We'll have to get up there before it really starts,' he said, pointing to the upper rim of the huge ice-field. He was right; there seemed to be at least a measure of cover under the jutting cliffs up there. We should take much longer by following that long curving rim than if we traversed diagonally, but –

'Look out! Something's coming!' Wolfi, six feet above me, reacted instantly, pressing himself hard into the ice. A host of little dots was coming down in a grotesque dance across the grey surface 300 feet higher up. They grew larger, bounding down towards us in great leaps, a grey army of them. Now! . . . that one's missed me, and that one, but what about this one? . . . sssst, ssst . . . Suddenly everything was quiet again. It was all over.

Wolfi straightened up slowly. 'Benediction over?' he asked. 'Then I'll lead on again. You keep watch and shout if you see anything coming.'

I cast an anxious eye up the face, the surface of the ice, the groove running up to the rocks above. Nothing stirred. The rope ran out quickly, as Wolfi went diagonally up the next 130 feet. He dispensed with step-cutting; we had to get out of the line of fire as quickly as possible. Tack . . . tack . . . tack, his crampons bit into the smooth surface, tilted at 50 degrees or more. It looked uncanny.

The view down the face had completely disappeared; all we could see was the lower edge of the second ice-field projecting over the abyss like a ski-jumping platform, with green ground beyond it, sending up a pale green reflection, mirrored by the surface up here, making the blue shadows look even colder.

The North Face of the Eiger

We wondered whether we had been spotted yet. Not that it makes the slightest difference. There is no place on earth where one is so utterly alone. I squinted up the runnel to where Wolfi stood, with only the frontal points of his crampons biting into the steep, bone-hard surface. I stooped and took a tighter hold on the rope.

Everything else had lost all meaning. Wolfi was standing up there on four steel spikes. Whether they held or slipped depended on his next movement . . .

We were alone . . . alone with the North Face of the Eiger. At that moment even our friends had ceased to exist for us.

Down at the Kleine Scheidegg, Herbert had his eye to the big telescope. 'I've got them,' he shouted. There, in the black circle of the lens, small and forlorn against the huge face, with a few cloud-tatters floating around it, he had seen two tiny dots against the grey belt of the second ice-field.

Fritz von Allmen, the hotel proprietor, one of the greatest Eiger-experts, who had followed our climb for a long time past, joined him. 'Midday – much the worst time for falling stones,' he commented.

'Yes, it's sensible of them to be keeping to the upper rim, in the shelter of the rocks, till they get out on to the Flatiron,' said Herbert, adding ruefully: 'I wish them better luck than we had!' Lothar was with him; they had come up from the valley as soon as they heard somebody was on the face. They did not know, of course, when we intended to start, but they were pretty sure that we were the two dots they had detected on the face . . .

We were now deep inside the great shell, working our way up to the end of the ice-field; in sunshine now, and it was warm. Water was trickling down the rocks, the ice was softer and had acquired a crust.

The hail of stones was nerve-racking, coming irregularly: short gaps, positive barrages, isolated salvoes, then utter silence once more; one never knew what to expect. We made use of every available inch of cover, pillars, pitches of rock, overhangs, crannies. Looking up for a moment at the crumbling bastions high overhead during some interval in the bombardment, we felt little surprise at the unnerving whistle of the falling stones, the sharp crack as they struck on rock, the dull thud when they hit the ice.

At this point the dirty grey surface of the ice-field looked like the face of a man scarred by small-pox. During the fearful minutes of the unprotected moves from one source of cover to another, we were painfully aware of every inch of our bodies. If it had been possible to hide ourselves completely under our helmets we would have felt a great deal better.

Our method of progress was an unusual one – a gigantic hanging-traverse of ice, on a rounded edge formed by the melting away of the ice-field's upper rim from the rock above it. For the most part we only supported ourselves against it, for it was by no means all of it solid enough to stand anyone leaning out from it. That traverse across the second ice-field is twenty rope's lengths – more than 800 yards long. You have to grab it a hundred times, move up a hundred times, always with the same extreme care.

I looked up. Bang! Something hit me in the face, blinding me. By sheer instinct I leaned forward against the face. 'It's finished', I thought.

My eyes opened again. There was blood running down my anorak. I put my hand tentatively to my face . . .

Wolfi had me on the taut rope, as I worked my way, bemused, up to a safe stance. Nothing much, he assured me, only a scratch. A small stone had hit me on the bridge of the nose. Just a small stone . . .

My head was buzzing. 'Come on! Off this damned ice-field!' I was still digesting my shock, but Wolfi was already balancing over the irregularities of the icy edge. No time for rest and recuperation sessions here, he said; it was the last thing I wanted, anyway! Wolfi led the next two rope's lengths.

By the time we were traversing out on to the Flatiron, I was quite myself again. At last we were off the second ice-field. For which relief much thanks.

The arête of the Flatiron, 250 feet high, jutting out like a regularly curved nose from the furrowed face, lies directly beneath the Spider and is, consequently, more than usually exposed to the hail of stones. Climbing simultaneously, we hurried up its easy rock and sat down, to get our breath back, under a small overhang near the top. Here we were really safe, and we could actually sit. We had now been engaged in fourteen unbroken hours of climbing.

We were ravenous, as we got bacon and bread out of the rucksack. There was even water, dripping down the rock. Now that we were sitting here and the tension was lifted, we could feel the weariness penetrating our bones. We had been on our feet since 1 a.m. and now it was half past four in the afternoon. We were not likely to get much farther today, but there seemed nothing to stop our reaching the summit tomorrow, if only the weather held.

That was the only question in our minds as we watched the little puffs of cloud all around us, climbing up the face, growing in size, disappearing – dissolving into thin air.

Shimmering curtains – as if the spirits of the air were engaged in a grotesque, swirling dance in the void all around us, accompanied by the thousand voices of the North Face, from the high, almost barking whirr of the smaller stones to the less frequent dull growling and roaring of the big lumps. And, somewhere, there was the sound of water pattering down the face.

We were climbing the steep Ramp, which slashes a way up the unbroken cliffs, anything from vertical to overhanging, below the Spider. It was getting late; soon it would be dark. We wanted to get to the good bivouac-site we had heard of, above the most difficult pitch in the Ramp, the famous chimney, which was either filled by a waterfall or by its frozen counterpart. It seemed a doubtful project. Behind us, through the mists, we looked across the tilted roofs of the two ice-fields to a fabulous view; but beyond it lay the veils of dusk. Here, on the steep Ramp, with nothing but sheer cliffs and a snow-gully all around us there wasn't even room to sit down. We should have to push on till we found a place. We got out our headlamps and our torches. By a stroke of luck we found a small hollow in the rock at the end of the first rope's length; there was just room for two people to sit, close together.

We made our preparations for the night very slowly and methodically (this is a long-standing item of bivouac-lore: the longer you take over the preliminaries, the shorter the night) hammered a couple of pitons firmly into the rock, bashed the sharper projections till they were more rounded, melted snow for a hot drink of fruit-juice. Ironically, there was water pattering down, a few feet above us in the darkness; but neither of us felt like climbing another inch. Before pulling the bag over our heads, we took a last look at the lights sparkling down in Grindelwald, more than 8,000 feet below; we agreed that it must be much more comfortable down there, and wondered whether we should be looking down on it from the summit tomorrow. Mists were creeping up from below; the lights wavered, grew dim, disappeared. The night air breathed coldly on us. We sat down and pulled our protective tent-covering over us.

The first light of a new day was filtering through our perlon shell. The night had been quite bearable, in spite of the stones which had refused to surrender their sharpness and the smallness of the sitting-room. Only once did I have to wake Wolfi up, when I heard him say: 'Uncomfortable here, I'm going out where it's level ground,' and saw him preparing to stand up. Otherwise, we slept almost all the time.

I lifted the perlon-casing a little and looked out. Fog! Everything was grey, water dripped down the rocks, a dull silence enveloped us. Water – not ice! No early morning frost, then. I didn't like it at all, and woke Wolfi up at once. We had to get on without wasting a moment. In all probability, the weather had broken.

All the same, we allowed ourselves a hot fruit-juice breakfast; then we started to climb again, stiff in every limb. In the very first chimney we ran into a lively waterfall. Damnable discomfort! The water got in everywhere, down our necks, up our sleeves, no matter how carefully we went. Our fleece jackets became cold compresses . . .

It grew darker and darker. At the top of the chimney, it began to snow. So the weather had broken, after all; for us, as for everyone before us. After this last chimney at the top that could be fatal. Visibility diminished and diminished. We simply must not miss the access to the 'Traverse of the Gods'. We got our photograph out, measured rope's lengths on it with the width of our fingers, remembering what Heini Harrer had told us: not to go all the way up the narrow ice-field above the Ramp, but out to the right, by the first opportunity offered – the only one that led to the traverse. We just *had* to find it; for we knew what lay above, if we went wrong, and what had happened there to others before us . . .

Clouds of powdery blown snow enveloped us. It must be that dark gap over there. We hurried across to it, to find that beyond it lay the crumbling black slates of a precipitous rock-band – yes, that must be the Brittle Band leading to the traverse itself. It tallied perfectly with the photograph, too.

Very cautiously, we worked our way across that ledge, bestrewn with loose slates and falling away precipitously below. There were one or two rock-pitches going straight up – and there we were, at the start of the traverse.

This could only be the famous Traverse of the Gods, but it did not look in the least like what we had expected. 'A route high above monstrous abysses, and giddyfying precipices,' said the description. We could see none of this – fog lay close to our right, above our heads and on this band ahead of us; a band covered with débris, sloping slightly outwards, not always clearly defined, and partly clothed in a grey, loose, soft crust. Not at all inviting.

We moved step by step, with the utmost caution, always carefully belayed by one another. Could we possibly get to the top today? It seemed essential that we should, for we shuddered at the

The North Face of the Eiger

thought of a second bivouac on the Face. But it was already almost midday . . .

A solitary stone swished past and disappeared into the grey. We did not hear it strike down below. The depths to our right, hidden in the fog were bottomless. Suddenly we are at the end of the band; a steep ice-slope loomed ahead of us, a gigantic many-armed funnel . . . we were at the Spider.

Down at the Kleine Scheidegg everyone was getting worried. There was nothing to be seen but clouds and storm; the mountain had drawn its curtains. Was there yet another disaster brewing?

Meanwhile, Salzburg and Vienna had become aware of what was going on, and who was involved. The papers were full of pessimistic comment: once on the face, rescue was impossible – the only chance was right at the top or right at the bottom. Anywhere in between, it all depended on the climbers themselves – a lesson painfully drummed in over the twenty years since the first successful ascent. Even Herbert and Lothar were worried. Fritz Von Allmen had telephoned them in Grindelwald to say visibility was nil: occasionally a strip of rock, a ledge, a patch of ice broke through the clouds . . . beyond that, not a trace . . .

Again and again Von Allmen trained the telescope on the pother of cloud in the boiling cauldron, between the Ramp, the Spider and the summit.

Stones came whistling down, but fewer than yesterday. On the other hand, we could see nothing. At the upper rim of the Spider's gigantic funnel we were met by the problem of a maze of interlacing gullies in the grey fog of cloud. Which of these exit-cracks was the right one? Not even our photograph of the face provided a definite answer.

At last we came across a piton; that must be it. We made good progress and found a second piton, so we carried on.

There was plenty of cover from 'shots'; but shots were few and far between and one could hear them coming from a long way off. The silence was mostly unbroken, and yesterday's showers of small stones seemed to have dried up. Perhaps the snow was immobilizing them. Anyway, it was all quite different from yesterday.

It had grown appreciably colder since noon. Could it be just because we were higher up, or merely because we were tired? The face seemed absolutely endless, this face that ends in a summit 13,000 feet high. Here we were in the fog and the clouds of the exit-cracks. Would we ever get out of them and up to the top?

Suddenly, there was no way of any kind to be seen ahead. An enormous overhang bulged out like a giant's forehead; farther to the left, a fearsome-looking crack shot up next to a rock-buttress. Were we expected to go up there? According to the route-description there ought to be a yellow crack, a 'rather difficult' pitch. Could this be it? But there was another one beyond it, which might be the way out of this blind corner; and yet another beyond that. They all looked exceedingly savage. It began to snow again.

Straight ahead of us, in the snow, we discovered a weathered rope. Could it have come down from above? We wondered what its history might be. Well, it couldn't reveal its secret; and Wolfi was already hanging from the yellow overhang of one of the cracks. 'Hopeless!' he panted and came down again. Then he tried again, only to fail a second time. In the end we were both standing together, utterly at a loss, in that horrible corner, with the wind whistling around the pillar above us. Suddenly I had an idea that something didn't make sense here . . . that old rope was a clue . . .

'Look after my rope,' I told Wolfi, 'I'm going to explore down below.'

It was pretty dicey; the rock was very brittle. A big lump hit me on the helmet, but luckily it hadn't come very far. I stopped for a moment, then traversed out to the right and immediately recognized the main couloir. Owing to the fog, we had strayed into a *cul-de-sac* – and lost two precious hours!

It seemed hardly possible that we should still get up to the top today; a bitterly disappointing thought. Everything was freezing up in the storm; everything was white now, cold and hostile. The cracks in the rock were filling up, our anoraks were covered in ice, and it was cruelly cold on the stances. Evening was drawing in.

We embarked on a race against time. We fought our desperate way up, foot by foot, our crampons digging into the ice in the bed of the gully, searching for a grip on the slabs of its containing walls. We gasped our way up an overhang. Suddenly there was nothing under my feet, and the rope ran taut; a moment later I felt lifted gently upwards and clawed on to a hand-hold. The piton had come adrift. I cast a grateful glance up at Wolfi, who had held my fall.

No time to waste! Which way now? Straight up, or over to that pulpit on our left? We could not afford to make another mistake; better examine the pulpit, to make sure. Cheers! A piton, an abseil piton . . . and below it, to the left, a narrow platform, an icy, splintered rock-bulge, and a steep gully shooting up from it . . .

Somehow the pitch seemed familiar . . . a picture in some book or other, with a man standing there. Down on the rope – this was it – now or never. This would settle the question: to bivouac or not to bivouac, indeed to get to the top still, or not, today. To get there, or not . . .

The North Face of the Eiger

Down we went on the rope. Now, up and on again: up through the couloir, full of water, up on stiff fingers. All of a sudden great loads of hail came rattling down, covering foot- and hand-holds, fusing with the water to form a slithery film. It was 7 o'clock by now, and getting uncomfortably dark.

Some kind of a ridge loomed up. We climbed out of the gully and on over slabby rock and snow. Wolfi had just climbed a rocky knob when —

A shout from above? Voices? People? A hallucination, of course, born of fog and weariness. There it was again: Herbert's voice . . .

Sure enough, it was our friends, shouting down through the storm; and, though we could not see them, we were overjoyed. We shouted back, and simply rushed up the dusk-dark slope of white above us. But remember to belay, said something in our minds, remember to belay! Then a figure loomed out of the fog – Herbert's figure, a rope's length below the ridge, from which the snow-banners were streaming. Up we went, on all fours, our axes in one hand, a piton in the other, drawing nearer and nearer to him up the steep slope. First one of us, then the other. Would the seconds never finish ticking?

We were on the last few feet of the Eiger's North Face.

We were shaking hands, embracing . . . the rim of the cornice . . . back-patting . . . the last step across it . . . 'Thank God you're here!' . . . Yes, off the North Face, up out of the bottomless abyss . . . 'And thank *you*, too.'

It was over, thirty-three hours of it. Over, at a quarter to eight on the evening of August 6th. Over, at nightfall, after thirty-three hours of climbing and one bivouac, after two days all alone with that giant Face. We were safely up here and talking to people again; here with Lothar, Herbert and Winkler, the Swiss climber, who had come up to wait for us, not knowing when – or whether – we should arrive. Simply because we might need help . . .

Oh, how glad we were that they were there! Not that we needed anything; but just because they *were* there.

Very soon we should have to settle down to a bivouac, somewhere on the descent, in wet clothes and ice-clad anoraks. But it wouldn't be on the North Face any more; and everything is more bearable if you are with friends.

In less than an hour it would be pitch dark. While the others were packing up their gear, Wolfi and I went on up the narrow, almost level crest of the final ridge, till a hummock of snow loomed up at our feet.

We were on the summit of the Eiger.

It was the first time we had really grasped the full implications. We stopped and shook hands again. Our Eiger! Wolfi, we have done it. You and I.

Postscript

The descent was no cake-walk, but nothing could bother us any more, now that Eiger was in our pockets. The thermometer fell to minus 12 degrees during the night, and it snowed right down into the valley. The gale screamed around the rocks and jammed every cranny with ice. We sat under our bivouac-sack and sang, almost all through the night, with breaks for brewing tea. In the morning, our friends, who had sat close by in the other sack, cast some very odd looks at us. Herbert confessed later that they had the impression that we might be just the least bit – you know! – light-headed. Not a bit; we simply sang to keep the cold out – it is warmer if you sing.

Moreover, we sat bolt upright and with our muscles tensed, for then you don't feel the wet shirt on your back nearly so much. And every now and then we brewed tea.

In the morning our anoraks rattled like cuirasses – everything was frozen solid. As we went down the West Face, we lost our way and found ourselves on limestone slabs; not very steep, but smooth and snow-covered. We were wearing crampons, and it was not particularly difficult; but there was the danger of a slip. So we thought it best to turn back, and that meant climbing up 300 feet we had just come down. However, we got down to the bottom at last and – remembering Wolfi's dream at the bivouac on the face – found ourselves going out 'to where it was level'.

How wonderful it was to be splashing in a hot, green foam-bath, to be lying in a newly-made bed, to be alive, and to be able to enjoy life – this wonderful life of ours . . .

Everything was splendid at the Kleine Scheidegg, and Fritz von Allmen saw to it that we lacked nothing; but we were soon busy packing up our tent, our sleeping-bags, a cardboard-box and everything. The great Walker Spur on the Grandes Jorasses was luring us away – and why not, in a summer which had brought so much luck?

There is not much more to say about our Eiger climb. Some people were angry with us because we did not give our photographs and reports away, free, gratis and for nothing, like good idealists. It is only now that I actually realize what bad businessmen we were: the sales did not cover a third of our climbing expenses that summer.

It was the others who did good business; the European Press made a picking. There was not a paper which did not carry a report, not a periodical which failed to produce a page of pictures. Perhaps that was because there had been so many failures and losses for years past and we were the first pair to come through safe and sound.

A climb like that can have the most unpredictable consequences. I discovered that the production of protective helmets had stopped or was on the point of stopping before our ascent. Now, all of a sudden, every picture-paper, for the first time, showed helmeted heads, our heads and those of our friends. Production started up again with a great, unexpected leap. Financially, we got nothing out of it; but if many of the 'extreme' climbers have seen fit to protect their skulls with PVC ever since 1958, it was definitely our climb which set the fashion. For nobody, not even climbers, can escape the stealthy, sublimenal influence of the advertising media. So, maybe, in the long run, the Eiger has saved as many lives as it has claimed!

I have been looking in the cabinet which houses all the old letters of that time; some of them were beyond price. Next to a letter of congratulations from the Austrian Embassy, I found a card from the *Rechter Bauer* Skittle Club of Düsseldorf. It reads: 'You idiots, do you really think you have done something remarkable, by climbing like monkeys on a stick?' This has the ring of true conviction about it.

Again: a textile firm in the Vorarlberg expresses its astonishment that when I was discussing the question of corduroy trousers as Eiger-wear, I said something about a 'sponge', which soaks up everything and never dries out again. I said it with deep conviction, too; for climbers and skittlers alike are no beaters about the bush. What I did not know then was that this firm had a very special corduroy cloth – a waterproof one, extremely solid, in all colours.

I clothed all my friends in the patterns.

And then there was my helmet. What became of my dear old helmet, which took such a drubbing on the Eiger, after seeing me up the North Face of the Matterhorn? Alas, it is no more. It disintegrated under the weight of a boulder somewhere in Turkey. That was its last service, and the head beneath it went unscathed . . . Bianca's head.

Bianca di Beaco from Trieste is one of Italy's finest women-climbers. When, on the way up to the hut on the Aiguille Noire, I suddenly fell backwards off an easy but exposed pitch, because a hand-hold gave way, she gave me a 'shove' and remarked: *'un litro di vino!'* – as is customary in Triestine climbing circles on such occasions.

She had undoubtedly saved my life; so I gave her my helmet.

. . . . .

That great Eiger summer was not over yet. We stood at the foot of the massive Walker Spur of the Grandes Jorasses, 4,000 feet of granite, hard as steel, bristling with difficulties up to Grade VI; a marvellous ladder leading to the mountain's highest summit, more than 13,000 feet high.

It is technically the severest of the three great north faces in the Alps, harder than the Eiger or the Matterhorn; but on it there are no falling stones, a most important difference. The slightly greater severity is thus much more acceptable in a climber's eyes, and it is indeed a climb one might even care to repeat.

The combined Eiger team had sprung into being. Wolfi and I, Herbert and Lothar did the buttress climb as a foursome – three long days of sunshine, cloud and blizzard, up that ladder to heaven, bivouacking on narrow ledges, with climbing passages where we looked down as much as 3,000 feet between our legs; enormously impressive, as we all agreed. As Wolfi and I shook hands at the top, we recalled how we had done the three great faces in partnership . . . .

Fate soon set our feet on different paths; Wolfi's engineering jobs took him first to Switzerland, then to Pakistan, but our times together are not finished. I look forward to the day when we shall tie up on the same rope again – even if it was only for a short climb on some practice-ground. Lothar lives in Munich and makes films – mountain-films and crime-films – you cannot make a living, he says, out of mountain-films alone. And Herbert, camera-man and world-tramp, is not very far away, for he married my sister. So one or other of us at least is at home from time to time . . .

Back for a moment to the summit of the Jorasses – that great summer of the Bernina ice-faces, the Eiger, the Walker Spur. Wasn't that enough?

I looked out over the cornice and away to my dream-climb, the great ridge over there, for me something even greater than the Eiger and the Jorasses – to where the glorious Peuterey Ridge swept up from the blue-green depths of the Val Veni, the greatest of all Alpine ridges. Hardly ever climbed in its entire length – five miles of rock-climbing, gigantic *abseils*, rock-pinnacles, ice-arêtes, mixed snow- and rock-work, every kind of difficulty, breaks in the weather, icy cold – climbing higher, day after day, above shimmering abysses, through cloud, storm and sunshine, up – up, to the summit of Mont Blanc.

The mightiest and finest climb in the Alps. Was I at last ready to try my luck on it?

In the autumn, maybe, when the weather is better and more dependable . . .

A Lesson in French

The Calanques – a Garden of Eden

What does an Alpine climber do when it is raining in Chamonix? He drives to Georges Livanos in Marseilles, or rather to his practice-climbing ground. Practice-ground? An understatement for the Calanques; they are a climber's paradise. For these are limestone cliffs, some of them hundreds of feet high, rising sheer from the sea; and there are some you can only get to in a boat.

In addition to all this, there are Morgiou and Sormiou, two small fishing-villages, with idyllic and alluring names; the only two places, locked in their dreams, on that twelve-mile-long coast – a hem of the land which is uncrossed by any road, and deeply indented by innumerable bays. Cactuses blossom there, and the hot sun beats down on a turquoise sky, perfectly mirrored in a sea-bed covered with red starfish, while shoals of glittering fishes flash in the crystal-clear water above it. There is no road to those two hamlets, only two pot-holed tracks, extremely difficult to find. This is a landscape in its original, primeval state.

Who would not wish to pitch his tent there? So – let us go.

We were at Livanos' home in Marseilles. We had actually tracked it down, and even found him there – a miracle, in view of our scanty acquaintance with the language, and a miracle in respect of the man himself, for he is never *at* home. This salesman, always on his travels, this specialist in Grade VI climbs, always on 'extreme' faces, takes his wife with him when he goes. Yet here they were, both of them, lively, gay, relaxed, as if we had always known them. Very soon eggs and tomatoes were sizzling in the kitchen, while Livanos cracked jokes and talked about the Calanques.

Later, over a strong cup of espresso coffee, he asked us what exactly we were looking for. Sipping the aromatic beverage reflectively, I told him: a climb on firm limestone, with a view of the sea, in some deserted corner, and redolent of the warm south. Livanos grinned. 'You German romantics!' he said and promptly drew a bold sketch, laughing happily as he did so, really enjoying himself. 'It's Morgiou you want,' he said. 'The *Grande Chandèle*, our tall candle. That's the best climb round there; highly romantic. And don't forget to do it by its Marseilles ridge – it's much the best thing on the Chandèle.' He hummed a few bars – could it have been the Marseillaise? – handed over the sketch, and off we went.

We had a job to find Morgiou, but we did, thanks to the sketch-map. One can rely on Livanos: from the Marseilles suburbs onwards, every road was correctly marked. We would have been completely lost without it, for I know about twenty words of French and Wolfi commands less. So we would have been hard put to it to find a recondite fishing-harbour.

Morgiou, a bay with brightly-coloured boats in it, under the hot sun. We decided to have a look at the Chandèle straight away and find a place for our tent. The scenery was savage, a coast of precipitous cliffs, below which we made our way; there were shrubs and trees growing out of the rock, and the air was keen with the tang of the sea.

It grew more and more lonely; the sea was glittering and moving; there were cactus flowers – and nobody. Just a small fishing-boat out there between the islands. In the middle of all this solitude, stood a notice-board – how very odd! It said: '*Occupé – les naturalistes de Marseille.*' It was all French to us, so we went on. Then we turned a corner. 'Oh . . . !' we said, and fell into a temporary silence.

The accent was unmistakably French: stalking gazelle-legs, swinging hips, and a lot of other things besides . . . at a distance, but not so far away as all that.

'H'm!' I remarked and looked at Wolfi, whose mouth was still wide open, whose eyes shone with the light of a boy-friend in a television commercial. . . . 'H'm,' he said, clearing his throat, for he had taken note of my look and had immediately assumed his toughest north-face expression: 'The "Naturalistes" must be nudists, then . . .' Was it only my fancy, or had his Viennese accent suddenly acquired a French *timbre*? 'Obviously,' I replied and, unhurriedly, took stock of the impressive landscape. It was a marvellous bay.

'What do we do now?' asked Wolfi as the next contribution to our voluble dialogue; moved no doubt by his mountaineering conscience, and pointing to the rock-tower of the Chandèle, beyond the marvellous bay . . .

'A typical Calanques feature, on superb rock, with views far out to sea, a magnificent climb': thus Livanos' description before handing the route-guide over to us. Oh, that Livanos . . . !

A Lesson in French

So much for the description. (This is where it ended.) Now what? Before our eyes, lovely, happy nudity . . . and, by heaven, this was obviously France!

'It's the only way through,' I said, summing up the situation, and trying to sound objective. To our left was a cliff, barring the way, with the breakers creaming at its feet – then a strip of sand, and sharp-edged, sloping slabs – the only sharp-edged objects to be seen in that direction . . .

That Livanos! I could just imagine him grinning over his 'route-description', specially designed for 'Romantics'.

'We must get across – but how?' growled Wolfi, wrinkling his forehead. We had never met a mountaineering difficulty of this kind before, and there is no mention of it in Paulcke's text-book on alpine dangers. But it has never been our habit to beat a retreat.

'There are only two ways about it,' I philosophized. 'To be noticeable or not to be noticeable. With, or without . . .'

Wolfi scratched his head. 'Oh, well,' he said, smiling contentedly. We decided for 'with'. The alternative would really have been too much bother, with all this climbing gear of ours. . . .

We were certainly noticed. The first looks cast upon us went through us like gimlets. We thought hard of the Grande Chandèle and continued on our way.

Now everybody was staring at us, the intruders, with many an inquisitive glance. Could we be members? Blushing, we looked, as indifferently as possible, away beyond slim shoulders, feeling the while appallingly 'dressed-up'. None the less we accomplished that exciting traverse. With stride unfaltering, our pitons clinking among French bosoms, our bodies hung about with ropes and climbing-hammers among French buttocks, dazzled by graceful contours, our pulses racing, but undeterred, we made our way through that shapely panorama set in the graceful coastal scenery of the Calanques; two tough sinewy alpine figures, their thoughts fixed only on the summits, the cynosure of all eyes, like models on a cat-walk . . . Suddenly, Wolfi begun to hum a Parisian ditty, unmusically, out of tune. I too slowed my pace as I crossed the big, sharp-edged, sun-drenched limestone slabs, with their outcrop of sheer loveliness. I had to, of course, because of the sharp edges . . .

I wondered if mountaineers could qualify for membership? My pace grew still slower. After all, Paulcke's book on alpine dangers says: 'Go slowly and you go well, and if you go well you go far.'* And if you go well . . . ! Ye gods, I was fairly dazzled the next moment; if I could only

* '*Che va piano, va sano: che va sano va lontano.*'

address that gorgeous creature! I groaned – oh, these language-difficulties! – and passed on in silence, broken-hearted. Passed on, left her . . . and if you go well – that ass Paulcke had no idea what 'well' means. 'Well' didn't mean the same thing, here and now. No, here, if you go slowly, all that happens – unfortunately – is that you still get on far too quickly. At this moment a deep sigh next to me announced the end of the 'Song of Paris'. If you go slowly, you get along too quickly and much too far; there was no doubt that we had irretrievably completed the traverse. I sat down, exhausted, on a boulder. Wolfi said not a word and passed the flask of peppermint-tea across to me; then he took a swig himself. From the last slab of paradise the strains of the Marseillaise came wafting over to us.

It was only later, from much higher up, that we observed quite a different approach-route to the Grande Chandèle. Livanos again – he never mentioned it!

Oh, well . . .

Sun, sea and sand – and, of course, rock. The weather had long ago turned fine again on Mont Blanc; but it was fine here too, and here stood our tent, on the sea-shore.

We balanced our delicate way up that lovely ridge. Down below lay the island-studded sea; a gentle breeze blew in from the distant horizon, the rock was firm, the water rippled and glinted, more than 1,500 feet beneath our feet. A splendid cliff, this Grande Chandèle, a marvellous tower, set in an enviably beautiful practice-ground, in the midst of a region that has neither roads nor houses – almost as it was in the beginning of things. . . .

We sat on top, blinking up at the sun, down to the sea.

'*C'est très joli ici*,' remarked Wolfi, for once in unexceptionable French.

'*Tu as raison*,' I replied. Then we went off for a swim.

The Great Peuterey Ridge

First: a black and white title, then a deep orange one, across a black-and-white picture. After that, grass, green or brownish in colour; a little lake, high above the Val Veni; the shining dome of Mont Blanc...

Words: '*A silence – almost absurd – a silence built of substance and tiny seconds... fashioned by this autumn sunshine...*'

Terenzio's voice quavered a little. Renato sat there, leaning forward, headphones on his ears, his hand on the volume control – a dark silhouette, like the others. Not a sound except Terenzio's speech. Not a movement, for the microphone picks up everything. There, on the top floor of our house in the Via Crispi, on the outskirts of Varese, at two in the morning, we were recording our film: 'The Great Ridge'. Action! Silently, I touch Terenzio's shoulder – the signal for him to start speaking: '*Every really great peak... demands its aura of silence...*'

It was going like a bomb, this time; we hoped it would be the last night of our recording sessions for Renato, Tona, Terenzio, Adriano, Gianluigi – the little team which could really take the credit if the film ever reached the Trento Festival. I had spent the whole summer cutting, joining sequence to sequence, excising again, swopping them round – arguing, defending, quarrelling, viewing, planning and reconsidering – with Tona and, particularly, with Renato. Anyone can shoot a film; to bring its idea to eventual fruition, to the point where the perforated reels constitute a film which projects what one had in mind, so that others can share in the experience, is quite another matter. I would never have succeeded but for my friends, but for Tona and, of course, my own obstinate head; for this was my first attempt at a film. I listened to Terenzio's rough, dark voice – so appropriate to this Odyssey on the Great Ridge; his elocution might at times be imperfect, but what mattered was that he was a climber, and therefore knew exactly what I wanted. So had they all – and they had all, long ago, lived through that adventure on the Great Ridge, high above the Val Veni ... in September, with hardly a breath ruffling the grasses, the air unimaginably clear, and not a sound invading it....

Words, once more: '*Space . . . seems to lose a dimension here . . . a flower, the summit of Mont Blanc . . . both infinitely near . . . or infinitely far . . .*'

The camera zooms slowly upwards – up the Aiguille Noire – the Aiguille Blanche – three seconds of Mont Blanc's summit (everything has to be timed to a split second) – now . . . I press Terenzio's shoulder again.

'*Trrrrrrrrreeeeng – Wumm – Trrreee. . . . !*'

'Curse all motor-cyclists! At two in the morning, of all things!'

Trrrreng – we could still hear it, disappearing in the distance. Everything washed out! This rider of a moped, at two in the morning, who had nothing better to do than choose the Via Crispi for his homeward journey, and with his throttle wide open at that, had wrecked everything. We had taken everything into account – even the bells of the near-by church – and now this . . . he had even broken the temporary padding of our 'recording-studio' under the roof. A good thing for him that we couldn't lay hands on him!

Adriano rewound the spool, cursing. Then we started all over again: '*A silence . . . almost absurd . . .* '

A glitter of snow-diamonds, a pale glimmer on the crest of Mont Blanc, under a yellowy-orange sky, and a figure moving up from the depths . . .

Words again: '*Aims, eyes, spirit – all focused on infinity . . .*'

As the figure came closer, Gianluigi plucked deep open-string notes, like the sound of bells, haphazard, and as he thought fitting for this moment, as if he himself were the central feature of the film. It could have been his dark-blue figure, moving across the glittering lights in the snow . . .

'*Buongiorno – and a good morrow be yours, too!*'

Well done, Terenzio. He had said it so feelingly – and how important that was, when there were a hundred ways of saying it; why, he might have said it in a voice that conveyed, 'to hell with it – I've had enough of this!' No, he had spoken the last words of the film in exactly the right way. Renato took off his headphones.

'My blessed infants,' he said, 'we've done it!'

We toasted Trento, the film, the Ridge, anything and everything. Anyone in the Via Crispi at 4 o'clock that morning might well have wondered what kind of a party was going on under the tiled roof up there.

We hardly dared to hope that the film would win a prize at Trento – where, this time, space would provide competition.

The longest ridge-traverse in the Alps is no simple tour, but a great mountaineering expedition. It was Tona who put the question which was in all our minds:

'Will the viewer understand the unfolding of this huge traverse, up over the ridges, up and down over towers and peaks? Above all, have we succeeded in conveying the spirit in which the climb was carried through? Have we been able – in three-quarters of an hour and 1,500 feet of film – to capture, for others, five miles of climbing, five days of it, the nightly bivouacs, the marvellous feeling of being up there, high above the world and outside time, the joy of it all ... ?'

She was right. The idea of making a film up there had meant a complete divorce from time, a traverse of that great ridge almost in the spirit of a hiker, day after day, content to wait in one place till the light and the clouds were right for the picture – even on so mighty a ridge.

We had, of course, no idea whether we could do it. Hermann Buhl and Gaston Rébuffat had tried before us to traverse the ridge in its entirety; both had failed, driven down by bad weather. The traverse had only been completed twice, once by a German party, once by a Polish. Of all the great climbs in the Alps, this one will remain the least often accomplished; for here the probabilities of success are lower than on the North Face of the Eiger or the Walker Spur of the Jorasses, both of which it exceeds in size and length – five miles of climbing, roping down, then climbing again, on the most varied of ground, as against about two miles on those famous Alpine north faces. The first sector alone, the South Ridge of the Noire, involves a mile and a half of climbing between Grades III and V, the second consists of a 1,600-foot *abseil* down that peak's vertical North Arête – a large imponderable in bad weather!

The final sector, the traverse of the Aiguille Blanche, the descent on to the broad saddle of the Col de Peuterey and the 3,000 foot ascent from there to the summit of Mont Blanc – this sector by itself is often called the Peuterey Ridge, though it only constitutes its upper half – is technically easier, but just as grand and impressive; here too a change in the weather has often dictated a retreat.

To make the route up this 'upper half' of the ridge easier, the Italian Alpine Club has established a small bivouac-box on the Brèche Nord at about 11,500 feet; many have spent storm-bound days in it, glad that it was there to give them shelter. (The ascent to it is a big climb in its own right – it is reached from the Fresnay Glacier up a couloir, after picking a route to its foot between veritable palaces of ice.)

Franz Lindner and I estimated that our traverse of the ridge, including all the preparations and a return to the Val Veni – where we had set up a kind of base camp – from the summit of Mont Blanc would require at least a fortnight. (Wolfi* wasn't very keen on the proposition on account of the gigantic *abseil* from the Noire. Not long before, during a winter attempt on the South Face of the Dachstein, a piton had come away as he was roping down, and he had fallen nearly 700 feet; by a miracle, and thanks to the depth of the snow, he had suffered nothing more than a horrid fright, but, understandably, he had ever since evinced a slight bias against *abseils*.) Franz and I established a first-ever supply dump close to the bivouac-box in the Brèche Nord; we also left the ice-equipment up there, so as to carry less weight during the rock-work on the Noire. Using two 'museum' ice-axes from the days of our grandfathers, and without crampons, we worked our way down to the Fresnay Glacier and back to the valley, across the Col Innominata. There we replaced the axes on the Guides' Monument (from which we had borrowed them in the first place), and climbed back to our base camp. Everything was now ready.

It was on a wonderful September afternoon that we set out for the little untented Noire hut, near the Fauteuil des Allemands.

Soundtrack: '*This scent of autumn pervading the air, this gentle sunshine, almost warm, augured good luck for our climb . . . how near was Mont Blanc's summit . . . how far, the summit of Mont Blanc . . .*'

The Great Ridge. For me this was much more than a climb, this ridge at which I had looked up so often. Today I still count it as the biggest and most rewarding of all the great alpine routes. It will remain so; for in it there lies combined, everything that can make a climber's heart beat faster.

We were roping-up. All our night-thoughts, our mountain-doubts, melted away. Only the present counted now. The pinnacles of the south ridge were already touched by the fingers of the dawn.

The South Ridge of the Noire . . .

The rock under our hands was gloriously rough, every hold, solid as steel. Up it went, up and up, slab after slab, cliff upon cliff, tower after tower, all of it steep, and always above the sheer abyss on either side. Mists came drifting up from the séracs of the Fresnay Glacier, to dance around the pinnacles and about us as we climbed on, drinking in the fresh clean autumn air.

All around us lay sunlight and valley and vast distances; the banks of cloud building slowly in the sky, the turquoise eye of the little Chécrouit lake far below, and the warm scent of autumn rising from the foothill meadows; the grey rubble-stream of the Miage Glacier, snaking deep

* Wolfgang Stefan.

The Great Peuterey Ridge

down into the valley, right into the green of the forests and the fields; the tiny houses along the Dora's banks – all far, far below.

The rock was beautifully varied. We met slabs whose rounded surfaces were covered with greyish-green lichens; white felspar crystals stuck out here and there, asking to be pocketed. There were ledges offering firm foot-hold for a groping boot, wrinkles in the rock inviting one to entrust the whole of one's body-weight to them and heave it up with one's arms. We came to a huge overhang and used each other's shoulders to overcome it. Then we were over the second tower and on our way to the next, the Pointe Welzenbach. We traversed out on to the right-hand face over ledges and slabs.

So we went on and up along the granite Jacob's ladder of the south ridge. And while our arms and legs were busy with the mechanics of climbing and our eyes engaged in searching out the way ahead, our thoughts went out over all the depths and distances around and about us. It goes without saying that we were happy beyond measure on our south ridge.

By the afternoon we were on the summit of the Pointe Welzenbach. There we sat down to rest and eat, and looked down on the way we had come. The first tower, the Pointe Gamba, looked like a small tooth, the pinnacles of the second lay far below us, and here we were, sitting on the third. Willo Welzenbach once got as far as this; it was some time after that before a way was found to the summit over the Pointe Brendel and the Bich. Looking up at the yellow and rust-coloured walls, we rated them at fully V – perhaps a bit more than that, though there is only one short traverse on the vertical face of the Bich, which is supposed to be from V to VI.

We were at a little flat place with a bivouac-wall all round it, a reminder that not everyone can do the South Ridge in a single day, and that we would probably find quite a few 'parapets' higher up.

We wondered whether we could still get to the top of the Pointe Brendel before nightfall. 'Let's get on with it,' said Franz, and we started off again. We now came to the first *abseil*, where we soon found a suitable block; the rope went whistling down and we followed comfortably enough in our 'Dülfer' seats. There followed a gently sloping step and a traverse to the left before we were at the foot of the Brendel's severe upthrust.

We craned our heads backwards to look up it, and spotted the route up the almost perpendicular slabs to the left, leading to the overhang above. This was another of the many things we wanted to film, but the difficulty was how to look after the rope at the same time? 'Leave it to me,' said Franz, taking the camera, and off I went. After a slightly overhanging start, I reached the first piton and could see the second, ahead of me. Of course, the rope had to jam plumb in between the two, just when I was not exactly comfortably placed. 'What's up?' I shouted down to Franz, 'give me some rope!' 'Lovely shooting,' he replied calmly and put the camera away. 'Now you'll have to wait a bit while I get the knot undone.' It didn't really take very long but, getting my breath back at the second piton, I thought to myself: 'No more safety knots in the rope, thank you. It's better just to rely on climbing carefully!'

Unfortunately the sun chose that moment to disappear behind a big cloud, so I had to wait. Not that it mattered, for we didn't care how far we got that day; but as the blessed light of the sun seemed to have gone for good, I decided to get on with the traverse. The moment I was across, of course the sun came out again. Up came Franz's voice: 'Get back again!' I couldn't very well refuse, and in any case, it was a nice traverse; so back I went and did it again. It all took ages, but I had to chuckle at the thought that for once we didn't mind about time, and what huge fun it was not to have to. Our journey up the great ridge would go on for days – just as many days as needed – all of them glorious days, as we simply climbed higher and higher up it.

We climbed the second pitch of the Brendel in the dusk. Presently it was quite dark, as we felt our way over easier rock to the spacious summit. There we found a splendid place for an overnight bivouac, in a hollow, where we could lie down and stretch full length, side by side; once again it was equipped with a protecting wall to break the wind. There was only one fly in the ointment; we were dreadfully thirsty. Naturally there isn't any water laid on on the south ridge, and nowhere on the way had we seen so much as a spot of snow. There was nothing to be done about it, and one can't have everything; perhaps we would find some tomorrow, on the summit.

The night was still, with only an occasional feeble stirring of the air about the peak, both only to die away almost at once. We were very happy with the day's work and looked forward to a night in the open worth remembering. It was very clear, and a thousand stars shone down on us with a rare brilliance. Soon I was welcoming my old friend Orion, as he came up over the horizon.

Then I suddenly noticed a patch of light shimmering between the rocks. I switched my torch on and there, miraculously, in autumn-time, up here, was some old snow. It must have been the only fragment of snow on the whole of the South Ridge. We took it in turns, without more ado, to lie on our stomachs sucking in the little trickle of melting water

The Great Peuterey Ridge

from that old snow, repeating the performance again and again. It was bliss, and now our happiness was complete. The only thing missing had been water.

It was a lovely night. We slept full length on our rocky bed, wrapped warmly in our fleece-bags, covered by the tent-sack. Every now and then I woke up to look up at the stars, to the glittering scarf of the Milky Way, and to watch the leisurely progress of Orion; happy in the knowledge that we would be continuing our journey up this great ridge for many another similar day.

Being autumn, it got a little chilly towards dawn. Slowly the sky lightened, yellow at first, then blue to eastwards; then the sun shot up and it was day again. The granite towers of our ridge were swathed in mists, turning our little summit to an island in the monotony of grey, through which the sun glimmered from time to time. At times the wind parted the curtains and we looked up at Mont Blanc, still remote and high above us. Down below, the cloud shadows were chasing across the crevassed surface of the Fresnay Glacier. We made breakfast and did some filming, before we realized it was 11 o'clock and time to be on the move.

Ahead of us lay the hardest sector on the whole climb, the precipitous surge up to the Pointe Bich, whose arête and ensuing traverse had moved even Hermann Buhl to respectful utterance. We wondered a little how we would fare on it with all our baggage. The passage of a few pinnacles in the next col brought us to the foot of the pitch. Baggage and all, it went better than we had expected; admittedly, we were reaping the fruits of an unbroken summer's climbing, and that helped a lot. Once up the steep arête, we tackled the traverse, which goes off to the right along a short airy rock-ledge above an overhang, offering only tiny finger-holds and forcing one's body out over nothingness. Short as it is, it made extreme demands on our fingers, while our packs did their best to pull us outwards off the mountain. It was soon over and we stopped for a breather before continuing for quite a time over easier ground. Now it would not be long before we were on the Noire's subsidiary summit. Then came another difficult rope's length, involving slabs and a small overhang. While Franz worked his way up from piton to piton, I filmed him and looked after his rope. Then we decided to put the camera away for a while, for it was time to be getting on to the summit of the Noire. On we went, over easy rock, to the subsidiary summit, and looked across to the true summit, on which the metal statue of the Madonna was reflecting the light of the setting sun. Below it, blazed the gigantic slabs of the West Face; and there, far down behind the Noire, where it was now getting dark, we thought we could make out the bivouac-box, and wondered whether we would get there tomorrow. We only stopped long enough to look at the vast panorama spread about us, then roped down into the next gap. Soon we were climbing over easy boulders, sometimes on the ridge, sometimes on the face, towards the summit.

A red sunset was flushing the sky as we reached the Madonna. There were isolated clouds floating above the mountain-tops, shaped like big fishes, raising sudden misgivings in our minds. What would we do if the weather chose this moment to turn sour on us? Ahead lay the tremendous *abseil* down the northern arête of the Noire, an undertaking to be treated with the greatest respect. It would be a serious blow if the weather broke here and now. We could only hope it would hold till the day after tomorrow and that we should be able to reach our provisions at the bivouac-box first. We found a sheltered place below the summit, with plenty of room to lie full length, and made everything snug for our second night out. The lights of Courmayeur twinkled up from the valley as the night passed slowly by.

A Break in the Weather

The summit of the Noire put on a halo of gold. A sky of unusual beauty, shot with every imaginable colour, heralded the rising of the sun. And the weather was still good.

We breakfasted on porridge, and packed up. We knew that very few parties had roped down the North Arête, and had brought plenty of pitons in case we went wrong. The *abseil* facilities at the summit did not look very safe to us, so we banged a heavy ring-piton into the rock just below its northern side; as it went in more firmly at every stroke, my grateful thoughts went out to Wolfgang Stefan, my companion through years of climbing, who had given it to me for this very purpose. We had climbed the South Ridge several years earlier up to this point, but no farther, thinking ourselves not yet ripe for the whole Peuterey Ridge.

The piton was home, down went our two 130-foot ropes, and I was soon on my way down over sloping slabs, and straight into thick fog, a not very helpful feature, which would make route-finding very much harder. However, the weather was still fine, even if things seemed to counsel greater speed than before. At the bottom of the rope I found some more pitons in the rock, and made myself fast, leaving the rope free for Franz's descent. We were soon heaving the ropes out into a white emptiness again and listening for them to 'slap' down below.

The Great Peuterey Ridge

For a few moments we caught a glimpse of the inclined slabs which would be our next landing-ground; then we tested the pitons and followed one another down through thin air. We were delighted to find the next launching platform, after swinging to and fro a little in our 'chairs'; there were three differently coloured loops of rope hanging there. All we had to do was to retrieve our own rope, thread it and go on down.

We could have done without the fog, though. Finding the right place for the next stage in the descent at the end of each rope's length was becoming quite a problem.

After another 'air-lift' we found ourselves jammed together on an exiguous stance in the crest of the arête. We could see a shelf thirty feet below us, with pitons and wood-pegs coming up towards us, new ones; so we must be bang on Jean Couzy's direct route. We heaved the ropes over the edge; they disappeared silently, drew taut, without so much as a 'slap'. All the indications were that we should be sitting suspended over the void at the end of our 130 feet. We dropped a stone and – after a longish time – could barely hear the sound of its impact; so there must be 200 to 250 feet of vertical and partly undercut rock beneath us. We had better go down the thirty feet to the shelf. We reached it soon enough and when I pushed myself along it, still in my sling, at last I came upon an *abseil*-piton, from which our ropes would touch the bottom.

That airy descent landed us on the great shoulder of the Noire's North Arête. From there we were left with the same distance down a chimney as we had already come from the summit. The first thing to do was to retrieve the rope. We tugged with all our strength, it wouldn't budge. It had stuck somewhere up there.

Stupid! We changed positions and tugged some more. Both of us, with might and main. All in vain: the rope just hung there, hopelessly stuck up above – 130 feet above, right at the top, of course. A nice kettle of fish, to be sure. The only solution was to climb all the way up in Prusik-slings and straighten things out.

Franz volunteered for that thankless job, saying he had been practising the technique only a little while ago. To some purpose, I must admit, when I saw him get up in under a quarter of an hour. Meanwhile it had started to snow. The weather had broken. Franz arranged the ropes in a different direction, tested their mobility and came down again. We both hauled anxiously on the rope, this time with better results than before. Cheers – the thing was moving!

The gigantic chimney, with its thousand feet of roping-down, was unmistakable in spite of the mist, and when, at the end of the first *abseil* we came upon a chock-stone with a rope-ring, we knew we were on the right road. Rope after rope, down and down we went. At times stones whistled past, dangerously near. After a time it stopped snowing. The chimney became a steep groove which we only left almost at its bottom, traversing out to the right between *abseil* stages every now and then, so as to reduce the height differential between us and the rift falling from the Brèche Sud to the Fresnay Glacier as much as possible.

It was halfway through the afternoon before we finally got into the rift. There was no time to waste if we were still to get to the bivouac-box on the Brèche Nord. We packed up the ropes and climbed up over slabby débris to the Brèche Sud. There we had to turn the pinnacles of the Dames Anglaises, rising in an irregular cluster ahead of us, on their left flank. We climbed a little way, then traversed slightly downwards, with frequent changes of direction, dictated by the nature of the ground. We had to go very carefully, for the rock, while not difficult, was unreliable and there were snow-patches in between. After much up and down and to and fro on the unstable stuff, we were very glad to reach the couloir leading up to the Brèche Nord. All that lay between us and the bivouac-box now was the upper arm of the couloir, consisting, unfortunately, of sheer smooth ice.

So near and yet so far! We were dog-tired, hungry, and it was growing dark. Otherwise we were perfectly happy. In spite of a day of bad weather, we had managed to traverse the Noire and reach our objective. The rest of the ridge was practically in the bag, for with enough provisions up there at the bivouac-box to enable us to face even a prolonged spell of bad weather, what could now prevent one going on, to the top of Mont Blanc?

I led, using the only crampon we had with us, while Franz belayed me with due care. While I was beating step on step in the smooth surface with my ice-hammer, it was suddenly pitch dark. At long last we got off the ice and reached the slabby saddle of the Brèche Nord, with the bivouac-box close at hand. Outside, the snow-flakes were whirling as we lay down, there and then, to sleep. How long, we wondered drowsily, before it turns fine again?

Our fourth day on the ridge dawned. We snuggled closer in our blankets with only one resolution in our minds – to have a day-off. All the same, we took a look at the weather through the door of the box; fresh snow was lying outside, but the sun was shining, newly risen. The fine weather was back again after the break. We would certainly have to wait a day for the layer of snow to settle. So we fetched everything out of the depot and had a good tuck-in after our days of scanty fare. We

The Great Peuterey Ridge

reconnoitred the next day's route for a short way and took a few feet of film. Our load for the following day was hugely inflated by provisions, ice-equipment, extra film gear, a tripod and all the rest, but we felt very fit. Still, if we were going to climb from 11,500 feet, where we stood, over the Aiguille Blanche and on to Mont Blanc's 15,782 feet summit, we should have to make an early start. A fine day gave way to a clear evening. We knew then that we could be sure of fine weather for the last stage of our long trek.

The Final Day

Autumn, in tune with our most secret desires, gave us, for our last day, her most perfect of all perfect days. As we climbed the Aiguille Blanche, our eyes ranged far and wide over innumerable peaks, in the warmth of the morning sun, under an immaculate blue sky. Down in the green valleys the houses of Entrèves and Courmayeur were small, beyond belief. It was sheer bliss to be alive.

Behind us the Noire diminished rapidly. We kept on thinking about its South Ridge, the night we had spent out on it, the exciting endless *abseil* down its northern arête, till at last the traverse of the triple-headed Blanche began to demand all our care and attention. From the summit we looked down on the huge saddle of the Col de Peuterey, lying nearly 1,000 feet below us – another long *abseil*. Once down, we jumped the bergschrund and tramped across the broad, smooth saddle; up over the opposing schrund, and then a short rest. The sun was already slanting down, so short are these September days. On, we went up the long, long 3,000 feet which separate the col from Mont Blanc's summit. Once on the ridge again, we were met by an icy blast, though the view and the sky remained clear. We made slow progress, taking care that the bitter gusts didn't unbalance us on the narrow white edge. Suddenly the great white mountains around us glowed red and Mont Blanc's monstrous shadow streamed out across the world. It was an overwhelming sight, even if the gale called for all our attention and our fingers had grown numb.

Presently there was nothing except a livid twilight. Moving together, we worked our way up without a pause. We did not belay, but each of us was on the alert, knowing that a slip on that narrow ladder to the sky could hardly be held. Then it was night. The abyss fell away beneath us, impalpable, illimitable, invisible. We only knew that it was there below us. Neither of us could see the other, obliterated by the uncanny darkness. And so we climbed, endlessly, onwards. Endlessly, straight up – up into the vague, dark nothingness overhead; but now we were belaying one another, rope after rope. The ridge gave way to a rounded slope, a kind of broad rib, getting steeper and steeper. The gigantic cornice of Mont Blanc de Courmayeur never seemed to want to put in an appearance.

We could see a sharp silhouette against the stars. It was the cornice, and soon we had found a way through a breach in it. We sat down thankfully in the snow. We had done it. We were up. What was left to do would be nothing by contrast with the last few hours.

We moved on again through the marvellous night. This was the last stage on the long journey from the valley to Mont Blanc's summit; and as we went, our thoughts were centred on the days behind us.

(Tona) 'To our surprise, the hall was full of applause. So the public had understood and identified itself with that long journey on which Kurt, Franz and all the rest of us had worked so hard! We were at the Eleventh Mountain-film Festival at Trento. Kurt was going up the steps to receive the prize. I was full of joy for him, for our friends, for everyone who may in future traverse the great Peuterey ridge. To have brought it off was a marvellous feeling. I had had the luck to contribute something – helping Kurt to share something of his passion, his mountain-magic, with others.

'He looks at his ridge with loving eyes, and it was perhaps a part of that love he had succeeded in giving us.'

The Great Ridge . . .

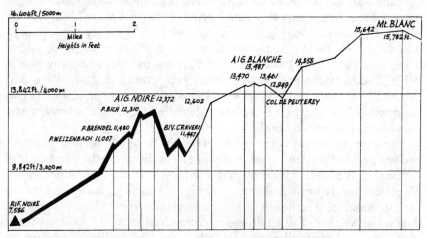

3. The Peuterey Ridge. That part of the route repeated is the bold line.

Alpine Geometry

Mont Blanc de Cheilon

'Mathematics are marvellous!' our maths-master used to pontificate, a sublime expression transfiguring his thin face.

We knew he meant it, and none of us dared to refute him; we nodded silently and thought about the next exercise we should have to do. He was very strict. Today I am sure he was right: mathematics *are* wonderful. They are clear and uncorruptible – especially in exercises, at school. I even taught mathematics myself for a year or two.

However what I set out to talk about is 'Alpine Geometry' – a very specialized subject. Every climber knows the thrill of his own trail up a face – the pleasure in its regularity (the final consequence of which idea is, of course, the *direttissima*). He knows the thrill, the unique inexplicable tension, which the regular shapes of the mountain world awake in him: huge pyramids, enormous rectangular slabs, piled-up triangles of rock, white circles, immense squares – the thrill of simplicity of shape and outline (and the excitement of mastering them, to an unbelievable extent, by his own efforts, his own power), the thrill of the straight line upwards . . . in fact, the Alpine Geometry . . . a thrill impossible to explain.

The first time I discovered something of the fascination of form was when, suddenly in a practical geometry session, cylinders, cones and pyramids started to turn on the papers, rolled through different 'eye-levels', threw their shadows on it. I was doing much more than required at the time, cutting imaginary pyramids open, letting the light fall into them, turning them, making clusters of triangles penetrate one another and throw shadows on each other. Often I was not at all sure if I would get a result, or what it would be, there on the white expanse of paper. It was often hard work, but highly fanciful.

Yes, I was doing more than required – for I started to draw the figures for some of my class mates; and the professor was very pleased with us.

A few errors, corresponding to the particular party, prevented him from noticing it. True, he seemed a little surprised when it came to oral tests – fortunately infrequent, but when they came fraught with minutes of shivering anxiety for those taking part. By doing practical geometry in this way I, again, avoided working on my thesis, a tedious essay in German on 'the treasures of the homeland'. We were a good team.

After I graduated I confessed to him. I admired him greatly not only because, in his own sphere, he was a past-master, but because I like people who not only have an enthusiasm, but actually put it into practice.

Remote, in the ranges of the lower Valais, at the end of the lofty Val des Dix, a tributary valley of the Val d'Hérens, stands a very unusual mountain. Seen from the north, it exhibits the shape of a huge pyramid, mathematical in its regularity. Its steep North Face is, by one of nature's freaks, an exactly constructed equilateral triangle. It is called the Mont Blanc de Cheilon.

One day in the thirties two daring young men stood at the foot of the face, sampling it – Ludwig Steinauer and Wolfgang Gorter. Then they climbed it, by a route as straight as Steinauer's braces and Gorter's natty tie – up the plumb-line. It was the first ascent of what was still now the single, finest and most direct line up that mighty triangle.

My 'geometrical' feelings sensed a challenge.

For thirty years there had been only one repetition of that first ascent – for obvious reasons. Not only was the face far from anywhere, but it was exceedingly steep, as witness the crowded contour-lines on the map. In fact, the slabs of smooth ice and the rock-shields of the final wall achieve a 70 degree pitch in places. The second climb had not been carried through to the summit, but had finished with a traverse out on to the ridge. There had been good reasons for that: right at the top, the crust – as elsewhere, too – is very thin, and getting thinner year by year; so the risk is increased and, at places, where polished rock has now made an appearance, so have the technical difficulties. It seems incredible, but Gorter and Steinauer on their first-ascent managed to find a bivouac-place up there, on that final wall. It must have been very uncomfortable.

Max and I had once again had our fill of desks and window-views on to a garden, of the harassing day-to-day preparatory work for our expedition to Dhaulagiri. This had meant hundreds of letters; arrangements for a glacier-aircraft; and, to raise the necessary funds, one of the

Alpine Geometry

biggest greetings-card operations ever mounted (we were later to dispatch 16,000 of them from Katmandu). The organization of an expedition demands strong nerves. We felt that if we didn't tackle a climb soon, we would cease to be human-beings. So we got into the car and headed for the Valais.

The guardian of the Cabane de Dix came into the dormitory and woke us at 2 a.m. Half asleep we staggered down to the common-room, packed the last essentials and had a hot drink. Then we stepped outside.

It was very cold and there was not even the tiniest of clouds in the sky. In the light of the full moon we did not need to switch on a lamp. Our mountain bulked up enormous ahead of us, seemingly quite inaccessible, and ghostly in the moonlight. We crossed the glacier in a wide curve from the right, making for a prominent pulpit of rock, projecting from the right-hand end of the mountain's base. It was the only place from which we could hope to gain access to the foot of the face, for to the left every approach was barred by a high barrier of séracs.

It was still dark when we got there, to find that it was hardly any distance down into the hollow beyond. We decided it would be best to rope up, and while we were doing so, the eastern sky began to brighten. A cutting wind had risen, stiffening our fingers; but it was an east wind – a good omen. For a little while Max had some trouble with a too-short crampon-strap. Daylight was coming swiftly now; we could see the mighty upsurge of our triangle, felt the thrill of the clean straight line, the excitement of following it up there, step by step . . .

We got down into the hollow and went up, over small avalanche-cones, to the bergschrund. It gaped wide open, but we found a place where it could be crossed quite easily. And then we were on the face.

There was hard grey ice in the avalanche-tracks, but we always found snow-covered ribs on which we could make upward progress. When, occasionally, they petered out all of a sudden, we had to traverse on to the next rib, now to the left, now to the right. It was quite an amusing game, picking out the best line. At the end of each rope's length we hammered in a belaying-piton. The second would then come up, climb through, and assume the lead till the next stance – fully two hundred feet each time. So we gained height rapidly.

Meanwhile, the sun had come up, its light appropriately matching our joy at this gorgeous climb. We felt sure that, with everything going so well down here, things wouldn't be half so bad as expected when it came to climbing out, up above. We might even be on the summit by midday!

Each time the leader hacked out a stance, a cloud of glittering crystals came tinkling down the face, raced past and disappeared in a rapidly thinning veil towards the abyss. There, on a hillock at the glacier's rim, stood the hut, small and forlorn. The light pricked out every wrinkle in the moraine. A few insignificant splinters of rock on the east bank had grown into gigantic shadow-fingers, clutching far across the glacier's surface. 'Like looking down from the rim of some mooncrater,' I couldn't help thinking: 'or like the echo-mountains of Saint Exupery's Little Prince, when he came to visit the Earth.' Yes, pictures of Mont Blanc de Cheilon hold something more than that for me: an utter feeling of release. The breath-taking sensation, the joy, of denying the vertical its verticality; of hanging poised between huge and different eye-levels; the experience of watching the earth's greatest shapes 'turning', beginning to change, raising up, sinking down into the depths – as if by some conjuring-trick – simply because a small human-being, taking thousands of strides, alters for himself that 'eye-level', freeing himself from the one basic eye-level of the plains.

The experience the climber and the man at the drawing-board share is the same sense of freedom and power, many times multiplied: a sense of mastery over all planes, the horizontal, the vertical and all the others, but in their actual reality. A gigantic practical geometry. The climber can make the greatest objects in the world turn for his inspection, so that he is able to grasp their form, simply because he has climbed above the usual plane on to a mountain. And once he has done that, all planes are his...

The higher we got, the more mightily did the Dent Blanche tower up to the east, its North Ridge savagely crenellated.

Our wall continued to get steeper and steeper. When we looked down to the bergschrund, the slope down there looked flat; yet we remembered clearly how, for the two hours spent on it, we had regarded its inclination as 'quite something'.

When Max was leading, all I could see of him as I looked up were his legs, his rucksack and the rope, falling free for a long way before it touched the snow. We were now on a white rib, barely a yard wide, which swept unbroken to the foot of the rocks above. With an ice-piton in our left hand and the hammer in our right, we made good progress up it. The snow, however, grew progressively more unstable and it was with mixed feelings that we gazed up at a tortuous couloir, overhead to the right, which led through the armour-plating of the summit wall's slabs and seemed to offer the only route. Now, too, as we approached the rocks, our ice-slope steepened again considerably. At every step we noticed that smooth ice lay under the continually thinning snow. The underlying layer often changed in the course of a few yards, and we tried to make the most of what offered by zig-zagging upwards.

At about 9 a.m. we reached the foot of a slabby rock-buttress, interrupted by small snow-patches, which rose towards the summit. At this point we had come up more than half the face, and its right-hand containing-ridge was much nearer now – the one whose shadow falls far across the face in the afternoon, just as now, in the morning, the buttress casts its shade from the other direction. If only we didn't run into bad snow just here...

We stopped, close to the right-hand base of the pillar, at a great block jutting out like a balcony, near a frozen waterfall. We were sure that there would be a practicable pillar of snow above it, though we could not see it from where we were. Then we moved very slowly upwards, to meet exactly what we had feared – loose-powder snow lying on polished ice.

At each step my left hand drove the piton, gripped very short, into tiny crevices in the steep face as hard as I could; my right hand, holding the ice-hammer propped my body away from the wall, and the front teeth of my twelve-pointer crampons dug into the ice – not very far, but just enough.

'Six feet more!' came up from below. Aha! at last the rope was running out. I hacked out a hand-hold and banged in a piton. Then I cleared a stance in the ice with my axe; the fragments went hurtling down to where Max, a rope's length lower down, pressed his body into the face, so as to escape them as much as possible. How glad he'll be that he has a helmet on, I thought.

Max came up and joined me at the stance. Where do we go now? Perhaps the rock above us to the left would go? The only other alternative was a dicey-looking traverse up to the right, to where the couloir began again. Let's try up to the left – after an overhanging rock-pitch there seemed to be a ledge running up to the pillar...

The ledge was an illusion; it turned out to be a steep slab with snow lying on it. However, after about thirty feet it looked much better than expected, for the next bit, anyway. I had to clear away whole masses of snow to get any kind of a hand-hold, then I moved a foot cautiously, my crampons found some kind of a purchase – but I couldn't see where, and was glad to get a belaying-piton in at once. On with the grind! No stance yet, but a crack, into which I could get my arms, and then a foot. So far, so good; but still no stance. I pressed on – it must get better soon. 'What's up?' Max called from below. 'Nothing,' I shouted back, gasping for breath and taking great care not to slide out of my snowed-up crack. At last I reached a knob of rock; I had arrived at the pillar. But where in heaven's name had I landed myself? Nothing but snowed-up slabs, 70-degrees steep, ahead. Suppose I took my crampons off? That would be lunacy, for there were continual snow-patches between the places where the wind had blown it away. No, my lad, you have committed a hopeless blunder this time!

I looked around me, resignedly. Over there on the right lay the traverse we had been so keen to avoid. From here it looked a novice's delight! True enough, it often happens that everything looks easier than just where one happens to be – but there was definitely no future where I was. So back we go again!

It took a long time to get down, and as soon as I got there Max tackled the traverse. I was somewhat depressed; our 'howler' had cost us a great deal of time. We would have to make up for it now, if we could – easier said than done... I could already hear Max's irons scratching on sheer rock under the snow. So there were slabs there too. Max came back a little way, climbed down about six feet and tried again. Anxiously I followed his every movement. I was able to give a little diagonal support with the rope, but it wasn't much help to him out there. He went down another three feet, then started to traverse. I held my breath, taking every step he took with him in my mind. Grab that boulder sticking out of the snow! He had hold of it. I breathed again; he was over the worst bit. Then he began to climb again. 'Fifteen feet more!' I shouted across to him. Very soon Max was hacking out a stance in the ice of the couloir and belaying with two pitons. I rejoined him on a comfortable stance, where he had made an extra step for me, and leaned against the wall. As it was by now midday we ate a snack, standing in our steps, and took a good swig at the tea-flask. The pencilled shadows had vanished from the glacier; only the crevasses – we were looking straight down into them – showed dark.

Thank goodness, we were now on ice again. We hoped it would continue for a long way up. We were certain of one thing: even the steepest of smooth ice was here preferable to the snow-covered rock, with its downward stratification.

Max went on, and cut a few steps. 'The ice is getting thinner again,' he called down, 'and pretty putrid into the bargain!' The rope ran out a foot at a time and there were long pauses in between. Small wonder, for the pitch of the couloir was fearsome and the crust of ice had dried out and become so thin that the hammer kept on striking through to the underlying rock; and the rock, thanks to the action of the ice was mostly smooth and totally inimical to pitons. Another rope's length farther up things didn't look quite so bad, however.

Alpine Geometry

Max went on working his way up for nearly half an hour. His belaying piton, dug into the rock, was not very reliable. I moved forward with the utmost caution, and didn't get on much better. Nothing but black ice, powder-snow, rock continually thrusting through. Meanwhile time simply raced away without our noticing it. It was well into the afternoon. The view into the abyss was fearsome. Slowly, terribly slowly, we gained height. Irritatingly, the summit's sharp ridge overhead seemed so close at hand. It could only be a couple of rope's lengths more...

Damn this final wall! Were we going to get stuck in it?

The sun was slanting down on the face, now. Clouds were slowly creeping up it from far down below. Evening was drawing in. We climbed on undeterred, but our progress could be measured in feet. The crest above our heads, which we had thought to be so near, drew nearer again. We must get there soon, now...

Yes, we had thought the same thing before – I don't know how long ago. Somewhere here those two bivouacked on the first ascent. I could not imagine where; for I could not see a level patch even the length of one's foot – everything was precipitous here . . . perhaps it had been still higher up.

Well, we had to get on. There were a couple of ice-hoses, some three feet wide, reaching up into the rocks of the final wall like spider's legs. It could only be three more rope's lengths and that should be possible before it got dark. A bivouac here on the slabs would be a penance – like monkeys on a stick. We chose the right-hand hose, but after about fifty feet further progress in it was impossible. I wallowed my way forward through powder-snow, unable to find a hand-hold anywhere. Then I found a crack for one foot-hold, but that exhausted all the possibilities. Well, there was a parallel groove over to the left; nothing but to traverse into it. To my astonishment, miraculously, there was a good crack facing me – just what was needed for a fine belay! I hammered a piton in and it held firm. Now to get into the groove...

Thirty feet up it, I was able to manufacture a stance. Just as Max joined me there, the sun finally disappeared behind a bright bank of clouds. We hoped our luck would hold. Max climbed on and disappeared above me behind a rock-arête. I could only pay out the rope foot by foot . . . evidently it hadn't got any easier.

I could no longer hear Max, though every now and then a shower of ice-chippings and snow came hurtling down over that rocky edge. A lump of ice hit me on the shoulder, but I was past caring; I crouched against the face and waited.

Slowly the twilight seeped in, with clouds mounting high into the sky. Suddenly I was back in one of my first geometry lessons. Our maths-master, full of enthusiasm, had just constructed an equilateral triangle on the blackboard, for us to copy into our exercise books. Spring was coming in, and I was watching the white clouds outside the window as they moved slowly towards the mountains. Next moment, those clouds were in my exercise-book, floating round my triangle, quickly converted by a little shading into the semblance of a mountain. I was just considering how to sketch in the immediate neighbourhood when the whole thing came to a sudden end . . . it seems that our mathematician had no feeling for 'art' . . .

The glacier, far below at the foot of the face, was a blue-grey shadow. Down in the valley, the first lights were twinkling.

There was another hailstorm of ice chippings, followed by a load of powder-snow. As they disappeared into the depths, Max called down to me. I was very glad to be on the move again.

The next rope's length brought me into darkness; the only glimmer of light was a pale streak in the western sky. 'There's a bivouac-place up to the left,' shouted Max. I climbed a slab and a few feet of smooth ice, and reached the top of a rocky knob. It wasn't even big enough for one man to sit on! It was now pitch dark, and I could only make out my immediate surroundings. The pinnacles of the summit-ridge looked like a cardboard cut-out. Bivouac – but where? Climb on by the light of our helmet-lamp?

I could not make out how far it still was; I only knew I was at the start of another gully. I felt my way gingerly up it. Snow – good, holding snow! I worked my way carefully upwards; it was loose, but perfectly sound climbing. I called to Max to come up, for he had the lamp. It *must* go now . . .

Max came up, climbed past me to a better stance. Here, it was possible to undo a rucksack. We turned the lamp on; its beam captured a big round spot on one of the pinnacles of the summit ridge – quite near, not more than 130 feet, and the rock up to it not at all difficult! We had won our fight. I could hardly wait to fasten the lamp to my helmet. As one rocky knob after another caught its glare, I pictured to myself what our feelings would have been in the morning, if we had settled for a miserable bivouac a rope's length farther down.

We were on top. 'No bivouac!' we said. We could sit down comfortably at last. Here on the summit of Mont Blanc de Cheilon, with its mighty face down there below us. We rummaged in the rucksack for everything eatable; there was even some tea left in the flask – a welcome surprise. And the light of our lamp threw a cosy circle around us.

Alpine Geometry

Then we climbed slowly down through the night. It was 2 a.m. when we sat on the wall outside the hut and took our boots off.

We woke to a brilliant morning; more truthfully a brilliant forenoon, when we stepped outside the hut. Under a clear blue sky stretched the long snowy comb of the Pigne d'Arolla; in the east, small and neat, rose the Aguille de la Tza, and down the valley ranged the shattered pinnacles of the Aiguilles Rouges. Far away to the east we could still see the tip of the Matterhorn. A gentle breeze was sighing round the hut, and the yellow and orange-coloured alpine poppies, growing thick on the knoll which houses the hut, were nodding their heads. A bee was humming hither and thither. We watched it and, every now and then, cast a glance up at our wall, humming – we too – any old song. On this glorious day, we felt as if everything – the air, the peaks and the glittering glacier – should join in.

We looked again to see whether the rope had dried out. Yes, it had. And what about our pitons, many of which had acquired a peculiar shape, like cracknels, since yesterday? They would need a bang or two with the hammer.

We packed our rucksacks and bade the hut-keeper 'Au Revoir!' Then we strolled along the lake, turning and turning again to where, at the valley's far head, Mont Blanc de Cheilon greeted our eyes. The Triangle.

The White Mountain of the Himalaya

DHAULAGIRI

High above the foothills of the Terai, flashes an enormous pyramid. From time immemorial the Nepalese have called it Dhaulagiri (Dawalagiri): *Dawala* is the Sanskrit for white, and *giri* is a mountain. So: 'The White Mountain.' Its gigantic flanks of rock and ice, high as the clouds which daily march on its ridges, gleam in a perpetual mantle of newly-fallen snow; they have done so just as long as clouds have been rising from Nepal's primeval forests, to envelop the mountain towards midday and then build up and up, to more than 26,000 feet, where they finally meet above the summit. Then that great mountain floats high above the world, in a cone of clouds.

This icy giant, standing solitary and unsheltered, might just as well have been called 'Peak of Storms', but no one thought of the name till, much later, men came to climb it, experienced its terrifying tempests and remembered them for the rest of their lives.

Dhaulagiri (26,795 feet) was the first of the fourteen eight-thousanders to be attempted by a modern expedition, the last but one to be climbed. Its fortress-keep defended itself for ten long years and fought off seven expeditions before finally falling to the eighth.

When the strolling minstrels, who have frequented the valleys of Nepal with their fiddles for hundreds of years, sing their famous ballad of Tensing – '*hamro Tensing Sherpa le tsaru himal tsutsura*' – they may by now have added a lay in honour of those two lucky 'Sunday's children', Nawang Dorje and Nima Dorje, who went to the summit of the great White Mountain.

Let me sketch the history of this great peak, the story of years of effort on the part of men who wanted to stand – for one short moment – high up there, 'where the Gods live'.

1949

An aeroplane was buzzing like a tiny insect among the icy giants of the Himalaya, one day in 1949 . . . A well-known scientist, Arnold Heim,

The White Mountain of the Himalaya

boarded a Dakota at Delhi. He was a Swiss, a geologist, interested rather in the structures and composition of the mountains than in routes and camp-sites on them. It was a flight of great importance, just as the year itself was an important landmark; for the gates of Nepal, so long barred to foreigners, had at last been thrown open.

The Dakota took off, gradually gained altitude, and, over Butwal, swung away to the north. Flying above the Terai plains, still in darkness, then over the low forest-clad ranges of the Siwaliks, it then followed the sombre trench of the Kali river, cutting deep into the glittering wall to the north – the untrodden thrones of the Gods. The plane flew on, between Dhaulagiri to the west and Annapurna to the east, out over Tibet and then back again. Arnold Heim was the first man to enjoy that pioneer's view of all the great summits, and he used his cameras to full advantage. The pictures he brought back were a unique documentation of the glory of those Himalayan giants. He was happy to reflect they they would doubtless fire the imagination of countless climbers, to whom Nepal had for so long been forbidden territory.

1950: *The French Reconnaissance*

In the very next year, a great snake of some 200 porters could be seen writhing its way over the Siwalik ranges into the Kali Gandaki valley, following the traditional trade-route to Tibet, along which flour and tea used to travel northwards, salt and borax down in the opposite direction. They were bound for Tukucha, a sizeable village of low, flat-roofed houses and inns, to the south-west of which Dhaulagiri towers some 20,000 feet above the valley-level. Here the expedition, consisting of the *élite* of the French Alpine Club – Lachenal, Ichac, Terray, Oudot, Rébuffat and Schatz, under the leadership of Maurice Herzog – were to establish their main base. For Tukucha, at 8,500 feet, halfway between the Dhaulagiri and Annapurna massifs, was the ideal starting-point for reconnaissances in all directions.

The objective was to climb the first eight-thousander ever. The French had not yet decided which of the two – Dhaulagiri or Annapurna. Reconnaissance parties went out daily and returned with their reports. Several of them explored Dhaulagiri's east glacier, streaming down to the valley straight ahead of them. 'Not exactly a stroll!' Rébuffat reported after the first visit. Later, they forced a way to within 1,000 feet of the ice-plateau which crowned the huge ice-fall. There, a thunderstorm, accompanied by heavy snow and the clatter of disintegrating séracs, drove them back to camp. In the end, Terray and Oudot reached the rim of the plateau, where they could see the north-east spur leaning like a white ladder against the sky. There was, however, no way of reaching its foot – it was as impossible for laden porters to cross the heavily-crevassed field of ice as to scale the ice-fall itself.

Yet another thrust brought the French to the foot of the enormous, crenellated South-east Ridge, or what they named 'the Frenchmen's ridge', whence they gazed up at the South Face, fully 13,000 feet high, one of the loftiest in the world.

The map furnished by the Survey of India aroused great hopes; it showed an easy access route to Dhaulagiri's North Face up the valley of the Dambush Khola, a small tributary of the Kali. Herzog and Ichac went up to reconnoitre it on April 24th. The valley rose far too steeply and held far too little water for one that was fed by the north glacier. Presently, a steep-sided cirque of cliffs terminating the valley put paid to the theory of an easy approach to the north face. Obviously, the map was wrong. Back they went to Tukucha.

This is an example of how, in the Himalayas, one might have to try desperately to locate and approach an unknown mountain before even getting to where the climb starts. And, even if things have since then improved vastly, it is something which the reader should be made aware of.

Reconnaissances continued – of Annapurna as well as Dhaulagiri. It was decided to try the Dambush valley again, and on April 26th Herzog and Ichac, joined this time by Terray, camped twice before reaching a pass, followed by a cauldron of snow and yet another pass, from which they could see an arid valley, with snow-patches in it, opening up towards the north. Once again Dhaulagiri was nowhere to be seen. So back once again to Tukucha.

It was not till May 5th that Oudot and Terray entered the 'Unknown Valley', as they called it. From this wide basin they climbed a 17,000 foot pass leading southwards, later to become permanently known as 'The French Col'. From it they obtained their first view of Dhaulagiri's North Face in all its immensity. They saw, too, that the glacier below them clearly fed the Mayangdi Khola which flowed south. The Cartographers' theory that the northern glaciers drained down the Tukucha side was scotched, once and for all.

And what about the prospects?

'I won't set another foot on this mountain,' Terray declared tersely at the council of war held at Tukucha on May 14th, which finally decided for Annapurna and against Dhaulagiri. 'Nobody will ever climb Dhaula . . . !'

The White Mountain of the Himalaya

1953: The Swiss attempt by way of the Mayangdi Valley and the 'Pear'

The French success in 1950 on Annapurna, the first eight-thousander to be climbed, turned the thoughts of Swiss climbers to the giant ice-peaks of Nepal. In spite of all, Oudot's picture of Dhaulagiri's north face inspired moderate hopes; accordingly, a very strong team was assembled under Bernhard Lauterburg.

They approached the mountain by the Mayangdi Khola, with its paddy-terraces, little hamlets, undulating track and suspension-bridges. Farther up, the dense bamboo thickets of the rain-fed jungle forced them to hack a way with mattocks; they were continually pushed up on to the slopes where, above a colourful rhododendron belt and the dark Himalayan pines, gleamed Dhaulagiri's flanks. Later, when there was nothing worse than a few birch trees on a tongue of moraine, they set up their base camp. To obtain a view, it was necessary to move farther, around a projecting spur. Before them lay the huge north glacier – known ever since as the Mayangdi Glacier. And, high up above, they saw the brown, débris-covered slopes of the 'French Col', but now of course, from its other side.

Straight opposite them rose the North Face of Dhaulagiri, some 11,000 feet high, with the ice-falls, ribs and couloirs that form its plinth. Above the mighty barrier of séracs, at about 20,000 feet, they could see a long glacier-terrace, on which a high-altitude camp could perhaps be sited. Above that, soared the gigantic smooth, unbroken face, which has fascinated and lured all those who have ever seen it – that mighty wall, pencilled with fine hatchings, as by some great artist, from which a few extraordinary islands of rock belly out, looking like monstrous pears.

The Swiss thought they could find a route up the 'pear' which reaches farthest down the face. The angle seemed to ease off above its upper rim, though the wall between it and the West Ridge was dauntingly steep. If they could only get up on to that ridge, the way to the summit must lie open to them.

They found a way through the savage ice-towers of the sérac-zone. They needed two camps before reaching the terrace and there, at 20,000 feet, they established their assault-base. Another camp was somehow clawed on to the rock below the 'pear'; but the horrific sweep of that feature from the terrace to the ridge above measured well over five thousand feet!

Every attempt to find another camp-site failed; the rocks of that immense wall were too steep and too polished. Yet they managed to push forward to within 200 feet of the ridge. They could find no way of climbing the final cliff.

They rounded off their gallant attempt with two reconnaissances, to the South- and North-east cols respectively. In the course of these they made one important discovery: Pfisterer established that an aircraft could land on the broad snow-plateau of the North-east Col, or at least drop material on it. Years later, the last Swiss Dhaulagiri expedition was to profit by this knowledge.

1954: *The Argentine Expedition – a near miss*

On May 21st of that year a most unusual thing happened on the 'Pear' face: the report of a blasting charge shook the cliffs, re-echoing like a thunderclap among them. Twenty-seven more followed. After the very first detonation, Felipe Godoy, an army sergeant-major, hurried from under cover near by to assess the results: the mountain had not disintegrated, no avalanche had been started, only a few lumps of rock were scattered around. It took three days to blast out a platform large enough to take two tents – Camp VI of the Argentine expedition to Dhaulagiri.

This was an enormous expedition. Its fourteen tons of baggage amounted to about 600 porter loads; but pack-animals were also used as far as they could go. For the actual climb there were fourteen experienced Sherpas, under Pasang Dawa Lama, the Sirdar. The leader of the expedition was Lieut. Francisco Ibañez, who had made a name for himself in the Andes, and had learned much about Dhaulagiri while acting as liaison officer on Lionel Terray's French expedition to Fitzroy. At the farewell-party at the Casa Rosada President Peron agreed to a proposal to sponsor an Argentine Dhaulagiri expedition, with the full support of the government and the army. The climbing party also included the Slovak Dinko Bertoncelj and Gerhard Watzl from the Tyrol, both naturalized Argentinians.

From Godoy's camp on the platform four parties started the climb towards the West Ridge on May 30th. The monsoon, which would put a stop to all activity on the mountain with its blizzards, was due very soon. By way of a gulley and a difficult chimney of loose rock they reached the ridge and at 25,000 feet sited their last and highest camp on it. Savage pinnacles barred the way ahead, towers which reminded them of those on the 'Catedral' at home; towers which masked the view forward to the summit and looked terribly difficult to turn.

Bertoncelj and Ibañez had come up, but Ibañez decided to wait in that high camp till a summit-party consisting of Magnani, Watzl, Pasang and his brother came back from their attempt. Bertoncelj and the remaining Sherpas went down again. June 1st proved to be the decisive day, when a mixture of courage and luck, both good and bad, brought the assault party past all the difficulties, and still robbed them, by a trick of fate, of the summit they felt was 'in the bag'.

Nobody foresaw the chain of events. The summit-party set out simply to reconnoitre the route ahead, leaving their loads and sleeping-bags in camp. 'I only had with me some chocolate and a tin of condensed milk,' said Watzl afterwards. Yet they succeeded in doing what nobody was ever to do again: moving on tiny ledges of extreme difficulty, with a drop of anything up to 13,000 feet below them, they turned the pinnacles.

By 4 p.m. they found themselves on a snow-ridge, put on their crampons and stamped their way up and up it till they were almost at the magic 8,000-metre level, over 26,000 feet. There they met with two great boulders with a small ice-cliff between them. Watzl climbed it and this is what he saw: 'A gently-rising crest about a mile long, without any difficulties in it.' The route to the summit lay at their mercy.

As the weather was unusually fine, they decided to bivouac and make the most of their unexpected luck. They finished digging an ice-cave by the last glimmer of daylight; the night they spent in it was a cold one and conversation turned time and again to Argentina's famous steaks. Well, they had none of those, but in the morning they would have something much more valuable – the summit of Dhaulagiri . . . !

At 5.30 a.m. they crawled out of their cave – to find two feet of freshly-fallen snow outside . . . no hope of the summit now without at least a second bivouac; and the descent of the smooth ledges behind them, newly covered in snow, as perilous as problematic . . .

Watzl took the cruel decision to retreat. The descent turned into a fight for their very lives. Pasang's brother was seriously injured when he fell and was checked by the rope, but in the end they all got safely back to camp.

Ibañez hoped to mount a second attempt, but it never materialized. He himself fell a victim to this series of misfortunes. By the time they managed to get him down several days later, from those icy altitudes to base camp, he was so severely frostbitten that it was clear there was no hope. After the long weeks of an agonizing journey back to Katmandu, he died there.

1955–58: Germans, Swiss and Argentines

Nobody ever got as high again on the 'Pear' route as that first Argentinian venture. Certainly not the so-called 'Vegetarian Expedition' of

Swiss and German climbers in 1955, under Martin Maier. One of the conditions of their financial support was a prescribed diet, in which meat played no part. Their official report stated that blizzards prevented their getting higher than 24,300 feet.

In 1956, the second Argentine expedition occupied the historic camp on the ridge as early as May 11th, but got very little farther. This time the monsoon arrived a month early and Col. Huerta, the leader, ordered a retreat. There were also complications caused by the fall of President Peron, who had promoted the expedition. For better or worse, his name was erased on the expedition's packing-cases. I have a photograph in my collection of a window-shutter in the Mayangdi valley fashioned from one such case. *Sic transit gloria mundi!*

Again, in 1958, the Swiss, under Werner Stäuble, got no farther. Detlef Hecker and a Sherpa made a last vain attempt on the pinnacles, then bad weather forced them down. The descent of the Pear face involved them in a dramatic avalanche incident, but happily without serious damage.

The Swiss camp V was a unique development in Himalayan history. Fearing that Godoy's platform would no longer be recognizable, the Swiss had, with their well-known attention to detail, built a contraption – a kind of grid-iron – rather like a bedstead with long legs, but only two of them. This they fixed to the steep slabs of the Pear at 23,600 feet. On that lofty frame they erected a tent. Two of these structures, swaying fearfully in Dhaulagiri's gales, mostly dictated sleepless nights. One can only imagine what it was like: the darkness, the fierce gusts of wind, the grating of the stilt-like legs on the slabs, and a precipice thousands of feet deep below the 'bedclothes'. '*Viel luft unterm födli*', in good Schwyzerdütsch: 'Plenty of air under your backside!'

Flinging great snow-banners into the sky as the gales raged, Dhaulagiri again won the verdict. The whole world waited for the expedition which would at last succeed in defeating the White Mountain. Many by now called it the most difficult of the eight-thousanders; for, one after another, the other great Himalayan giants had conceded defeat, while year by year, climbers of different nationalities came to the gigantic face of the 'Pear', to fail dismally. And still everybody clung to the same thought... the next one must be successful...

1959: *The Austrian Expedition*

This expedition, organized by the Austrian Himalayan Association, was under the leadership of Fritz Moravec, a bearded high-school teacher, who had already led a successful expedition of this kind when he climbed Gasherbrum II.

The Austrians were the first to tackle the mountain by its North-east Spur, that steep, straight route to the summit snow-cap of Dhaulagiri, which starts in the great hollow of the North-east Col. The French had already looked up at it during their reconnaissances of the east glacier; so had Pfisterer, the Swiss, when he pushed forward to the col from its other side. From there, westwards, a glacier-arm, broken up by steep cliffs, falls to meet the broad floor of the Mayangdi Glacier at about 14,400 feet. Passing beneath an enormous rock-triangle, which they named 'the Eiger', the Austrians forced a way, menaced at all times by falls of ice and rock, up towards the North-east Col. Camp II, sited on the col itself, was then equipped as their advanced base. There, they were still more than 8,000 feet below the summit.

From the saddle's wide snow-plateau, there first rises an ice-crest, after which the spur goes soaring straight up. Its steep, sharp crest is supported on the left by a colossal ice-face with an angle of from 40 to 60 degrees; on the right, by a narrow upturned triangle of rock. And so it rises steeply to 23,000 feet, where a rock-cliff at least 300 feet high and in places almost vertical, marks its termination. After that, the slope eases considerably till, at 24,300 feet, the snow- and rock-steps in the ridge steepen again, before, at 25,600 feet, it meets the Frenchman's marvellously crenellated, long-drawn South-east ridge (a 'dream-route', but endlessly long!). From the point where they fuse, the main ridge curves up towards the summit's final crest, broken only by a few isolated rock-patches.

Of course, the Austrians could not see the route in its entirety from the outset; the mountain would only reveal its secrets as they advanced step by step up it. However, they had seen enough to justify the following comparison of the two routes.

The Pear: its main difficulties high up on the mountain, particularly at the start of the summit-ridge; the whole face exposed to avalanche threats; camps mostly difficult to site.

The North-east Spur: technical difficulties in the steep ice below the spur and at the rock-cliff 23,000 feet up – in other words much lower down; no difficulty about camp-sites; avalanche-dangers far less; and delays on account of bad weather more acceptable on its ice than on rock.

Pasang Dawa Lama, whom we have already seen on the Pear, considered that the chances on the spur were better. The Swiss Eiselin, and the German Hecker, had already expressed that opinion. So Moravec decided for the North-east Spur.

Progress was swift: by April 21st, camp III was in being at 20,200 feet and on the 24th they started to establish camp IV at the foot of the ice-wall, a thousand feet higher up. The intention was to site a further camp at 23,000 feet on a high platform at the top of the rock-triangle.

It was at that moment that fate struck. April 29th had been decreed as a rest-day. Everybody in the little huddle of tents on the vast white expanse of the North-east Col was occupied in reading, writing letters or playing cards. Suddenly, someone noticed that Heini Roiss was missing; he had gone outside a little while earlier and now he could not be found in any of the tents. They followed his track away from the camp for about fifty yards, where it ended in a dark hole in the surface of the snow. There he had fallen into a crevasse; he was still alive, wedged far down in its depths. They worked frantically to widen the narrow rift, the only hope of getting him out alive; at last they managed to bring him to the surface, but he was dead.

A cross on a slope below the 'French Col' marks his resting place.

The expedition was never able to recover completely from the severe loss of one of its best members, which overshadowed everything that was to follow. All the same, they made a gallant attempt, digging themselves in, high up on the spur, where the gales had in the meantime ripped the tents to tatters, in an 'ice-parlour'. They safeguarded the whole 1,600 foot ice- and rock-aréte above camp IV with a chain of fixed ropes, toiling prodigiously, continually hampered by bad weather. When, on May 22nd, they at last established camp V at 23,000 feet on the tip of the rock triangle, they went straight on to prepare the difficult three-hundred foot wall which barred the way above. The monsoon was by now very near. On May 24th they pitched their last and highest camp, a little below 24,300 feet, hoping that there would still be time to tackle the summit. Next day, Karl Prein and Pasang Dawa Lama started out for it from that last high tent.

Up rock-pitches and snow-gullys they went, under a blue sky. Shining in the morning sun lay the ranges of the Dhaula-Himal, Tukucha Peak and the 'Breithorn', farther away, the icy peaks of the Nilgiri chain – the 'Blue Mountains' – and Annapurna's towering summits. To the north, a frozen brown sea of lower peaks stretched away into illimitable distance – Tibet. It was a marvellous view, and for a minute or two they were able to forget the terrible, icy fight to gain height, for, that day, Dhaulagiri's raging wind nearly uprooted them, robbing them of breath, freezing their stiff faces and the very blood in their veins. It was an appalling ordeal, as step by step, bent double against the blast, they struggled on upwards.

At about 25,600 feet they saw a ridge joining them from the left; to the right they thought they could make out the summit over the intervening humps. They were not far off now – another five or six hours should do it, if they could survive the murderous cold and the icy tempest.

It was an impossible task. They would have to try again tomorrow. So, back they went, down to the tent, only to find the gale had ripped open one side of it. They spent an icy night, with drifting snow building up inside the tent, till, by morning, their sleeping-bags were covered in a two-inch blanket of snow. However, Karl Prein was as tough as they come, and Pasang who had been up to 26,000 feet on the 'Pear', and who had stood on Cho Oyu's summit with Herbert Tichy and Sepp Jöchler, had dreamed for years of the summit of the White Mountain.

They tried again, and were beaten back again by the wind. They could not believe that all their efforts were in vain. After another night in their tattered tent, they tried a third time. All in vain – defeated again by that roaring tempest. Then it began to snow; the monsoon was knocking at the gates of the Himalaya. It had all been for nothing.

'We have no key to this mountain,' said Pasang Dawa Lama, with tears in his eyes, as they turned to go down. 'This is the third time I have reached so great a height on it, but the Gods are not willing for us to enter into their habitation.'

So far there had not been tragedies of a Nanga Parbat scale on the 'White Mountain'. They came, later, when in 1969 an ice-avalanche buried five Americans and two Sherpas in the ice-fall below that long, crenellated South-east Ridge and, a few months later, five members of an Austrian expedition perished on Dhaulagiri IV.

What made me go out there again, to attempt another eight-thousander, particularly this one – Dhaulagiri?

The hour I had spent on the summit of Broad Peak had made an ineradicable impression on my heart and mind. I often felt that nothing could happen to me again which could match it, not even on Himalayan heights. One cannot repeat such things – and yet...

Once one has climbed those distant white peaks, high as the clouds, remote even when you are close to their feet, their lure endures for ever, there is no escape, one dreams of them, of moving towards the summit, high above the outspread world, through a wide and frontierless sky, trusting that no storm will break that day – even though it should break.

Hermann Buhl went on from his Nanga Parbat to another eight-thousander, Broad Peak; then, on Chogolisa, he strayed out over the cornice in a blizzard. Gyaltsen Norbu, who had also stood on the summits of two eight-thousanders, perished under an ice-avalanche on

Langtang Lirung. Was I too, who could still not fully grasp that Chogolisa had not meant the end of everything for me, to try another of those mighty peaks at whose gleaming, all-compelling feet you feel their sheer inaccessibility?

Even today, with all the technical progress that has been made, no one can foretell the outcome of one of those attempts. Terrifying is the breath of those icy giants, when they awake, and man becomes a little living something, due to perish somewhere. They are still the 'Thrones of the Gods'. Nobody who has seen them can doubt it.

Yet, when Max Eiselin invited me to join his Dhaulagiri expedition, I could not possibly have refused. Was this not Nepal's glorious White Mountain – still untrodden by man – one of the world's highest peaks?

Sufficient was the very thought of being up there on that crest, high in the sky, more than 26,000 feet up, among the clouds themselves, unfettered and without an oxygen-mask, just as I am, moving towards an unknown frontier close above my head – a mere human-being high up in space, whose feet are still – unbelievably – in contact with the earth . . . moving on and up . . . till he stands on the summit.

Only to imagine it excited me hugely, for that is how I am. Yes, I would go and climb, and that mountain would belong to me. Would it, though? All I knew was that I would give my last ounce of effort to stand on its summit.

I knew the Gods might . . . maybe . . . but I had seen a picture of that mountain; what an indescribable thrill to be going to it.

The Gods . . . maybe . . . but I would have one more try.

When Herbert Tichy said goodbye to me in Vienna – that Herbert Tichy, who had journeyed through China, Nepal, Alaska, all over the earth's surface; who had once had his fingers frostbitten on Cho Oyu and still gone on to the summit; my friend who was holding my hand – he looked at me for a long time, before saying: 'I wish you all the best.'

Then he added this: 'And even if you should not come back, I still wish you joy of it.'

The International Swiss Expedition to Dhaulagiri, of which I was a member, started out in the spring of 1960. It was a huge expedition – thirteen climbers whose target was the ascent of the thirteenth eight-thousander; for only it and Shisha Pangma remained unclimbed. Max Eiselin's team included five other Swiss, Ernst Forrer, Albin Schelbert, Michel Vaucher, Hugo Weber and Jeanjacques Roussi, Peter Diener, a German, and two Poles, Adam Skoczylas and Dr Jerzy Hajdukiewicz, the expedition's doctor; like Max, a Dhaulagiri veteran of 1958; Norman Dyhrenfurth, who had come all the way from the USA to film and photograph the climb; and, finally, two very important people: Ernst Saxer, the glacier-pilot of the expedition's aircraft, and Emil Wick, his mechanic.

We were committed to the world's highest unclimbed peak, and prepared to do our utmost. This time we just *had* to pull it off. For our route we chose the North-east Spur.

Yeti's Flight to Dhaulagiri

Yeti was no abominable snowman, but our gaily-coloured glacier-aircraft; an amiable gnat, striped red and yellow, which floated tiny and forlorn, above the mighty valleys of the wide Himalaya, and hung between their great summits like some buzzing insect. Yeti had lifted us all from the depths of the Terai to the 16,500 foot snow-saddle of the Dapa Col, at the rim of the French explorers' 'Unknown Valley'. This was intended only as an intermediate station – for acclimatization purposes – *en route* to the proposed landing of the whole party on the North-east Col, 1,800 feet higher up. We could hardly wait for what would be the highest glacier touchdown ever made.

It was, of course, an experiment, just as everything we were doing was a unique 'first-time-ever' conception: nobody had ever tried to use a 'gnat' to leap-frog all the valleys in one swift bound and fly every man-jack of an expedition, baggage and all, up to over 16,000 feet on a Himalayan giant, and so avoid the long weeks of an approach-march with hundreds of porters. Nor had we forgotten Pfisterer's report on the North-east Col's saddle, half a mile wide: 'an ideal landing-place'. Even so it would be no child's play, for it lay at a height of more than 18,700 feet. We wondered how that would work out.

Ernst Forrer, the great gangling country-postman from the Toggenburg, who was used to a daily round of twelve miles at home, and I, who had previously gone up to great altitudes, were chosen as the first two to be landed up there, with a tent. We had both stood the first experimental leap of 16,500 feet from Bhairava very well, although we were at first confined to our tent with fearsome headaches and other unpleasant side-effects.

Eleven years had passed since Arnold Heim's memorable flight. Now an aircraft was once again to play its part in Dhaulagiri's history; and this time we were going to land! One of the greatest adventures in the opening-up of the Himalaya was under way, though we could of course not foresee that we were destined to return home minus our Yeti; that our bright butterfly, in which we had known the fantastic thrill of flying between those mighty peaks, would lie abandoned, its wings

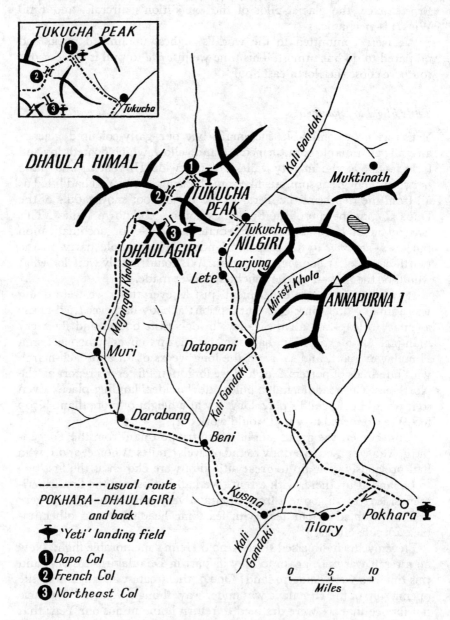

4. The Dhaulagiri–Annapurna Himal

broken, half-tilted towards the rocks, at the edge of a glacier-torrent high up in the 'Unknown Valley', having crashed during take-off, owing to a minor technical failure.

I think everyone of us has a bit of yellow or red metal hanging on a wall at home, as a memento of our Yeti...

On April 3rd the weather at the Dapa Col was glorious. Not a breath of wind stirred on its broad saddle of snow. The tents stood bright yellow and gay in the sunshine. Far away in the blue distance rose Annapurna; close at hand the ice-slopes of Tukucha Peak swept up to the sky. It really looked as if the hour, so long and impatiently awaited, for Forrer and me to be air-lifted to the South-east Col, had at last struck. Certainly Ernst Saxer was 'raring to go'; in weather like today's, in these air conditions, the first attempt to land on the col should definitely be 'on'.

First, however, he took-off in our wide-winged four-seater, unladen, and with only himself, the expedition's leader Max Eiselin, and his mechanic, Emil Wick, aboard, to test the wind conditions at the col. We watched them go, then packed our belongings, praying inwardly that there would be no reason to postpone our flight. We could hardly control our impatience to be up there at the foot of the gigantic Northeast Spur. From here, we could not see it, nor the vast snow-saddle of the col, nor even the summit of our eight-thousander; for, right in front of us, ice-armoured, scored by flutings, Tukucha Peak went winging to the sky – at 22,650 feet, far lower than Dhaulagiri, but effectively masking the whole view in that direction.

After a long time, Yeti was in sight again. Soon it was banking in a wide curve and landing elegantly close to the camp. We rushed across, eager to know if the flight was on. Definitely! 'In with all your gear and quick about it,' said Saxer. Equipment, food, gas for the cooker, a tent, more equipment, more provisions... then we ourselves got in and shut the door behind us. Good – all set to go!

A moment or two later our plane's broad runners were gliding down the slope, and down we tore at full throttle into the broad hollow, which seemed to come rushing up at us. Now... we had parted from the slope, airborne, in full flight, looking down at the wide floor of the hollow as it slipped quietly away beneath us.

We had taken-off on the Tukucha side of the col, and suddenly we were out beyond the rim of the hollow. Deep gorges went plunging abysmally below us, grey, black, their gullies filled with snow, all looking fearsomely steep. The 8,000-foot leap from the Kali Valley to Dapa Col looked like a ladder to the sky, first green, then grey and brown, finally white. We slid across a rocky, slabby buttress in Tukucha Peak's lower structure, and there we were hanging, far and free, out in thin air. Saxer was bent over the controls, we lay over sideways as we looked horizontally across to Annapurna while, on the other side, the steep slopes leading to the col swung across the windscreen and we felt pressed down into our seats – then the plane levelled out and we were flying back in the direction of Dapa Col. It all happened so quickly; I just caught sight of Dapa Peak, which Albin Schelbert and I had reconnoitred together; we were going too fast for me to be able to identify the tents of our camp; then we were over the huge snow-flecked groove of the 'Unknown Valley'. We were flying at about 100 m.p.h. The engine droned, we hardly exchanged a word. A whole veined network of water-courses and snow-gullies passed under us.

And then – there it was: *Dhaulagiri!* I touched Ernst on the shoulder and pointed up to the cloud-banners, the giant form straight ahead of us – exactly like the pictures from which I knew it – simple beyond words, mighty, unbelievably beautiful – Dhaulagiri. No, it was more than that; this enormous thing towering above us was more wonderful than the vision any mere picture could conjure up. This was the tremendous, the inaccessible mountain. I was shattered by what I saw. And the nearer we got to it, the smaller we felt.

Easily recognizable were the characteristic bands in its rocky faces, rising steeply next to one another, pear-shaped, from the white expanse of the snowfields and glaciers. There stood the dark, riven plinth, the smooth white belt of the middle zone above it, then the savage cliffs below the hanging-glacier high up, under the summit's huge crest.

That was our target – though at that moment I hardly dared to admit it to myself. All the same I sent a silent greeting up to the broad summit of that giant peak. 'Dhaulagiri, here I come!' I was possessed by a great joy.

Beneath us now lay the slopes leading up to the 'French Col', where ten years ago they had struggled before halting, staggered by their first sight of the 11,500 feet North Face of the White Mountain, as they stood down there on the saddle now rushing up to meet us . . . almost close enough to touch . . . across which we had already leaped, out and away. Next moment we were looking far down on to enormous débris-slopes pouring downwards into a glacier-cauldron – the Mayangdi Glacier, of course. And now we were flying straight as a dart towards the rocky base of our mountain. Great God! It was growing and growing, till it filled the whole of the sky. And still we flew on, straight into it. Dhaulagiri! It was absolutely horrifying. Surely we must be going to hit those rocks, so close ahead?

But Yeti was already banking steeply. I drew a deep breath as I looked through the window up to the clouds and snow-scarves high up

The White Mountain of the Himalaya

on the summit, while on the other side of our plane, now tilted at 45 degrees, there shot up, beyond the wing, a grim chaos of shattered ice, séracs, yawning crevasses – dear heaven, that was one of the ice-falls in the glacier which falls from the North-east Col! Before we could take a good look, Saxer was heading straight for the mountain again, only much higher this time, having gained altitude during that first wide sweep. This time the broad snow-fields of the middle zone were facing us, more or less flat. Even the stratified rocks of the 'Pear' looked less difficult now; though the cliff above them must be quite a problem. I took a quick look past my companion into the depths below, for we were banking again. A savage rock-spire swept up and past, then monstrous slabs, and far below, the ice-fall. Seconds later, Ernst and I were staring as if transfixed at the North-east Spur, now shooting up prodigiously straight before our eyes. We were flying almost straight into it, bearing a shade to its left. Good God! That was the thing we were proposing to climb? A Jacob's ladder, disappearing into grey clouds; perhaps that was what made it look so steep. In any case it looked savage – more of a buttress than a spur.

I leaned far over to my right. There lay the North-east Col – broad, white and soft. An enormous dip, or rather a plateau, miles wide. We were coming in very quickly, now.

To the left rose some rounded ice-summits and a sharp white snow-peak – the 'Breithorn' and Tukucha Peak, probably – with broad white glacier-hollows between them. Beneath us, the crevasses grew fewer and fewer, then we were over smooth white snow; we were flying over the saddle, straight towards Dhaulagiri's lovely, crenellated South-east Ridge. It was almost impossible to believe that anything like this vast natural arena could exist – it was so big that the plane could fly into it and then bank round in a wide curve without ever getting too near the south-east ridge. The right wing lifted slowly skywards, revealing a horizontal view across to distant Annapurna's many summits; then, suddenly, we were close to mounds of snow, the wing dipped gently and we were flying straight in, to touch down...

Nothing but snow below us, nearer and nearer, quite close, now. Tack! We were sliding on it, the engine roared, we lost speed, we stopped. A touchdown as soft as butter, as if on a feather-bed. We had arrived!

'Gorgeous, Ernst! Thanks a lot!' we cried. I would have liked to embrace him for sheer joy at that incomparable flight. And we had got here safely! He too was delighted, and no wonder; this marvellous landing-place, a perfect touchdown, and finally his: 'Altitude, 18,300 feet!' For our friend Ernst today had brought off the highest glacier-landing yet achieved; a source of great joy to our pilot. Wick was beaming, too, though he was, as usual, quiet and relaxed.

We jumped out on to the snow. It was unlikely that there were crevasses here, but we got the ropes out, just in case. The first thing I did was to tie Ernst Saxer to Yeti's front wheel-spar, greatly to the amusement of the other Ernst – the climbing one, who was going to share the tent with me up here. Saxer took pictures of his Yeti, then asked to go farther afield. I let some rope out, untied him from the wheel, pushed an ice-axe into his hand, grabbed one myself – and off went Ernst, at a murderous pace for such an altitude, straight across the wide, level saddle. It must have been half an hour before we got back to the plane.

It was time for them to take off again. Saxer and Wick climbed up into the cockpit, resuming oxygen-masks. Forrer and I planted ourselves to right and left under the wings and grasped the struts. The engine sprang to life, singing, screaming, droning; and at a signal from Saxer we rocked the aircraft up and down. The skis began to slide, we were caught in a whirlwind of blown snow-dust. We threw ourselves down, still in the whirling cloud of snow for some seconds, on our knees; then we got up, somewhat out of breath, and waved to Yeti, humming away rapidly into the distance. We were all alone.

It was by now mid-afternoon. We looked around for a suitable site for our high base camp, and very soon we had agreed on it. Then we dragged the sacks of equipment and food across to it and, as an icy wind got up and we were already in the shadow thrown by the peaks, we set up the camp's first tent and anchored it firmly. We panted a good deal for though this second flight in Yeti had, in spite of the distance covered, only brought us up some 1,800 feet, the difference was noticeable and we had still to get used to the new altitude. However, neither of us felt at all bad; but we were glad to crawl into our fleece-bags quite early.

By the time night fell, even the smallest of cloudlets had vanished, and the cold had grown intense. We leaned out of the tent-door, looking up at the gigantic dark mass of our mountain, with Orion shining directly above its summit. And, all around, thousands of stars sparkled in a beauty beyond all bounds of reality.

The Plateau in the Clouds

This vast natural arena, and the Jacob's ladder of the spur shooting up from it . . . everything was on so immense a scale that it almost passed belief.

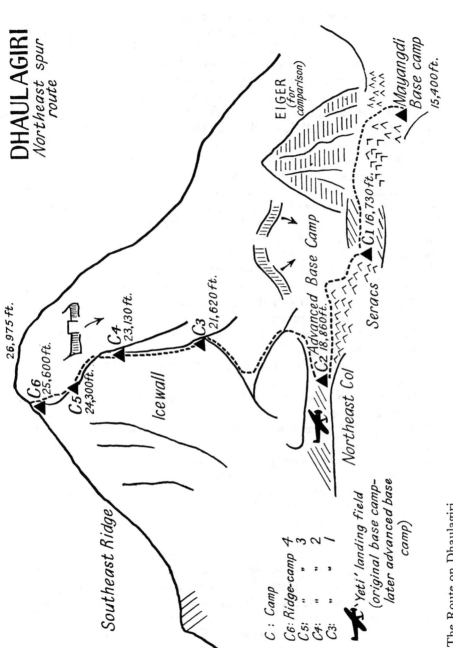

5. The Route on Dhaulagiri

Our little gnat visited us every day – announcing itself first of all by a gentle buzzing, then becoming visible as a tiny dot between those massive walls. It was usually quite near by the time we had spotted it and grew swiftly, to become recognizable as our bright-hued Yeti, roaring overhead and away, to dwindle again to a yellow streak against the ice-ribs of the 3,000-foot high, pinnacled wall of the South-east Ridge. Surely it must crash into it? But, no: it disappears somewhere into the white glare of the saddle's mile-wide curve. For a moment even its sound is lost; then, equally suddenly, it is here again as large as life, and touching down. Saxer and Wick jump out, waving; or, if we are still resting in the tent, they shout across to us.

We had settled down into a regular routine; dragging cases, sliding sacks over the snow, rocking Yeti. This exhausting exercise was indispensable on take-off, if our gnat was to become airborne in the rare atmosphere, for the friction of its two skis in the snow at the start could be considerable.

We could not risk leaving the cases and sacks scattered about the place; there were almost such masses of fresh snow that by next morning we might be unable to find them. North-east Col and Dapa Col were two very different places; up here the mountain made its icy breath felt. Besides, a packing-case buried in the snow could spell dire disaster to Yeti, as it came in to land.

Taking everything into account, life up here at 18,700 feet was a strenuous affair.

At first, we could not even spare a thought for the great white spur winging up above us.

We were glad when, on the day after our arrival, two Sherpas were flown up to assist us, but the older of the two was taken ill during the very first night, and Saxer had to fly him down all the way to Pokhara, in the plains. The younger one, Nawang Dorje, stayed up with us. Those first few days in the white desert of the col taught us what Dhaulagiri's might and mass, its cruelty and its beauty held in store for us.

Occasionally I scribbled a few notes in my diary, reflecting our feelings...

April 3rd (two days after landing on the col)
Yeti came up, bringing Georg, but he went down again. He complained of the length of time it takes to acclimatize. I am still very weak on my pins. I often sit down on a case and let my loads fall into the snow, without having to bend. A big drum calls for our united efforts.

'Much tougher than Dapa Col. Ernst stayed in tent all day. I sent the old Sherpa who fell sick straight down again. He had come to me in a very low state and with a confused look on his face, bringing all his belongings. High time he went down! The weather only stayed good till eleven o'clock. Then it deteriorated into a fearful storm all night. Moravec called it "the Pitiless Mountain". Very soon I shall believe it myself.'

April 6th
'Fantastic masses of fresh snow, at least three feet of it. Our equipment dumps have disappeared. Of the last batch only the big drum is now visible. Must do something. Put something on top of the drum and flags on that, for this snow is going on. There's a carton of millet-biscuits somewhere under the snow out there. Cigarettes for our plucky Sherpa.

'Over to the drum and back (just a stone's throw). It took an hour. The snow is bottomless.

'Suppose an avalanche came all the way down those 8,000 feet? We are quite a long way away. But a powder-snow avalanche might make this our last resting-place. We should hear the thunder of it, see the sky go dark above us, and be blown away, tent and all.

'The wind is screaming, the snow rattling on the tent-cloth, piling up higher all the time. You can feel it with your hand on the side wall. Cold.

'Terribly cold. The tent fabric grows lighter. The light of a pale moon. Up there, quite incredibly, the White Mountain, white, all white in the moonlight, soaring above delicate, shimmering mists. Uncanny, but magically beautiful. I called Ernst to look at it.

'What will happen tomorrow, if the sun gets on to those slopes above us?'

April 7th
'A golden light through the fabric of the tent. The sun. No more wind. We heard Yeti buzzing in and landing. No movement anywhere. No sound.

'I built a protective wall and a wedge-shaped windbreak. Ernst and Nawang Dorje dug the vanished material-dump out of its covering of snow.'

April 8th
'I told Ernst it looked like a break in the weather. No Yeti today. Once again we had to scrape the hoar-frost (it forms inside the tent during the night to a two-finger thickness). If you don't scrape it off, you get a snowfall in the tent as soon as it gets warm. Often there are tassels of frost hanging down on threads. In the evening there is a marvellous

flashing and glittering inside the tent, in the light of our miner's lamps. Makes you think of Christmas, somehow.

'By 11 o'clock clouds had come up and a strong wind had risen from all directions. The break in the weather had arrived. The gale howled and snow rattled on the fabric. It went on till evening. (This was the notorious Dhaulagiri weather with its nerve-racking regularity, and we were getting to know it at first hand.)

'At midday I cooked omelettes, peas and bacon.'

April 9th
'Only the tip of the Sherpa-tent is still visible. From it Nawang Dorje emerges like a mole. The gale gets fiercer and fiercer, shaking the tent as it screams across it. We feel sure that an unprotected tent would have been blown away long ago. Anything up to 100 m.p.h. The strip of light overhead gets narrower and narrower.

'Had to shovel the snow out of the tent. Didn't notice that my toes had lost all sensation. Not till a bit late, by which time they had sustained slight trouble. At midday Nawang and I cooked mushrooms, noodle soup and sausages.'

Just a few diary-entries, written by the light of a forehead-lamp in our glittering ice-palace, in the night, at 18,700 feet. Written when I was alone with my thoughts, with the storm, with my companion at my side; written when I found it impossible to sleep. Jottings full of hope on the one hand, uncertainty on the other. For even if there was the aircraft, here we were served up on a silver salver in the clouds; literally in the clouds, and a long way from the earth's good floor. We had no radio-link, no supporting-camp below us; not a soul between us and the Kali Valley, ten thousand feet away down there. Here, on our white platform, we were living as lonely and isolated a life as if we were on the moon. Here, with a huge white summit looming overhead, and only Yeti to provide an invisible bridge leading back to the world of men.

Saxer's Tour de Force
Our little plane came up again and again – sometimes from far away Pokhara out there beyond the Annapurna peaks, sometimes only from the Dapa Col out of sight behind Tukucha Peak, the expedition's first springboard. The material piled up in our depot and we were acclimatizing rapidly. Sometimes we even sang – with due pauses to get our breath back – some mountain-lay or other, accompanied by my ubiquitous guitar.

The White Mountain of the Himalaya

Then, suddenly, came the black day when for long moments we feared it was all up with us.

Yeti had landed once again. There was a great deal of snow, but everything was normal otherwise. We helped with the unloading, did our rocking act, gasping for breath and looking like Father Christmas, ducked down and watched Yeti move off, though the tail didn't seem to lift properly. Down over the snowy rim of the saddle went our little craft, as usual, into the cauldron beyond . . . But this time it didn't zoom up again. Full of foreboding, we followed its track to the rim of the saddle. Then we saw Yeti hanging at a slight angle on the slope down below. The tail-ski had never got clear of the snow and Yeti had failed to 'unstick'!

Saxer left us in no doubt as to the seriousness of the situation. It was only a hundred yards to the crevasses and séracs. We should have to stamp out a 'runway' – and a first-class one at that – to give Yeti a chance of getting airborne. If it didn't take off in that short distance, it would finish up in the big crevasses ahead.

I never saw Ernst Saxer so determined. As he said, this was the only possible chance. If it failed, that was the end. We all worked like demons – Forrer and I, Nawang, Saxer, Wick; and Peter Diener, who had been flown up for a short visit. We tramped up and down the slope, knee-deep in snow, panting and choking, till one or other of us had to lie down; we all gave everything we had, as we stamped out a runway at close on 20,000 feet. Finally the surface was smoothed with a pair of skis. Saxer jettisoned all but the essentials, heaving everything that weighed anything out of Yeti. A penny for his thoughts, as he looked at the ice of the séracs and crevasses, shimmering blue just ahead down the slope!

He decided to take off alone, full throttle at the séracs in front. A matter of only a few yards. We realized he was risking his life. Well, we should soon know the answer . . .

I had flattened out the last bit with my skis again and was coming up again when they signalled down that Ernst wanted to take off. I uttered a heartfelt prayer. The engine was roaring; the others were hanging on to the struts. The Yeti was off, hurtling down – rat-t-t-t – over the finely-ribbed runway, down the slope, straight for the crevasses. Fifty yards: still on the floor. Forty: for God's sake lift! Thirty: and there, just short of the chasm, the skis separated from the surface, and – scraping over the séracs by inches – Yeti was airborne.

Saxer had pulled it off! I had tears in my eyes as I watched. It had been a damnably narrow squeak. I shall never forget standing there watching Yeti roaring flat out towards the crevasses, with Ernst's head looking small in the cockpit, and the skis still ... still ... still glued to the snow ... and then, just before the runway's end, lifting clear ... Ernst, man, what a performance!

Our friendship lasted for years, till he crashed, flying in his own mountains, in Switzerland.

But on that day, April 10, 1960, Ernst Saxer, jet-fighter and glacier-pilot risked his life and saved our only link with the valley and the world outside – our Yeti.

6,000 Feet of North-east Spur

The three of us, Ernst Forrer, Albin Schelbert and I, were alone on our ladder to heaven, with four Sherpas in support; but we carried just as much as they did. Nothing stirred in our lonely world, except a big jet-black raven, which put in an appearance every now and then on the North-east Col.

We had suddenly been transformed into a lightweight expedition, cut-off in its advanced base; for the flight which had brought Albin up turned out to be the last. Since then, not a sight or sign of Yeti; not on the following day, nor the next, nor the third. There we were, waiting in vain.

They were probably doing running-repairs, as had already happened once. One of these days Yeti would be here again, bringing up the rest of the expedition and equipment. Yes, but when? This time it seemed to be something more serious. We could do nothing up here but wait and see ...

On the other hand, what would become of our intended ascent of the spur? The storms heralding the monsoon could break as early as mid-May, possibly even sooner. If we didn't put in some good, hard work on the mountain before the others came up, all our chances of reaching the summit would be gone.

So, we three, acting as a small, light group of the kind I had already experienced – without Sherpas – on Broad Peak, now tackled our mountain: an expedition consisting of only three climbers and four Sherpas, and again, as on Broad Peak, rejecting the use of oxygen. This 'Assault Party', at first with the Sherpas as porters, later on its own, forced its way higher and higher up the spur, and after long weeks of battle with the cold and the gales, established all the high-altitude camps up it.

Meanwhile, our fellow-members on Dapa Col, forming the second and larger group of the expedition, left high and dry by Yeti's default, had reached the North-east Col on foot, and managed, with much toil and sweat, to ferry most of the remaining material up to it by way of the

'French Col' and the Mayangdi Glacier. In the course of this toilsome operation, they established two new camps: a base camp on the floor of the Mayangdi Glacier's trough at 15,400 feet and an interim camp on the ascent from there to the North-east Col, where our aircraft-base was thus suddenly transformed into the expedition's camp II. So our plateau in the clouds had been fitted with a ladder from below. We had gone 'conventional'.

Yeti's disappearance from the scene had, incidentally, played havoc with the excellent-planned and ample provisioning of the expedition. As a result, one party was continually cooking different varieties of noodles and pasta, while hungering for chocolate and fruit-juice; while the other could no longer stomach the sight of chocolate and gradually spooned up their rice with diminishing enthusiasm. (Albin, our vegetarian, dreamed of corn-flakes and finished up by eating meat.)

The complete reversal of the basic plan fell hardest on Adam Skoczylas. Instead of being by now where he longed to be, on the great white ridge, he found himself saddled with the job of leading a column of coolies all the long way up from Pokhara, along the Mayangdi Khola – an endless valley-crawl, which meant for him an even longer postponement in acclimatization than the others were faced with on the transmigration from the Dapa to the South-east Col. Meanwhile, down in Pokhara itself, Max Eiselin, the leader of the expedition, joining Saxer and Wick, was occupying himself exclusively with Yeti's troubles.

We only learned what had happened when our colleagues came up from the Dapa Col during the first days of May. On April 13th a burst cylinder had forced Saxer to crash-land at Pokhara. Where in these parts could one get a replacement-engine quickly? Nowhere, but there was one coming – coming from Europe! Three weeks later, on the very day of our first summit attempt, May 4th, Yeti was in the air again. However, it looked as if the Gods had no great affection for our gay little butterfly; for on the very next day, it crashed, from no great height, while taking-off from the Dapa Col. It was a freak of ill-fortune – for the same type of aircraft later on proved itself highly reliable in regular use in Nepal – the grip of the thing called the 'Cloche' had come clean away in Saxer's hands. It was not all bad luck, though; for the pilot and co-pilot made their way, uninjured, on foot to the valley, although Yeti was a complete write-off.

Meanwhile, Ernst, Albin and I – suddenly isolated by a stroke of fate, with our Sherpas, high up in that white wilderness – were pushing on up the spur, a totally committed trio.

Better still, during those days of humping loads in furious storms with our Sherpas, we discovered that two of these sons of the Himalaya, displaying exceptional enthusiasm, were distinguishing themselves beyond all expectation. In short that our summit, for which we were expending such efforts, was 'their' summit too. Nima Dorje and Nawang Dorje, showed themselves genuine and completely competent rope-mates, with whom we became firm friends. Nawang, the tireless, we already knew from our days in the storm-swept tents on the North-east Col; Nima, the younger of the two, ever ready to help, always cheerful, had accompanied Herbert Tichy on one of his lengthy treks through Nepal.

The spur was steep, and it was difficult. Ernst, Albin and I meant to make our first attempt on the summit without Sherpas. Soon, too, we thought, for we managed, as early as April 15th, to establish a camp on the lower slopes of the ice-wall, just to the left of the crest of the spur. It was at 21,650 feet, tucked in under an impressive, slightly overhanging ice-step, the size of a family dwelling-house, which guaranteed our tent-community adequate protection from gales and avalanches. We were delighted at this first success – spur camp I, 2,800 feet higher up than the yellow fabric-blobs of our base camp, far away down there on the snow of the saddle.

And now to establish our next support camp, above the ice-wall, as soon as humanly possible. We were brim-full of energy. The very next day we pushed on up to nearly 23,000 feet, finding on our way the first traces of the previous expedition, a whole stair-rail of fixed ropes, which we dug out for the most part. We were full of hope that we would be able to establish spur camp II, above 23,000 feet, on the following day. But now, day after day, following a few bright early hours, the famous 'Dhaulagiri weather' struck, with gales and blizzards, which at times assumed terrifying proportions...

April 20th (all four Sherpas; supplies brought up from the col)
'Went with the Sherpas. Got to the crest of the spur where we met a very cold wind, which became a gale. Bursts of sunshine in between. Dhaulagiri frowned down on us out of huge veils and banners. Hands and feet cold. Climbing a torture. Gale increasingly furious. The Sherpas in despair. Nawang shouting: "My foot finish, sahib!" It was terrifying. I said: "Drop your loads and get up to camp I", but nobody was sensible enough any more to take any notice. Couldn't feel my own fingers and toes myself. Still, the only hope lay in help from camp I. I was almost all in as I forced myself upwards ... shouting, screaming ... Sherpas dark lumps in a white snow-cloud. Ernst and Albin didn't hear me. Knee-deep snow. On all fours towards the end. At last they heard me, and started down. All they found was the loads, the other two Sherpas

had already turned tail. Nima Dorje arrived. Pulled him up by his arm. Then Nawang, resting his face and arms in the snow again and again. Outside the tent, the tempest went on roaring over the ridge.'

Time and again we started up the ice-wall from our shelter; the storms hunted us back to our place of refuge every time, often before we had got halfway up. All there was to show for our labours were a few material-depots fixed to ice-pitons. It was now impossible to find the fixed ropes under a layer of hard-blown snow, and we gave up looking for them. That was the state of affairs when, on April 27th, we embarked on a decisive assault, determined this time to succeed. Once again we ran into appalling weather, but this time we did not turn back. At 22,800 feet, on a narrow pitch, where it was just possible, we dug our tent and ourselves into the mountain's flank. We christened it emergency camp II. Two days later we moved from that uncomfortable spot to a hardly less airy perch just below the remnants of the tents of a camp the Austrians had established the previous year. We had done it at last. On April 29th our spur camp II was in being, at 23,150 feet. It had taken us a fortnight to defeat the ice-wall.

On May 1st, I went up to reconnoitre the 300-foot rock-cliff immediately above. I found it very difficult and everywhere extremely exposed, but there were serviceable fixed ropes from the year before all the way up it. I worked my way up very carefully. Suddenly, at an almost vertical pitch, only some fifteen feet below the crest of the ridge, there was no fixed rope. I deliberated a while, then climbed it unbelayed and dumped the tent I had brought up with me at the top. At that moment I noticed that a menacing grey front was moving in. I only got back to the uppermost fixed rope at the second attempt. While taking a short breather there, I looked down the face's unbroken sweep of nearly 7,000 feet into the depths, where during the last few days tiny dots could be seen moving up towards the North-east Col – our colleagues from over there, 'outside'.

The first priority up here was to get a fixed rope hanging down that pitch!

The next morning was gloriously fine. The distant view all around us was clearer than we had ever seen it. It was possible to distinguish the farthest peaks in the Transhimalaya. Annapurna seemed quite close. We all agreed: this was summit-weather. Now, we only had to establish one more camp as quickly as possible. Then we could have a go . . .

It was after midnight, so it was already May 4th, as we lay in our tent at 24,450 feet, dozing or sleeping. I woke up at a quarter to three.

What with dressing, breakfast and the rest, time simply raced away. By the time we got outside the tent, the sun was just rising – there was a riot of gorgeous colour out there, a marvellous view, but the cold was terrific. When I touched my crampons my fingers burned like fire and I let go again in a hurry (in the evening I noticed that even so slight a contact had raised a blister on my finger; later on, it turned black and fell off).

We roped up and moved slowly off, along a band of rock towards the right, till we found a somewhat awkward place at which it could be surmounted. But the snow which succeeded it was deep and rotten, and we made pitifully slow progress. Ought we to take to the crest of the ridge instead? It looked most uninviting, with flakes and humps up above us, separated by broad couloirs. Still, there was no alternative – so, up on to the ridge...

We were up at 25,000 feet. We were now able to look down on the long, sloping hanging-glacier which falls down and across the whole North Face at this point, only a few hundred feet below the summit-ridge. The rib we had been climbing petered out, to be followed by another very steep couloir. The condition of the snow up here was no better; we were forced to toil laboriously up the flaky rock at one side of it. When we were within measurable distance of the first summit in the ridge overhead, the weather gradually turned grey. We were used to that, but it might, after all, not... on we went. After a short snow-crawl on all fours, the angle eased off again.

All of a sudden we were stuck in thick fog. In spite of it, we recognized at once where we were; for rising out of the abyss on our left we could see the vague shape of a huge white ridge, while, not more than fifty feet above us, there was a sharp little snow-summit, with nothing above it but grey mist. We had reached the junction point of the North-east Spur and the South-east Ridge, at a height of about 25,600 feet.

Should we press on? By now we could see absolutely nothing. The weather had disintegrated completely.

Although it was only midday, we decided to retreat. One cannot trifle with Dhaulagiri. As we were going down, it cleared up for a moment; we could see blue sky, and the surrounding peaks. We dithered briefly, but then the clouds closed down on us again and we soon ceased to regret our decision to withdraw, for the weather turned foul beyond words. The wind raged and it snowed hard. At times we had great difficulty in finding our way down. Finally, we reached our tent safely, and crawled into it with all possible dispatch. We had had enough for one day.

While we were massaging each other's toes and fingers, we drew up a balance sheet of our first attempt on the summit. It had taught us two important lessons. First, the apparently easier route over the hanging glacier and steep snow-slopes was impossible, the only way lay up the ridge itself. Secondly, it was essential to establish a bivouac-camp as high up as possible, so as to ensure reaching the summit in spite of what the 'Dhaulagiri Weather' might do. The summit had to be climbed before the almost inevitable midday break in the weather.

Meanwhile, the first requisite was a couple of days' rest and recovery at base camp on the col.

'*Dhaulagiri, Sahib, Dhaulagiri*'

Back at the col, we now had the company of our team-mates from 'over there', whom we had not seen for such a long time; there was much to talk about. Some of them were already at work on the spur in an effort to acclimatize to higher altitudes as quickly as possible, for they knew that time was running out. The monsoon storms might break any day now, and it was essential to use every moment of good weather.

On May 9th, Ernst, Albin and I, with our two trusty Sherpas, Nima and Nawang, started up the spur again on our second drive for the summit, taking with us the good wishes of all those remaining down at the col.

I knew from our experience on a no-less-difficult mountain, Broad Peak, where on the first day of both our summit-attempts we had climbed nearly 5,000 feet from base camp and still been able to climb again on the following day, that our present very fit party could tackle the 7,300 feet to our camp above the ice-wall here. So we leap-frogged the intervening camp.

We felt in wonderful form after our rest days down below and everything went as I had foreseen. We got straight up to our spur-camp II (now transformed into the expedition's camp IV, counting from the lower base on the Mayangdi Glacier) at 23,150 feet. There we found Peter Diener, who told us that the three Valaisian members of the expedition, Michel Vaucher, Hugo Weber and Jeanjacques Roussi, had gone on up that very morning to the next camp above, with a view to acclimatizing there. Although he had not yet got properly used to the altitude, he asked us to let him join us on our bid for the summit, and we agreed. Then we settled down to some much-needed sleep.

Next morning, May 10th, we went on up to camp V (24,450 feet), where the three Valaisian climbers were occupying the tent we had pitched there during our first attempt. Fortunately we had now brought two tents up with us, so there was a solution to the accommodation problem. That night nine of us slept in three two-man tents, pretty close quarters, but not impossible. We had, in any case, been used to uncomfortable nights for weeks past, and this one was no exception; the outer sleeping-bags soon turned to icy tubes owing to the hoar-frost, which continually formed on the lining of the tent walls.

May 11th brought with it a difficult problem. What would happen if we took one of the three tents with us for our intended bivouac-camp? Suppose our unpredictable Dhaulagiri, instead of yielding the prize of its summit, forced us to a dramatic retreat, and we had to abandon the tent up there? That would mean coming down to a camp with only two tents to house nine men – some of whom might well be frostbitten or utterly exhausted. It was a question which had already ruffled tempers yesterday, let alone this morning. In the end Michel, Hugo and Jean-jacques understood the situation and agreed to go down to the next camp and fetch up the tent whose absence might be so fatal. They started down at about 11 a.m., but failed to turn up again; it was only later that we knew the reason. Michel had been taken ill on the way down and they had consequently been forced down to the col.

On the 12th, after another day's climbing in an icy gale, we succeeded in establishing the bivouac-tent, according to plan, at about 25,600 feet, in a snow-cranny roofed over by a massive rock.

We thought the night of the 12th/13th would never end. The six of us squatted, crouched, and leaned against each other, all jammed together in our two-man tent. It was a long-drawn out torture, and we hardly slept a wink. From time to time a flicker of conversation would break out, the invariable topic being the lack of space and the general discomfort. Albin, for instance, was bent double between the tent-staves and the roof, with no means of stretching his legs, because the space was occupied by his neighbour. Nima Dorje had – comparatively speaking – the best place, close to the entrance. In the middle of the night Ernst and I asked him to make some tea, knowing how anxious he always was to help. Not this time, however; and suddenly – doubtless upset at being disturbed – he horrified us all by walking out and lying down in the open, where the temperature was at least minus 30 degrees Centigrade. None of our entreaties could persuade him inside again till morning – when he came in, not one atom the worse for his night out in the cold.

Morning came as a deliverance for us all.

Getting our boots on at such close quarters took ages and racked our nerves, but we finally dragged our stiff limbs outside the tent. All the view around lay clear and, so far as we could tell, the day promised to

The White Mountain of the Himalaya

be fine. The morning sun gilded Annapurna – the Nilgiris, now appreciably lower – Tukucha Peak and all the unnamed five- and six-thousanders stretching away into the Tibetan distances. I was filled with a great joy: the summit, only 1,300 feet above us, would fall to us today...

We roped up, put on our crampons and started slowly upwards, breathing deep at every step; for we were climbing without oxygen. As on the day before, I went with Nawang Dorje, that splendid type, tireless and always equable. Today there was joy written all over his face, because he was going to the summit; he kept on laughing and showing his flashing teeth. Out ahead, Ernst and Nima were moving slowly up towards the deep, dark-blue sky, while Albin and Peter, intending to follow a little later, were still at the tent. I carried my 16mm cine-camera in my breast-pocket, for I meant to shoot some film on the way up and, in particular, on the summit.

Step by step we made our way up the snow-crest, which was at times so narrow that, for safety, we had to plant our feet at right-angles to it. Immeasurable depths fell away directly below us: 7,000 feet to our right, and to our left, at our very toe-caps, we looked 13,000 feet down the South Face to a small glacier and low, greenish-brown foothills. We were left in no doubt that our path lay very high above the world.

Ernst was now stopping at the end of every rope's length and belaying Nima up to him; a false step here would have been fatal. Halfway up the ridge to the subsidiary summit, Nawang and I took over the lead. Very soon a step, with rock penetrating the snow, involved us in the utmost care and some precarious belaying. This was followed by a flatter sector of mixed rock and snow. The air grew appreciably rarer. We were climbing at the 26,000-foot level.

To avoid continual halts to get our breath back, I now throttled down our pace to well below what was possible. 'We go slow now, very slow,' I told Nawang, who seemed surprised at first, but soon got the idea.* Shortening the rope and climbing simultaneously, we hardly ever had to halt; and our even, leisurely pace made it possible to pick out the best line between boulders, snow-patches and slabs, our steps never having to deviate more than a yard. As a result, we made much more rapid progress than before, in spite of the increasing altitude.

What would the summit be like? Nobody had ever seen the rock flakes

---

* This intentional, drastic lowering of the tempo, almost down to 'slow-motion', produces an unbroken sequence of movement and rest combined; it is a little difficult to achieve at first – but soon brings relaxation and great conservation of energy, largely because of the regular rate of breathing which results. In my opinion it is the most efficient method of progress at and above the 26,000-foot level.—K.D.

on the arête from close at hand, and we wondered whether they would be easy or difficult. I soon noticed that the subsidiary summit was not a projection at all, but a mere kink in the crest of this huge ridge. Full of excitement, I looked beyond it. There it was, Dhaulagiri's summit! Between us and it, the back of a ridge covered in slabs, rather like the tiles on a roof, swung gently across to a solitary *gendarme*, beyond which there was a steep rise to a sharp, white summit, which one might have taken at first sight as the highest point; but beyond it there lay a notch, followed by a rocky step, which did not look exactly easy, and might possibly be a shade higher than the white peak. It must be the summit, because the humps and flakes of rock beyond it obviously fell away on its far side. We were standing at not less than 26,300 feet, so there were only four to five hundred feet more to go. And we still felt pretty good.

What fantastic luck we were having, too, with the weather! Though more and more cloud was building up below, it was exceptionally still up here; there was practically no wind at all. We sat down, got something to eat out of a rucksack and gazed at the surrounding prospect. Annapurna was still visible; the white triangle of Tukucha Peak almost submerged down there. Alas, more and more clouds were banking up...

Down in the depths, 10,000 feet below us, incredibly far off, lay the 'French Col'. That was where it had all started, ten years before...

And today? A sixty-mile-an-hour gale might just as well have been screaming across these fringed slabs of roof-tiling, interspersed by broken fragments, which almost looked as if they had been arranged in stripes. Yet, not a breath stirred. You had to say it out loud to yourself before you could believe it: today May 13th, the daemons of the storm were sound asleep!

I was happy beyond words at the marvellous way things were – so unexpectedly – going. Nawang's eyes, too, were shining and he was smiling all over his dark face. Ernst and Nima were no less thrilled when they came up and saw the summit. They sat down next to us. Then we moved on again, slowly ascending the easy slabby ridge, turning the *gendarme* on ledges without the slightest difficulty; but the steep snowslope beyond, up into a notch, was a breathtaking business. We were now once again on a narrow crest of snow straight above the South Face, up which clouds and mist were advancing. Albin suddenly joined us in the notch and explained that Peter was following a little way behind.

Gradually the tension increased. We could no longer see the summit, but it could not be far now. I knew we had to deal with the white peak first, and on the sharp arête leading up to it we had to exercise the utmost caution. We belayed from a stance on its first steep surge, then

The White Mountain of the Himalaya

Nawang, moving with exemplary assurance, and I went on again simultaneously – mostly one on either side of the crest, so that we had an automatic belay. We were soon on the white peak, and we could see that the next projection really was the summit – not more than 100 to 150 feet above us!

Untrodden rock, with mist swirling round it....

Something changed at that instant.

I heard Albin next to me, saying: 'Man, am I enjoying myself!' I asked him to go on ahead, and filmed him as he slowly moved up towards the summit.

On we went. A difficult boulder, plumb on the crest of the ridge, barred our way. As I pulled myself up by a small ledge – the only available hold – I said to myself: 'A Grade IV pitch, for full measure!'; and I thought of Albin who had just done it all on his own. I brought Nawang up on the rope. Only a little way to go now!

We traversed along a band, rather like a narrow path, moved out to the left for a short distance, up about six feet more – and Albin and I were shaking hands on the spacious summit. Nawang followed immediately, and we were soon joined by Ernst and Nima.

Overjoyed, we embraced one another, patted each other's backs...

We had been battling with storm and tempest for a whole month on this mountain, determined to get to the top, sustaining setback after setback, coming back at it again and again... and now, at last, we were here, on the summit.

It was 12.30 p.m. The ascent had taken just four and a half hours. The weather was still calm and fine, with hardly any wind. An incomparable feeling of peace and security lay upon us...

Great, bulging towers of cloud came rising like columns from below, swelling to cloud-castles high in the sky, now enveloping us, now clearing to let us see down to the 'French Col', Tukucha Peak, the North-east Col. From between the cloud-curtains, too, appeared the magnificent range of the Dhaula Himal, a little to the right of the curiously flaked and humped ridge of our eight-thousander, which stretched far away ahead.

We hoisted our pennants, among them my own country's colours, bright on Dhaulagiri's summit. The ice-axes and hammers we had brought up with us included two we had found on the way up in the camps of the 1959 pioneers. Our thoughts went back to the long battle for this peak; to Heini Roiss and Francisco Ibañez who gave their lives for it, and to all the others who had fought so long and hard... the summit was theirs, just as much as ours.

Presently Peter arrived and we all shook him by the hand. His performance had been an exceptional one, for he was markedly less well acclimatized than the rest of us.

Somewhere down in the depths, a thunderstorm was rumbling, the sound of the thunder-claps coming up faintly, almost imperceptibly. A painful prickling sensation of our scalps warned us that, here too, the air was becoming strongly charged with electricity and we started down without further delay.

It was about 5 p.m. when we got back to our top camp. We were very tired, but inexpressibly happy at the knowledge of our success. As we sat in our tent, with tea running comfortably down our throats, Nawang looked at me, grinned broadly and said: 'Dhaulagiri, Sahib... Dhaulagiri.' I knew just how he felt, and nodded back. Yes, Dhaulagiri ... a marvellous word to hear spoken.

Ten days later our team-mates Michel Vaucher and Hugo Weber repeated the ascent to the summit, starting from camp V and dispensing with a bivouac tent.

Then we went down – endlessly down, deeper and deeper down – 20,000 feet lie between the summit and the silver ribbon of the Kali Gandhaki – down into the valleys where men live, into Nepal's greenery. It was like being born anew. Grass, trees, rain, villages, rivers. We sang and drank *chang* in honour of our peak, as we strolled in leisurely fashion out towards Pokhara. Orchids bloomed, parrots played about, in the forests. And then we heard a cuckoo! Nawang, noticing my surprise at hearing that familiar sound, laughingly explained its meaning. 'Don't go up!' it meant; 'don't go up into the mountains – you stay here!' At least, he added, that was what the girls at home in Sola Khumbu said it meant, with a tell-tale gleam in his dark eyes.

'Cuckoo!' So that was it, then. 'Cuckoo!' Dhaulagiri shone white through the branches from high up in the sky.

Three of our party got married almost as soon as they got home.

Whenever I think of Nepal, the view from the Gorapani Pass – the 'Horse-water' Pass – leaps to my mind.

The summit of the pass is jungle-covered; lianas trail from the dark branches. Pale-mauve flowers blossom in the moss that clothes the trunks. Tree-ferns grow between them. And at the highest point on this immemorial road you will find prayer flags hanging.

As we were toiling up to the summit of that pass, close on 10,000 feet high, I saw Dhaulagiri once more. It was in the early morning. There it floated, utterly divorced from the earth and weightless as some mighty cloud.

Om Mani Padme Hum – Om Mani Padme Hum – *engraved on a stone tablet* – Om Mani Padme Hum.
Over and over again.
'Oh, thou Jewel in the Lotus!'
The prayer of those who worship Buddha. Just a prayer.

This stone tablet here comes from Nepal; from the foot of Dhaulagiri – from one of the stone monuments one continually meets by the wayside, fashioned out of the mountain's slate.
'Oh, thou Jewel in the Lotus!'
Somebody who wanted to use that form of prayer engraved the letters of those words and laid the tablet there, next to all the others bearing the same inscription.

It is supposed to be unlucky to remove one of those prayer-tablets; no native of Nepal would ever even think of doing such a thing. One of the climbers on the 1959 expedition had brought this one home with him.
Later he began to have misgivings. One day he brought it to me, which was a sensible solution.

Om Mani Padme Hum – *just a prayer.*
Sometimes it seems to come sounding right out of the stone.

Herbert Tichy

I looked at Herbert Tichy's postcard: a black-and-white photograph of flowers, grass, rocks, at whose feet great rollers were breaking in clouds of spray. Some island or other. 'This is what it looks like here,' he wrote; 'very impressive and noisy. The mountains here are steep and crumbling. I got up to a peak nearly 13,000 feet high, with a wonderful view, but very cold. So you are really working on your book? There are 7,000 islands; one of them must be the perfect subject, for it is high time I wrote another book...'

I had no idea where the island, or this mountain, from which the postcard came, might be. There was no clue to its whereabouts, no date on the card; but the island existed, with its high mountain, its lush vegetation and its storm-tossed sea. When Herbert came home, he would tell me about it. Or he might even write a book about it. It might still not explain exactly where the island lay; the important thing would be that, somewhere, it existed. When Herbert unfolds a tale, space and time become subservient to another dimension.

A leading cartographer once wanted to translate one of Tichy's eventful journeys through a little-known region of the Himalaya into the terms of a map; all he succeeded in doing was to produce a sketch-map full of question marks. He simply found it impossible to transfer Herbert Tichy's hidden dimension into the scale in which map-makers work – a complete tribute to the integrity of both conceptions.

In the accompanying text, the well-known compiler of a Himalayan Chronicle grudgingly growled out a few complimentary remarks about the wonderful powers of observation of human customs and the skill with which this geologist-errant portrayed them. (Actually his thesis for his doctorate, a study of the Himalaya, was the end of his programme as a geologist and the start of his career as an author.)

A great deal has been written about Tichy's life, so I will not try to do so. We are friends; so it is of no importance what we studied, where we went or how those years passed. The important thing is that we met.

Herbert Tichy

It is almost true to say that we met long before we came to know one another – for Herbert wrote books; and when I began to read about his years in China, about his pilgrimage to the holy peak of Kailas, about the hair-raising journey by motor-cycle to India, I realized more and more that here was a man who wrote about things I knew, though till then far less clearly. And I realized, too, that I really knew the man who wrote those words, although I had never seen him.

That is how, strangely enough, it turned out when Kurt Maix took me to see him. And after that? We have never been on an expedition together, nor shared a journey. When Herbert is away for a year, somewhere on the globe, he may write me a letter or a couple of cards; but when I go to Vienna to see him, it makes no difference whether a year or a month has elapsed. We talk all through the long afternoon, seeking the purpose of all this journeying hither and thither, of life itself, of lecture-tours, of being with other people; recalling the Himalayan peaks and skies. Very often we fail to find an answer.

I am sure every reader knows the importance of whom one meets – and that is why I have written these lines; for Herbert Tichy has clarified many things for me, if only by making me aware of what was previously unclear. He belongs in my life's orbit.

I know that in many ways we are very different people. I am a climber, while Herbert would never climb a mountain-face as an end in itself. This wanderer over the earth's surface says he is no climber; but that did not prevent his strolling up to above 26,000 feet, through tempest and icy cold, towards the wide Himalayan sky, even to the white dome of Cho Oyu. With only a Sherpa for company, he climbed higher and higher on that mighty Tibetan peak, Gurla Mandhata, without ever getting to the top – but because he had seen it he understood the Sadhu, deep in his meditations, to whom the summit belongs.

One should never describe anyone else's room, because it is his personal kingdom, every corner of which can contribute its aura. So I will only describe the floor of Tichy's – that generally unused plain, to which we Europeans merely accord a sterile existence, that empty space between desk, divan and chest, whose unreality we, at best, try to disguise with a resplendent parquet or a colourful carpet. (Though children have long known its true value and have, without restrictions or inhibitions, converted it to a private world of their own.) In Asia, too, the floor is part of the living-space and – coming back now to Herbert – everyone who writes books knows what a splendid place it is for scattering around the chapters of a manuscript, photographs, drawings, one's letters, maps, and mementoes of a journey; while the owner of the floor quietly surveys it all from on high, with the eyes of a traveller in space looking down on the earth's surface. I think it is a modern concept, though it may be a very ancient one – and certainly one no 'lady of the house' would willingly accept. Herbert, however, is a bachelor; and he who has trodden the floors of Asia, is an adept at floors.

It is impossible to talk about Herbert without recalling his quiet sense of humour. On his way back from the holy peak of Kailas in Tibet – he had made his journey to and around it dressed as a pilgrim – devout peasants of the locality kissed his feet and those of his native companions. 'No joy for us,' said Tichy, 'but certainly none for them, seeing that we had been on the march for several weeks.'

Herbert is tall, about six foot, fair-haired and very quiet. His stride betrays the many months of wandering through the valleys, over the passes and ridges of the Himalaya. I suppose he is about fifty, but I don't know, for there is about him a quality of agelessness. He has spent much time in Asia, going back again and again – sometimes for a few months, once, in China, for seven years. He always came home – to Vienna, to Nepal, to people living under unnamed ranges, or at the edge of the sea in the far north of Alaska – it didn't matter, he was at home anywhere where people were at home.

What happens to a man who has grasped in its entirety one truth, and then another, and another? He will wander the earth till the end of his life – where to, none can say.

The poet Wang Wei wrote:
'The Earth is everywhere the same
And eternal, eternal are the white clouds . . .'

Herbert journeyed on, with two Lamas he had met on the way, southwards. He wanted to get to the south of the clouds.

I went to Vienna.

Herbert was happy and radiated his pleasure. He had been in Africa for a year. No, he had not been lonely. He talked of the life down there and the people he had met. I asked him if he planned to go there again.

Two years later I was in Vienna again.

Herbert was unhappy. We talked about life, a whole long afternoon – all to no avail, for we could not change the things we talked about: they were hard facts. Still, it was better to have talked again.

Six months later I stopped at Vienna on my way to a lecture in Budapest. 'I think I must get away somewhere,' said Herbert.

When I saw him again, a month later, his trunks were in the middle of the room, packed and ready.

Herbert Tichy

'When do you leave?'
'In a month's time.'
'Where to?'
'I don't know yet, exactly. Might be Formosa . . . might even be Japan.'

We sat by those packed trunks, smoked a cigarette, drank a glass of whisky, to wish his journey well.

I called him up three weeks later. Herbert had gone. I had a card from Formosa, with greetings on it. How long will he be away? A year, two years? Nobody knows, not even Herbert himself.

One of these days he will be back in Vienna, as if he had left only yesterday.

That is the man who said to me, when I went off to climb Dhaulagiri: 'Come back safe. But even if you don't, I wish you joy!'

18 to 81

FINALS AND A POLICE-SERGEANT

I have passed my finals: my finals – I have passed them: my finals are – past!

My clothes are clinging to my body. I am dragging one foot, because I have only one shoelace in one shoe; the other must be somewhere in the police-station. My tie looks like a corkscrew. And I could embrace the whole world – even that fat police-sergeant. For I am a diploma'd Lecturer in Commerce. At last!

No more swotting! I'm free again – isn't life wonderful? Wonderful rain, proper, gorgeous, beneficent, torrential rain, running down all over one's face. Isn't life wonderful?

A few years ago, at the University of Commerce, Vienna, these had been the reflections of a grant-aided student-lectureship candidate: 'I am a mathematical genius, only it doesn't always show itself, because I always make mistakes in my arithmetic. Still, I belong to the higher IQ levels – I am a mathematician, not a reckoner. Arithmetic today is done by *machines*; mathematicians are the *men* of the future . . .'

This stupid business of arithmetic. Just practice stuff, fit only for morons. Anyone can learn it, if he goes on long enough. Why do I always get the wrong answer? I gave a groan.

'My friend,' said the soft voice of an obvious head book-keeper in the making, by my side. 'It is because you haven't had enough practice.' I said nothing and continued to stare at the example in front of me. 'I'll tell you what to do,' he went on, patiently and helpfully (by now he looked exactly like a doctor prescribing a medicine): 'You just take a bit of paper every day and do ten of these reckonings.' He took a piece of paper and, as I regarded him sceptically: 'Just watch,' he said, enthusiastically. Then he wrote down the figure 18 and draw a vertical line down from it. 'Let us take 18 as an example . . . now you multiply it by 2 . . . then the result by 3 . . . and so on, up to 15.'

'Don't you think 9 would do?' I interposed.

'All right, up to 9, then,' he said, with an indulgent smile. 'And now

Finals and a Police-sergeant

you start dividing, first by 2, then the result by 3, and so on, up to 9. If you haven't made a mistake, you get back in the end to the figure 18. You do ten such reckonings a day – in addition to your others, of course...'

I said, 'thanks' and gave a deep sigh. I remembered that kind of uncongenial task from the days of my O-level exams; about as useful as fifty knee-bends after the shrilling of the alarm clock in the morning (stated in mathematical terms = + 5 minutes' lie-in).

Finally, I said: 'It wouldn't be the least use – I should just go on making mistakes.' 'You go on doing it until you don't make mistakes any more,' he said quietly, with a slight grimace. So we were back where we started – just stupid practice-maths; didn't I know that commercial arithmetic was something for dolts? Why was the chap smiling so knowingly? He was beginning, somehow, to get on my nerves...

I packed up my bank-accounts and went to a coffee-shop. So, I was supposed to fritter a quarter of an hour of my time away, simply to start from 18 and get back to 18 again? Give me a piece of paper....

I needn't have worried: my result was 73.

I did it again... 26. Well, anyway, I was getting nearer.

I got it right the third time, and thought it over for a while.

All hope was not lost, then. In any case, the finals weren't till April.

Just for the record: the paternal state takes great thought for Lecturers in Commerce. It wants them all to be practical people. So it prescribes eighteen months of practical sales or book-keeping experience before they take their finals. I forgot a great deal during that time – perhaps others didn't suffer the same way, but I did.

I turned up with the gloomiest forebodings. I passed in book-keeping, business-correspondence, pedagogics (a 'v.g.' for that!), the theory of business management... I went down in arithmetic like a bomb. So did some of the others, not that that cheered me up any. Anyway, my time in Vienna was up: from now on I would do a bit of desultory study in arithmetic, so as to take the beastly subject again, from a discreet distance. For, in the interim, I had found – well, I was going to say a 'career' – I had become a climber! My life had begun to include lecturing, going far afield on expeditions, visiting the mountains. I lectured on the Alps and the Himalaya in Austria, Italy, England and Switzerland – my journeys were often long and marvellous; and I got to know a great many people. Then I got married – and still I hadn't passed my finals – at least, not in that confounded subject, arithmetic.

I would have taught already, but I said to myself: until they have let you pass in commercial arithmetic, you will not teach. There may be two points of view, I'm sure. I personally don't regret those years in the least – it was so definitely the life I was meant to live; and so many other people shared it with me.

But now let us take another flying visit to Vienna.

The next 'finals' were due in a few days.

I sat in the front row, taking up what is scientifically known as a 'showerbath' position. For our professor set much store by attendance at his lectures. There he was, looking around, looking at me ... and I heard him saying: 'Once I had a candidate who came regularly all the way from Linz to hear me lecture!' I bowed my head guiltily; I only came from Salzburg and by no means regularly.

Unfortunately, no luck again, that time ... but it went much better than the first attempt – I was only *just* ploughed. Ruefully, I had to admit that this just wouldn't do, the way I was playing it; study by remote-control wasn't the right answer – in spite of the notes a kindly nun had made for me. There was always something to distract me: mountains, lectures, everyday life. Unfortunately, a man cannot do only the things that give him pleasure – even if that *is* his real life.

One day I took the great decision: it has to be! I must say farewell to wife and child and go to Vienna, in deadly earnest, for two months.

Over my desk there was a framed calculation based on 18.

I studied like mad. Foreign exchange, calculation, current accounts, arbitrage – really quite interesting subjects. All the same, I was still making occasional arithmetical mistakes. But this time I felt much more confident.

The night before the viva, I sat in a lecture-room just under the roof of the University of Commerce. Here there were very few people, and there was at least peace and quiet. The view from there extends as far as the Prater. There was someone sitting a row in front of me, his head propped on his head. He was doing arithmetic. Suddenly he hurled his exercise book away. 'Wrong?' I asked, sympathetically. 'Yes – again!' he said.

'My friend,' I said, 'that's because you haven't had enough practice. I'll tell you what to do. Take the figure 18 as an example, and then you ...'

It so happened that police-sergeant Pomeisl was stumping his normal beat that evening in the suburb of Hietzing. Actually, he had

Finals and a Police-sergeant

nothing to do with the figure 18; but fate had decreed that we should meet on the morrow, over quite a different figure, just a quarter of an hour before the deadline for my viva. Of course, I didn't know that this evening, when I went for a nice walk, sure that at last everything would go well next day...

The clink of arms! The hosts marching to the decisive battle. Varus... Arminius of the Cherusci... an adding-machine... I had slept badly. Oh, it's only that damned alarm-clock!

... Hell! That's what happens when you lie in for only five minutes. Out you get, quick!

Houses went racing past, dark tunnels shut their cavernous jaws. The Vienna *Metro* went clattering and rattling along, first above the city, then under the city; the jolly old Vienna *Metro*.

It wasn't going nearly fast enough for me. Tense as a wire, I sat there, looking at the second hand of my watch, as it went round and round. Seven-thirty. My viva was at eight – oh, yes, I shall just make it. Not a minute to spare, though. I wondered whether the other chap was there already – there were to be two of us... armies on the march, the outcome could not be delayed now, the muffled sound of drums, the field of battle lay close ahead.

I hoped the other one wasn't too bright. (What an egoist you are!) Of course, I wanted him to pass – I just hoped he wasn't *too* bright. I mean: there were only two of us. If one of us boobed, that would be a fifty per cent failure. One really mustn't be as hard-hearted as that...

'Hietzing!'

Quickly, hop out! There's the tram, on the other side of the road. Don't let it get away, right under your very nose. I *know* the light's red; but I can't help it. *Got* to get across! Cars... very skilful, I am... there. I am safely in the tram. Somewhere in my subconscious – the sound of a whistle... not surprising, with all this traffic...

No sign of the tram starting. I'm not a Viennese; how was I to know it was a terminus? Heavens, time was running out, after all; a quarter to eight! Where on earth was my reminder-notice with the conversion-figures on it?

'That's 'im!' A tough, short, rose-red police-sergeant was peering into the tram. At me? Why at me?

'Out wiv yer!'

'Me?'

'Yus, you! You can't take no rise out o' me. Didncherear me whistling like mad? Cross on the red, you did. Outcher comes —!' He was as red as the traffic light.

'I hope it won't take long...' I was outside in a flash, pulling out my wallet. 'You see, inspector, I've got a viva. Quick, tell me what the fine is...'

'Ten schillings.'

Curse it, I hadn't any change. One, two, three, four schillings... not enough. A fifty-schilling note.

'Here's fifty schillings,' and I handed it to him. The conductor was boarding the tram.

'Ten schillings!... ain't got no change.' Hell and damnation!

'Please keep the fifty,' I begged. 'I have an all important exam – they are waiting for me. I'll fetch the change later!' The driver was getting aboard.

'P'raps I'd better get yer change now. Don't want no left-overs. Goin' inter shop fer change – then I gets ten schillings and don't owe no one nothing...'

'All aboard!' shouted the conductor; the tram-bell clanged.

'No!' I shouted to him. 'I've got to catch this tram and I'm going to (the board: my viva!). You can keep my passport (I *must* catch it). Keep the fifty schillings, the lot (what else could I do?) – but I *must* go on this tram!'

'You stay where y'are. You're under arrest!'

Everything began to go round and round, melting, wavering. Oh, no, not that – a whole year wasted! Perhaps never in such good form, ever again! No, not that! The tram was moving off – oh God, be merciful. The tram was moving on – merciful God... the tram... the sergeant... the Board... my viva. Tram, board, viva... *tram*!!

I was hanging on the step, my hands tight-gripped on the rail. The tram – despair, struggle, triumph...

The law was hanging on to my coat-tails. At the back of me. Useless. Good cloth this... but my police-friend wasn't a lightweight. However, I have strong hands. Of course, the strongest party concerned was the tram.

Something had to happen soon. I couldn't let go, now. I heard a seam rip. Titanic forces at work. I hung on desperately. So did he...

It turned into a superhuman display of strength, in which the tram was considerably involved. Seeing that my clothes were made in Austria and were therefore top-quality goods, and taking into account that while I am no giant, I am no weakling either, the odds against the arm of the law were three to one, and the tram – a good strong product of Semmering – won the national lottery.

Finals and a Police-sergeant

All of a sudden, I found myself free. I drew a deep breath of relief. My viva was safe!

Safe, for a few yards... surely not, surely not that?
There was a screeching, which cut deep into my soul – the trumpet of the day of Judgement... the tram was braking, coming to a halt.
This was the absolute end; I dared not turn round.
Very soon he had hold of me, panting, his face traffic-light red. 'Now, Y'come along of me!' he said, winding my tie round his arm. In front of all those people, too. I was being marched off. *Finis!*
I tried to explain things a bit. I was almost sorrier by now for him than for myself. He was covered in dust – through measuring his length in the road – so tight had his hold on me been. I couldn't have foreseen that – in any case, I couldn't have let go...
In a towering rage, he marched me off to the police station.
It was after 8 o'clock.
There was a telephone at the station. I rang the board up... I was in police-care... would be late...
'Have you been involved in a street-accident?'
'No – not directly (what could one say?).'
'Then be quick about it.'
Dear Lord, how much longer would they want me here?
Police-sergeant Pomeisl was there again (we were beginning to know one another). Again he wound my tie round his arm. 'Taking you to the district police station,' he announced.
Marched by the tie through respectable Hietzing, I didn't mind a hoot about the people: I minded a great deal about my viva.
By now he was only holding on to my coat. Should I chance it again? No – a sideways look reminded me that my sergeant had something of a Russian tank about him – yes, just that.

Officialdom was in full stride.
Another room, larger this time, with two officials in it. There was a telephone... I rang up the board.
'I'm afraid it'll take a little time. I have to clear one or two matters —'
'All right. But you'll have to be here in an hour at the latest.'
God willing, I would be.

'Sit down,' said an official, opening a book. He was tall, fair, polite, concise. 'How much money have you?' I counted it out. What on earth was all this about?
'Any offensive weapons – such as a pocket-knife? Put any pointed

articles on the table.' This was ridiculous. I wouldn't hurt a fly. All I want is to take my viva. I asked what this all meant. Politely and concisely, the official remarked: 'And now your shoe-laces and your tie.' ... Something was beginning to dawn on me: goodbye, viva!

'I forgot a tin-opener. I could cut a wrist-artery with that,' said I, bitingly, and dug savagely into my pocket (I am not very keen on *recherché* cooking). This was really the adjectival limit! Goodbye, viva!

One last hope. The station-superintendent. I want to see the superintendent. Now —!

I summoned up all my powers of persuasion and gave him my version of the dilemma. It worked; he understood me ... Proceedings suspended. My hour's grace was nearly over. The officer was concise, but not unfriendly. He had grasped what was at stake for me.

Of course, in the event, Pomeisl had only done his duty. (After all, what would happen to us in Austria if everyone who was in a hurry crossed on the red?) But the officer did more; he let me go in time for my viva!

I ran like a hare. The rain came down in torrents. I ran gasping round the blocks, then past trees, then two more streets. I made my appearance before the Board pale, breathless, soaked to the skin. Joy unalloyed! They were still there, and I was here. Water dripped from my suit on to the parquet-floor. Weren't they even annoyed with me? On the contrary, they were quite concerned about my state. 'But you can't take your viva like that; you are quite worn out!' they said. I sensed a great wave of sympathy – and I could have hugged friend Pomeisl. The police, I thought, your friends and helpers; I had them to thank for it. Out loud, I said: 'Of course I am fit to take my viva, I am used to great exertions; but (with a little bow) if the gentlemen of the board would be kind enough to give me five minutes, to sit down and collect myself— ?'

Not only did they give me five minutes, but they passed me with a 'Good' ...

Commercial arithmetic is a wonderful subject. A year or two later I made a submission to the directorate: '. . . I should be glad if, in the next syllabus, I could be allotted as many arithmetic classes as possible. For some reason or other I feel I have a special aptitude for the subject.' (And Susi, my new calculating machine, was a great help.)

The mills of justice grind slowly, but they do grind – not always a comfortable thought. In the end, my lawyer succeeded in getting the case transferred from Vienna to Salzburg. That was much more convenient; the court was in the next street.

There we were in a panelled room of the county court: the presiding magistrate, the public prosecutor, defending counsel, all in black robes... and, in the middle, on a slightly lower level, the defendant.

I was frankly anxious – you never know what may not happen. There was a picture of Justice hanging on the wall. I heard the words: 'You are charged, under paragraph 81 of the Act, of having offered open violence...'

'81 ... that's a wrong result', I thought.

'But, honestly, I couldn't have done anything else. If I had let go, I should have fallen on the back of my head, which is very dangerous; for, as everyone knows, looked at from any angle, the head is by far the most important part of the body...'

I was acquitted.

One more thing. I received a (not unexpected) official letter. 'On the –th day of — at Hietzing, during the performance of sergeant so-and-so's duty —' Pomeisl is a pseudonym – 'the officer's tunic suffered damage, for which you are duly held responsible. You are therefore required to pay a compensatory sum of S.50; in words, schillings fifty.'

I have learned something: always keep some change in your wallet.

PART IV

The Break-even

A rending and a splintering, as when a tall tree falls. Fear; stabbing pain ... I go hurtling through the air, impelled by some ungovernable force. My leg! Oh, you – *your* leg! One ski had bored deep into the ground. No! Oh, no! Bone-fragments, splinters ... I can see nothing, but I know well enough ... searing pain ...

I had had it.

... there was the tail-end of a ski in front of my eyes, the heel of a boot under my knee ... that heel belonged to me. So my leg must be twisted 180 degrees. I was on the point of passing out – thoughts: at least you have been on Dhaulagiri and Broad Peak ... searing pain ... fragments and fragments ... this was it ... I had had it ...

My brother-in-law Herbert and someone I didn't know dragged me to a hospital. I lay on a table while the doctors examined me. A rotational fracture, they pronounced.

'Are you on National Health?'

'No, private.'

'Too bad – in that case we haven't a bed for you at the moment ...'

God almighty! I was carted to another hospital, where there *was* room.

That day set its mark on three years of my life – years of hope, despair, doubts whether I should ever be able to go back to my mountains. Just a rotational fracture – not normally of any great account. Yet Bruno Winstersteller, who does Grade VI climbs on one leg, lost his that way; Carlo Mauri went limping around for years. It is possible to learn endless patience, to grit one's teeth, to live and see things differently, to hope and hope and hope ...

Even I could do that. In my case, callous refused to form where the broken ends of the bones had been set against each other, at least for a long time, and then not much. Finally, after six months, at first on my back with my leg in an elastic sling, later in a long plaster, they discharged me. Gingerly I put my weight on that poor little leg, grown thin and wooden as Pinocchio's, stiff in the knee and ankle, and half an inch shorter. Would it bear me?

At first it seemed to. I tottered my first hesitant steps, began to take long walks, got back on to rock. It was a very odd leg, but it held together. I even took it, treating it with the greatest solicitude, up the South Ridge of the Noire. Then I went to the post office where, with the feeblest of little reports, it broke again.

On my back once more; more plaster...

In spite of all, the period I spent in hospital was no all-time 'low'. A man who cannot walk a single step, who lies permanently fettered to the same spot, with the same window, the same wall before his eyes, lives a totally different life. He sees right through everything, transcending space and time, in a dimension not achieved by the swiftest voyager through space. Suddenly he realizes what a wonderful thing it is just to see the branch of a tree; and that others suffer pain more abominable than his own...

Only, one cannot stay in hospital for ever.

'The break-even ... is the moment in the course of a business venture when it shows neither profit nor loss. The business goes on, has no need to go into liquidation, but is unable to plough anything back; it simply maintains its entity. The only justification of its existence is the provision of its services...'

I had taken up a teaching post in business-management at a school outside Salzburg – a decision undoubtedly influenced by the disaster to my leg.

Not an easy decision to take for one who had lived 'free' to the age of thirty, without a 'boss', without a timetable drawn up by someone else; but also, of course, without security. To such a one it is damnably difficult to adopt what is called a 'regular routine', which provides that security at the expense of everything else. Yet, there comes a day when you ask yourself: 'What have you actually achieved?' And with the question comes the sudden feeling that only a 'normal career' is a career at all – and so you take a job.

It was autumn, and I was listening to the end-of-the-holidays address to the pupils:

The Break-even

'... to pick up your work again gladly and with strength renewed...'

All the same, the first year went well, and so did the second. I had my problems and dealt with them; after that, everything ran calmly along the same smooth track; and each year I was a year older and would be a year older each year – nothing else changing *en route* – till I was due for my retirement pension. I really enjoyed teaching; but my thoughts centred more and more on the knowledge that no pleasure, no improvisation, can permanently mitigate the monotonous burden of increasing regularity.

Ours is a ridiculous existence. Almost everyone today is a cog in an invisible machine, consisting almost entirely of bosses and employees. The boss is a lonely type. He is entirely pre-occupied with the morale of the workers in his business and the improvements required by that business; with bids, enquiries, turnovers. He nearly always ends up in splendid isolation – for few are they who bare their hearts to the boss...

And the employee? He watches everything being rationalized and does his own rationalization: trying to 'achieve a definite end with the slenderest means' instead of – and this is how the boss sees it – 'the greatest possible end with the means available'. Can the gulf between these concepts ever be bridged? Twenty-four hours are twenty-four hours for both men; the machinery is the same machinery. Is it possible, none the less, to garner enough satisfaction from that kind of daily round? I marvel at the imagination of those who think they can. But many fall by the wayside; they stick to their jobs and, gradually, their spirit grows rectangular – like the television screen, the container, the office bench, and their own bottoms, sitting on that bench. In fact, like the whole huge rectangular machine! But it is never too late for anyone to get up and go – for freedom of thought is always his, if he really wants freedom. And, above all, if he can still recognize the point where he has 'broken even'.

Just a day, a grey day – any day in the curriculum. I might have only five periods, or seven; in between them, gaps in the timetable, as in any occupation. I sit there, thinking and looking out: 'window-periods', like the air-spaces between the window-gratings. There they are, and they are no use to one. What have I done? What should I do? Security ... a living ... but time is passing; the sun circles in its course. There is a despairing entry in my diary: 'How much longer can I stand it?'

My young charges have no idea how I feel; we get on splendidly together. By now I have rationalized my work so well that I have a great deal of time in which to think – ample 'window-periods'. What am I to do?

I shut the next eight months away out of sight, waiting for the freedom of my next mountaineering expedition. But is that any solution? Time rotates slowly across the whole year, like the perforated dial of a musical clock, and there, day after day, one sits, between three pips of the mechanism, waiting for one's hour to strike. Perhaps I could write a book in those pauses? No, I have no feeling of freedom between the cogwheels of that clock.

And so I went on thinking and thinking: what am I to do? At times I tried to forget everything and to live just for the day. It was a kind of solution ... but for how long?

Then I found another. I told myself I would do one more year, and then go to a forestry school – a highly improbable pipe-dream. But now I knew that there was a term to my time here, and that made all the difference. Suddenly I felt that it did not matter greatly whether it was one year or two; what did matter was that I was not going to end my days here. That day I felt more free than for a long time past; I felt that school was a happy and sunny place, and my colourful tribe in great good humour. I managed to work in the business economics and financial aspects of a Himalayan expedition – not excluding the abominable snowman. In the evening I, the non-skittler, went with my class to a skittle-alley, and for the first time in my life took all nine. We discussed our various problems and – *Gaudeamus Igitur!* – were thoroughly happy. The whole world lay open to us – yes, to them and me, too.

Nothing could upset me very much at the school after that day; for I knew my days were numbered.

It was Christmas-time. My class had presented me with an eight-armed octopus made of black wool, with red eyes, inscribed: 'For our Yeti, on all steep climbs.' *I* was the Yeti, the snowman. I, who had told them I believed in it, who had seen photographs of its tracks.

I should hate leaving. We had all been bound together, as it were, by a common fate. But not by the one for me: not permanently. I had got to go, even though I did not know where to ... perhaps to some under-developed country?

I had spent five whole years of my life here ...

We celebrated the end of term; my class was leaving. It was a mixture of addresses, champagne, happy faces, the holiday atmosphere, gaiety. The blonde Elisabeth – spokeswoman for the whole 'mixed' class –

handed me a huge black cube. 'For our Yeti,' she laughed, and all the others grinned.

'Hm!' I wondered. 'What's all this about?'

I saw the glint of a catch and pressed it. Wumph! The lid flew open: a black ball, black as the very devil, leaped at me on the end of a coiled spring and swung backwards and forwards in front of my eyes. On it was 'A2', the name of my class. It was only then that I discovered what was written on the outside of the black box: ... 'The Break-even' ... because I had spoken of it so often.

It forms a feature of my furniture now; it stands in the middle of my table. The impression it makes is part serious, part cheerful.

The Fourth Dimension

I found the same pale-red flower, with four petals and a distinctive cross at its heart, near the edge of a glacier in the Hindu Kush and on the shore of a Greenland fjord teeming with icebergs.

What had borne it round the world?

Suddenly you find a link between two distant parts of the world. Mankind does not even need speech.

Then there was Bianca. What I have to tell of her is not a love-story. It is something quite different – something that lives among the grasses, between the waves of the sea at Duino and on the broad expanse of the Karst.* We called it the fourth dimension.

Love? I do not know if one can give the name to such an understanding as this. There is something more to it than that. And I believe it is something everyone is capable of finding.

The waves at Duino . . . Rilke wrote there, in the old walled castle, and he saw those waves as they are still to be seen today – differently by each beholder, different in themselves according to the day on which they are seen, yet always the same incomparable insurge of curving wave-forms, one overlaying the other.

There, below the old walls of the castle, below the trees and grasses that grow between the rain-eroded, skeletal limestone of the Karst, the huge twisted rock-faces of the peninsula plunge vertical to the sea.

The cliffs sweep up some 300 feet. At their base break the waves which come surging in from far out and surge back outwards again, with diminished force, curving, overlaying each other. Sometimes too, when the wind has set the thousand particles of deepest blue in swirling motion somewhere far out there, they themselves stay there. When, in the end, their motion, overleaping thousands of other particles, reaches the coast, this time to impinge obliquely, thrown back by slabs and buttresses, on the curves in the rock-face, and is flung back in the other

---

* The Karst is a broad limestone plateau, arid, scrub-covered, pot-holed, fringing the coast near Trieste. – Translator's note.

The Fourth Dimension

direction from the caves, over-running itself three and four times, obliquely at varying speeds – the matchless spectacle is such that the watcher, looking down on it 300-feet sheer, would do well to hold on to something for support. And yet, at the same time, there is a concept he can grasp; and, if he does so, he will gaze and gaze, unable to tear himself away...

The fourth dimension. Not only time, but many mingling dimensions. There, in the depths below, in the rise and fall of blue particles.

Bianca is a big girl and her eyes are dark. She comes from Istria. Always something of an enigma – she is for the most part fearfully energetic, as if she might lose one minute's-worth of life. Then again, she will be absolutely quiet – that is how she is. She has always a mass of things to do – her job, school, theatre; but when she climbs, rippling up the most difficult pitches with an incredibly natural lightness of movement – then she is quiet. Those are the two sides of Bianca. She can lead anything up to Grade VI, loves the mountains, the Karst and the sea; but she has no positive attitude towards the world – she says the difference is too great.

I had been lecturing in Trieste. I had spoken with enthusiasm of the mountains, looking up at my pictures on the screen – pictures of all the peaks I did not know whether I should ever be involved with again, because of my broken leg: not that it altered my love for them one whit.

Suddenly, there was Bianca facing me. She seized me by the arm, dragged me away through all the after-lecture confusion. 'Come along, let's drink a glass of beer,' she commanded; but before we could really start talking, all our friends joined us: Spiro, Walter, Fioretta, Erich, Violetta, and the evening turned into a cheery Trieste party.

All the same, next day, in the evening, we had our tête-à-tête talk. 'One shouldn't think...' she proclaimed. I wondered how much thinking she had done, before arriving at that thought.

'I believe one should think...' I countered. (I too had done a good deal of thinking.)

Between a 'yes' and a 'no' lie all the dimensions of this world.

The waters gulped and gurgled between the stones, the smell of the sea rose up to us – the delicate pink of the jellyfish shimmered and pulsated, multi-coloured, the mussels gleamed bright and black.

The grasses of the Karst. Clouds, trembling in the summer air. Greenish-black seaweed, greasy and heavy, feeling out into the moving waters like fingers.

This – all of it – was the present.

We went on across the Karst, over the rocky ribs at the heart of the Duino woods, till we stood at the edge, high above the waves. There they were, deep, deep below us – so that we had to hang on, craning far out to look down.

Suddenly I said: 'Look – over there – can you see it? – the waves, running over each other – more and more . . . ?'

'How can it be?' she cried.

Waves . . . waves . . . more waves . . . as we seemed to look into a gigantic globe.

'*E incredibile* – beyond all belief!' she breathed.

It was overpowering. We squeezed each other's hands.

The movement continued, sweeping over the transparent blue deeps with a compulsive regularity; cones of waves, of dimensions overlaying each other; a whole fine-spun web of time, unbelievably close-woven, pressing inwards from all directions. For long moments I felt that we were levitating at the heart of it – free of all contact with the ground beneath our feet.

'*La quarta dimensione*,' said Bianca. The fourth dimension. Or was it the fifth? Was it ours, or not only ours, but belonging to others as well? If so, to how many? Today it belonged to us, or we belonged to it. The difference was quite meaningless.

'It is ours,' she said, 'let us call it that and keep it so.'

We kept it so.

I have often wondered what it is that draws so many people to water. For there are countless numbers who watch the waves.

One day, suddenly, I realized something which started a new experience, into an unknown realm, into a line of thought more exciting for me than even a great voyage or climb. It suddenly dawned on me that time is only a part, perhaps only an expression of that higher dimension – even though time in itself is an unimaginable concept, so huge that none of us can understand it. Yet suppose one could grasp its meaning and, all unknowingly, most clearly of all just when one looks at the water and sees the waves over-running each other?

Over-running . . .

I have tried hard to solve the enigma.

I am standing on an enormous vertical slab of rock. From far away out there the waves come rolling in to break against the rocks at my feet and then roll away again in the opposite direction . . . lines that come, lines that go. The moment of impact against the cliff is a fact – the 'now' – the present time. Looked at in this way, the next wave, just

The Fourth Dimension

rolling in, brings the future; and the one thrown back outwards and receding, carries away with it the past. Successive waves represent the more distant future or the more distant past, and they are exactly superimposed; everywhere the past is rolling over the future, or the other way about. And they meet at the same point.

Is it such a fanciful vision? I do not think so. I can see the waves rolling farther and farther back towards the horizon, see the past meeting the future as it rolls in towards it, see that somewhere beyond that horizon the most distant past must meet the most distant future.

But then, the earth is round, isn't it?

Suppose it were completely covered by the sea and I were standing alone here on this slab, which springs from the ground like a shield, then that most distant past would come rolling in at my back, break against the rock and immediately hurry away, as the most distant future, towards the horizon, growing 'younger' – more immediate – till it came round again and broke, in front of me, at my feet – as the present.

That can only mean that here, on the slab beneath my feet, separated only by that thin sliver of rock, and approaching from both sides, the present and the remotest future – which, again, is born of the remotest past – meet one another.

Time encompasses even space.

And now some mountaineering friend will bang me on the head with my book. For my next question is this: what happens if the slab – the Stance – suddenly subsides, to be drowned in the waters – an alarming suggestion...?

Then, of course, the waves of the most distant past would, in that instant, sweep over you and your immediate present, just as the immediate future merges into the most remote. The very stance of your existence would have disappeared. Two eternal orbits would be turning in opposite directions.

Would they do so – sustained by divine tension? Or would they cancel each other out in a mutual Nirvana? Would all waves then roll in from one direction only? Would some new rock spring from the ground? Would you, as one who knows how to swim, be made eternal, or, as a materialist, drown out of hand? Or are you yourself the breath of one of those orbits?

I see a spider roping itself down from the ceiling on its exiguous thread. I love this earth of ours.

Something makes the blue particles of the waters ripple.

What makes them?
They do it.
What makes them?
They do it – whensoever the wind falls anywhere on the broad surface of the sea.

Ordeal by Fire

The Aiguille Noire is a magnificent peak. Sharp as a sword she cleaves the sky. Or a huge black sail.

The mountain exacts the ultimate from the climber, just because of its size. All its routes are steep and long. Even the East ridge, a Grade III climb, is not easy. The other ridges, South, West and North and the West Face, are huge, exciting climbs, Grades V and VI, on firm granite. Few are they who can climb any of these in a single day. No, it is not easy to reach the tip of that sail, high in the sky, up in the clouds; but that is what makes it so splendid – a dream peak.

And then, suddenly, something can happen which leaves you shaking every time it comes to memory.

For on some days the Aiguille Noire can transform itself, all of a sudden, into a terrible ship. And then, having battened down, beyond all means of escape, whomsoever she has lured on to her fatal deck, she sails away through timeless time with him on board, spewing electricity, shuddering under the hammer blows of the lightning, which races to earth down her steep sides, on every hand.

What then of him who is caught on the rocks of her summit? He sits at the heart of the storm-centre of some strange planet; trapped in the deadly labyrinth of invisible forces, whose laws he knows not; the victim of vindictive furies; shaken by shock after shock; faced by a black question, whose answer is beyond his comprehension; unable to do do anything about it. And so he is borne headlong, farther and farther through time, among the screaming clouds at the tip of that sail. Or, rather, perhaps, on an electric chair of gigantic proportions.

We ourselves have to thank blind luck and the strength of the bond between us all for our safe return to the world below...

Later, Bianca told her story:

'There were six of us on the South Ridge, climbing happily, light-heartedly, because the sun was warm and we were all friends together. Far below, the Val Veni shone green, dotted with the gay colours of the tents on the camping-site, a joy to look at. I felt like a new being, thinking of the lush, warm grass and the pleasure of treading it barefoot when I got down there again. I looked at the shining blue and white cataract of the Fresnay Glacier, and up at Mont Blanc. And, although this was my first time on this granite wedge of ours, I felt as if I had always known it. I would have been content to go on like this, moving upwards, gazing about me, for timeless ages, submerged in that sea of light under the taut, deep sky.'

I was climbing with Tona, behind the other ropes. We had not been to the mountains for a long time and we were glad to be back, even if my bad leg was still troublesome. Actually, I was disappointed about it, but, I thought, this was, after all, only the start; and I was happy in the knowledge that we were all together here on the ridge, and that it was I who had brought them here. Tona, her long fair hair escaping from her helmet, happily gripping the holds in the good granite, climbing up and up, hand-hold and foot-hold, along the 'Way of the Film', whose sequences we had once so laboriously edited. Terenzio – 'the Voice' – who had seen the film projected, and was now seeing it live. Mario, his partner, on this huge ridge for the first time. Walter and Bianca, shouting down cheerfully from above.

There we were, each of us experiencing the ridge in his own way, thinking his own thoughts; but our hands used the same holds, we enjoyed the same sunshine, and we were united by the bonds of friendship.

It was my third ascent of the South Ridge, and it was a marvellous day; I found new variants, recognized the old pitches, thought of Wolfi and Franz. Finally, we bivouacked on the third tower, the Pointe Welzenbach. It was a luxury bivouac; two comfortable granite beds, with clean little table-like slabs. We looked up at the vertical upthrust of the Pointe Brendel and the Pointe Bich. Above them glittered a thousand stars.

Towards evening, next day, we were close under the subsidiary summit, climbing on two ropes: Tona, Terenzio and Mario on ahead, Walter, Bianca and I about 300 feet behind.

Let Tona take up the tale:

'We had dealt with the difficult pitches of the Pointe Bich and knew we were quite close to the summit of the Noire. The subsidiary was just at the top of the next couloir. It was almost dusk, and we were moving quickly, for we intended to bivouac somewhere on the normal descent from the summit after crossing it. The sky had been wonderfully clear in the morning; but now it was being invaded by masses of cirrus, strangely-shaped and fantastic in colouring: flowers, fishes,

Ordeal by Fire

dragons... We ought to press on, for the weather would certainly be bad tomorrow. The clouds were coming in from the west, and we, on the south-east face of the mountain, watched them dissipating, as if by magic, just above our heads. And then, one of them failed to dissipate...'

There was an uncanny silence; it was suddenly dark, as a gigantic fish swam across the sky. Down in the valley the lights were going on: it was 8 o'clock. Time to find a bivouac site. Could we still catch the other up?

Suddenly we lay under an inexplicable threat, descending directly on us – a kind of tension, an invisible curtain, closing in all about us, closing inexorably down on the black rocks of the subsidiary summit...

A streak of fire split the firmament. There was a crash, which nearly lifted us off our feet, a hissing roar, as if a tidal wave were sweeping down the rocks, a fearful impact... right through our bodies it ran... the elements shook, in us, all around us... for long seconds chaos reigned... an electric salvo on an unprotected column...

The air echoed with shouts. 'Quick, on to that ledge!' 'Get down off the ridge!' 'The ironmongery – get rid of it!'

Then the next bludgeoning blow fell, in blinding light, with a rending crash. The distorted faces, the bowed figures of Walter and Bianca...

The whole ironmonger's shop came rattling down the rope to me on a carabiner. A nice present! Hell! Into a rock-cranny with it, somewhere. Dynamite in my hands...

Hailstorms, another blinding flash, another hammer-blow. The clatter of falling equipment, up above. A shout? My heart gave a stab. The others must be close under the summit up there. Great God – Tona ... why weren't we together?

There was no way up to her.

Walter, Bianca and I, and the bivouac-bag. We held hands. More crashes... Tona, Mario, Terenzio – suppose...?

'What is it, Kurt?' asked Bianca.

'Tona —'

The thought of that was worse than my fear for myself. Suppose?

'Terenzio and Mario are with her,' she said.

No way up. There, on the next pitch, millions of volts were racing to earth down the crest. No way up; no way back. Each successive crack went rumbling down the crest of the ridge with the crazy speed of a runaway train.

Dear God... there is nothing I can do.

· · · · ·

Tona, again:

'And then one cloud failed to dissipate. A rumbling blow struck and shook the face. "Lightning," said Terenzio, calmly.

'We bundled the pitons together as quickly as we could; sent every metal object flying down the face. We were almost at the summit, but who would risk crossing it at this moment? I put my down-jacket on. It was almost pitch-dark.

'I felt a whiplash crack in my back; my head was enveloped in flame. Hildegard! I thought: My Hildegard! Again that flame, another explosion, and I knew no more . . . Terenzio's face appearing out of the darkness, smiling. God knows why smiling: "Are you all right?" At all events, the three of us were alive, crushed hard against the face.

'It was snowing now. Thirty feet above our heads, the tongues of lightning were racing down the ridge. A crash to each lightning-flash. We tried to cover ourselves with the bivouac-bag. I couldn't move my right leg; it was quite numb. (Struck by lightning, of course.) Terenzio helped me. Mario was shattered, overwhelmed, behaving strangely. We stood upright all night long, for there was nowhere to sit, on that face.'

They had all three been struck, by various branches of that flaming shaft of lightning. It leaped into their bodies from the rock or out of the air, sweeping their faces and their clothing, running to earth through the soles of their boots. Tona had two burn-holes the size of florins in the palms of her hands, a larger one in her right ankle – burnt right through her sock – one of her bootnails was blackened. Mario had a similar wound in his back, Terenzio in his foot; his shoulder, like all their clothing, was punctured by innumerable barbs of lightning. The storm raged unbroken from 8 p.m. till 2 a.m. None of them knew then that it was only the beginning: that eight more thunderstorms were to follow, during thirty more hours. They killed five people in the Mont Blanc group.

Again Tona:

'We stood upright all night long . . . It was still snowing next morning, but the thunder had stopped for the time being. It was high time to quit our over-narrow stance, so we tried to make our way up the ridge overhead. The air was saturated with electricity; the rock was crackling with it. Our movements disturbed its equilibrium; a discharge exploded into light around us and a ball of fire went rolling down the ridge.

'We roped down a little way, till we reached a small ledge, just large enough to house the three of us, jammed close together. A great boulder

Ordeal by Fire

gave us protection from the direction of the summit. We used snow to heighten our protective cover, till we were in a little niche.' [It was not till then that they noticed their dark purple burns. Tona's leg slowly recovered sensation.]

'The thunder-storms succeeded one another, close on each other's heels. We tried to make ourselves as small as possible, to reduce ourselves to nothing, to disappear altogether.'

They were panic-smitten lest they should be struck again. Wouldn't it ever let up? Had the sun vanished for ever? It went on snowing, there were more lightning-flashes, and still the snow fell. A whole day passed; another night. Their faces were caked with ice, great shudders racked them. How much longer?

Were they going to die here, waiting in a niche, a few feet below the summit? In the end, that is what they came to believe.

Two of our friends, Gino and Silvia, overtaken by the storm, had managed to retreat, just in time, from the Innominata ridge of Mont Blanc...

They looked up at the Aiguille Noire, dazzling white, piercing the clouds like a sword – armour-plated, ethereal, a mountain from some other world, a huge glittering sail.

Suddenly the thought halted them in their tracks: hadn't Walter and Bianca, Kurt and Tona, Terenzio and Mario planned to — ? Could they still be up there? Oh, no – not that!

But they *were* still up there, they *must* be; two Englishmen, who had just managed to escape from the storm on the Noire, confirmed it. Gino and Silvia raised the alarm, rang through to Spiro dalla Porta in Trieste, managed, in the end, to get in touch with Walter Bonatti...

There was no hope of getting to the summit of the Noire in that storm – it would be sheer lunacy to try. The lightning would kill anyone on the ridge. But Walter Bonatti bit his lip and looked at Gallieni, standing by his side, remembering the tragedy on the Pillar Fresnay, which they had both survived: the endless days of that storm, the fearful lightning-flashes, the attempt to get down to the valley – which only he, Gallieni and Mazeaud had reached alive. The other four had all died, of exposure and exhaustion, one after another...

'Hell! It looks just the same as it did then for us!' said Gallieni.

Bonatti knew it, too, but he did not hesitate to mount an immediate rescue-operation. Meanwhile, Spiro had driven over from Trieste with a group of friends – one of them, Dumbo, just home after seven years in Africa...

Summits and Secrets

The summit of the Noire went winging, white, white from head to foot, into the dark, hurrying cloud-wrack. It looked uninhabited, uninhabitable by man...

On the crest of the ridge above our heads, the storm continued to rage – a dull, regular noise, only occasionally waxing and waning. The precipices below us shone bright in the pale light of the flashes. White all over, snow and ice plastered on every crack and cranny, the protuberances disappearing under a white pall.

Another detonation; the blast of it went through us as if we were a single body, and we groaned. This might have been the North Face of the Eiger in midwinter, under a network of electricity – escape? The lightning-flashes tore along the crest, down the gullies around us, everywhere, hurtling down from the summit, a deadly network. If we got up, that would be it; if we didn't, what then?

The snow kept on falling, piling up deeper and deeper. Everything around us was flattened out by it. Even ourselves. Every moment, survival was becoming more unlikely, even if we escaped being struck by lightning.

And what about the others? All we knew was that they were just beyond the subsidiary summit. We had heard their voices, so we knew they had survived the first storm. But, directly after the fearful crash generated by their movement, the second storm had come racing in. They were on their own, as we were on our own. We could only think – were they still alive? I didn't want to think, I only wanted to hope. Yet I had to think...

And what of Walter and Bianca, here with me?

This is what she said, later:

'I wanted to say something to my friends, but they were so motionless and silent, shut into themselves, each in a world of his own. So I didn't disturb them.

'It was I who had wanted to do the climb, and I knew that something like this could happen. I had come with my eyes open, and this must have all been decreed by time and fate. And now it had happened.'

The snow weighed heavy upon our bodies, now.

'To die is as natural as to be born... why did we find that simple fact as terrible as it was absurd? Perhaps, because it is logical when you only think of it, but becomes absurd when you experience it...' Another thunderstorm came rolling in.

'No, we shall never get out of this alive.'

· · · · ·

Ordeal by Fire

It had cleared for a moment. There was snow everywhere, the summit wintry-white. Beneath our feet lay the green of the valley, 7,000 feet below. Something out of the distant past: the Val Veni.

Look, way down there, an aircraft, skimming the ridges! Was it searching for someone – us?

A strong north-west wind was chasing clouds across all the peaks. It was thundering again behind Mont Blanc. The plane droned on across the ridges and was lost to sight. Walter was sobbing; he was the worst hit of our trio, having been struck glancing blows off the rock, on his shoulder and head. He was wearing a *portafortuna*, a charm, around his neck, a little gold charm; but we didn't profit by it till later on.

'Here comes the next one,' said Bianca, looking through a hole in the bivouac-bag.

Rumbumbum ... it came rolling in, exactly at our level, at the speed of a train. Clouds like phantom ships, black, convulsed, mocking, feeling round with dark arms that grew and then dissipated. Every atom of rock around us was alive, moving, disintegrating. The notion shot through my mind that we were water, a cone of water, rising up from the earth below – no wonder the lightning made use of it, I thought. We held hands hard. 'This is a nasty one,' said Walter. Then there was cloud around our peppered bivouac-bag, and, for a time, silence.

'**********, oh!' a moan, a flame and a shock, driving through every muscle of our bodies. That was a near thing! Plumb into the ridge next to us, on the rocky head of the Bich. And now what?

Now? ... nothing. We held hands.

Now? ... nothing. You ...

Now? ... nothing ... the rocks ...

Silence, silence, silence. But the lightning *must* come! What lightning? The next one, of course. Locked hands; mine, Bianca's, Walter's, tight-pressed in one another's ...

'*Xracks ... huiiiiiiii ...*' We were still alive ...

'*... pflob ... dump ... xssss*,' said the spirit-voices. Each flash was different. Electro-shocks, lifting us up, every time. Were they driving us mad? No sleep ...

There was one thing I have never quite understood to this day – in the end, I was enveloped by a sense of completely relaxed confidence, which included death itself. It may sound ridiculous, but I continued to make tea, and again tea. Just in case the thunder chose to stop some time; but also in case it lasted too long for us to survive it. I thought of Tona, hoping that she was still alive; I thought of a safe return to the valley and a resumption of life, down there. I also thought how it might be our fate to stay up here and never see each other again. All the same...

I made tea... and I made tea... it was the only thing I could do to keep a flicker of energy alive in us – even if it was to no purpose.

Gradually we began to believe we were becoming part of the snow and the rock.

Tona, once more:

'The fourth day dawned. The sky was grey; but, at last, it was quiet. Mario took the lead, as we started off, moving slowly and safely.

'We heard voices... they were here... Kurt... We looked at each other, and smiled. The six of us were together again, and we knew, then, that we should get down.'

We went on down the East ridge. Snow fell again, in heaps. We were mere animals now, capable of standing anything. Utterly weary, utterly resigned and patient. There was no other way, in spite of the cold and our failing limbs. One thought kept us going: we had traversed the summit, the lightning had stopped, there was one more day – tomorrow – to get through, then we would be back in the land of the living again. A fourth bivouac-night; then one more day to get through!

I made tea, hot tea, and again hot tea.

Wallop! A snow slide had buried Walter and Bianca in their bivouac-bag. Light, cold powder-snow. For the umpteenth time, the bivouac-bag shook itself like a dog.

'Tea! Tea coming up!'

Faint sunshine, driving mists. For a moment we could see the towers on the South ridge, before cloud closed down again. We attempted a sort of Indian dance, to get warm; breathless, we abandoned it as soon as started.

It was a good thing there were so many of us. We were a unity, slowly feeling its way down to earth, obeying its dictates, slowly and unflinchingly. Each of us, when he had to do something – actual climbing, belaying – was on the job; between times he retired into some spiritual vacuum. I noticed it myself: every time I was not safeguarding the rope or feeling for the next hand-hold, I dreamed of green fields, sunshine, its warmth on my skin. Actually, it would not have been painful to slip away into a twilight sleep – without a twilight, it would be – but we none of us wanted it. We would still get down below the snow-line today, down into the broad saddle, where the East ridge starts,

Ordeal by Fire

perhaps even farther down than that. We were not scared by the thought of yet another bivouac – it couldn't compare for horror with the last three. And it would be far down the mountain; there might even be some grass. And, now, it had, at last, turned fine . . .

Shouts? Surely, shouts? Someone was coming up from the depths. Was it really Walter Bonatti? Yes, it was Walter – down there on the snow-clad slabs – and someone else. I roared back at him, overcome with delight.

'*Siete tutti* – are you all there?' he was asking from down there.

'*Siamo tutti, e salvi*! Yes, all of us, all well!' (Even if that wasn't absolutely true – the lightning had stabbed three of us – but, for the time being . . .)

Our spirits shot up. Movement, life stirred afresh.

Suddenly, I felt indescribably weary.

Nothing excels the guides' technical skill in bringing a party down a skein of good. fixed ropes. At each piton I greeted another familiar face. Cosimo . . . Bertone . . . farther down, Gigi Panei. We gripped hands. Everyone, including those who waited down in the valley, Spiro, Aldo, Dumbo. Hands, and more hands . . .

We were overwhelmed with a sense of blissful security, comfort, gratitude . . . and sheer amazement, to have come back from that other world, down from that utterly different world.

Nobody may have noticed it, but once we were down in the meadow, we felt ourselves in the heady ambience of an angel-world. I am sure there were those who thought: 'How can they smile, after what they have been through?'

That was precisely why we could.

Higher than the Eagle Soars
HINDU KUSH

'Hindu Kush – what on earth's that?' Ten years ago most climbers would have asked the question, furrowing their brows; for that marvellous mountain range lay for many years in the shadow of the Himalaya and Karakorum. Though its summits rise to 23,000 feet and more, there are no eight-thousanders, so nobody noticed them.

In Britain's days of colonization, a few surveyors had penetrated those deeply-carved valleys. Troops gazed up at the peaks; British soldiers in the south-east, Russian Cossacks from the north-west. A British officer, Younghusband, even reported a clash with a Cossack squadron, which was cheerfully pushing on into Afghan territory, after the Russian annexation of the Pamirs. Finally, towards the end of last century, the narrow corridor of the Wakhan was constituted as Afghan territory, thus separating the two major powers from direct contact.

The wheel of time turned; after the Second World War, India and Pakistan emerged as independent nations and Chitral, in which stand the highest summits of the Hindu Kush, is today part of Pakistan. Yet the main mass of the range lies in Afghanistan, cutting through that country roughly from south-west to north-east; its wall of white peaks finally providing, to the south of the Oxus, which flows through the Wakhan, the frontier with Pakistan.

The Hindu Kush were already of importance in ancient times. They then bore the name of Parapomisus – meaning 'higher than the eagle soars'. Greek and Mongol armies bore down over its passes, and the caravans bringing the precious silk from China followed the course of the Oxus.

It was not till 1960 that climbers were to be seen passing through the Wakhan. Now the number of smaller or larger expeditions following the old silk-route grows steadily every year, on their way to the summits of the Hindu Kush.

Others again came from the south, by way of Chitral. There were a few early incursions, real pioneering enterprises, such as the attacks by British officers on Istor-o-Nal, 1929 and 1935 (Colonel Lawder) when it was very difficult to get porters, the local people being afraid of mountain ghosts. Later on there was the daring and successful Norwegian attempt in 1950 on Tirich Mir (25,263 feet and the highest peak in the range) and the ascent of Saraghrar also more than 23,000 feet high, by Fosco Maraini and his very large expedition in 1959. After that there began a real 'tribal-displacement' of Germans, Poles, Japanese, Austrians and, not the least among them, again British and Italians. More and more climbers were fascinated by the savage mountain-world of the Hindu Kush, by the tales they heard from those who had been there, by the pictures of mighty faces and ridges, sharp summits, raging torrents, which had to be crossed, secluded valleys, upland villages whose inhabitants were simple, friendly folk. The Hindu Kush had been 'discovered' and, within the space of a very few years, there followed an invasion almost impossible to keep under review.

My father, who had out of sheer personal interest involved himself in recording the events in this area – he has since been made an honorary member of the Himalayan Club – was soon the only person who really knew which summits had been climbed and which still offered a prize, where the most interesting objectives could be found, and how to get them. The paradox being, of course, that he has never been to the Hindu Kush. None the less, the walls of his room were covered to the ceiling with photographs of this world of glorious mountains: so he 'must have been everywhere'. With the advent of spring, not a week passed without some intended expedition appearing on his doorstep, wanting to know 'everything'. They left for their appointed target armed with maps, sketch-maps and all the information they needed...

What seems to me the most important feature is that they were mostly small undertakings, adventurous even in the matter of the outward journey; three or four climbers who just got together and said: 'Let's go!' People who might, for example, buy an old postal-bus in Germany, drive all the way in it, and sell it when they got there (to be seen plying on some out-of-the-way route today). People who obtained a permit to go as far as a village called Langar, and then proceeded to march the whole length of the Wakhan corridor because, at the other end of it, they knew there was another hamlet also called Langar. People who never reached their destination; people who, after travelling thousands of miles, had to watch their wrecked car being hoisted out of a ditch by camels, and towed away.

Definitely, this was the evolution of a new 'race' – the men of the Hindu Kush. Their characteristics: a strong taste for adventure, very little money, love of a gamble – the whole thing often rested on the turn of a card. If you are prepared to start out in an old car to cover 12,000 miles, there and back – half the distance round the world – and then to climb a mountain, and a high one at that – you have to be fairly happy-go-lucky and self-reliant.

We certainly were...

I will only try to sketch a brief picture of some of our experiences; they must needs be incompletely portrayed. I have been there twice, and I shall be going there again. I shall certainly have to write a book confined entirely to the Hindu Kush. One could write so much about them, quite apart from the things that happened to me personally.

'Inshallah' – in three-four time

A car, decorated with a large international 'A' for Austria, goes bumping through the Lut desert, on three cylinders: ... *ta tata* ... *ta tata* ... *ta tata* ...

It belongs to us – Franz, Tona, Herwig and me – though Franz, who did the Peuteret ridge with me is not with us; he will be coming out by air.

We others are driving to Pakistan in the firm's own delivery-van (we are a kind of Tirich Mir Co. Ltd., only without Articles of Association) with 1,000 lbs. of luggage aboard. The expertly stowed cases are covered by a couple of sorbo mats, on which we sleep, by turns, as the journey continues, day and night, without a break.

Who was this Herwig? He was the comfortable antithesis to the uncomfortable rhythm of our engine. Franz had introduced us to this strongly-built road-construction engineer from St Pölten, who had a fair knowledge of cars and machinery generally. So long as Herwig was happy, our expedition went rolling merrily along.

Ta tata ... ta tata ... ta tata ...

It was he, too, who had christened the car 'Murl'. As he said, an old car has a personality and deserves a name. 'Eh, Murl?'

I turned the fan on, and a succulent aroma of coffee came streaming in, accompanied by a furnace-like blast of heat. Coffee from real coffee beans – it isn't every car that can produce an atmosphere like that! No, our (at present) three-cylinder model was unique. It had delivered coffee for 60,000 miles and was now in retirement.

Ta tata ... ta tata ... ta tata ...

Why just Murl? Well, in Austria it is a favourite pet-name for those large flying beetles that make a buzzing noise, as well as for small, shaggy dogs; also, it sounds as round as a worn-out tyre, and so familiarly Austrian – like the present rhythm of our engine ... *ta tata ... ta tata ...*

6. The Road to Tirich Mir

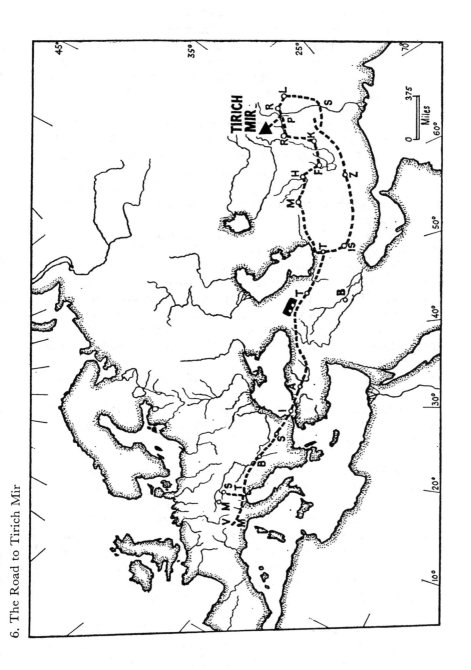

There was no element of haste about our progress – no doubt we should get there in due course. Tona drove by day, Herwig by night, and sometimes during the day as well. And I – I had as yet no assignment, for owing to so much mountaineering, I had so far neglected to pass my driving test. That was still to come, before our second trip. Meanwhile, I salved my conscience with the good intention of carrying more rucksacks than the others, when we got there.

Herwig was very good company, always calm and equable. We often sang – all through the night – it helped the driver to keep awake, a highly desirable objective. My guitar came in very handy, for our portable emitted nothing but oriental '*Jaiii, jaoooo, jaeee*' – liable to send the man at the wheel to sleep. When everything else failed, I just reminded Herwig of the dealer in Vienna who sold him Murl. That woke him up instantly.

When the morning sun climbed lemon-yellow out of the desert, Herwig knew his stint was finished, and Tona took over at the helm. Then the whole scene would gradually change colour. The pleasant early warmth swiftly increased to searing, blinding heat, which shook the ground into vibrating waves, making it impossible to touch the van's roof or to set a bare foot on the floor, even for an instant. It was July, the hottest time of the year. The countryside would change to a leaden hue, then rusty-brown, then yellow. We wondered what colour it really was.

There were plains, ridges of sandhills, mountains, and a vast emptiness...

The desert is a magnificent thing. I would never have believed it could offer so much to marvel at: the occasional oasis, an unexpected green field with a couple of trees, then suddenly in the midst of the sand – water.

Rain has become an old-time fairy-tale. Of course, such a thing exists, but it has grown impossible, here, to visualize what it is like, Rain? A figment of the imagination, a dispensation of fantasy, remote. remote, remote... And yet, we were continually surrounded by wide mirror-like sheets of water, out of which rose bright-yellow dunes, like flowers, quivering, floating, rising and falling, and then again suddenly taking on firm outlines; acquiring as we drove towards it hard reality, rising out of the solid ground which, a short time ago, was water. And then, behind us, where we had been driving, there stretched another wide, mirror-like expanse...

All sorts of other things, too. During a brief halt, I found in the sand what I took to be a feather; but it wasn't a feather, it was the seed of some plant, with a slightly-tilted corkscrew-like thread under it – the

20. Tona Sironi Diemberger after surviving a direct lightning hit near the summit of the Aiguille Noire in 1963 (see page 246). The lightning, not conducted by her helmet, skimmed her forehead, went into her hand, burnt her heel and sock and took its exit by a nail in her boot's rubber sole. Tona, the author's first wife, remains a keen climber and a close friend, and translates all his books into Italian.

21. (*right*) The Peuterey Ridge of Mont Blanc (seen here from the Grandes Jorasses) is the author's favourite alpine climb. The Aig. Noire (the pointed peak on extreme left) is best climbed by its classic South Ridge. A long series of abseils then lead down the North Ridge to the Dames Anglais. The Aig. Blanche is traversed and then a grand finale is provided by the majestic ice slopes and ridges of the highest mountain of Western Europe.
In 1958, partnered by Franz Lindner, the author filmed this great alpine classic and later won the main prize at the Trento Film Festival.

22. (*below*) The author leads on the steep, firm rock of the Pointe Bich on the South Ridge of the Aig.Noire during an earlier ascent.
Photo: Wolfgang Stefan.

23. (*lower right*) Filming the Aig. Noire at sunset from Punta Gugliermina. The North Ridge (used for the abseil descent) is the line of light and shade. *Photo: Franz. Lindner.*

DHAULAGIRI, 1960   24. The north-eastern aspect of Dhaulagiri with the North-East Ridge (the first ascent route) in the centre, the East Face to its left (climbed in 1981, alpine-style, by a Franco/Anglo Polish quartet)) and the dangerous South-East Ridge on the extreme left (climbed in 1978 by a large Japanese expedition – with four fatalities). The Pear Route takes the shadowy slopes on the right.

25. The 'Yeti' in which Ernst Saxer and Emil Wick ferried loads and climbers to the North-East Col – a key to the success of the 1960 expedition. Later it crashed (as seen here) on the Dapa (Dambush) Col.

26. Dhaulagiri was first tackled on the northern flank by way of one of its distinctive pear-shaped buttresses, but these were so steep and featureless that finding campsites became a major problem. In 1954 the Argentinians used explosives to try to enlarge ledges while in 1958 the Swiss supported their tents (seen here) by tubular alloy frames. *Photo: Detlef Hecker (Diemberger collection)*.

27. Dhaulagiri's North Face. The much-tried route up the pear buttress (far right) was not completed until 1983. The North-East Ridge is the left skyline. The central rock face succumbed in 1994.

28. From the south Dhaulagiri assumes it most majestic presence. This huge face, first tried in 1977, has been climbed by indirect lines by Polish (1986) and Yugoslav (1981) groups (neither reaching the summit). In 1988 a Czech trio made an alpine-style ascent by the South-West Pillar on the left. The South-East Ridge (Japanese, 1978) is on the right. *Photo: Leo Dickinson.*

29, 30 The final scenes during the first ascent of Dhaulagiri: *(below)* Ernst Forrer at 8000m on the summit crest and *(right)* Kurt Diemberger (displaying the Salzburg and D.A.V. pennants) with Albin Schelbert on the summit (plus four others). This is the world's sixth highest mountain and the highest where the first ascent was made without supplementary oxygen.

HINDU KUSH

In 1965 and 1967 the author explored the fascinating Tirich Mir group. In 1967, with Dietmar Proske, he put Buhl's *Westalpinstil* tactics to good use: after establishing a network of food dumps the climbers explored the mountains, using one lightweight tent for shelter. (pp. 252-287, 669-702).

31. *(right)* Tirich Mir seen from Noshaq. The Upper Tirich Glacier sweeps down from right to left. Tirich Mir (7706m) is in the top left with the four Tirich West summits to its right ("like the Grandes Jorasses"). Climbing with Proske or Masaaki Kondo the author made new routes on Tirich West IV and Tirich Mir. *Photo: Lucjan Sadus*

32. *(below)* Pitching the tent on Nobaison Zom (Pt.6999).

33. *(below right)* Dietmar Proske during the ascent of Tirich West IV's North Face.

wind had carried it far overland and screwed it firmly in the sandy ground.

That same wind, allied to the blown sand, acts as nature's blasting operation on the quartz surface of the sun-scorched rocks, which lie scattered around. Generally they exhibited the same larger or smaller wave-formations as the wind conjures into the desert sands.

There were few creatures to be seen by day. At night, we frequently saw scorpions and spiders in the beam of our headlights, and jerboas scampered across the eternal wash-board pattern of the ground – as familiar to us for many days now as the zebra stripes on hard asphalt. Only, to this one there was no end, as it rattled and shook and bumped together the packing-cases, the van and ourselves. We dared not exceed twenty-five miles an hour; our Murl would have taken umbrage.

One learned to be patient, as the savage spires of mountain ranges filed past in slow-motion, set one behind the other, like stage-scenery; brown, grey, blue, changing colour according to their distances and the time of day.

I even found time to sleep, occasionally.

Where had we got to? Oh, I remember, not very long ago we had enjoyed one of the most moving moments of the whole journey. After a thousand miles of desert tracks, sand, boulders, and a few oases, an amazing phenomenon had popped up out of the limitless wastes – a triangle mounted on a post. The nearer we drew to it, the more incredible it seemed: a traffic sign in the desert. 'Drive left,' it commanded.

'Drive to the left from now on: you are in Pakistan.' (In the Pakistan deserts one drives to the left, you see.) We danced around that lonely shield as if it were the Golden Calf, and when we were worn out with laughing, Herwig delivered a ceremonial address from the depths of his beard and his soul. 'My friends,' he said beaming, 'we shall get to the Hindu Kush, and we shall see our native land again. *Inshallah!*'

And so we drove out of the Persian desert into the desert of Pakistan. We had arrived. 'Drive left . . .'

Had we really arrived, though?

Ta tata . . . ta tata . . . ta tata . . .

For some time past we had been proceeding in three-four time. To start with, our Murl had been relatively modern, and normally functioned on four cylinders; but since a certain halt it had lost contact with the rhythmic haste of this day and age . . .

Ta tata . . . ta tata . . .

This desert was a very odd, dark one. Was it the Thalab, or still the

Lut; nobody knows where, in these parts, the boundaries lie? There was no longer any sign of life, except for a few stems sticking out of the black sand; they were dried-up and you could count them. Black desert, black rocks, black sand, and on the far horizon black mountains – the no-man's land between Persia and Pakistan. It was a week since the last car had passed this way.

It was then it happened. We had just had one of our halts – if we didn't stop fairly often, the oil in the engine would start to boil and lose its lubricating properties. Lords of all we surveyed, we had spread our tablecloth on 'our' road, laid our blanket in front of the wheels of the van (Bedouin are also know to take advantage of the shade thrown by their camels), and Tona was dividing a melon. We sat gazing into space, thinking of the snowy dream-peaks, of the limitless time at our disposal, the vast expanse of the landscape around us, utterly content with the world.

However, when we wanted to move on, our Murl refused to budge an inch. 'We'll soon fix that,' said Herwig and went to fetch his tool-kit. It was late in the day, the sun had dipped into the desert in a riot of colours, and Tona began to boil some soup. No need for alarm; this was by no means the first time Murl had declined to start.

This time, though, it seemed to be more serious. 'Damned nuisance!' growled Herwig. 'I shall have to take the engine down.' What on earth was the good of that? I merely said, 'oh yes'; but my knowledge about motors had once again been enriched. In the meantime, dusk had fallen, and a wind as hot as the breath of a baker's oven kept on coming from the north in isolated gusts...

'I mustn't let any sand get into the engine when I take it down,' said Herwig, adding: 'We'll all have to screen it.' He had suddenly become as serious as a surgeon before an operation. We were greatly impressed, and the wind in the silence of the desert had all of a sudden assumed unnatural proportions. As quickly as we could, we confined the area where Herwig was lying underneath the van with the back-rest from the bench-seat, blankets and other things.

Here we were, in no-man's land...

I tried to raise the morale of the party with a wisecrack. 'We have provisions for four weeks,' I said.

'Yes, and seventy litres of petrol in the jerrycan,' came Herwig's sarcastic rejoinder from underneath the engine. Tona didn't say anything; we were each of us holding a blanket round the space in which Herwig was working, as he lay on his back, his miner's lamp on his forehead, drawing a deep breath every now and then, his tool-kit by his side. We carried out his orders, handing him whatever he asked for –

hoping with the bleak hope of a man at death's door in the skill of a Barnard. Perhaps the situation was not quite so dire. Our water supply was sufficient, with care, for a week – possibly ten days, we reflected as we spooned up our soup. The engine still refused to work. In the middle of the night, some hours later, Herwig succeeded in eliminating one cylinder, thus allowing the other three to function. 'It's the only chance,' he said. I think we fell on his neck for joy.

Saved! We could drive on – at any rate till we met our first steep hill; and the next mountains we should meet were near Quetta. We would be coming across people before then...

Ta tata ... ta tata ... ta tata ...

Flat wadis stretched away to the south. Somewhere over there lay a salt lake.

A dancing dot appeared on the horizon; not a car, surely? No, for there was no dust-cloud. It stopped dancing and revealed itself as a house; then, as a cube adjoining some rails, here in the midst of Pakistan's boundless plain – in short, a railway-station!

An ancient, weatherbeaten, turbaned station-master presided over it, and there were hordes of children. 'My sons!' he explained, proudly. We presented him with a bundle of marker-pennants, and the desert was soon ringing with all the sounds of the hunt.

We asked him if we could ship our van to Quetta by train. He shook his head, informing us that special papers were required for that – but, of course! – and a special type of wagon; and in any case – excuse me, did we hear you correctly? – the next train wouldn't be going for a fortnight, no...

Oh well, we thanked him and re-embarked in our Murl. We looked back and saw the children waving their pennants, and we waved back. There seemed to be more of them than ever.

We came to the pass. Murl refused, on the very first rise. So we parked by the roadside and adopted hitch-hike techniques – one thumb in the direction we were going, the other on Murl. Traffic was relatively heavy hereabouts – there was a car almost every hour or so.

Then, an Arabian Nights fairytale – a lorry came along! (I ask forgiveness for the historical paradox; but the history of this kind of lorry must be colourful and rich in fantasy; its voyaging circuitous and exciting for an ordinary mortal – I have no doubt that the Khalif himself would have allotted an extra night to its story, had Scheherazade only known about it.) There was every kind of decoration, in all the colours of the rainbow, on that lorry: landscapes, faces – and, of course, the firm's telephone number. The warlike, turbaned figures of its two drivers might have come straight out of some ancient tale. With the aid of a rise in the ground, we succeeded in driving Murl, by way of two planks, up into the lorry. Then we ourselves climbed up in to the roomy driving-cabin and installed ourselves alongside the man at the wheel.

The place looked like a living room. There he was, bending over his hookah, and nodding to us. And when he started up, the windscreen rattled and rang and danced, with the glass beads, spangles, tiny bells and fringes that hung there, rather like the forehead-finery of some elephant in a fairy-story, moving at every step or, I should of course say, at every swell and fall in the road. Herwig was beaming with delight, the corners of his mouth tucked up into his beard. 'My friends,' he pontificated, slightly varying his favourite theme, 'we shall get to the Hindu Kush yet!' – and this time he omitted the *Inshallah!*

Trrrrrrrrrr . . . the lorry in fourth gear, and the turbaned one tearing hell-for-leather over everything, including the undulations in the ground. We might have been forgiven for losing all sense of vision and sound, but one thing we could still hear was Murl bouncing about behind us. . . .

Two hundred miles to Quetta . . . *Inshallah!*

The rest of the story – how there was no hump in the ground to enable us to get our Murl down out of the lorry again, how it nearly finished up in the bed of the river, and a few other similar trifles – is recorded elsewhere.

Dertona Peak

At this point, I propose to tell the story of a single climb on that first reconnaissance-trip of ours. It bears the name of an Italian city and also Tona's, according to how you read it. Der-tona Peak – which we climbed together. Since the Tortona Section of the Club Alpino Italiano had sponsored our expedition, and since the Latin name of that little city – whose enthusiastic climbers are to be found in every continent – was Dertona, the choice of the name for our mountain seemed doubly appropriate. She herself had originally opted for Hildegard Peak; but as the government would certainly have refused to sanction our daughter's name for a summit in the Hindu Kush, we dropped the idea.

It is not permissible nowadays cheerfully to label peaks in the Himalaya with people's names; though there was a time when you could. For instance, in Nepal there is a Gyaltzen Peak, so named because a

Scottish Women's expedition wanted to leave a permanent memorial to the devotion and skill of their Sherpa Sirdar. In the Hindu Kush, too, there are a few peaks named after cities, such as the Picco di Teramo, Citta di Milano and others; beyond all doubt, a Munich party achieved the ultimate with Koh-i-Batzenhäusl! It depends on the government in power whether those mountains will be allowed to keep the names given them in so happy-go-lucky fashion.

Hayat ud Din, our high-altitude porter, had come with us to the foot of the lovely pyramid, rising above the end of a great glacier coombe, four hours from camp. The snow was very deep all the way to our ice-plastered peak, in the centre of the Ghul lasht Zom group, whose summits bore some resemblance to the Lyskamm. (During the whole of four weeks, we had only five really fine days.) Yet, in spite of the depth of the snow, we had the delicious feeling that every step we took was on untrodden ground.

It is always interesting, too, to discover how wrong existing sketch-maps can be; the explorer of new ground derives from this source a deeply human satisfaction, difficult to describe in scientific terms (though it is well-known that science and truth approach one another ever more closely). Only very great scholars should get swollen-headed about such matters. At all events, with regard to the as-yet untrodden Ghul lasht Zom group, there were a great many discrepancies, and we enjoyed them.

Hayat trudged on ahead, carrying both our rucksacks. This blue-eyed steinbock-hunter from Shagrom had the strength of a bear, besides being a charming and sympathetic character. (He was almost as good at carrying rucksacks as I am; indeed he might have been my brother.) He was unaffected and always ready to help, too; and candid to the extent of one day bringing us Sahibs, without any trace of embarrassment, a bowl of hot water and making it clear, beyond any risk of misunderstanding, that washing was a good and healthy practice. Out there in Shagrom, in the Tirich Gol valley, below those steep and gigantic débris slopes which threaten to swallow everything up, he owned a field or two and a hut. We never saw his wife, even veiled; she must be very beautiful, for his children had something about them quite different from the others in the valley.

At the foot of the snowy face, Hayat shook hands with us, looked up at the rocky summit of our 20,000-foot peak and started on his journey back to camp. He would probably have liked to come with us, but it was out of the question. While we were roping up and getting everything ready, Tona told me how she had taken him up to a little peak, 19,000 feet high, just above the camp; the 'Viewpoint' – with a lovely view down on to the curving streams of the glacier, with the 25,000-foot crests of Tirich Mir and Istor-o-Nal opposite. Hayat had enjoyed it immensely, singing and laughing, and continually indicating that he had never been so high up before.

I was wallowing my way up, on all fours. The best description of what I was doing is to equate it with the activities of a mole. For I was boring my way up that exceptionally steep snow-face, straight up it, exactly like one of those delightful little beasts. Tona said I looked like Father Christmas. Well, there was no better method here; it was quite impossible to talk about breaking a trail. At places, the snow – all of it freshly-fallen – was up to our middles. So much for Gerald Gruber's wonderful Hindu Kush weather; how dared he advertise the range as a permanent fine-weather paradise! I could only hope it had been snowing as hard on him, over there at the foot of Buni Zom, as it had on us for the last few days. 'Geri', as they call him in the more intimate Hindu Kush circles (he has visited the range five times, and once drove the 5,500 miles from Graz to Peshawar in six days; though – this is not unusual among Hindu Kush drivers – he maintains a discreet silence about the fate of the first expedition's vehicle) must surely have choked every time he thought of us watching the snow-flakes whirling down and remembering his weather forecasts.

Tona shouted up to me: '*Guarda* – look!' and pointed up to the ridge of Ghul lasht Zom, curving white into the blue sky.
She was right – there they were, Herwig and Franz, two little dots, unbelievably small and unbelievably high up, there on the white ribbon of that ridge, close under the sky, moving almost imperceptibly towards the summit.
'Isn't it splendid?' I said to her. 'Two summit successes on the same day!' She smiled and nodded her agreement – '*si, e vero!*'
She looked charming: her small straight nose under her fur cap, her delicate mouth, now muffled in a scarf, and the joy of the climb – her climb – shining in her eyes. 'Let's go!' she said, and this girl called Tona – this strange combination of softness, energy and drive, of unselfishness and toughness – began to plunge energetically up through the snow again. She had rarely climbed a peak with me; mostly she stayed at home when I was climbing. But today we were climbing a six-thousander, together. And I could see how happy she was.
We were up at last on the ridge, a continuous chain of undulations,

Higher than the Eagle Soars

like the glossy belly of a snake, winding its way up to the summit. Snow, mostly, but some polished ice, too. There was a difficult spot where I had to use two ice-pitons. Close to us a spur fell away into the depths to where, fully 10,000 feet below, to the south-west there was a shimmer of green fields and streams; the Arkari valley. Beyond rose a sea of five-thousanders.

Our track up the ridge looked like a pearl necklace, as we drew near to the summit; we were now close to the 19,700-foot level.

'*Aspetta un po* – wait a minute,' came Tona's request. Yes, air was thinning rapidly. She waved up to me, her mouth open, gasping for breath, signalling to me not to move on yet. I waited. That gesture of her hand – it reminded me, suddenly of the concourse at the railway station in Milan, dark and grimy. Sure – what greater contrast could there be to the white world of peaks and glaciers around us here, outshining everything.

Then I knew why. It was the same movement of her hand, that brief, shy, half-doubtful, swift waving motion, twice repeated; exactly like at Milan's railway station, when we had first come to know one another and I had so often had to say goodbye, only to come back again and again...

What a wonderful day this was, today, with the peaks cradling everything in a white mantle of resplendent snow!

There were only a couple of rope's lengths to go now, with Tona taking the lead. Through the thin mist beyond the ridge rose a mighty fluted wall, like some wonderful panelling of white linenfold. There it stood, opposite us, higher and deeper than our mountain; and now the sun was shining full on it.

One more rope; then we should have to be careful, at the white rim up there. I spotted an excellent belaying-point in the sweep of the ridge, which was part snow, part rock. 'Stop at that boulder,' I told her. 'Right. Are you coming up?' Yes, at once! She had looped a belay round the rock and seen me safely up. Only a few feet more now: that wavy crest of snow just above us, that was the summit. 'Look out for cornices,' I advised, when she started off again and I watched her every moment, as I let the rope run through my hands. However, there were none, for firm rock lay beneath the snow. There she was, on top. She turned and looked down at me, smiling. Yes, there she was, on her summit. *Ciao!*

Dertona Peak, 20,000 feet: Hildegard's peak: my peak: her peak. It belonged to the Tortona Section, to our friends, the mountaineers, and of course, the mayor and all the chemists – in fact to everyone in Tortona.

We laughed and embraced. *Ciao!* Then we thought again of everyone to whom this mountain belonged. Only, today, it belonged, first and foremost, to us.

The summit consisted of two snow-domes of about equal height, with steep sides. It was a perfect arrangement for photographing each other with our various pennants, which we proceeded to do extensively. The green Reifenstein one, with its edelweiss, the one my dear old climbing friend 'Schorsch' had given me, the purple of Tortona, the sunshine gold of the Munich Bergländers, and again that one from Bruno and his little town on the slopes of the Appennines; finally – for the young skiers – the Mickey Mouse of the Topolinos. Exposure after exposure.

While we were busy photographing, great gusts of wind kept on coming up from below, covering us with glittering clouds of ice-darts, against the blue of the sky or the pale drifting mists. Gradually, the cold penetrated our clothing and we moved down a little to seek shelter and enjoy a summit snack. We hadn't had a bite all day – we had simply forgotten about it – and now it was only a trifle; for the wind was eddying ever more strongly, and it was getting uncomfortable. Clouds of snow-dust began to envelop us, and the ridges of Ghul lasht Zom were hidden from sight. It was already 5 o'clock, and time to be going down.

After an absolutely endless descent, we rejoined Hayat ud Din at about midnight. 'Tona Sahb! Kurt Sahb!' he cried, joyfully and obviously much relieved after his long wait. 'Tona Zom?' he enquired, shaking us by the hand. Yes, we had been to the summit. He dragged us into the tent; the thermos of tea he handed us tasted marvellous. 'What a treasure you are, Hayat ud Din!' we told him. He smiled. We wondered if he had understood? Of course, he had; he understood almost everything. Then he laid his head against his hands at an angle, looking at us enquiringly. Yes we nodded, back, definitely – sleep! We were dead dog tired.

We seemed to be sinking into a great void through drifting mist and white, shimmering snow.

When Herwig and Franz came back from Ghul lasht Zom, after a bivouac at 19,700 feet, we indulged in a tremendous victory celebration. The level of Franz's cognac bottle sank considerably, till we remembered that there were still other peaks to climb. Franz had not been with us very long. A few days earlier he had come, with the precious bottle in his rucksack, up the vast expanse of the Upper Tirich Glacier, like a voice crying in the wilderness, as he tried to locate us. He had followed us out to Pakistan by air and his further directions for the rendezvous were simple: Upper Tirich Glacier. So he had had to do a good deal of shouting and was pretty hoarse by the time we eventually met; but – a point greatly in his favour – that bottle had remained untouched. A man of character, we agreed.

'Chin! Chin! Four against Tirich Mir!' we toasted Franz, and as he described his long journey on foot and we told him of our adventures in the desert, the hoarseness gradually left his voice.

Yes, there was plenty for the four of us to do: the various white summits of the Ghul lasht Zom group, reconnaissances into remote, untrodden corners of the broad Tirich Glacier, our seven-day long attack on the huge spur of Tirich Nord, nearly 7,000 feet high – days packed with adventure, during which we were not always together but still formed a united party. We all loved Hayat ud Din and hated parting with him; likewise Aja Chan, that friendly old man who suddenly turned up at base camp with a basket full of apples, to pay a call on Hayat (Shagrom, his village, was three days away down there). The apples were a present for us.

Our time ran out all too quickly, and now we are at home again, going to our jobs every day. When, each morning, I put on my shiny town shoes, I think of Aja Chan climbing around in my fur boots, which I gave him as a farewell present; going out, maybe, into the bitter winter cold of the Tirich Gol to have a chat with Hayat, before he goes off to shoot a steinbock. While I go to catch my bus.

At the University of Milan they are busy estimating the age of one of our blocks of granite and preparing thin polished specimens. Oh yes, and in a backyard in St Pölten there stands a lonely coffee-delivery van, rusting and philosophizing about old age. Nobody ever disturbs its rest, and there seems no great danger that anybody will do so in the near future – for it remains unsold.

There were a few things before that which I should like to touch on briefly before closing this chapter – the memory of our eventful journey home, and of a Viennese butterfly-collector to whom we owe it that we and our Murl ever got home at all, in spite of a war, a typhus-quarantine and a broken-down engine.

As to Herwig, I believe that if we had only had one good cylinder left, he would have laughed as unconcernedly as ever into his beard, taken everything to pieces again, and made such a good job of the single one that the others, or at least half of them, would have thought better of it. Still, it was a very good thing that we ran into that Viennese collector of butterflies – Azad Vartian.

A great surprise awaited us when we emerged from the high valley; there was a war on – between Pakistan and India. We kept on seeing heavily-bearded and often very elderly volunteers leaving their valleys and heading for Peshawar, carrying drawn swords and age-old flintlocks. They gestured fiercely as they listened to the news about the fighting – bombs on Peshawar, tank-battles in the frontier areas. Next thing, we ourselves came within an ace of a bombardment, in Peshawar's bazaar. I don't know now what the outcome would have been, had not a policeman with a drawn pistol appeared at the critical moment and rescued me – for the crowd took me for, well, anything but an Austrian. There was nothing for it but to clear out. We spent the night sitting up with Hugo Kruschandl, the manager of Dean's Hotel, all of sixteen stone and a prince among men.

It was an unforgettable night: aircraft overhead, in front of us a whisky bottle to make do for the non-existent air-raid shelter, and Hugo telling us the story of his life . . . next day we were in Afghanistan. With the Khyber Pass behind us, we washed off the obligatory coat of camouflage (two buckets of water mixed with dirt and emptied over Murl). Murl, by the way was running in 4/4 time; but not for long. One night he went into a steep decline on to two cylinders – miles from the nearest habitation. And then the clutch started to misbehave. We trembled at every rise in the ground, ready to jump out and push. Finally, after a spectacular effort on the part of the whole crew, Murl stuck in a hollow; the opposing slope was too steep for us. It looked like the end. As we stood wiping away the sweat and panting, Herbert spoke. 'My friends,' he said, 'we shall see our homes again – *Inshallah!*' It did not sound very convincing.

Murl was on his way again.

We were a splendid 'rope'. Our rescuers were Azad, a dealer in carpets, and his wife, an artist; but their real passion was for Afghanistan's gaily-coloured butterflies – they even bred them in their car. Azad knew the valleys of the Hindu Kush well, and was worth listening to on the subject. We were a happy party, bumbling across the plain at 15 to 20 m.p.h., united by a rope between their vehicle and ours. How suddenly one's view of life can be completely changed!

I quote from my diary: 'No trouble with Murl. The bumper is standing up to it and the rope is in good condition. Our greatest problem, whenever we got to an oasis is: where do the caterpillars find leaves to live on?'

Higher than the Eagle Soars

Two years later I was back again. It was a unique expedition, during which I climbed more high peaks than in any previous enterprise. Renato Ceppâro, writing in Scarpone *called it 'the world's smallest expedition'. It consisted entirely of me, the leader and solitary member of the '1967 Austrian Hindu Kush Expedition'.*

The preparations were simple and successful. Once again I designed an impressive headed notepaper to full efficiency, and this time I was helped by considerable experience. There was another recognized Hindu Kush enterprise that summer, precisely the same as my own; it was the '1967 German Hindu Kush Expedition', for it came from Germany and consisted solely of its leader, Dietmar Proske. We did most of our climbs in each other's company, but – hardly knowing each other as yet – remained basically independent. Many of the larger expeditions cast somewhat sceptical glances on us two Chitral-hikers – for we were, like most of the visitors to the Hindu Kush during the last few years, mere tourists. During that summer, the 'tourists' bagged four six- and three seven-thousanders, including the highest peak in the Hindu Kush. They also garnered the first complete circuit of Tirich Mir, a great many moments of doubt and uncertainty, untold hours of delight and, in sum, a tremendous experience.

The North Face of Tirich West IV

There are many who say I have a weakness for north faces: how right they are!

When, on the afternoon of July 2nd, 'Didi' Proske and I stood on the summit of Ghul lasht Zom's southern summit, it was not only his first six-thousander, but also a fantastic 'presentation plate' for us to stand on and survey hundreds of peaks all around us. The finest prospect was to the south-east, where, directly opposite, the summits of Tirich Mir shot skywards.

There was a banner of cloud hanging on the very top of the main summit. Below it lay a whole gallery of precipices anything from seven to ten thousand feet high. There were rugged buttresses, slabs, hanging glaciers, all the way up to 24,000 and even to the summit's 25,263 feet. What a challenge!

We turned our attention to the north face of the farthest of the western summits. It is a little lower than the other three in Tirich Mir's western group, but it is the most impressive and carries its own quote of 24,073 feet. It forms the corner-stone of that gigantic wall, perhaps best comparable with the Grandes Jorasses, for in each case there is an immense granite face, interrupted by buttresses, on whose crest rises a row of separate summits relatively close to one another. Here the height of the summits increases in a south-easterly direction, towards Tirich Mir itself. West III, a corniced white crown of snow, can only be a few feet higher than our No. IV from which it is separated by the deepest saddle in the whole comb. West II, a sharply-ridged summit eventually leads to the highest point in the crest, which also bears a quotation of 24,427 feet. It can best be reached from Tirich Mir's north-west col, which it overtops by a mere 800 feet.

If the big Czech expedition besieging Tirich Mir took the route over that saddle, it would surely not miss the chance of so adjacent a first-ascent. We looked down; far below, fine-drawn as a hair, ran the trail the porters had beaten between the Czech camps, all the way up the glacier, till it made a wide curve around the rocky base of West IV and disappeared behind it in the direction of Tirich Mir.

Every day, they must have seen the ramp stabbing up into the lower half of the face, giving access to it; but they must also have seen what lay above it. So we felt sure our fortress over there was safely ours, and we need not worry. Safely? We might find we couldn't get up it, when the time came...

I watched the snow-banner on Tirich Mir's summit and wondered how long it would take the Czechs to get up there.

After a reconnaissance into the Anogol and the ascent of another six-thousander, we both felt in sufficiently good form to warrant an approach to our unknown wall and try to establish from close quarters the details which still remained unsolved in spite of binoculars; for many pitches looked different according to the point from which we were observing them and the time of day. Things that seemed possible one day looked quite impossible the following morning. Meanwhile, we had acclimatized splendidly, thanks to the continual humping of heavy loads.

I am leaving it to Didi to give his own account of his first-ascent of a seven-thousander:

'We had originally intended to climb the mountain with a larger party; but when the team did not show up in our area as planned, we had to readjust things for the two of us. To be honest, this huge 24,000-foot lump of granite, so difficult to survey from a distance, did not look exactly a sitting target for a two-man team.

'The first thing we did was to establish a new assault camp, at 19,350 feet on the southern arm of the Upper Tirich Glacier, specially sited at the foot of our Tirich West IV. With the assistance of Musheraf Din, our only porter, we lugged more than 200 lbs. of equipment and provisions from our lower-base camp to the new site, more than 3,000 feet higher up, in a forced march lasting eight hours. Musheraf then went down to Shagrom in the valley, with instructions to come back and meet us in fifteen days' time.

'We started our climb on July 31st. Kurt and I each humped a 45-lb. rucksack over disgusting pinnacle ice to the start of a broad ice-couloir. Our objective was the great ice-balcony, a long, narrow plateau in the midst of the steep face at about 20,700 feet. And this 1,300 foot couloir was the easiest way to it. After five hours under the drudgery of a 45-lb. burden we reached the top of the couloir. There we dumped our loads and went down again. Next day we went through whole procedure again, with one difference: this time we stayed up there.

'We managed to pitch our two-man tent at the beginning of the balcony, in the lee of a protecting tower of rock. A special luxury at this camp I was the "ice-lake", two yards long and mostly frozen over, which almost always spared us the tedious chore of melting snow. Unfortunately, this amenity involved a descent of 150 feet; we tossed up each time to decide who was to go down and whether this was to be late in the evening or in the bitter early-morning cold.

'As soon as we had the tent in position, we went on along the sloping balcony; presently it levelled out and broke away vertically to the Lower Tirich Glacier, far below. Opposite us, the northern face of Tirich Mir towered in all its immensity. We, from our fantastic vantage point, were the first to see this aspect of that mighty wall.

'The route ahead of us looked savage to a degree. The whole dauntingly steep north face of our own mountain was cut across by numerous superimposed veins of granite, from vertical to over-hanging, many of them 100-feet high, separated by ice-patches or roof-like, outward-sloping black slates. The whole constituted a geological contact, full of surprises and problems for us who wanted to climb it. We scanned it for a long time through binoculars, searching for ribs or gullies by which to penetrate those granite veins.

'One thing was greatly in our favour: this year the weather in the Hindu Kush had been uninterruptedly fine, and we felt we could reckon on continued luck with it for the days to come. (Kurt thought that, in the conditions he met in 1965, we should never have got even as far as this.) The risks attending a possible forced retreat were sizeably reduced, in the circumstances.

'Starting from camp I next day we both carried 35-lb. loads along the plateau and, beyond it, up a steep snow-slope in the face. Our intention was to lay down a depot of material on the face above at a distance of six hours from our first high camp.

'Everything was fearfully steep, hereabouts. On the very first traverse of the dark walls of slate we made very slow progress; one hold after another went clattering down into the abyss as soon as we put any weight on it, and it was almost impossible to use a piton. Overhead lay more than 3,000 feet of unexplored face...

'We managed it in due course, and were able to work our cautious way upwards rope's length by rope's length. Our morale rose appreciably. The granite veins we had to cross did not present any exceptional difficulties in spite of great altitude, the loads which weighted us down and our great thick boots; though there were one or two Grade IV pitches. It was afternoon when we laid down our depot at about 21,800 feet. Up till then we had not found a single level spot in the whole face large enough to house even a bivouac-tent; and now there was barely room to stow our equipment. Our descent to camp I was considerably easier, for we had marked the sector with pennants. The following day was spent in carrying more rope and provisions up to the depot. Our preparations were complete: we were ready to move up to the next storey of our granite castle. On August 4th, lightly laden, we climbed up to the depot. Once there, we had to lift a mass of material into and onto our rucksacks. Further progress was slow. Our intention was to go straight for the summit without a break.

'Just above our heads, everything was cut off by a vertical yellow barrier; we should have to traverse.

'It was a traverse full of dodgy passages: a sharp ridge, to be turned first to the right, then to the left, deep ice-gullies and bands of granite barring the way. On this face, the question is always whether, and more especially, where one will find a way up, so little of it can one see ahead at any given time. That traverse from right to left of the precipice, with its ups and its downs, must have been fully a quarter of a mile long. Finally, with the aid of pitons, we mastered a very strenuous Grade IV pitch and reached the lower rim of a hanging glacier. One particular moment of that traverse lives vividly in my memory; as I was strapping on my crampons, the huge block on which I was standing suddenly began to move – I just had time to get off before it went down the face.

'The sun was low in the sky as we now came to the upper part of the face, which consisted mainly of ice-slopes and granite buttresses. We had hoped it would be easier to find a place for our little bivouac-tent here, but our optimism was premature. Darkness fell, and we had to settle for a crevasse in the hanging-glacier. In it – remaining roped, of course –

we were able to put our tent up, if somewhat uncomfortably, on a snow-bridge. The work of hacking-out and levelling took all of two hours; during that time, in spite of circulation tablets, we said goodbye to our fingers and feet, and it took a long time and much effort before we got them back again.

'The cold – down to minus 30 degrees C. – was in fact the greatest problem we had to deal with during the whole undertaking. We had the very best equipment available (boots, clothes, food, medical aids), but somebody will have to invent even better ones!

'We had very little room in the tent, but the night was still a thousand times better than one spent in a bivouac-bag. Everything we didn't actually need we hung from ice-pitons all around outside the tent, to prevent it going down the mountain-side, for the surroundings were everywhere smooth and sheer. Fortunately, the darkness prevented our seeing how far things fell away below us – for we were at the very rim of the hanging-glacier.

'In the morning when we made tea and the sun eventually reached us in our perlon-home, we were subjected to the inevitable drip-bath, for the condensed ice on the lining melted or peeled off on us. To add to the joys of this "camp", a strong wind blew up; bringing, through the thin wall of the tent, a most unacceptable chill just where it is most uncomfortable to the man lying on the outer side. All through the next day, our dearest wish was to find a place for a comfortable camp.

'So on August 5th, we struck our bivouac-tent and went up the ice-field in a strong wind, feeling very hopeful, though the gale continually whipped ice-needles in our faces. After two hours there was not much left of this hope. Our thoughts were just going back to that camp II of ours, with its "comforts", when, at about 23,000 feet we found a splendid camp-site in a big, roomy crevasse, complete with a roof of ice over it and full protection from the wind. Even in that "ice-palace" with its fine panoramic view of the world below, we never unroped; for here there were just two alternatives – stay on, or come off...

'On the 6th we set out for the summit. The weather was lovely, though we suffered a great deal from the intense cold and the wind – not unexpectedly above 23,000 feet on the north side of our mountain. After every rope's length in steep, cold powder-snow we had to swing our feet vigorously to restore a vestige of feeling in them.

'We traversed upwards to the left for a long distance, below a wall of polished granite, till we came to a steep slope of hard ice which seemed to end in the blue sky itself.

'The drop below us was prodigious – we looked down sheer on to avalanche cones 7,000 feet below on the floor of the Lower Tirich Glacier. Our hearts were beating high in our throats. Every stride was taken with the utmost caution, with that breathtaking abyss beneath our feet.

'In the middle of all this verticality, a little island of rock invited us to rest and brew some tea. We were dying for a drop of something hot.

'After that tea-halt everything seemed to go twice as easily. We even began to take an interest in photography and I suddenly felt much as I would have done on a fine day climbing the north-west face of the Wiessbachhorn at home. Nor was our delight unjustified; for, as things turned out, the exit from this narrow ice-slope was actually the key to the summit, and we had found it first time. Whereas from down below, even with strong binoculars, we had never been able to establish whether, or where, there was a way through these vertical walls of granite and the rock-towers below the summit. Though we had tried from various viewpoints, it had all remained, till now, a matter of conjecture.

'And now, suddenly, we were standing on a little shoulder, from which – to our relief and suppressed delight – we could see, close in front of us, the top part of the West Face and, just above it, the spiny crest of the summit!

'A couple more rope's lengths up the slope, in sunshine, zig-zagging between enormous boulders lifting from the snow – we were breathless with altitude, excitement and impatience – then a last tower, a huge monolith, barring the ridge like some sentinel, frowning down upon us ... and at about 3 p.m. we were on the summit.

'I was overjoyed, for it was my first seven-thousander.'

That is how Didi saw it. I will take up the thread again. Darkness was falling by the time our long descent brought us down to our comfortable camp in the crevasse. On the following day we got down to camp I, at the 'ice-lake'. Our two-man tent looked as large and spacious as a room. That very evening it began to snow; the phenomenon was so unusual that we could hardly believe it. We realized that our summit would now be unclimbable for days to come, and rejoiced all the more at having done it just in time; also that we were safely back down here ...

On August 9th, ten days after our first ascent to the 'balcony', we climbed down to base camp with a mass of stuff on our backs. Our descent was rather like a ballet performed by two elephants.

An Apple on Tirich Mir

Little Masaaki was laughing and his dark eyes, set in a round sunburnt face, were dancing with joy. 'Very lucky,' he said; 'very happy,' and laughed again.

We were 'very happy': we hugged each other and patted each other's backs. Then we got out the pennants, which we had made of paper and bright red sticking-plaster stuck together: one red, white and red, the other displaying on its white background a big round blob of red plaster – the sun of Japan. I had to bend down a little to lay my arm round Masaaki's shoulders for the summit photograph Didi was trying to take – Pat and Patachon on the summit of 'Pyramid Peak', maybe? We had swopped the symbols of East and West in our hands. 'Cheers!' 'Yes, very happy.' And Didi pressed the shutter.

Masaaki Kondo was the Jonah of the Japanese Tirich Mir Expedition, but at that moment nobody would have known it. He was delighted to be standing on a summit, even if it was only the modest P 6778 (22,238 feet), already climbed by the Czechs. Besides which we were a happy party and the whole thing was only a day's outing from our highest camp to date (21,300 feet), our advanced assault camp for Tirich Mir.

During the descent, with the rocks and the clouds already turned to gold, Masaaki kept on looking up at Tirich Mir's summit (25,263 feet). His friends, who had started out some days before, must be somewhere up there. They had left him behind because, right at the start of proceedings, he had fallen sixty feet into a crevasse down on the Tirich Glacier, cracking a rib, and suffering other injuries. So they had thought it better to attempt that high summit without him. His rib was still hurting him, but having to be left behind hurt much more.

The Czechs had gone down in the meantime. They had climbed Tirich Mir by the North-west Col and Ridge, and also taken the first of the West summits from the col. From that saddle, they reported to the Japanese, they had taken twelve hours up and down for Tirich Mir, and ten for the other peak. They had left a tent up there on the col at 23,800 feet. They explained that it was terribly cold and stormy up there, which we had no difficulty in believing. Even on fine days, clouds might roll up in the mountain in the middle of the day, completely enveloping it – one could not doubt for a moment that then things were pretty unpleasant, and a sojourn in those regions, up there, not exactly an attractive proposition. When the peak emerged in the evening, it was often freshly-powdered white. According to the Czechs, the ridge-climb from the col to the top offered no great technical difficulties, but there was a vital key-point on the ascent from the forward assault camp to the col at about 23,000 feet: a 250-foot chimney, Grade IV, with a possible Grade V pitch in it. We kept on looking up through the glasses: the chimney looked exactly like that.

For the moment I meant to wait for the return of the Japanese summit-party. So there was our modest little tent, planted next to the comfortable spread of sunshine-golden perlon and bamboo of the Japanese camp. In it we could sit in comfort with the amiable, elderly Takahashi, the lively Nishina, and Masaaki, cheerful in spite of his setbacks – five of us on mats around the humming tea-kettle, talking about Japan and Europe, about mountains and a thousand other things. We acquired a taste for Japanese seaweed, pudding, coffee and whisky; and I sponsored an almost perfect Trieste fish-soup, made according to a secret recipe of my own, which I should not care to publish. They also got to like smoked ham and noodles; but not even oriental politeness could bridge the gap to my camp-special rice-pudding.

The summit-party should have returned by now, but there was no sign of them, except a slender trail on a snow-slope to the right of the col. They had left the walkie-talkie sets down here in order to minimize weight, and Nishina was beginning to get worried. In the circumstances I decided that we ought to make our own summit-push at once; we could take the radio along and one or other of us could report back, if anything was wrong.

Unfortunately, Didi's insides had failed to stomach the mixture of western and oriental diets. It might be days before he was all right again and nobody knew better than he that you have to be fighting-fit to climb a difficult peak, falling short by only 1,000 feet of being an eight-thousander. At first we could not think what to do; then, suddenly, we thought of Masaaki. He might like to? . . . *Would* he just! Of course, he wouldn't be able to carry a heavy pack – he pointed to his chest, shook his head and made a slight face, but smiled, as he almost always did. But I had seen how well he could go, he was fully acclimatized and, above all, he was such a good sort. On the previous day, he had come up with me to about 22,600 feet in the direction of the big chimney. We had left some food and a special thermos of tea hanging on a piton for the descending party. I had also imparted some Austrian ice-technique to Masaaki, the only difficulty being that his English was limited to about twenty words; however, he cheerfully said 'yes' to everything, and then did the exact opposite. He also greeted my occasional Austrian swearwords with a smile and an amiable 'yes' – so we got on splendidly.

Our sudden decision involved the necessary preparations, so it was not till about noon that we were ready to take leave of our friends. It was, of course, late to be starting out for one of the high seven-thousanders, but we pinned our hopes on reaching a little projection below the chimney, which might take our bivouac-tent. We stuffed our pockets full of small, green Shagrom apples, which Didi and Musheraf Din handed us out of the tent, as they wished us good luck. Then we were off.

We reached the projection – it was at about 23,000 feet – towards evening. On either side of it steep couloirs shot down through the vertical buttresses of granite. I climbed another rope's length up the steep one on the left-hand side, hoping to find a better site for our tent at its edge; but every apparent step turned out on close inspection to be smooth and sheer. So I fixed one rope and quickly returned down it to the projection. Not any too soon, for it was too small for our tent, and there was work to be done. The Japanese had sat the night out here – and I had no taste for that.

We went at the brittle rock with our ice-hammers, building two bays out into space at the sides, where it was too narrow; of course we were belayed as we worked. Our worst headache was getting the tent up – we had to fix some of the pitons directly underneath it, others out to right and left. Finally we got the two poles, which turn the perlon-tube into a tent, fixed, and pushed in two three-foot lengths of sorbo for a floor. Then followed the trapeze act of getting inside. At last we lay head to foot, gasping for breath, in our contraption and got some rest. The projection, plus our engineering work, was just large enough for the two of us, but we didn't dare to move much. In any case, it was nice to be lying still.

I had put one of my boots, with the cooker laced up inside, between my head and the rock-face. It worked, and a couple of lumps of ice melted slowly for a fine cup of Tokyo coffee. Through a little spy-hole we looked down on Pyramid Peak, pale in the moonlight.

We got up rather late. It took quite a time to undo everything and get it packed. Just as we were at last ready to start up the couloir, so as to get to grips with the chimney, which started immediately above – a dark, forbidding rift – a lump of rock came clattering down, making us jump for cover. Then we heard a voice, someone shouting, high up above. We answered. It was the Japanese, coming down.

An hour or two later we were all sitting together on boulders and ledges at the bivouac-place. They were tired and depressed, having failed to reach the summit, though by only a short distance, defeated by the cold and the wind. Fortunately all four were well and had escaped frostbite. During the tea-session I fixed two of the long Japanese ropes, to facilitate their descent; that would enable them to get down almost to our depot, after which there were no serious difficulties on the rest of the way down.

Later, when Masaaki and I were stuck in the big chimney, the sun was already pretty low in the sky. The fixed ropes helped a little but, unfortunately, they were very elastic and I had a 40-lb. rucksack on me. It was a horrid struggle. I swore and banged in another piton, while the ropes – stretched by the recent roping-down manoeuvres of the descending party – were now quite useless for my purposes. Darkness fell slowly.

I had found a stance in a niche, and the ropes were serviceable again, thank goodness, for I needed them. There was a short crack, its lower part overhanging, just above me. Two pitons were here; this must be the Grade V pitch. I wished I knew what the English for *Zug!* was, so as to get a lift on the rope; but then Masaaki probably didn't know either. I latched on and tried it on my own. I had almost got there, when I realized I couldn't quite do it; I gasped and fought to gain an inch. That blasted rucksack! Nothing for it but to retreat. I tried to bang in a piton, on which to hang my pack; it went ringing away. In the poor light I managed to find a crack, and the next piton held. As I was getting free of my rucksack, I heard a sudden clatter below me...

'Look out! Stone!' I roared down.

It went banging from one wall of the chimney to the other.

'Masaaki!'

'Yes.'

Everything was all right, then.

Without the rucksack it was quite a different matter; but it was dark by the time I got up. We were now above 23,000 feet. We could only go on by the light of Masaaki's 'searchlight'. That was in his pack.

This necessitated a lengthy manoeuvre. First, Masaaki had to come all the way up to the niche; then I had to get my rucksack up over the bulge below me, only a few feet, but a fearful effort; then Masaaki's rucksack and finally Masaaki himself, up from the niche, to join me. He seemed perfectly calm and collected, in spite of the darkness and our

An Apple on Tirich Mir

exposed position, which was very encouraging. We disentangled the ropes by the friendly light of the lamp; I kept my own, much the weakest, in reserve. Then the light went probing up the slabby face to our left and its cone revealed, right above us, a projecting flake of rock in a kind of groove; and there was the fixed rope, coming down it. This was another Grade IV problem and a pretty tough exercise, with one's feet against the slabs and the rucksack 'backing-up'. But now there was a shimmer of white, and things began to ease off. I have no idea how long it took before we got on to the snow-slope...

The moon was up now, and though we were in the shadow of the rocks above us to the right, we could see well enough, our finger-tips assessing the slope of the snow; we had put the lamp away.

We belayed from stance to stance. It was crushingly cold, and the one who was waiting shivered and counted the moments till the next reviving 130 feet of movement. We could have put on more clothing, but neither of us had the drive to unpack a rucksack. All we wanted to do was to get up another couple of rope's lengths. Up to our left there was a rock-comb leaning against the night sky. The col must be just above us. Everything became clearer; we were out in the moonlight now, and we felt much better.

Who can judge distances in these places? First of all we said: just two more rope's lengths – but it was always more. Then, suddenly, I realized it was only one more. In the silence of the moonlight, the wind above us was hissing over the snow-crest, powdering us with cold dust. We stamped hard into the wind-pressed snow, our crampon points grated on hard ice, and out of the pother of snow-dust there loomed a dark mass, a flapping structure of stuff, planted on this loneliest spot on earth: the tent the Czechs had left behind.

We were very glad that it was still standing and we should not have to use our own. The wind was howling across the little saddle, protected by a short three-foot high ice-barrier, slanting in sideways and giving scanty shelter. The tent was in a bad way – one stay gone and the entrance torn open; it fluttered like some black ghost. I managed to insert a stay . . . and we couldn't get inside soon enough.

We tied the entrance up somehow, and there we sat in a welter of cast-off tins, bags, equipment, powdered here and there by snow, which had forced its way in through a couple of holes in the tent wall. It was midnight, at 23,800 feet; but, at least, we were under cover.

We were separated from the gale outside by a single layer of cloth, on which the wind pressed, ballooning it far inwards because of the lack of tension, filling the air with a murderous rattling, shaking our heads mercilessly as we sat there; but it was a biggish tent and we were able to move away from the billowing wall. We cooked a bit, having discovered a bag of Czech biscuits, tidied things up and settled down. Wearing a fleece jacket you can feel comfortable even in an ice-shanty – one which has been erected by the hand of man, at that.

I had long ago realized that, having Masaaki Kondo with me, I was not at all alone. 'Masaaki!' I said, 'Tomorrow: nothing! After tomorrow ... summit!' He laughed. 'Now sleep,' he said. And that is just what we did.

It was dark and August 19th had already begun, the day when we were to attempt the summit. The cooker was humming. We had found two extra thermos-flasks; we were going to fill the lot with pudding, tea, Ovo, then we could really get going with the sun's first ray. We started up a second cooker, so as to have a meal now. The hours went by and the big yellow-tent-sack full of snow slowly emptied.

We had taken a long rest yesterday and then reconnoitred the route. First over to the left, eastwards, across the hanging-glacier on the north side; but that way up to the saddle between the east and main summits, with which I had, for special reasons, flirted from down below, looked very long and would mean hours of hard work on tough, blue ice. There was some of this terribly tough stuff just above the tent, barring access to the North-west Ridge; but we had found a way to turn it by circling to the east, and the ridge itself, from what we had seen yesterday, was good. We still could not make out how the Czechs had gone on up above. Perhaps we should find a solution satisfactory to ourselves. Perhaps the West Face? The upper part had looked very good, but we were separated from it by a deep gully; maybe we could get on to it higher up. Actually, the route I had reconnoitred in 1965, when Tona, Herwig and I caught our first discoverers' glimpse into this corner, ran over the lower part of the West Face and then up the South ridge. (Someday someone will do it, as well as the traverse of all four of the West Peaks, a huge climb. We at least proved that it is possible.)

Today all those high crests would sink far below us.

The icy gale kept on, though slightly less intense. Everything in the tent was frozen, and little heaps of powdery, fine snow had collected under the holes in the rim of the tent. Every now and then the entrance blew open. Outside, the tension was now better, in spite of the missing pole. Yesterday, we had fixed dark lenses and face-scarves to our ski-goggles – which we had in addition to ordinary glacier-glasses. Under our helmets, the masks were more reminiscent of space travel . . . but the icy bombardment was grim . . .

An Apple on Tirich Mir

We could make do with a couple of hours of sleep, later – cooking was, at the moment, much more important. In any case one doesn't sleep properly. Every nerve and sinew was concentrated on the coming day, as if it were the only day ever. Indeed, for the time being, it *was* the only day.

The question was would Masaaki's crampons stay on. Yesterday, on the reconnaissance, they had come off several times: a problem of his outer-boots. Could we dispense with them? No, neither of us. Meanwhile we had adjusted the crampons. I had sustained slightly frozen toes on Tirich West IV; I didn't want them to get properly frostbitten this time. So I had found a solution: I wrapped a sheet of sorbo round the whole boot, pulled the stuff-bag over it and then, using a little force, strapped the crampons on over the lot.

One thing we must not, repeat not, forget: to take one of the two cookers along. Otherwise, we were ready. We had drunk to satiety, and the three thermoses – one of them for the climb – were full. Now for a short nap . . .

The day was blue and clear. We had reached the ridge by the way we had pin-pointed yesterday; at present it was easy, a snow-crest of no great steepness, decorated with great boulders, around which the wind had shaped deep, semicircular hollows. Days ago, from the base, we could see the track of the Japanese summit-party, just here, high above. It all seemed a long time ago . . .

Masaaki and I went on up the ridge, towards the summit; slowly, very slowly, much more slowly than we were capable of going, but keeping the rhythm of our breathing absolutely even. My thoughts went back to Dhaulagiri: seven years ago Nawang Dorje and I had approached the summit in exactly the same way. I had told him : 'We go slow, very slow, now!' And so we had gone on up . . . one step – and breathing . . . another step – and breathing . . . a shorter step, because it was steeper now – and breathing . . . then a zig-zag – and breathing . . . never stopping altogether – and breathing. In an hour Nawang Dorje and I had got to 26,000 feet, all by ourselves, and not excessively exhausted; and there we sat down and waited for the others. They weren't any less good than we – we simply used a different method. Where does the limit lie for a man? It is all a question of 'how' – that is to say, of technique – of self-reliance and, of course, a combination of both. It is a basis which anyone can find, but not till then will he reach the limits of his capabilities, or the ability to approach them – and then only if fortune gives him his chance.

So now, on Tirich Mir, we went slowly upwards – in the end, when it got steep, in a ludicrous pattern of zig-zags. By taking this long way, we mastered the human body's fallibility, never stopping, with the least possible exertion. Masaaki and I, going on up. Today we would be standing on the summit – if we did everything the right way ... and I would see to it, every moment of the way, that we did. For fortune had given us our chance.

The wind had almost dropped, except when a sudden gust howled through the crags of the Czech ridge. We had reached the arête, which consists of rough, somewhat unstable blocks, from the north, by way of the face, on to which we had made a traverse. Our rhythmic progress was now at an end, and we belayed one another from one stance to another. We were already on a level with the first of the West Peaks, something like 24,600 feet, having started out at 8 o'clock, and it was now ten. There were still 700 feet, more difficult now, to the summit. A porridge carton and a red silk pennant marked the place where the Japanese had turned back after their bivouac in the icy gale. Far down in the valleys we could see a few little tatters of cloud. It was a grand day.

The peaks shone clear around us and beneath us, almost all below our own level now. In the depths the curving glaciers snaked their way down, repeated again and again by the yellowy-white and black lines of their moraines. Directly below us, the granite buttresses of the north group shot up, crowned by the white crest of Tirich Nord, but even that was far, far below us. Far over in the thin mists of morning ranged Afghanistan's myriad peaks, Koh-i-Bandakor dominating them all. There lay the Arkari valley, with Ghul lasht Zom, Noshaq and Istor-o-Nal soaring above. We had to press on, but which way?

The ridge of unstable boulders did not look attractive. I looked across to 'my' west face; once we were across the couloir just ahead of us and up the wall beyond it, the going would be perfect. There we could resume simultaneous movement, step by step, till we hit the South Ridge, and then on up its soft back, rather like an enormous roof of snow, to the summit. That's what we would do!

Crossing the brittle couloir proved tricky. It was a V-shaped, deeply scored gully, very steep, its bed only a few feet wide and filled at the bottom with snow. For safety's sake I fixed a piton, but the whole thing was not more than Grade III. The rock-cliff was no more difficult; once up it we allowed ourselves a short rest at the rim of the West Face. The way up to the South Ridge lay clear ...

We reached it at about midday, after a long ascent over fine scree, little patches of snow, and boulders, straight through the upper sector of the west face. Our attention was attracted by a few lightish-coloured

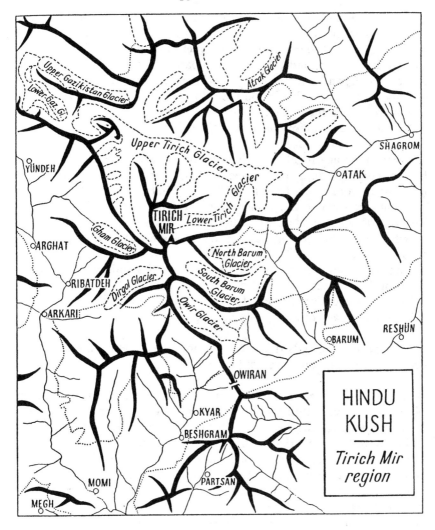

stones; dark tourmaline had overlaid them with a network of shining suns. My mind was by now completely at rest: we would get to the top. So we sat down for half an hour on a big flat stone at the edge of the South Ridge's broad white crest, ate a small meal and emptied the thermos. Wherever we looked now, our eyes travelled out over an endless sea of cloud. It was rising very slowly, but it was still far, far below us. And there, sitting next to me, was none other than the Jonah of the Japanese party – Masaaki – smiling.

Every now and then a hint of green showed through some hole in the cloud-carpet – a hamlet, 16,000 feet below. We had kept two apples for the summit, all these days – little green things which Musheraf Din, so eagerly awaited, had brought up to base camp the last time he went down to Shagrom. I decided I would leave mine up there on the summit.

Why do I have such luck on mountains? I do not know; all I know is that, at that moment, I was very grateful.

Yet, there's a question mark over all such matters . . .

We went on again. Though the summit was probably no more than a hundred or a hundred and fifty feet higher, the ridge had become almost level, so it would take time to get there. That didn't bother us – this strolling, high above the clouds, was marvellous. To our right, on the eastern side, I detected a cornice bordering our way, but the whale-back on which we were moving was broad and there was nothing to force us out towards it.

The ridge flattened out . . . at 1 p.m. we were standing on the white dome of the summit. Tirich Mir was ours.

What can one say? Masaaki looked at me and said: 'Very lucky . . .'

We hugged each other.

A page of Masaaki's diary with a hole, held before his chest . . . became the red gleaming sun of Japan.

What was there left for Didi and me to climb after I had done Tirich Mir? Obviously, nothing. But we were greatly attracted by a different kind of adventure: the crossing from the Tirich Glacier into Gazikistan, and then on into the Arkari valley. And after that, why not skirt Tirich Mir's southern flanks and come back into the Tirich Gol to rejoin our porter-friends at Shagrom? Our baggage could in the meantime be taken there, along the normal route, by some men led by Musheraf Din and stored in his hut. All around Tirich Mir: the prospect of strolling from village to village, with its white summit ever and again lifting a new aspect above the valleys, was highly attractive.

It was on August 25th that Didi and I started out from 'Koncordiaplatz', the name I had given, for private use, to the junction of the Upper Tirich Glacier's three arms. Once again we climbed over the scree-slope to the left of the ice-fall that bars the way to the Anogol* and pitched our bivouac-tent in the afternoon on the 'water-lily moraine', close to the provision-dump we had with such wise foresight established

* Anogol means 'valley of the pass', though there is no sign of any crossing of this glacier nowadays. – K.D.

there during our last reconnaissance (where, below a face with massive stratifications I had found rock fragments full of crinoids). The following day produced an unpleasant surprise; the pinnacles of ice in the upper basin of the glacier had grown considerably, and were now chest-high. We stumbled and cursed and fell about for hours, pushing a way through them, with Anogol Zom always before our eyes, but never appreciably nearer. In the end, we decided to steer as far as possible towards its east face, and to climb there; but before we could do that, we had to get through pinnacles of ice taller than ourselves. It turned into a veritable battle with these apparitions.

By evening our tent was up on the ridge at about 19,000 feet. Over a white fence of pinnacle ice we could look down into Gazikistan.

The next evening brought us sheer delight: flowers and grass, at the rim of a small tarn, which had formed between an old edge-moraine and the slope of the mountains, at about 13,000 feet. We had been on the march almost the whole day, climbing and making our way down and down; in the end to find the scent of grass and flowers. We slept out in the open, under a wide sky. What a lovely world this is!

For the next two days we were plagued by hunger – contrary to expectation there was no sign of human life here in Gazikistan – but we silenced it with wild rhubarb and onions. At first there was no kind of a track, and unstable scree-slopes made progress impossible at places. I chose an upper route, following a steinbock trail; while Didi climbed down to the glacier. So we went on for hours, with anything from three- to six-hundred feet of differential between us; while from time to time one or other of us would shout that it was 'better here'.

In spite of niggardly rhubarb-rations, I started to undertake an excursion on to the Upper Gazikistan Glacier, where I collected some geological specimens from its retaining wall. This also gave me the opportunity for a clear study of the 'crossing' from the Anogol into upper Gazikistan. This consisted of a pretty lofty ice-slope, which a climber could manage, maybe a Sherpa, but certainly not a local man without mountain equipment.

Till now, no expedition or reconnaissance had undertaken any of these crossings into Gazikistan. Even the inhabitants differ in their opinions. Judging by what we had seen, any such crossing must have been a very long time ago, for certainly nobody came up here nowadays. Yet what is the explanation of Musheraf Din's story: that long, long ago, people with horses used to cross from Afghanistan to Shagrom by way of the Anogol? Was it simply a legend? We had looked everywhere: nowhere had we seen even the possibility of such an 'extreme' route for horses. Even taking the alterations in the glaciers into account, the thing remains a riddle.

Didi, who had had to wait six hours for me because of my 'diversion', was rewarded by the spectacle of my trying to jump the full-flowing glacier-torrent between us, and – my leap curtailed by my heavy rucksack – falling right into it; it cooled my enthusiasm for 'diversions' for some time. That night we slept on sand under a thorn bush and dreamed of chapattis. We got them next day in that never-forgotten Arkari valley.

We were back with mother earth; and it was like a fairy-tale. At first there were just a boy and a girl standing on the path, their great eyes full of wonderment; then a bearded man came hurrying up, pointing enquiringly, asking where we had come from and shaking his head in unbelief. However, when we said 'chapattis' his astonishment at our *'bisi Tirich Mir'* soon turned to swift sympathy, as he patted us on the back and led us to his hut. We sat on the grass under two tall trees, whose branches bent, as the wind rustled through their leaves. An old man appeared, and a woman with a small child; she looked at us with marvellously clear eyes before departing, presumably to prepare the chapattis. It all seemed to us like a miracle. And the bearded man took down from the tree an age-old match-lock muzzle-loader and related with many words and gestures, how he had brought a steinbock down with it in Gazikistan. On the following day he came along with us as a porter.

Down at Arkari, we learned that two climbers had met their death on Tirich Mir. Next day, we met their companions and were given fuller details: they were the two Carinthian climbers, Hans Thomaser and Fritz Samonigg. They had set out for the summit on August 19th – just as we had done – quite unknown to us, be it said, and from a much lower camp than ours, on the other side of the mountain. At about 22,000 feet they had disappeared into the clouds – into that same sea of cloud on to which we had looked down and which, as it spread and spread, had that same day brought us a snow-storm and some critical moments in the choice of our line of descent. They were never seen again.

During the following days, as I watched the clouds continually mounting the flanks of that huge white peak, I kept on wondering whether our friends had reached the summit.

But the clouds keep their secret, and in any case, how would the answer alter anything?

There is a question-mark hanging over all things.

360 Million Years

Here in my hand I hold an unknown creature, which lived 360 million years ago. Its fossil still exists.

Three hundred and sixty million? I took a sheet of paper and tried somehow to get hold of the very idea. The thing was unbelievable; it sent shivers down my spine...

If I took a single forty-inch step every day, I would cover roughly 240 yards in a year. So in the thirty-six years of my life I would have gone five miles, and might expect – taking an optimistic view – to cover another four, or a little more, before I die. But if I wanted to go back to the time when this 'animal' I am holding in my hand was alive, I would – taking the prescribed single pace a day – have to cover a distance of 49,275,000 miles; in other words, farther than from this earth to Mars, or more than halfway to the sun – on foot.

One step a day for 360 million years...

In my hand lies a fossil, a thing that was once – unimaginably remote from me – alive.

Yes, farther from me than the orbit of Mars.

Nobody knows what this thing I am holding is, for no such living creature exists any more. It is one of the oldest, an inhabitant of the Devonian Sea, on whose bed waved whole forests of water-lilies.* In those days the first amphibians were invading the land which had already succumbed to ferns, shave-grass and licopodia. There were cuttle-fish and crabs, corals and mussels, strange types to some extent, but all identifiable today. And here, in the calm waters of a sea, whose surface the waves once ruffled, here where now cloud-topped mountains stand; here, between the delicate shapes of fronded sea-stars – those creatures so like 'miniature palms', for they look like plants, and have even been given the name 'water-lilies' – lived an absolutely unknown 'thing', unique and fascinatingly beautiful in its formation, about which nobody has the slightest notion...

Receptaculites Neptuni DEFRANCE, the scientists have named it. A resounding title for what? For a rare 'receptacle', about which no one is quite sure whether to class it as an animal or a plant. It appears to be

* Crinoids. – K.D.

several separate creatures, arranged in a marvellously regular pattern, enclosing a spherical space. No one has any idea how 'the thing' lived and functioned; but there it was – it existed.

It must have been a shallow sea which covered the original ground, where nowadays a track runs up to the 13,000-foot saddle of the Owir An; by its side there are still today single corals, countless stems of water-lilies, from the dawn of the earth's history.

I looked up at Tirich Mir, itself an instant in time. As Tona and I pushed forward along the southern arm of the Upper Tirich Glacier, we had seen revealed one of the great snapshots in the geological history of the earth – the 3,000-foot high intrusion of the Tirich Mir granite into the primeval black slate in the enormous plane of Tirich Mir West IV's western face. It was a whole chaos of light-coloured arms clawing into the dark slates, prising them apart, breaking them into clumps of strata – there were even great separate fragments, bigger than a row of houses, swimming like lost things in the weathered brown mass of the original bed-rock, once a fluid fiery mass in the tertiary period. They looked like dark lumps of sugar in dough. There they had remained unassimilated – for the granite had 'frozen' at that moment. A snapshot clocked, three thousand feet and more of it in height; the last sequence in a film shot millions of years ago.

You do not need to be a geologist to be impressed by it. It is an adventure from which, once introduced into it, you cannot escape. Tona and I regarded the Tirich Mir area as our own province. She was a qualified geologist; for me it was a serious though passionate hobby. Tona had made the first geological sketch-map of the mountains in this area. I broadened it, taking in a wider sweep, measuring strata, fetching samples, as yet not available, from remote corners. Nobody can imagine how delighted I was when, suddenly, on that lateral moraine of the Anogol Glacier, at about 16,500 feet, I came upon the stems of water-lilies, and at last the possibility of establishing the age of those dark layers moved within reasonable reach.

We were on the first complete circuit of Tirich Mir. My companion was a young native from the Arkari valley, Didi in the meantime had gone to Chitral and I pushed a fossil – a sea-lily stem found at the edge of the path below the Owir An – under my companion's nose. 'Look at that!' I said. He smiled, but shrugged his shoulders. I couldn't help thinking of the well-known Himalayan geologist whose porter took a very individual view about carrying 'stones'. When they reached their destination and the professor opened the case (which weighed the right amount) he found that its contents were ordinary stones from the bed of the last stream they had crossed. I understand that the porter had by then gone home.

When, after two hours, I was still breaking up boulders, my companion finally took such a waste of time amiss and pointed up to the saddle of the pass. However, we had not gone a hundred yards, when I suddenly discovered these rare, scarcely ever-seen creatures. They were beautifully circular, their pattern like some prehistoric jewellery. If they were corals, they were certainly very unusual ones. I had never before seen the base on which they lay, nor the surface – almost like a pineapple, or rather like a lepidendron, and yet not like that either. Some bryozoon, perhaps. Perhaps, after all, corals. Yet, a very special kind of coral...

Till this day not a soul knows how to classify these 'beings'. Only nine times have they been found anywhere in the world, only two of these in Asia. The nearest site where one has been found lies 600 miles away in Persia, the next nearest as far away as Western Australia. When I found mine, I at once felt sure that it was something extraordinary, and under the critical gaze of my porter packed all the marvellous-looking but somewhat heavy fragments I could lay hands on into my rucksack. (And, of course, not into *his* bag . . .) Then we strolled on towards the top of the pass and a new aspect of Tirich Mir, or of the clouds gathered about its crest.

'Higher than the eagle soars . . .'

I shall go back there again; many times, I rather suspect.

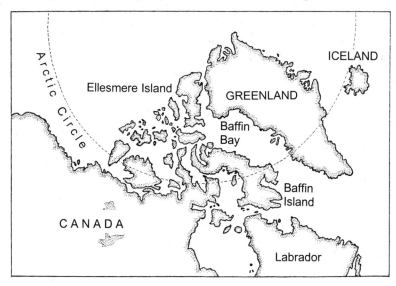

PART V

Three Words From Greenland

Tässa ... Susa ... Imaka ...

It is snowing. I am standing at my window in Salzburg, looking down on the rubble of the Salzach, with its big round boulders. The flakes go whirling by ...

A book grows rather like a snow-crystal. One doesn't write it from start to finish but, in greater or less degree, all at the same time – a bit here and a bit there; some of the star-points grow big, others remain rudimentary, some of them cut into each other – irregularly, as a snowflake forms, though it, too, follows its own laws.

The dry smell of the rope, the river and its stones down there, the echo of a Greenland song – that is why my book is not in chronological order; for everything is of the present, held in the moment when thought captures it. At times I have tried to preserve a chronology, so as to give the reader a picture of time's passage; but I have only succeeded in the broadest sense. So the jumble in these pages is not meant to be of time, but just as it comes to mind, now linked by strands of time, now suddenly timeless again. And for that reason, this book will never be a neatly-rounded whole – but it reflects a reality, which I am sure is not mine alone.

The echo of that song from Greenland – I hear it all of a sudden, and suddenly, in the midst of the city's densest traffic, Greenland is there, the great open spaces, the silence; until the next bus rumbles past. Or again, in the far Hindu Kush, by the rim of whose glaciers blow the same pale-red flowers as blow on the shores of the iceberg-cluttered Greenland fjords, I remember an evening when the cheerful native porters stamped in rhythmic unison on the ground, while Hayad ud Din, Musheraf, or Neap, clapped time with their hands till the air above

Three Words from Greenland

the camp fire trembled as if an iceberg were overturning. There they danced an uninhibited dance, like Greenlanders, to a tune, which my old guitar – four times broken and five times stuck together again – had transported from the northlands, just as if it were a song of their own. None of them knew a Greenland word, no one understood '*uchlok navok tachererpok sekinek*', nobody had any idea that it was all about the sun and the thunder of the icebergs; but they sang, and they clapped, and Greenland was there, though only I knew it. The fact that it was all in the past did not upset me. '*Tässa*' and '*Susa*' – Greenland was there. And would be again. '*Imaka*' – 'perhaps'.

Those three words are common in Greenland, and one hears them repeated every day. They are a sort of philosophy for those dwellers under the perpetual day and the long night of many months.

Greenland is an island. Geographers allot it to North America, politicians to Denmark. Basically, it is something quite unique; a kind of continent, on which human beings live, as hardly anywhere else on the earth's surface, in the midst of an all-powerful nature – and know it. It is peopled by roughly 30,000 souls, the population of a provincial town; yet so large is this island that, if laid out across Europe, it would stretch from Scandinavia to North Africa. The habitable ground is narrow, a coastal hem; the settlements lie at great distances from one another, with no road links, on the fringe of the ice-cap, at places 10,000 feet thick, which almost covers the island in its entirety. When you look above the Greenland peaks, the sky behind them is not blue like ours, but white – the *inlandsis*; higher than almost all the mightiest peaks in the island; it seems illimitable, and the loneliness of the traveller in this immensity of the white sky is unmeasurable, terrifying and compelling.

Fridtjof Nansen, Robert Peary, Alfred Wegener...

Winter in Greenland. The polar night endures for months; the nearer to the Pole you are, the longer it lasts. Icy cold and darkness reign, lightened only by the coloured glory of the Northern Lights, the moon and, at long last, by the reflection of the returning sun. A European is especially hard hit by the isolation from the world without. And the sea remains frozen long after the sunlight has come back. It is not till late in spring, rather the beginning of summer, that the supply vessels from Denmark fight their way, slowly, slowly, through the coastal ice. This is not so everywhere; but even in the south-west of this gigantic island, where, in the orbit of a branch of the Gulf Stream and mostly this side of the Polar Circle, the greater part of the 'towns' lie situated (Godthaab, the biggest, has 5,000 inhabitants), where living conditions are a little more favourable, a foreigner must love Greenland (or a fat salary) greatly before he can be persuaded to spend more than one winter there. And what about the Greenlanders themselves? They say their winter is lovely beyond compare. The foreigner, thinking perhaps of the endless journeys by sledge, can hardly understand that. The Greenlander just smiles: for him Greenland, in the grip of its long winter, is 'his' Greenland; even more than in the brilliant summer, when, under a flood of light, there is a universal explosion of green, with the sun continually circling the heavens, flowers of every hue show their bright faces, often springing from soil lying only inches deep over the smooth, polished rock below. Greenland – in truth the green land – as the Vikings found it, at the turn of the tenth century, on their incredibly daring voyage in their long boats, under Eric the Red. Green Land, as today's climber experiences it, flying in for a short visit from Copenhagen or Los Angeles, or coming by ship up the fjords, to reach unclimbed peaks on the rim of the ice-cap; and returning home, ere ever the twilight of winter's approach descends on the land and the sea stiffens in the grip of the first frost.

. . . There, below the aircraft's wing lay Iceland; the broad ice-field of the Vatna Jöku, fringed by a carpet of cloud, greyish-black lava-streams, then green, much green, overlaid with grey; brightly-coloured extinct volcanoes, red, yellow, ochre, dark brown; then clouds again and the darkness of the sea. That was Iceland. We were flying at 31,000 feet, almost at the speed of sound – Bruno, Pigi, Silvio, Mauro, Carlo and I. We represented the Greenland Expedition of the Tortona Italian Alpine Club, and had all been together before, in Africa. Our objective, the peaks of the Qioqe Peninsula far up the west coast, beyond the 71st parallel; great unclimbed mountains – only Mauri, Guaico and Ghiglione had ever visited the place, six years before, and had climbed wonderful Perserajoq.

How much longer? Look: little, sharp lumps of sugar, close together on the dark sea-surface below the clouds – drift-ice! We glued our noses to the windows – we could only be a matter of seconds from Greenland.

There it was – the east coast! A spiky wilderness of peaks, rising sheer out of the sea – behind an armour-plating of enormous floes. Blue fjords with millions of white dots on them, gigantic rivers of ice winding down to the sea, mountains and yet more mountains. The east coast, with its armour of floes, held for the greater part of the year in the icy grip of a cold stream from the north.

We could not tear ourselves from the windows; looking down to where, now, the shadow of our aircraft and its vapour-trails was etching

Three Words from Greenland

a black line across fjords, cloud-layers and peaks, as we drew ever nearer to the gigantic ice-cap. That streak which had grown in a matter of seconds – could that really be us? – was tearing across crevassed glaciers, jumping the very next moment, quicker than a heart-beat, from summit to summit, finally touching the last isolated crags still able to penetrate the ever-growing armour-plate of the ice – the so-called *nunatakker*...

Interruptions of blue-green lakes formed by the melting waters, miles broad. Then blinding brightness. White; nothing but white. So stark, so dazzling that it hurt the eyes. Light without outlines. During the next hour of the flight two passengers went snow-blind. I could only detect faint contours down there through doubled glare-glasses. Wavy contours...

Inlandsis. The great white desert. Enormous, indescribable.

We flew five hundred miles across it.

Sondre Strömfjord: the jet-strip close to the edge of the ice, on the west coast, at the start of the fjord of the same name, 130 miles long: a civil airport, sprung from an American base. And that is what it still is, though one may not see much of the installations, mostly underground, any more than of the other military posts which one hears are partly buried beneath the cuirass of *inlandsis*. We touched down.

We touched down. A reindeer was taking a walk on the runway, followed soon by an Arctic fox. Presently a jet took off for Los Angeles.

When would our helicopter arrive to take us to Egedesminde?

'Well, why don't you make an excursion to the inland ice today – it's very fine. Meanwhile we will do our best. You might be able to get away tomorrow; if not, the day after. Don't worry too much; you are in Greenland now, you know...' the fair-haired Dane gave a laugh. So the sun circled round the wooden huts – twice...

The red bus, seating twenty-eight, whose big shovel-bladed rotors whirled in the air as it slowly settled down, buzzed like a giant bumble-bee.

Then we were off. After two infuriating days of waiting (that is what one would have said in Europe: here they just shrugged their shoulders and said the single word, *susa*). For a moment I thought of Asia, whence these Greenlanders originally came from, and of its timelessness, as we swept across the land at 130 m.p.h. in our red 'jet-chopper'. I was told later that there are precisely three of these flying buses in all Greenland. One was always undergoing maintenance. The other two – well, there was a flight-plan for them...

Brilliant, bright green. Low humps, rock, grass, fjords. Hundreds of lakes – in the distance, the inland ice. A river with great, uncontrolled loops. Sand. Greyish-green reeds and mosses. Grey-green water . . . Violet-hued, milk-coloured, deep-blue water! Each lake a different colour. Bright light: everything clear and sharply defined. Ice-flakes on the water, a fine webbing of ice on the next lake. Another fjord. Islands, and more islands. Unpretentious, on one of them, lay our Egedesminde, with icebergs like toy dice in front of it. Like ships – no, much bigger . . .

We just escaped being made very unhappy that day at Egedesminde. The captain of the *Tikerak* explained to us, calmly and amiably, that he had never heard of us, his ship was full and that he would be very pleased to take us on his next trip, which would be in a fortnight. In a fortnight!

And what about our telegram from Italy? Damn it all! Some agitated moments ensued. We had to deal with heads no less tough than the iceberg-scored timbers of the ship. We did it at the top of our voices, using the whole range of the vocabulary, and we kept at it relentlessly. After all we were an Italian Expedition, and an official one at that! No, nothing could persuade us to go ashore from the *Tikerak* of our own freewill! And that telegram, where was it? Next morning everything was still as inconclusive as before . . .

We leaned on the rail as the ship headed northwards, leaving Egedesminde in her wake. Bruno thought solemnly of all Tortona's famous deeds of heroism, while we cleared our throats, and stood stiff as tall statues in the strong breeze, looking with resolute mien into the wind.

The wooden hull of our ship went bobbing up and down. Icebergs, innumerable ice-blocks went past. The sea was a bluish-black and there were white horses on it. Above it, under a pale sky, lay the ridges separating the fjords, brownish-grey, topped by a little snow. Soft and far they stretched, merging into one another.

Our good ship *Tikerak* was built for just such journeys as this. Round, all of wood, slow, comfortable. In Greenland language her name means: 'who comes for a short visit'.

The helmsman, a Dane, came to Greenland fifteen years ago, got caught up in it, and has been steaming along this coast, year by year, ever since. He kept on telling me proudly of his lovely Greenland daughter, whom he was going to take back to Denmark for the first time; she had just turned fourteen. He was pale, rather sloppy, looking more like some kind of an office-wallah somewhere. I wondered how many icebergs he had had to miss in the fog, in his time? He was a quiet man, and his every second word – when not actually talking about his daughter – was *susa*, which means, 'don't worry about it'. I have him to thank for that word.

The sky above our mast was deep and dark. There was a whole flotilla of icebergs ahead. Then – a heap of little dots, a cluster of gaily-coloured dabs along the shore, jolly, every kind of colour. Little wooden houses. A 'town'.

They were all of a pattern. There was a church (for both faiths) a school, various buildings of the KGH – the Royal Greenland Trade Department – a fish-processing factory, maybe, a small supermarket, even a motor-car for the two miles of road. It is very rare nowadays to find one of the old Greenland peat-igloos alongside the gay little wooden homes.

'. . . *Uchlok navok tachererpok sekinek pavanilo uchloriak kaamavok* . . .' To our ears, it sounded like a *conversazione* among wild ducks in the reeds. Karen, Eva and Louise were royally amused at our efforts to master the secrets of wild-duck talk, or rather to learn one of their Greenland songs by heart. It was quite a job. We captured the notes on the guitar; Louise wrote down the words; Karen produced a sort of translation. Karen was a delightful child, casting smiles or oblique glances from slanting Asiatic eyes; blue they were, and her round face was framed by two long reddish-brown plaits. The buxom Louise had pencilled eyebrows; she was dark as they come, like an actress in an Eskimo film. Eva evinced something of the jolliness of a young, female seal. Karen was a beauty of rare quality, though. Later, when my second daughter was born, I gave her that name, a piece of Greenland, to keep.

As it happened, we found out afterwards that the tune originated somewhere in Canada. Gaily strung together, with Greenland words, the song was a portrait of this coast: an entity which the timbers of our ship also embraced. People, met together by mere chance, utterly different people, each with his own goal in life, yet, under Greenland skies, constituting an entity. An ephemeral circle, to which each of them, if only by his presence, contributed something.

There was the old professor of geography from St Andrew's University in Scotland; a quiet man, who returned every year, for many years, to Greenland, to the unknown island off the west coast. There he had discovered a petrified forest, and was working on a map. He was mostly to be found leaning on the rail, alone. He was glad to be here again, and told me that he now had with him the material for setting up a small, permanent research hut at the perimeter of the native settlement on the island.

There was tall, black Michel, a sympathetic type, speaking fluent French, even understanding the Greenland tongue. He had been living on the island for two years, in one place or another. Greenland's only Negro, he was apparently working on a book. He liked it here, this possessor of all the vitality of Africa, all the charm of Paris – on this bleak coast, where one was responsive to charm. He really wanted to go to Thule, to the last of the racially-pure Eskimos, but had not been granted a permit. It was from him that I, the 'new boy' in Greenland, learned that *ab* and *namek* mean yes and no. Also the meaning of the continual *imaka*, which means 'perhaps', and often sounds like a Greenland version of *inshallah!* (As in: 'our ship will turn up in three days, imaka' – perhaps: God willing...)

I got to know the first officer, at midnight one night – it was of course daylight – as I wandered about the empty deck, my guitar under my arm. Suddenly I was confronted by this Dane with a huge, bushy beard. Very soon three of us, he, the helmsman and I, were sitting over beer and Danish ham in the cookhouse, guzzling like savages. Presently I reached for my guitar. When I started my song from Trieste, the bearded one leaped to his feet, banged his fist on the table and beamed with delight. '*Trieste – oh, bella Trieste!*' He stood there, bulking like a wardrobe and sang, full-throated. Trieste. Outside, the icebergs were bobbing. Then he explained that he had been there for a day, some years ago.

Mountaineering he held to be sheer lunacy...

Green is the emerald and its fire burns fiercer than ice. Mette's intelligence was ice-cold – a green laser-beam; a computer with the heart of a twenty-year-old girl. It was extraordinary; when she said anything, it was almost impossible to find an answer. She had come to Greenland for the winter. When I got back from the mountains of Qioqe I met her again at Umanak. She was off to Nepal next. I have never seen her since.

She told me much about the Greenlanders. She made me understand that our sojourn here was only a short visit, and I envied her the freedom of the great winter lying ahead of her – an experience barred to me.

On went our ship. Christianshaab, Jakobshaven, Qotligssat... new faces came aboard, old ones were missing. Yet, for a definite time, each of them belonged to the day's round, simply because they were on board.

Upernivik, Umanak... the journey lasted four days. Actually, it was always the same day.

Three Words from Greenland

Diary:

'Jakobshaven, ashore. The big fjord, spewing out thousands of icebergs. Up the hill . . . How low the sun stands in the sky . . . Utter stillness. The sea glints yellow. The rocks are rounded and firm. We go on up.

'The children find a bird. Joy! So many little hands reaching out, stroking, squeezing it . . . it will die. Love . . .

'We turned to go, and they wave to us: *Farvel – farvel – farvel* . . . the flowers, the crosses, the moss. The icebergs . . .

'"Tomorrow it will be dead – and it is love."

'The ship will be leaving soon.'

We came to Umanak on a dark, rainy day. A handful of houses on an island, consisting almost entirely of one great sharp-peaked mountain, winging up more than three thousand feet straight out of the waves. Many, many icebergs. A tiny harbour. And Pedersen waiting for us, here at the starting-point of our expedition.

'*Ragazzi, siamo arrivati* – here we are boys!' It was midnight, at the peninsula Qioqe. The mountain walls were dark in cloud, and it was raining. The bow of our small boat grated on shingle. Out we jumped, Bruno first, then the rest of us and the two Greenlanders, come to help us unload the heavy cases, labelled *Qioqe*. There was nothing to be seen in the filthy rain.

Pederson had brought us the sixty miles from Umanak, Pedersen, the resident agent of the government and the angelic helper of all expeditions. This man had already spent ten years in Greenland – oh, for his gift of complete relaxation! Everything in order: we, our cases, everything, safely on the rocks, in the teeming rain. The Greenland men pushed off from shore, laughing, pointing a finger to their foreheads: mountaineering, what a joke! One of them, a great bear of a Viking, the others short, dark, Mongolian types. '*Arrivederci!*' We waved, Pedersen raised a hand, the red boat shuddered and disappeared among the shadowy icebergs. We were to be here for weeks, all alone on the great, unpeopled peninsula. '*Arrivederci*, Pedersen!' Don't forget us . . .

This filthy rain! Quick, boys, up with the tent!

Our base camp was just twenty feet above sea level. The sun came breaking through the clouds. Up there, six thousand feet up, one marvellous peak, then another . . .

Qioqe: a veritable Piz Badile, a pyramid of a mountain, gently curving ice-peaks, like in the Bernina; a great wall, not unlike the Jorasses. And then an unbroken succession of peaks . . .

Qioqe. We spent weeks there, but months would not have sufficed. How infinite can a range of mountains be?

The peninsula reaches out thirty miles from the rim of the inland ice towards the Baffin Sea. A huge fjord to the north, another to the south; to the west, beyond the deeply-indented arm of a fjord, the mountainous island of Upernivik, uninhabited, as is all the realm of Qioqe. A huge glacier, flowing down from the ice-cap, ceaselessly calves icebergs into the forty-mile long north fjord; it is the some in the south. And then there are the peninsula's own glaciers. These do not all reach down to the fjord; but from 'Three Fjord Peak' the ice-avalanches thunder down, airborne for 5,000 feet, on to the surface of the sea. More icebergs . . .

Floating archways; a giant's boot; Monte Rosa – really, it looked just like Monte Rosa; a hat; a giantess's comb, shimmering, full of fine teeth; patches of green, blue, yellow light; crystals glittering in the light of the low sun; ships; castles, often three hundred feet long . . . all of them moving slowly down the fjord, or back up it, at the dictates of the daily current. We kept on seeing some of them, like Monte Rosa and the comb, over and over again. Others disappeared. Then there would be thunder, tremendous in the silence, as a berg suddenly disintegrated, or some colossus, higher than a house, lost its balance and, with the noise of a dying beast, began to turn over in the water, as chunks broke away or the whole edifice burst into pieces. Often, then, the great waves engendered by the dissolution pictured other fantastic images, as the thing tottered to destruction . . .

Qioqe, with its huge walls, shining yellow, sheer from the water's edge, mirrored below – 5,000 feet and more they shoot up from the sea. 'Ultimate problems.' Grey flanks. And, higher still, peaks running up to nearly 8,000 feet . . .

'Ultimate problems?' These have always existed, everywhere; but who thinks of them here?

My thoughts turn to the moon's overpowering landscape. Huge brownish-yellow craters against the blue, white-rimmed sky of the earth. Utter loneliness. Craters, mountains. Who would even think of climbing a face, there? That is too vast a landscape; and movement there is different, strange . . .

Something similar happens to the visitor to Greenland. In a boat, he moves over submerged valleys, glides past mountain walls, as in a dream, from one peak to another. Here they are, all the time, everywhere, the mountains. They have climbed down into the sea. Mountains and sea, fused in one another, in front of your eyes. This unity of height and breadth transforms the mountains; they are more omnipresent, stronger.

Three Words from Greenland

As the sun circles they never cease to vary their expression. A wall? Just part of a mountain, a trait of its face.

Everything here becomes more substantial, constitutes a unity. The rock-faces of Qioqe, gleaming yellow. Pale red blossoms with a cross at their heart. Strata of black tourmaline, thick as your arm. Red granite; yellowish-grey lichens. Knuckle-deep moss. The dark, white-flecked carpet of the harebell meadow. Icebergs. Glimmering muscovites. The bright light of day; the muted yellow light by night. The sharp black shadows thrown on the fjord-walls by the opposing peaks. Silence. Blue-green beryl crystals. Green ones? Emeralds? High excitement, fully justified from the human standpoint. However, the mighty pressure of the mountains has crushed them.

Shimmering bodies of many small fish, swarming to the surface like one body; a few big ones . . . We could not get them to bite. They played with the float, nibbled happily at the lead. We only caught one. Innumerable screaming gulls. Dark green water-plants. Layers of cyanide in the rock, shimmering a whitish-blue, like ice. And the icebergs . . .

I went out while the others were still asleep. It was a fabulous morning, that first one on Qioqe. I was avid to know what it all looked like behind the barrier of dark blocks, piled up perhaps, one fine day, by a landslide from 'Three Fjord Peak'. I found a valley there, leading from this western shore towards the interior of the peninsula. It was the only way, for great mounds of slabs went plumbing into the sea on either side of our base camp.

What kind of a valley – would there be cliffs in it, too? I moved on up, over a soft cushion of moss. It was a paradise. Deep and soft, like a carpet, underfoot. Lichens at every step, flowers; and among them the landslide's enormous boulders. It was a broad upland valley like those at home among the 10,000-foot peaks – yet I was not seven-hundred feet above sea level. Knuckle-deep moss, rust-brown peaks, streaked with fresh snow, ice-slopes thrusting to the blue vault, endless humps of moraines. All of it unexplored, untrodden till this day. I was content, happy. Here there would be plenty to do.

Was that a partridge? Or a pheasant? It was certainly a big bird, mottled black and brown, with a long neck . . . just like a picture in the cookery book. It was just two yards away. Trustfulness personified, it laid its head on one side and gave me a searching examination. No, this one had never seen a human being before! It was not till I got within three feet that he gave a little hop and stood, reluctantly, aside.

A partridge, eh? I am the first human being, thought I, the first in paradise; and that naturally connotes certain responsibilities. Happily, and with the lofty feeling of one who has exercised great renunciation, I went farther into paradise, the first human being . . .

There, cut into a boulder in front of me, stood that word *'Imaka'* – 'perhaps'. At first I could not grasp it. What, here? I stood there as though turned to stone. Was that a date – just a fortnight ago? I, Adam, the first man ever, breathed heavily. But – who?

'Eva – Hans,' I read. I swallowed hard.

But how was it possible? Umanak was sixty miles away. Qioqe uninhabited – hadn't Pedersen told us so? That hadn't bothered Eva. Suddenly I was looking at the region with different eyes – from the mountaineering angle, I told myself, the peninsula remained unexplored.

On my way down to camp I came upon another inscription. 'Eva-Knud', it ran. (My reconnaissance report began to assume a universal interest. During the many days we went on the peninsula, we went deeply and variedly into what Eva looked like; unfortunately, it all remained obscure – she never materialized.)

I had noticed something else: we had landed on the wrong side of the glacier tongue. Up its trough, every way was blocked, from here, by a deep gorge. Later, we erected a kind of emergency crossing in the icy water – the 'bridge' – built of slabs of rock. It took a long time. The gulls screeched and laughed 'he–he–he–he!' at us. 'They are laughing at us,' declares Mario, dragging rocks around (he is an insurance director).

At first we had nothing to laugh about. What distances! Heavy carries, reconnaissances – miles long – towards the centre of the peninsula. Moraine hummocks – up and down, up and down, down and up – then ice. Camp I at 1,400 feet; camp II at 3,300. The central glacier was a chaos of crevasses; gaping cracks full of water. The snow-bridges were so sloppy that one was prepared to see them cave in if one only looked hard enough. We began to wonder whether we would ever get to the centre of the peninsula, as Carlo and I crawled over the snow, on all fours, during our first attempt. That is the great handicap at this time of year: there is no frost at night and, under the sun that never ceases to circle, the glaciers seem to be visibly disintegrating into water, snow-slush and again water. There is no safe climbing 'daytime'; only near the summits do conditions improve.

'Avanti i mei prodi!' – onwards, my heroes! This was Bruno's stock exhortation. Definitely a memory of Tortona's famous history goes everywhere with him – Tortona, the 'strawberry city' in the Apennines. Bruno was the originator of our expedition, the inspiration of everything

undertaken by the Tortona Section of the CAI, but most of all a firecracker of ideas and humour. He is a doctor, and had served in Russia during the war. He wore a fierce red sou'-wester, and we called him Nansen. And it was he who climbed weighed down by bundles of tents, cases and gunny-bags. Like the others, Mauro, the insurance director, assured us that he had never spent a leave to match this one. He was our unconscious humorist. At Copenhagen, with a dead-pan face, he had wanted to declare his *Corriere della Sera* as our fourteenth item of baggage, because we had thirteen and he was superstitious. Meanwhile we still survived; though one day, horror written on his face, he discovered that we had pitched our base camp plumb on the burial ground of a long-vanished Greenland settlement.

Carlo – we called him 'Il Mulo' – said little and carted much. He was a patient man, married, and a sculptor. He deserved a hero's monument, rucksack and all, in the main square. He carried more than anyone else.

Pigi was the best groomed of us all: even in Qioqe he looked like an Italian. Seeing that he was the second doctor in the party, obviously nothing could happen to us.

All the same, something did happen. High up in the dangerous central glacier's chaos of crevasses, a snow-bridge collapsed under Silvio, pitching him head-first into the deep, water-filled rift and dislocating an arm. The united efforts of Pigi and Bruno got it back again, but for Silvio, unfortunately, this meant *finis*. Next time Pedersen came, he went back with him. Would we ever get to the centre of the peninsula, with the glacier 'running against us' like this? We had quite enough by the time we did...

'*Avanti i mei prodi!*' Bruno's eyes were bright with excitement at the overpowering impressions showering down on us. We were just 300-feet below the summit of Three Fjord Peak – the last 300 feet before it would be ours. We had finished the traverse of the hanging-glacier's rim – that hanging-glacier from which the ice-avalanches break away 5,000-feet sheer into the fjord. Now we could see down to the water, a breathtaking downward glance – deep and far below, dark as the dark-blue heavens, pointed with dazzling white stars, yes a heaven in itself.

I stood bemused, rooted to the spot, looking at that white-starred, blue expanse.

They were icebergs of course. One of them capsized, and the distant roar of thunder came rolling up from the abyss. Out of this world... if one could only stay here for ever. Astonishing what feelings every manifestation of heaven can awaken...

'Up, my heroes!' On again, up. Mountains and more mountains, grey, blue, white, all around. With a shout we pushed a ski-stick, with its pennants, up into the Greenland sky. We had climbed our first peak. We shook hands, hugged each other, laughing, full of joy.

Here we stood on the north-western cornerstone of Qioqe, at our feet the mighty north fjord, forty miles long; and nearly 6,000 feet below our toe-caps lay the wide mirror of the sea. A whole Eiger North Face! But this one was yellow, with vertical walls. And, over there, in the north – *sneepyramiden!* The outlines of a huge peak, fifteen hundred feet higher than ours. Then the sharp needles of Upernivik, the mountain walls of Qioqe. And deep indented arms of fjords . . .

We christened it Three Fjord Peak. A day of days, this. And the knowledge that night would not fall on this peak of ours gave that lofty, exposed place an indescribable air of friendliness and security. Under the slowly circling sun, we spent six hours up there.

Another capsizing iceberg, somewhere – that roar breaking the limitless silence, ever returning out of the peace of the blue heavens, surprising every time, yet familiar, often sounding like a sudden thunder-clap from the sun itself. It is as much a part of Greenland's long day as the hooting of cars is in our own. Could there be a greater contrast?

Lower and lower moved the sun, northwards now and closer to the horizon. The mountains changed their faces, the shadows lengthened, warmer grew the tints . . . Sea! Dazzling light! Black icebergs floating in the blinding gold of the waters. I closed my eyes. 'Yes – we will stay a while longer . . .'

Today, when any of us thinks back to the Peak of the Three Fjords, what he sees is that incredible sky, below him.

The stones came rolling and rattling down. We were high above the ice-plateau at the heart of the peninsula, on the central peak. It is a huge, regularly-shaped mountain, the highest or second highest in Qioqe, about 7,600-feet high. We were pushing on up the west face, with bivouac-equipment on our backs, Carlo, Pigi and I; we moved over steep, crumbling gullys, and rock-cliffs which hung, overlapping, above us. We talked in whispers, for fear of dislodging falling stones. There was a rumbling, crackling crash . . . 'Take cover!' And again. 'That's because you coughed,' said Carlo the silent, tersely. That disintegrating face is 2,500 feet tall, and quite a thing for the nerves; cat's-climbing, on velvet paws, always ready to jump. We zig-zagged up the confusion of grey and rust-red rock, where things could at any moment spring so suddenly to life. We took a breather on a shoulder of rock. It was evening; once again the sun was circling northwards. There was a castellated ridge above us. Should we take a short nap?

Three Words from Greenland

What an illimitable, universal thing is mountaineering here in Greenland – made for men of the daytime and men of the night! Anything is possible, all the time. I lay in my sleeping-bag in the sun, out in the open. Pigi crawled into the red bivouac-tent and Carlo, after smoking a cigarette, followed him. I woke up towards midnight, when the sun stood low and the light had turned yellow. It was an extraordinary scene. So we decided to climb our peak by night.

Midnight, an ochre sun. We climbed. The towers on the ridge were like cardboard cut-outs; we watched our own shadows moving against glaciers that glimmered yellow, themselves stroked by long shadow-fingers. The sun disappeared behind a cloud-bank and everything went blue and cold.

At 6,500 feet we took to our down-jackets and climbed on. Slowly the peaks sank away below us and the view grew wider, embracing *sneepyramiden* pyramids to the north, far across Upernivik's rock-teeth to the soft outlines of the hills in the Nugssuak peninsula, far to the south, farther even than Umanak. The fjords stabbed darkly into the land. Out to the east there lay an unnatural whiteness – the inland ice. There was tough, smooth ice close to my face. And now there was the cornice of a ridge; just below it, I was within an inch of falling into a totally unexpected crevasse.

We got to the top at 2 a.m., and named it '*Picco Centrale Gabriele Boccalatte*', in honour of that great Tortona climber who fell while climbing the Triolet. Our altimeter showed 7,700 feet. Before us lay the Südfjord, deep in the dusk, and the shimmering domes of Alfred Wegener-land, looking as if someone had poured yellow whipped-cream over them. A broad glacier flowed down to the sea. From its front, clean-cut as by a knife, a new-born iceberg was slowly floating out into the south fjord...

Would climbing – mountaineering – *downwards* be a crazy idea? If you have an objective the 'greatest nonsense in the world' knows no bounds of restraint. There was the Südfjord: there was the sea.

Suppose we were to cross all the ranges, all the glaciers of Qioqe right down to the sea, at the far side of the peninsula? My companions looked at me in astonishment; seconds later they were patting me on the back – what a splendid notion – *Che idea!* let's do it! It would be the first-ever traverse of Qioqe! So, while Bruno and Mauro set off on a reconnaissance to the north-east, we climbed, heavily laden, up into the central glacier's criss-cross of crevasses – Carlo, '*Il Mulo*', fully living up to his nickname, Pigi and I, carrying smaller 'sentry-boxes' on our backs.

Far out ahead of us stretched the white, untrodden plateau that was the peninsula's heart, with thin lines – hidden crevasses – drawn on its bright surface. We thought of Silvio and his crippling fall; the snow was soft and watery, here too; no frost to harden it by night. For all the magnificence of central Qioqe spread around us, those hidden crevasses left us with an uncomfortable feeling. One cautious stride after another, along an avalanche-cone. Was that a stream I could hear – the gurgling of a —

. . . Stream? Oh yes, it was a stream all right, gurgling noisily, a hundred and fifty feet below my dangling legs, at the bottom of a crevasse. I clung to the lip of the fissure, jamming myself into the snow, fighting to keep upright, pressed down by my heavy pack, beneath me the void. Not a damned thing to be found, to give me a foot-hold! In the end I found some support, somewhere, and stayed motionless on it for a matter of seconds; then, very carefully, I rammed in my axe, Carlo tightened the rope and I heaved myself sideways out on to the flat snow of the glacier, where I lay for a time, gasping for breath. Thanks, Carlo: a lucky get-away! I could easily have gone dangling down there, for the first time in my life.

The plateau seemed to go on for ever. We broke through more than once. It was not till evening that we came to a broad snow-saddle, with great ice-peaks above it; a breach flanked by towers like sky-scrapers. Ahead, where it fell away steeply into the depths, lay grey mists. Could the sea be somewhere down there? We waited six hours on a rock-rib at the saddle's edge, before the view cleared. There was the sea, 4,000 feet below us – the Südfjord.

Immediately, came the doubts. Could we climb all that way down, and then all the way up again? We had no boat, and there is not a living soul in the Südfjord. A few hundred feet below us, the glacier appeared to have been chopped-off abruptly; there must be an enormous ice-cliff down there. Much, much farther below, a brown snake of moraine poured out of a deep, steep-sided cauldron, on its long way down to the sea. Over it all presided a marvellous mountain, a peak such as one finds in the Andes.

Our objective was that sea down there.

At camp III, Pigi was all growls; he didn't think we could possibly do it. All the same, we said, let's go as far as we can, and then we can see what still lies ahead. Carlo thought we could do it. We decided to leave the tent here at 4,400 feet.

We managed it. For nine hours we climbed and clambered down rock-pitches, ledges and ice; lower down still, over the rubble of the moraines. Then – we ran the last hundred yards down to the shore, plunged our hands into the waters of the Südfjord. Everything about us was green, there were flowers everywhere – and that lovely coast was ours and ours alone for a whole hour. Delighted, we built a big cairn, strolled along the water's edge. Exactly where the glacier-stream cascades into the sea, we hoisted our pennants on a couple of boulders in the foaming brown water, to celebrate the first traverse of Qioqe. Our joy knew no bounds.

We were plagued by raging hunger; our provisions had run out. After a short bivouac a few hundred feet up from the sea we were climbing again. 'The second traverse of Qioqe!' growled Carlo, usually so silent, as we worked our weary way up towards the last tin of pork up on the saddle. We threw a longing glance back at the Andean peak . . . After thirty hours on end, we waded, more dead than alive, through the ice-cold water of the stream between us and base camp. Where the hell had that 'bridge' got to? The gulls mocked us overhead.

Curiously enough, the bridge was there next day.

'Apples! Have some apples!' cried Bruno, very excited. We were busy packing up, after a terrific celebration, during which we loosed-off all our remaining signal-rockets. 'Do eat some apples!' said Bruno, in a voice full of entreaty. Thereby hung a tale. Bruno had ordered them from Pedersen, who brought them. Fifty kilos, to replace the miserable five I had bought at the expensive luxury store of the KGH in Umanak. We fell upon them; in due course we chewed more slowly, finally just every now and then – at the North Pole even New Zealand apples lose their charm. 'You don't know how good apples are,' said Bruno, chewing ostentatiously and determinedly, and we thought of Pedersen, who would soon be here; it was a matter of honour that the load of apples he had delivered should have disappeared by then. How could Italians in Greenland fail to eat apples! But Bruno didn't get through them, so we hid them in a packing-case, where Pedersen immediately discovered them. 'Oh, look!' he said, with a grin, 'an apple!' and bit into one with enthusiasm. 'We haven't had any in Umanak for three weeks,' he remarked. 'You bought the lot.' Bruno heaved a sigh, and we tried to keep a straight face. And I blinked into the sun and considered that we were certainly the most important expedition on the west coast that summer, seeing that a whole town had been apple-less on our account.

The boat lurched forward. Qioqe faded astern. The peaks; the lovely lake, not marked on the map, discovered by Mauro and Bruno; the central plateau; the vertical walls of the fjord, and oh, a great many other things. Qioqe . . . '*Tässa*'. What had been, had been . . .

And now, I am bitten by a mosquito – a fact I forgot to register in my base-camp chronicle. Even that insect belongs to 'Eva's' paradise. '*Susa!*' Not to worry!

There was a yellow sunflower in a pot, against the background of a huge blue-and-white iceberg, framed in the window behind it; there was just room for that plant, growing a little crookedly. Then there was a polished, green tomato on the stem of a tomato-plant, in another flower-pot. All in front of the same bluish-white, icy background. The iceberg was bigger than the church, bigger than half of Umanak. 'Those are my window-plants, my garden!' said Mrs Pedersen, moving affectionately towards one of the tomato-pots. 'There are five now.' She smiled as she passed her hand over one of the shiny tomato-spheres in front of the iceberg. I nodded. We were to leave next day, on board the fast-steaming *Kununguak*. Fragments of conversation, in Italian, rose from the back of the room, and I heard the name 'Milano' . . . 'I envy you your window,' I said. She laughed. Then she said: 'Somebody once grew a cucumber in the window on Disko Island, but that wasn't easy.' I kept on looking at the odd garden under the crooked sunflower, and thought how the day when we would not bat an eyelid for a *pomodoro* lay close at hand. I looked straight through those green leaves and that blue ice to thick forests of trees, meadows full of green grass, fields of waving corn . . .

And I had no enthusiasm at all for what I saw. I wanted to stay here. Had I contracted a form of Greenland sickness? . . . The Pedersens had been here ten years. Ten whole years in Greenland: A handful of plants set against an iceberg. Those meaningful tomatoes: a fenced-in sunflower, reared with difficulty. Ten years! Ten years of winter gales and darkness; of people living at the rim of the ice, for whom the ice and icebergs lurk outside their front doors, cold and pitiless. Greenland, grim, vast, icy and overwhelming – where every feeling, even love, has to be outsize, or perish. Where light is really light, and shadow really darkness. Greenland, and its long night. The green and yellow polar lights, magic curtain in the void of space, covering the whole sky, moving, waxing and waning, fusing in iridescent changes, fading to pure green light in the ink-blue of the night, mysterious – and then, darkness again. The sun, returning out of the night, at first for a few minutes, later for an hour out of the twenty-four – until, in the end, it never sets all day. Greenland: a petrified forest and a ten-thousand-foot thick wedge of ice . . . I put the stone I held back on Pedersen's table-top; its structure was still that of the wood.

Now he was telling us about his sledge-journeys, hundreds of miles long, about the people in the tiny hamlets . . . Ten years. Not everyone

Three Words from Greenland

who lives in Greenland loves it, but many of them cannot bear to leave it. Pedersen loves it. He didn't say much, but what he did say amounted to something. Not that I needed its message – Greenland already had me in thrall.

I stood on one of the town's granite knolls, watching the *Kununguak* sail away. My companions of the expedition were aboard her, and I was thinking of them, returning home without me. I was thinking of home. 'I shall sail on the *Tikerak*,' I told myself. 'Later on.'

'*Uchlok navok tachererpok sekinek*' ... the day runs down and dies.
There was a pack of dogs, howling. Karen was walking her little brother by the hand. A father was upbraiding his son ... 'You codling, you!' A Greenlander, chewing at the roadside, offered me a slice of raw whale-fat – the best cut, close under the skin – so I sat down by him and we chewed fat. I played '*Uchlok navok*' on my guitar and he told me a long story in his native tongue. 'Ab,' said I – 'Yes!' I expect it was something to do with the whale. We shook hands.

An Italian paper printed: 'Diemberger continues his researches in the polar regions.' But I was living in Umanak and on the Nugssuak coast, the proud possessor of a Greenland song and perhaps twenty words of the language ... *Umanak, ab, namek, imaka, tässa, susa, ichli, uvanga, sermerssuak, kuja-nak, tikerak, kajak and more still ending in – ak.**

We hunted seals; sailed along the coast. '*Kassuta tamasa – skol!*' We understood one another. And something inside me fell away: something which had to some extent prevented my being myself. I counted each day as just one more, rejoicing in the clarity of things, the colours, life itself as they impinged upon me – that Greenland clarity for which there is no descriptive word ... vast, inexorable and – certainly, for one person utterly harmonious.

'What, you here?' said the computer. It was Mette, standing on the pier, wearing Mette-expression number one – a little meditative behind her glasses – a green iceberg, on a surprise visit from the Isle of Disko. 'Yes, it's me,' I said, concealing my pleasure at seeing her again, with some difficulty. 'I'm still here for a few days – this is my "winter".' The iceberg shook the long reddish-brown mane on its head: 'I never

---

* Later, in Basque country, hardly believing my eyes, I came upon similar words ending in – ak. Just chance? Then I learned that the language was as old as time itself – 'knife' was 'sharpened stone', cave-drawings showed ice-age reindeer. Is there a connection – starting in Asia – between the Pyrenees and Greenland? It is worth thinking about. K. D.

thought I should set eyes on you again,' it said. Then suddenly she, Mette, that abstraction of a fantasy, smiled. 'Splendid!' she said. 'Let's have a good time...'

Sledges on roofs, dogs, kayaks, little villages, Greenlanders, a whole community of life; so many children, so many dogs, so many fishes. The wooden racks for drying fish. The all-pervading smell: everything here smells of fish and dogs. It doesn't bother one much any more; one smells of them oneself.

The dogs are ravenous – ten to fifteen of them to every house. In summer they are not fed; they have to forage for themselves. They devour everything. That is why the fish are hung up so high, and even the kayaks are on stands. Mette knew a great deal about that coast. 'There are no cats or chickens in Greenland,' she told me: 'the dogs would have eaten them long ago. There is a cock and a hen at Jakobshaven, behind a fence, of course; the dogs sit outside the enclosure...' And the dogs will eat even one's camera-case, if one puts it down, I knew. They kill the dogs, when short of fur, often by strangling them, because the pelt is warmer and the hair stays erect, then.' Thus spake Mette, looking, as usual into the water.

An iceberg was moving past, semicircular like a theatre, wave-washed completely hollow inside, gulls occupying the dress-circle and the upper-circle. 'There are very few polar-bears left,' she went on, 'except far up in Thule. It's news in the Jakobshaven paper, when one gets shot.' Another berg went dipping past, one of those with slices hewn off it – to provide drinking water. Many villages get it that way, especially in the winter, that long darkness during which the sea is hard-frozen, the inhabitants build huts on it and fetch their fish up through a hole in the 'floor'.

Mette and I were as different as the hills and the sea are, here. We would often go into a village by widely divergent ways; then we would meet and tell each other what we had seen – or else say not a word.

There was a village called Niaqornat. The women were rolling casks up into the barns from the beach, for the winter. At Qaersut, the Danish flag was hoisted – I mean it! – in honour of our visit. The mayor, a friendly great sea-bear of a Dane, had an enchanting Greenland wife. The atmosphere was Japanese... As the fishing-smack sailed on, a Greenlander chanted the melody of *'Im Frühtau zu Berge'*. He had heard it just once, and memorized it...

They are musical – dance like dervishes – these Greenlanders. A party can last two whole days. In spite of the tough conditions in which they live, they are unbelievably light-hearted. Their gaiety can be noisy; yet it can be so quiet that you can hardly hear it. As at Niaqornat in the evenings.

'... It was only today that I understood. Here, alone with it all, when I was among the old fishermen's huts, below the rocky hill – it must have come to me then. When I could only hear my own footsteps, and found myself alone with the peat-walled huts, the people behind their windows, and the dogs...'

No one will ever be able to reveal the secret at the heart of Greenland.

We were on the ridge of a tower on the Umanak Mountain. Gorgeous climbing; but rain had driven us back. Then the rain stopped.

Below us lay the sea. We sat throwing little stones down into the twilight-blue inlet, caught between red-streaked rocks. They hit the surface of the water with a 'Click!' 'Click!' There were great rectangular boulders on the sea-bed, like drowned books. There was another 'click' on the surface as the next little stone went tumbling into the depths, swinging gently through the water, then lay still. Like seconds of time.

'We didn't get to the top,' I said, 'the rain —'

'*Ab*,' said Mette, which means 'yes'. She smiled; it was lovely. This was her first climb.

'Shall we have another go?'

'*Namek*,' said Mette, which means 'no'.

'Click'. Another little stone, swerving its way down, coming to rest. 'Click!'...

'In a couple of centuries we could throw the whole mountain into the sea,' said Mette.

Mette stayed on Disko till March. Then she went away, somewhere.

On the day after my arrival at Egedesminde, the *Tikerak* caught fire. It started in the engine-room, out there on the high seas. The fire gradually enveloped the whole ship. All Egedesminde stood on the shore, watching the spectacle. The timbers cracked, the hull shivered. Huge flames, the crashing mast, a sea yellow under the midnight sun, a shower of sparks – the good old *Tikerak*, that was.

Next day I met the helmsman. He had a pair of shoes in his hand and a cardboard box under his arm. I tried to find words. 'Oh, it's you, is it?' he laughed. 'You know, we shall get a new ship – next year. *Susa*: don't worry about it.'

'*Farvel*,' I said. He started to go, then turned and added: 'don't forget to look me up in Denmark. That's where I'm going now, with my daughter.'

The engines of the great jet hummed. There was a class of Greenland children on board, on their way to Copenhagen. Their school-mistress was telling them about the myriad lights of the great city; but the children were very quiet, and one girl kept on picking a photograph out of her little handbag. The Danish schoolmarm sobbed: 'they all find it so terribly hard to leave their island; it's only for them to learn a little Danish and see the country. They have given me a Greenland schoolmaster, to lend support during the flight. He was crying too, yesterday.'

The inland ice stretched endlessly below us. After that, leagues of cloud and sea. Then it gradually grew gloomier, a universal greyness closed down, hemming us in. Down we flew into an unfamiliar darkness, in which each day has a day, followed by a night.

Windbumps, rain...

And a thousand lights: Copenhagen.

My daughter Karen was born in Milan. She is as fair as Tona, her head is as hard as a Greenland iceberg, she climbs everything, is happy, and has a name that comes from the west coasts. We love each other very much.

A telephone call from Bologna? Why, Bernardi! Bernardi is a journalist, ex-bank clerk, a warrior of the Spanish war – in which he was nearly killed. He is also Bologna's liveliest grandfather.

What's that? Greenland? Winter in Greenland? A publisher wants an article? Of course I'll come!

Greenland in the winter...

'*Imaka* – maybe!'

Between the Gran Sasso, Salzburg and . . .

The Gran Sasso d'Italia – the Great Rock. A melody sounds over the savage mountains of the Abruzzi: '*Vulessi fa venir pe un ora sola . . .*' The villages are small, their houses huddle together, stone-walled. There are churches like fortresses, some of them with loopholes for firearms and battlements – relics of a bygone age. The people who inhabit that sterile land are simple and kindly folk . . . '*e vola, vola, vola, e vola lu pavone, se stai col cuore buone, bon . . .*' In wintertime you can hear the wolves howling below the Majella's peak. It is the very antithesis of anything a foreigner would expect to find in Italy.

I had driven all night, with my daughter Hildegard in her sleeping-bag, next to me on the bench-seat. I had told her: 'When you wake up with tomorrow morning's sun, we shall be at the foot of the Gran Sasso. . . .' This was to be her first mountain.

There was the sound of ice-axes clattering against rock. The wind had conjured up ice-crusts and snow-flowers. 'Look, Papa!' cried Hilde. She had shed all fear, and was determined to climb. She was just seven years old. Karen was only two; I could still see her eyes, above her comforter, looking at me over the garden gate: '*ed io?*' '*Domani – un altra volta.*' Later on, when you're bigger. '*Ciao!*' she said, raising her hand in farewell.

We were 8,500 feet up, the sun shone warmly above transparent blue veils, below which lay the countryside. While I took in the rope and Hildegard came nimbly up by hand- and foot-hold, Gigi, up above us on the ridge, sang the song of the Gran Sasso, from whose summit you can see the sea on both sides of Italy; while Bruno spoke of the three-thousand-foot faces, of the mushrooms that grow in the colourful autumn woods down there, and how he, who lived at its foot, had often climbed the Gran Sasso. But today, he said, beaming all over his wrinkled face, was a special day; and it was obvious how happy he was to be guiding the blonde young princess up his own mountain. Once the drudgery of the snowy coombe at the bottom was over, she climbed happily and easily. 'Say, Papa, I like climbing much better than walking,' she said. And now she decided that she wanted to stick her head into the 'gun-barrel', that black hole in the rock at 9,200 feet, a thing not even Bruno had ever done. What on earth for? But then Hilde had her own ideas; and while we were scrambling across to that dark cave, I recalled that the walls at home were papered with space-pictures, the cat was called Neil; and Hilde, determined to prepare herself for a flight in space, could tell one all about NASA, the astronauts, the flights of the various capsules. It was quite a relief to remember that she had expressed a wish merely to cross Iceland with me on horseback . . .

'Papa, we are higher up than the Corno Piccolo,' she cried, her eyes bright with excitement. Soon we would be higher than anything else in the Appenines . . .

The light fell gleaming on the autumn mists far below. Gigi was '*Me pareia che passu passu, se saliesse all'infinitu . . .!*'* And today, when we four had the Great Rock all to ourselves, and Hilde was climbing her first mountain, it really did seem as if we were going up into the heart of the limitless blue sky.

Hildegard has decorated the walls of our home in Varese with countless space-photographs – the Himalaya seen through the window of the Apollo capsule, an astonishing brown-and-white tapestry, fine-woven; the unruffled, dark curve of the ocean, with cloud-layers above it; the cratered landscape of the moon, over which the earth floats like some deep-blue soap-bubble. And then, hanging on our walls in Salzburg, there is a picture of one of this earth's craters . . . the crater of the summit Tona had climbed – her own photograph of it – Kilimanjaro, the 'High Snow'. A mountain of ice-slopes high above primeval forests, tree-ferns, lianas, giant heather and lobelia; a summit of lava and ash. A summit reached by trails you have to hack out for yourself, or by existing tracks, far from the normal route – through the forest, up over the mighty slopes, thousands of feet high. And Tona had been to the top, by the western flank.

There, at the rim of the gigantic Kibo crater, her companions had decided to halt; so Tona had gone on alone. She wanted to reach the 'Ash Pit'. Step by step, in the thin air at nearly 20,000 feet, she drove herself on till, at last, she stood at the mighty edge of the inner crater and could see down into it. That foray, all by herself, up in the skies, high above all Africa must have been an indescribable experience; and Tona has never said much about it. But there are times when such an experience – 'one crowded hour of glorious life' – can alter the whole

* 'Step by step into the Infinite.'

The Gran Sasso, Salzburg and . . .

course of one's existence. Now she is writing: a book about plants, and a children's story about the travels of a little fish.

Here I am in Salzburg, the festival city, looking out at the rubble in the bed of the Salzach and everything else one can see and share in the life going on all around: Mozart, the leaf of a tree and – the postman.

He brings greetings from Masaaki Kondo (memories of our Tirich Mir!); a postcard from Trieste – *saluti* from Spiro, Walter, Bianca, Fioretta. (Trieste, because of them, is my home from home.) A card from Ingher in Iceland, a place I have not yet managed to visit.

And here is a summons from the Association of Guides, for the following Sunday – yes, I will be there. For now I have yet another profession: guiding those who want to go up to the places where one becomes a 'different man' – and I enjoy doing it. Climbing a peak now has a new slant to it, even if it meant my being unable to carry out all my own plans, for sheer lack of time. (I cannot help thinking of Pierre in Paris, with whom I have for so long been meaning to do a big tour; and of Wolfi, now living in Pakistan.)

There is another postcard, too, from my ex-pupils. 'Greetings to our Yeti!' it reads . . .

I had left the school. If I had gone on sitting there, looking out of that window next to the directors' office, I would never have written this book; now, I have been working on it for nearly a year, and I am enjoying being an author. I am no longer ruled by a timetable, though it means that life is more unsure and unpredictable, less smooth and easy. On the other hand, I am now sitting on the cover of the 'machine', having lifted myself off its basic 'plan' – only, now there was another 'machine' in front of me – a typewriter. There is no way of escape; we are born into a world of plans and machines, they control and decide our existence. It is a fact of life. Still, I can use my freedom by tapping away at the keys: 'make life more human, humanize yourselves, each and every one of you. Don't let yourselves grow square; don't computerize your minds as well as everything else.' And that is not addressed only to my pupils, who will one day be bosses and employees . . .

Mountains, rock and ice – lovely shimmering ice. The lover of mountains must go to the mountains; otherwise he will cease to be a person, for others as well as for himself, and he will lose the very joy of life. But there are other things, too. I am watching a student preparing crabs for his collection (I take my typewriter all over the place with me in my car). The thought enters my mind that in a few milliards of years the sun will blow up and the earth will perish. What is the sense of it all? And yet, watching him, I find I have something to believe in.

I walked through the town, taking yesterday's rough pages to be copied-out fair by a secretary, then back over the Monchsberg, high above the city. It is a good place for thinking, and I thought about what I had done so far and what I was doing. An idea occurred to me, and at home I wrote it on the wall – or rather, not on the wall itself, but on the snowfield of a huge photograph hanging on the wall: 'For whatever I do, give me the true measure it deserves...'

Above the snow-field in that picture, soars K2, high as the heavens themselves. Where does that true measure lie?

To stand again above 26,000 feet ... *Imaka* ... perhaps. Certainly I will be going again – to Greenland, Nepal, the Andes. I must go there and live and discover things. Maybe make a book or a film of them; maybe just to live there a while and then come home – till the day arrives when I can take Hilde and, later on, Karen with me – wherever it may be that we go.

Rock, ice. Whenever I go up there the same miracle always happens: I feel as if that is where I was born. After twenty years of it, since the days of the lad who went crystal-hunting ...

When I look up from the keys of the typewriter to the green-and-red bilberry leaves on the slope between the drooping larch-branches, I see a limestone wall, bathed in sunshine ... a high wall: I have seen it for a long time, now.

Yes, I shall be going again; and when I do, I shall not have any more idea why, than I have ever had till this day.

Altamira

I was under the impression that I had written the closing chapter of this book. But now, again it has changed, this strange, unpredictable life, unforeseeable.

I had gone to Spain on a lecture-tour. My journey took me in winter through that wide and wild country – the Spaniards themselves call it *Savache* – so different from the rest of Europe.

At Altamira I went below ground.

Those unforeseen vicissitudes . . . Though one may not always know it, everything one does has an effect – on you, on someone else. The earth is continually dying and bringing forth something new: simply . . . just as grass may do.

Rain was falling softly on Santillana del Mar. Here on Spain's north coast, between the Pyrenees and the Bay of Biscay, lies one of Europe's heaviest rainfall areas; totally different from the heart of Spain, where in winter the icy wind whistles over the *Meseta*, and in summer the air quivers above the dry ground. But here, there seems to be a springy green carpet spread over the land – so green, so dense, so lush that the rain strikes one as a miracle, bringing life from the sky; or evoking it from the earth – or both. The rain is so much an integral part of this country that it no longer arouses any feeling of discomfort. It is just a fact; and man has accommodated himself to it. The inhabitants wear wooden clogs, with three stilt-like projections at the bottom; for if you leave the damp cushion of the meadows, you can find yourself ankle-deep in mud. In the course of thousands of years, the water has hollowed-out caves in the limestone which, during the ice-age, were the habitations of man. Many of them had been discovered, but who knows how many still lie beneath the surface, unbeknown to anyone? When you are driving across this hummocky land of the Province of Santander in your car, you notice, over and again, circular depressions, some of them funnel-shaped, in the ground; under many of them there might be hidden caves, though probably not habitable ones. One would only have to dig down a little, to find out.

It was in 1868, on a green slope near Santillana de Mar, that a hunter sent his dog into a fox's lair. He could not know that he was standing that day a few feet above a vault, which was later to be known as the Cathedral of the Ice Age. When the dog did not come back, the hunter started digging. That is how the cave was discovered.

Until that day, no air had touched the paintings in its roof; for the original entrance had been silted-up for time immemorial. Professor Herbert Kühn, explaining the reason for the immaculate preservation of the pictures, for the strength and freshness of their colours, wrote: 'And so, since the Ice Age, no one had seen the pictures, no breath of air had touched them, the temperature had remained even through thousands of years; one could really believe they had been painted yesterday...'

They are pictures of animals, mostly bison, but there are others, too. Animals that lived here then; and, miraculously, alive in these paintings today as they were then.

Was it the 'cult of the chase' that moved men to decorate the vault with the animal life, which populated those meadows – and maybe, at the time, those woods – of the hillocks of this coastal strip? Or was it an artist's sheer pleasure in painting: the urge to reproduce, to express life – and death?

Time and again, today, men go down below ground to Altamira; and when they come out again into the light of day, they seem bemused, overwhelmed. Altamira beggars description. If I should presently try to share the impressions of a visit, I know it can only be a feeble attempt. I can only hope to give a faint idea of what I experienced that day.

Anyone intending to go there should do so in winter. For then there are few visitors and it may be his luck to have the cave to himself, or be alone with just one person with whom he would care to share it. And then, in the silence of the cave, thousands of years will fade away and he will find himself able to identify himself, at its primeval springs, with the spirit of that human being who immortalized his vision on the roof of the vault with a paint-brush – as if it were himself, who had just come in from outside – he himself, that human being.

There is a road which leads from the continent of perception to an island of reality, outside. The road is intuition, the bridge, art. Where does it lead —?

Altamira

Altamira is the bridge built by the art of the Ice Age.

The vault is flat, some twenty yards long, ten wide, so low that there is no difficulty in touching the rock of the roof with one's fingers. There can be no doubt that it was the shrine of some cult. The living-quarters were apart, for there are several rooms in the cave. During the excavations, they found tools, made of stone and bone; flat mussels from the near-by sea, as large as plates, with holes bored in them . . . and little round mussels to act as containers for the colours, some of them with the paint still in them . . .

The animals painted on the roof are from three to six feet long, with smaller ones in between; but, as you look up at them, you are quite unaware of these dimensions. There are bisons, a running boar, a doe at rest, a horse, then more bisons. Some of the beasts are shown, rearing high into the air, in mortal combat. Others are static, beautifully at rest – all incredibly exciting. Some are overpainted – a new painting over the older, more faded one. Faded, or rubbed out? How many years between the two paintings – centuries, perhaps? I am no scientist; I have only my own way of recognizing something, of trying to put myself in the mind of the being who painted this or that picture. This takes no cognizance of time.

I think that many of the pictures are closely connected: I could specify them, but that is of no great importance here. There is one master who has spread the quiet shape of a bison over a shallow depression in the roof – almost in relief, concave. And here another bison – I think, from the same hand. But there, a very different matter – a wild, forceful character, who sought the circumference of the circle, in an effort to burst forth from it with his powers of expression; this one has composed of his brilliant surfaces, his economical, effective dark strokes, a dying bison, laid on a projection in the rock. In frantic movements, red and black, the beast bursts the bounds of space, of his own red-and-black space . . .

The animal is incredibly expressive.

'There are three of these pictures on rock-projections here – don't you see the similarity?'

'I think they are in the same style, springing from the same thought, but not from the same hand.'

In the dull light, the ochre paint flames red. The beast remains dumb.
'I think the same man did them.'

We remarked that the difference was irrelevant and sank back into contemplation of the pictures.

. . . . .

I was sitting somewhere, writing. Everything was still there, before my eyes. I wrote in chopped-up sentences, just as they came . . .

A few notes, on bits of paper in the glove-locker of the car. Written, not in Altamira, nor even in Santillana del Mar, but somewhere along the road.

Unnecessary, perhaps . . . it is all there for anyone to see . . . Why, then . . ?

All the same I have attempted it. There were those scraps of paper, my separate impressions on them, almost indecipherable . . . but perhaps the entirety was there?

Altamira! bigger . . . recognizable . . . but still possible to capture, but . . . for moments, for only a moment. It links us with eternity. 10,000 years, vanished at a stroke. It is the present time. The idea which motivated the brush, no not the brush; the hand which wielded the red chalk. Not the hand either, but the thought: 'How shall I draw this line, this reflection of my inner spirit, before my eyes, life, bursting the bounds of space, passing into death – immortal?' It dies, it lives as never before, I see it . . .

A sound of dripping in the cave, in the silence.

The Idea has come.

He wanted to perpetuate what he had seen. The beast, life, death. Red and black, the strokes go winging, the ruffled mane, the tensed muscles. He himself – the very beast itself. Up there on the roof, above me. You.

The grass grows. A dog looks along the street. The naked being, waiting, running, thinking. The bird sings; a voice. It lives, and clatters. No madness. No death. A thousand beings behind it . . . hundreds coming after. Perhaps.

Life. Death is unimportant. It is life that matters. Everything that has ever been, still exists.

That is the thing to know . . .

Life. Death is unimportant, a natural thing, inevitable. Life, a moment of existence. Why? Because of love. Being . . . all being. It is life that matters.

It endures; time is of no account.

The houses dissipate into thin air. The floor beneath my feet is his floor. The floor of the hillock above his cave. The trees are the same trees – a moment in the present – hundreds of trees, the past behind them. It is all here: the green knolls all around, the undulating contours of the

Altamira

horizon. Down in the depths under them, forests, and the beasts they house. Tomorrow one of them will die, . . . I am alive. We shall be leaving tomorrow. The aurochs, the bear, the stag, the doe. The forest. Tomorrow.

The floor beneath my feet. The horizon. Houses. God. The grass that grows. A few trees. A picture painted on the rock. An idea . . .

We live for a moment. That is a fact. My thanks to you, Beloved. Even if I didn't thank you, it would still be a fact. Just a day.

We stood outside the cave, looking at the grey sky, a few trees, the house that holds a museum. Should we go in? What for? Later . . .

'I'd like to be alone for a few minutes.'

'Yes – so would I.'

We walked over the meadows of Santillana del Mar, those meadows like a great green carpet, under a grey sky. We wandered up a path, then down again, back and forth, purposeless – everything was everywhere, where it has always been.

There was a small, low-built romanesque church and we went over to it.

A few hours later I was driving – unconsciously or by design? – at fifteen miles an hour – through the hillocky landscape . . .

'I felt it for a moment – the real thing – but only for a moment; when I tried to find it again, I couldn't.'

I know it. I sense it. It is the real thing. You knew it, too.

We had left Altamira far behind, and it was still there.

Everything is everywhere, where it has always been . . .

I drove on, over the wide *Meseta*, alone; the road ran straight as a die through that immense landscape. I was in the grip of a wild joy. I sang, to drown the gale that kept on buffeting the car.

Everything is everywhere, where it has always been . . .

The sierras stood white in the distance – did an ancestress of mine perhaps dwell somewhere on an arid mountainside, like those? – the distant Sierras . . .

Dazzling sunlight! There was sand blowing through the air; grey-green, dishevelled olive-copses; greyish-red, terraced hills in the wandering circles of light. It was like in the desert.

Everything was everywhere, where it always had been . . .

The gale had ripped round clumps of plants out of the soil; they rolled away across the *Meseta* tumbling oddly; continuously, like a *perpetuum mobile*; round clumps, cartwheels . . . the wings of the car rattled. My good old *Giovanna*, with nearly 120,000 miles tucked under her bonnet; rusty and battered ... (I wonder, shall I ever learn how to park properly?)

Everything is everywhere, where it has always been ...

Pot-holes, a curve ... dancing miles ... spots of light; the branches rustling ... I sang at the top of my voice, out of a full heart.

... it exists.

By the way, Lovell, after circling the moon, decided to stay on earth. Be it noted: *after* —

... after?

INDEX

Abruzzi, Duke of the,
  Expedition 121, 126
Abruzzi 309
Afghanistan 252-87
Aiguille Blanche de Peuterey
  62, 65, 164-76
Aiguille de la Tza 185
Aiguille Noire de Peuterey 62, 164-76, 243-51
Aiguilles Rouges 185
Alfred Wegener-land 302
Altamira 313-18
Annapurna 187, 188, 189, 194, 199, 200, 201, 206, 215, 216
Anogol 268, 282-83; Glacier 286; Zom 283
Apennines 309-10
Argentine Dhaulagiri Expedition (1954) 1190-91; (1956) 192
Arkari 284; Valley 263, 280-284,286
Austrian Dhaulagiri Expedition (1959) 192-97
Austrian Himalayan Association 192
Austrian Hindu Kush Expedition (1967) 267-72

Baltistan 104
Baltoro 102-29
Basque language 305
Beaco, Bianca di 159
Bernese Oberland 132-59
Bernina 71, 86, 138, 295
Bétemps Hut 78
Bhairava 197
Biancograt 71
Bich 249
Bockhardsee 16
Boë-spitze 39
Bonatti, Walter 244
Braldu River 105
Brandler, Lothar 136, 157
Bregaglia 51, 55, 59-60, 136
Breithorn (Baltoro) 109
Breithorn (Dhanla Himal) 194, 201
Breithorn (Zermatt) 44, 45, 65, 77, 201
Brenta Alta 58
Brenta Dolomites 51, 57-9, 65
Brenva Face 62, 65
Bride Peak see Chogolisa
Broad Peak 102-20, 121, 122, 123, 125, 129, 132, 195, 208, 213, 233
Buhl, Hermann 102-29, 167, 171, 195
Buni Zom 262
Busazza Arete 60

Calanques, the 161-63
Campanile Alto 58
Cengalo, 60
Chamonix 135, 160
Chécrouit Lake 168
Chitral 252, 286
Chogolisa (Bride Peak) 120-29, 195, 196
Chogori see K2
Cho Oyu 84, 195, 221

Christianshaab 294
Cima d'Ambiez 58
Cima degli Armi 58
Cima di Brenta 58
Cinque Torri 39
Civetta 39, 40, 60, 136
Col de Peuterey 165, 167, 175
Col Innominata 168
Copenhagen 290, 299, 307
Corno Piccolo 310
Cortina 38
Courmayeur 47, 135, 172, 179
Croz dell'Altissimo 57-8
Crystals 11-26
Czech expedition to Tirich, Mir (1967) 268

Dachstein Priest 42, 45, 168
Dambush Khola valley 188
Dames Anglaises (Peuteret) 174
Dangers of the Alps, The (Zsigmondy and Paulcke) 32
Dangl, Fritz 95, 96
Dapa Col 197, 199, 204, 206, 208 209
Dapa Peak 200
Defreggen Hut and Saddle 37
Denmark 289, 307
Dent Blanche 45, 68, 84, 180
Dent du Géant 47, 48, 61-62
Dent d'Hérens 65, 68
Dertona Peak 260, 263
Dhaulagiri 24, 178, 186-218, 223 233, 279
Diable, Arête du 62
Disco Island 304
Dolomites 11, 31, 37, 38-41, 55-61, 86 89, 147
Dorje, Nawang 186, 204, 279
Dorje, Nima 186, 210, 211
Drei Zinnen 11, 37, 59, 89, 134, 136
Dru, Aiguille du 96
Duino 238, 240
Dyhrenfurth, Prof G. O. 108, 121, 196

Edelweissklub 89
Egedesminde 292, 307
Eiger 96, 132, 133-59, 167, 248, 300
Eiselin, Max 179, 180, 181, 182, 183, 184, 196, 199
Entrèves 47, 175
Epidotes 13, 16, 25
Ertl, Hans 88
Everest 43

Fajdiga, Nadja 136
Falzarego Pass 38
Fauteuil des Allemands 168
Finsteraarhorn 138
Fossils 14-16, 285-7
Fourche de la Brenva 62
Franz Josefshohe 33, 34
French Alpine Club 187
French Col, the (Dhaulagiri) 188, 189, 194, 200, 209, 216, 217,
Fresney Glacier 62, 167, 168, 171, 174, 244

Furka Pass 43

Gasherbrum Glacier 121
Gasherbrum. 1, 11, Ill, IV 109, 116, 119, 121, 122, 193
Gazikistan 282-4
Geiger, Gross 19, 31, 36
Geiselspitze 31
Gemelli arête 96
German Hindu Kush Expedition (1967) 267
Ghul Lasht Zom group 2 61-72, 280
Giant Meringue, the (Konigsspitz) 85-101, 102
Glockner Gross 21, 32, 33, 34
Godoy, Felipe 190
Godthaab 289
Gorter, Wolfgang 178
Grande Chandèle 161-3
Grandes Jorasses 158, 160, 167, 268
Grands Charmoz 65
Gran Sasso d'Italia (Great Rock) 309
Greenland 16, 24, 26, 238, 288-308
Grindelwald 132
Gurla Mandhata 122, 221

Habachtal 13, 19, 21
Harrer, Heinrich 53, 137
Haunsberg 31
Heckmair, Anderl 137
Hedin, Sven 53
Heilmayer, Peter 38, 47
Heim, Arnold 187
Herligkoffer, Karl 108
Herzog, Maurice 187
Hidden Peak 124
Himalayas 16, 26, 68, 84, 102-29, 186-218, 221, 222, 225, 252, 310
Hindu Kush 238, 252-87, 288
Hintergrat Hut 95
Hohe Tauern 11-13, 15, 16, 21, 31
Hohen Zaun 37
Hollerbach valley 20, 21
Hörnli Hut and Ridge 70, 81

Ibañez, Lieut. Francisco 190
Iceland 290
Indus River 105, 129
Innominata Ridge 247
Iranian Desert 255-60
Istor-o-Nal 262, 280
Italian Alpine Club 167, 290
Jakobshaven 294, 306
Japanese Tirich Mir Expedition 272-280
Jotor-o-Nal 252

K2 (Chogori) 106, 109, 110, 113, 116, 118, 119, 123, 125, 129
Kaberi Saddle 122, 124, 128
Kali Gandaki 187, 199, 206, 218
Kangri (Baltoro) 123
Karakorum 102-29, 144, 252
Karst 238, 239, 240
Kasparek, Fritz 137
Katmandu 179, 191
Khyber Pass 266
Kibo crater 310

319

Kilimanjaro 310
Kleine Scheidegg 151, 155, 158
Koh-i-Bandakar 280
Koh-i-Batzenhaus 261
Kondo, Masaaki 272
Königsspitze 85-100
Kürsinger Hut 35, 37
Kurz, Toni 147
Kusma 198

Larmkogel. 21, 22
Latemar 40, 41
Lauteraarhorn 141
Lindner, Franz 137, 167, 264
Livanos, Georges 161
Lower Tirich Glacier 269, 272
Lyskamm 42, 45, 65, 78, 261

Maix, Kurt 67, 69, 74, 81, 82, 102, 103, 176, 221, 270
Makohta, Ante 135
Marmolata 11, 39, 40
Marseilles 51, 160, 161
Masherbrurn 116
Matterhorn 42-46, 50, 55, 65, 71-84, 103, 136, 145, 159, 160, 185
Maurertörl 37
Mayangdi Khola and Glacier 188, 189, 192, 193, 198, 199, 209, 213
Miage Glacier 168
Minnegerode, Graf 87
Miristi Khola 198
Mitre Peak 109, 116, 121, 122
Mitscherkopf 90
Mittelegi Ridge 132, 138
Mölltal 32
Mönch 137
Mont Blanc 27. 47, 50, 51, 55, 59, 62, 65, 84, 123, 137, 136, 160, 165-76, 243-51
Mont Blanc de Cheilon 177-85
Monte Cimone 55
Monte Rosa 45, 296
Mountain World, The 128
Mustagh Tower 109

Nanga Parbat 88, 102, 104, 105, 113, 114, 115, 116, 117, 129, 195
Nansen, Fridtjof 289
Nepal 186-218, 222, 260, 294, 312
Niaqornat 306
Nilgiris 194, 215
Noichl, Hias 135
Norby, Gyaltsen 195
Noshaq 281
Nugssuak 301, 305

Obergabelhorn 45, 65
Obersultzbachtal 12, 18
Ortler 87, 95
Ötztal Alps 37, 87
Owir An 286, 287
Oxus River 252
Paiju, 107, 116
Pakistan 104, 252, 254, 257, 311
Pamirs 252

Pasang Dawa Lama 190, 191, 193, 194, 195
Patternsattel 60
Pear, The (Dhaulagiri) 189
Peary, Robert 289
Pellegrino Pass 40
Perserajoq 290
Peshawar 262
Peuterey Ridge 62, 137, 160, 165-76, 243-51
Picco Centrale Gabriele Boccalatte 301
Picco di Terramo 261
Pigne d'Arolla 185
Pillar. Fresnay 247
Pinzgau 21
Piz Badile 59, 60, 295
Piz Bernina 138
Piz Palu 137
Piz Roseg 71, 138
Piz Scerscen 137
Pointe Bich *see* Peuterey Ridge
Pointe Brendel *see* Peuterey Ridge
Pointe Gamba *see* Peuterey Ridge
Pokhara 204, 206, 209, 218
Pordoi 39, 40
Preim, Karl 194, 195

Qaersut 306
Qioge 290-303
Qotligssat 294
Quader Saaed, Captain 109

Raditschnig, Herbert 135
Rainer, Kurt 109
Rainerhorn 37
Rakaposhi 123
Rawalpindi 104
Rébuffat, Gaston 61, 62, 167, 187
Receptaculites (fossils) 286
Reichensteiners 102
Roiss, Heini 194
Rote Fluh (Eiger) 145, 146
Rothorn Hut 66, 68

St Johann-in-Tirol ski-school 136
Salzack River 11, 14, 15, 27, 311
Salzburg 11, 14, 15, 16, 31, 38, 47, 56, 89, 104, 154, 231, 234, 289, 309, 310, 311
Salzburg - *cont.*
Samonigg, Fritz 284
Sandkopf 33
Saraghrar 253
Sarpa Laggo Pass and Glacier 106
Satillana del-Mar 313
Saxer, Ernst 199
Schaubach Hut 96
Schindeltal Chimney 55
Schmuck, Markus 104, 110, 112, 117
Schönthaler, Charlie 137
Schreckhorn 137, 141
Sciora di Fuori 60

Sella group 39
Sempach 75
Senn, Ernst 109
Shagrom 261, 265, 269, 283
Shigar River 105
Shish Pangma 196
Silbersattel 103
Siwalik ranges 187
Skardu 104
Sola Khumbu 218
Solvay Refuge 45, 46, 83
Spigolo Giallo 60
Steinauer, Ludwig 178
Steinerne Meer 21
Stefan, Wolfgang (Wolfi) 47, 48, 49, 51, 59, 60, 63, 64, 67, 71, 76-80, 95, 151, 156, 160, 168, 172, 241, 311
Sulden 86, 92, 93, 96, 97
Swiss Dhaulagiri Expedition (1953) 189-90; (1960) 196-218

Terai 186
Theodule Pass 70, 121
Three Fjord Peak 296, 297, 299, 300
Tibet 116, 119, 122, 187, 215
Tichy, Herbert 84, 122, 210, 220-25
Tikerak 292, 307
Tirich Mir 232, 246-7, 253, 261-72, 273-84, 286, 287, 311
Tofana 39
Torre di Brenta 58
Trango Towers 107, 121
Trieste 238, 239, 247, 294, 311
Tschierva Hut 71
Tukucha Peak 187, 188, 194, 199, 201, 215, 216, 217

Uli-Biaho group 107
Umanak 294, 295, 298, 301, 303, 304, 305, 307
Upernivik 294, 296, 300, 301
Urdokas 106

Val des Dix 178
Val d'Hérens 178
Val Veni 159, 164, 167, 243, 249
Varese 164
Vatna Jöku 290
Vegetarian Expedition (1955) 191-195
Venediger Gross 11, 16, 19, 21, 24, 25, 27, 31, 36, 37, 38
Vienna 51, 52, 73, 87, 154, 221, 224, 255
Vörg, Wiggerl 137

Wakhan 252-3
Walker Spur (Grandes Jorasses) 157, 159, 167
Wegener, Alfred 289
Weisshorn 45
Weisskugel 87

THE ENDLESS KNOT

For Julie,
and for all those who come to
touch these great mountains.

34. K2 seen from Broad Peak. The Abruzzi Route takes the spur on the right. *Photo: Doug Scott*

The Endless Knot
K2, MOUNTAIN OF DREAMS AND DESTINY

KURT DIEMBERGER

TRANSLATED BY AUDREY SALKELD

First published in Italy in 1989
First published in Great Britain
and the U.S.A. in 1991

ACKNOWLEDGEMENTS I could never have finished this book without thinking all the time of Julie and her wish, to pass on to others what we were living for. Besides herself it was Julie's understanding husband Terry, her early climbing partner Dennis Kemp and – perhaps in the most significant way – her martial arts teacher David Passmore who opened up a world for her that was very special.

To write about these events on K2 was hard and it took me almost two years to complete the book. I want to thank my wife, Teresa, for her incredible patience. Many others helped too: Audrey Salkeld who translated the book into English; Choi Chang Deok who helped me clear up some of the mystery hidden in Korean hieroglyphs; Charlie Clarke and Franz Berghold, high altitude illness specialists; Xavier Eguskitza, John Boothe, Peter Gillman, Judith Kendra and Dee Molenaar . . . even my daughters, Hildegard and Karen, have contributed to this work.

I must also thank those who made it possible for me to start writing at all: Gerhard Flora in Innsbruck and Hildegunde Piza in Vienna, who treated my frostbite, Enzo Raise in Bologna and the staff of Pembury Hospital in Sussex. Mrs Susi Kermauner in Salzburg took me to her rusty typewriter to start my first chapter and months later my little son Ceci taught me how to use the computor. There are many others who are not named.

Julie's book now has a companion – *The Endless Knot* – here it is.

Kurt Diemberger
March 1990

CONTENTS

Introduction	page 327
K2… The Peak We Most Desired	329
The Lonely Mountain – On the Baltoro with Hermann Buhl	331
The Boat – Meeting Julie	337
Dream Mountain – K2 From the North	344
England – Tunbridge Wells	361
Italy – Bologna	364
Raid on Broad Peak	367
Tashigang – Place of Happiness	385
Jinlab – the Magic of the Mountains	394
The Village on the Moraine	401
Threats Posed to Health by High Altitude	411
Success and Tragedy – Russian Roulette?	415
Julie Has Doubts	427
The Ice Avalanche and the Riddle of the Teapot	436
The Decision – We Go Together	443
Pushing to Great Heights	454
The Korean Tent	456
The Key Factor – a Tent	481
The Lost Day	484
The Summit – Our Dreams Come True	509
The Fall	523
Down to 8,000 metres	532
Blizzard at 8,000 metres	539
Flight from the Death Zone	555
Where is Mrufka?	564
Perpetuum Mobile	571
Clouds From Both Sides	579

APPENDICES
K2 – Expedition History; Summit Climbers; Those Who Died	581
Index	589

K2 from both sides, that was to have been the title of this book. Julie and I wanted to write it together. On my own, now, I find myself fighting shy of getting started.

Come on, Kurt!

Well then: testing, testing ... This typewriter seems all right, the ribbon is new and all the keys are functioning. The only thing that's needed is for the builders on the roof outside to stop their bloody noise. A neighbour on the other side was mowing his lawn all morning – that, at least, has finally stopped – unless he is simply taking a rest. Perhaps a nip of whisky will help me face all these distractions. I must type with my thumb because the fingers of my right hand are still too painful to use. Fingers, I say – I mean what's left of them after the frostbite.

Perhaps I can at least set my 'new' index finger to work – that's not too bad. I wonder if Susie has a finger-stall? Using only the thumb makes it hard to concentrate on what I want to say. I should try dictating into a tape recorder, I suppose, and then type it up – that way it would just be a mechanical action, and it wouldn't matter whether it was comfortable or not. But you do need peace and quiet to write on tape – not for the writing, exactly, I mean for the recorddddddddddddddddddddddddddddd dddddddddddddddddddddddddddddddddddddddddddddddddddding.

The 'd' got stuck. C'est la vie! *Difficulties are there to be overcome.* I fiddle the typewriter key backwards and forwards, until at last it moves freely again (the arm of the letter key, I mean.) Now ... where were we? Ah, yes ... I mean for the recording. The one person you could have in the room would be the person to whom you're telling the story – that's the only possibility. Otherwise, you have to be totally on your own, and with no interruptions, so that you can 'find the centre' – as Julie so often used to say – and which she explained best, perhaps, in connection with meditation – or with the martial arts like Aikido or Budo. There the 'centre' has its importance not only for your mind, but also your body. Oh, those damned builders! The noise of sawing boards chases all thoughts out of your head. Today, I can see, is going to be a battle against innocent opponents. But perhaps it will also reinforce my resolve, since this book is something I really want to write – for Julie, for me, for all those who understand. It seems senseless to have lived through all this only to have it disappear without trace.

Even then, it would not have been meaningless. It made sense for both of us at the time, representing the fulfilment of a lifetime ... It is about realisation I want to tell, a realisation that took place over only a few years, years during which K2 stood over us, remote and chill, yet more beautiful than any other mountain. A symbol, it seemed, of all that is unattainable.

An eternal temptation.

'Will we ever come back to K2? Of course we will.'
(Julie Tullis, 1984, in Urdokas on the Baltoro Glacier)

Introduction

A real book needs more than just a good writer. It needs a deep conviction, a promise to yourself, to others. I could never have finished this book without thinking all the time of Julie and her wish, to pass on to others what we were living for, to have them participate – and writing down our experiences made it real. It was a way of continuing our team, a conviction that grew during my lonely descent on the Abruzzi after the fatal blizzard. It was a promise. Thus, the mountain and our thoughts will be within these pages.

'Anything is possible', Julie used to say. She had a very strong will, was positive, determined and active. However, at times she would just sit still, listen to the sounds of nature, let her mind glide away into the space between the leaves of a tree, between the shimmering walls of ice towers, or up to the clouds beyond them. It was not only Julie herself who made our great days, those years – and with them, this book – possible. You almost never find that your achievements, your dreams, become real without the actions, influence or help of others. Besides herself, it was Julie's understanding husband Terry, her early climbing partner, Dennis Kemp, and – perhaps in the most significant way – her martial arts teacher David, who opened up the world for her very special, uncommon personality. Julie has dedicated several chapters of her beautiful book *Clouds From Both Sides* to them.

When I wrote this book I considered also how much it might mean to her friends. Our time in the Himalayas were her last years, bringing her the greatest fulfilment as a creative person, not only with the summit of K2, our dream mountain. It was a way of ascent to yet another realisation. Then it all ended abruptly in the blizzard at 8,000 metres.

To write about the events up there was hard, sometimes a real struggle, but it had to be. I'll never be able to accept what happened, but at least it should never be repeated. It took me almost two years to complete the book, and I want to thank Teresa, my wife, for her incredible patience, as well as Audrey Salkeld, who translated the book, for hers. Many people helped: Choi Chang Deok, a priest, was sent to me, perhaps by providence, to clear up the mystery of this tragedy, hidden in illegible Korean 'hieroglyphs'; Charlie Clarke and Franz Berghold, high altitude illness specialists; Xavier Eguskitza, the indefatigable chronicler, John Boothe, Peter Gillman, Judith Kendra, and Dee Molenaar ... even my daughters Hildegard and Karen have contributed to this work!

And I must not forget those who made it possible for me to start writing at all: Gerhard Flora in Innsbruck and Hildegunde Piza in Vienna, who treated my frostbite; the Pembury Hospital in Sussex which saved me from a sudden lung-embolism in the aftermath of K2; Enzo Raise in Bologna, who recognised at the last minute my totally unexpected malaria, probably caught on my way home in the aeroplane – I almost died from it. While I slowly recovered, Mrs Susie Kermauner in Salzburg took me to her rusty typewriter in that two-hundred-year-old house ... and I started the first chapter. Several months later, in Bologna, my little son Ceci interfered with tradition: he taught me how to use the computer! 'Oh, finally, Dad ...' he said.

Even if their names are not given, I want to thank many more people that Julie's book now has a companion, *The Endless Knot*; here it is.

Kurt Diemberger
Bologna, March 1990

K2... The Peak We Most Desired

A strange, filmy mist has settled over everything – a grey silk shroud cloaking the entire pyramid of the summit, fascinating and menacing at the same time. There is tension in the air: it runs through us, through this steep, snowy landscape with its undulations and ice cliffs. The weather is slowly worsening.

All the same, we keep climbing. It can't be much further now. If we're caught in a storm up here, up at almost 8,600 metres, we haven't a hope of surviving whatever we do. Whether we turn back or not. This way, at least, we shall have stood on the summit – 'our' summit – first.

A vertical wall of ice rears out of the silky light. With my ice-axe I turn a titanium screw into its hard surface. It creaks and grinds. Then I cut a couple of holds – no time to waste on artistic effect at this height. Will there be more obstacles above this? Or will we see the summit in a few minutes?

Julie belays me as I move up cautiously. Just a few metres and I am over the ice barrier. And there it is! In the soft, grey light, the highest billow of snow on this high mountain – the summit of K2. It looks so gentle – easy even – this final curve, after the terrible precipices below. A wave of happiness washes over me. 'Up you come, Julie! Come on, we're almost there!'

She appears over the edge, craning to see over its icy rim. Elbows in the snow, she stops to gaze upwards. 'Be still!' she whispers, and I see surprise and wonder in her eyes, those dark, familiar eyes under the frosted strands of hair. She seems to be in silent communion with the last smooth curve of snow.

What goes through her mind? I wonder. What is she telling those summit snows?

For three years we have lived with the dream of coming back to this, our mountain of mountains ... Now the elusive summit is within grasp. Nothing can take it away from us.

But it's late. And the weather is about to break. In a strange way, it seems to be holding its breath, granting us a few moments' grace. Yet, even though it looks a little brighter, the magic light cannot deceive us.

'Julie, let's go!' Suddenly I feel uncomfortable.

She looks up with a smile, as if returning from a distant world 'Yes, let's get a move on! Let's get up there!'

Within minutes, our three-year dream will be fulfilled.

The Lonely Mountain

THIRTY YEARS AGO – ON THE BALTORO WITH HERMANN BUHL

Shshsht! Shshsht! Shshsht! Shshsht! Our snowshoes glide over glistening, sunlit powder, across ribs of ice and the gently rolling curves of the glacier.

Ahead of me, still pushing strongly despite fatigue and moving with short, precise steps, is the small, almost delicate figure of Hermann Buhl, his energy clearly visible as he covers the irregular ground of the Godwin-Austen Glacier. I can see his grey, wide-brimmed felt hat above his rucksack, his fine-boned hands resting on the ski-sticks for balance each time he raises one of the oval, wooden snowshoes to take another, sliding step, but the expression in Hermann's ever-alert eyes as he scans the way ahead, I can only guess at. Thus, we make our way forward, past long rows of jagged ice-shapes, as if in an enchanted forest where everything has been frozen into immobility. Corridors between the towers lead us along the spine of the moraine, through freshly fallen snow.

We are alone – alone in the heart of the Karakoram, surrounded by mighty glaciers, in a savage world of contrasts, of ice and rock, of pointed mountains, granite towers, fantasy shapes rising a thousand metres or more into the sky, some very much more.

This spring (May 1957), besides Hermann and me and our three companions back in Base Camp, there are no other human beings on the whole of the Baltoro Glacier.

Marcus Schmuck and Fritz Wintersteller from Salzburg and Captain Quader Saeed, our liaison officer (who, having no one to liaise with, has been homesick for the more colourful life of Lahore for several weeks now), are fellow members of the only expedition this season within a radius of several hundred kilometres. We are alone on this giant river of ice, fifty-eight kilometres long, which with its fabulous mountains constitutes one of the remotest and most beautiful places on earth. Uncounted lateral glaciers fan out to peaks of breathtaking size and steepness – forming compositions of such harmony that they seem to emanate magic – to places where no one questions 'Why?' because the answer stands so plain to see. My great ambition, to go once in my life to the Himalayas and climb the highest peaks in the world, has been realised – at the age of twenty-five. Hermann Buhl invited me to join his team on the strength of my *direttissima* climb of the 'Giant meringue' on the Gran Zebru (Königsspitze), a sort of natural whipped-cream roll widely considered to be the boldest ice route in the Alps to date. I'm ecstatic. Everything I have, I will put into this one big chance.

Now, as we make tracks in the snow at almost 5,000 metres along one of the lateral glaciers (having set off from close to Concordia, the Baltoro's kilometre-wide glacier junction), my thoughts turn to the early explorers. The glacier we are on is named after the cartographer Godwin-Austen, one of the first to set eyes on the Baltoro in the middle of the last century; but Adolf Schlagintweit was probably the first non-local to get close to the Baltoro area and to reach one – the western – of the Mustagh Passes (Panmah Pass). He has not been commemorated by any name on the map. On the other hand, the beautiful, striated glacier across Concordia from us is dedicated to the traveller G. T. Vigne, who never set foot on it. Martin Conway, leader of an expedition in 1892, was the first to come to the Karakoram to mountaineer; he was later knighted and a snow-saddle he discovered was named after him.

We are not explorers in the same sense as those men, yet on a personal level that is exactly what we are. Going into an empty landscape like this, among giant mountains, your heart quickens and the prospect around the next corner is no less seductive to you than it was to the first people who were here. The same silence dominates the peaks, the same high tension arcs from mountain to mountain; days can still seem like a true gift from heaven. So it is with us on this morning.

Above us soars Broad Peak. No man has ever climbed its triple-headed summit, which rises into the sky like the scaled back of a gigantic dragon. For me, the very rocks breathe mystery: nobody has touched them. I am happy that this mountain, one of the eight-thousanders, is the target of our expedition. But today, Hermann and I are heading off towards K2.

The tallest pyramid on earth seems to grow steadily before our eyes in its unbelievable symmetry. Many years ago, British cartographers* computed the height as 8,611 metres: 237 metres lower than Everest. The second highest mountain in the world is, however, considerably the more difficult of the two to climb and is without doubt one of the most beautiful mountains in the world.

The international expedition of Oscar Eckenstein, which included the

* T. G. Montgomerie in 1856 (see Appendix 1). More recently, Professor Ardito Desio's 1987 expedition – which I accompanied as cameraman – remeasured the heights of several peaks in the Himalayas by GPS (Global Positioning System, using Navstar Satellite Signals), and found K2 to be 8,616 metres, and Everest 8,872 metres.

The Lonely Mountain

Austrians Hans Pfannl and Dr. Victor Wessely, made the first attempt in 1902 and managed to reach 6,525 metres on the North-East Ridge. But in 1909, a large-scale expedition led by the Duke of the Abruzzi opened up the South-East Spur (the Abruzzi Ridge or Rib), revealing that as the most favourable line of ascent. They only got to 6,250 metres, but on nearby Chogolisa (Bride Peak), the Duke and his mountain guides clambered to 7,500 metres, which stood as a world altitude record for many years. They were only 156 metres from the summit.

Hermann Buhl has stopped to look across towards Chogolisa, that shimmering trapeze of snow and ice, maybe thirty kilometres away. 'A lovely mountain,' he says.

To me, it looks like an enormous roof in the sky, but Hermann's attention is already back with K2. 'Such a pity that's been climbed already! But wouldn't a traverse be great; up the ridge on the left, then down to the right, by the Abruzzi?' And he tells me all he knows of the Abruzzi route, how the mountain was first climbed this way by a huge Italian expedition three years ago. They put in no fewer than nine high-altitude camps. And, it's said, fixed 5,000 metres of rope on the ridge itself. Ardito Desio, a professor of geology, was leader and the two summiteers among the eleven-man team were Lino Lacedelli and Achille Compagnoni. It was a national triumph, which threw the whole of Italy into a whirl of rejoicing. It is true that they used bottled oxygen, but it ran out towards the end. And they didn't give up! Hermann is laughing, 'So you see, it does work! You can do it without!' Then he tells of George Mallory and Sandy Irvine, who never came back from a summit attempt on Everest in 1924, despite taking oxygen. Nine years after their disappearance an ice-axe was found at 8,500 metres which can only have belonged to one of them, yet today we are no nearer knowing whether they made it to the top of the world or not. And he tells of Colonel Norton, who went very high on Everest without oxygen, and of Fritz Wiessner, who got within almost 200 metres of the top of K2 in 1939, also without using it.

I can see from his animation, from his eyes and gestures, that Hermann can hardly wait to have a go at K2, without oxygen or high-altitude porters. 'In West Alpine style' is the phrase he coined for it. 'Mmm! K2 *is* a beautiful mountain and no mistake,' he concludes, adding pensively, 'and the way to do it is definitely up that left ridge, down the right.'

But the mountain looks so high, like nothing else in the world. We are only tiny dots before this huge mass, which shines like crystal from the snow and ice on its faces. It arouses no desire in me. I am happy with our choice: Broad Peak is still virgin, and almost 600 metres lower than K2. Better for our 'West Alpine' enterprise – already considered crazy by a lot of people – better than the second highest mountain on earth!

With that, my thoughts turn to 'our' eight-thousander: the only time it was ever attempted was in 1954 by a German expedition under Dr Karl Herrligkoffer. They found it pretty hairy. Following a line under constant threat from avalanches, the climbers discovered that huge blocks of ice had stopped only inches short of their tent. One day the Austrian Ernst Senn fell down a sheer 500-metre ice wall, whistling along like a bobsleigh to land (by incredible good fortune) safely in the soft snow of a high plateau. At 7,000 metres, icy autumn storms drained the men's last reserves of energy, forcing them at length to abandon the attempt.

A few days ago, buried in the steep ice of the 'Wall', we discovered a German food dump with advocaat, angostura bitters, some equipment ... and a three-year-old salami, which still tasted all right. There was even a tin of tender, rolled, Italian ham, a well-travelled delicacy which quickly found its way into our stomachs. I have to confess that this side trip we're making to K2 is purely out of curiosity, to see what delicious titbits might still be lying around at the site of the Italian Base Camp!

A delusion: all our efforts to find the camp fail. The wide glacier is white and pristine, and there is no trace on the moraine either. Finally, we turn around and waddle on our snowshoes back the way we came.

It was curiosity, too, that led us to penetrate the avalanche cirque of Broad Peak. Hermann wanted to take a look at the route Herrligkoffer had chosen. The doctor had been his leader on Nanga Parbat and there was no love lost between the two men. Hermann himself had opted for a more direct line on the West Spur of Broad Peak, a line of greater difficulty, it's true, but very much safer, and one that had been recommended by the well-known 'Himalayan Professor', G. O. Dyhrenfurth. A straightforward and direct ascent like this is much more in Hermann's style.

As we approach Base Camp, tired now from dragging these legs with their wooden appendages, kaleidoscopic memories dance through my mind. I remember how, amid a swirl of dust, we touched down in the old Dakota on that sandy patch of ground near Skardu which serves as an airfield; remember crossing the Indus river in a big, square boat: the three-week-long walk-in, following first the wide Shigar valley with its blossoming apricot trees, then through the Braldu gorge, and finally trekking up the Baltoro Glacier with our sixty-eight porters ... remember being slowed down by snowstorms, so that our loads were dumped twelve kilometres short of Base Camp. The subsequent load-ferrying, backwards and forwards with 25-30 kilograms on our backs, went on day after day until Base Camp was at last established at 4,900 metres – that is higher than the summit of Mont Blanc. And Hermann's words of consolation, 'It's all good training for later on ... for the first eight-thousander to be climbed in West Alpine style.' Then the West Spur itself: up and down, up and down, plagued at first by headaches ... Later it went more easily. Whenever we set down our loads at Camp 1, we would squat on our haunches in the snow for a fast slide down into the depths again.

After a while, even taking every precaution, we could manage the 800-900 metres of descent on the seat of our pants in just half an hour!

Seen from Concordia, Broad Peak – this three-humped dragon – has the appearance of a mighty castle. From wherever you see it, it always looks different. You can never 'know' a mountain precisely ... When we finish here, Hermann hopes to have a go at Trango Tower, or one of the other fantastic granite spires in the lower Baltoro.

We are a modern expedition. Hermann has seen to it that we lack nothing progress has to offer. We have gas cylinders – huge ones like those for domestic use, each a full porter-load – and small ones of about 7 kilos for higher on the mountain. We have simple ridge tents, extremely stable. And advanced altitude boots of heavy, solid leather, made especially roomy to accommodate socks or felt slippers or whatever else we feel like using for insulation ... newspaper works quite well! Of course, walking on moraine in these Mickey Mouse boots is awkward – you feel like deep-sea divers. No doubt one day someone will come up with a custom-made boot-within-a-boot that is a lot better. But we are not ill-satisfied. Except for one thing: progress dogs us even on the West Spur in the form of a walkie-talkie apparatus weighing 11 kilos. We decide to dump it at Camp 1 (5,800 metres) and from there on use the time-honoured method of a piece of paper: write down what you want to say and leave it in the tent for the others to read when they get there.

Camp 2 is a natural snow hole, which we have enlarged, under the rim of a high plateau at 6,400 metres. We have even set up a kitchen there: Hermann has this weakness for potato dumplings, ox-tongue salad, mayonnaise, and buckthorn juice – in other words, for all things sour – and for beer. But the latter is only available at Base Camp. He calls it Nature's Own Sleeping Draught. His first 'dose' turned into a foaming fountain, a metre high, which only stopped gushing when the blue Bavarian tin was empty. Barometric pressure is quite different at 4,900 metres, and we soon learned to make only a tiny puncture and to keep a thumb over the hole so that the pressure could be released slowly and our nice sleeping draught not sprayed to the four winds.

The days pass. On 29 May, we push up from Camp 3 (just below 7,000 metres) towards the summit ridge. We make it as far as the northern end of the 'roof', that is to a height of about 8,030 metres. Only then do we discover that isn't the top: the opposite end of this enormous ridge is just a bit higher. But it's too late in the day. We descend. Back in Base Camp,

The Endless Knot

we know we have to retrace our steps all the way up the mountain again – just for those extra twenty metres of height at the other end of the ridge. There's no way round it: that is the summit!

Marcus and Hermann both have frostbite on their toes, and Hermann calls for the 'doctor'. That's me! Uncomfortable in the role, but using the calming words of a real doctor, I give him an injection. Then another one. Success! I was appointed expedition 'doctor' only a month before our departure. Hermann justified it by saying, 'Well, you've *studied*, haven't you?' My protestation, 'Yes – but commerce,' was not considered sufficiently valid an excuse for refusal. He must have great trust in me.

We had 27 kilos of pills and potions (assembled by a real medic) and a universal tool for pulling out teeth (which fortunately I, as Medicine Man, have not been called upon to use). During the long walk-in I have been approached by many of the locals for treatment. I did what I could, relying when in doubt on my bag of painkillers. Nobody should come to any harm, at least. (After all, we do have to go back the same way!)

The big day – 9 June. One after the other, all four of us reach the summit of Broad Peak. Even Hermann, in the end, despite his frostbite. He had given up at 7,900 metres, but afterwards changed his mind. On my way down from the top, I came across him still plodding upwards and turned to accompany him. As the day faded, this unique day, we stepped together onto the highest point ...

> It was about 7 p.m., the sun low in the sky, as we stood there ... a moment of truth. The silence of space surrounds and holds us. It is fulfilment. The trembling sun balances on the horizon. Down below, it is already night, over all the outstretched world. Here, only, and for us, is there still light. The Gasherbrum summits shine close by, and further away comes the shimmer off Chogolisa's heavenly roof. Straight ahead, against the last of the light, soars the dark profile of K2. The snow around us is tinged a deep orange, the sky a pure, clear azure. When I look behind me, an enormous pyramid of darkness is thrown across the endless space of Tibet. It is the shadow of Broad Peak! A beam of light reaches out above and across the darkness towards us, striking the summit. Amazed, we look at the snow at our feet: it seems aglow. Then the light disappears ...   (from *Summits and Secrets*)

It was the great sunset for Hermann Buhl, his last on any summit.

In all truth I admired K2 from up there, that massive wedge of deep blue, like a cut-out against the flood of light, But still I felt no desire. The mountain was too big, unapproachable, easy to leave alone. No thought crossed my mind then that it was to play such a decisive role in my life. Only much later did Eric Shipton's words draw me under its spell.

The Boat

MEETING JULIE

Can that be Sirius, that bright star?

No, not in summer. It must be one of the larger planets.

The way it twinkles, it seems almost to be dancing in the darkness behind the mainstay, mimicking the movements of the boat.

When the star moves too far from the dark line of the stay, I gently press the tiller until the catamaran is once more on the right course – for England. From time to time, after glancing at the illuminated compass, I look for a new star ... because everything turns endlessly, even the sky above the North Sea. I prefer taking my bearings from the stars, rather than referring constantly to the compass. With the voices of the sea, the rushing and gurgling of the water under the keel and the singing of the breeze in the rigging, the stars make up the world in which the boat moves, and my thoughts wander.

My sister Alfrun, who is supposed to be sharing the night watch with me, has dropped off to sleep. I sent her to lie down on a bunk that groans with each movement of the catamaran. This endless creaking is a reminder to me that the boat is rather old. Herbert bought it secondhand in Denmark recently. Herbert is Alfrun's husband, a successful cameraman, passionately fond of the sea. He has lured the whole family, and a friend too, into this adventure, because he is firmly convinced that the boat must be overhauled in the yard where it was built, close to the mouth of the Thames.

Herbert is a born optimist, and with his radiant smile and contagious enthusiasm managed in two days – back home in Salzburg – to involve me completely in this latest venture of his ... me a landlubber, who has always been suspicious of anything new ... though I had an ancestor from Helgoland.

However, I am happy now. I feel like a real sea-dog, and have completely got over the shock of the Limfjord – where we suddenly found the keel scraping the bottom and had to pull up the centreboards to free ourselves – counting the trip now as one of my 'happy-ending' adventures. There is something fascinating about steering a boat –

12 metres long, 8 metres wide, with two masts and two fibreglass hulls, providing living space for four people altogether. You can even sleep on it – if the waves aren't too big!

As I said, my brother-in-law is very proud of his boat, and yesterday, with the air of an expert, he calculated the meridian using sun and sextant, and with it our course. To us, it seemed like magic, even though we weren't convinced he'd got it right. After all we were in the middle of the sea. He became a little nervous when we came across some oil-rigs that weren't on the map, and I suppose I should not have remarked that navigation didn't usually depend on the location of oil-wells.

Now the cap'n is sleeping, having left instructions to be woken only if we see lights. But there haven't been any. The masts sway among stars slowly following their courses hour after hour – somehow it is just as when you sit in a bivouac on a clear night, keenly observing their steady circular progress. And, in the same way as the voices of the mountain bring overwhelming tranquillity, so here, the sea speaks to you.

Last year, I found a place where the two came together: rocks and the sea. Foamy crested waves rushed at vertical cliffs like wild stallions. 'A Dream of White Horses' is the name given by climbers to a route in Wales where you balance on delicate handholds directly above the crashing sea. Looking down, the frothy water beckons, and not until you have overcome your fear of it can you feel happy.

One English climber there clearly had no qualms. Slim and dark-haired, Julie moved up the rock smoothly, each movement expressing strength and a joy of living, just as an animal in its element expresses itself in movement. Her partner, Dennis, exhibited a similar harmony, white hair and beard, which framed sharp features, blowing wildly in the strong breeze. You could hear the roar of the sea, and the air was bitter with salt.

The two climbed so well together, it was easy to see they were in their element.

I learned later that Dennis was a photographer, specialising in quite stupendous nature pictures. Julie came from East Sussex, where she lived with her husband Terry, a ranger, a man of great strength and serenity. Julie and Terry, besides the forest, looked after their local sandstone rocks and ran climbing courses; they also had a coffee shop for climbers, where the relaxed and friendly Tullis atmosphere reigned supreme. Everybody loved Julie and Terry. It had come to them one day that learning to move on rocks could benefit handicapped children and the blind, and they began organising special courses for them. They never climbed together, perhaps because it made Julie nervous or because it led them to be over-critical of each other's style on rock.

The Boat

I met them for the first time when I was on a lecture tour in England many years ago, and again in 1975 when another trip took me to Wales, where Dennis lived. That was when I had seen him and Julie climbing together. The wild sea at the foot of the rocks made a very strong impression on me. Perhaps, by taking part in this boat trip, I wanted to overcome a fear that the unknown element, the fury of the sea, had generated in me. Perhaps I wanted to demonstrate that I was capable of 'dominating' something that had dominated me. But demonstrate to whom?

To myself certainly, but perhaps subconsciously also to Julie, whose own fearlessness I found so fascinating. It must have been that, or how else am I to explain to myself all that then followed?

After seeing Julie and Dennis so immersed in their element, I must have had a tentative desire to take part, even to add to the experience something of my own world.

Now, while I hold the helm and glide over the waves, up and down, up and down, I have the same feeling of strength I encountered there. And I even seem to know why I am approaching this coast.

I begin to dream: In the sky, among the stars, between the silhouettes of the sails, I imagine Lohengrin and his swan, and the legend blends into the sounds of the night. To be honest, I don't remember the story very well, but that doesn't stop me from elaborating a version of my own, tailored to the circumstances.

I want to go and find her, bring her onto this sea that surrounds her island, if only for a day.

'The one thing you must never do,' Herbert had said, 'is to leave the boat. You never give up!' The tone of his voice left no doubt how seriously he meant us to take this. Even though we have a canary-yellow dinghy on board, Herbert (who used to be a mountain guide) has fixed a belay line the whole length of the boat, to which he insists we attach ourselves if the sea is rough. We have to do this whenever we are 'outside' – that is, outside the two floating hulls. It makes sense, but will we really need it?

Herbert has dreams of a larger boat with all the necessary – and unnecessary – extras for ocean-going. (He will spend years building it – it still isn't finished yet.)

The storm! Here it is – hissing and whistling, and the boat groaning and squealing ...

'... It's not falling apart!' I cling to the captain's words, and to the helm.

The storm! In front of me, all I see is a huge wall of grey-green water ... it hoists up the little boat, but no sooner are we on top than the next wall appears, and down we plunge towards it ... Here comes the wall again ... It is never ending ... The sea is constantly renewing itself.

The sails vibrate in the whistling air. Everything trembles. Foam flies all around. The old catamaran moans. Each time we ride a wave it seems that the hull must break into a thousand pieces. 'Just the wood working,' Herbert declares airily in response to my worried expression. If he says so! We are sharing the helm now. Another wall of water ... a valley ... a wall ... on and on. Not a moment's rest. Before long we are as stiff as these never-ending, never-yielding walls. 'Not one of you is to stick his nose outside without first clipping onto the rope with the karabiner,' Herbert had shouted the minute the storm started. And he explained how impossible it is to find anyone who has fallen overboard in a rough sea. Nobody allowed out without a harness – you can see he was once a mountain guide.

'Wind force 6!' he shouts amid the uproar, his blue eyes dancing with excitement. 'Hey, Kurt ...' I make no comment. All I hope is it doesn't go up to 7.

I hold a diagonal course, as instructed, riding the mountains of water, up and down, just like an intrepid skier taking the humps of a rough slope in a straight line. Nobody can keep it up for long, however, and soon we change over. Having completed my stint, I stagger down into one of the hulls to try and find some rest despite the rolling and rocking. Even down there, everything creaks and squeaks, gurgles and snorts ... What on earth brings the Walker Spur into my mind all of a sudden, the Grandes Jorasses? Now of all times? It's a mystery. 1,200 metres of vertical granite, one of the most difficult climbing routes in the western Alps. 'Well, it's not as tiring as this,' I conclude. 'At least the Spur doesn't keep moving about.'

I am amazed how well my sister is coping with this turbulent environment. Having a husband like Herbert obviously toughens you up. Gerard, Herbert's friend, is looking green. 'It's the short North Sea waves,' Herbert comments. 'You can't do anything about it.' It was meant as reassurance. A day has passed and the storm is over. We feel a lot better, but where on earth are we? The last to be at the helm were Alfrun and I, and together we did our best to slice the waves at the right angle. Our poor captain, Herbert, despite himself, is doing battle with seasickness. Gerard, safely over his bout, now that the boat is once more moving peacefully, finds time for a nervous crisis. He has had enough! But you can't get off a boat in the middle of the ocean, not like on a mountain, where you can simply return to Base Camp. (That's not true, Kurt – sometimes you have to stick it out even up there!) All three of us try to calm poor Gerard until finally he smiles weakly, it is almost three

The Boat

days since we left the Danish coast. To tell the truth, I feel as if I have made three bivouacs. Nobody has managed to sleep, the best we have had are a few dozing rests. At this point I am convinced that ocean sailing is every bit as hard as a long mountain ascent. At the same time, however, I feel closer to the sea. The sea has become something special for me.

When you are on it, far from land like this, it takes on a different character; you feel in close contact with the water, not a bit like being on the deck of a large ship. It is as if you were absorbed by the essence of the water – the land, the coast, is only a distant, imaginary limit. You cannot appreciate what the sea is until you have experienced it like this.

We catch sight of a few large ships ... and feel reassured. At the same time, we worry over the danger of a collision. The automatically piloted giants might never notice a tiny sailing boat. The onus is on us to get ourselves out of the way. And soon we are alone again ...

'Land-ho!' A coastline has appeared.

Everybody is excited. But where are we?

'Switch on the Sonar!' I yell, remembering how we ran aground in the Limfjord.

'You and your Sonar! I'm amazed you didn't switch it on in the middle of the North Sea.' Herbert is sarcastic. He doesn't like to be reminded of the incident, but how can I help it if I like to know how much sea there is underneath me? 'The big ships have already shown us where the channel is.' With conviction, he declares, 'That's England ahead.'

'Oh, really?' I think to myself, and hazard – 'couldn't it be the Dutch coast?'

'For Heaven's sake, Kurt!' Herbert shuts me up with a ferocious glance and I mutter something about the unpredictability of marine currents. But he's right. It must be the English coast. Only where?

'We must wait until night,' says Herbert when we are a few kilometres off shore. We can just make out houses and trees; we drop anchor.

But why? Why wait until night-time? In the darkness you can see lighthouses and lightships, each with its own special signal. If we count the seconds between one impulse and the next, and look up the frequency on a chart we have on board, we can work out our location exactly.

Simple! However, when darkness falls the colour of the signals from the first lighthouse does not correspond with the chart, only the intervals do.

'Perhaps the lighthouse-keeper screwed in a red bulb when the last one burned out. Maybe he didn't have another white one.' That's my simplistic explanation. One thing is sure – and another of the lighthouses confirmed it, we are lying off the English coast, to the east of the Thames estuary.

London, Saint Katharine's Dock, Tower Bridge. We have sailed up the Thames.

Alfrun and Gerard go home – overland. Herbert and I stay a few days until everything is ready for the Swan's refit. Lohengrin Mark II – that's me – goes to make a phone call to Terry and Julie …

Will she say 'yes'? She hardly knows me, after all, and she doesn't know Herbert at all. Two Austrian mountain guides and film-makers. Are these trustworthy professions in the eyes of an Englishwoman? Or will we seem more like buccaneers to her? The only thing I want to do is to repay her for those wonderful days climbing in Wales by inviting her to come sailing with us, so that she can see how marvellous it is to dance on the waves in a catamaran. Maybe we'll even go as far as the French coast. For the weekend. It's all right with Herbert – but what about Julie?

Kurt, I tell myself, stop all this Swan nonsense. Who knows how the story of Lohengrin really turned out? On the phone, my nerve fails me. I pose the question finally when we meet – in the middle of Terry's birthday celebrations – and Julie turns down the proposition. But I'm not convinced. Next day we go climbing on a sandstone outcrop in the Sussex woods and I make another attempt, 'Why don't we sail across to France?'

You can sense whether or not a person possesses an adventurous spirit: there is some kind of special emanation – and Julie had this. I could feel very strongly that she was a born explorer. I believe she had the courage and the desire to try almost anything. Often, she felt obliged to stay quietly at home because of her family, but not always. Suddenly, she'd be off! She would run through the woods, climb her rocks, or dash up to Wales to climb with Dennis, or be on her way to some other place. Terry was understanding. He'd long got used to it, he said. So it didn't seem strange to me to be making a suggestion like this. But I was nervous. Shouldn't I have been? Sail in a catamaran to the French coast? Could I still convince her?

She looked at me thoughtfully. The air seemed to be vibrating, in small waves, dissolving into thousands of tiny dancing points, and I was sure that she wanted to come. In that moment she was on the boat and – I don't know why – I was held spellbound by her dark eyes. For several seconds I was incapable of thought, overcome by an emotion I could not recognise. Our gaze almost froze, and I felt sure that her voice could only say 'yes'. When she slowly opened her lips there was consent in her eyes, along with a shyness and reserve, as well as something else I did not recognise, something foreign …

The Boat

'It's not possible,' I heard her say. 'I have to go to see Dennis. He's ill.' She looked up at the gently swaying trees. Her climbing partner had angina, she explained, and she had promised to visit him. I knew from when we were in Wales how close they were to one another.

Timidly at first, then with increasing insistence, I pointed out that it would not take long to sail across to France. It was an opportunity that would not come again. Herbert was about to take the boat to the Mediterranean. I so much wanted to show her my 'ocean', the ocean I had just lived with. I could still feel the blue-green waves within me ... and I sensed how much Julie longed for this adventure. It had to be! But she said 'no', and that was that. Even Terry's encouragement served no purpose.

Much later she told me that her loyalty to Dennis was not the sole reason for refusing. She had a deep feeling – call it intuition – that this was not the right moment for us to get to know each other better.

I left, upset and disappointed. We didn't see each other again for three years.

Then, quite by chance, we bumped into one another in a restaurant at the Trento Film Festival. Julie was with Terry, and I with Teresa and our small son Ceci. We were even staying in the same hotel, we discovered, in adjacent rooms! Even now I find that hard to believe. Neither of us had been to a festival for years, and we had heard nothing of each other ...

Yet there we were, as if the stars had cast the dice.

And nothing had changed; we realised it right away. It was as if I had left England only the day before.

Yet, there was something different.

'I would go on the boat now!' Julie ventured.

'Let's go and climb the Alps,' I said.

The Alps turned into the Himalayas. It was the beginning of our adventures.

... Even the Himalayas were born of the ocean.

Dream Mountain – K2 from the North

FLOODWATERS – SINKIANG ON CAMELBACK

Floodwaters in the high Shaksgam valley: the sky is filled with tumult, a continuous agitation that dominates everything … the very air seems to tremble. My camel leans his full weight against the rushing current. Spume flies everywhere, and the deafening roar of the swollen Kaladjin river drowns out all other sound. I can feel the animal testing the sandy bottom with its feet, looking for hidden holes gouged by the power of the swirling floods.

Floodwaters – elemental, like an avalanche. You are impotent, completely at their mercy if the waters rise further. It's not like a storm on a mountain – then you can grasp what's happening. Here there is just fear … you listen to the roar and ask yourself all the time whether it's getting louder. It is as if somewhere above you, out of sight, tons of snow have broken off and begun rolling towards you – you hear it coming without knowing if or when it will engulf you.

Do Sinkiang camels have a sixth sense, I wonder? My animal seems totally calm as it leans into the water methodically prodding the river bed, moving, stopping, moving on. Just trust the camel, Kurt …

The Shaksgam Valley. Here, in its lower section, we are at 4,000 metres: the deep furrow cuts across uninhabited country, some of the most inaccessible on earth, a region of glaciers and high mountain desert. From one end to the other, the valley is about 200 kilometres, and nobody has ever covered its entire distance. Higher up, immense rivers of ice block it from side to side like giant dams. We have to leave it before we reach these, but now it offers the only possible route. For almost two months, practically the whole summer, any passage has been impossible because of the rushing meltwater coming down from the mountains and glaciers. Even now, at the end of August, the kilometre-wide valley floor is a close network of streams and islands, contained within the pale faces of the Kun Lun and the wild Karakoram mountains. For days we have been zigzagging our way through this huge, sinister valley.

Dream Mountain – K2 from the North

How often will we have to re-cross the waters, fight this current? Twenty times? Thirty times? In my memory I see the clear, shallow stream – marvellously pure spring water ... good to drink – that appeared so unexpectedly out of the interminable, barren gravels of the valley floor during the dry season last May when we were on our way in to K2. Now it is a tangle of glittering, tightly entwined loops, a confusion of meanders and bursting banks, one overlaying another, changing pattern from hour to hour in response to the sun's radiation or the clouds in the sky – and who knows what is happening fifty kilometres upstream? These braided serpents have control of the whole valley floor and hemmed in by the prohibitively steep walls on either side, their brittle rocks torn by heat, we are allowed no escape. There is only one way out: the Shaksgam.

My animal moves forward slowly, up to its belly in the foaming, brown water, the prow wave from its throat carried away by the current so that for some moments it seems we are speeding rapidly upriver, faster than the wind – an optical illusion that has already caused several of us to lose our equilibrium when trying to 'counterbalance' it. I cling to the ropes in the camel's thick fur, arched, tense, ready if the animal should suddenly stumble to throw my weight in whatever direction might be required. A half-strangled cry makes me look round and I'm horrified to see Rodolfo and Giorgio disappearing into the silty waters. Between them, their camel's head rides the surface. The beast was pulled off its legs by the force of the torrent. With frightening speed, my friends are carried downstream towards a vertical rock wall. Nobody can help them. I see them appear and disappear, paddling desperately with their arms. Just before the river smashes into the wall they manage to catch hold of some rocks on the bank. The camel, with its longer legs, had got out earlier. Certainly, without these incredibly resilient, near-indestructible beasts, we would have no hope of making it out of this mountain desert on the Chinese side of K2. Even so, yesterday four loads were lost in the river, and today three. We must be thankful nobody has drowned – there have been plenty of opportunities. The wild torrents of the Himalayas and Karakoram have claimed the lives of so many climbers over the years.

Right now, none of us wants to know about mountain summits – we are a worn out, dissolute crew, scorched in our minds after four months in the high Sinkiang desert. Our only thoughts are for home. This desperate longing drives us to plunge again and again into the muddy waters of the river which stands between us and our return – from stream to stream we go, island to island, day to day ... One of us has special cause to be afraid, little Agostino, our first summiteer on K2: he doesn't know how to swim! But without exception, all twenty-two members of this international (but mainly Italian) expedition have had their fill of the Shaksgam waters. Our bodies bear witness to the rigours of the past months on the mountain – rugged faces and baggy clothes flapping wraithlike around spindly limbs. One person has lost 15 kilos, another 20, and I am a full 23 kilos lighter. Julie, our British member who helped me with the filming up to 8,000 metres, has only shed 10 kilos, but however much she might have longed to be slim, she wouldn't win any beauty contests now, any more than would Christina, our doctor. Still, when you have been together on a mountain for so long, gone through so much, coped with all the disappointments, fears and joys, things like appearance matter very little. Helpfulness is so much more important.

Regardless of what she looks like, Julie has lost none of her energy and strength, nor the resilience that I so much admire. It's true her skin is a collection of wrinkles ... but the eyes in the thin, burned face are unchanged; and it's what's in them that counts. Sometimes, a fleeting, quiet smile lights her face, and under her tangled hair the eyes shine like the shimmer of mountain ice.

What we have brought back from one of the loneliest places on earth is happiness.

Our expedition team forged bonds of friendship, even if this was one of the toughest and longest enterprises I have ever been engaged in. Maybe, because of that.

Once or twice, as happens on expeditions, tensions arose but they never lasted long. Perhaps the Italian temperament is one of the best for getting over such things. And because we spent so long together, had to solve a variety of problems with no recourse to the outside world, we finished with a real understanding of one another.

A BOOK SPELLS DESTINY

The afternoon was fine, and nothing interrupted my view of the great amphitheatre about me. The cliffs and ridges of K2 rose out of the glacier in one stupendous sweep to the summit of the mountain, 12,000 feet above. The sight was beyond my comprehension, and I sat gazing at it, with a kind of timid fascination, watching wreaths of mist creep in and out of corries utterly remote. I saw ice avalanches, weighing perhaps hundreds of tons, break off from a glacier, nearly two miles above my head; the ice was ground to a fine powder and drifted away in the breeze long before it reached the foot of the precipice, nor did any sound reach my ears.

These words were written by Eric Shipton in 1937 in his *Blank on the Map*,

Dream Mountain – K2 from the North

a book I discovered in my collection years ago, and which was the start of everything for me. It is still a mystery how I came to have it: it was among things we inherited from an aunt who was fond of travelling but who had no particular interest in mountains and didn't speak a word of English. A note inside the cover revealed that she had bought it in India, a long time ago, even before I could walk. How on earth did she come to choose it? She died before I could ask. It must have been my father who put it into my 'library' (the shelf in the top of my wardrobe). Sometimes I wonder about the strange coincidence that brought this book to me ... without it, I would probably never have gone to the north side of K2, and K2 might never have become my mountain of dreams. Shipton's words caught the magic of the secret side of this mountain and I read them over and over again.

'Whatever you do, exploration is always the best part.' (That's an old explorers' saying.) It is definitely a greater adventure to discover unknown valleys and mountains than to climb a mountain by a known route, however high. But there is a link between discovery and climbing: to explore the hidden side of a mountain, to seek out a route, then to try to follow it to the top ... This is true also of 8,000-metre peaks – like K2's north side. Eric Shipton only wanted to see what was there, and was caught by its spell. It is as if the spirit of the mountain enters you there when you first gaze upon it. Shipton certainly felt it. And I think I absorbed the same feeling from his words; they aroused in me a deep longing to see this enchanted world for myself, to climb on this lonely mountain.

At 8,616 metres, K2 is the second highest mountain in the world. But if Everest stands higher (by a mere 256 metres), K2 is the more beautiful, more fascinating and quite the more difficult of the two. The Chinese call it Qogir, a variation of the local name Chogori, which means, simply, 'big mountain'. A perfect pyramid, it dominates the ocean of peaks around but remains somewhat obscured unless viewed from quite high up – as from an aeroplane, when you see its outstanding shape soaring far above anything else. On the Pakistan side, the mountain is generally known as *Kei tu* these days, a name derived directly from the topographical symbol 'K2' employed by Montgomerie in 1856 when he numbered the peaks for identification ('K' signifying Karakoram). From this side I had seen the peak first in 1957 with Hermann Buhl during our expedition to Broad Peak, and then again in 1979 when I stood on Gasherbrum II. The north side, however, Eric Shipton's 'magic' side, where the immense North Spur sweeps almost four kilometres into the sky in a straight line, I only saw with my own eyes in the spring of 1982, when I went with 'Bubu' Enzo de Menech, an Italian friend. We were making a reconnaissance – having a special permit from the Chinese – and were accompanied by four Chinese, six camels, two camel-drivers from an Uigur tribe (locals of Sinkiang and Chinese, too, by definition, but a minority group), and two donkeys.

That same year the north side was climbed for the first time, by a large Japanese expedition. At about 8,000 metres, the mountaineers left the main spur, traversed over a steep hanging glacier and climbed to the summit by way of a lateral ridge. Thus, the final 600 metres of spur were still virgin when Francesco Santon's Italian expedition (to which Julie and I belonged) arrived in the area with 120 camels at the beginning of May 1983.

We had passed through the harsh gorges of the Surukwat and the Aghil Daran, crossed the southern mountains of the Kun Lun ranges, had come over the Aghil Pass (4,780 metres) and descended into the Shaksgam, which, because it was spring, was dry.

Finally, we moved up a wide side valley, the Sarpo Laggo, an immense plain of gravel, where at 3,850 metres we came upon the paradise of Suget Jangal, a green patch of meadows and willow bushes about a kilometre at its greatest length, a natural wonder in this high desert. Shipton wrote of it with enthusiasm; Francis Younghusband and Ardito Desio visited it on their even earlier expeditions (1887 and 1929 respectively) otherwise this uninhabited place was known only to a few local herdsmen. No European had been there since Shipton. From Lower Base Camp, which we established there (calling it *Campo Casa*, Home Base), we could still take our camels on as far as the mouth of the K2 Glacier at 4,000 metres, but after that they were on holiday. Upper Base Camp was to be installed a thousand metres higher, on the glacier and closer to the mountain; but zigzagging through a maze of moraine hills and ice towers is too much even for Sinkiang camels. There was only one solution: if we were to get all the material we needed up to this place we had to ferry it ourselves.

A FAIRYLAND OF ICE TOWERS

Along more than 25 kilometres of gravel beds, over rocks, moraine humps, ice slabs, tacking between towers of ice as big as houses, sometimes hanging over raging torrents, unbalanced by the heavy packs on our shoulders, we toiled up and down this interminable glacier. Hump up 20-30 kilos – come down empty. It went on for several weeks. A thousand metres of height separated the end of the glacier and the site

Dream Mountain – K2 from the North

of Upper Base Camp at 5,000 metres – that is the painful reality of being human camels. It took three days to carry a load along the whole length of glacier. And so many loads! Some of us made the journey thirty times. Even with two intermediate camps, it was the hardest work I've ever been called upon to make on any of my expeditions – at least so far as transporting stores goes. Why didn't we have porters? The answer is simple: there aren't any in Sinkiang. Nepal has its Sherpas, Pakistan its Hunzas and Baltis, Tibet its Tibetans, but in Sinkiang the locals will go only as far as their pack animals. At the beginning we were helped by over twenty Italians, who had been 'invited' along specially just for this, but before they were properly acclimatized (and two were even on their honeymoon), they had to go back, together with the last of the 120 camels as it was already the middle of June and the floods could come down at any moment. By this time, too, the hay for the camels was exhausted.

Even if Sinkiang camels have no liking for glaciers, we did wonder if donkeys could be persuaded to go on them, and kept our two back with us – not without some anxiety. On a fine morning we tried to coax them from Home Base to the glacier. It was a real disaster. They simply would not grasp what it was we wanted them to do – or perhaps, they understood a bit too well!

But there are some creatures still to be encountered even above 5,000 metres. We saw butterflies happily circling between the ice towers, or visiting the flowers at the side of the glacier; there were spiders running over the moraine debris, there was an eagle, and high up, here and on the ledges of a smaller mountain, sometimes we were lucky enough to catch sight of a herd of *bharal*, mountain sheep.

And then there were the mice. They appeared out of nowhere on the moraine among the rocks in our kitchen. When we were eating, they would scurry between our legs and feet with no fear at all, so that Julie and I didn't dare move for fear of disturbing our droll little guests. They would be having their meal, too: poised on back legs, the better to be able to use their 'arms'; they would hold a long straw of uncooked spaghetti (much longer than themselves), chomping it up in record-quick time with sharp front teeth. There were only three at the beginning, but by the end of the summer we were playing host to seven 'regulars'.

Down at Home Base, plant and animal life was well represented – even to the temporary addition of new species: small gardens with spinach, salad, onion plants, radishes were planted by our Sinkiangese companions, thus enriching the customary expedition diet with unexpected delicacies. There was a flock of fifty sheep as well, placidly grazing between the bushes of the meadow – they too were destined for the cooking pots.

Such abundance could not pass unobserved. A big wolf, curious and hungry, came visiting several times from a nearby valley. His incursions reduced our hooved food reserves by at least seventeen units. All our defence strategy proved in vain – not even the battered old rifle belonging to our liaison officer, Liu, one of Mao's weathered old partisans, had any effect against him. The 'wolf' always managed to sneak away. Today I know better: it must have been a snow leopard.

With good old Liu, Julie and I had a special relationship – although he always regarded us suspiciously if we left with a rucksack, heading in an unaccustomed direction. Then he would set us strict time limits, and announce that other glaciers were not allowed. He was great! Quite soon, Julie and I had become real Sinkiang mountain marathoneers ... but usually we started, heavily loaded, towards the K2 Glacier. That summer we each wore out a pair of boots: between our glacier treks, film excursions and explorations we covered over a thousand kilometres. Every time we came back into the ice towers, it was like entering a new, though familiar world. We felt utter happiness: we loved this ice and its colours, its surprises.

Rising to sixty feet or more, ice towers develop a strange regularity of shape and positioning on the glacier surface, like a frozen procession of the Ku Klux Klan. A whole army, indeed. Sometimes you find a hollow tower, and if you shout into it, it produces a strange sound. They are constantly worn away by slow surface melting, but as the surrounding glacier for some reason melts faster than they do, they give the appearance of actually growing. The highest towers are usually found in the final section of the procession. Sometimes you can hear the thunder of one of them collapsing and breaking into thousands of pieces and blocks of white, blue and green ice. You should keep a respectful distance from them, but this is not always possible. The K2 Glacier is not the only one that has these towers. The mightiest 'processions' that Julie and I discovered were on the Gasherbrum Glacier. (We filmed there and reached, for the first time, the base of the unclimbed North Face of Gasherbrum II.) The tallest of these pointed towers I ever saw was in 1988 on the Singhié Glacier – some fifty metres in height. To walk in the corridors between the towers is to be in a fairyland. Only fantasy could create such shimmer, such a world of crystal. Yet it is real.

The first tents at the High Base Camp were in place at 5,000 metres by the end of May, but the load-ferrying to this place continued into the beginning of August, when all the high camps were established. One of the most original of these was Camp 1, tucked inside a crevasse at 5,800 metres on the sheer face close to the North Spur. Julie and I spent several

Dream Mountain – K2 from the North

days there, getting used to the altitude before going higher and (naturally, and just as importantly) doing some filming.

Julie had never been to 8,000 metres before. Now for the first time we were in direct contact with K2, could sense the great mass of the mountain, the vast sweep of the spur – an unimaginable 3,600 metres of vertical height. (The climbing distance is of course, much more.) But these are only figures, after all; they tell you very little about the thinning of the air as you climb higher, the great effort required, the increased hazards of altitude.

How would she fare up there? On Nanga Parbat, in 1982, Pierre Mazeaud, the expedition leader, didn't give her a chance. He is no sympathizer of women on expeditions and forbade her to go above 5,000 metres – a bitter pill for Julie to swallow when four years earlier she had climbed 6,768-metre Huascaran in the Andes. But regardless of any medical tests you take beforehand, you never know for sure – not even these days – how anyone will perform at altitude if they have not been high before. Marco Cortecolo, a first-class mountaineer on our expedition and an extreme-skier, found himself in Camp 2 suddenly fighting for his life. Only oxygen and the combined efforts of the whole team saved him from certain death; instead of filming a daring ski-descent down the steep face beside the lower third of the spur, Julie and I (from Camp 1) shot his rescue along the fixed ropes. He had no use of his legs, and without the uninterrupted sequence of ropes anchored to the face with rock pitons and ice screws, it is unlikely that any of us could have got him off the mountain in time.

Apart from this unfortunate incident, the atmosphere on the spur was usually happy.

LIVING IN A CREVASSE AT 5,800 METRES

'Watch out for those icicles when you operate the clapper board,' I (as film director) shout at Pierangelo, a bearded bear of a man from Bergamo. But it's just my little joke. He is standing outside the icicle curtain at Camp 1 in his bathing suit: out there the sun is merciless, while here inside the crevasse where we've set up home, the temperature is around zero. That is why we're not short of icicles: they grow faster than mushrooms in the woods (especially given the two hours a day of rain, or heavy dripping, that we get here, one of the drawbacks of this campsite). So you can always 'pick' them for icicle soup, icicle tea, and for mixing with the freeze-dried food: and if you sit long enough inside the cave, you even get icicles in your beard. I have just filmed the red tents inside the crevasse through a curtain of icicles, and Julie has fixed her microphone between two of them.

'Take one!' Pierangelo bellows through his mighty beard, then while the camera and recorder are running, provides the 'Action!' by leaping as fast as he can out of our ice-box cave and into the sunshine.

Altogether we shot 1,000 metres of film of the climb and life on the mountain itself, and we filmed many days on the North Spur: in four months we collected 11,000 metres of celluloid. It certainly needs strong faith to realise what you want to create under the circumstances of a major climb and most mountaineers do not concern themselves much with the mechanics of filming on a climb like this. Julie and I had already learned that the hard way on our Nanga Parbat trip. But here it is much better: tomorrow Luca wants to carry the big Arriflex camera up to Camp 2, which is about 900 metres higher than here. That means a wearisome oblique traverse over ice slabs, steep snowfields and rocks to the right of the ridge. Julie and I will carry our personal gear as well as our lightweight tent, the sound equipment and a summit camera. The unpredictable nature of filming often makes camera teams difficult to accommodate within normal expedition planning and routine. When the two of us reached this crevasse on the first occasion, for example, there was no room for us in the tents. Well, we shovelled out a snow hole and passed the night in our nylon bivouac bag comfortably enough. However, since then, we have preferred always to carry a super lightweight tent in the rucksack. If the weather gives us the chance, we could even dare a summit attempt (it's a secret dream of ours). But will fate grant us the chance?

As the number of loads carried up to Camp 1 grows, and more people visit it, the crevasse becomes increasingly comfortable. Alcoves for cooking have been carved out of the ice, and benches of snow: there are pitons in the walls on which to hang up equipment (but you do have to take care in choosing a good spot, not one where the icicles grow, or you may find all your gear frozen into a compacted lump that you may never get off the wall!).

Only the toilet facilities remain uncomfortable. Holding on to your ice-axe as a self-belay, you half hang, half lean over a vertical drop of fifty metres. We've all scratched our heads for a less exhausting solution, but so far no one has come up with one.

Even in bad weather, there is no shortage of humour on an Italian expedition. However, in Camp 1 when the avalanches sweep over you, you don't hear anyone laughing. There is this sudden sound, like a waterfall racing down the slope, and a mighty hissing across the mouth of the crevasse. Soft snow and powder comes in all over the place.

It's certainly frightening. We managed to partially close the opening with a sheet; even so, when the avalanches roll, it is not the best place to be.

Still, who would ever have thought you could get used to living inside a crevasse in the middle of a steep mountainside. But you do ...

7,000 METRES – GIVE UP OR GO ON?

'We've filmed enough with the big camera. From now on we'll only use the summit camera – and make our own attempt ...'

On 31 July, twenty-nine years to the day after the first ascent of K2 by Lino Lacedelli and Achille Compagnoni, our lead climbers, Agostino Da Polenza and Joska Rakoncaj, have reached the summit. Others, Sergio Martini and Fausto de Stefani, as well as Almo Giambisi and 'Gigio' Visentin, are in position for their try. None of them has been on the ideal direct line that we had dreamed of, but they have made the Japanese exit from the spur to the left and crossed the hanging glacier. All the same, the summit is the summit! Especially on K2 ... where you have to be really lucky with the weather and in extraordinarily good shape if you want to do it at all, particularly if you climb without bottled oxygen, as we did. (We had just three bottles of oxygen on the mountain, for medical purposes: they served well for mountain sickness and frostbite.)

What should we do, Julie and I, give up or go on? The question hung in the air for only a few minutes when Francesco Santon, the expedition's leader, came on the radio to ask why we were still filming on the spur. Hadn't we had that big camera up here for some while, long enough to get all we needed? Wouldn't it be a good idea to spend some time back at Home Base?

It sounded like a bad joke to us. Now of all times! No, we had no ideas of that kind. We wanted the summit, too! Or at least the chance to climb as high as possible. We had worked hard on this expedition, and we would still take film and sound while we made our attempt.

That's why we have come up even further with our lightweight tent and all the many things we need – climbing gear, food, stove, summit camera, sound-recorder – to an airy pulpit here at 7,000 metres beside the ridge. It juts out like a ski-jump, or rather a 'sky-jump', over an ocean of peaks. Immeasurable distances extend before our eyes, mountain to mountain, valleys filled with blue haze, glittering, shimmering belts of glaciers, like huge drowsy snakes.

Now that we have seen this, we know: the summit of K2 is not everything. Living way above the ocean of peaks like this is at least as good. Days when infinity belongs to you ...

The Endless Knot

And also, all that is close, below you: the small saddle above the Skyang Glacier, where we were not long ago ... and further out, in the wide gash of the Shaksgam valley, the round head of Tek-Ri, a place we know well.

'Nanga Parbat! Can you recognise it?' Julie wants to know.

'Yes, there on the horizon. All by itself.' That was our first expedition.

'And those high blue mountains, way to the west?'

'Rakaposhi, one of them. Kunyang Kish another. The Batura Wall – all those seven-thousanders above the Hunza valley.' Last year we were there ...

Today it is all ours. A day above the world. Far and wide, near and far – ours.

One of the mountains down there, a six-thousander, rising at the edge of K2 Glacier, is the one we have named Shipton Peak. It has to have been the one he used as his viewpoint.

During the night comes the storm. It seems impossible after a day like that. 'Never take anything for granted,' I think, and say as much to Julie. The wind pulls and rattles at the tent. There is not much space on our little 'sky-jump'. We are exposed to the full power of the storm. In such situations, you can't help thinking about the 2,000-metre drop beneath you, and wondering how strong the fabric of your tent is. Are the seams well stitched and shouldn't we have piled more rocks on the anchoring pegs? Such a high camp is always a gamble: if you go down because of the storm, you may lose the only possible day for the summit, yet if you stay and snowfall starts, avalanches could cut off all hope of retreat. There is no immediate solution, but at the same time, you know you wont give up: you have come here in full knowledge of the risks. These are the recurrent thoughts on stormy nights high in the Himalayas.

In the morning I have a headache, but it passes. The storm, however, goes on until the afternoon. We make the decision to sit it out. All of a sudden, from above, Agostino and Joska appear on their way back from the summit. And from below, Soro and Giuliano come up. Congratulations and big hugs all round. We are very happy to be together again.

Julie and I record the reunion for our film, but we are heart-and-soul mountaineers, too. Tomorrow we will go on up to camp 3!

Then to Camp 4 – and after that, who knows?

7,600 METRES – ON OUR OWN AND HEADING SKYWARDS

Camp 3 is situated in a horrible place. Two tents in the midst of a terribly

Dream Mountain – K2 from the North

steep snowfield, which extends up for at least another hundred metres. A slide of snow from up there could very easily wipe away the whole camp. You wouldn't stop falling for 2,500 metres. There is a fixed rope attached horizontally into the rocks of the spur, to which we can belay when in the tent, but it would still give you a nasty shock to wake up suddenly to find yourself hanging upside-down on it, all rolled up in the tent like a sleeping bat in its folded wings. No, I don't want to sleep in such a place. As soon as I arrive with Julie and Giorgio, who has joined us, obstinately I start looking for a better spot, but in vain. It is too late – I can't find one. But at least we could pitch at the edge of the snowfield, where we can belay more directly to a fixed rope anchored in the rocks above us. Giuliano doesn't spare himself in helping me shovel out a platform in the gathering darkness, and Julie gets the tent up while we're still recovering from the effort. We're all gasping for breath in the thin air.

Not a good night. There doesn't seem to be any end to all the brewing-up. The rule is that you should drink 6 litres of liquid a day at altitude, but whoever could melt that much snow? Even if there is no shortage of the damn stuff. To hell with it! I am very grumpy and completely done in.

Morning light: the weather is fine, but today all of us are late getting up. Julie, too, has spent a miserable night. Up here at 7,600 metres (where even sleeping takes so much energy), you feel life burning away all the time. As a precaution, two days ago I dumped an oxygen bottle a bit further down the ridge against emergency.

Good, friendly sunshine! Giuliano, without a shirt, is standing in the morning light wiring his chest up to an electrocardiograph. Then he and Soro, who is also up here, set off, to be followed a short while later by Julie and me. Giorgio wants to sleep in a bit longer. Only Luca decides to give up and go down. He has our sympathy: we were all impressed that he should even have wanted to give it a try – some weeks ago he was badly injured when a cooking stove blew up in his face, and the wounds have been slow to heal.

Above us the view is grim: the jutting ice cliffs of the hanging glacier, like a huge balcony clinging between the ridges of the summit pyramid. To its right, a fantastic row of towers – unusual for K2 – shaped from a pale yellow crystalline limestone, which I recognise from the Baltoro; it tends to build inspired formations. The ragged sequence of towers and notches up there, rising one above the other, is incredible, a Jacob's Ladder to heaven. Will anyone ever do the Direttissima?

Julie and I, despite feeling so low this morning, packed up our entire camp and are carrying it with us. We move slowly, one arduous step after another towards the first rock step. Gasping, we struggle over it – moving at slow motion, like robots. Again and again we stop just to be able to breathe. Nevertheless, we are back in condition, both of us feel well again and that encourages us.

Now we are on a steep slope of loose gravel, and there is nowhere to make a belay. We can only move with extreme caution. Then we tackle another steep step in the great rib to the right of the hanging glacier. We are on that yellow, metamorphosed limestone now. If only our packs were not so heavy! On a prominent rock among some broken slabs, ledges and snowpatches, we sit and take a break, have a bite to eat and drink from our bottle of tea. It's great to have everything with you like this, to push on completely on your own. Any time we wanted, we could set up camp and nothing would be missing.

Wherever is Camp 4? We should be close to it by now. Obliquely below us, back towards the hanging glacier, we discovered an oxygen bottle; it must mark an old Japanese campsite, perhaps their Camp 4? Agostino had told us about it, and also spoke of an old bivouac site around here somewhere.

Giorgio has come into view below us, climbing up from Camp 3. He's bringing bad weather with him, by the look of things: dark, heavy clouds are rolling in to the mountains below us from Pakistan, from the South-West. It looks worrying. Not long after, Giorgio shouts up to say he has decided to go back down ... and ... Julie? Might it not be better if she went with him? As she's never been this high before?

For a moment the question hangs in the air. I glance across at her and catch the silent, imploring look in her dark eyes. No, I can't face the thought that Julie might have to struggle down through a break in the weather, across those icefields, while I am still trying my luck up here.

'It's OK, Giorgio, thanks!' I shout down. 'Julie's all right!' We'll go on together, and if it's not possible, then we'll come down together. I hear Julie let out a deep breath, and I too feel relieved – despite the fact that below us the clouds are getting darker by the minute, and the huge billows, like weird helmets, roll up towards us. So much we have shared on this expedition: carried so many loads together, made this film together, dreamed (if all went well) of having a go at the Direttissima ... or at least to make it possible, the one for the other, to get to the top. Perhaps the weather will get better once more!

We zigzag further up the steep face, with the impressive towers looming over our heads. Then, suddenly, at the end of a ledge in the vertical rock of the spur, I see a natural windbreak of fallen blocks of snow protecting a little niche. A real swallow's nest. The afternoon sun shines right into it, and bathes the surrounding rocks in a golden glow. It's such a lovely, unique spot, we decide to stay. Even the clouds below us seem to have ceased their boiling. It's a good choice. We'll soon have our little tent up. No sooner have we settled down than we hear noises above us. Gigio is feeling his way down over the rocks, with strange jerky movements, and behind him, Almo. They had bivouacked on the hanging glacier, reached 8,200 metres – but no summit. Resignation, disappointment, exhaustion mark their faces.

We offer words of consolation – but what help are they? The pair continue their descent. Who knows how long they were up high …

We sit in front of our tent. 'It was a good day,' says Julie in a low voice. Indeed, it was. Later a beautiful sunset flushes thousands of peaks in a flood of golden light. We are so high above them, we must soon touch the sky.

8,000 METRES – OUR DREAM SHATTERED BY STORM

Places blessed with evening sunshine cannot expect to enjoy the first warming light of morning. We have to wait a long time next day before the sun reaches us. It is 5 August. We haven't far to go up today and the weather is beautiful, so we drape our frost-covered sleeping bags and all our damp clothes along the rim of our rock ledge to dry, and simply pass the time.

The scratching of crampons above us announces the arrival of Fausto and Sergio. And Soro is with them. Soon we know: the two reached the summit, but had a terrible bivouac the night before. The altitude has left its mark: Fausto's fingertips are frostbitten and Sergio has frozen toes. There is no happiness in their eyes, only utter tension. They will feel differently once they're down safely. Soro, good man, will accompany them.

The night in the open on the hanging glacier must have seemed interminable. Really it's quite remarkable that they went on after that. Sergio wishes us well for our attempt, gives us a friendly smile and they continue their descent.

It is almost 1 p.m, when we set off. The others told us that Giuliano and Adalberto hope to traverse out onto the hanging glacier today – with a tent. Tomorrow they will try for the summit from there … a wise solution. Days ago, when we were much further down and it was uncertain whether Julie could get as far as 8,000 metres – she suffered stomach trouble at Camp 2 – I wondered whether I might go for the top with Giuliano, my old friend from Everest 1980; but then Julie decided to go higher, and now I am convinced – she has proved it – that even great altitude is no barrier to her.

Fast clouds – low down, over there, from the west – advance towards us. Is the weather going to break today? We are climbing now towards an overhang of yellow rock, beside which there is a vertical wall. Disconcertingly close the towers soar above us ... the Direttissima.

Please God, give us one more day! No, two! Two days of fine weather. Then we can make our try and get back down again, and perhaps the summit will be ours.

At the very least we want to climb a few hundred metres up there, reconnoitre, touch rock that until now no hand has felt, no eyes seen; we want to know what is there ...

Another length of rope, and we reach a small rocky platform. Amid the rubble lies a crumpled tent – blue, shapeless – containing a few bits and pieces of equipment. There's nobody around. Then I spot Giuliano and Adalberto on the steep and exposed Japanese traverse, making their way out towards the hanging glacier. A breathtaking view from up here. '*Buona fortuna!*' I shout. Good luck! They wave back. But the atmosphere is growing more and more threatening. The sun has disappeared and patches of fog are drifting around the towers. It looks like trouble.

Julie is quick to put up our small blue tunnel tent, while I heave over every rock I can find to weight down the guys. Not more than a metre from the entrance there is a sheer drop, first to the hanging glacier (from our airy spot we can look straight onto the edge of the huge 'balcony'), then on down into the depths beyond. Hard to imagine in this grey mist that it is 3,000 metres to the bottom. I can't help thinking about the terrible fall taken by one of the Japanese mountaineers into that abyss, and pile more rocks onto our tent pegs. Please God, give us one more day before the storm breaks! But the air masses are bubbling up.

Would we be fit enough tomorrow to go higher in any case? At present we both feel well, despite having carried up our camp in one go. It doesn't look too difficult from here, even though the exposure is tremendous. The main problem of the direct route will doubtless be getting back down it. But what surprises are hidden by the next rocky upheaval? We've got pitons and rope ... We crawl into our sleeping bags and start melting snow – and, alas, tip it over. (I fell asleep for a moment while holding the pot.) *Porca miseria!* Chaos, water everywhere ... with handfuls of snow we try and mop it up as fast as possible. Julie stays calm, but I'm swearing. We start again, throw the wet chunks of snow in the pot and wait ... and wait ... minutes of exhausted silence ... then, finally, tea!

The first storm squalls hit us. Everything is grey now outside. (The others have taken shelter in a crevasse, higher up on the hanging glacier.) Snowflakes whirl through the air. Gusts of wind strike the tent with full force, and slither along it.

Time has become unimportant: up here at 8,000 metres what counts is the rising tide of snow around us, and the might of the wind. Our tent withstands the fury of the elements, thanks to its streamlined shape and the anchorage of heavy rocks, but we barely close an eye all night. It is pretty certain now that we shall have to abandon our attempt, and knowing that, we talk and talk and think about what we would have done *if* ... wonderful thoughts, nearer to the truth perhaps for us being so high, thoughts of the summit, of a push, of a reconnaissance into the last recesses of the mountain, of the Direttissima ... of the life we have begun to lead ... It is great to be here, to have reached this place – even if the storm will not grant us one step more. We have reached the upper storey of our 'dream mountain'. Having lived with K2 for so many days now

has made it 'ours', from its base to its highest ridges. Here we are, two hidden spiders, clinging to the edge of this giant, stormwracked crystal.

Will the summit be ours one day, too? Tomorrow? Another year? 'I wanted so much to know what it's like up there, around that corner,' says Julie.

Not until noon on the next day did the storm calm down sufficiently to allow us outside. We had been trapped in our tent for twenty hours. We looked about anxiously for our friends – and there they were, moving slowly back along the traverse! The weather was just good enough for starting the descent: the summit was out of the question.

It took the four of us two days to get down the 4,000 metres of rope, with strong currents of powder snow dragging at our knees and threatening to tip us down the face. Adalberto had altitude sickness; for half a day I helped him down the ridge until the air was thick enough for him to manage on his own. It was hard: three times the fixed rope anchors pulled out and we fell short distances. A year afterwards I still had a pain in my elbow to remind me. But all four of us made it without frostbite. Was it worth it? A strange question – it doesn't arise until you get back. With his frozen fingers, Fausto needed days before he could find an answer. 'Yes', – he said. 'I wouldn't have missed being up there, standing on top, not for anything.' To Julie and me, the four months of living in the mountain desert of Sinkiang brought more than reaching the summit of K2 could ever have done – even though we longed for it so much. The desire to return to this landscape would never forsake us. Exploring, discovering this fantasy glacier world and the endless ocean of peaks that faded into the blue of distance, the climb on the wild North Spur of K2 – all these were part now of our lives. We could never turn our back on them. Both of us had heard the siren voice of that empty land.

It also re-emphasised the importance of our film work, not just for us but for what it brought others too. This was a great joy to us – and after our return to Europe, we called ourselves 'the highest film team in the world'. Filming would be our path from now on. K2 itself, whose summit we had come so close to, remained our dream mountain, a symbol of everything that the magic world of glaciers and desert mountains had aroused in us.

England – Tunbridge Wells

THE HIGHEST FILM TEAM IN THE WORLD

'Look!' With large capable hands, Terry starts folding a letter-sized sheet of cardboard, humming softly to himself as he does so. I see it take the form of a triangle with side flaps. Now it gets a base as well. (I had never realised he had such a talent for origami!) I notice his satisfaction – he's obviously got it all worked out, and as he chews on his beard, engrossed in his creation, the first glimmer comes to me of what it is he's making. The white pyramid on the table can only be ...

'There!' declares Terry, surveying his work with the pride of an inventor. 'K2! Here, you write THE HIGHEST FILM TEAM ... on this side you put Julie's c.v. ... and yours on the other.' He points to the two side flaps, which keep K2 upright. Light dawns: it's a memo to put on the desks of television executives, carrying caricatures of both of us and highlights of our careers, along with our addresses ...

'That's fantastic!' Nobody would ever hide such an original piece of advertising in a filing cabinet.

Julie beams, leaping between the living room and the kitchen as she fetches wood for the fire – everything always at top speed. An enormous Newfoundland dog dozes unconcernedly in her path, a woolly mound, a metre high, practically unable to see out of his eyes for hair, a natural buffer of stoic calm.

Terry throws me a quick look. 'Man, how did you put up with her for five months in China?' How? I shrug. Well, the truth is I'm sorry it's over, I think to myself. Terry is in high spirits: Julie's climb on K2's North Spur was the highest a British woman had ever been. Supposing she had made it to the summit, too? That might yet come. He has nothing against this fresh start of hers: their son and daughter are grown up and away from home – Julie is free to travel the world if that is what she wants. But what does Julie feel about it? She told me once that Dennis and I had awakened in her a restlessness to see unknown places.

At the same time she loves her life at home: it has so many facets, between which she flits happily, sometimes turning in on herself, sometimes dedicating herself exclusively to a project, and at other times impatiently on the move. She and Terry have been married for twenty-five years, living in the Sussex woodlands. She climbed once in the Andes (with Norman Croucher, the mountaineer with two artificial legs); once in Yosemite with Dennis: now the Himalayas have captured her imagination – with a vengeance. Yet there is something else – a no lesser, indeed an all-penetrating force – something of which she said to me, 'You find it in the mountains in your own way – and it allows me to approach the big mountains.' She has discovered it, too, through the martial arts, budo and aikido. It is difficult to explain: to an outsider these warrior sports can seem brutal, more or less so according to which of them you are watching and how they are being practised, but from what I have seen, they appear more like a highly disciplined *ballade*, as an imagined opponent (who is not an enemy) is engaged and reacted to. It is an exercise in the deepest concentration, which in the end leads you to the real you, to it, the centre of your (and all) being, from which you

gain force and resistance beyond expectation, as well as something else for which no word exists ... I have experienced it in the mountains, have derived it from them and do so still, and it is this shared understanding that link Julie and me together so strongly. In a way I find it strange – but on the other hand, quite natural – I can somehow become part of the process, just sitting quietly and watching the martial artists as they 'fight' – or meditate. The whole space around them seems filled with an energy, as if a single spirit pervades their movements – I too can tap into it. David, the *Sensei* (or teacher), a man whom above all I admire for his simplicity and depth, not just for his ability, has tried several times to

England – Tunbridge Wells

encourage me on to the mat. But I always shake my head. My ice-bear shape and my phlegmatic constitution are not suited to it ... and whenever Julie (she wears the black belt of the masters) whirls somebody a dozen times through the air, or tumbles on the mat herself, like a runaway wheel, I say to myself: better just to absorb the essence! David is an extraordinary person. In Julie's life many things have been made possible by him. Several years ago it was discovered that he had cancer. Then, the disease halted by itself, quite suddenly ...

Julie is able to find a *dojo* anywhere, wherever she is, somewhere suitable for practising aikido. It might be a flat, sandy spot between the glacier and a mountain meadow, as on Nanga Parbat, or a great shield of ice at 5,000 metres between the seracs and the foot of K2 ... always it is a special place, you can feel it. There she meets and engages an imaginary opponent, fights or simply sits quietly on the sand between the ice towers, sunk in meditation – for an hour at a time, or even longer. It is not something I find I can explain – you either understand it, intuitively, or it remains totally incomprehensible, like climbing towards a summit. From it, Julie most surely derives her incredible strength and endurance in the Himalayas.

Italy – Bologna

ONCE MORE TO OUR DREAM MOUNTAIN

Of course. No question! Somehow we will make it possible. Gasping, I walk up a hill near Bologna – what is it, a hundred, a hundred and fifty metres? Again I am much too fat! In this country people seem to have heard of potatoes (my favourite vegetable) only from legend; instead there is pasta!: *tortellini in brodo, tagliatelle, lasagne al forno, spaghetti con le vongole*, et cetera, et cetera. Enough? What do you mean, enough? That was just the first course! I puff on. There is of course a perfectly respectable road up this hill, but I chose the steep slope for good reason. The next course will be *bocconcini* (small pieces of fried meat swimming in oil), *salsiccia, faraona, pollo, maiale, prosciutto* (ham), *grana* (Parmesan cheese) – a spicy aroma permeates everywhere, it sizzles and drips from all the kitchens in the area. The *vino* made by these farmers is *fantastico* and *genuino* – but you do need to know where to go for it.

'You know, it's true,' I think to myself, wiping the sweat from my brow, 'The Emilia-Romagna boasts the best kitchens in all Italy. That's why the people here have such nice rounded temperaments ... and not just temperaments ...'

I labour higher towards the round hilltop, where in this whole so-round world of Romagna, my round mother-in-law – a real symbol of the area – will doubtless have spread the (round) table with the latest of her oh-so-tasty culinary inventions, a real Italian 'square meal' for me, my wife Teresa, her two sisters, and for Ceci, my son.

I squint down at myself: it's high time I went on an expedition. I must be 20 kilos overweight again. Or I should move, for a week at least, to my relatively spartan home town of Salzburg, where I mostly do my own cooking.

At any rate, there the mountains rise before the door. Here, the highest things (since we came back from K2) are the phone bills.

Perhaps I should take up jogging? I cannot feel the slightest motivation for anything so uncomfortable. Skiing, then? There is this white bump not far from here which in winter swarms with a hundred thousand people – but either you are a slalom specialist, or you are not ...

Italy – Bologna

My son Ceci is great! A real champion skier. But the Alps are a long way away, you only see them on the far horizon on days of exceptional clarity.

Nevertheless, I am glad that we left the terrible plains of Portomaggiore a year ago, with their network of water channels, since when we have been living in the Apennines.

Mostly I am not here anyway, but off on lecture trips or in the Himalayas.

I am glad to have Ceci there to back me up sometimes – living in a house with four women! Not that I should complain: there's Teresa, my wife, who originally wanted to become a judge but has now settled for being a lawyer (it means I have to keep on my toes, too); Angela, an electronics engineer: Alida, a book-keeper (that has certain advantages) and, finally, mother-in-law – who, I really have to admit, is a superb cook.

But the mountains are such a long way away.

In Peking, Julie and I made the acquaintance of an energetic Swiss expedition leader, Stefan Wörner. 'How efficient he is,' she remarked 'and a really nice guy.' With him was the ever-cheerful Markus Itten. We all hit it off right away and agreed that we simply had to do a trip together. Stefan is really on the ball: last year his Baltoro expedition had the unprecedented success of climbing Hidden Peak, Gasherbrum II and Broad Peak – all three!

Stefan has that dry, irrepressible Swiss humour. 'Three eight-thousanders in a fortnight' was the title he came up with for his lecture programme – not out of swank, but because it was nice and snappy. All the same, there was a discernible twinkle in his eye and he gave a huge wink when he told me of a chat he'd had with Reinhold Messner. Having good-natured digs at one another is all part and parcel of the spirit of mountaineering (and no one else could claim the right to a lecture title like that, however hard he might try to figure it out.)

Stefan had a permit for K2, granted by the Pakistani government. Julie and I could go with him, he said – but how were we to finance it? Money, money! Always money! The telephone wires burned hot between London, Zurich and Bologna. Finally, it looked as if Julie had caught something in the net. But was it really going to come off?

Teresa is a good wife. When I am agitated, she smooths things with her calm. She has an angel's patience. You can't quarrel with her, anyway – try quarrelling with a lawyer! Moreover, Italians are always good-natured, especially towards foreigners (perhaps not so much amongst themselves: *avvocato* is a way of life in Italy). Teresa is no mountaineer, although she did enjoy coming to Everest Base Camp once. In some way, she is above all that, so balanced that the summits don't draw her. But she understands that I have to go ... my life up there, she knows, I can never give up. It will never be any different. Sometimes, when I come back home – like a Greenland polar bear returning from the icecap to the edge of the sea – I find there a quiet contentedness, a different happiness.

But now it has seized me again: K2. I could never have imagined that a mountain could bring so many sleepless nights, just not knowing whether you will get there or not. It has all to do with being there, not with the summit. You know that depends on a lot of things ... and there's no point in worrying your head about them in advance.

Zurich: spring 1984. At last, it's all settled: we shall go with Stefan Wörner's expedition ... In England they want a film about Julie for a series called Assignment Adventure. David South (originally a geologist) has worked out a treatment as thick as a thesis. We like him, and Julie is already on her way, backwards and forwards to Scotland, getting together the best possible mountaineering gear.

The air is vibrating again ... K2 ...

Will we? Won't we?

K2 ...

Finding out ... that is what makes life worthwhile.

The clever person that he is, Stefan Wörner has acquired permission for a second eight-thousander, one that is not all that high, one well-known to me – Broad Peak.

Raid on Broad Peak

Twenty-seven years after making the first ascent with the now legendary Hermann Buhl, I, who had been his last rope-mate, stood once more on the topmost point of the three-humped dragon – this time with England's 'highest woman', Julie Tullis.

Hermann Buhl's last summit proved an adventure for Julie and me that nearly cost us our lives. The challenge we had set ourselves was to climb this eight-thousander as a twosome, without a large expedition, without high-altitude porters or oxygen gear, just relying on each other. We were probably the oldest couple climbing in the Himalayas, but after two months on K2, we were at a peak of acclimatization and condition. Time and again the big mountains of the world have proved that being young is not the deciding factor, neither for making the climb, nor for surviving it. One thing, however, is the same for everyone: you cannot say the eight-thousander is yours until you are down from it safely; until then, it is 'you' who belong to the mountain ...

When, in the night that followed the 18 July, Julie and I finally crawled into our bivvy tent and sank into a deathlike sleep, we had not the slightest idea what the morning held in store for us.

THE AVALANCHE

From somewhere outside comes a strange hissing sound, like sliding snow. An avalanche?

'Strange,' I think muzzily, through my doze. Last night, when we crawled into this bivvy at 7,600 metres after so many hours of difficult descent from the summit and clinging to the rocks of the sharp ridge with a drop of 3,000 metres beneath our feet, only dimly able to make out the glaciers of China way down below, there had been stars in the sky. The doubtful weather seemed then to have taken a turn for the better. What a time we'd had of it, searching among those cliffs and snowribs in the faint beam from our one and only head-torch, moving so slowly, wondering which way on earth to go.

I pull my head down into my sleeping bag. Yes, it certainly was a tough descent. Coming down off an eight-thousander is always an escape, a return to life, to humankind – even though you have just given everything you have in the struggle to get up there, to where the summit touches the sky. And made it – for a few unforgettable moments.

The steep face of snow and ice below the gap at 7,800 metres had taken every last particle of energy as we belayed down, one rope's length after another, back towards an invisible bivouac tent – out in the darkness somewhere, attached to the face at the lower edge of a crevasse. It was only 200 metres below the gap, but in our weariness and the poor light, it seemed half an eternity away. Then we found it, an elongated darker patch in the overall darkness, an island of sanctuary on the steep slope. It was ten o'clock at night before our struggle for survival came to an end ...

There goes another *Whooosh!* outside somewhere, like sliding ...

And again! First pale light of dawn – 5.30 a.m. Surely there can't be avalanches at this hour? We are on a west-facing slope. Except there it goes again – I leap up as if from an electric shock, for all at once it is drumming over us, rushing down the tent entrance and on into the depths, drumming, drumming. I cling desperately to the fabric, press myself into the mountain. 'Julie! Wake up!'

But deep in her sleeping bag, she doesn't hear me. Thank God, we re-anchored the tent last night with the rope and our ice-axes, otherwise we would have been swept away by now. The drumming eases off. I am in such a state of agitation, I can hardly breathe. The tent has withstood the onslaught. With trembling fingers, I open the zip. There's a wall of snow outside – deep snow everywhere, and more falling silently ... the weather has obviously broken in the night. And we slept through the whole of it! We are in such a ghastly position here – with the 200-metre slope above us so heavy with snow it could come down at any moment – that for some seconds, I cannot utter a sound. My thoughts seem to have frozen, paralysed with the hopelessness of our plight, with the knowledge that we are sitting on Death's shovel and there's no way out. We may have only minutes left.

I don't know how to break it to Julie, I'm scared to tell her, but she must know the truth. 'Avalanches, Julie, everywhere! We have to leave at once! It might be too late already, but perhaps we can still get away if we move really fast!'

From her eyes I see she understands, but as she sits up, the next surge hits us, like a waterfall. I have jumped to my knees and, gasping, succeed with frantic arm movements in splitting the flow which is piling against the tent, diverting half of it downhill and the rest into the deep crevasse to our side. For a few minutes, this is our salvation, for we are in the direct path of the white flood. Our taut, firmly anchored nylon shelter, the mini-tube tent reinforced by metal hoops and designed, strictly speaking, just for one person, offers so little surface to the pressure that it quickly sloughs the snow into the crevasse before it can squash us flat – so that we make it through even this avalanche.

However, at the front of the tent where there is no crevasse, it is catastrophe. Against all my efforts, snow has come in that end, where Julie is struggling to gather up essentials or put on her boots I'm not sure which – and it's chaos. Several things have disappeared under the snow. We dig feverishly for the stove, that's vital, and yell a sort of countdown to each other, listing all the things we absolutely have to have if we are to get down this mountain alive – if by any stroke of fortune we don't finish up under an avalanche. Fat chance! Here comes the next torrent! I've only managed to get one boot on but hurl myself in the direction which it's coming, paddling like mad against the invading flood. 'Julie! Watch our boots don't disappear – or we're sunk!' We've got to get away from here, that's obvious, we can't survive much longer if we don't. Over – over – the cascade of snow has passed once more. I'm gasping for breath. Where's that boot? That second boot? We've not lost it down the mountain? The tent is half-filled with snow. Julie struggles free, breathing heavily. She must have her boots on already – how is it that she's so quick? Then panic seizes me: 'Julie! Where's my other boot? I can't find it anywhere!'

'It was just here a moment ago – no there!' She scrabbles in the snow inside the tent while I dig at the entrance. It's curtains for both of us if we don't find it. For a few minutes the horror of the avalanche danger fades ...

'Kurt, I've got it!'

Faced with setting out into this almost hopeless chaos of snow at 7,600 metres, finding a simple boot seems a miracle. It brings home to us, as do the ensuing events, that we either manage the descent together or we both perish. We abandon the tent, taking only our sleeping bags, stove, the barest essentials. And, as usual, we're roped together – luckily. Twenty minutes after the first snowslide, we are on our way, carefully probing the steep new snow above the blue serac walls of Broad Peak. We don't get far: at about 6.15 a big avalanche detaches right above us from a couloir between the rocky flutes of the ridge.

Everything is spinning: down is up, up is down; terrible forces against which all resistance is vain; they toss you, carry you, twist you, crush out your breath ... your mouth is stuffed with snow ... you grab another gulp of air, and then you're sucked in again ... moving down Broad Peak ... remorselessly. That's it ... the end ... I think, but ... no!

Not yet ... air. Don't give up! A pause. Then the tug of the rope again, pulling, pulling ... more of this terrible tumbling ... Oh, Julie! You, too ... caught somewhere in this never-ending whirl. Don't give up! We must not give up – never – even if this is the end ... air ... horrible twists ... somersaults ... bumps ... air ... there's no stopping this whirling ... until it stops by itself ... I don't want to d ... I have to try and stop ... need air ... a kick! Another impact ... the rope pulls onwards ... No! I won't give in. Hold on! ... Stop! ... It's stopped!

Stopped. I'm jammed between blocks of ice. The avalanche has moved on.

Sky up there. Blue. I can move, try and get up. Blocks of ice near me, the rope goes straight down ... Where is Julie?

... There's a figure, immobile on her back, arms widespread, head downhill, sprawled on the slope below me. I cannot see her face.

Julie!

Great God, let her be alive.

I yell: 'Are you hurt?'

Seconds of eternity. Answer, please answer.

'I'm all right, but I can't move. Please help me get up.'

Her voice. Alive.

Soon I have her freed from her awkward position. The avalanche, when I came to a halt, had carried Julie on, catapulting her head over heels into the slope, where she stuck on her back. We can hardly believe we are still here ... and unhurt. When we look up, we see a vertical wall of ice, as high as a house, over which the avalanche has carried us before depositing us onto this steep slope of ice blocks. We've come down more than 150 metres over the seracs and we're incredibly lucky to be still alive. The snowfall has stopped. There's blue sky looking down on us through a hole in the clouds ...

In the shelter of a huge ice tower we crouch in the snow, the events of the past minutes still etched in our faces. We are badly shaken, even if we appear to have got away unscathed. As we brew some tea, we slowly calm down. Julie is in some pain from a bruised thigh, and I have a haematoma above my left eye – small matters. I lost my snowgoggles and the avalanche pulled the gloves from Julie's hands (luckily she has spares in her rucksack), but such things do not bother us at present, when we think of what might have happened. We keep looking at each other in disbelief: here we are, both of us! If we hadn't been using the rope, we would each of us be, if not dead, on his own somewhere, without any possibility of help, and unaware whether the other was alive or not. We might never have found each other.

Raid on Broad Peak

That was how I lost Hermann on Chogolisa in 1957. We had no rope. 'When I was lying on the slope,' I hear Julie say, 'there was only silence all around me. I couldn't see anything – my goggles were choked with snow. Then suddenly your voice asked if I was hurt, and I knew you were alive …'

Reflectively, I sip my tea from the lid of the aluminium pot and my eyes slide up from Julie, who is now also engrossed in drinking, to the ridge of the mountain.

What made me want to climb Broad Peak again – after half a lifetime?

Did I want to recapture the memories of my first summit experience in the Himalayas? Or was it simply that I wanted to see the places again, stand there, where I had been with my companion – the ridge, the face with its seracs, the high gap and the view down into China, the summit with its cornice – to see if they were still the same, or whether Broad Peak had changed over the years? Did I perhaps want to know whether I could tackle an eight-thousander at the age of fifty-two as well as I had at twenty-five …?

Or was it a totally new challenge: for Julie and me as a team of two to make a 'lightning raid' on it – to climb it again in quite a different manner?

Probably it was a combination of all these things.

While we slowly sip our tea below the huge ice tower and gradually recover our composure after our devastating adventure, in my mind images of the first ascent in 1957 dissolve into those of the present. When Julie and I, a fortnight ago, during a first push got to 7,000 metres, I suddenly found something …

A twisted, rusty piton – a piton that I recognised. A heavy piton with a ring, both of solid iron, one of those pegs which long ago in the fifties were equally good for rock and ice but which nobody uses these days. I clearly remember Hermann hammering it into the rocks here – twenty-seven years ago – for anchoring our tent at Camp 3. He was swearing, as the piton did not want to grip in the friable limestone of the rocky island which we called the Eagle's Nest. Several pitons had to be used in the end. Finally, in the evening of that day, 28 May 1957, we had two tents up and our assault camp was ready for the first summit bid. Ready for the final stage of what others had so often called 'madness', the 'first eight-thousander in West Alpine style' – without high-altitude porters or oxygen respirators. A hard adventure: a true Buhl enterprise. One giant mountain and just four climbers: Hermann, Marcus Schmuck, Fritz Wintersteller and me, the 'Benjamin' of the expedition. God, what a lot we carried! But it was one of the last unclimbed eight-thousand-metre peaks. A dream – my first Himalayan trip. With the great Hermann Buhl ... so thin and frail he looked. But he was the idol of a whole climbing generation – not only in Germany and Austria: the whole world had been electrified when he got to the summit of Nanga Parbat on his own. At the time, that icy giant, the 'Naked Mountain', had already claimed nearly forty lives. Coming back down, he'd had to stand the whole night on a narrow ledge leaning against the rocks at 8,000 metres, a 'bivouac' few others could have withstood. Yet he made it. I still remember the famous picture: his face ravaged by sun and wind under the slouch hat, goggles pushed up onto his forehead, that staring gaze. In the forty-one hours of his summit ordeal Buhl's face had aged into that of an old, old man – it was an image that moved the world. And me with it: I worshipped him from that moment. And when, after going to one of his lectures, he wrote *'Bergheil'* on my Austrian Alpine Club membership card, I guarded it like a treasure. I was twenty-one and could never have imagined that in just four years I would be standing with him on the summit of Broad Peak watching the sun go down behind a savage sea of peaks.

When we climbed down the West Spur, I saw that face again – haggard from the struggle of the long, steep night-time descent and his own iron determination to return to life, just as he had been on Nanga Parbat. The unforgettable face of Hermann Buhl.

Our acquaintance was far too short. We only reached this one summit together. But we had great plans for the future ...

Neither of us could imagine that barely three weeks after that sunset on our eight-thousander, Hermann was to die on Chogolisa when he simply stepped out of this world, over a cornice in a storm ...

'We plan to stay on here for a while: make some excursions, perhaps do one or the other six- or seven-thousanders ...' Buhl wrote home. To me, it's as fresh as yesterday: after Broad Peak, the expedition divided – Marcus and Fritz dashed off to grab a lightweight Alpine-style ascent of Skilbrum, a seven-thousander in the nearby Savoia group; Hermann and I – moving with just one tent, which we planned to carry with us and set up day after day – had as our target the beautiful 'roof in the sky', 7,654-metre Chogolisa.

It all seemed to work well. Our 'mobile high-altitude camp' was fine. At 6,700 metres we left the tent on the ridge and set off towards the summit. It was 27 June 1957. Hermann was in fine form and really pleased with life: climbing such a high mountain in only three days, rather than three weeks, was like a dream, even for him.

But it was to turn out very differently ...

A little cloud came rolling up the slope below us. It grew larger,

Raid on Broad Peak

enveloping us, enveloping the peak. Without any warning, all hell broke loose. Grey veils of mist scurried across the ridge. We fought our way forward through clouds of blown snow, bending double to meet the fury of the gale. Yet such a deterioration in the weather seemed impossible after the glorious morning we had had.

'We must turn back at once. The storm is wiping out our tracks,' Hermann said suddenly. 'We'll end up over the cornices if we're not careful.' And he was right. Those were his last words at 7,300 metres. It was soon after that it happened.

'*Whummm!*' The noise ran through me like a shock. Everything shook and for a moment the surface of the snow seemed to sink. Terrified, I jumped out to the right.

It was the cornice breaking under Hermann Buhl. But I did not suspect that until later when he failed to join me, when I waited for him and he didn't come. I hurried back and discovered footprints, his last steps, leading to a fresh fracture line: at a bend in the ridge, he'd left the track and gone out towards the edge of the cornice …

And supposing we had been roped? Could I have held him, or would he have pulled me with him into the void?

I still do not know, and so often have thought about it. Hermann fell down the north face of Chogolisa, probably 500 metres – there was nothing to see on account of further avalanches. A later search revealed nothing. That I got down from there at all in that storm, I put down to a lucky star. And to myself – never giving up.

Hermann Buhl's face dissolves and the white roof of Chogolisa blurs into the distance: above me soars the huge ice tower, the sheer, vertical serac wall over which we have fallen. There is still a patch of blue sky above the rocky ridge of Broad Peak, but already the clouds are moving together to block it out.

Yes, I am infinitely grateful to the fate that has allowed Julie and me still to be here, sitting in the snow. It is nothing short of a miracle that we have both survived. It was the rope that prevented us from being separated by the torrent of snow …

I clasp the pot of tea in my hands, knowing that Julie and I need another lucky star to get us down to the place where I found that old piton; we have to descend at least another 400 metres across these avalanche slopes.

Julie smiles. The shock has evaporated from her face, and from the expression in her dark eyes, under her helmet, I can see that she has regained her concentration. We'll need plenty of that to get down. Julie is another of those who never gives up. Otherwise we would not be here now.

The Endless Knot

WILL WE MAKE IT DOWN?

Five hundred metres below the serac zone into which the avalanche threw us, Broad Peak's hanging glacier terminates in a vertical drop. Two thousand metres further down lies the Godwin-Austen Glacier. It would make no sense at all to climb down in a straight line from where we landed ...

We must traverse obliquely down towards the upper end of the West Spur, which offers the only feasible descent to the glacier bed. We came up this way, along the rib of rock and ice, in a day and a half – it was the first stage of our raid on Broad Peak. Two days later we reached the summit. This, now, is the fifth day we have spent on the mountain.

Shortly after 8 a.m. Julie and I leave our spot below the ice tower.

In the milky light, there's a slow-moving fog above us; below, the dull blue snow slopes sometimes change to brilliant white ...

Slowly, carefully, step by step, we feel our way down. Julie says nothing about her sore thigh, but she moves a little awkwardly. Is it giving her trouble? I don't ask. We have to focus all our attention on the slope. Curving away below us, the shimmering slope is cut diagonally across by a matt strip – the trail of an avalanche; we are going to have to cross it somewhere if we want to reach the West Spur. Everything is still, now, unbelievably still – no more snow slides – it is as if Broad Peak had fallen into an enchanted sleep.

But our hearts are far from still: the menace continues to lurk above us on the summit slopes, like a monster that might wake at any moment. And you can feel the tension in those blue slopes, know that one false step can destroy its precarious harmony. For it is all steep, fresh snow.

At first I hug the edge of the serac zone as it seems safer. It is like the bank of an invisible river, which we are going to have to cross sooner or later. Julie is behind me on the rope and, like me, thrusts her axe deeply into the snow with each step. Lucky for us we did not lose our axes during the fall in the avalanche – thanks to the wrist loops. They take some of the strain of descending, and also give us at least a chance of holding one another in the event of a slip. But in these conditions, it's the whole slope that could start moving ...

'We must play it by ear. It's the best way to go in this snow: test each step; sense what is the right line of descent. The risk of the whole lot sliding away with us on it would be less if we went straight down, rather than traversing, but we have no choice – we have to traverse, we dare not lose too much height.' A dilemma. I am going to have to leave the edge of the serac zone and launch into that immense snow slope.

Cast off, then! Leave the safe shore behind.

We cross the nearby avalanche runnel, holding our breaths, and step out onto the silent billows.

I suppose two hours have passed since then. We've slipped into slow motion. Every step needs probing with our feet: deep, soft, fathomless ground it sometimes seems. This is no invisible river – this is a tilted, frozen ocean that goes on for ever.

Only instinct can pilot you through its waves, tell you the best angle at which to cross the slope. Like mariners in slow motion, we sail the ocean of snow, and the prize to be gained is Life.

Another step.

After a while the sea starts to heave – in your mind, while you fight for balance – as your thoughts cut free and flow into the waves of snow.

One more step into the waves. And another. Hypnotic – so much regularity in white ... another step ... and another ... and another ... Yes, Julie, we're in our boat now – at 7,400 metres on Broad Peak, and everything is under the law of gravity. The waves ... the waves ... the waves ... Beyond are only dreams – and yourself in the middle. In the middle it's you.

Life ... these hundred thousand steps. Yes, life bounded by the laws of gravity! As are these waves of snow ... steps, waves, steps, everything living!

Only dreams range free. They are like light always floating free above. That's why we are here. Steps, waves, light, thoughts ... us. The life ... light and gravity. And dreams ... and you and you and you, in the middle. Love. Everywhere.

Another step. Many hours. The deep yielding snow, into which you sink as if in a dream. Tiredness, exhaustion – they take over the body, penetrate the spirit. The will: pull yourself together. Onwards! Keep going!

And we do keep going – for the sake of all that constitutes life. To save that. Our dreams, as well. It is they that have brought us this far.

Is there such a thing as a sixth sense? If so, you need it here on the avalanche slopes.

I've succeeded in forging a line across the slope so that now we are back on the route by which we came up – we struck it at the big crevasse. But now my eyes hurt from the strain: the constant concentration and all this deep snow have drained the last of my strength. It is increasingly difficult not to slip into apathy, not to give in to a paralysing indifference.

Behind the big crevasse I crouch down in the snow. Julie stops. 'Kurt, why don't you take my goggles? You'll end up being snowblind otherwise.' We hadn't been able to find the spare pair after the avalanche had ripped mine from me – we must have left them up in the buried tent.

'No, I'm OK, I just want to rest a bit. It can't be much further to Camp 3, and when we get there, I'm sure we can improvise something for my eyes.' I've been breaking trail for seven hours now, maybe more. Julie's sore thigh has improved, thank God. Really, I suppose I should take her goggles, but that would leave her without; besides, a kind of torpor has engulfed me. I just want to sit.

Grey patches of cloud well up from the depths – a fog creeping over the slopes – so that we can't see a thing around us, neither summits nor glaciers, just the cotton of the clouds. The weather's miserable. Is it going to snow again? That makes me sit up: we must find Camp 3 at 7,100 metres before it's too late. 'Julie – *vorwärts!* The fog …' More to myself, I say it.

Down and down we go. Bloody hell, not there yet? Already snowflakes are beginning to fall again. If only we could find it, the tent. Otherwise, we'll just have to sit it out in the snow in our sleeping bags, or find a crevasse, but it will be a miserable bivouac. Dig a snow hole … but which of us has the strength for that? I'm worn out, and perhaps that's why I'm hurrying so much now to get down. We must find this camp!

Julie is in better shape than I am. Since leaving the avalanche danger behind at the big crevasse, I have let go a bit. 'I want to sit down again, just for a moment …'

Fourteen hours after our narrow escape from the bivvy camp below Broad Peak's summit gap, we clamber down a wall of hard snow in the fog and make out the vague shape of the tent that constitutes Camp 3. Right up to the last moment we've been spared nothing – when, after many rests, we finally reached the right spot on the icy wall above our tent, we found we couldn't get down it for the huge amounts of fresh snow. The necessary detour drained our last reserves. But now, finally, we are safe.

Had we actually been frightened?

Certainly for some of the time, especially taking the first steps on these bottomless slopes, and when we had to cross the avalanche path, where every movement caused the snow to slide under our feet … and again, when the immense danger of our position suddenly struck home to us, and we realized how powerless we were against this mountain. But finally, you reach a state beyond fear, where you simply have to react, like a sailor, to the next wave or to the next squall striking the boat ... and you alter to a sort of destiny. You don't recognise it, but still you follow it because it is your path and because you know that only by doing all you can, will the path not be lost. You must not leave the boat.

SNOWED IN

It's as if this mountain will never let us go. Storm follows storm. Great clouds of ice crystals patter over the firn-wall onto the tent. We are so utterly relieved to have made it this far, where at least we can feel safe. Julie has just put a heaped pot of snow onto the stove and taken off her helmet, and her flattened hair frames her thin, finely cut face with the dark, expressive eyes, elegantly arched eyebrows and straight nose. She radiates strength of personality, and at the same time sensitivity. I watch her through the clouds of breath and steam as she chops up the snow in the pot with a knife, then leans her head back and closes her eyes. A sense of contentment washes over and warms me. No longer do I feel alone, neither in my thoughts nor in what is happening here – though my companion can often be as enigmatic and changeable as the mountain itself. Familiar, reliable, dependable – yet unpredictable – perhaps that is precisely what I like about her. Against my original belief that she was Anglo-German, she is, more properly, very European: she is Spanish (which one can see from her features), but she also has German and French blood, though she was born and brought up in England. When we have a difference of opinion, which does happen, I find myself dealing with several nationalities at once! Julie opens her eyes and looks at me quizzically. Did I say something? I reach across with a conciliatory smile and a piece of snow for the pot ... It took a while for us to come to a common understanding – Julie is as strong-willed as a snow leopard, and certainly has the endurance of a Sinkiang camel. For my own part, I can cope with being called the 'Ice Bear': I am every bit as persistent as she is, have equally strong convictions, can override any resistance on sheer obstinacy ... in other words, when we do have a clash of ideas, the result is a Gordian knot of some intricacy!

Fortunately, both of us have the same positive view towards life: obstacles and difficulties are there to be overcome ... thus, so far, we have always found a solution to the insoluble knot – a mutual comprehension. From the many winds that bore the love of her ancestors, Julie has inherited kindness and understanding; from the cocktail of nationalities a strong sense of justice and the will to fight for it. Not simple ...

The Endless Knot

Yet there has to be somewhere, some common ground where the soluble and insoluble can meet ...

One of the eight sacred emblems of Buddhism is the intricately interwoven 'Endless Knot', symbolising the unity of all things and the illusory nature of time. It could be our sign.

Julie and I, for the most part, think in completely the same way. Last year we carried our tent and all the gear we needed up to 8,000 metres on K2's North Spur and were poised for a summit bid when a break in the weather crushed our dream. Yet we did not give up. And what we started two years ago on Nanga Parbat, this shared and adventurous life of making films, we continued on the 'big mountain' where we founded 'the highest film team in the world': this year we shot another 9,000 metres of film there, with Julie doing the sound-recording, until eventually we had to retreat for the fifth time in one of K2's notorious storms, down the Abruzzi Ridge.

It takes an eternity to make a pot of tea. From a giant snowball you only get a thimbleful of water ... your tongue is glued to the roof of your mouth before it's ready. Julie throws more chunks of snow into the pan ... that might bring it up to a third full ... I close my eyes.

Again and again the summit of K2 faded into the clouds like an unattainable *fata morgana* – whenever we drew near, it vanished:

> Going up and down, up and down. Sometimes you don't even get as far as you did the time before. You come to hate the boring, repetitious, arduous climb up, and hate even more having to come back down. But something draws you back ... somehow it's part of the fascination.

This is how Julie described the two months on the Abruzzi Ridge in our film *K2, The Elusive Summit*.

Was all this yo-yoing a reason for our 'raid' on Broad Peak? Was it becoming inevitable? Like a steel-spring which you have wound and loosened many times, until it leaps, finally, whirring, out of its case?

Broad Peak was certainly a liberation for us. More than that: it was an emotional necessity. '... All is well, we are both very fit – but there is no conclusion. We took the dramatic decision to stay on,' wrote Julie in our film log afterwards. But the film itself was not really the reason.

When it finally became apparent that nobody was going to reach the summit of K2, the international Swiss expedition, of which we were members, went home. Julie and I, a couple of die-hards – were unwilling to accept such an ending, neither for the film nor for ourselves, and decided to stay behind to try our luck on Broad Peak. That was not even a week ago. And we had every intention, as soon as we were down again, of going back to K2 and climbing as high as possible – and not just because our cameras are still up at Camp 2 ... 'Something draws you back,' Julie had said.

Thus Broad Peak gave us fulfilment – our first eight-thousander together; and it was indeed liberating after the Abruzzi Ridge. But the summit of Chogori rises high above it: a mountain on top of a mountain. This year it seems bound to remain no more than a cherished dream. Snowed in as we are, who knows how long we will be here yet ...?

'Tea's ready!' Julie's voice breaks into my thoughts and I sit up with a jolt – not really possible in this cramped space. The precious pot topples off the stove. Luckily it falls into a downhill corner. I swallow drymouthed. That tea – I had already drunk it ten times in my mind! My tongue passes over sore, cracked lips. It is at times like this that thirst in the high camps reaches almost unbearable limits ... 'It could happen to anyone,' Julie commiserates, and using some absorbent fresh snow as a sponge, calmly mops up the mess. 'Anything is possible.' She smiles.

I give her a hand. Now we have to begin all over again.

Anything is possible: that's Julie's catch-phrase. In Nanga Parbat Base Camp, she offered to shorten a pair of blue jeans which I had inherited from a French expedition and, having no needle and thread, did the job with Pakistani Airlines stickers ... Julie is very practical, resourceful and determined. I always call this example to mind when she puts my own tolerance to the test. (I gave her a sewing kit after that, which she keeps by her like a talisman.)

Needlework is certainly not one of her strong points! On the other hand I admire her organisational skills: singlehandedly she collected together almost all the mountaineering equipment for our film expedition, the best and most lightweight available. Everything the two of us needed on the mountain ...

Crystals of snow patter monotonously against the roof of the tent, like the steady rhythm of Salzburg rain; I stretch my tired limbs and listen to the hypnotic sound – it's like lying on the bank of a stream, listening to the water ...

'Tea's ready!' Did I drop off? Greedily we slurp the hot liquid taking care not to spill it this time. My eyes hurt – I hope I'm not really in for a dose of snow-blindness. Julie makes some cold compresses for me out of the used teabags. She looks anxious. It was a hard day, yesterday, no mistake – we don't say much.

Snow fizzles in the pot again, Julie has wasted no time getting a fresh brew going. 'We must drink, drink, drink.' I remind myself of the constant refrain of Urs, our expedition doctor – now on his way home. The teabags bring some relief to my closed eyelids.

Are there such things as castles in the air? For two years K2 has been 'our' mountain, even if we haven't succeeded in reaching its summit. We live with it, dream of it – it is never out of our thoughts. Certainly, we will come back another year. But will we be any luckier? And if we're not, what then? This summit is not everything. Perhaps we never will stand on top. Perhaps, for us, K2 is meant to be an everlasting castle in the air, a vision, simply *there* above the sparkling glaciers – looking down on us while we discover hidden lakes and valleys with no names, while we peer into gorges and climb higher up untouched ridges, struggle through the dust of the northern deserts, and drink from the clear springs at the mountain's foot.

Perhaps that is the way it is meant to be. After all, haven't we just been given back the gift of life? Only yesterday. And we are not down yet.

Yes – we have found a second home in the clouds. It's there, our castle, and it doesn't have to be the summit. We would never want to give up this life.

Dream mountain, K2. You can win or lose everything on a big mountain. Do we have any idea what K2 still holds in store for us? Will we hear the voice?

Anything is possible. Always.

There is no let-up to this storm, and it is still snowing. The pallid light filtering into my eyes through the violent yellow of the fabric dims as the mass of snow outside rises steadily – a dark, narrow strip creeping up the tent. On the side closest to the mountain, the weight of snow threatens to overwhelm us. Quick, out! Shovel it free! For a while it's better. Then the dark line inches its way up the tent again.

During the night, I am suddenly seized with terrible pain in my eyes. Snowblindness. Desperate, I wake up Julie but when she turns on her torch, just for a couple of seconds, it is such absolute agony that I beg her to put it out. The irony of fate: as we grope in the rucksack, searching for eyedrops in the dark, we come across the spare goggles. We had them with us all the time. Like this, I can't possibly leave here, yet every hour that passes makes it less and less likely that we will be able to get down.

We are both silent, realisation slowly dawning that soon we won't have an escape any more. Julie takes care of me, and we wait. The weather has never been so bad; never before has the mountain slammed its door on us with such decisiveness. A whole day passes. And another night. We are at the mercy of the eight-thousander. We belong to it.

I think of the summit day. When we arrived at the gap between the middle and main summits at 7,800 metres, high above us the final ridge of Broad Peak's large roof came and went through racing clouds. It was noon, and we waited for two hours, hoping for an improvement in the weather. But it didn't come. I was on the point of giving up, my feet terribly cold. We decided to go a little higher, just to get out of the wind that was funnelling through the gap.

The night before had been awful. No room and hardly any sleep in the cramped bivvy tent ... but perhaps we were simply nervous. Although it is better to start high (7,600 metres), rather than from an assault camp at 7,000 metres – after our night descent in 1957, Buhl certainly thought so – the clear disadvantage is that if the weather breaks, you are trapped that much higher up. That was why we did not dare go much beyond the gap, which was already 200 metres above the high camp.

Then, suddenly, a miracle: the storm eased. We could hardly believe it: fantastic cumulus towers piled high on the Pakistani side, but over China, it was clear. Julie and I could continue towards the summit! I was full of joy and pleasure at the prospect of seeing that high place again – at least we had hope now. *Hinauf!* Up we go!

How the ridge had changed since I was here with Hermann ... where in 1957 we plodded with two ski-sticks, we now had to climb along a sharp and exposed rock ridge. There was less ice everywhere – in some places it had disappeared entirely. The ridge was much more difficult than it had been then. Twenty-seven years bring many changes – even to a mountain. Down at Camp 1 by the rock tooth, I had already noticed that the natural platform on which Hermann Buhl and I had pitched our tent was missing. There was another one now, a bit further away. Up here, on this serrated ridge, all the saddles and upthrusts have become more sharply incised over the years.

We approached a rounded top. It was just after five p.m. and we must now have been around 8,030 metres. Julie's face was shining with joy.

'We will be on the subsidiary summit soon ... and over there is the top,' I told her. She looked surprised. Did she think we had already made it, or was she shocked at how far we still had to go? My own heart was thumping with pleasure. Over there, the shimmering triangle of Broad

Peak's summit had appeared in view, just as I remembered it, just as it was all those years ago.

Another kilometre further on, perhaps ... bathed in sunlight and surrounded with fairytale clouds. Julie, too, quickly realised that despite the distance, nothing would now stop us getting to the summit that day.

An unexpected feeling of happiness overwhelmed me. The way over the enormous roof-ridge of Broad Peak was revealed as an indescribable walk in the sky. We kept to the upper edge, towers of cloud sailing slowly past us ... an ethereal shimmer in the air from millions of twinkling ice crystals, the sunlight ... shining veils of fog materialising and dematerialising around us ... It was summit magic. Quite different from when I was here with Hermann ... but undeniably there. I felt it.

The final cornice appeared. And very close now, just beyond the last rocks on the ridge, the snowfield of the summit. I was surprised: from the gap to here had taken little more than three and a half hours. Despite the altitude we both felt well, and merely knowing that filled us with pleasure. That didn't mean we hadn't noticed the thin air! Nearly there at last – with one of us always sitting on a rock, looking out at the shining dance of the crystals, the slow floating of clouds ... breathing deeply, while the other went to the end of the rope. It was unspeakably beautiful: to watch and breathe, to go and look ... with millions of flashing seconds of ice around you. At 17.45 we reached the highest patch of snow.

Julie – our Broad Peak.

The atmosphere is unreal. Low-angled sunlight. Joy. The summit snows. This is it! Hermann Buhl ... whirling crystals. Julie ... dark eyes shining with tears ... shimmering clouds ... wonder! The Gasherbrum peaks ... Then and now. Past and present embracing in a whirl of crystals, beyond time. The magic of this mountain.

'Just the two of us,' Julie says softly. The two of us, up here.

'Let's go out onto the rim of the cornice and look down into China – first you, then me. We can belay with the rope.'

The view is breathtaking. The marvellous sweep of the Gasherbrum Glacier, the barren, deep incision of the Shaksgam in the arid mountain wastes beyond, the countless thousand peaks of Sinkiang ... Down there, 3,000 metres below the snow at our feet, we were exploring last year. 'I can see the place the camels came to, there! By those glowing towers that look as if they should be in the Dolomites. And the great bend of the glacier that we couldn't reach because of all the ice towers in the way – that's there, look! Just below us! Goes in a different direction from what we thought, goes up between Broad Peak and the Camel-hump mountain.' Julie, above me at the edge of the cornice, points down, eyes shining ... That nameless, uninhabited land down there – how we love it, long for it. Why couldn't we go down and explore it right away? But the view alone is already a gift.

Looking back to where we have come from, we see, high above the long ridge, high above the slowly welling clouds, the huge pyramid of K2, towering into the sky. Our mountain. But when might that be?

High as the sky, the pyramid stands apart in all its crystalloid regularity, a symbol of all that is unattainable.

Nobody's mountain.

Yet wasn't it already our mountain? All those hours, two whole years! ... We knew it to its highest ridges, it was ours, even if we were never to reach its top.

Would we return? It was as if it held us in thrall: Mountain of mountains – yes, we are yours. Mountain of mountains, how beautiful you are. Of course we would come back ...

We started our way down along the summit ridge, above an ocean of clouds, the sun very low now, we had to hurry, a night descent would not be easy. Now that we'd been to the top, tiredness and thirst invaded our minds; still on the roof, near the subsidiary summit, I got out the stove and made a cup of Ovaltine for Julie. We sat there for some minutes, while the last light disappeared and twilight began. Then we headed down into the night.

Camp 3 above 7,000 metres. Julie and I were still snowed in, waiting. The pain in my eyes was much better. We would try to break out, down the spur, as soon as the weather gave us the chance. It was hopeless to imagine anybody coming up, there was far too much snow; there was no one on the mountain, even if there were still three expeditions waiting down at its foot.

Julie covered one of the lenses in my goggles with sticking plaster to protect the eye worst affected, but in the morning I noticed it was no longer necessary. We could start the last act of our Broad Peak odyssey, the 2,000-metre descent down the West Spur. There were still a lot of problems in front of us, but nothing we couldn't handle: in the deep snow it took us another one and a half days to get down. On 24 July, nine days after our start, we were back among the ice towers of the Godwin-Austen Glacier. Before returning to our 'mini base camp' below K2 (the whole place was ours: since our expedition had left we had just kept back two Balti porters), we allowed ourselves some time off at the foot of Broad Peak, wanting to look up friends and companions among the other teams. For two days we feasted our way through all three base camps.

WHY?

Adventure is beyond time and age.

Yet why the same mountain twice?

I remember the summit sunset with Hermann Buhl and the odyssey of the long descent with Julie. But that is not all.

Why? Because a mountain offers so much to discover, dimensions a person might otherwise never dream of.

How many times will we go to K2? Each time new facets of the crystal shine. Each step is a step into boundless possibility.

Julie says it more simply: wherever I go, anything is possible.

I say: where anything is possible, there I go. That's why we are together.

(Written in autumn 1984)

Tashigang – Place of Happiness

'It's a crazy life, but it's a good life.'
(*Julie writes in a letter*)

In two weeks we will meet again, this time in Vienna. Our life leads us all over the place: London, Paris, Venice, Frankfurt, Munich ... and the far Himalayas. It depends upon where an expedition is going, or a film is to be shot or edited – which sometimes takes several months. Last year, after taking part in an attempt on the North-East Ridge of Everest, we made a mad dash back to England via Peking and Hong Kong for a stay in Europe of only ten days – Julie wanted to organize a party for Terry's fiftieth birthday, a really big celebration. Then, with me coming from Bologna, we flew to Islamabad, and a week later were on the Diamir side of Nanga Parbat, ready to film for Lutz Maurer's TV series *Land der Berge*. But to be honest, we live this way because we like it. Neither of us suffers from any shortage of breath: in Lhasa, between us, we blew out 99 candles in one go – our birthdays are on following days in March, so we marked them together.

I used to be known as the 'cameraman of the eight-thousanders', now we are 'the highest film team in the world' and we're kept pretty busy.

That is one side of the coin – the other is that we must always be alert to every opportunity, ready to jump in order to hang on to this insecure, adventurous existence. It is like leaping from one island to another – and we don't always make it. But perhaps it is in our characters, never to give up, either of us ... And so we are content with a life that quite often becomes a dance on a tightrope.

This time the pan of destiny in which our eggs are sizzling is in Vienna – on the Küniglberg, where rises the modernist 'palace' belonging to the all-mighty Austrian Television, ORF. I regularly get lost in the galleries of this colossal building, which seem to have been designed to the harmonic principles of a superior but inscrutable brain. To find a way through the wildest icefall is nothing compared with finding a particular department within ORF. At least for me. Whenever I have to spend four weeks in the cutting room here, the fully air-conditioned atmosphere always fills me with a desperate urge to escape, and I dream longingly of bivouacs ... But the equable Austrian temperament can rise above even places like this – and I know several quite amiable people who work here! So the eggs of our fortunes are sizzling this time in the pan of the ORF, and the handle is held by no less a personage than the financial controller of the science division: Mr Peter 'Panhandle' (Pfannenstiel). His face has the calmness of the full moon, and his appearance is immovability itself, a quality present also in his soul. Julie and I warmed to him immediately (and it wasn't just because he approved our budget) as we did to his boss, Dr Alfred Payrleitner, who seemed on the one hand to be an exact scientist, and on the other a winged poet, radiating optimism and confidence. As also did the friendly, round woman with whom we used to have such nice chats over coffee. Julie and I indulged in dreams of how we would suggest lots more villages to this sympathetic trio, villages in which we wouldn't mind living and filming – in Tibet, with the Eskimos, in the jungle … somewhere at the end of the world.

It was obvious that our first production for them had to be absolutely first class … We invested it with all our enthusiasm.

With that alone, however, we could never have succeeded in making the film. Hildegard, one of my two daughters from my first marriage, to Tona, studied ethnology in Vienna. Together with Christian, a friend and colleague, she had immersed herself in the life of a Tibetan village in one of the remotest regions in the Himalayas. Its inhabitants for some unknown reason had emigrated several hundred years before from the province of Tingri and settled in the border area between Tibet, Nepal and India. Hilde and Christian spoke some Tibetan, were adopted by a family and soon learned to speak it fluently. Their life with the Tibetans and their discoveries would certainly fill a whole book on their own.

As I also knew this place – it was close to a holy mountain – we decided, the four of us, to make a documentary in which the scientific authority came from the two ethnologists and the technical and creative film work from Julie and me. It was a very fertile union – even if the film team were not 'adopted', in the village we did belong 'to the family'. This was of inestimable value to our work, and moreover, living with Tibetans was one of the most beautiful times of our life together.

At the last moment something almost got in between. A holy place in the nearby mountains, where there was a magic rhododendron grove, was the site of a fertility cult – it fell also into my daughter's field of study. That must have been a special twist of destiny: I was a bit surprised when we made the first of our two journeys to Tashigang – we intended to cover all the seasons – to see that the blessing of the holy place had not passed without effect on Hildegard … I was going to be a grandfather! Austrian science however closed one eye – having regard to the future

– and we rolled the cameras for the first part of the film with Christian alone. For the second part, however, Hildegard was with us very, very actively – while for two months Tona accepted the fate of grandmothers the world over; she babysat. I was in Everest Base Camp when I learned of the birth of my granddaughter Jana. We were sitting on boxes of Scottish whisky and within moments several of the bottles were on the table. With our British mountaineering friends, we raised our glasses to Jana, facing Chomolungma! So easy is it to become a grandfather!

Karen, Hildegard's sister, also studied in Vienna. She's married to a landscape architect. When I remarked to her she should take her time – and I wasn't referring to her studies – she seemed to me to be embarrassed. Moved, I stroked my grandfatherly beard. It was going to happen for the second time, obviously! This grandchild was called Rubi.

The first part of the film about the Tibetan village was in the can. Mr 'Panhandle''s smile almost split his round face in two: he pumped our hands and sent us off with his blessing – and money – back to Tashigang. Christian had already been there for seven months … he practically lived in the village full time.

Hildegard, Julie and I picked up our luggage in Varese, Bologna, in Tunbridge Wells, in London and Vienna … we met in Munich and on a sunny March day flew to Kathmandu.

Julie and I had with us all our gear for K2. Returning home after Tashigang was going to be out of the question, timewise. We would have to go directly to Karachi, and meet there the mountaineers of Quota 8,000 – to which our enterprise was attached. Most of them we already knew from our trip to the Chinese side of K2. They were our friends from the Italian expedition to the North Spur. While we sat in the aircraft, I thought of how difficult it had been to come up with an arrangement which made it possible for us to go back to K2 … It seemed jinxed, it simply didn't want to happen: when I heard of an American expedition, going to the north side of K2, I was very excited and ready to do anything they wanted! That was the place Julie and I dreamed of.

I wrote immediately to the leader, Lance Owens. I even received a call in reply from a mountaineer in Washington, but then it all fizzled out. Nothing – the connection seemed broken. My letters remained unanswered. It was a mystery. How often in life people could spare others so much heartache simply by giving a clear 'No'. Did they need or want a film team? Was it significant that their team included an American woman? So far no woman had been to the top of K2. Julie, who was so firmly against any form of competition, would never have tried to muscle in on being first … We were just very sad that our great hope of going back to K2 was withering from lack of nurture. The next shock was even greater: I got to hear of an Austrian mountain guides' expedition which had a K2 permit. Only three of them, as I learned later, had Himalayan experience, and as a mountain guide myself I saw an almost 100 per cent chance of attaching myself to them in a purely nominal way. For Pakistan rules for expeditions say that a team has to have at least four persons, thus no two-man expedition has any choice but to attach itself somehow or other to another.

I had made it clear to the Austrians that we would be self-financing, that we were an independent team and wanted to remain that way, with our own equipment, own food – everything – yes, we even offered a free film for their lecture tours. Their answer really shocked me: 'We don't want any stars.' That was what Hannes Wieser told me over the telephone after first – as he said – having discussed it with the 'powers that be'. I could not believe my ears. I didn't see myself as a star, even after having survived thirty years in the mountains of the world, and I have never behaved like one. My only concern was to find a way round a bureaucratic formality. It was totally incomprehensible. But there was something which up to then I had not appreciated: K2 had not had an Austrian ascent ... unfortunately. Perhaps that was the rabbit in the cabbage patch, as we Austrians say!

Some friends from Poland also had permission for K2. They would have loved to take us with them – but they needed dollars and no film.

We spoke next to Maurice and Liliane Barrard in Paris, and they too would have welcomed us into their mini-expedition – but they were leaving so early that we could never have finished in Tashigang in time. You cannot alter the customs of a village to fit in with a film, it has to be the other way round.

Then at that critical point Renato Casarotto offered to help us out of the hole. He was prepared to let us join his expedition; he had already done the same for Mari Abrego and Josema Casimiro, another two-man team who because of the damned regulations also found themselves in need of an 'umbrella'. We knew them both very well – Basque friends from Everest 1985 – and it would have been an ideal combination. However, again it seemed that the filming of Tashigang was very difficult to fit into the same timetable. At the very last I got to know that Agostino was also going to K2 – our friend Agostino Da Polenza from Bergamo. We had been with him in China; moreover, he was going out later. Agostino absorbed us with no problems at all. Julie and I were delighted with this solution. The thing that did astonish us was that half the world seemed to be gathering on K2 this year!

Kathmandu: bad luck strikes. An apparently harmless insect bite

Tashigang – Place of Happiness

during the airflight seems to have caused a dangerous infection and allergic reaction in Julie and her fingers are swelling. We hurry her to the Canadian hospital for treatment. The swelling goes down, but two of her fingers remain numb. This worries Julie for a while thinking of K2. Fortunately it later appears that the numbness is not linked to any increased sensitivity to cold, and will slowly get better. We also learned in Kathmandu that people have been dying of meningitis during the last month in the area to which we want to go, so we get ourselves vaccinated against it. Ten days later we finally reach Tashigang – and all else is forgotten.

The hills are blanketed in a thick mist of trees – black and dark green, and sometimes a shining green-yellow, according to the light that falls in this virgin forest: crimped silhouettes thrusting upwards, billowing storm clouds of twigs and leaves, strangely twisted trunks, moss covered, often tangled together, writhing bodies with arms uplifted on which delicate lilac orchids spread out the fingers of their leaves; curtains of ropey lianas dangling almost to the ground from these strange giant shapes. Here and there appear some steep, cleared slopes, a projecting shoulder – and there, in the midst of terraced fields, one above the other like a staircase, are a few clusters of low houses, pitched roofs constructed of several layers of bamboo matting, often reaching almost to the ground. They give the impression that a party of fishermen have upturned their boats on the terraces …

Even if the next big river in this mountain area, the Arun, is a full day's march away, there is water everywhere in Tashigang: the jungle ferns, the lichens and mosses hold it like sponges from rainfall to rainfall, and grey veils hang almost continually above the country … 'There's water all over my tape!' complained Julie after taking her first sound recordings in the village – but laughing as she said so, because it is too beautiful here to let any worries take root. All around there is rushing water: in green gorges, from dark walls of rock, down which the waterfalls pour their white ribbons, and from the deep, brown-green valley floor. Immediately behind the small corn-store, sturdily constructed of woven bamboo and supported above the ground on long legs in which Julie and I have made our home and stowed all our film gear, even there you have only to step around the corner between the rocks to reach a wonderfully clear stream of marvellous water. Then there are the shining red dots of sweet wild strawberries in between … '*Phagpa-lemu*,' grins Drugpa Aba, his dark eyes regarding us benevolently from his tanned-leather Tibetan face under its shock of black hair while the fruit dissolves on our tongues. Since Hilde and Christian were adopted here, he has been their 'brother' – and they live with him and his extended family in the house directly below our shelter. There, grandmother rules the roost – she is Drongpa Ama, which translates roughly as Mother-of-the-Household. The grandfather, a calm, still man, who – Hilde assures me – is a marvellous story-teller, lives for most of the year up in the high pastures – up at around 5,000 metres. As soon as spring comes this seventy-year-old man moves up with his herd, crossing a snowtopped mountain pass in his bare feet to get there. Sometimes his old wife pays him a visit up in the high valley. She brings 'Schnaps' and checks up whether he has made enough butter!

Drugpa Aba is their son. He has five children – but his name means Father-of-Drugpa ... referring to his firstborn, a son. Pasangphuti Ama, Mother-of-Pasangphuti, who became his second wife after he divorced the first, is a very resolute person. Her shrill laugh penetrates the bamboo walls and is the reason we dubbed her, not very politely, the Squealer. They are all great characters here. Kaili, who Hilde calls the Merry Widow – was even responsible for Julie getting out the sewing kit and mending my shirt; she feared a Tibetan *Love Story* would not look so good in the film. For when I was in desperate need of running repairs, strong, good-looking Kaili (she was a real picture when I filmed her ploughing with the bullocks) heard my cry for help from two houses lower down and came running. She nodded, looked carefully at the damage and ran an experienced hand over my chest, back and arms ... but then, as I said, Julie in the interest of the film came up with her sewing kit.

Unlike the ethnologists, who as a matter of principle want to live like the locals – and do – I took care to secrete into our lofty home some supplementary food, more appropriate to an Austrian mountain man (and a film-maker who has to wield his heavy Arriflex): a 'yak's' milk cheese from Kathmandu, as big as a wagonwheel, and several sides of good Austrian bacon. They are my consolation after sitting in the family circle around the fire, and out of politeness sharing with them the daily ration of millet gruel enlivened only slightly with a few vegetables.

My idea of making them a gift of a chicken – in the hope, I have to confess, of maybe catching a wing – was gratefully accepted. For five days our millet was flavoured with chicken juice and included millimetre-long fibres of meat ...

That was on the first trip. Now, on the second, like an old bear, I regularly retreat after supper to the privacy of our airy Eldorado where Julie shares my weakness for non-ethnological dishes. One day, when I appeared at the grandmother's with bacon, tuna fish and cheese for the whole family, I earned thanks but also an ethnological reproof – I was not to make a habit of it.

Well, then ...

Tashigang – Place of Happiness

Besides the *gonden* – as the thick, sticky millet porridge is called, and which together with a few potatoes forms the staple diet – grandmother also used millet or maize to make a sour alcoholic brew, *chang*. And from this again, she distils the schnaps-like *rakshi*. It is an adventurous spectacle: a metre-high, three-storeyed still made of pots and an inverted copper cone which is filled with cold water, around which the alcoholic vapours cool and condense.

Because of the *rakshi* I filmed only one sunrise. For at first light Drugpa Aba appears at the door of the airy grain shed with the morning song on his lips. He knocks for me and pushes in the steaming cup, the size of a small soup bowl, filled with hot *rakshi*.

Even if you play deaf there's no help for you, you have to empty it: Drugpa Aba smiles, we exchange some Tibetan words, we sip the hot schnaps, Julie offers me the cup, I offer it to her, she passes it back to me – and Drugpa Aba waits with the patience of an angel. After this 'mallet-blow' you sink muzzily into your sleeping bag, and blink finally and rather late into the sun of the new day ...

What shall I tell of our film work? It was interesting and extensive: two journeys to, and four seasons in, a paradise, which we could grasp because we were living it, far from the clamour of our everyday life. The only way it was possible. Here nature rules time: the people of Sepa – as this area is called – have a hard life, certainly, but they are in perfect harmony with their surroundings. They are a contented people. We have rarely laughed as much as with the people of Sepa. When Julie and I were not in Tashigang, Christian filmed events on his own – such as during the summer monsoon – because we wanted to cover the whole year. Over the space of three years Hilde and Christian came repeatedly to this place for anything up to eight months at a time, either alone or together, while they worked on their common thesis.

Phagpa-lemu, the local name for the wild strawberry, means 'pigs – good' however, as Hilde explained to me, it could just as well mean 'white man – good'. Whoever has tasted the fruit of Tashigang will understand why both like them so much.

I took Hildegard up the Gran Sasso (the highest peak in the Abruzzi Mountains) when she was only seven years old, and much later she came with me to the Base Camp of Mount Everest, where we climbed Island Peak (more than 6,000 metres); now my sometimes dreamy, sometimes resolute daughter speaks fluent Tibetan as her fourth language. The slim, blonde beauty has always had the spirit of adventure in her blue eyes and will not allow anyone to interfere with her plans. Tashigang has become a second home for her and Christian – it goes far beyond work;

they study the life of these villagers and their religion which is one of the oldest of the Tibetan people. In the village is a bearded *naksong* (one who goes in the dark) who is in contact with the powers of nature, the spirits which dwell in the rocks and trees and in the water; he is also a medicine man, healing not symptoms but the root of the disorder. There is also the lama – he belongs to the Red hat sect, followers of the oldest form of Buddhism in Tibet. The two men collaborate regularly – at marriages, pilgrimages to holy places. Both are married, have families, houses and fields. In this region you don't get monasteries or monks and nuns.

When somebody wants to know what will happen in the future he asks one of the 'oracles', three old Tibetan women who live in a neighbouring village. They read your hand; or – if they fall into a trance – the spirit of a mountain or the voice of a long-dead lama may speak through them … *In the dimness of the room, firelight flickers on the face of the* lakama; *her eyes are upraised, scanning the darkness, and a strange, high, rhythmical song comes from her mouth. She starts to tremble; her arms, head, her whole body shake as the trance takes hold of her. The lama poses the questions and she answers in a weird, unearthly voice* …

In these moments K2 seemed far away from Julie and me, as we from it. We both knew we would always want to come back to Tashigang. It had become a treasured part of us.

Many years ago I came under the spell of a holy place in one of the nearby high valleys, although I did not know then that it was a site of magical powers. Plagued by high-altitude cough and at the limits of my endurance, I had retreated from the final slopes of an eight-thousander to take refuge in the rhododendron forest below.

When I came to take stock, it was obvious what I should do: I had to come to terms with reality – with myself and the world. I had to give up high-altitude mountaineering. How could I have been so audacious as to tackle the fifth highest mountain in the world at the age of forty-six? And after a break of eighteen years, during which I had come to know many corners of our planet, but never once made another push up to the 8,000-metre mark?

For a week I lived alone with the blossoming rhododendrons and huge firs in that very special place I call the Enchanted Forest. There it happened. Not only did everything suddenly become clear, the prospect of renunciation no longer gave me a pain but I was physically restored to perfect health in a few days, strangely, once I had surrendered to the inevitable, strength flowed back into me sufficient to tackle anything.

I went back up and climbed Makalu; a little later, that autumn, Everest; and the next summer Gasherbrum II. Dedication to filming cost me

Tashigang – Place of Happiness

some summits, it's true to say, but even so I frequently climbed really high.

Julie and I were prepared now and again to relinquish the thrill of climbing to the highest point in order that others through our films might share the experience of the wild, crystalline, stormswept world of the Himalayas.

Julie was now forty-seven – even if she looked as if she were in her thirties – and I, well … I was fifty-four. But both of us still felt really well at altitude – it was as if the mountains themselves radiated energy to us upon which we drew to spend it with them. We intended to carry on climbing the highest peaks for several years yet. Nanga Parbat still beckoned, and Julie had thoughts of Everest, too. She even tried to talk me into climbing Makalu again with her, but Tashigang gave us pause … There was our future.

To bring home images of how people lived in places like this is totally different from making a film about an expedition: certainly it holds more significance for other people. That was confirmed some time later when Tashigang, *Tibetan Village Between the Worlds of Gods and Men* won first prize at the Trento Film Festival.

But our past was slow to release us. Julie once asked the 'oracle' about Makalu (the old Tibetan was not very clear in her answer: Julie would climb very, very high, she told us), and meanwhile in the far distance K2 was waiting for us. When I spoke with Hilde again about my mystical experience under Makalu she smiled and said that perhaps it had something to do with the *jinlab*. And then she told me what she had learned about the bountiful magic of the mountains from a Tibetan nun who lived at Rongbuk at the foot of Mount Everest.

Pelbe, the endless knot, one of the eight auspicious symbols of Buddhism. It signifies the infinite cycle of rebirth and the illusory nature of time. It is also sometimes called the life knot or love knot.

Jinlab – the Magic of the Mountains

My daughter, Hildegard, wrote a perceptive passage in her diary about mountain culture which she has allowed me to quote at this point:

The mountains, those bridges between heaven and earth, are the abode of the forces of fertility. To the people of Tashigang, Everest and Makalu are the Goddess Mother and the Great Father of the World. Mountains are believed to be the homes of giants and fairies – as is Nanga Parbat in Pakistan – or as the bold granite spire of Shivling in the Garhwal in India symbolizes the lingam of Shiva. Those who live among or at the root of mountains have always seen them as a border zone between the human world and the domain of gods. Mountains may even 'speak' to humans through the mouths of oracles.

Today they have become the target of mountaineering ventures, which often result in the defilement of sacred and secret sites – and are doubtless responsible, too, for changes in social and economic conditions, and probably for other things as well.

In the same way that each mountain has its own personality, its own emanation, so the way you perceive it depends upon who you are – be that Drugpa Aba, a farmer in Tashigang; or Sheraman Khan, a shepherd from Chanchal in Pakistan, driving his flock across flower-starred meadows at the foot of Nanga Parbat; or Sundra Nanda, spending his days as a yogi at the source of the Ganges river; or Kurt Diemberger or Benoît Chamoux, mountaineers from Europe … you experience the mountains within your cultural horizons, and your relationship with them depends deeply upon your relationship with yourself and with the world.

Perhaps climbing a mountain is the western way of experiencing transcendence, of relating to the border zone, whether consciously by total confrontation with yourself and with what the mountain offers in the way of beauty and drama, or by unconditional surrender without asking why.

Jinlab – the Magic of the Mountains

Once in a remote Himalayan valley, we spoke of this: Anila, a cheerful and learned Tibetan, nun and me, the young ethnologist adrift between too many questions and experiences and too few answers.

It was evening ... in a wooden hut: two simple plank-beds, two bowls of Tibetan butter-tea into which we stirred a handful of *tsampa* – the roasted barley flour was a present from Anila's former art master whom we had met on our way.

We were tired as always when we had done a lot of walking but the impressions of the long day would not let us sleep. Would the light plane for Kathmandu be able to take off tomorrow? Would the clouds lift? Anila took off her dark red cowl and stretching out on the planks of the bed began to tell her story.

Twenty years had passed since she was last here in this nunnery. She had met people she had not seen for a long time and had recognized familiar objects which whisked her thoughts back to the old days ... to the years she spent in Dza Rong Phug (Rongbuk), north of Everest, when she was a young girl ... and to those later years, after the Chinese occupation of Tibet, when she came to this new monastery in Nepal, Tubten Choling.

She spoke of her studies and experiences ...

After instruction from the lama in the Rongbuk monastery, she was often sent alone to one of the mountain caves that are found around 5,000 metres where she would then spend several days practising *chö* and *tsai lung*.

Up there at the foot of Everest she experienced *chö* – the ritual confrontation of all that frightens you – and *tsai lung*, the control of your energy through what is known as 'the channels of wind', a form of breathing which relates to the pulse of the universe.

Such consciousness and control over yourself and your own body allows you to develop warmth, energy, endurance, and resistance to an incredible degree – way beyond what is normally held to be possible. The aim is to dissolve all barriers between yourself and the cosmos, between one's own individual energy and the energies of the universe, to join the eternal flow ... cosmos into cosmos, one into the whole, emptiness, to tap the naked power of the creative forces ... *lung* is the breath of life; *lung* is the wind. The numerous prayer flags flapping in the wind at monasteries and on mountain passes at all the sacred places are the *lung ta* – the wind horses, but also the *pneuma* of the universe, the energy of life.

Anila was at last ready for the final test – which she passed. The one thing she particularly remembered was having to stay in an icy cave with snow all around and a thick wet cloth wrapped about her naked body: she was required to dry it by using sheer body energy produced in deep meditation and by the recitation of mantras.

Anila said: 'In Dza Rong Phug it is cold, so cold that if you don't drink your tea right away it turns to ice. It is different from here but oh, so beautiful! In the beginning I found life hard – I was only twelve years old when I was accepted into the nunnery – and was very embarrassed to stand there in front of the lama with the other girls, naked but for our red meditation ribbons for holding our yoga positions. As time passed you learned that in mystical experience there is no place for shame. You go beyond that ...'

For many generations in remote caves mystics have confronted the forces of life, death and being. Around Everest and Makalu in all the 'power places', all the *be yul* (sacred hidden valleys of the Himalayas which radiate power: 'navels of the earth' ... *sai lhe*), they have passed time in meditation.

These mystics are the ones who exceed the limits of the normal, the conventional; they withdraw from society in order to understand the energies, to control them, in order to transcend fear and cut free from ego, to capture the deepest essence of being. It is said that they were able to cover enormous distances on foot without resting, to levitate during deep meditation – to float – and to produce incredible energy with their bodies while standing immobile for days in front of a mountain. Extraordinary accomplishments, yet only the means, side effects even, on the road to enlightenment, for all living beings.

The barleymeal in my bowl did not mix well with the butter tea; I was not too adept at preparing it and as usual spilt most of it down the dark red skirt I was wearing. Flour-dust everywhere! Anila looked at me and laughed, then taking the bowl from my hand, with quick deft finger movements had it mixed in moments.

'This is the food we always take with us in Tibet when we go to the mountains', she said. 'It does not weigh much and provides plenty of energy. It's delicious with fresh cheese but good without too.'

That's true – maybe being so hungry had something to do with it, but I found the mixture fantastic.

Now it was my turn to tell a story ... How many adventures danced together in my mind like a kaleidoscope: the mountains – I have never learned to know them like a dedicated mountaineer, being always more interested in the ordinary people who live here up in the Himalayas. I have climbed sometimes, taken part in expeditions. So I have some experience of most perspectives that come together there – and sometimes clash with one another: the shepherd, the yogi, the mountaineer. They all cling to the mountain, all experience its power, its magic, can all learn fear from it. It's not by chance that the *ne* – those sacred places which radiate power – are mostly to be found in hidden valleys below the magic giants. To my surprise I found myself telling Anila all about Nanga Parbat – and my adventures with a small enthusiastic group of mountaineers enjoying a sympathetic relationship with those who lived there, the porters and high-pasture shepherds.

Base Camp was almost part of the mountain ... avalanches of powder snow silently swept the slopes above, then reared up with an enormous roar, before hissing to rest around the tents, plastering them in snow dust despite the protection of the moraine. Clouds and more clouds boiled and billowed in eternal movement as ice towers and seracs thundered one after the other over the rocky buttress at the end of the glacier – the voices of Nanga Parbat, the voices of Diamir. The 'Naked Mountain' in front of us, around us, was like a sleeping goddess – a massive and wilful deity forcing her everlasting presence upon us. Higher up, you could catch the shimmer of her loosened icy tresses – the wide, finely fluted slopes of the Bazhin. At her feet glowed a few small red dots – our tents – one on a little rocky bank. In that one sat Benoît, a young man of singular originality, a 'child', and above him his 'beloved', Nanga Parbat, – smooth of flank, naked-white ... bewitched.

At the critical moment, Benoît withdrew into himself for three or four days of the hardest concentration; he was learning to know and grow intimate with the mountain and its personality, to develop the deepest possible awareness of all his actions, to control the energies of his whole body. His strict vegetarian diet was regulated to produce the highest energy at the moment when his climb demanded the greatest physical exertion. And still he remained light-hearted ...

Then there was the question of selflessness, to be with and not against Nanga Parbat, to love and not seek to conquer or violate it. At eight o'clock in the evening Benoît started out – by himself with a tiny rucksack, a flashlight, some chocolate and six pistachio nuts in his pocket. At about 8,000 metres, he met his friends on their way down; at seven o'clock in the evening he reached the summit himself, twenty-three hours after setting off from Base Camp. It grew dark almost immediately ... the flashlight failed to work, and all night long Benoît wandered around the Bazhin, lost, only finding the right way down when dawn came up. Later that same morning he was back in Base Camp – totally exhausted, but possessed with the magic of the mountain ...

Anila interrupted: 'This is the *jinlab* of the mountain!' she said eagerly. 'This light, this warmth which the mountain gives you – if you love it offer yourself to it totally, if you "live" it deeply. Tibetans do not have a tradition of going to the tops of Himalayan mountains – except for Milarepa, he did – even though they seek ultimate inner enlightenment through meditation in the special power places below the mountains ...'

Yet whoever climbs high on the mountain for the merit of his soul (*sem ky don*), seems to me to have some experience of the *tsai lung*, to be perhaps also akin to the person who practises *chö*, who pits himself against himself, confronts his fears and with the released energy tries to overcome the gap between 'I' and 'it', between subject and object: it is unification, becoming one with the world, with the lover, with the mountain.

Once more I hear Anila's voice: 'If you are in harmony with yourself and with everything that you do, then you are light – your whole body is light and you can do incredible things. No doubt the reason why you actually climb mountains comes into it, too. People often go to the mountains to make a name for themselves or to earn money out of it – but that alters everything – then you become "heavy"...'

Hildegard Diemberger (diary entries)

RETURN TO K2

Karachi Airport 2 a.m., 15 May 1986:

'Agostino gave me a big hug ... and the warm greeting I got from the rest of the group made me feel I was in a big happy family.'

Julie is clearly moved to be meeting our friends from the North Spur again. Three years have passed since we saw one another but we still feel very close. We embrace. It will be great all being together again on K2. But there are new faces too: altogether the Quota 8,000 expedition has sixteen members – they fill a whole bus. (Quota 8,000 is a club which intends to climb all 8,000 metre peaks within the space of five years.) The atmosphere is happy and, as one would expect, noisily Italian!

A few days later we are batting along the notorious Karakoram Highway to Skardu – a 23-hour journey. And what a journey: 'The Pakistani driver disregarded potholes and corners, relying on his grip of the steering wheel to keep his seat. His unfortunate passengers were all bruised and battered by the time the journey was over and poor Kurt had also contracted a virulent form of flu,' Julie records in her notebook of our latest film trip, as usual keeping the log for both of us.

It was a bad beginning. I could hardly move my right arm and my shoulders were wracked with pain. Finally I had to stay in bed in Skardu with a high fever. Karl Herrligkoffer, the German expedition leader and doctor, was in Skardu with a large group of mountaineers and looked after me before setting off on his walk-in. He got me more or less on my

Jinlab – the Magic of the Mountains

feet, but I found the march through the Braldu Gorge, with its relentless ups and downs, such a painful struggle that Julie and I with a group of five porters dropped back to follow at our own pace, two days behind the rest of the expedition. This gave me time to recover and had the advantage of detaching us from the frantic rush to reach Base Camp.

'Part of Kurt's cure' Julie wrote in the log 'was to rest for an extra day at the natural hot springs just before Askole. We spent hours lying in the round rock bath tubs with the smell of sulphur in our nostrils, gazing up at snow-covered peaks all around. This would be our last soak for at least eight weeks and it really did ease away the lingering aches and pains.'

In the meantime Hildegard had arrived back in Europe with the heavy box of exposed film from Tashigang, leaving Christian sitting up there as usual in 'their' village. Julie and I had yet to make the transition: that gentle Tibetan atmosphere which had absorbed us so completely lingered still.

'Gradually we pulled ourselves back to our dream mountain ... a double journey back in time,' Julie said, 'first coming back to this side of K2, and secondly renewing the friendship with our Italian companions.' Of the many nationalities she had met on her enterprises she always held the Italians in special affection for their warmth and their ability to turn a group into a happy, caring family. 'It made no difference to them – or me – that I was not Italian. Nor that I was the only woman mountaineer.'

We were still within reach of villages. Bright shining green oases would emerge from time to time out of the barren mountains owing their existence to near-horizontal irrigation channels, some even 1,000 metres long, testament to the many generations who had dug into the stony flanks of this narrow valley. The water comes from the mountain torrents which find their source high in the snowfields and glaciers. Askole – at around 3,000 metres – is the last village on this difficult and sometimes dangerous approach to the Baltoro mountains. For more than one hundred kilometres you move a good deal along sandy goat-tracks, now and then passing beneath huge blocks of rock poised in precarious equilibrium on the shifting slopes; you proceed within reach of tall walls of compacted stones, loose conglomerate, and have to traverse enormous gravel slopes which slide under your feet without warning. You have to keep your eyes open! There are icy side streams to be crossed before the final forty-kilometre stretch on the mighty Baltoro glacier. Altogether, this approach to one of the wildest corners of the world takes between ten and fourteen days.

The local Baltis can earn about £5 a day as porters carrying loads for up to six to eight hours. Weighing 25-30 kilos each (50-60 pounds) the loads are made up of boxes, plastic drums or the duffelbags which hold the equipment and food for the walk-in. 'Their shoulders must ache where the mountaineering rope or homespun woollen twine bites through their thin cotton suits' – yet these people live on just chapatis, salt tea and sometimes a few lentils.

To get to K2 is an adventure in itself, as we knew from earlier expeditions. This time Julie said 'I am more scared of tripping and injuring myself on the walk-in than of the daunting prospect of climbing thousands of feet up the second highest mountain in the world.' Inexorably our mountain of mountains draws closer.

Julie again ... 'K2! K2! echoed through my thoughts with every footstep. K2! K2! Such a stupid name for the world's second highest mountain. I pushed it out of my brain with thoughts of my family and home half a world away but like a repetitive marching chant it always crept back to haunt me just as it has done for several years ... In my case it is a passion ... many people would argue that I must be mad to love a mountain but K2 is no ordinary peak.'

It was the most beautiful approach we had ever experienced. The five Baltis accompanying us were friendly and helpful. Now and then along the way when we encountered over two hundred porters of a big expedition, we would be more than ever delighted with the intimate atmosphere we enjoyed by being so small a group.

When at the wide circus that is Concordia, the junction of the giant rivers of ice, we saw K2 rise in front of us, contentment descended on us both.

We were home.

The Village on the Moraine

TODAY'S CLIMBING JUNGLE: GIANT EXPEDITIONS VERSUS SOLO SPEED MERCHANTS

Iridescent, blue-black bodies of giant bumble-bees cluster together, wings held out stiffly. They are drinking. With them on the damp, quartz sand are over a hundred brimstone butterflies, like yachts at a regatta, their wings barely moving and mostly folded. Only now and then does one butterfly open its delicately veined, lemon wings and gently adjust its position before closing them again. Thin proboscises uncoil to dip between the tiny fragments of rock that make up the sandy bar of the river. Here and there, single, much larger insects have settled, sleek as black velvet and with elegant sickle-curved wings, conspicuous by their darkness in the bright multitude. All might be exotic jungle blossoms around the river. The dense throng on the sandbank reflects the multiplicity of life in the forest beyond. And you don't think, in that moment, of the thousands that perish every time a forest giant falls to the ground, of the struggle for light, of the continuous growth and disappearance, of the birth of new species, the tenacious survival of old ones, of the balance of perpetual life which depends on, and evolves from, all this ...

The island of insects on the sandbank seems a haven of contentment. They are all drinking.

Base Camp at the foot of K2 was on the moraine, a long, curving sandbank in the kilometre-wide bed of the Godwin-Austen Glacier, at a height of 5,000 metres; and by its very altitude alone had nothing in common with swarming butterflies on an Orinoco sandbank in the Venezuelan jungle. Yet the gaudy tents shone happily among the rubble of the moraine, grouped in patterns of colour according to the expedition to which they belonged – as if different types of butterflies had lighted together on a favoured spot. The silent, crystal mountain world beamed its influence over the camp, just as the jungle held thrall over the sandy islet in the river.

It, too, appeared a haven of contentment: from tent to tent, mountaineers of different nationality invited each other to tea, were ready to offer assistance. They sat together, exchanging stories, drinking.

The Endless Knot

Everything had changed in the thirty years since Hermann Buhl and I made our lonely way up here. But the convivial picture on the moraine concealed deep division between opposing and conflicting styles of expedition. All were represented, from the classic to the most modern. People whose views on how to tackle a big mountain were at complete variance had come together: climbers with opposing ideas on strategy, risk and safety, climbers of varying degrees of 'hardness' and experience, according to their background and how they perceive the mountain scene. To call modern mountaineering a 'jungle' is not, I am convinced, overstating the sort of thing that is now happening in the Himalayas.

Will it ever find a natural balance? It is impossible to predict because the situation itself is an artificial one. People who don't like to delve too deeply into the causes of problems believe it can all be resolved through fraternal equability. But things are not usually that simple ... especially once you are on the mountain itself. Apart from the camaraderie engendered at Base Camp, there are few positive aspects to several expeditions sharing the same route.

It is only when climbers come to recognize the dangers inherent in too much togetherness – and to face them openly and with courage – that they will be able to drink their tea together as real companions, and not as victims of an illusion.

Even in 1979 when I went to Gasherbrum II, the sublime isolation of the Baltoro was already over: about a dozen expeditions gradually gathered at the foot of the big mountains. We visited one another from mountain to mountain, base camp to base camp, exchanging invitations to share Tyrolean bacon dumplings, Japanese fish, French delicacies, Spanish ham and red wine. The Baltoro had changed, but in a friendly way. Yet those who had known it in its pristine loveliness could not but help feel a little sad.

In 1984, when I returned again, twelve expeditions were to be found on just one of those mountains: Broad Peak. How astonished Hermann Buhl would have been to see his West Spur now: tents all over the place, and fixed ropes, too – and not just to safeguard the extremely steep and sheer ice wall, as we had them in 1957. The route itself had changed substantially and a good deal of the West Spur was laced with fixed belays ...

You couldn't rely on them, however. Even first-class mountaineers like Peter Habeler and Wojciech Kurtyka nearly came to grief when old fixed ropes gave way or anchors pulled out. On the other hand, the large number of climbers on the mountain provided an illusion of greater safety. Some felt it safe to wait in an improvised bivouac above the gap at 7,800 metres, only to finish up with heavy frostbite. Broad Peak, though

The Village on the Moraine

technically not a difficult mountain, had by no means become a safe one.

And the fact that it was *said* to be easy could well have had something to do with that.

Could a similar situation develop on K2? The multicoloured dots of the extended tent village, the island of butterflies, reminded me of the series of base camps at the foot of Broad Peak in 1984. But K2 was infinitely more difficult – and so much higher. A mountain on top of a mountain … What would happen? Most of the mountaineers were optimistic – the colourful Base Camp was a friendly, hospitable place to be in, never boring. It had its own, very positive, atmosphere.

We are sitting with the Casarottos – Renato, tall as a tree, and Goretta, his graceful wife – in their spacious grey-blue frame-tent. It is as large as a room and in the corner houses another, smaller tent, a shining red triangle – their bedroom. Along one of the walls stands a row of plastic drums full of gear and food. There is still space enough to sit comfortably in one corner and enjoy Goretta's home-baked cake (quite extraordinary at this height of about 5,000 metres). Renato talks of his past and why he has come to K2 this summer. He is among the world's best mountaineers, one of his famous first ascents being that of the difficult northern summit of Broad Peak in 1983, which he climbed solo. He has been to K2 before – in 1979 when he took part in an expedition led by Reinhold Messner. The very imaginative route they chose then followed first the SSW ridge, then ran up higher to the right. It had been 'discovered' by Messner, and christened by him the 'Magic Line'. For various reasons, however, and much against Renato's will, the expedition subsequently switched attention to the Abruzzi Ridge, by which Reinhold Messner and Michl Dacher finally made it to the summit. Renato, for whom the abandoned SSW Ridge remained the real goal, always felt there was an old score to settle: he wanted to climb it solo. But now he was faced with having to share the route not only with the Italians of Quota 8,000 and an American expedition which had diverted from its original objective, but also, last but not least – with a Polish expedition, expected shortly. For a soloist, the prospect of so many others moving up and down 'his' route was very frustrating – despite the fact he was on good terms with everyone involved, and that some of the climbers were friends of his. (This is where the image of the jungle leaps so vividly to mind: lianas fighting their way up a jungle tree, clinging to the trunk and to each other, obliviously.)

It is clear that two big groups working together can proceed more quickly and with less outlay than if they went independently. The practical advantage of such a joint enterprise is also felt by anyone who later follows the same route, for the fixed ropes are rarely, if ever, removed.

Whoever comes afterwards will at any rate find pitons in place and tent platforms left by his predecessors. You could say that the first ascent of the route results from the 'collaboration' of everyone who has ever been on it. Some people accept this combined system happily enough – others despise it and prefer to tackle unsullied mountains on their own; reality hardly ever satisfies everyone's expectations!

Similar problems and developments of routes can be found time and again in the history of the major first ascents in the Alps.

In 1979 a French team spent four months on the SSW Ridge and came very close to the summit. They failed by about 200 metres. In its upper section their route did not follow the 'Magic Line', going to the left of it – but all the same, the name stuck in the minds of many mountaineers.

Certainly, the position Renato found himself in on the overcrowded ridge held little attraction for him as a solo climber.

There was another party, too, which was not at all enthusiastic to find other people on 'its' route; this was the Austrian expedition which arrived later than most of the others. These climbers actually thought they would have the Abruzzi Ridge to themselves, and were amazed to see the huge village of tents at the foot of K2. Their first reaction was to stake out a perimeter fence, in the form of a light blue climbing rope, all around their patch, like a prospector's claim. The message was that everyone else should keep out. Other villagers watched with secret delight ...

However, the Austrian soul is quite adaptable. Soon Julie and the rebuffed 'star' Diemberger stepped over the blue line, bringing a guitar, and in a matter of minutes we were all sitting round, singing and drinking beer. And I let some of the young ones know how lonely and beautiful it had been here in the 'good old days'.

Austrian yodellers are an attraction all over the world. Immediately we were joined by the dark, stocky South Koreans (who also held a permit for the Abruzzi). Though they were shy at first, I managed to encourage them to some tentative yodelling – an Austro-Korean mixture is pretty exotic.

With nineteen members, the Koreans were the largest expedition in the place. They, too, came a little later than the rest, at the beginning of the fourth week of June. They put up a lot of tents, had high-altitude porters and intended to climb with oxygen. To our eyes, they were the epitome of the big classic expedition to an eight-thousander. At the same time, however, they were fully equipped with modern gear – not for nothing do the big sports equipment specialists from all over the world get their goods manufactured cheaply in Korea. Solar batteries fed three video cameras, which were operated by a TV crew from Seoul. You could

The Village on the Moraine

even 'go to the cinema' in the Korean quarter: they showed films of the history of K2 climbs and attempts, and later put on the James Bond movie, *Diamonds are Forever*. There was even an 'adult documentary' from California! The Koreans generously took their show on tour, moving up and down the moraine, from camp to camp – to see James Bond people even came down from the British Base Camp a quarter of an hour away at the edge of the Savoia Glacier, starting point for the North-West Ridge. If you spend two or three months in rock and ice, entertainment is always welcome. With increasing frequency, Alan Rouse, Jim Curran, the Burgess twins and other British climbers would come over from their splendid isolation behind the Gilkey Memorial to visit the rest of us on what they called 'The Strip'. Did they, I wonder, see anything there to remind them of Las Vegas besides the bright lights and colours?

Up to this point there had been no bad incidents, apart from when an Italian journalist, who wanted to take pictures of K2 from the Windy Gap, fell into a crevasse while wearing skis. He jammed on a bridge only five metres down. But he certainly had strong nerves: before he let Julie and me haul him out, he sent up a camera for us to take several pictures of him in his hole. 'After all,' he said enthusiastically, 'an occasion like this doesn't come along very often in life.'

All in all, there were fourteen different undertakings represented on K2 that season. Ten were expeditions: the Franco-international team of Maurice Barrard on the Abruzzi, as well as the Austrians and Koreans; Quota 8,000 had also paid for the Abruzzi Ridge along with the SSW Ridge. Renato Casarotto's solo attempt was destined for the SSW Ridge as well, as were American and Polish expeditions. Then there were the British on the North-West Ridge, and Herrligkoffer's international expedition, which was aiming for the South Face – all of these on the Pakistani side of K2! Only one expedition, the American, attempted K2 from the Chinese side.

In addition, there were three small independently operating teams on the Abruzzi: the two Basques, Julie and myself, and two Swiss, Fuster and Zemp. The latter really belonged to Herrligkoffer's expedition, but had decided to try the Abruzzi even though their permit did not allow them to. (They were not the only ones asked to pay a retrospective fee of 45,000 rupees in Islamabad!) Finally, there was the Yugoslav soloist, Tomo Cesen, who opted on sight to attempt a bold new route to the Shoulder* – and succeeded. It is understandable that the Ministry of

---

* Previously attempted, and nearly completed, in 1983 by Doug Scott, Jean Afanassièf, Andy Parkin and Roger Baxter-Jones. [Editor]

Tourism, faced with such a massive demand for permits (between a third and a half seek to climb 8,000-metre peaks), some years ago formulated strict rules and regulations for expeditions, in order to exercise control over the situation in conjunction with their liaison officers. However, some of these regulations seem to have been drafted on a 'green' table, as we say in Austria – that is, theoretically, with little regard to practicalities; others (really useful ones for the protection of wildlife and the environment) are very often only half-heartedly insisted upon, or neglected. The legal ramifications of this often yield strange fruit.

Take the case of the German encampment on the moraine, which found itself unintentionally breaking the rules. This group of tents served as Base Camp for K2, while one hour away, at the foot of Broad Peak, Dr Karl Maria Herrligkoffer had his main Base Camp, for the expedition held permits for both peaks. Under the terms of the rules, however, only one base camp is allowed per expedition! Their Pakistani liaison officer was very firm on that. It seemed insoluble – and then, Eureka! a way out suggested itself. The Base Camp for K2 could simply be officially renamed Camp 1 – whereupon the problem vanished! The tents were no longer 'unlawful'. Even on the Baltoro Glacier you can meet the galloping horse of bureaucracy!

Outside the Germans' large and comfortable mess tent, where we sometimes sat to enjoy fantastic dumplings, sauerkraut and delicious stewed bilberries, was parked a symbol of German efficiency, a special 'bicycle' – an ergometer. You could adjust it so that it required more or less energy to operate and then pedal away to your heart's content. It was one of Herrligkoffer's favourite toys – and I knew it of old. In 1978 the same machine had stood at 5,300 metres at the foot of Everest; good old Karl even allowed me a go on it – as an experiment. I see the eyes of doctors shine!

Even if you never caught him on the bicycle, present in this camp was the man who was without doubt the strongest on the Himalayan climbing scene: Jerzy Kukuczka. With his Polish ropemate Tadeusz Piotrowski, he was part of the international German expedition. In the race to be the first to climb all the eight-thousanders, Jurek, as he was known, was close on the heels of the great Reinhold; and even if each of them made out there was no competition, it was far from certain at that time which of the two would pull it off first.*

This friendly, rather silent Pole, with the fresh face of a country boy and clear eyes that reflected calm and circumspection, had a very special

---

* Reinhold Messner completed all fourteen that autumn, 1986; Kukuczka made it about a year later.

objective on K2: the unclimbed Direttissima, or Central Rib, on the South Face. His partner in this ambitious enterprise, the bearded Tadeusz Piotrowski, was even quieter, as silent as K2 itself: he was, as we say in Austria, a rock of a man, one of the best Polish winter-mountaineers, and quite imperturbable. Although the pair had for the moment the nominal support of the two Swiss, a German and 'Little Karim' (there has even been a film made about that legendary Hunza!), no one in Base Camp was under any illusions but that it would be the two Poles, on their own, who would solve the real problems of the route – and in pure Alpine style. Giant seracs threatened the central part of the route with falling ice and after that the angle became breathtakingly steep, up combined rock and ice, and leading directly to the 'exit' originally projected for the Magic Line, where icy couloirs and rust-coloured barriers of rock barred the way. 'A mousetrap, that exit, if the weather breaks,' commented that old fox of the Himalayas, Norman Dyhrenfurth. Yes, Norman! Such a pleasure to meet him again. We both 'live' in Salzburg, yet travel so much that we never see one another there. We went to Dhaulagiri together in 1960, when Norman shot the expedition film to which I contributed the summit sequences. It was an adventurous trip, in the course of which a ski-plane was used for the first time high in the Himalayas, to land supplies and people on the North East Col of Dhaulagiri. Ernst Saxer and Emil Wick successfully made the highest glacier landing of the world (at about 6,000 metres, according to the latest measurements). Not long after that, however, the aeroplane crashed, although luckily both pilots survived. Despite the resultant chaos, eight of us managed to reach the summit. At the time, this first ascent might well have been the highest without using oxygen (but we cannot know for sure, without knowing the full story of what happened to Mallory and Irvine on Everest).

This time Norman was filming the Herrligkoffer expedition. He was in good company. There were about a dozen cameramen and assistants at the foot of the mountain covering the various expeditions. Higher up, however, on the mountain, there were but few!

The strenuous and dangerous business of filming at high altitude requires not only considerable dedication, but also a special way of thinking and behaving that is not found in many mountaineers. You need to be able to withstand storms for longer, have a higher number of depots, and be prepared to move less hurriedly, with extreme patience and strength. You could compare it to being a sailor: you cannot leave the boat when the fun stops. To be creative when climbing a mountain needs a style of its own.

This is why Julie and I, while belonging to the Quota 8,000 expedition, have been granted total independence. Our goal is to climb K2 by the Abruzzi Ridge, and to make a film of the various aspects involved when so many expeditions jostle together on a mountain. Of course, our own climb will be part of it, as will the history of the mountain. Quota 8,000, on the other hand, has no other thought but to go all out for the SSW Ridge. At least, for the time being it hasn't.

Meanwhile, we are treated to a diversionary sensation: the young Frenchman Benoît Chamoux, who is also a member of our expedition, climbs Broad Peak in a single day. He is not the first to do so: the Pole Wielicki did the same in 1984. Julie and I were on the mountain when his team broke the trail. (There is no other way for such speed records: the 'mountain sprinter' can obviously carry hardly anything. Trail-breaking, high camps and back-up in the case of weather breakdown – all these are in the hands of the collaborating team ahead of him. Nevertheless, it is an enormous sporting achievement.)

Opinions differ over its relevance from a mountaineering point of view. An ascent like this can never, for instance, be compared with Reinhold Messner's solo climb of a new route up the Diamir Face of Nanga Parbat, nor indeed with Renato Casarotto's fiercely persistent, months-long struggle for the SSW Ridge of K2. The unladen sprinter follows a route prepared by mountaineers who without doubt did carry loads and therefore in all probability employed fixed ropes as well: for him the route is a measured race track, an uphill obstacle course. Freed of route-finding and weight-carrying, he can concentrate all his energies into finding his own most effective rhythm for optimal performance. Certainly it's adventurous, but it has little in common with mountaineering. At the same time, it can't be ignored that this obsessive preoccupation with speed for its own sake rubs off on everything else.

Benoît returned safely from his adventure, thinner than ever (if that is possible), and with his face alight with joy. The first thing he wanted was his picture taken with the Grandfather of Broad Peak! Of course, he got it. And the point I really want to make is that he never once lorded it over the rest of the team. Later, he produced an even more astonishing performance: he climbed K2 in similar manner by the Abruzzi Ridge, again in a single day. Not bad, for a scrap of a boy! I know other top mountaineers who are, like him, vegetarian. I go in for muesli myself, but I also pack my solid smoked bacon, my *Bresaola* (air-dried meat) and a block of hard Parmesan cheese, then I know I have the best basis to keep me in altitude trim. Mountain ibexes may live solely on grass, but the snow leopard – which has been seen as high as 6,000 metres – certainly doesn't go around just eating potatoes. Both ways of life have proved efficient at altitude, nutritionally.

The Village on the Moraine

What I find really remarkable are the incredible lengths to which Benoît will go to realize his ambitions. Sheer precision sets our youngest 'bloom' in the expedition jungle apart from many of his counterparts. He never improvises. The currently widely-held attitude, 'We'll make it – somehow' – whether in reference to acclimatization or to preparation for an ascent – is dangerous and hard to stop. So often climbers discuss different styles – whether to climb with or without oxygen, to go on big or small expeditions, take or reject high-altitude porters – ignoring the fact that all these styles work if they are properly applied. But if the attention to detail is not there, a lot will be in the hands of chance.

The Pakistani liaison officers in our 'township' may have felt this – regularly they all met together with their highest ranking officer, a major. And the expedition leaders? They can solve problems of collaboration and logistics on the mountain by discussion and consensus. Did they always? Sufficiently? Certainly everyone had the best intentions ... but a critical eye on the strategies applied in 1986 would discover more than one 'black hole', and the close proximity of different enterprises will always mean extra risk, however positive the human dimension. That was one of the lessons of this summer on K2.

Taking a stroll along the moraine – it is quite impossible to film for longer than an hour at a time – it was interesting to listen to the opinions of the medical doctors. That they can never agree I know from many expeditions. One thing is sure: back in 1957 (and later) we all regularly took Vitamin B12 for a fast increase of red blood cells, important for the transport of oxygen around the body; but now this has been discontinued because the blood becomes too thick, the haematocrit rises, and with it the danger of frostbite. Nowadays, the view is that it is better to give Vitamin E. Dilution of the blood, which about ten years ago was thought to be the key for better eight-thousander climbing, is no longer taken seriously by anyone: a French doctor once assured me that it was much too dangerous and would need a hospital on site to make sure it was done safely. And as for wonder drugs like Diamox, designed to speed up acclimatization and guard against mountain sickness, there was almost unanimous agreement at a recent medical congress in London that it would be unwise to take it if you had already had any degree of acclimatization. For then you would be likely to fall sick and become subject to a kind of over-acclimatization. The mountain doctor, Urs Wiget, told me that in case of a wrong diagnosis of oedema, taking a diuretic (which is what this is) could rob the body of precious liquid, already seriously diminished at altitude. This could so easily prove fatal to someone whose blood was already thicker than normal. I feel an obligation at least to warn against the thoughtless consumption of pills which a well-meaning friend might pull out of his pocket at 8,000 metres. That goes for all sorts of medicine – you should only ever take drugs under the direction of a doctor.

Once on Dhaulagiri, after taking some preparation to increase circulation, all of us felt the benefit of really warm feet, but in exchange, our fitness had totally gone. And I missed out on the summit of Nanga Parbat when in the dark I took some pills in mistake for aspirin. I cannot speak for medical science, but it is clear that how a person reacts at 8,000 metres and how much a body can endure, are still imperfectly known. In my opinion, medicines should only be taken at altitude if there is no other alternative, and above all, only for getting *down*, not up.

Acclimatization is of supreme importance. This takes at least three weeks for an eight-thousander. But let us hear what a well-known mountain doctor has to say on the subject . . .

Threats Posed to Health by High Altitude

In looking at the saga that follows it is useful to consider in detail the matter of high altitude physiology. In this I am indebted to Franz Berghold for the following summary:

Even if the human body is not fundamentally equipped for living and mountaineering at extreme heights, it can adapt astonishingly well and even accomplish remarkable physical performances – so long as one follows the 'rules of the game' governing climbing (and staying at) high altitude. But what happens in those cases where such adaptation cannot be achieved?

It is necessary to distinguish between *direct* and *indirect* damage or disturbance to a person's health.

A variety of disturbances that are collectively known as acute mountain sickness result directly from difficulties in adapting to the decreasing amount of oxygen which can be absorbed through respiration as one goes higher. In extreme cases a person may develop the very serious high-altitude pulmonary oedema (HAPE) or high-altitude cerebral oedema (HACE). Pulmonary oedema occurs most frequently between 3,500 and 5,000 metres, fluid from the tissues seeps into the lungs, from which a characteristic gurgling sound can be noticed; at the same time, the victim is desperately gasping for air, has difficulty remaining upright and becomes increasingly confused and unable to understand conversation. Swift transport to a lower altitude usually produces dramatic improvement.

Cerebral oedema, on the other hand, is usually met at very extreme altitude. It is characterized by dullness or lethargy, impaired co-ordination, confusion and ultimately unconsciousness. Unfortunately, even a rapid descent to lower altitude may not lead to improvement. This condition occurs less frequently than high-altitude pulmonary oedema, but is more likely to prove fatal. The immediate causes of both these high-altitude oedema conditions are so far improperly known, and no really convincing drug therapy exists. For instance, a doctor treating high-altitude pulmonary oedema in the same way as he would treat pulmonary oedema which has occurred in connection with other illnesses may find that not only does the patient not improve as normal, he may even get alarmingly worse.

Fortunately, however, and contrary to widespread belief, high-altitude pulmonary and cerebral oedema are not common. Much more frequent are several dangerous indirect disturbances, about which far too little is known and which are far too little taken into account. One is the inevitable and enormous loss of fluid from the body during high-altitude climbing, which poses a significantly greater threat than the lack of oxygen itself. By perspiration and, above all, by respiration, the body loses several litres of liquid per day; the consequence is an increasing thickening of the blood which can lead in turn to a series of extremely dangerous effects. I will list only the most frequent: strokes, pulmonary embolism/thrombosis, acute heart failure. At altitude, deaths from these causes occur more frequently than those from the better-known HAPE or HACE.

High-altitude deterioration, the slow 'dying' of the body at altitude, also probably derives primarily from an increased loss of fluid, even when in connection with persistent oxygen deficiency. There is no total agreement about this among specialists, but one thing is now clear: at extreme high altitude, the main cause of severe and fatal disturbances to health stem from the loss of liquid from the body. And it is a vicious circle: the increasing density of the blood due to fluid-loss slows down the delivery of oxygen to the body's cells. The lack of oxygen, already felt as a result of altitude, is made thereby worse. Yet oxygen is absolutely essential to all performance.

Lack of oxygen coupled with increasing density of the blood results more than anything in a dangerous decrease in efficiency. This affects not only the muscles but above all – and this is generally not given enough attention – it affects *mental performance*. The significantly *high accident risk at extreme altitude* (on the highest peaks of the world, nine times more people die from accidents than from altitude sickness) is more than likely due to the fact that at extreme heights the brain – in comparison to the muscles – is relatively poorly supplied with oxygen. This could explain why high altitude climbers often perform irrational acts, make wildly inaccurate estimates, and take alpinistic decisions that, lower down, would cause any mountaineer to shake his head. It goes without saying, therefore, that the risk of accident rises enormously, out of all proportion to the objective circumstances, extreme as these may be.

Finally, a brief mention of some of the relatively harmless disturbances that can be experienced at great height: *peripheral oedema* (fluid retention, causing swelling of an arm, a leg or the face, usually noticed on waking), *retinal haemorrhage, disturbed breathing patterns during sleep*. 'Harmless' in this context means 'not posing an immediate threat'. Such symptoms should at any rate be considered a warning that the sufferer is having difficulties adapting to high altitude. You cannot die from sub-cutaneous oedema, nor from disturbed breathing at night, however dramatic they may appear, nor do retinal haemorrhages presage blindness but people affected by these conditions should watch out that they do not later run into far more serious problems such as outlined above.

FRANZ BERGHOLD

More details on this subject can be obtained from Dr Charles Clarke at the Mountain Medicine Data Centre, St Bartholomew's Hospital, London EC1, or from the following books:

MEDICAL HANDBOOK FOR MOUNTAINEERS
Peter Steele (Constable, 1988)

GOING HIGHER, THE STORY OF MAN AND ALTITUDE
Charles S. Houston (American Alpine Club, 1988).

HIGH ALTITUDE AND MAN
John B. West and Sukhamay Lahiri (American Physiological Soc. 1984)

HIGH ALTITUDE MEDICINE AND PHYSIOLOGY
Michael Ward, James Milledge and John West (Chapman & Hall, 1989)

But back to 'natural medicine': remembering Hermann Buhl's sleeping draught', three weeks ago Julie and I mixed sugar and glacier water into the beer kit we had brought from England, and put the 24-litre barrel to ferment in the warmest place we could find – the Italian mess tent, a giant red and blue dome in which twenty people can sit together. We have three of these huge dome-tents with 'street lighting' in between – quite apart from the electric light inside the tents – all fed by silvery, shimmering solar cells. Then, like a row of small condominiums, come the colourful, peaked, individual tents of the Italians. It's all a bit too loud for Julie and me – we kept catching snatches of voices from Bergamo, Milan or Genoa on our tapes – so that we have set our tent some distance away on top of a conical moraine hill, with a wonderful view (day and night) over the Quota 8,000 centre, for all the world like a space station on Mars. Of course the electric extension cable was not long enough to reach us, and we have to make do with candlelight – but no matter.

The black barrel incubating our beer is a source of great interest to the whole village. Time and again someone will come, talk about the weather, K2 and the route – and then, casting an innocent glance in the direction of the barrel, enquire on the state of the brew. Willi Bauer insists on regular tastings to monitor its progress, so that we assume he must have been a food chemist in some other incarnation. Finally, our beer is ready and turns out to be a foaming, overwhelming success. From as far away as Chogolisa, people arrive to talk about the weather ... A good thing Julie brought along a second beer kit. We have enough time for another fermentation.

Sometimes, when I am sitting on top of the moraine hill at my tripod waiting for avalanche shots or taking long-lens views of camp life, I will notice that Julie is missing. Then I know that she has either walked over to the ice towers with her Japanese sword, to practise or to meditate, or wandered across to pass the time of day with Norman Dyhrenfurth, the old film-maker, whose stories of storms, Himalayan attempts, the search for the yeti, and many other adventures she enjoys so much. Norman is pleased to be visited by such an almost perennially cheerful butterfly, before she flutters on to see Goretta and Renato, or Mari and Josema – our Basque friends from Everest – or, helpful as always, gives some tips on sync-sound filming to the Italian cameraman who has not yet mastered it. Except for when aikido or budo draws her to the ice towers and the marvellous glacier tables, she is never gone for long. We'll meet sooner or later somewhere among the tents on the moraine. But if she takes the long Japanese sword and crosses the glacier stream in order to meditate, to sink into the core of her being amidst the icy landscape – or to perform the difficult, exacting martial arts moves, a ritualistic exchange with an invisible opponent – then I always leave her alone, I do not enter her circle.

Only once did she take me along.

'I have two passions,' she used to say. 'Mountains and the martial arts.'

It was good to be with her.

Success and Tragedy — Russian Roulette?

Seen from some angles, the contours of K2 exhibit the perfect harmony of a triangle with the dimensions of the 'golden section'. From above, it demonstrates the amazing symmetry of a cut diamond. Perhaps, indeed, one should call it the Himalayan Koh-i-noor after the celebrated diamond, the 'mountain of light', which similarly has been an instrument of fortune and disaster.

From a geographical point of view, the mountain rises from the centre of the highest mountain masses of Asia, and when you look on a map, the display of its ridges and spurs and ribs reminds you of nothing so much as a compass rose.

On 20 June the weather is beautiful and Julie and I sit looking out from our tent at Camp 1, at 6,150 metres on the South-East Rib, the steep Abruzzi Ridge. 'Good luck! All the best for the summit!' we shout after Mari and Josema, our Basque friends, as they set off up into the snow and stone desert of the wide ridge with slow, measured steps and bent under the weight of their enormous packs. They are carrying everything they need for an ascent of K2. It is an emotional moment. Julie and I originally hoped to go with them, and in our imaginations picture ourselves flanking our friends as they climb higher, fired by the same irresistible urge to stand on top of this mountain, the siren call which overrides all the stresses and struggles involved. What is it that makes us like this – have we been bewitched by the shimmer of the great crystal? Are we caught in its spell? Or are we simply happy in what we're doing? Why do people call this the mountain of mountains? Nobody can really explain, but Julie and I are not the only ones to have felt its pull ... this inexplicable lure which keeps drawing us back.

We are a little sad, as we watch our friends dwindling away in the wilderness of rust-coloured rocks and towers above us. It's a shame not to be with them, especially as we share the same style and attitude towards climbing, but we arrived at Base Camp three weeks later than Mari and

Josema, and are still insufficiently acclimatized. You need to build up to climbing at high altitude.

The view from here over the endless parallel ribbons which overlay the Karakoram glaciers, following their gentle curves and giving them their characteristic, regular pattern, is overwhelming and as familiar to us now as if we had always lived here. Two years ago we clambered up and down this spur so many times; and close by, we climbed our first eight-thousander together – there it stands, now, just in front of us. Yes, we are perfectly at home here. Yet we have to prepare for our ascent, have to establish points of support – supply depots, which we must keep pushing higher and higher and eventually turn into camps – before we dare venture beyond the 8,000-metre line. Our eyes continue to follow the two bowed figures ... are Mari and Josema embarking on one of the great days of their lives? Will they achieve their dream? And will they come back safely? We wish it from the bottom of our hearts.

Higher on the spur, a group of four are moving up together: Maurice and Liliane Barrard, Wanda Rutkiewicz and Michel Parmentier. They were the first this year to get started on the SE route. How long will they take? No new ropes have been fixed on the Abruzzi yet, and the old ones – if they are usable at all – will mostly be buried under snow. An ascent now, the way our friends are doing it, will be more or less in West Alpine style – even here. The effort required is infinitely greater than later on in the season when a big expedition will have newly roped the bulk of the spur. Then, even if climbing without the help of porters or the use of bottled oxygen, the alpine-style ascent only really starts below the mighty shoulder of K2, beyond Camp 3. Julie and I have experience of both methods and can appreciate the differences. In the circumstances, it is difficult to estimate how long it will take Maurice Barrard and his three companions, or indeed Mari and Josema. Nobody attempting a 'lightning dash' later in the season should compare his climbing time with that of earlier ascents when the route is in a very different state. For everyone, however, the trick is to try and co-ordinate his own performance, the conditions on the mountain and the weather to hit just the right day for going to the summit.

Luck in life almost always depends on being ready at the right moment. As Mari and Josema finally disappeared among the ramparts of the ridge, I remarked to Julie, 'Let's hope their summit day will be the right one.' And it was.

Choice of day, however, is not the only consideration.

'I have serious misgivings about the serac wall on that hanging glacier,'

Success and Tragedy – Russian Roulette?

Maurice had confided in Paris in the Spring, pointing to a photograph of the summit pyramid. 'It is definitely worse now than it was in 1979. Look at this latest shot: the fracture zone along this great balcony bit looks to have more cracks than ever. Heaven knows how much will come off and funnel down through the Bottleneck. My inclination is to try to the left, up that rock barrier – then, who knows ...' (he smiles enigmatically) '... afterwards we might be able to get from the summit onto the ridge along which we almost made it last time. I know the way down from there ...'

His big, searching eyes above the grey moustache in his chiselled features show no emotion: you would never guess he had just put forward the idea of doing the first traverse of K2. Maurice Barrard is a dyed-in-the-wool mountaineer, a man of enormous experience: in 1980 he climbed Hidden Peak (8,068 metres) with a single companion, by a new route, alpine-style; in 1982 he and his wife, Liliane, stood on top of another eight-thousander, Gasherbrum II; and in 1984 Nanga Parbat became their mountain. Over the last few years, they have made many great ascents. In 1985 he and Liliane came within a hair's breadth of the summit of Makalu: they were only about forty metres from the top, but there was such a storm, they did not dare enter the 'magic stronghold' of the summit itself. They would have been blown away.

Maurice is both audacious and cautious. He knows when he has to turn back. More than once he has proved that two people alone can climb well at altitude – even when one of them is a woman!

Your luck will hold as long as you follow your own rhythm ... but when that harmony is disturbed by the ripples of some outside force, then it can be threatened. Certainly he knows that.

Ever since we arrived at Base Camp, Julie and I have both had the feeling that something is wrong with Maurice. Liliane appears calm and strong, but Maurice is only a shadow of himself. We can't think what the reason can be. Perhaps he has overtaxed himself on the mountain? Is it having all these other people around that affects his rhythm? Is he disturbed by the obvious tension between Wanda and Michel?

One day, we were skiing up towards the icefall as they made their way back from the Abruzzi: they could not see us as we had just dropped off the normal 'track' to deposit our skis among the ice towers and, after a short rest, to pick up our two loads again to carry up to Advanced Base Camp (ABC) beyond the icefall. We caught a glimpse of them crossing the flat patch below the avalanche cone and were shocked at what we saw: not because Michel was moving quickly and Wanda was already way ahead – no, because trailing the calm, upright, walking figure of Liliane, came a stooped and tired Maurice, like an old man. That really did give us cause for alarm. We could not believe it was him – a man with all his successes. A mystery – and yet it seemed to us that he was the only person who could find the way to lift himself out of his 'trough'. Perhaps he simply did not have the opportunity, or did not allow himself to do so.

We had never met Michel Parmentier, a lively Parisian journalist, before. All we knew of him was that he had climbed Kangchenjunga. But Wanda Rutkiewicz – '*die* Wanda' – was a familiar face. I had first climbed with this tough, but always graceful, Polish woman on Everest in 1978. Time and again we have helped each other, as for instance on the South Col, when the day before her summit bid she found herself without a sleeping bag. I lent her mine and passed rather a cool night at 8,000 metres. The tables were reversed on Nanga Parbat, when Wanda left a tent for Julie and me above the Kinshofer Face. She did indeed reach the top of Nanga Parbat, and now her target was K2 – as yet still unclimbed by a woman. Wanda, ambitious and very determined, had Broad Peak on her shopping list this summer as well, and wanted to leave immediately after that to go on to Makalu! I got the impression that she had allowed herself to get caught in the eight-thousander race. But, well, if that's what she wants ...

One thing I did notice: she seemed lonely and less happy than on earlier occasions. The reason or the result of the way her life was going, I never knew. We never talked about it, even when we chatted together in Base Camp. It is just that when you have known someone for so long, you are aware of subtle changes.

The major difference was that Wanda was no longer part of her Polish women's team – as in 1984 and 1985 when she climbed with Krystyna Palmowska, Anna Czerwinska and 'Mrufka' Dobroslawa Wolf. She was now a lone operator, joining here and there where opportunity offered. In the past couple of years, Julie and I had enjoyed getting to know this happy, collaborative little group. We had been with them here on K2 and on Nanga Parbat. 'Mrufka', 'Anka' and 'Krysiu' should soon be arriving this summer, too, this time as part of a mixed Polish expedition under the leadership of Janusz Majer. Their target would be the SSW Ridge. We were looking forward to seeing them ... but then the dark shadow fell.

The first Black Day of the summer was the 21st of June.

All of a sudden, at 5.30 a.m., we hear a sinister roar from the direction of the Magic Line. Julie and I rush out of the tent and realize that an enormous avalanche has detached itself from the snow flank below the

Success and Tragedy – Russian Roulette?

Negrotto Saddle and swept down the entire face. Only grey ice remains. A ragged line marks the edge where the giant snow slab tore away. It goes right across the route! Was anybody on it? Who might have been up there? Base Camp is a hive of agitation ... soon we learn that two Americans, Alan Pennington and John Smolich, were climbing up the Negrotto Saddle. They have disappeared, buried under thousands of tons of snow in the basin at the foot of the wall.

Alan's body was discovered the same day, but no trace was ever found of John.

His friends buried Alan at the Gilkey memorial cairn, a rocky spot on top of a small hill near Base Camp where some flowers bloom and patches of moss grow in the sand. It was originally erected to the memory of Art Gilkey, who disappeared on the mountain in 1953, but it has since served as a cemetery for other victims, or more often as a memorial cairn with plaques for those who die or disappear in storms high on the mountain, and whose bodies are never recovered. K2 had claimed twelve lives before this summer, over the years. Much less, it's true, than Everest or Nanga Parbat but it still came as a shock to everyone. What would be the after-effects?

In my life, luckily, I have only rarely been confronted with death on the mountain, which considering the thirty years I have been climbing is remarkable. But I do know what it means.

If somebody dies during the course of an expedition, one of the first thoughts to emerge is, naturally, should one go on or not? On the one hand, you know that in the mountains, risk to life is ever-present. While on the other, the death of a person – how shall I put it? – shatters the dream with which you set out. What you eventually do depends on various factors – the same person may make different decisions given different circumstances: it certainly makes a difference whether the victim was your friend or somebody you hardly knew. Even if it is your best friend who dies on a mountain, you cannot foresee what you will do afterwards. If the summit for which you were striving was a treasured ambition of your friend, you may decide to go on just because of that. But you cannot say for sure: always, there are the two possibilities – turn back or go on. And everybody, when such a thing happens, reflects long and hard over what to do.

The Americans decided to break off their expedition. And Quota 8,000 decided as an immediate consequence of this terrible event to give up the SSW Ridge, its stated objective, and turn instead to the Abruzzi Ridge.

It seemed to me that all further climbing up towards the Negrotto

The Endless Knot

Saddle would be like Russian roulette for a while yet; there were still large sections of overhanging snow and ice higher on the route. Even if the same huge rock was no longer poised there to be loosened by the sun's first rays and come slicing down from above the Saddle, cutting through the surface tension, the equilibrium had doubtless been disturbed. (It had looked so safe, too: there were even fixed ropes attached to it.) Julie and I were happy, therefore, with the change of plan by our two leaders, Agostino da Polenza and Gianni Calcagno. Even without it, we would not have gone up this route again for filming.

Climbers know that reaching a summit always involves risk, but they do try to keep that risk to a minimum. If a certain danger is known, you can usually avoid it. But that still leaves the less definable hazards – some more or less so than others – and a certain residual risk has always to be accepted or no one would ever climb a mountain at all. I do not believe that those who have survived on big mountains are simply better than those who have died. Luck, certainly, comes into it. But errors committed do have their weight, as do caution and experience.

There are some situations where you cannot avoid the Russian roulette element – as for instance every step you take on the moving Khumbu Icefall on Everest – but they are, thank God, the exception rather than the rule. Those who've mastered the rules of the 'game' – for want of a better word – stand the best chance of surviving: yet without good fortune, nobody can make it. Fate is a vital ingredient.

The tense atmosphere that persisted after the disaster was aggravated by a completely unexpected turn of events: mail-runners arrived at Base Camp with instructions from the tourist authorities in Skardu to stop immediately any attempts on the Abruzzi Ridge for which permits were not held. It was a reasonable, tidy-minded intention, but everyone knew that in 1979 Reinhold Messner's Magic Line expedition had experienced no problems about changing their route – the royalty paid for the permit being considered a 'peak fee', rather than a 'route fee'. Those deemed 'illegal' amongst us were considerably agitated by the news: after all, they too had paid for K2. Even Quota 8,000 received one of the letters. However, since Agostino as well as Gianni had paid full K2 royalty fees – one was meant for the normal route – they believed themselves the victims of a mix-up in the paperwork at the Ministry of Tourism, and insisted that their switch to the Abruzzi Ridge was valid. They would clear up any misunderstanding on their way back through Islamabad (which they only succeeded in doing, in fact, thanks to the friendly intervention of General Qamar Ali Mirza, President of the Pakistan Alpine Club). If Quota 8,000 had given in, it would have hit our plans too.

Everyone wondered who was supplying the tourist authorities in

Success and Tragedy – Russian Roulette?

Skardu with their information about the Abruzzi Ridge. As a direct consequence of these events several climbers were banned from the mountains of Pakistan for four years.

Fortunately, Julie and I were on good terms with the liaison officers, none of whom objected to our presence on the Abruzzi. They also respected the film-work we were doing.

Then, 23 June brought the first summit successes – Wanda, Michel, Liliane and Maurice stood on the highest snow crest of K2. The weather was marvellous. They were rewarded with an indescribable view, thousands of peaks at their feet. And while they had been clambering to the top from a bivouac at 8,300 metres, Mari and Josema were making their own, quite separate summit attempt: from a final camp at 8,000 metres (which they considered a 'must' to get back to after their assault), they too – somewhat later on this radiant day – reached the top and there, overjoyed, hoisted aloft the Basque flag.

Later, Wanda told me that these were moments of sheer ecstasy for all of them, chasing everything else from their minds: a euphoria, impossible to describe, held them all ... Perhaps that was the reason why Wanda and her three companions – unlike the Basques – only came down 300 metres that day to pass another night at their bivouac site.

Considering what happened afterwards, this fatal decision appeared incomprehensible to everyone in Base Camp. But, then, we were not up there.

Tullio Vidoni, however, was high on the mountain at approximately 7,700 metres. With three companions from Quota 8,000 he had set out to attempt a summit dash, taking advantage of the initial fine weather period. In a report in *Alpinismo* (the journal of the Club Alpino Accademico Italiano) in 1987, he graphically recalls the later developments: 'Because of the squally conditions, we could barely make out the tents of the Barrard couple or of Michel Parmentier and Wanda Rutkiewicz, who had by now spent many days on the mountain: and when we reached the spot, there were Michel and Wanda coming down, both of them extremely tired. They told us they had been to the summit two days ago with the Barrards and two Spaniards ... They started descending this morning and had made it down despite the appalling weather conditions; the Barrards, however, were worn out and had decided to rest for some hours longer.' (Wanda told me later that she had seen them, for the last time, descending just below the balcony, the big ice overhang. She also said she was herself fighting the effects of two and a half sleeping pills, which she had taken during the night.) Tullio continues:

The Endless Knot

With the greatest difficulty, Gianni and I tried to set up our tent and, judging by the swearing, which was swallowed by the gusts of wind, it seemed that Agostino and Benoît were not having an easy time of it either. I couldn't help thinking of those two other poor people up there, higher than us, without gas or food. Once our shelter was up and we started arranging ourselves inside, Wanda appeared and asked us to climb up and search for her friends.

It was seven o'clock at night, quite dark, and in such an inferno it would have been madness to go out, and to no avail. We tried to make her see this, but she kept insisting for a long while more, before giving up on us. Though recognizing our impotence – there really was nothing we could do – we were beset by a feeling of guilt which nagged at us all night long. It was a sleepless night between the wind and snow lashing the tents, between the ever-diminishing hope of finding the Barrards still alive and, last but not least, worries about our own situation, for the snow was still falling and the danger increasing. Not only was it impossible to climb up, it was not going to be easy making it down.

Finally morning arrived: the weather was terrible. Snow was still coming down and it was foggy. Impossible to think of going up, and so we decided, all four of us, to descend. Wanda joined us, but Michel opted to stay: he still harboured slight hopes for the couple. His decision made us feel even worse: it seemed as if we were abandoning the situation. I descended last, with Wanda in front of me. She was moving so slowly that within a few moments I had completely lost sight of my other companions.

Wanda did not have any ski-sticks, so I gave her one of mine. After a few steps, she asked for the other one as well, but I refused. Now that the slope was so steep, we kept sinking in up to our waists; the densely falling snow cancelled out the tracks of my friends. We met the two Spaniards dismantling their tent, and Wanda sat down and announced she would descend with them, so I left them together and with great difficulty caught up with the others. At the end of the plateau, we now had to find the spur.

While we waited, hoping it would clear enough for us to see something, we picked out the indistinct figures of Wanda and the two Spaniards slowly coming down and then stopping. Meanwhile, we succeeded after some effort in finally finding the way onto the spur: after calling in vain back to Wanda and the others, we assumed they had decided to sit it out in the tent waiting for better weather and so we started to go down. However, I left my ski-stick pushed firmly into the snow to mark the beginning of the spur so that they would not have the same trouble we had in locating the right way to go.

That whole day long, snow and wind assailed the mountain – and us.

Success and Tragedy – Russian Roulette?

We reached Base Camp towards evening. Wanda and the two Spaniards came in exhausted two days later.

… Michel was still on the mountain, in radio contact with Benoît who performed a real miracle in talking him down across the snow plateau to the start of the spur.

Unfortunately, we don't know what happened to the Barrards …

Hesitatingly at first, but by and by with more conviction, we accepted that they would never come back. It was hard to come to terms with – a great shock to all of us. Everybody liked them. Was Maurice right in his belief that the balcony was coming down piece by piece – and were they hit by one such section? It is more likely that they lost their way in the storm coming over the Shoulder. Liliane's body was later discovered in avalanche debris at the foot of the mountain, directly below the Shoulder, but Maurice's has never been found.* I did not take part in the search which found Liliane. Later, an unauthorized picture of her body was printed in a magazine. In my mind I remember her only as she was, bright and lively.

In the course of a few years, Maurice and Liliane stood together on top of three beautiful mountains, among the highest in the world; they were a team of two, and their mountaineering had much in common with Julie's and mine. We felt very close to them and had hoped, one day, to climb with them. Neither of us felt like going to Liliane's funeral. Only later, in our own time and peace, did we visit the place. Something hung in the air, unsaid …

'They're coming! Mari and Josema! They'll be in camp in a couple of minutes!' The call echoes from tent to tent. Renato hurries towards them, the rest follow, we and many more. We are so relieved they have made it, overjoyed they are still alive.

But if it wasn't for their eyes and smiles, we would hardly recognize them. They're haggard and wrinkled, and must have lost a quarter of their weight. Walking prunes, the pair of them, two gnomes, horrible to behold and with almost no voices; yet at the same time, to us, so familiar, so dear and precious. They fell into Renato's arms, and now we hug them, too.

Next morning Mari whispers in a voice only slowly returning to normal: 'We have left our tent at Camp 2 for you. We knew you would have plenty to carry already with all the film gear.' It was a great gift, saving as it did the transport of one tent to 6,700 metres. But at the same

---

* Maurice Barrard's body was found in 1998. *[Editor]*

time, we still have three of our own tents on the ridge.

Mari tells me a good deal about the events higher up, yet there are still questions unanswered. Could sleeping pills have played a part in the fatal decision of the Barrard group to bivouac for a second time at 8,300 metres? What do we really know about the extent and duration of the effects (and side effects) of medication on people climbing without oxygen at extreme heights? How often may it have been chemistry that was ultimately responsible for people dying on high mountains – indirectly, without anyone being aware of it?

In the afternoon, Julie films an interview with our Basque friend:

ME: Mari, what was it like up there?

MARI: Up there? Hard to describe. Climbing up was such an exertion, and the thought that you had to get down again never left you. Thinking of the descent becomes such an obsession that you can't really imagine what the summit will be like. At any rate, when we got there, it was some summit – like a mountain on top of a mountain. It was wonderful! Because the weather was so gorgeous and – I don't know – the sensation I had most was that we'd made it come true, the greatest dream of my life, the high point of my mountaineering career. And perhaps, because I was so happy, that made me a little bit crazy …

ME (*pointing to the blue blisters on Mari's frostbitten fingers*): And that? Was it worth that?

MARI (*thinking hard before he speaks*): Yes, to me, it was worth it – for K2. Things like this: they'll get better. Perhaps if it had meant amputations, whole fingers lost, then I'm not so sure what I would think. It would certainly not be worth losing a whole hand, but something small like this, yes, it's worth that to have climbed K2. You might even be prepared to give more than that …

Quota 8,000 has another go, making the most of a few days of fine weather and first-class snow conditions. On 5 July Gianni Calcagno, Tullio Vidoni, Soro Dorotei, Martino Moretti, Joska Rakoncaj (his second time up, he climbed the North Spur two years ago) and Benoît Chamoux reach the summit. Benoît, as usual, started later than the others, climbing through the night, and joined up with his team-mates just as they headed for the summit: this way he succeeds in climbing K2 in an incredible twenty-three hours. Our Swiss friends Beda Fuster and Rolf Zemp also make it to the top.

On the same day, Julie and I reach the Shoulder of K2 and set up there our blue Ultimate tunnel-tent, ready for an attempt the following morning. We can see tiny figures moving above us incredibly slowly,

Success and Tragedy – Russian Roulette?

giving the impression of struggle in the extremely thin air. In preparation for their return, we open a sort of *osteria* on the Shoulder. For two hours, into that evening, we are brewing up for our summiteers who straggle in one by one, having stumbled down, taking plenty of rests on the way. They have raging thirsts and are totally dehydrated. Soro, who returns first, speaks of the incredible heat of the 'altitude sun' striking the steep face of the summit. He is the only one who does not stop for a drink, descending immediately over the nearby ice-barrier to the Italian assault camp below, set up for this dash.

The following day we gamble away our chance by making a late start and carrying too much (knowing that we will eventually need to bivouac). Eight people coming down the summit pyramid, in many places using the trail they had broken on the way up, have left something of a trench and quite often it is necessary to make new steps. Also, I waste some time putting in two awkward pitons, which I think will be necessary for belaying when we return along the traverse below the giant balcony. By four o'clock in the afternoon we have put the difficult part behind us and have a clear passage to the top. But now, with only a little more than 350 metres to go, we don't dare to risk a high bivouac; for a biting, icy cold has descended with the shadows and we turn back. Tired and disappointed, we reach our camp. Next day, the weather does not look good enough for the summit. We wait. But on 8 July it is no better. Ah, well, down we go then!

Shortly before we leave, we open our *osteria* once more, as Alfred Imitzer appears, the leader of the Austrian expedition. He is planning to make a solo attempt, but pretty soon he comes back, and quickly heads off down again. It is clear that the weather is about to break. We dismantle the camp, anchoring everything down to make a depot, and start the descent. It takes us to the 10th to fight our way through the heavy storm, unaware that high on the mountain, another tragedy is playing itself out.

Despite the bad weather, on 8 July, Jurek Kukuczka and Tadeusz Piotrowski both reached the summit of K2. It was the greatest success of the summer: the first climb of the South Face. They started on 3 July and after a straightforward climb set up their small lightweight tent under a vertical rock barrier, about the size of a house. Once above it, they had only to join the summit snow slopes of the Abruzzi Ridge. Back in Base Camp afterwards Jurek told us that the rock barrier was extremely difficult – Grade 5 or 6. In the end, they had no choice but to leave everything behind: tent, sleeping bags, equipment. In stiff winds and welling clouds, they finally stood on the summit and were able to make it down to the Barrard bivouac site at 8,300 metres. Next day they reached the

Shoulder, and on the morning of 10 July tried to continue to Camp 3, above the Abruzzi Ridge, hoping above all to find something there to drink: they had been without liquid for almost three days and had already spent two nights in the open.

They were slowly making their way down a steep ice slope below the Shoulder – Jurek ahead – when all of a sudden, Tadeusz lost one of his crampons. He tried to hold himself in the steep ice with his ice-axe, but before Jurek could do anything to help him, Tadeusz lost his second crampon as well while banging it into the wall in an attempt to get the front points to grip. He fell with full force onto Jurek, who braced, but could barely keep his own footing. Unable to catch his companion, Jurek watched with horror as Tadeusz hurtled into the depths. Shattered, Jurek finally reached Base Camp on 12 July. He and Tadeusz had achieved the finest climb of the summer, but at great cost.

I was curious to know how Tadeusz came to lose his crampons. Were they the modern quick-release type, which I know from experience do not always offer total security? For if you wear them over thickly iced gaiters, you may unexpectedly step out of them. But to my surprise Jurek said no, Tadeusz had been wearing the old classic strap bindings. There is then only one explanation: in his exhaustion he either did not fasten them properly or did not notice them working loose.

The two men had made a superhuman effort. Wanda remarked, 'The thing we always say about Jurek is that he can live for days on a diet of Himalayan rocks and come out fit the other end.' Just him, though. Tadeusz was never found.

Julie Has Doubts

After a push to 8,000 metres, you need at least a week in Base Camp to recover before you can begin to think of another summit attempt. That was something Hermann, Marcus, Fritz and I learned years ago on Broad Peak, when effectively we climbed the mountain twice – apart from the small difference in height between the two ends of the summit 'roof' – and it is something I have seen confirmed time and time again. It is nonsense to suggest that you are 'played out' for the rest of an expedition after once forcing your way above 8,000 metres. Quite the opposite: you usually feel much better the second time you go to those final heights. Many mountaineers will confirm this.

However, it is important to relax properly before your next try. And to do that in Base Camp, or even lower. The necessary interval between two attempts will vary from one individual to another, but it will rarely be less than a week.

Julie and I, on 8 July, had left our assault camp in place as a depot for another attempt. We had completed the very hard and difficult descent and arrived tired, but in reasonable shape, at the foot of the mountain. Route finding on the steep slopes below the Shoulder had been nerve-racking and we had spent two nights in storm-buffeted tents with hardly a wink of sleep, worrying about snowslides and the threat of avalanches. But after two expeditions on this spur we were on familiar ground. A high-altitude porter from the Korean expedition, who had fought his way down from Camp 2 through the same storm a little ahead of us, was sitting now in Base Camp with heavily bandaged hands having sustained bad frostbite to all his fingers. (Fortunately, the Korean doctor, Dr Duke Whan Chung, was eventually able to save them.)

No, getting fit again for another attempt was not a problem, especially as the unstable weather left more than enough time for rest and relaxation. Three weeks passed without offering any real promise.

But the mountain had claimed five victims. It made us all sit up and think very hard – Julie and me, no less than the others. We tried, as they did, to come to terms in some way with what had happened, to find explanations rather than to put it all down to an act of God. Mountains never 'want' to kill anybody, why should K2? It seemed incomprehensible. In 1984 Peter Habeler had called this icy giant a 'benign' mountain, and I must confess I had always had the same feeling. It was all very hard to understand. Was there suddenly some curse on the mountain?

Julie and I were nowhere near finished with our filming, even if our Quota 8,000 companions were now packing up. We would have to remain to do that at least, whether or not we got another chance at the summit.

I noticed that Julie showed less than her usual enthusiasm. She was withdrawn, and I could understand how she must be feeling. On the other hand ... there was the mountain, still standing there, enigmatically concealing itself with shifting veils, shimmering through the clouds.

Matters hung like that for a while.

Despite the shadow the dreadful events had cast over the camp, there were occasionally spontaneous good moments. People cannot suppress their positive characteristics indefinitely. Julie and I continued working on the film, trying to capture the atmosphere of this waiting period (which everyone handled in his own way). We shot the Koreans at their board games and various mountaineers endlessly checking their weight on rusty, unreliable scales (it is nothing to lose 15 or 20 kilos on an expedition): with synchronized sound, we filmed the two Austrians, Hannes Wieser and Alfred Imitzer, engaged in the long-winded process of moving their tent a few metres – as you have to after weeks of ice melting out from the stones all around but not from the shade of the tent, so that it finished up on a plinth, like a monument. The floor can be over a metre above the ground outside, and perched on this, your available space diminishes as the tent develops a list towards the south like a drunken castle.

Other things, too, told of the long time – close on two months now – that had elapsed since our arrival: mountaineers with scissors heroically tackling their matted, overhanging growths of hair, and 'Krysiu', our blonde Polish friend, who with a shy smile would always fill the vodka glasses whenever she saw me arriving so that I could drink a toast with the (unshaven) Old Man of the Mountains, the Polish leader Janusz Majer, or with 'Voytek', Wojciech Wroz, who had been to 8,000 metres on K2 twice in recent years, from different sides, or with the girls – small, active, dark-haired 'Mrufka' (the Ant), and quiet 'Anka', both of whom we knew from earlier enterprises. The Poles had their teeth well into the Magic Line – the SSW Ridge – and were making progress even during this bad weather ...

The only other person battling away up there was Renato – lone, indefatigable, Renato Casarotto. He began his third serious push for the summit on 12 July, promising Goretta that this would be his final attempt.

Julie Has Doubts

After that, they would return home. She remained, as ever, in their tent on the moraine, maintaining contact with him several times a day over the radio.

It was the beginning of the third week of July, and Renato was already high on his ridge, when Julie and I were able to record a discussion between him and his wife, which highlighted Renato Casarotto's drastic situation. Goretta was sitting in front of us, radio in hand, Renato himself could not be seen, up amongst the swirling clouds which encircled the sharp edge of the ridge and the streaming white banners issuing from the rust-coloured turrets ...

> RENATO (*over the walkie-talkie*): *Ciao*, Goretta. I arrived in Camp 3 at five o'clock. It's blowing a gale up here! The weather – well, let's hope it improves. Let's hope the wind from China clears the sky and gives me a chance of getting up this time. *Passo!* Over!
> GORETTA: Yes, but I don't really know. The altimeter looks good, but I can see that the wind is tremendous up there, where you are. We'll know better tomorrow.
> RENATO: Right. *Va bene.* But the little tent up here, it's full – absolutely stuffed full with snow and ice! It's taken me an hour to get it all out. A real epic: everything is soaked. I forgot to close the side-flaps last time, that's what did it, that's how all the snow got inside, *Cambio!*
> GORETTA: And you? How are you feeling, Renato?
> RENATO: I'm OK ... fine, really. So far. But I'm tired now, and so fed up with this whole business that I'd love to jack it in, come down, get away from here ...
> GORETTA: That has to be your decision, Renato. *Va bene*, Renato – let's speak again, later ...
> RENATO: *Va bene!* You call me!
> GORETTA: *Va bene! Ciao!*

Julie steps into frame and claps her hands to synchronize the sound and pictures (we did the same at the start of the discussion). 'End board!' she says (though we're not using the clapper-board), then turns to Goretta and whispers a gentle '*Grazie!*' That wraps it up for today. I put the camera away and go back, with Julie, to our tent.

It was one or two days after that, on 16 July, that we learned that Renato had definitely given up. It was a great shame – he was so high, something like 8,300 metres. All of us down in Base really felt for him, had been willing him to succeed on his SSW Ridge, but after two months even the indomitable Renato had now had enough. Would he be returning to Base Camp that night?

Goretta expected to hear over the evening radio link. She imagined him to be on the ridge above the Negrotto Col as he was still quite high the last time she had spoken to him. I was standing beside our tent with Michael Messner – perhaps we were talking about the weather, a frequent topic of conversation. Thoughtfully, I looked up towards the great glacier cirque at the foot of the steep slope coming down towards us from the Negrotto Col – it was a whole tangle of crevasses and threatening seracs, an elongated cone of large chunks of avalanched ice with narrow white passages between. No, the whole approach to the Magic Line has never held any attraction for me! All of a sudden, I fancied I could see a small dot in the middle of that chaos. It was moving fast as I squinted through half-closed lids towards the spot, about two kilometres away, and yes, the dot was actually more of a comma. Somebody was coming down at high speed from Camp 1 and heading towards the seracs, the humpy world of the icefall above the rock buttress about half an hour from Base Camp. Was that Renato?

Now the comma was moving forward almost horizontally across the plateau – there! Then, suddenly, it vanished. Wiped out. I rubbed my eyes in amazement and peered again. Nothing. Nothing at all. Yet I hadn't dreamt it, had I?

Alarm bells began ringing in my head. Why had that tiny figure disappeared so abruptly? There one minute, gone the next? When somebody is shielded from sight by the undulations of the glacier, it's not like that. Or were my eyes simply playing me tricks?

'Michei, did you see anyone – there?' I pointed to the spot, wanting to be sure.

'Yes – there's someone coming down, on the glacier.' So I hadn't imagined it – the figure.

'I think ... oh, I don't know ...' I faltered. 'He vanished so suddenly, that's all. As if he'd been swallowed up ... just as if he'd fallen into a crevasse.' There! I'd said it, and added, 'But I can't be sure.' Now at least the anxiety was shared.

'Whoever it was,' Michei sought to reassure me, 'He's bound to be down in half an hour. Perhaps a little bit more.' It was no good. The worry kept eating away.

It seemed absurd that I could have glanced up at the very moment someone disappeared: it was too much of a coincidence. Yet increasingly I felt that's what had happened. Could it have been Renato? I dared not tell Goretta my terrible suspicion – but at the same time, I could not just do nothing.

I hurried to her tent. She was sitting outside and looked up at my approach.

Julie Has Doubts

'*Ciao*, Kurt. What's the matter?'

'Renato – where is he now?' I tried to sound as calm as I could.

'Still on the ridge.'

For a moment, I felt relief. Then fear clutched at my heart again: *somebody* was on the glacier ... Michei saw it, too ... if not Renato, then who ...?

Something must have happened ...

'It's just that I saw someone, something, further down.' I didn't want to say more than that.

'No, it couldn't have been Renato.' Goretta was positive, but her clear blue eyes continued quietly to scan my face. 'I'll be speaking to him in a few minutes, anyway ... at seven o'clock.'

Was it a Pole, then, I had seen in the cirque? Should I run across to the Polish tents – tell them? Probably nothing had happened at all. In a short while, someone would come stumbling along the moraine. No! I have to tell them right away. Just in case ...

'Goretta, why don't you try now ... with the walkie talkie?'

She looked at me searchingly, a bit surprised. '*E va bene.*' she said, and picking up the handset, called Renato ...

The next moments will stay with me forever. Renato's words, desperate, tumbled over the receiver. He was at the bottom of a crevasse, in a very bad way. That much I gathered from the excited Veneto dialect. Tiny Goretta was shaking with tears. 'We'll get him out fast,' I tried to console her. 'I know exactly where he is ...' She could not be comforted. Grief-stricken, she kept repeating, 'He's dying!' Over and over: 'He's dying!' 'No, no, he won't die – we'll be up there in no time.' I took the walkie-talkie from her: 'Renato! Hold on, we're on our way. I know where you are!' '*Fai presto, Kurt, fai presto.*' Renato implored. Come quickly!

Perhaps he was jammed between the crevasse walls. If that was the case, there wasn't a moment to lose.

Within seconds Base Camp became an anthill. Everybody began running around gathering what was needed to help Renato. 'Rope! Where's a rope?' Then the desperate search. With the ever-increasing emphasis on unroped climbing in the Himalayas – apart, that is, from fixed rope belays – you can sometimes find yourself in the ridiculous position of not being able to find any rope in Base Camp once the rolls of fixed line have been taken to the foot of the mountain.

To rescue Renato, Julie and I took the only rope that was handy, our *Geh-seil* (the rope we used when we were climbing together), a couple of ice screws and ran off. Later, we gave it all to Agostino, who could move faster than we could.

The Endless Knot

We scrambled, gasping, across rocks in the twilight. Agostino, with the walkie-talkie in his hand, kept up a continuous conversation with Renato, talking to him like a father, willing him to live. He would not be alone for much longer, Agostino assured him, we were all running to help him ... as fast as it was possible to run at 5,000 metres. Not knowing how far down the crevasse we would find him, certain only that it was bad and he was injured, we forced ourselves on, stumbling, fighting for breath, up to the edge of the glacier. Every precious minute counted.

To get back to the question of ropes, it would be a good idea for expeditions to keep an emergency rescue kit always ready at Base Camp, so that time is not lost getting things together. In Renato's case, however, we were with him very quickly despite delays, hardly one hour after receiving his call for help from the crevasse. I told Gianni, who was quicker than I, where I thought Renato was, and he hurried ahead with Little Karim. They found him almost immediately when, in answer to their yells, a faint voice issued from a narrow and particularly deep crevasse.

Renato had broken through a snow bridge on the normal route we always took in that place. He was literally only five minutes from the end of the glacier. Moving so fast – as I had seen him – there was probably quite a weight of momentum behind each downward step, so that he thrust harder into the surface than he would have done if travelling more slowly. On the other hand, his speed was insufficient to carry him across to the other side of the crevasse. He probably did not see it coming up, his mind on other things, disappointed no doubt at having had to give up on the SSW Ridge, and in a hurry to get shot of the place now that the months of struggle and hope and disillusion were behind him. In conditions like those, how easy not to see the tell-tale depression in the surface of the snow, a faintly outlined, elongated groove which the path crossed. To one side the crevasse had always been open. The snow at that time of day was wet, heavy and deep, not yet reconsolidated by the evening cold.

As fast as we could, we built up an anchorage point, then Gianni went down on the rope – deeper and deeper. It could have been forty metres that Renato had fallen, going obliquely at first, and then straight down. It was an 'A-crevasse', that treacherous form of fissure you get in depressions and on even, flat glacier surfaces, where the opening is narrow but it gets wider and wider, the deeper it goes. As Gianni told it afterwards, Renato was crouching on the flat bottom of the crevasse, leaning against his rucksack in total darkness, with water running everywhere. He embraced Gianni – or tried to. It must have been a moment of indescribable relief for him.

Julie Has Doubts

In the light of his head-torch Gianni put the harness on Renato, who showed no obvious signs of injury. All the same, the force of so great a fall must surely have caused severe internal damage. He was dying, *tutto rotto*, he had told Goretta on the radio.

God knows, at that moment, hope lived once more in all of us. In Renato too, perhaps, when we started to pull him out. He was quite lucid talking to Gianni, helping himself as much as he could.

But this sense of relief that he was moving upwards out of the crevasse despite his pain, was the last he knew. Before he even reached the overhanging lip of the icy abyss, which we only managed to haul him over with the greatest struggle, he lost consciousness. Despite placing two ice-axes under the rope where it cut into the snow at the edge of the crevasse, it took us several attempts, and all our efforts, to get Renato to the surface. Immediately we muffled him in sleeping bags to keep him warm.

Finally, Gianni was back up beside us.

Renato lay perfectly still on his down bed. We feared the worst. Carefully, we shone the torch into his eyes. His pupils narrowed. He was alive!

Everyone apart from Gianni and me now descended to organize further help. Julie wanted to alert her British compatriots and take care of Goretta.

Shortly after they left, Gianni shone the torch once more into Renato's eyes.

He was dead.

All night long I stood or crouched there, gazing into the darkness, listening to the stones falling from the faces above the cirque, feeling the movements of air ...

Now and then Gianni would change position. Neither of us spoke. I could see the wandering of lights across the glacier, along the moraine, and another light which was moving slowly much higher up, on Broad Peak. Some time soon the British would arrive with their doctor, but it would be too late. Nothing could be done any more. Renato was a still, dark contour in the slope at our side. At some point in the night Gianni interrupted the silence to suggest that, if Goretta agreed, we should bury Renato here in the crevasse on his mountain.

I thought of his life. The only consolation was that he had really lived it. As he wanted to. Not many do that ... Poor Goretta – she does not know yet, but she probably senses what has happened. I'm glad Julie is with her.

Then I think of us, Julie and me: we have always had a tacit agreement that neither should press the other, if he, or she, did not want to go on. And we have kept it like that. I have the feeling too that now, after this night with Goretta, after Renato's death, that Julie might no longer want to continue ... And she shall not, if she doesn't want to. Everybody decides for himself.

Another thought presses in: if one of us at least were to get to the top this time, the thing would be finished. Otherwise K2 would remain the unattained dream: sooner or later we would come back and try again. In my heart, I now felt it was time for us to direct ourselves towards new targets ... beyond the great peaks. Could we do this without having satisfactorily concluded the past? I knew that Julie still had Everest in mind, she spoke also of Makalu: probably neither she nor I would ever escape from the charmed circle of big mountains. During the next five years, we would almost certainly still go now and then to the highest mountains in the world, but my understanding was that we had to go further, into the valleys between and beyond them, to the deserts, to the great forests, had to live with those people who are there, describing their existence with our films – as we had done with Tashigang ...

If just one of us, as a conclusion of our first years together, reached the summit of K2 – wouldn't that be fulfilment for both? Even if only one trod the dream summit? Only one made the dream come true?

I will try it.

As I expected, after Renato's death Julie had no further desire to climb K2 this year, not in this black summer. Did that mean never again, at all?

I was thinking a lot about it, but saw no direct connection between Renato's accident and an ascent by us of the Abruzzi Ridge. Come again next year? That would be our fourth expedition to K2. Again I told myself, if the weather grants you another chance, Kurt, go it alone. If one of us makes it, the mountain won't block our future any longer.

'Don't you think, with all these other people, the situation up there could get out of control?' Julie asked me this once when we were speaking about the possibilities of the ridge. How likely was it that an ascent of the Abruzzi could really get out of hand? Could anybody, after all these fatal accidents, embark on a gamble? I was optimistic. 'If you are self-sufficient,' I said, 'you just don't get yourself involved.' After all, if things snarl up too much, you can always go down. That was my belief. I was wrong. *Four* times, later, Julie and I tried to counter the developing tragedy, consciously or subconsciously, with everything in our power. Yet in vain. Was that fate? Can things happen no matter what you do? Thinking of K2, I still have not found a definite answer, not even today.

Sometimes I returned in my mind to 1984, and whenever I did, I saw us wandering in bright sunshine along the Baltoro Glacier towards Skardu,

Julie Has Doubts

having climbed Broad Peak after eight weeks of siege on K2, where we had been repulsed time and again by storms. Then, on our return, there was suddenly the most glorious weather, for two whole weeks. Yes, we could have climbed the mountain! In our joy of doing our first eight-thousander together, we had no regrets. Yet it is true: we could have done it – then. So what if we got the same conditions now …?

Certainly, most of me would have liked nothing better than to wander back into a green world … But I can't go away yet, I told myself. Whether in the end Julie decides to have another try or not, we can't leave yet. The film is not finished: we have only exposed about half our stock, 2,000 metres, so far. So we must stay for that, and, yes, if by the time that's finished, no other chance for a go at the summit comes up, I'll have to accept it. And I will, calmly. But supposing a chance does present itself, then I want to take it.

Did Julie know somehow in her heart of hearts that she would die up there? This was the only time in many years that she showed a hesitation to push into the unknown – even though, in the end, she still decided to go. I remember once on Nanga Parbat, just before setting out one day, having an urgent compulsion to make out my will – I only had time to scribble my signature on a piece of blank paper for my wife … and then I came back alive anyway. But is there a sixth sense that gives you a presentiment of the end, once you are close to it? As if a comet on collision course with a planet were conscious of the fact – or perhaps more aptly, a spaceship, conscious through its instruments before the crew were aware of the impending danger. Would the crew react to the warning – in time? The inner voices of individuals vary, even given the same situation, perhaps because their destined courses may be different. I am no fatalist, because most of what happens depends ultimately on decisions taken.

The Ice Avalanche and the Riddle of the Teapot

Bilberries are a wonderful fruit – especially on the Baltoro Glacier. Contentedly, I sit in my sleeping bag spooning them into my mouth.

Hey! What's that? A great rumble of thunder?

'Quick – an avalanche!' gasps Julie, ripping open the entrance to the tent.

'Coming ...' Drawing half a breath, I toss the bilberries into a corner and almost tumble headfirst out of the tent in my tiger-spring for the camera, which as always stands at the ready outside. Eye to the viewfinder ... press the button ... motor running ... clouds of snow powder, gigantic, thundering, welling, rolling, exploding out of themselves. Again and again, exploding.

Hundreds of metres high they are! This avalanche must have poured down all of two thousand metres and it is still growing, billowing around and below the Abruzzi. Now the swelling powder clouds blot out the ridge, gobble its features. Whew, it is a giant. Just what our film needs. In high excitement, I hold my breath and keep my finger on the button – not daring to move for fear of ruining the shot – until at last I am forced to struggle for air. 'That was gorgeous!' I pant to Julie, who is in the tent behind me.

'Mmm – wasn't it!' Her face has appeared in the entrance; she has her camera in her hand, and must surely have got some good pictures. She disappears again.

Only now I notice that I am barefoot, and in my underwear: in my giant leap through the tent door, I have stubbed two toes on the loose stones of the moraine.

Avalanches have an imperious command. Especially for cameramen. It's cool, I now realize. I climb back into the sleeping bag. The sky is covered. The avalanche is still mushrooming out of the clouds which wrap the Abruzzi Spur. But a cameraman can't be disturbed by bad weather. When avalanches come – any avalanche – then your finger must be on the button – even if the end of the world is on the way.

It's true, I grunt to myself, changing the magazine, the best a cameraman can hope is that his wedding night is safe from avalanches – then at least the light will not be good enough!

My bilberries! Did they survive?

'There are some cherries left,' Julie offers sweetly from inside the tent. 'Do you want any?'

Cherries, now? Didn't I just stuff myself with bilberries? But cherries on the Baltoro Glacier – who could refuse? Of course I want some!

The Germans bequeathed us all these wonderful delicacies when they left, since when Julie and I have really enjoyed ourselves. Mushrooms, goulash in gravy, casseroles, sauerkraut, sour pickles, cod's roe, anchovy rings, smoked herrings and other tins of fish, crispbread … a heavenly cranberry *compote*: I have to stop … my mouth is watering too much even as I remember it.

Not that we had any complaints about the catering of our Italian friends; they had fantastic ham, all sorts of olives, and always mountains of spaghetti; but regularly when Julie and I went to the Abruzzi Ridge where we looked after ourselves at ABC (Advanced Base Camp, at 5,300 metres, at the foot of the mountain), or even to the high-altitude camps, we felt much healthier. In Base Camp, sooner or later, we all went down with upset stomachs. Julie believed she had finally discovered the source in the brownish sediment at the bottom of the water drum; but Gianni, our second in command, has come to a rather different conclusion – he now thinks it must have been the cleaning-powder, which he says was used too liberally. As not all, but several of the Italians were hit, like us, with statistical regularity, it remains a mystery what it could have been. But perhaps it is possible to acclimatize, even to this?

Whatever the reason, we had now recovered, and felt increasingly better as each day passed. Steve Boyer, the doctor of the American expedition, had given us some green vitamin tablets – a poisonous green – as well as tiny white tablets which contained folic acid; without those, he said, it wouldn't matter what we swallowed, it would have no effect. So I don't know whether our physical uplift was due to the long rest in Base Camp, to the American pills, or to the first-class German cuisine. Perhaps it was a combination of all three.

There remained one shadow, however: sometimes Julie was homesick, it seemed to me. She kept pressing to order the porters for the trip out. So we did; with the gentle help of Captain Neer Khan, liaison officer to the Austrians, we fixed our departure for 5 August. I could sense Julie's relief. The matter was cleared, done, and her customary cheerfulness returned.

Base Camp was now smaller. In some way, you felt the loss of all those who had gone home. One of them was Norman – Norman Dyhrenfurth

– he had looked very tired when he left. Even though his expedition was successful, for him it had not been without personal disappointment: the leader, Dr Karl Herrligkoffer, before flying out from Base Camp (by helicopter), had deputed his personal major-domo, a Hunza who spoke quite good German, to be provisional leader in his stead. Being passed over like this must have given Norman several sleepless, angry nights.

For with his many years of Himalayan experience, Norman could certainly have handled a job like that. But perhaps old mountain lions are always a bit testy with one another. Julie and I got on well with both of them. We visited Herrligkoffer in the Broad Peak Base Camp on his seventieth birthday; and Norman I have held in high esteem ever since our Dhaulagiri expedition of 1960. Having never been on an expedition with Herrligkoffer, I cannot make any judgement, except to remark that he has given many mountaineers their first chance to go to the Himalayas.

It was a cordial goodbye. Julie and I were both sad to see Norman leave.

Whatever else happens, we have to finish the filming. For climbing footage, it will be enough that we can still go as far as Camp 2. We might not be able to get much higher anyway in this weather. But there are things to film, too, at the foot of the spur – like the old oxygen bottle from the year 1954, weathered now to a rusty orange, which we discovered between the ice and rocks there. It had, so the barely legible inscription informed us, belonged to the first climbers of the mountain, the 'Italian expedition under the leadership of Professor Ardito Desio'. On 31 July that year, Lino Lacedelli and Achille Compagnoni reached the summit of K2. Respectfully we weighed the elderly bottle in our hands, and carried it back to our tent at Advanced Base Camp. That we must certainly have on film, and the marvellous ice towers all around there!

... *Ratsch!* ... *ratsch!* ... *ratsch!* ... *ratsch!* go our skis on the wide glacier. We are on our way to the ice fall, climbing on special short skis with skins attached. Once there, we will leave the skis as usual close to the first ice towers, and continue on foot to ABC. When we come down, it is always such a pleasure to be able to shoot home from there and not to have to trudge all the way back.

It is darkish, with, here and there under the clouds, a glint of grey-blue ice on the massive flank of K2. We are now at the edge of the kilometre-wide surface from which the clouds of ice powder rose in the giant avalanche. I see a crushed gas cylinder lying on the ground, all bent and scratched. Enormous forces have been at work here – mighty

The Ice Avalanche and the Riddle of the Teapot

blocks litter the area, and everywhere are strewn bits of ice, small and large, with comet tails of snowdust behind them.

Ratsch, ratsch, ratsch, ratsch ... we hurry away; no place, this, to linger.

Hell, what's this lying here? An old teapot, squashed completely flat!

Ratsch, ratsch, ratsch, ratsch – I hurry on. Suddenly, an idea strikes me. That teapot could illustrate the power of an avalanche better than a hundred words. 'Julie, you go on,' I shout. 'I'll just nip back and get the teapot for the film.' 'OK!' She glides on.

I hurry back. The pot has been squashed very artistically. Aluminium: it really doesn't look that old. Anyway, it's good to have it – we'll film it up at ABC. I stuff it into my rucksack and race to catch up with Julie.

We have almost reached the end of the avalanche zone. As we clear the brow of a hillock we spot three figures spaced out along the foot of the avalanche cone. They are looking for something. They must be Balti porters on their way back to Base Camp. Their loads will have been deposited near the first ice cliff.

They must have found something – two appear to be carrying bits and pieces in their hands, but I can't tell what. Is it the remains of a tent? That is interesting. We stop and call across. The three porters approach us slowly.

There is no reason to be particularly concerned if bits of old expedition gear come down the mountain here – it happens all the time. But for some reason I am curious. Is it the orange piece of cloth which one of them is holding? I've seen something like that before, somewhere. Yes, on the other side of K2 at a height of 7,600 metres we found a torn Japanese tent, and each of us brought home a strip as a memento of the North Spur. Mine is hanging on the wall beside a big picture of K2.

But didn't Quota 8,000 also have such tents? The same colour?

Thoughtfully, I finger the piece of cloth handed to me by the first of the Balti porters, who now stands in front of me. Hmm, I hand it back to him, still uncertain what it can be.

'That looks like Austrian gear!' I hear Julie's clear voice. She is turning a red jersey over in her hands. The front is all ripped.

What's an Austrian pullover doing here – if that is what it is? Julie points emphatically towards the garment, 'It's theirs, I'm almost sure of it. Give it to the Austrians in Base Camp!' She hands it back to one of the three porters. We recognize him: one of the Balti cooks, a cheerful fellow we first met at ABC, where his favourite saying always was, 'The Koreans have everything; they are very, very rich.'

The third Balti on his way back towards Base Camp has nothing in his hands – and immediately after that he is not on his way back to Base Camp any more, either; because, to our surprise, we discover that his load is made up of our own gear from ABC – all stuff we still need! A misunderstanding: this morning we described to him a kitbag we wanted him to fetch down – for a princely bonus – and he has got the message confused, 'mixed it up with a Radetzky march,' as the saying goes in Salzburg. He is not at all pleased to have to carry the whole load back up to ABC again, but that has become his destiny. I wonder darkly what's in the heavy loads of the other two, but it is none of my business. They are porters to the Koreans.

Towards evening we reach ABC, and the Balti, no longer keen to carry down our kitbag, vanishes hastily. My mind is still trying to make sense of the torn pullover and the scrap of orange fabric, but we cannot be absolutely certain that the tent is Italian, nor the pullover Austrian. Why should they be?

We pass a marvellous evening, brew enormous quantities of tea and feast on cranberry *compote*. We are alone with the ice towers, content and happy.

Next day we film the old oxygen bottle. I 'find' it in the scree and, with 'astonishment', pick it up, turn it over slowly, weighing it in my hands and running my fingers up and down its weathered surface – that will do fine for voicing over the history of the first climb.

Similarly, you can juxtapose cookers or double boots – the old and the new – very effectively: my old heavy leather double boots from Everest which I am still wearing because they are so comfortable and because my left knee can't cope with the new man-made materials which haven't the flexibility of leather – set against Julie's modern, lightweight, plastic double boots. And with the film in mind, I have also brought along a petrol mini-stove developed decades ago by grand old master Borde for the Swiss army, and which my friends and I used back in the fifties when we did the Peuterey Ridge Integrale on Mont Blanc, the Eiger North Face, the Walker Spur and God knows what else. Even today, when your gas cartridges run out, there isn't a country anywhere in Asia where you can't find petrol, and so I can still cook with it.

Demonstrating that on film, in conjunction with a camping gaz cooker, is not difficult. We want to make tea anyway. Perhaps I should add that the petrol stove used to be known in mountaineering circles as the Borde Bomb, because if not treated with a proper respect it had the nasty habit of exploding in your face!

Finally, from the rucksack, I pull out the bashed teapot …

'Wow!' says Julie. 'That's really taken a beating!'

It certainly has: it looks as if a furious regiment of mountain goats had trampled on it or terrible claws mauled it; it has been crushed, kicked, bent, scratched. I let my camera roll as Julie scrutinizes it curiously. Her

The Ice Avalanche and the Riddle of the Teapot

concentration, as she tries to imagine its story (faithfully following the film director's instructions), looks real enough. 'OK, you can stop,' I tell her. 'That's enough.' But Julie doesn't look up. Her gaze seems to bore into the aluminium.

'There's a name written on this,' she says at last. And bites her lip.

'A name?' I, too, can now make out faint letters.

'M-A-N-D-I,' Julie reads slowly, a deep crease between her eyebrows. Mandi: that can't be anything but the name of who it belonged to. It sounds Italian, but I don't know anyone with that name. One of the earlier expeditions?

Suddenly I have the feeling I do know the name from somewhere. Could it be an Austrian surname? Does the teapot belong to the Austrians? A picture of the pullover we saw yesterday flashes into my mind – teapot and pullover, of course, there's a connection.

And the orange bits of cloth? Suddenly, I understand. The Quota 8,000 tents which had been under the ice barrier at about 7,750 metres, the tents of our friends which they left up there below the Shoulder, they were exactly this colour. The ice avalanche could easily have broken off from up there. All at once I remember an old Japanese fixed rope, black and yellow, frozen into the ice, on which I was able to put my weight carefully, yet which at a second try, without offering any resistance, came away in my hands. Obviously there were slow movements up there, continuously changing the ice, movements which even a strong rope could not resist. I remember also a crevasse in the ice barrier above that camp, and that enormous 'balcony' weighing many tons which hung over your head when you stood by the tents. Such a good wind-shelter it offered!

If the Austrians left gear up there, then the puzzle is solved. It is clear what happened: everything up there, left by any of us, will now have vanished. We must tell the Austrians right away.

Alfred Imitzer, Willi Bauer, Hannes Wieser, Manfred Ehrengruber ... all are deeply despondent. Their top camp has been wiped out. Willi's expensive cameras will all be smashed – they will obviously have lost everything they stashed up there in the Italian tents. This was to have been their highest support camp, essential to their plans, and the avalanche has smashed it. It's a terrible blow for them.

Nevertheless, they are grateful to us for bringing the news. The teapot question at least is solved: 'Mandi' refers to Manfred Ehrengruber, and he confirms he left it at the support camp, Camp 4.

At first nobody can find the pullover. Didn't the porters hand it over? Nothing seems to be known about it. Only after the Austrians' liaison officer conducts a lightning search among the kitchen personnel –

Hunzas and Baltis – does the thing show up. It turns out to belong to Willi Bauer.

A day later I am standing with him and Alfred Imitzer on the moraine, looking up at the mountain. From here only part of the route is visible. I am terribly worried that the avalanche might also have destroyed Camp 3. That, too, would have been in a direct line with falling ice from the seracs below the Shoulder. I try to convince Willi and Alfred that if they are planning a further attempt, they should take into account that Camp 3 might not be there either. I am most insistent. Something inside me tells me I have to get this home to them. Even at the risk of being thought an old prophet of doom with my admonishing finger, they must know my fears. Their next camp down is more than 2,000 metres from the summit – and without Camp 3 …

Alfred, I notice, hesitates; he has always given weight to what I have had to say. But Willi pooh-poohs the whole idea with an airy wave of his hand: 'If the avalanche had hit 3, then it would have taken quite a different line from where you found the pot.' 'But, Willi, avalanches can divide as well. Camp 3 could easily have been wiped out. ' I almost beg him to take notice. But in vain. When Willi Bauer makes up his mind, that's it.

Even Alfred now seems more inclined to listen to Willi.

We separate .. , none of us is very happy.

Perhaps it's a storm in a teapot anyway and there is no chance of going for the summit again – not in this miserable weather …

The ice avalanche. The debris suggested the destruction of both the high Austrian camps with the resulting likelihood of a tent shortage on their summit bid.

The Decision — We Go Together

Willi Bauer taps his altimeter. The weather is getting better. In the British camp they are packing to leave: only Alan Rouse and Jim Curran, the cameraman, will stay behind. Alan wants to have one more go at the mountain, this time by the Abruzzi Ridge, and with Mrufka, the Polish girl. If we are indeed to be granted one last chance, it looks as if it is coming up now. The Koreans are already preparing for another attempt. I am pleased that Alan will be on our route: I first met him on my lecture tours in Britain, and have always admired his dynamism. Julie knows him too, of course, he is one of the best British mountaineers. Secretly, I wonder whether this, together with the general renewal of activity, will influence her to change her mind about going up again. I love life no less than she does, and have no intention of risking my neck – not even for the mountain of my dreams – but we know this route well enough now, certainly as far as the Shoulder: it is only beyond that the question of 'yes' or 'no' arises. If we get that far, and things don't work out, well, we just come down again. If the weather breaks, we turn back . The only way it could go wrong is for there to be a sudden change during our summit bid, when we're already very high ... but, some degree of risk is inevitable – always.

I don't mention any of this to Julie – she knows it well enough herself – but I have the feeling that she is chewing things over. It could not be otherwise; I know her too well. Wouldn't it be best simply to take everything we need for our filming up to Camp 2 which we have to do anyway – and just in case, take along whatever else would be necessary for an attempt on the summit? That's what I think we should do. And, watching Julie out of the corner of my eye, I see that is what she seems to be doing ... Again, I tell myself that a decision does not have to be taken now; it will depend on the weather, on the circumstances ... in the last resort, it is up to how we feel when we're up there. Somehow, without Julie having said a word, I form the impression that she has had a change of heart.

Yesterday, when Willi Bauer asked me vaguely whether, if the worst came to the worst, he and I might tackle the summit together, I gave an equally vague response. But now I make the point of going over to speak to him. 'Willi, I think Julie probably wants to go after all.' He shakes his head thoughtfully, then laughs, 'Oh, well ...' and shrugs his shoulders. Later on, I see him heading out of Base Camp towards the Abruzzi with three other Austrians. It is 28 July. As for Julie and myself, we have a last-minute hitch: five porters suddenly turn up who could carry some of our gear out to Skardu. We ought not to miss this opportunity – you never know here whether you will really see porters when you expect them. Captain Neer Khan, liaison officer to the Austrians, one of the friendliest and most helpful people I have ever met on an expedition, helps us to negotiate with them. Finally, we see the small group on its way, under the charge of a wild-looking, bearded Balti, a giant of a man who carries, as a 'special load', the big movie camera in its metal case. No matter how we try to hurry, Julie and I do not get away until almost evening. And then, at the very last moment, I forget to bring my sunglasses, which are hanging at the entrance of our Phazor dome-tent. (I only notice it that night on our arrival at ABC. With the walkie-talkie out of order, there is no way of reaching Alfred, who might have brought them up for me when he comes later: however, Heli, an extreme skier in the Austrian party, is good enough to lend me his spare pair. He must have given up his plans for skiing down from the Shoulder, I suppose ... but not the summit apparently. I do have one pair of skier's dark storm goggles, but would never set out without a pair of normal snow goggles as a spare. So, I am very grateful to him for saving me a trek back.)

It is dusk when we climb through the icefall.

Julie says suddenly, 'I told Jim we had to get our cameras down from Camp 2 ... which isn't true.'

'That's all right – it's not his affair, what we do,' I reassure her. Julie ought not to worry over the odd white lie – she gave the diplomatic answer, that's all.

Maintaining an easy pace, we continue up through the icefall towards ABC.

We go on cooking late into the night. Again and again I feel my way down to the small stream at the foot of the boulder slope to fetch water. Stars are twinkling high above me ... I wonder what that means? Finally, we close the door of our tent and drop fast asleep in no time – so deeply asleep that we do not hear the Austrians make their early start. Clearly they want to climb straight up to 2, leapfrogging Camp 1. Some of them do not have much time before they are due to catch their return flight from Islamabad. We have a relaxed morning in the sun; I film the

The Decision – We Go Together

Austrians higher up on the spur, and Broad Peak bathed in sunshine, and the ice towers. To get to Camp 1, we don't have to leave until noon or early in the afternoon.

We will take along the small 16mm movie camera and maybe a dozen magazines for it ... but they are very heavy. Add all the other equipment, gas, food – even if we do have some stashed higher up – it's quite a load. We don't need sound, so I am surprised to see Julie loading her mini tape-recorder, and wonder if she intends dictating her diary into it, or something for the movie? Unless ... More and more, as she carefully checks, arranges, prepares everything with her usual precision, I become convinced that my companion, like me, has more in mind than a simple film trip to Camp 2. I have felt this ever since Base Camp, but have not dared pin hopes on it: now I can see with my eyes that it's true. We will go up together – as always. We will make our attempt together. I am deeply moved. So, in the end, she did decide to come after all.

Without realizing it, I have stopped my own packing to watch her: as if she feels my gaze, Julie suddenly says in a low voice, 'I know I didn't want to go up any more ... but I've changed my mind.'

I am silent, unable to find words. Now she has said it. There is no doubt any more. We shall attempt the summit together. The happiness that surges through me is beyond words, as if all the years of my life were concentrating here in this single moment. Everything that we have experienced together on K2 floods back to fuse with this moment – to create an entity, a oneness. I would have tried it alone, was ready to, but somehow that would have been absurd. Perhaps I would not have got far before turning back; I don't know ... Now I am just indescribably happy. We are no longer divided, as it seemed to me sometimes we were during this period of indecision. I know, too, that since we will now be together, it will be much easier to turn back, if there's a reason for it – that will be no problem; it is just that the two of us are together, on our way for a final try, and that alone makes me so happy.

'It may divide you forever ...' The thought comes like a bolt from the blue. For a moment, I am struck rigid with astonishment, then joy and high spirits drive away all forebodings: what on earth could separate us, since we will, as always, be on the one rope – and if the summit is not possible, we will turn around.

I put the thought out of my mind. Now, we have to concentrate very thoroughly and precisely. We have to be extremely realistic. Since the avalanche broke off at the ice barrier, below the Shoulder, we have to consider that associated shock waves might have caused other snowfields to collapse also. In the worst instance, it could have brought down everything right up onto the Shoulder. But even if Camp 3 has been destroyed,

The Endless Knot

it will not matter to us since we do not have anything there. Our depot – in a duffel bag at the foot of a bluish serac, a little further up – does not contain very much, either, and we know we have lost the few not very important items we had stowed inside the Italian tent which was torn away by the avalanche. None of these is very serious – but what about our depot on the Shoulder itself? Our whole Camp 4? Is that still intact?

To be on the safe side, we have to assume it no longer exists. So our green bivouac tunnel tent is hanging in the duffel bag at the rock tower below House's Chimney – we can get that from there; sleeping bags, however, we will have to bring along from here. Also from here, we must take our thick woollen balaclavas, the gloves, head-torches, batteries, a stove, enough gas, some food … Everything else is already on the spur.

But bigger and bigger grows the pile of things that should go with us. I left my warm Javelin over-gaiters up on the Shoulder in case of another try – they might have gone, I'll need some more. So I pack an orange pair of Japanese full-gaiters which we bought in the bazaar in Kathmandu on our way back from Tashigang. Julie's down trousers were up on the Shoulder too, so I see to it that we take mine along for her, just in case. Three pairs of gloves each, spare socks, the thin silk balaclavas. What a good thing we doubled up on almost everything. When I finally try and hoist my rucksack, I can hardly shift it off the ground. 'A pig of a bloody load!' Even Julie's pack is unbearably heavy. So we empty the bags and start again. Finally, we reduce the film magazines by half, but not much else can be jettisoned (it's only when we're climbing that I notice my down trousers were left behind in camp after all).

On top of everything, we take an extra load, just for today, to give us some luxury on the way up to Camp 1 – juices and tinned fruit salad. And since, just before we get there, there's a wall where we can get good pictures of ourselves struggling, heavily laden, through some rust-coloured, vertical rocks, with crampons scratching the slabs, we shoot off two of the magazines here. We can leave the exposed magazines behind in the next camp to be picked up on the way down. So, that only leaves three more for higher up … If we do go for the summit, how high will we tote the movie camera, anyway? We can always take slides.

Julie's familiar cheeky expression is back, the understanding between us, all as it ever has been – the crisis of uncertainty over, I take a deep breath, not just because of the heavy load on my shoulders … happiness goes with us. Whether or not we make it to the top, this will be a fitting ending. Even if the weather stops us going higher than the Shoulder, and the whole struggle is for nothing, we can return home then with no

The Decision – We Go Together

complaints. Better to have tried and not made it than to have not tried, and wasted the opportunity.

Good God! Is that Camp 1? The Korean tents topple forlornly like old toadstools. The sun's powerful rays have melted away much of the snow, including that underneath the tents. Our tent, too, has developed an alarming tilt; lying inside is like being in a bed from which somebody has stolen two of the legs. For security, I lash a rope to the nearest rock, passing it through the entrance, and we both sleep belayed in our harnesses. It doesn't seem worth the effort of taking it down and putting it up again, flattening out another platform and all that – and Julie says she doesn't mind. I simply stuff extra rocks under her side for support. We are used to a bit of discomfort.

It's a bit stormy during the night, but nothing too bad; higher up, however, as we learn in the morning, it must have been much worse. We can't believe our eyes suddenly to see two tired figures stumbling down across the steep slope of snow and rock beneath the towers, close to where House's Chimney makes a deep cleft in the shining yellow barrier of rock. They're Austrians ... not Willi – I would have recognized him immediately from his short, stocky figure – it must be two of the young lads. And yes – when they get closer we see it is Siegfried Wasserbauer and Helmut Steinmassl. They have both decided to pack it in. It was terribly stormy up there, they tell us, and anyway – one of them makes a deprecatory gesture – 'Enough is enough,' he says laconically. Julie and I make tea and the other two start taking down one of their tents to take back to Base Camp. Suddenly I hear '*Kreuzbirnbam!*', one of those all-purpose Austrian oaths, followed by laughter. 'The tent is full of water! It's unbelievable!' I jump to take a look and call Julie too. I certainly have never seen anything like this: the tent is like a filled bath-tub! Condensation? Powder snow – blown in and then melted? 'Well, there's one thing you *can* say: your tent's certainly waterproof!' I grin at my compatriots: 'Especially the lower half!'

How on earth to get rid of so much water? There must be nearly 30 litres in there. 'Seems a pity to waste it – you could take the highest bath in the world!' I ought not to joke at my friends' expense. 'Best thing would be to stab it with a knife, on the downhill side, close to the ground ...' As I offer my helpful advice, I'm already standing by with the movie camera ... The Swiss Army knife stabs at the swollen belly, then a jet of water spurts into space in a high curve, to finish as a stream running down the slope. Water sports above the Godwin-Austen Glacier. They couldn't have had more fun at the noble water games in Salzburg's Hellbrunn Castle, where Archbishop Markus Sittikus regularly soaked his guests. When the tent is finally drained, the two poor lads still have to scoop out armfuls of ice that the morning sun had not yet had the chance to melt. Only then could they roll up their no longer perfect, but still basically watertight, tent. Meanwhile the tea is ready and we all have a drink together before they begin their descent. As they leave, they present me with a burner from one of their Husch stoves; this will fit onto the extremely lightweight gas cylinder I got from Alfred in Base Camp, which I plan to use on the summit day. Alfred didn't have any burners in Base Camp and told me to keep my eye open for one on the mountain. After struggling with too much weight on our first summit attempt, this time I have worked everything out to the last gram, with the pedantry of a Benoît Chamoux.

A Husch cylinder with burner weighs far less than a camping Gaz stove – that will be our standby in case we bivouac on the summit assault. Julie will go with just a hip-bag for the final day, and I with a superlight Japanese rucksack, which will hold all we need (that, too, came from the bazaar in Kathmandu). For the time being, however, we are both pack mules. That's why we decide to leave the heavy 16mm camera here and to shoot off all the remaining film magazines before we go. Already another subject has presented himself. Hannes Wieser, twinkle-eyed and laughing as usual and wearing his customary black hat, swings into view over the crest of snow below camp. It means that Willi and Mandi (proprietor of the teapot) will soon have company – if they haven't already gone on. Alfred, too, has arrived, tall as a tree and full of energy (he was here even before Hannes). We film each other, drinking tea, and Julie looks up at 'her' Broad Peak. She seems a little tired after the night in our tilted tent, but her eyes shine with that imperturbable spirit, which has already seen her through so much. Soon we will climb up to our tent at Camp 2. We are collecting our stuff together. The camera and the films we will leave hanging inside a small bag under the roof of this dome tent, well up off the ground – heeding the warning of the Austrians' 'bath-tub'.

By the time we are about 100 metres above the camp and look back a multicoloured group has appeared. It must be the Koreans and their high-altitude porters. With so many people coming, we get a move on.

Having picked up the bivouac tent and some gas from our rocktower depot, I struggle under my heavy load through House's Chimney. I can understand why high-altitude porters often refuse to climb without fixed ropes. Only when you have done the job – for that's what it is – yourself, can you understand the problems. Anyone who is familiar with alpine-style climbing in the Himalayas knows from experience – from his own

The Decision – We Go Together

oversized rucksack – how much effort the mountaineer is spared by having a porter. Even with other styles of climbing, there is still plenty of opportunity to find out what ferrying loads is all about. Almost everyone who reaches a Himalayan summit has got there by dint of very hard work.

There is no doubt that without the help of high-altitude porters – above all, the Sherpas, but also the hardy Hunzas – many expeditions would never have reached their goals. These mountain people have a strength which would do credit to a mountain buffalo – were there such a thing. 'Himalayan tigers' is the traditional epithet for Sherpas, but nobody has yet come up with the perfect synonym, either for the men from the East (*Shar* = East, *pa* = people) who until the fifteenth century lived in Kham in eastern Tibet, from where after decades of migration – 2,000 kilometres across the high plateau – they came over the Himalayas to settle in the high valleys of Nepal and Sikkim; or for the wild Hunzas from the high valley of the same name in northwestern Pakistan, who defended their independence so fiercely and successfully for so long and were notorious until the end of the nineteenth century for making surprise raids on camel caravans crossing the Karakoram Pass. Courage as well as strength characterizes both Sherpas and Hunzas, and it's not surprising that quite often their bodies have developed an incredible tolerance to high altitude, exceeding that of many expedition mountaineers. There are Sherpas whose bravery has become legendary – several have died trying to rescue their 'sahibs' on Himalayan ventures. And still today, avalanches, storms, rescue missions regularly claim victims from among their number. In 1939, here on K2, Pasang Kikuli died together with two other Sherpas, after climbing the Abruzzi Spur in bad weather to bring down the sick and exhausted Dudley Wolfe from one of the high camps: they disappeared in the storm. These people look at mountains and at mountaineering with different eyes from us. I have already told of Nawang Tenzing, my friend and rope companion of several expeditions. With him I went to the summit of Makalu, and with Nawang Dorje I climbed Dhaulagiri. I am not certain whether my third indigenous partner for an ascent of an eight-thousander was a Hunza or not. Fayazz Hussain and I climbed Gasherbrum II together: he was our liaison officer – I feel quite sure that the dynamic Fayazz must have come from the mountain area in northwestern Pakistan. In all three cases we enjoyed a good relationship, were friends and remained so.

Unfortunately, attempts on the part of the expedition participants to understand the world of the locals remain sketchy – that's if any attempt is made at all. Only when you speak the language – even a little – when you try to understand their life and their religion, do certain things become clear in your mind; and you are not surprised when, for instance, someone like brave Pasang Dawa Lama (who later stood on the top of Cho Oyu with Herbert Tichy), having climbed to almost 8,400 metres here on K2 in 1939, resisted going any higher for fear of the evil spirits that come out at night – something which cost Fritz Wiessner the summit. You could say that fleeing from night demons indicates a very sound sense of self-preservation.

As well as such legendary figures, there are also some very ordinary mortals amongst these mountain people. Throughout one expedition, Julie and I couldn't help wondering whether the Balti who came with the glowing recommendation of one famous mountaineer was really the man he said he was – or his brother. At least he was happy and an outstanding singer!

High-altitude porters are paid according to rules laid down for expeditions by the government. Besides their wages they must be supplied with a complete mountaineering outfit: but if you give this too early, they scurry off to the bazaar and sell it all. Sometimes they show up with old tattered gear from other trips. You should not be angry – because these people are not rich – and of course it's natural to try to make good money out of the equipment. In fact, you can buy the most modern equipment the world has to offer in the bazaar in Kathmandu! In Pakistan, such things are more usually shared out within families: I did not find much in the bazaars there. For these people, the lure to possess things from the faraway and 'exotic' countries of the mountaineers, as well as curiosity and vanity, besides just simple poverty, leads to desires being awakened that are mostly impossible to satisfy – a shining tubular steel ski-stick here can give its owner a prestige akin to the possession of a Porsche ... at least he thinks so.

Except when you are on the mountain, in the real throes of the climb, you should not take it too tragically if things disappear. Such petty offences are the exception rather than the rule, and it is balanced by the fact that they themselves willingly offer you what little they have. Hunzas for instance are famous for the greatest generosity and honesty. Towards the end of an expedition, however, you can find on several Himalayan peaks that the mountain becomes a sort of goldmine for the locals ... the conservationists' target of a 'clean mountain' could easily become reality without much effort, provided a little time and encouragement were devoted to it. Travellers to the Himalayas will notice that the less an area has been visited by strangers, the less likely it is that they lose even the smallest items – quite the reverse, for often it is you that will be given gifts. At a later stage of a place being opened to outsiders, locals may be too timid to ask for items which to them seem to represent 'riches beyond measure', but which they would nevertheless like to have; perhaps then, something might disappear.

It didn't matter much that our good Hayat in the Hindu Kush filched a few packets of nuts for his children: he was a bit uncomfortable when Tona silently gave him a whole boxful. With Musheraf it was rather more difficult: he had an incredible talent for invention when it came to explanations of what had become of our ski-sticks: they fell into crevasses, into mountain streams, they rolled down the steep slopes – but he was such a fantastic man, so full of energy for our climbs, and again and again would generously bring us fresh apples from his village which was three days' walk away. He obviously had a good number of friends with fruit trees – all of whom had an insatiable need for ski-sticks! In the end we came to a mutual and good-natured understanding, overlooking his little foibles by regarding them rather as a 'ski-stick tax'. Musheraf turned a little red in the face when I told him that I should hang on to one stick at least for the journey back. Since then, I always carry an abundance of ski-sticks on expeditions.

Apropos of which, each of us, Julie and I, have one ski-stick firmly fixed onto our rucksacks! This certainly makes climbing up through House's Chimney very awkward, but the end is almost in sight now. Even though we both know it by heart (in two years we have climbed up here about a dozen times), the chimney remains a struggle when you are heavily loaded, despite the fixed ropes and the old metal caving ladder. Gasping for breath, I take another rest ...

In 1954, the Italians installed one of their winches here – a sort of rope hoist to ferry up their material. The rock barrier reaches a height of eighty metres, and the great chimney of ochre-coloured dolomitic rock cuts through it at this point in an oblique line; in difficulty, it is not dissimilar to a section of the big curving couloir on the Matterhorn North Face. Towards the end, it grows so narrow that my huge rucksack keeps snagging against the wall. Chunks of ice rain down into the depths.

At last I'm through, and call down to Julie that she can follow. She has been sheltering behind a projecting rock out of the line of fire of all those ice chunks and stones I have set off during my ascent. Her reply floats up – she's climbing. Apart from this almost vertical cliff, the Abruzzi Ridge has an average inclination of forty-three degrees. Above about 7,000 metres, on the slabs of the Black Pyramid, the angle steepens to fifty to fifty-five degrees, and only after 2,000 metres of height gain from the foot of the mountain, do you get the more gentle slopes of the so-called Shoulder. Today – as distinct from in 1954 – only the highest snow shoulder just below the summit pyramid (between about 7,800 and 8,000 metres) is referred to by this name. Higher up, it gets very steep again – all the way to the summit!

Camp 2 ... 6,700 metres ... we've almost made it! Already I can see the friendly red glow of our Basque tent up there, sheltering in the lee of a high rocky islet and dug into the fairly steep, packed snow which coats the gravel slope. Nowadays, this airy position with its panoramic views over Concordia and the wild Baltoro peaks serves as Camp 2 for most expeditions, although originally it used to be Camp 5. The first climbers established a total of nine camps, something which had advantages and disadvantages.

Julie and I climb the last few steps together and hurry towards the camp, full of anticipation – and relief that for today at least the effort is over.

Whatever's happened to our tent? Christopher Columbus! It's a Spanish caravel in full sail, run aground in the snow! Fantasy. 'Don't exaggerate,' I scold myself. 'When it's only the top sail you see.'

Blown snow, which the wind has collected from the mountainsides over the last three weeks, has built up against the tent, causing the fabric to yield, wherever possible, under the pressure; the top of the tent, however, being secured by a rope to an anchorage in the slope higher up, could not give – and now the whole structure is a series of undulating curves, between pressure and tension, like some untitled creation of a modern artist

Untitled? No – it has to be 'The Spanish Caravel'! In my time, I've seen an enormous variety of names given to the untitled works of great artists (artists who may or may not be a 'name' in their own right)! The only people who might possibly object to naming this particular opus after a Spanish sailing ship, could be our Basque friends from whom we acquired it.

'Half an hour's work,' says Julie drily then, laughing, she nods at the tent meaningfully. Half an hour of shovelling before we can live in here again ... that should do it. She knows how much I enjoy spade-work – even as a student in Vienna, long before we met, I often exhausted my energy in this way. Shovelling enlarges your breathing passages – essential for mountaineering, I console myself. Soon chunks of snow are flying out over the slope, blocks of snow are smashing and rolling down the mountain until they become smaller and smaller balls and in time they dissolve entirely to dust. While I am digging away, Julie pulls strongly at the fabric, readjusts the tent poles and guys: luckily, nothing is broken.

Finally, it's done: how beautiful, if you have really worked hard for your hours of peace, to be lying in your sleeping bag, sipping your soup, looking effortlessly from the door down over the whole world – we have left it open on purpose. Once more we are having a really good time.

But now we're tired: we lean our heads against the snow wall behind the fabric and fall asleep, content and happy. Quite early for us – it's only afternoon.

Herds of stampeding buffaloes? What is it? Alien yells disturb our idyll. Am I dreaming of a Western? Red River Raid, perhaps? An ambush?

'*Patsch!*' Swearing, I sit up; something has hit me on the head. '*Porca miseria!*' I yell out loud. Three more blocks of snow have thundered against the side of the tent.

'Calm down.' Julie soothes; 'it's the Koreans' altitude porters.' Outside, there is a moment's quiet, then comes the sound of loud laughter and foreign voices joking – at least now only small chunks are hitting the tent.

'The blessed shovel must needs serve the community ...' I do my best to remain objective, and bury my head in the sleeping bag. Of course, there are others, like me, who enjoy shovelling – but now, not a metre away from me, a Hunza's ice-axe begins pounding the ground. Closer and closer – he's already touching the tent, for goodness' sake – one false stroke and he'll have a hole in my head. I explode, leaping up again. '*Himmelkreuzdonnerwetter!* Watch out for the tent!' I bellow. Outside an invisible Korean intervenes, and the metallic hammering close to the tent ceases; I am grateful to him for that. But the general noise goes on for hours – the clattering of pots, shouts, slurping, laughing, moaning, snoring – a high-altitude symphony. At times it's overlaid by the reverberating movements of someone crossing the slope and hanging onto the tents and fixed ropes for support ... or hacking new snow for cooking.

Julie has long since disappeared deep inside her sleeping bag. She has a way of overcoming situations like this without losing her equanimity: an ability that I admire and envy. No sleep comes my way.

Then I remember something: up here in 1984 we had to sit out two days of violent storms, during which we read Herbert Tichy's *Weisse Wolken über Gelber Erde* (White Clouds over a Yellow Land), gusts battering the tent as I translated, and Julie listening as best she could over the clamour of the wind. K2 was giving us a good piece of its mind, then, on storm trumpets that were far louder than this.

With such thoughts, I finally drop asleep despite the Hunza symphony.

Pushing to Great Heights

Whichever way you climb, with or without high-altitude porters, whether or not you adopt alpine-style, you have to conserve all the energy you can. You should climb only after you have become totally acclimatized and without carrying too much weight. (The higher you are, the more you feel it.) If you share out a group's equipment in a sensible manner, and if you build up depots beforehand, you can reduce the average weight carried: the same applies to the division of exhausting work like trail-breaking, not only when you're going alpine-style, but also, for instance, when employing what is known as the Hanns-Schell technique, where the person in the lead makes use of the group's only oxygen apparatus, handing over the set when he hands over the lead. That way supplementary oxygen goes only to the person breaking trail.

On K2 I cannot see any disadvantage in climbing up slowly and conserving energy on the first half of the mountain: in my opinion you then arrive at a great height in better condition than if you had 'run'. However, from 7,000 to 7,500 metres onwards (the latter being the height at which the so-called Death Zone starts) the number of days given to climbing and descending should be kept as low as possible. The actual height at which you make the transition will vary a little from person to person. If someone has adopted a special tactic which involves carrying practically nothing, then he might do it in a different way – like Benoît Chamoux, who was working in tandem with a group that started a day ahead of him, so that going up to join his friends he climbed at a predetermined rate, with practically no stops at all, enabling him to maintain the same rhythm all the way to the top, climbing night and day. However, dire consequences would befall anyone wanting to break records in this way who had not made all the necessary preparations; blind dedication to speed alone is incompatible with safety and is, I feel, already having negative side effects.

But if you have to carry more to enable you safely to spend longer on the upper half of the mountain, you should – and will prefer to – climb more slowly. There is the danger that essential food and equipment will be left behind in the interests of gaining speed … and that actually reduces the safety of all the people on the mountain at that time.

Normally, an ascent using supplementary oxygen cannot be carried out, or does not make sense, without high-altitude porters. When climbing without oxygen and without such porters – in the West Alpine style of Hermann Buhl – everything that is going to be needed should be transported up and cached in depots or high camps before the top is stormed. Nowadays, the modern alpine-style mountaineer often tries to omit this phase (the pure West Alpine-style without fixed camps, as used on Chogolisa and Skilbrum in 1957, is referred to as alpine-style today) and so he sometimes arrives at great altitude insufficiently acclimatized. If a route is planned to be done in pure alpine-style, then you need to prepare yourself, train and practise on another route or another mountain beforehand. The much quoted ascent of Hidden Peak by Messner and Habeler in 1975 – two mountaineers on their own with a mobile high camp – was an admirable performance, but it was not pioneering: the technique they used was not new, nor was it correct to claim this as the first eight-thousander to be climbed in West Alpine style – for Hermann Buhl set both these precedents. He pioneered both the idea and the name for it. Even Reinhold Messner only followed the tracks of Hermann Buhl in that respect (the attempt on Chogolisa and the ascent of Skilbrum in 1957 were already examples of perfect alpine-style and somewhat purer than that used on Hidden Peak).*

That K2 with its great altitude and steepness deserves its title of 'mountain of mountains' has been proved many times over the years, not just because of its extraordinary beauty, but also for being 'a mountain above other mountains'. In comparison to K2, fellow eight-thousanders in the Karakoram – Broad Peak, Gasherbrum II and Hidden Peak – and all the higher seven-thousanders, are still a 'full storey below' this giant. Whatever applies for them is only part of the story for K2. There, the mountaineer experiences his few minutes' worth or half an hour of summit joy at the most only one or two rope-lengths above 8,000 metres, whereas on K2, an equivalent height just brings him to the last high camp. A decisive difference: it means that anyone on K2 has to be able to stay above 8,000 metres for very much longer – for days longer.

* This concern with style has been much debated, particularly during the race to be the first to complete ascents of all the 8,000m peaks. Any Himalayan ascent achieved in alpine or neo-alpine style is meritorious, be it a one-push success (with bivouacs or lightweight camps) or with climbers setting up and stocking one or two lower camps and then making a lightly-equipped summit bid. The lapse in ethical purity comes when fixed ropes are established to ease awkward sections (often in ice-falls but sometimes at technical sections on the route itself, e.g. House's Chimney) or when porters or other support climbers are used. The precise meaning of the word bivouac has, to some extent, been changed by the improvement in lightweight tent design – it being a moot point about when a bivouac sac becomes a tent, poles now being so light that the difference is marginal.
  The Messner/Habeler Gasherbrum 1 (Hidden Peak) climb was lauded not so much for its precise purity or innovation, but more as a dramatic re-affirmation, in the 1970s, about the way Himalayan climbing might develop at a time when the seige-style expedition had become dominant. *[Editor]*

The Korean Tent

The Black Pyramid: its rocks split by frost, glued back together by ice – a structure made up of fragments, and steep enough in places to lean against – shattered slabs, with here and there vertical breaks like giant steps.

The porter column scratches, clanks and pants its way across the rocks above us, punctuated every now and again by a shout, in a Korean voice or some Hunza dialect. We follow close on the heels of the porters, but don't intend climbing as far as Camp 3. We can imagine what the overcrowding will be like there – we won't find any of the peace and quiet a mountaineer needs just before an eight-thousander. There will be no opportunity for concentration, for imagination, for focusing every last fibre of being on what lies ahead. Hermann Buhl identified this phase as decisive before any big mountaineering effort – we often talked about it. The whole night before a big climb he sometimes spent in a state between waking and sleeping: a kind of trance, Hermann used to say, completely dedicated to the mountain.

For my own part, I prefer some sleep before setting out ... 'We will overnight in the 7,000-metre camp, and continue climbing tomorrow,' I tell myself. Michel Parmentier's lightweight *parapluie* tent, which he donated to us when he left, should be up there inside Wanda's tent; it's a little dome that you erect in the same way as opening an umbrella, and it holds two people – just. Julie is clearly already looking forward to this magic contraption – as if in some way it shared the Gallic allure of its owner. (The suave French journalist talks altogether too much to my way of thinking, but I guess that goes with the job – really I suppose I shouldn't mind.) I have more confidence in our own narrow but uncomplicated British bivouac tent – a streamlined, dark-green tunnel with a front extension in which you can cook – even if you have to lie down to do so – and this does not even weigh one and a half kilograms. Of course, it is a bit tight for two (very tight, Julie says!), but remarkably stable. It stood the test well on our Broad Peak climb, but Julie claims that you can't move once you're inside it. So I guess that for the summit, we will be exchanging this tent I have tied onto my rucksack for the one with the

The Korean Tent

French chic. If our depot on the Shoulder of K2 is still in existence, as we hope but rather doubt, then we will also have our blue Ultimate tunnel tent. This has proved itself stormproof, and in the event that it's there, we will certainly use that.

Suddenly the column stops in its tracks – dissent, a cacophony of voices. 'What's the matter?' I yell upwards.

'Camp 3, finish!' calls back a Hunza, letting his heavy load slide from his shoulders and crash on to the rocks; he has obviously lost all motivation. Camp 3, finish – gone!

Of course – the avalanche. The same thundering cloud of ice and snow that brought down Mandi's teapot, that squashed and battered it so unrecognizably under the force of the ice blocks, as well as ripping Willi's sweater, the same avalanche that carried away the tatters of the Italians' tents from the assault camp at 7,700 metres and dumped them in the valley had then also, as I feared, got as far as Camp 3, and devastated that.

A figure appears: it's Mandi – Mandi Ehrengruber. Pale, with a ravaged expression and rapid movements, as if fear still stalked him. He must have spent a sleepless night on the site of the destroyed camp up there at 7,350 metres, exposed no doubt to the full blast of the icy winds from China and worried all the time about what else might come down from higher up the mountain.

He sees us and stops. 'Camp 3 is gone, Camp 4 as well,' he says dully. 'The whole serac wall above the Italian tents has come down. My God, you can't imagine what that slope looks like.' We regard him silently – his face tells more than volumes of words. His eyes wander.

'I've had enough,' he says at last, turning to face Julie and me again and shrugging his shoulders in resignation – so far as his rucksack allows. 'Every bloody thing's gone from up there.' He breathes heavily, 'All that effort for nothing.' Utter disappointment and tiredness sound in his voice. It alarms me. 'And Willi – what's he doing?' I ask. 'He found a Korean tent – the only one to escape damage. He's going on.' Well – Willi, I think, a lot more has to happen before this one gives up!

'What are the chances of more stuff coming down?'

'Plenty, I should think. Snow-slips, I'm sure, are still possible. It's difficult to tell.' He turns to leave, taking hold of the fixed rope. 'I've had a bellyful, anyway ...'

'Safe journey, Mandi – take care!' Julie calls after him.

I bite my lip. It's going to be chaos ahead.

Above us a great commotion has started up, yelling voices cut the air. The news has hit everyone like a bomb. We work our way up towards the group of gesticulating porters and the stunned Koreans trying to calm them down. But the porters have good reason to be upset; they have not just thrown their bags into the snow on a whim – they're frightened. They're afraid that the whole place which they are trying to reach will be destroyed. One is worried that he will not find any shelter for the night, others that they will no longer make it down again before nightfall. Above us rears the Black Pyramid with its notorious slabs, the most difficult section of the Abruzzi Ridge.

The leader of the porters pleads to turn back, insisting to the Koreans with increasing urgency that it is madness to go on. When his entreaties fall on deaf ears, his frustration finally spills over.

'You will all die!' he yells.

Even today, writing these lines, I can still hear the cry: it was at once a shriek of fear and a terrible warning. Arms uplifted in supplication; the wide-eyed troubled stare; the note of pleading in the voice of the normally so cheerful and determined Mohammed Ali, as he begged and begged, 'Please, don't go on – you will all die!' That is something I will never forget.

The news from above had changed the situation at a stroke. Panic and desperation now reigned. Terror in the face of such forces of destruction as had been operating up there was written in almost every face. To know finally the full and devastating effect, the extent of the ice avalanche – which I had feared – was shattering. Even if Julie and I had no supply point within reach of the avalanche (apart from that almost empty duffel bag by the ice tower above Camp 3), we were still faced with the big question of what now should be done – and the Koreans, too, were scratching their heads. It was as if suddenly a dark star had risen over everybody on the ridge, as if its invisible light mingled with the sun's rays, which until a moment ago were playing so cheerfully on the steep ribs and crumbling towers of the Abruzzi. The ice of the serac cliffs far above us now took on a dangerous glint – the sunlight still beamed in the wide sky above the Baltoro mountains, but it no longer carried the promise of good fortune.

Had the falling ice been the pointing finger of Allah, warning the bearded leader of the porters? And why only him? Was the man a clairvoyant? My steps slowed. So compelling were his gestures, so vehement the words of Mohammed Ali, they certainly seemed like a voice from Beyond. I hesitated, glancing at Julie: 'We'll go as far as the 7,000-metre camp, shall we?' It was only a couple of ropes' lengths further on, tucked under a rock wall. My companion nodded earnestly, if a little thoughtfully. 'Of course,' she said. Both of us had now stopped.

Throughout the argument between the Koreans and their high-altitude porters – which language difficulties of necessity made a long-

The Korean Tent

winded business – and while the former desperately tried to reach a compromise, I was thinking to myself: so, the ice avalanche has wiped out Camps 4 and 3. Willi is sitting in possession of the only remaining tent – a Korean tent – up at the site of Camp 3; and he, I guess, even if it's too late now, must be remembering my warning. The only Austrian tents that remain intact are those below House's Chimney at about 6,500 metres – 2,100 metres below the summit. By placing their faith in a more limited reach of the ice avalanche, the Austrians neglected to carry up with them any other tents – and who knows how much, if any, of their gear still exists in Camp 4 and Camp 3?

The Koreans on the other hand, with such an array of porters, will surely have spare tents for the summit push – and they are helpful people. But if their porters refuse to go any further, the Korean attack is finished. And we, what about us? Do we want to go on?

I'm not so much shocked about being proved right – I sensed that anyway – as about the possibility of further avalanche danger. What is the state of the snow surface on the slope below the Shoulder? How much will it have been affected by the falling masses of ice? And what if a vertical drop has been created in the serac wall, which cannot be overcome and necessitates a long and complicated detour? There are a lot of unknown factors above us. However, you can't judge them from the troubled face of one fleeing climber. Especially as Willi Bauer has remained up there, and I have the feeling that the weather is improving all the time. Mandi was appalled at what he saw and decided to give up – not without good reasons, for the Austrian summit push is now almost certainly without a tent of its own and all its gear missing, swept away by the avalanche.

'Yes – this time I will see it through, however tough it turns out to be. It's the last chance!' Willi had said, down in Base Camp before setting out. That's why he is still up there ...

For Julie and me it makes the most sense if we take a look for ourselves and come to a decision after that.

The Koreans? They seem desperate, are still negotiating. 'If we go ahead' – Julie breaks into my thoughts – 'it may get their porters moving, too.' That's right, if we simply go on, it may be enough to budge the porters from this spot. They could at least climb up another section before turning round – some would make it up to Camp 3, almost certainly.

We say a few words of encouragement to the Koreans, then we tackle the mighty snow rib below the big, and in places vertical, rock wall on whose grey-black slabs further up swings a very ancient rope ladder. The snow rib is steep and continuous. We are breathing heavily under the weight of our overloaded packs. At the end of the second rope-length we traverse to the left, on to a snow-covered rock band, just below the wall – a bit to one side of the route. Looking back, we realize with satisfaction that the porters are on the move, they are climbing up.

'All sorted out!' Julie laughs . 'I think we gave them a hand, don't you?' She chuckles. A look of determination has come into her eyes. The Korean push continues, then! They overtake us with their porters, having passed the break-even point of the climb. For a while we still hear the scratching of their crampons, the shouts of the column, then silence settles. We are alone.

'Kurt – what do *you* think about the avalanche danger?' Julie asks out of the blue. I hesitate. 'I don't want to die, you know,' she says in a low voice – a moment of fear revealed in her eyes.

It touches me like a breath of the big mountain. 'Oh, Julie, we will go back immediately, if anything is wrong. I don't want to die, either!' I assure her, moved. Nobody must die!

The scene down there with the leader of the porters had its effect on her, too – I am still chewing it over myself. The avalanche danger? I don't feel I can comment on this until I have seen things at first hand; it's several days ago now since the ice fall happened. 'We'll take a look and decide then ...'

Julie seems reassured. I am, too, to some extent. We'll certainly not take any unnecessary risk ... equally, though, we don't want to give up too easily.

'He-ey! Let's pick up that French tent, then!' Julie says abruptly, eyes alight with expectation.

I growl assent ... the French tent of Michel Parmentier! Our gift horse – I had almost forgotten about it. He said we would find it inside Wanda's tent, up on this rocky ledge. 'You go and look,' commands Julie and points to the 7,000-metre Camp, as this intermediate post is called, with some overstatement. Wanda's dark green Goretex two-man tent, storm-crumpled and half-squashed by snow, sits on the narrow ledge at the foot of the vertical rock wall, carefully belayed. Immediately to one side of it there is a sheer drop down endless snowfields and ribs, about 1,700 metres to the Godwin-Austen Glacier. Exactly how far, nobody knows, because the given heights of camps on the Abruzzi Ridge vary from one expedition report to another, sometimes by as much as one or two hundred metres. The so-called 7,000-metre Camp is perhaps only 6,900 metres high. But who worries about that – barometric heights, which in the end depend on the atmospheric pressure, are unreliable. On the dark green fabric of Wanda's shelter there is the bleached, barely legible inscription: 'highest film team in the world' – Julie's and my logo. We

The Korean Tent

gave the tent to Wanda last summer on Nanga Parbat, after we had to give up only 600 metres below the summit when the weather broke and in our haste to get down had to abandon the tent Wanda had lent us then. Now – after her K2 success – Wanda doesn't need the tent any more: she told us to help ourselves to its contents. But for reasons of weight, we cannot take much; I find provisions, some gas, and *voilà!* – the carefully rolled-up, shining red French mini-tent! I see Julie's eyes shine as I pass it out to her, and cannot avoid thinking of the charming Michel, the noble benefactor. Truly, it can be set up with a couple of moves, very much like opening an umbrella which has a floor attached beneath it. The thing is light, you can sit inside and – if you first tuck your feet into the attached side-pocket specially designed for the purpose – even lie down. French *raffinement*, somewhat bizarre! To me, the spokes of the 'umbrella' seem a bit flimsy and the circular entrance-hole too small and close to the ground – all right perhaps for a svelte and elegant Frenchman (like Michel), but hardly adequate for a solid, unbendable, Austrian *Gugelhupf*-eater (like me)! However, during the long years with my rope-companion I have come to recognize that when there's something she really sets her heart on resistance is useless ... (a trait which, in the occasional 'tugs-of-war' between us, we attribute to each other!).

As I gasp my way on all fours through the ridiculous entrance, I think to myself: 'Love is to accept an awkward French tent – even when you have a perfectly good British one.'

While Julie is cooking and I am outside again, I suddenly see Hannes Wieser – unmistakable in his black hat – coming up at some speed. He's always cheerful is Hannes, everybody likes him. He tacks over towards us and I have the feeling that there's something on his mind. 'Have you a spare sleeping bag, by any chance? One of our people has stupidly taken two bags down with him!' he calls. We tell him no. 'But we can give you a bivvy tent, very good and very light. Considering that up there all your tents are gone ...' I add.

'No,' Hannes replies, 'I don't need the tent. Willi has agreed something with the Koreans over the radio. But do you have a stove? And gas?'

'Of course – a cooker and a gas cartridge you can have, the others we need ourselves, but provisions, if you need ...' In my mind's eye I see Camp 3 destroyed by the avalanche: anything, everything could have disappeared, been destroyed, swept away? It is clear Hannes and his friends plan to climb up to Camp 4 tomorrow – does he really not want the tent? As I hand him the cooker I say again, 'It's super light our bivvy tent, and we don't need it. Really, you're welcome to have it ... you never know ... with the situation up there ...' But Hannes waves it away; a kilo more is a kilo more – that's true enough and I don't insist. Alfred is already way ahead and so he shouldn't waste time, says Hannes, pulling tight the strings of his rucksack. Then he climbs on, speedily and cheerful as ever, his black hat pushed to the back of his head.

We don't envy him the chaos up there, inevitable with so many people trying to re-establish the derelict Camp 3. The Koreans will surely put everything into a decisive push towards the summit now that good weather, finally, seems to be on the way: it could well be the last chance of the season.

Optimism starts to fire us, too, despite all the setbacks the mountain seems bent on throwing in our way. No, we don't want to force anything that should not be – we'll leave a definite decision open – but the weather seems good, we are in fine shape, and if, against our expectation, the summit remains forbidden to us this time too, then at least we shall have tried. We can go home with a totally different feeling. As for the thoroughness of our planning, we could hardly have done more. To begin with we will pass a calm and undisturbed night here – 7,000 metres is still a good height, if you are acclimatized.

Later I often thought back to this stage of the ascent, back to this day. We had already then had three chances of escaping the subsequent tragedy: first, there was the warning of the sirdar. It was irrational – logic demands reasons why one should give up, and there were none. But did Mohammed Ali hear an inner voice? Only a few days later he was fatally hit by a falling stone. It was below Camp 1 on the same Abruzzi Ridge on which he had warned the others so earnestly. Isn't the choice of destiny sometimes absurd?

Why didn't we hear the voice? Perhaps we did – but we didn't believe in it. Still, I see in front of me the man with his uplifted hands, with the imploring gestures, hear his voice. *Allah o akbar*... we should have listened to him. But he was the one who died.

The second chance we might have had to escape fate came with the strike of the high-altitude porters. If they had persisted in their refusal to go on, it would have been unfortunate for the Koreans, for their attack would have failed: I hardly believe they would have entertained an Alpine-style push. (They were moving according to an exact plan, in the classic style of a big expedition, the strategy of which is determined from Base Camp.) The Austrians could then, without fuss or restriction, have simply taken over the only undamaged tent in Camp 3 – the Korean one – for their own summit push. The fateful overcrowding would never have happened.

The third way we might have avoided the disastrous constellation on the K2 Shoulder would have been the introduction up there of our small

The Korean Tent

bivvy tent, giving extra space for one or two people. The overcrowding would have been alleviated and the fatal consequences avoided. But who could have foreseen it? At that point – nobody. When Hannes Wieser refused our small tent, unwittingly we had all come one step closer to the deadly trap.

It was diabolic machinery, into the cogwheels of which all of us were imperceptibly but irretrievably being sucked – the mechanism being so complicated that it was not recognizable to the individual: every way that might have led us out eventually became blocked by the taking of single decisions, which by themselves would never have been so critical, but in their conjunction opened the death trap for seven people up at 8,000 metres. That two of them finally survived the hell of the days-long storm is a miracle – which ever way you look at it.

My hope is that by thinking through the individual elements in this chain reaction the lives of future mountaineers on K2 or on other mountains in the world may yet be saved. Perhaps they will realize in time that their situation is narrowing down in a similar way. It is for this reason that I go into all the detail, that I write about these events at all.

Julie and I spend a calm, recuperative afternoon and evening. It is so nice when you don't have to hurry, when you can really live with the mountain.

To live with the mountain – that's what always draws me back. It is something I have discovered with Julie, my rare companion, even if basically it is what I had been doing myself from the very beginning. Both of us have tried to understand how even among our best friends there is an increasing mania to make an expedition as short as possible, to climb the mountain as swiftly as possible, to start back as soon as possible. More and more people are caught by this disease: do they still love the mountain? They don't seem to 'live' it any more – or if they do, they 'live' it differently – perhaps only as an extension of themselves. It is understandable that sometimes for tactical reasons you have to move fast on the mountain – in certain situations, at certain sections during a climb or a descent. But with them, it seems to become a rule that dominates everything. Do we go to these wonderful places simply to fulfil a duty – and to get shot of them, the sooner the better?

Today is 1 August. A fantastic day. Luck is with us …

It has often proved the case on this great mountain that in order to put yourself into fine weather high up when going for the top, you have to commit yourself to the ascent in advance of it before you can be sure what the weather will do. Naturally, you may make a mistake and have started for nothing ... but if you hang on until it is absolutely fine, conditions may turn bad again before you are up there.

But this time, Julie, we've got it right! Her eyes shine with happiness; I think we both glow – like the ocean of glittering peaks and glaciers around us, from way below our feet out to the distant horizon. Its reflection has lit up our faces. Amid that dazzling flood of light, there soars in front of us, still considerably higher than we are, the striking profile of Broad Peak, which seen from here presents its narrow side. The summit we shared ... Through the pleasure that wells within me, seeing it like this, I anticipate how beautiful it will be to stand at last on the top of K2. While Julie, above me, tackles the vertical serac wall below Camp 3 – because of the sideways pull on the fixed rope, only one of us can move along it at a time – I look out into Sinkiang: there in those savage valleys is where it all started ... now we are climbing to the very apex of the giant crystal that dominates that land.

7,200 metres! Heavily loaded, we pant our way up the steep icy wall. In spite of the ropes, it's a bloody hard struggle. But that's all part of the game. If only we could know that our depot on the Shoulder was still there, we could dump a whole lot of this gear in Camp 3. Whether it is, or not, will depend on where exactly the ice avalanche broke off, I suppose.

Of course when you carry a whole altitude camp on your back like this, you are heavily loaded. At least, under the weight, we can feel assured that we are fit, that the long rest period in Base Camp has done us good: also our acclimatization after so long here is better than ever before.

Julie is first to reach the top of the ice cliff and waits for me there. Gasping, I muscle up the last few metres, one hand on the grip of the jumar clamp, which I push, move after move, higher along the fixed rope, while at the same time forcing the front points of my crampons into the wall and giving myself additional support with the ultra-lightweight titanium ice axe in my other hand. All the equipment is far less heavy than it was in Hermann Buhl's time – jumars didn't exist then at all. Nor had the figure-of-eight been invented, this compact metal device with two holes in it: when abseiling, you pull a loop of rope through one hole and then pass it over the opposite end and snap the karabiner of your seat-harness into the other hole. Gently braking by means of the friction of the rope in the figure-of-eight, you then slide graciously into the depths ... with hardly any effort at all. None of that existed.

We will deposit the two figures-of-eight in Camp 3 for our return. (Here we are at the last of the long sequence of fixed ropes on the Abruzzi.) I have reached the top now, too – and immediately notice that both the ski-sticks I left there last time I came down have disappeared. I curse –

The Korean Tent

but Julie shrugs her shoulders: we have each taken the precaution of bringing up an extra one. We detach them from the rucksacks. Up to here, a ski-stick is useless ballast, but from now on it is enormously important. Standing on the gentle snow slope above the ice wall while we rope up, I cast my eyes upwards: the Shoulder of the mountain looks unchanged – nothing has happened up there. Those tons of ice have detached themselves from the steep face just below it! Exactly there where the tents of Quota 8,000 stood at 7,700 metres, making up the camp which the Austrians took over as their highest stronghold after the return of the Italians. Before that, tucked into the sheltered position at the foot of the vertical to overhanging ice cliffs, there had been the tents of the two Swiss, as well as Michel Parmentier's, Wanda's, and that of the two Barrards. The entire ice barrier, the height of a house, has collapsed along its full width. It was sheer good fortune that nobody was up there when it happened ...

Critically, I observe the sheared surface left by the fall: it looks smooth enough and there are no new horizontal fractures visible above it. No apparent danger, then, at present ...

Everything must be buried beneath it, under blocks of ice several metres thick – if anything remained here at all, that is – and I think of Willi's torn pullover and Mandi's squashed teapot which we found 2,000 metres lower down, at the foot of the mountain, vivid testimony of the power with which the ice thundered down ...

Slowly we plod up the slope to Camp 3, oppressed by the realization of how destructive the ice avalanche had been, even here: all that is left of the Austrian camp are tattered rags. A grey-green block of ice, the size of a table, came to a halt just short of the campsite, leaving a deep, scoured track behind it: it stands lopsidedly now on the slope. The whole area looks terrible, as do the surfaces above: trenches, clefts ... missiles of ice must have raced into the abyss, hurtling over the snow like speedboats: dice, the size of houses, rolled down the steep slopes, breaking into thousands of fragments, leaving furrows and depressions in their wake ... The friendly slope we trudged up on our first attempt is now completely disfigured by scars and pock-marks.

It's a wonder that one of the Korean tents survived this inferno, probably only because it was rolled up, and not erected. But the prudent Koreans have now had new tents brought up with their high-altitude porters, and have put them up. They are in their camp now, but nothing can be seen of Willi, Hannes and Alfred, who must have gone on this morning, to the Shoulder.

In the snow I notice a bundle of bamboo wands, for marking the slope above Camp 3, and am surprised that no one has set them up yet. Maybe because the weather is so fine? I know how much store Kim, the expedition leader, sets by them: we will take care of it.

Kim Byung-Joon is thirty-seven years old, and has always appeared to me as an open, sympathetic character, a man of prudence and precision. Not a single decision does he take lightly; the events during the ascent, the decisive radio contacts between Base Camp and the mountain, his anxieties – all faithfully detailed in his book of the expedition – are proof of that. After the 'teapot avalanche', he too was highly worried about the fate of Camp 3: unlike 2, which remained unharmed, it could not be seen with binoculars. One of the Korean mountaineers gave it a 50 per cent chance of survival, but the deputy leader, Chang Bong-Wan, reckoned it had only 10 per cent and concluded from this: '... we have to change our plan.' Kim Byung-Joon, who had divided his members into an attack team and several support groups, therefore decided 'to have all necessary material carried up once more to Camp 3, in order to make sure that the attacking party has everything at its disposal above Camp 3.' The attitude of the Austrian members towards their last summit push cannot have been unanimous, otherwise much remains simply inexplicable: they all knew that the avalanche had carried important material to the foot of the mountain. 'Yet it appears that they did not carry up sufficient supplies to replace the loss when they made their summit try,' Adams Carter later adjudged in the *American Alpine Journal*. One other point worth making is that, according to their report, it was Willi Bauer who informed the Koreans that the highest camps on the mountain were probably wrecked.

Camp 3, 7,350 metres on 1 August: Julie and I discover an old, unused platform between two red Korean dome tents and have our French *parapluie* set up in no time at all. Perhaps it was not such a bad exchange after all – I start warming towards this intricate contraption. In our own tent, which we left at the intermediate camp, it would not have been possible to sit upright as we are now doing. In addition to our ice-axes, an ownerless snow piton serves to anchor the tent in place of my ski-sticks which disappeared from the edge of the ice cliff. But all this is little more than a morale booster. We obviously hope that after the avalanche, several days ago now, nothing much else should come down for a bit; nevertheless, I remember that I have never felt very easy in this place.

All of a sudden, I jump up: one of the Koreans is filming with a small 16mm summit camera. It is like a sting of conscience, for my own camera has been left lower down. Cameramen are all terribly jealous of each other, and it is the first time that I have seen the Koreans filming on the mountain. Then I calm down: you can't have everything! After all, there's only the two of us, and no high-altitude porters. We will use our shots

The Korean Tent

from the first summit push, backing them up with still photographs. There are more Koreans, all familiar faces from our time together in Base Camp, but with the exception of a very lively, curly-headed climber, I never remember who is who. Almost all of them are called Kim, or Chang, or Joon, with an additional name tacked on, difficult to keep in mind. They are dark-skinned and almost constantly smiling, their movements fluid, and without exception they are friendly and helpful – spitting images of one another to the unaccustomed eye …

Except for the one with the black curls! He nods in my direction cheerfully. 'Hello!' he beams, sparkling, impish eyes dancing with enthusiasm. Is it the summit he has in mind – or our beer barrel? Or the possibility of celebrating both in a forthcoming feast? He is the one who in Base Camp most frequently takes up our 'secret' invitations to beer-tasting – 'secret' only among the Koreans. After every sip, 'Curlyhead' casts a prudent glance over his shoulder towards Kim's tent because, conscious of his responsibility as expedition leader, Kim deposited all the team's alcohol in Paiju during the approach march. Since then, the Koreans have been sitting on the dry side of the moraine.

With the exception of this merry (and occasionally 'damp') curlyhead, then, it is difficult to distinguish one quicksilver Korean from another. How many of them are there up here – in and outside the tents? Four? Five? Six? Hard to say: if they are not all standing side by side, you have no idea.

To one of them, I hand a small nylon pouch containing our figures-of-eight for the descent along with some other bits and pieces, asking him if they would mind keeping them in the tent for us. 'No problem,' he smiles. I know I can rely on them: once they even brought my exposed films down from the mountain. I wonder if we shall go to the summit together? It rather looks like it. While we are shooting off photographs of one another – with seracs and the ocean of peaks in the background – one of them tells me: 'Austrians today Camp 4, tomorrow summit; we tomorrow Camp 4 … and next day summit … I think.' He smiles timidly. Yes, you can never be quite sure of that.

So that's the plan! Willi, Hannes and Alfred to have their summit day, followed by the Koreans a day later – on the same day as us, in other words, and the same day as Alan Rouse (who has meanwhile turned up, to the enthusiastic welcome of Julie) together with Mrufka, one of the Polish women. The slim, lively Briton and his diminutive companion have much in common: the same bright eyes and strong glance, the same determination and energy. I notice it as they install their tent on the slope diagonally above us, first shovelling free a space. They too have arrived heavily loaded, having all they need with them.

The Endless Knot

One question still burns in my soul: is our depot still on the Shoulder, or has it vanished? The avalanche broke off below there, but who knows? Thoughtfully, I look up.

'Three porters up there ... today ... coming down,' says a friendly Korean at my side, following my gaze. Fantastic! They will almost certainly have seen whether our depot is there or not. First-class high-altitude porters to go to 8,000 metres ... you won't find many around here. So, six people have climbed up today to establish Camp 4.

While Julie chats with Alan, I make tea. Suddenly, I hear a shout and raise my head – up there in a landscape of light and shadow, creeping veils of cloud and the wind-sculpted snow formations, three figures have appeared. They are coming back – the porters. We'll soon know about the depot! They approach fast: two powerful young Hunza lads and – I notice with slight misgivings – the Balti cook, who failed to hand over Willi's torn pullover to the Austrians and subsequently got a real dressing down from the liaison officer.

Panting, the three arrive and throw their packs to the ground to one side of the Korean tents, just a few metres from us, a space apparently set aside for the high-altitude porters. 'Did you see any material on the Shoulder?' I can hardly wait for the answer. It would save such a terrible sweat tomorrow if our things were still there.

But I am to be disappointed: 'No depot on the Shoulder,' replies the Balti cook with conviction. His ski-sticks look suspiciously like those which disappeared lower down. Forget it, Kurt ... The bad news is our depot is gone. It's true we have brought up enough spares to set up a new camp – but the sleeping bags we had left up there were better than these, and the tent bigger and more solid. Nothing we can do about it.

Probably all the stuff, cached near the rim of the Shoulder, was simply smothered by drifting snow. It will almost certainly still be there, somewhere; we anchored it so well, that I doubt it would have been blown off by a storm. All the same, we have to consider it lost ...

The presence of the Balti cook has caused me to think. There have been one or two instances where members of this basically honourable profession have damaged the reputation of Himalayan cooks. I know it from my own experience. It is definitely not a good idea to use cooks as high-altitude porters, even if sometimes you find exceptional men among them.

In the Himalayas, the profession of expedition cook is quite often practised by people who, thanks to their abilities not only in preparing dishes but also in procuring provisions as well as demonstrating very necessary and multi-faceted organizational talents, prefer to earn their money this way rather than by the highly strenuous chore of carrying

The Korean Tent

loads. Usually they are quite good businessmen, too, so it is as well to keep an eye on the Base Camp cook when you're close to villages: sometimes, on a return march, we've discovered we could buy a great deal of our own provisions in shops along the way! High-altitude porters, you will find, are usually honest and high camps not seriously endangered. Nevertheless, according to the principle that 'nothing must be wasted', depots on a mountain could be interpreted as abandoned, and may not be so safe.

I heard of one case where a whole high-altitude camp was cleared by people from the valley. On the Diamir Face of Nanga Parbat, it is worth protecting the fixed ropes on the lower third of the ascent route by striking a bargain to agree a date after which the agile shepherds of the villages at the foot of the mountain are allowed to come and cut them off.

All the same, I have not completely given up hope of finding our depot ...

Julie and I are quite naturally upset at the news of its loss; if we had not brought up all that extra gear three days ago, we would be left now with no option but to go down. Even so, instead of a 'light winged' ascent tomorrow, we have now to hump heavy loads again. But we have no idea that another and much worse shock awaits us on the Shoulder ...

Until this moment, I have not given a thought to any possible mix-up of the Austrian and Korean summit assaults, even though I knew that the Austrians no longer had a tent of their own up there.

Then we forget about all that! The morning comes up!

It is a dream day. There are high spirits all round. Such fantastic weather! It couldn't be better. Views into the farthest distances. I start to believe in Providence – this time we have guessed it right: tomorrow we really will be on top. The lost depot has become insignificant – all that counts is the weather.

At last – our K2! What we can see of it from here is little, but we sense the mountain. Julie's deep joy is apparent in her fast, determined movements as she packs the rucksack, as well as in the small, cheeky smile she throws at me – yes, it's trembling, vibrating in the air, happiness, luck, this is one of those days when the world is yours, when you think your whole life is worth it because such a day exists. Today ... it's sparkling and shining, twinkling from all sides in the morning sun – seracs, ice cliffs – it is a flood of light, everywhere, which catches, grasps you and carries you away, out to shimmering glaciers, glistening firn-shields, blue pinnacles; out into the sea of Karakoram peaks where countless tiny ice-patches gleam like silvery fishes, to ridges blown clear by storms, marvellously engraved, iridescent surfaces, frozen glacier lakes, fluted faces like delicate icy plumage; yes, it would be difficult to draw enough breath to enumerate all that flows towards you: there is the feeling of leaning against the big mountain, while at the same time floating high above the world and in the midst of it – almost as if you are at the centre of a crystal sphere, inside which images of life are mirroring, refracting, repeating themselves in bewitching variety.

On days like this you start to see things differently. Suddenly you understand how a mountain has come to be called Mother Goddess of the World, another the Fish's Tail or a third the Place of Giants, and the *why* – the laborious explanation – you don't even need, for all exists on a different plane.

These are the days of name-giving.

It was a lucky moment on such a magic day when man saw with his soul to the other side of things … when someone – nobody knows who or when – recognized in an ice-covered, shimmering, twin-headed peak of the Himalayas the two-pointed form of the Fish's Tail and named it accordingly: *Machapuchare*; even today, it is still a holy mountain. The villagers at the foot of Nanga Parbat call the icy massif, whose wide spaces echo repeatedly with the growl of enormous avalanches, as if from the sound of titanic voices, the Place of Giants – *Diamir*. So we were told by Sheraman Chan, the wild shepherd, one of few there who dare to climb the steep faces. And the distant peak, a pyramid in the dark sky of the Himalayas, regarded with awe by all who have seen it: Mother Goddess of the Earth, many Tibetans call it – *Chomolungma*. But it bears several names, as do other peaks in the 'Abode of Snow'.

And K2? This enormous, enigmatic mountain on which we creep higher – with its strict crystalline regularity? Today I feel intuitively that I understand why it is known merely as 'big mountain' *Chogori*: it is unapproachable, even for a name-giver.

And tomorrow? '*La tela khor re, e nyima che shar*', Drugpa Aba will have sung an hour ago, over a thousand kilometres to the east, in Tashigang – today, like every morning. Tomorrow, too. '… And so it is turning … the great sun is coming up … the sun of a great day … in the five colours … may nothing change … may luck remain … may nothing change … may everything bloom …' It is his prayer, this song.

The happy laughter of the Koreans preparing for their climb pulls me back into the present. Their child-like pleasure, manifested in a fast sequence of lively gestures and excited sounds, fits perfectly the atmosphere of this sunny day. And while the snow is sparkling and we sip the last cup of tea, the carousel of peaks, of which we are a part, 'turns' from minute to minute, slowly and imperceptibly in the light … *La tela khor re* …

The Korean Tent

Broad Peak, a dark-blue silhouette in the flood of morning sunlight, soars like the mighty fin of a jumping dolphin who has playfully dipped his smooth snout into the Godwin-Austen Glacier at our feet while his curved body suddenly, under some magic spell, remains frozen in the air between the Baltoro and K2.

The shimmering trapeze of Chogolisa, like an iceberg, could have drifted here from some northern sea. It's 'the great hunting ground' of the ibex hunters on its southern approaches. British explorers later called the shining apparition Bride Peak, clad from head to foot as it is in a fantastic, folded drapery of snow which flows down into gently billowing, silken waves.

Hang on a minute, Kurt! Haven't you forgotten that Broad Peak, your dolphin, has three dorsal fins? Pretty unusual, that, wouldn't you say? Yes, well, from this angle you only see one, the nearest, so hopefully no marine biologist will complain.

And what of the 'ocean' of peaks – is that sheer fantasy, too? During one of our excursions from Suget Jangal, Julie and I found thousands of sea-urchin spines on top of a brown hill; we discovered corals in the Shaksgam valley; a fossilized whelk at the edge of the northern Gasherbrum Glacier; I even came across a nautilus shell on the moraine of the Baltoro ... this really was once an ancient ocean.

Only the waves have changed: the crested ocean of peaks ...

Yet even they are not rigid. *La tela khor re* ... eternal motion.

Amid such a seascape, you may find the hermit crab – a mountaineer with his tent on his back. Several, in fact. So, not much changes. Sometimes two or three will be carrying one 'shell' between them.

Not far to the north rises Skyang Kangri, 7,544 metres, a shining yellow, three-tiered upheaval of crystalline marble, originally known as Staircase Peak – every step rises between three and five hundred metres. By its side – way down, yet even so at 6,000 metres – we see Windy Gap, from where in 1909 Vittorio Sella, expedition photographer to the Duke of the Abruzzi, took pictures of the still virgin K2. That year it was attempted for the first time by the Abruzzi Ridge route. Sella used sheet film, 20×25cm, rather than his celebrated 'Alpine Camera', which was as big and heavy as a beer-crate and operated with 30 × 40cm plates. Glass plates like these would never have survived seven weeks of transport through this rugged wilderness. Vittorio Sella's photographs have never been surpassed for sharpness nor – even today – for beauty. He has immortalized the spirit of this mountain, the indescribable essence of K2.

Looking out into the distance, I see to the north the ranges of the Kun Lun, pale yellow and grey, some of the peaks snow-covered; they are beyond the deeply incised Shaksgam trench, which separates the very individual mountain country of the Sinkiang desert from the Karakoram. Yet further out, like distant surf, lies a white, crested line on the horizon. Is that Tien Shan, the Celestial Mountains – or could it be the Pamir? Or is it just as likely to be clouds?

'Look!' Julie points over to the Shaksgam, to a certain corner of the valley, at a rusty brown, rather insignificant rocky pinnacle. Only we two know that we were the first humans to stand on top of it! This is our 'Heart Mountain'. Oh, good old Liu, with his worries about nameless, unclimbed peaks! Over there is 'Left Ear Peak', and there 'Right Ear Peak' – if you need good viewpoints for your camera, what on earth should you do but climb? Julie smiles roguishly: our name-giving had little in common with serious geography. And I had fallen in love up to my ears.

What are nameless mountains for ... on such a name-day? That was a day like today.

'Look!' This time Julie is pointing downwards. 'We are definitely higher now!' A nameless dark peak, which we know to be about 7,000 metres high, is now far below us, on the opposite side of the Godwin-Austen Glacier. We have had an eye on it for quite a while already. At its edge, at the base – even if we cannot see it from here – there is a small triangular lake, hemmed in by whalebacks of moraine. It is an intense green. We have wanted to go there for a long time – a really special, hidden lake it must be. It would only take a day. But how can we fit it in ... ? It will have to wait until next time, I guess – we have ordered porters to arrive on 5 August for the return march and already it is the 2nd.

So we have three days: just enough for the summit, for there is little sense in staying longer in the so-called Death Zone above 7,500 metres, where regeneration is impossible even for the fully acclimatized. As for the weather, this time I have no worries; tomorrow will almost certainly be fine, and probably the next day too – going by the K2 weather pattern – and after that, we will already be on our way down.

I glance up. Shining, glistening slopes, with others a matt white: a variegated surface with, above it, the mighty curve of the Shoulder.

Out of the corner of my eye, I notice a bundle of bamboo sticks outside the nearest Korean tent. They remind me that during a recent chat I had with Kim, the expedition leader, I stressed that I felt trail-marking up on to the Shoulder was absolutely essential if he had no plans to fix ropes, always such a time-consuming and soul-destroying task. He was of the same opinion: so far, everybody who has been caught in a storm up there has experienced problems finding the way out.

Thoughtfully, my eyes wander over the wide, snowy curves above us:

The Korean Tent

on those silent, still slopes, several people have already fought hard for their lives. Julie and I, too, struggled down with difficulty on our last attempt, and Wanda admitted to me that she had trouble steering herself through. It may well have been that Pasang Kikuli, Pasang Kitar and Pintso, who all disappeared after braving storm and snowfall in their vain attempt to rescue Dudley Wolfe from the 7,530-metre Camp, met their fate on these now-so-silent slopes. That was in 1939, on Fritz Wiessner's expedition. Tragedy also struck here in 1953: in a desperate battle against storm and gravity, American climbers tried to bring down their mortally sick comrade, Art Gilkey. A pulmonary embolism and thrombosis had left him unable to move. Before they could get him to the relative safety of Camp 7, he was swept away by an avalanche – and they, too, had a miraculous escape when Pete Schoening succeeded in holding his five companions after a multiple fall. Art Gilkey's death probably averted total tragedy.

I notice that only one of the bamboo sticks that the high-altitude porters have brought up bears a red pennant; the other marker flags have either been lost during the transport along the ridge or have not yet been fixed. No time to sort that out now ... in any case, with this gorgeous weather the temptation to leave the sticks behind is almost overwhelming. I look at the bundle thoughtfully: they're no protection against avalanches, that's for sure. To put them in now, so near to the end of our time here, seems almost pedantic, an over-scrupulous precaution in the circumstances ...

Then I think of Kim Byung-Joon: one of the difficulties on expeditions is that decisions taken down in Base Camp are not always executed higher up. Sometimes this is because it is impossible to do so under the prevailing conditions, but often, too, because at great height, people's priorities, their personal will, existing energy, the need to husband strength, are all different from those down at Base Camp. So it happens that in order to save effort, people tend to improvise in just those circumstances on the mountain where precision and pedantry would be of greatest importance. Kim Byung-Joon – we filmed this man with his impressive 'battle plan' – has taken care that the bamboo came up here; we will see to it that the markers are set out.

Among those getting ready for the ascent, I notice the two young Hunza porters who were on the Shoulder yesterday; the Balti cook is not with them – evidently he will go down. And again, I see the Korean with his movie camera – it makes my fingers itch: the morning scene is beautiful, the atmosphere one of anticipation, the bright colours of the moving figures in the sunshine call to mind a host of excited, coloured butterflies, about to take wing into the beckoning, dazzling mountain world, which today emanates only fortune and pleasure – I so regret my camera being down in Camp 1, imagine looking through the view-finder, following the gaudy yellow of our windsuits (sunflower colour – we both love it), like an inquisitive butterfly myself, then from the blue of the seracs I pan out into the distant Shaksgam, where perhaps in an oasis of that mountain desert the descendants of the thirteen sunflowers we planted are really blooming … I can almost see them.

Kurt, the most beautiful pans are those in one's head!

It's more important now that we make it up the mountain! Take the snow piton with you – you'll need that to anchor the tent. And pack the stove. Put on your crampons. Fold up the *parapluie*!

'Let's get this umbrella down, quick!' Julie, with a glance at the busy Koreans, echoes my thoughts. I temporarily interrupt my crampon-fixing: this umbrella is a real godsend – it's folded in a trice. The two little bears, our mascots which Julie has just tucked into her rucksack, have brought us luck indeed. Alan, too, has just taken down his small tent, and is busy packing up, together with Mrufka, 'the Ant'.

Julie and I are almost ready; the high-altitude porters are on their way and the Koreans just about to leave … Oh, the bamboos! What will we do about them? I nearly forgot them altogether.

'Really, we ought to mark the section up to the Shoulder,' I remark to Alan, as he bends over his rucksack. He looks up: 'Yeah, I think we should, too. Chances are we won't need them but it's worth doing … ' he fetches a bundle of bamboo wands, and Julie too brings a dozen. We will set them up at intervals as we climb higher. After all, you never know.

'I'm glad we're going to be with Al,' Julie says as we set off. I am, too: the little episode with the bamboos has reinforced my faith that here is somebody who is helpful, and who pays more than lip-service to the principles of safety – he doesn't shirk effort. Instinctively, I recognize Alan as someone with both imagination and integrity.

We are enveloped in the sound of our steps, single words in the air, the rustle of nylon suits as at every footfall, every move of the arm, the fabric rubs against itself … After a bit, you get so used to this accompaniment that you cease to notice it and the great silence of the slope enfolds you once more – utterly.

I am careful not to put the sticks too close together, and notice Alan is being equally sparing. The slope is approximately three hundred metres high – it would be marvellous if we could eke them out for the whole distance.

We are short of three sticks. Earlier, I had called out to a Korean who

The Korean Tent

was just about to start down from Camp 3, 'Please put *three sticks* in, till to *start of fix ropes*!' He looked at me, startled, and hesitated – probably not understanding my telegraphic English – and I stepped down towards him, pressing them into his hand. The rim above the drop, just below Camp 3, is lethal in fog; and even to locate the beginning of the fixed ropes, you really need markers, as we have all seen. Since Michel Parmentier's desperate odyssey in the fog, which he would never have survived without Benoît's cool-headed radio talk-down, we have all been acutely aware of that. The Korean needed no persuasion, therefore; we fumbled a few friendly words to one another, then he went down. As I turned to make my way upwards, I saw him planting the first stick.

One thing is clear to me: an Alpine-style climber could never bring anything more than the basic necessities up here, certainly not a bundle of bamboo sticks. For those, we must be thankful to the high-altitude porters.

There are ways that markers can help even when avalanches threaten: once a heavy snowfall has set in and you can see neither tracks nor surface features, you can – with their help – still evacuate swiftly. At the moment there is no avalanche danger, and the snow here has no real depth, but in the lee of the Shoulder, further up, it is bound to be deep: the six climbers who yesterday set up camp on the Shoulder for the Austrian and Korean summit attacks must have had to dig their way through for much of the route up there.

Here the slope offers no problems; it is only a moderate incline – a friendly ski slope in sunshine. The old scoring, left by the ice avalanche, doesn't seem all that menacing – if you don't think about it – and on a glorious day like this, it's hard to appreciate Mandi's panic. Naturally, everything always looks less serious with the sun on it – or was it the damaged camps that turned him back? Did it just suddenly come to him that by relying on their own means, the Austrians could not get any further? Or did he pick up a whiff of destiny ... ?

Events will always find different interpretations: and the good or bad outcome of a venture is all that is normally taken into account. Causality is so often ignored, the actual connections rarely being exposed. On the outcome alone – success or failure – a gambler might be made into a hero ... and another man branded as a fantasist, as having overreached himself. But there comes a point, even for the most meticulous engineer of a technical wonder, when all he can do is pray that when his invention is put to the test, no screw will work loose ... No amount of caution or precautions can divert the course of destiny or just 'switch it off'.

That is not to suggest that people should simply rely on destiny – hardly anybody does. When things go wrong, there are usually solid reasons why. It is certainly fate that determines the moment you join a motorway, but if, at that moment, somebody veers across the central reservation and rams into you because his steering has broken down, then technical failure has also come into play.

When Reinhold Messner and Jerzy Kukuczka survived fourteen eight-thousanders, it was principally thanks to their ability and experience. But they owed something to luck, too. Just how much, neither knew. Perhaps Mandi did hear 'the voice' – and interpreted the avalanche his own way. Perhaps he climbed down and is still alive today because of that. With the exception of Mandi, all the rest of us ended up in the invisible pull of the summit.

It seems to have been unstoppable – and in the centre of the fateful vortex stood a tent. Without the Korean tent – which remained undamaged in Camp 3 – there is every probability that everyone could have got out of the deadly whirl in time.

Today, I often ask myself: why didn't the ice avalanche tear that Korean tent into pieces, too …? That it did not, that the tent was spared – that was fate.

While we climb the slope, planting our sticks, I keep noticing half-closed cracks in the surface – as if almost everything had been on the move. Is it possible that a small earthquake played some part in all this? I experienced something similar once on Everest below the Khumbu Icefall: many ice towers lost their tips and in Base Camp a glacier 'table', almost as big as a house, collapsed without warning.

Yes, it must have been fate that spared the Korean tent. To the Austrians – other than Mandi – this I am sure must have looked like a good sign; nevertheless, I am still surprised that they did not consider fetching an Austrian tent up from Camp 2 before continuing with their assault. In one hour, two at the most, Willi could have been down to their camp below House's Chimney … It would have meant then that everyone would have gone up to the Shoulder together, all forces united. Clearly, the Austrians could not then have stayed in the lead, they would have become part of the mixed group moving towards the summit. Why didn't they do that? The only consequence was that they would have lost a day – but not one in the Death Zone.

Perhaps Willi and his companions simply wanted to prevent their 'First Austrian Ascent' losing a valuable day – at any cost. But the day they thought they had won – won through an agreement struck with the Koreans, saving them the effort of bringing up one of their own tents through House's Chimney – proved illusory in the fulfilment of that

The Korean Tent

agreement (which *according to Willi*, as well as allowing for the common use of the tent, also called for them to fix ropes '*for the Koreans in the Bottleneck*'): on 2 August, the Austrians *lost* a day! Had they gone down for their own tent, they could certainly have reached the summit on 3 August: all forces – Austrian, Korean, British and Polish – would have made a single assault.

Yet at the time, I didn't have any headaches on that score: the Austrians had obviously agreed something useful with the Koreans and wanted to attack the summit on subsequent days. With that number of people, I quite naturally assumed that a tent-camp of corresponding size would be established on the Shoulder as a base for the two summit attempts.

7,700 metres: and above us to our left is where the ice avalanche detached itself: the newly exposed scar is clearly visible. Looking upwards, the massive bulk of the Shoulder conceals the summit pyramid of K2. It resembles a castle: there are the ramparts – namely the Shoulder with the ice barrier below it, which now, since the collapse of the ice wall above the old Italian camp, can only be penetrated by a single passageway: almost a month ago Beda Fuster and Rolf Zemp climbed steeply up to the right of where we are now, while Julie and I were able to reach the Shoulder directly from the Italian camp. Once you have surmounted these outer walls, you are standing on the Shoulder in front of the highest part of the castle, the summit cone with its threatening balcony – the keep, or last defence of this ice castle.

This time, after the bad experience of our first attempt, Julie and I want to get as close as we can to the summit stronghold – setting up our tent at about 8,000 metres so that we don't lose time unnecessarily in approaching the steep face on the morning of the push. At this level it takes an hour to gain a hundred metres of height – further up, you manage even less.

I have only one stick left – the bamboo with the red pennant. I hesitate. Where shall I put it? The traverse to the right, close to the steep wall, passes a block of snow, like a huge pillow, standing as high as a man. From there, because of the curve in the slope, I cannot see any of our markers if I look back. It needs something here if we are to locate them. Past the snow pillow is the passageway. I plant my bamboo stick. That's it, then – Alan, too, unfortunately, has come to the end of his sticks.

Deep snow ... powder snow ... with my face to the wall, holding the ski-stick at mid-height and repeatedly ramming in the ice-axe to haul myself up on, I work my way up the deeply furrowed track which leads directly over the ramparts. This was made yesterday. Julie is behind me, but we are only two in a long, human snake which burrows its way higher, taking time and stopping for plenty of rests. The slope is not too high, fortunately: forty to sixty metres at this steepness, then it eases off. Labouring heavily under our loads, which at this altitude seem to weigh us down more and more oppressively, we reach a small hill just in front of a giant crevasse. Here the track does a loop – it was obviously not clear which was the best way to get across; then I see: there's a bridge, and immediately afterwards, another steep slope – a tricky route-finding problem, it occurs to me, if a storm should blow up suddenly. A pity we have no sticks left … but a warning bell must have tweaked somebody else's conscience, too, for in the steep slope above the crevasse, just to the side of the tracks, a lonely snow piton has been stuck. A placebo, I grumble to myself – no more than that. But whoever left it there obviously had nothing better to use, either. I thought originally that this way through would lead directly to the campsite, or to the back of the Shoulder, without making any detours, but we emerge much higher than where we had our tent a month ago. And our depot? I have not totally given up on that. It would be nice to find it, even if now that we have carried everything up again – it's of no great importance.

Suddenly I realize that the China Wind is blowing! Weakly, but there is it! Julie smiles when I tell her. The China Wind – it is like a sign of Providence – the good-weather wind.

Now we focus our whole attention on the snow rim of the Shoulder, which grows obviously closer with every step. Clearly I can see, a bit further down, the place where the white rim runs almost horizontally.

That's where our cache must be!

The summit pyramid, too, has now come into view and it begins to rise above us at each step … but I see nothing of the Austrians. It is 13.00 hours …

At last – we've reached the edge. I look up at the steep face of the summit and above the ascending Koreans spot three tiny figures traversing below the giant overhang of the hanging glacier. What? No higher than that? I am taken aback, but it is definitely Willi, Hannes and Alfred! They will have to bivouac – or come back without the summit. What can have happened?

An uneasy feeling creeps over me.

Then my gaze slides lower – and my heart almost stops beating. All these people moving up the Shoulder, and there, at the edge of a small snow plateau, at 8,000 metres, sits forlornly – I do not trust my eyes – only one single tent.

'Quick! Let's look for our depot!' I shout to Julie and throw my pack to the ground. Silently, she follows my example: with just our ice-axes, we storm down along the edge …

The Korean Tent

We must find that tent!

The ground levels off – this must be it. Even if there's no sign of our ski-stick marker. I ram my ice-axe up to its hilt in the snow. Nothing. Julie does the same. We probe again and again, all around the area, until we are totally breathless. Nothing.

Again, I look up at the traverse below the ice balcony, then to the plateau, which the Koreans have now reached. I stare hard at the silhouette of the camp, but I haven't been mistaken: there is only the one Korean dome tent, which would normally shelter just three people. Where will they all stay? I still cannot believe there aren't two tents.

'Come on Julie, let's look again ...' While, more intensely now than ever, we continue probing for our depot containing the blue tunnel tent, I reflect: I didn't see the porters bringing up a tent today, they had plenty to carry with other things for the Korean summiteers, including oxygen. The only other possibility is that the altitude porters brought up a second tent yesterday, which has not been erected yet. But nobody is doing anything about putting it up so, there can't be another one!

Will the Austrians bivouac on their way to the summit, or coming back? It seems unavoidable, one way or the other, at the speed they're going. Perhaps they are fixing ropes. What were they thinking about yesterday, only to carry up this Korean tent? Did they believe they might get down as far as Camp 3, after going to the summit? Back to 7,350 metres? Such a thing would be practically unheard of!

Frantically I continue thrusting my axe into the snow, while a few metres away, Julie does the same on the flat surface near the rim of the Shoulder. But it's useless. There is no resistance, no yielding of fabric below the axe point, even though I am certain this is the right place,

Julie too is silent and worried. The situation is clear to both of us: there are almost a dozen people above us on the mountain, and so far they have only one tent between them.

That's an exaggeration, I tell myself: the two high-altitude porters will go down, and Alan and Mrufka have their own two-man tent – so that's four people less. One of the Koreans will probably go down, too, but three of them are sure to remain for the summit attack – and that means the tent will be fully occupied. But if they don't want to be faced with dangerous overcrowding should the Austrians retreat suddenly – dangerous in view of the heavy day in front of us tomorrow – then somehow or another an extra tent has to materialize. I keep probing.

I can't understand why we find nothing, not even the two ski-sticks that so securely anchored our enormous rucksack (which also contained two special sleeping bags), when the yellow-stained pee patch can still faintly be seen in the snow surface a few metres from where our tent was pitched. We can't – just can't – be looking in the wrong place. I wonder darkly about the Balti cook, who went down from Camp 3 this morning, but there have also been three weeks of snowstorms. 'Anything is possible,' says Julie, breathing hard and plumping herself down in the snow, 'but one thing is sure: here is nothing!' We give up the search.

The Key Factor — A Tent

Looking back on the whole matter of the tents after the event I reached the following view of what happened:

Somehow, somewhere, there must have been a misunderstanding or a breakdown of logic in the Austrian-Korean agreement: it is a fact that on 1 August the three-man Austrian summit team were not the only ones climbing up to Camp 4; three of the Koreans' high-altitude porters also went up but returned to Camp 3 the same day. On 2 August two of the Koreans' porters climbed again to Camp 4; with them went the three-man Korean summit team, as well as one or two other Koreans. That all these people only carried one single three-man tent to Camp 4 seems to me remarkably under-prepared. In my opinion it was a tactical error which could perhaps be excused as an oversight of the moment, and which I feel sure had its roots in the sudden and amazing entry of the Austrians onto the Korean scene. Even if you start from the premise that the Korean mountaineers carried only personal gear up to Camp 4, that still leaves the load capacity of five porters as well as the carrying potential of the three Austrians. After all, it was they who had made the offer of carrying the Korean tent from Camp 3 to the site of Camp 4! The load comprising the ropes for fixing would have been managed by one porter, and the total of four oxygen bottles by two more. But even if you make some allowance for the weight of gas and provisions, I cannot believe that it was not possible to carry up a second tent – at least on the following day. With that array of people, I had taken it for granted that is what would have happened and it was only the evidence of my own eyes on the Shoulder of K2 that taught me differently. It seems to me that the Koreans' strategy was simply confined within the limitations of their own summit attack – and would have worked perfectly, as such, with only the one tent, had they not become involved with the Austrians. Their comradely help towards the latter really demanded an enlargement of the capacity of Camp 4 – either they did not realize that, or it was not possible.

The Endless Knot

The Austrians on the other hand were not just receivers of comradely help: they probably broke the majority of the trail from Camp 3 to the Shoulder. And the fixing of several Korean ropes below the ice balcony on the summit pyramid was doubtless very valuable. Neither of the two parties, however, can have done a calculation of the time involved, or, if they did, it was unrealistic. For the whole arrangement to have worked with the presence of only one Korean tent at Camp 4 at 8,000 metres, the three Austrians would have needed, on a single day, first to attach the fixed ropes, second to reach the summit, and third – on top of all that – to descend to Camp 3!

That this is hardly possible is obvious to anyone, even to those who are not familiar with K2. Nobody has ever tried such a thing.

Some light into the darkness of what happened up there is thrown now by the Koreans' expedition report, which has been written in minute detail: it not only documents movements on the mountain, but also the walkie-talkie discussions that took place with Base Camp.

Kim Byung-Joon, the leader, did not take decisions lightly. When the Austrian summit team (via Chang Bong-Wan) radioed down from the Abruzzi Ridge to ask whether they might have a hundred metres of rope and whether they could borrow the Korean tent for their summit attack, he reflected long and hard. For the request placed him in quite a dilemma: if he refused help, he feared for the good name of Korea; yet if he granted it, he saw risks developing which could threaten the Korean success. This did not affect the concession of rope – the Koreans had 800 metres of that up there! But the tent: even though it was undoubtedly a help to both parties if the Austrians carried it, Kim Byung-Joon feared that they might even take it up as far as 8,300 metres or use it too long in the event of bad weather; or they might – exhausted perhaps after their summit attack (made possible by this arrangement) – claim the help of the Korean assault team.

Kim, for this reason, wanted a safety guarantee: and only after Hannes Wieser had given him express reassurance that the Austrians would make use of the tent on the Shoulder for no more than one night did he declare himself in agreement. The cession of the ropes, however, was without condition.*

While the Austrian expedition was busy clearing up in anticipation of an imminent departure and at the same time three of their number attacked the summit, the Koreans had divided their team into an assault

---

* K2 1986 *Expedition Report* by Kim Byung-Joon (see Bibliography).

The Key Factor – A Tent

group and several support groups, who supplied the camps on the spur with all essentials, as well as restocking Camp 3 which was feared destroyed by the 'teapot avalanche'. Given this situation and taking into account the above-mentioned report of the Koreans, it appears to me totally incomprehensible that Willi Bauer (in his book) should subsequently express indignation that the Koreans had not carried another tent up to the Shoulder for themselves! Did Bauer not speak to Wieser?

Doubtless, by now, everybody has his own view of events.

The Lost Day

The 'mountain on top of the mountain'.
The summit pyramid of K2, rising from the Shoulder.
Both are in the Death Zone.

Reflections: By whatever manner a person arrives at such a critical height – whether it be fast or slowly – it is to a certain extent a matter of choice. It may also depend on the weather, the weight he is carrying, and other circumstances – on his style obviously, too … But once there, he has not much time: three days at most – with two nights in between; a third night would be cutting it fine. He would still be able to descend then, but any movement towards the summit would automatically involve a fourth day – and that's definitely too long. He would hardly be likely to achieve very much anyway.

Nevertheless, the fact that within such three-day periods at high altitude there have been mountaineers who have managed to venture twice towards the summit into the region above 8,000 metres – from Noel Odell on Everest, via Fritz Wiessner to Willi Bauer and Alfred Imitzer on K2 – proves that with exceptionally good acclimatization, even this is possible. Naturally not everybody can allow himself three days, and most would hope to make it in just two, but, really, somebody for whom these three days are too much should not even go up there in the first place. Oxygen can obviously change these basic timings, but it is over-valued and is no *carte blanche*. Basically, one should spend as little time as possible in the Death Zone and lose no day unnecessarily – not waste even an hour.

On the five 'big' eight-thousanders – Everest, K2, Kangchenjunga, Lhotse, Makalu – there is (apart from a couple of extraordinary feats performed under special circumstances) nothing that can be done in less than about two days; the third, the reserve day, you should hope not to use. Even if resting can relax you, can restore your strength, a real recuperation is no longer possible. The dangers of altitude are ever-present: embolism, oedema, the weather. That perfect physical shape and full acclimatization are prerequisites goes without saying.

The Lost Day

And something else, too, which is not easy to define: a 'compatibility with the universe', balance, harmony ... you feel it on certain special days ...

The China Wind is blowing! Its whisper along the snow rim, through the undulating formations which air turbulence has created almost everywhere on the surface of the Shoulder, sounds like a reassuring voice. 'Luck will go with you' – it says – 'Tomorrow you will go to the top.'

Yes, we've calmed down again. They've possibly reckoned with a bivouac up there. That must be it, otherwise they would have already turned back. After all, the weather is beautiful!

Out in the distance, far away, Nanga Parbat has appeared, immediately to the side of the SSW Ridge of K2. Considerably closer, in the same direction, just beyond the Baltoro Glacier, soars the Matterhorn-shape of Masherbrum, 7,821 metres high.

Julie and I have now reached Alan and Mrufka again. They have set up their tent on a moderate incline below a somewhat steeper slope – just within calling distance of the plateau above, at the edge of which the Korean tent can be seen standing. But I want to get up there – if the China Wind blows up more strongly, the Korean tent will offer a sort of windbreak for our small shelter. I wish Alan had set himself up there as well: it would make it easier for a common start tomorrow. Well, we can always shout! Was it Mrufka who chose this place, I wonder? She always has firm ideas about things. Perhaps she ruled out settling on the plateau because of the huge ice balcony which hangs above it from the summit face? Or did Alan want to be closer to the exit route through the Ring Wall? All he will say in response to my question is a laconic 'I like it better here ...'

And Mrufka? While she is tightening the guys of the British two-man tent, her keen eyes repeatedly turn towards the summit. She is small and delicate like an ant, busy like an ant ... yes, and as obstinate, too (that's something we have in common). This time the mercurial, energetic 'Ant' – in 1984 we often used to rock-and-roll together in our 'glacier disco' at 5,000 metres – is absolutely set on reaching the summit. Her expression is cheerful enough – but it masks strong determination. The summit of Nanga Parbat escaped her by only a few metres. She has no intention of letting that happen a second time!

Briefly we discuss arrangements for tomorrow with Alan, then we plod up the slope to the Korean tent.

While everybody on the Shoulder is preparing for a summit attack, 3,000 metres further down in the K2 Base Camp Alan's friend, Jim Curran, the British cameraman, is enduring considerable heartache over the way things are going on the mountain. 'Four days up and two down,' Alan had told him. A feasible estimate, if somewhat optimistic for a mountaineer who is carting everything he needs for a summit attack on his own shoulders up the full length of the Abruzzi Ridge. This was on 29 July – and in the evening of the same day Alan had started out with Mrufka. Since then, Jim has been trying in his mind to follow Alan's ascent; it is true there is a Korean radio link between the Abruzzi Spur and Base Camp, but because of language difficulties Jim seems unable to get in touch with his friend or to leave messages for him.

He is, however, in contact with the Poles; their leader Janusz Majer has put Jim personally in charge of the walkie-talkie connection between Base Camp and the SSW Ridge. Julie and I don't know yet that the Poles' summit assault on their 'Magic Line' is in full swing (Reinhold Messner's projected route, with a different upper section). There has been no news of its progress, but Alan must have been aware of Jim's unexpected commission: '… to act as Base Camp Manager, and more important, maintain radio contact each evening with their team … Weather forecasts each evening could be picked up from Radio Pakistan. We also arranged to open up the radio at eight each morning in case any message was necessary' is how he was later to outline his role in his book *K2, Triumph and Tragedy*. Radio Pakistan may or may not have proved helpful as regards the weather outlook, but Jim himself was a careful observer, as his notes describing these days reveal. Whether his conjectures were on target and whether or not his worries well founded – no doubt they carried the usual uncertainty inherent in all weather forecasting – none of us were in a position to judge, because up where we were we heard nothing from him. How much Jim agonized only appears from his tape-recordings. So, for instance, 2 August seems to him 'to have been a perfect summit day' for Alan, yet at the same time Jim has the greatest misgivings for the day after that, should Alan be late … 'I very much fear that the weather may be deteriorating and by tomorrow be bad again', he confides to his recorder with his next breath. The 2nd was the day we reached the Shoulder. Around us the China Wind was blowing – the fine weather wind.

Had we had any worries (then or later), any concern over the weather, we could easily have asked the Koreans for a walkie-talkie connection to Base Camp. Jim's silent reservations were no help to anybody on the Shoulder.

Not far from the gently rounded rim of the plateau Julie and I have trodden down a patch of snow to make a platform for our *parapluie* in the wind-shadow of the Korean tent. By ramming our ski-sticks deeply into the snow (we won't be needing them any more, higher up), we anchor the little French wonder. Its intense red shines cheekily in the sun. The snow piton we brought up from Camp 3 serves as another anchor, and then, near the ground, we connect our 'umbrella' to the massive dark blue dome of the Koreans at two points. How high are we? It's difficult to say, given the strongly differing figures quoted for altitudes on this mountain – around the 8,000-metre level at any rate. Judging by the scenery, we are not far from where Walter Bonatti's bivouac site must have been. In 1954 he spent an icy night in a snow scoop with the Hunza Mahdi, after the two of them (together with Eric Abram) had carried up oxygen destined for the summit assault of Lino Lacedelli and Achille Compagnoni. Their tiny shelter was somewhat higher than this, further up on a rocky step.

We've plunged our two ice-axes in the snow of the narrow space between the two tents, and attached to them our crampons and karabiners. Julie crawls into the tent, and I pass to her the short yellow mats (we have halved a normal one) which insulate against cold and humidity, then the rope, the rucksacks ... Astonished, I suddenly notice that one of the Koreans is starting to descend. The two Hunza lads are already off. What's the matter? Has a new walkie-talkie directive of Kim's arrived from Base Camp? With the Koreans, so it seems to me, all goes according to plan. And now? The Korean waves to me as he leaves the tent.

'No summit?' I ask him. 'Not possible. Three climbers in this tent. No space ...' is his answer. Was there a note of regret? He says it with a smile and shrugs his shoulders. Then he plods down along the wide white curve towards Camp 3.

So then, there are three Koreans in this tent – and they 'attack' tomorrow. Curlyhead is among them: I noticed that earlier.

Julie calls for snow! She pushes the empty plastic bag out through the entrance and I hurry to fill it with wind-pressed chunks ... thirstiness is a faithful companion in the cold dry air of high altitude. But until the tea is ready, I still have time on my hands. While she is brewing, I can tighten the guylines, arrange one more anchor (it's blowing, in fluctuating waves, this China Wind); some kind of step in the slope in front of the entrance wouldn't be a bad idea either ...

Occasionally I look up to the ice cliffs of the great balcony. Like ants, the three are attached below it. Yes, they are definitely fixing some ropes there ...

Don't lose too much time! Go on ...! I silently bid them. They must surely have looked down and seen what is happening here. One of them must have counted heads?

Possibly they are planning a bivouac, further up, there where Wanda and her companions passed the night ... 'Tea is ready!' Julie's hand with the steaming mug appears in the entrance and then she too emerges. 'What's the matter up there?' she asks, looking up with a frown. But I cannot give her a satisfactory answer ... Beside us, in the Korean tent, things have gone silent. The quiet before the summit storm.

Julie goes on cooking: soup with mushrooms. With it, we have *Bresaola* – air-dried meat – and crispbread; we cannot complain of lack of appetite. Next thing is to fill the drinking bottles – at least one for the night! Without porters, we have of course no Thermos bottles – they are heavy as well as being liable to break too easily; we'll have to leave cooking our tea for the summit assault until tomorrow morning – at least we can partially anticipate the time-consuming process of melting the snow. In the English aluminium bottles liquid stays hot for a long time, if you take them into your sleeping bag – and everyone loves hot-water bottles. On Nanga Parbat, I had ...

Hallo – things are moving up there at last! They are no longer fixing, they're climbing on! Slowly, it's true – but gaining height ... Announcing this to Julie, I crawl into the tent beside her. She smiles: for both of us it is as if 'a stone fell from our hearts' – the Austrians have gone beyond the crucial passage now; even the fragile French umbrella seems to draw breath, in the Sinkiang breeze.

I snuggle into the sleeping bag, continuing to spin my thread of thoughts: ... well then, on Nanga Parbat in 1982 I took a real rubber hot-water bottle up to the high camps – the contents of which I usually drank during the night, even if the taste wasn't that special. I rarely remind Julie of this expedition as she leaps into a fighting mood whenever she thinks of Pierre Mazeaud, the leader – he wouldn't allow her to go above 5,000 metres and even tried to imply she was lazy. Since then we have been to 8,000 metres three times – to err is human! 'I need more snow!' I am put out like a cat from my warm place ... (Never a moment's peace! Not that I complain ...)

And up there, how is it going now? Slowly my gaze sweeps over the wall. Neither beyond the compact rock barrier in the first third of the 600-metre high summit wall (which you can only overcome by climbing through the narrow, icy Bottleneck) nor on the difficult and terribly exposed traverse which follows, overshadowed by the giant ice balcony, is there anyone to be seen. Instead the three tiny figures are working their way in slow motion up close to the left edge of the ice overhang. It is less difficult there, just snow, but enormously steep ... I know that from our first attempt at this monstrous feature, a month ago. Its sheared end alone, with its dangerous lustre, beckoning and terrifying at one and the

The Lost Day

same time, must be 150 metres high. What is a human against such dimensions?

Willi, Hannes and Alfred could now be about 8,300 metres. Why do they keep going directly upwards, hugging the scalloped edge of the balcony?

Julie and I traversed that steep snowfield a bit lower down, at the end of the difficulties, before we turned back in order to avoid the risk of a bivouac ...

I collect chunks of snow, then crawl back with my bag through the sleeve entrance. It's still a tight fit – I haven't yet acquired the sleek lines of a Frenchman – but at least it's downhill, like the entrance of the Korean tent next door, which makes it somewhat easier; Julie passes me the last mug of tea from the previous brew. It's tepid. While drinking, I reflect ... even if they follow the edge of the overhang, from the top of the ice balcony, that heads summitwards as well! Soon they will be at 8,400 metres; yes, they can still make it to the top today. They should be up there by evening, they will certainly experience a beautiful sunset – tomorrow they can sleep it off down here. I don't begrudge them the 'first Austrian ascent', which means so much to Willi; Julie and I are an international rope, but we are here neither for Britain nor Austria, we simply climb for ourselves, it is our dream mountain, we are climbing beyond any classifications ...

What should we take with us tomorrow? I sip the last dregs of tea, at the same time gathering with one hand a couple of the things which we shall need; some I hand to Julie – now and then a word drops in between: we have done this so often, it is second nature to us. This time, we will go with the minimum of weight: there is the light, pink Japanese summit rucksack for me, and Julie can take the grey hip-bag, which will hold a full drinking bottle along with something else – there is the very light Husch cooker ... the alu-mug we can put in only after cooking tomorrow morning ... we'll only take one of our two head-torches, together with a spare battery ... the sunflower-coloured windsuits – they weigh next to nothing – the new long down jackets we're already wearing: it is all top-quality British equipment which Julie got this spring specially for K2. In addition we have gloves and spares, two titanium ice screws, two titanium pitons. Is it worth taking a rather heavy jumar for the sake of five or six fixed ropes? One, perhaps. Our two little bears? Hmm ... isn't it better for them to wait here? (Hey! – here Julie interferes! She wants to take them ...) A lighter – yes, we must have that, better, take two. But everything has its weight ... even the tiniest ... a spoon, for instance, would be a luxury; the two full drinking bottles are heavy enough. Every litre of water weighs a kilo (an absolute *must*). We'll leave those till tomorrow morning, but one thing goes into the rucksack right away: the space blanket for bivouacking. Essential too ... because you never know. We shall still do a countdown later on, check through everything once more – at this moment Julie's camera comes to mind, but she has that of course; the little recorder she will certainly leave here ... otherwise I shall do my best to dissuade her from taking it.

'Would you mind having a look to see how they're getting on?' Julie's voice betrays a slight unease. Well, it is to be hoped they do get on, I mean. I squeeze out of the door ...

Great God! They've turned round!

They're coming down, rather fast ...

'Julie!' I call into the tent, 'I am very worried – the Austrians are retreating – in a bit of a hurry ...' No summit. No bivouac. Descent.

Heavy silence. 'No accident,' I add. That much I can see. Nevertheless, the question hangs in the air like a menace: where do they intend going?

'I only hope they don't want to stay here ...' Julie says at length in a low voice. If they do, it will be chaos – there's no room!

They could still make it down to Camp 3, I think to myself, it's only afternoon. No problem, timewise. But will they want to? That is a different question! Without the summit? There is another solution: Willi, the strongest, stays here – at a pinch the Koreans might take one of them in. That way the 'first Austrian' on K2 could be assured.

The other two would have to go down to Camp 3 and try again a day later. And would they still want to do that? I am not convinced, one of them appeared to me rather slow today during the ascent. Soon we will know all!

'Get the stove going, Julie!' They will be thirsty for sure ...

'It's going already!' Of course it is. Idiot. The altitude ... I am nervous. My curiosity to know what brought about their failure up there combines with worry about the space problem: to be squashed together before a summit assault is a real *Krampf* – physical condition is bound to suffer, sleeplessness ... anything is possible. The three Koreans, it's true, have a bottle of oxygen between them for the night ... Silently I crawl back into the tent for a while.

Do I hear footsteps in the snow? The Austrians are coming – puffing and snorting, and at a good speed, like Alpine zebras making for the waterhole. Here they are: Willi Bauer, stocky, red-haired, iron-hard, a born endurer; Hannes Wieser, cheerful daredevil; Alfred Imitzer, consciously deliberate, the expedition leader.

It's impossible to tell with Willi how much he has been through, he seems as indestructible as ever. Expressions on the faces of the other two

The Lost Day

reflect what a hard day they have had. All three are totally dehydrated.

'Our next tea is just ready,' says Julie. 'They're lucky!' I call Alfred over. The other two squeeze in with the Koreans for a drink.

Something puzzles me a little: whereas Willi says they fixed ropes and in so doing made themselves too late, Alfred openly declares that he ordered a retreat from the summit attack because of deep and unsafe snow towards the top of the balcony – he wouldn't have wanted to take the responsibility of going any further. Alfred has a giant thirst. He is certainly a giant of a man – I realize that as I watch him greedily sipping his drink: his legs are outside, down the snowslope, even though he sits inside the tent. We are tightly pressed together in our small, flexing shelter. We can just manage to hold the steaming teapot between the three of us. While Alfred tells us more of their summit push, I wonder gloomily what his intentions might be now, and those of the other two …

We are not left in doubt for long. Soon, from next door, from the Koreans' tent, excited Asian voices can be heard … It's like a tidal wave, gaining in strength, getting louder and louder. Now and again I catch the pacifying voice of Willi Bauer … but it is soon blotted out by the angry babble. It doesn't take much imagination to guess the reason for this hubbub: it's not a tea-break the Austrians are after. They plan on staying overnight.

You don't have to understand Korean to gather that the 'amicable settlement', as Willi was later to call it, is a somewhat exaggerated way of describing what happened next – he must have been speaking from a very individual point of view. The way the Koreans saw it has since been described by Peter Gillman, quoting Chang Bong-Wan, the leader of the assault team:

> … But the Koreans' leader, Chang Bong-Wan confirms Kurt's account. 'After failing to reach the summit the Austrian team asked if they could sleep in our tent, he says. We refused their request as we had to try to reach the summit the following day. But they repeated their request. They begged us. There was no way to escape so two members of the Austrian team slept in our tent. It was very overcrowded …*

Unfortunately there are enormous discrepancies in the different descriptions of events, according to perspective. At stake in the argument were: the winning or losing of an important day; the possible saving of effort and struggle; how to find a solution, a way out of the cramped

---

* *Clouds from Both Sides* by Julie Tullis (with final chapter by Peter Gillman).

situation – and, of course, the summit. It was not an emergency situation: if it had been, everybody would have accepted it without question.

When, later, after endless terrible days I arrived at the foot of the mountain, clinging grimly to my last iota of life I never dreamed that I would need to speak about the argument on the Shoulder. I kept quiet about it. Everything that had happened up there bore down on me too heavily.

But there was the 3rd of August: the lost day. It was more than just Julie's and my planned summit day. It was a fact: *seven people idled the day away on the Shoulder of K2 in beautiful weather.* That could not pass unnoticed, it was inconceivable …

All around the world mountaineers racked their brains about it. And not only them. The most absurd explanations emerged – one even went so far as to make out that the strongest man up there in those days of the summit climb, namely Alan Rouse, was a fantasist with no ability to gauge the situation, and someone sadly out of shape into the bargain. Elsewhere, it was said that we all frittered away a day up there cooking tea because we were deluded by a sort of euphoric summit fever. Even when the real reasons slowly seeped through and became known, experts (so-called) preferred to air their own theories and to consider only the consequences, not the whole fatal chain of events that led up to them. However, the worst were – as they are always – those who instead of thinking and searching for the root causes, preferred to hide behind facile judgements and their own subjective views, people who were unwilling and incapable of putting themselves into similar situations. There are always those who could have 'told you so' (they exist in their thousands!); there are also others who, using respect for the dead as an excuse, want to draw the final line under every human tragedy – something only time can do. The voices of the dead do not demand reverential silence, but rather an appreciation of what happened to prevent it doing so again.

This 3rd of August – just a day. How much depends on a single day? On an eight-thousander … perhaps everything.

The evening before we were already plumb in the middle of a critical turning point – perhaps it would prove the most critical one of all:

Camp 4, on the Shoulder of K2 (from diary notes):

'What about that tent you left up here?' Willi calls over. 'Unfindable,' I answer shortly. Should somebody have another look, I wonder? This space problem will not magic itself away – even by tomorrow! But at 8,000 metres decisions seem hard to take …

The Lost Day

'We could all three sit in here overnight, even if it is narrow,' says Alfred, still sipping his tea. But it's already unbearably cramped: Julie and I – legs hugged to our chests – are not able to reach anything we want, cannot finish packing for the summit, to say nothing about cooking in the morning. And Alfred – his legs are still outside! He really is a giant! This tent, the smallest in Camp 4, is so meticulously worked out that the groundsheet even has a lateral pocket, extending outside, in which the two inhabitants have to stick their legs if they lie down. Otherwise they won't fit in. Through the vapours of hot tea and breath, I notice Julie's startled expression ...

'There's no way,' she murmurs.

I take courage: 'Alfred – it won't work; with the best will in the world it won't. I'm sorry you haven't made it to the top today, that's a pity – but we aren't here for the first time, like you. This is our third expedition to this mountain. Tomorrow is our summit day. We cannot accommodate you – we have to be fresh tomorrow.' Give up everything?

We've finally got the right day and the right weather! And in Alan and Mrufka have another strong rope to climb with – what the Koreans will do, we don't know, but anyway they will be using oxygen – it promises to be the best possible constellation. No, we will not simply sacrifice our planned summit day. Who knows how long the China Wind will keep blowing? I see Julie's worried face, which gives way more and more to an expression of determination. 'Alfred – you have to sort it out with the Koreans, we are not party to your agreement,' she says. However it came about, this problem has to be solved between those two teams. It is still not too late to go down lower. The question keeps coming back: was there a misunderstanding? Confusion in settling the details? Whatever it was, we are now all in the soup. 'Perhaps you might manage to squash in with the others – or take turns to be in the Korean tent? There's still time to establish an extra bivouac.' I can't resist adding. 'How on earth did you think it was going to work up here with the space?' 'We believed that after the summit we could still get down to Camp 3,' Alfred admits hesitantly. Is that the rabbit in the cabbages? But if that is the case ...

Alfred continues: 'Yes, I can see that ideally we ought to descend to Camp 3, but it was really hard work up there, you know. Tomorrow we will take a rest day here, then have another go at the summit.' A second summit attack? Hats off to his sublime obstinacy, but it is no comfort to Julie and me, and robs me of my last patience. 'Alfred, if you have failed today, and intend resting tomorrow anyway, you don't need to obstruct the summit attempts of everybody else! You'd do better to have your rest day lower down, in Camp 3! If you get yourself together, you can still make it – one or two of you at least should go down ...'

Alfred reflects. 'Yes', he replies, and takes a long pause – 'but perhaps it will still work the other way.'

'Tell him we'll dig a snow hole *and* cook him tea,' Julie chips in again. A solution! A snow hole! British mountaineers have lived for weeks on Everest in snow holes. There's no black magic to making them – we could all help. Put a sleeping bag inside and take turns in it … not the greatest of all pleasures, perhaps, but tomorrow all three can make up for their lack of sleep in the empty tents.

In vain: it seems that 'snow hole with tea' is nobody's dream of luxury up here. 'Just for this one night,' Julie persists – tomorrow we are prepared for that ourselves … Walter Bonatti 'survived' worse.

Alfred doesn't answer. Can he still squeeze in with the others? A three-man tent with five people – then a sixth? It seems almost impossible. Why in all heaven weren't two tents carried up here? I explode silently. With only one, everything has to run like clockwork – otherwise, it simply will not function. And with all due respect for the installation of some Korean ropes … a lost day is too high a price to pay. The discussion in the angry red, bending *parapluie* has not yet deteriorated into a scrap between French fighting cocks – this is not possible between Alfred and me – but what is the way out? Julie is at a loss, at the end of her proverbial helpfulness: she would even concede Michl's gift to the three Austrians – but not before our own summit attempt – no solution for tonight. We are at a dead end.

It's getting later and later – and it goes on, with pauses, here and in the other tent. Every preparation for tomorrow has ground to a halt. Slowly, I feel a fury growing within me: something has to happen soon! Otherwise, totally uninvolved people will end up footing the bill for a non-existent tent. Wherever the blame lies, either Julie and I or Alan and Mrufka will have to pay with tomorrow's summit. Adieu to our common ascent? No! Alan is one of the best British climbers – and Julie sets so much store on that, we must undertake the dangerous adventure with him – he is lucky that his small tent is situated further down the slope, so that he will not be drawn into this fracas …

Gone six o'clock already: for some while on the Shoulder of K2 we have been dipped in the cold shadow of the summit pyramid. How long has this tug-of-war been going on? One hour, two? … an eternity.

All of a sudden, it takes an unexpected turn. 'Yes – someone should go down – but there ought to be at least two of us,' says Alfred. 'We can always come back after a rest day in Camp 3; I'll go and see what the others say …' He squeezes out awkwardly. 'Can you let Alfred have five minutes of oxygen?' I yell loudly into the voices of the neighbouring tent. 'He needs a boost!' But what will the Koreans make of that? They will

The Lost Day

wonder what for ... 'No – they need the oxygen for the night and the summit,' Willi calls back at once. 'Only five minutes,' I insist. 'He's thinking of going down to Camp 3 with one of you – and that will give him the necessary impetus – otherwise, it means even more of you will have to squash in together. Or we have to dig a snow hole ...'

Then, everything happens with the speed of lightning: in a few moments the fateful decision is taken. The Koreans refuse to take a third person under any circumstances; Willi and Hannes don't want to give up their places; Alfred – the one left over – unwilling to descend alone to Camp 3, stands forlornly with his sleeping bag in front of the Korean tent. Suddenly, we catch the name 'Rouse' ... 'Try with Rouse ...' Only a few words.

It wasn't loud, but Julie heard it. As if bitten by a tarantula, she shoots up and shoves her way out through the tent entrance: 'There is no way you should do that,' she yells, trembling with protest. 'Alan needs his night's sleep. How can he go to the summit tomorrow, otherwise?' Julie has a strong sense of justice, she is terribly upset – not so much that our plans for a common ascent are being run into the ground, but more than that, by the way it is happening. 'You are not leaving him any choice!' she shouts, still shaking with anger. But Alfred, his sleeping bag under his arm, is already making his silent way down to Alan's tent.

What can a fair-minded person do if somebody suddenly appears outside his door with a sleeping bag at around 8,000 metres? I am shocked. Sympathetic as I am to Alfred's plight, I make no secret of the way I feel about the proposed solution – but it makes no difference. Instead of letting us dig a snow hole together or going down to Camp 3, without a second thought the Austrians are prepared to condemn the person spearheading the summit assault on the second highest mountain in the world to a miserable night in a narrow tent. Is there no respect any more for other people's plans, I ask myself, distraught. In that moment, I wanted nothing more than to go down – to be shot of the whole thing. And if Julie and I had not already spent three years trying to climb this mountain, I would certainly have done so.

My distress was not so much directed towards Alfred, who at least had shown a measure of understanding in the end: but the fact that nobody else was prepared to consider a solution that was acceptable to the others, I couldn't understand! It seems to me that great altitude temporarily damages people's judgement.

One thing is beyond question: caught in the machinations of fate at 8,000 metres, things are very different from on an Alpine peak. The sluggishness of decision-taking, temporary forgetfulness, an inclination to immobility, sometimes also a certain tunnel vision, and a quickness to temper – these are all effects of altitude which can strike everyone (and

I don't want to exempt myself). From a comfortable sofa, such situations can only be judged with difficulty ...

The argument on the Shoulder definitely tipped the balance. Later on, only the uninfluenceable forces of nature raised their voices. The 3rd of August was the last day on which we were not yet within their power. It was the last day on which somebody could reach the summit of K2 and still get down in good order.

With the decision of the Austrians not to descend to Camp 3, the dice had fallen again. Without knowing it, all three of them – Alfred as well (he was the last) – were caught in the merciless machinery of altitude, time and storm, from which there was virtually no escape. And along with Alfred, Alan and Mrufka had also been pulled into the invisible cogwheels. The next to go would be Julie and me. Although not necessarily! At that time, there was still a chance for things to have gone differently for us ...

But the following night and morning brought us, too, to a fateful juncture.

Night. Unease tortures me. What shall we do? My thoughts go backwards and forwards, round in circles; they persecute me. What shall we do? The spontaneous creation of a team of strong experienced people, brought together by coincidence (or predestination?) seems to have broken down. This time when even the weather was on our side; when 3 August, the day planned for the summit assault, finally seemed to be the right one – to suffer such a blow is doubly bitter. Alan Rouse, the British ace, and the indomitable Mrufka are hardly likely to start after a miserable night crammed together in such a tight space. The Koreans may overcome it better, thanks to their oxygen – nevertheless, the overcrowding can't have done them much good either. Julie and I are no longer directly involved – but we have suffered nervous stress as a result of it, too. One thing is sure, the failure of the Austrian summit attack has thrown us out of kilter.

Don't let yourself get involved! I remember now my talk with Julie in Base Camp. Still, we couldn't help getting involved ...

And now? What shall we do now? Something keeps resurfacing in the endless circle of thoughts – an inner voice, like an inner conviction, telling me ... you have to go tomorrow! That is Julie's and your day! Maintain it, whatever else happens – don't delay!

It is as if it were a categoric imperative.

Then there is another voice, which murmurs to similar purpose ... the Koreans are good guys, you get on with them ... no matter whether in Base Camp or on the mountain. They radiate friendliness and helpful-

The Lost Day

ness, they treat you like a 'father', and you for your part often find yourself advising them as if they were sons. You feel closer to them than to the speed-merchants, who may sometimes have a better chance of getting to the top, but what does the mountain itself really mean to them?

Go with the Koreans tomorrow! It whispers, this voice.

At the same moment a third voice interrupts, forcefully, like the command of a general – you do not know the Koreans! In a mountaineering sense, they are an unknown quantity. It's a gamble!

A fourth, gentle, voice – Kurt, if you two were really on your own, you would certainly try tomorrow. Go tomorrow, as if you were alone … (there it is again – it's the same voice that came before …).

But now a fifth voice joins in the debate – a voice devoid of all emotion, rational only – which says … If now, after three years, this is at last *the opportunity* that you have been waiting for, be sure and weigh all the factors carefully – you must be sensible about this. At this height, you only have one shot and that must be a 'hit' – to waste energy on a doubtful attack is the last thing you can allow yourself. Almost certainly, you won't get a second go on the following day – and even if you do, it will have less chance of success. Sound strategy is decisive on the mountain, as ever in life! Even here, where no war is waged – because the confrontation of man with great altitude and the mountain is on quite a different plane – sometimes the language of battle describes the situation of a summit attempt better than anything else, and here, too, there is truly life itself in play.

Certainly no summit in the Himalayas has ever been 'defeated', all the 'summit conquerors' are just humans who by virtue of intelligence, strength or sheer luck have won a special game. For many of them, however, it includes something unexplainable, a sense of their innermost being.

So, the rational voice – what does it tell me? That I don't really know the Koreans, but if they start early – and that is their intention (4.30 one of them said; better six o'clock, I suggested, because of the morning cold) – then it might still be good to go together. We could collaborate in trail-breaking, and should they give up, we might still continue alone. Most of our high-altitude climbing to date, Julie and I have done on our own, just the two of us. However, if the snow is as Alfred reported – heavy and deep – two people on their own could not manage the trail-breaking to the summit. Ergo: we *have* to start *with* the Koreans. That means, be ready in time.

What will Julie think about that? She is quiet – I don't wake her.

For a while I'm satisfied, I doze a bit and sleep. Then I can't help it, I have to let her know: I submit my proposal.

The answer is not very encouraging: 'If you really think we should …' No eager echo there to my Korean plan. 'I would prefer we go with Alan, but my fear is he'll be knackered in the morning – almost certainly after a night like this. It's a real shame.' she grumbles. 'I fear it, too,' I agree.

For a while there is silence, then Julie remarks: 'If Alan stays here – and we went a day later – it makes a much stronger team.' Is her countryman the deciding factor for her?

Something inside me bristles against this going-later variation. There is no exact reason for it, just that we ought not let this day slip by: tomorrow – our day! 'Julie – something tells me not to lose tomorrow …'

Again there is a silence. Both of us know too well how much can hinge on a single day on the great peaks of the Himalayas – summit luck, delusion, fulfilment of years of hope … even your life – the loss of a day at such altitude can be fatal.

'If we start with the Koreans early, we could see how it works out – then continue, or go back,' Julie concedes thoughtfully. Of course: that does not rule out the day after that. But there is a problem: they are going with oxygen and we without. Our speed could be totally different … Perhaps it will all run like clockwork – but what if their apparatus breaks down, or they run out of oxygen? I remember bad experiences with masks on Makalu – if we get stuck with the Koreans somewhere in the midst of it all, the chance may well be gone. Not everybody is a Compagnoni or a Lacedelli, able in such a case simply to continue 'without'.*

'Well,' Julie breaks into my silence with some hesitation, 'if you think we should attempt it with the Koreans – let's give it a try …'

She is not enthusiastic, but she would go; she has obviously decided – I still have to. But has she really? Dear God, let Alan get enough sleep! So then, I go on grinding the mill of my thoughts …

There are two unknown factors in the calculation for tomorrow, Alan on the one hand, and the Koreans on the other – and on top of that, there is the uncertainty of their starting times. When can they really hope to get going with all the overcrowding in their tent?

Also, there is a lot of snow up there …

---

* When Kim Chang-Sun – as Kim Byung-Joon reports in his book – checked his oxygen gear at six o'clock, he discovered a hissing, which he was unable to stop. Breathing two litres of oxygen per minute (which is remarkably little for ascending) he should have been able to reckon on his bottle lasting eleven and a half hours, but the pressure gauge told him he only had nine more hours. In spite of that, he started – intending to switch off the oxygen during his stops on the way. By twelve o'clock he was already at 8,400 metres: then – at 14.00 hours – the pernicious hissing finally stopped. Kim Chang-Sun continued towards the summit … (another Lacedelli?).

The Lost Day

After tomorrow, we'll know all about that: the situation will be clear, unambiguous ... that's if the weather holds, of course. It's a great temptation to wait.

In the end I tire of thinking: ... why are things building up against our ascent on the planned day – is it some sort of providence, perhaps? Should we not go? Will the Koreans fail tomorrow, and we with them? Once more the voice in me says no!

It will be best to keep one eye on Alan's tent and one on the Koreans at our side, then make a spot decision in the morning ...

Be ready, at any rate!

No better solution comes to me. Finally I fall asleep.

Sunshine on the tent! Light seeps through the fabric and I hear sounds of movement outside, coming from the Korean tent. Seized by a sense of duty, I start brewing up. Julie is still completely muffled inside her sleeping bag. I cannot see her face.

By the time the morning tea is ready, I wake her. We sip from the steaming mugs in silence. That really does you good! Hot liquid slipping down your dry throat. You breathe deeply, inhale the vapours, cough your lungs free. Julie looks at me and her dark eyes hold a question – but she says nothing.

Naturally, I have been keeping a careful eye through the entrance to see what's happening, especially down towards Alan's tent – but there's no sign of life there yet. It's probably as we feared.

'Let's get ready, Julie,' I say.

She does not answer. Slowly we prepare for a start. The weather – it does not surprise me – is still good. There are sounds of activity next door, of course, but it takes little imagination to figure that it must be quite a stew in there, with five people in a tent only designed for three. Five people means five sleeping bags, a heap of boots, to say nothing of the cooking and the preparation of oxygen gear. It will take them quite a while yet to be ready.

In fact, it turned out to be considerably more than 'quite a while' – it went on longer and longer. I kept shouting across and getting some sort of reassurance. Yes, soon they would be ready, soon they would go. But nothing of the sort happened. It was totally puzzling – what should I do? I didn't – couldn't – know that one of the three Koreans, Kim Chang-Sun, was feeling unwell. Another reason, in an overcrowded tent, not to get started.

At any rate, no matter what caused the delay, the effect on me was that I began to waver. It certainly did nothing to boost my confidence, and time continued to tick by unmercifully ...

It goes without saying that 'an early start' no longer came into it. Moreover, Julie showed no enthusiasm. It had become totally clear in the meantime that Alan was not going to make an attempt today. We saw him – just for a few moments, but enough to get the message. 'He's definitely not going,' Julie assured me.

It was seven o'clock when we gave up the day for lost.

There is no doubt about it: the Koreans had a very delayed start, but as to the exact time the summit team finally got away, there are differences of opinion. Peter Gillman, in *Clouds from Both Sides*, maintains that Chang Bong-Wan declared to him that they left at 6 a.m. But according to my recollection, this is way short of the real time: I had the impression it was nearer eight (see the interview I gave to *Climber* magazine in December 1986) ... and certainly no earlier than 7.30 a.m. The camp had already been in full sunshine for a long time when the last of the three Koreans made his departure. Before that, we organized his oxygen regulator to deliver three litres a minute, rather than the two he'd had it set for. Is it possible that a watch was wrong, or that a glance at the dial was perpetuated in memory over several actions, thus effectively 'freezing' time? At such a height, all sorts of things are possible. It's more likely, however, to have been an error in translation. Dennis Kemp, who recently returned from Korea, told me that a member of the summit team had been most emphatic to him that they were *preparing for their departure at six o'clock*. It would have been quite understandable, too, at that stage of the proceedings, for the Korean assault mountaineers to have been hesitant in admitting over the radio to their leader just how late they were in getting away. (They all held him in such enormous respect.) Indisputably they reached the summit at 16.15 – and if they really had left at six, that means they were climbing for ten and a quarter hours – longer than it took most of us to reach the summit, without oxygen, the following day! As each of them only had one bottle of oxygen for going to the top, it's worth considering, too, how long that lasted.

From a practical point of view, it is rather unimportant the precise time the Koreans made their start. Julie and I did not follow them – and for a number of reasons.

However much, and whatever has been written about the 3rd of August – and it is a colourful kaleidoscope of opinion – none of the authors has solved the enigma, the real 'why' of the *lost day* ... which passed now to no real purpose as far as most of us on the Shoulder were concerned. The Austrians' 'rest day' undeniably turned into one for everybody except the Koreans, who went to the top. Even Peter Gillman has no explanation and concludes drily: 'Whatever the reason, the loss of that day was to prove disastrous.'

Out of the clamour of voices in the night, it was the low one, the voice of my deepest instincts, to which I should have listened.

The day – 3 August – went by initially with no remarkable events. When, from inside the tent, I heard some of the others remarking that the Koreans were steadily gaining height, I disappeared into my sleeping bag with very mixed emotions. Should we have started despite everything? Never mind the delay? Was that low voice right which had urged me, 'Go today. Behave as if you were on your own'? Still I could hear it. But it was too late now to change anything. Even as I tried to console myself with the thought that we could not have made the same progress as the oxygen boys, for us it was simply too late. There was no getting away from the certainty that we had lost our summit day.

Soon afterwards, Julie spoke to Alan. He confirmed that he had passed a dreadful night: there was so little space that he hardly closed an eye; he wanted to make up for lost sleep now, during the day, and was planning on an early start tomorrow. Julie suggested he move his tent up nearer to ours so that we could keep in better contact in the morning. Accordingly, he and Mrufka carried all their things up the slope to our plateau and erected Alan's small two-man tent in the snow a few metres beyond the Korean dome. I had more or less calmed down about the side-effects that the Austrians' failed summit push would have on our own plans. Tomorrow we would all go to the top – we'd be a big and strong group – and yesterday's fight would be forgotten. So I told myself. Nevertheless, I saw clearly what a muddled kind of mountaineering this was. Travelling *en masse* along the same route, as we were doing this summer, was not at all to Julie's and my taste. It seemed just too obvious that chaos would be the inevitable result. We would take care in future, never to let the same thing happen to us again.

In our opinion, it was not simply that there were a lot of people on the mountain – after all, there had been quite a crowd of mountaineers in the one expedition when we climbed K2's North Spur. It was more the different atmosphere that prevailed, a different spirit. It seemed as if a different wind were blowing. Could the reason be found in the great variety of people and styles? In the colourful patchwork strewn over the mountain's ridges and faces extending towards the summit – which confuses the good spirits of the Himalayas and causes them to flee? Twilight of the gods? Twilight of mere mortals? Something is out of balance. It's not only to be found on K2 ... and the real cause cannot be attributed to any single individual.

I was longing for Tashigang. And for the loneliness of the glaciers and valleys to the north of here.

What do you do on a 'rest day' at 8,000 metres? Not much. You sleep, you cook. It occurred to Julie and me that the way things were now, our porters would arrive in Base Camp on 5 August for the return march before we could be back down. It wasn't something that worried us too much: we only needed a few men and the liaison officer would surely hold them back a day for us.

The change of plan did however bring another problem. On a rest day in particular, a day of inactivity, everybody uses substantially more gas and provisions than on a climbing day. Julie and I had done a careful calculation at the foot of the mountain – as we always did – to include contingency provisions, but now I was reluctant to start using something destined for the climb or descent. It crossed my mind that three days ago, before Hannes knew how things would turn out, I had given him a cooker and a gas cylinder. By now the Austrians had no more headaches on that score, they were sitting pretty on the Korean reserves, which would not now be needed as the Koreans had stuck to their plans.*

And thanks to their valuable assistance in fixing some of the Korean ropes during their initial summit attempt, the Austrians were first in line to 'inherit' them. So I took heart and explained to Hannes that because of the loss of the day, I could do with having the gas cylinder back. He at once understood – and a moment later gave us an Epigas stove. It was Korean, he said, not camping Gaz but we certainly didn't mind that. So our calculations, including spares, were back in balance again. They even came with a free gift – a packet of crispbread and a sachet of strange powder. This latter intrigued me greatly – it smelt of fish – what kind of delicacy might it be? Fish soup, perhaps, or some Asian 'energy powder'? With pleasurable anticipation we got the stove going – I really love fish soup! But the culinary delight was a delusion – the 'ocean brew' tasted foul! One sip – and we threw the rest away, making tea as fast as possible! Perhaps, in my eagerness, I had failed to dilute it sufficiently; perhaps it was not fish soup at all! Korean 'hieroglyphs' – who can read them? At any rate, afterwards I told Julie the famous story of Anderl Heckmair's sardines. They almost cost him the first ascent of the Eiger North Face. And we drank yet more tea.

---

* The Koreans had stocked their camp on the Shoulder with all essential provisions and gas for five days. However, as far as oxygen was concerned, only four of the five cylinders originally provided arrived in the camp – three of which were reserved for the summit ascent (one for each climber), the fourth was to share between them at night.

The Lost Day

Gradually, the bad atmosphere lifted. We were full of hope and looking forward to the following day. Out of the blue Julie confessed that she was happy now we had not gone that morning as she had no wish to reach the summit before Alan. She didn't want it to look as if the British ace was losing his edge. That would not be very good form on her part, she thought.

At a certain point I noticed that the freshening wind was no longer blowing from the Chinese side. It came now from Pakistan. At first I was worried – then I calmed down; we could not change it anyway. All we could do was hope that fate would grant us another day for the summit tomorrow.

Huge clouds had built up around, and the wind was moving the tent, inside which we were lying. The sun shone on the bright fabric, and we let our thoughts carry us where they would. Now and then we spoke of our plans and dreams. The most important was that we carried on, along the path we had come together. We were both content simply to exist, that the other was there. For a long while we'd had so little solitude, had not had a day like this of inner peace on a mountain – even the wind swaying the tent was like a familiar voice. Nobody wanted anything of us, we could simply relax here undisturbed, each for the other.

In the afternoon Alan told us that he believed the Poles who were climbing the SSW Ridge might reach the summit today or tomorrow. The Koreans, too, were very close to it now. He did not say anything about the weather – obviously there was no call for alarm. Wind from Pakistan, with clouds, is not infrequently encountered by would-be summiteers in the Karakoram. The China Wind is the exception, not the rule.

There may have been signs of a change in the weather that we missed by being inside the tent. I am not sure whether there was anything to notice or not. Certainly there was nothing to prevent four other groups of mountaineers in or near our vicinity from preparing an assault above 8,000 metres the following morning and to set out, just as we did. Around noon on 4 August Slovene climbers reached the summit of 8,035-metre Gasherbrum II, as well as that of Broad Peak (8,047 metres); the soloist Tomo Cesen began his seventeen-hour climb to K2 Shoulder; and the Americans on the North Spur of our mountain went to 8,100 metres before they – there were only two climbers – had to give up the exhausting struggle of trail-breaking in deep snow. They escaped the deadly high-altitude storm whereas we were caught by the change of weather when within reach of the summit. And while the Koreans on 3 August were

The Endless Knot

still heading upwards, the mountaineers of a French expedition hugged one another on top of the 8,068-metre Hidden Peak.

The 4th of August had now been established as our 'day', having taken over the role from the day before. It seems an irony of fate that even the Austrians could have had 3 August as their summit day, if only they had brought up one of their own tents from below House's Chimney. On 4 August now, at any rate, it *had* to work for them – if they eventually got off the Shoulder by midday on the fifth, they would then have passed four full days in the Death Zone.

Neither for them nor us, however, did the disastrous consequences of the lost day owe their origins to the *length of stay* in the Death Zone up to this time – we all endured one day's prolongation without any physical problems – but to the simple fact that the delay brought us into the storm's own fateful and unalterable 'timetable'.

At four o'clock in the afternoon a feeling of relief runs through the camp – the Koreans are about to stand on top of the mountain. We all enjoy their success with them, with Kim, and with the others in Base Camp and on the Abruzzi Spur as well. They've deserved it!

At 16.15, K2 is theirs. Julie and I think warmly of our curlyhaired friend; at this moment not even Kim would object if we were sitting near our barrel, clinking foaming mugs together …

If and when? But the weather on this late afternoon does not look bad. Sometimes in the Karakoram, a tug-of-war takes place between the various factors that influence the weather from the Chinese side and from the plains of Pakistan – out there will be monsoon now, which does not exist here, yet in some way its pressure is felt here, now and then. We shall see that tomorrow morning! It's windy …

We've rolled up like hedgehogs to conserve energy; we concentrate on tomorrow, completely focus our minds on it. All is ready. We have spent almost the whole day in the tent together.

Then, out of the blue, we hear about the Poles. It can only be them! Somebody else has appeared on the summit: the SSW Ridge is climbed! Incredible – everything is running like clockwork today …

Then, suddenly, someone observes drily: 'They are coming down …'

Coming down?

Here?

Normally I can keep a rein on my temper, and in my case I'm a fairly phlegmatic soul – people say I'm something of a stoic, even if they also say I speak my mind too much, which isn't easy for everyone to take. Agostino often remarks, 'Kurt, you are terrible … really terrible – but we like you!' I believe in still trying to find the reason why, even if a giraffe

The Lost Day

is looking in the window. But occasionally I don't understand something, can't accept it because it seems just so totally impossible ... and then, heaven help me, I blow up! Even among friends. This is one of those times.

'*Polnische Wirtschaft!* What kind of mess is this? How on earth do they think they can come down here? Nothing was agreed. The K2 Hilton is already overbooked ...!' I am swearing. I no longer understand the world at all! And with all respects to our mountain friends from Warsaw and Krakow and wherever else ... what is happening here?

It strikes Julie the same way. She grumbles, 'How can climbers come over the top of a mountain to other camps without having made any provision for their accommodation or support?'

It cannot be! They know we're going to the summit! They must be desperate! I calm Julie, so far as I succeed in calming myself. Mrufka, I'm sure, would have a walkie-talkie – amongst other things – if this had been pre-arranged. She would surely have known about it ... it can't have been planned?

But there's no getting away from the fact that chaos reigns up here on this mountain, and has done for the last two days. If it were a lower peak – you could go along with it – but here, on the mountain of mountains ...

Somehow it will have to be resolved, one way or another ... there will be thirteen people sitting here at 8,000 metres tonight. We won't be in clover, that's for sure,

But the most terrible event of this night – it far exceeded everything else – had not yet happened. It was Wojciech's death.

It was an event so grievous, the question 'why' was not asked at the time ... thus I can only relate what came out later.

The Poles reached the summit by six o'clock in the evening, not too late to embark on the descent. Willi told us about it as we lay in the tent; he had been keeping an eye on the situation up there and later fixed his head-torch onto the Korean tent, so that all the people descending could find the camp. But even before it got dark, when he could still see quite well, Willi had a sudden impression he had spotted somebody falling from below the top.

Whatever it was Willi saw remains unclear; but later, shortly before midnight (around 23.30), one of the Poles did fall – in the region of the Bottleneck. It was Wojciech Wroz, an experienced mountaineer who had already been twice to over 8,000 metres on K2 – on the North-West and on the North-East ridges. Julie and I knew the gritty-looking Pole with the sharp-cut features from our occasional perambulations around

The Endless Knot

Base Camp, which sometimes ended sipping vodka in the cheerful circle of those who 'only' have the wintry Tatra Mountains (and industrial chimneys) to train on, but who (along with the Slovenians) are nowadays considered to be the hardest Himalayan mountaineers in the world.

The assault team, which besides Wojciech comprised Przemyslaw Piasecki and the Czech climber Petr Bozik, all extremely tired after several very high bivouacs, were struggling down on the Abruzzi side of the summit pyramid, fighting not only the effects of altitude but latterly also those of darkness – and they did not know this face at all. Nevertheless they had opted to come down this way as it was easier than returning along their Magic Line.

Two of the Koreans, also now descending, were rather slow (one of them finally attached himself to a piton and bivouacked) and they, too, were present in the Bottleneck at the fatal moment. All of those involved were exhausted, and apart from the possible failure to pass on a warning, altitude alone can be blamed for what occurred.

It is not totally clear, however, what did happen, even today: on the extremely steep terrain which was provided with fixed ropes, some of them old, some newly installed, there was one unbelayed and dangerous gap in the line. According to reports, the Korean who descended first wanted to 'bridge' this gap with a length of rope, and in the course of so doing left the end of another rope hanging, which he had shortened for the purpose ... From there to the next belay was easy.

On the other hand, when Julie and I climbed up the next morning, we found at the foot of an almost vertical corner (the steepest section of the Bottleneck) not a gap in the fixed ropes but a new, free-hanging blue and white rope which led directly to the steep snowslope below. This rope had no restraining end-knot. It was lethal – and not only at night. We immediately tied a knot in it, one so thick it could not possibly slide through the karabiner of any climber coming down from above, and a hand-loop as well. When descending, this would be the very last of the sequence of ropes.

At this time, we were still under the impression that Wojciech had sustained his fall below the summit – as Willi believed he had seen. But Wojciech certainly got as far as the Bottleneck. His two companions, Petr and Przemyslaw, who after abseiling in the darkness had waited for their companion below the ropes at about 8,100 metres, heard a sudden dull sound as if somebody had fallen ... Did the unsuspecting Wojciech hurtle into the depths, just when he felt himself safe on a rope, because in the darkness and in his state of extreme tiredness, he did not notice the missing end-knot?

Here, in this place? Or further up? Did the piece of rope above have

The Lost Day

a knot, was it perhaps too small, or iced over, or was Wojciech himself simply not fully aware of what was happening? In that moment it was unimportant to the others which it was – Wojciech had fallen, disappeared, was dead – there is no chance if you fall up there. When all hope for his safety had gone, the survivors descended to Camp 4, where they arrived at two o'clock in the morning.

Thus, during the night between 3 and 4 August, there were finally *eleven* people in the Shoulder Camp. As the bivouacking Korean only came down at daybreak, Alfred was able to squeeze into his place in the Korean dome. And Alan Rouse? After the cramped night he had passed before, he was not willing to endure another like it. His solution was a snow hole. He invited Petr and Przemyslaw, who were in shock from the loss of their companion, to use his tent (that made three in there, with Mrufka) – and he himself bivouacked, half inside, half on the outside of his small shelter of fabric, in a snow-niche – uncomfortable, but at least he had air to breathe, even if it was cold.

It is an interesting fact that this did not affect him adversely. On the contrary: Alan proved to be the strongest on the summit day. He broke trail, leading most of the way to the top. Only perhaps a hundred metres short of the summit did Willi relieve him and take over the lead.

It is also worth remarking that Mrufka (who six days later still had energy enough for a descent) experienced a noticeable drop in performance during the following day after another night in the cramped tent.

In Camp 4, after the nights of overcrowding (ten to eleven people) several times there was somebody who suffered deterioration as a result of being packed tightly into a confined space: Alan Rouse and Kim Chang-Sun after the first night; Mrufka and Hannes Wieser after the second. (Despite Willi Bauer's assertion that Hannes gave up his climb on account of damp mittens, from the way he was moving for the hundred metres he did manage, it was patently clear that he could never have reached the summit even with dry ones. Julie and I predicted his turning back before it happened. This is to cast no aspersions; very few mountaineers have accomplished more than one summit assault within such a short time.) Kim Chang-Sun, after feeling unwell in the morning after his bad night, was nevertheless the strongest Korean on the summit climb, as Alan was on ours – and Mrufka, too, was still in good shape days afterwards. Were lack of sleep and tight confinement, or the lack of oxygen inside an overcrowded tent, reasons for the temporary wretchedness?

Condition is certainly no linear constant, it is all too easily influenced. The French theory that the physical shape of a mountaineer in the

Himalayas decreases continuously during the course of weeks while his acclimatization is increasing steadily is from a practical point of view rather odd to say the least. (A medical friend with a sense of humour said to me 'It's right enough if somebody has diarrhoea.') According to such calculations, we ought all to have been flat on our backs on the Shoulder from the word go, because all of us had already spent many weeks on K2.

'Despite their bad shape, X, Y and Z did reach the summit of K2!' asserted the author of the mathematically inspired French report – you are tempted to add, 'and, moreover, without oxygen.'

That this, as well as the fact that we endured many more days at high altitude afterwards, is clear evidence against the above *courbe de forme*, must have escaped the selective vision of the ardent theorist. He obviously did not want to see it: in reality, physical shape is a very individual and serpentine curve, dependent on many factors – not only on time.

The 3rd of August, the lost day, passed into the 4th with no marked separation. This passage was marked by a continuous sequence of events which were in some way all linked together apart from Wojciech's death, which rose lonely above them all.

There were now two walkie-talkie sets in Camp 4, a Polish and a Korean one, but it was the events which dominated the brief 'air time': as far as the next day's seven aspirants to the summit were concerned, there was no direct communication with Base Camp, nor any message received from below.

The mood here is subdued and tense at the same time. The last chance, the last effort … everybody reflects on what that entails, but everybody knows he will try it. You feel the immense might of the big mountain … You are scared of it, but you cannot leave it. And at the same time, you trust it.

The Summit
– Our Dreams Come True

… A tiny figure, and a whole sky of ice above …

The 'sky' has fissures, clefts – iridescent and glistening up there, silent in the light of the sun. And though you ask yourself how it can be possible that these thousands of tons of cantilevered ice don't come tumbling down, at the same time, you will them most urgently to cling together.

If this were not so, if they were not supporting one another, the giant 'balcony', this monster, would not be poised up there. But what if the mysterious forces should suddenly relent? Then, an enormous cloud of ice-dust would thunder down the steep slopes and ribs of K2, down the Abruzzi Ridge, gathering such momentum that it would not stop, but surge on, up Broad Peak on the other side of the valley.

Instead, the ice continues to hang there, as silent as sky above a tiny, hunched human figure, who approaches it on all fours – while the frozen forces remain quiet.

If you look at K2 from the valley, on your way perhaps to the Windy Gap, it is impossible from that distance to comprehend the dimensions of this icy projection. The mountain appears as a marvellously faceted and pure white crystal, but having – as the result of a whim of some giant – half a 'glass apple' stuck into its side just below the top (an apple complete with teeth-marks around the edge!). The whole summit pyramid, from down there, appears remote, floating, unconnected to the crystalline strength of its massive base: its multiplicity of lines, a tissue of buttresses and spires, seem to have grown together into one single heavenward swoop. The whole huge structure, about 2,000 metres high, rises out of the glacier surface from a height of about 5,300 metres, the busy upward thrust of its many lines calming finally in the wide expanses of snow spread over the gently curving slopes of the Shoulder like a smooth white cloth.

From the middle – as if on an altar – rises the main summit pediment. To stand before such harmony, such a conjunction of power and beauty, releases strange emotions, impossible to describe. This mountain radiates a force, coupled to remoteness, a greatness which in its simplicity overwhelms you completely.

When you're leaning into the wall below the 'glass apple', you have approached this highest sphere – and your eyes search and check it at close quarters. The image of an altar is reinforced, a mysterious altar housing equally mysterious offerings – and you stand in awe.

Or you might call it – fear. It is fear.

Nobody can escape this feeling when he climbs to the highest point of K2. The small, bent human figure creeping on all fours is Alan Rouse. A little lower is another shape – Mrufka. Further down still – Alfred. It is seven o'clock in the morning on 4 August. Julie and I have started too; below us we soon make out Hannes, and a little after him Willi coming up as last man. But Hannes meanwhile has turned back.

It is not long before Julie and I find ourselves last in the line. We are the only two to climb roped – it's safer, but it takes more time. However, we were only about an hour behind Alan when we started out, and we don't expect to increase that by very much on the way to the top.

How lucky we are with the weather! Dazzling brightness all around, glaring sunshine …

Step by step, we draw inexorably closer to the Ice Monster, feeling much as a mouse must feel, trying to crawl silently between the paws of a sleeping cat.

The only comfort to be drawn as we pass below the giant serac is that the fatal collapses seem to occur only irregularly and at considerable intervals. We don't like to think about it – nobody does – but to a certain extent, it is just a question of luck whether you are underneath it or not when it goes. We are all painfully aware of the danger, and hurry past the spot. It is one of those rare, unavoidable situations, where the risk is obvious and you accept it with your eyes open.

Not far above Camp 4 we saw traces of one such break-off, hundreds of half-melted blocks were piled under the balcony, covering a wide section of the slope.

Faced with the choice, whether to go up through the dangerous Bottleneck just below the ice balcony, or to tackle the difficult and time-consuming climb further left, through the vertical rock formation, most people would opt for the Bottleneck – because time is such a decisive factor in a summit assault. At an altitude like this, and with regard to the difficulty and steepness of K2, you cannot count on being able to gain as much as a hundred metres of height in an hour (something which presents no problem on Broad Peak or Gasherbrum II. Here, from a final high camp at about 8,000 metres, you may need from eight to ten to fourteen hours even to reach the summit of K2: the extraordinary

The Summit – Our Dreams Come True

variation depending on snow conditions, your own physical condition, the degree of acclimatization you have achieved, the weight of your load, the possibility of sharing the chore of trail-breaking, the quality of sleep the night before the summit, how much time you've already spent at 8,000 metres, the existence of or the necessary application of fixed belay points (and in critical places of fixed ropes as well), on whether it is an 'oxygen-free' ascent or you're climbing with the help of mask and respirators. Heat, cold and storm will also be major influences. Thus, with so many unknown, or only partly known factors, it is nearly impossible to gauge in advance how long it will take to climb the summit pyramid of K2. Sometimes it will not be possible to reach the top at all. Therefore, this variable time scale cannot even be considered as a rough guide.

The 'mountain on top of a mountain' remains sphinx-like, an enigma beyond human understanding.

On this same day – 4 August – at eleven o'clock in the morning, Slovenian mountaineers on nearby Broad Peak are approaching the summit. In the sky long veils of thin cloud have appeared, and just below the 8,000-metre level, puffier formations are building up. Only the summit block of K2 – the 'mountain on top of a mountain' – stands free in the sunshine. Half an hour later, the high veils have dissolved and the sky is blue with some large patches of transparent cloud. The fluffy layer, however, has settled itself around the Shoulder of K2 and become more dense …

Tomo Cesen, making a solo bid on K2, turns back in the fog from a height of about 7,800 metres. Later, light snow begins to fall there. The Koreans, as well as Petr and Przemyslaw, start their descent. The second group of Poles on their Magic Line has also been swallowed up in the 'grey soup' and opted to retreat in miserable weather.

The climbers on Broad Peak, however, reach the summit at about 11.30. Visibility above the sea of clouds is still good. At noon, their compatriots further east stand on top of another eight-thousander, Gasherbrum II. And even in the early afternoon, Willi Bauer photographs Al Rouse, who is still in the lead, against a cloudless, cobalt sky. Dressed completely in red, his dynamic figure can be seen below the last seracs, close to the summit. He is steadily breaking trail.

So the weather appears totally different on this day, according to your perspective. This is not unusual for an 8,000-metre peak, Julie and I witnessed similar conditions more than once on Nanga Parbat … and when I stepped onto the summit of Dhaulagiri with my Swiss companions on 13 May 1960, far below us, 2,000 metres down, a storm was raging: the roll of its thunder crept up to us from a great distance.

But – back to K2!

The Endless Knot

'Julie, it's only midday! This time, we'll make it!' I am in high spirits as we near the end of the traverse.

'Yes – this time we will ...' she replies in a low voice, and smiles. We are happy. Behind us, the bizarre ice formations of the hanging glacier glisten in the sunshine. Once past them, and with your ear no longer cocked nervously for sounds from above, once the huge sheets of ice, taller than houses, the blue-green daggers and splinters and cogs no longer threaten your head – well, then they are beautiful!

The weather is fine and we still have half the day in front of us. All the same, we don't want to be on the summit any later than 4 p.m. With the worst difficulties now behind us – the Bottleneck and the traverse – K2 will be ours! At last! Our spirits run high ...

Here is the last fixed rope! Alan Rouse or the Koreans must have put it across the flank, since Alfred, Willi and Hannes, when they climbed up the day before yesterday, chose to go straight up along the ice balcony, before getting stuck in deep snow over there, somewhere.

The last fixed rope ... it isn't really necessary here, I think. This ascending traverse is not difficult. Still, the snow is deep in places and it certainly provides a fantastic trail-marker in case of a storm, when visibility is poor. I know only too well how you are more than grateful for every little assistance provided at 8,000 metres! Nobody can be sure, up here, that his memory is not playing him tricks – especially when, in swirling winds and racing cloud, it all looks so different that you can't recognize a thing. These are hazards of the Death Zone. Once, long ago, during the first ascent of Shartse (7,502 metres), anticipating a stormy retreat, I marked the whole route with pieces of clothing: strips cut from my second pair of trousers (sacrificed especially), my spare yellow socks – one of the socks on a prominent boss of rock, the other further up, as the route was very complicated. We did not need them to save our lives then – Hermann Warth's and mine – but we might have done if we had suddenly disappeared into cloud.

8,300 metres! From the last piton, above a giant isolated boulder on the left edge of the steep snowslope, I belay Julie as she climbs to join me. We are now on the rocky rib, which Fritz Wiessner followed with Pasang Dawa Lama in 1939 during his attempt on what was still, then, a virgin summit. Pasang was one of the best Sherpas of all time. Both men climbed without oxygen and knew they were within reach of their goal. There was no doubt they could have made it, and Wiessner was prepared to spend the night out, but suddenly Pasang, usually so imperturbable, became paralysed with terror. He dared not continue for fear of evil spirits, which come out at dusk. Only 230 metres of height separated them from the summit.

The Summit – Our Dreams Come True

So, you never know, up here, what to expect. This is the third time that Julie and I have penetrated the final sanctuary of K2. Four years now this mountain has held us in its spell … invaded our dreams. We had almost given up hope of ever climbing it. Now the sun is shining! We feel great – better than ever before at this height on K2. The past weeks of relaxation at Base Camp have paid off. Above us, the mountain still towers into the sky, but is not as steep as the section below the ice balcony. A large, wide ridge stretches ahead, scoured and fluted by the tempests, its surface marked with hundreds of horizontal runnels carved by the elements; it is a white desert with thrusting dunes of ice and snow, and here and there isolated seracs. High up, just below the summit, outlined clearly against the blue of the sky, there stands the remarkable, shimmering ice cliff which Julie and I call the 'Shark's Fin'. Below it, a lonely red figure moves higher through the steep world of snow – slowly but inexorably gaining ground, undeterred it seems by anything: Alan Rouse. He is maybe a hundred or a hundred and fifty metres above us. The others have been swallowed by the enormous landscape, have disappeared somewhere between the dark pulpits of rock and the dazzling undulations.

The indefatigable figure, plugging higher and higher, seems the very symbol of hope … almost blurred by the blinding whiteness, and framed by the sinister, nearly black sky whose deep, velvety darkness threatens to engulf everything. The world of humans is so far away.

All of us up here are held within the power of the mountain. We feel it acutely. We cannot know how this will turn out, where this path is leading us – up here. But already we feel joy. This time we are so early that by any human reckoning the summit we have dreamed about for so long will really be ours, unbelievable as that seems. With the joy comes the sensation, however, the menace, that up here human judgement hardly counts for a thing.

Your companion is the only being up here that, amazingly, still derives from a far distant earthly life – she and your thoughts, and both of you are linked together like floating thoughts, linked by the rope … two islands in space.

And Pasang Dawa Lama's sleeping demons? Where are they, will they wake? Something urges us to hurry, an uneasiness which overshadows the pleasure, the joy at our good progress. Soon it will be one o'clock. How time is racing!

We still have some 300 metres to overcome before we reach the summit.

Should we leave my pack here – with the stove, bivvy gear, jumar clamp? Hang it on the last piton? Every kilo carried multiplies at this height.

Surely, we will have no trouble getting back this far, whatever happens? I consult Julie. She nods, pushing up her dark ski goggles to reveal her face. Her eyes are shining – with the excitement, I suppose, of being at last so close to our goal. 'Yes, one sip from the bottle, and then press on,' she says between the deep breaths, which, up here, accompany every move. Sure, a little drink and let's go! Spare gloves, a plastic bag with Ovaltine, the head-torch – we stuff them all into the pockets of our down jackets. I take along the two titanium ice-screws as well – you never know! The teabottle we drain and leave behind, but decide to hang on to our second one, which we pack in Julie's hip-bag.

Somehow we overlook the space blanket – a pocket-sized pack of foil fabric, weighing next to nothing; it gets left in the rucksack. Now we have to move as lightly and speedily as possible. Not that it is late, but … K2 is high, incredibly high. We feel that distinctly when we look back down at the puffy sea of cloud, into which the other eight-thousanders have now also sunk: Broad Peak, the Gasherbrums – all gone. A mingled sense of excitement and fear grips us now; I know no word for that!

Higher, and yet higher … Leaving our rucksack at that last piton means we have to get back that far today, no matter what.

It is almost half past one when we set off again. The sun is still shining, but the light seems a little weaker now. This might well be our last fine day. Again I tell myself – Kurt, we're doing fine, we're feeling fine, we've never been this good, this high! We're bound to make it this time!

Still, I feel a slight unease. But it passes.

Moving on a short rope over the rocks and snow of the rib, we reach a rocky outcrop, a vertical wall about ten metres high, rust-coloured streaked with sulphur yellow, and overhanging. The ground at the bottom – it seems absurd – is totally flat, and sheltered, large enough indeed for a small tent. To one side, on the lefthand edge, is a yawning drop – K2's South Face. Somewhere around here a month ago Kukuczka and Piotrowski struggled out after completing the Face, having had to abandon nearly all their gear because of the extreme difficulties encountered near the top. Certainly this must have been the spot where the Barrards had their bivouac – Maurice and Liliane, with Michel and Wanda.

We pass to the side of the rusty rock formation and continue between slabs of snow. Above us, a final rocky shoulder has appeared, from where we will traverse right onto the steep, wide vaulting that leads to the summit. For a while I catch sight of the half-hidden figures of Willi, Alfred and Mrufka moving behind a snow-barrier at the same height as the rocky shoulder – then they vanish again. Perhaps they have sat down for a rest.

Only Alan is visible now, further up, climbing over a steep snow wall.

The Summit – Our Dreams Come True

He has slowed down a lot ... it doesn't look too easy up there! Glancing up a little later, I notice Alfred and Willi right on his heels, but they have tackled the obstacle at a different spot, and not without difficulty. The strain of climbing for so many hours at such altitude shows in their every movement. They seem to be in slow motion. Everything now is bathed in a milky light. With blue shadows. But, good God! What about Mrufka? Where is she?

This terrain is unbelievably tough going. The snow has been all churned up. There are sinuous braids and ribbons of a marzipan-like consistency and slabs chiselled into fluid, fluted shapes by the wind, then fused to the bonehard surfaces beneath by the sheer force of moving currents of ice-cold air. There are shields fashioned in different thicknesses from crystal powder and often fallen across each other chaotically, like the ruins of a huge, collapsed slate roof. Most will hold your weight, but not all – you step between them or through them, and they shatter into fragments, or slide away ...

'Careful, Julie!'

'I know ... Don't worry!' Even with crampons we need to pay the utmost attention here.

After skirting a chest-high barrier of snow with an overhanging rim, we put the treacherous wind-ploughed landscape behind us ... only to find ourselves sinking at every step in deep, loose snow. Gasping for breath, I reluctantly track back towards the rounded spine of the ridge. The distance between us and the three figures above has widened, but they too are barely moving, hanging up there like marionettes on the slope beneath the final seracs. We must get on! There is obviously another struggle waiting for us up there! The time it takes to gain altitude increases dramatically in this last section below the summit – for everyone.

'Julie, how are you feeling?'

She smiles at me, 'Don't worry!'

'No headache? Not at all?' I need to know. After all, we are approaching an invisible barrier, which it is only possible to cross on certain days of your life, the very best days. The exaggeratedly slow movements of everyone up here is proof of how far we have already penetrated into the forbidden zone.

Julie's answer dispels my anxiety. 'No, Kurt. No headache – *kein Kopweh* at all!' She nods her head for emphasis. 'Go on, keep going. No time to lose!'

Up! 8,400 metres ... it will soon be three o'clock.

Soon after that we discover Mrufka.

She is leaning, immobile, into the steep slope above the small rocky shoulder. 'She's asleep!' says Julie, amazed. I don't trust my eyes. Can she really be sleeping here?

Before, earlier in the day, at the end of the traverse where the last fixed rope was, Mrufka had dozed off with her head on her arms. It is obviously not 'her day'. Willi took a picture of her in that position towards the edge of the ice balcony, in sunshine and with the clouds below. (Alfred is in the picture, too – you can recognize him by his rucksack.) Worried about her, Willi told Mrufka she ought to go down. But she was a long way from giving up. So Willi and Alfred continued in Alan's tracks with Mrufka following on her own.

I tentatively approach the huddled figure on the snow slope. She really is asleep! Her forehead, framed by dark blonde hair, is resting on her right arm. She has her hand in the sling of her ice-axe, which is anchored deeply in the snow to belay her. But what, I wonder, would happen were she to wake up suddenly?

'Mrufka – do you want a sweet?' I ask anxiously, clutching on to the back of her yellow anorak. She reacts with alarm, looking up full of surprise: 'No ... Up ... I have to go up!' That is what she wants.

I am startled, shocked. It's not the Mrufka I recognize. The good and helpful 'Ant' seems to be obsessed. There is no way of slowing down this bundle of energy – even if the lack of oxygen has put her in a strange state of mind – as is quickly demonstrated.

To Julie's consternation, Mrufka suddenly climbs up between us. At any moment she could stumble, grab at the rope and pull me down. Why not follow us, Julie suggests, adding, 'You can always go ahead when we get to the summit.' But Mrufka only increases her speed and retorts drily, 'I don't want to climb behind an old man.'

I cannot believe my ears. Is she bewitched? Don't take any notice, Kurt, I say to myself. Let her get in front! I stop and immediately Mrufka steams ahead. With much concern, I watch the hasty, uncontrolled movements of the Polish woman above us, as she swings hammer and ice-axe into the unsafe and uneven surface of the snowslab, working her way upwards. She is in a state halfway between sleep and waking. I am irritated, with a feeling of impotence: there is really nothing I can do about it. If nothing else, it urges her every fibre upwards. She is fighting for her summit. For her, turning back is out of the question, however much for the best it might be. Seconds later, a terrified Julie shouts from below, urging me to overtake her. If Mrufka should fall, she could tangle in our rope and sweep us all off the face. I try it, but it's completely out of the question to overtake by breaking a different trail. Every time I get close, Mrufka speeds up. Gasping for breath, I give up.

The Summit – Our Dreams Come True

'*Basta!*' I yell down to Julie – I'm fed up. We have to take the risk ... just as we would with any ice tower above us. But then I change my mind – keep a safe distance! It is the only thing we can do.

How much valuable time and energy has been wasted on this unexpected intermezzo? Hopefully it won't be long before Mrufka meets Alan. Perhaps she will listen to her partner.

'Let's have a rest and a drink,' I say to Julie. We need a breather, anyway.

Mrufka now climbs above us and to our right. We are out of her fall-line, thank God. The sky above has meanwhile paled. Clouds are welling up from below. It is happening very slowly, but it's still worrying. When I look out to the Baltoro, I see the outline of Masherbrum, and below it an ocean of peaks, but a soft, hazy greyness has spread over the whole landscape.

The weather is slowly worsening, that much is evident. It reminds me of my summit climb of Gasherbrum II. Then, seven years ago, the weather was almost exactly like this when I reached the highest point with my companions – worse, even, if anything: the sky grew steadily darker and the sun penetrated the leaden curtain with a sinister light. In the end, darkness lay over everything like a burden – *Götterdämmerung* on the Karakoram mountains – but nothing happened. Just a delicate veil of fog of an almost transparent greyness, which slowly grew denser, swaddling the enormous pyramid of K2 so that it rose, like a wraith, above all the other peaks. A mist like chiffon ... eerie and of ominous beauty ... but that was all. It stayed like that and we came down safely.

4 August 1979 ... and 1986. Is history repeating itself? The date is the same, just seven years later. Nobody knows – it could just as easily be different. We are too high to escape, that much is sure. In the event of a real breakdown in the weather, we are doomed – even if we turn back now.

I cling to my memories of Gasherbrum, try to calm down, while the mantle of greyness slowly, very slowly, increases. Another ingredient of danger? I guess we have to take the risk, the unavoidable sort of risk with any high climb like this, but I still have the feeling it will turn out as it did on Gasherbrum.*

I wonder what Julie feels about it?

---

* One thing confirmed by the subsequent course of events was that nothing would have changed for us, even had we turned around. We were as equally trapped as Hannes Wieser on the Shoulder, who did not even tackle the summit climb, as Mrufka, who turned back just below the summit, as Alan Rouse, Willi Bauer and Alfred Imitzer, who got to the top. There was no difference, it was not a question of hours, we were all too late by one whole day.

'Julie ...'

But she does not reply. She is staring up, fascinated. 'Look, there!' She points. On the soft skyline of the summit, at the dark edge of snow behind the serac immediately above our heads, is a figure! Now another! They are half-hidden by the edge, but now one raises his arms in triumph – the summit! That's got to be it, just beyond them. They are almost there!

It's an effort to hold back my excitement, to force myself to be calm, realistic. The summit seems quite close for us too, but appearances can be deceptive – we might still have another 200 metres of climbing to get there, and that's a lot up here.

'Yes, let's rest and drink something.' It does us good!

We empty the bottle. We are standing next to each other and have no idea that at this very moment Willi is taking a photograph of us from above, albeit unintentionally. We appear as two small figures further down the summit slope, behind his friend Alfred who is taking the final steps to the subsidiary summit. It is 3.15 p.m. Looking up a little later, I spot somebody else. That's three of them have made it. Onwards!

Like a giant suitcase, a projecting bulge of snow bars the way ahead. Mrufka went to the right here, which meant burrowing in deep snow for several steps. I prefer to put a titanium screw deep into a corner on the lefthand side, where I have found some good ice. Belayed by Julie, I climb obliquely to the edge above, then work my way along a steep hard rib on all fours, using the front points of my crampons and my ice-axe. It soon widens out. At a small crevasse, I set up a good belay and bring up Julie, who removes the titanium screw on the way. Above us, in the bluish-grey mixed light, we see a succession of steep convex snowslopes, a three-pointed sérac – which hides the summit from our view – and on the right, higher, but still so close you think you can touch it, a gleaming white shape – the mighty 'shark's fin' of ice. That, we know, is not far from the top.

It is four o'clock. That was to have been our limit for the summit but we are so near now, so near.

Suddenly Willi Bauer appears. He and Alfred are on their way down.

'Are you sure you still want to go up?' he asks me.

The question takes me by surprise. 'It shouldn't take us more than an hour at most,' I answer. What is he talking about?

'You're wrong,' says Willi. 'It took us four hours!'

'Come off it, Willi!' I object, reproachfully, and for a moment feel a sense of panic, wondering how such a thing could be possible. He must have misunderstood me.

'It took us four hours,' Willi continues, 'from down there.' And points in the direction of the ice traverse.

Ah, well. That's an entirely different thing!

The Summit – Our Dreams Come True

Nevertheless I am quite concerned, because I suddenly remember our rucksack is down there – with the stove and the bivouac gear. It takes far less energy to descend, but we'll need at least an hour to get back there from the summit. What shall we do if we cannot make it down in time?

At this moment Agostino and Joska come into my mind, our two friends who in 1983 found shelter near the summit and escaped with only minor frostbite.

'Are there any crevasses where you can bivouac?' I ask Willi. He nods: 'Yes, sure – and of course you'll reach the summit.' He follows after Alfred, who has by now climbed down the snow barrier.

A whirl of thoughts buzzes round my brain. It is close enough, the summit, but what bothers me now is not so much weather as time.

Willi, with his vague reply, was not a lot of help. But up here time is like a rubber band. You are so engrossed with what you're doing, paying attention to do everything correctly and precisely, all your concentration focused on the snow and ice, every step taken in this landscape dedicated to the climb – that you forget all about time. It is as if the whole dimension ceases to exist up here.

Heads down, we continue – every step requiring several breaths. 8,500 metres ... What's that – suddenly – as if something magic touched me? Aghast, I stop and look up. A weaving play of light and shadow, eddying, whirling, dancing above the last dark curves of snow ... Is this the prelude to a storm? A coquettish tease before all the forces of heaven start to roar?

Is it about to start? And we, will we be in it then, right in the heart of it? Or is it just the fluttering of the pale, silky folds of this mantle of mist which enshroud us and will eventually dissolve ...?

An inner wrangle between my faith in 'our' mountain and instinctive fear brings the lunatic response – Up! While it's still possible – let's go up! Even so, I would be prepared to turn round. If the occasion demanded it, if Julie wanted to ...

'Should we go on, or not? The summit is so close – there it is! But we can still turn around.' I notice Julie's tense expression. She has also seen the dancing veils.

'I'm feeling very fit!' she says.

'It can't be more than an hour ...

'If you think so – let's go on!' she replies decisively. Go! Go! We know everything is at stake. Once in a lifetime! Today! We are going into this thing with our eyes open, totally aware of what we're doing.

The dancing veils disappear. The air does not move at all. That's not the way a storm announces itself. The transparent greyness over the landscape indicates rather a gradual worsening of the weather. Will we manage to avoid a bivouac? We must be above 8,500 metres ...

Here's Mrufka again! She swings her ice-axe, thrusting it into the steep snowslope, a look of wild determination on her face. Without doubt she is driven by an unremitting will to get to the summit, but she has to rest every few steps now, stopping, sinking her head on her arm on the slope. I shudder, imagining her spending an icy night up here. It is obvious she should turn back, but how to convince her of that? If she will listen to anybody, it will only be to Alan, her partner. Where in all heavens is he? Julie has already remarked earlier that we would never be able to support an exhausted Mrufka to the summit and, more to the point, get her safely down again – a descent that without doubt would be partly in the dark. After all these years, we have a sense of what we can manage between us, the two of us, but we couldn't do it with three! At last Alan appears on the curved outline of snow above us, his slim silhouette against the grey of the sky. Alan Rouse, who has acted as saviour more than once in the chaotic situation on this mountain!

'Are there any crevasses we could bivouac in up there?' I ask him. A good bivouac site could be a matter of life and death. 'Yes, you'll find somewhere,' he tells us. 'And please, Alan ...' Julie implores, 'take care of Mrufka. She won't listen to us. But we think she ought to go down.' She indicates to where Mrufka is leaning into the snowslope, resting. Will Alan succeed in talking her into giving up? 'Whatever you agree, both of you,' Julie says, as Alan, very surprised, reaches his companion, 'stay with her.'

Not long afterwards we see the pair descending: it was a black day for one of Poland's best mountaineers. Even back in Camp 4, she still cried for her summit.

We are alone ... the snow around us, the ribbed surface, hundreds of lines. The Shark's Fin is now directly above us and very close. A thin transparent haze muffles everything. We climb towards the summit. The dice are cast.

It really isn't that far now! With every step, I feel it more strongly: we're not going to need a bivouac up here! But I notice a windcarved niche, directly below the huge, icy triangle and make a mental note, just in case. Tension is increasing. Our way ahead is suddenly blocked by a large, almost vertical ice barrier, about three metres high. We can't even see what lies ahead. Have we really got to climb that? There looked a much easier way on the other side of the big triangle, but I am loath to go back. The titanium ice-screw grinds as I turn it into the hard wall with my ice-axe. I chip some handholds with the pick (any energy saved is a help) – then, curious to see what waits on the other side, I push myself

The Summit – Our Dreams Come True

up. Glancing down at Julie, as she belays me, her eyes I see are big and questioning, her face full of excitement. I cut another two handholds in the ice, then pull myself over the edge ...

There is the smooth line of snow leading up to the summit with, below it, a moderate slope, a shallow depression. At once all seems ridiculously easy. 'We're almost there!' I shout down. 'We can leave the titanium screw in place for the way back.'

Over there, not much higher, the mountain ends. K2. Taking up the rope, I belay Julie. Our K2. A shine seems to come over her face as she raises her head above the edge and looks over. Just a few minutes more ...

I see she has brought the screw with her anyway. I spot another possibility for a bivouac, and glance along at the hole at the beginning of the depression almost with a smile. It is much brighter up here. A friendly place compared with the dark steepness of the enormous mountain flanks. But we won't sit here in a bivouac. Not without some irony I think about time: we have actually arrived here much earlier than we thought when we were so nervous about coming on.

One more crevasse, then we follow the smooth line of snow, gently leading us higher ...

The joy! The happiness! We cling to one another. For this one moment of eternity, K2 – beautiful K2 – is ours.

'Julie – the peak we most desired!' I feel my voice trembling as I look into the big, dark eyes under the yellow hood – eyes which can radiate so much power – the familiar glance and the little smile. 'Our very special mountain,' she whispers. It is, it is – our own and very special mountain.

Thousands of peaks lie at our feet, but we see none of them. They don't matter. Just to be here, together. Minutes in the snow, in the highest snows of K2 ...

It is just after 5.30 p.m. I notice as I glance at my watch. On the curved, rounded crest of snow, in the grey haze which surrounds us – now clearer, now darker, are propped some bulky yellow Korean oxygen bottles, and fixed between them, the large red-white-red Austrian flag (which used to fly in Base Camp): and, barely moving in the still air, a little triangular pennant from the *Naturfreunde*, and a British flag, smaller than a pocket handkerchief, which Alan must have placed there. I detach it and hand it to Julie ... 'For you,' I tell her, 'Alan won't mind if we take it down ...' Hesitating, she holds it in her hand for a moment, then stuffs it into the pocket of her down jacket ... 'You can have it later – or Alan, if he wants it ...' She doesn't seem to attach much importance to the flag, the summit of our dream mountain means more, much more.

At the same time, the all-enveloping mantle of grey prevents us from seeing very far. A small, but prominent, subsidiary summit of rock and ice over on the opposite side must mark where the Magic Line comes up. Below us, to the north, we can see an elongated bank of rock through the silky fog: it is a secondary top – just a step, really, but the highest on the North Face. A thought flashes through my mind, leads me down for a moment to where we turned back in 1983 – and a feeling of satisfaction rises inside me …

But the fog is darkening and a cool wind sweeps over the summit. It is like a warning. Quickly we shoot off some pictures, but Julie says, 'It's high time we left …' Anxiety flickers in her eyes. It's past six already. We really have to go!

The Fall

NIGHT ON THE HANGING GLACIER

We'll be able to move more quickly if I do the leading. My route finding is better and I have no qualms about Julie following on behind. She is in very good shape. I wouldn't dream of letting her come down second otherwise. There should be no problem about making it back to the top camp on the Shoulder without a bivouac, but unfortunately we'll not reach the rucksack we left hanging at the end of the fixed ropes before dark; it's still 300 metres further down. Good thing we have a head-torch.

'I'll go ahead, then – if that's OK?' I glance back at Julie, see her nod of agreement: she blinks at me from under hoar-covered hair.

'All right, but go! No time to waste!' Her voice follows me as I leave the summit. She's right. Every minute counts. I must hurry. There is still some light: we can see well enough. And only a light wind. But how long have we got before it's quite dark? Everything will become twice as hard then, every step a problem.

Don't rush, don't go any faster than is safe, a voice inside me keeps saying.

That's the subsidiary summit behind us. In the grey mist, I make for the icy silhouette of the Shark's Fin. Suddenly I remember that somewhere around here, there was a small crevasse. Accordingly, I detour a little to the right to be sure of avoiding it before going on towards the Fin. In the snow, I can see our tracks from the way up. I pause for a second and take another look round – and freeze. Oh, my God! At the other end of the rope, Julie in her haste has omitted to make the detour. She is coming directly at me in a straight line, and just in front of her – almost invisible – is the dark smudge of a depression. The crevasse!

'Stop! For God's sake, stop!' I yell just in time to bring her to a standstill.

I hadn't seen the crevasse from above, either: it was only my memory that warned me.

'Go back up, and follow my steps round,' I instruct her. But why hadn't I said anything before? I should have warned her. Can that be an effect of the extreme altitude? The thin air up here leads to all sorts of short circuits, even when you think you are behaving perfectly reasonably. If you don't do things the minute you think of them, you are apt to forget, or what is even worse, to think you have done them just because they occurred to you – thought becoming reality. No less disastrous, you may take the very thought of an action as sufficient to render the deed itself unnecessary ... 'Not now,' you tell yourself, 'later maybe.' Dangerous delusions!

I am quite sure that the two of us have not reached that state yet, but so narrowly avoiding the crevasse has set alarm bells ringing in my mind. Don't break your neck. It doesn't matter how slow and cautious you are. The descent is always the most dangerous part.

Julie stopped the moment I shouted. Now, carefully, she retraces several steps, reaches my tracks and follows them. I let out a deep, long-held breath – I don't dare to think of what might have happened if one of us had fallen into a crevasse up here at 8,600 metres ... Onwards!

Almost immediately, I reach the top of the short vertical step, make a stance, and belay Julie down. We are now at the same height as the Shark's Fin.

'Put the screw in at the bottom,' I call down to her as she descends.

Yes, even though it costs valuable time, it's worth putting in an ice-screw! Not that I think I will fall – but safety is worth those few minutes.

'Come on!' Julie's voice floats up to me, and I lower myself down while she takes in the rope. Only a few words are exchanged as I join her, and already she is removing the screw. Not for the first time, I notice the determination in her face. Yes! We still want to get down to that camp: we need to move as fast as possible, but at the same time we must do so with the utmost caution – we have to make the most of the last of the daylight to get over the seracs.

Onwards!

We move together now. My feeling is that, going down, we would do better to cross the lower ice and snow step at the place where Mrufka came up, rather than where we tackled it. Already we are just above the steep section where the two tracks divide. It is obvious from the trampled surface which way the others have gone. Again, going ahead alone, I sneak carefully down until I reach a small horizontal crevasse which lurks below me in the twilight, and I wait there, belaying Julie with my ice-axe rammed deeply into the snow. I am relieved – because Julie, having appeared at the edge above me, tackles the steep obstacle with surprising agility. Now she is with me.

'Take care. There's that little crevasse. Remember?'

With the reminder, I am anxious in some way to make good my sin of omission further up.

'Yeah. Sure!' she says, a bit breathlessly. Was that a smile?

The Fall

Of course, we both knew the crevasse! On the way up it was where we went to the left and Mrufka to the right ...

'Let's keep going. Down!'

I wonder if Mrufka and Alan have already reached camp? Meanwhile the daylight has faded more and more so that I can just make out nearby snow formations, but not much more than that. Peering into the depths I can faintly recognize by its dark silhouette the highest of the rock shoulders. That's where we have to get to.

That's the way.

We'll be at about 8,400 metres when we reach there and not very far from our rucksack. We should be able to manage that even when we have to move more slowly once it's dark. We'll need that head-torch pretty soon now.

Shall I get it out ready? I ask myself.

No. Let's not waste time. We can still see enough.

I grope my way over the slightly curved slope, stepping sideways, step after step, time and again thrusting in the ice-axe, my gaze resolutely directed downhill.

Here are those damned snow shields – irregular wind-pressed slabs. Don't take it too fast, Kurt. Take great care. Really, we can hardly see a thing now.

'Take care!' I call up to Julie. 'Great care. Go slow here ...'

But I know that she is prudent. Again I ask myself whether we should get the torch out now. It's in her down jacket. She put it in the pocket when we dumped our rucksack at midday. The surface of the snow here is very irregular – and what are these here – still tracks? The slope is not steep on this section and I know we are in the right direction, but never mind, let's get the torch out.

'Stop. We'll do it ...'

'Oh, Kuuuurt!!' The yell splits the darkness, loud, terrified, desperate. In the same moment, I spin round and ram the ice-axe with all my force into the slope, hurling myself on top of it. The rope! The rope! Here it is! Already, Julie, a dark bundle, hurtles by at incredible speed ...

Hang on, you *must* hang on, Kurt.

Terrified, I wait for the shock. Though it's hopeless, I still pray for that one in a thousand chance of being able to hold this unexpected fall.

Kurt, my head tells me, you haven't a hope. This is the end: you'll both fall 3,000 metres down K2.

With vicious suddenness, the shock comes on to the rope, and for a fraction of a second I succeed in holding it. Then I'm catapulted out and flung with incredible force down the mountainside, powerless, weightless, like a feather in an erupting volcano.

The Endless Knot

I am helpless ... helpless ... The speed is terrifying ... An overwhelming fear of impact grips me ... this endless tumbling ... head-over, head-under, down, down ... The slope! The slope! I clutch at it frantically, get a grip and hang on with all the force of desperation. Again, the shock: a giant fist rips me once more from the surface and flings me into the air. The tumbling goes on ...

Stopped! The giant fist has crushed me into the snow. In a sitting position, back to the wall, I am stuck upright in the snow, buried knee-deep, legs trapped in deep, heavy snow. The rope is still in one hand, but my axe gripped in the other is buried deep under the snow. Words fail to come ...

Julie? What's happened to Julie?

'Kurt!' Through a haze, the words float down the slope.

'Get your ice-axe in. Belay yourself!' I howl up into the darkness. My whole body is trembling uncontrollably.

At the same time, I press myself even deeper into the snow. By some miracle I have come to rest in a natural, safe belay position. Miraculously, too, Julie has stopped several metres higher up. I can just see her indistinct form on the slope above. Did she brake her fall?

'I can't get my ice-axe out ... I'm lying on top of it.'

If she's on top of her axe, then probably she did manage to brake. But why can't she pull it out? I have trouble understanding the whole thing properly – can't even grasp that we're still both alive, that we are not lying smashed at the foot of the mountain. It is truly a miracle.

'I'm trying to get my axe out now, but I'm in an awkward position. Watch out!' The voice from above sounds muffled.

Attention, Kurt!

What does she mean, in a bad position? Is she lying obliquely in the snow? Or with her head downhill, perhaps?

Whooshhh ...

The sound of sliding – eventually, Julie bumps into me with full force. Thanks to my bomb-proof position in the heavy, deep snow, I resist the impact. Once more it went well!

'Julie, are you all right?'

'Yes. Fine,' she replies matter-of-factly. 'But my ice-axe is still up there.' Only a deep sigh betrays the relief she feels to find herself still alive.

Ice-axe still up there? Uh-uh! But the main thing is she hasn't hurt herself. I climb up and get it.

What will happen now? It is almost totally dark. Nearby I recognize the indistinct outline of a crevasse in the gentle curve of the hanging glacier on which we have landed. We are at the beginning of the giant balcony in the upper half of the summit pyramid. The fall has thrown

The Fall

us off route and night is almost upon us. The best thing would be to bivouac over there. It ought not to be that cold as it is overcast and there's no wind. Perhaps this crevasse will make a good bivouac site? If we wait a couple of hours, we might be able to continue the descent ... but I doubt it. Although I can vaguely see the outline of the highest rock shoulder away off to one side, to get over there to rejoin the route in the middle of the night may not be that simple. We have to be content that we are still alive, thank God! After that, we can cope with all the rest. The weather certainly is not good, but neither is it really bad. We are in cloud – for a free bivouac that is better than an icy, star-clear night. But we're high. Very, very high. At a guess 8,400 metres – perhaps slightly less than that.

'Julie, we have to bivouac. Let's go over to that crevasse.'

We stamp through deep snow across the moderately inclined slope. By the time we reach the crevasse on the hanging glacier, it is almost pitch dark, yet it is still possible to pick out the main features. The icy trench looks an ideal place to bivouac, being perhaps two metres wide and with a ramp inside that leads down as if into a den. I feel how close we are to the edge of the giant balcony. Uncomfortably close. The snow here is hard and reliable. A good belaying place – Julie rams her ice-axe into it. The ramp then ought also to be of good hard snow: all the storms should have tamped a good, thick crystalline layer over everything, the same as is very often found on the wind-exposed sections of the summit pyramid. The crevasse is certainly chockful of snow. Nevertheless – perhaps just because everything does seem so perfect at first sight – I cannot suppress slight mistrust. And Pasang's evil demons come to mind – those demons who spring to life at night.

Haven't we just survived this fall by some enormous stroke of luck? Escaped certain death? All of a sudden, this miraculous shelter seems to me more like a trap.

'Julie, I have to check it out before we can go in. Please, get the flashlight, then belay me.'

Yes ... that's it, before we move into it, I must examine it carefully, probe all round with the ice-axe; I ought definitely to be well belayed for that. Julie rummages for the torch in the pocket of her jacket. Both of us lived for days in a crevasse like this on the North Spur of K2. The expedition set up a whole camp inside it. It offered a really safe refuge in the dangerous flank of the spur, while the avalanches kept sliding down over our heads. On Tirich West, too, in the Hindu Kush, Dietmar Proske and I occupied a similar crevasse-bivouac on the north face of that 7,000-metre peak. But such shelters are not always so benign.

Julie finds the torch. 'I'll need to turn the battery round,' she says with a sigh and fumbles with the casing. Perhaps our eyes have got used to the darkness, or is light coming off the snow itself? Whatever the explanation, there is a strange shimmer all round us, even in this cloud. It's not pitch-black, anyway. That's something. We can recognize shapes, and the task Julie is doing now, she has done a hundred times before. She always carries the battery back-to-front as a precaution against the torch being accidentally switched on and draining all the power; now she has it the other way round. Already I am beginning to regret that for reasons of weight we decided not to bring two torches with us.

With resignation in her voice Julie announces, 'It doesn't work!'

She tries the switch several times without success, opens the casing again, and fiddles some more with the battery. I feel a hot fury welling up inside me. Perhaps the nervous tension of the past few hours has finally proved too much.

Bloody hell! I think. That's all we need! Night! At 8,400 metres! We've had a fall, we're sitting on the highest balcony of the world, we're longing for any kind of shelter, and now ... *this*.

Julie has put the battery in again, closes the case and switches on. Nothing.

A wave of utter frustration overcomes me, robbing me suddenly of good sense. I tear the lamp from Julie's hands and hurl it into the night. Even as I do so, I am bitterly shaken by my outburst.

'Hell!' I mumble into my beard, shocked at the consequences of my sudden temper. This must be the altitude. Julie doesn't say a word, but it is obvious that we should have kept trying longer. Now, we're very definitely without any light. In the darkness in front of me yawns the black mouth of the crevasse. Inside, there is a sinister silence. Nevertheless I have to try it.

'Belay me!' I chew into my icy beard, then crawl slowly and carefully down the ramp, probing as I go. I'm in a square tunnel between the walls of the crevasse: the floor is quite firm, but much too steep yet for a bivouac. My optimism rises. Again I probe. The snow seems solid and carries me well. If only I could see something! It's still steep. For a moment, I stop and a sense of misgiving rises once more. Hadn't I better back out?

'Julie, belay me carefully.'

On my belly now, hand anchored on the ice-axe, I edge feet-first a little further into the tunnel, sliding along ... Now it's more even. This would be all right, but I want to make one final check. Then I notice: as far as my feet have reached, the ground is still firm, but testing sideways with my boot has revealed an open hole where the hard snow ramp fails to meet the edge of the wall. For God's sake! We can't stay here – there's nothing but air below this ramp!

The Fall

'Julie! Julie! Pull!'

Immediately the rope tightens, but in the meantime a huge chunk of the ramp has broken away and clatters into the void. There is no anchorage left for my feet any more.

Panting heavily, and with a frantic surge of energy, I slither upwards, back over my ice-axe, looking for some kind of hold to enable me to get a bit higher still. I succeed and force in the axe again in front of me.

'Julie Pull as hard as you can!' I yell, panic in my voice. 'It's a bridge and it's crumbling away!'

My breathing is desperate. I can hear the broken pieces echoing down into the crevasse. Somehow, I manage to stick my left crampon into something: but my right foot is still hanging in space. For a moment I don't dare move ... Damned, damned trap! Didn't I just know it? If any more of this stuff breaks away, I'll go down with it ... Scared, I think of the way Renato died ... Carefully, I wriggle a tiny bit more and succeed in bringing my foot up out of the hole and back on to the crumbling ramp, but I don't dare trust any weight to it. I can only pull up on my hands.

I scream: 'Julie!'

I'm finished. That's it. I can't do any more. Heart hammering, I'm wedged obliquely in a fragile equilibrium, sustained solely by the ice-axe, one crampon-tooth – and Julie. I try to collect my wits, muster some strength, tank up my lungs with oxygen. Heaven knows there is little enough of that up here. Then I have another try.

'Up again, Julie! Pull as hard as you can!'

Panting like a steam engine, I inch higher until at last I have found holds for the crampon-points of both feet, but my energy is totally spent.

'Stop pulling. Just hold me.' Mouth agape, I force out the words.

I rest my face in the snow of the ramp. All around me it's pitch-black. I can't make out a thing, but I can sense, below me, the pitiless emptiness of space, invisible, ever-present. I cling to the sides of my icy coffin. Exhaustion grips me, as do the long black arms of the chasm. Pasang's demons are on the loose! I am suddenly filled with indescribable panic unlike anything I have experienced in my whole life before. Will I ever get out of here, escape this icy crypt?

'What's the matter?' A voice from outside.

'I need to breathe,' I reply feebly. It's like a paralysis, like being under the influence of a spell.

At this very moment, and for no apparent reason, the whole edge collapses under my right foot. It cracks, breaks off and crashes into the depths. Terror strikes harder. Utter panic. There is no doubt about the spirits! My hand tightens like a claw around the ice-axe. No, no! You won't get me! 'Up!' I yell, and immediately feel the pull. For a moment practically my whole weight comes on to the rope. I jam a fist between the left wall and the snow, just enough so that with the other hand I can pull out the axe and thrust it in a little bit higher. 'Pull!' I *will* get out of here.

I can hear Julie's heavy breathing above me now. I dimly see her dark, hunched shape as she pulls at the rope with all her might. At last the demons are losing their grip. My teeth are clenched tight with effort. Push. I work myself higher. Again and again, gasping for breath like a fish out of water, I press the axe into the surface. I have hardly any strength left at all, but God, Yes! I am getting out! God, Julie, you held me!

'Don't panic. You won't die here.' Her dark silhouette looms over me. Her voice is very quiet, like an oracle.

No, I shall not die here. I am out! Lying outside with my face in the snow. Julie, you've saved my life.

'Thank you,' I gasp with my last breath. 'That was very close.'

Where will we stay?

I have an overwhelming desire to get away from the crevasse, even if there is safe snow around it. The terror is still in my bones. Where can we stay? Dig a snow hole somewhere on the face? That's the only option left. A little higher than we are is a steep section of snow with a hard crust. I start swinging the ice-axe, hollowing out a half circle, a place for two, tight together ... It's absurd! Our bivouac gear is hanging only a hundred metres lower in the small rucksack at that last piton. Everything seems to be running against us now.

Without a head-torch there is no way we can reach it. It's much further over, out on the spur. We'll have to wait till first light to find a way back from our hanging glacier, from the balcony, to the route. We are both working hard at the hole. We don't feel cold. An old bivouac rule says, the longer you prepare the bivouac, the shorter you need to spend in it.

Clang! The ice-axe hits hard ice. We try further up, further down, further everywhere – there's a hard wall below the snow. Bloody hell! So much for a snow hole.

We have to be satisfied with an open niche. At least I manage with the axe carefully to hollow a small hole behind the hard crust without breaking it. One of us – Julie – will have room to kneel or sit inside.

The ground is level in front of the hole and there is no wind, so the other can just crouch there, half sheltered by the curve of the niche. A Spartan luxury: some sweets and a small plastic bag with Ovaltine powder. All we have to sit on is the rope (for one of us), and Julie's hip-bag (for the other). We're wearing our long down jackets, the yellow anoraks and our over trousers, but we miss the warm down trousers which are down at ABC – not me so much, I'm fairly impervious to cold, but Julie. Otherwise, we're well enough protected here with our mittens and overgaiters. As it happens, neither of us sustains frostbite on our feet up here. Nor do I on my hands – not then. But the tip of Julie's nose suffers and possibly two fingers on one hand.

However, it is a terrible misfortune that we haven't been able to reach our bivouac material. What's more – and this error was surely to do with high-altitude absentmindedness – we've even left the foil space blanket, which weighs hardly anything, down in our rucksack at the last piton. I can't believe it. Desperately I search again and again through all my pockets ... but in vain, we really have left it behind in the rucksack.

It is a long, long night. Luckily the weather does not break, but towards morning it grows very cold and windy. We've tried, as best we could, to keep each other warm by hugging and rubbing each other and moving from time to time, but we're relieved when finally the thin light of dawn breaks through the veils of cloud, glad that the long night is over, and we are still alive and still possessed of sufficient strength for the complicated descent. Thank God the weather did not break down totally. Thankfully, we welcome even patches of sunlight as we start to search out our way down.

Down to 8,000 Metres

THE ILLUSION OF SAFETY

Where is the camp? The refuge at the end of our space odyssey? We have to find it!

The descent from the top of the ice balcony has cost us many hours of the utmost effort and concentration. It was the last act in our fight for survival on the summit pyramid – or so we thought. Now we are somewhere around 8,000 metres, and can't see a thing. A short while ago – but who knows, maybe it was as much as an hour since – I could still make out the Bottleneck and the ice overhang above us, and that gave me a clue to the direction we should follow: now we are caught in a grey soup and in real danger of passing clean by the camp without noticing it! We can't allow that to happen! I am uneasily aware that the descent has sapped almost all our reserves – and we felt so amazingly well this morning! For quite a while now Julie has been calling for a rest, but I've resisted, allowing us only time to catch our breath – just half a minute or so when we reach the end of the rope, Julie on a belay stance and me climbing down to join her from above. We move on all fours, facing into the slope.

We're in a real stew of clouds: filthy grey masses moving slowly, banks of fog, flurries of snow crystals that seem as lost as we are and are now roaming from one place to another. It's all white, or grey, or oppressively dark, according to the density of this icy cotton wool. The steepness of the slope and how well I can remember it from the way up are the only indications of where we are. A short while ago I mistook a rock for a tent, and the disillusion was almost unbearable. Still the shock shook me up and remobilized all my senses. We will find the right way. I'm known for my sixth sense when climbing at night or in fog – and not without reason; I would have been dead long since without it.

I see Julie's vague outline, filmy, grey, watch her slow movements. She knows as well as I do that it must have been somewhere around here that the Barrards – Liliane and Maurice – lost their way. 'Let's continue to zigzag,' I shout. 'We must find the plateau.' I say it as much to keep contact between us as anything else, although of course we do have to locate the small level section on which Camp 4 is situated. 'Yes, we have to find it,' she agrees. 'But the slope here is still too steep …' I notice the look of seriousness in her dark eyes between the frosted strands of hair. It's so gloomy now, dark twilight, that we have had to take off our goggles. She's right, the slope is too steep. A horrible thought flashes through my mind: we could miss the plateau completely and stray onto the China side, ending up among those giant cornices! They overhang enormous drops. Maybe that's where Maurice disappeared after he lost Liliane. Julie and I are on our rope: whatever happens, we're together: it is either our life or death.

It has to be our life. Let's give it another try to the right. Only by maintaining our downhill zigzag will we find this camp. 'To the right, now!' I call, praying in my heart that it is the right decision, and nurturing the absurd, crazy hope for a gust of wind to part the clouds – to open them if only for a few seconds.

Zigzagging, we make our way down, but we hardly seem to get any lower. We're wasting our last energies, yet it's our only chance. It's the only way not to miss the camp in this grey and white desert. Our anxiety increases … how much longer? We're tired … we have come through so much … will this mountain ever let us go? Surely, it would have taken us earlier if that is what it had wanted? We have been at its mercy ever since our fall.

The slope is easing off! Julie, by God, it's getting flatter! That has to be the plateau! Or couldn't it just as well be the top of a giant cornice? I can't see the curving mounds of ice debris, the rounded chunks, half-melted and then refrozen, glued together by the icy night winds and continually replenished from the giant hanging glacier on the summit wall above. The shards and fragments fall 200 metres before coming to rest on the easier angle … Where, then is this zone that should mark the upper edge of the plateau? It was such a feature, I remember, on the way up. Where on earth are we? Is this a cornice after all? Maybe everything has been covered by impacted snow, freighted in by the wind? Is or isn't this the start of the plateau?

It shoots through my mind that they should be able to hear us from the camp. If we are where I think we are, all we need to do is yell.

'Ha-a-ll-o-o-o!'

I holler into the fog, and with a glance to Julie, add, 'They should hear that!' She looks at me in astonishment. 'Are you calling for help?' 'No, just so that we don't miss the camp.' That's if there's anyone around here. There follows an anxious wait – and silence.

'Can I sit down now?' I hear my companion say. 'Of course.' I continue to listen out into the clouds. Then I call again. I'm beside myself with agitation. Is this day going to end in another bivouac? Again, no answer. Only clouds ... and silence ... and the low noise of the wind over the surface of the snow. 'We have to go on,' I tell Julie. Disappointment. Hopelessness. But then, a resurfacing of hope. Julie pulls herself together and gets up.

Suddenly I hear a yell through the fog. There is an answer! The next moment both of us are shouting back at the tops of our voices. Relief surges through us – it's as if a great weight of fear has lifted from us. The camp ...!

No more bivouacs! We hear the voice again. It sounds like Willi.

From its direction, I know we must be at the beginning of the plateau. Immediately afterwards, I come upon the first mound of ice chunks – so, then, this is the zone I remembered! Now the angle diminishes. We are standing on a gentle snowslope, which – as I know – leads to the camp we set up at the lower end of the plateau.

With all that has since been written about the tragedy, I cannot forbear to comment at least once – and it has to be here – on the many distortions that have emanated from a number of quarters concerning the whole course of events. I have to do it for Julie's sake and mine: we who fought our way down from the top of the mountain to the highest camp completely on our own, by our own efforts and relying solely on one another. It's not true, as several writers have said, that Julie crawled the last part of the way into camp. It is also not true – as Willi reported – that her nose and cheeks were black with frostbite and that shreds of flesh were hanging from one hand, that she was unable to stand and had to be dragged by him to the tents. The considerable discrepancies which recur again and again between our two accounts could, in my opinion, indicate that Willi was the victim of hallucinations, that he experienced visions and thoughts which bore no relation to reality. Nobody who reaches 8,000 metres can be sure of being immune against that. But when other writers, who were below the cloud layer at the time, grotesquely misrepresent the time Julie and I arrived on the summit, saying it was 7 p.m., I'm lost for words. That goes, too, for the last 'speech' accorded to Renato Casarotto on the rim of the crevasse – when in reality, he was unconscious and almost dead. It seems to me that artistic licence has been stretched to breaking point many, many times in the reports of what happened on K2.

'I definitely want to rest now.' says Julie, letting herself down onto the snow. Both of us are incredibly relieved to discover that the camp is so close.

Down to 8,000 Metres

Just for a moment, a breath of wind tears a spinning hole in the fog, a circle within which I can make out the coloured shapes of tents. They also appear to be turning. A second later they are gone. Keep the direction in mind, Kurt. Hang on to it. Which way? There? Straight down, that's where, it must have been. But we could do with another opening like that to be sure. I crouch on the snow next to Julie, put my arm around her shoulder. Tiredness and relief show in her face. We've made it. Made it down safely from the 'mountain on top of a mountain'. K2 is 'ours'. But it was a narrow escape this time. I think of the fall and the bivouac. I see the stamp of frostbite on the tip of Julie's nose, discoloured, brownish – but, thank God, we are alive and K2 is ours: We will never come here again. The final full stop has been added to our long association with this mountain – even if K2 will always be bound to us and we to it. We pushed to the very limits, but despite everything, I feel content that we got there. We are free to go another way now ...

It opens up again. I see the camp, the three coloured tents, see Willi standing there. We have to go across to them before it all closes in again. But Julie still wants to rest, sit a little longer. Can I pull her? Over there is tea, warmth and recuperation. There is the end of the terrible odyssey. I stand up. 'Come on, I'll pull you,' I tell her, taking her hand. Then I start yanking her down the slope. It's easier than expected, because she is wearing her shiny yellow nylon trousers and the snow, despite its corrugations, is pretty regular and angled slightly downhill. Julie puts out her other hand to steady herself during the slide, lifting her cramponed feet a little to keep clear of the surface. I remember there is a small crevasse somewhere here on the plateau – please God don't let us fall into it! I keep my eyes skinned. Gasping, I tug Julie towards the camp. After a while, I stop. 'Wouldn't you like to get up?' I pant, asking myself whether she just fancies this way of moving, or whether now that our ordeal is over, she has suddenly been smitten with fatigue. Surely she would rather walk into camp under her own steam especially since we managed so well all day coming down those really horrible slopes to the plateau? Wouldn't she?

'I can't see very well ... I'd rather stay on the ground.' Her answer catches me by surprise. Is there something wrong? She had no problems with her eyes before now. Is it the effort? Or the start of snowblindness?

'OK,' I tell her and lean forward to start pulling again. From somewhere I hear Willi's voice, but I know now where the camp is, even if for the moment it is lost in fog once more.

'My glove! My glove!' Julie cries out. She must have lost it while supporting herself in the snow. Hopeless trying to find anything now! 'We're almost there, hang on a moment!' I gasp. In front of me I recognize the tents, emerging from the fog, and Willi, who has started towards us from the Korean tent. I pull Julie up from the ground and we approach Willi together. We hug one another. We are returning to a different world, from a different world.

'Please make some tea for Julie,' I ask Willi. It is obvious to me that there is not enough space for both of us in their tent. And I'm glad there is somebody to take care of her. Now that we're here, I realize that I have given everything, all my strength and mind, to make it possible. Now I am tired to death and all I want is to sleep. The Austrians take Julie in, and I lie down in our small tent and soon drift away. I don't remember seeing Alan or Mrufka, but they must – be here. Nobody can go down with the visibility at zero like this.

As Willi told me later in Innsbruck, Julie soon recovered her strength, after some hot tea. Knowing she was safe must certainly have helped. The worst was over. That's what everybody thought. Julie's feet were not frostbitten, Willi discovered, but she had sustained an injury as well as frostbite on one hand. In Willi's opinion, there was no doubt at that point that she would manage the descent. Her eye problem was giving her headaches, though. 'When we gave her drinks, she kept missing the cup,' Willi later recalled. Hannes and Alfred began talking about getting a helicopter to pick her up from the lower part of the mountain, but Willi knew that helicopters could only operate up to 6,000 metres, and only then under perfect conditions. Julie did not take the idea of 'rescue' seriously, although she would not have turned her nose up at a helicopter flight – anywhere! She told Willi that General Mirza had promised her a ride in a helicopter if she reached the summit of K2. I remember we were in Base Camp when he made the offer and I saw her delight at the prospect – sooner or later she would get her flight! Julie had never been in a helicopter and it was another adventure she looked forward to – some time – with no less excitement than a trip in Concorde, even if, in the end, it proved only a sightseeing trip over London!

Willi has since assured me, several times, that on that first day nobody had any doubts but that Julie, who had now recovered, would cope with the descent. She stayed in the neighbouring tent with the Austrians all the rest of that day. Like me, she was making up for lost sleep – as I was told at one stage when I woke up and asked for her.

As I had observed in earlier years, there is often quite a variation in the weather on K2: it may be almost calm on the lower Abruzzi Ridge, while higher up storm clouds sweep horizontally across the rocky ridges; the

Down to 8,000 Metres

Shoulder can be stuck in dense cloud while the summit has different weather entirely.

Its great height places the top of K2 almost at the cruising level of jet planes. Passengers on flights from Islamabad to Peking often observe a remarkable pyramid floating in the sky above an ocean of cloud – the summit structure of K2; sometimes the highest tips of the Gasherbrums and the sharp roof and dorsal scales of Broad Peak will be there as well – when below everywhere is experiencing filthy (or at least unpleasant) weather.

On 4 August, the bad weather began to develop in layers during the course of the day. But the force of the gathering storm failed to strike the upper reaches of the mountain. Julie and I could never have survived the bivouac in the open niche at 8,400 metres otherwise.

Below 8,000 metres, however, by five o'clock in the afternoon of 4 August, swaths of snow had swept the whole south face of K2. It grew increasingly dark and the clouds muffling the upper part of the mountain soon reached right down to the glacier as well. Then it started to rain, very steadily, before finally turning to snowfall. Petr and Przemyslaw, the two survivors of the Magic Line party which had gone over the top of K2 and now were struggling slowly down the Abruzzi Ridge, noticed that the snowfall was not so heavy higher up.

At noon on 5 August – according to Jim Curran – you could even see a tiny bit of blue sky from Base Camp, but it was obvious how strong the wind was because of the swirls of cloud drifting away from K2. However, by half past one in the afternoon, the weather was worse than ever. Full of concern, Jim confided to his tape recorder: '... expect the worst. There are actually twelve people on K2 at the moment, all at or above 7,000 metres and the weather up there must be horrendous.'*

It was not until 8 August, two days after Petr and Przemyslaw, that the last climbers from the Magic Line route – leader Janusz Majer and the two Polish women, Krystyna Palmowska and Anna Czerwinska – made it back into Base Camp. The retreat down the difficult route had been a hard struggle for them. It was lucky there were fixed ropes.

Even if a rescue operation had been suggested for the seven of us marooned on the Shoulder, there was no chance at all of anybody getting there from Base Camp so long as the storm was raging. It wouldn't matter how many people were in the party, in those circumstances, nobody would have made it. Besides, all those left in Base Camp were either exhausted, or had frostbite or other troubles. Of the Austrians, only Michael Messner was still around, the others had already set off for

---

* *K2, Triumph and Tragedy.*

Islamabad some days before, bearing (in good faith) the exciting news that three Austrians had been to the summit of K2.

The Koreans, during their descent down the Abruzzi Ridge, left everything in their tents necessary for an emergency, and Julie and I had our own depots, too. But the big question for all of us on the Shoulder was: how could we actually get down onto the Ridge without killing ourselves on the way?

Jim, in Base Camp, observes the weather day after day and keeps hoping. But the chances for those high up decrease rapidly. No human can survive indefinitely in the Death Zone, even when fully acclimatized and given sufficient to drink. And they must by now have exhausted their Gaz supplies. What about oxygen? There wouldn't be any of that either. For a stay of such length, a whole truck-load of bottles would have been necessary. Could anybody still be alive?

The 8th of August and Jim Curran is desperate: he is firmly convinced by now that Al, Julie, Kurt, Mrufka and the three Austrians are probably all dead. Yet he doesn't give up hope entirely.

On 9 August, together with Michael Messner, he goes up to the Advanced Base Camp, but doesn't discover anything. He spends the night in our small dark green tent, the only one still there, where all night long the wind rattles the swaying shelter, beating torn guylines against the roof.

The roaring of the storm continues on into 10 August, although the weather looks better. Jim goes back to Base Camp.

On 11 August, the news that everyone has died is sent out to the world.

But let us return to 5 August – to that island at 8,000 metres, lost in the storm ...

Blizzard at 8,000 Metres

THE AGONY OF THE FIVE DAYS

Night. I hear the hissing of the wind, the repeated crackle of snow crystals against the fabric of the tent. I lie awake listening to the gusts: so long as the sound doesn't change, just keeps recurring like this, it is drifting snow. The wind picks it up from one place on the mountain and deposits it somewhere else! You can tell from the intervals that the snow is not coming down now, just being shunted around. That's not too much to worry about – even if our little tent is facing the wrong way now that the wind has changed direction. When Julie and I put it up, the wind was blowing in from China, so we erected our fragile-looking shelter in the lee of the Korean tent, close enough to gain protection from the massive Asiatic dome. But that was on 2 August, since when the wind has turned a full 180 degrees, coming now from Pakistan. So we catch the full force of it! There's nothing we can do about it: the anchorage points have long since disappeared deep beneath the snow and are frozen into the ground. We'll go down tomorrow morning if … Full of worry, I keep my ear cocked to the wind noise, but it's still only drifting snow …

In any high camp, you can tell at once when the real snowfall starts. The sound is steady and much softer. Avalanche danger and a forced and speedy retreat are usually the attendant consequences.

It's high time we got away from here. We *must* get away tomorrow. We lost one day – and still made it to the summit. But now 5 August is almost over. It's more than enough.

What about the visibility, though? That's a big problem: since the disastrous collapse of the serac barrier when the 'teapot avalanche' broke off below the Shoulder of K2, only a very narrow passage remains which was the way we came up here. If only there had been enough bamboo wands to mark it, we could have descended it even in fog, but they ran out at the end of the big slope above Camp 3 at 7,700 metres. Alan Rouse and I would have needed another ten to fifteen sticks to finish the job.

The weather was glorious when we came up – and most of the others probably thought we were being fanatically over-cautious to have used the sticks at all. Now we are marooned in this fog, and if only we had a line of markers, we could find our way down. Make one mistake here, and you are likely to fall over the edge of the seracs …

Nevertheless, we will have to try it. God, I hope we don't get a snowstorm as well. If that happens, then there's no way out – we really are in a trap. The risk of losing our way in the swirling mass of a blizzard is enormous; we probably wouldn't even find our tents again. It would be certain death. So, what do we do in such a case? Wait and hope?

I wonder how things are with Julie in the next tent?

Frightened, I listen in the darkness to the sound of the snow crystals. Still only drifting snow. I fall asleep again.

What's that at the front of the tent? 'Open up!' I hear Julie's thin voice. Dozily, I grumble into my beard. She could have come back earlier! I open the entrance sleeve and Julie crawls awkwardly inside. 'It's a job to get in,' she pants. No wonder, with all this packed snow! The entrance is small and very low, just above the floor of the tent. Not much good in rapidly growing snowdrifts! I remember thinking that down at intermediate camp at 7,000 metres.

'Why do you only come now, in the middle of the night?' I grumble.

'Willi was taking care of my fingers. He gave me his silk gloves.' I hear Julie's voice in the dark. Well … she will need them. At least she has recovered over there, drinking tea … and caught up on her lost sleep … and at least she's here now! We snuggle up in the down bags and sleep.

A ferocious rattling of the tent wakes us. What a storm … it has to be a blizzard. Hell, no! I feel a knot in my throat. We really are in it this time. Getting down's going to be a real swine now.

Our little tent buckles under the force of the wind as the atmosphere sucks and seethes outside, a dull thundering comes from the direction of the summit pyramid.

The wind is gusting at 100 kilometres an hour, pushing waves of blown snow against the tent. It builds up higher and higher outside, pressing into the fabric. Will the masses of snow smother our small shelter completely, as happened one night on Nanga Parbat? At least then we had a solid tent.

Instinctively I pull Julie close, hug her in a tight embrace. We survived then – that was 7,400 metres – but here we are at 8,000, considerably higher. Julie doesn't say a word, presses herself to me. I know her thoughts are running along the same lines.

Slowly the morning comes up, but here in the tent it stays gloomy. I feel really sorry for having been so grumpy last night – somehow I want to say something nice … 'We made it to the top of K2, Julie. We survived the fall and the bivouac. We'll come through this, too. K2 is ours – doesn't that make you happy?'

No reply. Her silence oppresses me.

'I don't know ...' Julie finally says hesitatingly, in a low voice. And after a pause, 'I can't see very well ...' My God! What does that mean – she doesn't see very well?

I'm shocked. I suddenly remember she said the same thing yesterday, when I pulled her over the snowslope. Quite out of the blue – and I thought then it was just tiredness. Something similar happened to me on Everest. But now?

'Do you have any pain?'

She shakes her head. 'No, no pain,' she answers softly. I look into her face. Her eyes, large, seem darker than usual. But this is probably due to the dim light in here.

Her lips are cold. It scares me, but I don't let her see that. Something is wrong, I know it. I have never known her as low as this ... It's certainly not snowblindness. Surely she will be a lot better tomorrow? If only we weren't up here, in this storm trap! One thing is clear: this is another reason why we can't leave yet. 'We'll wait here till tomorrow – then you'll be feeling better and we can go down!' I force myself to appear calm. A descent in this storm would be madness, anyway.

But something must be done to buck Julie up. Tea! Liquid! I hurry to get the stove going. How much can Julie still see? I mustn't let her know how worried I am. How can I find out how bad she is? An idea comes to me. 'Pass me the knife,' I say, 'for the snow ...' (I'll cut some chunks from by the entrance, for cooking.) Anxiously, I watch out of the corner of my eye. She hands me the knife. I let out a deep breath. It was lying around in the tent, near the side, but she must have seen something – she couldn't have known so precisely where it was, otherwise. Could she?

Tea's ready. Sipping it is a real pick-me-up, for both of us. Julie leans against me. Despite the blizzard raging away outside, it is not cold in here. The rising walls of snow at least keep us insulated. Finally, we even take off our down jackets; we stretch out and, still in our sleeping bags, push our feet into the strange lateral pocket, and wait. After a while we doze off.

I had taken a close look earlier at the fingers on Julie's right hand: they're a little brownish as is the tip of her nose. Frostbite, but not third degree. Two are not too good, but the third is only slightly damaged. I'm convinced this should not present any insuperable handicap. She is worried it might mean she will be unable to hold her sword ... not that she complains, but I know how much her martial arts mean to her.

I try to reassure her – but we always knew such a thing could happen one day. The snowstorm keeps howling ...

'Bloody hell!' I swear involuntarily in English. The tent! It is slowly bending forward. Masses of snow have accumulated on the uphill side and are pressing heavily into the dome. The flexible poles of the *parapluie* no longer seem strong enough to withstand the pressure, and in two places they're bending like snakes. I'm worried: how much longer can this French contraption bear the strain? There is only one solution: relieve the weight!

To do that, I have to get out. There is too much snow over the tent to clear it merely by punching energetically from the inside!

Indeed, in many storms over the years I have been out to free a tent from its burden of snow usually without taking the trouble to struggle into boots and overpants – I have enough spare socks, even up here! But the problem this time, as I soon learn, is not just limited to the weak struts: I can't even get out through the entrance! The opening, with its short nylon tube just above floor level, seems to have been designed with gentian-filled Alpine meadows in mind, not deep snow. Despite having pitched the tent with the entrance facing downhill, so much snow is weighing down the tube that I can't push my way through it. 'To hell with this umbrella!' I swear, gasping after my unsuccessful struggle. Here we are, trapped like two mice under a cheese-cover. Not quite as bad as that, perhaps, because in the last resort we could always cut a hole and step out but that would be a drastic solution, and not to be advised in this weather! Right now, I have some choice words for our French 'wonder tent', this funny umbrella with a floor in it. Instead of furiously clouting the walls, as I'm now obliged to, I would prefer to be stepping into the ring with the inventor. *Merde! Merde!* I pant, not without reason.

At this moment I hear Alan Rouse's voice outside. He seems to be talking to Willi.

'Al will help us,' says Julie. We yell to him to ask if he can free the entrance.

'Of course!' Ever helpful, Al digs away like a dachshund into the deep snow. I cannot see him, but hear his laboured breathing through the thin fabric. It's very hard work: he's using just his hands as there's no shovel in this camp.

'I have to stop,' pants Alan. 'I've dug a great pit, and I'm not there yet!' I can believe it. Now Willi gives it a try, first with his hands then with the ice-axe. One false stroke rips a hole in the tent, but at least the 'pit' has now reached the sleeve entrance. 'You'd better do the rest yourself!' Willi puffs like a hippopotamus, he's had enough. 'And hurry up,' he adds, 'or it will close in on you again!' I hear him crawling into the nearby tent with his companions. Alan, too, must have returned to his shelter. I cannot hear him any more.

Blizzard at 8,000 Metres

What now? Get into my boots? That will take far too long! My thick, woollen socks will be OK. I've got spares. In a few minutes I can be back inside ... clear the entrance, find a prop for the sagging poles – an ice-axe or a ski-stick – there's sure to be something I can improvise, then nip back.

And Julie? Can she help from inside? 'All right!' she replies and we discuss what each of us should do. She seems full of energy – again, positive. I look at her anxiously, but with more confidence now, as she sits, half upright in the sleeping bag, waiting for me to go. Julie, good Julie, I think ... we will make it! Then I start getting out...

Lying on my back, I push feet-first into the narrow entrance which, as I have already realized, slopes uphill. I wriggle like a worm, then once my legs are outside, turn over onto my belly and continue squirming up through the snow, my head still inside the tent. Gasping for breath, I finally arrive outside and stand upright on the slope, facing the tent and the funnel-shaped hollow our companions have made at the entrance. At the same moment, the storm catches me. There is snow in the air, swirling everywhere. Through the gloom, I can make out the silhouette of the Korean tent, shaking in the racing blasts. Of our own squashed red dome, only the top is visible ...

This is one hell of a storm! Snowflakes whip my face. God, mountains of snow are piling up out here! and it's bloody cold after being inside! But I'll warm up in a minute. I work like a beaver. The tent is buried so deeply. God knows where the guylines are. I cannot find a ski-stick! On the side nearest the mountain, the flat slope of the plateau has built up into a huge wave, level with the top of the tent. I burrow away as fast as I can at the downhill end in a bid to clear the entrance completely, but it is the work of Sisyphus and all the time I notice that the tent keeps leaning more and more towards the funnel.

Should I use the ice-axe to prop it up from the inside?

Dodgy.

And how long will it be before the entrance is blocked once more by drifting snow? By the look of things, not long. I am increasingly aware that nothing will keep this tent standing very much longer. The icy cold seeps into my body from all sides. I never intended to stay out here so long ... 'Try and lift the tent!' Julie's voice calls from inside. Lift the tent? What for? But with resignation, I grab it and heave upwards. Is she having much luck inside? I notice Julie working on the struts to the left of the entrance. 'I think we can make it!' Her voice sounds as positive as ever, full of hope ... Oh, brave Julie! I admire you ...

But a moment later the tent tilts crazily forward once more. Such a nonsense, to have been in such a hurry just now! Mad to have come out

The Endless Knot

without boots ... I should have taken the time to put them on. Let's get back in! Come on – fast! Can I still get in?

And who will dig us out again in half an hour?

And what if the tent collapses? Everything inside me resists having to tell Julie that we are left with only one possibility.

'I can't fix it.' Julie's disappointed voice comes from inside. Poor Julie. There's nothing that can be done about it.

'We're going to have to abandon the tent, Julie. It means splitting up!' The words sound strangled. There's no way we can get into another tent together.

It's horrible, but we have no other choice. This icy cold! I am shivering all over.

'Quick, give me my sleeping bag.' I beg her. 'Will you go to Alan and I to the Austrians?'

Julie, make up your mind fast in there – I'm shivering as if I've got malaria and I can't spend another minute here!

'No, let me go to the Austrians, you go with Alan.' The sleeping bag comes out through the entrance ...

'Willi! Quick! Our tent has had it – please take Julie in with you,' I scream at the dark dome. 'Can you help out? Now, immediately?'

Stinging flurries. Fractions of seconds pass – an eternity – Willi's massive bulk pushes through the entrance. 'Yes of course,' he says.

Now Julie's hand has appeared ... 'Please help me out!' I hear her calling. Already Willi passes me to give her a hand through the narrow passage. 'Julie!' I yell through the storm. 'I'm freezing. Willi is here to help you. I have to run ... see you later!' Trembling, and dusted all over with powder snow, my feet numb in the woollen socks, wooden, without any sensation at all. I am running through the deep snow to Alan's tent, sleeping bag in hand.

'Please, let me in!' I gasp ... but Alan has already opened the entrance. Looking back, I see Willi still outside our tent, bending forwards ...

No, Julie. We could not have saved that tent. We had to part. Crawling in with Alan and Mrufka, I feel thankfulness, warmth and yet at the same time an infinite bitterness rising in my heart.

I am leaning against the snow wall, which I can feel through the tent, cold and solid. By my side are Alan's legs. He is asleep, with his head at the entrance. With me in the back of the tent, half-sitting, is Mrufka: she is quiet and withdrawn, staring into space, railing silently perhaps against the fate that denied her the summit of K2. She was nearer the top than last year on Nanga Parbat. She seems not to be here at all.

Alan took touching care of me when I arrived, helping me into my

35. The Pilatus Porter aircraft (Yeti) passes Dhaulagiri's North-East Ridge while making one of many supply trips to the North-East Col during the 1960 Swiss Dhaulagiri Expedition (pages 197 and 207).

36. Masaaki Kondo with an improvised Japanese flag on the summit of Tirich Mir in 1967 (see page 684).

37. *(above left)* Kurt Diemberger and Nawang Tenzing on the final rocky couloir on Makalu during their ascent in 1978 (see page 816). *Photo: Hermann Warth*. 38. *(above right)* Julie Tullis abseiling down a steep section at the end of the Broad Peak climb in 1984. After their ascent Diemberger and Tullis, during a snowstorm, were forced to quit their high camp, survived an avalanche and then struggled to quit the mountain safely to complete a sustained nine-day climb (pages 367-384). 39. *(below)* Julie Tullis near the summit of Broad Peak. K2 is in the background.

42. Alan Rouse.

43. Mrufka Wolf.

44. *(right)* Julie Tullis moves up the lower slopes of K2's Shoulder heading to the site of the highest camp (c 8000m). This was positioned above the small ice overlap on the right.

40. Kurt Diemberger and Julie Tullis at K2 Base Camp in 1986.

41. Alfred Imitzer *(left)*, Willi Bauer *(rear)* and Hannes Wieser *(right)*.

45. *(top left)* The difficult final slopes of the Abruzzi Route on K2, the scene of many dramatic episodes in the mountain's history.

46. *(top right)* The Shoulder and upper slopes of K2 in the deteriorating conditions similar to those when the climbers completed their ascents on 4th August.

47, 48. *(above and left)* Descending the fixed ropes and ladders on K2 during poor weather – conditions like those encountered by Bauer, Wolf and Diemberger during their arduous retreat in 1986.

49. The Wizard, one of the fine granite pinnacles of The Needles in Southern California (see page 792)

sleeping bag – once I removed all my clothes. Everything was covered with powder snow. The only thing I have left to wear is my down jacket – apart from that I am lying naked in my sleeping bag, in this frightfully cramped space. We threw my wet things into the space between the tent and the flysheet, where they will surely freeze bone-hard in no time at all. All my other clothes are inside the *parapluie*, along with my boots. In our unplanned flight, there was no way of getting hold of them. Hot tea, prepared by Alan, revives my spirits and goes some way to soothing my bitterness about the whole miserable situation. I know Julie is being looked after in the next tent, even if there is no way of calling to her over the storm. It would mean going outside and shouting. When things ease off a bit, we'll be able to make contact from in here. I can't go out again without shoes and socks. Are Julie's eyes any better, I wonder?

I find it painfully sad that the two of us, who've always taken all our decisions together and who've come through so much, cannot now do a thing for each other – divided as we are by a few ridiculous feet of snow and these roaring masses of air. We still have our thoughts – but they don't help us much. I wonder if she will come over?

In the meantime Alan and Willi have made a shouted agreement that we will all descend together at the first possible opportunity – as fast as we can go. But in such a heavy storm, the risk of getting lost and then losing the tents as well is so immense that it is better to wait a day.

'Jesus Christ! So much snow ...' grumbles Alan, rising with difficulty and squeezing out through the entrance into the open. He is fully dressed. It is not the first time that his powerful, long arms flail like windmill-blades through the piles of white powder, trying to keep at least the down-hill side of the tent and the entrance clear. To the leeward, the banks of snow keep rebuilding themselves with alarming speed. Alan has already given up on the side nearest the mountain; there the snow drift is packed solid into a massive, rigid wall. But the sturdy little two-man tent bears the pressure well. I have nothing but admiration for this young British mountaineer: for his alert mind and seemingly endless energy, and for the fairness and helpfulness, which he, more than anyone else, has demonstrated on this climb. Four days ago he gave shelter to Alfred Imitzer and just three days ago gave up his place to exhausted climbers from the Magic Line. Where does he get so much strength? Of the Austrians, Willi is the one in best shape. He, too, is quite helpful now.

If only we can get out of this trap. That lost day: I don't want to think about it, but it remains like a bitter taste on my tongue. By now we could be descending the Abruzzi Ridge, be well down – maybe even as far as our tent at the foot of the mountain. I lean my head against the snow wall and listen to the storm.

The Endless Knot

What has been happening outside our confined world on the Shoulder, where we huddle like prisoners longing for release from the elements? Where every day we have hoped and believed it would be our last one up here?

The Slovenians, who stood on the summits of their two eight-thousanders around noon on 4 August, have meanwhile made it back down. The American contenders on the north side of the mountain have accepted that given all the deep snow, there was no point in pushing further and turned back from around 8,100 metres, retreating in worsening weather down their fixed ropes on the North Spur. They reached their Base Camp safely. The Koreans, too, made it down the fixed ropes on the Abruzzi on 4 August; but the Poles on the Magic Line have been fighting for days against bad weather and are still not down. Petr and Przemyslaw only left Camp 4 at 10.30 on 4 August, when the cloud layer was intensifying, but now they are safely off the mountain.

The rest of us are stranded high above.

On 5 August Jim finally called Camp 4 – but too late. Petr and Przemyslaw took their walkie-talkie down with them, as did the Koreans.

Our group, stormbound on the Shoulder, was now without radio communication. Seven people stuck in the clouds, unable to receive a message from Base Camp of any possible improvement in visibility. It was of no help to us then, that on the morning of the 7 August, Jim described a moment of hope.

'... K2 is clear up to the Shoulder and the pinnacle behind which Camp 4 lies is also visible, so the whole of the Abruzzi and the whole of the descent is out of cloud ...' and '... it's certainly not as windy as last night and anyone up there will, I imagine, be hot-footing it down. The big question is, is there anyone up there?'*

All this was unknown to us. We were aware during the night of 6 to 7 August that the storm was easing and planned to make a break for it, but there was no visibility on the following morning. With only the one line of escape, the risk of getting lost in thick fog or cloud on the Shoulder was great, especially when we did not know how far down the cloud extended: none of us could know that below the Shoulder the weather was clear! Thus, for want of information, the chance slipped by. A walkie-talkie at that moment could doubtless have saved lives.

'Let's hope our gas will last!' Breathlessly, Alan struggles at the entrance once more. He is very worried we may run out – his original calculation

---

* *K2, Triumph and Tragedy*, p. 141.

has been thrown out by all the loss of time. 'I still have another full cylinder.' I try to calm him. 'The one we kept for the summit push.' The unused Husch cartridge is in the pocket of my down jacket, and there's a nearly-full Epigas stove in our tent as well. Does he want to get that? Alan shakes his head. He doesn't feel like it right now. So bang goes my chance of having my boots and other clothes brought over at the same time! There are no worries yet about gas in the neighbouring tent, because of the provisions left by the Koreans. And all of us think: the storm cannot last forever. There is not much food left anywhere, but what really counts up here, is being able to drink.

I wonder how Julie is faring? I wish I had my boots ...

An attempt to get them picked up by Mrufka also fails: by the time she is outside, taking a turn at freeing the tent, she forgets all about it. Anyway, it's blowing a gale.

Night. All quiet. Quiet? Is the weather getting better? I hear voices outside. Willi. Are we going down? But after a while, the voices stop – so I guess we won't. If the weather is really improving, we'll wait for daylight I'm sure. Alan crawls in from outside. 'Looks a bit better. We can go down tomorrow.' That's it, then. Off in the morning!

This was the night, Willi told me later, when Julie said, 'It's quiet outside, we could go down.' But later still, in the Innsbruck hospital, his memory of the event changed ... Julie's words, he then said, were, 'It's quiet outside, you could go down.' She had not included herself apparently.

At any rate, I remember that I wasn't unhappy about delaying our start until morning; I still had no way of contacting Julie. (I was told once that she was sleeping – nothing else.) And all my necessary gear, including boots, was still in the abandoned tent.

I am lying in a rigid, cramped position in the furthermost corner of the tent. My neck hurts. This narrow squeeze is a torture. In my sleeping bag, I'm warm enough and it really doesn't matter that I have no clothes on. But the pressure of snow against the side of my head is really bad. Aching, I seek to ease my position. This immediately involves the other two – whether they like it or not. We are an exhausted tangle of limbs. Moaning ... laboured breathing ... then, again, silence. Why are the nights so dreadful? Why is the crampedness a hundred times worse at night than during the day?

From outside comes the low shuffle of the wind and now and then a hard pattering as crystals of snow strike the vault of the tent. It is daytime again. I guess it must already be quite late in the morning of 7 August. All grey outside, but a little brighter. So far, nobody has mentioned anything about going down. I feel worry and disappointment: obviously the weather has worsened again. No visibility! At least the storm is no longer roaring.

Do people think it's likely to clear up soon?

I'm still a prisoner in my sleeping bag, and leadenly tired after the nightly ordeal in a confined space. The intermittent crackling of the snow crystals, the whistle of the wind lull me back into my doze ...

Wasn't that Julie's voice? 'Hey, Kurt, Julie's calling you!' Alan shakes my arm. 'I think she's coming over.' I rise abruptly, unable to believe it. I am beside myself with joy. She's coming over – and if she can do that, she *must* be able to see!

'Julie!' I yell at the top of my voice.

'Oh, Kurt!' I hear the faint reply from the direction of the Korean tent. Then comes the sound of approaching steps. A moment later she bumps against the tent on the downhill side, beside Mrufka. 'No, Julie! The entrance is here, to the left!' And I tell her, 'It's great, you are coming ...' In a rush I realize how worried I have been for her, how much I missed her! I am so happy she is here, and feeling better. 'I just wanted to say hello,' she says and stoops over the high snowdrift which has accumulated at the entrance. 'How are you?'

I cannot see her; there is only a small opening left now – even the flysheet extension is half-filled with snow. I am stuck in the rear of the tent, with my feet to the entrance, legs half-wedged under Alan's body.

'Don't worry, I'm fine!' I lean forward as far as I can. 'But I want to see you. Can you bend down?'

The edge of her hair appears ...

'I still cannot see you – I want to see your face!' I insist. Can't she crouch lower? 'Look, you must see my hands!' I stretch my arms towards the entrance, towards her ...

'Here I am ... yes, I'm OK. But how are you? Are you all right with the Austrians?'

The fringe of hair lowers: it is like a tissue, a web, grey and brown in the fog, familiar but still so far away ...

It reminds me of something, a crystal pattern, something I have seen in the past, a long time ago ... yes, I remember ... it was on the Chinese side of K2, on the northern glacier ... we were happy then ... K2 above us, dream mountain for us then... On a flat spot in the loam at the edge of the glacier, a garden of ice crystals had grown overnight – long, thin, needles, a web of them, twinkling, shimmering – and all vanishing as the day warmed up ... They left a magic imprint on the ground: the crystals themselves disappeared every morning, yet still they were there! The image was so bewitching that we were suddenly caught by its beauty and clutched each other's hands as if under a spell: there it was ... gone, but still existing. And the next night would bring it back to the beginning ... the endless knot ...

'Kurt, I am feeling rather strange ...' Julie's voice floats in as if from a far distance, through the web of hair and ice crystals: it is as if she is speaking close by, but from somewhere else as well. What does she mean, feeling strange?

She came over on her own ... under her own steam.

She must drink ... drink, drink, drink ... And tomorrow we will all go down. It's not going to work today ... not any more. As soon as I have my boots I'll go across and see her. I tell her that, and urge, 'be strong, Julie! I'm thinking of you!'

Can I lift her spirits? I lean forward – as far as possible – but still I cannot get close enough to see her face. And now Julie's hair disappears, too. 'Bye, bye!' she says, and as she takes the first steps back, adds, 'I don't have your boots ...'

A strange answer. But while I listen to her steps receding. I think: at least she can see again! She must be seeing all right to find her way over here alone. She retreats back into the Austrian tent. I'll go and visit her later but first, I have to get those boots!

More than anything, I want to free myself from the back of this tent, pressed hard into the mountainside – why don't I turn round, get my head to the entrance – especially now I know that Julie might come over again?

It turns into rather a major undertaking: after about an hour of multiple disentangling and squirming, finally, I find myself lying with my head in the corner of the fly-sheet extension directly opposite Alan. His face is right in front of mine: sharp featured – the straight nose, the open clear-eyed look – sometimes a bit absent and dreamy, but always positive. Mrufka has decided to remain in her original position, on the downhill side, her head to the rear of the tent – like a marmot in its hole.

I offer to free the tent if anyone can fetch my things from 'over there'. Alan agrees, but then falls asleep. Alarm rises in me at the impotence of my position: I have no way out – quite literally.

'Alan,' I say, 'let me borrow your overtrousers and boots – just to visit Julie?' Then I can dig everything I need out of our tent, too. He mumbles his agreement, but then says, not to worry, he'll get my stuff later, today or tomorrow ... before we go down, anyway.

Something is wrong with Alan. He's no longer the same pillar of strength.

The Endless Knot

It is afternoon. The wind is blowing intermittently. They should be able to hear me now, over there. I sit up and yell at the top of my voice, making it clear that I want to come over for a few minutes. The reply is disappointing – no space! Absolutely no space! Besides – Julie is sleeping ... I am depressed. Slowly it gets dark. I will go over tomorrow.

The morning of 8 August. Another night over, slightly less cramped this way round. Alan is awake. I will ask him once more for my stuff. I can hear the wind – on and off, pauses between – it is not too strong.
  Is that Willi's voice?
  Yes, he's shouting something. I call back: should I go over?
  'Kurt!' Willi calls. 'Julie died last night.'

'If I could choose a place to die, it would be in the mountains. When we were falling in the avalanche on Broad Peak, I knew that I would not mind dying that way. There have been a number of other occasions in the mountains, when just to sit still and drift into an eternal sleep would have been an easy and pleasant thing to do, but hopefully the circle of nature will not close for me too soon. I have a lot to live for ...'*

It was like a hammer blow, and so totally unexpected. Alan, at my side, tried to comfort me. I heard his words without grasping their meaning – but in the end I was forced to believe it.
  Everything was different from that moment, totally changed – the days, the light, the darkness, everything. The rope binding the two of us had been severed – by the storm, by something ...
  Only gradually did I come to realize that the bond still existed.

* Julie's thoughts after the death of our Basque companion Juanjo, from a discussion in 1985 at the foot of Everest, and later included in her book *Clouds from Both Sides*.

Blizzard at 8,000 Metres

8 August. Camp 4, last days of the storm:
... flashes of light, thoughts ... adrift between this world and beyond, the present interrupted by dreams of the past. Reality is all these – the now, the then, together – up here, down there ...

Julie once said that perhaps the best way to die would be to fall asleep, high in the mountains. Is that, then, how it was? Did she know when the time arrived? How could she have died so suddenly? We should never have split up ... that was the real end. Was it destined to be? I don't think so. But now it has happened, it is irrevocable. For ever.

It's a strange thing ... since she died, something has taken hold of me, a force that isolates me from everything else, yet at the same time binds me to the earth. Whatever it is – it has unbelievable strength: the now and the then, united; the up and the below.

But as soon as I find myself no longer able to make the distinction between Then and Now, Up and Below, I won't be able to go down. For the moment, still, I can.

What if the blizzard persists many more days? Here, at 8,000 metres?

Notes from my diary:
When the gas in Rouse's tent had finished and my boots were still lying in the *parapluie*, I managed to talk Mrufka into fetching the lilac rucksack and the stove, too, from over there. Unfortunately, she again forgot the boots. But we had gas once more, three teabags, a few sweets, two and a half slices of crispbread (which we divided scrupulously, like treasure), having had nothing to eat for days. The three teabags offered only a little taste as we could no longer afford to boil water – but in our state of near apathy, they stimulated some interest, were an unexpected luxury. Unfortunately, we 'lost' two of them pretty soon – once it was Alan, and once Mrufka, who forgot to remove the teabag from the pot while urinating! (How we managed to do all these things in the restricted space is a mystery to me, but we had no choice. Outside the storm still raged. Now that I have time to reflect, I realize Mrufka must have been twice to the other tent – this must be so, because at the very last I got my boots. The exact time sequence of all the days we spent in that tomb has not stayed clear in my mind.)

Since Julie's visit on the second day, I have lain with my head to the entrance. This way I could easily reach the snow, and taking turns with Alan, operate the stove – for as long as the gas lasted. He and Mrufka freed the tent several times from the drifted snow, and Willi helped twice, too. But in the end, there was so little air in the tent that the flame floated like a ghostly halo above the burner and almost immediately vanished into the gloomy darkness before we managed to set the small pot of snow onto the stove. Only after many tries, and having forced an air-hole through the snow by the entrance (which was an awful exertion), did we succeed in melting water again.

Worst of all were the nights: the hipbones of your neighbour pressing into your muscles, until pain forced you to find a different position; but then, because of the crush, very little change was possible. As everyone had the same problem, the result was an interminable carousel, which only slowed to a halt in the morning (God knows why). Once, during our tangled nocturnal contortions, I realized gas was leaking from somewhere. Terrified, I hunted for the stove, and eventually found it underneath me and turned it off. I do not know how much we lost on that occasion, but I do know the gas had run out by the last day – or was it the day before? In the end, nobody had strength enough, nor will, to clear the entrance – the snow slowly poured in as if filling a hourglass. It would do so, steadily, I supposed, until our time ran out. Meanwhile, we simply grabbed handfuls of the stuff, and ate it.

9 August. Twelfth day on K2:
As I wake up, I notice that I have been asleep with my hand in the snow. All feeling has gone from several fingertips – they're frostbitten. I register the fact …

Kurt, I tell myself, you know you shouldn't fall asleep with your hands in the snow. Still, it's happened now … No other frostbite apart from that. Nothing like that has ever happened to you before. Is that how it's going to be from now on?

Sooner or later, I won't have any strength left.

There's nothing to do, but wait.

The wind decides.

The end of my middle finger has swollen into a huge, blueish blister … I guess that's had it. Not nice, to die off piecemeal, like this. Is that really how it will be? Outside, the storm is still roaring – there's not a hope of making a break for it.

I remember once asking somebody if an eight-thousander was worth a bit of frostbite. Oh, yes, he replied, this one was! That was at the foot of K2, and Julie was at my side. It was a beautiful day, the sun shining and the light flashing between the ice towers …

When I breathe I feel some sort of resistance, a blockage somewhere below the right shoulder-blade. Is it the lung? Slight discomfort, a resistance – I don't know how else to describe it. Is that a sign that the end is coming?

Blizzard at 8,000 Metres

How much longer?

How much longer will this storm last? Alan is going downhill. Last night was bad, he was thrashing about, agitated, like a chained animal. He would lunge suddenly, delirious, quarrelling with destiny. I tried in vain to calm him. Good, kind Alan, Alan who took my arm and sought to comfort me when Julie died, is fading away. His face is drawn with the fatigue of these last days; really, he is not here any more. He begs continuously for water, which we no longer have. I put a piece of slush to his lips, which he sucks at greedily. Alan – the question beats dully in my brain – Alan, how long can you hold out? Up here, if you lose the power of walking, you are doomed – even if the storm should end.

Mrufka, still huddled in the corner, is immobile: she seems to have drifted into a sort of hibernation.

Again I notice that slight resistance when I breathe – apart from that, and providing it isn't an indication of something really bad, I feel I could hold out for another day … but not much longer. I chew slush – only liquid and an end to the storm can save us now.

I am surprised that I am so calm about it. But it would not help to get agitated. It is all so simple, everything depends on how long the storm lasts. Meanwhile, I have to eat more snow, let it melt slowly in my mouth. I know I must have water, even if my stomach feels absolutely horrible. I push another piece of slush between Alan's lips. He slurps, sucks … his eyes are red, a network of little veins … they weren't like that yesterday. He looks up into the vault of the tent – 'Jesus Christ!' he murmurs. And again, 'Jesus Christ!'

Outside, the storm continues. Snow crystals rattle intermittently against the tent. In the background, you can hear the dull, sinister, steady roar of the air masses as they part around the bulk of K2 – an eternal, distant sound. I close my eyes …

Fields in sunshine … green barley swaying on the terraces … virgin forest all around with the fabulous silhouettes of giant trees, the village with its smooth roofs of bamboo matting, Tashigang – a Tibetan song – the song of the sun … *'la tela khor rhe – e nyima che shar'* … and so it turns and turns – the great sun is rising … thus Drugpa Aba, head of the family, 'father of Drugpa', welcomes every new day, and the light of the sun, this wonderful light, penetrates everything, penetrates the ears of barley and the shining leaves … it is a shining green, a wonderful light. It is the Light.

Night. The constricting torture of our prison. Bow to fate – but hang on. Exhaustion – but keep hanging on! Dreams … sunshine, meadows, dear ones at home, life … what is reality?

The Endless Knot

10 August. Thirteenth day on K2:
Pallid dawn. Inside the tent the bent shapes of bodies in sleeping bags. Exhaustion. Another night over. Outside, the air still roars, but at least it's no longer dark – be thankful for that. Even this cramped hell can be accepted more easily once you can see around you. It seems a little brighter than usual. Is life giving us one more chance? Is there still hope? The snow crystals continue to rattle relentlessly against the little patch of fabric above our heads – the only bit that has not been covered by the snow which has engulfed us. Up there, removed from us in some way, is the storm. Inside our tomb, we're no longer part of it. But is it brighter? Has it stopped snowing? Is there a break in the deadly clouds which have held us prisoner for so long, like blind men in a labyrinth; which have granted us only the sanctuary of this icy vault, this place of lingering death? Hardly one of us can last another day ...

If you no longer have strength left for the descent, all that remains are the last dreams ...

Sun – that is sunlight, isn't it, on the tent fabric? Dear God! I dig through the powder inside the doorway, stretch my arms, reaching up to the surface – there, there, through a tiny hole in the snow, blue sky looks in! There is the blue of the sky – scarred by the racing crystals of snow whipped by the storm across it – the blue of the sky bringing us one last hope of getting out of here alive!

It *is* real.

Flight from the Death Zone

There's movement, voices calling from tent to tent. The sun has awakened the camp from its deadly torpor. But Alan is delirious, mumbling for water – and there is none. And who knows what the position is in the other tent? All I can hear is Willi's voice. Go down: yes, it is our only, our last chance. It is impossible to tell how long we shall be able to see the way down, how long the clearing will last. And although we have sun at last, the storm is still blowing; it may take hours before we manage to get away as we are in a complete daze after our long incarceration at 8,000 metres. The flame of life flickers only in the innermost core of our souls.

Decision time. The situation is extreme. Whoever stays here any longer will die.

Mrufka prepares for the descent but in the oppressively cramped quarters, only one of us can move at a time. To give her as much room as possible, I press tightly against Alan, immobile in his corner. As she struggles into her boots, I notice that one of Mrufka's big toes is completely frostbitten – it's dark blue. But that shouldn't stop her making it down – and apart from this, little 'Ant' has weathered these last terrible days well. That is probably in part thanks to the warm water with which Alan kept plying her, so long as we still had gas. He and I mostly made do with cold water and slush. But Alan, who sacrificed all his energies in keeping others going during the days of the summit assault, has finally reached the limit of his incredible endurance. The terrible certainty already hangs in the air – in his condition, he will not make it down alive. Even if he will never know that.

The prospect of having to leave him up here is a ghastly one. While Mrufka, with painfully slow movements, puts on her gear, I gesture towards Alan – what shall we do about him? He is moaning in his sleep. I know it's a pointless question. Mrufka turns her eyes away. 'Life is down there,' she says in a low whisper. A little while ago we tried unsuccessfully to sit him up. He sank back and wanted water. It is his only wish. Yes, life is down there. And water is down there too. But it is impossible for us to carry Alan. There is no way we could do it – it would be too much.

The storm still rattles away at the tent. It must be icy cold outside. I need my boots! Mrufka knows it, but I remind her once more as she crawls out, 'Mrufka, don't forget my boots: they are over there in the tent, with the blue rucksack.' She mustn't forget!

'Do you need the rucksack?' she asks.

'No, I've got Julie's' …

'So I can have it for my sleeping bag?'

'Yes, of course …'

I am lying with my face on my boots. I must have fallen asleep. I remember Mrufka giving them to me. Now she is off, somewhere outside. I have to get dressed! The storm is howling … but there's still sunshine. How long will it last? It must be nearly noon.

Up! Get dressed! I raise my head, look around. Where are my trousers? Oh yes. I remember, here, the light down pants, they're folded up on my chest, tucked into my down jacket to keep dry. I'm still completely naked in my sleeping bag except for the jacket, just as I have been all these days since I took shelter in Alan's tent and had to get rid of all my snow-sodden clothes. Crazy that … but it was the only way to avoid soaking my sleeping bag too. I still have Julie's lilac rucksack from our summit bid, the yellow windsuit, a single glove, one mitten, and one orange overgaiter … everything else has disappeared in the chaos of snow in the half-collapsed tent. Three pairs of gloves? Yes, once upon a time – but now I have to fix myself up with whatever's left. It's enough. Alan groans next to me, 'Water!' It tears my heart. God, if only I could give him what he wants. Fulfil this one wish. Maybe I can find a drop somewhere – perhaps over in the other tent? Alan sinks back into his shadow world.

Slowly, stopping repeatedly to draw breath – one, two moves, pause – I get dressed. This inner boot is wet I notice; it was under my head on the ground – breathe! – no, there doesn't seem to be any frostbite on this foot – not yet at any rate – pause again for breath. That was lucky. Neither of them frostbitten – breathe! – the second inner boot is dry. Put on the harness. What a good job I put all the stuff into the rucksack after coming back from the summit. Breathe! Well, not everything – sadly – I've only got the one glove and one mitten – but at least my feet are OK …

So the harness is on. That gives me security for abseiling down the fixed ropes on the Abruzzi. Pause for breath … I will take the rope down too. It may be no use to anyone, but who knows …

Thank you, Mrufka, for getting this rucksack for me. I would not have dared to go over for it barefoot. Why on earth didn't I take the trouble to put my boots on before freeing the entrance of our tent? Because I had done it so often in socks before, I suppose. If only the entrance of that bloody tent hadn't been so narrow and the poles so flimsy – we would never have needed to split up ...

But what can I change? Nothing any more.

Mrufka has come back. She is outside the tent, wanting her sleeping bag. I have already stuffed my own damp, icy bag into Julie's rucksack. Better than nothing for a bivouac. I hand Mrufka hers out. Alan murmurs in his sleep. I still don't know what to do ... yet at the same time I know I have no choice. Except to stay up here and to die. Wouldn't it have been better to have remained with Julie in our tent forever? We should never have separated. So she died alone and nobody told me. Bitterness overwhelms me. Could it have changed anything if I had been with her? Maybe – yes. Certainly for her. Now here I am, but at the same time distant from all this, faraway, forcing myself with great difficulty to make one action follow the next, everything in slow motion, requiring all my concentration. I take the utmost care not to forget anything – because at heights like this you pay so dearly for every single mistake.

Perhaps I can still find a few drops of water for Alan. I squeeze outside to be immediately struck by the icy blast of the wind: enormously strong gusts chasing scudding clouds, lower than we are, lower even than the Shoulder of K2, down at a height maybe of 7,700 metres. Visibility is clear enough above them, but this terrible storm! Still, today is the only chance we have left of getting down. Without the visibility it would be as good as hopeless to find that one passage left by the ice avalanche between the seracs below the Shoulder.

It feels like having to learn to walk again as I take a few tottering steps into the storm.

Willi and Mrufka are outside, busy sorting out the ice-axes and ski-sticks. I take my ice-axe and notice the slow awkward movements of the other two: they are like robots. A moment later my axe seems suddenly to have vanished. Full of panic I search for it and find it sticking in the snow. Fragments of words toss in the air, mixing with the icy gusts ... I still feel dazed, as if in a dream. Then a clear thought – we have to reach Camp 3! We? Alan is finished, and who among us has strength enough to pull him? Willpower alone won't do it. I don't see anything of Hannes and Alfred, they must be in their tent. If they were still all right they would be out here by now. I seem to recall Willi trying to get them going before, bellowing at the top of his voice. Now he is somewhere down below the edge, down the steep slope – does he think they will follow him or is he just taking a look? The slope has a wind-scoured rather hard surface and is covered with drifted snow formations, imprinted by the force of the storm. It seems to be mostly slabs all the way down and out as far as the lower end of the Shoulder. There is no deep snow, but in order to find the passage we will have to drop down where it levels off on to the steep side in the wind shadow. Will we be able to make trail there? That could be what Willi is checking out.

Really it *is* just like learning to walk again. Stumbling I lurch through the storm to the other tent. Yes it must be that Willi is reconnoitring the critical section of the descent where it goes down to the large crevasse on the left-hand side – or has he simply made a start in the hope that the others will follow his example? I don't know. Nobody *has* followed him, that much is sure.

Coming into the storm-shaken Korean tent, I find Hannes sitting by the entrance. He recognizes me, makes his inimitable wink as if to say *Servus!* We'll make it OK! But I see his snow-white hand, which he is massaging in an endeavour to get the circulation going: the skin is absolutely white and bloodless, soft and wrinkled as if it has been soaking in water for days. Behind him Alfred is slurping chunks of snow from a big pot. His face is dreadfully ravaged, his eyes bloodshot. Sometimes he stares, sometimes he appears to be somewhere else – his condition reminds me of Alan's. I think he's confused too. It does not look as if either Alfred or Hannes want to leave the protection of the tent. Mrufka and I now squash in with them too to get out of the wind. We've got no more water for Alan I announce sadly looking at the remains of the snow in the pot. In my tent next to this, in which Julie is now lying, there's no water of course. In any case I feel shy about rummaging around in there. Now I see Willi puffing up the slope obviously annoyed that nobody has followed him. I have moved outside in the meantime.

'*Aussa! Aussa!*' Willi yells at his companions. Out! Out! He pulls them from the tent. It is the only sure way to get them going. Dazed and staggering, Hannes and Alfred start the descent with him and Mrufka. I stay back here – with Alan and Julie.

What can I do? Benumbed I go on looking for something for Alan but there is nothing.

For a while I sit silently in the Korean tent, reflecting.

I remember Julie's small pocket-recorder. Could she have ... could there be anything on it? I don't know a thing about her last hours. Almost nothing about her last two days. But there is nothing in the pockets of her down jacket, which is lying in a corner. Anyway it's unlikely she would have used it – the small camera must have been lost in the storm too. I give up dejected. I will never know. Timidly I approach our tent. Willi tore open the roof with his ice-axe when he put Julie in there – I know that from Mrufka.

Flight from the Death Zone

I cannot see her face. The tent is half caved-in but has not collapsed. I move the sleeping bag sealing the opening, and put the down jacket over her feet … see her mountain clothes, red and black. Julie … For the last time, I touch her – then I leave her alone. Somewhere inside the tent must be our two little bears, the mascots which coincidence brought together from a bus in Varese and a small village in southern England. They will stay with her. And I can still see Julie's proud smile in Base Camp after she had embroidered a new eye for one of the bears. The sleeping bag sealing the hole in the tent is completely dry – and remembering the dampness in Alan's tent I wonder whether to give it to him. Yes – stuffing the down jacket in its place I carry the bag over to Alan's tent. Every step I take is more reluctant … I have no water for him, nothing. The down sleeping bag is only a token because really I have nothing. I am just a helpless wanderer up here between my dead friend and another who will die. And I know that I have to go down.

Meanwhile down on the flat part of the Shoulder something terrible has happened. I registered it some moments ago from this distance. Alfred and Hannes, after little more than a hundred metres, came to the end of their strength. Willi and Mrufka tried desperately to support them helping up and holding first one then the other – but they kept falling into the snow. It was simply hopeless and they eventually had to give up the task.

Now I see Willi and Mrufka close together, two stooping silhouettes in the transparent grey of the fog on the lee-side of the Shoulder, barely moving. They seem to be up to their waists in deep snow. I hold the sleeping bag for Alan in my hands … He will want water from me. And I have none …

Dear Father, what shall I do? If ever you are still near me, it will be now! I know you are near me. At times when I have found myself in terrible situations and not known what to do, I have asked you.

Oh Alan. Down into your tent it's a dark hole: Do I see or just imagine the bewildered eyes, hear the rambling voice above the noise of the storm? Do I see the fingers reaching, moving, grasping after something in the air …? 'Alan!' I yell into the dark hollow, 'I have brought you a dry sleeping bag …'

No answer. Did he understand me? I push the sleeping bag down towards him. Frightened I notice that above me whirling clouds spin across the summit face, multiplying, thickening, reaching down towards me. Those scudding clouds lower down, they are creeping higher now – how much longer until they close together? Till the inferno of clouds smothers the whole mountain again?

'*Bua, du muasst abi.*' Yes Father, I know I have to go down. 'Alan, I have to go now.' But I cannot take away your hope for water – if you still understand me at all, that is. 'Alan, I will go and try to find some water.'

In the grey of the depths I can hardly distinguish the shapes of Willi and Mrufka. A thick felt of snowdust fills the air on the leeward side of the Shoulder, grey cotton wool swallowing everything – them and the way down.

Go Kurt, go! Clouds of snowdust … flashing sunlight … tablets of snow bursting under my feet. I am grasping my way down the slope.

Go more slowly! Don't trip!

Life is down there, is what Mrufka said. Up here, now, is only death. And it's still a big question whether we can escape it. Perhaps.

I reach Hannes. He is sitting in the snow with his back to me. A few metres further on Alfred is lying face down on the furrowed surface, completely still. He must be dead. Hannes moves his arms weakly, rowing the air in slow motion, while ice crystals bombard us unmercifully and I can hardly keep my footing for the fierce bursts of wind. Then I see his face. His eyes, blank, stare into space. He does not see me. I shout his name but he does not even move his head. Only his arms keep rowing through the air. He cannot hear me. Perhaps he is in another world – is already dead. It is as if he were listening to something far away. He is no longer here, yet still I think, how much better it would be if he were back in his tent now – a better place to die than here, even if he does no longer feel the cold. 'Hannes!' I shout, 'if you can manage somehow, go up to the tent!' But he does not move, does not even turn his head. Snowdust whips at the two figures on the wind-ploughed slope. Absurd sunshine – horror, impotence, resignation. Yet still from somewhere, the will to live. The sun still shines. I cannot help here any more.

I go on, passing along the snow edge. Somewhere here I have to go down to the left. Last steps in the light of the sun, already the grey is taking over. Here are the tracks of Willi and Mrufka – a small drop and snowslabs below. I climb down, spy their shapes ahead of me in the gloom further down, half immersed in a sea of powder snow and fog. They're clearly making progress but only very slowly. There's the track again – almost a channel.

Down there, Willi is ploughing through the snow like a tank. And Mrufka clings to him like a shadow. What a descent! If we survive this – then it will have been with the help of all the angels. Quickly I reach the others. Willi is the first to notice – he is clearly surprised to see me and asks suddenly, 'Do you have anything to eat?' 'Have you brought a stove?' How could I have done? Nobody has either any more! I am astonished at the question and reply, 'No, of course not.' Willi says nothing and con-

Flight from the Death Zone

tinues quietly breaking the trail, followed by Mrufka, slowly, step by step. It is fluffy, light snow but it is a fathomless ocean. It would be impossible to climb upwards through it; even if the guys in Base Camp thought we might still be alive, they couldn't help us here. We're in the soup and must rely on our own memory. The vague recollection of the ascent line must be reversed: the gentle incline, the seracs, the big crevasse with the bridge – those we have to find if we are to locate the only way through to the steep slope that follows, a slope that will be frightening, now under many tons of fresh snow.

Vague outlines, grey on grey, increasing steepness – a descent under such conditions is madness, but the alternative is to die. We all know that. All safety rules are only fairy tales – we either break our necks or we don't. Cautiously Willi pushes forward, infinitely slowly. Below us, faint and barely recognizable, the giant crevasse appears. It looks unreal in the empty greyness as if we were floating above it. But down there, that must be the bridge we came over on the way up. Will the slope hold our weight? Or will we thunder down the mountain in a cloud of powder? Will anybody down there ever know what happened to us? I hold my breath, call to Willi. We are agreed, there is no other possibility. This has to be the way to go.

While seconds stretch to eternity Willi pushes slowly downhill, through the powder, step after step, pause after pause. He seems to have become part of the snowscape, and as if we had earned a miracle after all these terrible days, the slope holds. We arrive at the bridge and get across the giant crevasse. For a few steps on the other side we go slightly uphill, then the steepest slope of all follows, leading down into the void.

But now we have faith. The snow is deep, and it is indescribably tiresome to wallow through, but it holds. It doesn't slide off. We can make it. We have only to concentrate like the very devil not to fall into the bergschrund which yawns below.

It's done – we're over! Even though visibility is nil now and we're floundering in snow up to the waist, we know from memory that we have to keep to the right. Mrufka relieves Willi for a short while in breaking trail then I plough the ditch for some time until the outline of the serac wall, from which the avalanche detached itself, appears hazily to the right. Below it the powder snow seems bottomless, it's an inhuman struggle and the output of energy results in a furious hunger. 'Hasn't anybody got a bite to eat?' I ask, but with little hope. 'Yes, there is a sweet,' says Mrufka, 'but I'm saving that for us tonight.' In vain I try to convince her that we could do with this last boost of 'fuel' now – splitting it between the three of us – because down in Camp 3 we should be able to find something anyway. But Mrufka is adamant.

The Endless Knot

The first bamboo sticks! The last that Alan and I planted on the way up. We are therefore at about 7,700 metres. So, not even 350 metres still to go to Camp 3! The ploughing through the snow is over, the slope has now been cleared by the force of the storm or partly covered in the usual hard-packed snowdrift formations. I remember several dangerous patches from the way up: some sheer ice and blocks of insecure snow. There is still no visibility at all, and even though the temptation is great to descend facing downwards, I turn into the slope and climb down on all fours. Doing it this way with ice-axe and crampons, is obviously safer, but inevitably slow.

Soon I am alone.

Another bamboo stick! Kurt, don't let the others hurry you …don't change this technique – it is the only safe way to go down in our state. And as we are not belaying one another, you only need to make one false step and it's down into the abyss! That's why I told Willi and Mrufka some while ago not to wait for me when they preferred to move faster facing downhill.

We must have been on the go for about four or five hours now. I wonder what state Camp 3 is in?

A metre down, another metre, and one more – snow formations, furrows in the cloudy fog. A voice! Somebody is calling! Sounds as if they are waiting for me after all. A moment later I discover Willi and Mrufka near the blue ice cliff, below which Julie and I put our tunnel tent in a small gap during our first summit bid.

'Keep on going, descend to 3,' I call down. 'It's not that far now.' I'm taking it slowly. Just a few more bamboo sticks.

Camp 3! 7,350 metres. It's devastated. We cannot stay here. It must have been the force of the blizzard that wrecked this recently rebuilt camp. All I find is a squashed Korean tent under the snow, barely visible, and rip into it with my ice-axe! Anything to eat? I have to find something to eat – also our figures-of-eight which Julie and I left here in the small bag. We'll need those to abseil down the fixed ropes. But nothing! I cannot find them! Disappointed I rummage through the meagre contents of the tent. Willi and Mrufka do the same at the Austrian tent – a little further down and also destroyed by the ice avalanche. As Willi told me later Mrufka found a gas cylinder for her stove (which she had brought down from Camp 4). The figures-of-eight don't seem to be anywhere! That is a severe blow – they save so much energy, give so much more security. What's this – orange sweets? No, effervescent pills! Something at least, the stuff fizzes in my mouth, mixed with slush … well it's something. I put the rest in my pocket, will give some to Willi and Mrufka. And what about these red mittens? They're great, these Korean mittens. My own single mitten (for my left hand) is wet – I could exchange it for one of these. But I'll hang on to the leather glove on my right hand for coping with the karabiners on the fixed ropes, for changing over at the stances. I only need one therefore – I'll leave the other here. (Today I curse such blind-eyed logic – an example of the linear step-by-step thinking which has taken over our brains since the high-altitude storm – that second mitten could have spared me nearly all the amputations on my right hand. Certainly I would have been slower on the fixed ropes, but it would have been enough to put it on from time to time instead of the leather glove. However, I was no longer capable of thinking that far ahead.)*

I give some of the fizzy stuff to Willi and Mrufka, still bemoaning the lost figures-of-eight. Willi hands me a grey screw-karabiner which I accept even though I have a blue one of my own already – it's always worth having a spare. So, sadly, not one of us has a figure-of-eight. Bad luck? Yes – to have one would have meant more than just making things easier.

---

* It was Kim Chang-Sun who left the two mittens in case one of us should need them on the descent. I am grateful to him. The tent which contained our figures-of-eight was probably destroyed and blown away by the storm.

Where is Mrufka?

7,250 metres: the serac wall below Camp 3 is an imposing cliff of blue opalescent ice, interspersed with near-vertical white slabs, almost like marzipan in texture, made of compressed granular powder mixed with crystalline fragments. This is where the fixed ropes start for the descent from Camp 3. Almost all have been renewed by the Koreans over the last month. They promise a safe retreat down the Abruzzi Ridge, but only of course if you make no mistake, and provided you can locate the start of them when descending in a storm. Seen from above, the steep snowslope below Camp 3 ends abruptly at the edge of this drop; the wall itself, you only see from below.

Now, in our desperate flight from the Death Zone, having survived there so miraculously for so many days, all three of us – Willi, Mrufka and myself – were convinced that we had won. What could happen to us now? Descending the fixed ropes was as familiar to us as ABC. Naturally, the technique a mountaineer employs depends upon what he is used to, but everyone knows alternative methods of abseiling in the event of the loss of a vital piece of equipment. So, even without figure-of-eights, roping down was not a gamble – all of us knew the Abruzzi well, had often gone up and down it. No, by any normal judgement, we should be safe enough now! Even the weather did not look too alarming, and although we were very tired, none of us was in a state of actual exhaustion. It was thirst and hunger that stressed us most. It is a complete mystery, therefore, why Mrufka did not make it to the foot of the mountain.

It is true that nobody had ever before survived as long at such a height as we had – we had been eight, in some cases nine, days at or above 8,000 metres, without artificial oxygen. None of us knew how seriously this had affected us, physically. Perhaps not only Mrufka but Willi and I were pushed so close to the limits of life when we were descending to Camp 2 that we were incapable even of registering the fact. Or did we feel something? In all of us, our blood had thickened like honey with the altitude, and probably we were each on the brink of an embolism. In that situation, the increase of oxygen as you get lower comes too late to have any effect – what you need is to drink, drink, drink … It is a race against time before a blood clot develops – was that the race that Mrufka lost?

Where is Mrufka?

Late afternoon, on 10 August, at the edge of the serac wall: here I dump the green and red rope we acquired from our Basque friends that's half a kilo less – it won't be of any use to us now. For a moment Juanjo's tomb on Everest is in my thoughts, up on the ridge there, high above the neighbouring peaks – where Julie and I stood with Juanjo's companions, Mari and Josema (the two who gave us the rope). Julie is half-Basque herself ... was, I mean. Again – something remains, something – of us, of her ... Standing, waiting here, is horrible. The cold makes me shudder suddenly. Isn't Mrufka down the wall yet?

You have to be very careful not to descend too far here – or you could find yourself hanging over sheer ice, from where it would be almost impossible to get on to the traverse which comes after this. Moreover, there is one rope too many. When the Koreans were fixing it, it must have been blown out by a high wind to snag in a wide loop, about forty metres out among the overhanging seracs. I remember, on the way up, Julie and I wanted to pull it in as it was so obviously a danger, but we were unable to free it from the blue points of ice.

The blue and white fixed rope at my feet has not moved for a while. It is anchored just in front of me at the edge of the drop; it and several other ropes are all on one massive snow piton. Does that mean Mrufka is down? Can I go now? I can't stop shivering – from the fog, the cold, the dampness. (I had to leave half of my clothes frozen solid at Camp 4.) Down! I need to get moving!

Feeling a bit dizzy, I move to the edge, bend forward and take hold of the rope ... Careful, Kurt! Get a grip – you can't afford any mistakes now, not while you're off the rope. The grey drop below me falls away for 2,000 metres, I know that ...

Snap the karabiner into the sling at the piton, Kurt, the self-belay! Then take the other karabiner, put in a friction loop, and screw it shut tightly. God, that's awkward – my fingers are so numb in this icy leather glove ... As I start sliding down the rope, I peer into the murk below me. There's no sign of Mrufka. Probably I waited up there too long.

Hurry up, Kurt. Get a move on, while daylight lasts. Crampons scratch and bite into the ice as I abseil down. Now I can see Mrufka – she's obliquely below me, pulling herself hand-over-hand along a transverse rope. Everywhere around is so bleak and gloomy – just fog, snow and ghostly shapes. I can't see Willi anywhere, whichever way I look. 'Willi gone!' I think, amazed. 'How come? He's the strongest of us. He must be running down to Camp 2. He can make some tea there – bet he's thirsty.' It's my own thirst making the assumptions! I hope to goodness nothing happens up here. But what could happen – on fixed ropes we have swarmed up and down so many times? Right – that's the vertical

The Endless Knot

wall of the séracs done. No, not completely. Kurt, don't forget the delicate section before the traverse. I lean into the blue ice, breathe and rest. Then I move the karabiner onto the next rope and pull myself towards the traverse – very hard work, this bit. Safely across, I draw several more deep breaths. It must be dreadful to make the mistake of going too low here when you are tired like this.

Mrufka seems to have disappeared again. She must be quite a way ahead. I hurry. It is easier now – you have only to loop the rope around your arm, snap in the karabiner, and off you go! There is the pink rope down the short vertical 'natural staircase'. It was loose. I remember from when we were here the first time that we had found it flopping down into empty space – probably due to ice or stonefall, or to the friction of the wind. Julie had tied the rope to another line. Suddenly I have the feeling that she is near me, here, as if she wanted to see me safely across the traverse. There is one section without a rope, across snow ... take care on that, Kurt!

This is the smooth slab with the chimney – the fissure. Yes, thirty metres lower down there's an overhang to be coped with. The black and yellow rope is a good one – we used that before ... now there is a Korean rope running down beside it. There's a flat spot, just above here, where one night in 1984 we hacked away at the snow in a vain bid to clear enough space for our little bivouac tent – but it didn't work out, and in spite of the late hour, we had to go on down to 7,000 metres with Wanda.

My crampons scrape and scratch on the smooth rock on either side of the crack ... careful ...

Suddenly, I slip ...

Hold on, Kurt! Hold on!

Flung backwards against the edge of the crack, I come to a standstill. My right arm hurts, the one taking all my weight; my hand still has a tight grip on the rope ... It was only a short fall, but one of my feet jammed inside the fissure, so that I was slammed around and into the edge. It takes some moments before I can move again. I hang there gasping, shocked at the unexpectedness of the incident. Then I pull myself up slowly. It was a good thing I had tightened the screw of the karabiner holding the friction loop – but I wish it had been a figure-of-eight. A figure-of-eight is unsurpassable – safety and speed together.

Julie and I left our spare one at the foot of House's Chimney in the duffel bag by the rock tower. Will that be gone, too, I wonder, like the others in Camp 3? Mrufka hasn't got a figure-of-eight either – she decided against bringing one because of the extra weight.

While I continue gliding carefully down past the black overhang, I discover Mrufka again, below me, and soon catch up with her. I watch and wait as she swaps from one rope to the next, busy in some way with her sticht plate. Actually, it's quite easy here, not at all dangerous. 'Wouldn't you prefer to go down by karabiner now?' I cannot really understand why she is bothering with this slow technique, however well it works. 'No,' she says – and I don't press it beyond remarking that she'd get along much faster with a karabiner. This is obviously the way she wants to do it, and up here everyone has to make up his or her own mind about what is best. 'Do you mind if I go ahead?' I ask her. It is a comfortable spot with no problems about changing over. She has no objection. A little further down there is a narrow horizontal shoulder, one on which we often used to rest when we were coming up. There, she joins me as I clip the karabiners onto the next rope. 'Would you mind putting my ice-hammer into my rucksack for me?' she asks. Fiddle with buckles, now? With my hands in this state? It seems a bizarre wish on her part in our present situation, a complete waste of time: she won't need the hammer any more, it is just a useless weight. And we haven't got much daylight left.

'I'll let you have mine, if you want it, when we get down. Don't let's waste time! Just leave it!' I'm in a hurry to get going.

There's no feeling left in the fingers of my right hand at all; the leather glove got completely soaked coming down the fixed ropes. Why on earth didn't I take that second mitten when I had the chance? But how could I have operated the karabiners with it? Logic, after a week in a storm at 8,000 metres, still exists, but it is decidedly narrow.

I can still see Mrufka above me, abseiling down over the slabs where there are several parallel ropes, some older ones with thick knots, others reduced to fibres by the battering storms, and covered in inches of frost. It's twilight now: dark clouds are approaching on the horizon, and veils of grey mist drift here and there. It's almost evening. This will be some descent in the dark!

A little later, I lean against the wall in the gloom, waiting for Mrufka. Gusts strike the rocks and after a while I give up. It is obvious that her technique is much slower, however safe, and I am shaking with cold. I have to move! You can't lose the route here anyway, the sequence of fixed ropes is uninterrupted.

Despite the stormy gusts, the snow holds off – luckily. At one point, feeling the call of nature, I realize there is no way (with my right hand stuck in this wet glove) of opening my over-trousers and unzipping the blue down pants underneath – to say nothing of the harness. So I pee down one side of the pants. It really doesn't matter. The main thing is not to remove the glove – I'm terrified of losing it. My fingers are already frostbitten, but perhaps something can yet be saved.

It's getting dark now; that spells the end of any fast descent.

I'm too tired to hurry now anyway, I just have to be careful not to make any mistake when changing over karabiners at the belay stances. All my attention is focused on the rope, the rock over which I move, and the snow in which I plant my feet. Even in the pitch-darkness, I still know where I am – but I just have to take it slowly. I can't afford a false step.

The most difficult section turns out to be the steel ladder – I have to rest on nearly every rung.

But the whole time I have the sensation that there is an invisible presence watching over me, a force around and within me, a guardian being. It has been with me for the last few days, up there in the tent. Is it Julie?

Gradually, I slip into a state of numbness, no feeling any more, only thoughts registering in slow motion ... oh, I recognize this rope ... that pulpit ... here is the beginning of the traverse ... the knot in the rope ... now turn round ... one step back onto the cliff – don't miss it ... the slab – that has a step, too ... was there a storm? I think one did blow up for a while, earlier ... now it has stopped. The air is rich and full of oxygen ... it is a pleasure to breathe it.

It must be ten o'clock when I arrive at Camp 2 at 6,700 metres. At first there seems to be nobody there, all I can see is the dark silhouette of our Basque tent. Then, as I turn a rocky corner, there appears the shining green glow of a Korean tent, tucked against the wall on the highest seam of snow. A view of pure magic promising light, warmth, life – a giant green Korean lantern, shining into the pitch-dark night. Like a picture from a fairy tale.

I open the entrance, and what greets me is like a fairy tale come true: Willi is squatting there like a sorcerer swathed in wreathing vapours, stirring a big pot filled with an indefinable, brownish brew! Whatever it might be – and there are thick, swollen grains floating around in it – it has been ages since I have seen so much liquid! Without a word, he passes me the steaming pot, and I drink.

How it flows, so warmly, so wonderfully down my dry and tortured throat! Heavens, I'm thirsty! Willi's face is a flaming red; it is like a steam bath in here, the gas stove hisses ...

'Where is Mrufka?' he asks suddenly.

'I think she'll be another hour,' I answer. Hard to say, now it's dark. It could be two.

When by midnight Mrufka has still not arrived, we start to worry. Is she bivouacking? I know she has her sleeping bag with her – in my blue rucksack. She also brought a stove down from Camp 4 and found a

Where is Mrufka?

gas cylinder to fit it, among the ruins of Camp 3. Didn't she say something during the descent that she might stop over in Wanda's tent at 7,000 metres, just below the ladder? That's a bit off the route, but there is food there. If not ...? We leave the light on, listen into the night, melt more snow ... but Mrufka does not appear. Willi has frostbite on both hands – all his fingertips are affected. As for me, my right hand looks terrible – one finger has a big blister, one nail is missing and all the other fingers are damaged – only the thumb seems to be intact and that even hurts a little, which is a good sign. My left foot is completely without sensation and swollen. I massage it long and intensely, without result ... the circulation must be quite blocked. It will have been the wet inner boot and the loss of one of my over-gaiters in the chaos of the assault camp that caused that. Depressed, I finally give up my futile attempts to bring it back to life, and turn my attention instead to my right foot. There I have more success: after a long, sustained massage, I recover all sensation. Of course, my right leg has always had the better circulation, ever since I broke the left one – twice (once while skiing and once on the marble steps of the post office). Willi's feet seem to have suffered no real damage – he wore plastic boots and his inners did not get wet.

We wait for Mrufka until almost noon, but she does not arrive. We're uneasy, full of foreboding. Today is 11 August: we have been on K2 for two weeks now, climbing up, down, being trapped in the tents. No one other than us has ever withstood so long a storm at 8,000 metres, a storm from which it was impossible to escape. Indeed, of the seven of us four died up there: can it be that the mountain has claimed another victim at the very last moment?

There only seem to be two possibilities: either Mrufka has reached the tent at 7,000 metres and is sleeping it off, or she has made some technical error on the fixed ropes and fallen. I keep thinking of that sticht plate and the small sling she was using – was it that? On the other hand, if she is sleeping in the tent, she could be up there two days.

Since neither of us has the strength to climb back and look, Willi decides to hurry on down to Base Camp as fast as he can and arrange for a rescue team. In the meantime I will continue down the Abruzzi at my own slow pace. In the end, Willi talks me into leaving my sleeping bag here as it is so icy and wet, offering me one of his from the camp below. After some hesitation I agree – even if I don't see much point in it. (I eventually carried his down, but never used it, and in the end had to borrow one from the Poles in Base Camp. No less than three versions of this story and the subsequent descent through the chimney were to appear later – all of them conflicting with each other.)

Willi sets off first. He wants to look through the Austrian tent at the foot of House's Chimney to see what is left there. He will wait there for me, he says. I struggle once more with my left foot, massaging it – but in vain. During the night I tried to dry the wet inner boot over the flame of the stove – it's well-scorched now. The large purple blister which had replaced the whole end of one finger has burst as a result of all these activities, but I feel no pain. Awkwardly – it's a strenuous job – I at last struggle into my boots and get going.

Some of the rungs of the metal caving ladder in House's Chimney have frozen into the ice at the back of the chimney, some are missing or damaged – I am forced into three pitches of demanding abseiling … When finally I reach Willi at the Austrian tent he hands me the sleeping bag and starts on his way again.

I am by myself on the spur.

Slowly climbing down the Jacob's Ladder of rocky steps, towers and snowfields, bringing me back to the more familiar lower levels, my thoughts keep returning to last night in Camp 2. I learned something then about Julie's death – she went to sleep and did not wake again.

And suddenly – I hear it still, above the sounds of the mountain, above the gusts of air blowing around our tent – suddenly Willi, in a faltering voice, emotion nearly robbing him of breath and with tears in his eyes, tells me, 'She just said …' He stops, struggling for composure, and then – faster and faster, while I feel my heart contract at every word, it sounds so like an outcry – 'She just said, "Willi, get Kurt down safely" …' He sobs.

So that is what she said. She knew then that the end was near. Emotion and waves of pain seize me: what else don't I know? Did she say anything else?

'… That was all … the last. She didn't speak any more … just slept …' mutters Willi.

I feel the darkness all around the tent, and the moving air. The night has suddenly found a voice … her voice.

So that is what she said.

I was only a few metres away, through the storm.

And still I did not know.

Why wasn't I allowed to be with her?

There is no answer.

Her last wish – that I should get down, for both of us.

Is that an answer?

It has to be. It is her answer to everything.

It is day. And I hear the voices of the night.

Julie …

Perpetuum Mobile

Whenever the pace was my own, things worked out fine. The result was never as good if someone else was urging me on. Mistakes, loss of control, burned reserves are all consequences of rushing.

The reason I am still alive today is because I have taken things at my own speed.

I seem to be a *perpetuum mobile* that has its own rhythm, a rhythm it can only find within itself, by day, at night, from sunrise to sunset, and again at night …

I came from somewhere, and I'm going somewhere … even if the form changes. This place, and the path I travel, are part of Pelbe, the endless knot.

(from my diary)

11 August, afternoon. Still making my way down.

… The sun is shining. Fine weather. At last I have the figure-of-eight that I was so desperate for, retrieved it from our dumpsack at the rock tower below House's Chimney … along with the hammer ice-axe, which will be useful tonight. There's another 1,000 metres to go to get to the bottom of the mountain. At least abseiling is a piece of cake now I have the *descendeur* – I lean back as if in some fantastic aerial armchair, my descent gently controlled by the loop of rope running through and around the figure-of-eight, and all I have to do is let my feet walk down the rock. But I'll be needing all my reserves during the night ahead – I can't hope to be down to the final big slopes before then.

Night itself does not frighten me. I have often climbed at night – even the modern fast men who 'run' up eight-thousanders include the night in their planning. But I don't run – my speed depends on different principles: my natural rhythm, and also the particular circumstances on the mountain.

I can't get over the difference the *descendeur* makes! What a good thing that Julie and I left depots on the ridge like that. At the foot of the mountain, too, in our tent at Advanced Base Camp, there is everything I need for a retreat or stopover. I shall certainly rest there until midday tomorrow, before going on to Base Camp.*

Already I am feeling the revitalizing effect of being lower – there is so much more oxygen to breathe at 6,000 metres!

Willi could be in Base Camp by about now and getting a search party together to try and rescue Mrufka. But what about Mrufka? Sometimes, leaning back in my harness during an abseil, I peer up to see if I can detect any sign of her, but it would be a miracle if she were coming now. Did she, I wonder, reach Wanda's tent at the 7,000-metre camp? If so, most likely she'll be sleeping all today to make up for last night. She's safe enough there, there's food and she can cook with her stove and the cylinder she found. If she didn't make it ... then something must have happened. And in that case, there's hardly any hope.

How ironic that the fine weather had to wait until now.

Camp 1. I look at it with bitter emotion: this is where Julie and I were sitting drinking tea with Hannes and Alfred before they went on to join Willi. Hanging inside the red dome tent should be the bag with our last film magazines, those showing Julie and me – with Hannes – holding the mugs of hot tea. Happy and optimistic we were then. Both of us knew that from there on the summit counted more for us than the film: we would definitely leave the camera behind. We had been given this one last chance; we should not let it go unused.

Everything is so different now. Tears well in my eyes as, with trembling hands, I undo the entrance to the silent tent.

My hand feels up under the dome. Yes, there it is! The bag with the movie camera and those last precious films is still hanging safe – the last testimony of our little team ... team that is no more.

They won't be left behind! While I stuff the bag into my rucksack, conviction rises in me like a vow – no, our spirit is not dead ... our ideas are still there ... so long as one of us remains alive, Julie, I will keep it going, the team, us ...

By the time I leave the camp, stepping down with the shadows of approaching evening to the last, steep section that still has to be descended, the ground seems to sink beneath my feet around me, I see whirling ridges, veils of cloud, all caressed with the still, shining light of

---

* I did not know of course that there was nothing left at the foot of the Abruzzi Spur: a week after we were last seen ascending during our summit bid, everything had been cleared. We had been given up for dead.

Perpetuum Mobile

Tashigang's green fields ... through tears, I see the blurred outline of a mountain, dreamlike, beautiful. It was ours ...

Night ... Tired stars, half washed away. A steep slope against which I lean to catch breath ... the last 500 metres down. I no longer bother with the fixed ropes, which are hard to pick out and in places have disappeared under all the snow that has come down since we've been away. In any case, because of the melting of the ice sheets, they are often too far into the rocks where they are anchored to the side of the great bulk of the Abruzzi Spur, which sleeps like a dark dragon at my side. It would be too much of a torture to have to move on to the rocks to find them.

Alone, therefore, alone with the night, the heads of my two ice-axes clutched in my fists, I embrace the steep snowslope. Axes held high, in front of my face, the abyss below ... alone with my thoughts and with the passing time, I inch my way slowly, steadily, down the snow, swinging first one heavy leather boot behind me, and then the other, reaching down and kicking hard so that the power of the foot's own weight drives the front points of my crampons into the steep slope – and all the while keeping myself in balance with the axes. Feet secure, then move the hands, one at a time to lower holds, matching the rhythm of the feet, plunging the axes with all force into the invisible snow surface once more. Inch by inch, step by step, in the darkness I creep towards the Godwin Austen Glacier far below. It is still hours away. However desperate I am to reach the bottom, it is more than ever essential to be vigilant now. Here, alone, and with no protection on that open face, no error would be forgiven.

Tak, tak...tak, tak...tak, tak, the sound of my crampons penetrates the night, together with the rhythmic crunch of the snow under the picks of my axes. Every twenty steps or so I take a rest, leaning forward into the slope, forehead on forearms, lost to the darkness. I think of that water down there, the little stream between the stones, the water between the ice patches, its trickling murmur. I think of the few clumps of green – you could count them on the fingers of one hand – hidden among the rocks, like secret, magic gardens that you sense rather than see. How we both loved that place with its backdrop of wild ice towers and a view towards the third summit pyramid of Broad Peak. From a height of 5,300 metres, you could look along the sinuous course of the Godwin Austen Glacier all the way down to Base Camp (still two hours' walk away), that little 'village' with its milling activity. But here, the foot of the Abruzzi Spur, is a homely place. Why, it even boasts a homesteader: a little hamster-like creature with black button-eyes. This must be his summer residence.

The Endless Knot

Snowdust brushes past me. I breathe in the cold night air. Should I move on? The thumb of my right hand is sore from repeatedly thrusting my ice-axe into the hard surface, the other fingers are reduced to rigid, bone-hard claws with no feeling left in them at all. A few stars flicker in the sky. I could rest here indefinitely.

... that animal was living solely on titbits it could scrounge from expeditions and those few green leaves. One day we noticed how carefully it treated the secret garden: it never ate the leaves totally, just nibbled here and there a bit, so that they could continue growing ... a clever animal ...

But how does a hamster climb through an icefall? And why?

... Darkness all around me and dominating everything, the face, indistinct rock figures rising from the Abruzzi. I lean towards the snow, rest my head on my arm and hear the rush of glacier water far below, the sound carried up to me on a draught of air. I wish I could be down there.

Tak, tak...tak, tak...tak, tak. I go on. The sound of my own steps rings like a *perpetuum mobile* through the night. A steady heartbeat rhythm ...

... When the Koreans came, tents sprang up like coloured mushrooms on the scree around our own small, dark-green dome (the same colour as the pointed leaftips). The little homesteader resented their intrusion at first and would not come out, but later he probably brought up all his family and friends as well, there was so much rice ...

Tak, tak...tak, tak...tak, tak... yes that garden overlooking the ice towers was a very special place for Julie. We both loved it: it was our place. It makes me happy to think about it.

Tak, tak...tak, tak...tak, tak...

There will be something of her there? She will be down there? When I touch the water, she will be there ...

Tak, tak...tak, tak...tak, tak...

The snow is deeper now, but less steep. Like a huge python, the ridge at my side winds into the depths. I can only guess where it ends.

Why did you have to stay up there, Julie? It's something I'll never be able to understand. Tak, tak.

I wonder if you knew in your heart that it might happen? Why didn't *I* sense it? Both of us, of course, were aware that something like that was always on the cards ...

We wanted to be with our dream mountain once more, try one last time for the summit together before giving up, perhaps for good. It was so great being linked by the rope again.

Tak, tak...tak, tak...tak, tak...tak...

Now I am alone. All that's left is this longing for that place down there. Perhaps I'll find you down there. At the water ...

Perpetuum Mobile

'I will be a little mouse and watch you,' you said to me in Tashigang once and smiled. It was the only time we ever mentioned the subject – what would happen if one of us were to be lost in the mountains? But the sun was shining over the roofs of the village, sunlight oozing from the green of the fields, we could feel its warmth on our skin and quickly spoke of something else. It was absurd to think of death. Unimaginable that only one of us might come back from the mountain. That would never happen.

Tak, tak...tak, tak...tak, tak.

But it has happened.

I am coming down from K2 alone.

We fulfilled our dream – and have given up everything else for it. We did not know ...

There is the whirr of a stone in the air. Then all is still again. How long have I been climbing through this darkness? Two hours? Three?

Tak, tak...tak, tak......tak...tak......tak...

Why this tiredness? What's happening to me? Shivering, I stop. A strange sensation runs through my body, through my brain. An awareness of unlimited distance. I must sleep for a while. No! Get it together, Kurt! If you sleep you'll fall! You have to get down now! It's not that far.

Tak, tak...tak......tak... but where are my usual steady movements? My confidence starts to crumble.

All of a sudden, it is finished. I can't go on any more ... darkness ... it's all empty around me. Fear takes hold of me. Below me, the deep – all of a sudden it seems bottomless. A never-ending abyss. Stay calm, Kurt. Take a rest – and then go on. Ram in the two axes firmly. Nothing will happen. Stay calm.

I sink my head on my arm ...

I am part of the night.

Time passes, infinite time.

I travel measureless distances.

What is that moving there? It looks like people, lights ... Lights! People! A lighted tent? Or a hallucination? One moment ago there was just darkness, I was alone in the vast night. It can't be people. Go slow, Kurt. Don't be taken in. Look into that slope in front of you.

Tak, tak... now I've reached where the avalanche debris spills in large lumps of packed ice across a boulder slope ... I find a clear way through, groping my way, still on all fours, crawling down, face to the slope. I should turn round now, but I'm frightened I'll fall on such uneven ground.

The Endless Knot

I rest again. The people below me have become a reality: they do exist. The lights are blinking with busy movement. They have not yet noticed me. A sensation of relief flows through me ... I *have* made it. In a few minutes, I will be at that place where the water is, will reach our Garden of Eden. Its little landlord must be fast asleep, deep between his stones.

Who are they – these people? I am in a kind of trance, not registering properly.

I keep climbing down, can feel with my feet the shallow depression at the edge of the snowfield. The dazzling beam of a lamp suddenly penetrates the darkness, reaching up towards me. Have they discovered me? I still feel that I belong to the night.

In that moment I look forward to meeting the people who are coming ...

Someone must have spotted me. I hear voices, calls, see lights moving out across the boulders just below me, but I give no sign.

Mutely, I step down, unchanged, not knowing how to break the pattern of the perpetual motion of this night. Tak...tak...tak...tak......infinitely slowly.

I'm caught in a cone of light. There is a figure approaching. Now he is at my side. Slowly I turn and stand upright.

'You're safe at last!' the words are Jim's. Jim Curran's. He grabs my arm and supports me firmly as all around the night slowly vanishes, this night of which I have been part, and which now only grudgingly releases me.

More lights. More people gathering round.

You're safe at last. Why did Jim say that? Of course I'm safe, here at the place of our garden. I've made it, yes. But, she ... Julie ... she is up there.

'I've lost Julie,' I tell Jim. There's nothing else to say.

It is midnight on 11 August. The 2,700-metre descent from the place of the fearful storm is over. Krystyna, Janusz, Jim ... they lead me across the boulders to a tent, to their tent which they have just erected. Now I realize: the whole camp – Julie's and my tent included – has disappeared. It has been cleared: for days now we have all been given up for dead.

It was two weeks ago that we set off from here on our climb ...

There's one thing I've almost forgotten to tell: I groped my way down, as if I wanted to fulfil a promise, all the way to our garden by the murmuring water. I tripped, fell over in the splintering ice – and drank and drank and drank.

I am lying in a double sleeping bag, belonging to one of the Poles – soft, cosy and warm as only Polish bags can be. And 'Krysiu', white-blonde

Perpetuum Mobile

like my daughter Karen, feeds me hot tea. Oh, it's good to be looked after so caringly! A few minutes ago Janusz took off my boots for me, and Jim tells how he came to find me.

'... There was this strange noise in the night, repeating itself over and over. Like a low, hesitant heartbeat – no, not quite like that – anyway, I couldn't make out what it was ... and then I heard it again ... it sounded like metal, and yet somehow human ... living ...'

A heartbeat that propelled thoughts, and arms and legs and my ice-axe! An inextinguishable energy that came out of the night. A *perpetuum mobile*. I feel it a miracle to be still alive.

Doctors and scientists say that everything has an end, that perpetual motion does not exist. Not inside you and not outside of you. But perhaps sometimes one participates in the wholeness of existence.

The next morning, completely unexpectedly, it was almost all over for me. With Jim, Krysiu and a high-altitude porter I was climbing down through the icefall. I was exhausted and moving gingerly because we were doing it without a rope, as most people did in those weeks, and because my frozen, swollen feet would no longer fit into my wet double boots which anyway weighed a ton, I had changed them for slippery moonboots. All of a sudden a handhold broke in the ice. I skidded, lost my balance, and it was only the quick action of Jim grabbing my arm that saved me from falling into a crevasse full of water, in which I would almost certainly have drowned.

A little later, hardly surprisingly, I was overcome with a terrible hunger and felt quite at the end of my strength until good Krysiu ran ahead and had a potful of hot soup sent up from Base Camp for me. Then, slowly, I went on again.

When, on the moraine about a mile from Base Camp, a group of mountaineers appeared with a stretcher, I made no fuss ...

The search for Mrufka, by the rescue party alerted by Willi on his arrival in Base Camp the day before, met with no success. She could not be found anywhere at the foot of the mountain, nor was she, as I had hoped, sleeping in the small tent at about 7,000 metres. That was as high as the rescuers could reach. A year later a Japanese expedition discovered her body on the fixed ropes, somewhat above the ladder that starts near the tent. Her hand still held the rope and, as I understand it, she was upright, leaning into the wall. She had a thin cord around the rope, the significance of which no one could explain. Did she die of an embolism? Or had she simply fallen asleep? It will always be a mystery.

Mrufka was buried near Advanced Base Camp.

Of the other victims on the Shoulder, nothing has been found. The snowstorms have covered them.

Whether or not you think it is possible to have any links with 'the beyond' during life, it can certainly never be visualized, nor ever explained. Logical people often dismiss it as so much moonshine, even though no logician has yet come up with a satisfactory explanation for the enigma of life and death. Nevertheless, even the driest of realists, the most sober of mathematicians, is sometimes confronted with signs or experiences which belong in a different world, which are inexplicable by normal standards. Yet they are still real – and merely to put them down to coincidence sounds like a cheap cop-out on the part of people who simply don't know.

Similarly, what I am going to tell next can never be explained.

A strange thing happened – I noticed – on my right foot, the one that was the least frostbitten. There appeared more and more visible from day to day in the nail of the big toe, as if inscribed there, a distinct number '11', blue at first, then turning to black ... a frightening mark. It was so clear, that I could not just put it down to a product of fantasy and began to brood upon it. (I had more than enough time to think in the Innsbruck hospital.) Did it mean I was destined to be the eleventh victim on K2? After Mohammed Ali, the leader of the high-altitude porters, who was hit by stonefall on 4 August near Camp 1, Julie, on 7 August, became the ninth victim of the terrible mountain summer on K2; Alfred Imitzer was the tenth, dying during the last desperate attempt to get down on 10 August, and he was followed by Hannes Wieser, Alan Rouse and finally Mrufka on the fixed ropes. It was 11 August, just before midnight, when I won the fight for survival by reaching the foot of the mountain after two days struggling down from 8,000 metres, most of which time I was completely on my own. It was 11 August, the end of that day, when on my last legs, I met the party coming up to look for Mrufka (and to rescue me, too, if necessary).

The 11th of August – was that to have been my last day? Or was I supposed to have died up there on the Shoulder as the eleventh victim?

However you looked at it, the black '11' was a sinister mark. I was under no doubt that I had escaped destiny.

50. *(above)* K2 from Windy Gap. The Abruzzi Route is in profile on the left. The technical climbing, starting from the Godwin-Austen Glacier, involves 3056m of ascent. The final camp on the highest level of the Shoulder at around 8000m leaves a summit climb of some 616m. Then, having regained the camp, some 2440m of continuously steep descent (with two or three intermediate camps) is needed to return to the glacier – a formidable escape route, especially when fatigued.

51. *(left)* Willi Bauer and Kurt Diemberger at Skurdu after their ordeal – the Korean doctor skilfully tending their frostbite injuries.

Clouds From Both Sides

Sometimes people say to me: You lost close friends up there, would you go back to climb in the Himalayas again?

They expect me to say 'No'. However, losing my friends was not all there was to it, I also lived with them up there. They found their *life* up there.

I couldn't, not now, change the way I live. I have been going to the Himalayas for thirty years; I cannot imagine any sort of future that doesn't involve going back there. I have to be with the big mountains – even if now only rarely do I get up to the summit.

August 1988: I'm sitting in a plane, on my way to Sinkiang. I am with Agostino, Gianni and the others. We will be exploring the mountain desert to the north of K2 – there, where the endless processions of green-blue ice towers march shoulder to shoulder down the lonely curving glaciers. Below the Gasherbrums, up behind Broad Peak ... maybe even into that corner which Julie and I burned with impatience to see. We will be there, where the two of us roamed with shining K2 high above our heads.

Yes, I know – happiness and sorrow will go with me. And I shall still be searching.

Outside, not far from the window of the plane, enormous towers of cloud have appeared: I see them growing, watch the fluted outlines expand and change ... we slide among them, through them; spectral threads of white cotton race by, weightless overhangs, meandering inlets, bays – into which we dive – giant, puffy shapes surround us, huge pillars and columns reaching up from the depths ... beautiful cloud formations. Clouds, as Julie loved them.

I remember what she once said about the faces of clouds: 'there is one side, the beautiful face, which imagination allows you to see – as a child I was always dreaming about those castles, seeing so many things in those silhouettes ...

'But they also have a dark face, which can destroy your dreams ...'
and she explained to me why she intended to call her book *Clouds from Both Sides* ...

The many faces of the clouds ... white towers, building and rebuilding, endlessly re-creating themselves, changing their form; avalanches of vapour which extend into the sky with the same might and power as snowdust ... with the same power of fantasy that will always transport inquisitive souls who yearn to understand, to feel and touch ... what they see in the clouds. Because in that lies a sense of being.

But may clouds not hide storms? May they not rise, threatening, mighty, incomprehensible – like immense dark birds ... storm birds, that tear away everything, that destroy not only dreams? When they are over you, when you are in their power, there is no light and shadow any more. And you must fight for all that constitutes life, for all that is dear to you and your companion – and you fight for him, for those at home, for yourself – until one day the time comes when you sink back silently – as Julie did.

Yet stormbirds, too, have their end.

The darkness, the all-encompassing dreariness, lasted for a long time after the return from K2 – as if the storm, like a bad spell, had not fully worked itself out. There were gaps in memory ... full of fantasies; there were heroic poems, and clichés. There were invented 'rescues' – when in fact nobody unable to climb down by himself could have survived. The most extreme opinions clashed together. But that time is over, it was a fight, but it was necessary for the truth, for all those who will climb in future.

Luckily, I learned to know a different side, too: friendship, people who really helped me, and had to bear a lot, like Teresa, Karen, Hildegard, Tona. Like Ceci, Inge and Dennis, Terry ... it takes a long time to clamber out of an abyss like that.

Today I am flying between Julie's white clouds. And she is not sitting by my side and watching them. She is with them.

'Love is no possession; it is everywhere.' She wrote that once on a small piece of paper for me during a flight through clouds.

The voice ... there it is, I can hear it.
Today I am flying between white clouds ...

The Endless Knot

APPENDIX I

K2 EXPEDITION HISTORY

(from the first reconnaissance to 1990)

Following the expeditions of 1835–8 (Vigne), 1856 (Schlagintweit), 1856 (Montgomerie), 1861 (Godwin-Austen) and 1887 (Younghusband) – that penetrated and made the initial surveys of the Karakoram, the first expedition to actually tackle K2 may date from 1890:

Year	Expedition	Leader / Route / (SE = Abruzzi Ridge) / Remarks
1890	Italian	Roberto Lerco He made the first reconnaissance of K2 (between May and October); also explorations around the Hunza Valley (see *Rivista Mensile* 1954); he appears to have climbed to 6,600m on the Abruzzi Ridge, but this is open to question.
1892	British	William Martin Conway An expedition with scientific and mountaineering objectives, and the first to penetrate the full length of the Baltoro glacier. (Conway gave the enormous glacier junction its name Concordia, being reminded of the Place de la Concorde in Paris.) First ascent of Pioneer Peak (6,890m) on Baltoro Kangri – a world altitude record at the time; valuable topographical work (Baltoro map), six 'explorers' (climber/scientists), an ornithologist, four Gurkha soldiers.
1902	International	Oscar Eckenstein NE Climbing attempt on North-East Ridge to 6,525m; six climbers – among them the notorious Aleister Crowley and the Austrian mountaineers Heinrich Pfannl and Victor Wessely.
1909	Italian	Luigi Amedeo de Savoia, Duke of the Abruzzi SE Exploration and attempt on K2's 'feasible' route, the Abruzzi Ridge or Spur to a height of 6,250m; twelve climbers.
1929	Italian	Prince Aimone di Savoia, Duke of Spoleto S/N Mountaineering attempt renounced in favour of important geographic and geological studies. Professor Ardito Desio took part as a geologist, exploring the Shaksgam Valley with three other members; on the Baltoro side his explorations included reaching the 'Possible Saddle' described by Conway, between the Baltoro and the Siachen glaciers (he named it after its discoverer).
1937	British	Eric Shipton N Exploration, scientific and topographical survey work, as well as climbs to the north of K2 in the region of several large glaciers and in the Shaksgam (four climbers and seven Sherpas).
1938	American	Charles S. Houston SE First concerted attempt to climb the Abruzzi Ridge; seven high camps erected and an altitude of 7,925m attained (six climbers).
1939	American	Fritz Wiessner SE A push to 8,382m – without artificial oxygen. Nine high camps. During the final retreat, despite a rescue attempt, three Sherpas and Dudley Wolfe, perished. (Members: six climbers and nine Sherpas.)
1953	American	Charles S. Houston SE Eight high camps erected and a height of 7,900m reached. A desperate bid to save the sick Art Gilkey failed and he was lost in an avalanche shortly after Pete Schoening astonishingly checked a mass fall. (Eight climbers.)
1953	Italian	Riccardo Cassin SE Reconnaissance expedition; Cassin and Desio went to the foot of the Abruzzi Ridge (September).
1954	Italian	Ardito Desio SE *First ascent of K2.* Nine high camps. Fixed ropes and oxygen apparatus employed. On 31 July at about 18.00 hours Lino Lacedelli and Achile Compagnoni reached the summit. Eleven climbers; Mario Puchoz died of pneumonia.
1960	German/ American	W. D. Hackett SE Bad weather made it impossible to surmount the 'Black Pyramid', a difficult and steep section of the Abruzzi Ridge (seven climbers).
1975	American	James Whittaker NW A new route, attempted from the Savoia Saddle; highest point reached – 6,700m (ten climbers including one woman).
1976	Polish	Janusz Kurczab NE The Poles surmounted the difficult North-East Ridge; an attempt on the summit pyramid by Chrobak and Wroz reached 8,400m. This route had originally been attempted in 1902 (nineteen members).
1976	Japanese	Takayoshi Takatsuka SE Reconnaissance. On 7 August three climbers attained 7,160m on the Abruzzi Ridge. (Six members.)

Appendix I

1977	Japanese	Ichiro Yoshizawa SE *Second Ascent of K2*. Mammoth expedition: fifty-two members, 1,500 porters. Six Japanese and a Pakistani reached the summit on 8 and 9 August. Oxygen used.
1978	American	James Whittaker NE/SE *Third ascent of K2*. The Polish NE Ridge route was followed to a height of 7,700m, then an oblique traverse made to the Abruzzi route. Four climbers reached the summit on 6 and 7 September – with little or no use of oxygen. (Fourteen members, among them three women.)
1978	British	Chris Bonington W First attempt on West Ridge (to 6,700m) abandoned after the death of Nick Estcourt in an avalanche. (Eight members.)
1979	French	Bernard Mellet SSW South-South-West Ridge attempted by massive expedition. One of the steepest and most difficult ridges on the mountain: five summit thrusts were made to a height of 8,400m. (Fourteen climbers; death of one high-altitude porter.)
1979	International	Reinhold Messner ML/SE *Fourth ascent of K2*. Reinhold Messner and Michl Dacher gained the summit without using oxygen on 12 July via the Abruzzi Ridge. Four high camps. An attempt on the projected 'Magic Line', the original objective, was earlier abandoned. (Seven members; one porter killed falling into a crevasse.)
1980	British	Peter Boardman W/SE After an attempt on the West Ridge to 7,000m, 7,900m was reached on the Abruzzi. (Four climbers.)
1981	Japanese	Teruoh Matsuura W *Fifth ascent of K2* (and first via the West Ridge). On 7 August one Japanese and one Pakistani stood on the summit. Oxygen employed.
1981	French/German	Yannick Seigneur S Attempt on a new route (on the South Face); 7,400m reached. (Four climbers.)
1982	Polish	Janusz Kurczab NW Attempt to force a new route without touching the Savoia Saddle; 8,200m finally gained on the Chinese side, where they were observed and ordered back! 3,500m of fixed rope employed (twenty-one climbers: fifteen Poles and six Mexicans).
1982	Japanese	Isaoh Shinkai N *Sixth ascent of K2*, and first from the Chinese side via North Ridge. Seven climbers reached summit on 14 and 15 August but Yukihiro Yanagisawa was killed during the descent. No oxygen (fourteen climbers).
1982	Austrian	(Hanns Schell) Georg Bachler SE 7,500m reached, and further attempts abandoned to help in the evacuation of dead Polish woman climber. Bachler was the effective leader since Schell remained in Austria! (Four members.)
1982	Polish	Wanda Rutkiewicz SE Polish women's expedition; death of Halina Krüger; they reached 7,100m (eleven women climbers, including one French, Christine de Colombel).
1983	Spanish	Antonio Trabado W A height of 8,200m reached via West Ridge and West Face (Juanjo San Sebastián and A. Trabado).
1983	International	Doug Scott S An attempt on a rib to the left of the Abruzzi by three Britons and one Frenchman, reached 7,500m.
1983	Spanish (Navarre)	Gregorio Ariz SE Mari Abrego and Roger Baxter-Jones – after their respective expeditions had given up – reached a height of 8,300m before bad weather turned them back. (Earlier the nine-person Navarre team had been to 7,700m.)
1983	Italian	Francesco Santon N *Seventh ascent of K2* (and second via the North Ridge). Summit reached by four members (three Italians, one Czech) on 31 July and 4 August, climbing without oxygen. Julie Tullis became the 'highest woman' on K2. (Twenty-three members in all.)
1984	International	Stefan Wörner SE 7,500m reached.
1985	Swiss	Erhard Loretan SE Five climbers reached the summit on two separate days. No oxygen.
1985	French	Eric Escoffier SE Three climbers reached summit. Daniel Lacroix lost during the descent. No oxygen.
1985	Japanese	Kazuoh Tobita SE Three Japanese reached summit – probably without oxygen.
1985	International	Wojciech Kurtyka SE Attempt foundered at 7,000m. (R. Schauer and Kurtyka later climbed West Face of Gasherbrum IV.)
1986	Italian/Basque	Renato Casarotto SE/SSW Mari Abrego and Josema Casimiro reached summit by Abruzzi Ridge. Casarotto died in a fall into a crevasse after attempting SSW Ridge.

The Endless Knot

1986	French	Maurice Barrard	SE Summit reached by all four members, Wanda Rutkiewicz and Liliane Barrard becoming the first women to climb K2. The Barrards, husband and wife, were lost during the descent.
1986	British	Alan Rouse/John Barry	NW/SE Attempted NW Ridge to 7,400m; Alan Rouse died after reaching summit via Abruzzi Ridge. (Eleven climbers.)
1986	American	John Smolich	SSW After Smolich and Al Pennington killed by avalanche, attempt abandoned. (Eight climbers.)
1986	Italian/ International	Agostino Da Polenza	SSW/SE Eight members reached summit by Abruzzi Ridge. Julie Tullis died during the descent. The attempt on the SSW Ridge was given up because of avalanche danger.
1986	International	Karl Herrligkoffer	S/SE Two Swiss reached summit by Abruzzi Ridge; Jerzy Kukuczka and Tadeusz Piotrowski made first ascent of South Face but Piotrowski killed during descent. (Sixteen members.)
1986	Austrian	Alfred Imitzer	SE Two members reached the summit, two deaths during the descent (Imitzer and H. Wieser) (seven climbers).
1986	South Korean	Kim Byung-Joon	SE Three climbers to summit, using oxygen. Death of sirdar in stonefall. (Nineteen members.)
1986	Polish	Janusz Majer	SSW/SE First ascent of SSW Ridge; death of W. Wroz during descent. 'Mrufka' Dobroslawa Wolf died during descent after attempt on Abruzzi. (Eight members, including three women.)
1986	American	Lance Owens	N Attempt on N Ridge to a height of 8,100m (eight climbers).
1986	Slovenian	Viki Grošelj	S Tomo Cesen soloed new line (essentially that nearly completed in 1983 by the Scott party) to left of Abruzzi Ridge, as far as the Shoulder, 7,800m.
1987	International	Doug Scott	S Another attempt (after that of 1983) on spur to the left of Abruzzi – 7,100m reached. Also 6,900m reached on the Abruzzi Route (six climbers).
1987	French	Martine Rolland	SE Attempt to 7,000m (six members).
1987	Polish/Swiss	Wojciech Kurtyka	W Attempt on West Face with Jean Troillet to 6,400m.
1987	Japanese	Haruyuki Endo	SE Attempt to 7,400m.
1987	Japanese/Pakistani	Kenshiro Otaki	SE Attempt to 8,300m; Akiri Suzuki killed in a fall (fourteen members).
1987	Spanish (Basque)	Juanjo San Sebastián	S Climbed the rib to the left of the Abruzzi as far as the Shoulder, then the normal route to 8,300m (seven climbers, plus a sirdar).
1987–8	Polish/International	Andrzej Zawada	SE Winter attempt to 7,350m (twenty climbers).
1988	Slovenian	Tomaz Jamnik	SSW/SE Attempt to 8,100m, then Abruzzi Ridge to 7,400m (fifteen members).
1988	American	Peter Athans	SE Attempt to 7,400m (five members).
1988	New Zealand	Rob Hall	SE Attempt to 7,400m (four members).
1988	Spanish (Catalan)	Jordi Magriñá	SE Attempt to 8,100m (twelve members).
1988	French	Pierre Béghin	N Attempt on North Spur to 8,000m (six members and a doctor).
1989	Polish/Swiss	Wojciech Kurtyka	NW An attempt to open new route on NW Face couldn't get started on account of bad weather (with Jean Troillet and Erhard Loretan).
1989	Austrian	Eduard Koblmüller	E/SE An attempt on unclimbed East Face reached 7,200m.
1989	Spanish (Basque)	Juanjo San Sebastián	SE Reached 7,400m (eleven members).
1990	American	Doug Dalquist	SE Reached 7,600m. Abandoned due to excessive soft snow.
1990	International	C. A. Pinelli	SE 'Free K2' international cleaning expedition organized by Mountain Wilderness with (deliberately) no summit attempts (nine members).
1990	Australian/ American	Steve Swenson	N North Spur climbed on 20 August at 8p.m. by Swenson, Greg Child and Greg Mortimer.
1990	Japanese	Tomoji Ueki	N Attempt of a new route (NW Face and N Spur). Hideji Nazuka and Hirotaka Imamura reached the summit on 9 August from the Chinese side (twelve members and eight Chinese helpers).

Appendix I

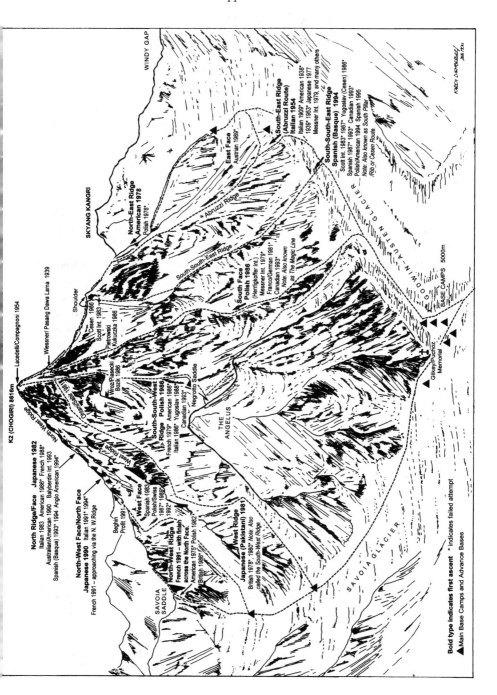

The Endless Knot

APPENDIX II

FATALITIES ON K2

Name	Nationality	Date	Cause	Route
Dudley Wolfe	American	30.7.39	Probably high altitude sickness, exhaustion: in Camp 7 (7,550m).	Abruzzi Ridge
Pasang Kikuli	Sherpa	31.7.39	Disappeared between Camps 6 and 7.	Abruzzi Ridge
Pasang Kitar	Sherpa	31.7.39	Disappeared between Camps 6 and 7.	Abruzzi Ridge
Pintso	Sherpa	31.7.39	Disappeared between Camps 6 and 7.	Abruzzi Ridge
Art Gilkey	American	10.8.53	Avalanche near Camp 7 (7,450m).	Abruzzi Ridge
Mario Puchoz	Italian	21.6.54	Pneumonia at Camp 2 (5,900m).	Abruzzi Ridge
Nick Estcourt	British	12.6.78	Avalanche near Camp 2 (6,500m).	West Ridge
Ali, son of Kazim	Pakistani	9.6.79	Fall into crevasse.	Savoia glacier
Laskhar Khan	Pakistani	19.8.79	Heart attack between Camps 3 and 4.	SSW Ridge
Halina Krüger	Polish	30.7.82	Heart attack at Camp 2 (6,700m).	Abruzzi Ridge
Yukihiro Yanagisawa	Japanese	15.8.82	Fell during descent.	North Ridge
Daniel Lacroix	French	7.7.85	Lost during descent.	Abruzzi Ridge
John Smolich	American	21.6.86	Avalanche death at 6,000m.	SSW Ridge
Alan Pennington	American	21.6.86	Avalanche death at 6,000m.	SSW Ridge
Liliane Barrard	French	24.6.86	Fall during descent.	Abruzzi Ridge
Maurice Barrard	French	24.6.86	Lost during descent.	Abruzzi Ridge
Tadeusz Piotrowski	Polish	10.7.86	Fall during descent.	Abruzzi Ridge
Renato Casarotto	Italian	16.7.86	Fall into crevasse at 5,100m.	SSW Ridge
Wojciech Wroz	Polish	3.8.86	Fall during descent.	Abruzzi Ridge
Mohammed Ali	Pakistani	4.8.86	Stonefall below Camp 1.	Abruzzi Ridge
Julie Tullis	British	7.8.86	Complex of causes, after fall, in Camp 4 (8,000m).	Abruzzi Ridge
Alan Rouse	British	10.8.86	Probably high altitude sickness and exhaustion, in Camp 4 (8,000m).	Abruzzi Ridge
Alfred Imitzer	Austrian	10.8.86	Probably high altitude sickness and exhaustion, below Camp 4 (8,000m).	Abruzzi Ridge
Hannes Wieser	Austrian	10.8.86	Probably high altitude sickness and exhaustion, below Camp 4 (8,000m).	Abruzzi Ridge
Dobroslawa Wolf	Polish	10.8.86	Unknown (embolism?) between Camps 3 and 2.	Abruzzi Ridge
Akira Suzuki	Japanese	24.8.87	Fall from c.8,200m.	Abruzzi Ridge
Hans Bärnthaler	Austrian	28.7.89	Fell with collapsing cornice while photographing E Face from a nearby peak.	East Face

Note by Xavier Eguskitza: of the twenty-seven mountaineers who reached the summit of K2 during 1986, seven died on the descent (as well as six others). Since then three more have also died: Michel Parmentier and Petr Bozik on Everest in the autumn of 1988, and Jerzy Kukuczka on the South Face of Lhotse in October 1989.

Appendix II

APPENDIX III

K2 SUMMIT CLIMBERS
by Xavier Eguskitza   † indicates died during descent

No.	Name	Nationality	Date	Route	Expedition	Leader
1	Achille Compagnoni	Italian	31.7.54	Abruzzi Ridge	Italian	Ardito Desio
2	Lino Lacedelli	Italian	31.7.54	Abruzzi Ridge	Italian	Ardito Desio
3	Shoji Nakamura	Japanese	8.8.77	Abruzzi Ridge	Japanese	Ichiro Yoshizawa
4	Tsuneoh Shigehiro	Japanese	8.8.77	Abruzzi Ridge	Japanese	Ichiro Yoshizawa
5	Takeyoshi Takatsuka	Japanese	8.8.77	Abruzzi Ridge	Japanese	Ichiro Yoshizawa
6	Mitsuo Hiroshima	Japanese	9.8.77	Abruzzi Ridge	Japanese	Ichiro Yoshizawa
7	Masahide Onodera	Japanese	9.8.77	Abruzzi Ridge	Japanese	Ichiro Yoshizawa
8	Hideo Yamamoto	Japanese	9.8.77	Abruzzi Ridge	Japanese	Ichiro Yoshizawa
9	Ashraf Aman	Pakistani	9.8.77	Abruzzi Ridge	Japanese	Ichiro Yoshizawa
10	James Wickwire	American	6.9.78	NE Ridge/Abruzzi	American	James Whittaker
11	Louis Reichardt	American	6.9.78	NE Ridge/Abruzzi	American	James Whittaker
12	John Roskelley	American	7.9.78	NE Ridge/Abruzzi	American	James Whittaker
13	Rick Ridgeway	American	7.9.78	NE Ridge/Abruzzi	American	James Whittaker
14	Reinhold Messner	Italian	12.7.79	Abruzzi Ridge	European	Reinhold Messner
15	Michl Dacher	W. German	12.7.79	Abruzzi Ridge	European	Reinhold Messner
16	Eiho Ohtani	Japanese	7.8.81	West Ridge/SW side	Japanese	Teruoh Matsuura
17	Nazir Sabir	Pakistani	7.8.81	West Ridge/SW side	Japanese	Teruoh Matsuura
18	Naoé Sakashita	Japanese	14.8.82	North Ridge	Japanese	Isao Shinkai
19	Yukihiro Yanagisawa†	Japanese	14.8.82	North Ridge	Japanese	Isao Shinkai
20	Hiroshi Yoshino	Japanese	14.8.82	North Ridge	Japanese	Isao Shinkai
21	Kazushige Takami	Japanese	15.8.82	North Ridge	Japanese	Isao Shinkai
22	Haruichi Kawamura	Japanese	15.8.82	North Ridge	Japanese	Isao Shinkai
23	Tatsuji Shigeno	Japanese	15.8.82	North Ridge	Japanese	Isao Shinkai
24	Hironobu Kamuro	Japanese	15.8.82	North Ridge	Japanese	Isao Shinkai
25	Agostino Da Polenza	Italian	31.7.83	North Ridge	Italian	Francesco Santon
26	Josef Fakoncaj	Czechoslovak	31.7.83	North Ridge	Italian	Francesco Santon
27	Sergio Martini	Italian	4.8.83	North Ridge	Italian	Francesco Santon
28	Fausto De Stefani	Italian	4.8.83	North Ridge	Italian	Francesco Santon
29	Marcel Ruedi	Swiss	19.6.85	Abruzzi Ridge	Swiss	Erhard Loretan
30	Norbert Joos	Swiss	19.6.85	Abruzzi Ridge	Swiss	Erhard Loretan
31	Erhard Loretan	Swiss	6.7.85	Abruzzi Ridge	Swiss	Erhard Loretan
32	Pierre Morand	Swiss	6.7.85	Abruzzi Ridge	Swiss	Erhard Loretan
33	Jean Troillet	Swiss	6.7.85	Abruzzi Ridge	Swiss	Erhard Loretan
34	Eric Escoffier	French	6.7.85	Abruzzi Ridge	French	–
35	Daniel Lacroix†	French	7.7.85	Abruzzi Ridge	French	–
36	Stéphane Schaffter	Swiss	7.7.85	Abruzzi Ridge	French	–
37	Noboru Yamada	Japanese	24.7.85	Abruzzi Ridge	Japanese	Kazuoh Tobita
38	Kenji Yoshida	Japanese	24.7.85	Abruzzi Ridge	Japanese	Kazuoh Tobita
39	Kazunari Murakami	Japanese	24.7.85	Abruzzi Ridge	Japanese	Kazuoh Tobita
40	Wanda Rutkiewicz	Polish	23.6.86	Abruzzi Ridge	French	Maurice Barrard
41	Michel Parmentier	French	23.6.86	Abruzzi Ridge	French	Maurice Barrard
42	Maurice Barrard†	French	23.6.86	Abruzzi Ridge	French	Maurice Barrard

The Endless Knot

43	Liliane Barrard†	French	23.6.86	Abruzzi Ridge	French	Maurice Barrard
44	Mari Abrego	Spanish	23.6.86	Abruzzi Ridge	Basque	(Renato Casarotto)
45	Josema Casimiro	Spanish	23.6.86	Abruzzi Ridge	Basque	(Renato Casarotto)
46	Gianni Calcagno	Italian	5.7.86	Abruzzi Ridge	Italian	Agostino Da Polenza
47	Tullio Vidoni	Italian	5.7.86	Abruzzi Ridge	Italian	Agostino Da Polenza
48	Soro Doroei	Italian	5.7.86	Abruzzi Ridge	Italian	Agostino Da Polenza
49	Martino Moretti	Italian	5.7.86	Abruzzi Ridge	Italian	Agostino Da Polenza
50	Josef Rakoncaj	Czechoslovak	5.7.86	Abruzzi Ridge	Italian	Agostino Da Polenza
51	Benoît Chamoux	French	5.7.86	Abruzzi Ridge	Italian	Agostino Da Polenza
52	Beda Fuster	Swiss	5.7.86	Abruzzi Ridge	Internat.	Karl Herrligkoffer
53	Rolf Zemp	Swiss	5.7.86	Abruzzi Ridge	Internat.	Karl Herrligkoffer
54	Jerzy Kukuczka	Polish	8.7.86	South Face	Internat.	Karl Herrligkoffer
55	Tadeusz Piotrowski†	Polish	8.7.86	South Face	Internat.	Karl Herrligkoffer
56	Chang Bong-Wan	S. Korean	3.8.86	Abruzzi Ridge	S. Korean	Kim Byung-Joon
57	Kim Chang-Sun	S. Korean	3.8.86	Abruzzi Ridge	S. Korean	Kim Byung-Joon
58	Chang Byong-Ho	S. Korean	3.8.86	Abruzzi Ridge	S. Korean	Kim Byung-Joon
59	Wojciec Wroz†	Polish	3.88.6	SSW Ridge	Polish	Janusz Majer
60	Przemyslaw Piasecki	Polish	3.8.86	SSW Ridge	Polish	Janusz Majer
61	Petr Bozik	Czechoslovak	3.8.86	SSW Ridge	Polish	Janusz Majer
62	Willi Bauer	Austrian	4.8.86	Abruzzi Ridge	Austrian	Alfred Imitzer
63	Alfred Imitzer†	Austrian	4.8.86	Abruzzi Ridge	Austrian	Alfred Imitzer
64	Alan Rouse†	British	4.8.86	Abruzzi Ridge	British	Alan Rouse
65	Kurt Diemberger	Austrian	4.8.86	Abruzzi Ridge	Italian	Agostino Da Polenza
66	Julie Tullis†	British	4.8.86	Abruzzi Ridge	Italian	Agostino Da Polenza
67	Hideji Nazuk	Japanese	9.8.90	North Side	Japanese	Tomoji Ueki
68	Hrotaka Imamura	Japanese	9.8.90	North Side	Japanese	Tomoji Ueki
69	Steve Swenson	American	20.8.90	North Spur	American	Steve Swenson
70	Greg Child	Australian	20.8.90	North Spur	American	Steve Swenson
71	Greg Mortimer	Australian	20.8.90	North Spur	American	Steve Swenson

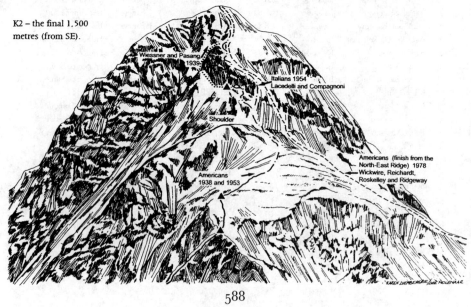

K2 – the final 1,500 metres (from SE).

Index

Abram, Eric, 487
Abrego, Mari, 388, 414, 415-416, 421, 423-474, 565
Abruzzi, Luigi Amedeo di Savoia, Duke of, 333
Abruzzi Ridge (K2), 333, 378-379, 403-405, 408, 415, 420-421, 434, 451
acclimatization, 409-410, 411-413
Ali, Mohammed (porter), 458, 462, 578
Alpinismo (journal), 421
Ancarani, Alida, 365
Ancarani, Angela, 365
Anila (Tibetan nun), 394-398
Argentero, Luca, 352, 355
Assignment Adventure (TV series), 366

Baltoro Glacier, 331, 332, 434
Baltoro mountains, 399, 402
Barrard, Maurice and Liliane, 388, 409, 416-417, 421, 465, 514,532
Bauer, Willi, 413, 441-444, 448, 457, 459-460, 465-466, 483, 484, 505, 507, 533-536, 543-544, 547, 550-551, 555, 557-566, 569, 570, 572
Berghold, Franz, 411-413
Black Pyramid (Abruzzi Ridge), 456, 458
Bonatti, Walter, 487, 494
Borde mini-stove, 440
Boyer, Dr Steve, 437
Bozik, Petr, 506-507, 511, 537, 546
Broad Peak, 332, 334-337, 347, 366, 367-376, 378-383, 402, 408, 435, 471, 503, 510-511
Buhl, Hermann, 331, 332, 333-335, 347, 367, 371-373, 381-382, 384, 402, 413, 427, 455, 456, 464
Burgess twins, Adrian and Alan, 405

Calcagno, Gianni, 420-421, 422, 431-433, 437, 580
Cappelletti, Rodolfo, 345
Carter, Adams, 466
Casarotto, Goretta, 403, 414, 429-434
Casarotto, Renato, 388, 403-405, 408, 414, 424, 428-433, 529, 534
Casimiro, Josema, 388, 414, 415-416, 420, 423-424, 565
Cesen, Tomo, 405, 414-416, 420
Chamoux, Benoit, 394, 397, 408-409, 422, 424, 454, 475
Chan, Sheraman, 470
Chang Bong-Wan, 466, 482, 491, 500

Chogolisa (Bride Peak), 333, 371-373, 455, 471
Chogori, see K2
Chung, Dr Duke Whan, 427
Clarke, Dr Charles, 413
Climber magazine, 500
Compagnoni, Achille, 333, 353, 438, 487, 498
Conway, Sir Martin, 332
Cortecolo, Marco, 351
Croucher, Norman, 362
Curran, Jim, 405, 444, 485-487, 537-538, 546
Czerwinska, Anna ('Anka'), 418, 428, 537

Dacher, Michl, 403
Dawa Lama, Pasang, 449, 512-513
De Marchi, Giuliano, 354-355, 357
Desio, Ardito, 333, 348, 438
Dhaulagiri, 407, 410, 449, 511
Diemberger, Ceci (Kurt's son), 343, 365, 581
Diemberger, Hildegard (Kurt's daughter), 386-387, 389, 391, 393-399, 581
Diemberger, Karen (Kurt's daughter), 387, 581
Diemberger, Kurt: as expedition doctor, 386, 370-371; sailing, 338-341; overweight, 364-365; caught in avalanche on Broad Peak, 367-370, 373-377; snow blindness, 380-381; grandchildren, 387; spiritual experience, 392-393; influenza on 1986 expedition, 398-399; brews beer, 413; temper, 504; at summit of K2, 521; trapped in crevasse, 528-529; stranded in storm at high-altitude camp, 539-554; and Julie's death, 248-51, 259: frostbite, 552, 568-570; continues descent, 559-577; rescued, 578; *Summits and Secrets*, 337
Diemberger, Teresa (Kurt's second wife), 343, 364-365, 581
Diemberger-Sironi, Tona (Kurt's first wife), 386-387, 451, 581
Dorje, Nawang, 449
Dorotei, Soro, 354, 357, 424
Drongpa Ama, 390
Drugpa Aba, 390-391, 394, 553
drugs and medication, 409-410
Dyhrenfurth, G. O., 334
Dyhrenfurth, Norman, 407, 414, 431

Eckenstein, Oscar, 333
Ehrengruber, Manfred ('Mandi'), 441, 448, 457-458, 475-476
Endless knot (*pelbe*), 393
Everest, Mt., 347, 385, 392

fluid-loss: at high altitude, 412
Fuster, Beda, 405, 425, 477

Gasherbrum Glacier, 350, 382
Gasherbrum II, 350, 365, 392, 402, 417, 449, 503, 511, 517
Giambisi, Almo, 353
Gilkey, Art, 73
Gillman, Peter, 491, 500
Godwin-Austen Glacier, 331
Gran Zebru (Königsspitze), 332

Habeler, Peter, 402, 428, 455
Hanns-Schell technique, 454
Hayat (porter), 457
health: at high altitude, 409-410, 411-413
Heckmair, Anderl, 502
Herrligkoffer, Karl Maria, 334, 398, 405, 406-407, 438
Hidden Peak, 365, 417, 455, 504
House's Chimney, 448, 451, 476
Houston, Charles S., 413
Hunzas, 449-450
Hussain, Fayazz, 449

Imitzer, Alfred, 425, 428, 441-442, 444-445, 448, 462, 465, 468, 478, 484, 489, 491-496, 497, 507, 545, 558-559, 573, 579
Irvine, Sandy, 333, 407
Itten, Markus, 365

Jana (Kurt's granddaughter), 387
jinlab, 393, 394, 398
Juanjo (Basque climber), 550, 565

K2 (Chogori): height, form and character, 332-333, 347, 415, 454, 471; Kurt approaches from Sinkiang (1983), 344-349; Swiss expedition fails on, 378-379; as aspiration, 378-379; seen from Broad Peak, 283; Quota 8,000 expedition to (1986), 387-389; base camp at, 401, 403, 413; multiplicity of expeditions to, 401, 405, 409; assault time on, 484; Koreans reach summit, 504; Kurt and Julie reach summit, 521; *K2, the Elusive Summit* (film), 378
Kaili (Tibetan woman), 390
Kangchenjunga, 416, 484
Karim, Little (Hunza), 407, 432
Kemp, Dennis, 339, 343, 361, 500, 581
Khan, Captain Neer, 438, 444
Khan, Sheraman, 394, 469
Khumbu Icefall (Everest), 420
Kikuli, Pasang, 449, 472
Kim Byung-Joon, 466, 472-473, 482, 487, 498, 504
Kim Chang-Sun, 498, 499, 507, 563
Kitar, Pasang, 472
Kukuczka, Jerzy ('Jurek'), 406, 476, 514
Kurtyka, Wojciech, 402

Lacedelli, Lino, 333, 353, 438, 487, 498

The Endless Knot

Lama, Pasang Dawa, see Dawa Lama Pasang
Land der Berge (TV film), 385
Lhotse, 484
Liu (Chinese liaison officer), 350, 472

Mahdi (Hunza porter), 487
Majer, Janusz, 418, 428, 486, 537, 577
Makalu, 392-393, 416, 450, 484
Mallory, George, 333, 407
Martini, Sergio, 353, 357
Masherbrum), 485, 517
Maurer, Lutz, 385
Mazeaud, Pierre, 351, 488
Menech, 'Bubu' Enzo de, 348
Messner, Michael, 430
Messner, Reinhold, 365, 403, 406, 408, 420, 455, 476, 486
Milledge, James, 413
Mirza, General Qamar Ali, 420, 536
Montgomerie, T. G., 332, 347
Moretti, Martino, 424
Mountain Wilderness Movement, 401-402
'Mrufka', see Wolf, Dobroslawa
Musheraf (porter), 450-451
Mustagh Passes, 332

Nanda, Sundra, 394
Nanga Parbat, 351, 352, 354, 372, 378, 393, 397, 416-417, 485, 488, 511, 540; Diamir Face, 408
Norton, Colonel Edward Felix, 333

Odell, Noel, 484
oedema, 411-413
Owens, Lance, 387

Pakistan, 405-406
Palmowska, Krystyna ('Krysiu'), 417-418, 428, 537, 578
Panmah Pass, 332
Parmentier, Michel, 415-418, 420-422, 456, 460, 465, 475, 514
Pasargphuti, Ama, 390
Passmore, David, 362
Payrleitner, Alfred, 386
Pennington, Alan, 419
Peretti, Giorgio, 345, 355-356
Pfannenstiel, Peter ('Panhandle'), 386
Pfannl, Heinrich 333
Piasecki, Przemyslaw, 506, 507, 511, 537, 546
Pintso (Sherpa), 473
Piotrowski, Tadeusz, 406, 425-426, 514
Polenza, Agostino Da, 345, 353-354, 356, 388, 398, 420-422, 431, 505, 519, 580
porters high altitude, 448-450
Proske, Dietmar, 527

Quota 8,000 (club and expedition), 387, 398, 403, 405, 407, 420-422, 439-441

Raditschnig, Alfrun, 338, 341, 342
Raditschnig, Herbert, 338-341
Rakoncaj, Joska, 353-354, 424, 519
Rouse, Alan, 405, 442, 467, 475, 477, 479, 485-487, 492, 493-494, 495-496, 497-503, 507, 511-513, 514, 517, 519-520, 521, 525, 538, 540, 543-550, 551-553
Rubi (Kurt's grandchild), 387
Rutkiewicz, Wanda, 416-417, 421-422, 426, 461, 465, 473, 488, 514

Saeed, Captain Quader, 331
Samton, Francesco, 348
Saxer, Ernst, 405
Schicklgruber, Christian, 386-387, 389, 391, 399
Schlagintweit, Adolf, 332
Schmuck, Marcus, 331, 336, 371-372, 427
Schoening, Pete, 473
Sella, Vittorio, 471
Senn, Ernst, 334
Sepa (mountain area), 391
Shaksgam Valley, 344-346, 348, 382
Shartse, 512
Sherpas, 448-450
Shipton, Eric, 337; *Blank on the Map*, 347-348
Singhie Glacier, 350
Sinkiang, 344, 349, 360
Sittikus, Archbishop Markus, 447
Skardu, 434, 442
Skilbrum (peak), 455
Skyang Kangri (Staircase Peak), 471
Smiderle, Christina, 346
Smolich, John, 419
Soncini, Adalberto, 358, 360
South, David, 366
Steele, Peter, 413
Stefanl, Fausto de, 353, 357
Steinmassl, Helmut ('Heli'), 444, 447
Suget Jangal, 348, 471

Tashigang (Tibetan village), 387, 389-393, 394
Tenzing, Nawang, 489
Tichy, Herbert, 450: *Weisse Wolken über Gelber Erde*, 453
Tirich West, 527
Trango Tower, 335
Tullis, Julie: on 'Dream of White Horses' route, 339; background, 339; Kurt invites to go sailing, 342-343; on K2 North Spur expedition, 346, 349-351, 353-361, 378, filming, 351-352, 354, 378, 385-387, 389, 392, 407; martial arts and meditation, 362, 414; on 1984 K2 expedition, 366, 378-379;

climbs Broad Peak, 367; caught in avalanche on Broad Peak, 367-370, 373-377, 378; character, 377, 379; reaches summit of Broad Peak, 381-383; travels, 385; on 1986 expedition, 388-389, 398-400, 407, 415; in Tashigang, 389-391; age, 392; brews beer at base camp, 413-414; unsuccessful attempt on K2, 424-425; death of Renato Casarotto, 432-434; presentiment of death, 435; decides to make further attempt, 443-446; on final attempt, 463-474, 477, 495, 498; on final climb, 509-520; reaches summit, 521-522; falls on descent, 524-527; night on ice balcony, 530-531; descends to high-altitude camp, 532-535; frostbite, 531, 533-535, 541; eye trouble, 535, 541; stranded in storm, 538-541; death, 550-551, 559, 570, 581; *Clouds From Both Sides*, 550, 581
Tullis Terry, 339, 361-362, 385, 581

Vidoni, Tullio, 421, 424
Vigne G. T., 332
Visentin, 'Gigio', 353, 356
vitamins, 409

Ward, Michael, 413
Warth, Hermann, 512
Wasserbauer, Siegfried, 447
Wessely, Victor, 333
West, John, 413
West, John B., and Lahiri Sukhamay, 413
Wick, Emil, 407
Wielicki, Krzysztof, 408
Wieser, Hannes, 388, 428, 441, 448, 461-462, 465, 467, 479, 482-483, 489, 490, 495, 502, 507, 510, 512, 517, 536, 558-560, 573, 579
Wiessner, Fritz, 334, 450, 473, 484, 572
Wiget, Dr. Urs, 380, 409
Wintersteller, Fritz, 331, 372
Wolf, Dobroslawa ('Mrufka'), 418, 428, 443, 467, 474, 479, 485, 493-494, 496, 501, 505, 507, 510, 514, 516-517, 518, 520, 525, 538, 544, 547, 551, 553
Wolfe, Dudley, 449, 473
Wondra, Inge, 581
Wörner, Stefan, 365-366
Wroz, Wojciech ('Voytek'), 428, 505-508

Younghusband, (Sir) Francis, 348

Zanga, Pierangelo, 351
Zemp, Rolf, 405, 424, 477

SPIRITS OF THE AIR

Spirits of the Air

KURT DIEMBERGER

TRANSLATED BY AUDREY SALKELD

First published in Italy, 1991
First published in Great Britain and the U.S.A., 1994

To my father

Only the Spirits of the Air know
What awaits me behind the mountains
But still I go on with my dogs,
Onwards and on . . .

This old Eskimo proverb defines my existence – and not only when I am in Greenland. I have been called 'the Nomad of the Great Heights' – certainly ever since I clambered to my first summit as a crystal-hunting boy, since I set out on my grandfather's bicycle with two friends to reach and climb the legendary Matterhorn, I have felt urged beyond the horizon in search of the unknown.

And that haven of peace behind the last mountain? Does such a thing exist? There is always a new enigma springing up to meet you. Some new secret. That never changes. However far you travel . . .

Only the Spirits of the Air know what lies in store for you, says the Eskimo on his dog sledge.

That is Life.

ACKNOWLEDGEMENTS Unless otherwise specified the illustrations are from the Kurt Diemberger archive: for collaboration in some cases I want to thank my companions named in the book. Professor Karl Weiken's historical pictures of the Alfred Wegener expedition were a great help and a notable contribution. Other photographs came from: Robert Kreuzinger, Sadamasa Takahashi, Doug Scott and Hermann Warth.

Most of my photographs were taken with Leica R3 and SL2.

Credits for the sketch maps are given, but I want to thank my son Igor and my daughter Karen for helping in their adaptation for *Spirits of the Air*.

A special thanks goes to my father for historical work in the Greenland chapter and to Professor Karl Weiken for checking my text and lending expedition reports. I am also very grateful to Axel Thorer for the permission to print his humorous story describing the atmosphere in a hotel bar in Kathmandu which appeared in May 1980 in the German edition of *Penthouse*.

Last but not least, I would like to thank Audrey Salkeld for her translation and Maggie Body my editor.

KURT DIEMBERGER, Bologna, 1994

CONTENTS

PART I

I Can Never Give Up the Mountains	page 597
The Second Birthday	604
Double Solo on Zebru	616
Crystals from Mont Blanc	625

PART II

The Magic Carpet – How I got involved with Filming	637
Blind Man's Buff	638
Friendly Margherita	650
Montserrat	664

PART III

Hindu Kush – The Tactics of a Mini-Expedition	669
Nudging Alpine-Style a Step Further	674
An Expedition Journal	678
Two Chickens Come Home to Roost	686
Neck and Neck with Reinhold – The Third Eight Thousander?	688
Climbing the 8,000 metre Peaks	692

PART IV

In the Eternal Ice – On the Trail of Alfred Wegener	703
Who was Alfred Wegener?	707
A Green Land?	707
Origins of an Expedition	709
The Voyage to Greenland	710
'Modern Times' in Umanak and Uvkusigsat	711
The Difficult Landing	715
Dogs? Propeller Sledges? Horses?	716
Ascent to the Inland Ice	717
First Finds	718
1930: Towards Station Eismitte	719
The Sledge Journeys	721
The Propeller Sledge Fiasco	722
Nunatak Scheideck, a Treasure Trove!	723
Alfred Wegener's Last Journey	725
Qioqe, Agpatat and – the Final Take	728

Spirits of the Air

PART V

A Night on Stromboli	735
'I Canali' – the Channels	743
The Millipede	746

PART VI

A New World	749
How to Catch a Millionaire	755
Milestones in California	760
Fifty-six Steps Around a General	762
Grand Canyon – A Sunken World	765
Atlanta – The Holy City	771
The Lake	784
In the Plane	786
Isis	786
The Wizard – Climbing the Needles of Sierra Nevada	792
On the Gulf	796

PART VII

Makalu (8481m) – The Turning Point	799
Yang Lhe – The Enchanted Forest	800
Through East Nepal	802
Strikes – Left With Nine Out of a Hundred	806
Chance and Mischance With the Oxygen	808
Makalu . . . With a Monkey Wrench	811
Depot Kurt	822
'Take One' . . . On the Summit of Everest	832
Death Valley in Winter	840

PART VIII

Hildegard Peak (6189m) – Island Peak	843
The Green Flash	846
Gasherbrum II	848
A New Horizon	849
Under the Spell of the Shaksgam	851

APPENDICES

Note on Heights	861
Chronology of Main Climbs and Expeditions	862
A Note on Terminology	864
A Selected Bibliography	865

PART I

I Can Never Give Up the Mountains

We are climbing up Nanga Parbat, my daughter Hildegard and I, entering the Great Couloir of the Diamir Face. Behind us rear the wild summits of the Mazeno Ridge, a fiercely serrated wing of blue ice and steep rock jutting from high on the main body of the mighty mountain. Way below, glints the green of the Diamir valley.

Here, all is steepness and shadow. We keep plunging our axes into the snow, and of course, we are wearing our crampons. Hildegard – blonde, twenty-five years old – is a confident climber, even if, as an ethnologist, her deeper interest lies with the people of the mountains. She has come with me this time to the peak that was Hermann Buhl's dream – and, who knows, the two of us may reach as far as 6000 metres. Perhaps, in a few days, I might even go to 7000 metres, but I am not pinning my hopes any higher. I have no idea how my K2 frostbite will bear up at altitude. It was only just before Christmas that I had the amputations to my right hand – and with my damaged toes I cannot entertain any hopes of the summit. Yet neither can I accept the prospect of staying down. There is no way I can give up climbing mountains.

Below us, on the slope, Benoît has just come into view, the young French speedclimber attached to our expedition . . . tack, tack, tack, tack . . . his movements are like clockwork, as is the rhythmic throb of his front-points and his axe in the steep ice of the couloir. He wants to climb the 8125 metres of Nanga Parbat in a single day. But not today – today he is only practising.

Quickly he draws nearer.

'Who goes slowly, goes well – who goes well, goes far . . .' Whatever became of that old proverb? The wisdom of the old mountain guides, it seems, is now out of date. Tack, tack – tack, tack, tack, tack – tack, tack . . . Benoît is a nice guy and has remained refreshingly modest, despite his prodigious skills; he is small, fine-boned, gentle. I like him, even if some of his opinions send shivers down my spine. Others I have reluctantly to accept (not wanting to start any arguments up here! But what is the point in all this *running*? What good are records up here?) It must make some sort of sense to him.

Here he is! Benoît Chamoux. The speed artist, the phenomenon! He pants a little, greets us, laughing, and we exchange news; then I fish in my rucksack for the 16 mm camera. My job is filming, but it's my pleasure, too. Showing other people what the world is like up here . . . that is part of what mountaineering means for me. Not this alone, of course . . .

Still, I want to bring down truth, not fiction! And if, for some bright spark, happiness is running up mountains – then he, too, is part of this world of Nanga Parbat. (My daughter, I must say, has thought so for quite some while – perhaps that's an ethnological observation?)

I film the young sprinter: well, it looks fantastic, I think, eye to the viewfinder, the way that guy comes up! So I have him do it three times more, up and back again – the way film-makers do, and he is in training, after all.

Before I can dream up further variations, big clouds start rolling in. A change in the weather? Nothing unusual for Nanga Parbat. We descend.

Base Camp, down where it's green . . .

Only the Spirits of the Air know – how this will turn out for me. I contemplate my discoloured toes – all red and blue – as I swish them round in a bowl of water. Our cook, the good Ali, has tipped at least half a kilo of salt into the water, anxious to do what is best for me. How long will it take till I am fit again? Months, or years?

This is not the first time I have felt all is nearly over, that I am stretching life thinly: coming down from Chogolisa after Hermann's death, or during the emergency landing I made with Charlie – what I call our 'second birthday'. But this time? This time it is different.

Do I still enjoy climbing? It can never be as it was before.

And I will never come to terms with what happened on K2. Up on our dream mountain I lost Julie, lost my climbing companion of so many years, sharer of storms and tempests, joys and hopes on the highest mountains of the world. How often did we count the stars together, or look for faces in the clouds?

And then, suddenly . . .

So many people died on K2 that summer. Julie and I had been in such fine form, we were perfectly acclimatised – we ought not to have lost a single day! But I've no wish to set off that spinning wheel of thoughts again . . . It's over. Nothing can be changed. The dream summit was ours – and then came the end.

I Can Never Give Up the Mountains

Life, somehow, goes on. The mountains, like dear friends, have always helped me before. Whenever it was possible. Where is the way forward now?

Agostino da Polenza, our expedition leader on K2, was here at Base Camp until a few days ago. Then he dashed off to get another project under way, one on which I am again to be cameraman: remeasuring Everest and K2 for the Italian Consortium of Research (CNR) – or, more accurately, for Ardito Desio, the remarkable ninety-year-old professor who, as long ago as 1929, pushed into the secret valley of the Shaksgam beyond the 8000-metre Karakorum peaks till he was stopped by the myriad ice towers of the Kyagar Glacier. Yes, it's true, the secrets are not only to be found on the summits . . .

They wait also behind the mountains. And I think of years that have long past, adventures in the jungle, in Greenland, but in more 'developed' areas, too, places like Canada; or the Grand Canyon with its rocky scenery – where time is turned into stone. I remember Death Valley. And expeditions to the Hindu Kush . . . that first glimpse into hidden corners of the glacier . . . the first circuit of Tirich Mir.

There was an eighteen-year gap between my second 8000-metre peak and my third. But I have no regrets about that: it was time well spent. Many chapters of this book bear witness to that.

'*Guarda lassù* – there they are!' Hildegard turns her head excitedly from the camera tripod, swinging her long blonde hair, 'Look!' She points up at Nanga Parbat, which even from this distance fills the sky above the treetops. 'They're almost up!' Her eyes are shining. We are in a small summer village in the Diamir valley, surrounded by cattle-sheds, herdsmen, women, many children . . . and goats, goats and more goats: two or three hundred of them! You can scarcely hear yourself speak over the sound of bleating. There are millions of flies, too, but they do not seem to bother Hildegard. I flick them irritably from my forehead and press my left eye to the viewfinder to peer through the 1200 mm lens: yes, I see them! Three tiny dots, and a fourth one, lower down, right in the middle of the steep summit trapezium. They are going to make it!

We are beside ourselves with joy. Those lucky sods – lucky mushrooms, as we say in Austria – just the right day they've picked for it! And I feel a twinge of sadness not to be up there with them. But not for long: as we watch our companions inch higher, happiness suffuses every other feeling. But one dot is missing up there. It worries us at first, then

Spirits of the Air

we tell ourselves it must be Benoît. He will not have left Base until the others reached their High Camp.

He is bound to catch up with them before long!

Then the clouds swallow everything.

We scoop up our belongings and hurry away, anxious to get to Base Camp before the others come down; we want to prepare a welcome-home party, a summit feast.

Two days later: they are all down. Soro, Gianni and Tullio all made it to the summit – shortly after the clouds cut them from our view. Only Giovanna, the lowest dot, turned back before then. And Benoît? He had a real epic up there . . .

At first all went well. He reached the summit as planned in a single day from Base Camp. (Normally – if you can speak of normality in terms of Nanga Parbat – it takes at least three days for an ascent.) But then began a chain of misfortune: during the descent, Benoît was overtaken by darkness and lost his way in the giant Bazhin basin. All night long he wandered backwards and forwards up there at around 7000 metres because, with his lightweight equipment, he dared not sit down for a bivouac. He did not discover his companions' final camp until morning . . .

Benoît looked thin and drawn, almost transparent, as he staggered finally into Base . . . but an incredible willpower still burned in his eyes. We flung our arms round him, so happy to have him back.

The sun is shining, its light reflecting off the small stream which runs across the sloping meadow on which our Base Camp stands. A good place: protected by a moraine bank from the air blast of the many enormous avalanches which thunder down from the upper slopes and teetering ice balconies of Nanga Parbat and the Mazeno peaks. Here, at 4500 metres, frost binds our little brook every night, covering it with an embroidery of wonderful ice crystals. But in the morning, when the sun appears behind the inky blue bulk of the mountain, it flashes and sparkles everywhere and, as the crystals and plates of ice crackle and split, gradually the murmur of the little stream starts up again between the tents. Gianni and Tullio, inseparable as ever, stroll across the grass and kneel on its bank, dipping their hands in the icy water and splashing it over their faces . . . they chatter and laugh; Soro and Giovanna stretch out in the sunshine; Hildegard, lost in thought, wanders over the moraine, and Benoît sleeps, and sleeps, and sleeps. He has earned it. The good Ali prepares breakfast, and Shah Jehan, our

I Can Never Give Up the Mountains

liaison officer, squints lazily into the sun above his enormous beard and tells again of all the ibex he has bagged in the Karakorum. This is the man we know could never hurt a fly. In the summer of 1982, on my first expedition here, I climbed with him to 6500 metres on the Diamir Face. Next time – 1985 – he was unfortunately not with us. That was when Julie and I went to 7600 metres: only another 500 metres or so would have seen us on top, but when we came to make our final attempt the weather turned against us . . .

I am looking up at the dark blue trapezium, in shadow now: some day I'd love to go up there. It will have to wait till I'm better, and that could be years yet. But look, there it is, the summit that Julie and I were so close to.

Will I get another crack at it?

Will I ever stand on the top?

And, if I do, will I come down again – or stay up there for ever?

Even if I never make it up there, I have to have the experience again, this moving up between the clouds . . .

Once you have started that . . .

'I climb mountains for such moments,' Julie had said, 'not just to reach the top – that is a bonus!'

I *will* go up again.

Then my thoughts turn to Makalu.

Many years ago that was, when I faced the question of whether or not to make one last try – knowing that, on whatever I should choose, would depend my whole future.

SPIRITS OF THE AIR

Strange eddies of cloud spill over the summit of Mount Everest, twisting veils, transparent fans, mysterious phantoms. Catching the light, they shimmer in all the colours of the rainbow – deep purple, radiant green, yellow, orange – a swiftly changing kaleidoscope.

Does it herald a storm?

As I watch, some of the clouds take on a mother-of-pearl lustre, others drain of all colour. It is a strange cavalry, galloping, multiplying, gradually filling the whole sky. The red granite summit of Makalu, just over 3000 metres above me, wears a wide-brimmed hat, like a gleaming fish. I have often seen such clouds in the Alps, on Mont Blanc, and again I'm prompted to wonder if a storm is on the way. Down here in Base Camp the air remains very still, with only an occasional limp

Spirits of the Air

flutter from Ang Chappal's prayer flags. He hung up two strings of them when we first arrived to keep favour with the mountain gods and spirits. I look beyond them and out over the stone cairn on its little hill to the side of camp: what should I do? Should I attempt Makalu? What hope have I got of reaching the summit? It is eighteen years since I last climbed an eight-thousander.

The prayer flags stir weakly, while high above, the wild clouds charge in every direction. The rainbow colours have disappeared, but light and shadow animate the spectacle. The sun – one minute a fiery ball, the next a pale disc – sinks slowly towards the ridge of Baruntse, the great seven-thousander on the far side of the valley. Down here it is still warm, even though we are above 5400 metres.

So what's it to be? Shall I give it a try, make a start?

Not today, certainly. But soon I have to come to a decision; we have already ordered porters for our return march. On the other side of the campsite Hans and Karl are sprawled on the ground. They staggered into camp two days ago with Hermann and the Sherpas, completely whacked after an incredibly painful descent from the mountain. They were changed men. Hans, who is usually so cheerful, wore a bleak, dead look behind his double goggles.

'I wish you luck for the top, Kurt,' he said gruffly, in a voice barely above a whisper, 'but no bivouac!'

All the toes on one of his feet are frostbitten, and Karl is in almost as bad a way. He can scarcely hobble, or even accept support from his friends because four of the fingertips on his left hand are blackened as well. He muttered something, too, but I can't now remember what it was. Those must have been horrific days, coming down from their bivouac at 8250 metres, step by painful step, down through four High Camps. Later, helping Karli with his bandages and medicines, I asked him whether the top had been worth all the anguish. He was silent for a while, then said, 'Oh, yes, it was worth it . . .' and, indicating his swollen foot with a bitter smile, the old Karli-smile, added, 'We've got this under control now, haven't we?' Certainly, it won't be long till the porters come, but Hans and Karl are in for a miserable journey back.

If I do still want to go for the summit, I dare not delay any longer. I should start tomorrow, or the day after at the latest. I sink back into the soft sand near our tents and gaze up at the chasing clouds. How many men, like me, have wondered what their tomorrow would bring, and known that on the decision of the moment, all the rest of their lives depended? Perhaps they have known that the decision could be avoided – perhaps they did sidestep it, but what is that for a solution? You never know what you'll encounter tomorrow. Only the Spirits of the Air know that . . . So what's to do? Looking up, I ponder that age-old question, and it is as if, while I am losing myself in the whirling clouds, an answer gradually reveals itself: an answer not in words, but in certainty. And I continue gazing at the weaving veils, follow their courses, their variations, while all questions dissolve away. I can feel the motion of the wheeling shapes, and if I surrender to it, I am no longer here, but there . . .

The Spirits of the Air: with what power they rise from nothing, secretively, and as quickly vanish once more. Rolling mists, tumbling cascades, weightlessly dancing on their way, multiplying as they go into strange new figures that reach out to embrace each other with their fluttering arms, sometimes succeeding in bringing an evanescent new creature into existence, but mostly melting away before they can touch. Spirits of the Air? Can they really know what tomorrow will bring? Where do they hide when the air is cold and clear, and when in the icy stillness mountains stand like blue crystal in the morning sun, when a pale full moon floats in the daylight sky until, sapped of all strength, it sinks to a mountain ridge and you imagine it rolling, like a barrel, down the hill.

Are they behind the mountains then? Somewhere they must be continuing their ballade. Where is certainty? The secrets are on the summit and beyond. 'Only the Spirits of the Air know what awaits me behind the mountains.' So runs the old Eskimo proverb. 'But I go on with my dogs, onward and on.' Some days ago, when I was lying sick, down below in the rainforest, I fully believed there was no future for me on big mountains, that my fate lay away from them, somewhere behind.

But now I know: it is up there, on the summit of Makalu. If I don't try this climb, I have no future. And if nobody wants to come with me, then I shall have to go alone. Sometimes there is no way forward for a man if he does not find the answer to his question.

The Spirits of the Air told me: Go up!

The Second Birthday

Whatever happens to me now is a bonus. By any normal standards my life should have ended several years ago . . . it all came about innocently enough.

'Charlie's bought an aeroplane!' – the news went round like wildfire. How come so fast?

Never imagine climbers to be strong, silent types, not given to chatter! Nothing could be further from the truth. The discussion over the placing of a single piton can rage for hours. And if, in putting up some great new route, a climber strays beyond the iron disciplines of the purists (let alone, he may not have done it at all) then the talk spreads faster than bush telegraph. Usually the sole topic is mountains but this news about Charlie was something extraordinary. It was common knowledge that he had started out as a modest ski instructor, then for some years shuttled between America, Australia and Europe before opening a small sports shop in Innsbruck. Nothing extraordinary. But now, all of a sudden, Charlie has surprised everyone.

'Hey, guys, heard the latest? Charlie's got himself wings!' Brandler tells Raditschnig, Nairz passes the word to Messner, Stitzinger phones up Sturm . . . Where did he get that kind of money? Does he know how to fly the thing? How long before he breaks his neck? These were the questions doing the rounds. But sooner or later almost everyone looked forward to a joyride. Only the more cautious of us preferred to wait and see. As one of Charlie's oldest friends, I knew some of the facts: one, that the machine was a single-engined Cessna 150; also that Charlie was not his real name. He had been born Karl Schönthaler, and cannot abide his nickname; nevertheless, 'Charlie from Innsbruck' is how everyone knows him, and if I refer to him differently, nobody will know who I'm talking about. Aeroplanes are easier: they have an identification number, and all those with the same number are similar. Charlie's, however, must have been something of a one-off, but I don't want to anticipate . . . He was delighted with it. At first.

'Fancy seeing you!' Charlie greets me on the fateful day, his blue eyes crinkled with pleasure. 'Hey, remember our Piz Roseg climb?' he says,

The Second Birthday

'I went and took a look at it the other day.' Easy for him, I think. Just a hop, here, there, wherever he wants . . .

'Come on, let's go there now, why don't we?' He pushes back his ski cap rakishly, and throws me a challenging look. The old devil doesn't change! Should I take up his offer? I am cautious by nature, but he has been flying for a year now, and I have always had complete faith in him as a mountaineer. I convince myself I trust him just as implicitly as a pilot . . . and that is how I come to be standing on Innsbruck airfield shortly afterwards, while Charlie squints up at a clear, blue sky. 'Okay,' He smiles, content. 'Let's go! Let's spin over to the Bernina and say hello to that route of ours.'* Seeing your old first ascents again is fun, especially from the air; you can congratulate yourself on how great you used to be. (Mountaineers are no less vain than anyone else – and certainly, we two are no exceptions.) Again, he says it, this time more solemnly: 'Come on then, back to the scene of our triumph,' and slipping on his gloves, he caresses the shining aircraft, at the same time casting me a stern glance. 'Flying is a serious business, Kurt,' he warns. 'You are not to make me nervous. No taking photographs the whole time and, *Kruiztuifl*! above all, don't bother me with a string of questions . . .'

Charlie comes from the South Tirol. He has this habit of lapsing into dialect at moments of great importance or stress. 'It's all right,' I try to calm him. 'I'll only take pictures from my side of the plane,' and I hug my two cameras to my chest. (The reader should know that many pilots have this obsessive fear of photographers getting in the way of the controls, besides wanting to know the name of every last garden shed on the ground. A flying doctor friend in Italy would grow very nervous when I used to persuade him to open the door for a better view of the fields and villages.) But if Charlie is worrying that I might block his view, at least he's keeping his eyes open, I think, not pinning all his hopes on his instruments.

That turns out to be true. As we take off, my friend continues his lecture: 'It's more important for me to catch a glimpse of the mountain, than that you get it in your viewfinder . . .' Okay, Charlie. I take the point.

We are already passing the crags of the Innsbrucker Nordkette – on my side, luckily. Charlie is whistling cheerfully, and seems utterly at

---

* It was the direct North-East Face of the Piz Roseg that Karl Schönthaler and I climbed in 1958, at that time the hardest route in the Bernina group. It still belongs in that category. The first direct exit from the Klucker route over the ice bulge of the North Summit also fell to us.

Spirits of the Air

peace with the world (with me, too). As he gently runs his snow-white gloves over the gleaming fittings of his beloved plane, I think how well he has done for himself. How good to have such friends! Who work so hard. Ski instructor to aeroplane proprietor – whoever would have thought it? But Charlie has always been one of those silent, unexpected geniuses.

I aim my tele-lens down into the Inn valley to capture a neat village – or small town – for my picture archive. 'Where's that, Charlie?' I ask, since a photograph isn't much good without a caption (publishers don't take kindly to invention . . .)

'There you go – at it already,' he answers with irritation. 'I don't know what it is. Isn't it enough that we're airborne, who cares what the village is called?' And he snorts, 'It's not a village, anyway – that's a town. Telfs, probably. Yes, it's Telfs!'

Don't ask a pilot about geography, I think to myself. (It comes as a surprise to learn that pilots don't always know exactly where they are. My Italian doctor friend once circled with me above the small town of 'Stradella'. Wasn't it curious, I ventured, how similar the big golden Madonna on the church tower was to the one in Tortona – which, as it turned out, was where we were. Clearly, my friend didn't open the door often enough!) It seems to me pilots are so busy taking care not to bump into another aircraft – that they are happy to just watch the ground go by, knowing only vaguely where they are.

Now, on Charlie's side, a wild valley appears, hemmed in by high peaks – even today, I am not sure if it was the Kaunertal or the Ötztal, everything looks so different from the air; Charlie will not commit himself beyond saying it is the Ötztal Alps. Not to worry, I tell myself, we should soon see the Wildspitze – and then we'll know where we are. The distinctive three-thousander is the highest mountain for miles around. Charlie confirms the Wildspitze will be coming up shortly, and I cannot resist a mock-polite cough. He glowers in my direction, remarking huffily that the main thing is not to bump into the mountain! (Motto for all Innsbruck pilots, that!) Then, after a pause, 'There was a bad incident recently, with a photographer . . . To be fair, he had more camera equipment than you . . .' This latter he says more kindly, and I am glad I have only brought two Leicas along. 'The guy insisted on flying to the end of a valley – the very end – and just when the pilot said "Enough!" and tried to pull the plane round, he found he couldn't because the telephoto-lens was caught under the joy-stick! They had to make an emergency landing, and it's nothing short of a miracle they didn't turn the thing over! That's another rule of flying, by the way, always keep your eyes skinned for emergency landing places.' My friend

The Second Birthday

is in lecture-mode again. He casts an exaggerated glance out of the window, then nods back at me, satisfied. Meanwhile I hurriedly scoop all the lenses on to my lap. He seems perfectly calm now. Slowly and steadily we gain height.

'Three thousand six hundred metres,' he advises cheerfully. 'Any minute now for the Wildspitze . . .'

From my window I can see right into a high valley filled with haybarns, a beautiful green valley running parallel to the Inn River, which by now has almost vanished into the distance. Such parallel valleys high in the mountains have an ancient, perhaps Celtic, name – 'Tschy'. (That this was the Pfundser Tschy I did not know at the time, any more than did Charlie. Nor were we aware that the farmers would be haymaking there, scything the grass and spreading it to dry across this wide green valley at 1500 metres, a valley hardly ever visited – perhaps no more than a couple of tourists go there in a summer . . . But, back to our flight!)

Impressive silhouettes of mountains and dark rocks float by on Charlie's side, just as if they had been cut out with scissors. This must be part of the Kaunergrat, and I cannot resist leaning over for a moment – just this once – for a closer look. Charlie growls, banks the plane to a steeper angle and, yes, there it is, the Wildspitze! Over there!

How fantastic, the glacier world of the Ötztal! The engine labours with what seems to me a slight change in tone, but Charlie gives no sign of alarm and I continue gazing out of the window: the Ötztal peaks! It is twenty years since I was last here, as a young lad. Soon, I will spot all the old places! Thanks to Charlie and his kite. The plane shows little enthusiasm for the shining Wildspitze – the motor definitely sounds different now, more hollow. Is it anything? Surely, Charlie would tell me if something was amiss? He sits silent, just a bit hunched, and not sparing a glance for the Wildspitze. I take a photo of it, and another into the depths where suddenly a small emerald-coloured lake has appeared, set in a rocky cirque and surrounded by weird, eroded ridges, thrusting upwards.

What an abyss! It makes you dizzy to look at it. Hey, that engine noise is really most peculiar now – although I know nothing about such things – and I see Charlie fiddling with various buttons, turning them this way and that. No wonder he has lost interest in the landscape! I feel the blood rising, hot to my head: something is wrong! Is it serious? Charlie confirms my anxieties. 'Get the bloody cameras out of the way,' he bursts out. 'The engine's in trouble!'

It's true, then. I swallow. Try to stay calm. 'I thought there was something,' I say. 'It sounds just like an old car before it claps out.'

'Don't talk nonsense,' my friend snaps. 'It's practically brand new – it can't clap out. I've probably just got to change the mixture.' He pulls another handle. (The reader, flying with us, must excuse the lack of technical precision: a cipher I am, merely, when it comes to things mechanical, having no idea how to fly a plane. You must rely on Charlie for that: after all he has been a pilot for a whole year. By now, even the most ignorant landlubber will have recognised we were in dire straits, with our stuttering *huppada-huppada – hupp*! Alarming, when that is all that holds you in the air.)

Charlie radios Innsbruck: 'Charlie-Mac-Alpha, Charlie-Mac-Alpha – engine trouble, we have engine trouble.' He has to speak English – all pilots do. Some practical advice obviously follows, which he tries out right away, and for a moment he succeeds in bringing the motor to a *huppuppupp-uppup* . . . but our hopes are soon dashed: we are hardly moving forward at all, even though we stopped trying to climb ages ago. The aircraft rocks from side to side, like a boat on Lake Como in a light swell. (Would we were on any lake, rather than up here.)

'Charlie,' I hear myself saying, 'let's turn round and try to get down to the Inn valley.'

'That's our only hope,' he retorts. 'Don't bother me now.' And he calls up Innsbruck again.

This is a moment I know will live with me for ever – the swaying aircraft, the motor on its last gasp, those sharp ridges below and, at my side, Charlie clinging to the microphone as if it holds the key to our salvation. My thumping heart feels as if it is shrinking. Are we going to fall out of the sky? Yet, even terror has its tragi-comic moments. Charlie, gabbling into his walkie-talkie, forgets the rules and breaks into Tyrolean. There must be a different controller at the other end, unaware of how critical our position is. 'Why don't you speak English, Charlie-Mac-Alpha?' the man says.

It is the last straw. 'Stuff your English!' yells a furious Charlie, as the propeller makes its last half-hearted revolutions – one, two . . . oone, twoo . . . o-n-e, t-w-w-o-o – then, quietly, as if it were the most natural thing in the world, coming to an oblique halt. 'The bloody crate has died on me!'

He roars into the mike in his broadest Tyrolean, and suddenly no one gives a fig about the rules. The propeller has given up the ghost: no time for niceties. The aeroplane is still rocking gently like a little boat, but it hasn't flipped over. Not yet. That means you won't be falling out of the sky right away, a small, rational voice announces from some uninvolved centre of my brain, bringing transitory relief. But then, how long before

The Second Birthday

you do fall once your engine cuts out? How many minutes have we got? Charlie is silent, hanging on to the steering with an abstracted expression. The plane continues its swaying. Seven hundred and fifty kilos it weighs, the same as a Volkswagen Beetle. A glance down reveals barren mountains, cirques, peaks rising from deep valleys, and over there, the Ötztal glaciers, shining, white . . .

No, the two of us are not in a rocking barque on any lake: we are 4000 metres up in the sky, in a Beetle-heavy plane without an engine, cutting through the air with a steady hiss. The slanting propeller, outlined against the white of the glaciers, slides gradually over the grey-green depths . . . A chaos of rocks appears below us, a basin with a little lake.

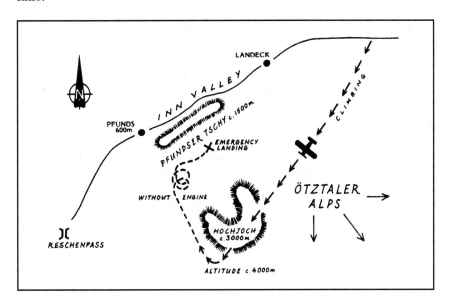

A map (not to scale) for the Second Birthday

'Nowhere for an emergency landing there,' Charlie says in a low voice.

If only we could get out of this thing.

How simple to break down in a car: with its last momentum, the driver can roll to the road side, then call out the rescue services. Seven hundred and fifty kilos would require a pretty strong guardian angel to hoist us out of trouble up here. How much longer now, before we hit the ground?

Spirits of the Air

As if in answer to my thoughts, I hear Charlie say, 'If we can maintain enough forward momentum, we can glide down.' Glide? With this weight? Glide like a cockchafer, I think. But so far it seems to be working. Hoarsely, Charlie radios our position to Innsbruck – in English. 'I'm trying to reach the Inn valley,' he tells them, then turns to me. 'Kurtl,' he says, 'I have practised this several times over the airfield. It's going to be all right . . . If we find somewhere to land . . . If we don't get caught in any turbulence . . . and if . . .'

The thought of 'coasting' this box of tricks down imbues me with new hope. 'The most important thing, Charlie,' I tell him, 'is to stay calm . . .' He is all for calling Innsbruck again, but I tell him that it is no use. We are on our own. Nobody on earth can help us. Our only hope now is to keep our heads, just as we did on Piz Roseg all those years ago, when eighty-metre séracs were poised above us, ready to break off!

Silence. Utter, utter silence . . . apart from the hiss of air around the wings. Charlie, my friend, stay calm . . . and I lay my hand briefly on his shoulder. We have everything to gain, everything to lose. I may not know how to fly this box of tricks, but I can help him not to panic.

What a strange coincidence that we should have bumped into each other today, that Charlie and I are together again, now, so many years after our big climb, linked once more as surely as by a rope, for better or worse.

What a stupid coincidence! Another voice intrudes in my mind: you would never have dreamt this morning that such a thing could happen. How come, after a year of flying, it should be today of all days that Charlie's plane breaks down, and on our first spin together? A couple more minutes and it could be all over . . . for good . . . Never mind the thousands of dangers we have survived in the mountains! What irony! I can just imagine what the newspapers will make of it: MOUNTAIN AIRCRASH, CLIMBERS DIE FIFTEEN YEARS AFTER FIRST ASCENT. There will be gruesome pictures of scattered wreckage alongside our portraits. Bloody hell, that's no way to be thinking! I have more important things to do . . .

'Charlie, you'll make it,' I shout through the hissing air. He nods, grimly, clinging tightly to the controls and peering towards the Inn valley, from which we are still separated by a high mountain ridge. The expression on his face suggests he is calculating our chances of 'leap-frogging' over it. Luckily, we had climbed to over 4000 metres earlier – now we are 'living' on that. The wings slice the air, we sink lower . . .

'Everyone makes it down!' That is a macabre piece of pilots' lore. But

The Second Birthday

down where? We are still over a rocky amphitheatre, though there is more and more green ahead now.

Deeper and deeper we sink.

I seriously doubt we will clear this ridge which guards the deep furrow of the Inn valley. But shouldn't there be that high valley pasture first, the one I noticed this morning? I look down, trembling with fear and anticipation. Never have I wanted anything so much as to be down there on firm ground, treading the sweet grass. Never have I been further from all that the earth means; only my thoughts touch it now: they want to melt into the ground, the rocks, the forests – all of which are coming closer by the moment. Yet though I long for this fusion, the moment of contact will almost certainly whisk me to infinity, into a world without space, beyond all that lies so far away, down there. My children . . .? I think only how glad I am they have no idea what is happening to me. Perhaps they are just enjoying a fine day, somewhere down in the green.

It makes me so happy merely that they exist.

'Charlie, I don't think we'll make it over that ridge!'

'Depends on the air currents. It's our only hope.'

No, no! Ahead of us, a bright green patch approaches, deep down, coming up now, rising above the jagged line of trees. It's getting bigger, down in that wide trough, just before the barrier of hills. The high valley! It's the Tschy! Look, look! Glinting up like a promise! I can make out wooden barns, see them quite clearly, sprinkled like tiny dice in the bottom of the valley. 'Charlie, we can land down there! We don't have to go over the ridge. It's not that we know what's on the other side anyway. Let's put down here!'

My friend hesitates for no more than a second. 'Right, here we go!' And already we are banking almost vertically, the air rushing and swishing around the plane, our downward wing pointing directly into the bottom of the Tschy. 'I'm going to spiral down now,' yells Charlie through the noise, leaving me lost for words at this sudden change. Then begins a slalom to play havoc with the senses. It's like being suspended inside a moving spiral staircase . . . a chaos of sight and sound as we descend into the green cirque of the valley. Charlie has suddenly become a wondrous ski-ace, launching himself into the unknown in quest of 'gold'. The 'game', increasingly difficult the lower we get, is played for life or death, countless spur-of-the-moment decisions where no error is permitted, swooping down a spiral staircase whose end is hidden from us – and where we need nothing short of the 'gold' to survive. From Charlie it demanded the utmost in ability and instinct, an almost overwhelming demand after only a single year's experience.

Tighter and tighter grow the spirals as we etch whistling circles between the mountain flanks. Ours is an oblique world, the wings of the plane continuously above and below us. Charlie's concentration remains absolute, his eyes staring fixedly ahead, his brow deeply wrinkled. Once I yell, 'Watch out! Mind we don't flip over!' and he snaps back at me to shut up, saying, 'You don't know a thing about aerodynamics. Of course we're not going to flip over.' Our weird spiral gouges on into the depths, into this gigantic green funnel. I cling to the seat as the forest rotates 500 metres below; watching the wheeling treetops, I am still unconvinced we will not end up nose-first. Charlie wears a frozen smile, or is it a grimace of effort? He has the joy-stick in an iron grip. 'You're doing fine,' I tell him. 'Keep it going!' And, however uncomfortable my position, it's a fact, we haven't dropped from the sky yet. We are still flying: increasingly it looks as if we might see this thing through. The earth appears much nearer now, and my longing for it has grown out of all bounds – as has my fear.

'I'm going to turn the plane on its head – see if the motor will restart,' Charlie announces suddenly. Every muscle in his face is tense.

'No, no, don't!' I yell. 'It'll never work!' Having come to terms with the spiral, I am reluctant to face another manoeuvre. But when Charlie is convinced of a thing, he does it: already we have gone into the headstand. Three hundred metres below are the roofs of the hay-barns, and small dots on the meadows – people – moving . . . the rush around the wings has risen to a roar as they slice the air, the roofs grow closer, the people bigger – they are running. God, I wish I was with them! Charlie tries the ignition, but the propeller makes only a couple of feeble turns . . . 'It's not going to work!' he curses. And down there, suddenly, the roofs disappear from view and the mountainside arcs steeply upwards in front of us, as we are pressed into our seats with full force. Blue sky? Clouds? Whatever is happening now? Panting, Charlie holds – no, leans with all his strength – against the steering. We've had it, then, I whisper to myself, just another couple of seconds . . . I want to say something to Charlie, but my throat narrows and nothing will come. I am suddenly overwhelmed by a sense of weightlessness, and at the same time, of helplessness . . .

'Charlie . . .' A glance across shows his face distorted, his eyes mere slits. That was it then, Charlie, was it? Suddenly the weightlessness vanishes and in its place an immense pressure seizes me: my arms are lead, my body is lead. The seat, the elbow-rests thrust up

The Second Birthday

at me with great force, countering gravity. But we must be falling . . . aren't we?

For a moment I do not know what's happening.

Charlie draws a deep breath. 'That was hairy,' he says. No, we aren't falling any longer, we are hanging once more sideways in the air. 'We must choose somewhere to put it down,' says my Charlie, 'there's not much time left.' He is maintaining the curve. I feel life has just been given back to me, I am thankful for every extra moment. But now, God, another decision! Those meadows, which looked so smooth from above, we see are full of bumps. And the valley is dotted with hay-sheds, fatal wooden cubes: we don't want to smash into them. There is a ditch, too, beside a narrow dust road.

'Go higher up the valley,' I call instinctively. 'Charlie, over there!' And I point ahead.

'Yes, that'll do,' he yells back and is flying now straight towards a meadow immediately above the dust road, which looks more promising. It is racing towards us – oh, hell! It is just as bumpy! 'Can't do anything about it now,' Charlie mumbles, 'I'm lowering the flaps.' A second later, I hear the rush of air. A couple more seconds, and all will be decided, one way or the other. It is almost a relief. The earth is close. I am full of hope.

The road! There's a farmer, running; he throws himself into the ditch, but already we have swooped over him. Again I hear Charlie. 'When we're down, try to get out right away. If that's possible.' His voice sounds urgent. Roofs skim past . . . a big grassy dome approaches – there? No, not there! That's it, no more choices . . . no time . . . The road! The road with the ditch – here too! We're still moving at a hundred kilometres per hour, we'll just get over it . . .

'Tuck in your legs! Any minute now . . .' Charlie roars over the noise. Fractions of seconds, fragments of time: the green dome, again . . . there are humps behind it, too! In between . . .

CRAAAAAASH! Then a wild kick, and we are flying again, thrown up with enormous force. We flop over the hill, an enormous jump of at least forty metres! CRAAAAAASH! I hug my legs, bent, hanging in the harness. And we're airborne again, like a football. Will it never end? CRAACK! That was very hard, that one! Another jump – into the air – PRANGGGGGG! At last we seem to have come to rest. GET OUT! QUICK, OUT, OUT! In a fraction of a second I am free of the harness, hurl open the door, and I am outside!

The world does not move any more.

The meadow. The grass. The flat, still ground.

My feet are planted back on earth. I feel it coming up through every fibre of my body, from the surface – life. It is a miracle.

'Kurtl!' Charlie laughs crazily, 'We're alive!' And I see him pulling at his hair and running round and round in the meadow, like a lunatic. And I'm running through the grass too, deliriously shouting and screaming. And we fall on each other's necks, hug one another and gallop round again. We are totally beside ourselves – over the edge with joy. Here we are, here we are . . . we are alive!

'Kurtl,' Charlie yells suddenly. 'You might not know how to fly, but you're the very best companion for a crash! Without you, I'd have been really nervous!'

'Charlie . . .' I say. But I cannot say anything: all of sudden I have no more words. Charlie, I think, without *you* . . .

To Charlie, I owe my life, my second life – that's why he is here, at the beginning of my book – even if his real name is Karl Schönthaler and not Charlie at all. Forgive me, Karl . . .

What else remains to be told?

A lot: we had been incredibly lucky. The aeroplane didn't catch fire, we didn't nosedive, or turn it over, we didn't even break any bones – nothing at all! Charlie walks round his plane in sheer disbelief: 'The only damage is to one of the struts. And at the back, there's a little bit torn away. That's all! And we are alive!'

Beside ourselves with happiness, we are standing in our flower-decked 'birthday meadow', 1500 metres above the sea, in this beautiful Pfundser Tschy, as the first farmers, men, women, boys and girls come flocking round. They look at us as if we had risen from the dead and shake our hands. Some shake their heads as well. A farmer's wife remarks with feeling that you would never catch her sitting in one of these contraptions . . .

Straightforward country people, who do not waste a lot of words; we are happy they came; we are happy about everything. Happy beyond measure, beyond words. Real birthday kids! And into this 'contraption' which Charlie has just coaxed safely out of the sky, this box with which he struck 'gold' for us – our lives – I, too, will never venture inside. Never again.

Everyone living in the high valley had to come and visit this meadow, of course. At first glance you would never know the plane had made an emergency landing, even if it was standing a little cock-eyed. Only closer inspection revealed the cracked strut and damaged rudder. By chance, in the afternoon, two German tourists dropped by – and they

The Second Birthday

had heard nothing of our drama. One of them, a well-fed man with a shaving-brush of chamois hair on his (new) hat, remarked to his wife, 'Did you realise, Wilhelmine, that these Austrian farmers are now *flying* in to harvest their hay?'

I guarded the plane next day, in case it became an irresistible 'toy' to the children of the valley, and there were even more visitors. I had to explain over and again what happened. But I didn't mind, I could have stayed for days in this meadow. Charlie had gone down to the Inn valley to find a mechanic and some heavy vehicle that could tow us. The whole plane would need dismantling screw by screw to load it on to a transporter and get it down to Innsbruck.

. . . Later, I have to say, Charlie preferred to buy a new plane.

Double Solo on Zebru

Monte Zebru (3735m)* looks like the raised fin of a giant fish. Sunlight, catching its north-east face obliquely, reveals a fine design like radiating bones. These are snow and ice ribs, varying in number according to the prevailing conditions on the face. Up to the right, the piscine image is fortified by an overall pattern of dark speckles – islands of rock penetrating the thin skin of snow and ice. The top edge of the fin runs more or less horizontally, though it carries a summit-point on either end. The face below the one to the right – the northern – was unclimbed from this side, although a route had been pushed to the South Summit, up a completely white flank which lies almost always in shadow, being inclined towards the north. There is a plinth of outcropping rock at the base of the fin, surmounted by a small hanging glacier – except that nothing is really 'small' here. The height of the face itself is some 700 metres. My two-fold climb of this giant fin took a full day, giving many adventurous hours: a first ascent to the North Summit, followed by a first descent from the Southern Summit, both solo.

In some way it was another birthday.

I was climbing on my own because my friend Albert Morokutti's leave had run out before I felt ready to go home. I don't really consider myself a soloist; I far prefer sharing an adventure with someone else. That is not to imply anything against solo mountaineering: it is just a different kind of experience, often more dangerous, sometimes more intense, and one which takes you to the limits of existence – no other human can help you find the answers, only the mountain . . . and yourself.

Thinking about this climb, I sat alone in the hayfields of the Pfundser Tschy, waiting for Charlie to organise recovery of the damaged plane.

What brought it into my mind? During my solo on Zebru all those

---

* Not to be confused with Gran Zebru or Königspitze (3851m) to its south.

Double Solo on Zebru

years ago, just as in the crippled aeroplane, there had been moments when I longed for some good flat earth beneath my feet. And it had been just as far away.

A thirty-metre hemp rope over my shoulder, some pitons in my rucksack and an ice axe in my hand: that's how lightly I set out for Zebru. The hut warden had thoughtfully provided a couple of sandwiches, but these weighed scarcely anything, and my rope was quite thin – sufficient only for a self-belay on some of the more difficult passages, or for abseiling if it became necessary to retreat – you never know.

It was still only half light as I approached the face. The pale bulk of the Ortler rose to my right with its snow patches and the rock bastions of the Hinter Grat; and to the left, the Königspitze soared into the sky. Only a few days ago I had climbed that great face with Albert; true, the Giant Meringue still beckoned, the impressive summit cornice which no one had yet managed to overcome, but as a soloist, without the possibility of help or belay, I saw no chance of doing that for the time being.

Thus, everything was uncertain, as so often in life, even today. But casting light into uncertainty, transforming it by degrees to clarity, is the adventure of the mountaineer, an adventure for life. I will never be able to do without it!

The first rays of sun come up as I put on my crampons, but the spectacle affects me less than usual: I am tense with anticipation. What lies in store for me on this Zebru North-East Face; and how will I cope with it, just on my own?

I feel in great shape. It is autumn now, and a whole summer of climbing lies behind me. Across the gently sloping glacier, I approach the steep face where it sweeps down from the North Summit. The snow surface sparkles all around, scattered with crystals from the overnight frost – but I keep my attention on all the troughs and hollows, which could indicate a hidden crevasse. Falling into one of these is a great danger of soloing, when you have no lifeline, no companion with a rope to haul you back to the surface. Usually, nobody even knows where you are. You might manage to extricate yourself if uninjured, but the odds remain against you. A big transverse crevasse bars the way. I had already noticed it from below, had even discovered a snow bridge – but now, close up, I don't fancy it at all. It is frozen bone-hard, but very flimsy. I probe around with my axe, but in the end I can see no other possibility and rush across it with momentum, catching a second's-long glimpse into the frigid blue depths. Otherwise, the glacier holds no problems, simply becomes increasingly steep. On all fours, I crawl up the white flank, plunging in the pick of the ice axe with every step. (I call it an axe, but it also has a hammer head.) The front points of my crampons, too, I thrust into the white surface, and I clutch a pointed ice piton in my left hand to make the fourth point of contact. I take great care always to have at least three points in contact with the mountain before making a movement: either two hands and one foot, or two feet and one hand . . .

To an outsider, this juggling of holds might sound a complicated and risky procedure, but when you have been climbing for years, it has long passed into your flesh and blood and you don't think about it. The precision demanded by each step becomes second nature. On a mountain, imprecision takes bitter revenge, sooner or later!

At last I reach a vertical barrier of grey rock. Friable limestone, very similar to that on the Ortler, or over there on the Königspitze. For a while, I pause to study the possibilities . . . Then, I inch my way carefully higher, testing every hold. No one has ever held this rock in his hand before! I am right to be cautious: a handhold crumbles away . . . Frozen with horror, I watch the jumping pieces disappear into the depths. If more than one hold comes away at a time, so much for my good shape!

With infinite care I retreat back to the foot of the rock barrier, find a fissure in sound rock, and hammer in a piton. Then, belaying myself to this with the rope, I start climbing again. Careful only to trust my weight to holds by pressure – pushing down, not pulling on them – I sneak up the wall, stopping just once on a small ledge to extend my rope belay. That's the way to secure myself with no partner gradually paying out the rope. At last, the rock band! There is a good crack. Bang! Bang! Bang! In goes another piton . . . give it a vigorous wiggle . . . it's solid. Then, descending the rope, I hammer out the first piton. With a rope from above and easier now in my mind, I clamber back across this unfriendly fragile wall. True, it is a long-winded technique, but perfectly secure if the pitons are well placed. Taking out the upper one, I reflect that, alone like this, somehow these pegs become companions. (I could not know then that many years later a sort of belaying device would be given the name 'Friend'.)

Coiling the rope, I take another look down the barrier . . . That was some circus act, and no mistake, only without an audience. I feel totally calm, in balance, not bothered at all by being on my own. My gaze sweeps over the mountains: how blue they are, on this silent autumn morning.

Double Solo on Zebru

And then it occurs to me that perhaps there is a spectator after all: Fritz Dangl, the warden of the Hinter Grat hut, the only person to whom I confided my intention, maybe he is watching through his telescope? It feels fine to be alone with the mountain – but it is good, too, to know that another soul shares your secret – even if only from outside.

But soon, climbing onwards, I forget all about Fritz and am conscious only, in this direct relationship with the face, of the overwhelming pleasure in discovering something new, a sense which increases by the minute. No, I don't feel lonely at all! The face and I. Then, having been on the go for perhaps three hours, I find myself among the rock islands which stud the upper part of the giant fin, below the North Summit. Every so often I can escape from the steep white snow to catch my breath in one of the faintly defined niches below the rocky islands. I am already high on the face, and totally content. The wall is surely mine! Yes, full of boyish presumption, I look across at the North Face of the Southern Summit: perhaps I could climb down that way instead of the normal route? Pig-steep, it looks, no interruption, no niche, no place to rest. Still . . . *Ma gia che si balla, balliamo davvero!* . . . since we are dancing, let's do it properly! I'll give it another look from above, from the top – without obligation. Mmm . . . but it would be very tempting to descend that way, clinging like a louse on a polished shovel, with everything around tilting away and plunging into the depths! Perhaps that's not such a good metaphor after all: a louse has the benefit of six legs, which must make everything safer . . . my goodness, imagine! Five points of contact . . .

A cool breeze! Does it mean the summit is close? A breath of wind that plays around the last rocks in this white world? The Ortler – over there – still rises above us, above me and my mountain. So it is higher, the Ortler, so what? What do height and size really matter? This is my mountain, my discovery – my route for all time.

Well, for a moment only.

Nothing lasts longer . . .

An edge, the sky above me – and I've arrived. The summit! I scramble up the last steps, happiness storming through me – here it is, my summit!

I stand on it.

Yes, I have reached you – and by a path which no one's eye had so closely beheld before; what streams through me may well be the joy of an explorer. What else? Contentedness, certainly, that the venture succeeded. And satisfaction, too, that I did possess the ability to move up here, to overcome the difficulties; in knowing for me mountaineering was not just a gamble. What else? A feeling of being part of nature. It surrounds you here, this nature, silently, with its greatest creations – the mountains.

Squatting on the summit, I look over at the Königspitze, soaring against the light – it is not yet noon, so it has taken me four and a half hours to climb the face. What a powerful cornice that Königspitze has! Will I ever succeed in climbing that? Not by myself, I won't.* But the big snow roll continues to bewitch me as I skip along the airy waves of the connecting ridge between Zebru's North and South Summits, a bridge of no sighs or problems, wonderful with plunging views on both sides and distant panoramas. Where does the normal route go down? I have completely forgotten to take any interest in that. Probably, the face absorbed me so much that I thought: you will find out when you are up there. A mistake. In the meantime, this is the South Summit! The whipped cream roll looks quite close from here. I lie down for a while to ponder it. When I rouse myself, it is time to start thinking about how to get down! What about the North Face of this Southern Summit? Coming up, didn't I flirt with its white steepness? From where I am now I cannot look into it. Towards its top, the face curves like a belly, and one would need to descend a bit before getting a good view down it. Gingerly, I step lower, turning in to face the mountain as it gets steeper, and continuing backwards on all fours, similar to the usual way of coming up on snow and firn. So far, so good. Finally, below my crooked arm, I catch a glimpse down . . . Heavens! It shoots off into nowhere! About 600 metres below, I recognise the small glacier where I started out this morning. Of course exposure is a feature of steep ice walls like this – you certainly do feel as if you're hanging on them, and no better than a louse on a steep polished shovel standing against the wall. I'll have another think about it – slowly I scramble back to the summit.

Whatever you do, you ought to have a rest first, my inner voice tells me. And so I lie down and it doesn't take long till I fall asleep, stroked by the light breeze which plays around the summit, warmed by the mild autumn sun . . . It is about an hour later when I wake up. Hop-la, time to go! If it takes as long to get down here as to come up the other face – this is going to turn into a very full day! There must be no more hanging around!

With no real relish, I set off down, into the abyss – it was so pleasant lying dreaming there on the summit. Yes, I definitely have to rediscipline myself to being on such steep ground again, to pay attention to

* See the chapter 'The Giant Meringue' in my *Summits and Secrets*.

every step and not make any mistakes. Sometimes, I glance through the gap between my arm and the wall, and the drop immediately concentrates my mind!

Zack! Zack! I ram the front points of my crampons into the steep and rather hard white surface. At the same time, I take my weight on my axe, the pick of which I press into the firn. With the other hand, I thrust in the long pointed ice piton, though it will not penetrate very far, so that I have to shorten my grip by putting a karabiner in the ring of the piton. I am wearing my hard hat, of course, since a small piece of ice or even a little stone could be fatal for a solo climber!

Zack, Zack . . .

Zack, Zack . . .

Zack, Zack . . . the way down is endless.

After about an hour of this, I peer to see if there's anywhere to rest. In vain. There is nothing. Everywhere, above and below me, is steepness.

So, go on. Zack, Zack . . .

Zack, Zack . . .

Finally, I hack a stance out of the wall, and take a breather.

How long I spend, leaning there, I don't know. At first, I don't look further than the snow in front of my nose. Then I try to estimate how far there is still to go. But it's hard to say. Several hundred metres below me the small hanging glacier projects like a ski jump, and then, further down I see the valley floor, and out in the distance the Hinter Grat hut. Once down on the hanging glacier, I should have almost made it. It should be possible from there to traverse to the bottom. Looking down, far beyond the points of my crampons, I notice some rock islands which appear to be just above the small hanging glacier. Could I rest there? But they are still a long, long way down. I sigh, and start off again with increasingly painful calf muscles. How different this descent is from my sunny climb this morning.

Zack, Zack . . . another two steps . . .

I am in shadow, here, and it's cold – and gloomy. And the depth doesn't want to come to an end.

Zack, Zack . . .

Can you ever get used to such monotony?

Is this how you lose attention . . . grow careless, don't give a damn?

It must be like that – all of a sudden one of my crampons slips and I am left hanging on the ice axe and the point of the ice piton. Blood is hammering in my temples! I go rigid.

Spirits of the Air

This face has been storing up even more suprises for me, I realise now – black ice below me! Hell! That makes a difference.

Already, on a steep ice face, it is even harder to go down than up. Especially when it's smooth and sheer like this. And on black ice? You need to have tried it to know what I mean – and not just for a short section . . .

I prefer to chip handholds here, and even several small notches for the front points of my crampons: that is not easy because the axe only has a short handle, so that I have to bend right down to fashion the notch for the next step. At the same time I am hanging with my fingers to another nick in the wall – a handhold which needs to be carefully chiselled out!

It is a lonely and acrobatic art, preparing this handhold, and the next, and the next, making them bombproof, so they don't come off under my weight when I'm hanging on them to carve the next foothold below. I say lonely because, despite knowing that the warden of the Hinter Grat hut is almost certainly watching now, I have for the first time the sensation of being really alone. Nothing else in the world counts, except how to get down. Out of minutes, grow hours . . . I have slowed right down, I'm very slow. But the hanging glacier down below, that white El Dorado, which even looks flat from up here, has inched a little bit closer! Its surface, down there, is, for me, the earth to which I return. I am looking down more often now, estimating more often how much is left to do. Fatigue, tense muscles, the continuous need for acute concentration . . . all this suffering will fly away like a bird once I'm sitting down there in the snow! I keep thinking of this moment with anticipated pleasure.

Don't rush it, take time, be precise! The message keeps flashing in my brain. Yet the temptation to hurry grows with every minute. Suddenly, something catches my eye: forty metres below me a black rock projects from the wall, like a pulpit, like an upholstered chair! A resting place, a gift from nature, by good heaven!

It was my greatest discovery on this face – the 'easy chair' on the North Wall of the southern Zebru. A crazy invention, a cosmic joke: somewhere to sit in this relentless steepness, the only place to draw breath on the whole face.

I take advantage of its hospitality for, I guess, half an hour; sitting and looking, stretching my overtired muscles and relaxing completely – in the end I like it so much here that I feel it to be the most beautiful place in the whole world; and its only disadvantage is that I have to leave it. Still, the very presence of this heavenly pulpit, in the end made the wall seem a wee bit friendly.

Double Solo on Zebru

Getting going again, after this long break, is a different matter. I am in high spirits, and the hanging glacier comes nearer. Here is the snow roof that leads to the bergschrund, but it's still separated from me by a steep cliff. I manage to climb down a short distance on rock and sheer ice – then the business seems too delicate. I bang in a belay piton. Will the doubled rope reach to the bottom? No! Hopeless. Well, then, how about single? I tie the rope to the piton and descend over ice slabs and broken rock. With a deep sigh of relief, I finally stand in the snow of the roof above the hanging glacier. A couple of chops at the rope with the ice axe – it's cut! I stuff the rest in my rucksack, (It's not normally my habit to be so brutal with ropes, but I'd had enough.)

Down now, down the sloping roof! Whew, I look forward to being able to sit down there in the snow. Still on all fours, I scramble down quickly – it is almost a joy to move here. Now I am at the upper lip of the bergschrund. Boy, that's a drop of all of five metres! But down there it's flat. The snow looks good, no ice. For a moment I hesitate. Then I jump. There's a flurry of powder; it's like landing on a feather bed. I sit and laugh and laugh, I am so happy. I have done it! I have done it!

All that remains now is to scamper down to the valley, and back down to the hut, to Fritz. I have so much to tell him!

For a moment, though, I stop at the bottom of the plinth, and look back up at the giant fin. Two firsts in a day: one up, one down! The summit and the abyss. Like the light and the dark side of the moon. I'll probably never do that again . . . not alone.

Even though I have climbed solo from time to time since then, hardly ever have I found myself forced to ask: Where is your place? The soloist experiences the entire might of the mountains, without the outline of someone else between him and his peak. So, he can go beyond limits which the presence of another would impose . . . But, in so doing, doesn't he run the risk of losing the measure of reality? Doesn't he build a surreal world for himself? What do people still mean to him?

Standing there at the foot of the Zebru face, it became clear to me again that my thoughts needed an echo . . . an altered, variegated echo – one which is not reflected just from a wall, but comes from the heart of another. I am no soloist.

While I was busy on Zebru, my friend Wolfi was in the Dolomites with his girlfriend – Wolfi Stefan from Vienna, my ropemate on almost all my climbs in the western and eastern Alps. We continued to be an indivisible partnership until our professional activities separated us. Amongst our friends there were some outstanding soloists; the one who most readily springs to mind was Dieter Marchart. We used to meet him often on the Peilstein, the outcrops in the Viennese Woods, and in other places, too. He climbed the Matterhorn North Face solo – in five hours, if I remember rightly. And then, he was hit by a pebble from the ice couloirs of the Eigerwand . . .

Wolfi Stefan and I have remained alive. Of course we have had our full share of luck. But we never envied the soloists their adventures.

I think of the Eiger: how much it meant to both of us to be roped to someone we'd known for years, finding the way together through stonefall, bad weather, and the vertical maze of slate which makes up this forbidding wall. Someone to lessen the hardship of bivouacs, to share a laugh with . . . Seeing plans come to fruition, and the joy of your friend, too, when you are blessed with success . . . All that, the soloist misses out on.

Perhaps some do it only because they have not yet found the right companion . . .

Having fallen asleep in the Pfundser Tschy meadows, I am awakened suddenly by two small boys wanting to know how the aeroplane's rudder works. I do my best and, not entirely satisfied, eventually they leave. The rudder, it must have been, which was responsible for that descending spiral we made, that weird spiral staircase ride that brought us to this place.

The sun is pleasurably warm . . . and soon I am dozing off again . . .

Séracs! A spinning icefall! Oh my, everything is going round again – at top speed. But what are all these shining towers? Crystal shapes of ice. What's happening here, Charlie? Oh-oh! that's not Charlie, that's Jay at the controls. He is a Californian who lives in Courmayeur near the foot of Mont Blanc, and he often goes flying. I met him once, guiding: a blond, open-faced lad. He flings the plane into another steep turn, laughing with excitement. The motor roars and the Brenva Face arches over in front of us like a spinnaker before a storm. Now the Aiguille Noire rotates above us, its pointed silhouette an immense dark crystal in the sky. Beyond it, barely moving at all, is Mont Blanc. My Mont Blanc.

Crystals from Mont Blanc

The dream bursts like a soap bubble. I am lying in the meadow, my eyes open now, unable to shake Mont Blanc from my mind. That summit – I did not reach it whenever I wanted; and when I went crystal-hunting there, would frequently return empty-handed – but what matter! I love that big white mountain.

Its beautiful Peuterey Ridge – which I consider the finest route in all the Alps – resembles a sequence of crystals rising from the valley. Eight kilometres of climbing it offers, if you follow the skyline with all its indentations. The first – dark – crystal is the Aiguille Noire with its stunning upwards stab; next, after a clutch of slender needles, comes the white, three-pointed Aiguille Blanche, more than 4000 metres high. Finally, the rhythmical line steepens from the Col de Peuterey to a shimmering crescendo, the dome of Mont Blanc itself, 4810 metres. A magic silhouette.

No, we didn't reach the summit the last time I was there, though we spent five days on that great ridge. In my mind's eye, I am still there.

The Aiguille Noire, steep and black like the prow of a ship, cleaves the storm winds. That's how it seems to me, looking down at the banners of cloud rising sharply from its crest. We are clinging to the ridge, surrounded by the rushing, roaring waves of tempest; tatters of cloud scurry and merge in whirling circles of light at the snow's edge.

Sepp, Walter, Edith. 'Never saw the Peuterey so wild, so powerful,' I shout to them over the wind. 'I hope we'll be able to make the Col today.' We have already endured one bivouac. Conditions up here at 4000 metres on the Aiguille Blanche could hardly be worse: fresh snow everywhere on the rocks and it is so cold – it may be only September, but – heavens! – it's like winter.

I remember Edith's creased face this morning; we had tucked her between us for protection through the long hours of the bivouac, and a chill breeze blew in steadily from the west all night. A crust of frost crept over our shoulders and 'ice flowers' blossomed on the stones all around ... Soon our faces were numb and our bodies stiff ... we sat out the night on our stone 'bench' above the swelling clouds. Lightning flashed above the distant Dauphiné peaks – a firework display lasting for hours. Anxiously, I watched the ocean of fire at just the same height as ourselves, willing it to stay where it was. How far away was that? What was the strength and direction of the wind? Bloody hell, we'd be in deep trouble if we had to move from here, down on to the steep slopes! Luckily, the storm finally blew itself out far behind the Barre des Ecrins . . . and the clouds were swaying again, gently up and down, as if the whole gliding coverlet of light and darkness was breathing under the touch of the moon. And we sat on, stiffly, listening to the low whisper of the air around us, watching the crystals grow, and huddling ever closer to one another.

Hours went by.

Something suddenly shook me from my icy torpor; a nocturnal phenomenon I shall never forget. Behind the palely gleaming Gran Paradiso – right in front of us, really close – a round, puffy tower of cloud emerged from nowhere, slowly, steadily, growing all the time. Menacing and cold in the moonlight . . . like a nuclear mushroom. And then it lit up, illuminated from within by the flickers of lightning . . . and nearby rose another mushroom, and over there, another . . . a whole colony of strange, expanding figures peering over the Gran Paradiso at us. Panic seized me: if they stepped over the crest, we would be done for. And with all my might, I begged the soft west wind to resist them: Do not desert us now, I pleaded. Fear is far too frail a word to describe how it feels to be crouched among the rocks, waiting for the next lightning strike . . . and then the next . . . and the next, the shock running through your limbs . . . and the next. Each one perhaps your last. You never forget that! Many years ago, down there, on the Noire – just below its black summit – we survived eight thunderstorms, one after the other: that was Tona, Terenzio, Sepp, Walter, Bianca and me. Tona suffered deep burns to her palms and heels; our down jackets were spattered with black spots from the sparks. For two days we counted the seconds in those electric clouds.

The big mushroom grows a hat, elongates, stretches eastwards; it becomes a giant ship, gliding across the Aosta valley, lit up repeatedly by sudden internal flashes. I take a deep breath. And then I think of Tona, who was my wife at the time we were fighting for survival in the firestorm on the Aiguille Noire. She still goes to the mountains, on expeditions too, even though we are not together any more. Perhaps, whenever she looks at the Aiguille Noire, she feels as I do. People who have been through something like that can never really separate. And, besides, there are our two daughters – we love them so much.

The great cloud ship had sailed away. 'How are we doing, troops?' I broke the silence. Walter, and Sepp and his wife, were cowering at my side. 'All right . . . but how about changing places? It's your turn to sit on the side of the wind.' We changed places. 'What about making some tea?' We made tea. They go on for ever, September nights.
 No more lightning shimmer. Anywhere. All gone. The fear was spent, the danger over. I had not sat on such a fine granite bench in a long while, with its ringside view over the cloudfields. What we had been through! What a fantastic night!

When daytime came at last, it brought a storm wind. The air was biting. On our way once more, now we were crossing the three heads of the Aiguille Blanche to reach the Col de Peuterey. We were moving at the shining edges of snow, past the curled ribbons of overhanging cornices, muffled in cloud, in an arabesque of light and shade. At times, when you touch the snow, or twist in an ice-screw, when you are waiting and belaying, you wonder how long this storm can last. One minute it gets fiercer, the next brings a lull. Mont Blanc looms ahead – immense. Squalls buffet its rocks. Glistening veils are sucked at fantastic speed up into the blue sky. We are going to have to bivouac on the col! There's no alternative: a snowhole in a bank on the saddle. Sitting on a ledge carved out of snow. We stay there for two whole days . . .

No way up! Even after that. Fresh snow lying waist-high. Higher up, the storm continues its raging. Good old Mont Blanc . . . Though the sky is an intense blue, it is midwinter here. We opt for retreat: abseil down the Gruber rocks. Five hundred metres to the bottom – many hours. We come across the old abseil slings left by Walter Bonatti, Pierre Mazeaud and their companions when they were fleeing from the Frêney Pillar – even find some cut pieces of a harness. Only three of those seven men survived the descent. We abseil down on their slings . . . a long day behind us. We did not make it to the top. It does not matter.

―――

A tractor rattles through the Pfundser Tschy, climbing up-valley. It is towing a long trailer. Then I see Charlie, waving. An hour later and our red and white flying machine has been completely dismantled and loaded aboard: we jolt down the mountain valley. Soon the beer mugs are clinking at Innsbruck Airport: Charlie's friends. '*Prosit*! Cheers! To your second birthday!' And this time, Charlie does not have to say it in English. Tired out, we slink off to his house to sleep. Life, that by rights should have ended, goes on. Nothing is predictable. And as I slowly drop off to sleep, I reflect on the phone call I made home to Italy, and the unexpected reception I received. 'What in God's name possessed you to go flying? You're never home – and then you go and nearly get yourself killed!'

Why, I wonder, did I marry again? A person like me, always off somewhere, up to something – heart in the mountains, sworn to adventure – I had no business embarking on it in the first place. That seems to be what most people think.

Maybe they have a point – in principle.

But there is this alleyway – I can still see (and smell) it – with its aroma of fresh bread. A dark passage near the bakery in Via Santo Stefano: the arcades, cars jolting over cobbled streets, students strolling to the university . . . a complete mélange of colour, skittishness, calm and vivacity . . . a spirit, indeed, which permeates the whole town, this town below its pair of silhouetted towers, le Due Torri, pointing obliquely into the sky. As if designed by a drunken architect, they lean towards each other, symbols of Bologna's friendliness.

At the end of the dark passageway lives Teresa. She is a student. Of the many students in Bologna, she is special. She *always* looks at you with such calm and disarming candour, and always says exactly what she thinks. Her eyes are huge and dark, and her features finely drawn. She wants to become a judge. Or a lawyer . . . Shouldn't a man know to beware of a woman with ambitions like that? In principle, yes. But some men choose to live dangerously, or at least find themselves drawn towards exposed situations. I felt drawn towards Teresa, this Teresa who wanted to become a judge. Those eyes were not on me for more than five minutes before subjecting me to an intense scrutiny; she was like a judge who, having first glanced around the people in the courtroom, tries to put himself into the psyche of the accused. '*Tu sei un po puttano*,' she announced. Those were her first words to me. They cannot be translated literally. To be a bit *puttano* means to be no real upholder of moral values! I was lost for words. '*Le puttane di Bologna*' are famous throughout Italy, those 'easy women' who line the avenues of town – and (occasionally) other roads and squares of importance as well. They are as much part of Bologna as its leaning towers. Well, *puttano* might not be exactly their male equivalent but, certainly, if a woman calls you this, she cannot be thinking you the most upright of fellows! So, I was dumbfounded. And wondered if she could be right ... It unnerved me that such a judgment should be reached on sight; and then articulated to my face – but it did induce me to look again into those dark big eyes, so calmly regarding me with an expression almost of irony and mockery ...

Who was this woman who spoke to me in this way?

We married.

Teresa loves nature, the rays of the sun, and the flowers; and she has endless patience. Without it, she would never have been able to put up with me. When I think how little I am at home ... Teresa is no mountaineer, but sometimes she comes with me – perhaps to hunt for crystals on Mont Blanc.

There is, for instance, a huge boulder, as tall as a house, just above the raspberry patches near the torrent of Dora Baltea. Nobody would imagine you could find crystals there! But there is a good chance you may. Unfortunately, now, a number of people know about it, but on my first visit there, I was amazed to find myself in front of a wall of crystals – beautiful smoky quartz. My daughter Hildegard was with me, and we christened this boulder the Treasure Chamber. It was marvellous, like a shrine. The great pity was, it did not remain a secret ... From the very start, the evidence of hammer and chisel marks showed that at least one other person knew of its existence. And he must have noticed our presence too, perhaps within days, for the next time we returned, large chunks of the crystal wall had gone. From then on we were like two mice, taking turns to gnaw at the same piece of cheese. And since the spot was so close to the footpath leading to the Dalmazi hut, our activity could not possibly pass unnoticed. There are still many crystals in the Treasure Chamber, even today, but being inside the rock, they require a lot of work to extract. Who knows how many gems are revealed each year on the faces of the big White Mountain, whenever the cold fractures the rocks?

There are prisms of pure quartz, absolutely transparent – white or rose, or tawny-coloured – tapering to hexagonal pyramids. Hunting for them becomes a real passion, hard to explain. Finding them brings even more excitement and happiness than possessing them; I have given many to my friends. However, it is a pity when such an exceptional boulder as the Treasure Chamber cannot be protected, unscathed. It never really had a chance, with the footpath so close. In the upper basin of a major Mont Blanc glacier, I have found similar rocks, covered in a lawn of crystals – myriads of flashing spikes – and only looked at them. You always know that what you take home are only fragments, that it is better just to move your head and enjoy the thousand-fold sparkle.

Spirits of the Air

Nature protects these blocks well up there: ice avalanches threaten the place, and very few people can reach it.

Several even more remote places exist among the wildest faces of Mont Blanc, which hardly anyone knows, and far from any route. No one lets on about them. The two Ollier brothers from Courmayeur, who in the past have brought home smoky quartz crystals of up to half a metre in length, only go out searching for them in the very worst weather, in fog, or at night . . . when nobody can see them. Mario, the cook at the Scoiattolo refuge, where I used to hang out in the light-hearted days when Orazio and Annie ran it, once imagined he had picked up a whiff of their trail. 'Kurt,' he whispered to me, 'yesterday someone spotted the two Olliers on the Dent du Géant, and at the Aiguilles Marbrées – and it occurred to me we ought to take a crawl into the bergschrund there.' Needless to say, Mario is an obsessed crystal hunter. I was not optimistic: plenty of people have attempted to locate secret Ollier-haunts, without success. However, Mario felt sure this was a hot tip. It might work, I reasoned, since erosion is always bringing new crystals to the light of day. If the brothers had been seen there, well . . . Soon, we had inflamed each other with dreams of crystal-lined chasms . . .

Full of expectation we approached the place, but wherever we stuck our noses, we found nothing. Finally, above the fabled bergschrund, I noticed an enigmatic hole in the wall. Using ice-screws, crampons and rope, we got ourselves up to it, and I placed a belay piton at the edge of a small cave. Fortunately, it was a solid, nay a very solid piton. Mario was digging like a mole in the hole. Nothing! Still, you are always hearing of people giving up just inches before striking a lucky vein . . . we were not going to let that happen to us! Next it was my turn, then Mario's again . . . each buoyed by our commonly woven crystal fantasies. After two hours, at last we are convinced we must be looking in the wrong place, and give up.

Half crouched at the entrance of the hole, I start belaying Mario's descent. I cannot see him, nor have I any idea how fast he is likely to go. For all I remember now, this may well have been the first time we climbed together. Suddenly, I hear him shout: '*Io vado*! I go!' And the rope snakes through my fingers like a bally trout-fisher's line. My goodness, but these Aostan guys are quick: he must be running down the wall! No, something is wrong! I brace myself . . . and almost immediately comes a gigantic jolt! From way down I hear a plaintive '*Porca miseria*!' and, craning towards the sound, I see Mario hanging in his celebrated bergschrund and wriggling like a frog. He must have slipped the minute he uttered his '*Io vado*'.

To this day, Mario's friends still tease him about his '*Aostan speed*' and his '*Io vado*'. Slowly, we made our way back to Courmayeur – with empty sacks.

Next morning, Alessio Ollier winks at me, 'I hear you had a productive day up there!' I mumble something and we go for a drink. Of course I never stoop to ask him where his secret spot is. He would not give me a straight answer, anyway. But the day will come when I discover for myself where he found his giant black Mont Blanc topaz . . . at night, and in the fog.

Fortune can smile on you unexpectedly: this I discover with my wife Teresa on the Triolet Glacier. We are at 2800 metres, skipping happily across little streams and crevasses, when suddenly we are rooted to the spot: in front of us, as if set there by magic, is a pyramid of granite, as tall as a man, and on top of it the most beautiful crystals. Rose-coloured, clear, shining in the sunlight . . . a fairytale splendour! '*Fantastico*,' murmurs Teresa, entranced.

Together we consider the best way to detach the upper part of the pyramid without breaking or chipping the individual crystals, which are several inches long. For two hours I chisel away, with lots of helpful advice from my wife – we even put sticking plaster over each crystal in an attempt to minimise vibrations and stop the tops splintering off.

A yippee of joy! The whole upper crust of the rock comes off without breaking! It is a big block, only just portable . . . but I don't want to tempt fate any more with the hammer. There follows a hard and heavy descent to the valley with a thunderstorm at the end of it. And to cap it all, Teresa sprains her ankle. By the time I get wife and druse down safely, I am exhausted.

Some of the magic comes back whenever we look at the stone.

The next time Teresa and I go there, little Ceci, our son, rides on my back, complete with cradle, up to the Miage Glacier lake . . . and it brings back memories of my father carrying me with him when he went hunting for mushrooms in the steep Austrian forests. Ceci gazed wide-eyed at the mountains, and they looked down on him . . .

Mont Blanc has given me many crystals – and not all of them quartz. There have been those flowers of ice which the wind sometimes fashions on rocks, and the gift of crystal-clear days; there have been thoughts which could never have come to me elsewhere – whether sheer fantasy, or endowed with the clarity of decision. And friendship, happiness and, perhaps, luck.

Will we ever know all that is contained in a crystal?

At the spectrum's other end, during those four storm days on the Peuterey Ridge, when the force of the air had staved in the wall of our bivouac, all of us nursed a secret fear of how it would end. But fear and uncertainty have their place in mountaineering, every bit as much as joy and luck. Life in the mountains is heightened, in all senses: it brings enhanced happiness and pleasure, as well as increased risk and the fear of losing all. It is an extreme way of living, but once you are used to it, you can never give it up.

I WIN A CAR

There are a number of very peculiar treasures which came to me from Mont Blanc: Franz Lindner and I, climbing the Peuterey Ridge *intégrale* in autumn 1958, filmed the whole traverse in 16 mm, an ambitious undertaking for two men, which had never succeeded before (nor has since). After five days we sat on top of Mont Blanc at midnight, with Franz saying, 'What a pity it's over – I've grown quite used to living on the ridge.' The documentary earned my first-ever film award, at the Trento Festival. The lucky streak continued when in 1971 a photo of Aiguille Noire in storm clouds presented me with a wonderful surprise – and that is a story in itself: at a friend's suggestion, I had entered the picture in a mountain photography competition in Munich – a big event with no fewer than 15,000 entries from around the world. Then I forgot about it and continued roaming around Europe in my old car – a ten-year-old Beetle with a respectable 300,000 kilometres on the clock. When it started letting in the rain, I drilled a hole in the bottom and solved the problem (Austrian vehicle testing has always been more lenient than in Germany). That old car ran and ran, until the day it would run no longer. It was the end, this time, no doubts about it. I rolled it into an Italian orchard, took the numberplate for a souvenir, and rang my father. 'Don't worry, my boy,' he told me. 'You had a letter today . . . you've just won yourself a brand-new BMW 1800! For a picture of Mont Blanc, it said. Must be some sort of competition.' The Grand Prize, it was, no less.

I was speechless as I put the receiver down, and my legs went wobbly. But I soon got over it, and continued my vagabond travels with 'Filippo' (as my daughter Karen christened the new car), and somehow it always remained linked to Mont Blanc in my mind – especially as I would regularly bring the mechanic a crystal whenever I brought it in for its annual MOT. Eventually, I clocked up more than 300,000 kilometres in that jalopy as well.

Crystals from Mont Blanc

Filippo's end, when it came, also had a twist in the tail. After many repairs, it was clear that my dear old friend would not get through even an Austrian vehicle check, forcing me to a sad decision. With heavy heart I drove the sorry heap to the scrap merchant's, but it was already late and the yard was closed. Parking Filippo outside, I bade a sentimental farewell and went home. In the middle of the night I was startled awake by the telephone. 'I'm sorry to have to tell you,' an official voice said, 'your car has been run into by a drunk-driver – he's not hurt, fortunately, but the vehicle's a write-off.'

Nothing but a cloud of rust in the road . . . be *assured*, dear reader, that sudden end was the best for Filippo (and for me)! I retrieved a piece of headlight from the ruins and nailed it to my wall. It has the same curve as a horseshoe – a lucky horseshoe from Mont Blanc (you could say that, I think, after so incredible a story!).

AS A MOUNTAIN GUIDE

Many years have passed since my first visit to Mont Blanc on Grandfather's bicycle, when I was twenty. Setting eyes on the white dome in July 1953, I had no idea that later on I would be linked to it professionally . . . The course my life took simply confirmed that I cannot live without the peaks, without feeling their breath close, or at least returning to their shade: after graduation at the University of Commerce in Vienna and five years of teaching at the Academy of International Tourism in Salzburg I turned the rudder through 180 degrees and became a mountain guide! Good old Kuno Rainer, the celebrated Peter Habeler and young Klaus Hoi were my examiners. That was in Austria, of course, but mostly I plied my trade in the Mont Blanc massif. I met with no jealousy from the local guides, since as often as not I turned up with my client from abroad. Sometimes, when an expedition came up suddenly, I would even pass him over to them.

Of my guiding experiences there, I could write a separate book. This kaleidoscope of local and imported characters created a special frame for my mountain, a world of its own . . . There was Don Pino, the 'Don Camillo' with his holiday camp for young people in the Val Ferret, just below the Grandes Jorasses . . . how many toasts did we drink in his favourite blackberry schnapps! Or Dr Bassi – the Courmayeur physician, another daredevil pilot – for whom, after he turned his plane on its nose, the guides created the limerick, 'Sooner or later with Dottor Bassi, you'll find yourself between "quattro assi"' – between four boards! (That is to cast no aspersions on his medical credentials: he is a very fine doctor, and has saved the lives of a number of mountaineers). We have met him before in this book – he is the pilot who dragged his heels at opening the door of his plane to allow me to take pictures of the landscape. Or Wanda, secretary of the local tourist office, who wanted so badly to know what it was like on the pointed tip of the Dent du Géant. She found out (with me) – but there, at 4000 metres above the sea, on a spot no bigger than a table, in the clouds, with a vertical drop of at least 1000 metres all round, was so overwhelmed, she could not stand upright – and on top of everything, suddenly wanted to spend a penny! Thank God, this mountain has two tops, so that I could retreat to the other, after establishing a complicated belay. Last, but not least, of all those many clients from outside Italy – one in particular I should not forget . . . though I have yet to guide him to the top of Mont Blanc. Never mind, Axel, I *shall* . . .

Whatever I say here, I like him enormously. How terrible the world would be if there were no critical journalists – people would simply do what they wanted without regard for others. It can be really bad if somebody big and influential hogs the media. What a good thing that free writers exist, like Axel Thorer. He has an original style, beyond imitation, for puncturing such inflated characters. How much they care depends on whether they have the hide of a hippopotamus or are sensitive mimosa blossoms. Axel himself, who has to be prepared to take as good as he dishes out, is one of the more resilient pachyderms. And not without some anxiety, I fear he will take me at my word one day and want to be guided to the summit of Mont Blanc. Why? He doesn't strike you as someone to lose his balance: he is as stout and upright as the sea-lion in the Salzburg House of Nature, and his handlebar moustache looks strong enough to hang ice axes from at each end – but supposing this mighty Axel should topple . . . All my three-point anchor belays would be as nothing – it would only remain for someone to put two nice 'crystals' on to our tombs in the valley . . . for once Axel is at full velocity nothing and no one can stop him. (We will find that out later in the book.)

Mont Blanc is not far from where I actually live, and there have been years when every season would find me on the faces or ridges of this great mountain massif. Even in the Himalaya, I am conscious that Mont Blanc is *the* alpine peak to bear comparison. This mountain, which has never released its hold over me, is the epitome of a great peak to me – in the same way that when I think of a climbing partnership, it is always Wolfi Stefan who springs to mind; with him I made most of my alpine climbs. No less important than the fascinating structure of rock and ice is a good understanding with your companion – such as I enjoyed with Wolfi in the Alps and – many years later, in the Himalaya – with Julie Tullis, the other half of my 'film crew'. In both cases we formed inseparable partnerships, linked by the rope. It is true that to find happiness on a mountain, you need more than simply a fine peak.

There is something else, too, which keeps bringing you back to the mountains, and which is almost impossible to explain: I call it their secrets. That something you feel when you see a tremendous sunset up there, or when you find yourself enveloped in a powerful storm . . . The peak, the companion, and those secrets – their merging into an entity is the real heart of it. That is what makes a person return, time and again.

Strolling through the Val Veni below Mont Blanc, I am aware of the smell of flowers, the rush of the torrent – I pick up a lump of quartz, and the sun shines through it . . . a luminous piece of Mont Blanc! And strangely, as I hold the stone against the light, a small hover-fly lights on my finger, as if to say: Hey! Don't forget me, I'm part of Mont Blanc, too.

―――

These are the Mont Blanc crystals: a mosaic of years, people, experiences – which is still evolving. Before I began going to the Himalaya year after year, this place had become my second mountain home. My first? That was the high ranges of the Hohe Tauern near Salzburg. There, the crystal-hunting boy climbed his first summit, and stared with awe at distant peaks and the horizon that bore a question to be answered. But 'Only the Spirits of the Air know what you will meet behind the mountains' – the proverb proved true yet again: on the Brenva Face and the Peuterey Ridge I carried a movie camera, without knowing what my later career would be. It had its roots on Mont Blanc, but then, all of a sudden, I plunged more deeply into the business of filming and it opened up all kinds of adventures, beyond the mountains . . .

PART II

The Magic Carpet

HOW I GOT INVOLVED WITH FILMING

The man sitting opposite me was clearly something of a character. As he spoke I noticed how he emphasised each word with flashes of his dark, somewhat slanting eyes. And, as I listened, I tried to think what it was he reminded me of. He was unusually tall, and extremely thin – and in that overcrowded Italian roadside restaurant he towered over his colourful and noisy surroundings; it was as if an ostrich had dropped in for dinner at a chicken farm. The strong bird-like resemblance was reinforced by a relatively small head. Mario Allegri wore his hair crew cut and an immaculately tailored corduroy suit. His movements were spare and contained, but impressive none the less by virtue of his size. He did not fit my preconception of an 'adventurer' in the least, although friends had told me at one of my Milan lectures how he had been several times to South America with Walter Bonatti. This was after Bonatti, the famous Italian mountaineer, had given up guiding in favour of a life of all-round adventure; he worked now as a features photographer for *Epoca* magazine. Mario Allegri lived, when he was at home, in Milan, but you could tell from his face and those unusual eyes that he was not pure Italian. He told me later that his family tree included a grandmother from the Mato Grosso.

My table companion, it soon transpired, had already organised several filming expeditions of his own. He had little patience, he told me, with large teams, for they would inevitably include someone who found the strain of adventure intolerable.

'Can you work with an Arriflex?' he demanded suddenly, the dark eyes scrutinising me keenly.

Arriflex, eh? The camera of professionals: you have to know it really well to get good results. My brother-in-law, Herbert Raditschnig, uses one all the time, and I'd seen it of course, but . . . A voice inside was warning, 'Kurt, this is your big chance. Don't blow it!' Mario was clearly looking for a one-man film-crew, who wouldn't be put off by danger or difficulty. And me? I wanted a springboard to the wider, adventurous world, wanted to get to know it not only as a mountaineer. 'Play it very carefully,' my voice whispered, as the question still hung in the air. 'If you want that job, don't give any hint of weakness!'

'Of course,' I replied, hoping I was pitching the right tone of confidence, 'of course I can work with an Arriflex.'

'*Benissimo*. All we have to do, then, is find one.'

'Well, it's true I don't have my own,' I ventured, 'but – given the right advance, of course – I'd be prepared to get one.'

I got the advance. Now I was an adventure cameraman! I could have leapt for joy. The fact that, apart from the camera, I would get nothing out of the enterprise, bothered me not one jot. I had the whole world at my feet, a totally new horizon. This would be the magic carpet to waft us from continent to continent . . .

Every day I practised with my new camera – new to me, that is: it was second-hand, of course, a well-preserved memento from an old Tibet hand.

At last the great moment arrived. The smallest film unit in the world set off from Milan, Mario and I: he the actor, and I the rest. And if we turned out not to be the smallest, certainly we would be the most 'adventurous'. First stop: Scandinavia.

BLIND MAN'S BUFF

Dandelions are blooming in Copenhagen. In Oslo everything is green. A wonderful town, I think, as we touch down. In the waiting room a TV-screen shows us snowploughs shovelling wall-like mounds of snow . . . Funny, I think, to be showing winter films now. Where is that? 'Oh, way up north,' A Norwegian passenger smiles reassuringly. 'A long way from here!' But could it be where we are heading, I wonder? More than likely.

A two-hour flight will take us to Tromsö . . . it is dark as we take off, and we see nothing of the mighty fjords and the many islands, nor the deeply troughed valleys of this ancient ice-fashioned landscape. We will look at it, when our magic carpet will be carrying us on to England and Newfoundland . . .

By and by, as we approach the Arctic Circle, dawn starts breaking . . . in the soft half-light we swoop along the Tromsö airstrip, whipping up sprays of grey ice. Whhoarrr, it's cold here! Midwinter! Soon we are

The Magic Carpet

in the air again, on our way to Alta: nothing to see but snow, snow and more snow – it might as well be Christmas! The sweltering heat of Milan, the dandelion meadows of Copenhagen seem surreal now, with this hummocky white landscape beneath us. Only the fjord water remains unfrozen – everything else is buried under deep drifts. No wonder the Scandinavian television was full of it.

We are well kitted out: you have to be prepared for anything on a world tour such as ours. Our boots and high gaiters, for instance, essential in deep snow, will serve as well in the jungle, and might even prove useful at sea – it is purely a matter of style and personal preference. Only in the desert might we find them too hot, despite their obvious protective qualities against cactus spines and rattlesnakes. But that's a long way from this – soon we will be with the reindeer, in the Land of Reindeer. Lapland is full of reindeer, every child knows that. The Lapps centre their lives around reindeer. They eat reindeer meat, make tools and other household objects from reindeer horns, and only keep a few small, rough-haired horses in order to be able to maintain control over their enormous herds of reindeer . . . I can remember the geography lesson clearly. I suppose they don't run around dressed entirely in reindeer fur, but they surely sit on it. And the tents of this nomadic people will consist of birch-pole frames with reindeer-skin canopies pulled over them, and more skins stuffed into the gaps to keep out the draughts.

We eat reindeer schnitzels in Alta's little airport restaurant. Dark meat – very tasty – and surprisingly expensive. There are antlers all over the walls – reindeer, naturally. 'We should be able to wrap up here in two days,' Mario tells me. The publisher who has commissioned the film is not after an in-depth scientific documentary, rather a series of glimpses of different places around the world, all featuring Mario as their (well-paid) hero. (To be fair, he incurs a lot of expenses in the process.) It is to be a publicity film, and, as such, needs to be as colourful and multi-faceted as we can make it. I call it the Magic Carpet since – besides taking Mario and me 30,000 kilometres, halfway around the globe – it must be woven in stripes of white, green and red – ice, jungle, and, perhaps, desert. Mario wants it finished as soon as possible . . . whereas I wish it could go on for ever. It seems such a pity to grab everything we need here in only two days. I so much wanted to reach the North Cape, to see more of the country . . . but to picture Mario with a herd of reindeer and a Lapp or two, whether I like it or not, cannot be blown up into a big production. Already, I envisage the first strip of the magic carpet: white, with black polka dots, like a punch card, or a spotted cravat . . . the dots being the reindeer, of course. I cannot resist a sigh at an enterprise more Laputan than Lappish.

Lunch over, Mario asks our host, 'Where are all the reindeer around here?' Instead of the prompt reply he was expecting, the man scratches his head reflectively before announcing at length that we would probably do best to drive to Karasjok. 'You're bound to find some there. It's a Lapp town . . . and all the animals belong to them.' A town? With houses? Well, we shouldn't be surprised: time does not stand still anywhere. We'll just have to find a way of rustling up a few tents from somewhere. Fancy having to drive more than 200 kilometres for the nearest guaranteeable reindeer herd! Mario pulls a sour face, but I am jubilant. Aha! I tell myself. See how it is: an Italian in Norway expecting to see lots of reindeer is no different from the American tourist thinking he'll find everyone wearing chamoix brushes in Austria and Lederhosen in Bavaria. Maybe I'll get to the North Cape yet, who knows? Except, of course, that Karasjok is in the opposite direction, almost on the Finnish border. Our host observes that if only we had landed in Lakselv, we would now need to drive just seventy kilometres. What's the odds? We need a rental car anyway. And soon we find one: an old black Beetle, somewhat rusty. 'You'll find two winter tyres and chains inside,' the car's owner tells us.

'We'll not be wanting those for just 200 kilometres,' Mario remarks under his breath, adding, 'I used to be a test-driver, you know.' And we were off!

Piles of snow everywhere, the road itself is really wintry. Mario drives like an Italian in summer. This must be what you call an occupational hazard, I think to myself and hang on grimly.

But soon I understand: Mario really can drive. Even with summer tyres in winter. I still have a lot to learn about my companion in adventure. So, how do you make small talk with a test-driver? 'I was with Ferrari,' Mario explains laconically, and lets the car glide round another bend. Hills are passing by, cloaked in birch saplings, all sticking out gauntly from the snow, and finally there comes a flat plain. The road is dead straight and Mario steps on the gas. He is a true artist, and I tell myself you should never begrudge an artist. Soon we have covered a hundred kilometres – halfway – and all I hope, as Mario begins telling me chapters of his life's story, is that we don't encounter an icy patch . . . What did I learn about him? Everything has slipped my memory, but for one moment. And that I see and hear as clearly as if it was happening right now: Mario had just remarked that test-driving was only one episode in his professional quest for adventure,

The Magic Carpet

'There was that business with Walter Bonatti . . .' he says, pausing for dramatic effect at the very moment we start a slide towards the edge of the road. Oooop, over we go, plunging down in a cloud of snow. We can see nothing, seem to be swimming . . . I cling to the doorhandle, feel a blow on my knee – and that's it – we have stopped. Silence. A rather exaggerated dramatic pause our storyteller made there, but he appears completely unmoved. 'These things happen,' he continues after the interruption; I, meanwhile, rub my bashed knee. We are stuck in deep snow, some six metres from the road.

I don't answer.

'Won't have done the car any harm,' Mario comments. 'German workmanship.'

'You're sure of that?' I grind my teeth, still hugging my knee, tempted to remark that while the car might be German, it's the bloody Italian stuntman's work that has brought us to this. Better to swallow it. At least we have not turned over. As we eventually scrabble our way out, I enquire wearily whether many of Mario's test runs proved as demanding as this.

'Oh, much harder,' he assures me. 'This was just a minor derailing – come on, put your back in it, push!' That's never going to move, I think, as I strain against the vehicle. And nor does it. The car will not budge an inch. We are stuck.

I am just wondering how we come to be having such bad luck on the very first day of our trip, when I notice the '13' on the car's number-plate. Usually I consider that my lucky number – have done so ever since making the thirteenth ascent of the Eigerwand. (Even when it later turned out to be the fifteenth!) At least, we can now be sure of an extra two days in Scandinavia! Thoughtfully, I regard the car: everything depends on how you look at it – even the number 13 . . .

Mario hunts for a shovel in the boot and, failing to find one, swears, '*Porca miseria!*' I am still weighing the mysteries of numbers – can any number be luckier or unluckier than others? A superstitious pessimist would have no doubts that was why we came off the road. I am just about to ask Mario whether in Italy test-pilots regard 13 as a good or bad omen when . . . tuck, tuck, tuck . . . across the solitude of this wintry landscape comes the welcome chug of a tractor. It is our lucky day after all! Apart from two snowploughs and five cars, we hadn't seen any other vehicle since we started. We beam delightedly at the tractor-driver as if he were the Redeemer himself . . . Mario jabbers away in Italian and English, I, at the same time, in German – but anyone can see what has befallen us. The man shakes his head, winks, clucks his tongue and mumbles something we, in our turn, cannot understand.

Spirits of the Air

Eventually, he clambers from his vehicle and produces a length of rope. I suppose he must be used to this sort of thing. Within minutes, the Beetle gently breasts the surface of the snow – leading its cloven wake like a swan on Lake Constance – and is returned to the road.

Mario drove on with considerably more caution, and in the small town of Lakselv we stopped to put on the winter tyres. Clouds covered the sky, engulfing everything in monochromous grey. We were still surrounded by thousands of birch trees. This was an incredibly lonely landscape, yet one of haunting beauty. I still could not get over how we had stepped from Italy's summer into this deepest of deep winters. Such abrupt transformations throw your feelings into havoc. We were in boisterous spirits, one adventure behind us already, and all the time drawing nearer to the enormous reindeer herds of Karasjok. Every so often I would peer concentratedly into the murk, to see if I could make out any of the animals yet.

Then, all of a sudden, after a bend in the road, the village materialised ahead: small houses, a neat red-roofed church, people. Not a reindeer in sight, anywhere. An old man was sitting on a stool beside a pile of antlers, carving . . . Taking a deep breath, we approached and enquired, with the liberal aid of sign language, where all the animals were. The Lapp smiled, reordering the crinkles on his friendly old face; sometimes nodding at our gesticulations, then he waved expansively towards the open landscape . . .

Not here, did he mean? Not now, or not at all? We pressed him again. The gesture was repeated with more precision. He pointed to the north, saying something that sounded like 'North Cape'. The reindeer were certainly not here: that much was clear. They were either at the cape or on their way there. Mario's face darkened for a moment, while I showed no emotion. Then, shrugging, my friend conceded: 'I guess that means we head for the North Cape. Come on.' Two hundred kilometres, and a ferry ride! Oh, Lapland, Land of Reindeer!

Just then, a small boy, who had been called over by the old man, tugged at my sleeve, pointing up the road . . . Full of expectation we followed him to a courtyard, where there really was a reindeer! The only one in all Karasjok, but here only because it was sick – so we understood from the many signs and words of a kindly Lapp woman in a red bonnet. I was ready with my camera to film Mario, the ailing reindeer and the helpful woman with her round and friendly face. But he would have none of it: 'It's not what we want at all,' he snapped, and his short hair appeared to bristle even more than usual. 'Come on, let's get out of here!'

Karasjok had indeed proved a disappointment – for Mario. Soon, we

The Magic Carpet

were racing along again at test-speed. Back towards Lakselv, where we had just come from. For it was clear that we would not reach the North Cape that day.

Honningsvog. Colourful houses, red, yellow, green, even blue, overlooked the grey, wide expanse of fjord, surrounded by rounded rocky hills. The mirrored images of the ships danced a weaving pattern of broken lines and colour-splashes on the water's surface. The ferryboat, which had brought us to this island of Mageroy, was tethered to the jetty. A Norwegian we met explained to us that the reindeer were able to swim across this narrow strait separating the island from the mainland. With dismay, we learned that they had done so only a couple of days ago and were now roaming somewhere in the mountains of the island. We might be able to find them, but only with luck on our side. We had simply arrived a few days too late.

So better reconcile ourselves to a longer stay: getting up into the snow-covered mountains with the cameras and all our paraphernalia was not going to be a picnic. And, anyway, where should we go? Where would the reindeer be hiding? Even if we found them, they were not likely to hang around till we got close with our cameras.

A German, I thought wryly to myself, would certainly have come better prepared than my happy-go-lucky Italian friend. A German would surely have contacted the appropriate local authorities beforehand . . . would never have found himself in a predicament like this. But Mario – I understand that now – likes to drop from the sky. He is an adventurer to the root of his soul. Later, I learned to admire him for his art of improvisation. His reaction in this instance was to assert, 'We'll work something out – with the help of these three bottles of cognac I bought in Copenhagen. Not to worry.' It's not that reindeer have a taste for cognac, you understand, but the Lapps might prove a different matter. In Norway, with its strict alcohol regulations, and where almost half the population moonshines, Mario's proposal sounded perfectly plausible. Especially since the Lapps surely wanted to catch their reindeer sooner or later, and knew well enough how to do so – I had no doubts about that. The problem was that so far we had not found any such Lapps.

That was the situation when Mario and I started for a small walk along the coast. We did not take our cameras, we were just stretching our legs, not expecting to find anything. It was night-time and very still, not a person on the road, but – of course – it was not dark. Here we were, just ten kilometres from the northernmost point of Europe, the North Cape, already well inside the Arctic Circle. Some readers will know from experience that when you first visit this area, you hardly shut an eye during the bright nights. The best thing, then, is to get up and do something positive, which is how Mario and I came to be walking along the coast, pondering Item 1 on our agenda, the reindeer problem. After half an hour we turned a corner to discover a small bay. The sloping shore on the other side shimmered in the twilight, a gleaming stripe punctuated with black dots. What's this? The punch-card strip of the magic carpet? It was! Almost exactly as I had imagined it!

'The reindeer!' Mario yelled at the same moment. We hugged one another, then speeded our steps. As expected, there was a Lapp close by – and we soon arranged with him everything for our filming.

However, the nearer we drew, the more peculiar this herd seemed. Strangely immobile. 'They are never reindeer!' Mario let out a curse, *'Porca miseria!'* And he had a point: the herd turned out to be . . . a graveyard. Nothing but identical dark headstones in the snow, with some coloured plastic flowers between, invisible from a distance. It seemed an inauspicious omen.

'Isn't it time we gave up on this story?' I suggested to Mario.

The two brothers were called Jakob and Knut. They lived with their families in a pair of low houses behind a hill above Honningsvog – and where they lived, the mountains began. Not big mountains, archaic stumps, smoothed and rounded by the great glaciers of the Ice Age. Ideal for ski-tourists and, of course, reindeer. Jakob and Knut would be happy to take us to the reindeer, or – if we preferred – the reindeer to us . . . which would take perhaps two days.

The brothers already had an enthusiastic gleam in their eye when I met them; Mario had spoken to them beforehand. 'This time, we really get the animals,' he whispered to me with a knowing nod. There was one bottle less in his box.

Ratta-tat-tat! The skidoo went racing over the slopes, leaving a rippled furrow like a miniature bulldozer track. Not a good comparison, perhaps: a skidoo, which is no bigger than a motorcycle, is no lumbering load-carrier, but swift and highly manoeuvrable. Ratta-tat-tat . . .

Lapps in houses, on skidoos, rather than living in tents and riding small, shaggy horses? Let us not dwell on that: this is no time for nostalgia – which of us, in the Lapps' position, would not seek to improve his lot? Luckily, one of our new friends spoke a smattering of German. Did they still have any horses, I wanted to know. 'Just two,'

The Magic Carpet

they told me. I could see how difficult it would be logistically to make a film about the way the Lapps used to be, and it was fortunate that was not our aim. A small 'expedition' was put together: two motor sledges (the skidoos) with crew (the brothers), two long low regular sledges, which would be hitched to the motorised ones, a dog who barked delightedly at the prospect of going into the mountains, and, of course, Mario and me. On to one of the sledges we packed the tripod, one big camera in its metal suitcase, fur skins and other material; the second carried tarpaulins, ropes (which later turned out to be lassos), food, more fur skins and dry birch branches. The power with which those two motor sledges finally pulled all that weight over the slopes was impressive. Mario was in high spirits. He had been watching the younger of the two brothers, Jakob, romping around on his skidoo before hitching the transport sledge to it, and he couldn't wait to try it for himself. I must say, it was spectacular. Jakob at once detached the heavy sledge, apparently honoured at our interest, and proceeded to give an acrobatic display with all manner of tricks. He even jumped the skidoo several times over a snow cornice. Mario, beside himself now, was desperate for a turn, but Jakob would have none of it. Hence, I still cannot tell you, even today, how a Canadian skidoo (for that's where they are made) would stand up to an Italian 'roadtest' . . .

The low sun bathed the slopes in soft light. It was a highly romantic atmosphere. Gold and purple clouds stood high in the sky, while below – in what strange contrast – the young tearaway roared his machine across the wastes.

Several kilometres to the west we could now see a peninsula reaching far out to sea before falling away abruptly in a sheer cliff. That must surely be the North Cape – I remembered it from pictures. Jakob rehitched the transport sledge to the skidoo and we moved higher up the gentle mountainside for a wide view over the sea and surrounding bays. Pulling to a halt on a broad flat patch, the two brothers gave us to understand that this would make a good campsite. They would take a skidoo in turn and go in search of reindeer, while the other waited here with us. Even if it irritated Mario and me to be left out in this way, it was clear that the Lapps would be better able to approach the animals without us. How long was it likely to take? Were we going to bivouac here for a whole day, perhaps? We tried to find out. But Jakob, the brother who could speak some words of German, explained to me that he did not know the answer – but here was Knut to stay with us. Then he leapt on to his skidoo and – ratta-tat-tat – made off at speed until he was nothing more than a tiny dot moving over the next hillock.

Knut now did something which seemed very peculiar to us: he began unloading both of the transport sledges. Why was everything to come off? We gave him a hand, without knowing what it was in aid of. He took one sledge and, with a single move, upended it in the snow. Then he did the same with the second, tilting it a bit so that the curved front-runners could be locked into a slot on the other. Immediately, we understood and at this point were impressed how simply and efficiently this Laplander was setting up a shelter – a solid wooden 'house' in a couple of easy moves! He adjusted the angle of the first sledge, so that not even a storm could dislodge it. (Was Don Whillans inspired by Lapps, I wondered, when he designed his famous bivouac box?) Already Knut was tugging a tarpaulin over the prepared framework. I had never heard of such a fantastic and simple invention, nor could I be sure even whether all Lapps knew of it.

Knut now clothed the floor of our little 'house' with reindeer skins, arranging them also up into the outer corners so that, in the end, the only snow you could see was a little in the entranceway. Meanwhile the light was fading. It was cold and humid and we were happy to crawl into the welcome warmth and snugness of the furs. The three of us fitted comfortably inside. Knut lit a small fire in front of him with a little bundle of birch twigs, taking care not to singe the furs. Soon its heat and smoke filled the enclosed space. We were lying on the ground, out of the worst of the smoke, which was drifting up through a hole in the roof. This accomplished, Knut yawned and uttered something which sounded like, 'So . . .' He looked first at Mario, and then – with a significant wink – at Mario's rucksack. And Mario, clearly picking up the signal, opened his bag, where I was surprised to see the other two bottles of cognac. Knut either knew this already, or had deduced it from the chinking of glass. For a while the reindeer were forgotten – we left them to Jakob as the first bottle circulated. Knut was taking the most touching care of us – and the spirit. He even prepared hot tea for everyone, laced with cognac. True we could not speak to each other for, unlike his brother, he knew no word of German or English. It did not seem to matter: we smiled at each other warmly, and when the silences became too long, saved ourselves from embarrassment by offering each other another sip from the bottle. The atmosphere became increasingly relaxed until, finally, I fell asleep. In my dreams thundering herds of reindeer flowed by, like seething waves, thousands of animals with immense, nay, truly gigantic antlers . . .

Ratta-tat-tat! The brother had returned. Reindeer? Well, he hadn't found them yet, but – and he beamed in at us, passing a handful of eggs through the entrance, beautifully speckled, black and green – he did

The Magic Carpet

have a pretty fair idea where they might be. He indicated into the distance before – ratta-tat-tat! – disappearing once more.

Knut smiled pensively. Should we have scrambled eggs with cognac, or make advocaat? Mario was snoring. Before anyone could come to a decision about the eggs, brother Jakob returned – ratta-tat-tat! He'd found the reindeer! Knut sighed. I shook Mario awake. The dog, curled in the snow outside the tent, also came back to life. It was all systems go! We crawled out of the shelter on all fours. I searched for a good place to set up my tripod, somewhere with a good field of vision, then, with a Hey-oop! hoisted the heavy camera on to it. Knut, panting, fished out his lasso, and at Mario's request donned a peculiar three-pointed hat, characteristic headgear of the Laplanders (though not, we were told firmly, when catching reindeer). Then we waited, breathless with tension.

Before long we see them coming! There, along the skyline and the gentle curve of the next hillock. They appear, one by one, so many, then more and more – all these reindeer at last! It is a Fata Morgana, a vision! No, it's real – they are there, the reindeer we have been searching for for days! A fairy tale . . .

I do not have to dream them now! In fact it's imperative that I don't dream at all. I must be wide awake now, make sure to do everything right; even the ground under my feet seems to be heaving (damned cognac!). Already I am picking up the deer in the long lens, am pressing the button . . . Now they are coming into the reach of my zoom. It looks fantastic as they draw closer . . . the midnight sun gilds the slopes all round and every animal casts a long shadow. Some have antlers, others not, some smaller deer – babies, they must be – move in between. It is difficult to describe them: the slowly approaching herd is so much part of this northern landscape. The brown fur of some of the animals echoes the rocks which randomly stud the smooth, snow-covered hills; the mild grey of shadowed snowslopes and the pale hue of the northern twilight are all reproduced in the fur of others; and in their profusion the deer are at one with the constantly recurrent forms of this landscape, with its harmony – it could be a painting . . . Kurt! Concentrate! You are here to film: action! Now, behind them, Jakob has appeared on his motor sledge, keeping his distance. He glides carefully in low gear closer to the animals, sometimes approaching from the left, then from the right. Close to me, I notice Knut, who has just begun moving towards them, too, with slow careful steps, the dog at his side, lasso in one hand. He keeps stopping and standing perfectly still. Mario stands a short way in front and to the side of me, since he is required to appear in at least one scene. Now the reindeer have stopped. They have apparently recognised Knut, who approaches them now without difficulty. A sudden swift move of his arm and the lasso hisses through the air. Some animals leap backwards, but, incredibly, the swaying figure of Knut has caught a reindeer at his first attempt! I am amazed that the other reindeer are not running away, but maybe they are used to this sort of thing. Meanwhile, I have already run out a lot of film, and I am really only missing a wild 'storming herd' sequence. But will I ever get that? Sooner than I think, as it turns out . . . Mario, all six feet of him and more, now makes his own gentle move towards the animals. But he must appear as some sort of monster to them, for the Lapps, who they are accustomed to, are a small people. Anyway, all of a sudden, there is a stirring in the throng and before we know it, the whole herd begins storming away! Drumming hooves, the sound muffled by snow, bodies streaking, head to head, horn to horn, passing across my lens – a beautiful shot! I keep pressing the button, eyes glued to the viewfinder, following them through the zoom and the tele-lens . . . Photographs? I have none. Not a single picture. How can you film and take pictures together? Impossible, as many readers will know from their own experience.

It was a fine and unexpected end to our game of Blind Man's Buff across the Arctic Circle. And Knut and Jakob kindly set us up a real Laplander's tent later on, nearer to their home. It was made of birch trunks, covered in reindeer skins, and the whole family came and sat inside. The children had a lot of fun – and so, too, did we, even if this was not, by a long chalk, as original as the brothers' traditional 'Whillans box' we had experienced the night before. For a long while the two families waved their goodbyes to the backs of the two strangers, as Mario and I, burdened with reindeer skins as well as our gear, returned to 'downtown' Honningsvog.

On the drive back to Alta, I have to say, three times reindeer jumped across the road! They are everywhere and nowhere . . .

I took home two skins, which I'd purchased from Jakob and Knut – one dark, the other white. Ever since, the house has been filled with wafting hairs – so many, they must outnumber all the reindeer in Scandinavia!

The next destination for our magic carpet was Newfoundland, followed by the 1000 kilometres of Labrador's coastline. One day I find myself

The Magic Carpet

sitting opposite an Eskimo, staring into a hole in the ice. He has cut it in the frozen sea on which he is standing. The line in his hand moves up and down, up and down as he waits for the next fish. And another, and another . . . Endless patience. Again, I have the feeling of having reached the edge of the world. A different edge . . .

It was a pity we could not stay longer. Soon it was on to South America.

Friendly Margherita

OUR BRUSH WITH AN ANACONDA

Whether she was really friendly or not is anybody's guess. For Margherita was a giant snake, strong, supple, six metres long, and as thick as a man's thigh. I jumped to the conclusion that she must be warmly disposed towards us simply because she had not crushed Mario in her coils. Admittedly, he was more than one third of her length – but, I mean, to any self-respecting boa constrictor, fresh from the jungle, he should have represented no more than a warm-up routine in her early morning work-out. Don't run away with the idea that I wished Mario any harm – he's a friendly enough character himself – though when I later discovered that my partner in film was getting sixteen million lire from our Italian producer, and I only one, then sometimes I thought . . . (well, maybe it is not necessary to tell all that one thinks) . . . just leave it that now and then fantasies would erupt in my mind, in which the friendly Margherita assisted me in putting the squeeze on Mario . . . I realise I am wandering off the point.

We were in Lima, lying on our beds in the Hotel Crillon, somewhere on the seventeenth floor of that skyscraper. Mario was telling me of his adventures with Walter Bonatti in the rainforests of South America: about the Indians, and an encounter they had had with some harlequin-coloured little frogs, which he only afterwards learned were the ones used for making lethal arrow poison . . . and how Walter Bonatti narrowly escaped being crushed to death by an anaconda.*

'By the way,' continued my companion, 'we will be needing to catch a giant snake of our own – they want us to film with one.' He said this as if it would be as easy a matter as going into the woods for a kilo of mushrooms. I did not answer immediately: this was the way Mario had dropped surprises on me before . . .

'Is it that easy to approach a giant snake?' I enquired at length.

---

* There are known cases of anacondas swallowing fully grown Indians (Grzimek's *Tierleben* (Animal Life). Whilst anacondas can reach a 'guaranteed' length of 8–9 metres, a boa constrictor only grows to 4½ metres according to all the books. Our 6-metre-long 'Margherita' belonged at any rate to the family of the boa snakes, even if it might have been another kind of anaconda. The animal dealer in Iquitos said it was a boa constrictor.

Friendly Margherita

'No problem at all,' Mario assured me. 'The Indios bring them out of the forest all the time. A friend of mine, Pedro, can get us one easily.'

'Where does this Pedro live?'

'In Iquitos, on the Amazon.'

'Send him a cable, then, so that he can reserve a fine specimen for us.'

'No need, Professor,' (that was my nickname from Mario) 'when we get to Pedro's he'll have an eight-metre anaconda for us within half an hour. No tame one, either, one just brought in by the Indios. We'll take it off into the jungle for a couple of days, let it go, then film it being caught again.'

'And who's going to catch this snake?'

'Me,' Mario replied airily.

Cheers, then, mate, I mutter to myself, knowing we're in for some fun and games. Better watch out!

EQUIPADO CON RADAR it says on all the Peruvian airline planes, making them sound reassuringly modern. Even so, the aircraft are not always as reliable as this device suggests – that is, if one is to believe Mario, who is tightening his seat belt at my side. 'Another one disappeared in the jungle, only recently,' he tells me with relish. What, I wonder, is the radar for, then? These aircraft have to cross the Andes to get to the Amazon from Lima.

Below us, the dark red desert coastline slips away, then come isolated snow peaks, rugged rock faces and deeply cut valleys, a wild mountain area, the highest points of which are all six-thousanders. The further east we go, the more clouds pile up, increasingly filling the airspace above the endless green canopy which shimmers up at us through vaporous cottonwool. Down there, rivers loop like snakes – we catch the glint of water among the greenery, and spot little ox-bow lakes, cut off from the main stream. The clouds through which we are flying – we are reasonably low – are constantly transfigured by marvellous rainbows, half and full circles. 'The Ucayali!' Mario calls suddenly, pointing to the bends of a big river, one of the headwaters that feed the Amazon. 'Soon we'll see the Marañon as well,' he continues. 'Bonatti and I tried to navigate that from its source – but we didn't make it. We took a bath.' A thousand kilometres lay between Lima and Iquitos. Shortly before we get there, the two headwaters join. If you include the length of the Ucayali, the Amazon is 6518 kilometres long. It is the greatest river of South America, the third largest on earth, and having the most extensive catchment area of all the rivers in the world.

We land on the small airfield of Iquitos in a violent cloudburst – within a few minutes we are soaked from head to toe. But, almost immediately, the sun shines again. Mario locates Pedro without any trouble, but he returns with a long face. 'There's been a cock-up with our snake,' he murmurs. 'Pedro says everything went with an animal shipment a few days ago. We have to find our own – I must have one at least eight metres long. It doesn't matter if it's a boa or an anaconda.' Drenched in sweat, we repair first to the hotel.

A full day is spent traipsing around, sometimes wet, sometimes dry – between one cloud and the next, from one animal dealer to another. Iquitos is the main settlement of the Peruvian Amazonas area. Ships keep docking, navigating the giant river without difficulty: it is 1800 metres (over a mile!) wide here.

Besides tourism, rainforest animals are an important source of income. It is incredible how many we see in a day: exotic fish of all kinds, circling in their aquariums, some big, but mainly an infinity of small flashing jewels – as if nature had overturned a treasure-chest, animating all the gems through some magical process. There is the squawking of hundreds of colourful jungle birds. Monkeys swing with grotesque twists of their limbs. A spotted jaguar hisses and jumps furiously against the bars of his crate. Fluttering on the outside of a big cage of birds with red shining head-feathers are others of the same species – trying in vain to get in . . . the sad consequence of human intervention with the freedom of the forest; here at the jungle's edge – because Iquitos is an island of civilisation – all these creatures face deportation. Do they sense that? All of a sudden I seem to feel the invisible shadow outstretched above so much colourful vitality. Our snake – I promise myself – will regain its freedom afterwards!

So far, however, we have no snake, neither boa nor anaconda. 'Too small,' Mario says every time an animal dealer shows us his best wares: pompously striped, patterned with curves, eyes, tangled lines, the markings seem to convey a hint of the immense power of these snakes. However passive they might look, is our two-man team equipped to cope with one of these creatures? Mario – the chief player (and in my thoughts, I already see him wrestling a writhing anaconda!) – and . . . well . . . me? I remember the Saint-Exupéry sketch of a well-satisfied boa, who has just swallowed an elephant, whole: the elastic-sided snake looks like a domed hat, viewed from the side, the brim on one side representing the tail; and that on the other, the snake's head, which is relatively small. It is left to your imagination how so big a meal passed through such narrow jaws: the jungle is full of secrets . . . Would a whole film team fit inside a boa? Or, having swallowed the larger of its

Friendly Margherita

two components, would the snake remain sated for the next few weeks and merely sleep? At least, I have never seen an 'Exupéry-hat' with *two* bumps . . .

But the jungle, as I said, is full of secrets.

'Mario,' I ask prudently, 'if I choose the right lens, couldn't we make do with a four-metre snake?'

'No way! She has to be eight metres,' insists the 'dominant half' of our film partnership. I sigh, but then calm down: at any rate my partner, with all his extra height, is going to seem the 'better half', in the snake's eyes also!

Finally, we found her: A BOA CONSTRICTOR. She was asleep, and measured six metres. Her body, at its thickest, you could not encircle with your two hands – but her head was no bigger than a dog's. She had wonderful markings, extending all over her scaly body, and Mario, well content, purchased her. The dealer assured us that she had just eaten a couple of mice. She really looked satisfied and peaceful – and I was about to put Saint Exupéry's 'hat' from my mind, when I remembered the saying, 'One swallow does not a summer make'. Nor do a couple of mice fill a hat! But then, I said to myself, a snake from the Amazon could not possibly know this European proverb.

'Let us call her Margherita,' said Mario. Then we went down to the harbour to Pedro's home.

Our boat divides the earth-coloured waters of the giant river. Above the green stripe of jungle on the opposite bank, which passes monotonously by, black thunderclouds build; here, in midstream, the sun strikes the boat with full force, but we do not notice it. We have a shady roof above our heads. Our craft is a primitive houseboat, which we have hired together with its three-man crew – dark-skinned locals, darker by far than the dark, earthy river, and dressed in an assortment of faded, well-worn garments. Pedro, Mario's friend and our manager, is *mestizo*, the colour of his skin considerably lighter than that of the others. He has cultivated a small moustache, of which he is obviously very proud; his sunburnt face with the dark eyes is usually half hidden below a wide-peaked baseball hat – now he has lifted the brim. I can more or less understand his Spanish; he has just told me of a giant fish, very rare now. It looks like a monster and the local hunters kill it with a harpoon. Its name is the Paiche; I had already heard about it from Mario. Hunting this beast has so far never been filmed. The legendary predatory fish is very shy. Nevertheless, you can often find its exquisite

Spirits of the Air

scales, which can be as much as five or more centimetres in diameter, and prized here for necklaces ... usually strung with colourful seeds and snail shells. The bony tongue of the fish was – perhaps still is – used as a file by primitive Indian tribes. But the Indians hunt the Paiche mainly for its meat. It can reach four and a half metres and weigh as much as 180 kilos. To catch it, with just a harpoon, must be a violent and dangerous adventure. Will we ever see that fish? Now, the most important passenger on board is doubtless our Margherita! She is tied in a big jute sack, and unless you knew she was there, you would think we simply had a harmless load of sweet potatoes. It is understood that nobody will sit on that bag ... So, Margherita, are you still asleep?

All of a sudden, behind the boat grey bodies flash from the water, describe a majestic circle in the air, and disappear into the splashing flood, again and again, playfully. 'Dolphins,' says Pedro. 'You often see them here.' Five thousand kilometres from the mouth of the river where it flows into the Atlantic Ocean, here are tumbling dolphins! At the same time, entire islands of uprooted trees and water plants drift towards the distant ocean. The water plants have bright lilac flowers, which reminded me at first of periwinkle, but they have large bubbly airsacs and can, as I noticed during a rest ashore, continue to grow

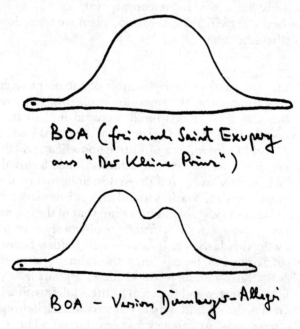

Boa according to St Exupéry and the Diemberger-Allegri version

Friendly Margherita

perfectly well on firm ground. A whole carpet of bladders and blooms cover water and land . . . An amphibious plant, tailor-made for this mighty river, with its ever-changing water levels and extensive floods. Later on, a botanist will tell me that these are water hyacinths and they exist in many places across the world.

We travel well into the dark, through sunshine and pelting rain – most of the boats we encounter have roofs like ours. When we spot the glow of fires on shore, we tie up. Hospitable Indians allow us to pass the night with them. Dog-tired, we spread our mosquito nets above the wooden grille which forms the floor of one of the huts, all of which stand on four poles. As I slide into sleep, I still feel the continuous rocking of the water, and my heart glows at the sensation of shelter under a friendly roof, of people in the forest.

For three days we go upriver, following first the Amazon, then a smaller tributary, the Rio Maniti; our target is not only to film this snake, but as much as possible of its natural surroundings as well. Once here, on the Maniti, we do not meet any more boats and the walls of the forest on either side have crept closer. They have accepted us between them. In the evening we hack out a small space with our machetes, light a fire and sleep in hammocks – inasmuch as one can sleep amidst the multitude of animal sounds. It is like a living curtain descending and enfolding you into itself. Given several more pages, I could perhaps attempt a description, but it really would not help; I could never capture the unification of this flood of nocturnal sound, its *togetherness*, neither its synchronisation, nor the rhythmic, monotonous way it rises and falls in intensity. And this strange sensation of being part of it all.

It takes possession of you, courses through your veins, puts every fibre of your being under tension. Nowhere in the world is life created so abundantly, nor exists so closely together as here in the rainforest. Death is an ever-present constituent, but in the face of this thousandfold prodigality it has lost its horror, simply because here everything lives; death is only a smile, which in the moment of fading is already being born anew.

All my senses are alert because in the forest, so full of dangers, you are never permitted to dream. You need to be able to react quickly, to understand so much; it is a confusing world, one which needs your full consciousness to comprehend it. Even the apparent calmness of the forest people masks their ever-present vigilance. The dreaming, the smiling, the feeling at home in the jungle is a gift, but one which is offered to nobody from today to tomorrow.

Spirits of the Air

A quick brightness invades the sky: the day returns, as suddenly as it went. In between lay eternity.

In the morning Pedro tells me that Margherita woke up, but a couple of mice had quickly pacified her. Our silent companion in the big jute sack would seem to be of phlegmatic disposition – so I think – but Pedro assures us the boa will become lively enough as soon as we open the bag at the forest margin. Several Indians will be needed for the safety of the film team, and we should choose a spot carefully, where the giant snake can be easily recaptured.

That day we arrive at a little Indian village, its huts standing on stilts in a clearing of the forest by the river's shore. On the opposite bank are two further pile dwellings, near where we land. Pedro knows the old headman here, and after a warm welcome, it is obvious that this is where we'll stay. Mario hopes also to be able to film crocodiles, and whatever else might turn up. We see a crocodile for a short while the next night – but not with a camera; Pedro, who feels obliged to shoot at everything, does not hit it, luckily. Instead, with two shots, he brings down a thorn-pig or tree porcupine from the top of a forest giant: the animal splashes into the water only a short distance from Pedro. It is a doubly valuable trophy with its spines of more than thirty centimetres long – like black knitting needles. The 'pig roast' which the chief's wife prepares next day tastes great, despite the sinister fact that without its spines, the animal closely resembles a baby. It takes a great effort of will to bite into this grilled infant.

But you get used to it. Some things the Indians consume never cease to revolt you: bird-eating spiders, as big as a man's hand; ants with fat honey-yellow abdomens; and creepie-crawlies of various kinds . . . The ants taste of earth, and the spiders – well, I only managed to nibble at one leg; they are considered delicacies, but obviously I have not yet spent long enough in the forest. Porcupines from the grill, I can recommend, however, notwithstanding their appearance! The same goes for another speciality which from now on becomes our daily fare: fried piranhas! These notoriously bloodthirsty little fish still bare their teeth on the fire as if they wanted to strip an ox to its carcass, but of course they are harmless in this state. Even in the water, they pose only a limited threat – limited to the concurrence of blood being spilt. Given that, it is true everything happens with lightning speed: hundreds of little jaws with their razor-teeth snap and snarl, the water boils . . . and soon only the bones of the victim are left. Even so, I cannot conceal the fact that on this trip up the Maniti, and later too, several times I saw Indios bathing without fear in the forest rivers. Mario swam across the

Friendly Margherita

Rio Maniti and for a long time in the middle of the river eagerly struck out against the flow. But Mario, well, is Mario. He is not to be put off by crocodiles or piranhas – whereas I prefer to keep a tight hold of the side of the boat whenever I cool myself in the river. I do not let my bare feet touch the bottom if I can help it, and never take off my bathing suit, having been warned by my companion about two unsavoury inhabitants of such waters: one is a fish which lies around on the riverbed and you run the risk of stepping on its poisoned spine; the other – covered in sharp bristles – deliberately seeks out orifices in the bodies of larger animals, in which to enter as a parasite, and from which it is almost impossible to extricate as its points are barbed like a harpoon.

You can take it from me that it had to be really hot before I let myself slip into the water.

Next day, we head upstream in a dugout canoe; we have been told of a little lake nearby, and Mario wants to see if we'll be able to shoot our giant snake scenes there. This is a tipsy form of travel, and you have to pay some attention to equilibrium. In front of me an Indian is crouching with a short paddle, behind me sits Mario, and then Pedro, who also has a paddle. For some days the Rio Maniti has flooded its banks, enabling us to travel the whole way to the little lake in the canoe – even across the rainforest!

It becomes a strange journey.

Sometimes Pedro points to one animal or another which has saved itself by clambering into the high branches of a tree. Mostly, you can recognise them only by a sound, or movement. The treetops, and indeed the different layers of branches, are worlds in themselves, and after we leave the river and penetrate the drowned forest in our canoe, this becomes even more obvious. We zigzag between dense vegetation, then high tree-trunks. There is no noticeable flow, and everywhere smells of mud and the rotting leaves which are drifting on the water. I am filled with apprehension: even as a tenderfoot in the forest, I recognise how abnormal it is to be canoeing right across the forest floor like this. Besides gliding so mysteriously through the magic world of trees, you are moving in a different perspective, too, from at ground level. More than once I am tempted to ask the Indian in front of me to stop as we pass within reach of one of the fantastic red orchids with their darkly gleaming flutes, sitting on what would normally be the high branches. . . But it is just a whim; he passes by unmoved – to him it's just an everyday thing. The water is getting shallower and the tree formations sticking out of the water become increasingly bizarre. Indeed, can you still call such contorted figures trees? There is no word for this multitude of tangled roots and trunks and stems, all from the same plant, holding each other in tight, inescapable embrace, as if the participants in a wrestle for life and death had suddenly become frozen by a spell. Colourful orchids and ferns peek from the crooks and hollows. Aerial roots dangle down, and lianas . . . our dugout slides silently amongst these 'sculptures' – that is what they seem to be – groups of entangled Laocoon figures in ever-changing permutations, reminding me of the unsuccessful struggle of the father-priest and his sons of Greek myth, enmeshed by snakes. Sometimes the water gurgles gently at the dip of the paddle – the mirages of the tree-figures start to move and dissolve . . .

In front of us appears a clearing: the lake! A circular surface, surrounded by the walls of ancient forest giants, black water, like a lead mirror. All around it is still. Beside the boat, where the sunlight falls into the water, a transparency of dark brown to olive green dissolves into the black of the depths. You cannot see the bottom, and no animals are moving in this water . . . A sinister black hole.

Suddenly a swarm of parrots, with hellish squawking and whirling wingbeats, flap like beginners across the gap in the forest . . .

Mario decided this place was not suitable for our film. I had no objection. On the way back the man with the paddle sitting in front of me – speaking through Pedro – told us that a friend of his had died here recently, and he pointed vaguely to one of the twisted tree-sculptures: he was just ducking below the invasive canopy of leaves, when a little snake bit his head and it was too late to help him, it was a very poisonous one . . . The Indian's tale went on vividly, and all of a sudden Pedro laughed, explaining to us, 'The man did not suffer very much – he was drunk.' When I think back, I do not like this day at all. But that is how it was.

Finding a suitable location for the film turned out to be difficult, but then luck stepped in. At the edge of the clearing a new house was being built – that means a couple of poles had been erected with two cross logs fixed between. These provided a platform where our helpers could keep guard while Mario attempted to catch the snake below them.

On the day in question, even he seemed uncharacteristically tense and thoughtful, more irascible – not his usual prankish self. He knew that at the critical moment he dared not stumble, knew that the snake would only be subdued if he succeeded in grabbing it with both hands just behind its head, and pressed firmly. Until this moment, he had to beware at all costs of getting into an embrace! A bite from the reptile would hardly be worse than that of a dog – but a clinch could spell death. Why such a giant snake loses most of its force if you succeed in getting the correct grip around its neck is a puzzle to me. But all snake handlers know the trick. And what Mario needed to help him was a

Friendly Margherita

long, forked stick. He quickly cut himself one from the forest with his machete. I would also keep one of these sharp knives within reach during the ensuing film session; if things went wrong, I could enter the fray – and fast! That such swift assistance might be necessary was understood by the Indians as well. Even though they are accustomed to catching anacondas and boas from time to time, it doesn't always work out to plan – a man on his own is a weak opponent to a giant reptile!

I set up the big camera on its tripod about one and a half metres above the ground on the slatted wooden floor of a hut close to the one that was being built. I was four metres away from the ominous jute bag, lying now at the side of one of the new house-poles. From where I stood, I hoped to catch the whole scene with my zoom lens, secure a good overview from obliquely above and still be able to follow all the details of the action. In emergency I could easily leap down and weigh in with the machete – or, preferably, with my hand camera. Of course I felt some sympathy for Mario – at that moment he seemed a true hero to me, the essence of courage! And the sixteen million lire of his contract no longer seemed such a giant sum; safely atop my wooden grille, I felt quite content with my million. It is amazing how completely a metre and a half of extra height can change your perspective!

Not that you could say, of course, that you were really in a safe place up there: boas and anacondas are agile climbers and often found in trees.

The closer the moment approached, the more the white space of sky above the clearing seemed to disappear. The chattering of the natives died away. Even the forest itself stepped back . . . all my concentration was focused on what would happen in front of me.

It was the same for Mario: we had discussed all the eventualities and clearly knew what had to be done. Three Indians were sitting on the cross-tie of the new house. They would pitch in only once Mario had succeeded in locking the head of the snake in his special grip – he had hoped they might have been on the ground sooner, but they refused. Pedro was standing with a machete in the shadows behind another hut, ready to rush to assistance . . . We could start!

An Indian slowly and carefully loosed the string of the jute bag . . . and disappeared behind the next hut. The bag was lying so that its opening faced the forest and Mario.

For some seconds nothing happens. Then the brown fabric starts to move: evidently Margherita has noticed the glimmer of light penetrating the darkness of her prison. Slowly, hesitantly, she pushes her head into the open, as if dazzled by the brightness of the day.

Spirits of the Air

I watch Mario: his face has frozen to a mask, his black eyes fixed, immobile, his glance nailed to the slowly emergent boa five paces in front of him. He has crouched forward slightly, like an animal about to spring . . . in his right hand he holds the two-metre pole with its forked end. Margherita suddenly stops. Has she noticed Mario? A forked tongue appears and flickers several times in front of the brown head with its shiny scales, licking the air above the ground. It is as if she is checking for hidden danger, and warning anybody from preventing her return to her forest. Mario still arches forward like a statue, 'frozen' in the sticky heat, sweat running down his face, eyes rivetted on the motionless snake. In the shade of the hut's roof, I too am bathed in sweat over my whole body – from excitement, from heat, from the effort of filming, from the concentration on what was about to happen next.

All is still and I can feel everybody holding his breath – even the Indios on the log; suddenly Margherita's decision is clear: with an agility and speed I could never have credited to a giant snake, she shoots towards the forest, not by the shortest way, but in a sideways loop, to outreach Mario . . . already I see her escape!

But Mario is not to be caught offguard: with a quick bound he blocks her path, standing in front of her once more, ready to thrust down the raised forked stick . . . And Margherita? Without hesitation, she adroitly changes direction, in a way which makes it impossible for Mario to realise his intention: her head slides back over the coils of her body, so that if Mario were to dive for it now, he would surely be caught in a suffocating grip. His situation has become unexpectedly tangled – taut and tangled in every sense of the words! He circles the sliding spirals at a respectful distance, yet close enough to take advantage of the moment when Margherita, in whatever direction, makes another break for the forest . . .

The boa has become slower now. Or is it simply an illusion caused by the many overlapping, overlooping coils of the scaly body? Now, at last, the giant snake must have understood that Mario is her enemy . . . more than a mere obstacle on her way to the forest . . . slowly, she now slides directly towards Mario, whose face betrays that he has understood . . .

Does he falter? Will he keep his nerve? Step by step, he retreats slowly and I see his hand clenching the stick so tightly that the knuckles have gone white – obliquely beneath me I hear the rustle of a sudden move as Pedro draws in from the side, but my full concentration is with Mario: he has lifted the forked stick and brings it down with all his force. Into the sand. He has missed the snake's head! The reptile makes a sudden

Friendly Margherita

move – Mario pants, he has lifted the stick again, I see how he trembles with tension in this uneven duel. He knows that he is not allowed another mistake like that! Again, he thrusts down – and this time he gets the fork exactly above the neck of the boa, nailing the head of the mighty animal to the ground. The six-metre scaly body starts to wind like a giant screw – a terrible sight . . .

Everything then followed at such flashing speed that it is all but impossible to describe it in sequence. A confusion of events, simultaneous, one after another and overlapping between: I see how Mario, hand over hand, comes down the stick as quick as a flash to the head of the snake. There comes a rough yell, from Mario or Pedro I cannot tell which. The Indios slide down from the log. Mario, having successfully secured the neck of the snake, now grips the boa tightly behind her head and, with all the strength of his arms and fingers, presses as hard as he can. He holds her head sideways now, half a metre above the ground. The Indios collect the still-writhing spirals of the reptile – but it is as if the energy behind the immense power of the animal has vanished under Mario's grip. Working in fours, the men now drag the snake to a large basket. I draw breath, but mentally only, because my filming goes on – it is truly unbelievable how the men succeed in stuffing the coils of the thick body into the basket, beginning at the tail. At last, Mario, with one swift gesture, tosses the head in on top of the giant skein – he had been holding the boa 'in grip' all this time. Swiftly, the lid is slapped over the wickerwork and tied securely. To me, it is inexplicable why such a strong snake does not simply burst or bite through a jute bag or a basket. But Pedro has repeatedly assured me that, cut off from daylight, these animals immediately curl up, as they would in nature in a hollow tree. Nobody has ever thought with the mind of a snake. I take a breath. Mario sinks exhausted on to a rush-mat: he is running with sweat, marked with strain.

'You did that well,' I tell him.

He nods and pants. After a pause, he suddenly says, 'And you? Did you do your bit well?'

The events of the last ten minutes flash past my mental eye. Exciting scenes, certainly an enthralling story . . . but every conscientious cameraman knows that you can never have enough material; such a truth one should not hide, not even in the case of a giant snake . . . 'Fantastic scenes,' I reply, seeing Mario visibly relieved, then – after a pause – I add, 'All the same, I could do with a couple of close-ups with my hand camera.' Silence.

'Are you serious?' Wide-eyed, Mario looks at me as if I'm a lunatic.

'You can never have enough material,' I insist, according to my conscience, and then I add with a benevolent voice, 'You can rest for a while!'

What Mario thought I don't know – at any rate, in the end he said, 'Okay, once more!'

Secretly, I want to add, at the back of my intention was the hope that Margherita might this time perhaps succeed in reaching the forest. I did not expect Mario to prevent her with the same resolution as before. But I was wrong: Mario subdued the snake a second time with his special grip! This time I was really close with my hand camera, 'skin-close'. Nevertheless, it all went so fast that I still needed one more take. After that, we were all exhausted. And poor Margherita? She had gambled away her third and last chance of freedom.

We stayed on a few more days in the jungle. We filmed the Indios, orchids, and several other things. Finally, we returned to Iquitos.

And Margherita?

Despite my protestations, Mario had presented her to the Indios as a gift. They killed and ate her. Mario said, 'We would have committed an unforgivable sin in their eyes if we had let her go.'

One of the laws of the jungle is never let yourself fall into the power of another.

I know this story of Margherita could have ended differently. Perhaps in a zoo in Europe, if we had brought her back to Iquitos. In those circumstances, I think what really happened was better. But why did we not let her go somewhere on the way back?

She had been promised to the Indians – and, once more, the rules of the humans prevailed over the rights of the animal.

It would be a pity not to tell how things went on with Mario . . .

We never did work together again. Not because of any flaws in the films we made. Well content with our success, we returned to Milan after our magic carpet had carried us 30,000 kilometres around the world. But there was a big catch to Mario's next project: not that we were supposed to spend a day with crocodiles on a sandy islet in some African river; nor even that on Kilimanjaro I was temporarily to pass my camera to my companion and perform a stunt as the star of the show – the script requiring one of us to fall over the edge of a snow or ice face (not to the bottom of course, we could use a rope. That was more

Friendly Margherita

my department, Mario said. It would be better for him to hold the rope). No, the real snag was that at the very start of the journey Mario wanted us to penetrate the Danakil Desert of Ethiopia. This, he hoped, would bring us into contact with an unchanged aboriginal tribe with some pretty strange habits. He had some telling photographs of women wearing necklaces made from the highly prized 'noble parts' of enemies of the tribe. This, I have to confess, did not endear these people to me. It may well be that they had now abandoned the practice, as was said, or that none of their trophies had ever come from Europeans . . . but it was enough: I had the uncomfortable feeling that my beloved Arriflex was not all I might lose there. Bloodthirsty stories abound in Ethiopian history: it is said that during the Abyssinian War some 3000 Italian prisoners were emasculated! Of course, that was a good while ago now, but even in 1969, when I traversed the highlands of Semyen just to the west of the Danakil, we heard from a very reliable source of one such act of revenge at the end of a fight between two locals. Mario, intrepid to the core, made out that his ruling principle in life would be compromised if he did not attempt to seek out this tribe, but by the time I had come to terms with the idea, and wanted a contract to cover all risks, Mario became suspicious. It rubbed him the wrong way, and when our wives then entered the argument, he became even more furious. One day I heard he was about to leave with a different partner. It wounded and grieved me, but I rang him to wish him good luck, even so.

Mario and his companion crossed the Danakil Desert, were captured at one stage, but got free again. Destiny caught up with them on Kilimanjaro, where they were forced to bivouac in a terrible snowstorm at almost 6000 metres. The end was bad – not for Mario, he has nine lives, but his companion had to be flown back to Europe with very severe frostbite. Mario called off the rest of the journey.

One fine day I was sitting in a pizzeria in Rome with Carlo Alberti Pinelli, a film director who wanted to visit the Indians at the source of the Orinoco River. Turning round, my eye was caught by an unusually lengthy corduroy suit, topped by a small rounded head. The man had his back to me, but that bristly haircut . . . the ostrich! It was indeed Mario. We had a pizza together soon afterwards and Mario told me that he was planning very shortly to parachute into the rainforests of South America. He believed he had finally discovered the lost city he had been hunting for so long. He said this with that same nonchalant smile with which he had once told me we were to capture a giant snake. It must make some difference, I think, if your grandmother comes from the Mato Grosso.

Perhaps I should add, by the way, that both of us ordered a Pizza Margherita.

Montserrat

ON THE PUDDINGSTONE WITH
JORDI PONS AND JOSE MANUEL ANGLADA

'The serrated mountain' was how the practical Catalan farmers described these saw-toothed hills, long before scientists understood about the effects of erosion. Not a romantic name, perhaps, for such an outstanding work of nature, a composition of forms and figurines, shapes and silhouettes, unique in the world. Clusters of tall beings with curiously rounded heads, like a giant puppet show, some dormant, others in wild movement, all frozen to the spot by some mighty and irrevocable command.

The Romans built a temple to Venus here, the love goddess. And Catalan shepherds discovered a mysterious black Madonna in the year AD 880, which became the patron saint of all Spain. For more than 1000 years this place has held deep religious significance. At the bottom of a long row of rocky figures, there is a road leading to the monastery, whose church and the black Madonna are important sites of pilgrimage. Archaeologists think Montserrat has been a sacred place since primeval times. These strange and patently phallic rocks could have held only one meaning for our ancestors: a manifestation of the eternal creative force which maintains life on earth. A pagan fertility spot, no less. And so mystical, so holy, that its significance has transcended religious evolution, and even today, young couples – Catalans and other Spaniards – still come from far and wide to be married here, that their union may be blessed and fruitful.

To the climbers of Barcelona, of Manresa and other places around, the giant puppet theatre is a wonderful playground. What a joy, to hang between sky and earth as if amid the invisible threads of marionettes, what a lark to be played with gravity!

At first glance you would think the rocks of Montserrat were nothing but a mass of hand- and footholds, but a second look reveals that all the little rugosities are rounded, that hardly a grip is to be had on any of the violet, white, grey or brown pebbles which make up the reddish conglomerate of the mountain. This is 'puddingstone', resembling nothing more than a well-crammed cherry cake. And if, sometimes, with two or three fingers, you are able to gain temporary lodgement in one of the holes where a 'cherry' has fallen out, the general verticality or convex nature of the compact rock, and above all those rounded pebble-holds, demand an acute sense of balance and superlative finger strength. Moreover, the last resort of banging in a piton when free climbing fails, is scarcely an option here: the conglomerate is far too dense for that. Who climbs at Montserrat needs a thorough mastery of his craft, and a rock-solid nerve. No wonder the area enjoys an international reputation in the climbing world.*

I could not help but be reminded of this requirement for steely nerve all the time on my first visit, inching my way up a vertiginous wall, my fingers clinging to two pebbles in airy space, the tip of my boot perched on another pebble, while with my free foot I groped for some 'cherry hole' in that perpendicular cake. All around wafted the marzipan-sweet smell of acacia, waves of it welling up on the breeze from the foot of the rock towers. Hey! Another pebble! The sun was beating down, and the rocks reflecting the heat, as I fingered my way higher, surrounded by a landscape which Picasso might have designed. Climbers were calling each other from one hundred-metre puppet, 'la Bola', to another, just slightly lower, which resembled an oil bottle: or from the tip of a giant finger which held aloft an 'Easter egg' of many tons in weight (how long had it balanced there?), to a comparatively small cube, which none the less still occupies the space of a sizeable house.

'*Aixo es el Daiet – lo vuoi provare?*' says José, my companion, half in Catalan, his mother language, half in Italian, knowing I understand that better, and he laughs as if at some great joke. Then, he explains in German, his eyes twinkling with roguish fun as he indicates down towards the house-sized cube, that this Daiet goes by the innocent name of the *Würfelchen,* or 'nice little cubelet'. Did I want to try it? And still he grins all the while as if trying to conceal something.

Well, why not, I think, and agree. At this moment we are standing atop the rounded head of the Bidglia, a skittle-pin some eighty metres high, and the petty cubelet down there fails to inspire me with great respect. And of course to my partner, the well-known expedition mountaineer and international businessman, José Manuel Anglada,

---

* Later I learned that even here some people have drilled straight up-and-down lines of bolt-holes. Spattered with artificial anchorages practically anything becomes possible, and such gloriously fortuitous 'puppets' are relegated to little more than designer climbing walls. Of course, a number of extreme and interesting moves will be created, but at what cost? Of destroying a mountain's identity.

whom you can often find climbing on these walls with his wife Elli, or with the film-maker Jordi Pons, and who of course naturally himself got married in the Church of Montserrat, certainly to him this cube should not represent any big deal. He has made a number of first ascents around here.

As we stand in front of it, the cube does look a little more commanding. 'É un buon quinto,' José winks, 'it's a good 5:1 or more!' and he approaches one of its facets. 'Not at all easy,' he adds, groping for the first hold. 'A friend of mine came off here recently,' and he raises his eyebrows, nodding emphatically. 'Two weeks in hospital, it cost him. He fell the full length of the rope; landed, luckily, in the bushes. But you met him, yesterday, didn't you, at your lecture?' Already he is hanging by one finger, and stuffing the next into a hole above, then, maintaining the tip of his suede boot on a small white pebble, he wriggles and winds himself higher in serpentine fashion . . .

'Ah, mmm,' I answer, watching carefully – and recall the guy with the plaster cast. José is climbing in shirt sleeves and braces, easily, fluently, seeming to put no more effort into it than a stroll in the woods. But he is all attention. The hospital . . . José's braces seem to bounce, he'll be up in no time . . . It is true, I think to myself, people who wear braces usually exude spirit, humour – and security – even on the vertical walls of Montserrat. But it may well be just that the owner of the braces was called José Manuel Anglada, and I was reacting intuitively to that. Anyway, it helped to know that the braces were above me at that moment, and I was not required to lead this pitch. I chewed over the problems of the cherrystone wall, and eventually worked my way up it.

Anglada looked at me with a crooked smile, 'So, how do you like our cubelet?'

The climb that I long for, even today, is a thirty-metre sphere, perched upon a sixty-metre pillar. That I covet. I would love to stand on its top, but it has never happened. Something always got in the way. But perhaps, after all, it is always politic to retain an unfulfilled wish at all the best places life offers.

Spain is one of the best places that I know. A wide, open country, full of colour, a harsh beauty. The sky above the Meseta's immense plains seems closer, and the clouds (if there are any) lower in the blue than elsewhere; I remember pale desert areas and meadows full of red poppies, and I return often to the Basque country – as green as our Austrian Styria. It feels familiar and yet different. The songs of the Basques, their yodels and dances, these I treasure, and the feasts we have enjoyed together. And the hours in the mountains, in Spain as further afield with Mari Abrego or Josema Casimiro on K2 and Everest. I can see the round, near-Styrian face of Patxi, President of the local mountaineering club, and hear his calming 'siempre tranquillo' amid the wildest, most rumbustious revels and at blow-out 'banquets' in high places protected with barbed wire . . . When it comes to calmness, only 'little Pedruccio' surpasses Patxi. The whole world seems to revolve around his prodigious form (well over a hundred kilos!). Only his wife is exempt from this revolution: she, too, weighs more than a hundred kilos. Together, these Basque stalwarts are what we in Austria would call 'true human souls'.

Home is not simply that place or country where you were born, or lived as a child. It widens . . . and as life passes, your roots penetrate the ground in a number of places. This becomes both a gift and a burden. The more and better you understand, contentment and longing become your inseparable companions.

I am sitting on the boulders beside the pier in Barcelona harbour. The waves approach, break and retreat . . . and my thoughts wander far beyond the sea . . .

PART III

Hindu Kush — Two Men and Nineteen Camps

THE TACTICS OF A MINI-EXPEDITION

Mountaineering expeditions these days almost always have a definite summit in mind. Accordingly, all their planning is directed towards climbing it. If the peak happens to be in the Himalaya, the Karakorum or the Hindu Kush, then they are restricted to the terms of a permit, which must be obtained in advance from the government concerned – Nepal, Pakistan, China. They are obliged to keep to certain areas and named peaks. The small but extended Hindu Kush enterprise which Dietmar Proske and I undertook in 1967 was an altogether different proposition. In the first place, there were just two of us and we were not, officially, an expedition, but simply travelling as 'sporting tourists'. Secondly, in spirit, this was a wide-ranging foray involving climbing and reconnaissance. For Dietmar, it was his first experience of the mountains of High Asia; I had been three times already and, besides, knew the Hindu Kush from an earlier, similar journey to the mountains of Chitral. However, since my first visit to the Tirich area, things were beginning to change and to be without a permit now could land you in big trouble. This was the end of the era when you could climb wonderful peaks and explore unknown valleys without asking anyone.

In some ways, I consider this mini-enterprise to have been my most successful expedition. Hermann Buhl's alpine-style thinking, with which I became familiar on Broad Peak and Chogolisa in 1957, had left its influence on me. The concept, I believed, could be expanded to apply to a whole mountain area.

I do not intend a full narrative of events, but want to demonstrate, by means of a compressed expedition diary and a sketch map, the complete comings and goings of our trip, with its repeated setting-up of camps (and depots) for our various objectives. On top of that I will endeavour to give the thinking behind the preparations we made for all this activity to show how a small two-man expedition with multiple aims can work and, depending on circumstances, could be repeated. Of course, there were times when Dietmar and I had to make the best of our situation, and times when luck played no small part in the outcome – but then, on any trip, you will always need some luck.

Looking north from Chitral – the main settlement in the area of that name in north-west Pakistan – you see the shining snows of Tirich Mir, high above the valleys. This mountain massif is the highest in the Hindu Kush, a range that includes several 7000-metre peaks. Tirich Mir itself is 7706 metres. Like a bastion, the massif thrusts south from the main spine of the Hindu Kush which forms the boundary between the Wakhan in Afghanistan and Chitral in Pakistan. On closer inspection the bulk resolves into crests, groups and single peaks, embracing mighty glaciers. Glacial tongues push out even into the barren brown mountain valleys to its east, south and west.

The second highest peak of the Hindu Kush, Noshaq (7492 m), and also the precipitous Istor-o-Nal (7403 m) are both linked to this system of crests, which encircles the multi-branched Upper Tirich Glacier like a framework. This glacier is essentially the heart of the area.

It is not surprising that the seven-thousanders of the Hindu Kush and other fine peaks of lesser height in the area captured the interest of climbers, albeit relatively late. Not until 1960 was it possible to launch attempts on the main range from the Wakhan Corridor – that narrow strip of land bordering the Oxus River, and created as a sort of *cordon sanitaire*, a buffer zone between two areas of political interest, two empires, the Russian and the British-Indian. Well before this, however, British officers, maintaining the Gilgit Frontier, and surveyors explored the mountain world of the Hindu Kush from Chitral, which then came under British influence. And as early as 1929 and 1935 there had been attempts on Istor-o-Nal by British officers, although it was 1955 before an American team reached what it thought was the summit.* On Tirich Mir itself an attempt from the Owir Glacier in 1939 led by Miles Smeeton was accompanied by the twenty-five-year-old Tenzing Norgay, but the first ascent was achieved only in 1950 when a Norwegian expedition led by Arne Naess approached from the south.

* The real first ascent was made fourteen years later by a Spanish team. See Adolf Diemberger's article in *Himalayan Journal* 29. My father was fascinated by the rugged mountains of the Hindu Kush, becoming eventually a specialist on the range, even though he had never been there!

Hindu Kush

When, in 1965, with Herwig Handler, Franz Lindner and my wife Tona, I pushed beyond Istor-o-Nal to the heart of the mountains of the Upper Tirich Glacier, we were pioneers from an alpinistic point of view. Only Reginald Schomberg before us had made a geographical exploration of the area in the 1930s.

We found ourselves entering a wide glacier floor within what could best be described as a circle of mountains, beginning with the Tirich North group to our left. From where we were standing, the long southerly arm of the Upper Tirich Glacier continued up towards the pre-eminent Tirich Mir, bypassing the granite castles of the Tirich West group. Rising beyond this glacier arm, to the west, were the white peaks of the Ghul Lasht Zom group, almost in front of us. To our right, Istor-o-Nal, with its steep flanks and flying buttresses, bounded the outgoing (eastern) stream of the glacier, which finally dispatched its meltwaters through the broad U-shaped valley of the Tirich Gol into the main river of Chitral. (This river changes its name from stretch to stretch: here it is the Mastuj.) A further arm of this intricately branched glacier system extended up between Istor-o-Nal and its close neighbour, Nobaisum Zom; another, in a wide sweep, flowed from the foot of the southern flanks of Noshaq and Shingeik Zom. The Anogol Glacier (yet another branch) derived from the watershed between the Tirich basin and the two Gazikistan glaciers to its west. I wondered if, in the old days, people used to cross a pass here, down into the Arkari valley?

We christened the confluence of all these sidestreams of the Tirich Glacier with a name borrowed from a similar, but more famous landmark on the Baltoro in the Karakorum, Concordia or, as we preferred it, Konkordiaplatz. Our 1965 expedition was crowned not only with the first ascent of the 6732-metre Tirich North, but of three further six-thousanders in the nearby Ghul Lasht Zom group. We also gained some remarkable scientific results: Tona, a geologist, did the preliminary research for the first geological map of the area. We discovered enormous intrusions of granite in the dark slates (which turned out to be Paleozoic); they had forced crystalline dykes into the sedimentary rocks which had once been an ancient ocean bed (we found fossils in some places). Beautiful minerals formed from this conjunction of rocks lay everywhere around: black-rayed 'suns' of tourmaline and rose-coloured flakes of mica, shimmering like silk. My heart, like Tona's, quickened at such fantastic finds – after all, had not my own path to the mountains begun as a young rock-hound so many moons ago? Alpinistic objectives apart, we could see there were geological enigmas in plenty awaiting resolution: clearly, a return visit was called for. Two years later I managed to come back.

But this time everything was different. Whereas before we had been the only people on the Upper Tirich Glacier, now, in 1967, the Tirich area was attracting the attention of many mountaineers. Two strong expeditions penetrated the southern branch of the Upper Tirich Glacier, one behind the other: Czechoslovaks, under Vladimir Sedivy, and Japanese, with K. Takahashi as leader. Both intended an attempt on Tirich Mir from the west (this would be a new route: the Norwegian first ascent in 1950 had been via the South Ridge).

Also busy in the massif was an Austrian group from Carinthia, led by Hans Thomaser. They wanted to open a steep route on Tirich Mir from the south-west, from the Dirgol valley. The leader and his companion died during the summit attempt, and it was not until 1971 that a Japanese team succeeded from this direction.

A three-man party from Salzburg exploring on the Upper Tirich Glacier, our area, included my friend Kurt Lapuch. This group climbed the North Peak of Istor-o-Nal; and Kurt and I stood together on the first seven-thousander of my Austrian Hindu Kush Reconnaissance, 1967. Technically, I was a one-man expedition – as lightweight as you could get – but I should quickly add that another solo party, the German Hindu Kush Reconnaissance, 1967 – namely, Dietmar Proske – was active at the same time. The two of us had made separate plans to come here, although we agreed to travel together. Not knowing each other beforehand, it seemed prudent to remain basically independent, leaving each of us free to team up with other parties or make solo ascents. In the event, apart from a couple of days, Didi and I were always together and the collaboration worked so happily that you might just as well consider us a two-man expedition.

And our goals?

One strong reason for my coming back was because the West Peaks of Tirich Mir, still untouched by man, beckoned along the southern branch of the glacier. Beautiful, wild seven-thousanders! There in 1965 we had cast the first exploring glances into the far reaches of the Tirich Glacier – and, not least, at the West Face of Tirich Mir. In consequence, Didi and I hoped gradually to penetrate this east-curving glacier arm, and climb several of the surrounding peaks in the process: in particular we set our sights on the beautiful pyramid of Dirgol Zom (6778 m) and one or two of the Achar Peaks – a silhouetted crescent of six-thousanders which separated the western rim of the Upper Tirich Glacier from the deeply cut furrow of the Arkari valley, 3000 metres

52. The South Face of K2 seen from Broad Peak North. Though the upper slopes are still foreshortened to some degree, the various sections of the mountain are seen in more comparable scale from this high viewpoint. Of particular note is the steepness and size of the upper part of the peak

53. K2 from Skyang Kangri. The North Face is in profile on the right, with the steep upper slopes of the Abruzzi route on the left (scene of the Diemberger/Tullis fall). *Photo: Gakushuin University Expedition*

54. Hermann Warth climbing Shartse in 1974 with Lhotse Shar in the background (pages 689-681). The author saw this as the start of a grand Everest traverse, a futuristic enterprise that remains unattempted.

55. *(above)* The North Face of K2. The 1982–1983 attempts took the central ridge (pages 344-360).

56. The author climbed Gasherbrum II *(right)* with Fayazz Hussain in 1979 – his fifth 8000m peak. The slightly lower Gasherbrum III *(left)* is notable as the highest summit (also the world's highest unclimbed peak) where women made the first ascent (Wanda Rutkeiwicz's 1975 Exp.). *Photo: Ewa Abgarowicz*

GREENLAND

57. *(left)* During the first traverse of the Qioqe Peninsula in 1965 (see pages 288-308).

58. *(lower left)* Umanak Fjord – a fisherman's boat works through icebergs.

59. *(right)* A member of Alfred Wegener's 1930/31 Expedition crossing the frozen sea near Umanak (see pages 709-728). *Photo: Diemberger collection.*

60. *(right)* Mario Allegri and Kurt Diemberger (proudly holding the box containing his newly acquired Arriflex camera – "it cost the same as the fee I received") setting off from Milan in 1959 *en route* to Lapland. This was the first of a number of film/reportage trips they made together (see pages 637-663). This marked the start of the author's professional film making, a development that was to change his life.

61. *(left)* A youthful Diemberger on an early lecture assignment in Vienna. His multi-lingual skills have since allowed him to become one of the world's most active and entertaining mountaineering lecturers.

62. *(lower left)* During a Polish lecture tour – at the offices of the Polish climbing magazine *Taternik*, the author poses with his wife Teresa (centre) – a Bologna lawyer. On the left is Wanda Rutkeiwicz, their host and long-standing friend, who became one of the most experienced mountaineers in the world before her sad demise high on Kangchenjunga in 1992.

63. Exemplars of two generations of Himalayan and Alpine achievement: Kurt Diemberger with Reinhold Messner outside a bar in Kathmandu. Even though they hold different views they remain on good terms and frequently collaborate on matters of mutual interest.

V.I.P.s MEET CLIMBERS

64. Members of Ardito Desio's Karakorum Survey Expedition (to re-check peak heights) with Pakistani leader General Zia ul Haq in Islamabad in 1987. Professor Desio and General Qamar Ali Mirza (head of the Pakistan Alpine Club) are right of Zia, with Agostino da Polenza and an Italian Embassy official on the left. The author stands behind Polenza.

65. San Francisco's Mayor, Diane Feinstein, with her husband Dick Blum, with the author and fellow film-maker Mike Reynolds *(left)* in 1981 prior to their departure on the American Everest East Face Expedition. Their film later won an Emmy Award.

below. It goes without saying that we also hoped for the chance to climb Tirich Mir itself – either by a route being pioneered by the big expeditions or, better still, a new one of our own. To our dismay, as I said, bureaucratic difficulties had arisen since 1965: the Pakistani government now demanded an official expedition permit for Tirich Mir. We wondered if, perhaps, it would be possible to ride on the coat tails of the Czechs or Japanese. We had no wish to upset the government, but my oh my! Tirich Mir was a most beautiful mountain . . .

What about the other peaks? No problems, there: as 'sporting tourists' the authorities in Peshawar had granted us a fine permit, rubber-stamped to allow us to fish, roam freely so long as our wanderlust held out – including in snow and glacier areas (be it noted!), and to explore possible ski areas (they said this would be good for tourism). I took it that we could also climb all those peaks which were not on the special list prepared by the Ministry of Tourism as requiring the standard expedition permit. But what peaks these were was for us then a matter of conjecture, and we were wary of asking too many questions. Unfortunately, everyone knew that Tirich Mir was an official mountain . . .

This, then, was the transitional period, with many things left open to individual interpretation. Were we an illicit enterprise? No, no, God forbid! Even so, there was the risk of surprises: my friend Gerald Gruber, a geographer from Graz and a dedicated Hindu Kush hand, found himself one fine morning in a village where the local police would not allow his porters to go on. He had to call off his exploration. That is why Didi and I treated the liaison officers of the big official expeditions with the utmost respect. Twelve years later, in 1979, linked by friendship and a rope to our liaison officer Major Fayazz Hussain, I would break trail for many hours with him through the deep snow of an eight-thousander to share the joy of a summit success on Gasherbrum II. But in 1967, Didi and I could not bank on such harmony, nor hope that our happy-go-lucky wide-ranging (and, we hoped, high-reaching) sporting activities would be seen as a reasonable interpretation of our special permit. Hence, we hesitated before accepting the invitation 'Please come for tea' from a liaison officer down at the bottom of the Tirich Gol valley. That is to say, we accepted, yes, from the safety of our inaccessible glacier world, but then had to postpone the date, over and again, because of 'sickness'. We strung it out until we had 'hooked' all our 'fish' . . . In the end I did 'come for tea', but from the other direction, up-valley, having fulfilled my wish to encompass the whole Tirich Mir massif.

Spirits of the Air

NUDGING ALPINE-STYLE A STEP FURTHER

Back to our plans! I wanted our climbs and exploration to include the opportunity to collect more rock samples for widening the geological map; I developed a special interest in the Ghul Lasht Zom group, because the old *kammkarte* of the area to the north of there, towards the Anogol Glacier, was definitely wrong. Also, the southern peak of that group, a six-thousander, was still virgin – the only one we had failed to bag in 1965. And incidentally, what was on the other side of the Anogol – could you climb down there?

So far, nobody had ever succeeded on the South Face of Noshaq. Nearby soared the virgin and nameless P6999 and you could elevate that to a seven-thousander with your own body. Aims upon aims, possibilities without end . . .

Ever since I was on the Baltoro Glacier with Hermann Buhl, I have been committed to alpine-style, even when, as on Dhaulagiri in 1960, I could not put it into practice. (The oxygen at least remained unused on that trip.) What handicapped us in achieving multiple alpine-style successes in 1957 were the many miles of moraine rubble and glaciers over which all the necessary gear and food for other mountains would have needed to be carried. But given the acceptance of a multitude of targets from the beginning of an expedition – and accepting, too, the premise that in the Himalaya all alpine-style mountaineers employ porters to help get gear and food to their Base Camp below the mountain – then it is clear what should be done: create an appropriate depot system at the outset.

As I said, in 1967 we had no shortage of aims or possibilities capable of being realised by just two climbers in alpine-style. The term nowadays is usually only applied to the *ascent* of a mountain; for us, it included exploration and discovery as well. To explore more than one massif, and include successful quality climbing, you have to push the style even further. You need a network of depots for your intended camps, that still allows you the option of adjustment where necessary. The better you plan this beforehand, the less will land on your back later!

For our multiple targets, we required elastic planning. We only had a very limited number of tents: a couple of bigger ones for normal camps and a lightweight tent for moving around at high level on steep mountainsides – a Desmaison design with two vertical tentpoles. This latter gave us extreme mobility. We could proceed for days, setting it up night after night at a higher – or at least different – place, saving ourselves from dangerous bivouacs. Hermann Buhl and I had already employed such a 'wandering high camp' in 1957 on Chogolisa, his last climb: it represented the lightweight extreme of our *west alpine-style* (no high-altitude porters or oxygen gear for the climb), and corresponded to the purest alpine-style, even by today's definition. This dynamic climbing technique – often embellished with the term 'bivouac', although the use of the tent demonstrates it cannot be that – proves wonderfully effective as well for traverses of every kind, and for far-reaching exploration. We used our lightweight tent in making the grand circuit of Tirich Mir, and it was equally useful during the climb of the mountain itself, as well as on Tirich West IV, another seven-thousander, and the aforementioned P. 6999. It would in any case have been utterly impossible for us to set up a chain of camps, in the way that big expeditions do. In a sense, we got close to the 'capsule-style' concept advocated by Chris Bonington, the British master of strategy.

Our self-sufficient little team made frequent use of depots. We cached a duffel bag or an aluminium box with food and equipment on the Anogol Glacier; on the southern branch of the Upper Tirich Glacier; two such caches on the Konkordiaplatz; another on the North Face of Tirich West IV; and yet another below Noshaq; as well as several more. The addition of a tent to any of these depots meant instant transformation into a camp. Conversely, if a tent was needed elsewhere, returning a camp to a cache was equally simple. Even a reader inexperienced in mountain craft will see how flexible an expedition can be with the aid of such relay-stations. It is incredible how much distance can be covered when the layout of these stations follows a logical pattern.

In the course of our two months' stay in the Tirich area we only employed a single porter, Musheraf Din and, even then, sent him back to his village for a holiday every so often! It did mean a lot of carrying ourselves. There had been twelve porters on the march in; they deposited our gear in more than one place and the subsequent redistribution we did ourselves. Obviously, the honesty of the porters is an integral requirement of this system, but that was guaranteed for us by Musheraf Din and his people. No less important was the fact that the porters of every other expedition came from the same village – Shagrom Tirich – and Musheraf Din was their mayor!

But now: how to proceed? More precisely: how to extend the lightweight strategy for a chosen climb? In the centre of your field of action – for example where the southern branch of the Tirich Glacier flows into the Konkordiaplatz – you convert a depot into a main camp. (Alternatively, the necessary gear can be brought from the nearest cache, or from the last point of action. There's no danger that things might become too easy – you'll always find some load or other that needs ferrying! Logistics can never be that fail-safe, especially when you have a limited amount of equipment. Once, we were faced with gathering what we needed from three different spots.)

After setting up the new main camp, you add a small 'high base' at the foot of your desired peak, a miniaturised ABC (the Advance Base Camp of a large expedition). From there, you either start the climb in purest alpine-style, carrying just your lightweight tent, the 'ladder' of camps being reduced to a single mobile rung. Or, what is usually advisable, make a higher cache first, in order to reconnoitre before the final assault; and if circumstances or safety require it, to set up a high tent beforehand and start the 'mobile rung' climb from there. Common sense has to outweigh doctrine in the mountains – if you want to live to tell the tale. Whether and where to put a cache should depend on the situation. Tirich West IV (7338 m), this beautiful granite castle, was explored and climbed by us in this manner, taking seven days from the bottom. We chose a giant ice ramp and the north buttress for this first ascent.

During our seven weeks on the Upper Tirich Glacier we employed the following 'Base Camps' in turn: one at the foot of Istor-o-Nal (facing Noshaq and Nobaisum Zom); the next to the east of the Ghul Lasht Zom peaks; a third at the start of the southern branch of the Tirich Glacier; and finally a sort of permanent satellite in the remote AnoGol basin. Altogether we established nineteen camps, and once occupied the abandoned tent of another party.

This elasticity worked well: we succeeded on three seven-thousanders – including Tirich Mir itself (7706 m). The other two of them were first ascents: Tirich West IV and Nobaisum Zom (the freshly christened P6999, which we found to be 7070 metres.) And to these, we added four six-thousanders. It cost us a lot of sweat and on-the-spot reckoning.

As a tiny team to have 'conquered' – or rather, made ours – the mountains of a whole area and, ultimately, to have circled the main massif; to have succeeded on a row of beautiful peaks on the Upper Tirich Glacier, with remarkable distances to cover; and to overcome all the logistical barriers in the course of this mini-enterprise – that was an adventure which, today, fills me with more satisfaction than if Dietmar and I had climbed an eight-thousander somewhere else. Several hundred more metres of altitude are fine, – but taking everything into

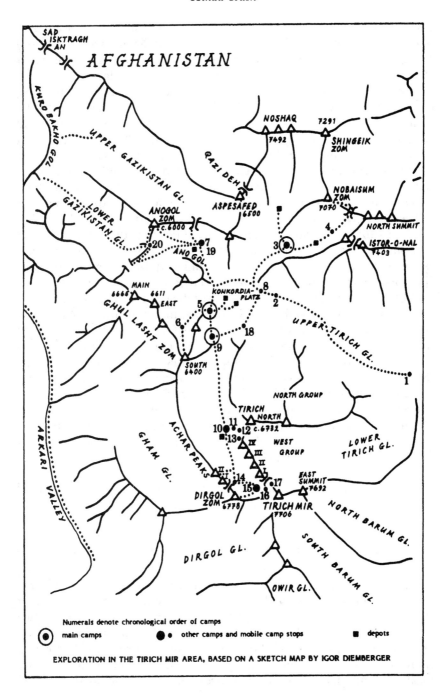

EXPLORATION IN THE TIRICH MIR AREA, BASED ON A SKETCH MAP BY IGOR DIEMBERGER

consideration, that would have been less interesting, less original – and much simpler! Reinhold Messner's Challenge, which he and Peter Habeler undertook on Hidden Peak (8068 m) some years later, produced a great climb that was widely acclaimed as innovative. But the principle had been enacted earlier – more than once, on 7000-metre peaks, whereas Reinhold's 'bivouacs' were practically camps: the highest offered a double-fabric silk and perlon tent and sleeping-bags. Reflecting on the summer Dietmar Proske and I spent in the Hindu Kush, the difference, it seems to me, was merely a few pitches of rope, given the fact that Hidden Peak only just exceeds the magic 8000-metre line and its logistical difficulties were nothing by comparison. Reinhold, for his part, drew a not so apt comparison between his climb and the first ascent of Broad Peak in 1957. His 1975 expedition, he said, required only a tenth of the total weight in equipment and food that ours had done. Moreover, he had not taken a doctor. I could not resist a smile at that remark, at least. But for the mathematics, we had been four climbers, not two; we had been utterly alone on the Baltoro Glacier; and moreover, it had been almost two decades earlier. How many changes had taken place in that time, in equipment alone! On top of that, Reinhold used twelve porters to get to his starting point – just as we did in 1967 in the Hindu Kush. Of course Hermann Buhl's *west alpine-style* on Broad Peak was heavier and less elegant than Reinhold and Peter's method of climbing Hidden Peak, but the revolutionary concept was *his* and crystallised soon afterwards in the purest alpine-style employed on Chogolisa and Skil Brum. On Hidden Peak, an old style and an old concept had been applied – without question in a brilliant way!

After this 'spiritual excursion' to the Baltoro, let us return to the relative quiet of the Hindu Kush. Three eventful months – a great time!

AN EXPEDITION JOURNAL

Dietmar and I met in early June to assemble the equipment. After three days the total weight of 500 kilos had been reduced to 420 kilos and strong rear-wheel shock absorbers fitted to the car. We drove for two weeks across Turkey, Iran and Afghanistan. At Dir, in Pakistan, we 'garaged' the car in what we hoped was a burglar-proof way by driving it on to someone's verandah up a ramp of planks knocked together by local men and then removed. We proceeded by Jeep for two days, hired donkeys for two more, then set off on foot with twelve porters to Shagrom and the Tirich valley.

Our objective was the Rhubarb Patch, known locally as Chur Baisum, where the Lower Tirich Glacier enters the valley of the Upper Tirich Glacier. The Lower Tirich is small and narrow, squeezed in between the North Face of Tirich Mir and the Tirich North group. This Rhubarb spot could be a good base for a first ascent of Tirich Mir's North Face!

The diary continues:

5 July Didi and Kurt pitch their tents some distance before the Base Camp already established by the Czechs.

6 July While Kurt is chatting in the Czech mess tent with them and their liaison officer, Didi, who has made an early start, passes with our porters. We march along the south flank of Istor-o-Nal to a spot shortly beyond called Nal, or Horseshoe. Years ago, according to the locals, one used to be able to take horses through from here to Afghanistan. Today the glaciers don't allow that.

7 July Didi and Kurt head on, turning right at the western edge of Istor-o-Nal to the northern arm of the Upper Tirich Glacier. This is where Kurt Lapuch's Salzburgers had their Base Camp for climbing the North Summit of Istor-o-Nal; they have now marched off to Shagrom. We set up our tents, and Lapuch arrives, following an invitation from Kurt. Nobaisum Zom (P6999) will be tackled from here by the two of them. After establishing a depot at Konkordiaplatz all porters except Musheraf Din are sent home. This depot will supply further depots to the south and west.

8 July Starting from Nobaisum Base Camp a high cache is established at 5800 metres.

9 July Lapuch and Kurt depart from Base Camp for their summit attempt and set up the lightweight tent at 6050 metres. The route for Nobaisum Zom will take the gap between this mountain and Istor-o-Nal, then follow the ridge to the summit. Didi makes a reconnaissance towards Noshaq – another possible objective of our enterprise – and sets up a depot.

10 July First ascent of Nobaisum Zom (7070m by aneroid).*

11 July Descent to Nobaisum Base Camp.

12 July Lapuch marches off. A little later a gigantic rockfall roars

---

* For me this was a hard struggle as I was not yet sufficiently acclimatised to such high altitude. In the same season (1967) Doug Scott, on his first expedition to Asia, was experiencing similar difficulties in the Hindu Kush in Afghanistan.

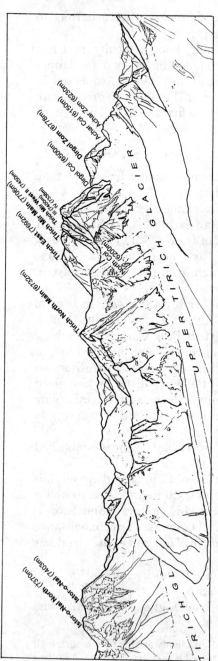

Sketch panorama of the Tirich Mir area from the Ghul Lasht Zom (NNW) by Josep Paytubi, from photographs by Kurt Diemberger

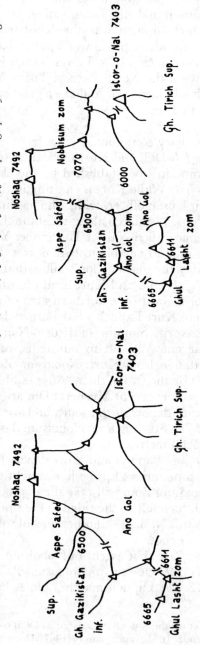

Sketch map of the Upper Tirich Glacier area before (left) and after (right) our 1967 expedition

Hindu Kush

down the granite wall of Istor-o-Nal near Base Camp. Musheraf Din fetches the rucksack with our food, which had been deposited for the ascent of Noshaq. The reconnaissance has revealed the approach to the face to be too complicated and dangerous; Noshaq will not be climbed this time.

13 July Now the push into the Ghul Lasht Zom group must be prepared. Kurt will stay a short while at the Nobaisum Base because of phlebitis in one leg which has become worryingly thick. Didi and Musheraf Din are bringing material from the depot at Konkordiaplatz to the foot of the Ghul Lasht Zom peaks. Establish Ghul Lasht Zom Base Camp (4950 m).

14 July Same procedure. Musheraf Din afterwards goes off for a 'holiday' to Shagrom. Kurt's leg luckily is getting better after treatment with several medicines. No ill effects. Later he admits rushing up a 7000-metre peak immediately on arrival is a dangerous error.

15 July Didi climbs Panorama Peak (about 5600m), first ascended in 1965). Kurt arrives from Nobaisum Base Camp.

16 July Kurt and Didi, on ski and skins, ascend the south branch of the Upper Tirich Glacier, to a height of 5500 metres, then ski down it for several kilometres. The run is very difficult and not worth it on account of a long stretch of small *penitentes*. In 1965 there had been good snow conditions on the southern branch, but we had no skis then.

17 July Departure for exploring the Ano Gol, the north-west branch of the Upper Tirich Glacier. The access to Ano Gol is barred by an enormous icefall, which can be bypassed on the left (southern) side over a steep rock section. The *penitentes* make very heavy going. Climbing up to the saddle between Ano Gol and the Upper Gazikistan Glacier, the latter belonging to the Arkari valley side of the watershed. From the saddle (*c.* 5500m) a knoll (5600m) is ascended. This gives a very illuminating view: a descent from Ano Gol to the Upper Gazikistan Glacier could be possible, but very difficult. According to Schomberg, there might once have been a passage here for shepherds or smugglers down to the Arkari valley, and on into Afghanistan. Maybe ice conditions were better then. Another revelation is that between the Ano Gol and the glacier at the northern foot of the Ghul Lasht Zom group, there appears to be no barrier. Its ice flows for the most part down to the Ano Gol Glacier, and consequently into the Upper Tirich. Only a small amount finds its way into the Lower Gazikistan Glacier. The old *kammkarte* is wrong here. Interesting finds are blocks crammed with paleozoic crinoids on the left-hand-side moraine of the Ano Gol Glacier, originating from the southern precipices of the Asp-e-Safed group. Return to Ghul Lasht Zom Base Camp the same day.

Spirits of the Air

18 July Day off. Didi gets some provisions from Konkordiaplatz.

19 July Start for the Ghul Lasht Zom group. Set up a High Camp (5700 m) in a glacial basin which is surrounded by Panorama Peak, Ghul Lasht Zom South, Dertona Peak and Ghul Lasht Zom East.

20 July First ascent of Ghul Lasht Zom South (6400m) by Didi and Kurt from the High Camp. Great view of Tirich Mir and all the peaks around the Upper Tirich Glacier [see page 680].

21 July Descent to Base. Here Musheraf Din, back from his holidays, is waiting. He brought apples and needs new ski sticks.

22 July Start for first ascent of Ano Gol Zom. (The view from the top could be extremely revealing.) We set up a High Camp on Ano Gol Glacier (5700 m).

23 July From Ano Gol Camp to the saddle between Ano Gol and Lower Gazikistan Glacier, then ascent of Ano Gol Zom (6000m), via southern ridge. Discovery of a promising descent possibility towards Gazikistan from the southern ridge. Whereas the saddle ends in a gigantic icefall, a passage seems to exist – though its lower end is not visible. Return by night, descending the east flank after an impressive view from the top towards Noshaq, Tirich Mir, Ghul Lasht Zom and to the Afghanistan peaks. Maybe a descent to the Upper Gazikistan Glacier would be possible, too, via a small peak and the north-west flank from the saddle we reached on 17 July. (Steep. Some crevasses.) Very late return to Ano Gol Camp.

24 July Establishment of a depot (Alu box) at the Ano Gol campsite for a planned crossing to the Arkari valley at the end of our activities. Return to Konkordia and establish another depot there near the Ghul Lasht Zom group and then ascend to our old Nobaisum Base Camp.

25 July Make two heavy carries from Nobaisum Base Camp to Babu Camp (at the south-west foot of Istor-o-Nal, a very favourable position). Flowers, grass, sun, a little spring. Height about 4900 metres. Babu was here as an Englishman's companion, so Musheraf Din tells us. Sleep at Babu Camp.

26 July Departure from Babu Camp to Konkordia, and then along the western moraine of the Tirich Glacier to the foot of Panorama Peak, erecting there a depot for our subsequent Tirich Mir Base Camp. Return to Babu Camp.

27 July Same procedure as yesterday. Now the Tirich Mir Base Camp is in place, and occupied.

28 July Rest day. Musheraf Din brings the duffel bag from Konkordia. Moreover, all the remaining material is brought from the abandoned Ghul Lasht Zom Base Camp to our new Tirich Mir Base Camp.

29 July We arrive with nearly a hundred kilos of material at the foot of Tirich West IV and establish a High Base there.

30 July Musheraf Din takes material from Tirich Mir Base Camp and carries it halfway up, from where Didi and Kurt transport it to High Base. Musheraf Din goes back to Shagrom again, another holiday.

31 July Ascend with heavy loads (twenty kilos each) from the Tirich West IV High Base (or ABC) through a broad snow and ice couloir to the beginning of the big ice balcony, leaving a cache for our Camp 1 (and return).

1 August After dismantling our High Base, we climb to our cache and set up our two-man tent at 6350 metres, protected by a rock tower. An ice lake, some two metres long, and fifty metres below saves us having to melt snow! Explore along the big balcony to where it drops away at its eastern end towards the Lower Tirich Glacier. Impressive views down to the glacier, to the back of the Tirich North group and into the north faces of Tirich Mir and Tirich West. Spend a long time with binoculars scanning for a route between steep black slate and granite veins above us. The geological contact zone is like a huge spider's web made of dykes. Sleep in Camp 1.

2 August A reconnaissance push up the North Face (partly Grade IV), leaving a depot at 6650 metres. Return to Camp 1.

3 August Transport material to the depot. Return to Camp 1.

4 August Departure from there for a summit attack. With the light-weight tent, equipment and food, we climb to the depot, and then, with heavier loads, make a long traverse on to the hanging glacier. Benighted, we stay at a very uncomfortable place (6900m) in a crevasse.

5 August Transfer everything into a capacious bergschrund (High Camp 2 at about 7000m), there being absolutely no other possible site for our little tent.

6 August Go for the summit. First ascent. Difficult passage around the granite bulwarks on their east side and a steep firn flank. We reach the top (about 7300m) in the afternoon at around 4 pm. Fine view to Afghanistan and closer Hindu Kush peaks. Take important photographs of the area and build a big cairn, Kurt finds some beautiful quartz crystals. Return to High Camp 2 in the bergschrund.

7 August Descend to High Camp 1.

8 August Bad weather, a real exception, not to see the sun. Extensive snowfall. Rest day.

9 August Descent from High Camp 1 with everything to the bottom of Tirich West IV. Leaving only a depot there, continue to the Japanese camp in the saddle between Dirgol Zom and Achar Zom I. Establish our own camp (nearly 6000 m) there.

10 August Rest day. Acquaintance/conversation with the Japanese.

Spirits of the Air

11 August From the camp in the saddle ascend Achar Zom II (probably the highest in the long row of Achar Zoms, or perhaps equal in height to Achar Zom I, about 6300m). Kurt – without Didi but together with two of the Japanese, Nishina and Takahashi (who is fifty-five years old) – makes the second ascent (after the Czechs). At the very top Kurt has a short fall through a breaking ice crust and is stopped by Nishina with the rope. He in turn holds Takahashi twice when he slips in the dark. Returns in bad mood to saddle camp.

12 August Kurt descends to Tirich Mir Base Camp for provisions. Nocturnal return to our camp.

13 August We go on to the High Base of the Japanese (6500m) at the end of the southern branch and set up our own 'High Base' (One tent) close by. The Japanese politely decline an invitation to Kurt's sweet milk and rice pudding.

14 August Ascent of Dirgol Zom (6778m) by Kurt, Didi and Masaaki Kondo, a strong mountaineer not included in the Japanese summit team for Tirich Mir owing to a broken rib, sustained in a crevasse fall. Return to High Base.

15 August Didi brings up supplies from the saddle camp depot. Kurt and Kondo establish a depot for the summit push on Tirich Mir at about 6900 metres on the slope which comes down from the gap between Tirich Mir and Tirich West I.

16 August Kurt and Kondo climb up to the depot and onto a 'pulpit' between two couloirs at about 7000 metres, where they spend the night in the lightweight tent. Didi was prevented by dysentery from taking part in the attempt.

17 August Encounter descending Japanese assault team after their fruitless summit attempt. Taking care of them delayed departure until 5 p.m. Difficult climbing in the eighty-metre chimney (IV, V), completed in darkness. Then by moonlight push up to the abandoned Czech tent on the saddle (7250m) between Tirich Mir and the West group. Thus, no need to pitch our own tent, just crawled in theirs.

18 August Stay on the saddle. Short reconnaissance for the ascent. Masaaki barely understands English, but we manage somehow.

19 August Start at 8 a.m. for Tirich Mir summit. First follow the Czech ridge (North-West Ridge) to a height of 7400 metres, then traverse a couloir, climb a rocky face (III) to the western flank, traverse snow and blocks of rock diagonally to the right, up through the whole upper flank to join the Southern Ridge (where it makes its last kink), rest there for half an hour, then continue over the snowy ridge easily to the summit (but there were cornices!). Summit reached at 1 p.m. Stay there 1–1½ hours. Great view over highest peaks and an ocean of clouds. Descend by the same route, getting back to Czech tent at 6 p.m.

20 August Descend to our Tirich Mir High Base.

21 August Descend to our Tirich Mir Base Camp.

22 August Descend, just the two of us, with ninety kilos from our now-dismantled Tirich Mir Base Camp to the Japanese camp at the south-east rim of Konkordiaplatz (4900m).

23 August From there, to Babu Camp, and pack up. We prepare a box for the transport back to Shagrom. It remains temporarily at Babu as a cache. The remaining material is brought by us to the Japanese camp.

24 August Packing up everything at the Japanese camp.

25 August Musheraf Din appears with four porters from Shagrom and carries our luggage back there, where it is to be stored in his house until Kurt comes back from the other direction after his trip around Tirich Mir. Didi and Kurt depart for their crossing to the Arkari valley, arriving heavily laden at the depot on the Ano Gol Glacier. The Ano Gol camp is set up again (with the lightweight tent).

26 August The camp is dismantled. We move everything, tiresomely struggling across big *penitentes* to the southern ridge of the Ano Gol Zom, and up it to about 5800 metres. The tent is erected again.

27 August Pulling down the camp, descend over a long rib of slate to the Lower Gazikistan Glacier. Along it and on to its northern moraine, to a small pool with flowers (altimeter 4250m). Sleep without a tent for the first time in eight weeks!

28 August Descend to the valley of Kurobakho Gol. Kurt goes up the valley alone and climbs on the Upper Gazikistan Glacier to 4300 metres to collect geological specimens and to photograph in order to clarify the question of the old crossing from Ano Gol to Upper Gazikistan Glacier. (It clearly is possible with crampons and good snow conditions. Impossible for horses. Steep.) Overnight stay in Kurobakho Gol. Food almost finished and no other humans for miles. We live on thin soup, rhubarb and wild onions.

29 August Descend out of the valley to Wanakach (3300m). First inhabited settlement. Food! People are very surprised to see us.

Didi met up with the Japanese again a few days later, and when I also reached Chitral they obligingly included me as Masaaki's companion on their official paperwork for the Tirich Mir climb.

It had been an expedition with a broad range of success: we had achieved the first ski descent of the Upper Tirich Glacier and the first circumambulation of the Tirich Mir massif. We had corrected the map in the Ghul Lasht Zom area and made some important fossil finds – crinoids and the extremely rare Receptaculite, so far encountered in only nine places in the world. As for the climbing, I had made the third ascent of Tirich Mir, on a partially new route, with Masaaki Kondo; and with Didi achieved first ascents of Tirich West IV by a difficult route from the north, Ghul Lasht Zom South and Anogol Zom; the pair of us also did the second ascent of Dirgol Zom with Masaaki Kondo; and I made the first ascent of Nobaisum Zom (P. 6999) with Kurt Lapuch and the second ascent of Achar Zom II with Nishina and Takahashi. The total duration of the expedition had been three and a half months. However, on our return to Chitral we had every reason to fear it might take longer . . .

TWO CHICKENS COME HOME TO ROOST

Sooner or later all the knots in a thread will arrive at the comb – that is an old weaver's saying in Italy. Sooner or later, boy, if you are up to mischief, they'll find you out! It's like British chickens coming home to roost though I confess, as an Austrian hearing that one over the phone for the first time, I thought it was 'roast' rather than 'roost' – what we would call a Wienerwalder Version. Audrey Salkeld at the other end of the line felt the Italian comb version more aptly described Didi's and my touristic foray in the Hindu Kush, although when it came to our return to Chitral, it really seemed that all three of them fitted.

We had lived – one could modestly say – as if in the good old Age of Exploration. Even my eventual encounter with the Japanese liaison officer at the end of my circumperegrination of Tirich Mir had not gone too badly: the storm, when it burst about my head, was dignified and flowery, while the local Chitrali were grinning and nodding at me, mumbling an appreciative *sot zom* . . . We had become famous with the ibex hunters and smugglers of the area. *Sot zom* – that means 'seven peaks'.

However, on my arrival at Chitral, where Didi was already waiting for me, I sensed that something was smouldering. The political agent could not have been more friendly; he gave me the necessary signature and all good wishes for our return, but one of the other authorities was not so well disposed towards us. The Japanese may have helpfully declared me as one of themselves so far as Tirich Mir was concerned, but the fact that someone had climbed all over these 'hills', and then afterwards even gone round them, that had never happened before and appeared highly suspicious. Somebody wanted to pick a chicken, and we had just come home to roost! Or a roasting! I immediately began to tremble for my beloved stones and the photographs I had taken for the geological map – would all that effort be in vain? It was clear that we were not going to be allowed to leave here. No Jeep driver in the whole village would agree to be hired. A guard was posted outside our room. We were two quietly roosted mountaineers with a sentinel.

I was furious about the whole business, for what in the end was our mischief? I shaped a plan – and it worked. Outside the village, I engaged a lorry-driver with his vehicle, just coming up the valley, and told him that he must load all our stuff in a matter of seconds and leave immediately. There would be a bonus for this. The baffled sentry was quieted by the political agent's signature, which I thrust under his nose, then our bags and boxes were hurled on to the lorry and we took off. The two chickens escaped! We were jubilant . . . In Drosh, though, a small village further down, we found ourselves stopped by the police. After an hour of discussions, during which we refused all requests to get out of the lorry, finally the barriers were cleared. Mountaineers in Chitral had declared – thank God – that we were personal friends of the Austrian President. Apparently the telephone works in Chitral too – extremely well, indeed! The poor guard was badly punished, so we afterwards learned – but why had we been held? Did somebody suspect us of being spies? Who knows what goes on in the minds of military people. Of course, they only do their duty. I was later to be highly praised by Pakistani scientists, and a whole box of rocks – precious samples – now resides with the venerable Professor Desio in Milan.

Whenever I think of this expedition, a well-known Viennese joke springs to my mind . . .

A man enters a pub in a great hurry and calls, 'Quick! Quick! Give me a gin before the fun starts!' The bartender quickly fetches him a glass, and in no time the man has drained it. 'Quick, another one!' he shouts, 'before the balloon goes up!' And he swallows that one down as swiftly as the first. Feeling better now, he smiles at the host and says, 'Could I have just one more before all hell breaks loose?' And the puzzled barman fills the glass again. 'What is all this fuss you keep on about?' With the third glass empty, the man-in-a-hurry wipes his mouth with his hand and fixes the host with an even stare. 'The fuss is just about to start: I am afraid I do not have the money to pay you . . .'

In place of money – or the lack of it – we had a very dubious sporting permit – and the question which we put to ourselves, up there in the glacier world, was: Do we go down now or later for 'tea' with the liaison officer? My advice was, 'Let's wait a bit. Let's grab another one before the balloon goes up. Better still, make that a double . . .' Tirich Mir!

Neck and Neck with Reinhold

THE THIRD EIGHT-THOUSANDER?

'Kurtl, our third eight-thousander, let's do it together!' said Reinhold Messner at the Trento mountaineering film festival, always a good place to catch up with old friends. That was before the 1974 summer season. Wolfi Nairz was there as well, the Tyrolean climber and expedition leader. We were discussing an attempt on Makalu's South Face, which – if it succeeded – would mean a third eight-thousander each for Reinhold and me. The two of us had recently given a marathon joint lecture – organised by Charlie of Innsbruck – and entitled 'Four Eight-Thousanders' (Reinhold's two and my two).

That had proved very interesting, if long. I was convinced that with the exception of some experts, by the end of the evening nobody in the hall could have stood a further ascent, wanting, then, only to get home 'by fair means'! I think the lecture had lasted four hours. (The British have more endurance in these matters: at the mountaineering conference in Buxton in 1976, I delivered a six-hour non-stop slide and film lecture on my own, the longest so far in my career. It was, by the way, a very exciting meeting. At that time Cesare Maestri had just climbed the extremely difficult South American granite tower of Cerro Torre placing bolts with a compressed-air drill. He was there in Buxton, as well and, not surprisingly, stimulated a really animated discussion.)

In Trento, before the mountain summer of 1974, it certainly looked as if Reinhold and I would be climbing the South Face of Makalu together ('together', or one after the other . . . that would remain to be seen), but then one morning soon afterwards I received an official letter (and one could feel from its tone how hard it had been for Wolfi Nairz to write); it was an 'ex-vitation' (or whatever is the best word to describe a revoked invitation). Somebody on the expedition (or several) clearly did not want my presence. For me – who already saw the shining Makalu so close – this was a black day. It does not help very much now to go on about my thoughts then – the fact was it left me with very little time to wrestle the tiller . . . but I succeeded: I became instead a member of Gerhard Lenser's Lhotse expedition, which from the beginning was beset with bad luck and difficulties.

A big Spanish expedition held the permit for Everest, and did not

Neck and Neck with Reinhold

want to share its climbing route with anyone – and the standard approach for the highest mountain of the world is essentially the same as that for its satellite, the 8511-metre-high Lhotse. (Only a saddle separates the two peaks.) This was a rich and influential expedition: the battery firm Tximist in Navarra was picking up the tab. Our protestations that we could peacefully coexist on the route were dismissed by the prestige-conscious Spanish, who feared a one-sided success. In the end, the Ministry of Tourism in Kathmandu told us: you have the permit for Lhotse, fine, but try the mountain from another side!

Hell, what kind of concession was that! Two years before, Gerhard Lenser had deposited in Lukla all the equipment suitable for a normal ascent of the eight-thousander.

. . . Or indeed, no less useful even for the South Face.

None of us, however, felt ready to venture on to this deadly face. Avalanches, avalanches, avalanches . . . a Russian roulette. And so we came to the decision to try the Great Ridge: one of the greatest traverses in the Himalaya – not attempted hitherto, though perhaps possible – the Lhotse Ridge starting from the Barun Glacier. Given good weather, we reckoned we stood a real chance of getting over the two virgin 7000-metre peaks, Shartse (7502m) and Peak 38 (7589m), at least as far as Lhotse Shar (8383m) . . . It filled us with renewed enthusiasm: such a wonderful route and – if it succeeded – a fantastic achievement! So we told ourselves.

We felt a little like pioneers for the future – even if we succeeded only in taking the first tentative steps towards what would doubtless be the ultimate, and far-distant challenge of this great ridge . . . You could project the line further, from Lhotse over to Everest, and from there down into Tibet to give you the greatest 8000-metre traverse in history. And including three seven-thousanders into the bargain. Such a feat would certainly need multifaceted military-style organisation, working on a number of different levels. Music for the future . . .

Our dream of doing the great Lhotse Ridge came true only in part – we experienced one of the worst pre-monsoon periods ever in Nepal. Scarcely any expedition was able to realise its high-flying project. The Spanish had to go home without Everest (which we wasted no tears over!) and Reinhold Messner was rebuffed on Makalu. I didn't reach Lhotse or Lhotse Shar. Neither Messner nor I got his 'third'.

But one mountain success did bless our expedition: Shartse – the first of the two virgin seven-thousanders on the ridge – the eastern corner of the Everest massif (Shar = east, Tse = corner, summit). It was the

Spirits of the Air

highest first ascent that season in Nepal, and proved extremely dangerous as well as much more difficult than I had thought. What I carried home from this expedition were friendships and the memory of storms and sickness. Extracts from my diary:

> 'If it goes on like this, we'll use up all our tents,' moans Gerhard Lenser. Never before has he experienced such a series of bad luck:
>
> In Camp 2 on a day of tempest there came a sudden retort, like a shot, and a wonderful Jamet Tent ripped open along its full length . . . a stray gust had found its way in through the entrance, which happened to be open.
>
> In Camp 3 wind-borne drift crushed everything, broke all the poles, and tore the tent. So often before, we had carefully collapsed it when we left, but this time, for some reason, did not.
>
> In Camp 4 devils were on the loose. A cornice collapse destroyed the camp, burying it under tons of snow and ice. It was good luck only that nobody was there when it happened.
>
> In Camp 5 the Schwabian, Hermann Warth and his companion Nawang Tenzing were buried during the night by a snow slide. Even though they extricated themselves, they had terrible hours till morning. All the tentpoles were broken by the force of the impact. 'Many danger,' smiles the strong little Tibetan, whenever the conversation comes back to that night. 'Camp 5, no die.' Perhaps we can repair the tent for a further summit attempt.

Only in Base Camp were no tents broken. A bad sandstorm had flattened them all – but it was not disastrous.

'In all truth, it was the most terrible season for weather,' complained Gerhard Lenser, and he should know if anyone does. He is more at home in Nepal than in Europe, so often does he go over there. It was no exaggeration: how many thunderstorms had we seen that set the whole night sky aglow over Makalu with continuous lightning-flicker – lasting hours at a time – a breathtaking firework display around that black silhouette. Around us on Shartse, fantastic snow shapes formed, magically created by this extraordinary winter: nuns' hats, on the ridge, all white and starched, fresh from the laundry, and forty metres high.

There was a giant snowdrop, and from Lhotse Shar you could see it clearly – floating like an angel with spread wings.

Further down on our wild ridge, the wind played another of its jokes: a snowman was wringing his hands.

I railed at cruel fate because I was sick: was that the fault of the weather, or the big cornice which fell on my head at 6300 metres? 'My right lung feels like a sandbag, I am breathing mostly through the left side. But I don't have any fever. Nevertheless, it stabs so much . . .' I wrote. As it turned out, I had a broken rib, but that certainly was not the only thing. Even so, on 23 May 1974, Hermann Warth and I stood on the summit of the 7000-metre peak, 'our' Shartse, the first mountain on that mighty Lhotse Ridge. Our faces were bedecked with icicles (see jacket). We looked more like monsters than men and Hermann had two of his fingertips frostbitten during the summit climb.

This difficult mountain is only the 'first obstacle' on the Lhotse Ridge – we were happy that we had at least managed to bag that.

What else had this expedition given us? So much. The fact that four years later Hermann Warth, Nawang Tenzing and I were able to stand on Makalu is in no small part thanks to our epic on Shartse (I can't call it anything else), which left us such friends. Day after day we had pitted ourselves against an unkind destiny, that simply didn't want us to win through – against tempests and cornices. We had to endure so much. But we also experienced wonderful moments during this wild adventure. Sometimes, when towards evening the clouds were rising, that giant granite monolith with the name of Mahakala – a dark godhead – burnt like a sacrificial fire in the sky. Then we would urge each other to the entrance of the tent and look up through the icy silence of the evening till the light went out.

. . . Makalu . . . Mahakala . . .

At such moments this mountain is the most secretive place in the world.

One day before we got back to Tumlingtar – into the wide valley of the Arun River – as we were ambling along the path through the bramble bushes, stopping from time to time to pick a couple of the sweet, yellow fruits which are so full of taste, and when once again I was asking myself why in Nepal the blackberries are yellow – along comes the postman.

Mail from home! We bury our heads in the letters and read and read – at the same time I am still half-thinking about the blackberries because I know that Teresa, my wife, is coming for her first visit to Nepal, to wander with me, and she is crazy about blackberries. I will lead her into a great yellow bramble-heaven.

There, it is written: she has obtained her visa. In ten days she arrives! I open the next letter. Whoaa . . . What's this? I have been engaged to make a film in Greenland – in two weeks' time.

Oh, oh! Poor Teresa . . .

When will we finally wander through Nepal?

(We did succeed – many years later!)

Spirits of the Air

CLIMBING THE 8,000 METRE PEAKS

Before I bring the reader to Greenland, let us stay for some pages in the great Himalaya. Five years after my return from the epic on the Great Ridge – I jotted the following reflections:

> Shartse: So much for my 'third eight-thousander' – it was not to be. Could a person climb all fourteen, I wonder? Nowadays I think it is possible. A lot of things and circumstances have to work together, but lighter weight equipment and shorter approaches have increased the probability. Luck you will still need.

Thinking it over today – and assuming survival – I could already have climbed all fourteen eight-thousanders quite a while ago. In the eighteen years' pause between the last 'young man's' eight-thousander (Dhaulagiri 1960, at the age of twenty-eight) and the first 'latter-day eight-thousander' (Makalu 1978, at forty-six) I would have needed to climb one every two years in order to accomplish the nine I lacked . . . such a thing is perfectly possible. Reinhold Messner has shown, as I have, that you can climb three eight-thousanders within fifteen months. Yes, at such a rate, theoretically you could snap up all fourteen in a little less than six years.* But I doubt if it would be much pleasure any more.

Nevertheless, I am sure there will be people who will succeed in making the complete 'collection'. People who have enough time and money, and certainly also a prevailing sporting attitude to the problem. I think that Messner and I have already given the broad indication that it is possible. For my part, I do not for a minute regret my eighteen eight-thousander-less years during the long pause between Dhaulagiri and Makalu. How much I lived in that time . . .

I wrote that in my diary in 1979, having within a short while 'bagged' Everest, Makalu and Gasherbrum II – all, as I said, within fifteen months! At the time I could have entertained a race with Reinhold Messner, but I lacked the passion for it, as well as the necessary organisation and the money. It would have meant the end of a free life for me, and my untamed spirit would never have accepted such a bridle. I can well understand that many years later, when Wanda Rutkiewicz had attained eight of the highest peaks, she should want to cut the matter short by her 'caravan of dreams' – finishing off the rest in

---

* As a matter of fact, Jerzy Kukuczka needed just eight years. My forecast was almost spot on.

just one year. But she died on Kangchenjunga. And Messner himself, after reaching the goal in 1986, admitted to feeling 'freer than ever before'!

At the stage when each of us had five (different) eight-thousanders, the fact did not pass unobserved by the public (in the insider circle of the mountaineers, most already knew it). Moreover, my sudden, belated success on the eight-thousanders must have struck a little too close to home. How otherwise can I explain to myself that after Makalu my partner Hermann Warth (whose second eight-thousander it had been), was invited by Reinhold Messner to go to K2, but I, who had climbed my fourth, wasn't. Hermann did not accept the invitation. To both of us it smacked of politics. Doubtless Reinhold was already taking into account the possibility of becoming first up all fourteen eight-thousanders, rather than simply being a master mountaineer. He has always been an outstanding calculator, planner and organiser.

A journalist picked on the subject and wrote an amusing satire – through the eyes of an absolute non-climber – at the same time poking fun at the overall climbing scene. In the name of truth and objectivity, I have omitted a couple of the more unrealistic passages and below-the-belt fouls. Reinhold at any rate is well used to wrangles with journalists. But between its lines, this little set piece casts an amusing light on the situation in which we found ourselves then. Over a glass of wine on the moraine at the foot of Everest, Reinhold and I also spoke of the matter in autumn 1980. His suspicion, he told me, was that the journalists wanted to set us against each other: both of us had just suffered a defeat (neither he nor I were granted the summit of Lhotse). But we clinked glasses and drank to the future!

This intuitive piece of contemporary non-climbing writing was called: 'The Secret Fear of Reinhold Messner: has Kurt Diemberger been there already?' and sub-titled: 'Imagine the scene if the two best mountaineers in the world should run into each other'. It appeared under the byline 'Michael P. Winkler' in May 1980 in the German edition of *Penthouse* magazine. Having encountered the journalist Axel Thorer – who knows both Reinhold and me personally – in the bar of the Hotel Narayani I was convinced the story must have been propagated from his fertiliser! He has recently confessed as much, and allowed me to reprint it. Here, then, is the story of the journalist who was waiting to interview 'the best mountaineer in the world':

> 'Let us meet in the Hotel Narayani in Kathmandu,' he had said on the telephone. The Narayani in Patan is the starting point for most Himalayan

expeditions. It is where the 'boys' kip in their last real bed before exchanging soft quilts for sleeping-bags for months on end.

In the bar of the Narayani all rules are dictated by a dark-eyed human penguin in a wine-red jacket, who whistles for taxis, and who greets you (as if by clockwork), 'Good morning, Monsieur.' In earlier times he used to include 'Mister' and 'Mein Herr', but that was before Pierre Mazeaud, the ex-Sports Minister of France, arrived from Paris with his Mount Everest entourage. Since 1978 it has been 'Monsieur'.

The Narayani Bar is square, and positioned close to the windows on one side, so that, after their tenth beer the climbing stars can belay themselves securely to the curtains. Coming in from the right in the half-darkness (low light is chic; almost no light is very chic, in Nepal) you presume, rather than make out the little tables, chairs and benches in the room. And you surmise rightly.

Some people are sitting there. They wear corduroy knickerbockers and bright red knee stockings. If one of them gets up to go through the glass door into the hotel lobby in search of the loos, it sounds as if a freshly shod carthorse is clopping over cobbles. Aha, nailed boots!

They will have been wearing them since Munich, even in the tropical heat of Delhi where they broke their journey. At worst, this will have cost them a few blisters, but think of the excess baggage saved! Yes, they are true lads of nature.

'Gin and tonic,' I shout. Devendra, the bartender, looks at me with astonishment while swiftly whipping away half a bottle of gin and three small tonic waters and concealing them in the ice under the counter.

'Hey, hey,' I warn him, 'I saw that. What are you doing?'

'Sorry, mister,' he excuses himself, 'Those are reserved for the best mountaineer in the world.' Who's that? I feel tempted to ask, but I let it go. No point in starting an argument this early in the evening. Besides, several Italians are already looking up with interest. The world's best mountaineer, eh . . . theirs, or the one from Austria?

Toni Hiebeler's 'Lexicon of the Alps' cites two! On page 124: 'Kurt Diemberger, Austrian mountaineer and guide, born 16.3.32, from Salzburg. In the Alps he has mastered all the big north faces of Eiger, Matterhorn and Grandes Jorasses. Has climbed five eight-thousanders, among them the first ascents of Broad Peak and Dhaulagiri.' And on page 277: 'Reinhold Messner, Italian mountain guide from South Tyrol, born 17.11.44 in Brixen. About 20 solo climbs in the 5th and 6th grade of difficulty. Also, six big winter first ascents.'

Devendra, hardened by years of dispensing alcoholic treatment to mountaineers – like a football-masseur oiling muscles and limbs of the league champions – slides a beer towards me, foam spilling over the edge and dribbling in small rivulets down the counter. The beer is called Pink

Neck and Neck with Reinhold

Pelican, and I feel really happy to be in a country which can apply such a name to a beer, even if there are no pelicans in Nepal.

From the ceiling three lamps dangle over the corner of the wooden bar. Their lampshades of woven wickerwork swallow half the light which the dim bulbs push out. Energy crisis on the roof of the world: more than three miserable forty-watt lamps and all the lights of Patan go out.

A few climbers are pressing in, others trying to get out. It's like a mustering: those in the lobby are staring through the glass door into the bar, and those inside keep looking out to see if they can recognise a familiar face. ('Ah! Old so-and-so from Innsbruck in here!') Every newcomer does what all the others did when they came in – set down their rucksacks at the entrance and raise a finger, 'Beer, please!'

Devendra in all seriousness asks, 'Pelican or Lion?' It seems in Nepal there are only zoological kinds of beer.

The air is getting thin. I am waiting for someone, who has decided to renounce all manner of oxygen gear for the rest of his life, from the highest peaks to the deepest valley. Thank God that every time one of the climbing stars comes in through the glass door, he fans some fresh air from the lobby into the bar. The buzz of voices in here is a babel of German-English-Italian-Nepalese-Japanese-French. Then, suddenly, everything stops as a reverent hush fills the room. The manager proudly leads a guest in through the glass door. At once, the whirr of voices starts up again, so that the newcomer does not immediately know he has been recognised. One admires him, but . . .

I had been told to expect a 'six-footer' and, supposing this to be the secret of his success, was disappointed to learn that in English this merely represents a measure of height rather than hexapodous endowment. The newcomer, then, is tall and lanky, and he wears modish 'New Man' jeans, a cotton shirt over his tee-shirt (leaving only letters 'rgst' visible), and embroidered slippers. The wide-brimmed hat, his trademark, he lets dangle from his left hand. Obviously he has no fear of excess baggage. The guy looks around, comes across and asks if the stool beside me is free; when I say 'Help yourself', he stands behind it. He has a slight lisp and a look of studied earnestness.

I would have liked to lift the fringe and peer behind the beard to see what he really looks like. Later, some associations spring to mind: a civilised yeti, perhaps, or a beautiful young man after a hunger strike. Some of the guests in the bar cannot contain themselves. Germans. They are storming out of the niches, boots aclopping, to surround the man. 'Reinhold!' one of them cries, 'Look – it's Messner in person!' 'What are you doing here?'

In impeccable High German he lisps, 'Holiday.'

Someone says, 'Did you hear about Hannelore?'

Reinhold looks really sad: 'Yes, but no details.'

Spirits of the Air

I remember: Hannelore Schmatz, thirty-five years old, wife of a lawyer from Neu-Ulm; she was part of a group of three to climb Mount Everest on 2 October 1979, but died of cold on the way back, along with the American, Ray Genet . . .

I take a gulp of beer and timidly address the face behind the hair: 'Excuse me, what did they die of up there, those two?'

'Too old,' he replies, and strokes his beard. 'Genet was forty-eight, far too long in the tooth for such an undertaking.'

So that was it.

I look about. The people clustering around – are they all too old for the highest mountain in the world?

By and by I realise I have penetrated an elite group. You don't hear any surnames: they are all called Peter, Pietro, Pete, Pierre, Pedro. Or Luke, Jean-Luc or Luigi. Many of them seem to have invisible labels around their necks: 'First winter ascent of the Matterhorn East Face.' And: 'Three seven- and two eight-thousanders.' One calls to another: 'How was it on Lhotse?'

'I guess,' says the shock-haired lisper, 'that here in this bar' – and he revolves on his heels like the official valuer in a dead man's flat – 'there must be about fifteen eight-thousanders.' Pause. 'Without counting my six.' Six?

That must be a dig at the man I am waiting for . . . Kurt Diemberger.

Devendra takes away the empties and serves new Pelicans. I ask: 'Is it really cold up there?' and I point like an idiot at the ceiling of the bar as if Everest was lying just outside the hotel. The bearded façade with the peeling stucco of sunburnt skin replies that if the sun is shining during the day, and there is not too strong a wind, then with luck the thermometer might creep up to as much as +25C. Encouraged, I decide I will go and give it a try myself.

Then Reinhold continues: 'During the night it is somewhat cooler. Down to, maybe, minus 40.'

I grasp my fresh beer. It feels like an icy rock wall. I try to withdraw my hand, but my fingers are already stuck fast, as if to frozen metal.

At such temperatures,' Reinhold recalls, 'you lose all sensation. My feet have frozen at minus 30.' He looks down at me. My own right leg has gone numb, all the way to the knee. One of the Italians is taking interest and addresses the beard in his mother language. Reinhold answers in the same tongue. So, he is a South Tyrolean.

'That was on Nanga Parbat,' Reinhold continues, 'on 9 August 1978.' My right upper leg has now lost all feeling. I keep kicking it with the left. Nothing. And my hand is still frozen to the beer glass. That's it, then, I have got frostbite from listening.

'I am just down from K2, over in Pakistan,' lisps the beard, pulling a nut from his pocket and hanging it around my beer glass – clearly to give me something to hold on to if I should fall. Then he goes on. 'That was in July,

Neck and Neck with Reinhold

12 July, actually, I reached the top without oxygen.'

I draw a deep breath. 'Without oxygen?'

'Mmmm, that's right. It's 8611 metres, quite high. Over 6500 metres the oxygen ration in the air is too low to sustain life in an unacclimatised person.'

'Oh . . .' I say.

'If you have bad luck,' he lisps on, 'your brain cells die away like flies on the wall. That's why mountaineers normally use artificial oxygen at these heights.'

'But not you?'

He sees that I have understood, and continues my education. 'I have trained my body so well, that I can renounce this technical aid for a long time. Before K2 I climbed Mount Everest without oxygen. All in all, I have been up five eight-thousanders, and one of them even twice . . .'

I start to lie: 'No one will repeat that in a hurry, will they?'

Before Reinhold can answer there is some movement in the throng. Pushing through the glass door comes a small compact figure. He has receding hair, a bushy beard and the look of a crucifix carver who has fallen on hard times. The rucksack over his shoulder hangs as shapelessly on his back as do the cord trousers around his legs. Almost unnoticed, secretively even, he steers himself towards the last free stool at my side. Barkeeper Devendra pulls out the half-full gin bottle and the tonic water and fills a glass. 'Here,' he says, 'your drink.' Bald-pate smiles happily, thanks him, and puts it away in a gulp. I guess he must be fifty and wonder if that is perhaps the guy with whom I made an appointment in Kathmandu over the telephone in Munich.

A group of English, French and Japanese now surrounds Reinhold to my right. Five – sorry, six – eight-thousanders this guy has climbed. So often he's been to that altitude, which a normal earthling only ventures into by plane. Eight thousand metres. And every time without air. Beg your pardon: without oxygen.

Devendra tries to pull two pieces of chewing gum out of his hair, put there by a drunken American. The Christ-carver to my left demolishes his second gin and tonic with proficiency. 'Can you imagine,' I ask him, 'climbing an 8000-metre mountain and not carrying oxygen?'

'Sure,' he says, taking another slug. 'That's nothing unusual. This chap called Dacher from Germany climbed Lhotse solo without oxygen. But he did not beat the drum about it.' Pause. Then – a little louder – 'Reinhold is rather better in that department.'

An arrow has been released that is now sailing through the bar of the Narayani like a UFO before a surprise attack.

'Germany', the Christ-carver had said. Which makes him a foreigner.

And 'Reinhold', he also said. So he knows him, perhaps? This really must be the Diemberger I am waiting for.

Just before setting out for Nepal, I met the Africa-explorer Heinrich Harrer, one of the first conquerors of the Eiger North Face; he was about to board a plane in Munich for Tanzania. He told me, 'This Kurt Diemberger from Salzburg was already climbing without oxygen twenty years ago. Not from any love of adventure, but because he could not afford the expensive oxygen bottles.'

About 800 Deutschmarks such a bottle costs today. And it lasts five hours. If you only take ten cylinders with you to Everest, you're still breathing a fortune! Dispensing with the genie in the bottle has become a matter of ideology among mountain stars and their fans.

I reflect whether I should ask this elderly gentleman at my side whether he is Diemberger, and whether he climbs without oxygen. But Reinhold Messner's words come into my mind and I don't want to be tactless. 'At forty-eight you are too old for Everest,' he had said.

A young climber from Tyrol, who told me yesterday that he had already climbed three eight-thousanders, joins me. 'You only managed your eight-thousanders because you are not yet thirty,' I venture.

'Mountaineering is not a question of age,' he corrects me. 'Messner is thirty-six now and has climbed five eight-thousanders.'

'Six,' I say.

'Yes, yes,' he answers, 'but one was twice.'

'I know,' I say, 'Nanga Parbat.'

'Diemberger, on the other hand,' he continues (the old man, that I take to be Diemberger, has meanwhile retired into a dark window corner) 'is forty-nine, and has also done five eight-thousanders. The last, Gasherbrum II, only this last August.' The Tyrolean is swallowed up again in the throng, but at the name of Diemberger, the elderly man re-emerges from his dark recess and is again at my side. Perhaps he likes me?

Fifty years old and still clambering around at 8000 metres in icy conditions. Fantastic.

'Fantastic,' I shout. 'Can you imagine that?' I yell into the ear of the gin and tonic guy.

'Sure' he answers quietly, pushing his glass forward for a refill.

'But without oxygen?' I forget my manners. 'Would you ever go without oxygen?'

'Why not?' he says. 'But with oxygen you get more out of being up there, because the fourteen million brain cells are more receptive.' This man understands something of medicine.

The fans have directed their attention away from Reinhold. He turns around, raising his glass to his lips – then, abruptly, sets it down.

'Kurtl,' he yells, 'Diemberger, Kurtl, where did you spring from?'
'*Servus* Reinhold! Nice to see you.'
Now I know for sure that the Reinhold is Reinhold Messner and the Christ-carver Kurt Diemberger. The youngest and the oldest best mountaineer in the world hug one another enthusiastically. Both, as I said, with five eight-thousanders behind them. Their closest rival only has three. Never have the two men climbed together. Each has Mount Everest in his swag-bag: but none of their others are in common. The last time Messner and Diemberger met was eight years ago, lecturing in Innsbruck. That was when they had each climbed two eight-thousanders and so split the evening between them. Afterwards, they swore to attempt the next Himalayan giant together.

'It should have been Makalu, 8475 metres high,' Diemberger remembers, 'but then your expedition dumped me, Reinhold.'

'That was a bit mean,' I say to Messner.

'Ach, leave it,' Kurtl interrupts me, 'they didn't climb it, anyway.' Diemberger has meanwhile added it to his tally, Messner still waits to.

With the appearance of Diemberger, which has been noticed by others in the Narayani Bar as well, a chillier, more combative atmosphere has descended, and this sense of an impending prize fight overflows from the bar, through the glass door and into the lobby . . . More knickerbocker-wearers, hitherto uninvolved, draw closer. They are expecting something to happen. It really is a historic moment when two such eminent alpine stars confront each other – even if no gorge separates them, only a hotel bar.

Messner, as the young climbers know – several of whom are now squatting at his feet so that the people at the back can also participate – this Reinhold Messner has climbed his five eight-thousanders without oxygen, Diemberger only has three gasless ascents.

'True,' admits the old man, 'but my record can never be broken: I have climbed two eight-thousanders as first ascents.' (None of the fourteen remains virgin now.)

A profound reverence charges the air. The lads cluster round with shining eyes – as happy as football fans suddenly caught in the same sauna as Kevin Keegan and Pelé, perhaps.

With this, in the international climbing standards, Diemberger has been elevated to the mountaineers' Valhalla, whatever Messner might still do . . .

Diemberger leans closer, sloshes gin and tonic on my trousers, and remarks innocently, 'Broad Peak and Dhaulagiri.' I don't understand.

Somebody else whispers: 'Those are the two summits he has climbed as first ascents.'

Ah, yes?

A stentorian shout issues from the darkness of the niche: 'Grö-ö-öbaz!'

Gröbaz? I know 'Gröfaz', the 'Greatest Field Marshall of all time' – it's code for Hitler. But Gröbaz?

Then it dawns on me: the 'Greatest Bergsteiger of all time' – Messner. The man who called must be from the Diemberger camp. His acclamation has stirred the fans of both factions into frenzy. They are trampling on each other's feet. Why, can't be clearly made out; perhaps they have all risen at once, or is it because the hand-to-hand phase has started?

In another dark corner a muscular and chauvinistic Austrian adds his voice against Messner, the Italian. Taking the beer glass from his face, he hisses, 'Bivouac-merchant . . .'

Messner has not heard him. But Diemberger did, though he does not react. Something, therefore, must be hanging on that, or Diemberger would not accept a public detraction of his colleague.

In the bar the Messner supporters now crowd Diemberger and start having a go at him. 'You must speak slowly, friends,' he says, 'I have climbed too many eight-thousanders without oxygen.'

I am flirting with danger, here, because sudden laughter causes me to slap my hand on the counter and almost fall off my stool.

Did or did not Diemberger just insinuate that his competitor has suffered slight 'roof damage' from rushing without oxygen up the eight-thousanders? Including himself in that, too. For, if Diemberger claims roof damage after only three gasless eight-thousanders, and Messner has climbed five . . . I don't dare to think further.

[Note by K.D: I didn't mean it that way; if Reinhold really lost brain cells – they regenerated very swiftly!]

'What are the two of you doing here?' I ask.

Diemberger says he is earning money guiding a tourist group to the foot of Everest. Messner replies that he is exhausted from writing, and the endless driving from one lecture to another. 'Far worse, this rushing about,' he says, 'than any approach-march.'

Kurtl laughs, 'How would you know that? You always fly in by helicopter to Base Camp.' Touché!

The counter-blow comes from a Messner fan: 'And you have seventeen kilos of excess baggage when you set out.'

'Yes,' says Kurtl, and gets his glass filled again. 'But after fifteen days of foot-slogging and carrying forty kilos of luggage on my back up to 5400 metres, I am match-fit.'

The beer glass in my hand has meanwhile warmed sufficiently for me to free it easily.

'It's amazing that you can still climb so well at your age,' I praise Diemberger. 'What did you do last year?'

Diemberger starts counting them off: 'Gasherbrum II: that was on 4 August . . .'

Neck and Neck with Reinhold

'When I had just come down from K2,' Messner chips in.
'Diemberger continues: 'In spring '78 I was on Makalu.'
Messner moves in closer: 'That's when I was on Everest.'
The division of the Himalaya to the Kings of the Mountains continues briskly. Any more bids? Messner? Diemberger! 'Autumn 1978, I stood on Everest.'
A fan from the Messner side: 'When Reinhold was on Nanga Parbat for the second time.'
A further eye-witness chips in: 'Then, Messner was on Manaslu and Hidden Peak,' he declares.
Promptly from a niche, the echo arrives: 'But Hidden Peak is only sixty-eight metres above 8000.'
I stifle a sneeze. 'Anyone got a handkerchief?' I force out the words with my hand in front of my nose.
'Yes, here!' says Kurtl, fishing in his trouser pocket and bringing out a handful of coloured pennants from all nations.
'What use are those?' I ask, helpless, and rescue myself with a serviette from the table.
'Other people collect stamps,' says Diemberger, 'I collect pennants.'
'Which some poor sods have carried dutifully up an eight-thousander to record which country's sons have been up there?'
'Yes,' crows Kurtl, and blows his nose into my serviette.
Without doubt – this man in front of me is the most sacrilegious magpie of the mountain world. An American leans over to me. 'Believe, me, he doesn't just collect pennants, he passes them on as presents. Two months ago, he gave me one which I had myself stuck on the top of Makalu three years before!'
Kurtl tips more drink on my trousers and endeavours to order a new one, but the bottle which Devandra had reserved for him is empty, so he wants to leave. But through the glass door – the only way of escape – another tee-shirt walks in. This one, with the words: 'Joggers make better lovers'. A suntanned Tyrolean en route for Ama Dablam which, though not that high, is said to be the most beautiful mountain of the world, an over-iced Matterhorn. Messner – who sports a cryptic 'rgst' on his tee-shirt – also wants to go to Ama Dablam. Perhaps the two are together?
I grab Kurtl by his trouser belt as a witness and ask Messner the significance of his tee-shirt motto. 'It's a printing error,' he lisps. 'The shirt comes from the USA.'
Now everyone wants to see what comes before and after the 'rgst'. Reinhold unbuttons his shirt to reveal the chest, held by many young ladies to be the most desirable bivouac site of the world. 'Bergsteiger,' I read, 'make the very best lovers.'
Now Diemberger feels obliged to counter. He unbuttons, to reveal no

bivouac paradise, but a somewhat portly form, on which is written: 'Just a dirty tee-shirt'. Well, that's the way he is, Kurtl.

The Tyrolean with the competing shirt to Messner – Joggers v. Bergsteigers – moves towards me and asks: 'Can I have your autograph?'

My God! What embarrassment . . .

I ask the reader: after this piece of theatre, should we guide the said Axel Thorer up Mont Blanc and fulfil his secret dream? I, the 'pennant-pilferer' and Reinhold, 'the civilised yeti' . . .

I think we should agree in advance to procure some adventure for him on the way. Though we can expect to chew our nails awaiting his report of the climb . . .

Perhaps we had better take that old print-devil up.

PART IV

In the Eternal Ice

ON THE TRAIL OF ALFRED WEGENER

The helicopter thunders, it sings, as below us the outlines of mighty ridges and faces flow into one another, then extricate themselves once more. Oh, oh, you wonderful mountainland at the edge of the inland ice cap! Land of my heart! Another of those places in the world where I am at home.

A massive rock cliff appears. Qingarssuaq . . . the Summit above the Three Fjords . . . How fine it is! Suddenly an idea strikes me: I wonder if my cairn, my stoneman, is still there on top? 'Can we land on that summit?' I bellow through the helicopter's roar, shaking the pilot's shoulder to catch his attention and pointing downwards. Like a cathedral with yellow walls, the mountain rises vertically 1700 metres from the greeny-blue waters of the Kangerdlugssuaq Fjord, its finely detailed upper section dissolving into pulpits, ribs, flying buttresses . . .

The friendly Dane nods and gestures his agreement and already the motor begins hammering as we sink towards the peak.

The spire of the cathedral reaches out to us, daunting, incredible. These pilots are such gladiators, they can land anywhere! Squeaks of alarm issue from Anne at the start of our unscheduled descent, but her husband Robert, squashed in beside me, lets forth an enthusiastic roar. The tip of the spire draws closer.

'He's a crazy man, this Kurt!' Anne shrieks. 'One mad idea after another!' But I only laugh: I know the cathedral is not as sharp as it seems. Nevertheless, for a moment before we touch down, the aircraft tilts so steeply that all we see are the fjords which half surround us, and icebergs – looking no bigger than tiny sugar cubes, though they must be at least the size of apartment blocks. Heaven, I think as I stare into those dark sugar-studded waters, let there be no gusts.

A soft jolt: and we have alighted on the brink of the abyss. 'Watch yourselves, getting out!' I shout superfluously. But that applies only to one side – from the other, the summit can be reached easily. And there he is: my stoneman! I had already spotted him as we came down, and with a surge of sentiment – I am not ashamed to admit it – I watched eagerly as he drew closer, like a greeting, something of myself in this place – the memory of a happy day.

For some minutes I forget my friends, the pilot, the helicopter, everything. Approaching the cairn, I am tugged back into the past. We could have just built it – Bruno, Carlo, myself . . . the others. Gently, I slide away one of the rocks and the lady winks out at me, the little Madonna of Tortona, that strawberry town in the Apennines. Another greeting from the friendly earth. A small piece of Italy here in Greenland above the expanse of blue fjords. I nod to the stoneman: it is like dropping in unannounced on an old friend, and finding him as glad to see you. It is easy to imagine the stoneman happy to have company. He has been on his own for eight years.

This is my third expedition to this part of Greenland. I came first in 1966, with the Italians – and I have told about that in my earlier book, *Summits and Secrets*; next was with Germans in 1971, the year I got to know Robert and Anne. We were wanting to climb other big mountains on the long Qioqe Peninsula, on which we now stand. This time – summer 1974 – one of our targets is the inland ice shield, where we hope to find traces of Alfred Wegener's last expedition.

Officially, we are the Second Hessian Greenland Expedition, and our leader is Robert Kreuzinger. Before we came, I spent weeks trawling through the yellowed pages of two old books in his library: *SOS Eisberg*!* about a film expedition made by Dr Arnold Fanck to this area, and *Alfred Wegeners Letzte Groenlandfahrt*.† Kreuzinger wrote to all the survivors from the explorer's last enterprise of 1930–31, and I, in my role as film director and cameraman for the German television company ZDF, took myself to Düsseldorf to visit the white-haired professor, Dr Karl Weiken. This remarkably vigorous octogenarian gave me an eye-witness account of those dramatic days. Subsequently, every expedition box we found at the edge of the inland ice, every pemmican tin, every horse skeleton rekindled the long-gone events for us, and posed riddles . . . In Germany, Kurt Schif was able to furnish valuable

---

* Dr Ernst Sorge, *With Plane, Boat, and Camera in Greenland*, Hurst and Blackett, 1935.
† Else Wegener with Dr Fritz Loewe (ed), *Greenland Journey: The Story of Wegener's German Expedition to Greenland in 1930–31* as told by members of the expedition and the leader's diary, Blackie, 1939.

information about the peculiar propeller sledges which were without doubt a fateful element in the course of Wegener's expedition. And BIBO-Film of Rüdesheim, who produced our ZDF film, even unearthed some ancient, faded but incredibly breathtaking fragments of film from the expedition itself! All these, associated with our own experiences, conjured up – and still conjure! – a 'word-film' before my spiritual eye, which I will try to realise in this chapter. (In order to make my mental leaps easier on the reader, I put historical events and all that is concerned with them in seperate sub-chapters.) My admiration for the deeds of the old explorers is profound, and I am of the opinion that what we mountaineers do now on our expeditions to Greenland and the Polar regions does not remotely measure up to the achievements of those men, nor do we know anything of the privations they endured. They must not be allowed to fall into oblivion!

So, here we were, on a reconnaissance flight for the filming of *Im ewigen Eis* – having just made our unscheduled pause on Qingarssuaq summit. It was a happy day and I could not foresee that only a month later, while taking some of the final shots to illustrate Alfred Wegener's last journey, I would almost lose my own life. On this cathedral I felt only that something was linking me to the great explorer, perhaps the feeling of being at home in this barren, wonderful loneliness that is Greenland. Surely he felt that way about the inland ice, returning to it, as he did, time and again . . .

The helicopter lifts off again, Three-Fjord Mountain falls away, the ice cap extends immeasurably, limitlessly, appearing ever wider the higher we climb; firn basins shimmer, crevasse carpets spread, cloudshadows wander. The earth is full of secrets – to hold you in thrall for a lifetime.
   The inland ice, the white desert . . .
   I think back to that vanished time when our century had not yet run a third of its course . . .

On an afternoon in May 1931, a column of sledges stops some 190 kilometres from the western rim of the inland ice. Two skis have been stuck into the snow, about three metres apart. Between them lies a splintered ski stick. The men of the sledge column leave their dogs and with picks and shovels start digging close to the skis, which obviously represent some kind of memorial, or a marker, for a wayfarer perhaps trying to cross the inland ice . . .

Spirits of the Air

A reindeer skin is uncovered. Below it are more pelts, and a sleeping-bag cover. And below them lies the body of a man, sewn into two sleeping-bag covers. After cutting away the shroud they see he is fully dressed, wearing fur boots, dog-skin trousers, a blue ski tunic, blue waistcoat, a woollen jacket, wind-jacket, woollen balaclava and a hood.

The face of the dead man is peaceful, relaxed, his eyes open. He has been given a careful burial by someone who was a good comrade and forced to leave him behind.

Those who opened the dead man's grave are also his companions. They waited long for his return, then set out in search of him. He is their expedition leader, Alfred Wegener. Now, they re-inter him in the ice, building a memorial from blocks of firn over the spot. The skis are stuck back in the snow and a black flag attached to them. Then the men head back westwards. They want to finish the great scientific programme which their leader had planned and partially carried out.

Let us flash forward to the start of our expedition: after a four-hour flight from Copenhagen we landed in West Greenland. On the airstrip of Sondrestroemfjord, a staging place for Polar flights and the most important civil airport on the island, we stand before a signpost which points to the four winds and proclaims optimistically how, in just a few hours, you could get from here to most of the big cities of the world. But that is not what we want: we have been waiting since 8 o'clock this morning for the scheduled twenty-eight person helicopter to take us to Umanak, 500 kilometres away. We – eight men and a woman, hailing mostly from Hesse but including also one Austrian and two Bavarians – are all enthusiastic alpinists with Greenland experience. Our intention is to follow in the footsteps of the biggest German Greenland expedition to date, that epoch-making venture which explored the island in the early thirties under the leadership of Professor Alfred Wegener. At the same time our mountaineering ambitions are not to be denied: we hope to make the first ascent of Agpatat, a mountain rising almost 2000 metres above sea level! (And that really does mean 2000 metres – unlike the Alps.) Agpatat is situated in the Umanak area and has already defeated two Italian attempts. We are sitting in the hall of the wide, low airport hotel, waiting and waiting. This is normal: Greenland schedules are rarely followed exactly. (I have been here for three days already!) I keep flicking through the folder of archive photographs which Robert has collected; one, more recent than the rest, shows a memorial plaque to Alfred Wegener, erected by his Austrian friends from Graz on rocks below the inland ice at the head of Qaumarujuk Fjord. Thoughtfully, I look at the picture of the explorer . . .

In the Eternal Ice

WHO WAS ALFRED WEGENER?

Alfred Wegener, born on 1 November 1880 in Berlin, was a professor of geophysics and meteorology at the University of Graz.

The name Wegener became famous in 1912, when he sprang his 'Hypothesis of Continental Drift' on a startled scientific world. America, Europe, Africa and Asia were originally part of a single land mass, he postulated, only later drifting apart: America floating west, while part of India along with Australia and Antarctica headed east. Wegener's hypothesis was at first ridiculed by a conservative establishment, but later, as geologist H. P. Cornelius put it, proved the 'magic wand by which a number of partially heavyweight problems of geology itself, as well as various adjacent fields, could be seen in a totally new light'.

Alfred Wegener, however, was no mere desk-man; as a meteorologist and glacier explorer, he felt drawn to the eternal ice of the largest island on earth, to Greenland. Here were problems enough to satisfy not only glaciologists, but meteorologists too. The southern part of Greenland lies in the so-called 'Polar front zone', where cold and warm currents of air collide, creating vortices which move on towards Europe and greatly influence its weather.

Alfred Wegener went three times to Greenland, dying there on his third expedition.

The helicopter descends like a giant bumble bee. We clamber aboard, and soon see the land beneath us passing by in humps and waves, all smoothed and rounded by the action of ice – indication that the icy armour of Greenland once covered this south-west area also, aeons ago. Now, though, it is green, beautifully green! Reindeer throng down there; and arctic foxes, not that I can see any this time round – I just know Reynard's home is there as well! From the distance comes the gleam of the inland ice – yellowish-white, whitish-grey, with hints of blue here and there; a person might certainly ask himself how Greenland came to be so called.

A GREEN LAND?

People say Greenland acquired its name through a trick. A thousand years ago Eric the Red propagated the notion of a green and verdant land to attract Icelandic settlers to the country. In fact, the wedge-shaped island with a north–south length corresponding to the distance from London to the Sahara is anything but green. More than eighty per cent is covered by the inland ice, an ice cap which spares only a narrow coastal strip. Inner Greenland is a shallow bowl, and the ice contained within it is gently domed, achieving a thickness of as much as 3000 metres in the centre. Flowing slowly from this centre to the coasts, the ice becomes heavily crevassed towards its edges, before either breaking off directly into the ocean or sending glacial floes into the long fjords which articulate the coastline. What are known as nunataks – narrow hogs' backs of rock, or domes, or little spires – project here and there from the ice cap, though they are not usually very high. Around the coast, on the other hand, ranges of alpine peaks rise to as much as 2000 metres in the west, and more than 3000 metres in the east.

Thunderous roars accompany the famous 'calving' of the glaciers, when great masses of ice detach themselves to give birth to icebergs, and huge waves ram the coastline, sometimes causing havoc even in the villages. Icebergs drift through the fjords on carpets of broken ice, created under the shattering force of the calving waves.

The small town of Egedesminde has appeared in front of us, its painted houses tossed like coloured dice along the edge of sea. There are no big towns in Greenland, the whole island having only 50,000 inhabitants. Soon we are in the air again, flying on to the north. Below us now, in Disko Bay, numerous icebergs appear like floating castles – or like toys cast on the water by a fractious baby giant. I am delighted, even though I know that none will remain there.

Ocean currents carry the icebergs away, most notably the Labrador Current which flows southwards between Labrador and Greenland. Where it encounters the warm Gulf Stream waters, enormous banks of fog are created, especially around Newfoundland, compounding a notorious navigational danger. This is where the International Ice Patrol begins its operations, keeping drifting icebergs under surveillance on behalf of aircraft and shipping. It was an iceberg, appearing suddenly out of the night in 1912, that brought death to 1500 souls aboard the liner *Titanic*.

Doubtless the earliest inhabitants of Greenland observed the icebergs, too, understanding them perhaps better than we do. Nobody, however, calls these men explorers, even if, in their everyday struggle against the forces of nature, they were in many ways true discoverers. But scientific exploration also penetrates into those areas which are avoided by the settlers, and in doing so, takes advantage of local experience, where that can be useful to the realisation of its projects. Kayaks, fur clothing, igloos, skin tents and the winter huts of the natives

In the Eternal Ice

all proved of great value to the pioneer Greenland explorers.

For science, crossing the big island was naturally a prime consideration. Fritjof Nansen was the first to succeed, on snowshoes, in 1888. Next came the crossings by Peary (1892–5), Rasmussen and De Quervain (1912) and the Koch-Wegener expedition (1913).

ORIGINS OF AN EXPEDITION

Alfred Wegener, the greatest expert of his day on Greenland's inland ice, was asked in 1928 if he would lead a summer enterprise to attempt to measure the thickness of the ice cap. It was to be financed by the Notgemeinschaft der Deutschen Wissenschaft, an association founded in 1920 to benefit science during the post-war economic difficulties in Germany.

Professor Weiken explained to us how this work was achieved: 'By means of an explosion on the surface, you could create shock waves which penetrated through the ice to the rockbed below, from where they were reflected and returned. From the time it took for the waves to come back to the surface, it was possible to calculate the depth of ice . . . We made such measurements in many places.' Why it was deemed so important to know the thickness of the ice sheet in Greenland was because geophysicists at the time wanted to extend their seismic techniques to prospect for mineral deposits in the earth's crust.*

Alfred Wegener – who was under the spell of Greenland more perhaps even than he was of science – grabbed the opportunity. His own agenda went even wider: with the help of kites and balloons, he wanted meteorologists to explore the temperature and movement of the air masses above Greenland. Glaciologists, besides taking their measurements of the ice, should also ascertain its structure and temperature at various depths. A very important point in Wegener's programme was to take gravity readings. This was to determine whether the Greenland massif was rising or not. If a measurement in a certain area shows a higher value of gravity than that calculated as normal for this point of the earth's surface, then a surplus of mass exists: in other words, the area is sinking. A smaller value signifies a deficiency of mass: the area is rising.

Wegener was fortunate: it was accepted that one summer in the field would be insufficient to accomplish his programme; almost two years

---

* Later, similar methods came to be used by geological surveyors in Austria and other places to locate oil deposits.

would be needed. A special team would even make observations of the inland ice during the winter.

One of the proposed centres for scientific exploration was, as mentioned, in the middle of the ice cap (the Eismitte), at about 71° latitude. Furthermore, there were to be stations established on the east and west coasts. One of these two coastal stations would have to serve as the base for a push towards the interior and for the creation of Station Eismitte.

Only the West Station could support such an operation. Why? It was a question of time and distance. The provisions, fuel, scientific material had to be ferried over 400 kilometres to Eismitte, which meant starting the transport journeys as early as possible in the year. The west coast was known to be regularly free of ice earlier than the east. For this reason, the East Station was not established until later and worked totally independently of the other two bases. But that is to leap ahead: first, from where on the west coast should the push on to the inland ice be made? Wegener favoured the area around Umanak, but the decision over exactly where would be most suitable would have to be determined on the spot – before anything else could be done. The resultant pre-expedition comprised, besides Wegener, a further three scientists: Dr Johannes Georgi from the Seewarte (Marine Observatory), Hamburg, intended to be the leader of the central firn station (Eismitte), Dr Fritz Loewe from the aeronautic meteorological station in Berlin, later organiser of the sledge journeys, Dr Ernst Sorge, who assisted Georgi in Eismitte as a glaciologist.

They were looking for a glacier that should not be too fast-flowing – not like the Rink Glacier, for instance, which according to Sorge's observations dispatched 400 to 600 millions of cubic metres of ice every ten to twenty days in mighty calvings! Moreover, for laying the ascent route it did not want to be too steep, because sharp steps create crevasses and séracs. Finally, the snout of the glacier should not be too far from the coast, since an approach over boulderfields and sand would be extremely tiring. The most appropriate glacier turned out to be the Qaumarujuk Glacier, which flowed in a south-westerly direction towards the sea. It was, unfortunately, also possessed of a sérac zone, but that had to be accepted. Access to the inland ice had been found. The main expedition could start the following year!

THE VOYAGE TO GREENLAND

How different it was then! Today you step into a jet in Copenhagen and in a mere four hours are over in Greenland. Then? Well, everything ran

In the Eternal Ice

to plan, at first at least – even if it was different from today: on 1 April 1930, the 'Disko', the biggest ship in the Royal Greenland Trade Department fleet, set out from Copenhagen, taking aboard twenty-five Icelandic ponies in Reykjavik, steaming around Cape Farewell, then north along the west coast of Greenland, to anchor in Holsteinsborg. From there, the journey to Baffin Bay continued on board the 'Gustav Holm', which was able to negotiate the drift-ice. The destination was to be Umanak, a small fishing village on an island at about 71° N. In order to reach it, the vessel had to turn east from Baffin Bay and enter the Umanak Fjord.

This is no simple fjord, rather an enormous bay limited to the north by two islands, Ubekjendt Eiland and Upernivik. From the east several peninsulas reach into the bay, amongst them the Qioqe and what

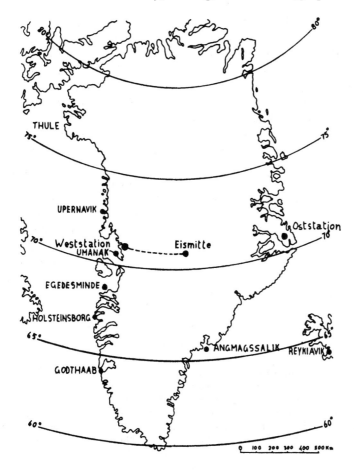

would later be called Alfred Wegener Land. Everywhere are summits reminiscent of the Alps: a playground for mountaineers of the future, stepping into the footsteps of the scientific pioneers. Uvkusigsat, a small village at the end of a long headland, dominates the access to the Qaumarujuk Fjord. It was to prove an important base for the expedition. However, then, in the beginning, on 4 May 1930, none of the islands, peninsulas and inlets could be reached by the 'Gustav Holm'. The sea was frozen! Still on 15 May the edge of the ice ran in a northerly direction to the west of Umanak, then curved sharply westward south of Qioqe towards Ubekjendt Eiland.

'MODERN TIMES' IN UMANAK AND UVKUSIGSAT

Umanak Mountain has appeared. I spotted it – my face pressed to the window of the helicopter; over there, it is diagonally ahead of us – a Greenland Matterhorn! A mountain on an island, the island consisting almost totally of this mountain. Greenlanders call the bold rocky shape 'the heart of a seal'. You need imagination to see that – something the Greenlanders have in plenty. Only minutes now separate me from that place which, on my first Greenland visit in 1966, could not be reached except by ship. Next time I came there was a helicopter pad. Everything here is in a continual state of flux . . .

Greenland has come a long way since the days of Alfred Wegener. As a base for the Allied Forces during the Second World War, it saw swift economic development, thanks to American aid. Few true Eskimos exist any longer. Plastic kayaks are part of the cultural evolution. And you hardly ever see turf huts any more: the Greenlanders live in prefabricated wooden houses, the raw materials for which are supplied by Denmark. One consequence of systematic commercialisation in sheep breeding and the fishing industry has been the replacement of small scattered hamlets by larger villages. The population has tripled in the decade and a half preceding our visit. Most of the Greenlanders live around the west coast, on peninsulas or nearby islands, like here in Umanak. All children must now go to school.*

---

* Postscript, 1994: Since 1953 Greenland, instead of being a Danish colony, has been an integral part of the Kingdom of Denmark, sending delegates to the parliament in Copenhagen; and in 1985 it was granted the status of an 'autonomous region', but with Denmark still being responsible for foreign policy and defence. In 1988 the inhabitants numbered about 54,000, the capital Godthaab, (Nûk in the Greenland language) accounting for 11,000. The most recent census of 1993 puts the total population at 55,000.

Already I can make out the houses! Red, blue, yellow, green, orange – all colours, as if a slap-happy artist had been flicking his brush over the brown granite of the island! In front of the houses, on the coast, there is a small and miraculously sheltered natural harbour, which nonetheless cannot prevent some icebergs sneaking in to anchor alongside the ships. You find them in all shapes and sizes drifting over the wide surface of the Umanak Fjord!

A fairytale image!

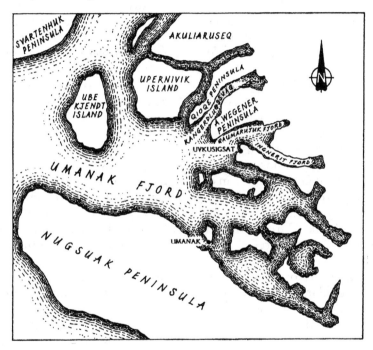

Umanak, once a tiny settlement, has become one of the district capitals of Greenland with 1000 inhabitants. Ice conditions mean the harbour can only be used from June to October, but it is nevertheless (in 1974) an important transshipment depot for the KGH, the Royal Greenland Trade Department which controls almost all business in Greenland.

Unlike Wegener, when he arrived in 1930, we can look down from the helicopter on to an open sea at the beginning of July; he was confronted by an ice-locked coastline after an ocean voyage of five weeks.

The rotor blades whirr, the motor stutters loudly, and we sink down. We are here – Umanak – the starting point for our expedition!

Word of our arrival spreads quickly, attracting the curious. Above all, countless children with their lively clacking-chatter (to me, Greenlandic sounds like a wild duck language) observe how the combined efforts of the eight of us eventually transfer our one and a half tonnes of expedition luggage on to a fishing boat. (The Wegener expedition, by contrast, had a hundred tonnes, the equivalent of ten railway waggons full! To be sure, they also had bigger aims than we do.) This boat has been procured for us by the ever-present trading company, and our smooth transit to the small village of Uvkusigsat, our next objective, does not come about by chance, of course. Long before being able to tread the Greenland soil, we had to obtain a visa and fix our expedition's route inside the country; moreover, we were obliged to raise a considerable insurance stake. The officials demand this safety deposit because all too often helicopters and rescue teams have to be called out to help expeditions in distress. The Wegener team in 1930 were reliant solely on their own resources – their safety lay in the knowledge and experience of their leader.

Our voyage to Uvkusigsat takes us through some fantastic ice formations – pyramids, archways, shining combs for fairy hair, armchairs, a giant grand piano, an enormous whale of ice . . . and whatever else you care to imagine (some people, it is true, may see only ice!). Before setting out, the fisherman in charge of our boat took aboard a sizeable chunk of fresh white whaleskin with its meat and blubber attached – and, with relish, he now chews on a mouthful of skin: it is a delicacy – for Greenlanders.

Uvkusigsat is to be a sort of central base for our ventures. We will set off for the inland ice from there, and for Agpatat peak and the Qioqe Peninsula (where we will of course have further camps; in all these places there will be no other people besides us). We are greeted in Uvkusigsat by a wave of friendliness, and an overwhelming smell of fish, which is everywhere hanging up to dry on high wooden frames. Large packs of sledge-dogs yowl and scrap – they are always hungry! And children, children, children, rampaging and laughing – Greenland is a happy island. Children make up about half its population. This may have something to do with the long winter nights, which counterbalance the endless days of summer.

As in Umanak, much has changed here since Wegener's day. Hardly a turf house remains. And the fish hall belongs to the Royal Greenland Trade Department, which buys all the catch – for vouchers, which the fishermen can use in self-service stores belonging to the company. Alfred Wegener had to bring in all his provisions, but we can go shopping around the corner – and find practically everything! The local luxuries are liquor, tobacco and cigarettes. A bottle of whisky costs about double what we would pay, but other food costs much the same as at home.

A fisherman in Umanak told Robert Kreuzinger that a Greenlander from the Wegener expedition still lives here in Uvkusigsat. We go to see him. The small, white-haired, seventy-two year old Fredriksen and his wife are round-eyed with astonishment and hardly able to contain themselves when they see the photos of expedition members taken by Weiken and Schif over forty years ago. In some of the shots they recognise their friends, relatives and children! They have never seen these pictures before.

It is on one of these days in Uvkusigsat that Robert, Anne and I are taken in a small helicopter belonging to the nearby lead and zinc Black Angels Mine and piloted by a friendly Dane for the recce-flight described earlier. By this time, I have already shot many reels for our Wegener film. And how did things progress on that expedition in 1930? The reader will remember we have left Wegener and his team at the edge of the frozen sea outside Umanak . . .

THE DIFFICULT LANDING

The 'Gustav Holm' could reach neither Umanak nor the Qaumarujuk Bay. Instead, the ship rammed into the edge of the ice to create a provisional harbour for herself. Unloading was done directly on to the ice, whence dog sledges and horses carried all the gear to Uvkusigsat. The night of 9–10 May was the first passed on Greenland soil. The propeller sledges had been brought 'overland', by dog-power, directly across the sea-ice into the Qaumarujuk Bay. But the weakening ice could scarcely bear them. There was no way, either by water or over the ice, that all the Base Camp material could be ferried up into the innermost corner of the Qaumarujuk Fjord. From 10 May began a series of idle, nerve-racking days, spelling loss of precious time to the expedition. The men waited for thirty-eight days! It was 17 June before the expedition's 2500 boxes, chests and drums stood on the beach. These contained provisions, fuel, even blasting material for the seismologists, scientific apparatus, balloon envelopes, kite parts, and last but not least, hay for the horses. The team comprised eighteen members – German scientists, engineers and helpers – with some ten Icelandic ponymen, and a number of locals. Of particular significance to the further course of the expedition were its two technicians, Franz Kelbl and Manfred Kraus, who drove the motorised propeller sledges and doubled as radio operators.

Kelbl, after the transports were finished, was to man the radio station of the western party, Kraus the one at Eismitte – but neither radio operator Kraus nor his wireless gear reached Eismitte in 1930. Was this double-function role envisaged for Kelbl and Kraus one of the factors contributing to the tragic outcome of the expedition?

That was something we mountaineers of the German Greenland expedition of 1974 thought about often as we ascended towards the remnants of the West Station.

We gather in front of the Wegener memorial plaque in Qaumarujuk Bay. This is where the ship's captain has set us down after the short trip from Uvkusigsat. It will be our Base Camp for the forthcoming days while we establish a further camp about 1000 metres higher, from which to start the search for the relics of the Wegener expedition. We have small lightweight walkie-talkies with a range of a few kilometres only, but enough for us.

Eismitte Station, some 400 kilometres distant, lay beyond radio contact . . . was that the disastrous ingredient for the pioneers, or was it those new-fangled propeller sledges?

DOGS? PROPELLER SLEDGES? HORSES?

Kurt Schif, engineer, leader of the propeller sledge operations, had a meeting with Alfred Wegener before the expedition in the little Berlin hotel Westfalia to discuss his ideas for a mechanically driven snow vehicle.

Schif can vividly remember this first encounter: 'From the very start, I was impressed by this man with his shining blue eyes and direct gaze. He had modesty written all over his face, and you would never have known from looking at him that he already had two major Greenland enterprises behind him, and enjoyed such high prestige in the scientific world.'

What did the two men talk about? It was known that the Greenlanders managed to take their dog sledges over almost every kind of terrain, even if they preferred travelling over the flat frozen sea. Wegener had used horses for his Greenland crossing, and would employ them again this time as pack animals. But on top of this, he wanted to use mechanically powered vehicles. So far, though, all vehicles whose motive force acted directly on the ground (that is, via wheels) had failed in the snow, and contemporary caterpillar-tracked vehicles were too heavy for the inland ice. So why not employ propeller-driven motor transport over the snow surface?

There were already a number of propeller sledges in use in Finland. They were manufactured by the Finnish state aeroplane factory in Helsingfors, and employed during the winter months as a transport link between offshore islands. After his discussions with Wegener, Schif got in touch with the factory, which eventually agreed to design and make two propeller sledges especially for the expedition. A few weeks before the date fixed for departure, Schif went to Helsingfors to try to speed up their construction.

Spick and span at last, they stood there: red, shiny, awaiting only their final trials before disappearing into enormous packing crates for the journey. The bodywork was extremly solid, notwithstanding the lightweight construction: streamlined, with a cabin and seat for the driver and a roomy luggage compartment, the motor and propeller were mounted on the rear. Four broad strong skids of hickory wood were arranged in pairs on the two axles and well sprung on a rubber suspension. The front pair of skids could be turned, like the front wheels on a car. The air-cooled Siemens Sh 12 aero-engine had a horsepower of 112, and its fuel tank would hold 200 kilos (63 gallons). Would they work efficiently in Greenland? Before knowing that, they had first to be carried up on to the ice cap – with all the problems that entailed . . .

ASCENT TO THE INLAND ICE

Their route was to take them to a nunatak of brownish rock, which divided two glaciers and probably for this reason acquired its name, Scheideck (*Scheiden* is to split or divide). These were the Qaumarujuk Glacier, up which the ascent was to be made, and the Kangerdluarssuk Glacier, upon which they would later erect the winter quarters.

'There was a serious obstacle on the Qaumarujuk Glacier,' Professor Weiken recalled, 'a heavily crevassed icefall which we couldn't get past. We had to construct a way through – had to keep on hacking and blasting a passageway through the ice – in order to get the heavy loads up, particularly the two propeller sledges, their motors and the winch. No sooner would we have it made, than it would be ruined again because of the sun melting the glacial ice, and have to be abandoned.' Transport through the icefall was a test of power and patience for man and horse. Afterwards, the route was transferred on to a side moraine, but this route, too, had to be tailored to provide wide enough turning circles for the horses to negotiate. Above the icefall the loads were transferred from the horses and carried on by dog sledge.

To start with, at Scheideck, there was only the meteorologists' tent with those of a dog-sledge team nearby. Schif, Kraus and Kelbl started out in a camp south of the Scheideck nunatak, where the two propeller sledges were to be reassembled and made ready. It had taken six weeks to get them up here from the fjord. Later, to avoid constant negotiation of the crevassed edge of the inland ice, the sledge team moved to a depot which Karl Weiken had established twelve kilometres east of Scheideck. Here everything destined for Eismitte was cached, and it was from this depot, called Start, that the propeller sledges set out in 1930. Later on, the winter hut of the scattered West Station was situated a good two kilometres north of Scheideck on the Kangerdluarssuk Glacier, and this provided the base for the inland ice journeys of 1931.

FIRST FINDS

Ahead of us lies a 1000-metre climb to Scheideck [in 1974]. At the back of the valley we see the tongue of the Qaumarujuk Glacier and the steep step up on to it, but neither will give us any problems! During the last four decades changes have taken place in the ice. We will carry provisions for five days, four lightweight tents and skis for a push on to the inland ice. Our backpacks are heavy – each of us is humping thirty to forty kilos! That is not counting the film gear, which nobody wants to be burdened with. Karli Landvogt, our doctor, volunteers to take the heavy tripod. 'A training exercise,' he says with a grin. You can hear the others sigh with relief. After a while everything is divided and we can start. That is just what Reynard, the polar fox, has been waiting for. As soon as we are off, he comes visiting the tents of our Base Camp. We know him well by now: usually, he turns up with the twilight, looking for something to eat – and he is quite successful. His weakness is for tinned meat, but one enigma remains unsolved: why on earth does he keep stealing rolls of toilet paper? Now we wave goodbye to the slim, trusting little fellow, and are soon making our way around the strange collapsed ice bubbles of a fibrous structure which have formed over the valley floor to an impressive diameter of nearly ten metres. Then the gradient sharpens. Glacier ice and tiring loose moraine debris . . . blocks roll away under our feet . . . After two and a half hours of climbing Wolfgang Rauschl finds the first positive trace of the Wegener expedition: a petroleum can, probably lost in the transport. A few minutes later we are lucky again: Robert and Anne Kreuzinger discover a huge hydrogen cylinder, as tall as a man. It is astonishingly well preserved. Hydrogen was needed by the meteorologists for filling both the tethered and the mobile (pilot) weather balloons.

Our steps grow slower, our burdens heavier. It is hard to imagine that 100,000 kilos of material were conveyed up here by Wegener's pioneers. And what a much more difficult job it was then – I remember old film reels showing columns of men hacking routes through the ice, and the propeller sledges being hauled by winch up the steep sections, the men beating the horses to induce the monster sledges just a few more metres closer to the inland ice!

Of course, we make many pauses in our own ascent because of my filming. Towards evening we reach Land's End, at the edge of the inland ice, and spot a protruding dome of rock to the north-east. This can only be the nunatak Scheideck! It is too late to reach it today. We put up our tents.

Breakfast! We fortify ourselves for a dream of a day – the sun shines out of a cloudless sky, and we are full of expectation: ahead of us beckons the inland ice, surging into the distance in wide waves. But we can also see a barrier of crevasses. Four of us will venture on to the ice cap today. Somewhere around here must be the route the dog and propeller sledges took towards Eismitte.

After struggling through a real morass at the edge of the ice, our skis glide well. We have little hope of finding anything on the ice itself – like the winter quarters: too much time has passed. But perhaps our comrades who intend to search the rocky area at the nunatak will be more lucky . . . It will not be an easy job: they are without skis and will have to find their way there on foot through the deep watery slush. We see them become smaller and smaller dots behind us the further we press into the white of the ice cap . . . What a pity that there is not really such a thing as a time machine – we can only think ourselves back to those earlier days. How did it go, then?

1930: TOWARDS STATION EISMITTE

Station Eismitte was to be established about 400 kilometres from the westerly rim of the ice cap. It would need to be equipped with provisions, fuel and instruments so that a working team could overwinter there. Various calculations needed to be made: How much material had to be transported to Eismitte? How many sledge journeys would be necessary? Could the propeller sledges make a significant contribution to the effort?

Alfred Wegener had already pondered these matters back in 1929. He reckoned on a payload of 3500 kilos, which would have to be delivered to Eismitte between June and October.

Professor Weiken: 'Alfred Wegener had worked it out very precisely: three dog-sledge journeys would be required to take in all items essential for overwintering at Eismitte. The propeller sledges could carry extra items. Of course, further journeys would be needed the following spring to re-equip Station Eismitte for the summer ahead. These three dog-sledge journeys duly took place: the first in July and August, another during August, and the third from the end of August to 21 September. The propeller sledges were there primarily as an experiment – to see whether they could operate on the inland ice; Wegener warned everybody not to rely on them. That is why the essentials for Eismitte were to be entrusted to the dogs.'

As it turned out, however, far more material was found to be needed at Eismitte than had been originally assumed (particularly petroleum), and hopes were then pinned on the propeller sledges. They were incomparably faster than dogs and apart from fuel needed no 'food'.

We have reached 1050 metres above sea level! Robert glances at his altimeter. The surface of the inland ice is changing all the time, and we have to be very wary of crevasses. The wind has covered many of them with snow, so that frequently we only notice the dangers at the last moment. Naturally, we have been travelling roped for a while now. It is easy to envisage the difficulties the dog and propeller sledges must have experienced in this area. That is why most of the journeys started beyond the crevasse zone.

A slight mist rolls in towards evening – our altimeter now registers 1115 metres. We are increasingly overwhelmed by a sense of utter loneliness. Something similar, I imagine, to what it must feel to be on a small sailboat in the middle of a wide ocean. Here it is an immense ocean of ice which surrounds us, rigid, solid – but given a gentle dynamic by the slowly sliding shadows of clouds, and the ever-changing light, by waves of mist which form and dissolve again. Inland ice: home of the spirits, so the Greenlanders believe, and you feel tempted to believe it . . .

It can easily take you over, become an addiction, compelling you to go ever further into it, step after step, day after day.

A yearning.

But we turn back after twenty kilometres. For one day only we have felt ourselves the loneliest of people, surrounded by the eternal ice.

In the Eternal Ice

THE SLEDGE JOURNEYS

Reports of expeditions to the highest summits of the world very often carry charts illustrating their logistics on the mountain. Such a diagram is presented as a horizontal band of time, along which the heights achieved by individual members in their various ascents and descents are plotted vertically. There is a similar chart in the book of Wegener's expedition, but it shows, besides time, not heights but the distances covered by teams from the West Station.

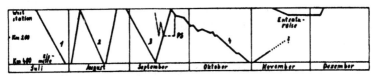

Extract of a diagram from the 1930 expedition by Dr Kurt Wegener (simplified).

You can see from the above the journeys made to Station Eismitte: 1, 2, 3, 4 represent four dog-sledge journeys and PS the soon-to-be-interrupted attempt by the propeller sledges. The Entsatzreise is the rescue journey in November–December. The line for the return of the fourth dog-sledge journey to Eismitte is a dotted one and cut short abruptly.

It was the end of the drama.

In the beginning, despite time lost on account of the pack ice, everything ran more or less according to programme. On 5 July the first dog-sledge journey headed out towards Eismitte. Loewe, Georgi and Weiken went with it, waymarking the route. They put in black pennants every 500 metres, and every five kilometres built snowmen with black fabric hoods. As much as anything, these were to pacify the Greenlanders among the party, since none of them had travelled on the feared inland ice before. Loewe turned back at the Depot Kilometre 200, as planned. Georgi and Weiken reached the middle of the ice cap on 30 July, along with four Greenlanders. Weiken then also said goodbye, leaving Georgi alone and out of contact with the rest of the expedition to establish Station Eismitte. At 3000 metres above sea level, this proved fatiguing work, but if men were to overwinter there it was important to make all necessary preparations. Wegener's plan called for him and Sorge, as well as a radio operator, to remain in the middle of this ice desert until spring 1931.

The second sledge train bringing material for Eismitte started out at the beginning of August. Wegener now had serious worries. The first trip had only delivered 750 kilos to its destination and, according to his estimate, almost five times that amount was needed. Under no circumstances did he want to relinquish this base, which was to be the heart of the expedition. Guided by Loewe, the second sledge party arrived on 18 August with a 1000-kilo payload. Ten more sledges set off on 30 August, accompanied by Sorge, Woelken and Jülg. They reached Eismitte on 13 September, where Sorge was to remain. Earlier, as they were leaving the Western Station, the men had seen the propeller sledges making their way to the Depot Start. They appeared to be functioning well. Everybody was optimistic that it would not be long before they were welcomed at Station Eismitte. But they never arrived.

THE PROPELLER SLEDGE FIASCO

Broken down into sections, the propeller sledges and their motors had been brought over the icefall to the assembling tent, and then put back together. The matron of a sanatorium (was that a bad omen?) had christened the two sledges Ice Bear and Snow Bunting when she came for a visit to Scheideck. Snowballs substituted for the usual bottles of champagne on that occasion.

Kurt Schif recalls: 'We were unlucky to encounter snow and surface conditions on the ice cap which were quite different from Wegener's predictions, based on a crossing made with horses at a totally different time of year. We experienced very uneven terrain, shot through with crevasses, presenting very variable surface quality – one moment it would be needle ice, then powder snow, and somewhere else snow swamp. One look was enough to make me doubt that our propeller sledges would prove as revolutionary as we had hoped. Initially, we had no idea how we ought to address these difficulties, and quickly decided to establish the starting point for the propeller sledges on the inland ice itself, at a distance of some twelve kilometres from its crevassed edge. Test runs showed that the sledges could only operate when weather conditions were kind to us.'

The gained speeds were, according to Schif, thirty to forty kilometres per hour, and it was impossible to reach Eismitte on a single, full tank. Petrol depots would have to be laid in advance along the route. During the seven days it took to do this, the sledges covered a total of 800 kilometres. The depot at Kilometre 200 was especially well equipped, holding also the reserves destined for Eismitte.

On 17 September the propeller sledges left for the decisive push towards Eismitte: 'We reached speeds of seventy kilometres an hour, got to Kilometre 200 and passed the night there with Woelken and Jülg, who were on their way back from Eismitte. We hoped to continue next day at the same speed to Eismitte, but during the night there was a terrible break in the weather – temperatures fell to minus 36° Celsius and we found to our consternation that the sledges simply could not move any further. Nevertheless we sat it out, expecting an improvement in the weather. Only when our rations had dwindled so much that we had food for just two more days, did we decide to unload the sledges and dejectedly to start back.'

But it got even worse. Within thirty-nine kilometres of Depot Start the motor of the Snow Bunting packed up: piston damage was diagnosed, caused by insufficient cooling. Everyone piled into Ice Bear, but eight kilometres further on, that, too, konked out. Piston damage again! They were benighted on the spot. In the morning, Wegener and Loewe suddenly appeared in front of their tent. They were on their way with the fourth sledge journey to Eismitte. Wegener now knew that he could no longer count on the propeller sledges for this year, and that his fourth provision run for Eismitte was all the more vital.

But the fiasco with the propeller sledges was still not over. There was no hope of encouraging Ice Bear an inch further. Two dogs collected on the way back were tied in front of a small emergency sledge, on to which a tent, sleeping-bags, some fuel and food were loaded. Severe blizzards hampered progress. It was 27 September before the team regained Station Start. They were absolutely exhausted.

Twice that year they tried to rescue the abandoned sledges, but failed to budge either of them: the ice held them fast. They would be there now until the spring of 1931.

NUNATAK SCHEIDECK, A TREASURE TROVE!

Sunshine on the glacier. The soft curves of the inland ice dazzle and shimmer, all around. Standing on the rounded head of the nunatak, you feel like the captain on the bridge of a ship sailing into a white ocean. The gnarled patches of swampy snow around the ice rim could be the foamy hollows between waves pressing towards the coast, just before impact. In one respect, however, the comparison falls down: the coastline here is lower than the sea. The white ocean in front of you – were it in movement – would sweep over you! It rises slowly, but steadily to a height of 3000 metres.

That is the feeling you get, looking over the prow of a nunatak.

The four of us returning from our inland ice ski trip rejoin Hans, Wolf, Karl and Wolfgang – our foot patrol. They had made a discovery while we were gone: a place marked with coal, in the ice just near the nunatak. Enthusiastically we all start to dig. We know that a year ago Danish search teams recovered one of the two propeller sledges for a museum, and afterwards marked the spot where they had found it. This is surely it! The second sledge must still be here, buried in the ice! We work fast, like moles who suddenly find themselves caught out in the sunshine. Soon, an edge of rusty metal appears. With renewed excitement, we dig further, but the deeper we get, the more difficult the digging becomes – it could take days to excavate the whole sledge. That at least is what the 'non-Austrian' majority thinks! Exasperated, all I can film is part of the engine-mounting at the rear.

But already, buoyed by the find, Hessians and Bavarians join forces and set themselves to work on the rocky hill and the blocks at its base. Shouts ring out! Every moment yields some new discovery: here is the winch for the kites and balloons – it must be! Karli and Wolfgang joyfully wind the handle – the thing squeaks terribly, but turns perfectly! You couldn't expect more of it after forty years . . . Just as I am about to remind my energetic companions of the little matter of a buried and, to me, at least, magic propeller sledge – I did so want it on film in all its glory – Wolf Reute comes running over with a dog's pemmican tin. I sigh. Anne hauls over broken pieces of boxes bearing the inscription of the Wegener expedition. Will Kurt now, finally, forget about that damned sledge? Wolfgang procures horse skeletons, even discovers the foundations of a stable with some real hay in it. This country really is a fridge! The second biggest in the world after Antarctica. At any rate, that little rocky hill keeps us busy throughout the next day and the one after that – many finds and many rolls of film. Despite searching in the direction of the winter hut, we find no trace of it. The fast-moving glacier has engulfed it and in the intervening decades carried it God knows where . . . Sic transit gloria mundi. Thoughtfully, I look at one of the old photographs: expedition members and a smiling Greenland girl in front of the winter hut. The old white-haired man in Uvkusigsat, Jonathan Fredriksen, had recognised her as his sister-in-law Sarah, who was the caretaker. She's been dead a long time, as has his brother, who stood beside her in the picture. We gave him the photograph. I still remember how he took it back to his old turf hut, the only one left in the village.

Evening has come, the beginning of a bright night, which you cannot really call a night at all. I am standing on top of the nunatak, looking east over the inland ice . . .

ALFRED WEGENER'S LAST JOURNEY

Would the propeller sledges make it as far as Eismitte? Wegener had some doubts about this after participating in their first test runs. Shortly after Sorge started on the third dog sledge journey, therefore, he decided to organise a fourth. He would undertake it himself, together with Loewe, with the main objective of carrying to Eismitte from Kilometre 200 the paraffin and other items still lacking there. Very soon after setting out they met Woelken and Jülg returning from the third sledge journey (Sorge had stayed behind at Eismitte). They brought two letters with them: in one Sorge gave a detailed description of the provisions at the base, and Georgi wrote that if they didn't get more paraffin and other essentials before 20 October, they would leave the station on foot with a *Handschlitten*, a man-hauled sledge, and return to the Western Station. (Later on, the two changed their minds: the rooms of Eismitte which were excavated in the firn below the surface could be heated sufficiently with the existing paraffin; moreover, a return journey with just a man-hauled sledge seemed too risky. Wegener never learned of this change of plan. No radio message was possible because the apparatus and the operator were not there.)

Wegener (as we have seen) encountered the Snow Bunting and Ice Bear stuck in the snow. All the more urgent now, he felt, to get his column to Eismitte!

But at that moment his Greenlanders went on strike, eight of them returning to the west. Four stayed with him for the time being, though he himself was later to send back another three. The reduced group that trekked towards Eismitte thus comprised just Alfred Wegener, Fritz Loewe and the Greenlander Rasmus Villumsen.

Wegener sent back letters for Karl Weiken with both of the returning Greenlander groups: in the first (dated 28 September) he still hoped to be able to ferry the necessary paraffin from Kilometre 200 to Eismitte, but in the second (of 6 October) he declares his desire to push on to Eismitte, even without a payload, so that he can at least bring dogs to Georgi and Sorge. Sorge's plan to leave Eismitte on 20 October by man-hauled sledge was held by Wegener to be unfeasible. They would never make it through, and freeze to death on the way. He and Loewe, he hoped, would eventually relieve Sorge and Georgi. Eismitte had to be manned over the winter at all costs!

In his last letter, Wegener requested that a small relief team go to Kilometre 62 to wait – until no later than 1 December – for the men coming back from Eismitte.

The relief journey took place: Weiken, Kraus and two Greenlanders set off on 15 November from Depot Start. At Kilometre 62 they built a snow igloo. They also set up two tight lines of marker flags, ten kilometres long, one towards the north-east, the other to the south-east, forming a rough right-angle and thus making it possible for anyone coming from the east to be guided into this 'corner' where the igloo stood, even in thick fog.

Every afternoon, as darkness began to fall, they would light a paraffin flare, which would burn for three hours.

However, on 7 December the relief mission was called off. It was impossible that anyone could still come from Eismitte. Storms were raging and temperatures had dropped to minus 42° Celsius.

The winter meant a long break in all activity outside the stations.

Did Wegener, with Loewe and Villumsen, make it through to Eismitte?

Yes, by 30 October, Alfred Wegener, Fritz Loewe and Rasmus Villumsen had reached the station. The temperature by this time had sunk to minus 50° and Loewe had suffered heavy frostbite; in his state a return journey was out of the question. However, inside the roomy 'cave-dwelling' which Sorge and Georgi had hollowed out below the firn surface the temperature was bearable. Here, they could continue their scientific tasks throughout the winter!

The 30 October was the only rest day for Wegener: it was as if he didn't feel comfortable in the firn-cave without any wind or snowdrifts, without the bitter cold. The extreme hardships of a journey lasting more than four weeks had failed to exhaust him. New projects for 1931 were discussed – two Greenland crossings! On 1 November, his fiftieth birthday, Wegener started out with Villumsen for the Western Station. Loewe could not go with them. All his toes were frostbitten. Some time afterwards they were amputated by Georgi – with a pocket knife and wirecutters. Loewe was obliged to sit in his sleeping-bag the whole winter, right into May, because it was too cold in the room for his damaged feet.

What was the situation meanwhile at the ice rim, at the Western Station? Karl Weiken continues his description: 'Wegener never arrived with us; we waited for him in vain – and we all hoped, therefore, that Wegener, Loewe and Rasmus had remained in Eismitte with Georgi and Sorge. If they lived frugally and also ate the dogs they had brought with them, they could last out there till May, even five of them.'

Spring 1931: At the Western Station operations for the current year were being organised. The propeller sledges were meanwhile functioning without any problems. Everybody was oppressed by a single worry: Alfred Wegener – what had happened to him?

The first sledge journey of the year, therefore, had to be to Eismitte: a dog-sledge group led by Weiken set off on 23 April. The propeller sledges caught up with them at Kilometre 330, just short of their common destination. They spent the night there together. On 7 May the propeller sledges were the first to reach Station Eismitte . . . Where was Wegener?

'He left last year with Rasmus Villumsen, on 1 November; he was heading for the Western Station . . .'

Only then do the men of Eismitte and Western Station understand that Alfred Wegener and his companion must have died on the inland ice.

The search started immediately . . . Wegener and Rasmus had left Eismitte with two sledges and seventeen dogs. If they lost a considerable number of dogs on the journey, they intended to go on from Kilometre 200 with only one sledge. Rasmus was to drive it, Wegener follow on skis.

At Kilometre 285 a box of pemmican was found, at Kilometre 255 a sledge, at Kilometre 189 Wegener's skis standing in the snow. A preliminary dig when the earlier team passed this spot on their way to Eismitte had turned up only a pemmican box. This time they dug deeper and found Alfred Wegener's grave. He had died, they supposed, from exhaustion.

Rasmus probably took Wegener's diary, gloves, pipe and tobacco with him. After burying him, he would almost certainly have continued westwards.

They found two of his campsites. At Kilometre 170 he might have spent a longer time. An axe from Eismitte was found on the spot. After that, nothing.

Kraus had established a small radio transmitter in Eismitte. On 8 May he radioed the message homeward: Wegener and his companion had perished on the ice cap.

The work of the expedition continued. Kurt Wegener, the dead man's brother, took over the lead. Even today in Greenland the name of the peninsula Alfred Wegener Land commemorates the great explorer.

QIOQE, AGPATAT AND – THE FINAL TAKE

1974: We packed up and abandoned Scheideck. During our days there we had found much, even if not all that we wanted – the events of a long-gone time had woven themselves into our consciousness. Robert and I, in our thoughts, were still decades back on the inland ice when we descended to Qaumarujuk Bay. We had so identified with the events surrounding the last journey of the great explorer that it was hard to put it behind us. It almost seemed absurd that from now on there would simply be normal mountaineering.

When we reached Base Camp our friendly Reynard, the arctic fox, was waiting, already impatient. Wolfgang immediately opened a tin of meat for him! Next day we left the bay on board the cutter. Reynard stood on the beach and followed us with his gaze. I believe he thought it unfair of us to go . . .

Increasing numbers of small mountaineering expeditions visit Greenland nowadays for its carefree climbing on fascinating coastal mountains – so different from the Alps, with the climbing from sea level, on uninhabited peninsulas and islands, and in the everlasting daylight of the Greenland summer. Under the low rays of the sun at midnight, when it stands in the north – and during the bright day when the seagulls circle above the fjord and dive for fish.

You could write a whole book simply on the fascination of climbing in Greenland.

It has its special adventures: just pull an iceberg ashore and melt it down if you cannot find fresh water. Or sit on a summit, as if it were the middle of a sundial, and watch the shadow of your mountain circling way below, like the hand of the clock – hour by hour over icebergs, sea, glaciers . . .

When we reached the Qioqe Peninsula we experienced all that. It was the third time I had been here. And it was, as I said in the beginning, a piece of home to me.

In the Eternal Ice

After several first ascents we turned to our last objective.

Agpatat is the highest point in Alfred Wegener Land. Its summit, 1922 'true' metres above sea level, was still unclimbed. Twice it had been attempted. It is a mountain of many ridges, subsidiary summits, buttresses and enormous fins and flakes – which quite often conceal the main summit from the fjord. A strange, complicated structure, as we had already ascertained from the aerial pictures given us by the geodetic institute in Copenhagen. However, we finally worked out a possible line of ascent from the south – where we are now.

Colourful flowers bloom in the rocks of the cliffs – daisies, willowherb, bellflowers . . . lichen, bilberries and pillows of moss higher up . . . after that for two hours we encounter nothing but boulders: and what boulders! Extremely steep moraine debris. Stones keep rumbling away into the depths. Today I have given the tripod to Anne – as everybody takes good care of her – the camera I carry myself. When we arrive at the base of a massive, vertical corbel of eroded, rotten rock, suddenly, lit from above, it glows beautifully green: malachite probably. A really big patch of it. Unfortunately, it is not possible to get at it. We penetrate a high valley, a sort of amphitheatre: rising in the background, above a steep snow and rock face, is a pinnacle that could well be the summit. There is a glacier in front of it. Before going on to the ice we find a flat spot, dotted with mighty blocks, an ideal place for a high camp – and with water, too! Eleven hundred metres above the fjord we erect four lightweight tents, pop into them our sleeping mats and bags and the camp is ready. Tomorrow, the summit of Agpatat will be ours! Eight hundred metres more – no problem. Tomorrow, we will build another stoneman on the highest mountain of the Wegener Land and feel happy . . .

Brilliant sunshine, indescribably clear air, the unspoiled nature of Greenland. Already we are being treated to summit views. Of course there are still riddles to be solved, alpinistic ones; we can see that . . . but that is part of the fun!

It turns out to be no fun at all. The next day begins with bad weather. Humid, cold winds, dark banks of cloud; and then it snows, and it snows, and it continues to snow – for fourteen hours. You are tempted to forget this is summer in Greenland. Finally, things look brighter, and I set off at once with Wolfgang in order to film the 'bad weather version' for the end of our film – in case we do not make it up Agpatat. Our companions consider that a bad omen. They are right, of course: within a short while the weather is again so foul that the scenes of 'the retreat' look very authentic!

And so, Wolfgang and I lie down in our camp fairly well satisfied, under the circumstances.

It lasts four days . . . Mostly, we sleep or toss from one side to the other. Then, even the most optimistic among us are fed up. Defeated, we descend to the sea. There, it is raining. Sometimes for long stretches, sometimes shorter. I work away imperturbably at my bad-weather ending. Most of my companions have started to swear whenever I call them for the next take. Suddenly, I hit on one last, grand idea. Please, good friends, it really will be the last! It's Joerg who makes the sacrifice: he agrees to descend on a rope from an overhanging wall, directly towards me, coming to a standstill exactly in the focus of the big camera lens! Not a problem for him: he climbs from the other side until he's at the top of the wall, hammers in a piton, passes the rope through, and rides down the doubled rope in a sit-sling. And I? Of course, I am not standing below him for reasons of safety. Joerg comes down twice more, kicking out every loose stone on his abseil route – I had always hoped I would grow old . . . Right! Everything is ready. Joerg is sailing down, directly into the camera. 'That was no good,' I yell at him. 'We need more action,' and I keep looking through the viewfinder. Now even Joerg is swearing – it is the fourth time he's come down the rope. Normally he is always so patient – it must be the weather. Still, he runs up again, mumbling to himself that this time he'd show me. He seizes the rope. I'm convinced that now he'll come down elegantly – just like Rébuffat – you only have to activate those energies which lie sleeping in everybody. Already I see the silhouette in the viewfinder. (I am ignorant of the rock poised obliquely over my head, six metres further up the wall, as big and heavy as a typewriter.) 'Bravo, Joerg. Bravo. That was good!' (Not really like Rébuffat, more a wild horse in a harness, but never mind . . .) I keep my finger on the button, the camera whirrs, Joerg's outline in my viewfinder swings out sideways, comes in again . . . Suddenly: all is black! CRAAACK! A terrible blow in my face knocks me down, and it feels as if I have lost my head, an unbelievable impact, an enormous weight – I sink to the ground, dropping the camera at my side – Joerg bends over me, I hear yells from the camp, running footsteps – then nothing. Almost immediately, it seems, I am awake again: see Karli, our doctor, and feel blood running down my face. I cannot see anything out of one eye. It is as if the violent blow had frozen into my face; it is still there, particularly on the upper jaw . . . Ah, there is a faint gleam, fuzzy shapes . . . Yes, I can make out something with my left eye. 'What's the matter with my eye, Karli?' I blurt out – I think I'm wafting off again.

'Don't worry. Your eye's fine, but you're a lucky sod: without that

In the Eternal Ice

camera in front of your face, you'd be stone dead by now,' he says, and bandages me up. 'We must give you an eye patch for a while. My, that looks elegant.' And he doesn't know how much he calms me with that; if Karli is launching into his Bavarian good cheer, then he must think I'll be okay.

In the background I hear somebody mutter: 'My God, look at the camera. Total write-off . . .'

The Arriflex which saved my life was cracked through; two of the optics looked like squashed top hats. Joerg was devastated, not because of the camera – that was insured – but because of me. It wasn't his fault. His fatal sideways leap had really been caused by me. From the distance comes the throb of an engine. The fishing boat, thank God! But I cannot manage to lie down on board: throughout the whole journey I remain on my feet in the cooling wind, as the pain hammers away in my eye and my jaw.

My companions are kind to me, helpful as never before. I think now they would even excavate the propeller sledge. It is good to experience such care. But I also notice that obviously as a self-made film director, I must have been too hard on them sometimes. Because, as I am lying on the divan in our room in Umanak, already feeling better, Robert turns up: 'If one doesn't have to carry your tripod, you are a nice bloke,' he says, and gently adjusts my head to the correct position on the cushion.

Karli joins us with a grin. 'Take Six,' he says, and puts a new tape over my eye.

'This cup of tea – I hope I only have to bring it to you once!' says Wolfgang drily, but one could guess what he meant. (How many takes did I put him through again?)

And Anne? Anne strokes my face kindly and asks, 'How are you? Better?' Even if this had nothing to do with the film, it was very, very pleasant.

But then, what does she say? I hear her laugh softly. 'Kurt, it is a fact that since you stopped filming, we all like you much better.'

There must be some truth in that.

And by the way – just because there is a grain of truth in it – I want to describe one small episode of this film production. We needed a crevasse fall. (Why in films do they always want crevasse falls? Just one of those things? Whatever, there it was in the script which the production company had given me: Scene 15 – crevasse fall.) I decided to film it on the inland ice. That's where it was supposed to happen in the film.

After some research we found a suitable place about a mile from the spot where the Hessians and Bavarians had refused to dig out the sledge. (During my fevered dreams after the accident, sometimes the expedition appeared coming home in a triumphal procession; marching in tight double rows, two and two together, and carrying on their shoulders a golden propeller sledge!) So, anyway: I had the crevasse – blue, neat, commodious, ideal – but neither Hessian nor Bavarian wanted to jump inside it. You can understand why. Jumping with crampons is dangerous; to jump without them . . . can be quite uncomfortable afterwards. Best not to jump at all. That's what my companions thought, too. But finally, Wolfgang Rauschl sacrificed himself – give the guy a medal! While he was hanging in the crevasse and being held by Hans, the latter yelling into the abyss (a tremble of excitement in his voice: I am a tough director), 'Wolfgang – I've got you!', at exactly that moment, the batteries of my recorder ran out. Damn. Not now! There is no other solution than to fake this scene later on.

Although it goes without saying that the whole accident was phoney (did you ever hear of anyone filming a non-intentional fall into a crevasse?), it embarrasses me to have to confess to additional fakery with camera and sound. But when, a fortnight later on the Qioqe Peninsula seventy kilometres away, Hans was standing 'at the edge of the crevasse' (actually, at the edge of a granite boulder above a green meadow by the beach) and in his trembling voice yelled towards the crevasse victim (who was relaxing in the grass), 'Wolfgang – I've got you!', a sudden suspicion came into my mind that perhaps Hans had worn a hat in the original take. Bloody hell! (There are no patron saints for film directors to call upon.) I tell him, 'Hans, we must shoot the whole thing again. Weren't you wearing a hat?'

Hans, who already had pearls of sweat on his forehead (he was at 1000 metres on the ice rim, and heavily clothed), stuttered, 'I have three different hats . . .' and as if my misfortune wasn't sufficient, he continued, '. . . and I cannot remember whether I was wearing my goggles or not either.'

The tumultuous laughter of the Hessians and Bavarians echoed from wall to wall along the Kangerdluarssuk Fjord, and no doubt all the way to the inland ice. Various more or less 'ambitious', more or less volunteer tripod- and film-box porters made pointed remarks about film directors – I was destroyed. By the sweat of our brows (mainly of Hans Lautensach's, but also my own) I committed all possible permutations on to several rolls of film (Hans, a person of pedantic precision, only a bit distracted, had meanwhile remembered something else: did he wear gloves, or not?)

In the Eternal Ice

The subsequent laughter in Rüdesheim carried from the studio across the Rhine. You couldn't hear it from the inland ice, but certainly as far away as Mainz. On the cutting table: Hans with fur hat, without goggles, with gloves . . . trembling: 'Wolfgang, I've got you!' Hans, with beloved woollen Peruvian bonnet, with goggles, without gloves: 'Wolfgang, I've got you!' Hans, dripping with sweat, without hat, without goggles, with gloves: 'Wolfgang . . .'

Now I always carry a notebook in the pocket of my jacket. But only the spirits of the air know whether I'm wearing the right jacket.

PART V

A Night on Stromboli

... AND EVERYDAY LIFE IN ITALY

Stromboli – the only continuously active volcano in Europe. Also one of the seven Aeolian Islands to the north of Sicily. The island bears the same name as the volcano, since that is all there is: the steep cone rises straight out of the sea. Its top is 980 metres high, but what the visitor sees, approaching by ship, is no more than the very tip of the cone: the roots lie 2000 metres lower, on the bed of the Mediterranean.

Stromboli will disappoint nobody. Like a kind of 'Old Faithful', its craters spew thundering fire fountains into the air as regularly and reliably as the whistle on an overheated pressure cooker. Anyone on the summit is treated to a spectacle of indescribable power, so frightening and fascinating as to touch one's innermost being. The intention may have been to spend just an hour there, but one finds oneself staying a full night.

Sometimes though, the fiery soul of the mountain is stirred with an overwhelming force, which sends a glowing lava flow racing down the black burned slopes of the Sciara del Fuoco and into the sea. At those times it is better not to make an attempt on the otherwise benign summit. The local guides know the moods of their mountain and will certainly warn anyone when it is unsafe.

A number of fishermen and their families live on the island. More precisely, there are two small villages – San Vincenzo on the northern coast and Ginostra in the south-west. They are built on old lava flows – and, sitting in their squat houses spooning their fish soup, folk often hear above them the rumble of the mountain. They have got used to it.

To a rock climber, Stromboli is of no interest. It is for the adventurer. British mountaineers attempted the traverse of the steep north-westerly coast, from one fishing village to the other, at sea level, passing below the Sciara del Fuoco, the 'course of fire'. Threatened by lapilli slides, they struggled forward, sometimes in, sometimes out of the water, through niches and caves, moving across sand and ashes until, blackened but happy, they finally reached the other side. It was never repeated. For their part, the fishermen hold such goings-on as madness, and prefer to travel by boat. Only very rarely does anyone cross the island by climbing over the mountain.

I met one of the British 'madmen' once on the cliffs of the Welsh coast: Dennis Kemp, an excellent climber and mountaineer with a lot of experience behind him, though white-haired, was full of youthful enthusiasm. We spoke about the beauty of different places around the world, where the sea and the mountains meet, and while we were sitting on our airy pulpit, with the surf pounding the slabs below us, he told me about Stromboli. Near us, meanwhile, a pair of climbers moved slowly on tiny holds across 'A Dream of White Horses', the famous traverse high above the foaming crests of the waves. Surrounded by all these impressions, a plan ripened gently in my mind: I would experience the volcano for myself. The opportunity came sooner than I expected. When I returned, somewhat battered, from Greenland, my daughters hugged me and scolded: 'Papa, we're not letting you go off again for a while.' Teresa thought the same. No doubt they were right: it was time to stay at home. But hardly a week had gone by before I was conspiring to make my convalescence rather more eventful . . .

Black sand, glittering and overlaid with a yellow-gold shimmer when viewed into the sun; black, rotten lava monsters emerging from the foam of boiling waters. The dazzling houses of San Vincenzo, the narrow coastline around the island. Higher, the dominating mountain skyline, rusty and black, with patches of dark green on the lower slopes. Fast moving clouds – drifts of smoke? A distant rumble, echoing down from the sky . . . the volcano.

'. . . è normale!' It's normal, an Italian fisherman comments with a smile. Another wears an apron, which boasts in big red letters: I TALK ENGLISH EVERY INFORMATION. A handful of tourists cluster round him – the old sailor (I take him for that), home from the sea, has managed to find a way of using his experience to augment the meagre livelihood of an islander. But the tourists soon return to the ship which brought us here from Naples, and continue on to Lipari, to Panarea, to Vulcano . . . Only a few remain on Stromboli.

We find a room to stay, very cheap, with old bedsteads and mattresses, but breakfast is included. What luxury! We spread out our sleeping-bags – Karen and Hilde, my two daughters, only eight and fourteen years old, Teresa from Bologna, and me. We are very excited, delighted with the island, and do not hide from our hosts that we want

A Night on Stromboli

to go to the top of Stromboli tomorrow, and overnight there. Overnight, as of course in the dark you can watch the eruptions so much better.

Our hosts, though, meet this announcement with an expression of sorrow: only last week there had been an accident. A boy lost his way, coming back in the dark. He fell over a cliff. Dead.

Fall to one's death on this mountain? Such a possibility had never crossed my mind. We have hard hats with us, sleeping-bags, a bivvi bag, a stove, torches . . . but no rope.

Next morning we buy a hemp line from a fisherman, not very long, but tough . . .

Clouds are racing over the ridge up there, sailing by incredibly fast. There's a strong wind from the west. Patches of sunlight and shadow dance across the steep slopes. It looks unfriendly. Some tiny dots are moving up on the skyline. Somebody, then, has gone up . . .

We don't get away till afternoon. The wind has died down and the sun is now shining pleasantly, warmly. A comfortable mule track leads through the tight Mediterranean scrub . . . Spanish broom; metre-high spheres of spurge, what we call Wolf's Milk; and in between, the countless blue and white flowers of rosemary, with its characteristic scent; pink blooms, too, and greenery . . .

The black sand and the lava cliffs become inkier and inkier as they recede into the depths, and the sounds of the sea soften to a murmur. In the end, only the hum of insects and the sweet smell of the maquis surround us. We meet some islanders descending to their village, and a group of young lads with enormous rucksacks and colourful anoraks overtake us as we move leisurely upwards. Clearly, they want to pass the night up there, too. Soon they are lost to view. A jungle of tall, yellowish cane, which covers the slopes now, has swallowed them up.

It is getting steeper. The mule track has given way to a narrow path which winds in a tight zigzag up between the shrub and cane. Sometimes it is deeply incised in the soft ground, then dissipates into vague traces across loose rubble and dark volcanic rock. Leaning on our sticks and ice axes, we gradually work our way up, following a rounded ridge that is flanked on its right-hand side by a sheer drop. Obliquely below us, we can see the steep, grey course of the Sciara del Fuoco. The sea is shrouded in a yellowish haze, and to the west a grey bank of cloud has built, getting darker all the time. 'What do you think about the weather?' Teresa asks anxiously.

'Not much,' I reply, but continue upwards. When we stop for a breather I address my little crew: 'You had better know that I'm in no mind to carry this enormous pack up, down, then up again. We have got everything we need for a fine bivouac, and if the weather turns bad, we wait till it gets better.' No objections are raised to that. They have never bivouacked before, anyway – high time they did!

The strong wind blows up into a storm. Whenever we draw close to the exposed edge, sand whirls about our ears, blown uphill from the depths of the Sciara del Fuoco. We put on our pullovers and anoraks. The branches of the bushes bow low before the wind's blast and Hildegard's long blonde hair streams like a battle standard. She leans into the wind with all her might, but little Karen has pulled her hood over her ears and does not look at all convinced . . . Teresa takes her hand and coaxes her gently upwards, quietly, patiently, as always. Coming from a big Italian family, she is used to having other people to take into account, many others, and is resigned to not always being able to do what she wants. Probably she would prefer to be down at the bottom now. But – turn around here?

Shouts from above, trampling in the bushes, two figures appear. One of them, a bearded guy, stops. 'You're not going up now?' he yells at me, staring at the children. 'Not in this storm, for heaven's sake?'

I protest that he doesn't understand. 'We're keeping an eye on things. If it doesn't improve, we can still go down!' The bearded man throws me a glance as if I were mad, and hurries after his companion.

'These people obviously haven't come prepared with bivouac gear,' I reassure my troops. Maybe they have, I think, and just don't like bivouacking . . . but I keep that to myself. It is good for the children to get used to storms.

Another group clatters down. '*Mamma mia!*' and '*Padre impossibile!*' yells a dark Italian woman, regarding our slow-moving party with wide eyes. An impossible father . . . But my children, of course, know that already. 'Papa, perhaps we had better go down,' a small voice issues from under Karen's hood.

'Wait a bit, sweetheart. It's not raining yet.'

Is that more trampling and shouting from above? Somebody else about to undermine our resolve? 'Come on, let's tuck ourselves in the bushes for a rest. We can wait till they've all gone.' And I distribute nuts and – chocolate – a good father. (I'm having to polish up my image.) As we sit in the scrub, the last group scampers downhill. Now we have the mountain – and the storm – to ourselves. All possibilities open.

Perhaps we can still find somewhere to bivouac that has a view of the eruptions, as we planned to. Some little niche higher up, out of the wind? I rather doubt it: already it's beginning to get dark. But to sit it

A Night on Stromboli

out here and see nothing – that would be totally boring. We're all agreed on that. So then, higher! Unfortunately, it really is dark now. We get out the torches . . . A little later, at a steep rocky section, the hard hats and fisherman's rope are pressed into service as well. With care, we manage to get across, but it's worse on the other side: no bushes, not even smaller plants, nothing to slow down the wind, and no trace at all of somewhere to bivouac. In these gusts, the occasional rumble of the volcano can hardly be heard, it sounds like collapsing séracs on a glacier . . . I admit defeat! 'Okay, gang. We'd better go back. We can't stay here . . .'

Down in the groove of the path, we find a spot where it is horizontal and smooth, sheltered from the wind among the canes, and tucked into our sleeping-bags, down jackets and bivvy bag, preparing something hot to drink becomes more interesting to everybody than any eruption . . .

The moon draws a glittering ribbon across the sea. Incredible. The wind has vanished, and the sky is clear! Suddenly, just like that. How long was I asleep? 'Isn't it beautiful, Papa!' whispers Hildegard. She has raised herself on to her elbow and looks down. Karen and Teresa do not stir. Above, a thunder-roll makes the air tremble. A small cloud takes on a red glow for a second or two.

'Wait! I'll creep over to the edge and take a look!' Another thunderclap . . . followed by a whoosh! Beyond the black silhouette of the ridge glowing spheres rise into the sky, silent, then gently float down again. I grope my way back. 'Hilde, come . . .'

The spectacle bewitches her. 'Papa, we must get higher!'

Stromboli's craters lie on the north-west side of the mountain, somewhat below the summit and directly above the Sciara del Fuoco. The higher we can climb this ridge, which is blocking the view to them, the closer and better we should be able to see the eruptions. I wake Teresa. 'The weather is fine now! Hildegard and I will go up a bit higher. We'll be back in a couple of hours. Then I'll take you and Karen up. We couldn't go all together, not in the dark. You sleep for now. *Buona notte!*'

How different everything is without the storm. Hildegard and I are roped up, it is true, and we are wearing our helmets, but the difficulties are minimal, elementary you might even say. Nevertheless, we must not fall. To each other we seem only unreal shadows, as we feel our way up the black rocky step which stopped us before. Again, I can't help thinking: how different without storm! How lucky we are . . .

We gain height briskly. Even at fourteen, Hilde is almost as tall as I am. She was only seven when we climbed the Gran Sasso; later other interests took over. With mounting excitement we grope higher towards the invisible thunder, which emanates from somewhere behind the dark rock. What will we see? Above us, the outline of the ridge stands out clearly, so it cannot be far now. Another loud rumble. Instinctively, we quicken our steps, as if we might be missing something irretrievable, and pant up the last few metres, moving as fast we can.

The ridge. All is quiet. We are standing on a horizontal shelf. Soft moonlight bathes the dark bulk of the mountain, as it does us; it draws our shadows out as silent companions on to the rocky, sandy ground. Deep down, almost intuitively, we sense a mighty semicircular cauldron, which must be where the Sciara del Fuoco begins. Beyond it, considerably higher than we are now, is the summit. It still seems a long way off, unattainable and dream-like. In a wide curve, our ridge, seamed with black shadows and indistinct obstacles, leads up to it. As far as that? I am surprised.

Suddenly there appears below it something like a giant flower of fire, trembling, opening, blossoming within seconds high into the night sky! A thunderous roar . . .

We are both speechless.

It is so beautiful that at this moment I feel no regret that we failed to establish our bivouac on the summit; on that so distant spot . . .

Although . . .

'Papa, that is magic! We have to get up there!' whispers Hildegard.

'Much too far at night.'

'But I want to get to the top!' she insists. 'We've got this far . . . and there's still plenty of night left.'

Perhaps my daughter is right. Nothing is unattainable, except what you have already relinquished. 'Okay, then. Let's give it a try!'

I realise something, and it touches me in a strange way. I was almost prepared to accept the situation, to give in . . . Not Hildegard! Joy seizes me, a sort of exultation that I cannot explain to myself – as if something would come of this night, something to link her and me in a vitally new way, different from before. It is true I am in front, leading, but for the first time I feel my daughter is an equal ropemate. More than that, it was she who made us continue.

We are feeling our way along the ridge. It is wider than we expected. Many of the obstacles turn out to be shadows only, and we are able to detour a real rocky barrier. To our left, the ground plunges away,

A Night on Stromboli

down, one imagines, to the fishermen's village of San Vincenzo. All of a sudden the earth below our feet changes to a fine, soft, yielding sand! It gives the sensation of trudging uphill through heavy snow. Above us, the summit outline has noticeably altered. Another few steps and it has changed again! That means it cannot be much further now – it is just the moonlight that makes it seem so far away!

'Hilde, another half an hour and I think we will be up . . .!'

We whoop for joy. The mountain is ours, already it's ours . . . has been all the time!

And the magic of this night. Again and again the explosions come, every quarter of an hour . . . In between, the volcano bubbles and sloshes in its mighty pots: liquid lava, the red glare of fire in the darkness. We see them diagonally ahead, and much nearer now. Phew! What a stench of sulphur! Acrid fumes engulf us, blowing over the sandy ridge from the craterfield. And there is a prickle on the skin, like a million fine needles. We hurry on through it. Steeply now we are plodding up the last few metres. The outline is quite different now – it can only be a few more minutes . . .

A fire fountain, very close. We stop. It is so beautiful; you could never get used to it.

It is two o'clock in the morning: the ground becomes hard again. Lava slabs, a curving crust above the void. We take the last steps to the summit.

Here it is!

Who could have imagined that we would still make it up to this spot tonight? The moon, the sea, the silhouetted coastline of the whole island below us, the red glow from the craterfield, the tangled contours of the mountain . . . over there, on the other side, outlines of ridges and troughs. Far to the south some twinkling lights and a shadowy line of coast: Sicily! A cold wind is blowing up here. We might even walk over to the other side of the crater rim . . .

We follow a sort of track that appears to lead down into the craterfield. It is a real temptation to keep going closer – but at a bivouac wall with inviting stone 'seats', we stop. The mighty pots are simmering and hissing – still some distance away. Nevertheless, the next explosion almost yanks us from our perches in fear and excitement . . . With a deafening thunder-roar, a cascade of liquid rock, white-hot, one or two thousand degrees in temperature and weighing many tons, shoots skyward just in front of us, splitting into a giant bundle of rays, parabolas, and a hundred ribbons of light, arcing back to earth. Rocks patter as they strike the edge of the crater, a fiery rain that continues to glimmer on the ground, changing from white-yellow to orange to red, to crimson – till all the dots of light go out, disappear, and only the dull glow of the bubbling lava, reflected up from the depth of the craters, penetrates the darkness.

We wait for the next eruption.

Somewhere deep down on the ridge Teresa and Karen are sleeping in their bivouac. They cannot imagine what we are experiencing at this moment . . . but, they could not have made it this far at night. Perhaps tomorrow morning?

It is such a pity they don't see this.

Of the five craters down there, three are active – and the largest of them erupts regularly about every ten to fifteen minutes. This is the one we are specially waiting for! Its fire fountains may reach one or two hundred metres high. The second crater only erupts now and then. And the third is a real character: we call him the Swindler. This hooligan is the noisiest of the lot: he roars like a jet testing its engines, only louder – he roars, and roars . . . yet nothing appears, until shortly before the end of his performance, he spits, one by one, three or four red glowing tennis balls at crazy speed, diagonally into the dark, where they rise higher than all the other missiles from the craters. It looks so funny for all that noise to produce so ridiculously little, and whenever he does it, we can't help laughing. For all its otherwise fantastic show, the Stromboli Theatre has its clown, too. Once, he even seems to respond to Hilde's shouted encouragement and spits five balls!

Cold creeps into our bones, but how can we ever drag ourselves away from here? Every so often we reassure each other that it is not that bad – but next time we will bring a sleeping-bag with us. Next time? Who knows when that will be?

One thing is certain: never in our lives had we dreamed of such a night. Perhaps it is the more impressive because we are here totally on our own. And because we had to fight our way up here. And . . .

Many things are possible only once in life – you have to seize the opportunity when it comes.

While we descend to Teresa and Karen, it is as if we walked slowly out of a strange dream. We have to keep telling ourselves it is still true. For how long? Words and pictures encompass only a space; inside that, reality gradually dissolves, like smoke.

Later on, while Hildegard catches up on some sleep at our bivouac, I climb up with Teresa and Karen to the shoulder of the ridge. We see a couple of wonderful eruptions – and Karen hugs us both with delight.

But the dawn is gradually creeping in, covering mountain and sky in pale blue, draining the shine from the glowing shells . . .

There is no point in going on to the summit any more. 'From up there,' Teresa says wistfully, 'it must be even more beautiful.'

Another time.

'I CANALI' – THE CHANNELS

There is one landscape in Italy that could be called a mountaineer's nightmare: the channel country near the mouth of the Po River . . . For centuries people here have been draining the swampy ground, tough people reclaiming land while the mighty river continues dismantling Alps and carrying them to the Adriatic, pushing the coastline further and further eastwards. Porto Maggiore, as its name implies, once the biggest harbour, is now a small rural town more than thirty kilometres inland – as the crow flies . . .

And crows, that's another thing. There are literally hundreds of them in this land of pulverised peaks. Normally I like birds and their songs, and I certainly don't go along with those people who see the crow as a bird of ill omen, but even I consider there are perhaps too many in this flat land, which has unexpectedly become an important station along my life's way, and very much a proving ground. Here is where Teresa was born, grew up. Her mother, too.

And the channels? This is a landscape you cannot hurry through: wherever you walk, wherever you go, you soon come to a dyke or channel far too wide to leap across.

A weird sensation for a mountaineer.

There is something else, too: the *Padrona di casa* – a special and peculiarly Italian figure. The literal translation 'patroness of the house' does not really get you very far. Since I have had the benefit of a growing personal experience, I will attempt to describe the phenomenon more exactly.

In appearance, usually as solid as the farmhouse she rules over.

Once you have entered the house, you are in her domain. Woe to the person who dares sneak something out of the fridge at night (admittedly a shortcoming of mine!). It is for the *Padrona* to decide when people eat. She keeps all objects and subjects under her control. Night and day.

Never wash the dishes, nor the plate or cup you have just used. Don't

Spirits of the Air

try to be helpful – leave well alone; thus you avoid offending the *Padrona*.

She does not care whether Mount Everest is in Africa or Asia, or if India is in South America – or not; just so long as the borders of her property are right (and respected).

No matter how the watchdog howls and lunges on his chain, do not set him free. The animal might dig up the lettuces, or even run into the house . . . a terrible thought for the *Padrona*.

She is busy in the house from morning to evening, cleaning, cooking (great!), and dealing with the laundry. Like the Forth Bridge, as she finishes one end, she starts again at the other. Anyone who expects to find a speck of dust in the *Padrona's* house is sadly mistaken.

Entertainment during the day for an Italian *Padrona di casa* is provided by visits from the scattered clan of relatives, the network of which is almost as intricate in the surrounding area as that of the channels. On these occasions, the normally sacrosanct 'best' rooms are thrown open.

And, finally, since anyone who comes within her circle of might will do his utmost to follow the *Padrona's* unwritten laws, for fear of provoking her indignation, inevitably all outside connections, contracts and relationships cease at once to be valid. As the husband of a *Padrona's* daughter, you are not competent to make decisions – indoors or out – however much you grind your teeth. It is the *Padrona* who has an absolute claim over love and respect.

On the other hand, if you manage to observe all her rules, you can be sure she will do everything for you . . .

For a mountaineer, that is not, as we in Austria say, an easy tart to swallow. Knowing what to do in a sudden breakdown of weather, or how to avoid stonefall, to face the dangers of a mountain – none of these prepares you to cope with a *Padrona di casa* in the network of channels of the Emilia-Romagna (a district, incidentally, where Mussolini was born).

To be sure, my mother-in-law is a helpful person, but I do not think she considers me much of a catch for her daughter . . . and one has to understand that. In this channel landscape, I fit about as well as a Matterhorn in a cabbage patch.

So, we are not always in harmony: especially when she keeps the shutters closed all day long . . . she loves the dark, and I the sunshine. It must provide an entertaining spectacle for an observer: a house where the venetian blinds snap up and down continuously. Two tough characters fighting for the light of day.

A Night on Stromboli

These were my impressions, recorded in my diary, in 1980. Thinking back now, I realise how much better things have become since we built a big, new, roomy house on top of a hill near Bologna, a house for six people, including Teresa's sisters! Half of the shutters stay closed and the other half open, and we respect an invisible borderline, as it were between England and Scotland. Two dogs run freely together and mother-in-law generously feeds everyone in style, tends her flowers and, well, is the boss on her side of the house. We can smile now at the old trench warfare. Still, anyone who imagines the Italians as an easy-going people, knows only half the truth. And a Padrona di casa is a very special regional delicacy . . . In the interest of my fellow mountaineers, who might find themselves marrying in Italy, let me return once more to the entrenchments (as described in my diary) . . .

Besides my wife, there was the dog who demonstrated himself in favour of my visits: he jumped for joy whenever I arrived, knowing I would cast off his chain, at the same time urging him not to exhume any more lettuces! Of course, I wouldn't leave the door open and give him the opportunity of slipping into the house – I was full of high endeavour to keep the peace! And, though things changed only slowly . . . my wife assisted me and I admired her for her patience. I knew she would never turn into a Padrona di casa (at least, Good heavens, I hope not!). Two full summers I endured in the landscape of the channels for her!

It was not just stoicism that kept me there, we were extremely fond of each other. Even so, I felt that the striped pattern of the venetian blinds so perfectly echoed the watery network outside. That I did not end up a 'pulverised' mountaineer, is simply because I could not give up the hills.

Even today, in Bologna, I live far from real mountains – they are in these pages as I write, and frequently I long for them. Months and years are in these pages – you give up a lot of present for the past. But in the channel landscape I learned fortitude.

Ceci, my son, was born there – he is stubborn and full of fantasy . . .

Some things never change, even today: without warning the Peuterey Ridge suddenly erupts out of the vegetable garden over the hills . . . and I am off again! Teresa and Ceci know that I have to go whenever too much time has passed. It is the other life. Father will come back, sooner or later. That is the way it is with mountain guides, sailors, cameramen – their home has no walls and no fence.

(Will mother-in-law still feed me? Perhaps I had better scrap these pages in the Italian edition! After all, in Italy, they know well enough what a Padrona di casa is . . .)

The Millipede

It is huge, living amongst us, and proliferating with the speed of a swarm of locusts; it munches, munches everything before it . . . The legs of this replicated monster cast long shadows across valleys and forests, into once lonely cirques, over alpine meadows, plateaux, even over the summits of some peaks. Or the monster turns into an apparently harmless slow-worm, winding its way steadily, and gently covering more and more of the green with grey. Highway millipedes with concrete legs, asphalt snakes with their offspring, parallel and diagonal links, countless poles of cableways . . . entire 'zip-fasteners' opening up our alpine homeland. And not only there: the millipede threatens the forest areas of Germany, no less than the mountain world and high valleys of Austria, Switzerland, Italy, France. Stay away from a place for ten years, or even less, and you will be surprised when you return. If we do not act quickly, the millipede scourge will march inexorably on. You can always find a reason for it, be it a wish for comfort or the commercial interest of a group of people – local or urban outsiders. It might satisfy some person's justifiable need, or the country's economy, or the image of a politician, seeking to improve his chances in the next election; sometimes, people merely feel left behind by the burgeoning progress they see all around them. There is increasing art and cunning in the destruction of our landscape: people have no trouble finding more than one justification for their own pet millipede: economic, touristic, development, redressing competitive disadvantage, capitalistic – for investment, or because it deserves to be done – or to bring full employment . . . And at the back of it is always a political motive, because somebody will have a personal agenda. Consequently politicians either have little regard for landscape (especially mountains), or at best find themselves in a big dilemma – more bluntly, you could say their personal freedom of choice is compromised.

So, we should not be surprised when yet another fresh weal disfigures the earth's countenance, another cord is added to the ever-constricting network that strangles air and liberty and living space. It is like a fungal disease ravaging a face, and spreading relentlessly – fed by an amalgam of power, greed, technical progress and indolence. It is the cancer on the skin of the world.

On this increasingly comfortable globe, where today you can travel almost anywhere quickly and without effort – but where in so many places it is no longer worthwhile to go since everywhere begins to look the same – if we do not stop and protect what remains, all that in the end will be left are apathetic idiots and a handful of specialists. Should we then be surprised, and would it even matter, if one fine morning the second Big Bang overtook the lot of us?

Does it have to come to that?

Who is there to help, disinterestedly and honestly, pushing personal interest aside? In the summer of 1980, when I entered these thoughts in my diary, I came to the rather sceptical conclusion: Except for some single outstanding individuals, statistics show that people's trust in the honesty of others is very far from encouraging. I quote from the *Neue Kronenzeitung*:

> The American psychologist Dr Julian Rotter interviewed 4000 people in New York on what they thought of the honesty of those engaged in twenty different professions. He found that doctors and judges were considered to be the most sincere. Then priests and teachers. At the end of the honesty scale were ranked television technicians, plumbers, second-hand car dealers. The least trustworthy of all, in his researches, were – the politicians.

As I said, not an encouraging picture. Along with the vested interests of industrial and agricultural development, it is the politicians who, in the end, decide the matter by making laws and directing funds. Without engaging their interest, no one will get anywhere . . . True, Dr Rotter's was a North American statistic, but it makes you worry about the situation in Europe, too. At least there is some hope: in my Salzburg country, thanks to politicians, a high mountain plateau has been saved from development. But, recently, I heard of a project for a new cableway on the Grossvenediger. It makes you weep . . . Heavens above, don't we have far too many cableways already?

One of my friends from Canada – Herbert Kariel, a professor of economic geography at Calgary University – studied the alpine situation. As a result, he issued a terrified warning to the Canadian Alpine Club, begging them to ensure that development was never allowed to get that far in their own country.

Spirits of the Air

Thank God that today such voices can be heard in increasing numbers on both sides of the Atlantic, as well as in the Himalaya, and a general conscience for the protection of the environment has begun to take shape. Yet it will be a continuous battle, with some successes, but many defeats. I remember my own fight against Russian helicopter transport of tourists to K2 from the Chinese side, as well as against a cableway project in Spain. I was supporting my friends of the *Collectivo Montañero por la defensa de los Picos de Europa*, who with the sterling help of a British climber, Robin Walker, finally defeated the financial interests.

The growing number of expeditions and treks also contribute to the despoliation of some of the most beautiful places in the Himalaya. New roads and a number of accompanying facilities increasingly erode the natural barrier of fatigue; no wonder that more and more people arrive. In Biella, in 1987, at an international meeting of mountaineers in which Lord Hunt and other eminent climbers participated, we founded the movement Mountain Wilderness for the protection of the mountain environment. Along with Chris Bonington, I am still one of its guarantors. A number of interventions have taken place since then – in the Alps, the Apennines, on K2 and other places of the mountain world. For too long we climbers have taken insufficient care of our mountains, have committed desecration simply by going to them and opening up the area to outsiders.

PART VI

A New World

IMPRESSIONS GAINED DURING
AN EXTENDED NORTH AMERICAN LECTURE TOUR

Beside me, Chic Scott gnawed on his pipe and gazed over Salzburg's many churches, its fortress, and the grey-green ribbon of the Salzach River flowing through a scattered sea of houses. The town lies plumb in the centre of a wide bowl which stretches from the gently undulating plain and alpine foothills to the north to the massive limestone outcrops of the Kalkalpen. We were standing in a meadow on top of the Gaisberg, a hill of about 1000 metres, and my silent friend, who is Canadian and had been working in Europe as a climbing guide for a year now, was letting his eyes range back and forth over my home town and out to the abrupt line of the Untersberg plateau, with the dark woods at its foot. 'It's nice here,' he said at length, taking the pipe from his mouth and pointing to the dusky rim of flat land below the limestone cliffs. 'See that forest?' He drew a deep reflective breath, which sounded more like a sigh, before continuing, 'Where I live, the forest just goes on and on and on, if you can imagine that. In the Rocky Mountains, everything is so much bigger . . .' Then he clamped his teeth around his pipe once more, not appearing to notice that it had gone out long since. He was homesick. That evening, when we were climbing up from the banks of the Salzach to the rocky fortress of Hohensalzburg, he spoke of Canada again.

Considering the many expeditions I had made around the world, it may sound strange that the North American continent was a blank on the map to me then. I had trodden its margins years ago when filming the Labrador Eskimos with Mario. That was all. Today, when I feel perfectly at home in the Grand Canyon and have flown many times through the skies over New York, it is hard to imagine that my knowledge of America at that time came solely from books, postcards, and a few Westerns. Of course, I knew this was a gap in my experience, a serious neglect on my part, but I could see no practical way of rectifying it. Apart from Alaska, North America is not somewhere you make expeditions to, and where was the adventure in going with a group of tourists? How was I to get there? Everything changed for me when I met Chic Scott.

He found Europe attractive, and sympathetic, but very small, very limiting. After his visit to Salzburg, I drove him back to Leysin in Switzerland, where he was working. Karen and Hildegard, my daughters, came along for the ride, and Mama Tona was alerted to pop one of her special giant pizzas in the oven. We would take the route via Varese, even if this was by no means the shortest way to Leysin. During the long ride the conversation ranged over all manner of things. We spoke of *The Eiger Sanction*, the latest Clint Eastwood thriller, which was pulling in audiences on the other side of the Atlantic, and making the Eiger's notorious North Wall even more infamous. Chic had worked on the shoot for this film along with a Salzburg friend of mine, Norman Dyhrenfurth. We spoke, too, of the Himalaya (which Chic had yet to visit), and about Canada (which I told him I regretted not having seen).

Suddenly he said, 'Why don't you come to Canada, and tell us about your expeditions?'

Could I do that? Was that the way? 'I'd love to,' I told him, 'really love to! But how would I go about it?'

'Oh, I'll take care of that,' Chic replied, and he said it with such nonchalance, you would think it the easiest thing in the world. Even though the North American continent was so large, he told me, Canadian climbers, from the east coast to the west, all knew each other. The Alpine Club of Canada was an extremely well-knit association, its sections keeping in close touch with one another. That certainly proved to be true. But, as I found later, it can be a different story in the United States. You are made just as welcome around that enormous country but, to arrange a lecture tour, have to negotiate individually with all the local clubs along the way. It becomes very difficult to plan a rational and cost-covering route with the vast distances involved.

Chic Scott returned to Canada soon afterwards, and I waited on tenterhooks for news. Would he be able to pull it off? Would I get to tell of my adventures in that land of opportunity between two oceans? Months went by . . . while in Banff, right in the heart of the Rocky Mountains, Chic and Evelyn, the Alpine Club of Canada's

A New World

secretary, worked on my itinerary. When the letter finally arrived, I could not believe my eyes. I was invited to travel all over the continent, from Toronto to Vancouver, with a trip to Los Angeles thrown in. I had mentioned to Evelyn over the phone that I knew a philatelist there, and by chance he turned out to be the main organiser of events for a local climbing and rambling club, the Vagmarken – or Milestones. But more of them later.

I was overjoyed! Never had I believed such a thing possible. Now I burned with excited impatience. Once more, I had seen living proof of how doors open up for someone with foreign languages. If you know five, even if you do not speak them all perfectly, you can regard yourself as a citizen of the world – even three may be sufficient to get you by. I was interested in more than just 'getting by'. When you give up a secure life in favour of freedom and uncertainty, among the advantages to this often difficult freedom is being able to talk to people of other nationalities about their lives and perceptions, besides enjoying the opportunity to convey something of your own experience. It is quite wrong to say that in a civilised country, there is nothing left to discover – the jungle and the Arctic are not the only places where you can go exploring!

A new world! As far as I knew, Gaston Rébuffat had been the only other European mountaineer to make a lecture tour in North America, but that was many years ago. Later, I learned that Dougal Haston, too, organised an extensive circuit in 1974. My visit was in 1975, when I proudly presented my 'show', *Summits and Secrets*. From one lecture venue to the next, I covered enormous distances: the equivalent of several times across Central Europe! Altogether, from my departure to return, I travelled 29,980 kilometres. The tour did not end as planned, just kept extending and extending . . . Even if the earnings were melting away under the southern sun before I could get them home, it was an adventure I would never have missed. To feel in tune with a whole continent – is a wonderful thing! For that, I shall always have Chic and Evelyn to thank.

A glittering sea of lights below the plane's wings, a carpet of twinkling lights, some amber, others nearly white, like luminous pinheads closely packed on a dark pincushion. Street blocks become strange trinkets and there are bright islands down there – impossible now to say what they may be . . . New York is sliding away . . . I am already on my way to Toronto. I have lost all track of time. I don't care. I'm here now. The shiny red Beetle outside the little airport in Luxembourg, my friends Klaus and Brigitte, who had driven me there, waving and waving . . . I can still see them . . . Then Iceland, with its fog banks and dark grey-green patches of land between . . . the east coast of Greenland, a Milky Way of broken pack ice along its length, like disintegrating nebulae seen from up here at 10,000 metres . . . Greenland's chilly peaks, the inland ice, fjords . . . so many hours jumble in my head.

Gradually, the chain of images sorts itself out in my brain, and I am landing in Toronto. Skyscrapers, spattered with lights, thronging streets, yet a strange calm at the heart of it all – it's like one of the Wonders of the World, comprising a quiet Austrian engineer who whisks me home to stay with him. Next day, like a sleepwalker, I take my first steps through a suburb. The trees are in bloom. Springtime in Canada! But towards evening it turns cool, and grey, and a few snowflakes tumble from the sky. 'There's a blizzard on the way,' the engineer announces drily. More snowflakes flutter down, and more. I deliver my lecture, experiencing a little stage fright at the beginning. 'Jolly good! Super!' the people say and begin to stream out of the hall . . . we follow them out, the engineer, some American friends and I – to find it snowing in the streets, just like Christmas! Tomorrow I have to give my talk in Ottawa.

A blizzard rages outside as I stand in the departure hall of Toronto Airport. Everything is white, except for the small dash of colour provided by the maple-leaf device on the Air Canada planes – all of which are grounded. There's no doubt about it: Ottawa is cut off by train, road and air. I have to cancel the lecture. Springtime in Canada!

Two days later I am in Montreal. A train managed to plough its way through the snowdrifts, often barely able to move at all. A friendly Canadian in a fur flying cap, down jacket, and a pipe in his mouth, picks me up at the station, saying, 'There's been a newsflash on radio and TV, telling everyone to stay at home!' Cars have been abandoned all over the place, almost buried under snow. Most of the stores are closed since nobody could get into them anyway with snow up to their doorhandles. But I give my lecture – fifty people turn out for it! Not a lot for a town the size of Montreal. This is a good start, I think to myself. The New World is certainly full of surprises!

I am in high spirits. Below me unfolds the country of the Great Lakes. Like oceans, they epitomise the spaciousness of this Canadian landscape. I am getting into the spirit of it now, taking in more, and more: these endless dark woods, studded with thousands of little lakes, and huge fields – one after the other – like a snowed-in chessboard. For

A New World

hours and hours, they slip below me. Somewhere in the middle is my next stop, Winnipeg. Mountaineers here always complain about how far it is to the Rocky Mountains. No wonder, even in a straight line they are some 1000 kilometres away. And to get here from Montreal has been 1500 . . .

I am taken on a short cross-country skiing trip while I am here, along a frozen river. All is flat, as far as the eye can see. This country wouldn't suit me at all.

On again. Endless farmland beneath the jet's silver wings: this is where all the Canadian wheat comes from, and cattle, too. At last, the Rocky Mountains! A dark indigo ramp on the horizon – not a series of peaks like our Alps, but a multitude of parallel ranges, one behind the other, great arcs of mountains, each with its own name – the Selkirks, the Coast Ranges – until you get to the Pacific Ocean. The main spine of the Rockies, however, towering up here to the west of the Great Plains, extends from north to south throughout almost the whole continent, from the Yukon to New Mexico. It is about 4000 kilometres long. Here on the prairie, where the buffalo herds have long since vanished except for sad remnants, surrounded by fertile agricultural land, lies Calgary and, a hundred kilometres to the west, among the limestone peaks of the Rockies, Banff, main settlement in a large and famous national park, seat of the Canadian Alpine Club and later, home to a great festival for mountain films. Most of my Canadian friends live here – Herb, a geography professor, Pete and Judy, and, above all, Chic and Evelyn, who were responsible for my tour. In those first days after I landed in Calgary, of course I could not have foreseen that I would come back here time and again, that the mysterious curves of the Rocky Mountains would resolve for me into peaks with individual characteristics and very special adventures of their own – just like my summits in the Alps. I have now seen the Rocky Mountains in every season: I know they have their own Matterhorn, Mount Assiniboine; that the rocky citadel of Castle Mountain could easily be in the Dolomites; and that Mount Temple richly deserves its name. They rise from the dark pine forests and I can understand why Chic Scott was so homesick in Europe for his native, immeasurable woods.

Chic was waiting at the airport to drive me to Banff. He stopped off to show me a tiny church on the way, near the Bow River, introducing it proudly as a 'historical monument, very ancient'. Perhaps seeing me had reminded him of the many churches in Salzburg. This modest chapel was called the McDougall Memorial Church and was built in 1875, one of the first churches in this whole area. Chic explained how it was originally intended for the Indians of the Stony Tribe.

Spirits of the Air

When, a little later, we came to a railway line taking trains across the Rockies to Vancouver, he told me how important the opening of this communication link had been at the end of the last century, adding – again, not without pride – that his grandfather was an engine driver on the line back around 1910. I was touched by how gently, step by step, he was presenting his homeland to me, to this Austrian confronting the wide-open spaces of Canada for the first time, having travelled so far to be here, with what seemed only short airdrops into the other cities on the way. Driving towards Banff felt a little like approaching the Salzburg 'basin' from the plain, only to find everything changed. But, as Chic found something to tell me about every landmark on the way, I fancied we were merely continuing the conversation about the great Canadian forests that we had begun on the Gaisberg. Pine woods – spruces and fir trees – were the dominant features, with small maple woods in between, and my friend conjured up for me visions of rich autumn tints in these blue limestone mountains. But here on the Bow River, it was springtime at last, even there banks of ice still stood beside the water and isolated patches of old snow dotted the bright landscape. There was no trace of the blizzard that had struck the east of the country. It was sunny and warm.

In Banff, to my great surprise, Evelyn – dark-haired, shapely – sat down at a grand piano and played Chopin. Maybe one pays more attention when you are a long way from home, but in any case I was enchanted by this melody in the heart of the Rocky Mountains. It seemed strange to be hearing the familiar notes in this Canadian wilderness, where frozen cascades still hung from the mountain walls, where one peak followed another among the infinite forests. The notes pearled away carrying us out of time . . .

The mood was interrupted by the sudden arrival of Evelyn's sister, a wiry grey-eyed woman with dark blonde hair and an extremely dynamic personality. I at once declared her the archetypal Canadian Woman, which prompted some hilarity. Later on, she and Evelyn took me for some fantastic white-water canoeing trips. Certainly, you could traverse all Canada with a woman like this! Definitely an original. I spent several days in the area, lecturing at Banff and Calgary, from where Herb took me off into the prairie to a place where dinosaur bones had been found. Imagine the ecstasies of an old fossil-hunter presented with that! But my programme tugged me on to the West Coast, with its deep bays and countless islands – to Vancouver, Victoria, Seattle (the stronghold of alpinism in the Pacific north-west, where more than 800 people came to hear me and afterwards I climbed with Bill Sumner, Dusan Jagersky, and fourteen-year-old John on their local crag –

A New World

Mount Rainier, a 4393-metre extinct volcano. From a distance it looks like a *Gugelhupf*, covered in whipped cream, rising above the immense pine forests. We reached the top, with one bivouac, by the Liberty Ridge). Later, I moved on to Los Angeles, 1500 kilometres away, then in three days was back another 2300 kilometres to Edmonton – only 300 kilometres, a catspring away, from Banff, my Canadian 'Salzburg'. There, I gave some hard thought to what I should do next. My final lecture was only a month away – a restaging of the one cancelled because of the blizzard in Ottawa, back another 3000 kilometres therefore to the east coast. Meanwhile, I had developed a taste for this country: couldn't there be something for me, too, in the Land of Opportunity? But what? Lectures . . . adventures . . . mountains . . . The American west lay open before me, and I had the feeling of a good time waiting there for me, if only I looked hard enough.

HOW TO CATCH A MILLIONAIRE

Whether Gordon from Nevada is really a millionaire or not, I cannot say with my hand on my heart, but he certainly looks the part. Greying slightly at the temples, a high, intelligent brow, and an air of cool determination. He can be pensive, then suddenly become more full of beans than you would credit a man in his late fifties. He has that certain something, a combination of sensitivity with the raw toughness of a penetrating intellect, which marks out the real businessman. I don't know what his business is – he used to run a flying school. He is a self-made man and, as I said, projects an air of great wealth. He certainly owns a mountain, and an observatory, and he lives with his young and pretty wife and their family in a wonderful house, built of sweet-smelling wood, and overlooking the deep blue Lake Tahoe. Because of prodigious snowfalls that hit the Sierra Nevada, it is often impossible to get to his house by any conventional means of transport. The nearest road is miles away. Gordon has equipped himself with three huge caterpillar-tractor snowmobiles to maintain supplies; on one of these his son is driven every day to school. The boy could take one of Gordon's many horses instead, but with those masses of snow and the humid air blowing in from the Pacific, the snowmobile is probably safer.

I am staying in the house for the time being, but, knowing myself, realise it will be for only a few days. Before this I was in Colorado, where the indefatigable Steve Komito repairs boots for all the mountaineers in the American west in his shop near Denver, and where Michael Covington and his mountain guides take hundreds of people every year to the summits of the Rockies, some by extremely ticklish routes. It has been snowing there a lot, too. When I climbed the East Face of Long's Peak with Michael (a crest more than 4000 metres high), it was more like a winter ascent. And it's partly on account of the snow that I am living now in the millionaire's house . . .

Flashback to Banff: Mountain Holidays, a wilderness outfit run by a couple of Austrians, invite me to go heli-skiing in the Selkirk Mountains. 'That's a rich man's sport,' Evelyn tells me. All the better that it's gratis, then, I think – and we both go. I take a box of slides with me. In case . . .

And so we abandon the hard climbers – all away at the moment, climbing frozen waterfalls – for a life of luxury. (Incidentally, some of those waterfalls are incredible formations – like the Pilsner Pillar, a column of ice some eighty metres high. You can walk right round the bottom of it, a cascade paralysed by frost. It is climbed with the aid of crampons, ice-screws, and most particularly, short axes. You have to stop the minute the weather warms, otherwise the whole flimsy chandelier might suddenly collapse, along with its human pendants.) Another speciality here is skiing on slopes of just a hundred metres high: you have to keep clambering up on skins – very tough and traditional, very Canadian. But, today, Evelyn and I are on easy street. The helicopter, which in the crowded Alps is seen as such a disturbing nuisance, causes little intrusion here in the expanse of the Canadian Rockies. The Bugaboos would hardly be accessible without it, because of the avalanche danger in narrow V-shaped valleys. A splendid, comfortable lodge greets us – you could not call it a mountain hut – ski instructors, a few helicopters, and long, beautiful downhill runs all round us, up to thirty kilometres at our disposal – including the glaciers.

'Try and get in as much downhill as you can manage,' Leo, the stockier of the two Austrians, advises, nodding in my direction. He's going to stay in the lodge. I certainly will! I'll keep it up until my knees turn to jelly.

Which they did.

Seven thousand downhill metres in a single day! I had no idea where I was at the end of it, and that's the truth. You can put that down completely to the helicopter. No sooner are you at the bottom of the hill than it whisks you off somewhere else, up among the peaks – and you peer around you, trying to make out where you have just been. But already, you cannot work it out. The helicopter sets you down again, its powerful rotorblades churning the air. People rush out, ducking low into the snow – despite the need for speed, no one wants to lose his head! Then, off you go again, down a different run, behind an ace instructor, over pristine snow where no one has been for weeks – because the area is so massive. You can enjoy powder snow or firn, and have it to yourself all day! A skier's paradise! No wonder it is not cheap . . . a day here would even then cost you 200 dollars. But there is no shortage of takers. They come from all over America: some are certainly mountaineers, others could be honeymooners – I try to sneak a good look at my fellows during the short breaks, but there's so little time. Over there, another helicopter touches down on a peak. And it's downhill again, down, down! Bend your knees . . . There's snowdust in the air, flashes of crystals. Don't lose sight of the others, most of them racing like champions! Bend those knees! Peter Habeler was rude about my style when I took the guides' course – 'archaic', he called it – but at least it keeps me on my feet. Watch those knees! . . . And we're down. Another trice, we're up again! And once more it's: Remember to bend those knees! and, Keep your head low, watch out for the rotorblades – you don't want it sliced off! How many times have I heard that today? Always somebody says it. A grey-haired man from Nevada whispers it to a pretty young thing next to me in the snow. She is Janice, he Gordon – a nice couple. Then there are the honeymooners: a helicopter ride is scarcely long enough for a kiss . . . but there are plenty of them! Evelyn is streaming down the hill like a goddess – no wonder, with that long Canadian winter!

My knees increasingly feel the strain. That's no wonder either. Perhaps I should have listened to Peter and changed my style? I can't seem to make it work today. Back in the helicopter again; it roars, and up we go. The honeymooner is kissing her millionaire; she beams with joy, no doubt, congratulating herself on her fortune. My God, I suddenly think, that is just what I need. A millionaire. But how to catch one? Then I have an idea (America prompts good ideas): remembering how *The Eiger Sanction* has been enjoying such success in all the cinemas, I think: I know! I'll give a free lecture at the lodge tonight on the Eiger North Wall! I've got some of the slides in my box, and my other pictures can just set them in context. Only today, I won't play it modestly: I'll be a real hero! Superman on the Eiger!   So, I give my lecture that evening, in a style I would never dare at home, and hardly have I finished when the gentleman with the distinguished greying hair sidles over. He comes from Nevada, he says, near Reno: where there are no mountaineers, but it would be extraordinarily interesting if I could give a lecture there. (My heart leapfrogs for joy.) And, why not at Lake Tahoe as well? I am aware that this is the area where the big ski centres are, as well as all the casinos . . . I ask him about the gambling casinos – he doesn't sound too happy that I brought them up – yes, there are plenty, but I am not to worry that it might affect the attendance: he will personally guarantee a respectable minimum fee! He eyes me expectantly, and after a short deliberation, I accept his offer.

Aha! – I think to myself – here's my millionaire! Now, *I* have one. It's something to sing about – not a woman's prerogative! And the mind dreams up untold possibilities: pretty soon it is raining dollars! From now on, the only way is up: America will lie at your feet! But gold does not rub off easily, it says in the old proverb, and you need more than luck and good connections to become a millionaire. You must practically be born to it, for it means hard, very hard work, and always being on your guard. You have to sacrifice a lot. That I don't find so appealing.

So my golden Icarus-dreams are doomed from the start. And besides, it would be too boring in the long run. Really, it is more interesting to dip into all manner of lives around the world, making your own at the same time. But you are allowed to dream: my new friend Gordon could not know what raptures of imagination his timid request unleashed in me – I took care not to let it show (I didn't want that to lower the price!). Later on, I manage to arrange an evening in the American Midwest, 1500 kilometres from Banff, and I seem on an inexorable rise: it's Hollywood, Los Angeles next stop. (And speaking of Los Angeles, the Titian-haired club chairman has already enrolled me as a member of the Vagmarken, the Milestones.)

Will I have to act as my own agent when I get there? I wonder with a sigh. Maybe, I am not born to be a millionaire. Steffi, the Vagmarken redhead, has fabulous hair that reaches to her knees, full and thick – a striking chairman she makes. What a club! A long way from the *Alpenverein*!

'It's a long way from LA to Denver . . .' John Denver sings on the radio, homesick for Colorado . . . indeed it is – about 1600 kilometres. He is singing of Aspen, of the forests of the Rockies, of the waterfalls and the white bark of the aspens.

Sixteen hundred kilometres, then, the other way round, from Denver to LA. Perhaps I should visit my club?

Meanwhile I am staying at Gordon's, in Nevada, with him and his family. They are very friendly and kind, and hardly ever talk business or money. All that seems to belong to some former life of Gordon's. We speak of the universe, and on clear nights observe sparkling clusters of stars and spiral nebulae above the Sierra Nevada. Thousands of wonders up in the sky and thousands of questions to ask. What about

A New World

black holes? Will a new universe develop after this one has gone?

We are sitting in Gordon's observatory, looking up at stars which perhaps do not exist any more; we are surrounded by pricks of light, each one standing for another time, depending on whether they are near or far in the cosmos. We are posing unanswerable questions in a web of light-years, worlds apart. I want to say that in the end, here at Gordon's place, my dream of a new career appears futile – so insignificant in view of the fact that is constantly borne home to me: the sheer fortuitousness of being alive!

After all the different kinds of skiing I encountered in the last weeks – with sealskins, cross-country, with helicopters – here I become acquainted with a new one: Gordon loads the whole family into one of the big snowmobiles and rattles up to the top of his mountain. There is a fine vista over the undulating crests of the Sierra, down to the deep blue surface of Lake Tahoe, that marvellous stretch of water in the mountains, its far bank in California. There are only young trees in the landscape; Gordon explains that the forests all vanished down the pit shafts during the gold and silver rushes. He points eastwards to the brown hilly country of the Nevada Desert.

Some days later I go into the desert with a new friend, a college lecturer. Near Virginia City, a ghost town, we discover an old gallery, bearing the nameplate HOWARD HUGHES. We can't resist it and drag ourselves along on our hands and knees into the bowels of the earth. Three hours go by before we blink back into the daylight again, covered in dust from head to toe, and not a single crumb of silver or gold the better off. Still, a nugget as big as a man's fist was found by a daytripper last week in a nearby shaft.

In the meantime, the leaves of my calendar are falling as the day of my lecture approaches! At Reno and Lake Tahoe, my *Summits and Secrets* is up in coloured lights. Many people must see it as they hustle to the casinos below, but of course the throbbing illuminations for The Golden Nugget and other such attractions also exert their pull on the passers-by. I am anxious to see what the outcome will be. The great day comes. In the red plush seats – fifty people only. Nearly a black hole. The Golden Nugget has won. Gordon sighs, and says that it is a hard lecture to start with in this part of the country, compared to the Eiger thriller, but I should not abandon hope. Nor should he, I tell him, we can try it again some other time. And he nods sympathetically.

Then, he hands over my agreed minimum fee.

A few days later we are passing the packed gambling halls of Lake Tahoe, just before my lecture; regiments of slot-machines rattle and jingle and occasionally spit out money with a great fanfare, but most of the time swallow it up relatively soundlessly . . . We are prepared for the worst . . . it turns out to be a very pleasant, if intimate evening. Gordon and I exchange smiles. 'Not to worry,' he says calmly. All the same, I don't think we'll be taking it to Vegas.

MILESTONES IN CALIFORNIA

'Hi Kurt, can you hear me? How are you?' On the phone is the chairman with the red and wondrous hair. 'We'll be delighted to see you in Los Angeles again,' she tells me. 'Listen, we'll pick you up in Jack's plane at noon, at the Carson City Airfield. Be there!' I am overwhelmed, overjoyed that my suggestion to return to Los Angeles has been taken up, even if there is to be no lecture. Who cares about that! This is almost too much to take in straight away: only in this Land of Opportunity could anyone say they would pick you up by plane! It's a distance of – I don't know – it must be at least 1000 kilometres, yet to them, it seems, no more than we might say at home, 'Wait on the corner, I'll grab a taxi and be right there.' My heart leaps sky-high. The chairman of the Vagmarkens, those oh-so-sympathetic Milestones, is still giving me details about where we are to meet. In the background I can make out a deeper voice, her husband, sending me greetings. It is the voice of a big man, gruff, bear-like. I sigh. Nothing is perfect!

I bid farewell to my millionaire, to Janice and the children. It was so nice staying with them. An hour and a half later and this Austrian mountain-adventurer stands expectantly on Carson City airstrip in the Nevada Desert, heart thumping, hopes high, a rucksack full of slides, and head craned back, scouring the skies for his 'lift'. It comes! Twin-engined, with twin tail booms, an odd-looking craft, one engine in front and the other behind the passenger's cockpit – a Cessna Skymaster, Steffi had said. It loses height, touches down and taxis to a standstill. The Milestones tumble out – a representative selection at least, nothing in the least 'stony' about any of them, or at all angular. Besides Steffi-the-Red, there is brunette Donna and blonde Renata. The pilot, Jack, clambers down, too, tall, smiling, waving cheerily. It is his plane. I could not wish anyone a warmer welcome. The Milestones hug me, relieve me of my backpack and usher me aboard.

Yippee! California, here I come!

The blue surface of Lake Tahoe disappears behind us, as ever more grandiose mountains march past. Looming ahead, the Sierra Nevada! Valleys filled with forest, mountain wilderness, the dark eyes of little

A New World

lakes – then a magnificently incised valley – Yosemite! That fantastic dreamland of granite, beloved of climbers . . .

As an extra treat, Jack flies us in close to the Nose of El Capitan, we skim over Half Dome's bald pate, see a gigantic cascade pouring in to the 1000-metre-deep valley. And then? (Even today, a flush of vertigo washes over me as I remember that ride, such electrifying havoc was played with the senses.) Jack whisks us the full length of the Sierra Nevada, swooping over towers and minarets, soaring around a Californian 'Matterhorn', showing us proud Mount Whitney, one of the four-thousanders and the highest summit of the United States outside Alaska.

Those mountains of Sierra Nevada are so beautiful. Now, that – I think to myself – is somewhere I could live! At the time I had no inkling that for the next few years California would turn out to be my second home, almost indeed a second life, quite separate from the one on the other side of the Atlantic. How often are you reborn, once you have come into the world?

A dismal valley, with only meagre splashes of green, passes below the wings as we head east from the mountains. Steffi explains that Owen's Valley was a verdant paradise until the people there began selling water to Los Angeles. The thirsty megalopolis, pushing out its boundaries and growing thirstier all the time, has so lowered the water table that today almost nothing remains of its once-green splendour. Owen's Valley. Lawsuits rumble on, and you can still see pieces of waterpipe, blown up by demonstrators. Soon we will be landing on the outskirts of Los Angeles.

'Seven million people!' Donna says. She is small, dark-haired and with an Italian air about her. 'That's more, isn't it, than all the inhabitants in Austria?' chips in Renata, in German. She is a new American. It is certainly difficult to grasp how vast Los Angeles is, for you never see all of it, on account of its size, and there are very few skyscrapers. They emerge, two or three stumps here and there, from an immense field of lower houses. The buildings are light, simple and uncomplicated, the majority single-storey or at most one other floor. That is enough with the earthquake danger. The San Andreas Fault runs to the north of the city, that great dislocation in the earth's crust between San Francisco and Los Angeles, rendering the whole area seismically unstable.

We have landed. In one of the many districts of this urban sprawl. My companions deliver me to the home of my philatelist friend, Gordon, a retired postmaster. It is thanks to my long correspondence with him that I met up with the Vagmarken. (I do not collect stamps myself.) So, now I know two Gordons here: a millionaire and a former postal official – how different life can be! The night grows cold, as it does in the desert, but there's nothing to be seen of the desert here. Yet the Mojave begins just outside Los Angeles.

Gordon's wife Norma, a friendly motherly woman, has put an electric blanket on the bed for me. I snuggle under it, switch it to the top setting, and dream of Madam President.

FIFTY-SIX STEPS AROUND A GENERAL

Ever since I was in California, all other generals in the world have lost something of their stature, no matter what decorations on their chest or how many stars on their epaulettes. There, it took fifty-six steps to walk around a general, touching him all the time. Nowhere else will you find a brass hat to match that! General Sherman in the Sequoia National Park.

It was the middle of the night when we arrived at the big trees. Steffi had this idea that nobody could comprehend just how big they were merely by looking at them. It was something much better achieved by touch, by walking round them in the dark.

A strange idea, maybe, but that is Steffi: she is herself a natural wonder . . .

How she managed to get away, I'll never know . . . from all those down parkas she has to sew – and from her husband (whose giant presence kept intruding in my mind). Bud, his name is. He reminded me of the calm and well-weathered hero in those romantic old Westerns with bodies all over the place, the tough guy who never loses his cool, and still manages, in a matter of a moment, to fell three men with a single move of his hand. His grey eyes, set between impressive side-whiskers, looked friendly enough, rather thoughtful if anything, but it would clearly be no joke to have him mad at you. Steffi always treated him with the greatest respect, I had noticed that. John Wayne or not, those dominating whiskers commanded deference!

I wonder why natural wonders have been distributed so unevenly?

Natural wonders: vast tracts of country can boast nothing of consequence – just fields, fields and more fields . . . Of course I know it is possible to see something in every blade of grass . . . but, well, in the long run . . . it is a pity, I think, that the real phenomena are sometimes

A New World

so close together. This was to give me a bit of a headache later on. But that is still in the future, and another story.

So, it is night and Steffi has suddenly stopped the car on the winding uphill road. 'Out you get,' she says. 'See if you can find the big tree. Then, walk round it. And touch it – don't forget to touch it!' She sends me off with a sweet smile. That's how I come to be going round in circles in the dark, all round an invisible monarch.

Steffi is full of ideas.

Though I can hardly see a thing, I succeed in finding the tree, and set off walking. Round and round, careful to maintain contact with the rough, fibrous bark. It feels like fur, or the hide of a horse – and more like being beside an animal than a tree, a calm, docile animal that lets you stroke it. Something huge, a dinosaur, almost – no, bigger even than that! Fourteen steps bring me back to where I can see the rearlights of the car once more. Steffi has left them on to give me one point of constancy in this pitch blackness. Fourteen steps around a tree! 'Why, that's only a baby!' she sings, and I hear her laughing.

A baby, eh? So how big is this General Sherman? After that night I knew it: fifty-six steps it took, my hand on the general, till I was back where I started. This time there were no backlights to guide me, but Steffi waiting in the darkness. We called them the friendly giants, these trees. Each one was an individual. You could imagine them talking to each other at night – and even to crazy visitors like us.

Monorock. A spire of granite. A giant figure with a weathered face. (No whiskers, though!) We parked the car close by, just as dawn came up, reclined the seats and fell asleep. Next thing I knew, the sun was high . . . Steffi slumbered on beside me. I looked at her . . . soft and warm in her wonderful down parka . . . and so close. I had sunk into those downy billows when I fell asleep, and even now remained comfortably afloat, supremely content with America (as you can imagine) – oblivious, then, of its darker sides. Steffi stirred lightly. 'Whaaat's the time?' she blinked, still heavy with sleep.

'Nine o'clock,' I lied, and she whispered, 'That's all right, then. We can sleep a bit longer,' and, with that, my down-swaddled wonder snuggled against me once more, devastating me with her soft eiderdown warmth, and those long, straight, beautiful red tresses, winding and smooth. Ah, Steffi! And I sank again into the blissful softness, wishing that every time I wrapped myself in eiderdown concoctions on the high summits in future, it could be like this. Some while later I sensed somebody peering in the car window at us, some visitor to the National Park, no doubt, but I kept my eyes tight-closed.

It was around noon when we woke properly. Steffi flung the door open with fierce energy. 'Dammit! How could we sleep that long?' She commanded respect, too, did Steffi . . . definitely a no-nonsense gal. When you are married to John Wayne, that's how you have to be. Even her strength was impressive. And she had that swing of the hips, which in Italy we call *la mossa*, a scintillating move of southern women, which switches the heart of the dark cavalier to high frequency . . . she not only knew how to achieve this swing, but to such effect that it could be dangerous to be standing next to her at the time – *la mossa* could toss you against the nearest wall! I dare say John Wayne, that rock of a man, never found himself hurled to the wall, but with lesser guys Steffi is not so pernickety. No wonder they made her chairman. But the last thing I want to do is convey the impression that she lacks charm. She is very feminine and graceful.

In these American forests, which to a newcomer from Europe seem to burst with wildlife, I never felt anything but safe in Steffi's company. It was as if all the animals respected her. Even bears? Well, if there were bears in Sequoia National Park, I am sure even they would have been teddies that day. In her home Steffi has a great raven flying about the place: he bit me on the finger at first sight, but with Steffi he is as gentle as a canary.

We came to a grove of sequoias some way from the others, five or six giants towering above the universal conifer canopy – which here seemed mere brushwood by comparison – and we sat down among them, cradled in their friendly atmosphere. Their rusty bark, I noticed, exactly matched the colour of Steffi's hair . . . I risked a sideways glance, then ran my hand over those marvellous locks, which here, among the giants, were so completely part of nature. Slowly, the big trees moved their massive arms . . .

One of them triggered something in my mind. Dark beards of moss trailed from its branches, grey, intermingling fronds . . . looming over me, like side-whiskers . . .

'Watch out!' Steffi warned me at that moment. 'If one of those sequoia cones clocks you after falling sixty metres, you'll think you've been shot by John Wayne!' She said it in a low voice, gentle as the breeze stirring the branches over our heads. But there he was – John Wayne again! What prompted her to bring him into it?

'I think we had better go,' I said. 'This particular monster is not as friendly as the others.'

In the years that followed we returned several times to our friends in the grove, the friendly giants. We spoke to, or listened to them. But that first time – perhaps because I had never before made the acquaintance of such beings – I was a bit nervous. A crackling in the undergrowth made me jump out of my skin! A bear? No, a bulky figure in a brown uniform: a warden. 'They patrol the National Park,' Steffi explained, 'to see nothing happens that shouldn't.' I took a deep breath. The man passed by, smiling and waving in sociable fashion. He had a weather-beaten face and side-whiskers. And he moved with a slow rolling gait. Like John Wayne.

Later on, in California, I wasn't so twitchy.

GRAND CANYON – A SUNKEN WORLD

A dense grey fog hangs over 'the Valley' (as the inhabitants of Los Angeles like to call their home territory). It is not always obvious to the seven million people who live under this noxious canopy, because of the sheer extent of the city, but you get a better idea from the air, from where it appears as a brownish, barely transparent stain, enshrouding the whole town. In the distance, mountains and knolls rise from it, like a coastline. Sometimes the smog covers them, too. To be sure, there will be rare days when you are able to see the impressive ocean of houses, Los Angeles clear and distinct, like an interminable field. Then you are treated to the best view as the jet makes a wide loop over the Pacific before descending into Santa Monica. The majority of the time, though, only the roofs of enormous industrial complexes, aeroplane factories and other bright reflective structures glint up through this cover of haze. Most people here have never seen the Grand Canyon, only 400 kilometres away as the crow flies.

We are sitting in Jack's Skymaster, passing over the barren brown landscape of the Mojave Desert. A short while earlier Jack dived towards a green oasis in the midst of this pale sandy expanse and landed on a small, clean concrete strip to refuel. Around us are brown hills and black mountain ranges – probably solidified lava. We still have a long way to go: to fly the full length of the canyon means another 300 kilometres each way. So we crowd back into the plane, where I am sitting next to Chuck, a young Vagmarken climber, who is supporting his hand rather awkwardly. It was put in plaster last weekend after he attempted something ambitious at the local outcrop. The pilot, Jack, sits diagonally in front of me, a man coming up for forty now, I guess. His sharp aquiline nose has the effect of accentuating all the checking glances he casts out of the window, between giving his eighteen-year-old daughter some advice about flying. She already holds a licence, but her father thinks there remains room for improvement. At the moment, one of his three planes languishes, wingless, in the cellar of his house – but that is not something daughter Beverley likes to be reminded about.

Word has it that she was doing fine until a friend kept her waiting at an aerial rendezvous. When, suddenly, she realised her fuel was running low, there was barely time to put down in a cornfield, which is where her troubles started. The corn was unusually tall, much taller, it seems in this field than in any of the others, and when the plane came to a standstill . . . Whoops! No wings! Completely sheared off by the cornstalks! She must have been coming in at one hell of a lick!

'It's no problem,' Jack had said when I coaxed the story out of a reluctant Beverley recently, 'I can fix it.' He is an aeronautical engineer – or, more properly, was: now he produces sporting goods, designing new models with a refinement that only an aircraft engineer can give. He makes streamlined tents, all gleaming and metallic, which in their styling and fabric look like futuristic flying machines. And sophisticated sleeping-bags, with built-in mattresses, yet still ultra-light. Multi-layered clothing systems to meet almost any requirement, the ingenuity of which only Jack can explain. You think, surely there has to be some button that serves no practical purpose, but no! Every feature is vital and performs a variety of functions. Jack, in short, is an inspired inventor. Though he does not consider himself well-off – three planes notwithstanding – that doesn't bother him. He is one of life's realists. I sincerely believe that anyone who feels at all depressed or mixed up would only need to meet him for things to resolve themselves immediately. He radiates convincing optimism, and however much we Europeans may scoff at what we see as the American laid back attitude, Jack, inventor and philosopher, could prove in a few words (or a lot, maybe, if that's what the occasion demanded) that everything would come right in the end. You will get through, if you want to, if you are prepared to rationalise your way out. Jack laughs a lot; you rarely see him without a smile on his face – as if this in itself were part of his philosophy – unless he is lost in thought.

Now, as Jack talks to his daughter and Chuck dozes, it is my turn to be buried in my own thoughts. A perfectly straight line runs below us across the desert, like a double black thread – we have been following it for most of the flight so far: it is the highway from Los Angeles to Las Vegas. Microscopic cars move along it. Occasionally, you see houses by the wayside, or a square or circular green patch, and for the rest, just pale, desolate sandy plains, shimmering in the heat, with mountains of shattered rock like ruins in an endless brown sea. The great spaces of North America with their diversity of scenery, like their people, are

A New World

difficult to describe in just a few pages. A single visit gives only a small idea, but it does show what a cramped world we inhabit in Europe, where so much has become impossible. Gazing out into these endless spaces, you feel you have stepped from what was your life into another, wider one. Even as a visitor, here only for a short time before returning home, the door never closes. The fascination which this continent exerts – despite the darker aspects of the American way of life – few European can deny who have been there.

The plane is shaken by some hefty turbulence. Father and daughter – both of them? – busy themselves at the controls, minimising its influence. 'The desert!' Jack laughs shortly, casting a glance back at me. I nod back. Yes, the desert! Hot air currents rise from every mountain ridge – here comes another to rattle the plane, and another. It must be an oven down there. I cannot help remembering how yesterday we were sitting in Jack's Jacuzzi, the whole family: Jack's wife Joan, with her long sleek hair, and several young men – not all at once, of course: the family is very big. This circular hot tub, about three metres across, is set into the floor of the living room at just the right depth for you to be able, sitting in hot water up to your chest, to reach over your shoulder and pick up a drink. If you wanted to eat a meal in it, the water would have to be lowered slightly but, basically, anything is possible, says Jack. You could even wear a swimsuit, if you had a mind to, but that seems a rarity in this house. When I walked in with Jack the first time, I was taken aback at being introduced to an Austrian pilot and his fiancée soaking in the pool. 'Servus!' I stuttered, bowing to the naked nymph. But a few more minutes saw us exchanging all the Austrian gossip, as if we were in a Viennese café.

Jack's latest invention is another pleasure pool, which he has constructed from an old boat. This small craft penetrates the outer wall of the third floor of the wooden five-storeyed house which he and his family have been sawing and hammering away at for two years now. The stern projects into the open air, while the bulk of the boat resides in the living room. Every evening, this cheerful family and their guests relax in the airy and unusual construction. 'Well, I couldn't fit the whole boat in the room,' Jack explained to me. What would our building regulations make of that? I wondered. But the house that Jack builds stands in the beautiful maple woods of New England on the East Coast. (Yes, like so many Americans, Jack has moved home once more!)

Las Vegas has come into view! By the bright light of day, the sparkling gambling town with its famous shows looks disappointing.

Spirits of the Air

Small pale squares in the brown of the desert – nothing more. But a short while later we see a stretch of the most heavenly deep blue: a lake pushing its many fingers into the desert valleys, like a skeleton-leaf of blue water. 'Lake Mead,' Jack tells me. Small boats are buzzing about on its surface. How big, how branched this lake is – incredible! The course of the old river and its tributaries have been flooded by the waters of the Colorado behind the colossal Hoover Dam. The main valley has long since vanished under the immense reservoir – so many indignities this Colorado must suffer on the long journey from its source in the Rocky Mountains to the Gulf of California, 2000 kilometres away in Mexico. From the reservoirs, water is drawn off for irrigation; the biggest vegetable-garden in the world, the Imperial Valley in California, is exclusively nourished by Colorado water. Only a fraction of the river, a pathetic remnant, reaches the Gulf of California not least because of the enormous evaporation during its long passage through the deserts.

The famous Grand Canyon of the Rio Colorado would not exist today, would probably have been filled with water like Lake Mead, had it not been protected from economic exploitation in the past by being granted national monument status. Most people are unaware that Lake Mead is a drowned canyon of the Colorado.

The Grand Canyon . . . 'We'll be there in a moment!' Jack sings out and starts nosing down. We are gliding over a bay, an arm of the lake, towards the entrance to a gigantic chasm.

I am staggered! Overwhelmed is no word for it! And anyway, there's no time to be overwhelmed when new sensations are continually bombarding you, shaking you, grabbing your attention, whetting your appetite for even more unexpected thrills. You are looking ahead, back, down, as gigantic buttresses sweep past, pillars and palaces of red rock, side valleys opening and closing, the terrific gorge agape below you . . . You are flying through the biggest trough on earth. All the pictures I have ever seen of the Grand Canyon are forgotten. They are tiny facets, mosaic pieces, nothing more – I see that now. No human brain can comprehend this intricate labyrinth which is the Grand Canyon. It is a world.

'A sunken mountain range . . . a submerged land', is how Indian tribes in ancient times are said to have described the colossal chasm. We are flying now at low altitude over an immense, wide valley, bordered to left and right by relatively small walls . . . flying like a midge over a blanket.

The bluffs on either side sometimes draw more closely together, then pull apart, periodically yielding to tributary valleys – in places there may be fifteen or twenty kilometres between the two sides of the canyon . . .

'The outer rim,' I hear Jack say, indicating the upper edge of the canyon, to our left and right, just a little higher than we are flying. Then he points obliquely downwards, where a deeply incised chasm running more or less in the direction we are following, creates a jagged edge in the wide red bedrock below, 'And that is the inner rim.' He pulls the aircraft closer to this incision, so that the view into its depths really opens up. You could imagine an angry giant having slashed the ground with an axe, in a frenzied, zigzagging fashion. Steep vertical walls drop away to bottomless depths: it is a terrible abyss, at least 1000 metres down to the Colorado River, which appears now, far far below, as a small greenish ribbon, filling the narrow base of the cleft. Jack banks steeply into the chasm and we follow its direction as best we can. This inner gorge of the river has many twists and side valleys, cutting the rocky surface of the Esplanade, as the wide course between the outer rims is known. Table-like mesas, which occur in many places as a result of the erosive action of the side canyons into the Esplanade, are sometimes several kilometres across, so that our little plane, in its low-level flight, one minute skims the surface with its rare green bushes, and the next leaps the open air above a deep and narrow cleft, or niche, or amphitheatre, as it approaches another near-brush with the following red mesa. Jack (understandably in the circumstances) is now in sole control of the aeroplane; his daughter is glued to the window, just like Chuck and me. We take some pictures, naturally, but above all we are looking, looking, looking . . .

For 300 kilometres we fly through the Grand Canyon – and then back again, higher up, to give a totally different perspective. How can that be expressed? Words? Music? A painting perhaps?

I met people who were utterly under the spell of the canyon, like John, an old ranger in the Thuweep valley, whom I have now visited so often. The last time I saw him he winked at me and said, 'He got you too, the canyon!' Since then I have climbed down to the bottom and to little-known places which Steffi told me were 'summits' of the sunken mountain range, and later shared the adventure again with Chuck and my blonde daughter Karen. I have listened to the frogs in the crevices of the Esplanade, and more than once frozen with sudden shock at the sound of a rattlesnake. I remember the night when a strange supple animal came several times to our camp – a soft ringtail-cat. He was after the foodbag, which of course I did not deny to such a rare visitor. And one day, with the help of Tom and Bonnie, I hope to succeed at last in performing a full 'Eskimo Roll' in a kayak – so far I have only managed to get halfway, leaving me head under water. It must be a great thing to achieve, and especially because a great dream of mine is to descend the whole canyon in a kayak.

... A volcanic landscape! Black lava flows slide now below the wings of our plane, flows that issued from conical dark mountains millions of years ago, and still cleave to the walls of the canyon. 'That's Vulcan's Throne.' Jack points out a perfect cone of grey and rust colour. Scientists have worked out that this volcano was last active 1.2 million years ago, when its lava cascaded into the canyon. Compared to the age of the canyon, which the Colorado River slowly carved over a period of six million years in the wide plateau of what is today Arizona, that is only 'yesterday'. The rocks of the canyon walls, exposed to the light of day by continuous erosion, contain the whole history of our earth's crust in their multiple forms and unusual colours. The 'Vishnu-layer' inside the 'inner granite gorge' of the canyon (about the deepest spot, almost 2000 metres below the upper rim) is amongst the oldest rocks known anywhere on the planet – 2000 million years old. When, 'yesterday', the volcano erupted, no humans saw it. There were no humans. But what a spectacle it would have been: the shiny red, glowing lava flow tumbling for more than 1000 metres to the river, eventually creating a natural dam to stem the flow of waters, while on the other side the liquid lava ran on a further fifty kilometres down the dry gorge. How many more stories does this canyon hold?

... Snow! Everything gleams white over there! A whole forest, extending for miles along the upper rim of the canyon – trees under snow. We are still in the plane, and seem to have emerged into winter now ...

Later on, Steffi would explain to me how the climate is so different at different levels in the canyon. There may be burning heat at the bottom, while a cold wind whistles around the upper rim. I discovered woods on the north rim, with deer, fir trees and mountain meadows ... just like Bavaria, it was, or Austria. But 1000 metres lower we had just hiked and climbed through a desert landscape with metre-high cactuses.

In front of us now, the wide plains of the Painted Desert have appeared, home of the Navajo Indians, the former masters of this land ... Jack swings the nose of the plane into an upward curve and we start back. Inside my head, as I write, I still see walls and terraces, moving plains, castles and gorges in swift succession. I feel as if I was allowed a glimpse into the inner structure of a gigantic crystalline lattice. One hour later, from high above, I take a last look at the volcanic landscape we passed earlier in the day, unaware that this would one day become my favourite place in the whole canyon. Toroweap.

Hardly anybody knows it. Only John, the ranger, lives there. Occasionally a visitor will come by, having made the bumpy, hundred-kilometre detour up a dirt road. But to arrive at the edge of the canyon makes the long journey worth while. Carefully, on all fours, you approach the edge of the drop. Then you lie there and look down, down and down 1000 metres to the bottom.

ATLANTA – THE HOLY CITY

'And what wonders of nature do you intend photographing this time?' Teresa asked, her eyes flashing.

'Only a town in America,' I protested wearily. 'Really, just a town with skyscrapers.' For some while now I had been avoiding all talk of natural wonders – ever since the fine morning Teresa found my box of slides of the giant trees in California. To accentuate their unbelievable scale, I had inserted red-haired Steffi between their trunks . . . more than once . . . so much more graphic, I thought, than flat wooden signposts with prosaic explanations. But try explaining the principles of living photography to a judge! Especially a would-be judge from Italy, who happens to be your wife . . .

In any case, the States are a good deal more than just California . . . more than Los Angeles – 'that town of the angels', as my wife would insist on calling it, with a certain edge to her voice. Having the most honest of all intentions (sorry, the most honest intentions of all), I took a plane to Georgia . . .

Atlanta – the holy city . . .

Odd title, isn't it? Most good Christian people (like this Austrian Catholic) know that the Holy City can only be Rome. Even so, I have to say, nowhere have I met so many ardent 'believers' as in Atlanta – they believe in progress, in religion, are convinced they have found the positive solution to race problems, and they are sworn to extraordinarily bold building concepts. If that were not enough, the United States had Atlanta to thank for a positive-minded President. For that alone, I feel hesitant in starting this story.

'Bring me back some compelling shots of Atlanta's famous *megastructures* when you are next in America,' my publisher had asked me –

referring to the unusual skyscrapers for which the town is famous, superlatives of modern architecture . . . That explains why I was there now. With the best intentions of all, and only two days to go before my return ticket to Europe expired (I had stayed too long in Colorado and at the Grand Canyon!) Buoyed with optimism, I stepped on to the Atlanta plane at Kennedy Airport in bright sunshine . . . Now it was raining, and almost impossible to see anything. As we touched down, I could only dimly make out the grass at the edge of the runway.

How are you even going to find the right skyscrapers in this? I growled to myself as I boarded the bus at the terminal. They all looked alike. Some sort of concrete Dolomites in horrible weather. Still, I made a plan: today, explore the situation, tomorrow take the pictures – if the sun comes out! But would it? The situation was desperate. And equally desperate must have been the forlorn expression I directed towards a charming young lady, sitting opposite. She was surrounded by parcels and the only passenger on the bus besides me. She answered my look with one of compassion. Clearly, she was possessed of a heart full of understanding for the predicaments of others . . .

All very innocent. Nothing more . . . I swear by the Saints of Atlanta – and by Holy Saint Rupert of Salzburg, too – that this is not going to be a frivolous story, even if it threatens to start out that way. So, here I was, caught by surprise at such a sympathetic gaze. One is always pleased to be understood.

'Are you from Atlanta?' I asked the friendly being.

'Sure – you here for a vacation?' She beamed at me, an angel under this desolate, shrouded sky. And a native of this town! A sensation of relief ran through me, as if she would be able to blow away these heavyweight clouds in an instant . . . Immediately, the day was less grey. And I lost no time letting her know that I was by no means on holiday, as she supposed, rather . . . (what should I say? Something impressive! A little white lie?) . . . rather on an important assignment for an Austrian university . . . which . . . er, which needed photographic documentation of famous Atlanta! (To tell the truth, my publisher was Italian, and Saint Rupert – well, hopefully he was still back in Salzburg and didn't hear that!) Bemoaning my bad luck with the weather, I told her how lost I felt in this enormous town. That at least was true. With an expert eye, I had assessed the weight of her luggage: it looked as if there was the possibility of lending a hand here – I had been a Boy Scout when young, and none of my Scouting virtues (nor skills) has gone to waste since. Moreover, it was clear to

A New World

me that, as a local, she could scout out my options and possibilities better than I!

If she had a mind to.

Pearlstrings of lights were strewn through the branches of trees in an avenue between mighty skyscrapers, whose walls reared into the fog above us. Just before they vanished from view, high up, I could make out cross-connections between them, floating tunnels from one building to another. And, on the sidewalk, a multitude of colourful reflections shone from the wet asphalt. A dynamic mosaic, like the ever-renewing patterns of stained glass chips in a shaken kaleidoscope. Such beautiful pictures. Only my 'megas' – the tall ones – eluded me in this weather! 'Tomorrow, perhaps,' comforted Barbara (that was her name). But I no longer needed consoling: I was in high spirits . . . it's always a thrill to drop in somewhere from the sky and continue living as if you had always been there! Whenever it happens, you feel as if the earth is welcoming you . . .

Two hours I have been in Atlanta, and before that knew nothing about the place, never met anyone who lived there – yet here I am, choosing gifts with this blithe spirit for a feast-day that exists for me, too, somewhere else in the world – for Christmas! I carry parcels, advise on whether we should take this or that . . . She smiles, nods. True, I find myself wondering occasionally what I am up to, my bewilderment emerging now and then – but, on the other hand, it is as if I had always been here; that's how it is. I am at home.

Turning a corner, I notice a sign: bright red writing, letters as big as houses, dazzling out of the murk: COCA-COLA! Mega-Cola. It's no surprise to find it dominating everything, here: Atlanta is the headquarters of the multinational company. This is where the brown, foaming fluid started its victorious course . . .

I am surprised to see so many black faces: my companion guide Barbara tells me that about a third of the inhabitants of this town are black; there is even a black mayor. A black couple under a brightly coloured umbrella – presenting a composition of yellow, blue, red and green triangles – flirt happily, leaning on the railing of a bridge as we pass. Black consciousness here appears to me quite different from in New York, freer, more relaxed – am I right? Barbara replies that much is happening here, and the ghettos are disappearing.

So, what about 'Underground Atlanta'? I had already heard about that. Oh, that is just for the tourists, with souvenir shops, cheap entertainment, cafés, bars . . . not worth your while at all to go there! says Barbara, almost primly. Okay, okay, I feel tempted to soothe, but decide to keep quiet. She seems rather high-principled, which is a pity, really. Being so nice, otherwise. Then I think back, to how on the bus she said, 'Of course, you could always come with me. I'll do my Christmas shopping and show you all the important places.' What a lucky strike, I thought – such a delightful lady, and so helpful and understanding right away. Maybe I even radiated triumph – glorying in how easy it was to get by as an Austrian in the States!

While we continue to walk down the street a whirl of ideas spins through my brain: how exciting, to help such a person to do her shopping, how useful that she is willing to show me all the important . . . Ah! but not Underground Atlanta! Alas, she seems really serious about that . . . might one change her mind? Bend it a bit? ('Kurt,' an inner voice warns me, 'you are not in California, here. Behave yourself!') The parcels and string bags begin to weigh heavy: a good deed every day – sure, that's what I am already accomplishing, brave Boy Scout that I am . . . But what about a second one? At this critical moment, with goatee beard and broad-brimmed hat, Baden-Powell floats before me – he raises three fingers, in international salute . . . I take it as a sign: it doesn't have to be just one!

Frowning, the apparition vanishes back into spiritual fog: apparently that wasn't quite what he meant. (I have since found out that B-P's three fingers stand for duty to God, Country and helping one's Fellow Man – or Woman. So I was not totally wrong! But some days are full of misunderstandings . . . which would soon be confirmed.)

My good deed is getting more and more ponderous: now I am carrying five string bags and cardboard boxes. However, I don't blame my good fairy, and think of Baden-Powell. If destiny provides you with a strapping mountaineer from Austria for Christmas . . . She only hangs on to the full black shopping bag she was already carrying on the bus, 'Christmas tree balls – watch out, they're glass!' she explains with a dismissive gesture when I attempt to take it. 'And peaches,' she adds with a sweet smile, 'peaches from Georgia are the best in the United States!' From her clear eyes shines deep conviction. Really, the best? What can be the secret of those convincing peaches from Georgia? But I don't rack my brain over it for long. Atlanta is altogether a convincing town, I think to myself – and cannot foresee that next morning it will appear to me holier than Rome. At present, that is not in question. Barbara speaks of Georgia's peanuts. Their popularity has diminished. For political reasons? Perhaps. Nobody, however, could say that of Coca-Cola; on the contrary . . . Triumphantly red, another giant neon sign glows out between the grey-blue silhouettes of the mega-buildings. Is it the same one I noticed before? I turn around on my heels . . . Could be. I am a bit confused in this glittering, glistening metropolis . . . What if Barbara were to lose her way? No, she would never go astray . . . I feel pretty sure one could never lead her from her strict path.

Coca-Cola. I have personal experience of that. A sort of passion. I was almost addicted to it. But then I kicked the habit. Does that happen to Americans, too? How come today I keep noticing advertisements for it everywhere, to which normally I would not pay any attention? But this is an unusual day anyway. Even the gentle rain tickles pleasantly on the skin. Another laughing Cola poster! At the same time I notice a vending machine. Barbara has seen it too. We could have a Coke, she suggests. Oh, tempting Atlanta! Why not? And, though I do not really want one, I draw two from the machine. It tickles pleasantly in the throat, and we smile at one another. How could we otherwise, with all that publicity; but is Barbara's smile merely dutiful? Cheers, I say to myself, glancing at my companion: no, it is genuine! Cheers – for this brimming city, Atlanta, bubbling over with surprises . . . Cheers (and I steal another look) for this sweet girl's great Coca Cola town . . . By the way, I could use another one! Am I going to become addicted all over again?

I pull Barbara into a bar – she does not object. Before we enter, I peer up at the sky and think that it still looks like the thumbs down for my photo-mission. Still, is it my fault these damned megastructures are lost in the clouds? In any case, there are some pretty enthralling compositions down at this level, some very shapely images . . . and so close to hand! Sneaking another look at my companion, I feel tempted to say something. We sit down. The waiter arrives and, hissing, a fresh Coca-Cola shoots into the glass – my third today! (I had already been given one by the stewardess, shortly before landing in Atlanta.) I really should stop now, otherwise it all starts again – Barbara is on her second glass. She looks delightful.

What a craving! Can I help it if Coca-Cola makes me high? It is a dangerous drink for me. I have heard it can dissolve one's teeth – a whole set of false teeth – within two weeks, but such stories are of course fairy tales. I, for one, can still boast a wolf's full dental pride as my own! What would my Little Red Riding Hood say to that? Does Barbara know her Brothers Grimm? ('Kurt!' I am warned again. My patron saint, Rupert himself this time? Too late! Under the effects of the brown elixir, my fantasies are working overtime. Everything appears highly positive to me. And Barbara?) She now casts a wide-eyed, almost innocent glance at me, and smiles – encouraging, no, inciting, 'You don't speak much . . .'

True – it is quite a while since I have said a word! Oh, good Little Red Riding Hood. 'Sorry,' I answer pensively, sucking air through my wolf's teeth, 'I am a person who thinks a lot,' and while she nods, admiringly: 'I was still worrying about the megastructures.' She is wearing a claret-coloured dress, flatteringly cut, front and back. All is mega! I become absorbed in the image. 'Really, nature is responsible for the best work,' I add, 'think what an eternal structure the Grand Canyon is!' Her wide, deep eyes, are enlightened, and profound as the skies of Utah.

All of a sudden, a chance movement yanks me abruptly back to Georgia. The black shopping bag tips over. Those peaches! I jump up to help, but am rejected: 'It's all right. Take it easy!' And bending forward, Barbara sets the bag upright again. A short, insignificant gesture, but offering such a delicious and confusing view! Oh, Georgia – the Peach State! She smiles at me as if nothing had happened. And of course, it hadn't. Thoughtfully, I regard the claret-coloured dress. Wine or Coca-Cola? That is now the question.

'By the way, where do we have to go with all these parcels?' I ask quietly. (Oh, good Saint Rupertus, I feel your warning gaze! But am I not allowed to discover Georgia with heart and soul? Please stay in Austria's apple orchards tonight and turn a blind eye to my reconnaissance. Aren't you supposed to be a vegetarian?)

Barbara throws me a long glance, and for an instant seems confused by my question. With full reason: it is already evening. 'Well, actually, yes . . .' she replies, rather shyly, and smiles. 'The best thing will be if we go to my home.'

(Holy Saint Rupert, don't blame me!)

That was my last Coca-Cola today, I tell myself, as we glide through the thousand vibrating, flickering lights of Atlanta. Now for the wine.

(Saint Rupert remained hidden.)

We enter the house. Does she live alone? I am apprehensive that our promising acquaintance might be disturbed by outsiders. I remember a similar situation, where there was a wild and jealous dog . . . but that is a different story.

As she opens her apartment door, there is neither a stern-faced, six-foot fiancé, nor a slavering wolfhound – instead, a voice, clear as a little bell, rings out, 'Hello-o-o!' . . . and two friendly blue eyes under neatly coiffured, red-blonde hair scrutinise me frankly. Barbara introduces me, 'This is an Austrian photographer, Wendy,' I am treated to a magic smile. Heavens above! Almost too much of a good thing! Another ethereal being! I feel myself wavering: should I be happy or sad? On balance, I was sad. What a complicated situation . . .

Still, I had not the slightest inkling of the series of body blows which were heading in my direction.

At least I had found a home, I thought, and looking around, wondered: where will they put me? But that was not important. Not yet. 'It is wonderful for a stranger to find friends and assistance when he arrives in a big town for the first time,' I said, and meant it truly, as I stretched out my legs. They were feeling the strain of Atlanta's long avenues, and my arms were stiff from the weight of my pretty companion's parcels. We were sitting in the kitchen.

The answer caught me totally unprepared . . .

'We are a religious household, and one of our aims is always to help people,' the red-blonde smiled warmly; both of them nodded. Barbara offered me one of her peaches – all orderly, on a plate.

My face must have spoken volumes, and my spiritual flag dipped immediately to half mast. What a blow! The pretty young lady, whom I had accompanied all afternoon, from shop to shop, who had been so charming and brought me to her house, had not done so, as I supposed, in reponse to my irresistible appearance, but out of 'love for one's fellow man' – Christian charity!

I fancied the insipid taste of watered wine on my lips – I needed a Coca-Cola, urgently. I got it. 'Wine or Coke . . .' I remembered, upset, and stared at the ceiling. But the bubbling elixir coaxed me from my sad considerations. Everything could be rationalised: hadn't I seen far worse matters through? In my mind, in this hour of disappointment, suddenly appears my father . . . Fathers will always help their sons. Didn't Father graduate in Theology during the time he was studying Biology before becoming a high school teacher? There is a proverb: 'Nothing you learn is ever wasted.' Even if only your sons apply it.

Barbara unpacked the other mega-peaches from her shopping bag and put them on the table. I sighed: everything had entered a different phase, somehow. Yet: hope dies slow. Following the principle 'Father will sort it out,' I entered the field of Theology myself, telling them how he was an expert on different religions, had graduated twice – and how, even with so many flawed interpretations of the Christian doctrine which exist today, he could still see through them perfectly well.

The girls smile and nod politely – they say, Atlanta too is a religious town. I then start talking about Saint Rupert: I scrape together all my Catholic knowledge, feel like a participant in some religious quiz, who despite diabolic buffets of fate, is finally making headway again, and growing optimistic once more. Even so, by and by I get the feeling that something is wrong. Difficulties of comprehension? The red-blonde girl looks at me with almost a touch of challenge . . . Then she says, still amicably, but somewhat reservedly: 'We are a Baptist community.'

There is a great silence. I gasp for breath, in deep desperation.

'You are an Austrian, therefore Catholic, and it is not your fault,' says my pretty young lady consolingly, Barbara, my Little Red Riding Hood from the bar where the Cola-revelation took place. At this moment, I feel like a scorched and toothless old wolf.

Even so, at the same time, I recognise the clear need to prove myself a valuable member of human society. While I am brooding over how to rebuild my damaged status in this house, a young man – another Baptist – blows through the door and announces that he has been discussing metaphysical questions with his friend upstairs. I grasp the opportunity with both hands and escape to the first floor, to converse with the Baptists. I expect to return in a short while.

In our discussions we even reached an acceptable compromise! Meanwhile, however, down on the floor below, all discussion centred round where the Catholic should sleep. And before I could explain that he was happy with little comfort, they had booked me into a hotel. That's how it goes, if you don't, like a devil, keep your hoof in the door . . . *Himmelkreuzdonnerwetter! Himmelkreuzbirnbaum! Zum Teufel nochmal!* . . .

How did the story go on from this point? As a matter of fact it went surprisingly well (looked at with a cleansed mind). A photographer appeared: Oliver. Not only did he take me to a simple motel, but wanted to accompany me the following day . . . 'to all the important places'.

There was to be a Baptist meeting, too, late in the morning – which I was invited to attend. Barbara and Wendy were working in a hospital, and Oliver had free time only after noon – before that I would scout around on my own.

And my patron saint from Salzburg, who had disappeared so abruptly during my chat with Barbara? I have to confess, I saw him again. The night after, I had a terrible dream: Coca-Cola, Barbara, and Saint Rupertus – it was a nightmare, a revolting mixture,

A New World

bubbling in my brain! But by and by, things cleared up, purified: the face of the saint rose above the sin. And I called out to him from the depths: 'Saint Rupert! You should have told me right away . . .!'

Then I woke up. I don't know whether saints take malicious pleasure in others' discomfiture. Surely not. But before he disappeared, I swear my Saint Rupert was grinning . . .

I rose early, grabbed my cameras – but it was raining. After a while, it stopped, though the sky remained covered with low-moving clouds, damp fog and streaks of mist reaching down . . . Oliver, the photographer, had given me some tips where to go for my 'megas'. For want of time, I turned down a visit to the Cyclorama. This is a circular painting, with a circumference of 122 metres, a height of 15 metres and – wait for it! – weighing 8164 kilos. It is, I confess, the only picture whose weight I know. To be serious, it is one of the three biggest paintings in the world, a breathtaking depiction of the Battle of Atlanta in 1864, during the Civil War, when the town was almost totally destroyed. Rebuilt, Atlanta today is the only real metropolis between Washington and New Orleans, situated at 300 metres above sea level in softly undulating countryside below the southern Appalachians. It is the economic and cultural focus of the American south-east. Practically every big enterprise in this area has its head offices in the town with its near two million inhabitants. A friendly lifestyle, pulsating vigour and futuristic buildings characterise the capital of Georgia.

Besides their architecture, the mega-buildings were interesting to me, above all, for what they offered to the people living inside – and their effects upon them. That is why I was on my way this morning to the Colony Square complex. Oliver had recommended one particular 'monster' of interconnected skyscrapers! I found it contrasted sharply with surrounding low villas, set in gardens, and some old houses tucked in front of it. A friendly man in the porter's lodge of one of the skyscrapers explained the layout to me, by means of a model in the entrance hall: 'Here is our hotel, this is the bank, these two buildings are apartment blocks, this one too – in part, at least – but inside there is also the library, the post office and the hair salon; our swimming pool is right here, ice rink there, and over this side are all the stores: food, clothes, and a drug store . . .' He pointed first to this, then to that building – incredible: nothing, absolutely nothing had been forgotten! I looked at him with wide eyes – then asked, where hereabouts I could find a Coke machine. 'Just back there!' – he gestured.

I fetched a can, and sat down on a bench in front of the post office, in order to reflect upon all I had seen. It was my sixth can this morning –

already I was well on my way. I put it down to the multitude of home-made chapatis I have consumed throughout much of my life in the Hindu Kush, the Himalaya, the Karakorum: their effect has been to make my stomach elastic – like that of a boa constrictor – and for days I can stay without food . . . but then I have to eat a lot. It works the other way round, too! And applies to drinking as well. I am familiar with it from other periods in my life when I was into peanuts besides Coca-Cola. It becomes a big effort to stop. The Americans, I notice, drink the brown elixir like their daily water, not needing even to burp. Admirable.

After a visit to the library, a look at a skating class, I take the high-speed elevator to a rooftop restaurant which the porter had recommended. What a hurly-burly! Cooks in high hats, elegantly dressed guests – an exclusive high society meeting? A feast? A marriage? Some binge evidently, judging from the giant cakes! Am I allowed to take pictures? I tell them I am on a commission for (how did it go?) – an Austro-Italian university . . . 'No problem!' A piece of cake and a Coca-Cola – that makes the seventh today. As I go down from the seventeenth floor with the flashing special express lift, I cannot restrain a loud and extended burp when the cabin brakes sharply and comes to a halt at the tenth floor. I am still at it when the door opens – and the gentleman who joins me, apparently calibrated by steady consumption of the local brew, looks in my direction, astonished: 'You come from abroad, don't you?' Embarrassed, I have to admit that is so, just as the fast lift sets off, squashing my intestines once more, 'I am from A-a-u-u-stria' – and once more I can hardly contain the rising fizz as I aspirate the name of my home country. We are down now, thank God! No more Coke today, I swear an oath. My over-expanded chapati stomach is – after seven cans – obviously at loggerheads with it.

Altogether, though, I am very impressed by this fine complex. What scale! What mind-blowing variety! Here, you really can find everything on one and the same spot.

Back at the porter's lodge, I thank the man for his tips. Suddenly, he says, drily, 'We are going bankrupt.' Bankrupt? Yes, bankrupt, he nods. I cannot help feeling sorry for him.

Forgetting my resolution, I say, 'Let's have a Coca-Cola together?'

'No, I hate it!' He shudders with disgust. I stare at him as if he were the First American in person . . .

What the man in the porter's lodge revealed was – as I found out later – typical of the financial situation of other mega-complexes, too. Is

A New World

that absurd? How many people want to live in a place where they can find everything, absolutely everything within easy reach of their home? Whether or not the constructions might be true superlatives of mega and modernity. On the flight back to New York, I would read in a newspaper about the economic problems of the megastructures: some were used to no more than 25 per cent of their capacity. That could be a proof of the psychological problems which arise from living in a concrete mega-world.

Almost with a bad conscience, now, I felt thirsty once more for the elixir. I found a machine at the next corner. The last can! Really, the very last today, I told myself.

Kurt, it is raining again! Have you still not come to terms with your Saint?

An hour later I arrive at the Baptist community. A religious ceremony in a small plain church. Many people. A man in the pulpit with a large golden book open in front of him speaks, tells, reads. The building is very simple. I sit down on one of the benches, stay till the end. Oliver, the photographer, is not in here. As the people pour out into the open, one of them asks, 'Are you the Austrian?' Yes, I say. 'Oliver is at the Hyatt Regency. We'll take you over,' and he points to a small group of devout Baptists. That's fine – the famous luxury hotel is one of my objectives anyway.

Suddenly, an elderly Baptist lady asks me: 'Have you already thanked Jesus for this day?'

I catch my breath abruptly. Dear Lady, I am tempted to reply, that's quite something to ask of an Austrian Catholic. But the truth was I hadn't, yet. Instead, waking up to rain this morning, I had already, quite early in the day, combined several Austrian pear trees with the heavens, bringing in crosses and thunderstorms in good measure (our native swearwords are famous for their adaptability!). On the other hand, while I wrangled with the holy weather-maker, Saint Petrus, the farmers of Georgia must have been thanking God for the water on their fields.

There was no need for me to do that. 'I haven't yet found time for it,' I answer the white-haired lady.

Everyone was staring at me now, as the woman said, 'Well, you are a Catholic... but we will pray for your soul,' and, turning to the others, in a loud voice enjoined them: 'Let us pray for Kurt!' They began right away, all of them praying for my soul. Such a thing had never happened to me before, neither in Rome nor Salzburg – I was moved

Spirits of the Air

to the bottom of my profound Austrian heart. Now they began to sing a psalm, and with all this conviction around me, I timidly wiped away a tear. The sky had cleared a bit, a sun ray beamed . . . in front of my mind's eye my publisher at once appeared! My pictures . . . as fast as possible, get to the Hyatt Regency! Carefully, I plucked at the sleeve of the singing lady: 'Can we go now?' It was not very tactful to disturb her. The sunbeam went out . . .

Off to the Hyatt Regency, Kurt! Oliver was there already. Who knows how long he had been waiting but he seemed not to be impatient, merely said; 'Hurry up, we must get to the next intersection! The fog has lifted and we don't know for how long! The Peachtree Plaza is over there. Maybe you will get to see it in its full glory. We can come back to the Hyatt Regency later, and have a look at the inside.' That sounded reasonable, it wasn't quite as high. Off we went, and despite our hurry, I noticed how the reflections of several high buildings were curving in strange distortions in the mirror-walls of others; in the sky above us light and dark grey clouds intermingled.

'Here we are – step over and don't look up till then,' said Oliver, taking my hand; I followed him to a certain spot on the sidewalk. Then I raised my eyes.

A gigantic tube of metallic shimmering glass stood an unbelievable seventy floors high . . .

The Peachtree Plaza Hotel. One of the most impressive buildings I ever saw. An awe-inspiring architectural masterpiece, it is the highest hotel in the world – but even if under today's obsession for records another, higher one were put up somewhere else, such harmony and elegance could hardly be surpassed. I am standing at the base of the metal and glass cylinder, the summit of which is still in the clouds, though faintly visible now and then – and I am awestruck. I tilt back my head, as if standing at the bottom of the Guglia di Brenta, wanting to look to its very top – exactly so! The Guglia, that beautiful column of rock in the Brenta Dolomites, is close to 300 metres high – the Peachtree Plaza is almost the same size . . . perhaps one rope's length less.

Amongst the rock towers on earth it is one of the most outstanding, in every sense of the term, with a shape of magic regularity, a harmony in outline – an elegance that enthrals not only climbers. To my mind, amongst man-made structures, the Peachtree Plaza most closely approaches it. Oliver, standing at my side, explains that there is not much point in reaching the top of the giant cylinder, since we would then simply find ourselves in the grey of fog, in the clouds. The word

A New World

'skyscraper' has become very hackneyed nowadays, no longer evoking emotion – but anyone standing with us on the pavement that day below this mega-building, would have seen and felt how, in the true sense of the word, it was truly 'scraping' the sky.

Later, I learned some more interesting details: the dance hall of the hotel can hold 3500 people and there are 1100 rooms! The Hyatt Regency also has 1100 rooms, but is built in a different way; it has a revolving restaurant on top, but its main attraction is its enormous lobby . . . which we entered soon afterwards. Usually, when you go into a hotel, you see a reception lobby of medium height, with more or less furniture, according to the category of establishment – here, however, after I had passed the hall porter, I was rendered breathless. This was a lobby eighteen floors high!

What a welcome – what a 'reception' – I thought. Then, I started counting the floors which surrounded it, like a giant court, but did not come to an end before my attention was drawn to the gigantic, shimmering illumination in the middle of the hall, easily twenty metres high: a column of bundled strip lights, opening out higher up into a sort of circular fan – like the spokes of an inverted, half-open giant umbrella, stuck into a spindle. In between, there was a glimmering, like reflections of water – perhaps a fountain – you could hear its gentle sound coming from somewhere in this big space. In the soft light of this enormous fitting, I discovered a circular café in the background, which was apparently hanging on a rope – but then, while Oliver, a photographer like myself, had gone for a walk in response to my 'I have to stay here for a while', my wandering eyes focused on something else: a dark, multi-angled column protruding from the wall to my right. It was not only its enormous dimensions, but more particularly what was happening on it, that captured my whole attention and made a slight shudder go down my spine . . .

Attached to the column were three elevators, incredibly exposed . . . the whole thing was such a bold structure that it seemed more a device of science-fiction, or belonging to a spaceship of the distant future. Somewhere up around the eighteenth floor of the lobby a lift-cabin, made of glass, and spangled with lights, appeared glued to the dark column. It looked terrifying! Just as I marvelled at the lack of vertigo exhibited by the riders of these cabins, two of the odd, longish shapes began to move like 'glow-woodlice' up the trunk of a big tree (I apologise for the comparison – of course no sort of louse at all is thinkable inside the Hyatt Regency!). One might perhaps call them 'glow-worms', since part of their bodies did indeed emit light, but these strange contraptions, sliding up and down at considerable speed, had nothing romantic about them: I thought them programmed and weird. Gigantic woodworms from another world, ovoid and shining, crawling along the edges of the column, their legs hidden. One of the three shining 'insects' had stopped now at the fourteenth floor, another was just coming down, the third disappeared through a hole in the ceiling . . . to the floors higher up. To regain my equilibrium, I needed a Coca-Cola – but this is one place, strangely, where there was not a can to be had; from the suspended café, I heard the pop of a champagne cork . . .

Throwing a last glance at the glittering spindle with its neon umbrella spokes, I went outside. This time I did not look for the receptionist.

The same day, I saw the Omni-Sport Arena, the Atlanta Memorial Arts Center and still more structures that all borrowed from the world of fantasy. I, for one, think that in no other town have architects realised futuristic buildings with such imagination and flair. It needs much conviction to do that. And religion? Perhaps, that too. At any rate a great conviction. To an artist, creation is also his religion.

Oliver got me to the airport early next morning. He and the two girls, Wendy and Barbara, along with the other members of the Baptist community, had been so friendly to this curious being from another part of the world – this Catholic Austrian! To whom, on the other hand, their world appeared strange and full of surprises. Hopefully, my friends will one day come to Salzburg!

What will I show them? Our own megastructures of course: Hohensalzburg, our big castle, then the domed cathedral, followed by the Franciscan Church, and the Church of Saint Peter, then . . . good heavens, I realise now, we have no church for holy Saint Rupert, our patron, whom I have called on so often in this story . . .

But before that, by the way, we will have a feast in Saint Peter's Cellar. With wine from mega-wine-siphons and . . . Peach Melba!

Will I succeed in cracking the secret of the giant peaches of Georgia – next time round?

THE LAKE

'All space is but a nut-shell.' I found that written on a piece of paper in my pocket, thought it sounded like *Hamlet*, though I cannot remember putting it there. I used to do that – on a climb, sometimes, or a walk, even in a bus . . . the ideas were not always legible, not always right,

A New World

but better than not being captured at all. What you are told by a moment – its truth – can be unique. Later, you may only be able to find a shadow.

Star space . . . Milky Ways . . . Oceans . . .

My 'ocean' is to be found in the Bavarian foothills. It is only a little lake. And I do not propose betraying its name.

It changes its face as the year progresses: covered with ice in winter, and in spring by a dusting of pollen from the fir trees. During summer thunderstorms a hundred thousand little spheres of water dance on its surface, and afterwards, the sun lights up its ripples again, or the moon rocks on its swaying surface, or the lake holds a whole skyful of stars.

On certain days in autumn, when the air is so still you think you could touch it, when fresh snow in the mountains lies without melting, and when in the moorlands the sedge and mosses have changed their colour to yellows and russets – then something peculiar happens to the lake: it becomes a flawless mirror, absolutely calm. So immobile is it then, so smooth its surface, that you don't see it any more . . . If you approach gently, planting your steps lightly, so as not to set up a tremble in the swaying bog, then it seems that the trees at the rim grow towards a sky in the depths, and their lowest branches, reaching out towards the invisible water, are granted entry into this magical space which has opened at your feet, reach on down in an endeavour to touch the echoed branches stretching up vainly from below.

As you watch, no longer can you be sure which branches are real; there seems only to be a tree growing into the sky above and below . . . and you must take care not to overbalance into eternity if you lose your footing.

Because on such a day, the whole world is in a nut-shell.

What my little lake told me was right, in essence, even if – as I later learned – my Shakespeare 'quote' was flawed*. For a mere in a bog, as well as for the North Sea around the British coast with its thundering white horses . . . words are only the shell around a core of feelings and facts . . . What is inside could well be the same . . . whether it is a simple man who speaks, or a great poet.

---

* 'I have checked your *Hamlet* quotation. It is from Act II, Scene 2, and should read: 'O God, I could be bounded in a nutshell and count myself a King of infinite space' . . . So you just turned it around a bit. Just.' (From a letter written to me by Julie.)

Spirits of the Air

IN THE PLANE

When I hang in the skies somewhere, travelling from continent to continent, and it is night, I am happy with the beautiful jewels that are granted me from the deep. They are like greetings from the earth, after the black of the oceans. And what glittering treasures have been mine, for moments only . . . The juxtaposition of the hundreds of lights in a village, or the many thousands in a town, under the starry vault are never repeated. And as the plane moves onwards, these ever-changing patterns have just enough in common to remind you of earlier delights. And that too makes you happy.

It is like with the crystals of Mont Blanc: since finding my very first as a boy, they all are mine, even though I don't hold them in my hands. I know they are there.

The same with the desert floor at night under the invisible rays of Rick's 'blacklight' – an ultra-violet prospector's lamp which created a dazzling fluorescence from certain minerals: when you walked through the dark, suddenly a feast of 'emeralds' would light up the black night, and enormous 'rubies', and gems with no name . . . You held your breath and plucked beaming stars from the ground.

A fairy tale come true: that was this walk with Rick through the midnight desert. And later, at Klaus's house, we spread the seemingly insignificant collection of stones over the carpet, and with the aid of Rick's magic lantern, transformed ourselves for a few minutes into proprietors of shining treasures, of unimaginable wealth. Klaus himself is an engineer, sober-minded you might think, but no! Otherwise he would not have said: 'There must be poets, too!'

Swathes of light from Los Angeles: down there, too, I am at home, where the desert begins. And I have to go again . . . even if Rick has now stashed his prospector's lamp somewhere in a corner. (Having married Marcia, a real-estate agent, he finally struck a lucky vein.)

I will go back, nevertheless.

Thoughts in an aeroplane, lights in the night, towns – they are no different from the desert floor.

ISIS

Mojave Desert. Brown hills, pale silhouettes – still dark; day is only just breaking. Renata and I have driven through the night from Los

A New World

Angeles. We are bound for Death Valley . . . which is said to be one of the most bewitching places on earth. Only later did I learn the story of its ominous name . . .

It was in the winter of 1849–50, at the time of the Great Trek to the American west, when two families with their ox carts decided to take a short cut across the wilderness of the Great American Desert in order to get to Los Angeles, from where they wanted to head north to the Californian goldfields. As the season was already well advanced, they believed it would be impossible to cross the Sierra Nevada on account of the snow.

The fabulous gold strike of James Marshall at Sutter's Mill on the American River on 24 January 1848 had set in process a mass migration, unique in history. Up to 1849 15,000 people had travelled the Oregon Trail to northern California, and another 4600, mostly Mormons, had arrived in the Salt Lake valley, where they decided to stop and found their new Zion. But in 1849, the first year of the Gold Rush, no fewer than 25,000 overlanders reached California. They came for a variety of reasons: some to find new land to settle, others hoped to get rich quickly and without difficulty, and still others sought adventure and new horizons.

Thus, by the late autumn of that year, a colourful mix of peoples* with more than a hundred ox wagons had started from Hobble Creek, some hundred kilometres south of the Great Salt Lake. They knew almost nothing of the Southern Route (the old Spanish trail to Pueblo de los Angeles) and so its dangers – namely, lack of water and of forage for the draught animals – were of lesser significance when weighed against the notorious blizzards which threatened a late Sierra Nevada crossing.

After a hard month, travelling through Utah, controversy divided the party: a sketch map was produced which promised a much shorter way to the west, whereas another described this area as 'unexplored'. The group separated. Almost all the wagons headed westwards, but upon encountering a bluff, difficult for the oxen to negotiate, seventy-five of them, the majority, returned to the Southern Route. Only four family groups, led by William Lewis Manly, pressed on to reach the Amargosa Desert, to the east of Death Valley. By this time they had very little food left and, between finding one spring and the next, were

---

* 'A truly American composite,' Leroy Johnson told me when I joined him during his search for the historical escape route of the people stranded in Death Valley. For his book on this story see the Bibliography.

almost dying of thirst. Wearily, they entered the immense and nameless valley only to find a high mountain ridge blocked all forward progress. While Manly and his friend Rogers set off on foot in search of a way over the mountains, hoping to be able to return with food and horses for their women and children imprisoned in the desert, those left behind were obliged to slaughter their scrawny cattle to stay alive.

When the two men finally returned – with a single mule and the knowledge of a way out – having covered in four weeks more than 700 kilometres, it must have seemed a miracle to their waiting families.

From a point which today is still called 'Manly Lookout', and which Manly and Rogers reached with one of the survivors three days after they began their escape, they saw the snow-covered peaks of the Sierra Nevada ahead of them, and the deep valley and desert behind, which they had just crossed. The three men took off their hats.

'Goodbye, Death Valley,' one of them said.

Since then, the valley has borne this name.

Less than a century and a half has passed since then . . . and almost everything has changed. The Indians, who tried with their bows and arrows to kill some of the oxen of the stranded trekkers, have long disappeared. An asphalt road now leads down and across the desert. Nobody today can imagine the indescribable fatigue and desperation of the involuntary discoverers of Death Valley – unless he, too, has left the road, lost all sense of direction and finished his water.

Because of its natural beauty, the valley was declared a national monument. For some visitors it is one of the most beautiful places on earth.

We have been driving for many hours now, through the night. I peer out ahead, at the pale sky in the east. Faint, glimmering desert shapes pass by outside. Renata sits beside me, her white-blonde hair glimmering too in this dawn light, long, smooth strands hanging beyond her shoulders. I can hardly make out her blue-green eyes with their dreamy expression, which can give way so suddenly to determination. She is special and contradictory. Her ancestors came from Russia . . . but not only from there. In some way, it seems to me, her personality embodies all the contrasts of the world. Yet she can be so clear and straightforward.

We two want to get to know this strange place we have only heard about, Death Valley. Renata, like most people who live in Los Angeles, has never been there. 'You won't find it dead at all, this valley. It's alive,' insisted our friend, good old Campy, a real desert fox, one of the Vagmarken. 'If you go there in springtime,' he said, 'you'll see flowers sprouting everywhere from the sand, splendid flowering cactuses, a real place of wonder . . .' and he smiled all over his leathery, sun-tanned face, adding with a warning twinkle, 'You may even fall under its spell.' And he gave us a long look.

Well, then, this is spring! A time for snap decisions and doing things straightforwardly. Like visiting Disneyland (the Los Angeles Kindergarten, as I so disrespectfully called it). We did that yesterday, on a whim of Renata's, and I must confess we were like children at a fair. All at once I realised the enormous art that had gone into the intricate working models, and the so-skilfully produced puppets – three times we went underground on the Caribbean pirate ship. I would never have expected it of myself! Now we are on our way to discover another place.

The desert shapes pass, pale as the ash-blonde strands of my companion's hair. She is serious now, contrary Renata, yet I remember how she can be playful as a child. Her presence envelops me, even in silence, and I do not know how I could ever escape her strange wiles.

The road leads us directly towards the long ranges which hide Death Valley. Behind their black silhouettes the whole sky starts to burn with orange flames. Everything shines, glowing around us. Any minute now the sun must come up. We brake the car, drive into a clump of Cat's-claw bushes dotted with yellow blossoms. Quick! Quick! We throw the doors open, jump out.

There it is! The sun! Sliding above the mountain rim, flaming, flaring, with cosmic might! We are mesmerised, transformed by the trembling, incandescent sphere floating above the desert . . . a force to ensnare the soul . . . and, suddenly, something is born from this power that touches the core, that creates dreams and reality.

Isis.

A goddess of nature.

Since that day, that is the name I have given my companion. Something, somehow, had changed. It lasted for a long time. We carried the sun inside ourselves.

And I returned there time and again.

A soft haze over the salt flats. A strange, mellow, intangible spell emanates from the landscape of death. Almost hypnotic . . . We are on the mountain ridge about 2000 metres above the valley floor, looking down, and it is as if something is reaching up to us. What can it be? The spirits of the desert? Perhaps it is the essence of Death Valley that is touching us and which is in all these things here around. Tall yellow flowers, like marguerites. Tender rose-coloured blooms that have opened on the cactuses. Yellow-red, and even green soft rocks and soil, just like the colours on a giant artist's palette. Eroded ochre mushrooms of rock between, as large as houses. Strange weird tufts of grass, a foot and a half high, like corn-stooks . . . 'the Devil's Cornfield'. Waves of sand dunes behind . . . imperceptibly wandering shapes. Bushes, once engulfed by the moving crests, have emerged years later on the opposite slope as wooden skeletons, spreading stiff branches – like fingers in hopeless defence. Tracks of the little animals that have scampered across the surface, and giant curls of rocks, like spellbound snakes, high across a mountain face. Desert lizards, lightning quick, and placid island peaks protruding from enormous fans of gravel. Black and orange gorges, and small volcanoes that once, eons ago, filled the valley with their thunderous roar. Barren salt flats . . . looking as if they have been violently hoed. Some old carts, relics from when borax used to be extracted here; people also searched for gold and silver. One old-time swindler, a plausible rogue remembered as 'Death Valley Scotty', even built a castle in a side canyon – with money he charmed from the banks on the strength of gold-strikes he never made.

Oh yes, if Death Valley could speak . . .

About 200 kilometres long, the valley is, and very wide – during the Ice Age it was a big lake, which has almost evaporated now. A couple of fish still live in it – more precisely, a certain species of fish has survived all that time; they have multiplied and adapted . . . over many thousands of years, thanks to a little spring. At the deepest point of the salt basin, eighty-four metres below sea level, there is still a bit of water left, not potable of course, which is why it is called Bad Water today. Almost unbelievable that it survives, considering the valley is the hottest place in the western hemisphere.

But the glaring heat of the summer has not yet started . . . the red tufts of flowers of the Indian Paint Brush are nodding their heads, whenever the warm, gentle breeze caresses them. Springtime . . .

We approach the dunes. From far away they had seemed just an insignificant flaxen patch in the blue-grey expanse of valley – bare of outline. Only as we get closer do crests and shadows appear, a rippled pattern of bright yellow waves, expands before our eyes between the high dark mountain ridges that bound the valley on either side.

Cautiously we enter this landscape of sand, curious to know what we

might find. With a mounting prickle of anticipation, we enter the maze
. . . Waves of an unknown ocean under the desert's smile – below dark
blue mountain silhouettes. What will we discover? At every step the
contours of the maze subtly shift, a new furrow opens, a basin, a new
billow rising in front of us. A butterfly sails through on the breeze: 'I
want to know,' it seems to say. The same wish has burned in us all day
long. What waits behind the next sandhill? As if an old, teasing question
would release its secret . . .

Another furrow, another ridge, another view from higher up: shimmering dark forms in the vibrating air . . . plants, bushes, an immense, seemingly infinite plain, tiny dots in the distance, melting in the haze.

We learn nothing else but to be in the valley. Yet this answer fills our hearts with joy, and still more longing. We go on.

Soft, yielding sand under our steps, and the late afternoon sun is projecting our shadows onto the waves of our ocean, growing, stretching, jumping, merging . . . What is it that makes us so happy? Just the sense of being?

There is more, we know there is more . . . It pushes us onwards. And the desert voices promise: yes, yes, be sure you will find it . . .

And then it happens, strong as a scream yet totally silent, with that suddenness peculiar to Death Valley: somewhere colours start to bloom, bizarre lines emerge, where nothing but brown or grey existed before – fantasy shapes materialise in a moment, stand there, shining, woken by the sun, by the light, still and secretive.

Death Valley . . .

A hundred times you may pass a place and nothing is there – nothing of significance to move you – and you go on. Then, all at once, it is exactly on that spot the desert flower opens so astonishingly – and you stand, entranced, unable to believe it was there all the time . . . You may come again and again, it will never be the same, and you can never know whether or where it will happen.

Will it, will it happen again?

Dusk is approaching, twilight stalking over the hills. We stop. I take Isis by the hand. We will go no further today.

As we leave, we carry the certainty with us that we have consorted with the spirits of the desert.

Will it happen again?

One thing is true: you may return, and return, and return . . . never will the valley appear the same to you. Yet it is. You just feel it. But never can you foresee which reality you will encounter, and whether magic – just for a moment – will call from the sand, from the rocks.

THE WIZARD –
CLIMBING THE NEEDLES OF SIERRA NEVADA

A young lad appears from the dark of the conifer forest and enters the bright green of the manzanita, the infamous scrub which covers the ground here so densely that sometimes you have a real fight to get through it. He is tall, athletically built, but he moves slowly towards us, and he stops again and again. He has a dark expression on his face. Something must be wrong.

'What's the matter, Joe?' Herb asks him. (My companion was the rock climbing 'King' of the Vagmarken, a dedicated Needles climber.)

With no change of expression, the other muttered, 'Mike took a screamer. He's coming now,' and he nodded glumly behind him. There was his friend moving painfully round a bend in the path, step by slow step, his clothes torn to pieces down one side – the skin, too, probably, for he was all bandaged up.

There was not much we could do for him; it had happened, and now they were on the way back to their car, their weekend at the Needles over. We wished them luck.

While we moved on, Herb pointed over the trees to one of the monstrous granite spires that make up the Needles. 'That's what Mike was leading when he came off,' he told me, 'Fell fifteen metres.'

Giant slabs soared through the branches, bright in the sunshine, some of them completely yellow with a rough and abrasive lichen. I could picture how it would be to come off on one of these. Your clothes would be eroded off first, then your skin, then more. 'I'm not surprised it is called a screamer – you wouldn't stop screaming.'

'That's about the size of it,' Herb nodded. 'But it only happens to the leader.'

Obviously the second man never falls far enough. Looking at the compact granite slabs my thoughts wandered back to the steep ice faces of the Alps – those were what I understood . . . 'Herb,' I said, 'these are your mountains, you are the Needles expert, you lead today . . .'

He smiled, then said he had no taste for screamers either, and why

A New World

didn't we do a little bouldering . . . And immediately he shot off, up on some knife-edge, performing a solo ballade, jumping across to another boulder, doing several pull-ups. 'Don't you want a go?' he asked.

'No, Herb,' I replied, 'I think I'd better save my energy for the Wizard. I don't want to wear myself out before that.'

He understood. And I have to confess that delivering all those lectures in the preceding months had left me in no great shape, really. Several times that day, attached to some tiny feldspar crystal or other on these impressive granite slabs, I would find my mind wandering back to the screamer Mike took in the morning.

First of all, we climbed the Witch. She is another of the granite personalities here, about ninety metres tall and with a strange bonnet on her head. Her normal route is only Grade IV. No problem there, I thought, as I felt my way cautiously up towards the bonnet, even for an Austrian ice-specialist . . . Nature used all her magic when shaping these Sierran Needles over endless time for us to enjoy today. There is a Hermit, a Warlock, the Witch, even a White Lady, who really does proffer the profile of an elegant woman. Last, not least, there is the Wizard. He is the most uncanny of the whole eerie crew. Really sinister, like a giant gorilla in a hat, his tongue lolling from an open mouth. He is tall, perhaps ninety metres. When I first saw him, I was seized with a desire to stand right on top of his hat – so wonderful that must be, I thought, really wonderful. Oh, I did so want to do it! 'Where does the route go?' I asked Herb.

He was delighted at my interest, grinning. 'You see the waistcoat? See the thin fissure? Up that! There's a chimney to get there' – he shrugged disparagingly – 'but it's no problem at all.'

The crack running up the waistcoat was a thin, straight line, thirty metres or more with no interruption at all. 'Is there a good belay up there?' I tried to sound jocular, light-hearted.

'Nope.' Herb went on drily, 'None. You have to go right up through to the collar without stopping. And then there is the gorilla's face . . .' He smiled now, 'The eyebrow is quite interesting!' At this his expression melted into ecstasy.

'How difficult?' I wanted to know. '5.8.'

The Californians are a precise people. In my earlier days I had climbed European Grade VI. Here free climbers had arrived at 5.11, even 5.12! Of course, they put in plenty of practice – weekend after weekend in one of the desert Klettergartens, or on boulders just on the outskirts of Los Angeles, even within the town itself. And San Francisco, too – Yosemite is only a drive away.

Spirits of the Air

You need special soft boots to be able to jam your feet into the cracks, and you need to jam your hands or fists in as well, otherwise your feet could slide out. You turn your foot as much as ninety degrees in a crack to hold it in there. It hurts sometimes, of course, and by evening, unless you are one of the really hard men, everything hurts: feet, fingers, hands, arms! But when the sun sinks behind the mountains in the Mojave Desert – or wherever – the 'American Lake District' empties and during the long drive home, one climber will work on another – massaging feet, neck muscles, arms – a wonderful thing is this Californian buddy system!

Steffi is a dab hand at it, superb; everyone agrees she is surpassed only by Chuck. If he works on your toes, he does it with a vibrating high frequency that no one else can match. Your legs, your feet are soon as good as new, and you are ready for more cracks in Californian granite.

Back to Herb. He is sitting on a granite boulder, sorting out the gear we shall need. Free climbing means climbing without artificial aid, but it does not mean going naked up the rock, like a squirrel. Herb creates a pile of slings, karabiners, and an assortment of aluminum cubes or 'nuts' – some small, some larger. An appropriate one of these in a crack will provide a belay so secure that the second climber, whose job is to take it out, may find the want of a special hooked tool for the job. Just as the old-style burglar needed his big bunch of keys, the rock climber cannot go anywhere without arming himself with an enormous bundle of slings and nuts in all shapes and sizes (less if he uses Friends).

Meanwhile, I almost forgot, Steffi has appeared on the scene; a helpful angel, she will sit patiently at the bottom, guarding our things and taking pictures of the climb.

Herb is ready. We leave the trees and crawl down through a gorge. After a fight with some bushes, a few easy rock passages, we approach the Wizard. He looks down at us – I can feel it – his great tongue lolling, an enigmatic look on his face. (The expression is always changing, according to the sun's position and the shadows moving across the rock.) We arrive at a niche at the bottom, and off Herb goes, swinging, with incredible lightness, around an edge. Belaying him, I think: It won't look the same when I do it. I'm up to ninety-two kilos again, though I will certainly lose some today. Herb scuttles up the chimney, Grade IV only, and there he is, on a little ledge, selecting a nut from his bundle. Soon he calls down for me to follow. Light-footed, I twinkle round the edge in a dance of pure joy – or, should I say, I pressed myself into a crack and groped blindly round, trying to find some hold or other on the other side. Then comes the chimney, vertical as all chimneys are, but with good handholds. Right! Here I am, Herb! I fix a good anchor,

Herb augments it with two additional nuts in separate fissures, quelling my surprise with a dry, 'You can't be too careful with Europeans! You still climb with pitons there!' I sighed. At least I was firmly attached, like a statue of Abraham Lincoln.

'Now, be sure and belay me damned well!' Herb says. 'If you want to take a picture, do it now, not later. If I fall off up there on the waistcoat, then it's no joke. You really have to hold me!' He smiles, but I know it is serious.

Herb starts off up the rock gorilla's waistcoat which is splashed here and there with patches of intense yellow, the lichen. I wonder it wasn't called King Kong, rather than the Wizard. He moves up sound rock directly above my head, on tiny, but good holds . . . but then they run out. I see how he has just his fingertips in the long fine fissure we had spotted earlier. He tries to get some grip with the rubber soles of his rock boots on the vertical slab to his right. There are no holds anywhere, but the sole grips by pure pressure. It's a technique which of course he knows well, but this vertical dièdre – the narrow groove in the enormous slab – is impressive. He is a very good climber . . . sometimes I see his face, his tensed muscles, hear the chink of his climbing gear. Otherwise, it is quiet, still, but for the whisper of a light breeze now and then out there in the trees of the Sierra – or is that just my imagination? I try to memorise the moves Herb makes, the contortions and steps, remembering I have to get up there, too, and on my own! I have also got to take out all the mini-nuts on their thin wire slings, jammed deeply in the waistcoat's crease. Herb has inserted them as he climbs, as quickly as he could, but very accurately. He is now twenty-five metres above my head on a vertical slab, and for the first time calls down to me: this is where the fissure runs out, he will have to turn a corner to find the next crease in the garment. I can see the soles of his boots carefully edge round high above me. I hold my breath. A fast move now, fluid, elastic, he is round, disappears. Soon he calls from somewhere up there. It is my turn now. I start on up.

The sky seems full of nuts to me – and none of them wants to come out! Keep the legs wide, stay in balance, pull, fumble, fiddle with the 'fire hook', streams of sweat running down my face. I swear, then pull again . . . some of the nuts are held absolutely fast. 'Don't you dare leave any nuts behind,' comes faintly from above. 'It's a matter of honour here, to get them all out!' Can't have that, I think. The next guy up finding one of Herb Laeger's nuts! He would never hear the end of it. Sweating, I strive to maintain our climbing honour. Finally, I am two-thirds of the way up the dièdre, spread uncomfortably between two granite walls which meet at a wide angle, when, suddenly, I have to grab hold of a nut to save myself slipping: it holds well, but that is probably why afterwards it absolutely refuses to come out. I work and work away at it, streams of sweat pouring from my whole body – it is a hot country, this, it really is – and then (I hardly dare commit it to paper) I say, 'To hell with it!' and leave the nut where it sticks. Herb has so far not realised this.

When I reach him, I am decorated with slings like a Christmas tree; he sits happily on a little ledge, whistling a melody. He has taken off his shirt, which is hanging on a sling with a nut in a crack. Three more nuts go in for me – the old business, Herb having regard for my bulkier outline – and thus, secured, we both sit on this beautiful ledge, looking over the fantastic granite spires to the woods beyond. What a wonderful range, this Sierra Nevada . . .

The Wizard's eyebrow! Everyone knows what beetling brows gorillas have – this one has a real overhang – 5.8, no less! Herb leans backwards horizontally, feet in a niche below, then suddenly pulls out one leg and sets the foot carefully on to the edge of the eyebrow! For a second he almost does the splits, but immediately pulls up his body, to attach himself completely to the eyebrow. Soon he is disappearing beyond the overhang.

The rope runs in short jerks through my hands, through the karabiners in the nutted slings, then I hear his shout from above, while Steffi yells from below: the summit! Herb is standing on top of the gorilla's hat – right on top of the Wizard of stone! It takes me somewhat longer to heave my ninety-two kilos over the eyebrow, and as I do so I vow to lose more weight in future – but a wide crack in the hat makes the end of this pitch a dance. I put in a special *Variante* of my own, drawing a grin and a shake of the head from Herb. Two worlds – old and new – so happy together on this day. I hope one day to exchange the hospitality and show him 'my' Mont Blanc! '*Berg Heil!*' says Herb, with an American accent, and we shake hands on it.

Two men on top of the Wizard.

ON THE GULF

A day between Europe and Asia . . . a boat in the far distance, almost lost in the hazy grey glitter of the Gulf of California, off Mexico.

A New World

Lines in the sand around us – lots of lines with gaps between.

'What are you doing?' Isis asks.

'I draw seconds.'

'Seconds?'

'That's right. Every line is time, that passes; and where I don't draw a line, time passes, too, but somewhere else for someone else . . . I shall come back here and make some more seconds for you to see. Think of these lines sometimes, when I'm gone . . .' I answer.

A whole pattern of lines covers the sand, straight ones, curved ones, semicircles, braids and cables, but never a circle.

As we walked on towards the water, suddenly I saw the design again. The sea had made it! We were crossing a flat open stretch of beach covered by an incalculable number of ripple marks, straight and curved, some in parallel, small elevations and depressions in the fine sand left by the retreating waves . . . we were walking across hundreds of seconds, which the sea had drawn. Before we reached the water, the shoreline behind us had become a thin, narrow band in the distance.

The closer we approached to the water, the more distinctly could be heard a peculiar rushing, a sound composed of a million individual sounds, a tone that approached and retreated, went off to the side, that gradually enshrouded and inundated us. There was no understanding its pattern for hundreds of smaller and bigger waves and currents were running and lapping across each other . . . it was a mysterious sound, enticing beyond words. A hypnotic spell.

Further and further we venture into it, this vault of sound. We enter the water, the sand strangely hard and smooth underfoot – quite different from before. Holding each other's hands, we cling together as the many currents gently buffet our bodies, and all the while we are engulfed in this spellbinding rushing, are touched by the countless ripples, dancing around us like a pattern of small, sharp peaks, and the thousandfold dazzle of light flashing in our eyes, many, many suns. No more coast, no more sky, only the rush, rush, rush in a space of dancing suns, in which the seconds close into circles. We are in a space without gravity, no longer aware that our feet touch the ground anywhere.

We remain wrapped in each other's arms.

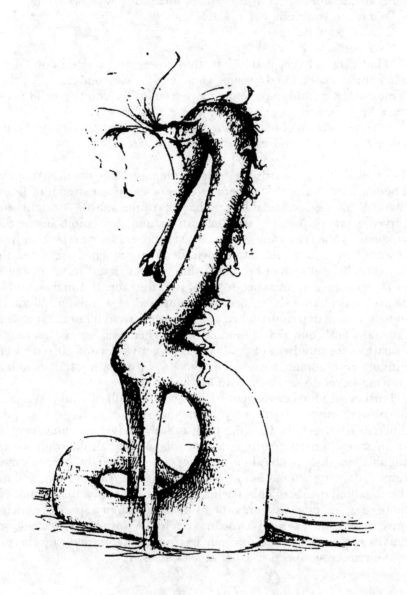

PART VII

Makalu (8481m) — the Turning Point

'But why that, Kurt? Why does it have to be that?' The question came from my old friend and expedition companion Markus Schmuck, whom I had just bumped into navigating through the crowds of tourists in Salzburg's famous Getreidegasse. He had evidently heard of my proposed trip to Makalu, or he would not have been treating me to such long and earnest scrutiny. Of course he meant well and only wanted to be sure I did not embark on anything foolish. I knew that.

It had been twenty years since Markus and I made the first ascent of Broad Peak with Hermann Buhl and Fritz Wintersteller, the first of the eight-thousanders to be climbed alpine-style. The climb was judged by many at the time to be a crazy enterprise – no oxygen, no porters, just the four of us.

Well, we had succeeded. But that was then. No one can deny that twenty years is a long time: you only get older.

So here was Markus trying to talk me out of going to Makalu. And he was not the only one. Helmut Wihan, the best pulmonary specialist in Salzburg, who was treating me for a bronchitic allergy I had almost certainly picked up from staying too long in town, was adamant that I should not venture an inch higher than Base Camp. Another doctor friend simply said, 'Kurt, you can't expect to go on for ever. It's time to call it a day.' But I wanted to do it! Wanted to have a go! I needed to know what it would be like – this beautiful Makalu – could not bear the thought of life without it. I had seen it from Shartse when I was with Hermann Warth and Nawang Tenzing. They would both be coming on this expedition, too, and there would also be Karli Landvogt, our doctor from Greenland in 1974; Hans von Känel, an ebullient Bernese climber; Dietlinde, Hermann's wife, and two other Sherpas, Ang Chappal and Nga Temba.

'You should think it over,' Markus repeated anxiously as we said goodbye, and he hung on to my hand as he shook it, giving me another of his long and concerned looks – as if he did not expect to see me again.

YANG LHE – THE ENCHANTED FOREST

Between the trunks of the Himalayan firs, rhododendrons are a riot of bloom. As far as the eye can see, splashes of every colour from white, through rose to a deep, deep red, and all mingled with yellow and mauve . . . a living Impressionist painting. It is spring, a perfect dream-like spring. The whole forest seems to be under a magic spell. Wafting gently from the fir branches long fronds of green lichen weave a mobile and intricate web of three-dimensional lace. Caught in the web are the crystal notes of birdsong from many, many birds. A waterfall, like white satin ribbon, hangs from a granite wall, so high that the water is transformed to a fine spray long before reaching the ground. A small log hut in a clearing amongst the trees is surrounded by prayer flags on long wands of bamboo; they stir gently in the breeze. Om, mani padme hum, om mani padme hum . . .

It is a sacred place.

Between the prayer flags I come upon a rock bearing the traces of a carved outline. Buddha, perhaps? I cannot tell, but instinctively feel that this precious place with its fabulous trees is enchanted, the enchanted forest of an unknown deity. There seems no other way to explain my remarkable recovery . . .

I arrived down here racked by such terrible coughing spasms I thought they would never leave me. I had already abandoned all hope of going high on the mountain, and had left Base Camp, on my own, to drop down to around 3500 metres. That was three days ago – or was it four? I have lost all sense of time. Few people ever come here. Two or three times a year, perhaps, the inhabitants of Shedua on the other side of the Kongma La Pass make the journey to celebrate a religious feast, and during the monsoon you occasionally meet a herdsman with a small flock of sheep or goats, or a couple of cows roaming along the Barun valley from pasture to pasture. Otherwise, the place is deserted. Dangerous gorges separate it from the villages of the great Arun valley. So, I am quite alone here.

High altitude cough is a pernicious disability which has struck down many a Himalayan climber. The French, when they made the first ascent of Makalu in 1955, suffered badly from it during the early stages of the expedition. If you have never experienced it, it is hard to imagine

Makalu (8481m)

what a convulsive cough it is: a few days ago Dietlinde fractured one of her ribs in a coughing fit and Karli had to strap her up with a huge sticking-plaster bandage. Nawang Tenzing was another victim, but he managed to shake it off. Not me! I saw my only chance in getting down to a lower level, into the rhododendron jungle. I felt so dejected, desperate. When you have spent all your life in mountains, and suddenly, on such a beautiful peak as Makalu, you are forced to give up, it takes some adjustment. Had I really grown too old, or was it just this accursed cough? Was Markus right after all when he warned me the time had come to pack it in? How do you accept you may never climb again on the great heights of the world? How can you come to terms with that? I endeavoured to calm my mounting panic, persuade myself it would not be too bad: Kurt, I said, I know it's hard, but even without big mountains, life can be worth living.

There are plenty of secrets beyond the mountains, not only on the top? Everywhere there are thousands of secrets, wherever you go in the world.

But that doesn't stop it being heart-rending to accept you will be excluded from the one deepest experience of all, for all the time that is left to you.

Then I felt the forest around me, this magic forest with all its beauty. And only then did I begin to experience solace. It was as if love was streaming towards me from all sides. I can find no other way of describing it. I do not consider myself superstitious, but there is so much in this world which nobody can explain. The conviction began to grow in my mind that the forest of Yang Lhe must be sacred. I wondered if a clue might be found in the very name Makalu, the origins of which are uncertain although there are a number of theories about it; but then I thought that forest perhaps has nothing to do with Makalu at all. It is simply here.

Yet, there is something in the branches.

Is it the Isis of another world?

Am I meeting something I have encountered somewhere before? In my mind everything seems connected.

Even today, I do not know what happened to me during those days in the magic forest of Yang Lhe. I cannot explain it. But when I started back up the mountain, I was a different person. What is more, I was completely restored to health. It was not long before I could tackle Makalu in such good form that my friends could only shake their heads in disbelief.

I was grateful to the unknown goddess. A little bell, which I had brought with me from Mont Blanc, may still hang there among the tree branches near the prayer flags.

THROUGH EAST NEPAL

The drizzle started on the way up yesterday. Every so often, one or other of our heavily laden porters would lose his footing on the slippery red clay and slither back down the path to the laughter of the others and yelps of Yahoo! Thanks to the high-profile tread on our boots, Hermann, Hans and I were instantly delegated to be 'protecting fathers' (as some of the women porters called us). We did not spare ourselves, struggling up the steep slopes with a Sherpani or two under our wings.

So, despite the pouring rain, we arrived at our day's destination in the high spirits that characterise this country, Nepal. Khandbari, at about 800 metres in the foothills of the Himalaya, was the first village on the long and rugged approach to Makalu. Our joy at having arrived there had a deeper reason. Only those familiar with the standard expedition scrimmage in Kathmandu, the 'Zermatt' of the Himalaya, can appreciate what competition there is each year for the few available charter planes. The team leaders who come off worst arrive at their mountains too late in the season, running the risk of being overtaken by the monsoon just as they are about to make their summit bids.

Humid monsoon winds, sweeping in across the Bay of Bengal, bring welcome rains for the farmers of India and Nepal. But to the mountaineer, they spell thunderstorms, excessive new snow, avalanches – in short, an end to the expedition! There is only a brief weather window for mountaineering activities between the end of winter in the Himalaya, and the onset of the monsoon – from mid-March until late in May. The post-monsoon season is even shorter.

Hermann Warth, who for three years had headed the German Development Service in Nepal with his wife Dietlinde, shared joint leadership of this Makalu venture with me. Our first expedition boxes had arrived into the care of Nepalese friends in Khandbari two years ago, before ever we obtained permission for our climb. But as a mountaineer you must be an optimist, otherwise you could never keep rekindling summit dreams from one venture to the next, especially when you know that an objective like this is one of the most dangerous you could undertake. We received our permit for Makalu from the government of Nepal against payment of an official peak fee of 14,000 rupees (about £1000; today it would cost more than six times as much).

Makalu (8481m)

The previous November Dietlinde had set out on foot for Khandbari in east Nepal with forty Sherpas and Sherpanis and a total of 1100 kilos of baggage left over from a previous expedition, which had been stored in Namche Bazar near Everest. It took twelve days to get there and, ever since, all seventeen members of the Shresta family have been obliged to live their lives around our Makalu boxes and sacks, which took over a large part of their house, our base in Khandbari. They endured it with their usual unshakeable cheerfulness.

Hermann, meanwhile, as a half-Nepali himself, was fully aware of the battle for charter planes that took place each March in Kathmandu, and – while three 'Europeans' of our international team (namely Karl Landvogt from Germany, Hans von Känel from Switzerland and myself from Austria) handled the organisation at our end – he booked a cargo flight for us on a Twin-Otter to Tumlingtar for 10 March; in other words, the day before yesterday. Still, alpinists all have to be aware of the proverb which says that in Asia, nothing happens as you expect it to. It applies especially to charter flights from Kathmandu in March.

Although mountaineering fellowship is said to span the world, any leader of an expedition in Kathmandu at that time would prefer to be the only one there – until his plane has taken off. So when Hermann passed on to me greetings from Wolfi Nairz who had been in town a few days before, I had only one question. 'How many planes does he need?' 'Three Twin-Otters,' Hermann replied, 'but don't worry. Ours is already booked.' I think of the mountaineer's proverb and cross my fingers. March 10 comes and we load all our baggage on to a Land-Rover: glorious weather, perfect for flying. The phone shrills. Hermann's face drops as he picks up the receiver: our flight is cancelled – some damage to the aeroplane.

Hell! Anything can happen in Asia! But then again, *really* anything can happen in Asia, and instead of waiting for a week, which we could have expected, we find ourselves taking off the very next morning, even though it is raining and you can hardly see any mountains for the grey haze. By the time we are in the air, I have the uncomfortable feeling that it won't be long before we turn back. Pilots here navigate entirely on visibility, and ahead of us nothing can be seen but grey entangled in grey, carpets of cloud amongst mountains. I take out my small plastic compass – a freebie from an earlier flight – seeking to know at least in what direction we are heading. Lieutenant Deepak Kumar Gurung, the liaison officer appointed to us by the government, has noticed my expression of concern and smiles encouragingly. 'The pilot is a cousin of mine,' he says.

Spirits of the Air

So I put my compass away. Hermann winks at me. 'If there is any chance at all of getting there, we will. The pilot won't want to make a fool of himself before his relatives.' I'm sure that's right. It is presumably why we are flying at all.

We seem to be heading south, towards India. Ah, I think, he is going to sneak in the back door, from the Nepalese lowlands, the Terai, which so seamlessly share a frontier with India.

Large streams of rubble, like winding snakes, glimmer up from a hill country almost obscured by mists – the Siwaliks. We are flying at lower level now, groping our way from one rubble stream to the next. To our left, in the distance, are long ridges, greyish-blue whalebacks leading east, waymarkers which constantly disappear then re-emerge. The plane now makes a turn above a boa constrictor of debris of a pale and glowing yellow. A wide ribbon of water comes into view. Can it be the Arun, the large river which flows through the mountains of eastern Nepal?

Hermann Warth and I travelled along the Arun in 1974 on our way to Shartse, beyond Makalu. That was when we first set eyes on the mountain we are going to now, and where we got to know each other and the inimitable Nawa Tenzing, our 'Sherpa' friend from the other side of Everest – not really a Nepali at all, but a full-blooded Tibetan. Indestructible, resolutely good-humoured, he would crack jokes even throughout the terrible tempests on the corniced ridge of Shartse. He is a member of this Makalu expedition, but under the flag of Nepal, together with two true Sherpas, Nga Temba and Ang Chappal, our Sirdar, both of whom had impressed Hermann with their skill and fellowship in 1977 on Lhotse.

These two are with us on the plane, sitting together and looking intently through the windows at the river below. Nawang Tenzing has been waiting in Tumlingtar for a week now, guarding our Makalu boxes at the edge of the airstrip. He will be surprised to see us arriving in this weather! The pilot is turning the machine to the north – then this must indeed be the Arun! Already we are floating along steeper mountain flanks with outcropping rocky ribs. Gorges are opening up, valleys . . .

Below us appears a wide valley with a longish oval of green, framed in a bend of the river . . . the meadow which is used as a runway. We spiral down towards it. Houses of the hill-people slide under the wings, terraced fields, one above the other, single trees . . . There follows a thunderous rumbling, such a juddering and jolting, a thrust and a moaning of wheels . . . we are rattled and jounced, but . . . we are on the ground . . . jogging over grass and dirt . . . we have arrived!

Makalu (8481m)

That was some Nepalese navigation – a zero-visibility flight, following an experienced nose! We break out into cheers for the pilot, clapping till our palms hurt, while the machine slows to a final halt. All out! We are in high spirits under the overcast sky. We made it! A major hurdle on the way to Makalu is passed.

Now, a day later, the rain is pummelling wildly on the tin roof above us and a reddish silt-heavy brook sluices down the village street . . . This is no Salzburg drizzle: this looks like the monsoon.

Seeing such torrents emptying on to Khandbari awakens our worst misgivings: will the way to Makalu be open, or will snowdrifts prevent our porters getting over the mountain barrier in to the Barun Sanctuary? This lot will mean a metre of new snow at least on the Kongma La, a pass of more than 4000 metres over which we have to coax more than a hundred porters and our three tonnes of gear. The outcome of our expedition could be determined up there before ever reaching Makalu with its 8481 metres.

But you need a cool head as a Himalayan climber, or you might as well stay at home. You know things never turn out as you expect – so best keep smiling! Be sure that when the sun comes out, it will melt the snow, so we carry on gaining height with our singing band of porters. Loaded with duffel bags, boxes, a ladder and plastic drums, they mount the terraced hillsides towards a rounded ridge that will bring us to nearly 2000 metres. From there it will be downhill on the other side all the way to the Arun River, 1000 metres below.

Just as we are putting up our tents that evening on the pass, on a grassy patch among some bushes, hailstones rattle down on us from fast-moving black clouds. Within moments everything is white. The porters scuttle into one of the hastily pitched large tents, abandoning their loads in pools of melted hailstones . . . Quick! Quick! Get everything off the ground! Stand stuff on the ladder, or on stones, or hitch it up in the branches! Only then, in all this confused antlike activity does it become apparent that not all the loads are here. Hell and damnation! Ang Chappal and Nawang Tenzing scamper back along the wet, skiddy path as fast as they can, darkness closing in around them. What can have happened? It turns out that some porters simply dumped their loads by the wayside and trotted off to stay in the surrounding villages. Finally, very late, we have everything back together and the campfires burning. The storm passes, stars come out . . . and familiar faces smile out of the glowing firelight, as one suddenly recognises this or that lad again from when he was with us four years ago on the way to Lhotse and Shartse.

The morning of a long day dawns clear and wonderful; a day in which we shall press on relentlessly, following the jungle-covered ridges high above the valley of the Arun. The mountain range opposite begins to quiver in the first pale light – five six-thousanders and the 7000-metre Chamlang. Behind them rears a gigantic, regular pyramid, its summit already rosy with sunlight. It is Makalu.

STRIKES – LEFT WITH NINE OUT OF A HUNDRED

Nowadays, to speak of the 'battle' for peaks is no longer fashionable. But if the game is to get three tonnes of expedition equipment on the backs of a hundred porters through storm and tempest, over snowed-in mountain passes, one may justly speak of struggling with elemental forces – and as far as the inhabitants of the villages of Shedua and Num could remember, there had never been such quantities of snow as fell last winter. Add to that all the fresh snow that has come down in the last few weeks . . .

The gap in the mountains we want to negotiate, the Kongma La, is 4200 metres high – and, strictly speaking, it comprises two passes. At the beginning of summer, wonderful rhododendrons bloom up there, and there is a little lake with prayer flags . . . but at present everything is buried under several metres of deep snow.

Having left the Arun behind us and dismissed our porters who came from the hill country beyond the river, we hire a hundred mountain men and women at the last jungle clearing below the pass, people from Shedua, Tashigang and Bungim. Then, together with two Naikes (porter chiefs), we set off again. The first day's climb passes uneventfully, apart from a few early season leeches in the jungle trying to suck our life-juices and invading our tents at night. We notice them in time, and snip them in half with scissors. More humane treatment only brings its own revenge: toss them out of doors and the creatures merely cling to the tent wall to come visiting again in the higher camps when you least expect them. (When we return after the expedition there will be countless numbers of them lurking in wait for us in the trees and bushes by the wayside.)

On the second day of ascent we meet the first snow in the rhododendron forest – old, rotten snow in great heaps. The men and women from Shedua, carrying as much as twenty-seven kilos each, have to

Makalu (8481m)

battle through it continually, often up to their waists – it is the most toilsome labour, torture you could say, for a mere twenty-eight rupees a day (about £1.20). You can understand how they would prefer to go home. We have distributed gym shoes, blankets, snow goggles, and just pray they will stay with us. The crossing, they keep telling us, has never been so bad. For us, everything is at stake. Up near the Kongma rock, the second leg of this stage, where expeditions usually wander over wonderful meadows, the snow is almost two metres deep in places. We decide to pitch all the tents we have to get our shivering army of workers out of the cold.

I man the modest field kitchen with our expedition cook, and we work till 2 a.m., seeing that everyone gets warm tea inside him (or her).

In vain. The next morning more than fifty porters desert us. We struggle on with the rest. Hans and I break trail almost to the top of the pass. The men behind us are still up to their waists in snow, but seem cheerful, laughing and joking about it (we truly do have the crème de la crème of these hill people now). But just before the pass they fling down their loads, and start back, most of them saying they will return in the morning: they are only going as far as the forest. We have no idea if we will see any of them again. Hermann prudently opens the trail to the top of the pass while Dietlinde – still down at the Kongma rock – guards the abandoned boxes and sacks, half of the total loads. It can be imagined how grateful we are the next morning to see black dots slowly pulling out of the grey layers of cloud below us, and moving along the white, undulating edge of the mountain . . . we count them. Yes! Nearly all are back!

Hot tea is handed round – then comes another half-hour of racking suspense. Will they stay, or go down after all? Our Sirdar, together with the liaison officer, implores the men and women to continue with us, pointing out that the trail is already broken as far as the pass. It is a very steep slope, but Hermann's tracks are clearly visible. They decide they will come on. Thank heavens!

That same evening, the first fifty loads arrive at a small pine forest on the Barun side of the Kongma La. There is nothing to be seen of the little lake and its rhododendrons but a dark watery patch in the snow desert. This is where the prayer flags stand, but only the highest of them peep out of the snow now.

Just as I am taking a photograph, a Sherpani passes by with her load. '*Tulo pani*,' I say, Big water! And I point at the sorry little puddle. She laughs, sets down her load and rummages in a little bag which she draws from the folds of her clothes. Then, murmuring a prayer, she tosses a coin into the water.

I grope in my own pockets, but I have no money on me. I find the beautiful stripey, silver and blue crystal of cyanite, which I picked up a few days ago in a field, wanting to take it home because it was so unusual. 'Makalu,' I say, and throw that into the water as well.

The next day, while the remaining fifty porters trudge back over the pass to fetch the other half of the loads, I cannot resist the temptation to wing down these slopes, which have cost us so much agony and effort. I carry my skis on up to 4000 metres, then whizz, deliciously, downhill.

In the Barun valley, nearly all the porters leave us, and we spend many days with the nine faithful who remain of our hundred, ferrying loads from there to Base Camp. That is after it has snowed for sixty hours without stopping. At least this gives me the chance of more skiing every time I go down to pick up my daily load from the Barun forest. After three weeks of approach, finally the mountain stands before us.

CHANCE AND MISCHANCE WITH THE OXYGEN – MY FRIENDS' SUMMIT

A weird droning emanates from the blue sky above us like a distant express train, a monotonous, eerie sound . . . incessant. No less strange is the reflected light which bounces off Makalu's rust-coloured granite, from a shining shield that rears in front of us, tilting into the sky. There is a difference of more than 3000 metres in height between here and the shield's upper rim; it is gigantic, unimaginably huge, and yet seems almost close on this clear day. The storm batters the edges of the giant shield, high, high up, while here in Base Camp the air remains calm and still. Banners of snow are sometimes flung from that gleaming rim; they circle a while then disappear . . . Only the sound, the unearthly droning of the high-altitude storm, the Makalu Express, rumbles on.

The top edge of the giant shield has a deep notch – the Makalu La, a saddle at about 7400 metres. To the left of it rises Kangchungtse (7678 m), which is known also as 'Little Makalu'; and to the right, rising in several steep and vaulting upthrusts, another 1000 metres of height to the summit of Makalu itself (8481 m).

Twenty-three years before our visit, French climbers found a way up this side to the summit – the first ascent. Since then, despite a number of attempts, nobody else has been able to repeat it, partly in view of the mountain's enormous height, but also because of the constant rearrangement of its snow and rock features under the battering of fierce storms, effectively renewing its virginity.

A New Zealander, Peter Mulgrew, who had suffered amputations to

Makalu (8481m)

his legs after sustaining serious frostbite on Makalu, called this eight-thousander (in his book of the same name), No Place For Men. Nevertheless, men have gradually solved one problem after another on this difficult mountain: the French Ridge, the South Face, the Czech Buttress, the South-East Ridge are all great, immense routes. But they have claimed their victims.

No traverse of Makalu has yet been done, but, having lost so much time in the terrible snowstorms on the Kongma La and afterwards, and realising the bad conditions on the south-east side of the mountain, we have almost stopped speaking of such a possibility. But perhaps, if we get up the north-west side quickly and the monsoon holds off until late . . . ?

Our Northern Base Camp was established on 4 April on top of a sandy shoulder at 5400 metres, and the little party remaining after the porters' departure has been working day after day on Makalu's steep flank, in an attempt to reach the aforementioned saddle, the Makalu La. Starting from our High Base, we can leapfrog campsites of earlier expeditions, and have already (on 8 April) put in our Camp 1 800 metres higher between the crevasses of a glacier plateau. Feverishly, we press on. It was Hans and I set up Camp 1, and Hermann with Ang Chappal who install Camp 2 on 13 April at 7000 metres.

To approach this camp is a steep and exposed climb, on which we have fixed 200 metres of rope. Anyone coming up heavily loaded must take special care since a false step here could send you plunging into the void.

Time and again the Makalu Express roars . . . gusts are so fierce that it would be impossible to reach or leave this Camp 2 without our safety line. Sleepless nights in rattling tents erode our nerves, but one day, finally, and again caught by a storm, Hermann, Ang Chappal and I, after a steep climb on granite slabs and snow, anchor two tiny tents with ice-screws into the sheer mirror of ice that covers the saddle at 7400 metres. Camp 3 on the Makalu La is standing and it is only 24 April. Does that mean we are still in with a chance for the traverse?

We hug one another, buffeted by the gusts: a first victory! Only 1000 metres from here to the summit; we can scarcely believe it!

Things continue more speedily than we expected. First, we must fix a line for belaying the access to this saddle, then Hans pushes the route onwards with Temba, then I with Nawang: at 7700 metres we cache five bottles of oxygen for our first summit team, Hermann and Ang Chappal. They are the fittest of us all.

And what next? The traverse? Not without some preparation on the south-east side of the mountain. I can't help asking myself during these days: Is Makalu asleep? Is this mountain really going to allow us tiny ants to crawl from bottom to top in less than a month? The prospect seems incredible, but our luck holds out.

Nawang gives Hermann and Ang Chappal a hand establishing Camp 4 at 7950 metres, breaking most of the trail and carrying an enormous pack without using any of the oxygen. Then he returns to Camp 3. Both of us are knackered, suffering from terrible high-altitude coughs and from our strenuous exertions up there. We descend, while Hans comes up with Karl (our indefatigable doctor, who has ferried loads like everyone else), and Hermann and Ang Chappal gain the pointed summit of Makalu – happy, on top of the world, for all of us. It is May Day, 2.45 in the afternoon. Hermann, as planned, used oxygen above Camp 4. The Sherpa went without.

On 10 May, in the evening, I am sitting in our Southern Base Camp, at 4800 metres, beside a crackling campfire with some porters who have brought up wood for us. The flames enliven the twilight, giving out a wonderful warmth. The last rays of the sun have set Makalu's summit pyramid aglow, high, high above our heads. Soon, the icy cold will rule up there. Spellbound, I watch as swathes of cloud play gently below the tipmost ruby rocks. It is a calm beautiful evening, and the light so beguiling that it makes you long to be on top at this minute but to hurry away with the last ray before the night can bind you in its terrible space-cold. It calls to mind that similar evening, twenty-one years ago, when Hermann Buhl and I stood at sunset on top of Broad Peak, 8047 metres, bathed in ethereal light, indescribably happy . . .

I have no idea as I gaze up at Makalu's rosy summit that Hans, Karl and Temba are standing up there . . . and that their view and mine and our thoughts meet in these last sun's rays.

But the cruel night lies in wait.

They are late, too late, not intentionally so, no more than Hermann Buhl and I intended to be on our summit at that hour. Afterwards, one is bound to ask how it came about, what one could have done differently, but meanwhile nothing can change the course of events.

Pensively Karl regards his black fingertips and swollen toes. In the two days since he came down, we have tried our best with injections and everything possible to help him. Hans, after days of snow blindness, sees the blue toes on his left foot for the first time . . . yet despite the

Makalu (8481m)

excruciating pain which wells over him from time to time, he does not question that the summit of Makalu was worth the price.

We were lucky, he says. It could have been much worse. And we all know that is true . . . After an open bivouac at 8250 metres, if all you lose are the tips of one or two fingers or toes, you have been lucky!

They might so easily never have resurfaced from the death-like sleep which overtook them when they finally arrived back in Camp 4; they could have gradually slid from semi-consciousness into eternity. Instead, they are here! And the first jokes come from their lips.

What actually happened? When I was on 'sick leave' down in the magic forest, trying to shake off my racking altitude cough, the second summit party ventured their luck: Hans, Karl and Nga Temba. With back-up from the others, everything at first appeared to go well. However, shortly before setting off for the top, all the evil spirits went on the rampage! One oxygen set after the other broke down. Attempts to repair them only led to loss of energy and time. Finally, all three, with Hans in the lead, moved off determinedly for the summit without artificial oxygen. At 6 p.m., they were on top, convinced they could still get down to Camp 4 before dark. But as night came, they realised that the cold had drained their headlamp batteries. The result was an ice-cold bivouac in a narrow alcove at the bottom of the final couloir, at 8250 metres, just below the steep face which rises beneath the summit ridge . . . Only Sherpa Nga Temba came through without frostbite – and as early as possible next day, he descended from Camp 4, helped down by Ang Chappal. Hans and Karl radioed that they, too, would be descending from there that day, but instead, they fell asleep as soon as they reached the tent. The bivouac had exhausted them terribly.

At the end of their strength, they staggered in to Camp 3 (7400 m) the following day where Hermann and Nawang did their utmost to persuade them to continue, finally physically conducting them down, despite protestations that all they wanted was to continue their sleep.

They may never have woken again.

MAKALU . . . WITH A MONKEY WRENCH

'Tea's ready!' sings out Ang Rita, our kitchen boy, in a voice loud enough to be heard all over the little tent city that is our Northern Base Camp in a sandy hollow at 5400 metres. With no sense of hurry, the small crew gathers in the spacious tent we call 'Alex'. Its fabric, once white, is now a venerable grey from several expeditions' service. Approaching, I catch the sound of laughter and joking. Even Karl,

Spirits of the Air

our doctor, hobbling in beside me on his two sticks, has lost none of his sense of humour. He comes from Bavaria, after all! And Hans, who we call 'the Bernese Lightning-streak', reflects wryly that so long as his toes hurt, they must still be alive.

I am the only one who is a bit subdued. The day after tomorrow, I shall set off with Hermann and Nawang Tenzing to attempt the highest peak of my career. It is eighteen years since I climbed one of the Himalayan giants – Dhaulagiri (8222 m) – and almost twenty-one since I stood on the top of Broad Peak in the sunset with Hermann Buhl. A third of my life has passed since then, a life of climbing, adventure and discovery. Will my luck hold over the next few days? That is why I am so quiet and preoccupied. The others too, of course, are well aware of the unpredictability which attends this, as any summit attack.

Everything worked like clockwork when the first two went to the top, Hermann Warth and Sirdar Ang Chappal. Hermann had no trouble with his oxygen set and Ang Chappal, by choice, climbed without. But the second attempt was disastrous – and since coming back from the forest, I am only now getting more details. Of the five oxygen sets we had brought, three failed to work at all, and the reserve would not function properly, notwithstanding that all the equipment – which had already performed successfully on a Kangchenjunga expedition in 1976, and on Lhotse the following year – had been put through stringent scientific testing in Switzerland before we set out. Obviously the apparatus preferred a neutral Swiss atmosphere to the thin icy air about 8000 metres. Luckily, Hans is something of a Mr Fixit, and has been able to locate one of the faults at least and cure it, miraculously, with a simple spanner. But for how long? He himself is not optimistic it will last. Hans reinforced his reputation as a technical genius on Lhotse last year; finding his oxygen flow blocked suddenly above 8000 metres by a build-up of ice crystals inside the apparatus, he calmly stopped and urinated through the tube and mask, instantly clearing the trouble!

Repairing oxygen sets at high altitudes is not usually accomplished so simply, however, and as a precaution we shall take two spanners with us in our rucksacks.

Nawang Tenzing, the good-natured Tibetan who now lives in Nepal, the one who struggled along the cornices on Shartse with Hermann and me in the storms, is also giving cause for concern. He cannot decide whether he really wants to go to the summit or not. He says he hates the cold, is reluctant to disturb the mountain gods, does not want to set himself up as an object of envy among his neighbours back home, yet we know he longs so much for another glimpse of his lost homeland – and how fantastic it must look from up there! I know how much it

Makalu (8481m)

means to him: I saw how he danced in the snow below Camp 2, when he first got high enough to see into Tibet.

It was Nawang's indecision that finally resolved Hermann to join us, even though he had been up once already. 'It would be marvellous if you could make it, too, Kurt,' he told me, adding that if he did make it again, he could bring back the stone from the top that he had promised his wife and forgotten to pick up the first time round!

Ever since shaking off my altitude cough a week ago, I have felt in tremendous form. I suggest to the other two that we make a lightning dash, bypassing Camp 2, and getting to the top and back in just a few days, like we did on Broad Peak twenty-one years ago. We would use oxygen from 7950 metres – although if it should fail again, I'd be quite prepared to try without, alone if necessary. None of us is interested in haemo-dilution. On the expedition, only the doctor, Karl, has tried thinning his own blood and that of Sherpa Nga Temba before their summit climb, but it is questionable whether it had any appreciable effect. For my part, I absolutely refuse to manipulate my body to enable me to reach the top. If my own blood is not good enough to get me up there, well then, I don't go.

And oxygen? It is true I climbed Dhaulagiri and Broad Peak without it, but now on the world's fifth highest mountain I will take the apparatus, and use it if I must; with or without it, I do not intend to push beyond my limits. I can see no sense in reaching the summit of a mountain at *any* price and by *whatever* means. No summit can ever be worth the lives of your companions, or yourself, or your ability to think and feel clearly in future. To sacrifice even part of that ability for success, makes of that success a failure.

Will you get closer to an understanding of the Why by climbing without oxygen to the greatest heights of the Himalaya? Or is the comprehension of why we are always drawn back to these mountains anyway beyond our intellectual grasp? Himalayan expert Elizabeth Hawley in Kathmandu told me an interesting thing. When Reinhold Messner listened to the tape recording he made of himself after struggling to the summit of Everest, he had to confess, 'It made no kind of sense at all.' He may have hoped, I guess, to have captured the sensations of another world. In vain. But this is one of the reasons why we mountaineers have to return. One thing I don't believe is that people who reach these high places feel nothing beyond the basic satisfaction of having made it. Even if some say that's all there was to it. Perhaps they have forgotten or don't know how to speak about an emotion that goes beyond words.

Certainly everybody has had the experience of their most wonderful dreams vanishing the very moment you want to keep hold of them for ever.

On 17 May, we set off: Hermann, Nawang and I, supported by Nga Temba and Ang Chappal who will accompany us as far as Camp 4, and Ang Rita who is to stay behind in Camp 1.

To start with, everything runs according to plan. And on our second day we manage the whole steep climb to the Makalu La, where our Camp 3 stands. The weather is splendid. But then, on the third day, a terrible storm blows up out of a blue sky, and continuing on to Camp 4 is out of the question. With horror, we realise that the high winds of the last few days have completely polished away all the snow from the slopes and surfaces below Camp 4. There is nothing but gleaming blue ice all the way to 7900 metres. This will make it extremely dangerous coming back from the summit unless we can fix some ropes for our protection. We are not prepared for anything like that. In the thick of the storm, I go out and cut what rope I can from the easier sections below the Makalu La, to help us higher up. The next day, 20 May, we luckily succeed in reaching Camp 4 – during the early afternoon.

The sight which greets us there is one of devastation: the tentpoles of a crushed three-man tunnel tent protrude from masses of blown snow like broken ribs. Nobody has been here for eleven days. The small igloo tent has fared better, but is not big enough to house all three of us.

I will not accept that this is the end to all our hopes! With the Sherpas, we extract the remnants of the buried tent, splint its ribs and patch it up as best we can. It should make an emergency shelter for Hermann and me. Nawang can have the red igloo. Ang Chappal and Nga Temba wish us luck and disappear round the corner of our little camping niche to head off down the fixed ropes on the steep blank ice.

It is a long night, very long. At the first glimmer of day we start our preparations for leaving, an irksome business in the makeshift tent. We can only move one at a time, and even putting on boots involves lying down and wriggling in a complicated sequence of acrobatics. Nawang prepares breakfast as we sort out the oxygen gear. As I am to be the trail-blazer, I set off ahead of the others at 6 o'clock, with just one bottle of oxygen. Hermann and Nawang will follow shortly, bringing two bottles each. After I have gone, however, their apparatus gives them some problems and they do not get away until 7 o'clock. Meanwhile I stamp laboriously up into the white solitude. Sporadic eddies of air spatter me with cold powder snow. On the steeper slopes, the surface has been compacted by storms and shatters into angular flakes at every

Makalu (8481m)

just the occasional little gust twirling wisps of spindrift around, but there's no time to waste admiring the view. Up! Up! Every moment could be precious. We cannot know how long our oxygen sets will last, and the higher we are if they do pack up, the greater our chances. We won't need them coming down, that's something . . .

As I belay, I ponder again the pros and cons of climbing 'by fair means', and it is easy to convince myself not to use oxygen another time when heavy equipment proves little more than a talisman!

At a vertical rock step where a dangling rope remains from the first summit attempt Nawang signals urgently that he is again experiencing difficulty with his oxygen. I yank my mask away from my mouth and shout to him. Does he want to try this steep pitch without it? He shakes his head. So we struggle our way up around the right-hand side, like two proboscideans. The fixed rope is clearly just for the descent. Suddenly I notice something wrong with my own breathing, and rip the mask off again. Far from coming as a shock to my system, the thin, cold air outside is a blessed relief! I swallow deep draughts of it, like a thirsty man gulping water – pure, clear . . . and it is only a couple of pitches further on that I realise part of the reason I feel so light-headed is the paucity of oxygen. Nawang joins me on a little ledge – he, too, is climbing without his mask now – and we sit down to take stock. What are we going to do? It cannot be far up to the ridge – why don't we dump all the superfluous weight here and climb on without it? And as we deliberate and fiddle, we find ourselves striking the offending masks and tubes with our fists. To our amazement, in so doing, we obviously loosen some of the ice that has built up inside, for when we shake them, small fragments tumble out. To my surprised relief I find I am able to breathe through my mask as well as before. The rough treatment has also helped Nawang's set, although whether he sets it to deliver one or four litres a minute, he gets the same amount – or rather, not quite enough. All the same, he prefers to go on with it, than without. We leave a thermos flask and an ice hammer behind, and set off again, up between some rocky blocks towards the summit ridge. This at least I feel sure that we will reach. Perhaps the summit, too, but I dare not let myself believe that yet, even though reason tells me there is not much in the way to stop us. Still, at this height every single step you make is a gift – you have no right to it.

We reach the summit ridge! So that's 8400 metres! A gentle, almost horizontal ridge it is, along which we can easily walk side by side, as if on a sloping roofhang, but we know that above the ridgepole to our left, the ground must certainly fall away to nothingness.

Spirits of the Air

In front of us now rises – no, floats above the 3000-metre chasm of the Barun – a magical creation, to which we come closer by the minute. It is a true castle of the gods – the highest, final pinnacle of Makalu! My companion lets out a startled shriek – or was it a cry of astonishment? – some muffled words of Tibetan under his mask.

'Nawang,' I seek to reassure him with a calming gesture, 'we can do it!' My words belie the fact that I, too, am deeply moved at the sight of this fierce, lonely, beautiful ice-covered structure, rising nakedly into the clear blue sky and wrapped around by the intermittent sparkle of thousands of tiny, floating ice crystals. It might not have been the right response to Nawang's call, but our masks hide every expression on our faces, make words unintelligible.

We take the last steps along the flat ridge. Then stop. The summit! There it is, right before us!

The final seventy metres are incredibly exposed. Steep flutings of snow rear up like surf from the blue depths, to connect, as a thin hanging bridge, the first, lower, summit with the second, which towers a full fifty metres higher. The rusty-brown rocks beneath are clad in a tracery of shimmering ice. The snow has been blown up by storms from the giant walls of the mountain, extending them skywards, so that the two sides now meet in a piped seam, so fine that in places you could pinch it between your fingers. I cast a glance back at Nawang – and he nods, silently.

Up we go!

The first summit is safely behind us: in the steep crystalline surface below the white piping I hack out a place large enough for Nawang and me to stand in. It is quite exposed: I cannot resist the temptation to look over the other side. Through a tiny gap, I see clouds, and beyond them, directly below me, the characteristic outline of P 8010, a pinnacle on Makalu's South-East Ridge, first climbed by two Czechoslovaks in 1976. There, too, is the steep final wall of Makalu, scene of a tragic Czech–Spanish ascent and the way by which a strong Japanese party earlier reached the top. This is momentary. My main concern is Nawang: now that he is close to this unearthly summit, this abode of the gods which so affected him lower down on the ridge, will he revert to his earlier confusion . . . and not want to climb it?

With this in mind, I had not stopped on the first summit, but run out the rope to its end. I need not have worried: on reaching the fore-summit, he regards the airy ridge, this Jacob's Ladder of snow leading across deep immeasurable space to the loftier summit, warily and with unconcealed amazement, but he does not falter for a moment. And as he comes across it, balancing his every step by thrusting his ice axe firmly in the snow, I am struck by how quickly and confidently he moves.

Two days ago, Nawang had told me: 'If we get to the summit, you will be very happy – and I some.' Now, to my astonishment, he exuberantly flings his arms around me on the narrow stance, exclaiming how happy he is! It gives me more pleasure than I can say.

Very slowly, every nerve in me tight, step by cautious step, hold by hard-won hold, I carve us out a passage with my axe up along the white rim, to reach a small rocky patch. With a sound belay, I carefully watch Nawang across, then go on . . . Suddenly, I am aware of an apex of snow against the blue sky only five metres above my head, a perfectly regular form out of which, to right and left, stick thin wands of bamboo.

My surprise lasts a moment only. Like a flash it hits me: this is the summit!

I inch towards it. The intangible gift of sky and earth has become reality. MAKALU! Here, in front of me. I sink to my knees, and clutch the highest tip of the snow with both hands. This point where all the ridges of the mountain come together, this Makalu is mine!

A wave of unbelievable joy washes over me, and I am strangely excited before this unique summit, this icy point in the sky.

I make room for Nawang, I have to move to the other side of the summit. There, beside a yellow oxygen bottle which was probably left by the Czech–Spanish expedition, I thrust in my axe and belay my companion. Up he comes! Just a couple of metres apart, we stand facing each other, the white summit of Makalu between us, and below us the ridges of the mountain, and clouds and peaks, and the silhouette of Everest in the distance. More clouds are moving in from the west . . .

We should not stay up here too long. I want to embrace Nawang, to shake hands with him and say *'Berg Heil!'* but he is ignorant of summit rites, and has in any case already conveyed his joy to me, lower down. Now he takes off his oxygen mask and stands mutely regarding the scene, eyes filled with wonder. Finally, he unscrews the regulator before ramming his near-empty cylinder into the summit snow; I follow suit, except that first I must rummage in my sack for the monkey wrench. Neither of us thinks to look at the gauges: regardless of how much gas we have left, we don't intend to use any going down. Then, as if in silent understanding, we press each other's hand, and I take a few photographs – close-ups, for you could not step back.

Perhaps it was the racing clouds, fear that a storm might catch us out up here; or maybe it was the euphoria of reaching the summit – impossible as that had seemed only a few days ago when I was coughing my heart out down below – I don't know why, but I forgot all about the flags I was carrying in my pocket and which I meant to photograph up here. So much had happened . . . since I fled to the jungle in such desperation, convinced beyond all doubt that my dreams could no longer come true . . . now, to be standing here, above the world, not just in my thoughts, but in flesh and blood, body and soul . . . this was like the wingbeats of destiny, a magical floating feeling, against which the everyday world had no place.

Not until we are below the lower summit again do I realise my omission. Oh, Lordy! What will they say back home when there are no pictures of the Austrian flag, or the Alpenverein flag, or any of the others, on the summit? Hastily, I press my camera into Nawang's hands so that at least we shall get a picture of the flags on the summit ridge! One thing we did not forget: the stone from the top for Dietlinde! From the last rocks under the snow summit, we have brought several samples: granite, quartz and a kind of dark slate. But now we must hurry off the ridge as fast as we can, for the storm, heralded by the wild clouds, is already upon us. We urgently need to get into the shelter of the couloir. We reached the top at 1.30 p.m., and have every hope of making it all the way down to our camp on the Makalu La this evening.

We manage it: at around 5 p.m. our Sherpa friends Ang Chappal and Nga Temba embrace us in the ruins of Camp 4, and at around 8 o'clock, after an exhausting descent to the saddle, a beaming Hermann welcomes us into Camp 3. The first 1000 metres lie behind us. But the night is a calamitous one for me: I am awakened by the tormenting pains of snow blindness, my penalty for taking off my goggles several times when climbing the rocks of the couloir. I treat myself right away with a variety of eye drops, and Hermann concocts some special goggles for me using sticking plaster, with narrow slits to see through. Wearing these, I stumble off next morning, with him belaying me. The cold air seems to help the pain – I can see slightly better – and after a few hours, following first the fixed ropes then retracing the familiar route across the glacier, we reach Camp 1, 1200 metres lower. I sleep there for a couple of hours, the sleep of the dead, lying in the snow outside the tents – and then we put another 800 metres behind us to arrive in Base Camp. Now, as I peer up through the thickening dusk with my least-affected eye, it seems like a dream that only yesterday afternoon I was standing up there on top with Nawang Tenzing.

A few days later, on 25 May, our porters having come from Tashigang for us, we set off on the return march. No longer is this a journey

Makalu (8481m)

through deep snow, but one taking us through rhododendron forests in bloom . . .

In Yang Lhe the birds are singing. I feel so happy and thankful. For everything. An inexpressible energy will accompany me from now on. What it is, I don't know. We all leave here changed. We were in the palace of the gods – and that, perhaps, is what alters our lives.

It was surprising, with how much courage and humour Hans and Karl managed their painful return across the mountain passes. They knew that was the price for the top. To the rest of us, it meant a lot to see that for them, too, the blossoming trees were a splendour, and the chang-parties put on for us by the locals, a pleasure. We had every reason to feel happy. Even if we had not achieved the traverse we desired, each of us had fulfilled a life's wish: to stand on top of Makalu. And Didi, Dietlinde, smiled too, hugging her summit stone; she had never envisaged going to the top herself.

Even if it does not appear so at first glance, this had been quite a special enterprise: between the first party reaching the summit and the last, three full weeks elapsed. We had all helped each other, and in that way everybody had his chance.

Moreover, Hermann had put into practice, for the first time on an expedition to an eight-thousander, his idea of including Sherpas as totally equal partners in the venture, with their own claims to the summit and the load-ferrying being the business of everyone, with no exceptions.

It may seem remarkable, too, that our food provisions came almost entirely from Nepal. And oxygen? Today, I think that with such a team, we would have been much better off without it, particularly considering our good acclimatisation.

For myself, Makalu proved an unexpected turning point: within the space of fifteen months I was to stand on the summits of three eight-thousanders.

Depot Kurt

This was the name given to me by Pierre – Pierre Mazeaud, the one-time Sports Minister of France who led the 1978 French Everest Expedition, on which I took part as mountaineer and cameraman. We were sitting having breakfast one radiant morning in the Valley of Silence, in the spacious communal tent of Camp 2 at about 6500 metres. Suddenly, the Sports Minister wrinkled his nose. '*Dieu, quelle odeur de fromage!*' he exclaimed. 'My God, Kurt, what is that terrible cheesy smell?' He sniffed the air around him. '*Ça ne vient pas de la France.* It's certainly not a French one!' And he threw a sharp glance in my direction. '*Impossible!* It seems to be coming from these boxes. Kurt . . .?'

I retreated into deep silence, for he did have a point: the cheese in question was mine.

Good relations with Himalyan spirits continued beyond this mountain.

By rights, it ought not to have been up here at all: these boxes were supposed to contain only my official film equipment. One, however, was highly unofficial, and anything but FRAGILE, as it boldly maintained. Even back in Base Camp the French had been funny about the Nepalese yak-milk cheese (as big as a waggonwheel) which I had bought at the Takshindu dairy, refusing to allow it to enter the Valley of Silence. 'We can't waste Sherpa power carrying it. If you want it you can roll it up the glacier!' Jean Afanassieff had been quite

Depot Kurt

sarcastic, and the whole expedition was quick to point out, 'We have our own cheese, Kurt – French cheese!' at which they all nodded emphatically. But these dainty French cheeses were such minuscule mouthfuls that you could easily juggle several in one hand: nothing like enough for an Austrian appetite! (Otherwise, I had no complaints about their excellent food. Only in the upper camps were you aware of the relentless modern tendency towards 'ever lighter, ever faster' . . . An excess of superlight freeze-dried packets certainly kept you running, converting the slogan into drastic reality . . . by way of tummy ache . . . 'ever lighter, ever faster!') As I am a champion of genuine, natural provisions on the mountain, I agonised long over my gigantic cheese wheel. Eureka! Wasn't I entitled to a film Sherpa? A film box was emptied out . . . and half the waggonwheel stowed inside; a second film box accommodated the second half of the nutritious round . . . then the Sherpa marched towards Camp 2. He carried the valuable load with the utmost care (valuable, that is, to me, even if not as fragile as he was led to believe). I couldn't prevent Mazeaud's nephew, our doctor (anxious to declare his goodwill for the film) from carrying the other box up into the Valley of Silence, but I hoped he would never discover what he had done. All these thoughts passed through my mind, while Pierre Mazeaud, head down like a bloodhound, snuffled his way round the tent, remarking as he did so, 'That smells *(sniff, sniff)* like *Nepalese cheese. Kurt, what do you know about this?'*

I remain mum. To crown it all, he's a lawyer, I thought. What will I say? Because one thing was clear: the moment of truth was very close now . . .

'Halte-là!' It's coming from this box!' Pierre was triumphant. 'One of your film boxes, Kurt!' And he skewered me to the tent wall with a glance, as only a lawyer can who has just driven his victim into a blind corner. I made a clean breast of it, opened the box, cut off a slice of yak cheese for Pierre, saw with satisfaction how he munched into it, even with a short laugh – so then, it was not that bad an idea . . . was it?

But suddenly his expression is back as it was. He pontificates: 'Kurt, you have more gear than anyone else on this expedition. Look around you! Boxes everywhere. Wherever we sit, wherever we stand: everywhere, it says KURT DIEMBERGER – FRAGILE . . . *ou pas!*' And he pointed to the clearly far from delicate cheese.

'Oh, come, steady on,' I tried to calm my explosive Gallic friend. 'You know I have to make the film.' But I knew that bringing in the film was only part of the story; really, I did have a lot of things.

Unfortunately, here in Camp 2, this was becoming so evident because my well-proven 'depot system' had not had a real chance to get going. (I can't tell you if I invented it, but the idea is always and everywhere to have personal depots – on Everest that means a box in Camp 1, another in Camp 2, a bag in Camp 3 . . . so that wherever you arrive, your gear is waiting; but, as I said, for the moment it had all bottlenecked in Camp 2.) Pierre Mazeaud – with a wide move of his hand, as if delivering a great speech to parliament – affected not to have heard my justification. 'Kurt,' he said, 'you cannot deny that it is true . . . You need the Place de la Concorde for all your paraphernalia . . . and even that wouldn't be big enough.' He took a deep breath (no wonder, for such a tirade at 6500 metres of altitude). 'I mean,' he continued, 'that besides my logistics for this expedition, which is to put France on the summit of Everest, I need a separate logistical plan for the depots of Kurt Diemberger . . .'

I was contrite. It is true that I like to have a down jacket waiting for me in Camp 3 and, let us say, another one in Camp 1 or 2, and – of course – one in Base Camp as well; moreover, if possible, a sleeping – no, *two* sleeping-bags in Base Camp, a further one in Camp 1 and then one that stays in Camp 4 – because I hate to be running uphill and downhill all the time, overloaded with gear, sleeping-bags, mattresses! Anybody can see that mine is a good system! Let me just add, for all those who might be saying, 'We never would have thought that Diemberger is so lazy,' that when you're making a mountain film, you are already quite loaded – simply having to carry the movie camera – and, far more than any other expedition member, you are obliged to keep clambering up and down, to and fro.

So, please excuse my depot habits . . . (apparently, I have not fully digested Pierre's parliamentary preaching). But I also want to toss another positive aspect on to the balance. I had already initiated this system of depots long before I ever dared to dream of getting to the Himalaya. I was even using it back when I was a crystal hunter and needed to shoulder the weight of hammers and chisels and of course the heavy burden of rock samples and crystals which I found high up on the mountain.

To save always having to carry the heavy tools up to the same parts of the massif, I told myself the best thing would be to simply squirrel them away up there. Thus was my system born on Mont Blanc. (There are several good crystal sites and almost all of them high up; between guiding trips or when the weather was too bad for a big climb, I used to like going up there. Crystal-hunting is something marvellous!)

But we are only at the beginning: enter the marmots! (Or, more precisely, their burrows.) Because there is no better place to hide a hammer than a marmot hole – safe from avalanches, out of sight, and

Depot Kurt

moreover no effort involved. Hammer and chisel into one burrow, the stove into the next, a bottle of whisky into a third and . . . no problem, there are enough of these holes! The first time I went back, not long afterwards, I ran into a problem: I found the right place easily enough, but then I had to search like a dachshund – there were almost a hundred holes in the slope, and everything, everywhere looked very similar. Remedy: I carved a mark into a rock above the hammer hole when I eventually found it, and bore in mind that the whisky hole was five steps to the left, and the stove was stuffed into the tube of another dwelling eight steps to the right, while obliquely below . . . It is clear that every system must first be developed, it doesn't simply fall from the sky.

Ever since then the depot system has worked brilliantly. I was so convinced of it (and still am) that eventually I applied it to my everyday life as well. However, as this became more extensive and complicated, the more years that passed, I have to confess that the system also had its drawbacks: either you are lucky enough to find a wife who is *au fait* with everything, or you conscientiously feed every move into a computer – otherwise it can happen that you don't always know where is what or what is where.

For example, I am still searching – two years on – for one of my Leica cameras. No small thing, really, but it has been two years already . . . And it is not the only thing I'm after. Such a search can be full of emotions – and the pleasure, if you strike the motherlode, is great. I enter now into the 'thoughtful' part of this chapter – it reveals all the pros and cons of the depot method, which I still favour – even if I haven't yet located the Leica. I recommend it to the reader who wants to follow me in my search for something lost, to rope up with me – we will range worldwide . . .

To begin with, I think: Now where is it likely to be (whatever it is)?

But it doesn't come to mind. Which, as we all know, is destined to step up the pulse rate.

So again, more heatedly, the age-old question, such as was demanded no doubt by a Stone Age ancestor hunting for his flint axe: Where on earth can the bally thing be? (Variations like 'In heaven's name . . .', or 'Where the bloody hell is it . . .' may be of more recent vintage, but are nevertheless equally ineffective.)

Now, there is only one remedy: to calm down, and think.

So, I make a start and work through the most probable places where the thing could be. That is – at home, naturally, which means in

Spirits of the Air

Salzburg, or Bologna, or Portomaggiore.

> In Salzburg is my father.
> In Bologna is my wife.
> In Portomaggiore is my mother-in-law.

As the year passes, all these places are in turn my home. Therefore, if I'm searching for something, I know that books and slides and mountaineering equipment are most probably in Salzburg. In Bologna, where my wife lives, things do not usually go astray. And in Portomaggiore, at Mother-in-law's place, I have to look around if it's a case of missing garments or things to be mended. (My wife loves decentralisation of work; basically, her own depot system, in a wider sense.)

If I don't find what I'm looking for in any of these three places, then it gets more complicated. The thing may then lie anywhere in the world between Kathmandu and Hawaii. And if I want to dig it out of my subconscious memory, I must take to a couch (psychologists work to the same method), and ponder for some hours . . .

This business of order, or should I say, the instinct for order, is inherent to our family. My father and I are fanatics for order. This may be the very reason we mislay so much. It is why my father passes hours engineering new systems for locating items more easily. I, for one, think he's a genius – he is always dreaming up some new and logical system, but mostly in my absence. When I return home, he proudly shows off his latest scheme – and I groan, for I couldn't find things before. My father knows that – and therefore he attempts somehow to work universal principles into the programme: last time I came home I found the contents of two wardrobes carefully distributed according to the specific gravity of each item! What have I been looking for since then? Everything. But that's by the way.

While I am floating on my couch across countries and continents, I visit many friends; and thus can now introduce the reader to the surprises in store for a depot-being.

The system, as I've already hinted, does have its weak points: when, after two years of exploring the recesses of my mind, I went to fetch my suit from Herbert Tichy's house in Vienna, he said to me: 'I've given it to the postman.' How come? 'I racked my brains for quite a while about this mysterious suit. It didn't fit me. But the postman looks brilliant in it.'

Depot Kurt

You do have to be careful with writers: they are always so lost in their own stories . . .

Vienna, one way or another, has not proved the most satisfactory location for me: recently some mountaineering gear, a couple of books, and other personal items arrived from there in a cardboard box. Inge had got married. Yes – time doesn't stand still! (Everybody will understand the practicality of keeping a climbing rope elsewhere – not always having to fetch it from Italy.) Oh yes, another rope is sitting at José Manuel Anglada's pad in Barcelona, my Spanish depot. By the way, recently I brought him a key, a very big key, two feet long! I bought it at a flea market in Bologna because I knew that José collects keys. However, after a short glance at the antique piece, he said to me, it was a beautiful key, very fine craftsmanship, but, well . . . from Italy . . . not genuine; even so, he was pleased to have it. I wonder perhaps when I brought him the fake artefact, whether I put the real Leica in the bottom of his wardrobe? Perhaps it sleeps snugly there, as if in a marmot's tunnel? You see, in Barcelona, you hide everything. It is like a Spanish Naples. The fact that Anglada still has his valuable key collection is certainly due to the three special locks on his door. What lies there, lies safely; so if that's where my Leica is, it will be all right.

By the way: you can also get pleasant surprises with this system.

Not long ago, I was 'presented' with a pair of skis out of the blue; Orazio and Annie from the Squirrel Albergo in Courmayeur had dug them out of their cellar, and discovered 'KURT' written on them. Now I remember: those were the skis with which I descended the Tirich Glacier in the Hindu Kush thirteen years ago . . . My God, where things end up!

Another reliable place is the Black Forest. Even if I don't know precisely what I have deposited there. That is where Trudy lives; she is sixty-nine and comes from Berlin . . . she always transforms my loose-knit Austrian soul into military shape . . . for days I sit there framing and cleaning my slides. Moreover, she knows everything as far as the natural sciences are concerned; I can listen to her for hours. Thirty years ago we stood on top of the Gross Venediger in the Austrian Alps . . . It is true, when you stay at her place you have to get up as early as at the Kürsinger mountain hut – every day an alpine start!

But let us get closer to home: Munich . . . a traffic-node in all my journeyings. There, at Uli's, resides my film gear, thus saving me from fastidiously declaring it to our brave Austrian Customs officials every time I make a frontier crossing. (Perhaps the big business conglomerates with their multinational branches have also learned from the marmots?) Yes, and a projector and God knows what else is stashed near a Bavarian lake with Gerda and Volkmar. There I was recently shown the 'yellow card' because their lobby door could hardly be made to close any more – so a part of my gear is lying now over the road with my artist friend Herbert Finster. In the near future, I shall carry some miniature paintings up Everest for him (as a sort of a 'pennant' for art) – so that he can know his is the highest art of all, even if the exhibition attracts the least number of visitors.

Further to the north, into the Pfalz: there in Kaiserslautern in Klaus and Brigitte's cellar I have, besides a trunk of amethysts and agates from the nearby volcanic area, a whole row of boxes filled with copies of my book *Summits and Secrets*. From there, it is not far to Luxembourg with its cheap flights to America . . . my next depot is in New Jersey at my cousin Elke's. The depot in London, however, at Ken Wilson's, had to be dispersed. When his wife had their second baby, he needed the space himself.

Back across the ocean – Hawaii! A box of slides, forgotten after a lecture to the former King's family, the Kawananakoas. *Auf Wiedersehen*, Carol and Dudie, Phil and Fran, Elelule . . . I need the slides again – and not by post! See you next year . . .

Estes Park, Colorado: a pair of mountain boots – but I'm not quite sure. Are they still with Michael Covington and Steve Komito? (With Steve, who sold and soled boots for all the mountaineers in the west?) Or did I leave them with Gordon-the-millionaire in Nevada? I'll have to write a card.

Canada, Banff: a box of dinosaur bones in Evelyn's bedroom. They'll be all right there a bit longer.

Los Angeles: different things at different places.

Not to forget! Kathmandu: aluminium cases full of Himalayan gear with Miss Hawley and duffel bags at Mr Kalikote's. I can start a small expedition at any time at short notice. Before heading off I would then sit again with the 'living archive', Miss Hawley. This charming lady, who you would be justified in calling a landmark of Kathmandu, and who knows really everything that's happened in the Himalaya, having painstakingly recorded it over many years – such as the 'horse race', as I called the legendary page from her archives which we have discussed from time to time. She keeps a table of all the mountaineers who have climbed 8000-metre peaks. You can see quite clearly how they are proceeding from year to year – this one has two, that in the meantime has three, one has four . . . And then there are two who have five each: Reinhold Messner and myself. We have been running neck and neck for some time . . .

Depot Kurt

This will certainly have changed again by next year, because at this moment Reinhold is on his way to Mount Everest, and for my part, it's only two weeks till I go as well – I don't know why destiny requires us to be stumbling over each other's legs all the time. It's not intentional, although we have always been on good terms and in the past have enjoyed talking about mountaineering. I even think that for a while I once had a suitcase at his home in Villnöss.

(from my Diary, 1980)

But on to other places. In Warsaw, this wonderful, vital town – artists; museums; courageous lovely people, full of ideas – there, sadly, I have no depot. When I was lecturing and travelling around the country, I wanted to leave various bits and pieces behind, but my wife, who was with me, meticulously packed everything away, down to the last sock . . . Now my Leica flashes into my mind again, which I am still hunting for – before this book appears in Italian, I must run through my list of depots carefully, otherwise my wife won't be asking where I left the Leica, but: Why did he leave it there?

Düsseldorf: High Camps 3 and 5 – if you're overweight I recommend the latter, rather than the glorified jogging through the woods adopted by my colleagues – since the brave Amazonian Erica, in her fifth-floor apartment, has no elevator. At Wolfgang's (Camp 3), however, I have been working for two years already on a non-urgent soundtrack. Every time the wind blows me into town. (I've got two boxes there: perhaps the Leica is in Düsseldorf?)

Mon Dieu! How could I forget France in my round-the-world couch trip? I have not yet conjured up the *Petit Bateau*, the little boat in Cazères! Louis Audoubert, Marc Galy, the two Pyrenean specialists, are now more often travelling in the big mountains of the world. Louis, small, compact, blue-eyed, always laughing, a bundle of energy, soloing the Brouillard Ridge to the top of Mont Blanc in six hours; twice up the entire Peuterey Ridge, once even in winter – the 'wildest priest of the Alps'! In the end, he was left with only one crampon on the Peuterey Ridge – and his faith. It is true he had held a mass on the summit of Aiguille Noire just before. Now he is not allowed to do that any more – he got married. He has a lovely wife, and still his faith, this Louis! When he was a priest, I became godfather to his sister's baby son – and left my copy of good old Dyhrenfurth's book *Baltoro* there. It is said to have journeyed into Spain where mountaineers are preparing a new expedition with it. Yes, in the Pyrenees at the time I picked up French and Spanish, and puffed Gauloises for three months – although I was a non-smoker. (But that is a different story.) Altogether, it's incredible

Spirits of the Air

how useful this depot system proves to be – fantastically so, despite several flaws. I want to thank all my depot-managers – and manageresses.

Back to Italy: I haven't been in Trieste for a long time, even though I'm a member of the local Club Alpino. Bianca, my agile ropemate on several climbs, is unfortunately now always on the road herself, never there. In Treviso, however, where a kind elderly lady lives, Telene, who makes really outstanding spaghetti, there I stop quite often before I visit Gianni in his shoe factory, who has equipped my expeditions from the very beginning with mountain boots – there are always boots of mine at his place.

And so, I get to Varese once more, to Tona and the children, take a pair of skis and mountain equipment for Mont Blanc because I've got some tourists to guide; we are having a pizza in the garden, looking through the trees at our dear Monte Rosa. *Arrivederci*, darlings . . .

When the Mont Blanc trip is over, I want to take another look at my marmot holes up there on the mountain, before returning home to Bologna!

To Teresa, my patient wife.

Apropos Mont Blanc: I was there again recently, back where I learned the crystal hunter's wisdom, the principle of the depots, right at the place of its discovery. By the marmot holes below the Aiguille de Triolet. I found the mark on the rock without difficulty. And the hole with the hammer, too. It had grown quite rusty, but – I mean – two years had passed since the last time. Immediately, I start looking for the stove, the chisel and the whisky bottle . . . Nothing. Have I got it wrong? Impossible. Then it dawns on me: these diligent marmots! The wretches have dug so many new holes in two years. I am wandering over the slope, to and fro, up and down . . . where is the whisky, where is the chisel, where is the stove? How many metres to the left and right have I got to go? Surely the whisky will have matured nicely in the meantime? In vain: I didn't find it. If you come across it, remember to toast me. The stove didn't show up, either. Perhaps a marmot with a flair for invention has incorporated it into the architecture of his larder. So, well, I'm sipping cold water from the stream. At least I found the rusty hammer.

But something else besides I haven't yet found. What was it? Something else in the marmot holes? What was the reason for this voyage down memory lane? Oh yes . . . if anybody knows where my Leica is – I haven't yet given up hope!

PS: I would ask all my friends who read this book, please don't start digging in your wardrobes and cellars and then send me an avalanche of parcels!

Depot Kurt

Already one has told me on the phone he found some old mountain trousers at his place, and might they perhaps be mine? I told him, please, see if they fit the postman first!

PPS: Two weeks before going to press, quite unexpectedly I bumped into Pierre Mazeaud on his way up to Mont Blanc – the ancien ministre des sports et des loisirs carried a mighty rucksack. I was surprised – despite his charming companion. '*Seulement une petite tente* . . . just a high camp,' explains my friend, after greeting me cordially. Then he quickly climbs higher, too fast for me to follow him with my client.

Next day I'm looking everywhere on Mont Blanc for a high camp – I cannot find one: has my friend secretly become a convert to my depot system? 'DEPOT PIERRE'?

(from my Diary)

'Take One'

ON THE SUMMIT OF EVEREST

Eight thousand five hundred metres. Rotten rocks, shattered by the extreme temperatures of high altitude, crumble as I lean back against them, breathing deeply, rucksack at my side, camera on my knees. I am not so much sitting as crouching in a wind-sculpted open scoop in the snow. Across its edge, I gaze down the icy roof of the highest mountain on earth, and along the flutes of the East Face. In the depths, some three or four thousand metres below me, lies the Kangshung Glacier. An irregular pattern of mainly snow-covered moraine, it flows eastwards, past the silhouettes of Shartse and Pethangtse, and on towards the last granite spires of Chomo Lönzo. Above them, dominating everything on this side and masking the indigo shadow of the Arun valley, rises the beautiful pyramid of Makalu, the only 'big' mountain till my eyes reach Kangchenjunga, far out on the horizon . . . A beautiful day! The day of the century – a gift from the gods one might be tempted to say – a gift to whoever is climbing to the top of Everest today! For me, it is.

I am alone. Nearby, Lhotse, 8511 metres high, thrusts up like a crystal, the fourth highest mountain on earth, steep, brusque, cold. Silence and no wind at all . . . not here at least, where I am . . .

You must film! The thought tugs me from just quietly allowing my mind to slide from peak to peak, floating through this enormous space below . . . That is bound to happen more often this day, for on the one hand, here I am, climbing to the top of Chomolungma to fulfil a great wish – it seems incredible to me, even up here at 8500 metres, that it can yet come true, but logic says, 'Yes, it will' – and on the other, I am here to record the ascent of my French comrades on film, and even sound on the summit . . . I am cameraman to the French.

Where are the boys, by the way?

Kurt, shoot! Coming up, outlined against the Western Cwm, I can see their orange shapes, and I manoeuvre the figures into the frame of the viewfinder – Jean and Nicolas with, in front of them, a Sherpa. Obliquely above them, closer to me, I capture Pierre – Pierre Mazeaud, my ropemate, though we will not be using the rope until we get higher up, somewhere around the South Summit, certainly for the traverse of the sharp, exposed ridge to the very top. At present, it is every man for himself as we move unbelayed. No fall, not the slightest stumble, is permitted here without sending you irretrievably down into the depths.

To move freely is essential for me anyway. On a rope, I could never traverse off the route, as I have here, in order to film the others when they climb through the horizon's jagged blue line. It is an overwhelming horizon . . . peak following peak, and to the south the shimmering ocean of clouds with, beyond them – India!

A super shot! Despite the difficulty of holding my breath in the thin air so as not to joggle the picture, I feel happy, content, like a fisherman with a great catch! The camera whirrs, and my comrades pass by, heading on further, up towards the deep blue sky . . . Aah, hell – the film magazine is finished! I need to put a new one in . . . from my rucksack, beside me in the niche . . . Panting, I open the lid, albeit too late for another shot. While I am rummaging I remember how, with such high hopes, Pierre Mazeaud and I climbed up to this place yesterday, along with Ang Dawa, the faithful Sherpa, the only one to remain with us in the storm two days ago. It was a tiring struggle, not least because of the filming and getting higher at the same time, a heavy load of nearly twenty kilos on your back. Besides smaller items, the three of us carried two bottles of oxygen each – one for breathing, and the second for . . . at long last, Pierre and I decided to dump our ambitions and the bottles here and to descend to the South Col at about 8000 metres; we had been breathing only two litres a minute – not enough for what we were doing, a truth that dawned on us when it was too late. Thus, the desired summit was out of the question.

Today, we are again at this place, where all previous expeditions established their highest camp – around 8500 metres. We decided against such a shelter and so did the Germans of Dr Karl Herrligkoffer's expedition. Three of them reached the top yesterday – Hans Engl, Hubert Hillmaier and Sepp Maag. In any case, Pierre and I would never have been able to establish a camp here, with only the help of Ang Dawa. That is why we thought to come up this morning on a single bottle each from the South Col, and then continue to the top with the second one from our cache. Hopefully, that would last till we get back here, though that is not so critical: descending you need incredibly less air and effort at high altitude. Meanwhile, we are no longer alone: a couple of Sherpas have decided to join us, with Jean Afanassieff and

Spirits of the Air

Nicolas Jaeger, our two 'youngsters'. The Sherpas will accompany our group to about 8600 metres, where the gradient rises steeply to the South Summit, then they will go down.

High time to move, Kurt! Already the figures above you are too small in the viewfinder! I get my things together, deposit the used bottle, connect the full one to the oxygen regulator, go through the awkward process of putting on the mask again, which I had taken off to be able to film better, and continue, step by step, diagonally upwards towards my friends, carefully thrusting the ice axe into the snow at every move . . .

There was no way I could foresee, at this moment, that this day was to decide my further career and life – that after it I would continue as 'the cameraman of the eight-thousanders', a title given me by the French. These pages can only be a snatch, a day out of many days on Everest. Five expeditions I have made there, and several other visits to the people of the area. Only once did I reach the top. Which does not matter: 'I go to the mountains for moments like these . . .' Julie Tullis's words might have applied to those minutes spent in the niche on the ridge, looking down over all the peaks and hollows. We thought very much alike, and she was to become my film- and climbing-partner. In her book *Clouds from Both Sides* Julie included our later experiences on Everest.

Since catching my first glimpse of the mountain in 1974, and capturing on celluloid the giant cornices and our icicle-framed faces as Hermann Warth, Nawang Tenzing and I fought our way higher along Shartse's ridge – the East Peak of Everest – I have made six more films about Chomolungma and its people, the most recent in the winter of 1993 with my daughter Hildegard, on Tibetans and their customs to the north-east of the mountain. The twenty years in between have brought many changes in the Himalaya – I have been witness to those now for thirty-five years. There has been true development as well as the odd side-shoots, like speed or competition climbing on big mountains, but you can still find all styles on Everest, mixed like a bouquet of flowers! To enter discussion on them here would lead too far, especially when a brilliant book compiled by Peter Gillman appeared for the fortieth anniversary of the first ascent,* but I think some brief jottings from personal experience and thoughts on the matter might stand well here:

---

* Peter Gillman, *Everest, The Best Writing and Pictures of Seventy Years of Human Endeavour*, Little Brown, 1993.

'Take One'

of luck – whichever name you know her by. A strong feeling comes through the air. Yang Lhe? From there her magic blessing reached to the very summit of the big mountain. Does it reach over here, too?

Then Pierre snatches me back from my thoughts. He wants to know if that is really the summit above us, definitely the highest point? I nod in affirmation, for it is as if I had stood up here before: the view is so familiar to me from pictures I had seen. The final ridge, rimmed with cornices above the last rocks and the short, but impressive upthrust of the Hillary Step. Right now, clear against the sky, our two 'youngsters' appear: Jean and Nicolas, who went on ahead, are high on the summit ridge, two tiny figures . . .

Pierre and I rope up. We look at each other. Does he think, as I do, that in the end Everest is actually our 'Mont Blanc'? We have known each other for fifteen years now, so many times planned to climb the White Mountain together and it never worked out. Everest will be our first shared summit . . . We start. Pierre takes the lead. Deep, dark and blue, the sky curves like a dome above the highest point on earth. Out over the immeasurable spaces of Tibet.

Eight thousand eight hundred and forty-eight metres: we are standing on the roof of the world. We are speaking, coughing, embracing each other. We laugh, walk (rather wonkily) from one rim of the summit snows to the other, look down: Tibet, the grey-brown highlands scattered with snow-capped mountains as if they were floating islets of cloud. And at its edge, above long jagged waves of ice rising from blue depths like a swell of surf, Cho Oyu soars in the west, and further still, Shisha Pangma. Makalu, to the south-east, and Kangchenjunga far beyond it at the horizon – thousands of summits in between and hundreds of valleys – yes, it is like the coastline of an ocean.

We look down to earth from the heavens. And we feel in heaven. A day of days!

We have taken off the masks, switched off the oxygen taps; a couple of metres below the highest point, on the southern slope in the wind's shadow, one does not feel the cold. Only on the icy, horizontal crest of the summit, where you can sit as if on a bench, are you hit by a chill, steady draught from the north, blowing off the Tibetan Plateau. The Chinese tripod? Invisible, maybe gone. My French companions are speaking by walkie-talkie to Base Camp, and the radio operators are relaying their words (and our shared happiness) via space to Paris. Pierre, his beard encrusted in frost, excitedly tells his story – complete with gestures, as if he were making a speech in parliament – to all France. Only fractions of a second later his countrymen learn what it is like up here, a 'world first' live transmission from the top of Everest . . . we used a satellite.

A strange 'bridge' then, in 1978.

There was another world-first on top of Everest that day: the first cinematic 'clap', or, as those in the business would say, 'Take One!' Nobody had ever before made a film with people speaking, laughing, telling what they were thinking up there. The means I used were simple: a Mini-Nagra-SN recorder and my 16 mm Bell & Howell magazine camera, which I had to wind up by hand, as it ran by clockwork. At 8600 metres we split some of the weight between us. We took no clapperboard with us to the summit, but did not expect this to present a problem. In an alpine meadow you can just clap your hands to give a signal for synchronising sound to pictures. But now on top of the world, none of the good fellows wants to take off his gloves! Wisely, but an eiderdown 'clap' is imperceptible to the little mike we have. So, I let them keep their gloves on and, instead, yell '*Chac*!' with a single big wave of the arm in front of their faces at the start of a scene on sound. That worked, up to a point . . . but, combined with the jerkiness of the cold camera mechanism, gave the cutting editors in Paris something to get their teeth into. Still, the outcome was great! You can see and hear the joy of those guys, stumbling, beaming, waving and panting their *Chacs*! And Pierre's enthusiastic words . . . Certainly, with delicate art, much of the coughing has been removed from the French sound version, but, I mean, please, that was the first time Frenchmen had stood on the rooftop of the world!

Take One! Take Two! Take Three!

Among the scenes I shot up there is the shadow of my waving hand at the rim of the summit snows, above Tibet. It was a bit of a joke, but great to wave to the world. Perhaps I was influenced by the minister's performance.

We spent at least an hour on top. For a while I was sitting on the highest – and coldest – park bench in the world, just looking and thinking. It was then that I noticed a lingering expression of disbelief on Pierre's face – but we were here, really here, above the world on a day of days!

It comes hard on you to leave such a fantastic place. I want to carry it with me for ever! Up, Kurt! I say, and turn around on my heels to

'Take One'

gather the whole, immense panorama from the top of the world into my lens . . . to Makalu, India, Nepal, Tibet . . . and back to Makalu. Still, I don't want to leave it.

But I must! Soon . . . Something like a frenzy has seized me in an endeavour to retain it all by means of my cameras as the moment of descent draws nearer. Take Six! Take Seven! Take Eight! Take it all with you, every moment. Can you?

Only then, as we leave, the very last minute I find time for it . . . I press my face against the summit-snows and thank the gods.

Om mani padme hum

Death Valley in Winter

Pale grass, like white-blonde hair above the salt flats. Snow in the depths. Snow, or salt?

Silky sheen.

It rustles every time the wind passes over, the tufts yield to the pressure of the wave of air then stand up again immediately; only some stalks continue to sway uncertainly to and fro.

The air is cold up here at 2000 metres, here, at the mountain's edge above Death Valley, and in the shade of the rocks there remains even a trace of snow – like a veil, which the diligent Californian sun will soon melt away.

We are sitting, sheltered from the wind, in a niche open to the valley and the sun. Renata is wearing the down jacket. On our faces we feel the thin warmth of the December light. A little bit of warmth up here, existing only where the wandering rays touch briefly.

The desert mountains on the other side of the valley are white with snow – and also the salt flats deep down, deep below the level of the sea, seem to be nothing else but snow.

The gentle, soft haze, which in a summer past shrouded the valley floor – this indefinite something which seemed to reach out to us, has disappeared. It has given way to a clarity, hard to comprehend. This landscape under the invading blue of the sky is full of precision, engraved, every rib of rock, every mountain, every ray in the wide fans of gravel is picked out, as if in pen and ink.

Have I come here from Europe for this?

Convincing clarity. Still impressive, yet – 'It has turned into a landscape of almost German exactness,' I say.

Renata gives a light laugh, but says nothing.

I step out on to a projecting rock to take a panoramic sequence of photographs – it is the first time I've done that in Death Valley. Somehow I want to keep hold of the valley, not let it go. Is it ours still? Are we losing it?

Death Valley in Winter

'Let's go down there.'
I sense that the valley we know still exists somewhere, hidden.

A few burros, wild donkeys – fairly tame they seem to be – look at us as we drive through a barren canyon towards the valley floor. Are they 'ours' . . . those of Aguereberry Point? As we stop, one of the animals comes to the window. Yes, we've got something for you! While the creature chomps contentedly – Renata is offering it biscuits – I think of the braying we heard last night, over there in the Panamint valley where we had stopped during the long approach near the old gold-digger's hut. There, the snow-covered silhouettes of the highest ridges of Telescope Peak looked dreamy in the moonlight, and the dark valley below only revealed its width and depth through the distant calls of the burros.

We have reached the floor of Death Valley, pass northwards along the sea of dunes.

To the source.

It is the last place we have come to see. The only one, where I still hope now, in December, to rediscover my old Death Valley. Our Death Valley . . .

Whenever I think of the source, then that means for me not only water which appears from the earth in the middle of a side canyon of the desert. It means both the water and the tree. Even if there are a couple of other trees not far away, doubtless over a hidden waterway – they are nothing unusual.

But this tree . . .

It surrounds the source.

At first glance you think it's many different trees – then you realise: none of them is coming out of the ground, but – like mighty branches, like great shoots from a recumbent trunk – they rear up, all coming from one and the same, almost metre-thick, tree body, which lies on the ground, or sometimes free above it, in many coils, like a sleeping reptile, around the place of the spring. A strange being – the roof of leaves seems to belong to a forest when you look up, and yet it is that of a single tree.

The ground is covered with a thick layer of dry leaves into which you sink with every step. They swish loudly with every movement, rushing almost like a wave when you cross them. It is true it could as well be a sinister place – but it isn't. To me, it means absolute concord, a little universe – in the centre of which there is the spring. Sometimes a bird appears, touches down at the edge of the water, which seeps almost imperceptibly out of a dark patch of ground from between the leathery

Spirits of the Air

brown leaves; it only takes a short way to reach close to the tree body, then it disappears again into the layer of dried leaves. This little water is very special, absolutely silent – it comes out of the ground like the elixir of life; totally clear. And that's what it is.

The grey-green leaves of this strange tree beat against each other with their hard edges – yes, the wind from the wintry-blue heights has arrived down here too: but it is not cold. Another wave of air – and I hear the pummelling of the leaves like a slow rainshower that moves from branch to branch, stem to stem of the tree-being, which flows and ebbs – sometimes surrounding us here, then approaching again, rustling, from another direction, sometimes shaking the whole tree in a cascade of sound.

We dip our hands into the water, look down on to the black bottom, only a couple of inches deep. 'In winter, Death Valley is not the same,' says Renata, wiping a damp hand across her face. It is completely still now. Silently, the water oozes from the floor.

'Nothing has changed here, but we have been away so long,' I say, and look up; slowly the leaves in the deep blue sky start to move again, a shower runs through the tree. I myself have been long and far away – I think of the Himalaya.

'Perhaps it's we who've changed.'

The leaves play their clapper-game. How many days? When they fall, there are new ones. As long as the water comes out of the ground. The tree must be ages old – and has always been in this spot.

Do you still want to tell me something?

Have you nothing else to say?

. . .

Be still, don't you hear it? The leaves!

Don't say a word. Listen.

In this sound is love. And it rises, every moment, beyond the rustling leaves out into the infinite blue.

Death Valley, in winter. Valley of Death?

The valley of – Always.

PART VIII

Hildegard Peak (6189m) – Island Peak

Many years ago I stood with Tona on the summit of a nameless six-thousander in the Hindu Kush. It was a first ascent and we wanted to call it Hildegard Peak after our little daughter. But unfortunately that was not possible. Today, tall, blonde Hildegard climbs her own summits, and asserts that a mountain's name is not so relevant. The mountain is yours for the moment you stand on its top. For her, the people who live at its foot are much more important. But I remember on her first six-thousander she was really keen. Island Peak, which stands like an icy cliff in the airspace above the wide valley of the Imja Khola, is surrounded by mountain giants, which completely dominate it in size but cannot compete with its location, plumb in the centre of this valley of glaciers, moraine ribbons and meadows.

It is almost sunset when Pasang and I arrive beneath Island Peak. Hildegard comes running up to me enthusiastically, her tall figure distinguishable from way off by her long yellow hair and the faded blue down jacket, an honoured relic from Hermann Buhl's last expedition. She tells me all sorts of stories about what she has seen, and the new words she has learned from Gyaltsen, Nga Temba and the three Sherpanis; and she is so much looking forward to the summit; I can see it in her eyes, feel it from her questions. For a moment I am reminded of setting off with Tona for her first six-thousander . . .

Both Hans Englert and Erhard Spiller are in good form, the two Hessian mountaineer-clients with whom I will try the summit the day after tomorrow as a guided rope of three. I know that I can trust my daughter to Pasang Phutar's care on the other rope. Gyaltsen and Nga Temba, along with our three Sherpanis, will accompany us to a higher camp tomorrow, which only Pasang knows: he has been to the summit

843

of Island Peak twice already. The men will wait there till the rest of us come back from the climb with Pasang.

A little fire of gleaned twigs crackles as twilight fades and the moon rises, and the Sherpa voices pipe up, telling each other stories and jokes. Suddenly my daughter remarks that it is so wonderful here, so perfect, she cannot begin to contemplate that it will all be over in just three days when we need to start back. She has learned so much from and about the Sherpas, and of their life, that she quite emphatically has to come back again; and she gives me that entreating, conspiratorial look daughters reserve for their fathers when they want to win them round to something (. . . she became an ethnologist later!).

Kantschi, one of the three Sherpanis, combs her long black hair. Tomorrow she will be carrying twenty kilos up the mountainside, as will her two female companions. I think back to my Makalu expedition and the approach to Shartse; on both occasions the Sherpas and Sherpanis carried the same weight loads. They were from a village far from here. But in the Everest region much has changed under the influence of so many expeditions. The Sherpa can work his way up from porter, to high-altitude porter and finally, if he has the spirit for it and an aptitude for organisation, to Sirdar. But Sherpanis do not have access to the same career structure; they continue to be porters and they hardly learn any English. It would certainly be very little use to them since the foreigner prefers Sherpa men for the higher work and is happy to relegate the organisation to them. And so Pasang, who carries the heaviest loads up to the South Col of Everest, is here blithely climbing through the steep rocks with a light day pack and an easy conscience while his sister follows, bent under her weighty burden. She is a porter after all . . .

We have arrived at an airy shoulder at 5600 metres, close to the edge of a hanging glacier. Gyaltsen and Nga Temba put up two tents and Pasang goes for a basketful of ice from the glacier. It is not easy to get, but no problem for him. Finally, we have water, tea, soup! Hildegard and the handsome young Gyaltsen have prepared it. It is delightful, I think, how interested she is in the lives of the Sherpa people. She has already told me the family background of some of them. The tea runs easily down the throat, cosy, warm, while we stretch out our legs comfortably on the foam mats, admiring the wonderful mountains beyond our toes and the rubble-strewn glaciers extending from beneath their mighty walls. Brown, green and blue glacial lakes glint up in the last sunshine. We can go for the top tomorrow – everybody is fine! The Sherpanis go down in the fading light, and soon Erhard's usual snoring is slicing the nocturnal silence.

Hildegard Peak (6189m)

'Put on your crampons. Here is a good place,' I call to my companions. We have arrived at the last crags of the boulder crest on Island Peak. It takes time, but finally we set foot on the glacial surface in two ropes. Pasang with Hildegard, and I leading Erhard and Hans.

Six thousand metres! Hildegard has glowing cheeks and her eyes shine – I know that her heart is leaping! We arrive at the last slope. It looks steep. A forty-five-degree gradient for about 150 metres. Island Peak is not as easy as it is often made out to be, not at all! Of course, the leader could string a fixed rope from the bottom to the top of the face and make it safe . . . but to climb a steep snowfield just in crampons requires some skill. I do not employ a fixed rope to the top, and we move slowly uphill. I am able to belay securely, first with an ice-screw, then with a snow piton and, finally, another snow piton.

Pasang and Hilde do their job well. Erhard, who is quite heavy, puffs a bit, but will make it. Hans, of lighter build, has less trouble. Then just below the ridge comes a very steep powder snow section, of uncertain but considerable depth. Poor Erhard is at a disadvantage with his weight, but I have secured a fine belay on the crest and, heeeeave-ho! hoist the protesting solicitor's clerk swiftly up the last few metres. There is enough space on the ridge for us to take a breather. The last ten minutes are then a real pleasure, there being no further difficulties and stunning views into the valley on either side of this rounded edge, and out far away to Ama Dablam and Makalu. Above us, blonde Hilde and little Pasang arrive on the summit. They wave down at us and hug one another. Then they hug one another again . . . and again! That's enough, Hildegard! Or you'll ram poor Pasang into the summit!

We know you are on top! Eighty-nine metres higher than your mama once climbed on her Peak Dertona. But what don't I know? Why does my daughter continue embracing Pasang? Secrets of the summits . . . yes, only the Spirits of the Air know who you will go hand in hand with beyond the mountains!

A few steps more and we are all on top. It is ours, this Pasang Peak, Hildegard Peak, Hans Peak, Erhard Peak and my peak, too, of course . . . our Island Peak.

Even a small summit can bring great happiness.

The Green Flash

It is close to sundown, and the wide Pacific burns before me in the evening light. Through shining palm leaves and orchids flushed orange in the soft glow, I gaze down over an immeasurable expanse of ocean. Here I am only a few hundred metres above the water but, close by, the gentle slopes of Mauna Loa rise to over 4000 metres.

I stood on that summit a few days ago, on that 'Long Wide Mountain' of Hawaii, after making what seemed an interminably lonely walk across a lunar landscape, climbing solidified lava flows, bare of any vegetation, in a primeval world of volcanic shapes, a frozen-to-the-spot army of petrified figures. The icy night I spent crouched in a pockmark of rock close to its top was one of the coldest bivouacs I have made anywhere. Unimaginably for Hawaii, ice crystals sprouted from narrow cracks – as I discovered to my amazement on emerging next morning from my night in the 'honeycomb' of the most enormous volcano in the world, dressed only in windcheater and shorts (and carrying an umbrella!). This mountain, if measured from its roots beneath the sea, would outstrip even Everest with a height of more than 10,000 metres. The brown lava streams, pitted with hundreds of cavities, over which I walked with such caution, listening to the echo of my steps (for hidden 'bubbles' as big as a room are not unusual here), gave way at last to the black surface of a petrified lava lake within the immense crater. I stayed over-long, forgot the time. Everything was lonely beyond words, impressive in its scale and monotony, its perpetual repetition, its silence. Later, when I groped my way back, down towards the big saddle linking Mauna Loa with Mauna Kea, in the scorching heat of a new day, the air quivering between the lava figures, I stumbled over a palette of stones: violet, green, red, bluish-green, even the glint and sparkle of silver and gold! Lost in astonishment and excitement, I picked up a nugget as large as a man's head, only to find it weighed – next to nothing at all! Pumice . . . With a sigh, I let it go again – I wouldn't be making my million that day.

I think of all those colours now, as the sun slides into the Pacific, and I stand on the slopes of the huge mountain which here at sea level boasts

The Green Flash

a diameter of a hundred kilometres, but down on the sea bed is 400 kilometres across. And no longer am I alone.

'Maybe in a minute you will see the green lightning flash,' whispers Elelule, a native of these islands. She lives in Oahu, is spending a few days on the main island, but her heart – she confesses – belongs to Kauai, an island of absolute green, the wettest place in all the archipelago. Many bays, it has, and luxuriant vegetation covering every inch of rock. Elelule has never been to the top of Mauna Loa: that is another world, up there! Not her world . . . she smiles. I can believe it: her tall figure, her flowing, unhurried gestures, the generous mouth in that sweet, dark face, everything about her cries contrast to the abstract ferocity of that eviscerated landscape with its enigmatic frozen lava figures. She knows so much about Hawaii . . .

So what is this green lightning? I only learnt about it a couple of minutes ago: on rare days when the sky above the ocean is cloudless as far as the eye can see, split seconds after the last blazing fragment of sun slips below the horizon, a single beam of light pierces the ocean with a brilliant green flash. Just for an instant, if it happens at all.

'I think you are going to be lucky,' Elelule says suddenly in a low voice. Her dark hair seems to glow in the radiant atmosphere – only the black eyes remain motionless and unchanged, looking out to sea. She has only seen the green flash once herself.

The sun! Its last rim is drowning in the waters. Will it happen? Impossible to tell if there is a small cloud far, far out there to interrupt the endless line of sight.

The great orb is gone – only the after-image glimmers before my eyes. Then, suddenly! I see it! The flash! Green as green, emerald green!

Like a laser, it penetrates the brain, enters the very soul . . . for a moment . . . it clutches . . . binds you . . . to everything.

I feel the breath at my side.

A secret . . . The sea and the sun unite.

Gasherbrum II

SPIRITS OF THE AIR

Gasherbrum, 'the beautiful shining wall' . . . that's what the name means. It derives from the fantastic face of golden crystalline limestone which mirrors the rays of the late afternoon sun when you look at it from the Baltoro Glacier. Gasherbrum IV is not the highest peak of this group, but has given its name to all of them.

My fifth eight-thousander belongs here, in this family of peaks, which comprise four summits around the magic 8000-metre mark, as well as a band of 'kids', several seven-thousanders.

Gasherbrum II is 8035 metres . . . a beautiful pyramid of perfect symmetry. I still find it hard to believe that I have now been up there, my third eight-thousander in fifteen months after Makalu last spring and Everest in the autumn. A magic run of luck . . .

Only a few days ago I stood on top, together with my companions from Austria, Bavaria and 'that other part of Germany' (as my neighbours insist on calling Germany beyond Bavaria). Well, that 'other part' had contributed no less than Reinhard Karl to the enterprise, an expedition organised by dyed-in-the-wool Himalayan hand, my friend Hanns Schell. Reinhard was obsessed with the idea of a Baltoro Marathon (an idea nobody else shared) and he was dreaming of a solo ascent of Hidden Peak, which rises right next to our mountain. Reinhard was a man full of ideas ahead of his time . . . It made for a lot of discussion! We also made the acquaintance of many other people, for the solitude which characterised the fifties was over. Almost as a symbol for the new epoch Jean-Marc Boivin floated under his hang-glider high in the sky above the Baltoro Glacier . . . much to the amazement of hundreds of Balti porters.

However, we did not tackle our mountain very differently from the way our party climbed Broad Peak twenty-two years ago – without the boost of oxygen or the help of high-altitude porters. Luckily, our walkie-talkies did not weigh eleven kilos, as they had then, and also the double-boot had been invented. Nevertheless, the Karakorum weather was as unpredictable as ever and we had quite a struggle, being beaten back more than once by storms.

'But now all fatigue is forgotten. Gasherbrum II is ours, and when I

Gasherbrum II

think back to Broad Peak, it seems to me that a whole lifetime has passed since then . . .' I write in my diary.

When will I stand again below a big mountain and demand of the clouds whether I should climb it, as I did that time on Makalu?

Today is the last day here, the last morning – and a strange thing happens: suddenly in the clear blue of the sky above the big mountains delicate loops, skeins and ribbons appear – then disappear – in a slow flowing movement, a surge. The beautiful pyramid of Gasherbrum is shrouded in a fairy veil of fantastic shape which continues to change as if bewitched. Now, Hidden Peak too wears a curved hat comprised of countless shimmering fibres, which slowly flow beyond its bounds and dissolve away.

Perhaps there's a storm coming?

Now, above Sia Kangri, it starts to shine in all colours . . . green, violet, orange . . .

I gaze at the dance of the veils, deeply moved . . .

Spirits of the Air. Greeting me.

A NEW HORIZON

The view from the summit of Gasherbrum into the mountain desert on the Chinese side of the peak, with its deserted valleys and the big ice floes with thousands of pointed towers, changed my world. A new longing was born: I must get down into that place!

How did that happen . . .?

Götterdämmerung in the Karakorum – that is what I wrote in 1979 in my diary of climbing this eight-thousander:

> Never in my life have I arrived on a summit in such gloom. We struggle higher, full of fatigue, stopping time and again – this Gasherbrum II is after all an eight-thousander! Really, we should be ascending one of the most enthralling peaks on earth. But today? Clear view into the distance, but with a strange twilight above overlaying everything, like a burden . . . I cannot help thinking of the fantastic sunset display Hermann Buhl and I experienced over there on the summit we shared, an unearthly play of light that seemed to penetrate our very souls. The gods were close to us then. Not now. Did they flee from the many people into the distant spaces of Sinkiang, this immense mountain world stretching to the horizon, empty of people as at the beginning of creation . . .

Spirits of the Air

Behind me, on the Pakistani side, I knew of a dozen expeditions on this Baltoro Glacier where Hermann and I had enjoyed total solitude. The place I came to know when I was twenty-five no longer existed. And I was searching for a new horizon. I found it up there, at the age of forty-seven, gazing out into Sinkiang with the Shaksgam valley at my feet, a deep furrow in a field of hundreds and hundreds of peaks . . .

That same year my life changed course, quite subtly. I met Julie again, who I had known briefly over a number of years, and this time we became rope-partners, not to be separated any more: in the same way as Wolfi Stefan and Kurt Diemberger 'conquered' the Alps as a recognised team in the fifties, so it was now with Julie Tullis from England and me, except that we went to the Himalaya and Karakorum. And instead of the old student lifestyle of my great years in the Alps, there was now a different impetus – our film-making. Soon we would be the highest film team in the world. I did the camerawork, Julie the sound recording, and as for ideas – we found them together. When we made our first joint documentary on Nanga Parbat in 1982 (it earned three international awards) we were, in the eyes of many, no spring chickens: I was just fifty and Julie forty-three. But that did not matter to us. The horizons were open . . .

Under the Spell of the Shaksgam

A low, dull sound reverberates in the air. It is weird in its steadiness and enigmatic, here in the total isolation of the enormous valley with its steep walls, which to me are like something from the Dolomites. So unusual is this sound above the wide spills of gravel in the river bed that both of us stop almost simultaneously, just as we round the corner of the embankment of dirty ice, sand and mud which marks the end of the Northern Gasherbrum Glacier. This mighty bulwark along the foot of which we walk lies at about 4200 metres above sea level and is more than two kilometres wide. The considerable force of the masses of ice behind it (the glacier is about twenty kilometres long) has pushed the front almost to the mountain wall opposite. Through the narrow passage the Shaksgam River meanders like a snake, sometimes forking into several branches. Some days ago, when we passed here early in the morning, we could only hear the gentle murmur of the waters. But now? This strange, hollow sound. . .

'What is it?' Julie asks and looks at me with a puzzled expression in her dark eyes.

'Never heard it before,' I reply. Is it something to do with the river? Now, late in the afternoon, the murmur has given way to an intense rushing. Or maybe the wind is trapped somewhere, high above us on these walls?

Slowly we go on, passing the sometimes vertical front of the glacier at a respectful distance for there is danger of sudden rock and icefall. The dull sound increases, until it dominates every other voice in the valley . . .

'Look!' Julie says suddenly, pointing ahead: behind a rampart of scree, a strange 'plant' has appeared, a tumbling, foaming mushroom, a mighty, stocky fountain which hurls stones and sand into the air . . . filling the space with its sinister voice, like a being from another world. It is so bizarre, so unreal, that for some seconds we simply freeze from nervousness and alarm, something indeed akin to awe, as if we had crept in unnoticed to a place where water and glacier spirits meet, a place far from humans where they still appear.

'Come on, let's get closer to it,' I say, when finally I manage to speak, and softly we approach the apparition, as carefully as we can on the loose scree, while the low sound which seems to penetrate everything, increasingly enshrouds us, making the whole air vibrate. The countless hurled pebbles drum loudly back down on to the river bed, a swarm of shiny black dots, as the glacier water fountain clears a path for itself. Amazed, we watch the birth of a new branch of the mysterious Shaksgam River!

For some while we remain spellbound in front of the tumbling, roaring, stone-spitting monster and the relentlessly advancing waters, which soon join another foaming flood that has burst from a dark vault in the steep icy façade – water everywhere! I feel rising doubts whether we will be able to make it through here to our camp with all that water, even if it is only half an hour further downriver. What other surprises are in store for us? A bivouac?

Soon afterwards we spot Pierangelo, our friend from Bergamo, who is as strong as a bear; he carries a rope in his hands and signals to us from the opposite bank of the swollen tributary, which now separates us from the glacier edge. Well done that man! Pierangelo wants to help us; he has come up to meet us from our little base camp. Who knows how long he has been waiting already? He knots a longish stone into one end of the rope and hurls it across to us. We anchor it as best we can, and then I hold it – as Pierangelo does from the other side – while Julie steps into the rushing water and begins to cross, hand over hand. (We are also linked by our ordinary rope.) After a few steps, however, she returns, panting and spluttering – it is impossible! The current all but pulled her legs from beneath her. So then, I indicate first upstream and again at the glacier, yelling to Pierangelo, 'See you later!'

And, that's how we did it: went back to the 'water-mushroom', and beyond until we came to a spot where we could climb the icy ramp on to the glacier, then on, up and down, up and down, in the last light of day over moraine hills and bumps in the glacier . . .

Breathless, wet and tired, we finally reached our small base camp. We had gone a long, long way. After many hours between the ice towers, we had still climbed a fine rock cliff high above the glacier. 'It was a good day,' smiled Julie, while our companions took care of us with mugs of tea, with biscuits and Bresaola. A fantastic group was our little exploratory party. The big Italian K2 expedition, to which we belonged, was five days' march away and somewhere to the west of us, establishing an Advanced Base Camp.

While the chilly night drives us into our sleeping-bags, in the distance there is an indistinct shimmer from the mighty Gasherbrum Wall.

Under the Spell of the Shaksgam

Nobody has ever climbed it. It stretches from Hidden Peak to Gasherbrums II and III and on towards Broad Peak . . . All mountains around the 8000-metre mark. Also K2 can be seen, pale, and soaring between the intricate dark silhouettes of closer six-thousanders. Unmistakable, the shape of the giant crystal in the night sky . . .

This is our last night, the end of our time on this glacier. During our five days here we penetrated right up under the North Face of Gasherbrum II – and further, in another direction. It was a great experience to be the first humans to set foot into such a hidden corner, even to find a spot where we might later – perhaps years later – set up the tents for a big and difficult climb.

When we realised that, owing to the complicated nature of the glacier surface, neither our time nor our food would hold out long enough for us to penetrate the last hidden corner of the glacier, which must be at least twenty kilometres long (oh! how much we would have liked to do that!), we ascended just a bit further towards the 'camel humps', two distinct mountains, probably seven-thousanders. God, yes, we swore to come back to this place by whatever means!

Now we are squatting in our sleeping-bags at the tent entrance, looking out into the night with all its shapes, which in our minds are mingling with the images of our days on the Gasherbrum Glacier. A kaleidoscope of floating summits, of glinting needles of ice, turquoise steeples of ice, rows of roofs, points, teeth and dice, with small lakes in between, entire processions of shining figures . . . and of the seemingly endless, curved ribbons of the moraines, brown and grey and black. Wild onions and flowers are dotted here and there at the edge of the glacier. We discover a massive fossilised whelk, which lived here millions of years ago in an ancient ocean. We found it under a huge tower of rock, and wondered if perhaps that had been a reef . . . no water now . . .

The next night was totally different: wrapped in the bivvy bag, we lay between the rocks of a moraine, close together, uncomfortable, but warm – even if when morning came, crusted ice crumbled off us at every move. My beard looked like that of the mountain sprite Rübezahl in winter, and Julie's hair was so full of frost that she could have been a Christmas angel. But to watch how the sun's rays first lit up K2, while everything else was still dark in icy blue shadow, then to see how the light gently edged further and further down until it touched even us . . . to think about where and how one might force a route up this giant wall of seven- and eight-thousanders in front of us . . .

. . . And that, too: the difficult decision to turn back, the acknowledgment that our time here had come to an end . . . on this occasion . . .

Together came question and certainty: Will we come back? We will certainly come back!

There are places, where you know what 'the Endless Knot' means.
The light and dark ribbons of this glacier landscape have bound us for ever.
We sat a long time at the spot where we turned back, and looked at wonderful jewels of ice – like transparent amulets, standing on fine thin stems and twinkling in the sun.

Three years later, when Julie and I climbed to the shoulder of K2 in fantastic weather, on the day before our planned summit attempt, the great glacier with its curved ribbons appeared in the distance behind Broad Peak. We saw it, and from the depths it reached up to us, hanging in the air: Will we come again? We most certainly will . . .

Six years have gone by since then. And I have returned to the Shaksgam, the place of our hearts' longing. I am ascending a steep spur, and below me march out the mile-long lines of ice towers, the thousands and thousands of tall spikes, one behind the other, a frozen procession. Above me there is a snow saddle, or rather, the shoulder of a big white mountain which doesn't have a name and which soars above rotten, steep flanks of dark rock towards the sky. From up there, I ought to be able to see K2, quite closely . . . no, it is still beyond the Sella Pass, the gap in the big mountain wall which here forms the frontier between Pakistan and China, a possible crossing place, over 6000 metres high, though never yet reached from this side by anybody. Nevertheless, I feel the Mountain of Mountains to be so close . . . Julie is there, remains there for ever – that takes away all distance. I hear the sound of my steps in the steep snow whenever my boots break through its crust. Blue shadows all around me, and an icy chill.

Diagonally above me a concealed crevasse leads from the flank towards the rounded spur along which I am ascending . . . a feeble horizontal depression in the surface disappearing before it reaches the curve of the spur. By any normal judgment the route should be safe, but as a soloist one cannot be careful enough.

I keep stopping. My eyes follow the serrated line of mountain shadows, painting fantastic jags on the glacier way below, dark mountain-shapes enlarging all the time as if they wanted to merge with the wild rock formations and gentle snow edges on the other side; and my gaze wanders far to the prominent furrow of the Shaksgam valley, and back into our hidden glacier corner, which nine years ago –

as long as that! – had been hidden from our view behind the soaring silhouettes of the 6000- and almost 7000-metre-high 'Camels', as we christened these nameless peaks in the manner of blithe discoverers. It is the secret valley below Broad Peak, which we had longed so much to see. What a desire we felt as the first humans to look around the corner, to enter this strange sanctuary with all its secrets, where nobody had been before, and into which I could now look down from above . . . how much we burned, Julie and I, with the yen to know what was there . . .

I hear my steps crunch higher. Alone. Ice axe in my hand, space all round me. Here I am. My eyes follow the thin rim of sunlight, outlining the ridge above, then sweep down to the curved moraine ribbons, with their jagged lines of ice between – and something like contentment rises to meet me. The sensation of loneliness, which so often burdens me, is gone. Last spring, in Catalonia, when I revealed the possibility of a route up the unknown face of Broad Peak, I knew well enough that, as the oldest member of an expedition, I was unlikely to be chosen for the summit of the 8000-metre peak, but that was not so important, I just wanted to be here again, in the Shaksgam; simply to return and fulfil our old idea, make it come true, what Julie and I had recognised, realise it for her, too. I stop to take a look at the giant ramp of snow, broken by séracs, which leads up to the high plateau of the Central Peak, across the ice wilderness of the east and north-east walls, a magic route, our route . . . somewhere up there, tiny beyond vision, are my companions: the bearded Jordi, always so spontaneous (whether cordial or abrupt) – Jordi Magriña with whom in 1991 I initiated the first Catalan expedition to this place, during the course of which we reached the Hidden Valley; Oscar Cadiach, generally reflective and calm, friendly . . . a great organiser and mountaineer; Alberto Soncini, our 'ice artist', a colourful Italian; and Lluis Rafols, the youngest, with his laughing eyes, mop of hair, a headful of ideas; last but not least the slim, tough Enric Dalmau, desperately anxious for his first eight-thousander! And Mingma, Dorje, Tenzing – our Sherpas – have they managed to get up? I cannot help taking the walkie-talkie from my rucksack and calling up Broad Peak. No answer. I try Joan Gelabert, our radio technician, far out in the Shaksgam valley, but he doesn't hear me either. So I pack the radio away again. One day soon I want to climb up as far as the plateau at 7000 metres: looking over the ocean of Sinkiang peaks from this vantage point half in the skies must be overwhelming . . . However today I will concentrate on taking pictures, which none of my friends could get: the Hidden Valley and our mountain above it; and perhaps a new perspective on to the unclimbed Gasherbrum Wall? To solve an enigma? No, it isn't that alone which pushes me onwards. It is K2, above the Sella Saddle! Will I see it? And, can you get up to the saddle from this side?

It is late. Some of the dark shadow-summits cast into the valley are already pushing their way up between the glowing peaks, higher and higher. Don't stop, Kurt. Otherwise you will not be able to get up as far as the ridge.

My feet have become icily cold in my lightweight boots, which were more suited to walking on the moraine. I must have climbed nearly 1000 metres up here – when I turn around I can already see over the 'Little Camel', which is a six-thousander. There is not much further to go – the cornice-roll above my head draws closer . . . I must aim for that, dare not go directly out on to the shoulder, for fear of another crevasse across the flank.

Yet very clearly, there is no possibility of getting to the ridge over the cornice . . . it is overhanging and possibly ten metres high, but I might be able to traverse below it – I must get out to the shoulder in order to look over to the other side – that is what I want!

Powder snow, icy powder. Up to my waist. Blue shadows. I grind my teeth. My feet hurt. Can I still feel all my toes? No time to worry about that now. The roll is hanging directly over my head. Carefully, and with great effort, I edge sideways in the steep powder. Slow, prudent moves require several breaths each time, and at every step I must work my foot down a few times before the yielding, insecure white stuff will carry my weight. I plunge the ice axe deeply into the bottomless snow. My heart beats up into my neck: the steep slope beneath me drops abruptly away to nothing – in the blue twilight the couloir winds down into far depths. Take care, Kurt! Only move very slowly. Is there no end to it? Sunlight, suddenly! A dazzling brightness! I emerge from the icy shadows . . .

And K2 appears!

Another step. And one more. The snow is better and not so steep. I am standing in the warming light, just in front of a crevasse and gasping for air, trembling from effort and emotion . . .

The mighty pyramid . . .

K2, there it is! And close to it, the sun.

You are up there, I think, so far – and so near!

Very much closer, here. Entirely close.

In front of me is the snow surface of the ridge's shoulder, bathed in the bright light. Above it, beyond a tremendous chasm – the whole glacier valley – soars the Sella Saddle. Over 6000 metres high. And behind it, as high as the sky, K2!

A whole cascade of ice blocks in all sizes, jumbled one atop the other, seals the access to a depression, a sort of a basin with steep walls below the saddle. But hey, look! At the very right-hand end, there is a possibility of getting through. Deep in my heart the temptation rises to try it . . . to cross the saddle. Why? To get closer to K2? To stand just across from it? No, it must be something else. Must be the inexplicable urge to push beyond, to the other side – even if I know what's there. Perhaps because a part of my life remains there. Or maybe K2 is still the reason, that which was once the eternal dream for us?

I don't know. I follow the route up to the saddle with my eyes, in all its details . . . and while I am looking, I feel a contentment in knowing it – I will go there – and if not this time, at least I know now where and how . . .

Before the sun disappears behind K2 and the cold blue of the approaching evening enshrouds me, I take some photographs of this stupendous landscape in the last slanting rays of sunshine. They fill me with deep pleasure. Everything is shining and alive. The lines of shadows are like chiselled artwork, the light is weaving designs into the flanks of the mountains, and while my eyes feast on this plenty, scrutinise new tasks, I say to myself: the delay is irritating, but it will be worth it. Return here for as long as your time lasts.

Almost intoxicated, I find myself dipped suddenly into the icy shadow of K2. And talking of time . . . be quick, now, get down! Down 1000 metres of mountainside as fast as you can!

It is almost dark . . . I race to gain seconds, but still treating the snow spur with extreme caution, taking it step by step in my own tracks. Then nothing can stop me any more! 'Skating' across gravel fields, bounding down the slopes of debris and over rocks in giant leaps, down, down following a steep trough with a small torrent – new land for me, because it is impossible to climb back down the way I got on to the flank this morning, along a rib of friable schisty fragments marking the edge of the ice. The important thing now is to find the quickest way on to the glacier – and to locate an escape route between the ice towers before it is too late.

However, darkness is swifter. It reaches me at the edge of the glacier, just after I have managed to slide down a wall of debris. Here I am, then: night. Ice towers. Morass. Out of the darkness comes the sound of water – it gurgles, drips, rushes. Blank ice walls, dead ends, chaos all around. Even in daylight it would be a problem to get through here – it took a concerted effort to find a way to approach our Base Camp tents a mile further down the valley, but I cannot reach that route from here. It is like being in a forest of Christmas trees made of ice, in amongst the trunks. Utterly confusing. Will I ever be able to get out? Fantasy knows no bounds, especially at night. Reality, however, is different: hovering between hope and doubt I have already climbed two of the towers by the light of my head-torch only to have to retreat once more, have discovered a lake which bars further passage, and finally bypassed it behind another formation of ice. Now I have landed in a steep basin, which can only be escaped by three steep runnels. Luckily some years ago I acquired one of the most modern ice axes – that is a bright spark at least, even at night: one blow with it and already you have a bombproof hold! If only we'd had something like that in the old days!

Tense with expectation, I inch my way up the steep, shorter runnel and raise my head over the rim: the cone of light hits water. The whole cleft in front of me houses a pond, from wall to wall. Back down I climb. If I cannot find a way out here, the only thing to do is to wait in my bivvy bag until morning. I squat down, chew some nuts and rest for a while. But I still have not abandoned hope – really the whole crazy situation is at the same time somehow fascinating. So far, at least. Meanwhile, two hours quickly pass. It suddenly strikes me that perhaps Joan, our radio man, might be worrying. But my walkie-talkie call again goes unanswered. Perhaps he is already asleep. What about trying the second ice tube? I direct a beam of light into it. Really, it is quite high!

. . . I reach a crest which leads onwards. Is hope in order? Gingerly, I place my crampons, step after step. On both sides water rushes down to invisible depths. Like a tightrope walker I follow my 'bridge' in the light of the headlamp – it is getting wider . . . heavens! Am I getting out of this labyrinth?

Down again, up, a switchback ridge of ice. In the starry sky I can make out the silhouette of the 'Little Camel' in front of me. Good, I am going in the right direction! And it is no longer that difficult. A dark hogsback appears, indistinctly, behind the last glittering shapes. The central moraine! Out! I am out! Now all I have to do is find the camp.

. . . A gleam of light through tent fabric penetrates the darkness! An illuminated dome. It is close to midnight. I hear my own stumbling

Under the Spell of the Shaksgam

among the stones, and the voices of the Sherpas from inside. Tenzing's head appears in the tent entrance: 'Papa! You here? We making tea.'

A month later. The summit! The icy Kafka-castle has been climbed. Four of our team made it: Oscar, Lluis, Alberto, Enric. And did so at the very last moment, when our camels for the return journey had already arrived in Base Camp. At the fourth attempt. They staked everything on one last card, in the end climbing at night, and bivouacking at 8000 metres shortly before reaching the Central Summit. The unpredictable weather was about to break again – shortly after beginning their descent they were caught in another snowstorm. This climb was a milestone in the history of the Shaksgam. Ten years before, when the Japanese climbed K2 from the north, it was the first great new climb on the Chinese side of the Karakorum. That was 1982. In August 1992 another one came into being: our route up the secretive East Face of Broad Peak.

Extreme difficulty in ice, and considerable avalanche danger could not frighten off my companions. I myself went once as far as Camp 2, but a breakdown in the weather foiled my attempt to reach the desired plateau at 7000 metres, so I returned to my explorations, leaving the youngsters to bring an old idea to an honourable conclusion. During the final risky dash – I can hardly call it anything else – I prayed for them. To God and to all the Spirits of the Air. Also to Julie. Because on these great mountains so much of the fate of people depends on circumstances beyond themselves.

Our four are back down again, safely!

Sometimes I find myself remembering an hour on the crest of a peak in the Shaksgam Dolomites, high above the glacier world. A butterfly dances around me in the warm light of the sun. It circles many times, alighting at last and opening its pale white wings to reveal strange eye-markings: large black circles around dark red.
  What does it hope to find up here?
  Perhaps it is wondering the same about me . . .
  'I want to know . . .' it seems to say.

What brings me here?
  Because I want to know something, too.
  And I am not alone. We have met one another.

APPENDICES

A Chronology of Main Climbs and Expeditions

1948	Larmkogl (3014 m) in the Hohe Tauern, Austria, my first mountain climb, when I decided to go for the top instead of making a crystal hunt (alone), at the age of sixteen.
1952	Matterhorn, Breithorn, Monte Rosa, Bernina-Biancograt, Piz Roseg, with two companions, Erich Warta and Gundl Jabornik, travelling on my grandfather's robust 1909 bicycle.
1953–55	Many difficult climbs in the Alps on rock and ice with my friend Wolfgang Stefan as a steady team of two.
1956	Matterhorn North Face (among others), first climb of the Königswand Direttissima. The Giant Meringue was the most difficult crux on snow and ice at the time in the Alps.
1957	My first Himalayan expedition to Broad Peak (8047 m) with Hermann Buhl, Markus Schmuck, Fritz Wintersteller; this was the first ascent of an eight-thousander in *Westalpenstil* (no high-altitude porters, no oxygen-aided climbing). The term, as well as the idea, was created by Hermann Buhl.
1958	Eiger Nordwand, Jorasses Nordwand (Walker Spur) and integral Peuterey Ridge of Mont Blanc, filming with Franz Lindner, still the only existing documentary of the five-day traverse of the greatest ridge in the Alps; first award at the International Trento Film Festival, 1962.
1960	First ascent of Dhaulagiri (8167 m) with an international Swiss expedition; climbed without oxygen apparatus. The assisting Pilatus-Porter aircraft crashed without loss of life.
1965–69	Himalaya and Karakorum unavailable for mountaineering. Expeditions to Africa (Mount Kenya and High Semyen mountains), to Greenland (three times), to the Hindu Kush (twice); in 1967 several two-man alpine-style enterprises, including the first ascent of Tirich West IV (7338 m) from the north; also Tirich Mir (7706 m) and five other peaks.
1974	First ascent of Shartse or Junction Peak (c.7500 m).
1978	Ascent of Makalu (8481 m) in the spring and of Everest (8848 m) in the autumn.
1979	Ascent of Gasherbrum II (8035 m).

A Chronology of Main Climbs and Expeditions

1980   Another Everest expedition, filming as far as the South Col. Because of my film work I missed out on the possible ascent of Lhotse. Since the first sync-sound filming from the top of Everest two years earlier, I had become the cameraman of the eight-thousanders.

1981   Film director of the American Everest Expedition to the unclimbed East Face. Received Emmy Award 1982–83.

1982   Exploration of K2 (8611 m) and the Gasherbrums from the Shaksgam, afterwards filming the French Nanga Parbat Expedition. This was the first film I made with Julie Tullis; its awards included the Grand Prix of the Diablerets Film Festival, 1983.

1983   Italian K2 Expedition from the Shaksgam side; Julie and I established ourselves as the highest film team in the world, climbing and working together up to 8000 metres; another exploration of the Gasherbrums from the north.

1984   Filming and climbing with Julie to 7350 metres on the Abruzzi Ridge of K2, making the film *K2, the Elusive Summit*, and climbing Broad Peak again with her.

1985   Filming and climbing with Julie on Everest North-East and North Ridge, and later on Nanga Parbat (8125 m) up to 7600 metres; filming Tashigang, a Tibetan village.

1986   Filming Tashigang again, then went to K2 with Julie, the third expedition together to our dream mountain. At the second attempt we reach the summit, but – for the loss of one day – we end up imprisoned by a terrible blizzard at 8000 metres. Julie and four other mountaineers die.

1987–90   Mainly scientific expeditions and exploration in the Himalaya and Karakorum. Filming the GPS-Measurement of K2 and Everest (to establish which is the highest mountain in the world) of Prof Ardito Desio's Everest-K2-CNR Expedition 1987 and returning to the Shaksgam and Nanga Parbat.

1991–92   Participating in two expeditions with Catalan mountaineers to the Shaksgam, first exploration and then first ascent of East Face of Broad Peak. I also explored for the future in this area. Filming an Italian Expedition to the top of Cristobal Colon (5,800m) in Columbia.

1993   Filming with daughter Hildegard in winter on ethnological research in Tibet.

1994   China, Shaksgam: first traverse from the North Gasherbrum Glacier over a nameless saddle and unexplored glacier area to the Northern K2 Glacier. Exploring also the possibilities of climbing the Gasherbrum Wall from China.

1998   Taking part as a photographer in an Italian Nanga Parbat expedition to the Diamir Face. Soloed to c.6000m on the Kinshofer Wall.

A Note on Terminology

Abseiling is the friction technique of descending a steep face on a rope.

Bivouac means passing a night or waiting out a storm in the open without the protection of a tent. A bivvi bag or a snowhole can provide a valuable shelter. But using a tent (including a so-called bivvi tent) is not bivouacking, and a mobile lightweight camp should not be confused with a bivouac.

Blacklight: geologists and prospectors use this device when searching for certain minerals in the night, which in daylight would hardly be noticed because of their insignificant appearance (for instance Scheelite, a valuable Wolfram ore, which under the ultraviolet rays of the prospector's lamp gives an extraordinary reflected glow).

Nuts are made of metal (threaded with wire or rope) and, inserted into cracks, can be used to protect a leader against a fall. An important environmental and sporting factor is that they are removed by the second climber thus leaving no permanent, tell-tale fixture in the cliff.

Friends are camming devices used for protection in the same way as nuts.

'Penitentes': a Spanish term for penitents. Refers to peculiar pointed forms of ice on the glacier surface in the Andes, the Hindu Kush and other high places where, during the melting process of ice, a combination of temperature factors create hundreds of pin-sharp and often slightly bent figures, sometimes so close together that they become an almost impenetrable obstacle.

Prusik slings are loops of thin cord fixed by a special sliding knot on to the main rope (under weight, the knot tightens and you can stand in the sling; without weight it can be easily pushed upwards on the rope – thus using two Prusik loops you can ascend vertically through the air on the main rope).

Sérac is an ice tower or ice cliff.

Westalpenstil/West Alpine Style was a new way for climbing an 8000-metre peak – which Hermann Buhl devised in 1957. This approach was without the help of high-altitude porters and without using oxygen apparatus. Fixed camps and a limited number of fixed ropes were permissible. Broad Peak became the first 8000-metre peak to be climbed in this 'alpine-style', which was a true pioneering achievement and still remains the only first ascent of an eight-thousander by this technique. Today what climbers call alpine-style implies also a refusal to use fixed camps and ropes. In fact, Buhl and Diemberger attempted Chogolisa in modern alpine-style, and Wintersteller and Schmuck climbed Skilbrum that way immediately after the first ascent of Broad Peak in 1957, without inventing a separate label for a method which they saw as simply a lightweight version of *Westalpenstil*.

A Selected Bibliography

Hermann Buhl *Nanga Parbat Pilgrimage* Hodder and Stoughton, London 1956.
Benoît Chamoux, *Le vertige de l'infini*, Albin Michel, Paris 1988
Miles Clark, *High Endeavours* (life of Miles and Beryl Smeeton), Grafton Books, London 1991
George Cockerill, *Pioneer Exploration in Hunza and Chitral* (in *The Himalayan Journal* 11), 1939
H. P. Cornelius, *Grundzüge der allgemeinen Geologie*, Vienna 1953
Adolf Diemberger, *The Problem of Istor-o-Nal* (in *The Himalayan Journal* 29), 1970
Hildegard Diemberger, *Beyul Khenbalung – the Hidden Valley of the Artemisia*, Institut für Völkerkunde, University of Vienna 1991
Hildegard Diemberger in, *Von fremden Frauen* (proceedings of the *Arbeitsgruppe Ethnologie Wien*), Suhrkamp, Frankfurt 1989
Kurt Diemberger, *Some Climbs from the Upper Tirich Glacier* (in *The Alpine Journal* 71), London 1966
Günter Oskar Dyhrenfurth, *To the Third Pole* Werner Laurie, London, 1955 (first published as *Zum Dritten Pol* Nymphenburger, Munich 1952 and later updated as *Der Dritte Pol*, 1960).
Peter Gillman, *Everest, the Best Writing and Pictures of Seventy Years of Human Endeavour*, Little Brown, London 1993
Leroy and Jean Johnson, *Escape from Death Valley* (from accounts of William Lewis Manly and other 49ers), University of Nevada Press, Reno, Nevada 1987
Reinhold Messner, *All 14 Eight-thousanders*, Crowood Press, Marlborough 1988
Reinhold Messner, *The Challenge*, Kaye & Ward, London 1977
Pierre Mazeaud, *Everest 78*, Editions Denoël, Paris 1978
Arne Naess, *The Norwegian Expedition to Tirich Mir* (in *The Alpine Journal* 58) 1951/52
Jill Neate, *High Asia – An Illustrated History of the 7000-metre Peaks*, Unwin Hyman, London 1989
Josep Paytubi, *Tirich Mir*, Quaderns d'alpinisme Nr 5; Servei General d'Informacio de Muntanya, Sabadell 1994
Reginald Schomberg, *Derdi and Chapursan Valleys: Mountains of NW Chitral* (in *The Alpine Journal* 48), Nov. 1936
Reginald Schomberg *Between the Oxus and the Indus* Hopkinson, London, 1935
Reginald Schomberg *Kafirs and Glaciers: Travels in Chitral* Hopkinson, London, 1938

Spirits of the Air

Eric Shipton, *Blank on the Map*, Hodder & Stoughton, London 1938
Ernst Sorge, *With Plane, Boat & Camera in Greenland*, Hurst & Blackett, London 1935
Julie Tullis, *Clouds from Both Sides*, Grafton Books, London 1986
R. Vogeltanz, M. A. Sironi-Diemberger, *Receptaculites neptuni DEFRANCE* from *Devon des Hindu Kusch* in Anz. Österr. Akad.d. Wiss., math,-naturwiss, Klasse.Jg. 1968, Nr.5
Hermann and Dietlinde Warth, *Makalu, Expedition in die Stille*, EOS Verlag, St Otilien 1979
Else Wegener with Fritz Loewe (ed), *Greenland Journey: the story of Wegener's German Expedition to Greenland in 1930–31*, as told by members of the expedition and the leader's diary, Blackie, London 1939

Note on Heights

Summit heights of Himalayan peaks vary on maps and in expedition literature. For example, Makalu appears variously as 8481, 8475 and 8463 metres, and Everest was for a long time given as 8848 metres; but a measurement in 1987 by the Global Positioning System apparatus (using Navstar satellite data) established 8872 metres as a new height, until in 1993 another GPS measurement came to 8846 metres. Not to worry, peaks will always be measured again!

CONVERSION TABLE METRES TO FEET (from the *American Alpine Journal*)

3,300	10,827	4,700	15,420	6,100	20,013	7,500	24,607
3,400	11,155	4,800	15,748	6,200	20,342	7,600	24,935
3,500	11,483	4,900	16,076	6,300	20,670	7,700	25,263
3,600	11,811	5,000	16,404	6,400	20,998	7,800	25,591
3,700	12,139	5,100	16,733	6,500	21,326	7,900	25,919
3,800	12,467	5,200	17,061	6,600	21,654	8,000	26,247
3,900	12,795	5,300	17,389	6,700	21,982	8,100	26,575
4,000	13,124	5,400	17,717	6,800	22,310	8,200	26,903
4,100	13,452	5,500	18,045	6,900	22,638	8,300	27,231
4,200	13,780	5,600	18,373	7,000	22,966	8,400	27,560
4,300	14,108	5,700	18,701	7,100	23,294	8,500	27,888
4,400	14,436	5,800	19,029	7,200	23,622	8,600	28,216
4,500	14,764	5,900	19,357	7,300	23,951	8,700	28,544
4,600	15,092	6,000	19,685	7,400	24,279	8,800	28,872